CASES AND MATERIALS

LITIGATION WITH THE FEDERAL GOVERNMENT

SECOND EDITION

by

GREGORY C. SISK
Orestes A. Brownson Professor of Law
University of St. Thomas School of Law

FOUNDATION PRESS

2008

© 2000 FOUNDATION PRESS
© 2008 By FOUNDATION PRESS
      395 Hudson Street
      New York, NY 10014
      Phone Toll Free 1–877–888–1330
      Fax (212) 367–6799
      foundation–press.com
Printed in the United States of America

ISBN 978–1–59941–181–1

TEXT IS PRINTED ON 10% POST CONSUMER RECYCLED PAPER

To my wife, Mindy, and my daughter, Caitlin,
for their unfailing love and uncommon patience

To my mother, Roberta Sisk,
for helping me become who I am

To the memory of my beloved father,
James Sisk

*

PREFACE

I

Although every lawyer, law teacher, and law student recognizes that the United States government obviously is involved in every federal criminal case, fewer appreciate that, over the past decade, the federal government has been a party, as plaintiff or defendant, to between one-fifth and one-quarter of all civil cases in the federal courts. As political scientist Christopher J.W. Zorn has observed, because of its ubiquitous presence in federal litigation, "more than any other entity, the federal government plays a central role in the development of law and policy in the United States courts." Christopher J.W. Zorn, U.S. Government Litigation Strategies in the Federal Appellate Courts 1 (1997 Ph.D dissertation). Moreover, the United States is hardly a typical litigant, as it benefits from a plethora of special procedures, defenses, and limitations on liability not available to others. Indeed, the federal government may not be subjected to suit at all absent its own express consent—a concept of federal sovereign immunity that rests somewhat uneasily within the jurisprudence of a democratic society.

As a concrete indication of the importance of this field of law, the United States Supreme Court continues to devote substantial attention to recurring questions of sovereign immunity, the distinctive jurisdictional statutes governing litigation with the United States, special forums for adjudication of particular types of governmental disputes, the limitations on governmental liability in tort and contract, and the availability of and standards for awards of attorney's fees against the national government and its agencies. Many of these cases are included in this casebook and most of the others are cited or briefly discussed in note material. These topics have also occupied the attention of many authors in the law reviews in recent years, a robust literature that reveals the lively controversies surrounding the subject, lends scholarly depth to the field, and establishes a reliable source of further information and critical analysis. Again, many of these articles are excerpted, discussed, or cited in this casebook.

Because it is the quintessential repeat-player in federal litigation, and because its litigation strategy generally is coordinated by the Department of Justice across the entire range of government cases, the federal government exerts a powerful influence on the federal courts. Moreover, "court cases involving the United States typically involve the most consequential issues for people's lives," Zorn, supra, at 3—through claims involving personal injury;

civil rights; welfare; Social Security; health, safety, and environmental regulation; immigration; governmental expropriation of property; and contractual obligations. David Schwartz and Sidney Jacoby, the pioneers in this field of law, wrote almost 40 years ago:

> Those who deal with the Government can do so capably only with some knowledge of the available remedies both by and against the Government, and with some understanding of the possible untoward consequences if the parties fall out and require the intervention of courts to settle their differences. . . . Moreover, litigation with the Government, whether studied or practiced, soon leads to the realization that the degree to which a state provides that justice be done in the settlement of the civil and even the petty commercial disputes between citizen and government is one of the indicia of the ethical character of that government. (David Schwartz & Sidney Jacoby, Government Litigation Casebook (tentative casebook 1960).

Accordingly, any student of federal litigation or of our system of government should develop a critical understanding of the unique principles and statutes that govern when the federal sovereign becomes a party to a civil action.

II

Moreover, a course on "Litigation With the Federal Government" should provide practical advantages to students. The agencies and departments of the federal government offer a wide variety of employment opportunities for young lawyers.* A student who can demonstrate an advanced understanding of the unique legal issues involved in governmental litigation should have a lead in the competition for federal government law jobs. Attorney supervisors and officials I worked with at the Department of Justice and other governmental agencies have responded with enthusiasm to law school instruction on this subject. Over the years, government attorneys in several offices have bemoaned to me the unfortunate fact that candidates for federal legal positions, both in trial and non-litigation divisions, generally lack even minimal familiarity with the basic concepts underlying federal government civil litigation.

Comprehension of the legal principles governing federal government litigation should also be helpful with respect to employment opportunities beyond the federal government itself. Students may seek employment with companies or law firms working on government contract issues. Law firms practicing in labor and employment law or personal injury litigation likely will encounter the federal government as an employer or a tort defendant. Employment with public interest organizations frequently will involve pursuing claims in court against government entities. A course on "Litigation With the Federal Government" should be designed to provide not only the tools that future govern-

---

* As reported by the Association for Legal Career Professionals, governments at all levels have employed from a high of 19.3% in 1975 to a low of 11.4% in 1989 of new law school graduates (specifically excluding judicial clerkships). NALP, Ass'n for Legal Career Professionals, Jobs & JD's: Employment and Salaries of New Law Graduates: Class of 2005, at 33 (Washington, D.C., 2006). In 2005, more than a quarter of these government jobs were at the federal level, accounting for more than a thousand positions that year for new lawyers. See *id.*

ment lawyers may use to defend the government but also to examine the issues from the perspective of those seeking relief against the federal government.

Finally, the course should be of direct value to students who aspire to federal judicial clerkships. One need only pick up a couple of volumes of the Federal Reporter or Federal Supplement to find new opinions interpreting and applying the various waivers of sovereign immunity authorizing suit against the federal government, its agencies, or its officers. And, of course, published opinions reflect only a small portion of the filed cases. As stated earlier, civil litigation involving the federal government is regular grist for the federal court mill. A federal court law clerk with an understanding of the basic framework of statutes governing litigation with the federal government is likely to find ample occasion for application of that knowledge while serving in chambers.

III

We begin in Chapter I with an examination of the federal government as a civil litigator, looking at the roles of the Attorney General and the Solicitor General, ethical expectations of government lawyers, subject matter jurisdiction and venue for federal government cases, discovery in government cases, the availability of jury trials in suits against the government, settlement of government cases, and judgments against the federal government.

In Chapter II, the course addresses the principle of sovereign immunity, which is the foundation for the rest of the course. We review the evolution of federal sovereign immunity in Supreme Court decisions, consider critical analysis by scholars of the concept of sovereign immunity, examine modern judicial construction of waivers of sovereign immunity, and take a brief comparative tour of how suits against the government and sovereign immunity are regarded in some other countries.

Through cases, statutes, and other materials, Chapter III surveys certain specific statutory waivers of sovereign immunity, including the Federal Tort Claims Act (its prerequisites, standards, exceptions, and limitations on damages and covered claimants), the Suits in Admiralty Act, Title VII of the Civil Rights Act, the Freedom of Information Act, the Social Security Act, agencies with "sue and be sued" clauses, government corporations, and various miscellaneous statutory waivers of sovereign immunity. Because of the necessarily finite coverage that can be achieved in any single course, and in light of the wide range of federal statutes that today permit prosecution of lawsuits against federal government entities, the survey is necessarily a brief one that focuses upon those particular statutes that, in my judgment, are most important to a generalist understanding of the subject.

Chapter IV looks at the two more general statutory waivers of sovereign immunity: the Tucker Act and the Administrative Procedure Act (APA). The Tucker Act governs various types of non-tort monetary claims against the United States, while the APA authorizes claims against the government for relief other than money damages. With respect to the Tucker Act, we study jurisdiction over Tucker Act claims, monetary claims founded upon statutes and regulations, the Indian Tucker Act and Indian trust claims, contract claims (including the Contract Disputes Act which supersedes most Tucker Act contract claims), and monetary claims founded upon the Constitution, including takings claims under the Fifth Amendment. Recognizing that the APA is covered in detail in the course on administrative law, this course offers but a short overview of the APA. This overview is followed by a more detailed examination of the relationship and overlap between the Tucker Act and the APA and the consequent implications for choice of forum (as APA claims are brought in district court, while Tucker Act claims for more than $10,000 are reserved to the Court of Federal Claims).

The course next considers in Chapter V those suits brought against individual officers of the federal government, for both equitable relief and damages, including an examination of official immunity.

The restrictive rules for binding the federal government, including such matters as equitable estoppel and collateral estoppel, are reviewed in Chapter VI.

In Chapter VII, the course (1) examines statutory limitations on the fees that a private attorney may charge a client who prevails against the government, and (2) surveys statutes that permit the shifting of legal fees by an award of attorney's fees against the federal government, including Title VII of the Civil Rights Act, the Freedom of Information Act, and the general provision for fee awards against the federal government under the Equal Access to Justice Act.

The course materials conclude in Chapter VIII with a brief look at the United States as a plaintiff in civil litigation, including the power to sue, application of statutes of limitations to the federal government, and the availability of counterclaims in response to governmental lawsuits.

For those wishing to explore these subjects further, I recently have authored the fourth edition of the standard treatise, at the generous invitation of Professors Michael F. Noone and Urban A. Lester (who passed away this past year) of the Catholic University School of Law who had prepared the third edition. Gregory C. Sisk, Litigation With the Federal Government (ALI-ABA, 4th ed. 2006). Given that my own understanding of the field inevitably determines the path by which I approach the study of litigation with the federal government, the treatise shares the same general structure and organization of topics as this casebook.

IV

These course materials are drawn from leading and illustrative decisions of the United States Supreme Court, United States Courts of Appeals, United States Court of Federal Claims, and United States District Courts, as well as scholarship and commentary, on the subject of civil litigation against the United States government and its agencies and officers. The materials have been edited, in some instances heavily; citations and footnotes often have been omitted without indication. When footnotes have been retained, I have used the original numbering. With respect to case material, I have frequently deleted or condensed material not directly relevant to the topic at hand. Some dissenting opinions have also been omitted or significantly edited. Omissions usually have been indicated by three asterisks, i.e., * * * or by bracketed notations. In sum, the cases and materials included are not verbatim reproduction of the originals. In addition, note that the pertinent statutory material is included in the text, rather than in a separate statutory supplement. By placing the statutory language immediately adjacent in the text to the cases interpreting the statute, I mean to emphasize to students that it is important to read the statute itself before turning the cases.

V

Finally, a word about the author, so that both teachers and students may feel some confidence in my qualifications to design and teach this course. I worked as a lawyer in all three branches of the federal government. I began my legal career as a legislative assistant to a United States Senator, employed primarily to draft legislation, and next served as law clerk to a judge on the United States Court of Appeals for the Ninth Circuit. Most importantly for present purposes, my years as an appellate attorney with the Civil Division of the United States Department of Justice afforded me an inside look at the manner in which federal government litigation is initiated, directed, and settled, from the trial level in federal district court or the Court of Federal Claims through appeal in the courts of appeals to final review in the Supreme Court. In addition to briefing and arguing federal government appeals in ten of the thirteen federal circuits, I participated in making settlement decisions, in making recommendations to the Solicitor General's office on whether to pursue appeals from adverse district court rulings or to petition for Supreme Court review after unsuccessful appellate litigation, and in drafting Supreme Court documents at both the certiorari and merits stages. In that capacity, I litigated cases touching upon almost all of the general topics which comprise the substance of a course on "Litigation With the Federal Government." Over the past sixteen years in the legal academy, civil litigation with the federal government has been one of the primary focuses of my scholarly writing, as revealed by the probably too-frequent excerpts from and citations to my own works in this casebook.

GREGORY C. SISK
Orestes A. Brownson
Professor of Law
University of St. Thomas
School of Law

June, 2007

*

ACKNOWLEDGMENTS

I wish to express my thanks to many people who generously contributed time and expertise to this project, in either the first edition or the second edition (or both):

- Chief Judge Edward Damich and the judges of the United States Court of Federal Claims have honored me on multiple occasions with opportunities to participate in meetings and conferences with the judges and practitioners before the court, from which I have learned so very much and which have been of invaluable assistance to me in trying to stay abreast of developments related to that important judicial body.

- Judges Eric Bruggink and Francis Allegra of the Court of Federal Claims have used these materials in teaching courses on litigation with the federal government and provided thoughtful comments.

- Professor Michael Noone of the Catholic University School of Law has taught me to better appreciate the history of this field as an area of study and generously invited me to author the latest edition of the standard treatise in the field that he and Professor Urban Lester had carried forward so well for many years.

- Professor William Luneburg at the University of Pittsburgh School of Law who has now taught the course on several occasions has offered regular encouragement as well as posing thoughtful questions and insightful comments that have influenced my continuing thinking and research.

- Over the years, many people reviewed discrete portions of the materials related to their areas of expertise, including Professor Joshua Schwartz, Co-Director of the Government Procurement Law Program at George Washington University National Law Center; Professor Sandi Zellmer, University of Toledo College of Law; Lt. Commander Chris Donovan, Judge Advocate General Corps, General Litigation Division, Department of the Navy; C. Stanley Dees of McKenna & Cuneo in Washington, D.C.; and many former colleagues at the United States Department of Justice, Civil Division, Appellate Staff.

- I also appreciate the support of student research assistants at two law schools, including Robert Muenchrath, Drake University Law School Class of 1994, who assisted in formatting the original draft of the first edition of this casebook; Julie Bettenhausen, Krista Carlson, Hayley Hanson, and Bruce Stanfield of the Drake University Law School classes of 1998, 2000, 2000, and 2001, respectively, who assisted in updating and reviewing material and editing the final product for the first edition; and Nicholas Polasky, Gerald Fornwald, and Lael Veldhouse Robertson of the University of St. Thomas School of Law classes of 2006, 2005, and 2005 respectively, who provided cite-checking, proofreading, and editorial assistance on the treatise and thus which also served as the essential background for this second edition of the casebook.

Of course, any errors or weaknesses that remain in these materials are my responsibility alone and likely reflect my failure to follow the wise advice of reviewers and commentators.

Permissions have been granted to reproduce excerpts of the following works:

Griffin B. Bell, The Attorney General: The Federal Government's Chief Litigator or One Among Many, 46 Fordham L. Rev. 1049, 1057-1061 (1978). Copyright © 1978, Griffin B. Bell. Reprinted by permission of the author and the Fordham Law Review.

Kenneth Culp Davis, Sovereign Immunity Must Go, 22 Admin. L. Rev. 383, 383-385, 392-394, 401-402 (1970). Copyright © 1970, Administrative Law Section, American Bar Association. Reprinted by permission of the American Bar Association and the author.

Drew S. Days, III, The Solicitor General and the American Legal Ideal, 49 SMU L. Rev. 73, 76-78 (1995). Copyright © 1995, Southern Methodist University Law Review and Drew S. Days, III. Reprinted by permission of the Southern Methodist University Law Review and the author.

Charles Fried, Order & Law 14 (1991). Copyright © 1991, Charles Fried. Reprinted by permission of Charles Fried.

Lester S. Jayson & Robert C. Longstreth, Handling Federal Tort Claims § 2.01 (1999). Copyright © 1999, Matthew Bender & Co., Inc. Reprinted by permission of Matthew Bender & Co., Inc.

Harold J. Krent, Reconceptualizing Sovereign Immunity, 45 Vand. L. Rev. 1529, 1529-1533 (1992). Copyright © 1992, Vanderbilt Law Review, Vanderbilt University School of Law. Reprinted by permission of the Vanderbilt Law Review and the author.

Douglas Letter, Lawyering and Judging on Behalf of the United States: All I Ask for Is a Little Respect, 61 Geo. Wash. L. Rev. 1295, 1297-1300 (1993). Copyright © 1993, Douglas Letter. Reprinted by permission of the author and with the permission of The George Washington Law Review.

Susan M. Olson, Challenges To the Gatekeeper: The Debate Over Federal Litigating Authority, 68 Judicature 71, 72-73, 78-81 (1984). Copyright © 1984, American Judicature Society. Reprinted by permission of Judicature, the journal of the American Judicature Society and the author.

Theodore B. Olson, The Advocate as Friend: The Solicitor General's Stewardship Through the Example of Rex E. Lee, 2003 Brigham Young University Law Review 2, 11-13. Copyright © 2003, Brigham Young University Law Review and Theodore B. Olson. Reprinted by permission of the Brigham Young University Law Review and the author.

H. W. Perry, Jr., United States Attorneys—Whom Shall They Serve?, 61 Law & Contemp. Probs. 129, 139 (Winter 1998). Copyright © 1998, by Law and Contemporary Problems. Reprinted by permission of Law and Contemporary Problems and the author.

James E. Pfander, Governmental Accountability in Europe: A Comparative Assessment, 35 George Washington International Law Review 611, 611-619, 623-625, 649-650 (2003). Copyright © 2003, The George Washington International Law Review. Reprinted by permission of the George Washington International Law Review and the author.

Richard H. Seamon, The Provenance of the Federal Courts Improvement Act of 1982, 71 George Washington Law Review 543, 551-54 (2003). Copyright © 2003, by George Washington Law Review; Richard H. Seamon. Reprinted by permission of the George Washington Law Review and Richard H. Seamon.

Gregory C. Sisk, The Essentials of the Equal Access to Justice Act: Court Awards of Attorney's Fees for Unreasonable Government Conduct (Part One), 55 La. L. Rev. 217 (1994). Copyright © 1994, Gregory C. Sisk.

Gregory C. Sisk, Interim Attorney's Fees Awards Against the Federal Government, 68 N.C.L. Rev. 117, 120-123, 139-140, 142-145, 147-151 (1989). Copyright © 1989, North Carolina Law Review. The author reserved the right to reprint the article as part of any book of which he was an author.

Gregory C. Sisk, A Primer on Awards of Attorney's Fees Against the Federal Government, 25 Ariz. St. L.J. 733, 735-736, 756-762 (1993). Copyright © 1993, Gregory C. Sisk.

Gregory C. Sisk, The Tapestry Unravels: Statutory Waivers of Sovereign Immunity and Money Claims Against the United States, 71 George Washington Law Review 602, 606-11 (2003). Copyright © 2003, George Washington Law Review and Gregory C. Sisk. The author reserved the right to reprint the article as part of any book of which he was an author.

Gregory C. Sisk, The Trial Courts of the Federal Circuit: Diversity by Design, 13 Federal Circuit Bar Journal 241, 259-63 (2003). Copyright © 2003, Federal Circuit Bar Association and Gregory C. Sisk. The author reserved the right to reprint the article as part of any book of which he was an author.

Gregory C. Sisk, Tucker Act Appeals to the Federal Circuit, 36 Fed. Bar News & J. 41, 41-42, 45 (1989). Copyright © 1989, Federal Bar Association and Gregory C. Sisk. The author reserved the right to reprint the article as part of any book of which he was an author.

XiXin Wang, Suing the Sovereign Observed From the Chinese Perspective: The Idea and Practice of State Compensation in China, 35 George Washington International Law Review 681, 681-82, 684-686, 689 (2003). Copyright © 2003, George Washington International Law Review. Reprinted by permission of the George Washington International Law Review and the author.

Seth P. Waxman, Foreword: Does the Solicitor General Matter?, 53 Stanford Law Review 1115, 1117-18 (2001). Copyright © 2001, Stanford Law Review and Seth P. Waxman. Reprinted by permission of the Stanford Law Review and the author.

Stanley Weintraub, The Last Great Victory 294 (1995). Copyright © 1995, Stanley Weintraub. Reprinted by permission of the author.

Richard K. Willard, How to Settle Your Government Case, in 3 Department of Justice Manual § 4-3.200A, at 4-48 to 4-48.7 (Prentice-Hall, 1994). Copyright © 1994, Prentice Hall Law & Business, Assigned to Aspen Law &

Business, A Division of Aspen Publishers, Inc. Reprinted by permission of Aspen Law & Business and the author.

SUMMARY OF CONTENTS

*

TABLE OF CONTENTS

TABLE OF CASES

Principal cases are in bold type. Non-principal cases are in roman type. References are to Pages.

TABLE OF STATUTES

xlv

POPULAR NAME ACTS

————

*

TABLE OF BOOK AND JOURNAL CITATIONS

Principal sources are in bold type. Non-principal sources are in roman type. References are to Pages.

CASES AND MATERIALS

LITIGATION WITH THE FEDERAL GOVERNMENT

*

CHAPTER I

THE FEDERAL GOVERNMENT AS A CIVIL LITIGANT

SECTION A. THE FEDERAL GOVERNMENT IN THE COURTS

Because it is the quintessential repeat-player in federal litigation, and because its litigation strategy generally is coordinated by the United States Department of Justice across the entire range of government cases, the federal government exerts a powerful influence on the federal courts and the development of legal doctrine. As political scientist Christopher J.W. Zorn has observed, because of its ubiquitous presence in federal litigation, "more than any other entity, the federal government plays a central role in the development of law and policy in the United States courts." Christopher J.W. Zorn, U.S. Government Litigation Strategies in the Federal Appellate Courts, Ph.D. Dissertation, pages 1–3 (1997).

Both in quantity (the federal government being a party to about one-fifth of all the civil cases filed in the federal courts) and in quality (the substantial impact of many of these cases upon the real lives of people and to public policy), federal government litigation is exceptional in its importance:

For the first four calendar years of the new century, the Administrative Office of the United States Courts reports that the federal government was a plaintiff or defendant in 23.1 percent (2001), 20.7 percent (2002), 18.8 percent (2003), and 18.3 percent (2004) of civil cases commenced in the United States District Courts. In addition, in certain specialized federal courts, most particularly the United States Court of Federal Claims and the United States Court of Appeals for Veterans Claims, the federal government is a party to every case on the docket.

Moreover, "court cases involving the United States typically involve the most consequential issues for people's lives" (Zorn, *supra*, at 3)—through claims involving personal injury; civil rights; welfare; Social Security; health, safety, and environmental regulation; immigration; governmental expropriation of property; and contractual obligations. As David Schwartz and Sidney Jacoby, the pioneers in this field of law, wrote more than 40 years ago:

Those who deal with the Government can do so capably only with some knowledge of the available remedies both by and against the Government, and with some understanding of the possible untoward consequences if the parties fall out and require the intervention of courts to settle their differences. ... Moreover, litigation with the Government,

1

whether studied or practiced, soon leads to the realization that the degree to which a state provides that justice be done in the settlement of the civil and even the petty commercial disputes between citizen and government is one of the indicia of the ethical character of that government.

David Schwartz & Sidney Jacoby, Government Litigation Casebook (tentative casebook 1960).

 This category of litigation is distinctive in the special rules that govern and limit the liability of the sovereign United States. To fully appreciate these limitations, we of course must examine the statutory waivers of sovereign immunity that set the boundaries on the government's amenability to suit, the exploration of which occupies most of the substance of this casebook. However, we must begin by looking at the federal government as a civil litigator, that is, the government as an institutional actor before the courts. As will be seen, certain features about the federal government make it quite different in the way in which it handles civil litigation and in the procedures that apply to it. These unique characteristics in turn affect the means by which civil litigation involving the government proceeds and the manner in which the federal sovereign can be held to suit. Because these points apply generally to most government cases, we should have them well in mind before moving on to consider specific types of claims.

———

SECTION B.   THE ATTORNEY GENERAL AND THE DEPARTMENT OF JUSTICE

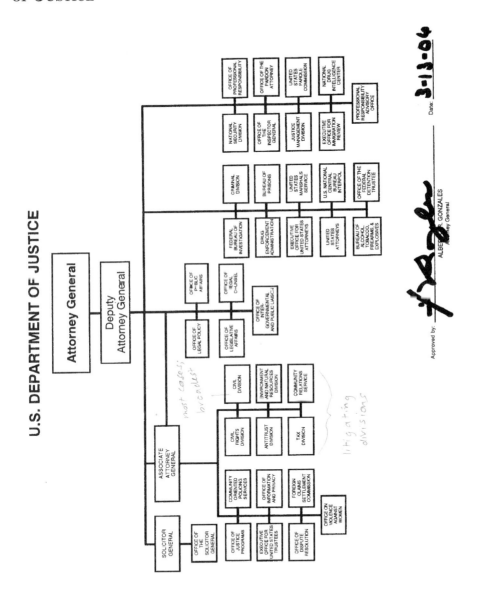

1.   THE ATTORNEY GENERAL

United States Attorneys' Manual

§ 4–1.100 (Responsibilities of the Attorney General Re Civil Litigation) (2007).

[handwritten margin note: JA 1789 statutory auth'ty]

The Office of the Attorney General was established by the Judiciary Act of 1789. Act of September 24, 1789, 1 Stat. 73. Section 35 of that Act vested the Attorney General (AG) with plenary authority to "prosecute and conduct all suits in the Supreme Court in which the United States shall be concerned" and to give advice and opinions upon questions of law when requested by the President or the heads of various Departments.

[handwritten margin note: 1870 – expanded statutory auth'ty]

The AG's statutory authority to conduct litigation to which the United States, its departments or agencies is a party was expanded and more fully developed by Congress in 1870 in the same legislation that provided for the creation of the Department of Justice. Act of June 22, 1870, 16 Stat. 162. Among other things, the Act forbade the Secretaries of the Executive Departments to employ other attorneys or outside counsel at government expense, and required them to

> call upon the Department of Justice ... and no counsel or attorney fees shall hereafter be allowed to any person ... besides the respective district attorneys ... for services in such capacity to the United States ... unless hereafter authorized by law, and then only on the certificate of the Attorney–General that such services could not be performed by the Attorney–General ... or the officers of the Department of Justice....

[handwritten margin note: 1870 – Purpose of Act]

The initial motivation for this legislation was the desire to centralize the conduct and supervision of all litigation in which the government was involved, as well as to eliminate the need for highly-paid outside counsel when government-trained attorneys could perform the same function. Other objectives of the legislation advanced in the congressional debates were to ensure the presentation of uniform positions with respect to the laws of the United States ("a unity of decision, a unity of jurisprudence in the executive law of the United States"), and to provide the AG with authority over lower court proceedings involving the United States so that litigation would be better handled on appeal, and before the Supreme Court. See Cong.Globe, 41st Cong., 2d Sess. 3035–39, 3065–66 (1870). *See generally* Bell, "The Attorney General: The Federal Government's Chief Lawyer and Chief Litigator, Or One Among Many?", 46 Fordham L.Rev. 1049 (1978).

[handwritten margin note: • uniform federal litig. policy • facilitate handling case on appeal]

The present statutory authority vesting plenary litigating authority with the Attorney General, including 28 U.S.C. §§ 516, 519 and 5 U.S.C. § 3106, parallels that found in the 1870 Act. Except as otherwise authorized by law, only attorneys of the Department of Justice under the supervision of the Attorney General may represent the United States or its agencies or officers in litigation. Counsel for other government agencies may not be heard in opposition. Nor, in the absence of statutes to the contrary, may any suit be brought on behalf of the United States except by the Attorney General or an attorney under his/her superintendence. *ICC v. Southern Railway Co.*, 543 F.2d 534 (5th Cir. 1976), reh. en banc denied, 551 F.2d 95 (5th Cir. 1977). The completeness of the Attorney General's authority is further illustrated by the fact that once a matter has been referred to the Department of Justice, the referring agency ceases to have control over it.

———

28 United States Code § 516

Except as otherwise authorized by law, the conduct of litigation in which the United States, an agency, or officer thereof is a party, or is interested, and securing evidence therefor, is reserved to officers of the Department of Justice, under the direction of the Attorney General.

———

28 United States Code § 519

Except as otherwise authorized by law, the Attorney General shall supervise all litigation to which the United States, an agency, or officer thereof is a party, and shall direct all United States attorneys, assistant United States attorneys, and special attorneys appointed under section 543 of this title in the discharge of their respective duties.

———

Mehle v. American Management Systems, Inc.

United States District Court for the District of Columbia.
172 F.Supp.2d 203 (D.D.C. 2001).

◼ ROBERTSON, DISTRICT JUDGE.

On July 17, 2001, the Federal Retirement Thrift Investment Board terminated its computer software development contract with American Management Systems for default. On the same day, Board executive director Roger W. Mehle brought this action against AMS for fraud, breach of contract, negligent misrepresentation, and unjust enrichment. The suit was not brought in the name of the contracting party, but in Mr. Mehle's name, in his capacity as executive director. AMS has moved to dismiss for want of subject matter jurisdiction. Because Mr. Mehle has not obtained Department of Justice approval to sue and is not authorized by statute to litigate independently, the motion must be granted.

Background

The Federal Retirement Thrift Investment Board operates the federal Thrift Savings Fund, which provides retirement savings programs similar to private-sector 401(k) plans for approximately five million federal civilian and military employees. The Board contracted with AMS in 1997 for the creation of a new recordkeeping system based on a commercial software program used by many 401(k) plans. The project was expected to cost $30 million and to be installed by May 1, 2000, but it ran into technical problems. When the Board cancelled the contract in July 2001, AMS had not yet delivered even a limited-functioning system and was estimating that another $57 million would be needed to complete the work.

Mr. Mehle filed this suit using private counsel and without seeking approval by the Attorney General. He asserts that AMS affirmatively misled the Board concerning the caliber of personnel that it would use in completing the contract and that it wrote about five times as much customized computer code as would be expected for a project of this size. Noting that AMS recently agreed to a $185 million post-trial settlement with the State of Mississippi after a jury found it liable for bad faith breach of contract and misrepresentation, Mr. Mehle claims that the Fund has been the victim of corrupt business practices.

Mr. Mehle invokes this Court's diversity jurisdiction based on his residence in the District of Columbia and AMS's citizenship in Delaware and Virginia. His attorney made it clear at oral argument that the reason Mr. Mehle wants to be in federal district court is to have a jury trial.

Analysis

The AMS motion to dismiss argues that the Contract Dispute Act gives the Court of Federal Claims exclusive jurisdiction over this case, that there is no diversity between the parties, and that Mr. Mehle has no authority to bring this suit. The Court of Federal Claims question is murky (and is, in any event, now before that court for decision in a contract claim brought by AMS against the Board). The diversity question is also vexing because the controlling authority on which Mr. Mehle's claim rests is an anomalous, 25–year-old decision that has been strongly criticized and may no longer be good law.[1] Without that questionable authority, there would be no diversity jurisdiction, because federal agencies are not considered "citizens of a state."

It is unnecessary to decide whether the Court of Federal Claims has exclusive jurisdiction or whether Mr. Mehle may properly invoke this Court's diversity jurisdiction, however, because it is clear that Mr. Mehle is not authorized to bring this action for his agency.[2]

---

1. *Trans–Bay Engineers & Builders, Inc. v. Hills,* 551 F.2d 370, 376 (D.C.Cir. 1976), held that the Secretary of Housing and Urban Development could be sued in diversity in her official capacity. The decision is criticized in *General Ry. Signal Co. v. Corcoran,* 921 F.2d 700, 703–05 (7th Cir.1991) as expanding the scope of diversity jurisdiction by allowing litigants to sue a federal official by name (or to bring suit in an official's name).

2. This argument has been advanced both by AMS and by the Department of Justice. DOJ has lodged two "notices" in this case, both suggesting that Mr. Mehle did not have authority to file suit. Because the Department has neither intervened nor sought *amicus* status, however, its arguments are not of record.

"Except as otherwise authorized by law, the conduct of litigation in which the United States, an agency, or officer thereof is a party, or is interested ... is reserved to officers of the Department of Justice, under the direction of the Attorney General." 28 U.S.C. § 516. Actions that are brought by government officials or agencies who are not authorized to represent the United States must be dismissed for lack of jurisdiction. Only explicit statutory language vesting independent litigation authority in another agency creates an exception to § 516.

Mr. Mehle cannot identify a statute explicitly authorizing him to sue or be sued or to act independently of the Attorney General. Instead, he relies on a long chain of inferences. First, based largely on statutory language stating that all moneys contributed by government employees and their employing agencies "are held in [the Thrift Savings Fund] in trust for such employee[s]," 5 U.S.C. § 8437(g), Mr. Mehle argues that the Fund is a private trust. Next, he argues that he must be the Fund's sole trustee, because he has management responsibilities and fiduciary duties. Next, he argues that, as trustee, he has an implied right under common law to bring litigation to protect fund assets. Finally, because the Attorney General is clearly assigned duties with regard to litigation against the Fund's fiduciaries, 5 U.S.C. § 8477(e)(4), Mr. Mehle invokes the principle of expressio unius est exclusio alterius to argue that the Attorney General's authority does not extend to this matter.

That reasoning does not stand up to close scrutiny. Even assuming that the Fund is a private trust, Mr. Mehle's claim to be the sole trustee is highly suspect. The United States itself may serve as a trustee, and Congress frequently designates boards of trustees in creating federal trust funds. If it is indeed necessary to identify the trustees of the Thrift Savings Fund, the members of the Federal Retirement Thrift Investment Board are much more likely candidates than Mr. Mehle. They are presidentially appointed and responsible for hiring and firing the executive director. They are responsible for setting the investment, management, and administration policies that the executive director must carry out. They are also fiduciaries, like the executive director. And, although Mr. Mehle has some responsibilities regarding asset management and disposal that the Board does not, his discretion over Fund assets is also quite limited by statute.

In any case, labeling the Thrift Savings Fund a trust and identifying a trustee or trustees does nothing to undercut the statutory, and plenary, grant of litigation authority to the Attorney General. Mr. Mehle's argument that 5 U.S.C. § 8477(e)(4) negates the Attorney General's authority except with respect to breaches of duty by Fund fiduciaries is not persuasive. If there is an exception to 28 U.S.C. § 516 in section 8477(e), it comports with the case law by explicitly giving litigation authority to the Secretary of Labor and creating a private cause of action for beneficiaries. 5 U.S.C. § 8477(e)(3). Subsection (e)(4) then spells out the Attorney General's responsibilities and authority in such cases. Thus, when Fund assets may have been jeopardized by a fiduciary's breach of duty, the Secretary of Labor is authorized to bring suit, but the Board and executive director are not. Even in such a situation, Department of Labor attorneys are subject to the Attorney General's direction and control. *Id.* § 8477(e)(4)(A).

An appropriate order accompanies this memorandum.

ORDER

Disp: AMS' M to dismiss for lack of SMJD granted: fed ct's can't hear suits brought by AM Fund officers purportedly on behalf of U.S. gov't, ~~onto AG's~~

For the reasons set forth in a memorandum issued contemporaneously herewith, the motion to dismiss of defendant American Management Systems, Inc. is granted.

———

AMS

Notes and Questions

Note who raises the objection to the commencement of the lawsuit in *Mehle v. American Management Systems, Inc.* (Although the Department of Justice lodged a "notice" that Mehle had no authority to pursue the litigation, the court concludes those arguments are not properly of record, so who else did object?) Throughout our study of litigation with the federal government, we frequently will encounter special doctrines and limitations that generally work to the disadvantage of those encountering the federal government in litigation. Here those limitations actually work to the benefit of a party sued by a federal government entity/official—even to the point of bringing about a dismissal.

Civ. Pro.

General Rule: exclusive & plenary authity to sue vested in AG

28 USC 516
28 USC 843X9) +(3)
5 USC 8477 (e)(4)

On the question of the validity of the lawsuit, the court begins with the general statutes granting litigation authority in federal government cases to the Attorney General. The question is whether the specific statutes governing litigation involving the Federal Retirement Thrift Investment Board and the associated Thrift Savings Trust create an exception to the general rule. Outline each of those statutes. What do these statutes say? Are there any exceptions to the Attorney General's plenary authority over litigation involving federal government entities? Do they apply here? And doesn't the Attorney General continue to hold the reins of power even in the case of such an exception?

———

Griffin B. Bell, The Attorney General: The Federal Government's Chief Litigator or One Among Many?

46 Fordham Law Review 1049, 1057–1059 (1978).*

The basic statutory scheme today is the same as in 1870: Except as otherwise authorized by Congress, the conduct of litigation in which the

* This article is reproduced with permission from *Fordham Law Review* and the author.

United States or an agency or officer thereof is a party, or is interested, is reserved to officers of the Department of Justice, under the direction of the Attorney General. The problem is the number of exceptions authorized by Congress. Professor John Davis has aptly characterized the situation as follows:

> a continuing effort by Attorneys General to centralize responsibility for all government litigation in Justice, a continuing effort by many agencies to escape from that control with respect to civil litigation, and a practice by Congress of accepting the positions of the Attorneys General in principle and then cutting them to pieces by exceptions.[30]

Prosecution of all criminal violations is controlled by the Department of Justice, and I do not understand that authority to be seriously challenged; but there is no consistent or rational statutory scheme applicable to agencies in civil litigation. The curious patchwork of civil litigation authority cannot be explained in terms of a congressional conception of the role of the Justice Department. Grants of separate litigating authority seem to have been enacted simply because of loud and persistent complaints from the agencies seeking such authority. Others seem designed to increase the control of particular congressional committees or subcommittees over particular agencies or programs. Neither a congressional body which works closely with an agency, nor the agency itself, wants the Justice Department making decisions counter to its desires. Fiefdoms have been created, and the Justice Department's efforts to ensure uniformity in government litigating postures can constitute a real threat to them. * * *

I recognize that Congress intended some regulatory agencies and government corporations to be independent of the executive branch and the President. That independence has extended to independence from the Department of Justice in legal matters, including litigation. The price of such independence is high, as it can and sometimes does result in two sets of government lawyers opposing each other at taxpayer expense. More importantly, it requires the judicial branch to decide interagency disputes that might be resolved more easily and better through the mediation of the Department of Justice.

I do not favor the independence of these regulatory agencies and government corporations in legal matters. I think it is unseemly for two government agencies to sue each other. It requires the judicial branch to decide questions of government policy, a role never envisioned by our country's Founding Fathers. It is time-consuming and expensive. I believe it would be possible to preserve the independence of these bodies even if they were represented by the Justice Department. Such a system would be more efficient and would reduce the amount of judicial intrusion into intragovernmental disputes. The Department of Justice can exercise a

---

30. Davis, Department of Justice Control of Agency Litigation 17 (Report to the U.S. Administrative Conference Aug. 14, 1975).

Bell's solution :

review and supervisory function in an effort to bring uniformity to government legal positions and still recognize the independence of the regulatory agencies' enforcement efforts.

My predecessors as Attorney General have shared my view that the Justice Department should represent the regulatory agencies. To date, however, Congress has been willing to pay the price of independent litigating authority for those agencies.

If separation persists, at least have rational system . . .

If separate litigating authority is going to continue for independent regulatory agencies and government corporations, then we should at least devise a rational system for the conduct of such litigation. One agency's case often will affect other regulatory agencies or executive branch departments. At the least, an agency should be required to alert the Justice Department in such cases so that the views of the executive branch could also be presented to the court. If a case could affect the entire government, such as an employment discrimination claim or a Freedom of Information Act complaint, the Justice Department should have control of the litigation rather than the single agency which is party to the case. The position taken by a single agency on a question of general concern should not bind the entire federal government.

It is my view that the Justice Department should represent all executive branch departments and agencies. The Department must, of course, work closely with its clients in a cooperative effort, recognizing the peculiar expertise and abilities of agency lawyers and delegating authority to agency lawyers in certain circumstances, but always retaining final control in the Justice Department.

———

Notes and Questions

Writing as the then-Attorney General, Griffin Bell not surprisingly advocated control of civil litigation within his Department of Justice. Attorneys General have consistently taken this position. From an outside perspective, do you believe he persuasively makes the case for that position?

In the essay excerpted below, Professor Susan Olson describes the continuing contest between the Department of Justice and the various agencies and departments over litigation authority and outlines the justifications offered by each side of that debate for their respective positions.

———

Susan M. Olson, Challenges to the Gatekeeper: The Debate Over Federal Litigating Authority

68 Judicature 71, 72–73, 78–81 (1984).*

The Role of the Justice Department

In private civil litigation the role of the lawyer as a gatekeeper between the client and the courts has been frequently noted. For federal government litigation, the U.S. Department of Justice plays an analogous role. Federal law makes the Justice Department the gatekeeper to the courts for federal officials and agencies. * * *

For civil litigation concerning the regulatory programs of administrative agencies, the Civil Division of the Justice Department usually provides the representation for the federal agency. Some district court litigation is delegated to local United States attorneys, but this is not common with significant regulatory cases.[7] A few agencies and departments, such as the Environmental Protection Agency and the Department of the Interior, work more with the Land and Natural Resources Division [now the Environment and Natural Resources Division] than with the Civil Division. see p. 3

The agencies have lawyers of their own, of course, who work in what is most often called the general counsel's office. These lawyers draft regulations, advise the nonlawyer program staff on how their programs affect and are affected by the law, and, in some agencies, represent the agency before administrative tribunals. When an agency is "contemplating" litigation, however, it becomes a client of the Justice Department.

The agency lawyers are supposed to cooperate with the Justice Department lawyers in preparing a case by assembling background information, helping the Justice lawyer learn the law specific to the case, and, sometimes, doing initial drafts of briefs or other legal papers. The Justice lawyers, for their part, are expected to "take care not to interfere with the policy prerogatives of our agency clients," in the words of recent Attorney General Griffin Bell.[9] When conflicts arise, however, about whether to bring a case or how to argue one, the dispute is appealed to higher officials in the Justice Department and, ultimately, the Attorney General gets the final word. At this point the situation deviates from the private lawyer-client relationship because the agency is not free to fire the lawyer and hire another one who will present its views the way it wants them presented. The agencies are thus "captive clients." Bell's speech continued: "An agency's views should be presented to a court unless they are inconsistent with overall governmental interests, or cannot fairly be argued."

---

* This article is reprinted by permission of *Judicature*, the Journal of the American Judicature Society, and the author.

7. In contrast, most criminal prosecutions are delegated to local U.S. attorneys, where a range of conflicts with the referring agencies, much like those discussed here, can occur. This article will focus on civil litigation at the national level.

9. Bell, *The Attorney General: The Federal Government's Chief Lawyer and Chief Litigator, or One Among Many?* 46 Fordham L. Rev. 1049, 1061 (1978).

This picture of how federal litigation is conducted is significantly modified, however, by the phrase in Sec. 516 "except as otherwise authorized." This phrase alludes to a number of federal departments, agencies, boards, and commissions that have statutory authorization to conduct at least some of their own civil litigation. As of 1982 this included some 35 different federal entities.[12] Those which have the most extensive grants of independent authority tend to be specialized commissions and corporations or independent regulatory agencies, but some executive branch agencies have also been granted degrees of litigation autonomy. * * *

Justice Department Arguments

In a 1980 speech sponsored by the Federal Bar Association, Associate Attorney General Robert Ford outlined the Department of Justice's arguments in favor of centralized litigating authority. He stressed that centralization maximizes five distinct but interrelated values: economy and efficiency, uniformity, rational priority setting, expertise, and objectivity. These same major points were consistently reiterated in interviews with all persons favoring Justice Department control.

First, the Justice Department sees the development of litigation expertise in more than one agency as unnecessary duplication. This is particularly true for legal issues common to all agencies, such as personnel matters, contract disputes, or Freedom of Information Act suits. Lawyers in any given agency rarely handle enough of these cases to become as familiar with them as the Justice Department lawyers, who do similar cases from many agencies.

Secondly, the argument goes, the very existence of a Department of Justice indicates the intent to ensure the uniformity of legal positions argued in court by the federal government. That this was one of the major motivations of Congress in establishing the department in 1870 is evident from the report of the debate over the new agency:

12. Advisory Council on Historic Preservation, Department of Agriculture, Commodity Futures Trading Commission, Comptroller of the Currency, Comptroller General, Consumer Product Safety Commission, Department of Defense, Environmental Protection Agency, Equal Employment Opportunity Commission, Export–Import Bank, Federal Communications Commission, Federal Deposit Insurance Corporation, Federal Election Commission, Federal Home Loan Bank Board, Federal Labor Relations Authority, Federal Maritime Commission, Federal Energy Regulatory Commission, Federal Reserve System, Federal Trade Commission, Department of Health and Human Services, United States International Trade Commission, Interstate Commerce Commission, Department of Labor, Merit System Protection Board, National Credit Union Administration, National Labor Relations Board, Nuclear Regulatory Commission, Pension Benefit Guaranty Corporation, Securities and Exchange Commission, Securities Investor Protection Corporation, Department of State (Overseas Private Investment Corporation), Student Loan Marketing Association, H.S. Synthetic Fuels Corporation, Tennessee Valley Authority [The language of its statutory authorization provides notably less specific authorization to litigate independently than the statutes governing other agencies, but in light of TVA's corporate status, the Justice Department has traditionally not challenged its representing itself.], Department of Transportation, Department of the Treasury.

[W]e have found that there has been a most unfortunate result from this separation of law powers. We find one interpretation of the laws of the United States in one Department and another interpretation in another Department.... It is for the purpose of having a unity of decision, a unity of jurisprudence ... in the executive law of the United States, that this bill proposes that all the law officers therein provided for shall be subordinate to one head.[43]

Congress historical vision for DOJ

Advocates of centralized authority today repeatedly invoke the theme that the federal government ought to speak with one voice. For one thing, it is claimed to be better for the average citizen to know what to expect from the government than to face the possibility that two different federal agencies might take him or her to court and demand inconsistent things. Furthermore, the argument goes, the courts, too, expect a uniform policy position from the government. They do not like to find government agencies arguing different positions on the same point of law. This is especially important because many cases involve issues of government-wide significance.

Another aspect of the uniformity argument is that uniformity is necessary for political accountability. In the words of a former Justice Department official, the Justice Department is where the President's policy and the courts "interface." Centralizing litigating authority improves the public's ability to know whom to praise or blame for the positions taken. This argument is fully applicable only to executive branch agencies because the independent regulatory agencies were created in part specifically to ensure their independence from presidential control.

Political Acctability

The third value which centralized litigation arguably supports—setting litigation priorities—has both a quantitative and a qualitative aspect. Some Justice Department lawyers feel that the responsibility to protect the courts from being overloaded with cases extends not only to the Supreme Court, but also to lower courts. * * *

Rational Priority Setting

Presumably the quantitative screening is based on qualitative criteria. The Justice Department believes that it can best determine which issues are the most important among the government's various interests that could be litigated. It sees itself as screening cases both for their substantive importance and for their legal soundness.

DOJ as smartest priority setter

The Justice Department's fourth argument emphasizes its greater expertise—expertise in the specialized skill of litigation. Only a fulltime litigator, they argue, appears in court frequently enough to become familiar with the proclivities of different judges. A litigator can tailor arguments to be the most persuasive both because he or she knows the personal idiosyncrasies of individual judges, but also because a lawyer who is a generalist, and not wrapped up in the details of a program, knows best how to translate that program for a generalist judge.

Expertise

43. Cong. Globe, 41st Cong., 2d Sess. 3036 (1870).

Broad expertise under one roof

Furthermore, litigators must be familiar with legal developments in all areas of law because judges are likely to use points from quite different substantive areas. The Justice Department is at a great advantage in having the resources of experienced litigators in many areas under one roof. Also, by litigating similar cases that come up in many agencies, Justice Department lawyers become substantive experts in issues of government-wide relevance, such as personnel problems, contract disputes, and tort claims.

Objectivity

By far the most frequent argument made in favor of control of litigation by the Justice Department, but also the most intangible one, was the department's greater objectivity. Again and again the claim was made that the Justice Department could and would better represent the "public interest" or the "broader governmental interest" beyond one case or one program.

Best decides which cases to bring

The value of objectivity arises in arguing a case, as well as deciding which to bring. The ability to translate the details of an arcane program for a generalist judge is one such example. Good litigation is also claimed to require a lawyer with enough distance from a program, with a sufficiently "jaundiced eye," to take a novel approach to it.

DOJ: Agency lawyers have blinders, narrow perspective, fiefdoms...

can't appreciate uniformity...

Not only does the Department of Justice consider uniformity, priority setting, expertise, and objectivity to be its strong points, but it also considers these same values to be weakly maintained in the agencies. Justice Department lawyers tend to see agency lawyers as dominated by "parochial interest." They are immersed in the programs of their agencies to the exclusion of government-wide interests and thus have a low appreciation for the need for uniformity in legal positions across agencies.

DOJ: Agency lawyers don't know how to be selective,

objective...

Accompanying this perception is the belief that agency lawyers are unable to say "no" to their nonlawyer program managers even when the program managers want them to take legally unwise actions. At worst, in Justice Department eyes, this may lead to the lawyers' being more accountable to political forces outside the agency than they are to the President's policies, which they are supposed to be implementing. Concern was expressed about agencies being "captured" by the interests they are supposedly regulating or having to "spill their guts" to Congress to protect their budgets. At the very least, this lack of objectivity makes them unable to set priorities and distinguish more important from less important cases.

Finally, Justice Department lawyers believe that many agency lawyers lack even minimal litigation skills. General counsels are political appointees, and some have never litigated. While they may be experts in the substantive area of law, their experiences are too narrow, and they may make poor arguments because they are not aware of the broader trends in legal development.

Agency Arguments

Needless to say, the agencies see the world (and especially the Department of Justice) very differently. The following discussion represents typical agency responses to the Justice Department's views of economy and efficiency, expertise, objectivity, inappropriate political influences, and uniformity.

Agencies also emphasize the need for economy and efficiency, but they see unnecessary duplication in having to educate Justice Department lawyers to litigate the cases agency counsel are already familiar with. Secondly, the agencies also recognize the need for expertise, but they mean substantive knowledge of their programs' regulatory law. Especially when the majority of litigation over regulatory programs is defensive (as it certainly is for most agencies for which the Civil Division litigates), the quality of defense raised is more important than the ability to choose which cases to bring. Furthermore, as one general counsel claimed, administrative law has changed and the days of the old technical defenses that the Justice Department knew so well (i.e., mootness, exhaustion, etc.) are dead; most cases now are argued on the merits. Justice Department lawyers, who have only hastily learned the law of the program they are defending, are unable to answer judges' questions and end up presenting a weaker case than the private legal specialists arguing for the other side.

Some agency critics go further and attack the Department of Justice on its own ground. Some do not believe that litigation is really such a unique skill that it cannot be learned easily enough for any substantive specialist to become a litigator. Except for jury trials, the argument goes, trial court work is not that different from practice before administrative tribunals, which many agency lawyers do routinely. In fact, Justice Department lawyers know much less about administrative practice than agency lawyers do, and many of their cases going to court are reviews of decisions made in the administrative process.

Furthermore, some argue that because of its hiring practices the Department of Justice is not as strong in litigation as it claims it is. The Department tends to hire young lawyers straight out of law school, and many of them move on before they have acquired that much experience. Complaints of inexperienced and arrogant young lawyers coming from the Justice Department and trying to tell old hands in agency counsels' or United States Attorneys' offices what to do are common.

A few agencies can claim expertise of their own on the same grounds as the Justice Department. For example, the office of the Solicitor of Labor has had an extensive trial and appellate practice since the 1930s. Noting its longstanding degree of independence and authority, the Solicitor of Labor's office tends to agree with the Justice Department's view of the need for objectivity, but believes that it possesses the appropriate lawyerly detachment from program managers.

Some agencies interpret the Justice Department's claim of greater objectivity as a lack of vigor in enforcement. The Department leaves itself vulnerable to this criticism with comments it has made about buffering citizens from overzealous agency officials. The agencies charge that it is not the Department's proper role to selectively enforce statutes. While the Justice Department may believe it is a matter of simple priority setting to

. The insignificant "little guy" is no statutory exception

. DOJ "priorities"

let the "little guy" go in the interest of pursuing the big offender, one agency lawyer commented that if an offender was too minor to be concerned about, then Congress should rewrite the statute and exempt persons of that sort.

Occasionally more serious charges about Justice Department decisions not to pursue violations are made. A Congressional staff aide critical of the Department's proportion of settlements to tried cases referred to the Justice lawyers as "white knuckle flyers," meaning that they are so concerned about their conviction rates that they would delay inordinately in hopes of a settlement when they ought to proceed to trial. Another person mentioned a problem with having to work through U.S. attorneys in district court—that their priorities are often more attuned to local political considerations than to the merits of cases or the demands of a program.

Separation of functions = less (practical) enforcement

Regardless of alleged shortcomings of the Justice Department's will to enforce vigorously, one agency lawyer believes that less enforcement will occur simply as a result of separating the functions of preparing cases and taking them to court. A former EPA lawyer talked about the terrible inefficiency of the "inverted U," by which local EPA officials must refer cases to their national office, which refers them to the Lands Division of the Justice Department, which then refers them back to the local U.S. attorney.

. Variety of cases shoved off onto the Civil Div., which lacks expertise, Funds, & good management

Complaints of long delays after referring cases to the Justice Department are common. All parties will acknowledge that this is to some extent due to a shortage of resources. The Civil Division, which handles the litigation for most executive branch agencies, is in one person's words, the "stepchild" of the Justice Department. It lacks prestige and the interest of Congress, and thus the resources that go to the Antitrust, the Criminal, or the Civil Rights Divisions. There is, however, some evidence of management problems other than a lack of resources. Respondents from a client agency, a Congressional office, and the Carter administration project which studied the federal legal representation system all independently mentioned poor case management as a perennial Justice Department problem, even when they were complimentary about the legal skills of Justice lawyers. In the words of one: "They just get overloaded and drop the ball without regard to priorities." *Example?.*

Note

For other recent scholarly commentary on the centralization of litigation authority under the Attorney General, see Nicholas S. Zeppos, *Resources Shortfalls in Government Litigation: Externalizing Costs and Searching for Subsidies*, 61 Law & Contemp. Probs. 171 (Spring 1998) (arguing that the "near monopoly DOJ maintains over litigation" is an effective use of limited government litigation resources because the Department of Justice, through screening of all government cases, is better able to create goodwill and credibility with the courts than would the multitude of agencies); Neal Devins & Michael Herz, *The Battle That Never Was: Congress, the White House, and Agency Litigation Authority,* 61 Law & Contemp. Probs. 205 (Winter 1998) (observing that centralization of litigation control in the Department of Justice enhances White House control over legal policymaking and thus has been of intense concern to presidential administrations); Neal Devins, *Unitariness and Independence: Solicitor General Control of Independent Agency Litigation,* 82 Cal. L. Rev. 255, 263–73 (1994) (stating that, despite vigorous and somewhat successful efforts by recent presidential administration to centralize litigating authority, numerous legislative "exceptions to Department of Justice control [have] severely eaten into the Attorney General's role as chief litigator for the United States"); Neal Devins & Michael Herz, *The Uneasy Case for Department of Justice Control of Federal Litigation,* 5 U. Pa. J. Const. L. 558, 558, 574, 603–606 (2003) (arguing that the case for Department of Justice control of litigation is "not nearly as compelling as generally assumed," and advocating "a modest reconfiguration of lawyering tasks" in which cases arising from an agency's regulatory program would be handled by agency attorneys while Department of Justice lawyers would handle other lawsuits raising issues that arise throughout the government or that involve constitutional challenges).

proposal

The centralization of litigation authority in the Department of Justice is reflected in the allocation of attorney resources within the federal government. According to the Office of Personnel Management, in March, 2002, there were 8,949 general schedule attorneys employed by the Department of Justice. This is more than three times the number of attorneys at the Department of the Treasury (2,514), which is second on the list. *See Where the Government Jobs Are,* Legal Times, at 13, July 29, 2002.

Allocation of Resources

———

Structure;
Arguments;

2.   THE CIVIL DIVISION

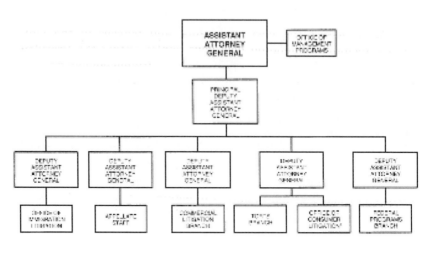

U.S. Department of Justice, Organization, Mission and Functions Manual—Civil Division (2006)

1868

In 1868, Congress gave the Attorney General the responsibility of representing the United States in all cases brought before the Court of Claims for any contract, agreement, or transaction with the executive departments, bureaus, or offices of executive departments. After the creation of the Department of Justice in 1870, a unit evolved within it that became known as the division for the defense of claims against the United States or the Court of Claims Division.

1870

1933 - consolidation

1953 - "Claims" Div.

what it litigates

The Attorney General created a new Claims Division in 1933 that consolidated responsibility for most of the litigating areas that comprise the present day Civil Division. In 1953, Attorney General Herbert Brownell, Jr., changed the name of the Claims Division to the Civil Division and broadened its responsibilities to include the litigation of the disbanded Customs Division.

In 1983, the Civil Division received additional responsibility for immigration and consumer protection litigation. With respect to its responsibility for consumer protection, the Civil Division litigates both criminal and civil actions under a number of federal statutes that are set out in 28 C.F.R. § 0.45(j). In 1986, Congress enacted the National Childhood Vaccine Injury Act, and in 1990, it enacted the Radiation Exposure Compensation Act. The Attorney General delegated implementation of these programs to the Civil Division.

more examples of what it litigates

The Civil Division represents the United States in any civil or criminal matter within its scope of responsibility—protecting the United States

what is that?

Treasury, ensuring that the federal government speaks with one voice in its view of the law, preserving the intent of Congress, and advancing the credibility of the government before the courts.

The major functions of the Division are to:

- Defend or assert the laws, programs, and policies of the United States, including defending new laws implementing the President's domestic and foreign agenda against constitutional challenges.

- Recover monies owed to the United States and victims as the result of fraud, loan default, bankruptcy, injury, damage to federal property, violation of consumer laws, or unsatisfied judgments.

- Defend the interests of the U.S. Treasury, prevailing against unwarranted monetary claims, while resolving fairly those claims with merit.

- Fight terrorism through litigation to detain and remove alien terrorists; defend immigration laws and policies, including determinations to expel criminal aliens.

- Enforce consumer protection laws and defend agency policies affecting public health and safety.

- Defend the government and its officers and employees in lawsuits seeking damages from the U.S. Treasury or from individuals personally.

- Implement compensation programs, such as the Childhood Vaccine and Radiation Exposure programs; support viable alternatives to litigation when appropriate.

- Represent the United States in foreign courts through foreign counsel supervised and instructed by attorney staff in Washington and London.

- Represent the interests of the United States in civil and criminal litigation in foreign courts.

[The matters assigned to the Civil Division are set out in 28 C.F.R. § 0.45.]

28 C.F.R. § .45

Note

As illustrated by the organizational chart included near the beginning of this Chapter, the Department of Justice includes a plethora of divisions and subordinate organizations, ranging from the Federal Bureau of Investigation and the Bureau of Prisons to the Office of Information and Privacy and the Office of Legislative Affairs. As this is a course on litigation, and "civil" litigation to be specific, our primary focus is upon the "litigating divisions" of the Department and, most particularly, upon the Civil Divi-

The 6 litigating divisions

sion.* The litigating divisions of the Department are the Antitrust Division, the Civil Division, the Civil Rights Division, the Criminal Division, the Environment and Natural Resources Division, and the Tax Division. Of these, the Civil Division has supervisory authority over the largest and most diverse categories of litigation matters. The organizational chart and description of the Civil Division set out above outlines the diversity of its mission. As a general rule, the Civil Division represents the government on any matter that does not fall into the specialized agenda of one of the other litigating divisions.

For purposes of this course, we generally will leave antitrust and tax issues to one side, assuming that they are better covered in courses devoted to those subjects, along with criminal matters which are outside the scope of this course altogether. The Civil Rights Division enforces civil rights claims against non-federal government actors, while civil rights claims against the federal government—such as employment discrimination claims by federal employees or claims alleging deprivation of constitutional rights by federal officers—are defended by the Civil Division. From time to time, we will consider matters that would be handled by the Environment and Natural Resources Division. The topic of environmental law itself, as to which that division generally acts to enforce the environmental statutes against private parties or state and local governments, will arise only occasionally in this course and will not be a focus of study, on the assumption that an understanding of environmental law demands a separate course. However, the Environment and Natural Resources Division is also responsible for cases involving federal lands (indeed, until the George H.W. Bush Administration, this division was known as the Lands and Natural Resources Division), which will be a subject of our attention.

Our focus is on Civ. Div.

Accordingly, the element of the Department of Justice that will be at the center of our study is the Civil Division. The vast majority of the cases that we will study fall within its jurisdiction. Thus, as you read a case involving the Federal Tort Claims Act (see Chapter III.A), the Freedom of Information Act (see Chapter III.C), federal civilian or military employment claims (see Chapter IV.A.2), or contract claims against the federal government (see Chapter IV.A.4), a Civil Division attorney or an attorney acting under the authority and supervision of the Civil Division will have advocated the government's position before the court.

As Professor H. W. Perry, Jr. describes it in the excerpt from his essay that is set out in the next subsection of this casebook, "the Civil Division is the most highly centralized and hierarchical Division in Justice." H. W.

---

e.g.

* Although our primary focus is upon the "litigating divisions," the non-litigating divisions of the Department of Justice significantly influence the positions taken by the government in litigation as well. Among these, the Office of Legal Counsel perhaps is most influential, as it provides formal and informal opinions on legal issues of general concern to the Executive Branch, which are authoritative sources for Department attorneys encountering those legal issues in litigation. In cases of political sensitivity or where members of Congress have expressed concern, the Office of Legislative Affairs may become involved either as an intermediary or to participate in efforts to resolve a problem by legislative rather than judicial means.

Perry, *United States Attorneys—Whom Shall They Serve?*, 61 Law & Contemp. Probs. 129, 139 (Winter 1998). By this, he means that cases which fall within the mission of the Civil Division are most likely either to be directly handled by Civil Division attorneys from "Main Justice" in Washington, D.C. or to be closely supervised by the Division's directors. The Civil Division traditionally has kept a tighter leash on government attorneys handling civil cases, even if those attorneys are located in the various United States Attorneys offices around the country. That is not the tradition and practice with respect to other areas of the law, most notably criminal prosecution, where the United States Attorneys operate with a high degree of autonomy. As you read the materials below on the United States Attorney, keep in mind that local autonomy is more closely cabined in the context of civil cases, although even then, the Civil Division strives to maintain a balance between asserting its superior authority and respecting the important position and role of the United States Attorney.

3. THE UNITED STATES ATTORNEY

United States Attorneys' Manual

§ 3–2.100 (United States Attorneys) (2007).

The United States Attorney serves as the chief law enforcement officer in each judicial district and is responsible for coordinating multiple agency investigations within that district.

There are currently 93 United States Attorneys stationed throughout the United States, Puerto Rico, Guam and the Northern Marianas. One United States Attorney is assigned to each judicial district with the exception of Guam and the Northern Marianas, where a single United States Attorney serves in both districts.

3–2.110 **History**

The Office of the United States Attorney was created by the Judiciary Act of 1789 which provided for the appointment "in each district of a meet person learned in the law to act as attorney for the United States ... whose duty it shall be to prosecute in each district all delinquents for crimes and offenses, recognizable under the authority of the United States, and all civil actions in which the United States shall be concerned." 1 Stat. 92. Initially, United States Attorneys were not supervised by the Attorney General but Congress, in the Act of August 2, 1861, (Ch. 37, 12 Stat. 185) charged the Attorney General with the "general superintendence and direction duties...." While the precise nature of the superintendence and direction was not defined, the Department of Justice Act of June 22, 1870 (Ch. 150, 16 Stat. 164) and the Act of June 30, 1906 (Ch. 39, 35, 34 Stat. 816) clearly established the power of the Attorney General to supervise criminal and civil proceedings in any district. Today, as in 1789, the United

· J. Act 1789

· Act of 1861

· DOJ Act of 1870
  "   of 1906

States Attorney retains, among other responsibilities, the duty to "prosecute for all offenses against the United States." See 28 U.S.C. Sec. 547(1). This duty is to be discharged under the supervision of the Attorney General. See 28 U.S.C. Sec. 519.

3–2.120 **Appointment**

United States Attorneys are appointed by the President with the advice and consent of the Senate for a four-year term. See 28 U.S.C. Sec. 541. Upon expiration of this term, the United States Attorney continues to perform the duties of the office until a successor is confirmed. United States Attorneys are subject to removal at the will of the President.

3–2.130 **Residence**

All United States Attorneys must reside in the district of their appointment except that in the District of Columbia and the Southern and Eastern Districts of New York, they may reside within 20 miles of their district. These provisions do not apply to a United States Attorney appointed for the Northern Mariana Islands who at the same time is serving in the same capacity in another district. See 28 U.S.C. Sec. 545.

3–2.140 **Authority**

Although the Attorney General has supervision over all litigation to which the United States or any agency thereof is a party, and has direction of all United States Attorneys, and their assistants, in the discharge of their respective duties (28 U.S.C. Secs. 514, 515, 519), each United States Attorney, within his/her district, has the responsibility and authority to: (a) prosecute for all offenses against the United States; (b) prosecute or defend, for the government, all civil actions, suits, or proceedings in which the United States is concerned; (c) appear on behalf of the defendants in all civil actions, suits or proceedings pending in the district against collectors, or other officers of the revenue or customs for any act done by them or for the recovery of any money exacted by or paid to such officers, and by them paid into the Treasury; (d) institute and prosecute proceedings for the collection of fines, penalties, and forfeitures incurred for violation of any revenue law unless satisfied upon investigation that justice does not require such proceedings; (e) make such reports as the Attorney General shall direct. See 28 U.S.C. Sec. 547.

By virtue of this grant of statutory authority and the practical realities of representing the United States throughout the country, United States Attorneys conduct most of the trial work in which the United States is a party. They are the principal federal law enforcement officers in their judicial districts. In the exercise of their prosecutorial discretion, United States Attorneys construe and implement the policy of the Department of Justice. Their professional abilities and the need for their impartiality in administering justice directly affect the public's perception of federal law enforcement.

H. W. Perry, Jr., United States Attorneys—Whom Shall They Serve?

61 Law and Contemporary Problems 129, 135–36, 137–40 (Winter 1998).

The Department of Justice could not begin to handle effectively the legal work of the United States from Washington. Much of the work done by the Department of Justice is done by U.S. Attorneys. Operating at a local level is not simply a logistics issue, however. As any lawyer knows, one can usually be more effective when one understands, and is seen as a part of, the local legal culture. U.S. Attorneys have and develop local expertise. Principal/agent theory posits that by delegating authority to agents who have more time or expertise, principals accomplish their goals more fully. * * *

Technically, the Attorney General sets the priorities for the Department. The official reports by U.S. Attorneys inevitably wax eloquent about how they are fulfilling the administration's priorities, but a close examination of the activity of individual districts shows that there is substantial variance in local priorities because of the discretion that lies with each individual local U.S. Attorney. Drug enforcement may be the priority of the Attorney General, but if civil rights enforcement is the U.S. Attorney's priority, there is little that can be done. There are potentially huge incentives to depart from the administration's agenda. This headquarters/field disparity phenomenon is not unique to the Justice Department, but the ability to control it may be. As presidential appointees, the Attorney General cannot fire the U.S. Attorneys, and for a President to do so over a disagreement over priorities is unlikely.

The power of U.S. Attorneys is far greater than an organizational chart would imply. While Justice Department organizational charts are careful not to spell out hierarchy too clearly, one might conclude from looking at manuals and procedures that U.S. Attorneys are near the bottom. But that does not begin to describe reality. Granted, many of the decisions of U.S. Attorneys require approval from "Main Justice," at least in theory. For example, civil settlements over a certain dollar amount require Main Justice approval. Often the person who actually does the approving is a civil servant, even if the signature of a higher official is required, so there are several layers of Justice Department officials "under" the Attorney General and "over" the U.S. Attorney. But few presidential appointees see themselves as subservient to civil servants, no matter what organizational charts or standard operating procedures may dictate. Some U.S. Attorneys even question where they fit in the hierarchy *vis-à-vis* other presidential appointees at Main Justice. Many U.S. Attorneys see themselves as really subordinate only to the Attorney General, and even that relationship is complex. It is not simply an issue of how U.S. Attorneys see themselves; there is a political reality that adds to their power. U.S. Attorneys are presidential appointees plus: Not only is a U.S. Attorney a presidential appointee, but his or her prime sponsor is usually a U.S. Senator. There-

[Handwritten margin note: The misleading hierarchical organizational chart -- Reasons why, practically speaking, US Atty's aren't really "at the bottom"]

fore, a U.S. Attorney's political strength at times can cause headaches for the Attorney General—not to mention the Deputy, Associate, or Assistant who tries to rein him or her in. This is not to say that all or even many U.S. Attorneys are power-hungry, or rampant questioners of authority structures, or that they are frequently out of sync with Main Justice. It does suggest that looking at an organizational chart of the Justice Department or reading the *U.S. Attorneys Manual*, with all of its requirements for coordination and approval by Main Justice, will do little to help one understand the true power of U.S. Attorneys. * * *

according to the Manual, Civ. Div. holds the power...

In short, it is difficult to know exactly where power lies. For example, the *Attorney Deskbook* for the Civil Division in the Bush Administration states quite emphatically and tersely who is the boss:

> Upon receipt of a new matter, the Director of each branch or his/her designee will make the initial decision on whether the case should be personally handled within the Civil Division, jointly handled with the United States Attorney for the district where the case is or will be brought, sent to the U.S. Attorney with the Division retaining supervisory jurisdiction, or delegated to the U.S. Attorney.... Civil Division attorneys work closely with the U.S. Attorneys' Offices. As previously noted, the Division determines who will bear primary responsibility for defending the Government in the litigation.

contrast the 'hierarchical Cv. Div.'s lack of authority over US Atty to less hierarchical divisions...

However, a later section seems to assure U.S. Attorneys that decisions affecting them are not coming from someone less important than they: "typically all correspondence with the U.S. Attorney * * * is by letter addressed to the U.S. Attorney and signed on behalf of the [Associate Attorney General] by a Director.... Correspondence addressed to U.S. Attorneys must always include 'Honorable' in their title." Somehow one gets the impression that this is not simply a tutorial in proper forms of address. And the Civil Division is the most highly centralized and hierarchical Division in Justice. On criminal matters, U.S. Attorneys have far greater discretion. The Criminal Division may have official authority over U.S. Attorneys, but in reality, decisions are usually made at the local level. In many ways, of course, this difference between the Civil and Criminal Divisions makes sense given the nature of the two areas, but the explanation is not simply good bureaucratic organization. It is crime that most U.S. Attorneys really care about. Not only does criminal work account for most of the time spent in U.S. Attorney offices, it is also usually the highest profile area. Prosecuting crime is especially important for those U.S. Attorneys with political ambitions, for reasons easily imaginable. * * * Whatever the official hierarchy, "Main Justice," like all "headquarters," is largely dependent upon the "field" U.S. Attorneys to carry out their mission. And hell hath no greater fury than a U.S. Attorney scorned when it comes to a case that he or she really cares about.

4.   THE SOLICITOR GENERAL

United States Attorneys' Manual
§ 1–2.104 (Office of the Solicitor General) (2007).

A principal function of the Office of the Solicitor General is to represent the federal government before the Supreme Court. *See* 28 C.F.R. § 0.20. As such, this office is responsible for:

A.   The review and revision of, briefs on the merits in cases in which the government is a party or in which it participates as amicus curiae (either on its own motion or at the request of the court); petitions for certiorari; jurisdictional statements; briefs in opposition; and, amicus curiae filings at the petition stage.

B.   Preparation of miscellaneous papers filed in the Supreme Court such as, applications for and oppositions to stays; and, oppositions to bail, etc.;

C.   The arguing of cases in the Supreme Court; and

D.   The determination whether to seek Supreme Court review in cases that the government has lost in the lower courts.

Except for a few situations in which administrative agencies have statutory authority to take certain of their own cases to the Supreme Court, neither the United States nor its agencies may file a petition for certiorari or take a direct appeal to the Supreme Court unless the Solicitor General authorizes it. *See* 28 U.S.C. §§ 516, 518(a); 28 C.F.R. § 0.20(a). Although the Solicitor General reviews every case handled by the Department that the Department has lost in the appellate courts to decide whether to seek Supreme Court review, the Solicitor General reviews such cases handled by independent regulatory agencies only if requested to file a petition for certiorari.   *[margin note: - whether to appeal to USSC]*

Another major function of the office is to determine, in all cases where the United States loses in the trial courts, whether the government should appeal to the intermediate appellate courts. See 28 C.F.R. § 0.20(b). The office also must approve requests for the courts of appeals for mandamus, prohibition and other extraordinary writs, and requests for rehearing en banc. The office also determines whether the government will file a brief amicus curiae or intervene in any appellate court. 28 C.F.R. § 0.20(c). In cases handled by independent regulatory agencies rather than by the Department, however, the Solicitor General has no control over their appeal to intermediate appellate courts.   *[margin note: - whether to appeal to intermed. cts.]* *[margin note: - mandamus/writs/ en banc hearings..]*

Finally, the Solicitor General may, in consultation with each agency or official concerned, authorize intervention by the government in cases involving the constitutionality of acts of Congress; and assist the Attorney General, the Deputy Attorney General, and the Associate Attorney General in the development of broad Department program policy.   *[margin note: - interventions]* *[margin note: - policy development]*

Charles Fried, Order and Law

14 (1991).

Jua. Act 1870

"What does the Solicitor General do?" sounds like a Trivial Pursuit question, yet the Solicitor General has always been a crucial member of the President's establishment. In this century two Chief Justices and several Associate Justices have had the job. The office was created in the Judiciary Act of 1870: "There shall be an officer, learned in the law, to assist the Attorney General." Because of the massive shift of authority to the national government during the Civil War and Reconstruction, the Attorney General gradually became not just the legal adviser to the President but the administrative head of a vast establishment that today includes the FBI, the Immigration Service, the Border Patrol, the Marshall Service, the Bureau of Prisons—in all some seventy thousand persons. But the Solicitor General's job has hardly changed since 1870. He still goes to the Supreme Court in morning coat and striped trousers as the principal spokesman there of the government. It is his job to approve what the government will say in any appellate court in the country. His staff is small (about twenty lawyers), and he takes personal, not just bureaucratic, responsibility for every decision, every brief he signs. In a real sense the Solicitor General is responsible for the government's legal theories, its legal philosophy.

————

Drew S. Days, III, The Solicitor General and the American Legal Ideal

49 SMU Law Review 73, 76–78 (1995).*

Ever since I was nominated to become the Solicitor General of the United States almost two years ago, hardly a day has gone by that I have not been told by another lawyer that I have the best lawyer's job in America. Now, there may be many explanations for why this is said. Clearly, most lawyers do not have their pick of interesting, important cases to handle or the opportunity to argue a half-dozen times a term before the Supreme Court. And being the Government's top lawyer has its other privileges. But I think that such comments are motivated by other considerations.

Perhaps unconsciously, lawyers may covet the job of Solicitor General because they believe it offers those who occupy that position the opportunity to act in ways that come closest to their version of what the ideal lawyer should be and demands qualities that the ideal lawyer should possess. Whether any particular incumbent rises to the occasion is another matter; the important point is that the office is rightfully perceived to provide the *possibilities* for lawyering unlikely to be found elsewhere in the profession.

* Originally appearing in Vol. 49, No. 1 of the *SMU Law Review*. Reprinted with permission from the *SMU Law Review*, the Southern Methodist University School of Law, and Drew S. Days, III.

I do not intend to recite the history of my office. Suffice it to say, the Office of the Solicitor General was established in 1870 in order to provide the Attorney General with assistance in the discharging of his official duties. Over the intervening one hundred and twenty-five years, however, a tradition of independence, both within the Department of Justice and the Executive Branch as a whole, has developed with respect to the Solicitor General's role. Although the Solicitor General is appointed by the President and works for the Attorney General, it is rare for his decisions to be overruled by either of his superiors. Consequently, for most purposes, the Solicitor General has the last word with respect to whether and on what grounds the United States will seek review in the Supreme Court and determines what cases from the federal trial courts the Government will seek to appeal.

In this process, the Solicitor General is not a "hired gun." Indeed, he has a captive client, who may not seek new counsel if he receives disagreeable legal advice. * * * [H]is responsibility is ultimately not to any particular agency or person in the federal government but rather "the interests of the United States" which may, on occasion, conflict with the short-term programmatic goals of an affected governmental entity. * * *

requires broader perspective

In so many ways, the Solicitor General is invited by tradition, as well as statute and regulation, to step out from the role of partisan advocate to assist in the orderly development of the law and to insist that justice be done even where the immediate interests of the federal government may not appear to benefit. For, as it is inscribed on the walls of the Department of Justice, "The United States wins its point whenever justice is done its citizens in the courts."

Seth P. Waxman, Foreword: Does the Solicitor General Matter?

53 Stanford Law Review 1115, 1117–18 (2001).

We all know that the Solicitor General is popularly termed the "Tenth Justice." We know that many legendary figures have held the position. And we know that for most of its venerable history the office has earned and enjoyed a unique respect in the Supreme Court. But does that matter? Does the Solicitor General have any special ability to influence the development of Supreme Court doctrine?

Sometimes—and sometimes often—the answer is yes. Representing a client that is a party in approximately one-half of all cases pending in the federal courts, the Solicitor General is responsible both for determining what position the United States will take on many important questions of federal law and often for choosing the specific cases in which to advance that position. No other lawyer superintends thousands of cases at a time, and none other has the authority to decline to pursue cases solely because

Distinct job traits

doing so would not promote the orderly development of the law. These two facts carry the potential to mean a great deal.

It is possible, I submit, to discern periods in the legal history of the United States, and substantive areas of the law, in which government advocacy—both substantive and procedural—influenced the decisionmaking of the Supreme Court. Let me explain what I mean by this and give some examples. I realize, this being the academy, that I am addressing an audience preternaturally skeptical of any assertion that advocacy plays an important role in the development of doctrine—particularly constitutional doctrine in the Supreme Court. But I come from a different world, and I think it often matters a great deal—particularly at the margins.

When I speak of substantive influence, I mean that the Supreme Court should, and in fact does, take seriously the expressed views of the United States. When the Solicitor General speaks about the needs of the national economy, when he warns of the real-world consequences of interpreting statutes or structuring remedies in a particular way, when he explains the context in which laws are executed, the Court properly takes heed. Not because Solicitors General are uniquely persuasive, or because they wear a funny costume. But rather because the views they express constitute a distillation—a reconciliation—of the often-disparate long-term interests of a national, representative government.

When I speak of procedural influence, I am referring in part to the ability of the Solicitor General—on occasion—to affect which cases come to the Court on a particular issue, and in what order. Why should this matter? Well, for one thing, because judges are human beings: Facts and context influence not just the outcome, but sometimes also the reasoning of a decision. For another thing, judges in the common law tradition are incrementalists. They are generally more comfortable moving the law in small steps rather than in a gigantic leap. Considering cases in incremental fashion permits the Court, over time, both to address the content of constitutional doctrine and to explore in step-by-step fashion its logical limits. And it permits developments in constitutional doctrine to develop momentum. It's important that each journey start out on the right foot. And sometimes the Solicitor General can help.

———

Theodore B. Olson, The Advocate as Friend: The Solicitor General's Stewardship Through the Example of Rex E. Lee

2003 Brigham Young University Law Review 2, 11–13.

As Rex [Lee] once put it:

[T]here is a widely held, and I believe substantially accurate, impression that the Solicitor General's Office provides the Court from one administration to another—and largely without regard to either the political party or the personality of the particular Solicitor General—

with advocacy which is more objective, more dispassionate, more competent, and more respectful of the Court as an institution than it gets from any other lawyer or group of lawyers.

Rex identified "[t]he advantage to the Court" that such advocacy confers. "[I]n more than half of its cases," he wrote, "it has a highly-skilled lawyer on whom it can count consistently for dependable analysis rendered against the background of an unusual understanding and respect for the Court as an institution."

The government now participates in a greater percentage of cases than it did when Rex was solicitor general. As I mentioned earlier, the Justices heard argument seventy-eight times in eighty-eight cases last term (some of the cases were consolidated), and the United States participated as a party or amicus in eighty-three percent of the docket. * * *

U.S. was party or amicus in 83% of cases b/f USSC..

In that regard, the government's increased rate of participation makes it all the more important that the solicitor general make responsible use of his role as the government's litigation gatekeeper. He must reconcile the positions of the components within the Department of Justice, the U.S. attorneys, the other executive departments, and the administrative agencies, and he must exercise restraint in seeking to invoke the Court's jurisdiction to ensure that only the most important cases in which the government has an interest will receive the Court's close scrutiny. He thus conveys important information to the Court that would be obscured if he were too aggressive in seeking Supreme Court review. He also helps them to maintain control over a caseload that remains daunting.

But determining which of the government's cases deserve further review is not easy. The problem the solicitor general faces is that most entities within the executive branch will want to appeal cases that the government has lost. In those circumstances, the solicitor general must judiciously exercise several different skills, all of which Rex possessed in abundance. Indeed, even in the relatively few cases in which the solicitor general agrees that review is warranted, agencies with different mandates and constituencies will often disagree about the government's position on appeal. * * *

[Rex Lee was] a faithful servant of the Supreme Court. As all solicitors general must, he respected the principle of stare decisis, resisting calls that he ask the Court to move too far too fast when his highly informed legal judgment counseled him that the Court was not prepared to be so moved. As Rex memorably explained in responding to a question regarding whether the solicitor general should make arguments he knows the Court will reject, "He is not the Pamphleteer General."

Indeed, one of Rex's special contributions as solicitor general was his remarkable ability to resolve the paradox of the solicitor general's role in situations where he experienced pressure to advocate positions that he believed would jeopardize his special relationship with the Supreme Court. I use the word "paradox," and not "contradiction," because of the depth of Rex's appreciation of the nature of the problem and its solution: although certain goals of the administration might be in tension with his duty to the Court in a particular case, he understood that success in realizing the president's overall litigation objectives ultimately depended on his preserving the solicitor general's special relationship with the Court. As Rex put it, "[A] wholesale departure from the role whose performance has led to the special status that the Solicitor General enjoys would unduly impair that status itself. In the process, the ability of the Solicitor General to serve any of the President's objectives would suffer." * * *

There has been built up, over 115 years since this office was first created in 1870, a reservoir of credibility on which the incumbent Solicitor General may draw to his immediate adversarial advantage. But if he draws too deeply, too greedily, or too indiscriminately, then he jeopardizes not only that advantage in that particular case, but also an important institution of government. The preservation of both—and striking just the right balance between their sometimes competing demands—lies at the heart of the Solicitor General's stewardship. "One of the most important jobs I have," Rex said while he was solicitor general, "is protecting the tradition of John W. Davis, Robert H. Jackson, Charles Fahy, and Thurgood Marshall."

Notes and Questions

Given the importance of the Solicitor General in formulating the government's position before the Supreme Court and the fact that the government is involved in such a high percentage of cases before the Court, controversy about the legal philosophy or agenda of a presidential administration will naturally focus upon the Solicitor General. For example, critics accused the Solicitor General's office during the Reagan Administration of becoming politicized, compromising its traditional independence, and taking stances on constitutional and other legal issues that were outside the jurisprudential mainstream, thereby losing the respect ordinarily given to the Solicitor General by the Supreme Court Justices. *See, e.g.*, Lincoln Caplan, *The Tenth Justice: The Solicitor General and the Rule of Law* (1987). Others argued that the Solicitor General's office under President Reagan was no more attuned to the political views of the Executive than under previous administrations and that, as a member of the President's administration, a Solicitor General properly advocates the considered legal philosophy of the elected administration. *See, e.g.*, Charles Fried, *Order and Law* (1991); John O. McGinnis, *Principles Versus Politics: The Solicitor General's Office in Constitutional and Bureaucratic Theory*, 44 Stan. L. Rev. 799 (1992). Professor Rebecca Salokar concludes that, despite the oft-stated ideal of the Solicitor General as neutral and independent, bound only by fidelity to the law and immune to politics, "the solicitor general has historically been a political actor in the arena of legal policy-making" and his "most important client is necessarily the President of the United States." Rebecca Mae Salokar, *Politics, Law, and the Office of the Solicitor*

General, in *Government Lawyers* 59, 62, 76 (Cornell W. Clayton, ed., 1994). For a variety of viewpoints on the proper role and behavior of the Solicitor General, see generally Rebecca M. Salokar, *The Solicitor General: The Politics of Law* (1992); David A. Strauss, *The Solicitor General and the Interests of the United States*, 61 Law & Contemp. Probs. 165 (Winter 1998), *Symposium: The Role and Function of the United States Solicitor General*, 21 Loy. L.A. L. Rev. 1045 (1988); Joshua I. Schwartz, *The President's Lawyer as Frie[n]d*, 60 Geo. Wash. L. Rev. 1081 (1992) (critically reviewing former Solicitor General Charles Fried's book).

Then-professor and now-Judge Michael McConnell identifies three different models of the Solicitor General's responsibilities: (1) the "independence" approach, under which the Solicitor General makes only "those arguments that he believes to be substantively valid"; (2) the "precedent" approach, under which the Solicitor General carefully advances only positions that conform to existing Supreme Court caselaw; and (3) the "government interests" approach, under which the Solicitor General zealously advocates the interests of the government and the agencies involved in the litigation. Michael W. McConnell, *The Rule of Law and the Role of the Solicitor General*, 21 Loy. L.A. L. Rev. 1105, 1105–07 (1988). Professor Steven Calabresi outlines a slightly different set of principles for Solicitor General behavior: (1) a "departmentalist" approach under which the Solicitor General takes his or her lead from the president and thus promotes the present administration's legal agenda, (2) a "Court-centered" approach under which the Solicitor General takes his or her lead from the Supreme Court and thus manifests significant respect and deference to judicial precedents interpreting or applying the Constitution and other law, and (3) "Burkean-representationalism" in which the Solicitor General is a partially independent representative or ambassador from the presidential administration to the Supreme Court. Steven G. Calabresi, *The President, the Supreme Court, and the Constitution: A Brief Positive Account of the Role of Government Lawyers in the Development of Constitutional Law*, 61 Law & Contemp. Probs. 61, 62, 73–77 (Winter 1998).

Of course, in actual practice, Solicitors General are likely to consider and reflect in their decisions all such approaches and strategies, although they may differ in the weight given to a particular understanding of their role. Consider where each of the commentators excerpted above fits in terms of a primary theory of the role of the Solicitor General. What do they say that leads you to that conclusion? (Charles Fried was Solicitor General in the Reagan Administration; Drew Days and Seth Waxman were Solicitors General in the Clinton Administration; and Ted Olson was Solicitor General in the George W. Bush Administration.) In *United States v. Providence Journal Company*, the next case in this casebook, how does the Supreme Court view the role and responsibility of the Solicitor General?

E.g.'s of "models" of S. G. behavior...

How does the USSC here view role & responsibility of S.G.?

United States v. Providence Journal Company

Supreme Court of the United States.
485 U.S. 693 (1988).

■ JUSTICE BLACKMUN delivered the opinion of the Court.

Conc.

The United States seeks reinstatement of a judgment of contempt against a newspaper and its executive editor for violating an invalid temporary restraining order against publication. Having concluded that the court-appointed prosecutor who sought certiorari and briefed and argued the case without the authorization of the Solicitor General may not represent the United States before this Court, we dismiss the writ of certiorari.

I

On November 8, 1985, Raymond J. Patriarca, son of Raymond L.S. Patriarca, by then deceased, filed suit against the Federal Bureau of Investigation (FBI), its Director, the Department of Justice, the Attorney General of the United States, the Providence Journal Company (Journal), and WJAR Television Ten (WJAR), seeking to enjoin further dissemination of logs and memoranda compiled from 1962 to 1965 during the course of illegal electronic surveillance of the plaintiff's father. The complaint, as amended, was based on the Freedom of Information Act (FOIA), 5 U.S.C. § 552, Title III of the Omnibus Crime Control and Safe Streets Act of 1968 (Title III), 18 U.S.C. § 2510 et seq., and the Fourth Amendment, and alleged that the FBI had improperly released the logs and memoranda to the Journal and WJAR pursuant to a FOIA request following the death of the senior Patriarca. The summons, complaint, and a motion for a temporary restraining order were served on the Journal on November 12, 1985. The next day counsel for the various parties gathered for a conference with the Chief Judge of the United States District Court for the District of Rhode Island. During that conference, of which, apparently, there is no transcript, the Chief Judge entered a temporary restraining order barring publication of the logs and memoranda and set a hearing for Friday, November 15. Counsel for both the Journal and the federal defendants objected to the order.

US Atty represents them

11/13/85

During the evening of November 13, respondent Charles M. Hauser, executive editor of the Journal, was first advised of the restraining order. After discussing with other Journal executives the perils of noncompliance, Hauser decided to publish a story based on the logs and memoranda. The following day, November 14, the Journal published one article about the Patriarcas and another about the "clash" between the District Court and the Journal. Patriarca forthwith filed a motion to have the Journal and Hauser adjudged in criminal contempt.

Journal disregards TRO

Patriarca, however, declined to prosecute the contempt motion,[3] and the District Court decided not to ask the United States Attorney to pursue

---

3. Our decision in *Young v. United States ex rel. Vuitton et Fils* S.A., 481 U.S. 787 (1987), in any event, would have prohibited Patriarca from taking such action. In

the matter because of his representation of the federal defendants in the underlying civil action. Invoking Federal Rule of Criminal Procedure 42(b), the District Court appointed William A. Curran of the Rhode Island Bar as "prosecuting attorney with full authority to prosecute" the pending contempt motion. On Curran's application, the District Court then ordered respondents to show cause why they should not be adjudged in criminal contempt.

Prosecution of the charge of crim. contempt by Curran
· fine
· probation

Following a hearing on February 10, 1986, the District Court found respondents in criminal contempt of the order entered on November 13. * * * The District Court fined the Journal $100,000 and suspended a jail sentence for Hauser, placing him on probation for 18 months and ordering that he perform 200 hours of public service.

Respondents appealed, and the United States Court of Appeals for the First Circuit reversed the judgment of contempt. In re Providence Journal Co., 820 F.2d 1342 (1986). The court found that the temporary restraining order was "transparently invalid" under the First Amendment, and thus its constitutionality could be collaterally challenged in the contempt proceedings. According to the court, none of the grounds asserted in support of the order, including FOIA, Title III, and the Fourth Amendment, provided even a colorable basis for the prior restraint ordered by the District Court.

Δs appeal
1st cir Reverses:
No factual basis for prior restraint of speech

The Court of Appeals, then sitting en banc, summarily modified the panel's opinion, holding that even those subject to a transparently invalid order must make a good-faith effort to seek emergency appellate relief. It ruled, however, that the publisher may proceed to publish and challenge the constitutionality of the order in the contempt proceeding if timely access to the appellate court is not available or if a timely decision is not forthcoming. The court was not convinced that respondents could have obtained emergency relief before the publisher had to make a final decision whether to run the story the following day, and found it unfair to subject respondents to substantial sanctions for failing to follow the newly announced procedures. *In re Providence Journal Co.*, 820 F.2d 1354 (1987).

Because of the importance of the issues, we granted certiorari.

II

Whether to grant Δs M to Dismiss writ of cert.

Before we can decide whether respondents could properly be held in contempt for violating the District Court's subsequently invalidated restraining order, we must consider respondents' motion to dismiss the writ of certiorari. It appears that the manner in which this unusual case reached us departed significantly from established practice. After the Court of Appeals reversed the judgment of contempt and, sitting en banc, modified the panel's opinion, the special prosecutor sought authorization from the Solicitor General to file a petition here for a writ of certiorari. By letter

How this case came b/f USSC:

Can an officer federal prosecuting a case on behalf of the judiciary file for writ of cert on behalf of federal gov't?
Can S.G. authorize that power?

Young, we instructed courts to request the United States Attorney to prosecute the criminal contempt charge, and, if the United States Attorney declined, to appoint as a special prosecutor a private attorney other than the attorney for an interested party.

S. G. denied

dated July 2, 1987, the Solicitor General denied that authorization. * * * [W]e conclude that the special prosecutor lacks the authority to represent the United States before this Court. Because he is not a [party] entitled to petition for certiorari under 28 U.S.C. § 1254(1), we must dismiss the heretofore-granted writ of certiorari for want of jurisdiction.

Statutory & Precedent Basis For Decision

A

Title 28 U.S.C. § 518(a) provides in relevant part:

"Except when the Attorney General in a particular case directs otherwise, the Attorney General and the Solicitor General shall conduct and argue suits and appeals in the Supreme Court ... in which the United States is interested."

AG → SG

The Attorney General by regulation has delegated authority to the Solicitor General:

"The following-described matters are assigned to, and shall be conducted, handled, or supervised by, the Solicitor General, in consultation with each agency or official concerned:

"(a) Conducting, or assigning and supervising, all Supreme Court cases, including appeals, petitions for and in opposition to certiorari, briefs and arguments, and ... settlement thereof." 28 CFR § 0.20.

Thus, unless this is a case other than one "in which the United States is interested," § 518(a), it must be conducted and argued in this Court by the Solicitor General or his designee.

B

The present case clearly is one "in which the United States is interested." The action was initiated in vindication of the "judicial Power *of the United States,*" U.S. Const., Art. III, § 1 (emphasis added), and it is that interest, unique to the sovereign, that continues now to be litigated in this Court. The special prosecutor seeks to reinstate a judgment of criminal contempt in a federal court, including a possible prison sentence for the individual defendant and a substantial fine for the newspaper defendant. The fact that the allegedly criminal conduct concerns the violation of a court order instead of common law or a statutory prohibition does not render the prosecution any less an exercise of the sovereign power of the United States. * * *

The special prosecutor and the Solicitor General argue that this case is not one "in which the United States is interested" because that phrase, as used in § 518(a), refers solely to those cases where the interests of the Executive Branch of the United States are at issue. In this litigation, the argument goes, the special prosecutor acted in support of the power of the Judicial Branch, rather than in furtherance of the Executive's constitutional responsibility, U.S. Const., Art. II, § 3, to "take Care that the Laws be faithfully executed." This suggested interpretation of § 518(a), however, presumes that there is more than one "United States" that may appear before this Court, and that the United States is something other than "the sovereign composed of the three branches. . . ." *United States v. Nixon*, 418 U.S. 683, 696 (1974).

We find such a proposition somewhat startling, particularly when supported by the office whose authority would be substantially diminished by its adoption, and we reject that construction as inconsistent with the plain meaning of § 518(a). It seems to be elementary that even when exercising distinct and jealously separated powers, the three branches are but "co-ordinate parts of one government." Congress is familiar enough with the language of separation of powers that we shall not assume it intended, without saying so, to exclude the Judicial Branch when it referred to the "interest of the United States." Moreover, while there may well be matters that are uniquely Executive Branch concerns, we do not think they would be fairly described by the broad statutory language of § 518(a).

In *Young* [*v. United States ex rel. Vuitton et Fils* S.A., 481 U.S. 787 (1987)], we reaffirmed the inherent authority of a federal court to initiate a criminal contempt proceeding for disobedience of its order, and its ability to appoint a private attorney to prosecute the contempt action. This power, considered to be a part of the judicial function, is grounded first and foremost upon necessity: "The ability to punish disobedience to judicial orders is regarded as essential to ensuring that the Judiciary has a means to vindicate its own authority without complete dependence on other branches." *Id.*, at 796. The special prosecutor claims his appearance before this Court is necessary for the vindication of the District Court's authority. For just as the District Court would be "at the mercy of another branch in deciding whether such proceedings should be initiated," if it lacked the power to appoint a private attorney to prosecute a contempt charge, the judgment vindicating the District Court's authority would be vulnerable to the Attorney General's withholding of authorization to defend it. This argument, however, overlooks the circumstances under which the special prosecutor actually came to be in a position to seek review in this Court.

'Inherent' Authority' of Jud.

When, as here, a district court's judgment of contempt has been reversed on appeal, a special prosecutor may decide to seek a writ of certiorari on the basis of his professional judgment that the court of appeals' decision merits review. Sometimes, as apparently occurred here, the special prosecutor and the Solicitor General will disagree with respect to whether the case presents issues worthy of review by this Court. That kind of disagreement actually arises on a regular basis between the Solicitor General and attorneys representing various agencies of the United States.[7] But that disagreement does not interfere with the Judiciary's

whose decision to seek review on the merits. . .

---

7. In fact, this Court relies on the Solicitor General to exercise such independent judgment and to decline to authorize petitions for review in this Court in the majority of the cases the Government has lost in the courts of appeals. See *Andres v. United States*, 333 U.S. 740, 764–765, n. 9 (1948) (Frankfurter, J., concurring); McCree, The Solicitor General and His Client, 59 Wash. U.L.Q. 337, 341 (1981). See also Griswold, The Office of the Solicitor General—Representing the Interests of the United States Before the Supreme Court, 34 Mo.L.Rev. 527, 535 (1969) ("The Solicitor General has a

power to protect itself. In this very case, before the consent of the Solicitor General ever became relevant, members of the Judiciary had decided that the District Judge erred in adjudging the defendants in contempt. Where the majority of a panel of a court of appeals or perhaps, as here, a majority of an en banc court, itself has decided in favor of the alleged contemner, the necessity that required the appointment of an independent prosecutor has faded and, indeed, is no longer present.

When, on the other hand, a district court has adjudged a party in contempt, and the appellate court has affirmed, a special prosecutor has little need of the services of this Court to fulfill his or her duties. It is only if the contemner petitions this Court for a writ of certiorari that the Solicitor General need be consulted and his authorization or participation obtained to oppose the petition and defend the judgment. Under such circumstances, if the Solicitor General declines to authorize a defense of the judgment and if § 518(a) prevented the special prosecutor from proceeding, the independent ability of the Judiciary to vindicate its authority might appear to be threatened: both courts would have agreed that the contemner had disobeyed an order of the court, but the Executive's judgment to the contrary would threaten to undermine those judicial decisions. This threat, however, is inconsequential, for it is this Court, a part of the Judicial Branch, that must decide whether to exercise its discretion to review the judgment below, and it is well within this Court's authority to appoint an amicus curiae to file briefs and present oral argument in support of that judgment.

The Solicitor General argues that § 518(a) does not apply to a contempt proceeding that is initiated unilaterally by a federal court, because in *Young* this Court sustained the power of the court to appoint a private attorney to prosecute a criminal contempt charge, despite the fact that 28 U.S.C. § 516, in language certainly somewhat similar to that of § 518(a), requires such litigation to be conducted by a Government attorney:

> "Except as otherwise authorized by law, the conduct of litigation in which the United States, an agency, or officer thereof is a party, or is interested, ... is reserved to officers of the Department of Justice, under the direction of the Attorney General."

Also, 28 U.S.C. § 547 requires: "Except as otherwise provided by law, each United States attorney, within his district, shall ... prosecute for all offenses against the United States." The Solicitor General concludes that *Young* necessarily implies that these broadly worded reservations of litigating authority, including § 518(a), do not apply to the case at hand.

Young neither expressed nor implied any such special consideration for a judicially initiated contempt proceeding. Both statutes implicated but not discussed in *Young* provide for the Attorney General's exclusive control over specified litigation *except as otherwise provided or authorized by law*. A

special obligation to aid the Court as well as to serve his client.... In providing for the Solicitor General, subject to the direction of the Attorney General, to attend to the 'interests of the United States' in litigation, the statutes have always been understood to mean the long-range interests of the United States, not simply in terms of its fisc, or its success in the particular litigation, but as a government, as a people").

fair reading of Young indicates that a federal court's inherent authority to punish disobedience and vindicate its authority is an excepted provision or authorization within the meaning of §§ 516 and 547. The "power to punish for contempts is inherent in all courts," and was not first recognized by this Court in *Young*; rather, it "has been many times decided and may be regarded as settled law." *Young*, 481 U.S., at 795. Thus, contrary to the Solicitor General's intimation, *Young* did not read an exception into §§ 516 and 547; instead, *Young* is consistent with the plain language of the provisos to those sections. Section 518(a), by way of vivid contrast, contains no such proviso.

C

Policy Basis for Decision

If the plain statutory language of § 518(a) were not reason enough to persuade us to accept respondents' objections and dismiss the writ of certiorari, we observe that the salutory policies that support § 518(a) could be undermined by, and anomalous consequences could result from, the approach urged upon the Court by the special prosecutor and the Solicitor General. Among the reasons for reserving litigation in this Court to the Attorney General and the Solicitor General, is the concern that the United States usually should speak with one voice before this Court, and with a voice that reflects not the parochial interests of a particular agency, but the common interests of the Government and therefore of all the people. Without the centralization of the decision whether to seek certiorari, this Court might well be deluged with petitions from every federal prosecutor, agency, or instrumentality, urging as the position of the United States, a variety of inconsistent positions shaped by the immediate demands of the case *sub judice*, rather than by longer term interests in the development of the law. * * *

· unitary voice
· centralization
· jud. economy

III

We conclude that a criminal contempt prosecution brought to vindicate the authority of the Judiciary and to punish disobedience of a court order is a suit "in which the United States is interested," within the meaning of § 518(a), regardless of who is appointed by the district court to prosecute the action. In this case, the special prosecutor filed a petition for a writ of certiorari without the authorization of the Solicitor General, and thus without authorization to appear on behalf of the United States. Absent a proper representative of the Government as a petitioner in this criminal prosecution, jurisdiction is lacking and the writ of certiorari, heretofore granted, is now dismissed.

It is so ordered.

■ JUSTICE KENNEDY took no part in the consideration or decision of this case.

■ JUSTICE SCALIA, concurring.

I join the opinion of the Court, which ably demonstrates that according 28 U.S.C. § 518(a) its plain meaning is fully consistent with the opinion of the Court in *Young v. United States ex rel. Vuitton et Fils* S.A., 481 U.S. 787 (1987). I continue to believe, however, that district courts possess no power, inherent or otherwise, to prosecute contemners for disobedience of court

· No inherent power of jud. to prosecute contemners or appt. prosecutors to do so

judgments and no derivative power to appoint an attorney to conduct contempt prosecutions. See id., at 825 (Scalia, J., concurring in judgment).

■ JUSTICE STEVENS, with whom THE CHIEF JUSTICE joins, dissenting.

Dissent:

JA 1789

A statute enacted by the First Congress in 1789 created the office of Attorney General of the United States and described some of the responsibilities of that office. That statute provided:

> "... And there shall also be appointed a meet person, learned in the law, to act as attorney-general for the United States, who shall be sworn or affirmed to a faithful execution of his office; *whose duty it shall be to prosecute and conduct all suits in the Supreme Court in which the United States shall be concerned*, and to give his advice and opinion upon questions of law when required by the President of the United States, or when requested by the heads of any of the departments, touching any matters that may concern their departments, and shall receive such compensation for his services as shall by law be provided." Judiciary Act of 1789, ch. 20, § 35, 1 Stat. 93 (emphasis supplied).

The 1789 Act has been amended to make it clear that the Solicitor General has essentially the same authority to conduct litigation in this Court as does the Attorney General and that such authority may be delegated to others. In substance, however, the provision has remained unaltered for nearly 200 years; the Attorney General—and now the Solicitor General as well—is charged with conducting all litigation before this Court in which the United States is "concerned" or "interested."

Executive conducting litigation vs. Legislative / Jud. Branches conducting legislation

Most litigation in which the United States is interested is, of course, conducted by the Executive Branch of the Government. Orderly administration requires that such litigation be conducted under the supervision and direction of a single office. Congress therefore wisely granted the Attorney General broad enough authority to accomplish that mission. It is unlikely, however, that when this statute was enacted Congress foresaw the possibility that matters such as judicial contempts, legislative contempts, or the need to defend a legislative veto, would present justiciable controversies in which the Congress or the Judiciary might have interests that diverge from those of the Executive Branch of the Government, but nevertheless be cases "in which the United States shall be concerned." It is equally unlikely that Congress, through amendment and more recent consideration of the provision, has perceived, much less endorsed, the view that § 518(a) should be read to place control of such litigation exclusively in the hands of the Executive Branch. Although the texts of the statutes that Congress enacted can be read to foreclose either the Congress or the Judiciary from appointing counsel to participate in litigation in this Court, we have long held that in construing a statute, we are not bound to follow the literal language of the statute—"however clear the words may appear on 'superficial examination' "—when doing so leads to "absurd," or even "unreasonable," results. * * *

* * * Section 518(a) directs that "[e]xcept when the Attorney General in a particular case directs otherwise, the Attorney General and the Solicitor General shall conduct and argue suits and appeals in the Supreme

Court … in which the United States is interested." The language is mandatory. In any case in which the United States is interested, the Solicitor General *shall* argue an appeal in the Supreme Court. Of course, and quite properly so, the Solicitor General does not seek certiorari in every case adversely affecting an interest of the United States. Instead, the Solicitor General acts strategically, choosing the most important cases and the cases in which the United States is most likely to prevail. In thus separating the wheat from the chaff, the Solicitor General makes a series of judgments as to what is in the United States' interest. As an executive officer, the Solicitor General may reasonably weigh and consider the interests of the executive agencies. When faced with a difference of view between the Executive Branch and a coordinate branch of government, however, the Solicitor General faces a conflict of interest that undeniably would be intolerable if encountered in the private sector. In essence, he or she is asked to resolve conflicting interests between clients. Common sense dictates that Congress did not intend to create such a conflict in the Office of the Solicitor General. Moreover, and even more compellingly so, it is unreasonable to conclude that Congress intended to abdicate to the Solicitor General and the Department of Justice the function of determining what is in the interest of the Congress or the Judiciary. Certainly, Congress did not intend that these executive offices be charged with weighing competing executive and congressional or Judicial interests, with authority—absent further legislation—to deny Congress and the Judiciary access to this Court.

[margin note: ..The other branches must also be able to seek review from & argue b/f the S. Ct.]

Not only is our prior practice consistent with a common-sense reading of § 518, but it is also significant that the officer most interested in a correct interpretation of that provision—the Solicitor General—places this interpretation on its text. In his brief in this case, he submits:

> "[Title] 28 U.S.C. 518(a), like the other statutes that vest the Attorney General with exclusive control over litigation, applies to cases in which the United States is 'interested' by virtue of the constitutional and statutory responsibilities of the Executive Branch—the Branch in which the Attorney General serves."

[margin note: ' The Executive isn't interested in it, but other Branches might be…]

Because I agree with that interpretation of the statute, I respectfully dissent.

---

5. THE ROLE OF THE GOVERNMENT ATTORNEY: POLITICS, THE PUBLIC INTEREST, AND A HIGHER ETHICAL STANDARD?

Douglas Letter, Lawyering and Judging on Behalf of the United States: All I Ask for Is a Little Respect

61 George Washington Law Review 1295, 1297–1300 (1993).

There is an inescapable fact that differentiates Department of Justice and other federal government lawyers from the overwhelming number of litigators in private practice. Government lawyers are paid a salary set and appropriated by Congress and the Executive solely in order to carry out their duties and responsibilities as employees of a democratically elected government. Business development is not one of their concerns. * * *

By contrast, a private legal practitioner serves almost exclusively an individual private client and that client's interests, regardless of what these interests might be and whether, in any particular instance, they might be antithetical to the established law or current government policy. This statement is a simplification because a private lawyer also has obligations to other entities—such as her law firm or the courts—and must follow certain ethical restrictions, such as not participating in or concealing planned crimes. Moreover, in order to be effective litigators, most of the time private counsel must comport themselves in ways that are acceptable to, or respected by, the courts. * * *

One of the clearest demonstrations of the difference between the role of the Department of Justice lawyer and that of a private practitioner is revealed by words written on one wall of the Department of Justice headquarters, near the office of the Attorney General: "The United States wins its point whenever justice is done its citizens in Court." This means that, if a government attorney litigates a case on behalf of the United States and loses in a just way, the client served has won regardless of the seemingly unfavorable result. This maxim is not true for a private practitioner, who rarely will be able to convince a client that it has actually prevailed if judgment is rendered against it. * * *

For example, I was assigned to a case some years ago in the D.C. Circuit in which an attorney from one of the most prominent firms in Washington, D.C. represented the other side—a major newspaper. That firm had made a technical error in perfecting an appeal from an adverse judgment. While assessing the case, I realized that I could have made a respectable argument that the appeal should be dismissed. Despite the harshness of that result, I thought there was a possibility that the court would grant the dismissal.

One of the opposing counsel, having realized the error, called me to say that she assumed that the United States would not attempt to take advantage of such a technical argument to dismiss an appeal involving an issue of substantive importance. As I spoke to her, I knew that if I were representing a private party, she would not have made the telephone call. Moreover, I would have committed gross malpractice through violation of my duty of loyalty to the client in such a situation if I had decided not to attempt to gain a dismissal under those circumstances.

In this instance, however, neither she nor I viewed her plea to me as improper or futile. Nevertheless, because her firm is notorious for its hardball litigation tactics, I could not resist asking her what she would have done had I been the one who had made the technical error on behalf of the government. I am sure that we both knew the answer, and that we both understood that each of us worked under a different obligation. My office ultimately raised the point for the D.C. Circuit in our appellate brief and won on the merits in the Supreme Court.

* * * Justice Department attorneys serve a special role because we litigate on behalf of the United States. In particular, we are in an odd situation because we almost always litigate against the people of the United States, who are the very people that we ultimately serve. Thus, if we prevail, it is usually only because one of the citizens of the United States, or their corporations or associations, has lost. This fact can and should be sobering.

Litigating against a segment of the group being represented raises a number of problems for public service attorneys. One is the recurring dilemma regarding the duty of the public service attorney when opposing counsel make mistakes that could be remedied if the opposing attorneys were aware of them. That this dilemma even arises reveals that the Justice Department has a very different role from the private firm representing a private client. On several occasions of which I am aware government attorneys have notified opposing counsel of technical problems so that they can be fixed before jurisdictional limits make a remedy impossible. This action would be obvious malpractice if followed while representing a private party.

Because of the interests that government attorneys must serve, it is not surprising that the D.C. Circuit and other federal courts impose special obligations on government lawyers. D.C. Circuit judges quite reasonably assume that government lawyers bear responsibilities—of fair dealing, full disclosure, and allegiance to the court system—that are not shared by private practitioners.

––––––

Notes and Questions

1. Both former Solicitor General Drew Days (in the prior subsection of this casebook) and Justice Department attorney Douglas Letter in the excerpt immediately above quote the words inscribed on one wall of the Department of Justice Building: "The United States wins its point whenever justice is done its citizens in Court." Can this maxim serve as a standard of ethical behavior for government lawyers? Can this ideal be translated into actual practice on a day-to-day basis, and if so, how?

If the government attorney is to consider the "public interest," how does he or she determine what that interest is? Professor Barbara Babcock, who served as Assistant Attorney General for the Civil Division in the Carter Administration, believes that "the government lawyer should take her definition of the public interest from the presidential administration in which she serves." Barbara A. Babcock, *Defending the Government: Justice and the Civil Division*, 23 J. Marshall L. Rev. 181, 191 (1990); *see also* Geoffrey P. Miller, *Government Lawyers' Ethics in a System of Checks and Balances*, 54 U. Chi. L. Rev. 1293, 1294–98 (1987) (arguing that the "the

Defining "public interest" . . .

Loyalty to Executive?.

notion that government attorneys represent some transcendental 'public interest' is * * * incoherent," that government lawyers are not empowered "to substitute their individual conceptions of the good" for the objectives established through the political process, and thus that government lawyers are ultimately responsible "to the Executive Branch as a whole and to the President as its head").

Personal Ideal of Pub. Interest?.

Other commentators insist that the concept of a "public interest," beyond slavishly following the agency political line, is intelligible and indeed can "provide a workable guidepost for government attorneys with regard to the choices and decisions that they must make in their professional roles." See Steven K. Berenson, *Public Lawyers, Private Values: Can, Should, and Will Government Lawyers Serve the Public Interest*, 41 B.C. L. Rev. 789, 790 (2000). While agreeing that "it is unlikely that government lawyers will be able to identify some sort of overarching, all-purpose definition of the public interest that will apply generally across the full range of human affairs," Professor Steven Berenson contends that government lawyers can resolve particular legal problems by deriving public values through "the familiar tools of legal practice, such as interpreting and applying judicial decisions, statutory and constitutional interpretation, and understanding applying the broader norms of legal culture." *Id.* at 814, 817. Moreover, he argues, the public interest can be better served through a participatory model of bureaucracy that involves citizens in the administrative decision-making process. *Id.* at 818–21. Similarly, a recent student note in the Harvard Law Review places the government lawyer in the role of mediating democratic values and conflicting interests rather than being a "partisan advocate[] for any single position." Note, *Rethinking the Professional Responsibilities of Federal Agency Lawyers*, 115 Harv. L. Rev. 1170, 1181 (2002). In this student author's view, rather than adhering to any particular position on a disputed legal point within the government, "the government lawyer's primary goal should always be reconciliation—or at least accommodation—of as many interests as possible, rather than vindication of any single interest." *Id.* Thus, the government lawyer must

Balancing the notions

balance the agency's policy interests, the "abstract notion of the public good," and the interests of other actors to reach a mediated position that promotes democratic values and makes the lawyer and agency accountable to the public. Id. at 1181–83. *See also* Daniel S. Jacobs, *The Role of the Federal Government in Defending Public Interest Litigation*, 44 Santa Clara L. Rev. 1, 1, 44, 48 (2003) (arguing that the government tends to move into a "defensive, not reflective, mode" when it is sued, and that, the Department of Justice, not so much the individual lawyer, should adopt reforms for evaluation of cases in "a concerted effort ... and resolve, rather than litigate, meritorious public interest cases," which are defined as those "challeng[ing] a program, policy, or action as unlawful, and seek[] remedies intended to insure to the benefit of a broad class of persons rather than simply the individual plaintiff(s)").

2. What if a government lawyer disagrees with the policy or political goals of the present administration or agency leaders? Professor Neal Devins speaks bluntly to this question in describing his work as assistant

general counsel to the United States Civil Rights Commission during the Reagan Administration:

> In large part, [my job] meant telling careerist attorneys—most of whom opposed the goals of the Reagan Administration—to toe the agency line. Consequently, when careerists sought to undermine official agency views (by invoking their duty either to the law or the public interest), I suggested that their duty was to do the agency's bidding (until they could find a new job).

Neal Devins, *Foreword, Government Lawyering Symposium*, 61 Law & Contemp. Probs. 1, 2 (Winter 1998). Does that mean that, as a practical matter, the high-minded rhetoric of "justice" and "public interest" mean nothing to the government "line" attorney who holds no political appointment in the administration? For them, is the duty only to "obey orders"?

In a provocative, controversial, and poignantly personal description of a conflict between one government attorney's moral conscience and his professional obligation of loyalty, Professor Michael Paulsen relates the dilemma he faced when, as an attorney within the Department of Justice in 1990, he obtained prior and confidential information that David Souter was soon to be nominated to the Supreme Court by President Bush. Michael Stokes Paulsen, *Hell, Handbaskets, and Government Lawyers: The Duty of Loyalty and Its Limits*, 61 Law & Contemp. Probs. 83 (Winter 1998). As a strong opponent of legalized abortion, as enshrined in the Supreme Court's decision in *Roe v. Wade*, 410 U.S. 113 (1973), Paulsen considered violating his duty of confidentiality and leaking to "pro-life" groups his advance knowledge of Souter's likely nomination, so that these organizations could mobilize in opposition and either persuade the President to reconsider the nomination or lobby members of the Senate to oppose it. As one of the government attorneys involved in researching potential judicial nominees during the Bush Administration, Paulsen had come to the conclusion that Souter likely would "vote to uphold Roe—a case I personally found morally and jurisprudentially criminal." *Id.* at 91. (Indeed, two years later, by a single-vote margin, the Supreme Court reaffirmed *Roe* in *Planned Parenthood v. Casey*, 505 U.S. 833 (1992), with Justice Souter joining the slender majority.) Paulsen asks in his essay: "Is it ever proper for an executive branch government lawyer to sabotage or undermine the lawful policies or decisions of the administration in which he or she serves?" *Id.* at 85. He acknowledges that revealing the information would have been a violation of his duties as a lawyer and perhaps even a crime. *Id.* at 92. Yet Paulsen concludes that he did the *"wrong* thing" in failing to take action:

> There are few issues about which I believe strongly enough to violate the duty of loyalty and confidentiality owed by a government attorney to the administration he or she serves—duties that in themselves have substantial moral weight. Abortion is one of those very few issues. * * * I was personally convinced, largely from my own reading of the Souter record, that there was a huge risk—indeed a substantial likelihood—that Souter would be a complete disaster on what I regard as

the most important, life-and-death issue to confront the legal system in my lifetime. That should have justified leaking.

Id. at 93.

What would you have done?

What would you have done, assuming you shared Paulsen's strong moral abhorrence of abortion? Or consider how you would act if you had a similar opportunity as an "insider" government attorney to "sabotage" a government decision that would ensure either the end or continuation of the death penalty, affirmative action, private ownership of handguns, or some other policy or practice that implicates your most deeply-held beliefs? Consider also what the consequence to Paulsen would have been had he acted? Isn't he simply suggesting a form of civil disobedience? Should individuals have the right, based upon personal moral beliefs not shared or not as firmly held by others, to obstruct a governmental decision that is legal, politically justified, and procedurally proper?

Historical e.g.

When it comes to questions of conscience and integrity, Professor Randy Lee reminds government lawyers of the example of Sir Thomas More, who resigned as Lord Chancellor of England rather than endorse the actions of King Henry VIII in challenging the authority of the Pope over the Church of England when the Pope denied the king's request to divorce his wife, Catherine of Aragon, to marry Anne Boleyn. Randy Lee, *Robert Bolt's* A Man for All Seasons *and the Art of Discerning Integrity,* 9 Widener J. Pub. L. 305, 305–06 (2000). When More then refused to take an oath required under the Act of Succession of 1534, which also rejected the Pope's authority over the church, he was imprisoned and eventually executed for treason. *Id.* at 306. As Lee explains, Robert Bolt's famous play about More, *A Man for All Seasons,* was "a story about how people in government respond when the issue is simple, but the choice can hardly be called easy." Lee, *supra,* at 306. By refusing to surrender even "in the face of dire consequences or grand temptations," More demonstrated "the highest level of integrity" and acted in a selfless manner. *Id.* at 306, 318. Lee concludes that, as depicted in the play, More as a government lawyer acted with integrity with respect to the laws of society, by "remaining faithful to one's conscience but accepting the law's protections and penalties as they apply." *Id.* at 333. (St. Thomas More, long patron saint of lawyers for Catholics, was elevated by Pope John Paul II to be patron of statesmen and political leaders as well.)

Accomodation for an individual lawyer's conscience

Fortunately, the scenario described by Paulsen and the dire consequences experienced by Sir Thomas More are not typical. *See* Marcia E. Mulkey, *A Crisis of Conscience and the Government Lawyer,* 14 Temp. Pol. & Civ. Rts. L. Rev. 649, 651 (2005) ("Happily, most government attorneys go through our entire careers without facing a true 'crisis of conscience' on the jog."). Indeed, one of the benefits of government legal service is a greater tendency by superiors to accommodate, within reason of course, the conflicts of conscience that a lawyer may have on a particular case or issue. As Judge Patricia Wald of the United States Court of Appeals for the District of Columbia Circuit explains:

With changes in administrations, many government counsel understand that, at least in DOJ, lawyers are not required, at the peril of ending their careers, to represent government policy that collides with their most fundamental beliefs. (The "don't ask, don't tell" policy on gays in the military is one example, I am told, where lawyers sincerely opposed to the policy are excused from defending it.) This kind of leeway is wise policy for an agency; given that the government is a vast enterprise required to take on a multitude of subjects, the possibilities of both conflict and substitution are greater. It is also wise for government counsel to take their employer up on the offer: Their discomfort is often discernible to the court, and no government counsel should be asked to ignore deeply felt convictions (so long as he does not have too many).

Patricia M. Wald, *"For the United States": Government Lawyers in Court*, 61 Law & Contemp. Probs. 107, 121 (Winter 1998); *see also* Ralph Nader & Alan Hirsch, *A Proposed Right of Conscience for Government Attorneys*, 55 Hastings L.J. 311, 330 (2003) (proposing that, either by statute or ethical canon developed by bar associations, that a government attorney be permitted to "decline an assignment if he believes it will force him to act unlawfully or otherwise violate his oath of office or conscience").

When the course of avoidance through reassignment is not available (indeed, even when it is) and yet the government lawyer determines not to resign or engage in civil disobedience, the government attorney should not neglect the rules-sanctioned approach of moral counseling of the client. For reasons both of professional survival and of "rule of law" principle, the government lawyer rightly should be hesitant to obstruct a governmental decision that is lawfully made by political leaders. But while the government lawyer must defer to political superiors on the ultimate decision as matter of democratic governance, he or she retains the prerogative, indeed the arguable duty of conscience, to raise moral objections and counsel a contrary course by the government client. To be sure, the right to choose a course of action based upon non-legal factors belongs to the client. Still, Rule 2.1 of the Model Rules of Professional Conduct expressly reminds the lawyer: "In rendering advice, a lawyer may refer not only to law but to other considerations such as moral, economic, social and political factors, that may be relevant to the client's situation." Indeed, Professor Gerald Postema argues that not only is a lawyer authorized to raise moral issues with the client, he has a professional responsibility to do so—and a duty that fully comports with the idea of zealous loyalty to the client:

> "[C]ut off from sound moral judgment, the lawyer's ability to do his job well—to determine the applicable law and effectively advise his clients—is likely to be seriously affected. * * * [T]he lawyer who must detach professional judgment from his own moral judgment is deprived of the resources from which arguments regarding his client's legal rights and duties can be fashioned. In effect, the ideal of neutrality and detachment wars against its companion ideal of zealous pursuit of the client interests."

[handwritten margin note: Rules—sanctioned moral counseling of the client]

Gerald J. Postema, *Moral Responsibility in Professional Ethics*, 55 N.Y.U. L. REV. 63, 79 (1980).

3. Let us turn from the politically sensitive to the more pedestrian type of case and consider the government lawyer's ethical responsibilities. If the government lawyer is obligated to follow the political guidance provided by higher level government legal officials on high visibility issues, is there still room to consider questions of justice or fairness in the run-of-the-mill case? What about the government "line" attorney handling the ordinary tort or contract dispute? Is there a role for "public interest" or "justice" concerns in ordinary litigation decision-making? What of the government litigator's professional responsibilities in behavior toward other litigants and accountability to the court?

"Justice" in run of the mill cases?

As an aspirational exhortation, Ethical Consideration 7–14 of the former Model Code of Professional Responsibility advised:

> A government lawyer who has discretionary power relative to litigation should refrain from instituting or continuing litigation that is obviously unfair. A government lawyer not having such discretionary power who believes there is lack of merit in a controversy submitted to him should so advise his superiors and recommend the avoidance of unfair litigation. A government lawyer in a civil action or administrative proceeding has the responsibility to seek justice and to develop a full and fair record, and he should not use his position or the economic power of the government to harass or to bring about unjust settlements or results.

Higher ethical std. for gov't attys.

The above excerpt from Douglas Letter's essay concludes by suggesting that government attorneys are and should be held to a higher ethical standard in court than private practitioners. Judge Patricia Wald affirms that judges have higher expectations for government lawyers appearing in court, and outlines that "higher standard" as including a higher level of competence, greater candor with the court, credibility by virtue of the attorney's enthusiasm for and confidence in the position advocated, a greater concern for civility, and consistency in government positions taken before the courts. Wald, *supra*, at 109–10, 119–27.

Likewise, Professor Bruce Green argues that, just as it is well established that prosecutors must "seek justice" in criminal cases, so also government lawyers in civil litigation have a "distinctive professional role." Bruce A. Green, *Must Government Lawyers "Seek Justice" in Civil Litigation?*, 9 Widener J. Pub. L. 235, 279 (2000). Because the client government agency or official "owes fiduciary duties to the public," Green suggests that the government lawyer "owes some derivative duties to the public." *Id.* at 269. Thus, in contrast with the standard of zealous advocacy and the partisan nature of the lawyer's role on behalf of private clients, the government lawyer has "public-regarding obligations" and should not "assert every plausible claim or defense, or [] otherwise engage in every method permitted by law to prevail in litigation." *Id.* at 235, 273–74. Like government lawyers in criminal prosecution, government lawyers in civil litigation should refrain from "bringing 'bad' or undeserving cases," a

Application

higher standard than merely avoiding taking frivolous positions, and are more restricted than private lawyers in exploiting legal and factual errors made by the court or the opposing party. *See id.* at 240–41.

Somewhat in contrast, Professor Catherine Lanctot argues, that in applying mandatory ethical codes, government lawyers are subject to the same standards as other members of the bar and are fully entitled to serve as zealous advocates on behalf of the government. Catherine J. Lanctot, *The Duty of Zealous Advocacy and the Ethics of the Federal Government Lawyer: The Three Hardest Questions*, 64 S. Cal. L. Rev. 951 (1991). With respect to raising technical defenses, candor to the courts, and presentation of weak (but not frivolous) arguments, she concludes that "under the Model Code and the Model Rules, the government lawyer may represent the government client the same way that a private lawyer represents a private client. * * * In short, the ethical codes draw no distinctions between the duty of the government lawyer and the duty of the private lawyer to defend a civil case zealously." *Id.* at 957–58.

However, Lanctot also points out that, because private practitioners are permitted to provide moral advice to clients, and because "the duty to consider the public good is a duty of all public servants, not just lawyers," the government lawyer may discuss with the government client the issues of justice and fairness. *Id.* at 985–86. Still, like other commentators discussed above, she concludes that government lawyers have little leeway to implement their personal view of the public interest:

> As government officials and as lawyers representing clients, government lawyers should participate in this decision-making process. Ultimately, however, in the American political system, the decision as to which governmental action will benefit "the people" or "the public interest" is vested in elected officials or those to whom they have delegated their decision-making authority. Once that policy decision has been made, the government lawyer may ethically defend it, even if the lawyer believes that the public interest may not be served by that decision. The government lawyer, after all, is not employed by the federal government to represent personal interests, and it is virtually impossible for anyone to determine where a neutral view of the "public interest" ends and one's own personal opinions begin.

Id. at 1015.

Consider these views of the ethical responsibilities of government lawyers in light of the following case:

———

Freeport–McMoRan Oil & Gas Co. v. Federal Energy Regulatory Commission

United States Court of Appeals for the District of Columbia Circuit.
962 F.2d 45 (D.C.Cir. 1992).

■ MIKVA, CHIEF JUDGE:

This case is plainly moot. The challenged orders of the Federal Energy Regulatory Commission were superseded by a subsequent FERC order, and while the challenged orders were in effect petitioners suffered no injury this court can redress. At oral argument, for the first time, FERC's counsel said the Commission had no objection to petitioners' request that we vacate the challenged orders. Accordingly, we vacate them.

Ct's commentary on the ethic & comport of gov't attys

Ordinarily, we would handle such a matter in an unpublished order. We write, however, to express our displeasure with FERC counsel's failure to take easy and obvious steps to avoid needless litigation. We also pause to address FERC counsel's remarkable assertion at oral argument that government attorneys ought not be held to higher standards than attorneys for private litigants. * * *

what the gov't atty failed to do

At several points before oral argument, FERC's counsel should have seen that vacating the orders would likely settle this litigation, saving time, energy, and money * * *, and allowing the court to focus on live cases and controversies instead of this moot one. Many lawyers would have seen the possibility of settlement as soon as FERC issued its [superseding] order, mooting the pending challenge. The ease of settlement became obvious when petitioners, in their reply brief, explained their concern that the unreviewed orders might prejudice their position in other litigation and asked the court to vacate the orders. Despite the benefits of settlement and the pointlessness of proceeding, FERC's counsel did not try to contact opposing counsel to explore whether vacating the orders would resolve the case; nor did FERC's counsel recommend that the Commission file a motion to have this court remand the orders so that FERC could vacate them unilaterally. FERC's counsel did not even disclose in the brief he drafted and filed with this court the Commission's position on vacating the challenged orders, leaving the impression that the Commission might oppose vacating them.

We understand that what seems obvious in hindsight might not have occurred at the time to a busy agency lawyer. We do not understand, however, FERC counsel's repeated insistence at oral argument that he had no obligation at all to take any of the steps we have mentioned. "I don't think we had to do that," counsel said in response to a suggestion that a phone call to opposing counsel might have put an end to the case; "the burden is on him." When a member of the panel submitted that counsel for a public agency has special obligations, FERC's counsel replied that "I think we can agree to disagree on that point." At the close of oral argument, FERC's counsel summed up his position: "All I can say is that I think you're holding us to a different standard here."

Criminal & Civil!

The notion that government lawyers have obligations beyond those of private lawyers did not originate in oral argument in this case. A government lawyer "is the representative not of an ordinary party to a controversy," the Supreme Court said long ago in a statement chiseled on the walls of the Justice Department, "but of a sovereignty whose obligation ... is not that it shall win a case, but that justice shall be done." *Berger v. United States*, 295 U.S. 78, 88 (1935). The Supreme Court was speaking of government prosecutors in *Berger*, but no one, to our knowledge (at least prior to oral argument), has suggested that the principle does not apply with equal force to the government's civil lawyers. In fact, the American Bar Association's Model Code of Professional Responsibility expressly holds a "government lawyer in a civil action or administrative proceeding" to higher standards than private lawyers, stating that government lawyers have "the responsibility to seek justice," and "should refrain from instituting or continuing litigation that is obviously unfair." Model Code of Professional Responsibility EC 7–14 (1981).

Government lawyers, we have no doubt, should also refrain from continuing litigation that is obviously pointless, that could easily be resolved, and that wastes Court time and taxpayer money. "[T]he United States," as President Bush stated in an Executive Order, "sets an example for private litigation by adhering to higher standards than those required by the rules of procedure in the conduct of Government litigation in Federal court." Executive Order on Civil Justice Reform, 27 Weekly Comp. Pres. Doc. (October 23, 1991). The Executive Order, designed in part "to reduce needless litigation," requires government attorneys to attempt to settle cases whenever possible. Although we express no views on the applicability of the Executive Order to counsel for administrative agencies, and although we think a government lawyer's obligation to avoid needless litigation precedes the Executive Order, the Order plainly propounds the very proposition FERC's counsel challenged at oral argument.

We stress, to conclude, that we are concerned not so much with the failings of FERC's counsel in this case, but with the underlying view of a government lawyer's responsibilities that counsel revealed at oral argument. We find it astonishing that an attorney for a federal administrative agency could so unblushingly deny that a government lawyer has obligations that might sometimes trump the desire to pound an opponent into submission.

The challenged orders are

vacated.

Note

Federal government lawyers in general and Department of Justice attorneys in particular are subject to government-wide standards of conduct promulgated by the Office of Government Ethics at 5 C.F.R. Chap. XVI, Department of Justice Order 1735.1A, and Department of Justice regulations at 5 C.F.R. §§ 3801.101–106. These standards concern such matters as financial disclosure reports; receipt of gifts; private gain that might be realized from official action; restrictions on outside activities that might conflict with official duties, such as teaching, speaking, and writing, participation in civic organizations, pro bono work, and political activities; and restrictions on post-employment activities. The Office of Professional

O. P. R

(civil &
criminal)

Responsibility within the Department of Justice investigates charges of serious misconduct by Department attorneys that relate to the exercise of their authority to investigate, litigate, and provide legal advice.

Moreover, the Citizens Protection Act of 1998, 28 U.S.C. § 530B, makes state ethics rules and local federal rules applicable to federal government attorneys:

> An attorney for the Government shall be subject to State laws and rules, and local Federal court rules, governing attorneys in each state where such attorney engages in that attorney's duties, to the same extent and in the same manner as other attorneys in that State.

Thus, for example, a federal government attorney is bound by the professional conduct rules that have been adopted in the state or states where he or she practices.

Because this statute restricts the ability of federal prosecutors to conduct undercover operations and interview persons who have retained attorneys—by reason of state professional ethics rules that prohibit a lawyer from making a direct contact with a represented person (sometimes called the "no-contact rule")—it has been controversial from the outset and was vehemently opposed by the Department of Justice. Since 1998, various bills have been introduced in Congress to grant greater freedom to federal prosecutors to communicate with represented persons, at least prior to arrest or indictment, notwithstanding conflicting state rules. Whether or not the statute is repealed or revised, it is unlikely to have a significant effect upon most attorneys engaged in a government civil practice, although the Citizens Protection Act does apply to *all* government attorneys and would have more direct consequences for those government civil lawyers who conduct investigations for purposes of pursuing civil or administrative sanctions against regulatory violators.

———

SECTION C. JURISDICTION, VENUE, AND JUSTICIABILITY IN FEDERAL GOVERNMENT CASES

Because the jurisdictional rules governing litigation against the federal government tend to be interwoven with the particular statutory waivers of sovereign immunity, a more detailed discussion of each pertinent jurisdictional provision will come at later points in this casebook. As we look at specific statutory waivers of sovereign immunity in subsequent chapters, these individual jurisdictional and venue statutes will be more closely examined in the context of particular causes of action against the federal government. At this point, look at this material for the big-picture and don't worry about parsing the intricate details of these statutes. The important point to take away for now is that the federal government benefits from specially crafted jurisdictional and venue statutes, one further indication that the government is not treated as an ordinary party in litigation.

———

1. SUBJECT MATTER JURISDICTION AND VENUE STATUTES

28 United States Code § 1345

Except as otherwise provided by Act of Congress, the district courts shall have original jurisdiction of all civil actions, suits or proceedings commenced by the United States, or by any agency or officer thereof expressly authorized to sue by Act of Congress.

action by U.S. . .

———

28 United States Code § 1346

(a) The district courts shall have original jurisdiction, concurrent with the United States Court of Federal Claims, of:

(1) Any civil action against the United States for the recovery of any internal-revenue tax alleged to have been erroneously or illegally assessed or collected, or any penalty claimed to have been collected without authority or any sum alleged to have been excessive or in any manner wrongfully collected under the internal-revenue laws;

(2) Any other civil action or claim against the United States, not exceeding $10,000 in amount, founded either upon the Constitution, or any Act of Congress, or any regulation of an executive department, or upon any express or implied contract with the United States, or for liquidated or unliquidated damages in cases not sounding in tort, except that the district courts shall not have jurisdiction of any civil action or claim against the United States <u>founded upon</u> any express or implied contract with the United States or for liquidated or unliquidated damages in cases not sounding in tort which are subject to sections 8(g)(1) and 10(a)(1) of the Contract Disputes Act of 1978. For the purpose of this paragraph, an express or implied contract with the Army and Air Force Exchange Service, Navy Exchanges, Marine Corps Exchanges, Coast Guard Exchanges, or Exchange Councils of the National Aeronautics and Space Administration shall be considered an express or implied contract with the United States.

(b)(1) Subject to the provisions of chapter 171 of this title, the district courts, together with the United States District Court for the District of the Canal Zone and the District Court of the Virgin Islands, shall have exclusive jurisdiction of civil actions on claims against the United States, for money damages, accruing <u>on and after</u> January 1, 1945, for <u>injury or loss</u> of <u>property</u>, or <u>personal injury</u> or <u>death</u> caused by the negligent or wrongful act or omission of any employee of the Government while acting within the scope of his office or employment, under circumstances where the United States, if a private person, would be liable to the claimant in accordance with the law of the place where the act or omission occurred.

Disqualifies certain potential plaintiffs

(2) No person convicted of a felony who is incarcerated while awaiting sentencing or while serving a sentence may bring a civil action against the United States or an agency, officer, or employee of the Government, for mental or emotional injury suffered while in custody without a prior showing of physical injury.

(c) The jurisdiction conferred by this section includes jurisdiction of any set-off, counterclaim, or other claim or demand whatever on the part of the United States against any plaintiff commencing an action under this section.

No pension claims heard in fed. dist. cts.

(d) The district courts shall not have jurisdiction under this section of any civil action or claim for a pension.

(e) The district courts shall have original jurisdiction of any civil action against the United States provided in section 6226, 6228(a), 7426, or 7428 *²* (in the case of the United States district court for the District of Columbia) or section 7429 of the Internal Revenue Code of 1986.

(f) The district courts shall have exclusive original jurisdiction of civil actions under section 2409a to quiet title to an estate or interest in real property in which an interest is claimed by the United States.

(g) Subject to the provisions of chapter 179, the district courts of the United States shall have exclusive jurisdiction over any civil action commenced under section 453(2) of title 3, by a covered employee under chapter 5 of such title [employment discrimination suits involving presidential offices].

———

action vs. Δ (officer of U.S.)

— venue

28 United States Code § 1391(e)

(e) A civil action in which a defendant is an officer or employee of the United States or any agency thereof acting in his official capacity or under color of legal authority, or an agency of the United States, or the United States, may, except as otherwise provided by law, be brought in any judicial district in which (1) a defendant in the action resides, (2) a substantial part of the events or omissions giving rise to the claim occurred, or a substantial part of property that is the subject of the action is situated, or (3) the plaintiff resides if no real property is involved in the action. Additional persons may be joined as parties to any such action in accordance with the Federal Rules of Civil Procedure and with such other venue requirements as would be applicable if the United States or one of its officers, employees, or agencies were not a party. * * *

———

28 United States Code § 1402

(a) Any civil action in a district court against the United States under subsection (a) of section 1346 of this title may be prosecuted only:

(1) Except as provided in paragraph (2), in the judicial district where the plaintiff resides;

_ specific venues

(2) In the case of a civil action by a corporation under paragraph (1) of subsection (a) of section 1346, in the judicial district in which is located the principal place of business or principal office or agency of the corporation; or if it has no principal place of business or principal officer or agency in any judicial district (A) in the judicial district in which is located the office to which was made the return of the tax in respect of which the claim is made, or (B) if no return was made, in the judicial district in which lies the District of Columbia. Notwithstanding the foregoing provisions of this paragraph a district court, for the convenience of the parties and witnesses, in the interest of justice, may transfer any such action to any other district or division.

(b) Any civil action on a tort claim against the United States under subsection (b) of section 1346 of this title may be prosecuted only in the judicial district where the plaintiff resides or wherein the act or omission complained of occurred.

(c) Any civil action against the United States under subsection (e) of section 1346 of this title may be prosecuted only in the judicial district where the property is situated at the time of levy, or if no levy is made, in the judicial district in which the event occurred which gave rise to the cause of action.

(d) Any civil action under section 2409a to quiet title to an estate or interest in real property in which an interest is claimed by the United States shall be brought in the district court of the district where the property is located or, if located in different districts, in any of such districts.

----

2.   STANDING, RIPENESS, AND POLITICAL QUESTION DOCTRINE

In addition to the statutory limitations on subject matter jurisdiction over federal government cases set out above, as well as the requirement of a statutory waiver of sovereign immunity (which will be the subject of Chapter II and an underlying theme to the rest of the course), there are certain jurisdictional or justiciability obstacles to suits against the federal government that flow from the very nature of the federal courts:

Initially, a plaintiff must establish standing by showing that a defendant has personally injured her. Furthermore, the case must be ripe (*i.e.*, well-developed factually and legally) but not moot (*i.e.*, irrelevant because the parties' dispute has ended). Finally, the question presented cannot be "political," but instead must be capable of "judicial" resolution.

Robert J. Pushaw, *Justiciability and Separation of Powers: A Neo-Federalist Approach*, 81 Cornell. L. Rev. 393, 395 (1996). Under Article III, § 2 of the United States Constitution, the judicial power extends to certain "Cases" and "Controversies." Thus, the federal courts may not offer advisory opinions on issues that are of only theoretical or abstract interest to the parties in a lawsuit. Rather, the courts may take jurisdiction only of concrete disputes in which the complaining party has suffered an actual and present injury and will realize a practical and significant consequence from resolution of the lawsuit. The doctrines of *standing* and *ripeness* have been derived from this understanding of the limited constitutional authority of the judiciary. Moreover, recognizing that the courts may lack legitimacy or competence when speaking on certain matters, the courts will refuse to hear complaints when the decision is viewed as being constitutionally committed to the political branches of government or beyond the expertise of the courts to resolve. This lack of justiciability is called the *political question doctrine*.

Standing. Although legal historians report that the modern doctrines of justiciability are of relatively recent vintage, the Supreme Court in this century has construed the "case" and "controversy" language in Article III to limit the judicial power to adjudication of those lawsuits that raise live disputes in which the parties have a personal and concrete interest. *See* Pushaw, *supra*. In the context of public law questions, the Supreme Court has held that "[o]ne element of the 'bedrock' case-or-controversy requirement is that plaintiffs must establish that they have standing to sue," that is standing to invoke the power of a federal court to review the conduct of government. *McConnell v. Federal Election Commission*, 540 U.S. 93, 225 (2003); *see also Whitmore v. Arkansas*, 495 U.S. 149, 155 (1990) ("[T]he doctrine of standing serves to identify those disputes which are appropriately resolved through the judicial process."). Standing requires the plaintiff to have "such a personal stake in the outcome of the controversy as to assure the concrete adverseness which sharpens the presentation of issues." *Baker v. Carr*, 369 U.S. 186, 204 (1962).

To satisfy the constitutional requirements for standing, a plaintiff must allege a personal stake in the outcome of the litigation, *Sierra Club v. Morton*, 405 U.S. 727 (1972), in the form of "some direct injury" which is "real and immediate," *City of Los Angeles v. Lyons*, 461 U.S. 95, 102 (1983). The injury alleged must be "distinct and palpable," and not "abstract," "conjectural," or "hypothetical." *Allen v. Wright*, 468 U.S. 737, 751 (1984). Moreover, this "injury in fact" suffered by the plaintiff must be "fairly traceable to the defendant's allegedly unlawful conduct and likely to be addressed by the requested relief." *Allen v. Wright*, 468 U.S. at 751; *see also* Lujan v. Defenders of Wildlife, 504 U.S. 555, 560–61 (1992). Thus, there are three interrelated constitutional components of standing—injury in fact, causation, and redressability by the courts. Lujan, 504 U.S. at 560–61.

As a prudential matter of judicial self-restraint, the Supreme Court has further restricted standing to those cases in which the plaintiff can show that the interest sought to be protected in the lawsuit is arguably within the zone of interests to be protected by the statutory or constitutional provision upon which the plaintiff depends. *National Credit Union Admin. v. First Nat'l Bank & Trust Co.*, 522 U.S. 479, 488 (1998); *Association of Data Processing Service Organizations, Inc. v. Camp*, 397 U.S. 150 (1970). However, Congress by legislation may expressly negate the zone-of-interests test or expand the zone of interests to more generously authorize suits against the federal government. *Bennett v. Spear*, 520 U.S. 154, 163–65 (1997); *see also Raines v. Byrd*, 521 U.S. 811, 820 n. 3 (1997) (holding that an explicit grant of authority by Congress to bring suit "eliminates any prudential standing limitations and significantly lessens the risk of unwanted conflict with the Legislative Branch").

Under these standing restrictions, generalized and abstract grievances about the conduct of the government are insufficient to establish the personal injury required for standing. *United States v. Richardson*, 418 U.S. 166, 173–74 (1974). Thus, an asserted right to have the government act in accordance with law is not sufficient, standing alone, to confer federal court jurisdiction. *Allen v. Wright*, 468 U.S. at 754. Nor will the mere assertion of a right " 'to a particular kind of government conduct, which the Government has violated by acting differently,' " satisfy the Article III requirements for standing. Id. (quoting *Valley Forge Christian College v. Americans United for Separation of Church and State, Inc.*, 454 U.S. 464, 483 (1982)).

The Supreme Court has long held that "standing to sue may not be predicated upon an interest of the kind * * * which is held in common by all members of the public." *Schlesinger v. Reservists Comm. to Stop the War*, 418 U.S. 208, 220 (1974). However, the Court recently has clarified that, where a harm is sufficiently concrete and specific—especially if it implicates fundamental rights, such as voting—standing may be found, even if the asserted harm is widely shared by other citizens. *Federal Election Comm'n v. Akins*, 524 U.S. 11, 22–24 (1998). Nonetheless, abstract or indefinite harm, such as a common concern that the government obey the law, remains insufficient for standing. Id. at 1785.

For more detailed discussions of standing, see Richard J. Pierce, Jr., Sidney A. Shapiro & Paul R. Verkuil, *Administrative Law and Process*, § 5.4, at 139–71 (4th ed. 2004); Charles Alan Wright, *Federal Courts*, § 13, at 67–83 (5th ed. 1994); Alfred C. Aman, Jr. & William T. Mayton, *Administrative Law*, § 12.7, at 379–412 (2d ed. 2001).

Ripeness. The doctrine of ripeness also limits the jurisdiction of the federal courts by precluding adjudication of abstract controversies in the absence of present and concrete hardship. If the harm that a plaintiff claims he will suffer remains contingent on future events, that are far from certain to occur, or the government has not yet rendered a final decision on the matter at issue, the case is not yet ripe for judicial consideration. In

Abbott Laboratories v. Gardner, 387 U.S. 136 (1967), the Supreme Court explained that the basic rationale of the ripeness doctrine is

> to prevent the courts, through avoidance of premature adjudication, from entangling themselves in abstract disagreements over administrative policies, and also to protect the agencies from judicial interference until an administrative decision has been formalized and its effects felt in a concrete way by the challenging parties.

Id. at 148–49; *see also Ohio Forestry Ass'n v. Sierra Club*, 523 U.S. 726, 732 (1998).

The Supreme Court has set out a two-part test for determining ripeness, requiring evaluation of both (1) "the fitness of the issues for judicial decision" at this time and (2) "the hardship to the parties of withholding court consideration." *Ohio Forestry Ass'n*, 523 U.S. at 733; *Abbott Laboratories*, 387 U.S. at 149.

First, in terms of the *fitness* of the issue for adjudication, the courts look to whether the issue is fully developed in the context of a concrete and present dispute. The Court is reluctant to hear a facial challenge to a regulation or rule that has not yet been applied, because "judicial appraisal * * * is likely to stand on a much surer footing in the context of a specific application of [the] regulation." *Toilet Goods Ass'n v. Gardner*, 387 U.S. 158, 164 (1967). (However, preenforcement relief is not always barred, if the party challenging the government rule can make a compelling showing on the second prong of the test, for example, that the party will endure high costs in complying with the rule or risks substantial civil or criminal penalties if the rule is violated. *See, e.g., Abbott Laboratories, supra.*)

Second, with respect to the showing of *hardship* by delaying adjudication, the courts consider "the degree and nature of the [government rule's] present effect on those seeking relief." *Id.* Thus, "[a] case may lack ripeness * * * even when it involves a final agency action presenting a purely legal question," where the action has no "sufficiently direct and immediate" impact on the parties. *Alascom, Inc. v. Federal Communications Comm'n*, 727 F.2d 1212, 1217 (D.C. Cir. 1984).

For a more detailed discussion of ripeness, see Pierce, Shapiro & Verkuil, *supra*, §§ 5.7.3 to 5.7.5, at 200–212; Aman & Mayton, *supra*, § 12.9, at 413–21.

Political Question Doctrine. That certain political decisions are, by their nature, committed to the political branches of the federal government has been recognized by the Supreme Court since *Marbury v. Madison*, 5 U.S. (1 Cranch.) 137, 164 (1803), in which Chief Justice Marshall acknowledged a class of cases that involve a "mere political act belonging to the executive department alone." The political question doctrine is founded on the separation of powers and precludes judicial review when any one of several "formulations" arise. *Baker v. Carr*, 369 U.S. 186, 210–11, 217 (1962). These "formulations" have been grouped into three relevant inquires:

(i) Does the issue involve resolution of questions committed by the text of the Constitution to a coordinate branch of Government? (ii) Would resolution of the question demand that a court move beyond areas of judicial expertise? (iii) Do prudential considerations counsel against judicial intervention?

Goldwater v. Carter, 444 U.S. 996, 998 (1979) (Powell, J., concurring).

The Court applies the political question doctrine sparingly and is more likely to do so in the narrow context of military and foreign affairs, wherein the Constitution confers substantial discretion upon the President. While not every case touching on foreign affairs lies beyond judicial review, *Baker v. Carr*, 369 U.S. at 211, the Supreme Court has repeatedly emphasized that "foreign relations are specifically committed by the Constitution to the political branches." *United States v. Balsys*, 524 U.S. 666, 695 (1998). In *Chicago & Southern Air Lines, Inc. v. Waterman Steamship Corp.*, 333 U.S. 103, 111 (1948), the Court said:

> [T]he very nature of executive decisions as to foreign policy is political, not judicial. Such decisions are wholly confided by our Constitution to the political departments of the government, Executive and Legislative. They are delicate, complex, and involve large elements of prophecy. * * * They are decisions of a kind for which the Judiciary has neither the aptitude, facilities nor responsibility and which has long been held to belong to the domain of political power not subject to judicial intrusion or inquiry.

For a more detailed discussion of the political question doctrine, see Wright, *supra*, § 14, at 83–91.

    * * *

The above summaries of three justiciability doctrines hardly do justice to these complex concepts or to the continuing debates concerning their proper breadth and application. Nor is an appreciation of black-letter law alone sufficient to a complete understanding of the controversies entailed by these modern doctrines of justiciability. For example, critics of the standing rules assert that the standards can be too easily manipulated to political ends, allowing judges to confer standing on those whose ideological goals they endorse while denying access to the courts for those whose views are disapproved. Richard J. Pierce, Jr., *Is Standing Law or Politics*, 77 N.C. L. Rev. 1741 (1999).

For two reasons, however, these brief synopses should be sufficient to our purposes in this course. First, standing, ripeness, and the political question doctrine should be central topics of study in such courses as Administrative Law, Federal Courts, and perhaps Constitutional Law. Given that this course on Litigation With the Federal Government is designed to address subjects not covered in other parts of the law school curriculum, a more thorough treatment of these topics is properly left to those existing educational venues.

Second, standing and ripeness issues tend to arise in the regulatory context of administrative law, when citizens are challenging a policy decision made by agency administrators with respect to regulatory or benefit programs. By contrast, the principal focus of this course is upon the government as a primary actor, that is, when the government has taken action as a sovereign entity that causes direct consequences of harm to others. Thus, if a private plaintiff alleges that the government has negligently injured him or her (a tort claim) or has breached a formal agreement with him or her (a contract claim), standing and ripeness are almost invariably satisfied and uncontroverted. When we study claims under the Federal Tort Claims Act (FTCA) in Chapter III.A, for example, we will not encounter questions of standing and ripeness, although we will find that the FTCA has its own standards for determining when a tort claim is ready for court consideration. The line between the government as a primary actor and the government acting as a regulator of private conduct admittedly is an uncertain one, and issues concerning the government in a regulatory capacity will frequently intrude upon our study in this course. Nonetheless, we will have little occasion to return to the subjects of standing and ripeness.

By contrast, the political question doctrine *will* re-surface later in this course, although sometimes in disguise. As we turn to sovereign immunity as a doctrine in Chapter II, the question of judicial competence to evaluate policy-making decisions by the other branches of government will underlie the discussion. Moreover, when we study certain exceptions to waivers of sovereign immunity, separation of powers concerns and judicial deference to sensitive political decisions will be central to the analysis. Indeed, when we discover that the "discretionary function exception" to the FTCA (addressed in Chapter III.A.4) is grounded in separation of powers concerns, you should ask whether the exception is, in sum and substance, the political question doctrine in another form and context.

SECTION D.   SERVICE OF PROCESS UPON THE FEDERAL GOVERNMENT

28 United States Code § 1391(e)

* * * The summons and complaint in [an action against a federal officer in his official capacity, an agency of the United States, or the United States] shall be served as provided by the Federal Rules of Civil Procedure except that the delivery of the summons and complaint to the officer or agency as required by the rules may be made by certified mail beyond the territorial limits of the district in which the action is brought.

Federal Rule of Civil Procedure 4(i)

(i) Serving the United States, Its Agencies, Corporations, Officers, or Employees.

(1) Service upon the United States shall be effected

(A) by delivering a copy of the summons and of the complaint to the United States attorney for the district in which the action is brought or to an assistant United States attorney or clerical employee designated by the United States attorney in a writing filed with the clerk of the court or by sending a copy of the summons and of the complaint by registered or certified mail addressed to the civil process clerk at the office of the United States Attorney and

(B) by also sending a copy of the summons and of the complaint by registered or certified mail to the Attorney General of the United States at Washington, District of Columbia, and

(C) in any action attacking the validity of an order of an officer or agency of the United States not made a party, by also sending a copy of the summons and of the complaint by registered or certified mail to the officer or agency.

(2)   *— Agency; Corp.; Officer/Employee... Official Capacity —*

(A) Service on an agency or corporation of the United States, or an officer or employee of the United States sued only in an official capacity, is effected by serving the United States in the manner prescribed by Rule 4(i)(1) and by also sending a copy of the summons and complaint by registered or certified mail to the officer, employee, agency, or corporation   , *individual capacity*

(B) Service on an officer or employee of the United States sued in an individual capacity for acts or omissions occurring in connection with the performance of duties on behalf of the United States— whether or not the officer or employee is sued also in an official capacity—is effected by serving the United States in the manner prescribed by Rule 4(i)(1) and by serving the officer or employee in the manner prescribed by Rule 4 (e), (f), or (g).

(3) The court shall allow a reasonable time to serve process under Rule 4(i) for the purpose of curing the failure to serve:

(A) all persons required to be served in an action governed by Rule 4(i)(2)(A), if the plaintiff has served either the United States attorney or the Attorney General of the United States, or

(B) the United States in an action governed by Rule 4(i)(2)(B), if the plaintiff has served an officer or employee of the United States sued in an individual capacity.

Note

Under Rule 4(i) of the Federal Rules of Civil Procedure, when the United States is a party to the lawsuit, effective service requires proper delivery or mailing to both the United States Attorney for the district in which the suit is filed and the Attorney General in Washington, D.C. As one court has said, a plaintiff must comply with both prongs of Rule 4(i)(1)

2 prongs

"[f]or good reason: that's what the rule says." *Tuke v. United States*, 76 F.3d 155, 157 (7th Cir. 1996). If suit is brought against a federal government agency, government corporation, or an officer or employee of the United States in an individual capacity, then service must be effected by serving the United States in the manner set out above and serving the agency, corporation, officer, or employee. Under Rule 4(i)(3), certain errors in accomplishing the multiple services required by the rule for service upon government agencies, officers, or employees may be cured "within a reasonable time." But proper service is required:

> While a court must give a plaintiff reasonable time to cure a defect in service under Rule 4(i)(3) or grant an appropriate extension of time for service under Rule 4(m), nothing in the Federal Rules of Civil Procedure allows a judge to excuse service altogether. Actual notice to the defendant is insufficient; the plaintiff must comply with the directives of Rule 4.

McMasters v. United States, 260 F.3d 814, 817 (7th Cir. 2001). On service of process against the federal government, its officers, or agencies, see generally Gregory C. Sisk, *Litigation With the Federal Government* § 1.06, at 36–38 (ALI–ABA, 4th ed. 2006).

———

SECTION E.   DISCOVERY AND THE FEDERAL GOVERNMENT

United States v. Weber Aircraft Corporation

Supreme Court of the United States.
465 U.S. 792 (1984).

■ JUSTICE STEVENS delivered the opinion of the Court.

The Freedom of Information Act (FOIA), 5 U.S.C. § 552 (1982 ed.), requires federal agencies to disclose records that do not fall into one of nine exempt categories. The question presented is whether confidential statements obtained during an Air Force investigation of an air crash are protected from disclosure by Exemption 5, which exempts "inter-agency or intra-agency memorandums or letters which would not be available by law to a party other than an agency in litigation with the agency."

I

On October 9, 1973, the engine of an Air Force F–106B aircraft failed in flight. Captain Richard Hoover, the pilot, was severely injured when he ejected from the plane. Under Air Force regulations, the incident was a significant air crash that required two separate investigations: a "collateral investigation" and a "safety investigation."

The collateral investigation is conducted "to preserve available evidence for use in claims, litigation, disciplinary actions, administrative proceedings, and all other purposes." Witnesses in a collateral investigation testify under oath and generally are protected by the procedural safeguards that are applicable in other formal hearings. The record of the collateral investigation is public.

The "safety investigation" is quite different. It is conducted by a specially appointed tribunal which prepares a report that is intended for "the sole purpose of taking corrective action in the interest of accident prevention." To encourage witnesses to speak fully and frankly, they are not sworn and receive an assurance that their statements will not be used for any purpose other than accident prevention. Air Force regulations contain a general prohibition against the release of safety investigation reports and their attachments, subject to an exception which allows the Judge Advocate General to release specified categories of "factual information" and "nonpersonal evidence."

After the collateral and safety investigations had been completed, Captain Hoover filed a damages action against various entities responsible for the design and manufacture of his plane's ejection equipment. During pretrial discovery in that litigation, two of the parties (respondents Weber and Mills) sought discovery of all Air Force investigative reports pertaining to the accident. The Air Force released the entire record of the collateral investigation, as well as certain factual portions of the safety investigation, but it refused to release the confidential portions of the safety investigation.

Confidential statements made to air crash safety investigators were held to be privileged with respect to pretrial discovery over 20 years ago. *Machin v. Zuckert*, 316 F.2d 336 (D.C.Cir.), cert. denied, 375 U.S. 896 (1963). That holding effectively prevented respondents from obtaining the pretrial discovery they sought—specifically the unsworn statements given by Captain Hoover and by the airman who had rigged and maintained his parachute equipment. Respondents therefore filed requests for those statements under the FOIA, and when the Air Force refused production, they commenced this action.

In the District Court the Government filed an affidavit executed by the General responsible for Air Force safety investigations, explaining that the material that had been withheld contained "conclusions, speculations, findings and recommendations made by the Aircraft Mishap Investigators" as well as "testimony presented by witnesses under a pledge of confidentiality." The affidavit explained why the General believed that the national security would be adversely affected by the disclosure of such material.[11]

11. "[T]he release of the withheld portions of the Aircraft Mishap Investigation for litigation purposes would be harmful to our national security. The strength of the United States Air Force, upon which our national security is greatly dependent, is seriously affected by the number of major aircraft accidents which occur. The successful flight safe-ty program of the United States Air Force has contributed greatly to the continuously decreasing rate of such accidents. The effectiveness of this program depends to a large extent upon our ability to obtain full and candid information on the cause of each aircraft accident. Much of the information received from persons giving testimony in the

Dist. Ct.
decision

Ct. Appeals REV'D

The District Court held that the material at issue would not be available by law to a party other than an agency in litigation with an agency, and hence need not be disclosed by virtue of Exemption 5. The Court of Appeals reversed, 688 F.2d 638. It agreed that the requested documents were "intra-agency memorandums" within the meaning of Exemption 5, and that they were protected from civil discovery under the *Machin* privilege. It held, however, that the statutory phrase "would not be available by law" did not encompass every civil discovery privilege but rather reached only those privileges explicitly recognized in the legislative history of FOIA. It read that history as accepting an executive privilege for predecisional documents containing advice, opinions or recommendations of government agents, but as not extending to the Machin civil discovery privilege for official government information. It accordingly remanded the case with directions to disclose the factual portions of the witnesses' statements.

e.g.'s of
privileged stuff
in the L.H. of
FOIA

II

"intra-agency"
+
Machin privilege =
AF doesn't need
to disclose

The plain language of the statute itself, as construed by our prior decisions, is sufficient to resolve the question presented. The statements of the two witnesses are unquestionably "intra-agency memorandums or letters" and, since the *Machin* privilege normally protects them from discovery in civil litigation, they "would not be available by law to a party other than [the Air Force] in litigation with [the Air Force]."[14]

Last Term, in *FTC v. Grolier, Inc.*, 462 U.S. 19 (1983), we held that Exemption 5 simply incorporates civil discovery privileges: "The test under Exemption 5 is whether the documents would be 'routinely' or 'normally'

'The witnesses
are candid only
because they are
assured no
repurcussions
will come from their
disclosure'

course of an aircraft mishap investigation is conjecture, speculation and opinion. Such full and frank disclosure is not only encouraged but is imperative to a successful flight safety program. Open and candid testimony is received because witnesses are promised that for the particular investigation their testimony will be used solely for the purpose of flight safety and will not be disclosed outside of the Air Force. Lacking authority to subpoena witnesses, accident investigators must rely on such assurances in order to obtain full and frank discussion concerning all the circumstances surrounding an accident. Witnesses are encouraged to express personal criticisms concerning the accident.

. . . .

"If aircraft mishap investigators were unable to give such assurances, or if it were felt that such promises were hollow, testimony and input from witnesses and from manufacturers in many instances would be less than factual and a determination of the exact cause factors of accidents would be jeopardized. This would seriously hinder the accom-

plishment of prompt corrective action designed to preclude the occurrence of a similar accident. This privilege, properly accorded to the described portions of an United States Air Force Mishap Report of Investigation, including those portions reflecting the deliberations of the Investigating Board, is the very foundation of a successful Air Force flight safety program."

14. Weber contends that the material at issue is not privileged because it was not obtained pursuant to a promise of confidentiality. However, the District Court found otherwise, and since that finding is supported by an uncontroverted affidavit submitted by the Government to the District Court, there is no basis for setting it aside. In all other respects, respondents concede that the requested material is covered by the *Machin* privilege, and did not file a cross-petition for certiorari challenging the Court of Appeals' conclusion that the requested material was privileged. Thus, we assume without deciding that the material respondents seek is privileged, and do not consider the arguments of amici that no privilege is applicable here.

Effect of
Non-disclosure. . .

disclosed upon a showing of relevance." Thus, since the *Machin* privilege is well recognized in the case law as precluding routine disclosure of the statements, the statements are covered by Exemption 5.

Grolier was consistent with our prior cases. For example, *Grolier* itself relied on *Renegotiation Board v. Grumman Aircraft Engineering Corp.*, 421 U.S. 168 (1975), which Grolier quoted on the scope of Exemption 5: "Exemption 5 incorporates the privileges which the government enjoys under the relevant statutory and *case law* in the pretrial discovery context." 462 U.S., at 26–27 (emphasis in original) (quoting 421 U.S., at 184). Similarly, in *NLRB v. Sears, Roebuck & Co.*, 421 U.S. 132 (1975), we wrote: "Exemption 5 withholds from a member of the public documents which a private party could not discover in litigation with the agency." *Id.*, at 148. In *Federal Open Market Committee v. Merrill*, 443 U.S. 340 (1979), we wrote: "The House Report [on the FOIA] states that Exemption 5 was intended to allow an agency to withhold intra-agency memoranda which would not be 'routinely disclosed to a private party through the discovery process in litigation with the agency....' " *Id.*, at 353 (quoting H. R. Rep. No. 1497, 89th Cong., 2d Sess., 10 (1966)). And in *EPA v. Mink*, 410 U.S. 73 (1973), the Court observed: "This language clearly contemplates that the public is entitled to all such memoranda or letters that a private party could discover in litigation with the agency." *Id.*, at 86.

Respondents read *Merrill* as limiting the scope of Exemption 5 to privileges explicitly identified by Congress in the legislative history of the FOIA. But in *Merrill* we were confronted with a claimed exemption that was not clearly covered by a recognized pretrial discovery privilege. We held that Exemption 5 protected the Federal Open Market Committee's Domestic Policy Directives although it was not entirely clear that they fell within any recognized civil discovery privilege because statements in the legislative history supported an inference that Congress intended to recognize such a privilege. Thus, the holding of *Merrill* was that a privilege that was mentioned in the legislative history of Exemption 5 is incorporated by the exemption—not that all privileges not mentioned are excluded. Moreover, the *Merrill* dictum upon which respondents rely merely indicates "that it is not clear that Exemption 5 was intended to incorporate every privilege known to civil discovery." It is one thing to say that recognition under Exemption 5 of a novel privilege, or one that has found less than universal acceptance, might not fall within Exemption 5 if not discussed in its legislative history. It is quite another to say that the *Machin* privilege, which has been well-settled for some two decades, need be viewed with the same degree of skepticism. In any event, the *Merrill* dictum concludes only that "a claim that a privilege other than executive privilege or the attorney privilege is covered by Exemption 5 must be viewed with caution." The claim of privilege sustained in *Machin* was denominated as one of executive privilege. See 316 F.2d, at 338. Hence the dictum is of little aid to respondents.

Moreover, respondents' contention that they can obtain through the FOIA material that is normally privileged would create an anomaly in that the FOIA could be used to supplement civil discovery. We have consistently rejected such a construction of the FOIA. We do not think that Congress could have intended that the weighty policies underlying discovery privileges could be so easily circumvented.[20]

Finally, the legislative history of Exemption 5 does not contain the kind of compelling evidence of congressional intent that would be necessary to persuade us to look beyond the plain statutory language. Because of the difficulty inherent in compiling an exhaustive list of evidentiary privileges, it would be impractical to treat the legislative history of Exemption 5 as containing a comprehensive list of all privileges Congress intended to adopt. Rather, the history of Exemption 5 can be understood by means of "rough analogies." *EPA v. Mink*, supra, at 86. The legislative history of Exemption 5 indicates that Congress intended to incorporate governmental privileges analogous to the *Machin* privilege. That history recognizes a need for claims of privilege when confidentiality is necessary to ensure frank and open discussion and hence efficient governmental operations. The *Machin* privilege was recognized for precisely this reason.[23] Thus, the *Machin* privilege is sufficiently related to the concerns expressed in the legislative history that we cannot say that the legislative history demonstrates that the statute should not be construed to mean what it says with respect to the *Machin* privilege.

We therefore simply interpret Exemption 5 to mean what it says. The judgment of the Court of Appeals is

Reversed.

Notes and Questions

1. In general, the discovery process under the Federal Rules of Civil Procedure applies to the United States in the same manner as to a private

---

20. Respondents also argue that their need for the requested material is great and that it would be unfair to expect them to defend the litigation brought against them by Captain Hoover without access to it. We answered this argument in *Grolier*, noting that the fact that in particular litigation a party's particularized showing of need may on occasion justify discovery of privileged material in order to avoid unfairness does not mean that such material is routinely discoverable and hence outside the scope of Exemption 5. Respondents must make their claim of particularized need in their litigation with Captain Hoover, since it is not a claim under the FOIA.

23. "We agree with the Government that when disclosure of investigative reports obtained in large part through promises of confidentiality would hamper the efficient op-eration of an important Government program and perhaps even, as the Secretary here claims, impair the national security by weakening a branch of the military, the reports should be considered privileged." 316 F.2d, at 339.

It follows that recognition of the *Machin* privilege would not be inconsistent with the fundamental goals of the FOIA since it does not necessarily reduce the amount of information available to the public. The privilege is recognized because the Government would not be able to obtain the information but for its assurance of confidentiality. Thus, much if not all of the information covered by the *Machin* privilege would not find its way into the public realm even if we refused to recognize the privilege, since under those circumstances the information would not be obtained by the Government in the first place.

litigant. *See generally* Gregory C. Sisk, *A Primer on the Civil Discovery Against the Federal Government*, 52 Fed. Lawyer 28 (June, 2005). Thus, ordinary discovery devices, such as interrogatories and depositions, may be used. However, the courts often restrict efforts to examine or otherwise obtain discovery from senior officers of the Government. In *Cheney v. United States District Court*, 542 U.S. 367, 383–91 (2004), the Supreme Court held that broad requests for civil discovery directed against the most senior officials in the Executive Branch, such as the Vice President, raise serious constitutional separation of powers concerns even without a formal assertion of executive privilege. When information is sought from the highest level of the government, the Court emphasized that the burden imposed upon the government weighs against permitting discovery given "the Executive Branch's interests in maintaining the autonomy of its office and safeguarding the confidentiality of its communications." *Id.* at 385. Even below the presidential level, the courts recognize that an "official's time and the exigencies of his everyday business would be severely impeded" if every plaintiff filing a suit against the federal government were permitted to depose the head of an agency. *Union Sav. Bank v. Saxon*, 209 F.Supp. 319, 319–20 (D.D.C. 1962). Thus, a head of a department will not be required to testify when deposition of a subordinate officer would serve as well.

2.   Discovery of information from the federal government for use in civil litigation does have a couple of different twists from private litigation. First, litigants in private litigation are limited to use of formal discovery and informal investigation to uncover information. But the federal government is also subject to a general duty to disclose information under the Freedom of Information Act. However, after *United States v. Weber Aircraft Corp.*, is there any advantage to a litigant against the federal government in resorting to this alternative system? Indeed, could discovery be more advantageous under certain circumstances? Consider whether there are situations in which information might be obtained in discovery, but would be withheld from disclosure under the Freedom of Information Act? What does the *Weber Aircraft* decision suggest in this regard (review footnote 20 of the opinion)?

Some commentators have observed that, even after *Weber Aircraft*, attorneys may effectively use the Freedom of Information Act to supplement discovery by (1) seeking documents before a lawsuit has been started and discovery is available, (2) obtaining documents that may not be "relevant" within the meaning of discovery rules but might still be helpful in litigation, or (3) submitting duplicate requests in the hope that government employees will accidentally disclose exempt materials, although this last practice has been challenged as abusive or unethical. Richard J. Pierce, Jr., Sidney A. Shapiro & Paul R. Verkuil, *Administrative Law and Process*, § 8.6, at 465–68 (4th ed. 2004); Edward A. Tomlinson, *Use of the Freedom of Information Act for Discovery Purposes*, 43 Md. L. Rev. 119 (1984) (arguing that a party in litigation with the government is obliged to provide notice to government counsel of litigation-related FOIA requests).

But...

Exemption 5 incorporates the limits on civil disc...

3.   In *Department of Interior v. Klamath Water Users Protective Association*, 532 U.S. 1 (2001), the Supreme Court described its precedent on Exemption 5 of the Freedom of Information Act as incorporating limitations on civil discovery:

> Exemption 5 protects from disclosure "inter-agency or intra-agency memorandums or letters which would not be available by law to a party other than an agency in litigation with the agency." 5 U.S.C. § 552(b)(5). To qualify, a document must thus satisfy two conditions: its source must be a Government agency, and it must fall within the ambit of a privilege against discovery under judicial standards that would govern litigation against the agency that holds it.

traditional limits:
- atty work product
- deliberative process

> Our prior cases on Exemption 5 have addressed the second condition, incorporating civil discovery privileges. See, *e.g., United States v. Weber Aircraft Corp.*, 465 U.S. 792, 799–800 (1984); *NLRB v. Sears, Roebuck & Co.*, 421 U.S. 132, 148 (1975) ("Exemption 5 withholds from a member of the public documents which a private party could not discover in litigation with the agency"). So far as they might matter here, those privileges include the privilege for attorney work-product and what is sometimes called the "deliberative process" privilege. Work product protects "mental processes of the attorney," *United States v. Nobles*, 422 U.S. 225, 238 (1975), while deliberative process covers "documents reflecting advisory opinions, recommendations and deliberations comprising part of a process by which governmental decisions and policies are formulated," *Sears, Roebuck & Co.*, 421 U.S., at 150. The deliberative process privilege rests on the obvious realization that officials will not communicate candidly among themselves if each remark is a potential item of discovery and front page news, and its object is to enhance "the quality of agency decisions," *id.*, at 151, by protecting open and frank discussion among those who make them within the Government, see also *Weber Aircraft Corp., supra*, at 802.

Id. at 8–9.

Inherent in FOIA

4.   As noted by the Supreme Court in *Department of Interior v. Klamath Water Users Protective Association*, the government also has the benefit of the traditional protection against disclosure of attorney work-product through discovery and thus concomitantly is protected from disclosure of work-product materials under the Freedom of Information Act by Exemption 5. As you undoubtedly learned in the first-year course on civil procedure, Federal Rule of Civil Procedure 26(b)(3) protects from discovery those materials prepared "in anticipation of litigation."

Recently, the United States Court of Appeals for the First Circuit initially appeared to significantly limit the availability of the work-product protection to the government as a basis for non-disclosure under Exemption 5 of the Freedom of Information Act. In its first opinion in *Maine v. U.S. Department of the Interior*, published in the advance sheets at 285 F.3d 126 (1st Cir. 2002), the court of appeals held that, to avoid disclosure under the Freedom of Information Act, the federal agency must show that such a document was created "primarily for" litigation purposes, that is,

The 1st Cir. put requirements for gov't to satisfy b/f apply work product privilege...

the primary motivation for creating the document was to assist in litigation and not for another governmental purpose. However, in response to a government petition for rehearing, the court ordered that opinion withdrawn from the bound volume of the Federal Reporter. Subsequently, the First Circuit issued a revised opinion which clarified that an agency need only make the somewhat lesser showing that a document was prepared "because of" the prospect of litigation in order to be afforded both work-product protection and exemption from disclosure under the Freedom of Information Act. *Maine v. U.S. Department of the Interior*, 298 F.3d 60, 68 (1st Cir. 2002). However, in that particular case, the court found that the government had failed its burden of showing that each withheld document was correlated with a lawsuit for which the documents were created and thus had failed to show that the documents would not have been created through routine administrative action in substantially the same form irrespective of litigation. *Id.* at 69–70.

5.   As a second twist on ordinary discovery, there are certain privileges from discovery that are available only to the federal government. Indeed, these privileges are designed solely with the government's institutional interests in mind. For example, the *Machin* privilege discussed in the *Weber Aircraft* opinion protects confidential communications to government investigators in a safety investigation following a military aircraft accident. By contrast, a mere promise of confidentiality would not protect against discovery in most non-federal government contexts.

Exclusive gov't privileges
. absolute vs. qualified

- machin

In addition, a well-nigh absolute privilege exists for military, diplomatic, and comparable secrets. *See* Sisk, *supra*, at 32. This "state secrets" privilege has been sparingly invoked since in recognition more than half a century ago. However, some observers complain that it has been invoked with increasing frequency in the aftermath of the terrorist attacks of September 11, 2001. *See, e.g.*, Louis Fisher, *In the Name of National Security: Unchecked Presidential Power and the Reynolds Case* 212, 245 (2006); Amanda Frost, *The State Secrets Privilege and Separation of Powers*, 75 Fordham L. Rev. 1931, 1938–40 (2007); William G. Weaver & Robert M. Pallitto, *State Secrets and Executive Power*, 120 Pol. Sci. Q. 85, 109 (2005); Dahlia Lithwick, *The Uncle Sam You Can't See*, Legal Times, Dec. 11, 2006, at 54). *But see* Robert M. Chesney, *State Secrets and the Limits of National Security Litigation*, 75 Geo. Wash. L. Rev. (forthcoming 2007) (concluding that the number of cases in which the state secrets privilege has been invoked is not significantly higher than in the past).

" state secrets "

In *United States v. Reynolds*, 345 U.S. 1, 7–8 (1953), the Supreme Court held that "[t]here must be a formal claim of privilege, lodged by the head of the department which has control over the matter, after actual personal consideration by that officer." While the judiciary must determine whether the assertion of the state secrets privilege is valid, the court is "subject to a standard mandating restraint in the exercise of its authority" and "is obliged to accord the 'utmost deference' to the responsibilities of the executive branch." *El–Masri v. United States*, 479 F.3d 296, 304–05 (4th Cir. 2007); *see also* Weaver & Pallitto, *supra*, at 98 (stating that the

.. How the court assesses invocation of " state secrets "

"clear message of the *Reynolds* ruling is that courts are to show utmost deference to executive assertions of privilege").

In contrast with many other privileges, when properly invoked, the state secrets privilege is absolute, "render[ing] the information unavailable." *In re Under Seal*, 945 F.2d 1285, 1287 n.2 (4th Cir. 1991). No balancing of interests occurs, indeed "[t]hat balance has already been struck" in favor of the government, *Halkin v. Helms*, 690 F.2d 977, 990 (D.C. Cir. 1982), and thus "[n]o competing public or private interest can be advanced to compel disclosure of information found to be protected" by this privilege, *Ellsberg v. Mitchell*, 709 F.2d 51, 57 (D.C. Cir. 1983). "Although harsh, the presence of a properly invoked state secrets privilege requires dismissal of the claim [or preclusion of the defense] that cannot prevail without the privileged information." *McDonnell Douglas Corp. v. United States*, 323 F.3d 1006, 1021–22 (Fed. Cir. 2003); *see also Farnsworth Cannon v. Grimes*, 635 F.2d 268, 281 (4th Cir. 1980) (en banc).

In *United States v. Nixon*, 418 U.S. 683 (1974), the famous "Watergate tapes" case, the Supreme Court recognized a "presidential privilege." However, in that case, the Court concluded that the privilege was outweighed by the constitutional demands of the criminal justice system and the need for the evidence on the White House tapes in a criminal trial. Shortly after this forced disclosure of the tapes, President Nixon resigned.

The contours of the "presidential privilege" and its legal sibling, "executive privilege," remain somewhat unclear. On the various forms of executive privilege, including a discussion of *United States v. Nixon,* the state secrets doctrine, and the *Dellums v. Powell* case which immediately follows, see generally 1 Laurence H. Tribe, *American Constitutional Law* § 4–15, at 769–83 (3d ed. 2000). The following case is one example of the assertion of the presidential privilege in civil litigation.

Dellums v. Powell (Appeal of Richard Nixon)

United States Court of Appeals for the District of Columbia Circuit.
561 F.2d 242 (D.C.Cir.), cert. denied, 434 U.S. 880 (1977).

■ LEVENTHAL, CIRCUIT JUDGE:

This appeal concerns the validity of an order of the District Court for the District of Columbia (Judge William Bryant) denying the motion of appellant, former President Richard M. Nixon, to quash a subpoena duces tecum served on Philip Buchen, Counsel to President Ford by plaintiffs-appellees.[1] The challenged subpoena demands production of "all tapes and transcripts of White House conversations during the period of April 16 through May 10, 1971, at which 'May Day' demonstrations ... were

---

1. The named plaintiffs-appellees, representing themselves and a class of approximately 1,200 individuals, are Congressman Ronald V. Dellums, Bruce Aldrich, Edward J. Cannon, Frederick J. Deterle, Janis L. McDonald, LaDuska Monaco, David L. Preiss, Gary M. Regan, Michael J. Roche, and Dorothy Strong.

discussed." Plaintiffs seek this material in connection with their civil action in District Court for damages ascribed to alleged violations of their constitutional rights.[2] The underlying facts refer to the arrest of plaintiffs and their class on the grounds of the Capitol on May 5, 1971, and their subsequent detention, during the "May Day" demonstrations held to protest American military involvement in Southeast Asia. The class action has already gone to trial as against all defendants other than former Attorney General John Mitchell, and the judgment of the District Court (also Judge Bryant) awarding damages to plaintiffs has been appealed.[4] The challenged subpoena is presently designed to obtain information for use only in the action remaining against Mr. Mitchell, whose case was severed on his motion.

[handwritten: → Constitutional claims]

The subpoena was originally served by plaintiffs in October, 1974. Mr. Buchen, the person who has actual physical control over Mr. Nixon's "White House tapes," filed a motion to quash the subpoena on the ground that he was not the custodian of the tapes, and alternatively that the material sought was not relevant to the case. The District Court denied Mr. Buchen's motion on November 14, 1974, and ordered him to produce the subpoenaed material. Shortly thereafter, counsel for Mr. Nixon learned of the production order and immediately filed a motion for stay of the November 14 order. He also filed his own motion to quash the subpoena, in which he asserted that the materials sought in the subpoena were subject to the presidential privilege of confidentiality recognized by the Supreme Court in *United States v. Nixon*, 418 U.S. 683 (1974), and that this privilege was absolute in the context of civil litigation. On December 2, 1974, the same date the District Court ordered severance as to Mr. Mitchell, it granted Mr. Nixon's motion for stay, without ruling on his motion to quash. The action against all but Mr. Mitchell proceeded to judgment without further material reference to the subpoena.

[handwritten: Buchen files M to Stay judgment ordering subpoena]

The subpoena thereafter remained in limbo until plaintiffs began making preparation to proceed with their action against Mr. Mitchell. * * * The District Court, on March 10, 1976, issued a Memorandum and Order denying the motion to quash, vacating the stay order of December 2, 1974, and directing Mr. Buchen to advise the Court of the time necessary for compliance with the subpoena. This court has stayed the District Court's order pending consideration of its validity.

[handwritten: 3/10/1976 Court vacates stay & wants compliance w/ s.p.]

2. Plaintiffs-appellees essentially charged that defendants deprived them of liberty without due process of law in violation of the Fifth Amendment, and infringed their rights to freedom of assembly, freedom of speech and freedom to petition the government for redress of grievances in violation of the First Amendment.

4. Mr. Mitchell was originally made a codefendant with the District of Columbia, the former Chief of the Capitol Police, the former Chief of the Metropolitan Police Department, and Mr. Richard Kleindienst. Mr. Mitchell was granted a severance on December 2, 1974, because of his involvement with other judicial proceedings. The remaining defendants went to trial and plaintiffs were awarded damages of twelve million dollars from the District of Columbia and the two former police chiefs; Mr. Kleindienst was granted a directed verdict because of insufficient evidence. Those judgments are currently on appeal before this Court. Mr. Nixon has never been a defendant in the suit.

Dist. cts reason for denying M to quash

In denying this motion to quash, the District Court assumed *arguendo* that a former President could assert a presidential privilege based on a generalized interest in confidentiality, but held that it was not an absolute privilege in the context of civil litigation and that it was entitled to a lesser weight than a claim of presidential privilege asserted by an incumbent President. The court found that the privilege had been <u>overcome</u> in this case, and that Mr. Nixon's Fourth Amendment privacy <u>rights</u> would not be infringed by a search of the materials by Mr. Buchen.

These holdings are vigorously challenged on appeal. Mr. Nixon asserts that the privilege must be absolute when asserted in civil litigation, and that a <u>formal claim</u> of privilege is entitled to the same weight whether asserted by a <u>former or an incumbent</u> President. He additionally urges that the District Court erred in holding that his privacy claim was frivolous.

Rev'd as to . . .

Affirm as to

We reverse the District Court, in part, and remand the case with instructions intended to give further protection to Mr. Nixon's interest in the privacy of his personal documents and communications. As to the claim of presidential privilege, however, with the interest of personal privacy put to one side, we affirm the District Court's ruling. That ruling was based on the inaction of Gerald Ford, President when the District Court made its ruling, and when this opinion was sent to press. If a different approach by Jimmy Carter, as President, should develop, this would be a basis for counsel to seek reconsideration by the District Court.

I.

This case does not require us to rule on the issue of law whether a former President has the requisite interest to assert a presidential confidentiality privilege. <u>Assuming</u> *arguendo* a former President <u>may</u> present a claim of presidential privilege, we agree with the District Court both that it is entitled to lesser weight than that assigned the privilege asserted by an incumbent President, and that it has been overcome in the present case by plaintiffs' showing.

. former vs. present
. weight

We begin our discussion by rejecting Mr. Nixon's contention that a formal claim of privilege based on the generalized interest of presidential confidentiality, without more, works an absolute bar to discovery of presidential conversations in civil litigation, regardless of the relevancy or necessity of the information sought. It is the province and duty of the judiciary "to say what the law is" with respect to the claim of privilege in a particular case, even when the claim is one of presidential privilege. *Marbury v. Madison*, 1 Cranch 137, 177 (1803); *United States v. Nixon*, 418 U.S. 683, 705 (1974). The privilege asserted in the case at bar is not premised on a claim of a need to protect national security, military or diplomatic secrets; it is, rather, premised on the needs of present and future Presidents to maintain the confidentiality of communications with their advisors in order to encourage the candid advice necessary for effective decisionmaking. The privilege rooted in confidential communications with the President is constitutionally based, and entitled to great weight, *United States v. Nixon, supra*, but it has been consistently viewed

Nixon's Basis: confidential Executive communications

as presumptive only. The various decisions considering the privilege reflect a balancing approach, weighing "the detrimental effects of disclosure against the necessity for production shown." In Judge McGowan's phrase, there is a "need for particularized analysis rather than [the] mechanistic formalism" inherent in a claim of executive absolutism. *Nixon v. Administrator [of General Services]*, 408 F. Supp. [321], 342 [(D.D.C.1976) (three judge court)].

The question before us was left open in *United States v. Nixon*, for in that case, as the Court noted, it had no occasion to consider the "need for relevant evidence in civil litigation."[10] Mr. Nixon argued that the recognition for civil litigation of a presidential privilege that is not conclusive, but only "presumptive," would effectively destroy the privilege. It is urged that recognition of a rebuttable presumption would open the floodgates: those on whom a President relies for advice would be foolish indeed to discuss the demands of executive decisionmaking with candor, when every proposal would be subject to public disclosure through civil discovery.

An advisor to the President has no guarantee of confidentiality. His advice may be disclosed by the President or a successor. As to disclosure by a court, the need for confidentiality is in large measure secured and protected by the relatively infrequent occasions when an assertion of the privilege may be overcome.[12] And so it is, and should be, that the "presumptive" privilege embodies a strong presumption, and not merely a lip-service reference.

Appellant's counsel stresses that in the 1974 *Nixon* case the court referred to the constitutional demands of the criminal justice system as identifying a need for disclosure. That is so. But there is also a strong constitutional value in the need for disclosure in order to provide the kind of enforcement of constitutional rights that is presented by a civil action for damages, at least where, as here, the action is tantamount to a charge of civil conspiracy among high officers of government to deny a class of citizens their constitutional rights and where there has been sufficient evidentiary substantiation to avoid the inference that the demand reflects mere harassment. The possibility of disclosure in such instances is not unlike the possibility of disclosure in criminal cases—the infrequent occa-

---

10. In United States v. Nixon, supra, 418 U.S. at 712, n. 19, the Court noted:

We are not here concerned with the balance between the President's generalized interest in confidentiality and the need for relevant evidence in civil litigation, nor with that between the confidentiality interest and congressional demands for information, nor with the President's interest in preserving state secrets. We address only the conflict between the President's assertion of a generalized privilege of confidentiality and the constitutional need for relevant evidence in criminal trials.

12.
The interest in preserving confidentiality is weighty indeed and entitled to great respect. However, we cannot conclude that advisers will be moved to temper the candor of their remarks by the infrequent occasions of disclosure because of the possibility that such conversations will be called for in the context of a criminal prosecution.

United States v. Nixon, supra, 418 U.S. at 712.

sions of such disclosure militate against any substantial fear that the candor of Presidential advisers will be imperiled.

It is of cardinal significance, in the controversy now before this court, that the claim of privilege is being urged solely by a former president, and there has been no assertion of privilege by an incumbent president, whose appearance had a distinctly different stance.[13] Absence of support from the incumbent at least indicates that "the risk of impairing necessary confidentiality is attenuated." * * *

* * * On a transfer of information and documents material to the carrying on of presidential functions, it is the new President who has the information and attendant duty of executing the laws in the light of current facts and circumstances, and who has the primary, if not the exclusive, responsibility of deciding when presidential privilege must be claimed, when in his opinion the need of maintaining confidentiality in communications, in which of course it is he who has the on-going interest, outweighs whatever public interest or need may reside in disclosure. There is a presumptive privilege that attaches to the communications, submissions and deliberations essential to the conduct of the office of the president. Obviously, the privilege does not disappear merely because the president who made or received the communication dies, resigns, or has completed his term. The question is, by whom must the privilege be claimed. Analytically, there is much to be said for the proposition that the state secret privilege must be claimed by some official authorized to speak for the state (the government), and the presidential privilege must be claimed by the president or an official authorized to speak for the president. As already noted, however, it is not necessary for us to decide that issue in this case. Assuming it may be asserted by someone other than the sitting president, conceivably by the court itself, the significance of the assertion by a former president is diminished when the succeeding president does not assert that the document is of the kind whose nondisclosure is necessary to the protection of the presidential office and its ongoing operation. The former president's assertion has a cast of history—at first recent history, and ultimately mere history—and his claim has less significance as an assertion of the current needs of the office. Such lesser significance does not open the door to public disclosure, but only to consideration whether the claim is overcome by a showing of other need, here litigating need.

II.

The District Court here found that plaintiffs-appellees had made a showing of need sufficient to overcome the claim of presidential privilege. This was not a rote, conclusory or perfunctory finding. The court presented the basis for its finding in a considered analysis:

13. When the Counsel to President Ford attempted to quash the subpoena no claim of privilege was asserted. Rather, he claimed that the subpoena should not be di-rected to him, and alternatively urged simply that the requested materials were not relevant to the litigation.

The Court believes plaintiffs have demonstrated a very strong entitlement to discovery of the tapes in question. Plaintiffs claim that a policy or plan was devised by the defendants in this case, including defendant Mitchell, which led to and instigated the allegedly unlawful arrest and detention of plaintiffs on May 5, 1971. Other discovery has established that high-level meetings were held at the Justice Department to plan for the May Day demonstrations. Defendant Mitchell, according to deposition testimony, was briefed on these meetings. At least one top-level White House aide was present at each of these meetings after April 16, the initial date with which the subpoena is concerned. The almost certain inference must be that these aides reported to Nixon on the progress of their planning, and took his reactions and directions back to the Justice Department. It is quite possible, as plaintiffs suggest, especially given the close relationship between Nixon and Mitchell, that the two men discussed the matter either personally or by telephone. If so, the conversations will be among those subpoenaed. And whatever recorded conversations occurred in the White House with regard to the Administration's plans for dealing with the demonstrators could constitute the most direct and central sort of evidence for plaintiffs' case. The Court can scarcely imagine what could be more relevant to the grave allegations in the present case than the actual words of those alleged to have been the conspirators. Nor can the Court perceive any alternative means by which plaintiffs could obtain comparable discovery. They have had considerable difficulty, in particular, in arranging to depose Mitchell, and even should they do so the results are bound to be far inferior to the actual contemporaneous record of the planning for the demonstrations. In short, the showing made by plaintiffs completely overcomes whatever presumptive executive privilege may attach to the former President's interest in the tapes.

We affirm the District Court ruling. Concededly, plaintiffs-appellees have not established with absolute certainty that conversations concerning the demonstrations actually took place between Mr. Nixon and those with whom he consulted during the time frame embraced by the subpoena. It is enough for present purposes that it is highly likely that such conversations did take place and were recorded, and there is a substantial possibility that Mr. Nixon discussed the matter with Mr. Mitchell, who was both his attorney general and a person who enjoyed a close working relationship with the President. Only if such recorded conversations do exist, will plaintiffs have access to any record. If they do not exist, the assumed privilege will remain intact and there will be no public disclosure.

We are also in accord with the ruling of the District Court that plaintiffs-appellees established a specific need for the requested information sufficient to overcome the rebuttable presumption of privilege of a former President, assuming such a privilege exists. Their need is beyond the routine desire of every party to discover relevant information to assist in the preparation of a case. The District Judge was acting on the premise that the lengthy trial held before him as to the other defendants established that the Department of Justice played a leading role in the executive's efforts to cope with the May Day demonstrations, and that there had ensued substantial violations of fundamental constitutional rights on May 5, 1971. What had not yet been established was whether, or to what extent, former Attorney General Mitchell was involved in the particular constitutional violations of May 5, 1971. Given the substantial violations of constitutional rights sought to be vindicated, given the high-level meeting at the Justice Department to prepare for the May Day demonstration, the attendance of a White House aide and briefing of Mr. Mitchell as attorney general on these matters, plaintiffs have made a showing of substantial need, in their attempt to establish Mr. Mitchell's responsibility for the violations, for overcoming the presumption of the privilege assumed to exist for former Presidents.

In sum, plaintiffs-appellees have certainly made at least a "preliminary showing of necessity" for information that is not merely "demonstrably relevant" but indeed substantially material to their case.

Qualifications to the Court's conclusion→

To obviate any misunderstanding, and in view of the importance of the considerations involved, we add a word concerning protective orders, even though not specified in appellant's papers. Disclosure because of the potential needs of litigation need not be made to the public, and indeed in a case of this kind should be restricted to counsel, unless and until the documents are made part of the public trial record. Former President Nixon would be entitled to a protective order, that before any documents are disclosed in a public proceeding or record there would be due and ample notice to Mr. Nixon, and an opportunity to litigate the issue of need for public disclosure, on a determination to be made in the light of the actual litigating posture of the case and the contents of the document(s). Our affirmance of the district court's order on this aspect of the case is to be taken as without prejudice to any request for or claim of right to a suitable protective order.

III.

We find, however, that the District Court erred in failing to provide adequate protection for Mr. Nixon's personal privacy interests in the materials subpoenaed.

The breadth of the subpoena

The court directed Counsel to the President to review the designated tape recordings to determine if conversations pertaining to May Day demonstrations were included therein, and thereafter to turn over such recordings directly to counsel for plaintiffs. Mr. Nixon claims initially that the subpoena amounts to nothing more than a wide-ranging "fishing expedition" designed to disclose to the public conversations covering 25 days. If the subpoena is read, as it is capable of being read if taken literally, as requiring an entire tape to be produced if any portion of it relates to the May Day demonstrations, plaintiffs would be entitled to discover all conversations recorded on such a day, including those of an intensely personal nature some of which would be subject to an independent common law privilege. At oral argument plaintiffs disclaimed any interest in such materials. The District Court's memorandum opinion indicates an intention to limit discovery to those portions of the recordings dealing with the demonstrations, but the accompanying order denying the motion to quash does not so explicitly limit the subpoena. While the memorandum opinion could fairly be interpreted as impliedly narrowing the apparently unintended scope of the subpoena, to avoid any possible misunderstanding we remand with direction to the District Court to make such limitation explicit in its order.

In addition, Mr. Buchen's review of the recordings in compliance with the District Court order implicates Mr. Nixon's privacy rights in a manner not contemplated by the Presidential Recordings and Materials Preservation Act. An essential element of the Act is review of the materials by a disinterested, professional archivist, and not by Counsel to an incumbent President, however conscientious he may be. Even under procedures of the Act, the invasion of Mr. Nixon's privacy is "not insignificant."

* * * In directing Mr. Buchen immediately to undertake review of the subpoenaed documents, the District Court rejected Mr. Nixon's privacy claims as frivolous. In our view, the privacy interests of a former President must be safeguarded.

Our resolution of the problem is a ruling that the District Court should appoint a professional Government archivist as a Special Master to the Court pursuant to Fed.R.Civ.P. 53(a) for the limited purpose of reviewing the designated tape recordings, transcribing those portions of conversations relating to the May Day activities, and transmitting such isolated transcripts to the court. At all times during the review, Mr. Nixon or his representative shall have an absolute and unqualified right to be present; however, the determination of what constitutes material in compliance with the subpoena shall be left with the Special Master. Following transmittal of relevant materials to the Court, and before they are to be turned over to counsel for plaintiffs, Mr. Nixon shall be afforded the right to assert "any rights, defenses or privileges" whatever they might be in accordance with the appropriate implementing regulation of the Act.

Under such circumstances, we contemplate a procedure in the District Court identical to that outlined in this court's en banc opinion in Nixon v. Sirica, 159 U.S.App.D.C. [58,] 79, 487 F.2d [700,] 721 [(1973) (en banc)]. While the parties are directed to that order, we think it sufficient to indicate that the procedure there developed contemplates in camera review of the challenged material at which time Mr. Nixon will be able to assert any claims of privilege with particularity. Counsel for plaintiffs will be entitled to inspect the materials in chambers to assist the Court in determining the validity of any claim of privilege. Any ruling adverse to Mr. Nixon is subject to appeal, if that course of action is deemed appropriate. See, id. at n. 100.

For the reasons stated above, the memorandum and order of the District Court is affirmed in part, reversed in part, and remanded for modification consistent with this opinion. Thereafter the subpoena may issue.

[handwritten margin notes: "discovery Ct's proposal to protect Nixon's privacy interest"]

[handwritten margin note: ".. just like ←"]

[handwritten margin note: "DISPOSITION"]

So ordered.

■ MacKinnon, Circuit Judge, concurring in part and dissenting in part:

In my view the majority opinion does not give full consideration to the true basis upon which the privilege rests. The presidential privilege is not something that is completely personal, but is something that adheres to the *office* of the Presidency. It is a privilege which exists to benefit the public, not to benefit a particular public official past or present. Its purpose is to assure that the nation will receive the benefit of honest, untrammeled advice from its officers as rendered to the President. Thus, whether the privilege is claimed by an incumbent or former President does not address the basic purpose for the existence of the privilege. To assert that the privilege shall be interpreted so as to protect incumbent presidents more than former presidents is to inject considerations that are almost completely foreign to the intended purpose of the privilege and ignores the true reason for the existence of the privilege. The true test should be, regardless of who raises it, whether the disclosure of the particular information *at the particular time it is demanded* would be injurious to the public interest considerations that the privilege is designed to protect.

In applying this standard it must be recognized that eventual disclosure of the advice of a Government official, even though the President to whom the advice was given had left office, might be just as injurious in the future to the nation as disclosure during the incumbency of the President who received the advice. Presidents of opposite parties often succeed each other. If the access to confidential advice given to one President is to be subjected substantially to the post-hoc determination of his successor, the assurance of completely competent advice is likely to be lost entirely. The President to whom the advice was given should be in the best position to state whether the expectation of confidentiality enhanced the advice given to him when he was the incumbent of the office.

Every President inexorably leaves office some time and if every President after he leaves office is to be forced to have his confidential conversations with his trusted advisors treated by some lesser standard than they would while he held office, then every advisor who has a confidential conversation with an incumbent President will always temper his advise by the eventual standard that will be applied to its disclosure. The suit will be cut to fit the cloth. Thus, the nation's public interest will suffer by trimmed advice from confidential consultants who no longer can be relied upon to give completely frank advice. Treating confidential advice to presidents by this double standard will operate to substantially depreciate the values that the privilege is designed to protect.

It would be a mistake to place greater emphasis on the privilege on the particular status of any President and that he alone can claim it. Since it is intended to protect the nation, others with a proper interest should be able to enforce it.

Of course, there is no doubt that time somewhat erodes the privilege with respect to some factual situations, but the erosion should not be substantially influenced by the fact that the President who received the advice has left office.

This is not to say that individual privacy claims in some circumstances might not differ between incumbents and former presidents, but such privacy claims are something different from executive privilege. * * *

SUPPLEMENTAL OPINION

Appellant Richard Nixon has filed a petition for rehearing which for the most part repeats arguments already made and rejected. One aspect merits a further word, and that is the objection to that part of this court's opinion that states that the District Court should appoint a professional Government archivist as a "master". We developed this in view of appellant's objection to screening by the counselor to the President. In the petition filed February 11, appellant asserts that he has objections to our alternative—he complains of a conflict of interest because of other litigation pending with GSA, and lack of pertinent expertise. Appellant asserts that he would even prefer screening by the counselor to the President. We do not probe these matters. We will revise our opinion to change "should" to "may", to make it clear that the procedure we have outlined is permissive, not mandatory. If appellant's contentions have merit, the district court can make other arrangements, including reference to the successor to the counsel to the President. In the sound exercise of discretion, after considering suggestions by the parties, the district court may appoint another master. To the extent indicated, the petition for rehearing is granted; otherwise it is denied.

———

Note and Questions

In *Cheney v. United States District Court*, 542 U.S. 367, 383–91 (2004), although not involving a formal invocation of executive privilege, the Supreme Court emphasized that discovery against senior officials in the Executive Branch, such as the Vice President, raise serious constitutional separation of powers concerns. The Court held that "the public interest requires that a coequal branch of government [the Judiciary] 'afford Presidential confidentiality the greatest protection consistent with the fair administration of justice.' " *Id*. at 382 (quoting *United States v. Nixon*, 418 U.S. 683, 715 (1974)). The Court observed that a request for information in a criminal case implicates constitutional considerations of production of relevant evidence to achieve justice and "the court's ability to fulfill its constitutional responsibility to resolve cases and controversies within its jurisdiction" that may in certain circumstances override the Executive's concerns for confidentiality. *Id*. at 383–85. By contrast, "[t]he need for information for use in civil cases, while far from negligible, does not share the urgency or significance of the criminal subpoena requests." *Id*. at 384. In sum, the Court explained, the "right to production of relevant evidence in civil proceedings does not have the same 'constitutional dimensions.' "

Id. The Court thus remanded the matter for the court of appeals to determine how to control "the overly broad discovery requests" made by the plaintiffs about the activities of and alleged participation of industry representatives on a energy policy development group headed by the Vice President and including other senior government officials. *Id.* at 386, 391–92. The Court held that the government was not obliged to invoke executive privilege or make particularized objections on a document-by-document basis in order to question and be able to appeal the legitimate scope of discovery against senior government officials. *Id.* at 388–90.

If the *Dellums v. Powell* case were to arise today, would the *Cheney* decision change the outcome? Why or why not? Even if the outcome of the discovery dispute in *Dellums* remained the same, would *Cheney* mandate a reconsideration of any of the reasoning in that decision? Compare the *Cheney* and *Dellums* opinions in terms of the significance that each places upon the difference between a subpoena for evidence in a criminal case and a request for discovery in a civil case. Consider as well the importance of the constitutional principles at stake on the merits of the *Dellums* case, including the fact that the claim of a conspiracy to violate civil rights was supported by more than mere allegations and whether that factor make *Dellums* a particularly appropriate case for overriding the interest of presidential confidentiality otherwise protected by executive privilege.

———

SECTION F.   JURY TRIALS IN FEDERAL GOVERNMENT CASES

28 United States Code § 2402

Subject to chapter 179 of this title [employment discrimination suits involving presidential offices], any action against the United States under section 1346 shall be tried by the court without a jury, except that any action against the United States under section 1346(a)(1) shall, at the request of either party to such action, be tried by the court with a jury.

———

Lehman, Secretary of the Navy v. Nakshian   5-4

Supreme Court of the United States.
453 U.S. 156 (1981).

■ JUSTICE STEWART delivered the opinion of the Court.

The question presented by this case is whether a plaintiff in an action against the United States under § 15(c) of the Age Discrimination in Employment Act is entitled to trial by jury.

Is this under 1346(a)(1)?

I

The 1974 amendments to the Age Discrimination in Employment Act of 1967 added a new § 15,[2] which brought the Federal Government within the scope of the Act for the first time. Section 15(a) prohibits the Federal Government from discrimination based on age in most of its civilian employment decisions concerning persons over 40 years of age. Section 15(b) provides that enforcement of § 15(a) in most agencies, including military departments, is the responsibility of the Equal Employment Opportunity Commission. The Commission is directed to "issue such rules, regulations, orders and instructions as [the Commission] deems necessary and appropriate" to carry out that responsibility. Section 15(c)[5] provides:

> "Any person aggrieved may bring a civil action in any Federal district court of competent jurisdiction for such legal or equitable relief as will effectuate the purposes of this Act."

In 1978, respondent Alice Nakshian, who was then a 62–year-old civilian employee of the United States Department of the Navy, brought an age discrimination suit against the Navy under § 15(c). She requested a jury trial. The defendant moved to strike the request, and the District Court denied the motion. *Nakshian v. Claytor*, 481 F.Supp. 159 (DC). The court stressed that the "legal or equitable relief" language used by Congress to establish a right to sue the Federal Government for age discrimination was identical to the language Congress had previously used in § 7(c) of the Act to authorize private ADEA suits. That language, the District Court said, was an important basis for this Court's holding in *Lorillard v. Pons*, 434 U.S. 575, that § 7(c) permits jury trials in private suits under the Act. The court stated that "if Congress had intended its consent to ADEA suits [against the Government] to be limited to non-jury trials, it could have easily said as much." 481 F.Supp., at 161. Recognizing that as a result of 1978 amendments to the ADEA § 7(c)(2) expressly confers a right to jury trial, whereas no such language exists in § 15, 481 F.Supp., at 161, the court found no "explicit refusal" by Congress to grant the right to jury trial against the Government, and noted that the legislative history of the 1978 amendments spoke in general terms about a right to jury trial in ADEA suits.

On interlocutory appeal under 28 U.S.C. § 1292(b), a divided panel of the Court of Appeals affirmed, *Nakshian v. Claytor*, 202 U.S.App.D.C. 59, 628 F.2d 59. The appellate court rejected the Secretary's argument that a plaintiff is entitled to trial by jury in a suit against the United States only when such a trial has been expressly authorized. Instead, the court viewed the question as "an ordinary question of statutory interpretation," and found sufficient evidence of legislative intent to provide for trial by jury in cases such as this. Noting that Congress had conferred jurisdiction over ADEA suits upon the federal district courts, rather than the Court of Claims, the Court of Appeals concluded that "absent a provision as to the method of trial, a grant of jurisdiction to a district court as a court of law

---

2. 29 U.S.C. § 633a.   **5.** 29 U.S.C. § 633a(c).

carries with it a right of jury trial." *Id.*, at 63. The Court of Appeals also adopted the District Court's view of the "legal ... relief" language in § 15(c). Further, it was the court's view that the existence of the explicit statutory right to jury trial in suits against private employers does not negate the existence of a right to jury trial in suits against the Government, since the provision for jury trials in private suits was added only to resolve a conflict in the Court of Appeals on that issue and to confirm the correctness of this Court's decision in the *Lorillard* case.

We granted certiorari to consider the issue presented.

II

It has long been settled that the Seventh Amendment right to trial by jury does not apply in actions against the Federal Government. In *Galloway v. United States*, 319 U.S. 372, 388–389, the Court observed:

> "The suit is one to enforce a monetary claim against the United States. It hardly can be maintained that under the common law in 1791 jury trial was a matter of right for persons asserting claims against the sovereign. Whatever force the Amendment has therefore is derived because Congress, in the legislation cited, has made it applicable."

Moreover, the Court has recognized the general principle that "the United States, as sovereign, 'is immune from suit save as it consents to be sued ... and the terms of its consent to be sued in any court define that court's jurisdiction to entertain the suit.' " *United States v. Testan*, 424 U.S. 392, 399, quoting *United States v. Sherwood*, 312 U.S. 584, 586. See also *United States v. Mitchell*, 445 U.S. 535, 538. Thus, if Congress waives the Government's immunity from suit, as it has in the ADEA, 29 U.S.C. § 633a, the plaintiff has a right to a trial by jury only where that right is one of "the terms of [the Government's] consent to be sued." *Testan, supra*, at 399. Like a waiver of immunity itself, which must be "unequivocally expressed," *United States v. Mitchell*, supra, at 538, "this Court has long decided that limitations and conditions upon which the Government consents to be sued must be strictly observed and exceptions thereto are not to be implied." *Soriano v. United States*, 352 U.S. 270, 276.

When Congress has waived the sovereign immunity of the United States, it has almost always conditioned that waiver upon a plaintiff's relinquishing any claim to a jury trial. Jury trials, for example, have not been made available in the Court of Claims for the broad range of cases within its jurisdiction under 28 U.S.C. § 1491—*i.e.*, all claims against the United States "founded either upon the Constitution, or any Act of Congress, ... or upon any express or implied contract with the United States, or for liquidated or unliquidated damages in cases not sounding in tort." And there is no jury trial right in this same range of cases when the federal district courts have concurrent jurisdiction. See 28 U.S.C. §§ 1346(a)(2) and 2402. Finally, in tort actions against the United States, see 28 U.S.C. § 1346(b), Congress has similarly provided that trials shall be to the court without a jury. 28 U.S.C. § 2402.[8]

The appropriate inquiry, therefore, is whether Congress clearly and unequivocally departed from its usual practice in this area, and granted a right to trial by jury when it amended the ADEA.[9]

A

Section 15 of the ADEA, 29 U.S.C. § 633a, prohibits age discrimination in federal employment. Section 15(c) provides the means for judicial enforcement of this guarantee: any person aggrieved "may bring a civil action in any Federal district court of competent jurisdiction for such legal or equitable relief as will effectuate the purposes" of the Act. Section 15 contrasts with § 7(c) of the Act, 29 U.S.C. § 626(c), which authorizes civil actions against private employers and state and local governments, and which expressly provides for jury trials. Congress accordingly demonstrated that it knew how to provide a statutory right to a jury trial when it wished to do so elsewhere in the very "legislation cited," *Galloway, supra,* at 389. But in § 15 it failed explicitly to do so.

The respondent infers statutory intent from the language in § 15(c) providing for the award of "legal or equitable relief," relying on *Lorillard v. Pons,* 434 U.S. 575, for the proposition that the authorization of "legal" relief supports a statutory jury trial right. But *Lorillard* has no application in this context. In the first place, the word "legal" cannot be deemed to be what the *Lorillard* Court described as "a term of art" with respect to the availability of jury trials in cases where the defendant is the Federal Government. In *Lorillard,* the authorization for the award of "legal" relief was significant largely because of the presence of a constitutional question. The Court observed that where legal relief is granted in litigation between private parties, the Seventh Amendment guarantees the right to a jury, and

---

8. It is not difficult to appreciate Congress' reluctance to provide for jury trials against the United States. When fashioning a narrow exception to permit jury trials in tax refund cases in federal district courts under 28 U.S.C. § 1346(a)(1), in legislation that Congress recognized established a "wholly new precedent," H.R.Rep.No.659, 83d Cong., 1st Sess., 3 (1953), Congress expressed its concern that juries "might tend to be overly generous because of the virtually unlimited ability of the Government to pay the verdict." Indeed, because of their firm opposition to breaking with precedent, the House conferees took almost a year before acceding to passage of the bill containing that exception. Only after much debate, and after the conferees became convinced that there would be no danger of excessive verdicts as a result of jury trials in that unique context—because recoveries would be limited to the amount of taxes illegally or erroneously collected—was the bill passed. See H. R. Conf. Rep. No.2276, 83d Cong., 2d Sess., 2 (1954).

9. The respondent argues that the strong presumption against the waiver of sovereign immunity has no relevance to the question of a right to trial by jury. But, it is clear that the doctrine of sovereign immunity — and its attendant presumptions must inform the Court's decision in this case. The reason that the Seventh Amendment presumption in favor of jury trials does not apply in actions at law against the United States is that the United States is immune from suit, and the Seventh Amendment right to a jury trial, therefore, never existed with respect to a suit against the United States. Since there is no generally applicable jury trial right that attaches when the United States consents to suit, the accepted principles of sovereign immunity require that a jury trial right be clearly provided in the legislation creating the cause of action.

reasoned that Congress must have been aware of the significance of the word "legal" in that context. But the Seventh Amendment has no application in actions at law against the Government, as Congress and this Court have always recognized. Thus no particular significance can be attributed to the word "legal" in § 15(c). * * *

The respondent also infers a right to trial by jury from the fact that Congress conferred jurisdiction over ADEA suits upon the federal district courts, where jury trials are ordinarily available, rather than upon the Court of Claims, where they are not. Not only is there little logical support for this inference, but the legislative history offers no support for it either. Moreover, Rule 38(a) of the Federal Rules of Civil Procedure provides that the right to a jury trial "as declared by the Seventh Amendment to the Constitution or as *given by a statute of the United States* shall be preserved to the parties inviolate" (emphasis added). This language hardly states a general rule that jury trials are to be presumed whenever Congress provides for cases to be brought in federal district courts. Indeed, Rule 38(a) requires an affirmative statutory grant of the right where, as in this case, the Seventh Amendment does not apply.

B

As already indicated, it is unnecessary to go beyond the language of the statute itself to conclude that Congress did not intend to confer a right to trial by jury on ADEA plaintiffs proceeding against the Federal Government. But it is helpful briefly to explore the legislative history, if only to demonstrate that it no more supports the holding of the Court of Appeals than does the statutory language itself.

The respondent cannot point to a single reference in the legislative history to the subject of jury trials in cases brought against the Federal Government. There is none. And there is nothing to indicate that Congress did not mean what it plainly indicated when it expressly provided for jury trials in § 7(c) cases but not in § 15(c) cases. In fact, the few inferences that may be drawn from the legislative history are inconsistent with the respondent's position.

The ADEA originally applied only to actions against private employers. Section 7 incorporated the enforcement scheme used in employee actions against private employers under the [Fair Labor Standards Act]. In *Lorillard*, the Court found that the incorporation of the FLSA scheme into § 7 indicated that the FLSA right to trial by jury should also be incorporated. The *Lorillard* holding was codified in 1978 when § 7(c) was amended to provide expressly for jury trials in actions brought under that section.

Congress expanded the scope of ADEA in 1974 to include state and local governments and Federal Government employers. State and local governments were added as potential defendants by a simple expansion of the term "employer" in the ADEA. The existing substantive and procedural provisions of the Act, including § 7(c), were thereby extended to cover state and local government employees. In contrast, Congress added an entirely new section, § 15, to address the problems of age discrimination in federal employment. Here Congress deliberately prescribed a distinct statutory scheme applicable only to the federal sector, and one based not on the FLSA but on Title VII [of the Civil Rights Act of 1964], where, unlike the FLSA, there was no right to trial by jury. * * *

C

But even if the legislative history were ambiguous, that would not affect the proper resolution of this case, because the plaintiff in an action against the United States has a right to trial by jury only where Congress has affirmatively and unambiguously granted that right by statute. Congress has most obviously not done so here. Neither the provision for federal employer cases to be brought in district courts rather than the Court of Claims, nor the use of the word "legal" in that section, evinces a congressional intent that ADEA plaintiffs who proceed to trial against the Federal Government may do so before a jury. Congress expressly provided for jury trials in the section of the Act applicable to private-sector employers, and to state and local governmental entities. It did not do so in the section applicable to the Federal Government as an employer, and indeed, patterned that section after provisions in another Act under which there is no right to trial by jury. The conclusion is inescapable that Congress did not depart from its normal practice of not providing a right to trial by jury when it waived the sovereign immunity of the United States.

For these reasons, the judgment of the Court of Appeals is reversed.

It is so ordered.

[The dissenting opinion of JUSTICE BRENNAN, with whom JUSTICE MARSHALL, JUSTICE BLACKMUN, and JUSTICE STEVENS joined, is omitted.]

————

Notes and Questions

1.   Why do you suppose that a claimant against the federal government is not ordinarily entitled to present the claim to a jury? What accounts for the deliberate reluctance of Congress to waive sovereign immunity to include jury trials? Read footnote 8 in the *Lehman v. Nakshian* opinion. Are you convinced? Why are claims for tax refunds the principal exception to the general no-jury rule?

2.   In addition to tax refund claims, Congress in 1991 amended Title VII of the Civil Rights Act of 1964, 42 U.S.C. § 1981a(c), to provide for a right to a jury when damages are sought in employment discrimination cases (as a jury right previously had not been available to parties in employment discrimination cases involving either private or public employers). Section 1981a of Title 42 of the United States Code, which grants this right to trial by jury, includes a cross-reference to the section of the Title VII that extends employment discrimination to federal employees. *Id.* § 2000e–16. The Supreme Court and several Courts of Appeals have assumed that a jury trial is now available in a Title VII suit with a federal

government defendant. *See, e.g., West v. Gibson*, 527 U.S. 212, 221–22 (1999); *Hudson v. Reno*, 130 F.3d 1193, 1196 & n.1 (6th Cir. 1997); *Yamaguchi v. United States Dep't of Air Force*, 109 F.3d 1475, 1481–82 (9th Cir. 1997). (Still, Congress has not provided for a right to a jury trial under other employment discrimination provisions involving the federal government.)

Section G.   Settlement of Government Cases

1.   Negotiating a Settlement

Richard K. Willard, How to Settle Your Civil Case With the Government

In 3 Department of Justice Manual § 4–3.200a, at 4–48 to 4–48.7 (© 1994, Prentice Hall Law & Business, Assigned to Aspen Law & Business, a Division of Aspen Publishers, Inc.).

Attorneys who engage in civil litigation with the federal government may feel that they confront an impenetrable bureaucracy. And, with tens of thousands of pending civil cases, it does take a small army of lawyers to represent the government's interests.

The purpose of this article is to explain the way the settlement process operates. A better understanding of this process should assist you in settling your case with the government and thus relieving the burden of litigation for all concerned.

Litigation and Settlement Authority

The authority to conduct civil litigation on behalf of the United States is generally vested in the Attorney General. 28 U.S.C. §§ 516–519. But the Government's civil litigation is actually conducted by attorneys in the Department's litigating divisions, the United States Attorneys' offices, and attorneys at the various federal agencies. The regulations and directives that effectuate these delegations of authority are found in title 28 of the Code of Federal Regulations.

The Client Agency

In most government civil cases, there is a department or agency that has a particular interest in the matter and is referred to as "the client agency." Thus for example:

- In a Social Security benefits case, the Department of Health and Human Services is the client agency;*

---

* [In 1994, the Social Security Administration was removed from the Department of   Health and Human Services and established as an independent agency in the executive

- In a shipbuilding contract dispute the Department of the Navy is the client agency; and

- In a case seeking damages for alleged negligence by a national park employee, the Department of the Interior is the client agency.

Sometimes more than one agency will be regarded as the client, and occasionally the Government's interest is so general that there is no client agency as such.

Some agencies have the statutory authority to litigate particular cases through their own counsel, but most cases fall under the Attorney General's general litigation authority. Even in this large category, attorneys from client agencies may be substantially involved in the litigation pursuant to a memorandum of understanding or some less formal arrangement.

involvement vs. authority

Agencies often have the authority to settle claims administratively. For example, an administrative claim is a jurisdictional prerequisite to suit against the government under the Federal Tort Claims Act. Such claims can be resolved without litigation, although settlements above $25,000 require approval of the Department of Justice. 28 U.S.C. § 2672.

When a case is in litigation, the client agency continues to have substantial influence regarding settlement. The agency may be able to block a proposed settlement or at least require higher-level approval at the Department of Justice.

Has the agency can influence settlement

The Litigating Divisions

At the Department of Justice, responsibility for civil litigation is divided among the six litigating divisions: Antitrust, Civil, Civil Rights, Criminal, Environment and Natural Resources, and Tax. (Yes, some categories of civil cases are handled by the Criminal Division.) The respective jurisdiction of these litigating divisions are set forth in 28 CFR § 0.40–0.71. Within the litigating divisions, there are numerous sections and offices that handle particular kinds of cases. — Asst. Atty Gen.—

respective jurisdictions

delegation to the AAG of each division

The authority of the Assistant Attorney General in charge of a division to settle cases is set forth at 28 CFR § 0.160. In general, it permits these officials to approve any nonmonetary settlement and any settlement involving payment by the government of up to $2 million. In affirmative litigation, they may accept payments when the difference between the original claim and the settlement amount is no more than $2 million or 15 percent of the original claims, whichever is greater.

who Approves Settlement?

All cases exceeding these limits, and any case involving a particularly significant issue of law or policy, must be approved by the Deputy Attorney General, who has been given the full authority of the Attorney General regarding civil settlements. 28 CFR § 0.161.

exceeding AAG's auth'ty . . .

branch. Thus, in a Social Security benefits case, the Social Security Administration is now the client agency.]

Delegation
of Asst. A.G.
authority

Within these limits, the Assistant Attorney Generals have delegated portions of their settlement authority to their subordinates and to the U.S. Attorney's offices. These subdelegations appear in a series of directives that are published as an appendix to Subpart Y of 28 C.F.R.

The United States Attorneys

The vast majority of civil cases are actually handled by Assistant U.S. Attorneys. Attorneys in the litigating divisions generally handle cases involving specialized expertise or nationally important issues. Litigating division attorneys sometimes work together with Assistant U.S. Attorneys on particular cases.

Generally

In general, the U.S. Attorney or a supervisor in that office has the authority to settle cases by paying up to $500,000 or, in an affirmative case, by accepting an amount within $500,000 or 15 percent of the government's original claim, whichever is greater. Other settlements must go back to a litigating division for approval or review prior to submission to the Deputy Attorney General.**

The Solicitor General

When the government loses a case in the district court, an appeal can be taken only if approved by the Solicitor General. The Solicitor General also represents the government in the Supreme Court. 28 C.F.R. § 0.20. A concomitant of this authority is that the Solicitor General must approve any settlement of a case which is in the Supreme Court or in which an appeal by the Government has been authorized. 28 C.F.R. § 0.163.

Considerations Affecting the Exercise of Settlement Authority

The general test for approving a proposed settlement is whether it is in the interest of the United States. Some of the considerations that enter into this determination are much like those involved in the settlement of private litigation. Other considerations are unique to Government litigation.

Likely Outcome if Litigated

As in private litigation, the most important factor in settling government litigation is the expectation of the parties about the likely outcome if the case is not settled. Usually, this involves a range of outcomes, each of which has a possibility of occurring.

Private attorneys are sometimes surprised that this sort of practical calculus is employed by the government, but it is. Of course, opposing

---

** [Through redelegation by the Assistant Attorney General for the Civil Division of the Attorney General's settlement authority, the United States Attorney now has the authority (1) to settle cases by paying up to $1 million, or, (2) in affirmative cases by the government, to compromise or close cases where (a) the original claim does not exceed $1 million or (b) the original claim does not exceed $5 million and the government accepts an amount within $1 million or 15 percent of the original claim, whichever is greater. United States Attorney's Manual, § 4–3.120 (General Redelegation of the Attorney General's Authority to Compromise and Close) (2007).]

attorneys often have quite different perceptions of the strength of their cases. But this step of the analysis cannot be omitted.

Consequently, a major step of the settlement process has to be the effort to reach a consensus—or at least narrow the range of disagreement—regarding the likely outcome of the litigation.

Among the factors that must be considered in evaluating possible outcomes is the likely resolution of points of law, both by the trial court and ultimately on appeal.

> Example A: A plaintiff seeks damages for personal injury under the Federal Tort Claims Act. The plaintiff has about a 50 percent chance of establishing that his injury was caused by the negligence of a government employee. The typical damage award for this kind of injury runs about $600,000 to $800,000. The government also has a statute-of-limitations defense, which has about a 50 percent chance of succeeding in the trial court or on appeal. Therefore, the expected outcome of this case, discounted for litigation risk, is $150,000 to $200,000.

In a case such as Example A, it is unrealistic for a plaintiff to expect settlement equal to the typical damage award when there is so much litigation risk. If the plaintiff wants to settle for substantially more than $200,000, then it will be necessary to convince the Government attorneys that the possible range of damages is higher than they think or that there is a greater likelihood that the case will turn out favorably to the plaintiff.

The Cost to Litigate

Private attorneys sometimes assume that the litigation resources of the Government are inexhaustible. Nothing could be further from the truth. Government attorneys do not bill by the hour, but their resources are limited by their annual appropriations.

Ltd. resources

In fact, the federal caseload has grown much more rapidly in the past decade than the resources appropriated for Government litigation. This creates a strong incentive for the Government to handle its cases efficiently and to settle as many as possible.

Indeed, the Government may from time to time be required to settle cases when it would be more cost-effective to litigate, but there are insufficient resources to do so. This is because costs of settlement often come from the Judgment Fund, which is not subject to the annual appropriations process.

Not always enough resources to settle!

Moreover, as with any case, if you are better prepared to try the case than your adversary, then you are also in a position to obtain a favorable settlement. Because of high caseloads and rapid personnel turnover, Government counsel may be poorly prepared for trial in some cases and have no realistic alternative to settlement.

Impact on Other Cases — *Policy Concern*

The government has such a large volume of litigation that it must be particularly concerned about how the resolution of one case will affect other cases. For this reason, the government will from time to time take a position regarding settlement that does not seem to make sense in the context of a specific case but is part of a broader policy. _

> Example B: The Government is sued in hundreds of cases alleging injuries from exposure to a chemical used in a Government facility. Government attorneys do not believe that the alleged injuries were actually caused by the chemical. However, in an individual case, it may be possible to settle for much less than the cost of litigation.

In such a case as Example B, the practical effect of settling some cases would be to require settlements of others that are similarly situated. To a greater extent than private parties, the Government may feel an obligation to adopt a consistent approach to settlement of cases that involve the same issues. And, in any event, settlement of one case encourages others like it to litigate to achieve the same result. Therefore, the Government may adopt a policy of not settling any cases of this type.

making your case different from the standard "settled" case

In this situation, the best way to achieve settlement is to try to distinguish your case from the others. A legal or factual difference may allow the case to be viewed as a valid exception to the general no-settlement policy. Otherwise, your burden is to convince the Government that it faces such litigation risk that it should change its no-settlement policy for all similar cases.

The "Test Case"

A variant of the foregoing category is the case selected by Government counsel to try to establish a particular legal precedent. A test case is often selected because the facts are perceived to be favorable to the proposition that the Government is trying to establish or because it is pending in a favorable jurisdiction.

It can be frustrating to represent a private party in a test case if you have no interest in the legal issue beyond its impact on your case. The best way to settle such a case is to convince the Government that for some reason your case is not a good test case; i.e., that there are extraneous legal issues or that the facts are unfavorable to the Government's legal objective.

Programmatic Impact

Another factor that influences the Government's approach to settlement is its impact on Government programs and policies. This factor is particularly important in nonmonetary settlements but may also be considered in cases involving damages.

> Example C: A lawsuit seeks payment of benefits from a Government program based upon an interpretation of the statute that has been rejected by the administering agency. The agency claims that such an interpretation would be unworkable and burdensome.

In this situation, settlement is unlikely as long as the agency adheres to its view of how the statute should be interpreted. Unless you convince the agency that yours is a bad "test case," as discussed above, then the litigating attorneys are unlikely to be in a position to settle over the agency's objections.

The Mechanics of Settlement

Settlement discussions originate in a variety of ways in Government litigation, as they do in private litigation. The best way to conduct these negotiations will vary depending upon the posture of the case and the personalities of the lawyers. Some general advice may be helpful, however.

The Line Attorney

The Government attorney primarily responsible for litigating the case is the most important person in the process. All decisions regarding settlement will be based at least in part on this attorney's recommendation. If the line attorney wants to settle the case, you are well on your way.

Once you have convinced the line attorney that the case should be settled, the next step is to obtain approval from higher-level supervisors. At this point, the line attorney generally prepares a settlement memorandum. This document can be critical in obtaining approval for the settlement.

The settlement memorandum will vary in length and content, depending upon the complexity of the case and the size of the proposed settlement. It will normally summarize the facts and legal issues in the case, describe the prospects for litigation, outline the proposed settlement, and discuss why the proposal is in the Government's interest.

The quality of the settlement memorandum may suffer if the line attorney is busy with other cases. Therefore, it may be in your interest to provide the line attorney with information that will assist in preparing the memorandum, such as data concerning comparable damage awards or settlements.

Higher Level Approval

A proposed settlement goes through channels to the higher-level authority who is required to approve it. If a case is being handled in a U.S. Attorney's office but requires approval from a litigating division, the settlement memorandum goes back to Washington, D.C., for review.

Proposed settlements are sometimes bounced back to the line attorney for further information and documentation. This process can take time, especially if there are strong disagreements within the Government about the wisdom of a proposed settlement.

Problems in the Settlement Process

If a line attorney is recalcitrant about settlement, then the next step is to contact the supervisory attorney. Similarly, if a settlement is bogged down in the approval process, then it may be necessary to try to communicate with a higher-level official to get a favorable result. These situations are tricky, however, because they involve you in the internal processes of the Department.

One way to deal with these situations is a written settlement proposal. This way you do not have to depend upon Government attorneys to understand and advocate the merits of a settlement. Your written proposal can present your view of the facts and applicable law as well as why you believe the Government should settle.

Meetings and telephone conversations with higher-level officials are often not very helpful. Government officials in such situations may not be very familiar with your case and may be inclined to back up their subordinates anyway. For this reason, a well-prepared written proposal may be more effective in communicating your position.

If you do meet with a higher-level official regarding settlement, keep the discussion objective. Avoid threats or emotional appeal. Try to find out if additional information about the factual or legal issues in your case would be helpful and, if so, follow up with a letter providing the information. Such "new information" may provide a face-saving way to go ahead and approve your settlement.

Political Influence

Lawyers who cannot convince the Government to accept a settlement sometimes contact members of Congress or other political officials in an effort to obtain favorable consideration. Such tactics are rarely helpful and are often counterproductive.

The normal impact of a political inquiry during settlement discussions is to cause the attorneys involved to become extremely cautious. The result may be to lock these attorneys into their prior position and make them fear that any change would be perceived as giving in to political pressure. Consideration of settlement may also be delayed, as everyone in the process makes an extra effort to protect themselves by documenting the deliberations in great detail.

Conclusion

Convincing the Government to settle a case involves the same ultimate consideration as for any litigant—whether it is in their interest to settle. The Government is not any more altruistic than another party. It will not settle a case just because you want it to.

Therefore, the best approach to settling your case is to look at it from the perspective of the Government. The more you can understand the considerations that affect Government counsel, the better off you will be. Convincing the Government to accept a settlement proposal is a particular form of advocacy, in which understanding your audience is a fundamental requirement.

_____

2. GOVERNMENT SETTLEMENT AUTHORITY

United States v. Walcott

United States Court of Appeals for the Eleventh Circuit.
972 F.2d 323 (11th Cir. 1992).

■ WELLFORD, SENIOR CIRCUIT JUDGE:

This dispute arises from a $500,000 loan from the Small Business Administration ("SBA") to the husband of the defendant, Patricia Walcott.

The defendant guaranteed the loan upon which her husband soon defaulted. The defendant, claiming insufficient funds to pay the entire guaranteed debt, settled the SBA's claim with its purported representative for $75,000. Later, the United States sued defendant Walcott, claiming that the settlement agreement was void because SBA did not have the authority to settle the claim. The district court upheld the settlement agreement, concluding that the United States was estopped from denying the validity of the agreement. We REVERSE.

On June 23, 1981, Holland International Food, Inc. ("Holland"), then operated by Richard Sperring ("Sperring"), borrowed $500,000 from a bank in participation with SBA. To assist her husband, Sperring, in qualifying for this SBA loan, the defendant signed as guarantor. Less than a year later, Holland defaulted on the loan. * * * In divorce proceedings while default was occurring, Sperring was required to pay the SBA debt. Despite his obligations, Sperring moved to England without repaying the loan.

On July 28, 1988, the United States, on behalf of the SBA, sued the defendant and two other guarantors[1] for the outstanding debt. In April, 1989, the defendant retained an attorney, Mary Grace Diehl ("Diehl"), to represent her. Diehl contacted Michael C. Daniel ("Daniel"), an assistant United States Attorney, regarding a settlement. Diehl then sent the SBA Walcott's financial forms along with a settlement offer of $35,000 cash. Settlement negotiations were thereafter conducted by the SBA, through its loan specialist David Mitchell. The SBA rejected the $35,000 settlement offer and stated: "considering the assets of [the defendant], the [SBA] recovery should be approximately ten (10) percent," or $90,000. A copy of that letter was sent to Daniel. To permit further negotiations, the pending court proceedings were stayed by consent of both Daniel and Diehl.

Walcott then offered to pay to the SBA $50,000 cash plus $40,000 in quarterly payments over a four-year term. The SBA rejected this second offer, and on December 15, 1989, the defendant offered $75,000 cash, asserting that this was the maximum amount that she could borrow.[3] Mitchell recommended acceptance to the SBA Claims Review Committee, which was informed that the Department of Justice concurred in the settlement recommendation. In actuality, the Department of Justice did not concur and was not even aware of the settlement negotiations.

Shortly thereafter, the SBA committee accepted the defendant's offer. Diehl was advised by letter from Mitchell dated February 15, 1990, that her client's offer had been accepted. Diehl then sent a draft of a proposed covenant not to sue to the SBA and to Daniel. Upon Mitchell's advice that the terms of the covenant were acceptable to the SBA, Diehl sent a letter,

---

1. The other two guarantors had each guaranteed $75,000 of the original loan amount, and both discharged their indebtedness.

3. The defendant took out a home equity loan for $55,000, borrowed $10,000 from her father, and secured $10,000 from "other sources."

with a copy to Daniel, and a $75,000 money order to the SBA stating that the payment was "per our settlement agreement." On March 16, Mitchell received the money order and executed the covenant not to sue as a representative of the SBA.

Despite all these negotiations and the payment, Daniel informed Diehl within a few days that the settlement was void. Daniel also informed Diehl that the defendant's check would be refunded, but this did not occur for about four months. Diehl was subsequently informed that the Department of Justice in Washington, D.C., had declined to approve the $75,000 settlement.

In the suit below, the district court held that the government was equitably estopped from denying the validity of the $75,000 settlement. It ordered that the government accept Walcott's second check in that amount. On appeal to this court, the government maintains that the settlement was void without specific Justice Department approval, and that the United States is not properly subject to equitable estoppel. * * *

The district court held that, although the Supreme Court has held that the United States cannot be estopped "on the same terms as any other litigant, [the Court] has clearly recognized the 'interest of citizens in some minimum standard of decency, honor, and reliability in their dealings with their Government.'" Opinion p. 7 (quoting *Heckler v. Community Health Services of Crawford County, Inc.*, 467 U.S. 51 (1984), and relying also upon *United States v. Vonderau*, 837 F.2d 1540 (11th Cir.1988)). * * *

The government cites *Vonderau* to the effect that "[t]he Government cannot be estopped by the action of its agent when that agent acts without authority or contrary to law." *Vonderau*, 837 F.2d at 1541. Its argument follows that equitable estoppel cannot lie against the United States in this case because the SBA agent clearly acted outside the scope of his authority.

* * * In *Vonderau*, the defendant argued that a contractual time limitation for filing suit had run, based on oral representations made by an agency employee. The court held that, because the agent acted outside his authority in waiving the debt of the defendant, estoppel did not lie against the federal government as a matter of law. The court acknowledged the harshness of its holding, but reasoned that anyone who enters into an agreement with the government "'takes the risk of having accurately ascertained that he who purports to act for the Government stays within the bounds of his authority.'"Id. at 1452 (quoting *[Federal Crop Insurance Corp. v.] Merrill*, 332 U.S. [380,] 384 [(1947)]).

We cannot escape the application of *Vonderau* to the facts of this case. Therefore, if the SBA agent who negotiated the settlement acted outside the scope of his authority, the United States cannot properly be held to be estopped from repudiating that agent's actions and the $75,000 settlement.

The United States asserts that neither the SBA agent nor the assistant United States Attorney had the requisite authority to settle the claim with Walcott or her guaranty, because the exclusive authority to conduct and control litigation involving the United States is vested ultimately in the

Attorney General. The government relies on two statutes to support its position:

> Except as otherwise authorized by law, the conduct of litigation in which the United States, an agency, or officer thereof is a party . . . is reserved to officers of the Department of Justice, under the direction of the Attorney General.

Statutory Basis

Is settlement 'conduct of litigation'?

28 U.S.C. § 516.

> Except as otherwise authorized by law, the Attorney General shall supervise all litigation to which the United States, an agency, or officer thereof is a party, and shall direct all United States attorneys, assistant United States attorneys, and special attorneys appointed under section 543 of this title in the discharge of their respective duties.

Was the settlement under the supervision & direction of AG?

28 U.S.C. § 519.

Under these two statutes, "the Attorney General is the chief legal officer of the United States and absent express congressional directive to the contrary he is vested with plenary power over all litigation to which the United States or one of its agencies is a party." *FDIC v. Irwin,* 727 F.Supp. 1073, 1074 (N.D.Tex.1989), *aff'd,* 916 F.2d 1051 (5th Cir.1990). * * *

where has it?

According to 28 U.S.C. §§ 516 and 519, and under the authorities cited, we conclude that the Attorney General was vested with the exclusive authority to settle the suit at bar. Although Congress could have "otherwise authorized" the SBA to conduct its own litigation, neither the court nor the defendant has suggested that such congressional authorization exists. The defendant does not argue that the SBA or the Assistant United States Attorney had the requisite authority; she essentially relies instead on the argument that the defendant "reasonably concluded that the Government's agent was acting within the scope of his authority. . . ." In any event, the defendant's perception about the authority of Mitchell and Daniel do not support a legal argument that the government agents possessed the actual authority to effectuate the settlement. The ultimate issue essentially is one of law, not one of fact, or even one of equity. There is no legal basis, then, to indicate that the SBA had authority to execute the settlement agreement with the defendant, absent approval of the Attorney General. Nor is there any legal basis indicating Daniel's authority so to settle. * * *

Holding ✓

Δ only made a detrimental reliance argument

apparent authority

ask Curtis

Ct: This is an issue of law -- so estoppel doesn't apply -- and we must look to statutes for the purported agent's auth'ty

Further, the Supreme Court has recently held that equitable estoppel cannot apply against the United States in a suit to recover "public funds." *See Office of Personnel Management v. Richmond,* 496 U.S. 414 (1990). In *Richmond,* the respondent received erroneous information from a federal employee regarding the statutory limit on earnings in order to receive a disability annuity. As a result, he earned too much money within a six-month period, and was disallowed the disability benefits for that period of time. He appealed the disallowance, claiming that the United States was estopped from enforcing the statutory limit because of the false representations made to him. The Court endorsed the "strict approach to estoppel [in] claims involving public funds." Denial of equitable estoppel claims in such cases is "to assure that public funds will be spent according to the letter of the difficult judgments reached by Congress as to the common good, and not according to the individual favor of Government agents or the individual pleas of litigants."

Here, the defendant's loan was made out of a congressionally appropriated fund, and the funds that the government seeks to recover are "public funds." As an alternative basis for our holding, we find that under the rule in *Richmond*, equitable estoppel cannot lie against the government in this case.

We are sympathetic to defendant's contentions in this case under the circumstances. We agree with the district court that the government handled the case and dealt with Walcott in a "shabby" fashion.[5] We find no alternative, however, but to enforce the law and the explicit statutes we have cited and find that the district court erred in applying equitable estoppel against the United States. The settlement must be set aside. In the ultimate determination of defendant's liability, however, she is to be given a credit adjustment for interest during the period that the government had the use of the $75,000 tendered by Walcott, and utilized by the government. The United States must also refund the payment made promptly unless the parties otherwise agree.

We REVERSE the decision of the district court and REMAND for further proceedings consistent with this opinion.

———

Notes and Questions

In the article excerpted above by Richard Willard, who was Assistant Attorney for the Civil Division at the Department of Justice during the Reagan Administration, he describes the regulations specifying which officials within the Department of Justice have authority for settlement of federal government cases. In *United States v. Walcott*, the settlement purportedly reached with the Small Business Administration had not been approved by the Department of Justice pursuant to these regulations. What is the consequence? Once again, as we saw earlier with such cases as *Mehle v. American Management Systems, Inc.* (see Chapter I.B.1) and *United States v. Providence Journal Company* (see Chapter I.B.4), we find that who has the authority to represent the United States—that is, who is properly acting as counsel for the government as a party—has a significant impact on the viability of the litigation or the attempted resolution of it.

Who is at fault here? Yes, the officials in the Small Business Administration certainly bear a substantial share of the blame; the court says they have treated Patricia Walcott in a "shabby" fashion. They certainly knew they were acting without Department of Justice approval and should have

---

5. At the same time, we take note that Walcott herself was earning $120,000 annual- ly at the time of the default.

known better than to unilaterally approve a settlement. But what about Walcott's attorney? What steps should she have taken to ensure a proper settlement? The court quotes the Supreme Court's decision in *Federal Crop Insurance Corp. v. Merrill*, 332 U.S. 380, 384 (1947), for the proposition that anyone entering into an agreement with the government "takes the risk of having accurately ascertained that he who purports to act for the Government stays within the bounds of his authority." How might the attorney have done so in this case? Do you see now why it is vitally important for those handling litigation against the federal government to understand the Department of Justice and its litigating and settlement authority?

from the private side ···

———

3. COURT SETTLEMENT CONFERENCES

Balancing test
- *convenience*
- *Gov't as unique litigant & anthy*
- *Centralized settlement makes it hard to comply*
- *Huge case load std.*
- *Abuse of discretion*

In re Stone

United States Court of Appeals for the Fifth Circuit.
986 F.2d 898 (5th Cir. 1993).

■ PER CURIAM:

(evidentiary & Art III)
Issue

In these petitions seeking writs of mandamus, we decide whether a federal district judge has the power, by a standing order, to direct the federal government to send a representative with full settlement authority to settlement conferences and, if so, whether he abused his discretion by so doing in these routine civil lawsuits involving the United States. In addition to requiring counsel to attend these conferences, the court also requires the attendance of a designated representative of each party with full authority to settle the case; that representative must appear in person—availability by telephone is not sufficient. We conclude that although the district judge possesses the ultimate power to require the attendance at issue, it is a power to be very sparingly used, and here the district judge, albeit with the best of intentions, has abused his discretion.

Holding

I.

In each of the petitions before us, the federal government objects to this order as applied to it. By statute, the Attorney General of the United States has the power to conduct all litigation on behalf of the United States, its agencies, and its officers, unless otherwise provided by law. 28 U.S.C. § 519. Pursuant to authority given by 28 U.S.C. § 510, the Attorney General has developed a set of regulations delegating settlement authority to various officials. See 28 C.F.R. §§ 0.160–0.172; *see also* directives reprinted at 28 C.F.R. pt. 0, subpt. Y app.

As we read these regulations, United States Attorneys often will be able to settle a case without approval from a higher authority, as the regulations provide that each local United States Attorney has settlement authority up to $500,000. If the client agency disagrees with the United

ROLs

States Attorney over the terms of the settlement, however, an Assistant Attorney General must approve the settlement. 28 C.F.R. § 0.168(a). In addition, settlements in various classes of important cases always must be approved by the Deputy Attorney General or one of the Assistant Attorneys General.[1]

II.

Although it is historically reserved for "extraordinary" cases, we have used the writ of mandamus as a "one-time-only device to 'settle new and important problems' that might have otherwise evaded expeditious review." *In re Equal Employment Opportunity Comm'n*, 709 F.2d 392, 394 (5th Cir.1983) (quoting *Schlagenhauf v. Holder*, 379 U.S. 104 (1964)). As district courts continue to become more heavily involved in the pretrial process, appellate courts may be asked more often to issue writs of mandamus to protect the asserted rights of litigants. Pretrial orders such as the ones before us raise important issues but are ill-suited for review after final judgment. * * *

C.

We are able to conclude * * * that, subject to the abuse-of-discretion standard, district courts have the general inherent power to require a party to have a representative with full settlement authority present—or at least reasonably and promptly accessible—at pretrial conferences. This applies to the government as well as private litigants. We find no statute or rule that attempts to regulate the court's use of that inherent power. But a district court must consider the unique position of the government as a litigant in determining whether to exercise its discretion in favor of issuing such an order.[5]

1. Even if a case is to be settled for not more than $500,000, so that a United States Attorney could settle it under the regulations, his settlement authority disappears upon disagreement over the terms of the settlement by the client agency.

5. As we noted above, the Attorney General has power to develop regulations dealing with the settlement of lawsuits involving the federal government. The government contends that the district court's order interferes with those regulations; it makes the bold assertion that a court may never compel the Department of Justice to alter its regulations governing its procedures for handling litigation. We disagree. If that were the case, the executive branch could use the courts as it pleased. The executive branch is not above the law. United States v. Nixon, 418 U.S. 683 (1974). Moreover, the government misinterprets Touhy v. Ragen, 340 U.S. 462 (1951), the authority relied upon for this argument.

In Touhy, a low-level official of the Department of Justice, obeying an internal departmental regulation, refused to produce papers demanded by a subpoena. Given the potentially sensitive nature of Justice Department documents, the Court held that he properly could refuse to turn over the documents. At best, this case stands for the proposition that courts should observe reasonable regulations of the Executive Branch that have strong underlying policy justifications. The Court's opinion and Justice Frankfurter's concurrence explain that the Court did not decide whether a district court could force the Attorney General to turn over documents. 340 U.S. at 469–73. Our holding today allows us to avoid deciding whether forcing the Attorney General to alter the settlement regulations would run afoul of the doctrine of separation of powers. * * *

As the Supreme Court recently has observed, the executive branch's "most important constitutional duty [is] to 'take Care that the Laws be faithfully executed.'" *Lujan v. Defenders of Wildlife*, 504 U.S. 555, 576 (1992). The purpose of the structure established by the Attorney General is to promote centralized decisionmaking on important questions. The Supreme Court has recognized the value of such centralized decisionmaking in the executive branch.

Centralized decisionmaking promotes three important objectives. First, it allows the government to act consistently in important cases, a value more or less recognized by the Equal Protection Clause. Second, centralized decisionmaking allows the executive branch to pursue policy goals more effectively by placing ultimate authority in the hands of a few officials. Third, by giving authority to high-ranking officials, centralized decisionmaking better promotes political accountability.

Given the reasonable policy justifications for the Justice Department's settlement regulations and the insignificant interference with the operation of the courts, the district court abused its discretion in not respecting those regulations. Where the interference with the courts is slight, courts should not risk becoming "monitors of the wisdom and soundness of Executive action." *Laird v. Tatum*, 408 U.S. 1, 15 (1972). The order at issue here imposes a major inconvenience on at least one of the parties without the showing of a real and palpable need.

The district court contends that the government is not special and should not be treated differently from private litigants. The government is in a special category in a number of respects, however, in addition to its need for centralized decisionmaking. "It is not open to serious dispute that the Government is a party to a far greater number of cases on a nationwide basis tha[n] even the most litigious private entity...." *United States v. Mendoza*, 464 U.S. 154, 159 (1984).

This court, as well, has recognized that the government sometimes must be treated differently. Obviously, high-ranking officials of cabinet agencies could never do their jobs if they could be subpoenaed for every case involving their agency. As a result, we have held that such subpoenas are appropriate only in egregious cases. *See, e.g., In re Office of Inspector Gen.*, 933 F.2d 276, 278 (5th Cir.1991); *In re Equal Employment Opportunity Comm'n*, 709 F.2d 392, 398 (5th Cir.1983). "[T]he efficiency of the EEOC would suffer terribly if its commissioners were subject to depositions in every routine subpoena enforcement proceeding." *Id.*

In determining whether to require the government (or, for that matter, a private party) to send a representative to a pretrial conference with full authority to settle, a district court should take a practical approach. The court must be permitted to conduct its business in a reasonably efficient manner; it need not allow the parties or counsel to waste valuable judicial resources unnecessarily. On the other hand, the court should recognize that parties have a host of problems beyond the immediate case that is set for pretrial conference. This is particularly true of the government. We have outlined above, in some detail, the peculiar position of the Attorney

General and the special problems the Department of Justice faces in handling the government's ever-increasing volume of litigation.

We conclude that the district court abused its discretion in routinely requiring a representative of the government with ultimate settlement authority to be present at all pretrial or settlement conferences. We do not suggest that the district court can never issue such an order, but it should consider less drastic steps before doing so.

For example, the court could require the government to declare whether the case can be settled within the authority of the local United States Attorney. If so, the court could issue an order requiring the United States Attorney to either attend the conference personally or be available by telephone to discuss settlement at the time of the conference.

According to the government at argument, most of its routine litigation can be settled within the United States Attorney's authority. Where that is not so, and failure of the government to extend settlement authority is a serious, persistent problem, substantially hampering the operations of the docket, the court could take additional action, such as requiring the government to advise it of the identity of the person or persons who hold such authority and directing those persons to consider settlement in advance of the conference and be fully prepared and available by telephone to discuss settlement at the time of the conference. Finally, if the district court's reasonable efforts to conduct an informed settlement discussion in a particular case are thwarted because the government official with settlement authority will not communicate with government counsel or the court in a timely manner, the court, as a last resort, can require the appropriate officials with full settlement authority to attend a pretrial conference.

The measures we outline above are intended to be exemplary, and we express no ultimate view as to such hypothetical situations except to point out that there are many steps that reasonably can be taken, far short of the standing order at issue here. We include these scenarios to demonstrate that the district court, before issuing an order such as the directive under review here, must give individualized attention to the hardship that order will create. The court must then exercise its discretion in light of the circumstances of that case. We believe that such practical measures will enable the courts to administer their dockets efficiently while allowing the Department of Justice to handle effectively the burdensome volume of litigation thrust upon it.

IV.

In summary, we conclude that the district court abused its discretion in these cases. We find it unnecessary to issue writs of mandamus, however. The able district judge has indicated that he welcomes this court's exposition of this issue, and we are confident that he will abide by our decision and adjust his directives accordingly. Thus, the petitions for writs of mandamus are DENIED without prejudice.

Notes and Questions

The district court in the *In re Stone* case had ordered the federal government to send a representative with full settlement authority to every settlement conference held before the court. Why does the government object to that order? Consider what would be the consequence if every district court in the nation adopted a similar order. Would the Deputy Attorney General and the Assistant Attorney General have time to perform their other duties if they were required to fly around the country for the myriad of government settlement conferences held in the various federal district courts every week? Of course, as the United States Court of Appeals for the Fifth Circuit recognizes, the United States Attorney often has settlement authority, although the district court's order would also significantly impose on his or her time if obliged to attend a settlement conference in every civil case pending in the district.

The court of appeals asks two questions: (1) Did the district court have the power to order the government to have a representative with full settlement authority, however high up the chain of command within the Department of Justice, to attend a settlement conference? (2) If the court has the power, was it an abuse of discretion to exercise that power in every routine case? How does the Fifth Circuit answer each of these questions. The district court opined that the government was not special and should be treated no differently than other litigants. What is the response of the court of appeals? How does the Fifth Circuit suggest that settlement conferences involving the federal government should be conducted in the future?

————

4.   ALTERNATIVE DISPUTE RESOLUTION

Over the past two decades, the federal government has taken initiatives to encourage alternative means of dispute resolution (ADR). In 1991, President George H.W. Bush issued an executive order to encourage prelitigation settlement of potential civil suits by the government. Civil Justice Reform, Executive Order 12,778 (Oct. 23, 1991) revoked by Executive Order 12,988 (Feb. 7, 1996). In 1992, the Department of Justice issued preliminary guidance to federal agencies to implement President Bush's order. Memorandum of Preliminary Guidance on Implementation of the Litigation Reforms of Executive Order No. 12778, 57 Fed. Reg. 3640 (Jan. 30, 1992). Subsequently, during the Clinton Administration, Attorney General Janet Reno directed "each of the civil litigating components to provide their attorneys with policy guidance on the use of Alternative Dispute Resolution techniques and * * * to develop case selection criteria for using ADR in appropriate cases," which resulted in publication in 1996 of an extensive set of guidelines. Department of Justice, Office of the Senior Counsel for Alternative Dispute Resolution, Policy on the Use of Alternative Dispute Resolution, and Case Identification Criteria for Alternative Dispute Resolution, 61 Fed. Reg. 36,895 (July 15, 1996).

As the litigating division most pertinent to our study, the Civil Division's guidelines offer the following introduction to ADR from the federal government's perspective:

ADR is any consensual dispute resolution process facilitated by third-party neutrals which can be utilized prior to or during litigation. ADR is not meant to replace traditional litigation or unassisted negotiation, but rather is meant to supplement them. In other words, ADR is another tool to resolve disputes and can provide unique advantages. ADR can be used when traditional negotiation is likely to be unsuccessful, has already been unsuccessful, or when it can expedite negotiations and/or allow them to proceed more efficiently. ADR can be used to resolve discrete parts of a particular case or, a series of cases; it can help narrow and/or eliminate issues; it can expedite critical discovery; and can help the parties gain a better understanding of the strengths and weaknesses of the case. ADR provides flexibility by allowing the parties to fashion their own resolutions to disputes—creative resolutions beyond what courts can offer.

In a similar vein, ADR allows the parties to fashion their procedures for resolving disputes. There are as many ADR processes as the parties can create. The most widely used ADR techniques are mediation, early neutral case evaluation, arbitration, mini-trial and summary jury trial * * *.

Civil Division–Statement on Alternative Dispute Resolution, 61 Fed. Reg. 36,899 (1996).

In a manner parallel to the guidelines of the other litigating divisions as well, the Civil Division guidelines set forth for each category of case (1) those factors that counsel in favor of use of ADR (e.g., continuing relationships between plaintiffs and agency; case involves largely a factual dispute; relief sought is money damages; personality conflicts or poor communication between opposing counsel adversely affects settlement negotiations; there is a need to avoid adverse precedent but traditional settlement negotiations have reached an impasse, etc.) *versus* (2) those factors that counsel against use of ADR (e.g., case involves significant legal, policy, or constitutional issues; judicial resolution is necessary for precedential value; case can likely be efficiently disposed of by summary judgment or other dispositive motion, etc.). The guidelines also suggest which ADR techniques are appropriate for a case (e.g., mediation, early neutral case evaluator/expert, non-binding arbitration, or a mini-trial).

Because the government cannot be forced to resort to any particular ADR method and will not agree to be bound by any ADR result, ADR is only an adjunct to settlement negotiations and thus should be considered in that vein. Indeed, Attorney General Reno's statement upon issuance of the published guidelines emphasized that "[t]hese criteria relate to the government's voluntary participation in ADR" and further stated that nothing in the guidelines "shall be construed to create any right or benefit, substantive or procedural, enforceable at law or in equity, by a party against the

United States, its agencies, its officers or any other person." *See supra* 61 Fed. Reg. 36,895.

SECTION H.   JUDGMENTS AGAINST THE FEDERAL GOVERNMENT

[handwritten: what are the statutory sources]
[handwritten: strict conditions/terms for payment]

Gregory C. Sisk, Interim Attorney's Fees Awards Against the Federal Government

68 North Carolina Law Review 117, 120–123 (1989).

[handwritten margin: ad hoc]

Prior to 1956, judgments awarded against the United States generally could not be paid until Congress enacted specific appropriations legislation for that purpose. As a consequence, payments of money judgments were frequently long delayed. With the enactment of the Judgment Fund statutes, 31 U.S.C. § 1304 and 28 U.S.C. § 2414, Congress established a procedure to permit timely payment of money awards *after* the judgment became final upon the exhaustion of appellate rights.

[handwritten margin: J Fund]
[handwritten margin: Fund procedure]
[handwritten margin: procedure]

Subsection 1304(a) of Title 31, United States Code, which establishes the Judgment Fund, provides a general waiver of immunity for payment of money judgments and awards rendered against the United States and its agencies, when "payment is not otherwise provided for" by another statute.[20] The Judgment Fund is a permanent and continuing appropriation, separate and distinct from any agency operating appropriations. It provides the sole source for payment of court awards and judgments against the United States and its agencies, except when another statute designates a different payment source that is legally available to pay judgments. Because appropriations of agency funds rarely provide for use of such funds in the payment of judgments, as a general rule, awards and judgments are payable only from the Judgment Fund.

[handwritten margin: A.G. certifies finality to Treasury]
[handwritten margin: ✳]

Subsection 1304(a) authorizes payment from the Judgment Fund only on the terms and conditions set forth in that provision. Section 2414 of Title 28, United States Code, referred to in Subsection 1304(a)(3)(A), establishes one of the primary conditions on payments from the Judgment

---

20. Subsection 1304(a) reads in pertinent part:

Necessary amounts are appropriated to pay final judgments, awards, compromise settlements, and interest and costs specified in the judgments or otherwise authorized by law when—

(1) payment is not otherwise provided for;

(2) payment is certified by the Comptroller General; and

(3) the judgment, award, or settlement is payable

(A) under section 2414 . . . of title 28 *[handwritten: ← a primary cond'n. on payment from J Fund]*

. . .

31 U.S.C. § 1304(a) (1982).

Fund.[23] Section 2414 provides that "payment of *final judgments* rendered by a district court ... shall be made on settlement by the General Accounting Office." The statute deems a judgment to be final "[w]henever the Attorney General determines that no appeal shall be taken from a judgment or that no further review will be sought from a decision affirming the same." In addition, Subsection 1304(a)(2) requires that the Comptroller General of the General Accounting Office certify the award for payment. The Comptroller General may not make this certification properly until the underlying judgment is final and no longer subject to modification upon appeal. In an official ruling, the Comptroller General has explained:

> In order for a judgment to be paid from the permanent appropriation, it must be certified by the Comptroller General to the Treasury Department for payment. This cannot be done until we have been furnished the amount to be certified for payment, with the assurance that it is not subject to further litigation.[27]

> In sum, Sections 1304 and 2414 permit payment of a monetary award against the United States only after the Attorney General has notified the Comptroller General that the government has exhausted the appeal process or does not contemplate further appeal and the Comptroller General has certified the award's finality.

The manifest purpose of these statutes is to protect the public Treasury. Congress has determined that the United States ought not to pay unreviewed awards by district courts when the United States contemplates appellate action, because a successful appeal will render such payments unjustified. Moreover, the finality requirement protects the United States from expending additional resources to recoup monies that a court might improperly direct the government to pay at an interlocutory stage.

Note

In 1996, the Judgment Fund statutes discussed above were amended to substitute "Secretary of the Treasury" (1) for "General Accounting Office" in performing the account settlement function under Section 2414, and (2)

---

23. Section 2414 reads, in pertinent part, as follows:

> Except as provided by the Contract Disputes Act of 1978, payment of final judgments rendered by a district court or the Court of International Trade against the United States shall be made on settlements by the General Accounting Office....

> Whenever the Attorney General determines that no appeal shall be taken from a judgment or that no further review will be sought from a decision affirming the same, he shall so certify and the judgment shall be deemed final.

28 U.S.C. § 2414 (1982).

27. In re Payment of Judgments Under Back Pay Act and Title VII of Civil Rights Act, 58 Comp. Gen. 311, 314 (1979) (citations omitted) * * *.

for "Comptroller General" in certifying payment under Section 1304. Pub. L. No. 104–316, Title II, §§ 202(k), (m), 110 Stat. 3843. Other than transferring these functions from the Comptroller General and the General Accounting Office to the Secretary of the Treasury, the pertinent substance of these statutes was not revised and thus the interpretation and application of these statutes presumably remain unaffected.

CHAPTER II

THE DOCTRINE OF FEDERAL SOVEREIGN IMMUNITY

SECTION A. THE EVOLUTION OF FEDERAL SOVEREIGN IMMUNITY IN THE SUPREME COURT

The concept of "sovereign immunity"—that is the immunity of the government from suit without its express permission—underlies and permeates the entire course. It lies in the background of every decision we study and every statute we explore. Even when the government has waived sovereign immunity through legislation, the doctrine influences the manner in which the courts interpret and apply such statutes.

In this chapter, we ask the basic questions: May the sovereign government be sued without its consent? Why or why not? What justification is there for holding the government immune from suit? Should the government be treated differently from any other ordinary litigant in federal court? Is sovereign immunity an archaic holdover from the era of monarchy and the autocratic view that the king could do no wrong? Can the concept be defended in the context of a republican democracy? If so, how? What are the historical origins of the concept? How has sovereign immunity evolved as a doctrine? How should the doctrine of sovereign immunity influence the basic approach or attitude of courts toward a statute purportedly authorizing government liability in a particular context? Should it be construed in the same manner as any ordinary statute or instead be interpreted strictly and narrowly? How do other nations approach the question of governmental liability?

We begin by outlining the development of the concept of sovereign immunity in a series of three landmark Supreme Court decisions. You will note that in none of these cases is the government itself actually named as defendant to the lawsuits (at least by the time the case reaches the Supreme Court). In each case, the plaintiffs attempt to avoid the bar of sovereign immunity by framing their complaints against individual government officers. Does the attempt succeed? Should it? Consider whether the government itself would be affected by a ruling in the plaintiff's favor. If so, then wouldn't the Court be indulging a legal fiction to pretend the suit is one against an individual government officer rather than against the government itself?

104

[handwritten: what is the nature of pl's action?]

United States v. Lee   *[handwritten: 5-4]*

Supreme Court of the United States.
106 U.S. 196 (1882).

■ MR. JUSTICE MILLER delivered the opinion of the court.

These are two writs of error to the same judgment: one prosecuted by the United States, *eo nomine;* and the other by the Attorney–General of the United States in the names of Frederick Kaufman and Richard P. Strong, the defendants against whom judgment was rendered in the circuit court.

The action was originally commenced in the circuit court for the county of Alexandria, in the state of Virginia, by the present defendant in error, against Kaufman and Strong and a great number of others, to recover possession of a parcel of land of about eleven hundred acres, known as the Arlington estate. * * * *[handwritten: Natl Cemetery]*

As soon as the declaration was filed in that court the case was removed into the circuit court of the United States by writ of *certiorari,* where all the subsequent proceedings took place. It was tried by a jury, and during its progress an order was made at the request of the plaintiff dismissing the suit as to all of the defendants except Kaufman and Strong. Against each of these a judgment was rendered for separate parcels of the land in controversy; namely, against Kaufman for about two hundred acres of it, constituting the National Cemetery and included within its walls, and against Strong for the remainder of the tract, except seventeen acres in the possession of Maria Syphax.   *[handwritten margin: Removed to U.S. cir. ct.]*

As the United States was not a party to the suit below, and, while defending the action by its proper law officers, expressly declined to submit itself as a defendant to the jurisdiction of the court, there may exist some doubt whether it has a right to prosecute the writ of error in its own name; but as the judgment against Kaufman and Strong is here on their writ of error, under which all the questions are raised which can be raised under the other, their writ being prosecuted in the interest of the United States, and argued here by the Solicitor–General, the point is immaterial, and the question has not been mooted.

The first step taken in the case, after it came into the Circuit Court of the United States, was the filing in the clerk's office of that court of the following paper by the Attorney–General:

"George W. C. Lee

v.

Frederick Kaufman, R. P. Strong,
and others. (In ejectment.)

"And now comes the Attorney General of the United States and suggests to the court and gives it to understand and be informed (appearing only for the purpose of this motion) that the property in controversy in this suit has been for more than ten years and now is held, occupied, and possessed by the United States, through its officers and agents, charged in   *[handwritten margin: Gov't's filing in U.S. cir. ct.]*

behalf of the government of the United States with the control of the property, and who are in the actual possession thereof, as public property of the United States, for public uses, in the exercise of their sovereign and constitutional powers, as a military station, and as a national cemetery established for the burial of deceased soldiers and sailors, and known and designated as the 'Arlington Cemetery,' and for the uses and purposes set forth in the certificate of sale, a copy of which, as stated and prepared by the plaintiff, and which is a true copy thereof, is annexed hereto and filed herewith, under claim of title, as appears by the said certificate of sale, and which was executed, delivered, and recorded as therein appears.

"Wherefore, without submitting the rights of the government of the United States to the jurisdiction of the court, but respectfully insisting that the court has no jurisdiction of the subject in controversy, he moves that the declaration in said suit be set aside, and all the proceedings be stayed and dismissed, and for such other order as may be proper in the premises.

"CHAS. DEVENS,

Atty. Gen. U. S."

The plaintiff demurred to this suggestion, and on hearing the demurrer was sustained.

The case was thereupon tried before a jury on the general issue pleaded by defendants Kaufman and Strong, in the course of which the question raised by this suggestion of the Attorney–General was again presented to the court by prayers for instruction, which were rejected, and exceptions taken.

The plaintiff offered evidence establishing title in himself by the will of his grandfather, George Washington Parke Custis, who devised the Arlington estate to his daughter, the wife of Gen. Robert E. Lee, for life, and after her death to the plaintiff. This, with the long possession under that title, made a *prima facie* right of recovery in the plaintiff.

The title relied on by defendants is a tax-sale certificate made by the commissioners appointed under the act of Congress of June 7, 1862, c. 98, entitled "An Act for the collection of direct taxes in the insurrectionary districts within the United States," as amended by the act of February 6, 1863, c.21. At this sale the land was bid in for the United States by the commissioners, who gave a certificate of that fact, which was introduced on the trial as evidence by defendants.

If this sale was valid and the certificate conveyed a valid title, then the title of plaintiff was thereby divested, and he could not recover. If the proceedings evidenced by the tax sale did not transfer the title of the property to the United States, then it remained in the plaintiff, and so far as the question of title was concerned, his recovery was a rightful one.

We have then two questions presented to the court and jury below, and the same questions arise in this court on the record:

1. Could any action be maintained against the defendants for the possession of the land in controversy under the circumstances of the

relation of that possession to the United States, however clear the legal right to that possession might be in plaintiff?

2) If such an action could be maintained, was the *prima facie* title of plaintiff divested by the tax sale and the certificate given by the commissioners?

It is believed that no division of opinion exists among the members of this court on the proposition that the rulings of law under which the latter question was submitted by the court to the jury was sound, and that the jury were authorized to find, as they evidently did find, that the tax certificate and the sale which it recited did not divest the plaintiff of his title to the property. * * *

In approaching the other question which we are called on to decide, it is proper to make a clear statement of what it is.

The counsel for plaintiffs in error and in behalf of the United States assert the proposition, that though it has been ascertained by the verdict of the jury, in which no error is found, that the plaintiff has the title to the land in controversy, and that what is set up in behalf of the United States is no title at all, the court can render no judgment in favor of the plaintiff against the defendants in the action, because the latter hold the property as officers and agents of the United States, and it is appropriated to lawful public uses.

This proposition rests on the principle that the United States cannot be lawfully sued without its consent in any case, and that no action can be maintained against any individual without such consent, where the judgment must depend on the right of the United States to property held by such persons as officers or agents for the government.

The first branch of this proposition is conceded to be the established law of this country and of this court at the present day; the second, as a necessary or proper deduction from the first, is denied.

In order to decide whether the inference is justified from what is conceded, it is necessary to ascertain, if we can, on what principle the exemption of the United States from a suit by one of its citizens is founded, and what limitations surround this exemption. In this, as in most other cases of like character, it will be found that the doctrine is derived from the laws and practices of our English ancestors; and while it is beyond question that from the time of Edward the First until now the king of England was not suable in the courts of that country, except where his consent had been given on petition of right, it is a matter of great uncertainty whether prior to that time he was not suable in his own courts and in his kingly character as other persons were. We have the authority of Chief Baron Comyns and of the Mirror of Justices, that such was the law; and of Bracton and Lord Holt, that the king never was suable of common right. It is certain, however, that after the establishment of the petition of right about that time, as the appropriate manner of seeking relief where the ascertainment of the parties' rights required a suit against the king, no attempt has been made to sue the king in any court except as allowed on such petition.

It is believed that this petition of right, as it has been practiced and observed in the administration of justice in England, has been as efficient in securing the rights of suitors against the crown in all cases appropriate to judicial proceedings, as that which the law affords in legal controversies between the subjects of the king among themselves. "If the mode of proceeding to enforce it be formal and ceremonious, it is, nevertheless, a practical and efficient remedy for the invasion by the sovereign power of individual rights." *United States v. O'Keefe,* 11 Wall. 178.

There is in this country, however, no such thing as the petition of right, as there is no such thing as a kingly head to the nation, or to any of the states which compose it. There is vested in no officer or body the authority to consent that the state shall be sued except in the law-making power, which may give such consent on the terms it may choose to impose. Congress has created a court in which it has authorized suits to be brought against the United States, but has limited such suits to those arising on contract, with a few unimportant exceptions.

What were the reasons which forbid that the king should be sued in his own court, and how do these reasons apply to the political body corporate which we call the United States of America? As regards the king, one reason given by the old judges was the absurdity of the king's sending a writ to himself to command the king to appear in the king's court. No such reason exists in our government, as process runs in the name of the president and may be served on the Attorney General * * * . Nor can it be said that the dignity of the government is degraded by appearing as a defendant in the courts of its own creation, because it is constantly appearing as a party in such courts, and submitting its rights as against the citizens to their judgment.

Mr. Justice Gray, of the Supreme Court of Massachusetts, in an able and learned opinion which exhausts the sources of information on this subject, says: "The broader reason is that it would be inconsistent with the very idea of supreme executive power, and would endanger the performance of the public duties of the sovereign, to subject him to repeated suits as a matter of right, at the will of any citizen, and to submit to the judicial tribunals the control and disposition of his public property, his instruments and means of carrying on his government in war and in peace, and the money in his treasury." *Briggs & Another v. Light Boat,* 11 Allen, 162. As we have no person in this government who exercises supreme executive power or performs the public duties of a sovereign, it is difficult to see on what solid foundation of principle the exemption from liability to suit rests. It seems most probable that it has been adopted in our courts as a part of the general doctrine of publicists, that the supreme power in every state, wherever it may reside, shall not be compelled, by process of courts of its own creation, to defend itself from assaults in those courts.

It is obvious that in our system of jurisprudence, the principle is as applicable to each of the states as it is to the United States, except in those cases where by the constitution a state of the Union may be sued in this court.

That the doctrine met with a doubtful reception in the early history of this court may be seen from the opinions of two of its justices in the case of *Chisholm v. Georgia* [2 Dall. 419], where Mr. Justice Wilson, a member of the convention which framed our constitution, after a learned examination of the laws of England and other states and kingdoms, sums up the result by saying: "We see nothing against, but much in favor of, the jurisdiction of this court over the state of Georgia, a party to this cause." Mr. Chief Justice Jay also considered the question as affected by the difference between a republican state like ours, and a personal sovereign, and held that there is no reason why a state should not be sued, though doubting whether the United States would be subject to the same rule.

The first recognition of the general doctrine by this court is to be found in the case of *Cohens v. Virginia,* 6 Wheat. 264.

The terms in which Chief Justice Marshall there gives assent to the principle does not add much to its force. "The counsel for the defendant," he says, "has laid down the general proposition that a sovereign independent state is not suable except by its own consent." This general proposition, he adds, will not be controverted.

And while the exemption of the United States and of the several states from being subjected as defendants to ordinary actions in the courts has since that time been repeatedly asserted here, the principle has never been discussed or the reasons for it given, but it has always been treated as an established doctrine.

On the other hand, while acceding to the general proposition that in no court can the United States be sued directly by original process as a defendant, there is abundant evidence in the decisions of this court that the doctrine, if not absolutely limited to cases in which the United States are made defendants by name, is not permitted to interfere with the judicial enforcement of the established rights of plaintiffs when the United States is not a defendant or a necessary party to the suit.

But little weight can be given to the decisions of the English courts on this branch of the subject, for two reasons:

1. In all cases where the title to property came into controversy between the crown and a subject, whether held in right of the person who was king or as representative of the nation, the petition of right presented a judicial remedy,—a remedy which this court, on full examination in a case which required it, held to be practical and efficient. There has been, therefore, no necessity for suing the officers or servants of the king who held possession of such property, when the issue could be made with the King himself as defendant.

2. Another reason of much greater weight is found in the vast difference in the essential character of the two governments as regards the source and the depositaries of power.

Notwithstanding the progress which has been made since the days of the Stuarts in stripping the crown of its powers and prerogatives, it remains true to-day that the monarch is looked upon with too much

*England's,
Attitude &
reverence for
the Crown*

vs.

United States --

- People as the Sovereign

reverence to be subjected to the demands of the law as ordinary persons are, and the king-loving nation would be shocked at the spectacle of their Queen being turned out of her pleasure garden by a writ of ejectment against the gardener. The crown remains the fountain of honor, and the surroundings which give dignity and majesty to its possessor are cherished and enforced all the more strictly because of the loss of real power in the government.

It is not to be expected, therefore, that the courts will permit their process to disturb the possession of the crown by acting on its officers or agents.

Under our system the *people,* who are there called *subjects,* are the sovereign. Their rights, whether collective or individual, are not bound to give way to a sentiment of loyalty to the person of the monarch. The citizen here knows no person, however near to those in power, or however powerful himself, to whom he need yield the rights which the law secures to him when it is well administered. When he, in one of the courts of competent jurisdiction, has established his right to property, there is no reason why deference to any person, natural or artificial, not even the United States, should prevent him from using the means which the law gives him for the protection and enforcement of that right.

*In cases of
foreign sovereigns having
disputes w/ the Crown
its political/diplomatic
branches settle the
dispute, not courts
(avoids the sovereign
immunity issue)*

Another class of cases in the English courts, in which attempts have been made to subject the public ships and other property of foreign and independent nations found within English territory to their jurisdiction, is also inapplicable to this case; for, both by the English courts and ours, it has been uniformly held that these were questions, the decisions of which, as they might involve war or peace, must be primarily dealt with by those departments of the government which had the power to adjust them by negotiation, or to enforce the rights of the citizen by war. In such cases the judicial department of this government follows the action of the political branch, and will not embarrass the latter by assuming an antagonistic jurisdiction. * * *

*what the
fed gov't
wants →*

The case before us is a suit against Strong and Kaufman, as individuals, to recover possession of property. The suggestion was made that it was the property of the United States, and that the court, without inquiring into the truth of this suggestion, should proceed no further; and in this case, as in that, after a judicial inquiry had made it clear that the property belonged to plaintiff and not to the United States, we are still asked to forbid the court below to proceed further, and to reverse and set aside what it has done, and thus refuse to perform the duty of deciding suits properly brought before us by citizens of the United States. * * *

* * * [An] examination of the cases in this court establishes clearly this result: that the proposition that when an individual is sued in regard to property which he holds as officer or agent of the United States, his possession cannot be disturbed when that fact is brought to the attention of the court, has been overruled and denied in every case where it has been necessary to decide it, and that in many others where the record shows that the case as tried below actually and clearly presented that defense, it was

neither urged by counsel nor considered by the court here, though, if it had been a good defense, it would have avoided the necessity of a long inquiry into plaintiff's title and of other perplexing questions, and have quickly disposed of the case. * * *

The fact that the property which is the subject of this controversy is devoted to public uses, is strongly urged as a reason why those who are so using it under the authority of the United States shall not be sued for its possession even by one who proves a clear title to that possession. In this connection many cases of imaginary evils have been suggested, if the contrary doctrine should prevail. Among these are a supposed seizure of vessels of war, invasions of forts and arsenals of the United States. Hypothetical cases of great evils may be suggested by a particularly fruitful imagination in regard to almost every law upon which depends the rights of the individual or of the government, and if the existence of laws is to depend upon their capacity to withstand such criticism, the whole fabric of the law must fail. * * *

The objection is * * * inconsistent with the principle involved in the last two clauses of article 5 of the amendments to the Constitution of the United States, whose language is: "That no person ... shall be deprived of life, liberty, or property without due process of law, nor shall private property be taken for public use without just compensation."

Conceding that the property in controversy in this case is devoted to a proper public use, and that this has been done by those having authority to establish a cemetery and a fort, the verdict of the jury finds that it is and was the private property of the plaintiff, and was taken without any process of law and without any compensation. Undoubtedly those provisions of the Constitution are of that character which it is intended the courts shall enforce, when cases involving their operation and effect are brought before them. The instances in which the life and liberty of the citizen have been protected by the judicial writ of habeas corpus are too familiar to need citation, and many of these cases, indeed indeed almost all of them, are those in which life or liberty was invaded by persons assuming to act under the authority of the government.

If this constitutional provision is a sufficient authority for the court to interfere to rescue a prisoner from the hands of those holding him under the asserted authority of the government, what reason is there that the same courts shall not give remedy to the citizen whose property has been seized without due process of law and devoted to public use without just compensation?

Looking at the question upon principle, and apart from the authority of adjudged cases, we think it still clearer that this branch of the defense cannot be maintained. It seems to be opposed to all the principles upon which the rights of the citizen, when brought in collision with the acts of the government, must be determined. In such cases there is no safety for the citizen, except in the protection of the judicial tribunals, for rights which have been invaded by the officers of the government, professing to act in its name. There remains to him but the alternative of resistance,

e.g. habeas corpus is enforced ag. fed. gov't

which principle? Absolutely no suit w/o express consent?

To base amenability to suit solely on consent of the sovereign overlooks role of court as arbiter & enforcer of rights guaranteed

courts   resistance

[margin note: Gov't's argument]

which may amount to crime. The position assumed here is that, however clear his rights, no remedy can be afforded to him when it is seen that his opponent is an officer of the United States, claiming to act under its authority; (for, as Mr. Chief Justice Marshall says, to examine whether this authority is rightfully assumed is the exercise of jurisdiction, and must lead to the decision of the merits of the question) The objection of the plaintiffs in error necessarily forbids any inquiry into the truth of the assumption that the parties setting up such authority are lawfully possessed of it; for the argument is that the formal suggestion of the existence of such authority forbids any inquiry into the truth of the suggestion.

But why should not the truth of the suggestion and the lawfulness of the authority be made the subject of judicial investigation?

[margin note: Jurisdictional analysis "Case or Controversy"]

In the case supposed, the court has before it a plaintiff capable of *[margin note: capacity]* suing, a defendant who has no personal exemption from suit, and a cause of *[margin note: sueability]* action cognizable in the court,—a *case* within the meaning of that term, as *[margin note: Cause of action]* employed in the Constitution and defined by the decisions of this court. It is to be presumed in favor of the jurisdiction of the court that the plaintiff may be able to prove the right which he asserts in his declaration.

[margin note: Right.]

What is that right as established by the verdict of the jury in this case? It is the right to the possession of the homestead of plaintiff. A right to recover that which has been taken from him by force and violence, and detained by the strong hand. This right being clearly established, we are told that the court can proceed no further, because it appears that certain military officers, acting under the orders of the President, have seized this estate, and converted one part of it into a military fort and another into a cemetery.

[margin note: Gov't does not defend the seizure under Constitutional powers or as compensated]

It is not pretended, as the case now stands, that the President had any lawful authority to do this, or that the legislative body could give him any such authority except upon payment of just compensation. The defence stands here solely upon the absolute immunity from judicial inquiry of every one who *asserts* authority from the executive branch of the government, however clear it may be made that the executive possessed no such power. Not only that no such power is given, but that it is absolutely *[margin note: Constitutional prohibition]* prohibited, both to the executive and the legislative, to deprive any one of life, liberty, or property without due process of law, or to take private property without just compensation.

These provisions for the security of the rights of the citizen stand in the Constitution in the same connection and upon the same ground as they regard his liberty and his property. It cannot be denied that both were intended to be enforced by the judiciary as one of the departments of the government established by that constitution. As we have already said, the writ of *habeas corpus* has been often used to defend the liberty of the citizen, and even his life, against the assertion of unlawful authority on the part of the executive and the legislative branches of the government.

No man in this country is so high that he is above the law. No officer of the law may set that law at defiance with impunity. All the officers of the government, from the highest to the lowest, are creatures of the law, and are bound to obey it.

It is the only supreme power in our system of government, and every man who by accepting office participates in its functions is only the more strongly bound to submit to that supremacy, and to observe the limitations which it imposes upon the exercise of the authority which it gives.

Courts of justice are established, not only to decide upon the controverted rights of the citizens as against each other, but also upon rights in controversy between them and the government; and the docket of this court is crowded with controversies of the latter class.

Shall it be said, in the face of all this, and of the acknowledged right of the judiciary to decide in proper cases, statutes which have been passed by both branches of Congress and approved by the President to be unconstitutional, that the courts cannot give remedy when the citizen has been deprived of his property by force, his estate seized and converted to the use of the government without any lawful authority, without any process of law, and without any compensation, because the President has ordered it and his officers are in possession?

If such be the law of this country, it sanctions a tyranny which has no existence in the monarchies of Europe, nor in any other government which has a just claim to well-regulated liberty and the protection of personal rights.

It cannot be, then, that when in a suit between two citizens for the ownership of real estate, one of them has established his right to the possession of the property according to all the forms of judicial procedure, and by the verdict of a jury and the judgment of the court, the wrongful possessor can say successfully to the court, Stop, here, I hold by order of the President, and the progress of justice must be stayed. That, though the nature of the controversy is one peculiarly appropriate to the judicial function, though the United States is no party to the suit, though one of the three great branches of the government to which by the Constitution this duty has been assigned has declared its judgment after a fair trial, the unsuccessful party can interpose 'an absolute veto' upon that judgment by the production of an order of the Secretary of War, which that officer had no more authority to make than the humblest private citizen.

The evils supposed to grow out of the possible interference of judicial action with the exercise of powers of the government essential to some of its most important operations will be seen to be small indeed compared to this evil, and much diminished, if they do not wholly disappear, upon a recurrence to a few considerations.

One of these, of no little significance, is that during the existence of the government for now nearly a century under the present Constitution, with this principle and the practice under it well established, no injury from it has come to that government. During this time at least two wars, so serious as to call into exercise all the powers and all the resources of the government, have been conducted to a successful issue. One of these was a great

[handwritten margin notes: "The Law as supreme Power in our system" and "Courts decide on relationship b/t gov't & citizen..."]

civil war, such as the world has seldom known, which strained the powers of the national government to their utmost tension. In the course of this war persons hostile to the Union did not hesitate to invoke the powers of the courts for their protection as citizens, in order to cripple the exercise of the authority necessary to put down the rebellion; yet no improper interference with the exercise of that authority was permitted or attempted by the courts.

Another consideration is that since the United States cannot be made a defendant to a suit concerning its property, and no judgment in any suit against an individual who has possession or control of such property can bind or conclude the government, * * * the government is always at liberty, notwithstanding any such judgment, to avail itself of all the remedies which the law allows to every person, natural or artificial, for the vindication and assertion of its rights. Hence, taking the present case as an illustration, the United States may proceed by a bill in chancery to quiet its title, in aid of which, if a proper case is made, a writ of injunction may be obtained. Or it may bring an action of ejectment, in which, on a direct issue between the United States as plaintiff and the present plaintiff as defendant, the title of the United States could be judicially determined. Or, if satisfied that its title has been shown to be invalid, and it still desires to use the property, or any part of it, for the purposes to which it is now devoted, it may purchase such property by fair negotiation, or condemn it by a judicial proceeding, in which a just compensation shall be ascertained and paid according to the constitution.

If it be said that the proposition here established may subject the property, the officers of the United States, and the performance of their indispensable functions to hostile proceedings in the State courts, the answer is, that no case can arise in a State court where the interests, the property, the rights, or the authority of the federal government may come in question, which cannot be removed into a court of the United States under existing laws. In all cases, therefore, where such questions can arise, they are to be decided, at the option of the parties representing the United States, in courts which are the creation of the Federal government.

The slightest consideration of the nature, the character, the organization, and the powers of these courts will dispel any fear of serious injury to the government at their hands.

While by the Constitution the judicial department is recognized as one of the three great branches among which all the powers and functions of the government are distributed, it is inherently the weakest of them all.

Dependent as its courts are for the enforcement of their judgments upon officers appointed by the executive, and removable at his pleasure, with no patronage and no control of purse or sword, their power and influence rests solely upon the public sense of the necessity for the existence of a tribunal to which all may appeal for the assertion and protection of rights guaranteed by the Constitution and by the laws of the land, and on the confidence reposed in the soundness of their decisions and the purity of their motives.

From such a tribunal no well-founded fear can be entertained of injustice to the government or purpose to obstruct or diminish its just authority.

The Circuit Court was competent to decide the issues in this case before the parties that were before it. In the principles on which these issues were decided no error has been found, and its judgment is

Affirmed.

■ MR. JUSTICE GRAY, with whom concurred MR. CHIEF JUSTICE WAITE, MR. JUSTICE BRADLEY, and MR. JUSTICE WOODS, dissenting.

■ MR. JUSTICE GRAY. The Chief Justice, Mr. Justice Bradley, Mr. Justice Woods, and myself are unable to concur in the judgment of the majority of the court. The case so deeply affects the sovereignty of the United States, and its relations to the citizen, that it is fit to announce the grounds of our dissent.

The action is ejectment, originally brought by George W. P. C. Lee against Frederick Kaufman and Richard P. Strong in a court of the State of Virginia, to recover possession of a tract of land known as Arlington, of which the plaintiff alleged that he was seized in fee.

The whole tract, having been advertised for sale for non-payment of direct taxes lawfully assessed upon it, and having been selected for government use for war, military, charitable, and educational purposes by the President of the United States under the power conferred on him by the act of Congress of Feb. 6, 1863, c. 21, was accordingly, in 1864, bid off to the United States at the tax sale; and for many years has been, and now is, held and occupied by the United States, through Kaufman and Strong in charge thereof, under the certificate of sale of the tax commissioners, and for the purposes aforesaid, and also under orders of the Secretary of War, part of it for a military station, and the rest as a national cemetery for the burial of deceased soldiers and sailors. * * *

This is not an action of trespass to recover damages only, nor is it an action to recover property violently and suddenly wrested from the owner by officers of the government without its directions and without color of title in the government. But it is brought to recover possession of land which the United States have for years held, and still hold, for military and other public purposes, claiming title under a certificate of sale for direct taxes, which is declared by the act of Congress of June 7, 1862, c. 98, sect. 7, to be *prima facie* evidence of the regularity and validity of the sale and of the title of the purchaser, and which has been defined by this court as a "public act which is the equivalent of office found." *Bennett v. Hunter,* 9 Wall. 326, 336.

The principles upon which we are of opinion that the court below had no authority to try the question of the validity of the title of the United States in this action, and that this court has therefore no authority to pass upon that question, may be briefly stated.

The sovereign is not liable to be sued in any judicial tribunal without its consent. The sovereign cannot hold property except by agents. To maintain an action for the recovery of possession of property held by the sovereign through its agents, not claiming any title or right in themselves, but only as the representatives of the sovereign and in its behalf, is to maintain an action to recover possession of the property against the sovereign; and to invade such possession of the agents, by execution or other judicial process, is to invade the possession of the sovereign, and to violate the fundamental maxim that the sovereign cannot be sued.

That maxim is not limited to a monarchy, but is of equal force in a republic. In the one, as in the other, it is essential to the common defence and general welfare, that the sovereign should not, without its consent, be dispossessed by judicial process of forts, arsenals, military posts, and ships of war necessary to guard the national existence against insurrection and invasion; of custom houses and revenue cutters, employed in the collection of the revenue; or of light-houses and light-ships, established for the security of commerce with foreign nations and among the different parts of the country.

These principles appear to us to be axioms of public law, which would need no reference to authorities in their support, were it not for the exceeding importance and interest of the case, the great ability with which it has been argued, and the difference of opinion that has been manifested as to the extent and application of the precedents.

The exemption of the United States from being impleaded without their consent is, as has often been affirmed by this court, as absolute as that of the Crown of England or any other sovereign. In *Cohens v. Virginia,* 6 Wheat. 264, 411, Mr. Chief Justice Marshall said: "The universally-received opinion is, that no suit can be commenced or prosecuted against the United States." In *Beers v. Arkansas,* 20 How. 527, 529, Mr. Chief Justice Taney said: "It is an established principle of jurisprudence, in all civilized nations, that the sovereign cannot be sued in its own courts, or in any other, without its consent and permission; but it may, if it thinks proper, waive this privilege, and permit itself to be made a defendant in a suit by individuals, or by another state. And as this permission is altogether voluntary on the part of the sovereignty, it follows that it may prescribe the terms and conditions on which it consents to be sued, and the manner in which the suit shall be conducted, and may withdraw its consent whenever it may suppose that justice to the public requires it." In the same spirit, Mr. Justice Davis, delivering the judgment of the court in *Nichols v. United States,* 7 Wall. 122, 126, said: "Every government has an inherent right to protect itself against suits, and if, in the liberality of legislation they are permitted, it is only on such terms and conditions as are prescribed by statute. The principle is fundamental, applies to every sovereign power, and, but for the protection which it affords, the government would be unable to perform the various duties for which it was created."

The English authorities from the earliest to the latest times show that no action can be maintained to recover the title or possession of land held by the crown by its officers or servants, and leave no doubt that in a case like the one before us the proceedings would be stayed at the suggestion of the attorney general in behalf of the crown. * * *

If it is proper that the United States should allow themselves to be sued in such a case as this, public policy requires that it should rest with Congress to define the mode of proceeding, the conditions on which it may be maintained, and the manner in which the decision shall be enforced— none of which can be done if the citizen has an absolute right to maintain the action. * * *

* * * [W]e are of opinion that the court had no authority to proceed to trial and judgment; because the suit, which had been commenced against the individual defendants, was thenceforth prosecuted against the United States; because in ejectment, as in other actions at law, a court has no authority to render a judgment on which it has no power to issue execution; because * * * no judgment against the defendants can bind or estop the United States; because the possession of the defendants is in fact and in law the possession of the United States, and the defendants may at any moment be displaced and removed by the executive, and other custodians appointed and installed in their stead; because to issue an execution against them would be to issue an execution against the United States, and to turn the United States out of possession of land held by the United States, under claim of title and color of right for public purposes; and because to maintain a suit which has that object and that result is to violate the fundamental principle that the sovereign cannot be sued without its consent, and to encroach upon the powers intrusted by the constitution to the legislative and executive departments of the government. * * *

Notes and Questions

1. Upon reading the opinions in *United States v. Lee,* you will discover that the dispute concerns a parcel of land that is permeated with historical significance and is now preserved as hallowed ground—what is today known as the Arlington National Cemetery. Some additional background, beyond that provided in the opinion (but undoubtedly well-known to the members of the Court), may help put the case in fuller context:

In 1778, John Parke Custis—the adopted son of George Washington (who married John's mother, Martha Custis, a widow)—purchased a tract of land along the Potomac River in Virginia. Upon John's untimely death as a young man, his six-month-old son—George Washington Parke Custis— was adopted by the grandparents, George and Martha Washington. At the age of 21, young George assumed ownership of the land, which he named "Arlington," and built the family mansion upon it. In 1831, his daughter, Mary Anna, was married in the main hall of Arlington House to a young Army lieutenant named Robert E. Lee. Upon the death of George Washington Parke Custis in 1857, the estate was inherited by his daughter and became the Lee family home.

union Occupation

After General Lee accepted command of the Confederate Army of Northern Virginia upon the outbreak of the Civil War in 1861, the Lee family was forced to flee the Arlington estate. Federal troops occupied the estate and a Union general used the mansion as his headquarters. Unionists regarded the mansion looking down over the river at Washington, D.C. as a defiant symbol of the Confederate military leader whom they regarded as a traitor. In 1864, General Montgomery Meigs recommended that a portion of the property around the Arlington mansion be used as a military graveyard for Northern war dead, making the property uninhabitable should the Lee family ever return. Although it may be an apocryphal story, General Meigs—whose own son later was killed in the war and is buried at Arlington—is reported to have said that if Mrs. Lee returned to the house and looked out of her window, she would see the graves of the Union soldiers her husband had killed, buried in her rose garden.

'Failure of Custis-Lee to pay taxes'

The Arlington estate had been transferred to the United States through purchase at a tax sale after the Custis–Lee family allegedly failed to pay taxes on the property. In fact, Mrs. Lee was quite willing to pay the taxes due on the property (only about $100) and sent an agent with the necessary funds to the federal commissioners collecting the taxes. The federal commissioners refused to accept payment and insisted that the taxpayer must appear in person to pay the taxes. Not surprisingly the wife of General Lee was unwilling to travel behind Union lines to appear before the federal commissioners. However, when this legal question arose in a previous case, the Supreme Court interpreted the pertinent statute to permit payment of the taxes by an agent, which accounts for the government's loss on the merits regarding the validity of the transfer of the Arlington estate at the tax sale. When the eldest son of General and Mrs. Lee—George Washington Custis Lee—ultimately filed the lawsuit for ejectment that is before the Supreme Court in this case, the jury concluded that the tender of payment had been sufficient and thus the tax sale had been improper and failed to transfer title to the government. Following the Supreme Court's decision in *United States v. Lee,* the federal government legally purchased the property from George Washington Custis Lee for the sum of $150,000, and today it of course remains a national military cemetery and military installation.

For further discussion of the historical background (from which much of the above is drawn) and the significance of the decision in *United States v. Lee,* see generally Jonathan R. Siegel, *Suing the President: Nonstatutory Review Revisited,* 97 Colum. L. Rev. 1612, 1634–36 (1997); Enoch Aquila Chase, *The Arlington Case,* 15 Va. L. Rev. 207 (1929).

2. Turning to the legal holding of the case, is the sovereign United States affected by the outcome of the suit in *United States v. Lee*? Will the outcome really affect the individual defendants in any manner other than as agents of the government? If a judgment for the plaintiffs will directly affect the interests of the United States, and will have no substantial effect on the defendants in their individual capacities, then isn't the majority indulging in an indefensible fiction by stating that this case is not against

the government and thus does not implicate sovereign immunity? What does this reveal about the attitude of the majority toward the very concept of sovereign immunity? Indeed, how strong does the majority regard the case for sovereign immunity in a democratic republic? Why does the dissent disagree? Consider the significance of what Professor Vicki C. Jackson has noted, that "[i]n 1882, ... nearly a century after adoption of the Constitution, the Court was split five to four on the reasons for and scope of the doctrine of federal sovereign immunity." Vicki C. Jackson, *Suing the Federal Government: Sovereignty, Immunity, and Judicial Independence,* 35 Geo. Wash. Int'l. L. Rev. 521, 534 (2003).

3. Evaluate the breadth of the holding in *United States v. Lee.* Does it stand for the proposition that any suit that is formally framed against a government official rather than against the United States—no matter what relief is sought or the circumstances of the case or the impact on the government itself—falls outside of sovereign immunity? If you were to construe the holding more narrowly, what circumstances in the *Lee* case would you cite to argue that the precedent should be understood in a more limited manner in future cases? Is there a constitutional basis for overcoming sovereign immunity in this context? What is it? But does the *Lee* majority treat the constitutional guarantee as an exception to sovereign immunity or merely as one more reason not to regard the case as one directly against the government itself?   *Q. what relief is π seeking ?*

power to decide merits vs. power to hear it at all

Larson v. Domestic & Foreign Commerce Corporation   6-3

Supreme Court of the United States.
337 U.S. 682 (1949).

■ MR. CHIEF JUSTICE VINSON delivered the opinion of the Court.

This suit was brought in the United States District Court for the District of Columbia by the Domestic & Foreign Commerce Corporation against Robert M. Littlejohn, the then head of the War Assets Administration. The complaint alleged that the Administration had sold certain surplus coal to the plaintiff; that the Administrator refused to deliver the coal but, on the contrary, had entered into a new contract to sell it to others. The prayer was for an injunction prohibiting the Administrator from selling or delivering the coal to any one other than the plaintiff and for a declaration that the sale to the plaintiff was valid and the sale to the second purchaser invalid.

A temporary restraining order was issued *ex parte.* At the subsequent hearing on the issuance of a preliminary injunction, the defendant moved to dismiss the complaint on the ground, among others, that the court did not have jurisdiction because the suit was one against the United States. The motion was granted. The Court of Appeals reversed, holding that the jurisdictional capacity of the court depended on whether or not title to the coal had passed. Since this was also one of the questions on the merits, it remanded the case for trial. We granted certiorari.

The controversy on the merits concerns the interpretation to be given to the contract of sale. The War Assets Administration construed the contract as requiring the plaintiff to deposit funds to pay for the coal in advance and, when an unsatisfactory letter of credit was offered in place of a deposit, it considered that the contract was breached. The respondent, on the other hand, construed the contract as requiring payment only on delivery of the documents covering the coal shipment. In its view, it was not obliged to deposit any funds in advance of shipment and, therefore, had not breached the contract by failing to do so.

A second question, related to but different from the question of breach, was whether legal title to the coal had passed to the respondent when the contract was made. If the contract required the deposit of funds then, of course, title could not pass until the contract terms were complied with. If, on the other hand, the contract required payment only on the delivery of documents, a question remained as to whether title nevertheless passed at the time the contract was made.

Since these questions were not decided by the courts below we do not pass on them here. They are important only insofar as they illuminate the basis on which it was claimed that the district court had jurisdiction over the suit. It was not alleged that the contract for the sale of the coal was a contract with the officer personally. The basis of the action, on the contrary, was that a contract had been entered into with the United States. Nor was it claimed that the Administrator had any personal interest in this coal or, indeed, that he himself had taken any wrongful action. The complaint was directed against him because of his official function as chief of the War Assets Administration. It asked for an injunction against him in that capacity, and against "his agents, assistants, deputies and employees and all persons acting or assuming to act under their direction." The relief sought was, in short, relief against the Administration for wrongs allegedly committed by subordinate officials in that Administration. The question presented to the courts below was whether such an injunction was barred by the sovereign's immunity from suit.

Before answering that question it is perhaps advisable to state clearly what is and what is not involved. There is not involved any question of the immunization of Government officers against responsibility for their wrongful actions. If those actions are such as to create a personal liability, whether sounding in tort or in contract, the fact that the officer is an instrumentality of the sovereign does not, of course, forbid a court from taking jurisdiction over a suit against him. As was said in *Brady v. Roosevelt S.S. Co.*, 317 U.S. 575, 580 (1943), the principle that an agent is liable for his own torts "is an ancient one and applies even to certain acts of public officers or public instrumentalities." But the existence of a right to sue the officer is not the issue in this case. The issue here is whether this particular suit is not also, in effect, a suit against the sovereign. If it is, it must fail, whether or not the officer might otherwise be suable.

If the denomination of the party defendant by the plaintiff were the sole test of whether a suit was against the officer individually or against his principal, the sovereign, our task would be easy. Our decision then would be that the United States is not being sued here because it is not named as a party. This would be simple and would not leave room for controversy. But controversy there has been, in this field above all others, because it has long been established that the crucial question is whether the relief sought in a suit nominally addressed to the officer is relief against the sovereign. In a suit against the officer to recover damages for the agent's personal actions that question is easily answered. The judgment sought will not require action by the sovereign or disturb the sovereign's property. There is, therefore, no jurisdictional difficulty.[7] The question becomes difficult and the area of controversy is entered when the suit is not one for damages but for specific relief: *i.e.,* the recovery of specific property or monies, ejectment from land, or injunction either directing or restraining the defendant officer's actions. In each such case the question is directly posed as to whether, by obtaining relief against the officer, relief will not, in effect, be obtained against the sovereign. For the sovereign can act only through agents and, when the agents' actions are restrained, the sovereign itself may, through him, be restrained. As indicated, this question does not arise because of any distinction between law and equity. It arises whenever suit is brought against an officer of the sovereign in which the relief sought from him is not compensation for an alleged wrong but, rather, the prevention or discontinuance, *in rem,* of the wrong. In each such case the compulsion, which the court is asked to impose, may be compulsion against the sovereign, although nominally directed against the individual officer. If it is, then the suit is barred, not because it is a suit against an officer of the Government, but because it is, in substance, a suit against the Government over which the court, in the absence of consent, has no jurisdiction.

The relief sought in this case was not the payment of damages by the individual defendant. To the contrary, it was asked that the court order the War Assets Administrator, his agents, assistants, deputies and employees and all persons acting under their direction, not to sell the coal involved and not to deliver it to anyone other than the respondent. The district court held that this was relief against the sovereign and therefore dismissed the suit. We agree.

There may be, of course, suits for specific relief against officers of the sovereign which are not suits against the sovereign. If the officer purports to act as an individual and not as an official, a suit directed against that action is not a suit against the sovereign. If the War Assets Administrator had completed a sale of his personal home, he presumably could be enjoined from later conveying it to a third person. On a similar theory, where the

---

7. There are, of course, limitations on the right to recover damages from public officers. These limitations are matters of substantive law, applicable in suits indubitably addressed to the officer, not the sovereign. They are not necessarily coincidental with the limitations on the court's jurisdiction to hear a suit directed against the sovereign. * * *

officer's powers are limited by statute, his actions beyond those limitations are considered individual and not sovereign actions. The officer is not doing the business which the sovereign has empowered him to do or he is doing it in a way which the sovereign has forbidden. His actions are *ultra vires* his authority and therefore may be made the object of specific relief. It is important to note that in such cases the relief can be granted, without impleading the sovereign, only because of the officer's lack of delegated power. A claim of error in the exercise of that power is therefore not sufficient. And, since the jurisdiction of the court to hear the case may depend * * * upon the decision which it ultimately reaches on the merits, it is necessary that the plaintiff set out in his complaint the statutory limitation on which he relies.

Pleading Requirement

e.g. #2

A second type of case is that in which the statute or order conferring power upon the officer to take action in the sovereign's name is claimed to be unconstitutional. Actions for *habeas corpus* against a warden and injunctions against the threatened enforcement of unconstitutional statutes are familiar examples of this type. Here, too, the conduct against which specific relief is sought is beyond the officer's powers and is, therefore, not the conduct of the sovereign. The only difference is that in this case the power has been conferred in form but the grant is lacking in substance because of its constitutional invalidity.

These two types have frequently been recognized by this court as the only ones in which a restraint may be obtained against the conduct of government officials. The rule was stated by Mr. Justice Hughes in *Philadelphia Co. v. Stimson*, 223 U.S. 605, 620 (1912), where he said: "... in case of an injury threatened by his illegal action, the officer cannot claim immunity from injunction process. The principle has frequently been applied with respect to state officers seeking to enforce unconstitutional enactments. [citing cases.] And it is equally applicable to a federal officer acting in excess of his authority or under an authority not validly conferred."[11]

Ct: Π doesn't contend that his case is #1 or #2

It is not contended by the respondent that the present case falls within either of these categories. There was no claim made that the Administrator and his agents, etc., were acting unconstitutionally or pursuant to an unconstitutional grant of power. Nor was there any allegation of a limitation on the Administrator's delegated power to refuse shipment in cases in which he believed the United States was not obliged to deliver. There was, it is true, an allegation that the Administrator was acting "illegally," and that the refusal to deliver was "unauthorized." But these allegations were not based and did not purport to be based upon any lack of delegated power. Nor could they be, since the Administrator was empowered by the sovereign to administer a general sales program encompassing the negotia-

need to allege 'Lack of power'

---

11. Of course, a suit may fail, as one against the sovereign, even if it is claimed that the officer being sued has acted unconstitutionally or beyond his statutory powers, if the relief requested cannot be granted by merely ordering the cessation of the conduct complained of but will require affirmative action by the sovereign or the disposition of unquestionably sovereign property.

tion of contracts, the shipment of goods and the receipt of payment. A normal concomitant of such powers, as a matter of general agency law, is the power to refuse delivery when, in the agent's view, delivery is not called for under a contract and the power to sell goods which the agent believes are still his principal's to sell.

'Agency' notions...

The respondent's contention, which the Court of Appeals sustained, was that there exists a third category of cases in which the action of a Government official may be restrained or directed. If, says the respondent, an officer of the Government wrongly takes or holds specific property to which the plaintiff has title then his taking or holding is a tort, and "illegal" as a matter of general law, whether or not it be within his delegated powers. He may therefore be sued individually to prevent the "illegal" taking or to recover the property "illegally" held. * * *

D & F's contention (misuse of U.S. v. Lee)

We believe the theory to be erroneous. It confuses the doctrine of sovereign immunity with the requirement that a plaintiff state a cause of action. It is a prerequisite to the maintenance of any action for specific relief that the plaintiff claim an invasion of his legal rights, either past or threatened. He must, therefore, allege conduct which is "illegal" in the sense that the respondent suggests. If he does not, he has not stated a cause of action. This is true whether the conduct complained of is sovereign or individual. In a suit against an agency of the sovereign, as in any other suit, it is therefore necessary that the plaintiff claim an invasion of his recognized legal rights. If he does not do so, the suit must fail even if he alleges that the agent acted beyond statutory authority or unconstitutionally. But, in a suit against an agency of the sovereign, it is not sufficient that he make such a claim. Since the sovereign may not be sued, it must also appear that the action to be restrained or directed is not action of the sovereign. The mere allegation that the officer, acting officially, wrongfully holds property to which the plaintiff has title does not meet that requirement. True, it establishes a wrong to the plaintiff. But it does not establish that the officer, in committing that wrong, is not exercising the powers delegated to him by the sovereign. If he is exercising such powers the action is the sovereign's and a suit to enjoin it may not be brought unless the sovereign has consented. * * *

The complaint must describe the cause of the wrong so the court can ascertain whether it's a suit against the officer (personally) or the sovereign directly, or against sovereign via the officers.

* * * We hold that if the actions of an officer do not conflict with the terms of his valid statutory authority, then they are the actions of the sovereign, whether or not they are tortious under general law, if they would be regarded as the actions of a private principal under the normal rules of agency. A Government officer is not thereby necessarily immunized from liability, if his action is such that a liability would be imposed by the general law of torts. But the action itself cannot be enjoined or directed, since it is also the action of the sovereign.

personal liability

United States v. Lee, 106 U.S. 196 (1882), is said to have established the rule for which the respondent contends. It did not. It represents, rather, a specific application of the constitutional exception to the doctrine of sovereign immunity. The suit there was against federal officers to recover land held by them, within the scope of their authority, as a United

Limits Lee's rul & reach

States military station and cemetery. The question at issue was the validity of a tax sale under which the United States, at least in the view of the officers, had obtained title to the property. The plaintiff alleged that the sale was invalid and that title to the land was in him. The Court held that if he was right the defendants' possession of the land was illegal and a suit against them was not a suit against the sovereign. *Prima facie,* this holding would appear to support the contention of the plaintiff. Examination of the *Lee* case, however, indicates that the basis of the decision was the assumed lack of the defendants' constitutional authority to hold the land against the plaintiff. The Court said (106 U.S. at 219):

> "It is not pretended, as the case now stands, that the President had any lawful authority to (take the land), or that the legislative body could give him any such authority except upon payment of just compensation. The defense stands here solely upon the absolute immunity from judicial inquiry of every one who *asserts* authority from the executive branch of the government, however clear it may be made that the executive possessed no such power. Not only that no such power is given, but that it is absolutely prohibited, both to the executive and the legislative, to deprive any one of life, liberty, or property without due process of law, or to take private property without just compensation.
>
> . . .
>
> "Shall it be said ... that the courts cannot give a remedy when the citizen has been deprived of his property by force, his estate seized and converted to the use of the government without any lawful authority, without any process of law, and without any compensation, because the President has ordered it and his officers are in possession?"

The Court thus assumed that if title had been in the plaintiff the taking of the property by the defendants would be a taking without just compensation and, therefore, an unconstitutional action.[17] On that assumption, and only on that assumption, the defendants' possession of the property was an unconstitutional use of their power and was, therefore, not validly authorized by the sovereign. For that reason, a suit for specific relief, to obtain the property, was not a suit against the sovereign and could be maintained against the defendants as individuals.

The *Lee* case, therefore, offers no support to the contention that a claim of title to property held by an officer of the sovereign is, of itself, sufficient to demonstrate that the officer holding the property is not validly empowered by the sovereign to do so. Only where there is a claim that the holding constitutes an unconstitutional taking of property without just compensation does the *Lee* case require that conclusion.[18] * * *

---

17. The *Lee* case was decided in 1882. At that time there clearly was no remedy available by which he could have obtained compensation for the taking of his land. Whether compensation could be obtained to-day in such a case is, of course, not the issue here.

18. For this reason the availability of a remedy in the Court of Claims may, in some cases, be relevant to the question of sovereign

* * * [We adhere to the following rule]: the action of an officer of the sovereign (be it holding, taking or otherwise legally affecting the plaintiff's property) can be regarded as so "illegal" as to permit a suit for a specific relief against the officer as an individual only if it is not within the officer's statutory powers or, if within those powers, only if the powers, or their exercise in the particular case, are constitutionally void.

Rule

rationales :
outside what the sovereign authorized -- so the suit is challenging the sovereign's grant, nor can officers

The sovereign cannot do what is unconstitutional,

The application of this principle to the present case is clear. The very basis of the respondent's action is that the Administrator was an officer of the Government, validly appointed to administer its sales program and therefore authorized to enter, through his subordinates, into a binding contract concerning the sale of the Government's coal. There is no allegation of any statutory limitation on his powers as a sales agent. In the absence of such a limitation he, like any other sales agent, had the power and the duty to construe such contracts and to refuse delivery in cases in which he believed that the contract terms had not been complied with. His action in so doing in this case was, therefore, within his authority even if, for purposes of decision here, we assume that his construction was wrong and that title to the coal had, in fact, passed to the respondent under the contract. There is no claim that his [action] constituted an unconstitutional taking.[27] It was, therefore, inescapably the action of the United States and the effort to enjoin it must fail as an effort to enjoin the United States.

Application

TTs didn't allege their case fell into #1 or #2

It is argued that the principle of sovereign immunity is an archaic hangover not consonant with modern morality and that it should therefore be limited wherever possible. There may be substance in such a viewpoint as applied to suits for damages. The Congress has increasingly permitted such suits to be maintained against the sovereign and we should give hospitable scope to that trend. But the reasoning is not applicable to suits for specific relief. For, it is one thing to provide a method by which a citizen may be compensated for a wrong done to him by the Government. It is a far different matter to permit a court to exercise its compulsive powers to restrain the Government from acting, or to compel it to act. There are the strongest reasons of public policy for the rule that such relief cannot be had against the sovereign. The Government as representative of the community as a whole, cannot be stopped in its tracks by any plaintiff who presents a disputed question of property or contract right. As was early recognized, "The interference of the Courts with the performance of the ordinary

Damages vs. Specific Relief

immunity. Where the action against which specific relief is sought is a taking, or holding, of the plaintiffs' property, the availability of a suit for compensation against the sovereign will defeat a contention that the action is unconstitutional as a violation of the Fifth Amendment.

27. There could not be since the respondent admittedly has a remedy, in a suit for breach of contract, in the Court of Claims. Such a suit, indeed, would be based on the theory that the action of the Administrator in refusing to deliver was the action of the United States and thus created a cause of action against it for breach of contract. Only if the Administrator's action was within his authority could such a suit be maintained. It has never been suggested that a suit in the Court of Claims for breach of an express contract could be defeated because the action of the officer in breaching it constituted a tort and was therefore "unauthorized."

duties of the executive departments of the government, would be productive of nothing but mischief. . . .''

There are limits, of course. Under our constitutional system, certain rights are protected against governmental action and, if such rights are infringed by the actions of officers of the Government, it is proper that the courts have the power to grant relief against those actions. But in the absence of a claim of constitutional limitation, the necessity of permitting the Government to carry out its functions unhampered by direct judicial intervention outweighs the possible disadvantage to the citizen in being relegated to the recovery of money damages after the event.

It is argued that a sales agency such as the War Assets Administration, is not the type of agency which requires the protection from direct judicial interference which the doctrine of sovereign immunity confers. We do not doubt that there may be some activities of the Government which do not require such protection. There are others in which the necessity of immunity is apparent. But it is not for this Court to examine the necessity in each case. That is a function of the Congress. The Congress has, in many cases, entrusted the business of the Government to agencies which may contract in their own names and which are subject to suit in their own names. In other cases it has permitted suits for damages, but, significantly, not for specific relief, in the Court of Claims. The differentiations as to remedy which the Congress has erected would be rendered nugatory if the basis on which they rest—the assumed immunity of the sovereign from suit in the absence of consent—were undermined by an unwarranted extension of the *Lee* doctrine.

The cause is reversed with directions that the complaint be dismissed.

It is so ordered.

■ MR. JUSTICE DOUGLAS.

I think that the principles announced by the Court are the ones which should govern the selling of government property. Less strict applications of those principles would cause intolerable interference with public administration. To make the right to sue the officer turn on whether by the law of sales title had passed to the buyer would clog this governmental function with intolerable burdens. So I have joined the Court's opinion.

■ MR. JUSTICE RUTLEDGE concurs in the result.

■ MR. JUSTICE JACKSON dissents.

■ MR. JUSTICE FRANKFURTER, with whom MR. JUSTICE BURTON concurs, dissenting.

Case-by-case adjudication gives to the judicial process the impact of actuality and thereby saves it from the hazards of generalizations insufficiently nourished by experience. There is, however, an attendant weakness to a system that purports to pass merely on what are deemed to be the particular circumstances of a case. Consciously or unconsciously the pronouncements in an opinion too often exceed the justification of the circumstances on which they are based, or, contrariwise, judicial preoccupation with the claims of the immediate leads to a succession of *ad hoc* determinations making for eventual confusion and conflict. There comes a time when the general considerations underlying each specific situation must be exposed in order to bring the too unruly instances into more fruitful harmony. The case before us presents one of those problems for the rational solution of which it becomes necessary, as a matter of judicial self-respect, to take soundings in order to know where we are and whither we are going. * * *

The course of decisions concerning sovereign immunity is a good illustration of the conflicting considerations that often struggle for mastery in the judicial process, at least implicitly. In varying degrees, at different times, the momentum of the historic doctrine is arrested or deflected by an unexpressed feeling that governmental immunity runs counter to prevailing notions of reason and justice. Legal concepts are then found available to give effect to this feeling, and one of its results is the multitude of decisions in which this Court has refused to permit an agent of the government to claim that he is *pro tanto* the government and therefore sheltered by its immunity. Multitudinous as are these cases and the seeming inconsistencies among them, analysis reveals certain common considerations. The cases in which claim was made that a suit against one who holds public office is in fact a suit against the government fall into well defined categories. Though our opinions have not always been consciously directed toward this classification, it is supported not only by what was actually decided but also by much that is expressly said.

Our decisions fall under these heads:

(1) Cases in which the plaintiff seeks an interest in property which concededly, even under the allegation of the complaint, belongs to the government, or calls for an assertion of what is unquestionably official authority.

(2) Cases in which action to the legal detriment of a plaintiff is taken by an official justifying his action under an unconstitutional statute.

(3) Cases in which a plaintiff suffers a legal detriment through action of an officer who has exceeded his statutory authority.

(4) Cases in which an officer seeks shelter behind statutory authority or some other sovereign command for the commission of a common-law tort. * * *

* * * The fourth category of cases brings us to the controversy immediately before the Court and demands detailed analysis. These are the cases, it will be recalled, in which an official seeks to screen himself behind the sovereign in a suit against him based on the commission of a common-law tort. A plaintiff's right "under general law to recover possession of specific property wrongfully withheld" may be enforced against an official and he cannot plead the sovereign's immunity against the court's power to afford a remedy.

The starting point of this line of cases is, *United States v. Lee,* 106 U.S. 196. Familiar as that case is, its controlling facts bear rehearsal. The

Arlington estate of General Robert E. Lee was seized for nonpayment of taxes. These taxes had in fact been tendered by a friend, but the official had interpreted his authority as permitting payment of the taxes only by the record owner. After seizure, the United States established a fort and cemetery on the land. The plaintiff, in whom title to the Arlington estate vested if its seizure could not be justified, brought an action of ejectment against the governmental custodians of the estate. After the overruling of a suggestion by the Attorney General of the United States that the Circuit Court was without jurisdiction because the property was in possession of the United States, the action was sustained against the defendants since they could not justify their possession by proof of a valid title in the Government. This Court affirmed, holding that the lower court was competent to decide the issues between the parties without the need of impleading the Government whose consent was withheld.

While there was some talk in the *Lee* opinion, as well as in some of the cases which followed that decision, about taking property without compensation, the basis of the action was that the defendants were ordinary tortfeasors, not immunized for their wrongful invasion of the plaintiff's property by the fact that they claimed to have acted on behalf of the Government. This group of cases is quite different from those in which the plaintiff claimed that the defendant, purporting to act in an official capacity, exceeded the authority which a statute conferred upon him, or that the statute under which he justified his action exceeded the power of the legislature to confer such authority. In this class of cases the governmental agent had valid statutory authority but he determined erroneously the condition which had to exist before he could exercise it. The basis of action in this class of cases is the defendant's personal responsibility for the commission of a tort, which makes it irrelevant that by waiving the case against the governmental agent the plaintiff might choose to sue the Government as for a contract. * * *

"Sovereign immunity" carries an august sound. But very recently we recognized that the doctrine is in "disfavor." *Federal Housing Administration v. Burr,* 309 U.S. 242, 245. It ought not to be extended by discrediting a long line of decisions. No considerations of policy warrant the overruling of *United States v. Lee, supra,* and the cases which have applied it in giving a remedy for wrongdoing without harm to any public interest that deserves protection. To overrule the *Lee* case would at least have the merit of candor. To attempt to explain it on the ground that the Government itself was not suable for the wrongdoing at the time of the *Lee* decision is to invent a new theory to explain away a decision which has held its ground for nearly seventy years.

This liability for torts committed by defendants even though they conceive themselves to be acting as officials and for the public good, rests ultimately on the conviction that the policy behind the immunity of the sovereign from suit without its consent does not call for disregard of a citizen's right to pursue an agent of the government for a wrongful invasion of a recognized legal right unless the legislature deems it appropriate to displace the right of suing the individual defendant with the right to sue the Government. The fact that the governmental agent cannot claim the immunity of the sovereign of course does not spell liability, under all circumstances, for the discharge of what he conceived to be his duty. Similarly, equitable considerations bearing on the propriety of granting the extraordinary remedy of an injunction may here come into play as is true whenever a private claim cuts across the public interest. But these are matters wholly beside the issue of sovereign immunity.

Of course where the United States is the owner in possession of property a court cannot interfere without the Government's consent. But if it is to be denied that a court cannot decide the question, when properly presented, whether property held by an official belongs to the plaintiff, [a long line of cases following *Lee*] must be overruled. * * *

As is true of the present case, the right of control over property may depend on compliance with the terms of a contract. The fact of compliance may rest, certainly in the first instance, in the judgment of a particular official. But that would not authorize him to rescind a valid contract if there had been full compliance. Of course, even that power may be conferred by agreement or by statute. But in the absence of such an agreement, or such a provision in a statute, a plaintiff may have redress against a defendant who has wrongfully rescinded a valid contract fully performed if a property right of the plaintiff is thereby tortiously affected. He may also have his day in court if he denies the right of an official to determine definitively want of compliance, when the issue of compliance is decisive of the defendant's alleged wrongdoing. And these are precisely the issues tendered by this complaint. It is no answer at this stage of the case, to say that it was in fact within the agent's authority to do what he did. If a valid statute gives him power to withhold property which belongs to another, or if he has the power to revest title in the Government after a valid contract has vested it in another then of course he is free from liability. But these are matters that go to the merits. The very purpose of this suit is to determine whether what the governmental agent did here was within his power. To decide whether the "authority is rightfully assumed is the exercise of jurisdiction, and must lead to the decision of the merits of the question." *United States v. Lee,* 106 U.S. 196, 219. The issues outlined above are issues which may be contested against a defendant, even though he hold office.

The District Court therefore had jurisdiction over the controversy because only after a consideration of the merits of the respondent's claim could it be determined whether the decree would affect Government property. Since that court has jurisdiction it can also determine whether a cause of action was stated and whether there are any considerations which would cause a court of equity not to grant the relief requested.

I would affirm the judgment of the Court of Appeals.

———

[Handwritten margin notes:]

Even if we rolled sovereign immunity back somewhat, other factors would limit the liability of the officers...

If the Court is to have power to decide whether Govt as owner in possession is sueable, we need to overrule [CASE].

(court has implied j.d. to hear them)

... had jd because it needed to determine whether was Larson did was grounds to ~~stop~~ seek specific relief against him.

TJ drafts complaint pursuant to Lee, but Ct. says Larson controls

Malone v. Bowdoin

5-2 - 2 didn't take part

(US Dept 4.)

Supreme Court of the United States.

369 U.S. 643 (1962).

■ MR. JUSTICE STEWART delivered the opinion of the Court.

This litigation began in a Georgia court when the respondents filed a common law action of ejectment against the petitioner, a Forest Service Officer of the United States Department of Agriculture. The basis for the suit was the respondents' claim that they were the rightful owners of certain land occupied by the petitioner. The action was removed to a Federal District Court under the provisions of 28 U.S.C. § 1442(a). The removal petition stated that the action "involves lands that were acquired by the United States of America by deed on June 6, 1936," that the petitioner's "official duties as a Forest Service Officer required him to be, and he was, in charge and in possession of the land described in said ejectment suit," and that "all his acts in connection with the matters charged in said complaint were committed by him under color of his said office."

Malone's motion pretrial: The petitioner filed a motion to dismiss upon the ground that the suit was in substance and effect one against the United States, which had not consented to be sued or waived its immunity from suit. Noting that the respondents had conceded in a pretrial conference that the petitioner in occupying the land was acting solely as an official or employee of the United States, the District Court granted the motion to dismiss, relying upon *Larson v. Domestic & Foreign Corp.,* 337 U.S. 682. On appeal, the judgment was reversed, one judge dissenting, 5 Cir., 284 F.2d 95. We granted certiorari to consider the scope of sovereign immunity in suits of this kind. We agree with the District Court that the doctrine of the *Larson* case required dismissal of this action, and we therefore reverse the judgment of the Court of Appeals.

Ct. of Appeals based its decision on U.S. v. Lee

For its view that the sovereign immunity of the United States did not bar the maintenance of this suit, the Court of Appeals found principal support in *United States v. Lee,* 106 U.S. 196. In that case the Virginia estate of General Robert E. Lee had been acquired by the United States for nonpayment of taxes, although the taxes had in fact been tendered by a third party. An ejectment action was brought against the governmental custodians of the land, upon which a federal military installation and a cemetery had been established. The trial court found that the tax sale had been invalid, and that title to the land was in the plaintiff. This Court upheld a judgment in favor of the plaintiff upon the trial court's finding that the defendants' possession of the land was illegal, holding that a suit against them under such circumstances was not a suit against the sovereign.

Lee: suit against gov't agent alleging the illegality of his act ≠ suit against the sovereign

In a number of later cases, arising over the years in a variety of factual situations, the principles of the *Lee* case were approved. But in several other cases which came to the Court during the same period, it was held that suits against government agents, specifically affecting property in

Specific Relief vs. Damages

which the United States claimed an interest, were barred by the doctrine of sovereign immunity. While it is possible to differentiate many of these cases upon their individualized facts, it is fair to say that to reconcile completely all the decisions of the Court in this field prior to 1949 would be a Procrustean task.

Many cases followed Lee's principle... we could distinguish them... we aren't going to try to make sense of them...

The Court's 1949 *Larson* decision makes it unnecessary, however, to undertake that task here. For in *Larson* the Court, aware that it was called upon to "resolve the conflict in doctrine" (337 U.S., at 701), thoroughly reviewed the many prior decisions, and made an informed and carefully considered choice between the seemingly conflicting precedents.

... b/c Larson controls

In that case a suit had been brought against the War Assets Administrator to enjoin him from selling surplus coal which, it was alleged, the Administrator had already sold to the plaintiff. The theory of the action was that where "an officer of the Government wrongly takes or holds specific property to which the plaintiff has title then his taking or holding is a tort, and 'illegal' as a matter of general law, whether or not it be within his delegated powers," and that the officer 'may therefore be sued individually to prevent the "illegal" taking or to recover the property " 'illegally' held." 337 U.S., at 692. The Court held that this theory was not adequate to support a conclusion that the relief asked was not relief against the sovereign.

Larson ΠΤ's theory

Cutting through the tangle of previous decisions, the Court expressly postulated the rule that the action of a federal officer affecting property claimed by a plaintiff can be made the basis of a suit for specific relief against the officer as an individual only if the officer's action is "not within the officer's statutory powers or, if within those powers, only if the powers, or their exercise in the particular case, are constitutionally void." 337 U.S., at 702. Since the plaintiff had not made an affirmative allegation of any relevant statutory limitation upon the Administrator's powers, and had made no claim that the Administrator's action amounted to an unconstitutional taking, the Court ruled that the suit must fail as an effort to enjoin the United States.

'Larson distinguished Lee'

ΠΤ's complaint was deficient

Not Fully
While not expressly overruling *United States v. Lee, supra,* the Court in *Larson* limited that decision in such a way as to make it inapplicable to the case before us. Pointing out that at the time of the *Lee* decision there was no remedy by which the plaintiff could have recovered compensation for the taking of his land,[8] the Court interpreted *Lee* as simply "a specific application of the constitutional exception to the doctrine of sovereign immunity." 337 U.S., at 696. So construed, the *Lee* case has continuing validity only "where there is a claim that the holding constitutes an unconstitutional taking of property without just compensation." *Id.,* at 697.

Larson limited Lee's reach.
· Must allege unconstitutional act
· holding of property

---

8. See 337 U.S., at 697, n. 17. Unlike the situation in the *Lee* case, there has been at all relevant times a tribunal where the respondents could seek just compensation for the taking of their land by the United States. That tribunal is the Court of Claims. *United States v. Causby,* 328 U.S. 256, 267.

No such claim has been advanced in the present case. Nor has it been asserted that the petitioner was exceeding his delegated powers as an officer of the United States in occupying the land in question,[9] or that he was in possession of the land in anything other than his official capacity. This suit, therefore, is not within the class of cases in which, under *Larson,* specific relief can be obtained against a government officer. Accordingly, it was rightly dismissed by the District Court as an action which in substance and effect was one against the United States without its consent.

Reversed.

■ MR. JUSTICE FRANKFURTER took no part in the decision of this case.

■ MR. JUSTICE WHITE took no part in the consideration or decision of this case.

■ MR. JUSTICE DOUGLAS, dissenting.

United States v. Lee, 106 U.S. 196, serves a useful function and should be followed here. There, as here, the contest was over real estate which an officer of the Federal Government held against the claim of the plaintiff. Here, as there, if the federal agent's possession of the land is illegal the suit is not against the sovereign. * * *

Ejectment * * * is the classic form of action to try title. It takes place in the locality where the land is located. No judges are better qualified to try it than the local judges. It is a convenient and ready form of remedy for possession of land. Moreover, the United States, not being a party, is not bound by the state court decree. If it is aggrieved by the state or federal court ruling on title, it can bring its arsenal of power into play. Eminent domain—with the power immediately to take possession—is available.

If, however, the citizen must bow to the doctrine of sovereign immunity, he is precluded from any relief except a suit for damages under 28 U.S.C. § 1346(b) or 28 U.S.C. § 1346(a)(2), or 28 U.S.C. § 1491. This places the advantage with an all-powerful Government, not with the citizen. He may, as the Court says go into court and get the value of his property. But he does not get his property, even though we assume, as we must, that the Government is not the rightful claimant. * * *

What Mr. Justice Miller said in *United States v. Lee, supra,* 106 U.S. 220, 221, needs repeating:

> "No man in this country is so high that he is above the law. No officer of the law may set that law at defiance with impunity. All the officers of the government, from the highest to the lowest, are creatures of the law and are bound to obey it.
>
> . . .
>
> "It cannot be, then, that when in a suit between two citizens for the ownership of real estate, one of them has established his right to the

---

9. If such a claim is to be made, "it is necessary that the plaintiff set out in his complaint the statutory limitation on which he relies." *Larson v. Domestic & Foreign Corp.,* 337 U.S. 682, 690. * * *

Lee :

The π must allege the statutory limit of the officer's powers

possession of the property according to all the forms of judicial procedure, and by the verdict of a jury and the judgment of the court, the wrongful possessor can say successfully to the court, Stop, here; I hold by order of the President, and the progress of justice must be stayed. That, though the nature of the controversy is one peculiarly appropriate to the judicial function, though the United States is no party to the suit, though one of the three great branches of the government to which by the Constitution this duty has been assigned has declared its judgment after a fair trial, the unsuccessful party can interpose an absolute veto upon that judgment by the production of an order of the Secretary of War, which that officer had no more authority to make than the humblest private citizen.''

Sovereign immunity has become more and more out of date, as the powers of the Government and its vast bureaucracy have increased. To give the agent immunity from suit is, to use the words of Mr. Justice Holmes:

"a very dangerous departure from one of the first principles of our system of law. The sovereign properly so called is superior to suit for reasons that often have been explained. But the general rule is that any person within the jurisdiction always is amenable to the law. If he is sued for conduct harmful to the plaintiff his only shield is a constitutional rule of law that exonerates him. Supposing the powers of the Fleet Corporation to have been given to a single man we doubt if anyone would contend that the acts of Congress and the delegations of authority from the President left him any less liable than other grantees of the power of eminent domain to be called upon to defend himself in court. An instrumentality of Government he might be and for the greatest ends, but the agent, because he is agent, does not cease to be answerable for his acts.'' *Sloan Shipyards v. United States Fleet Corp.,* 258 U.S. 549, 566–567.

← Immunity shields him from being answerable

The balance between the convenience of the citizen and the management of public affairs is a recurring consideration in suits determining when and where a citizen can sue a governmental official. The balance is, in my view, on the side of the citizen where he claims realty in the Government's possession and where there are ready means of adjudicating the title. If legal title is actually in the claimant, if the action of the official in taking possession under authority of the United States is *ultra vires,* what objectionable interference with governmental functions can be said to exist?

Balance of citizen vs. gov't admin.

· The place of property

I am authorized to say that MR. JUSTICE HARLAN agrees with this opinion.

––––––

Notes and Questions

1. In *Larson v. Domestic & Foreign Commerce Corp.* and *Malone v. Bowdoin,* what happened to the apparent fiction established in *United*

States v. Lee of treating a lawsuit against a government officer in his official capacity as though it were not against the government itself? Now when may a government officer be sued without implicating sovereign immunity? Doesn't *Malone* arise on nearly identical facts as *Lee*? How are the two decisions distinguished? What remains of *United States v. Lee* as a precedent? Did the *Larson* and *Malone* Courts faithfully interpret *Lee*? Would the *Lee* majority have agreed with the analysis in *Larson* and *Malone*? Or do these decisions reflect a shift in attitudes among the members of the Supreme Court on the legitimacy of sovereign immunity as a concept in a democratic republic?

2. In *Larson* and *Malone,* the Supreme Court held that an action could be maintained against a government officer when, although he acts pursuant to a statutory delegation of authority, his actions violate constitutional limitations. The *Larson* Court offers two alternative ways of understanding the principle behind this power to bring a suit against a government officer who has acted in an unconstitutional manner. First, the Court states that a suit is permitted against a federal officer under this circumstance because "the powers [of the officer], or their exercise in the particular case are constitutionally void." This suggests that the "unconstitutional conduct" rule is a species of the *ultra vires* concept. Under this concept, a government officer whose authority is not validly conferred because of a constitutional limitation is not truly acting as an agent of the government, because the government may not authorize an agent to violate the Constitution. Second, the Court describes the rule permitting suit against a government officer acting in violation of the Constitution as "the constitutional exception to the doctrine of sovereign immunity." This statement appears to acknowledge that the action of the government agent is indeed attributable to the government, but that the doctrine of sovereign immunity is not available to the government when it behaves unconstitutionally through its agents. In other words, the first understanding preserves sovereign immunity inviolate, but only through the fiction that a government officer acting unconstitutionally loses his status as an agent of the sovereign and acts *ultra vires.* The second understanding does treat the actions of the agent as those of the government principal, but pierces through sovereign immunity itself to hold the government liable for unconstitutional actions. Which do you believe is the better understanding? Does it make any substantive or practical difference (to the plaintiff, the defendant officer, or the government)?

For post-*Larson* and *Malone* scholarship on the question of when a suit is against a federal officer or really against the federal government, and on the more general issue of sovereign immunity, see generally Antonin Scalia, *Sovereign Immunity and Nonstatutory Review of Federal Administrative Action: Some Conclusions from the Public–Lands Cases,* 68 Mich. L. Rev. 867 (1970); Kenneth Culp Davis, *Suing the Government by Falsely Pretending to Sue an Officer,* 29 U. Chi. L. Rev. 435 (1962).

3. In *Larson,* the plaintiff sought something analogous to specific performance in contract against the government. In *Malone,* the plaintiff

sought to eject the government officer from land to which he claimed title. In both cases, the plaintiffs sought specific or affirmative relief from the government. Although the Court held that the actions were barred by sovereign immunity, Congress may of course waive that immunity and consent to suit. As we shall see in a later chapter, Congress has generally waived the sovereign immunity of the government to authorize suits against government officers for specific relief under the Administrative Procedure Act, 5 U.S.C. § 701–06 (see Chapter IV.B). However, specific relief is not available under all circumstances. In contract cases, such as *Larson,* specific performance traditionally may not be sought from the federal government; instead, an aggrieved party must maintain an action for damages for breach of contract (see Chapter IV.A.1.c, IV.A.4, and IV.C). *See generally* Richard H. Seamon, *Separation of Powers and the Separate Treatment of Contract Claims Against the Federal Government for Specific Performance,* 43 Vill. L. Rev. 155 (1998); Harold J. Krent, *Reconceptualizing Sovereign Immunity,* 45 Vanderbilt L. Rev. 1529, 1566 (1992). Similarly, in cases alleging a taking of property without just compensation in violation of the Fifth Amendment, a plaintiff is generally relegated to an action for recovery of the compensation (see Chapter IV.A.5.a).

———

SECTION B.   CRITICAL ANALYSIS OF THE CONCEPT OF SOVEREIGN IMMUNITY

Kenneth Culp Davis, Sovereign Immunity Must Go

22 Administrative Law Review 383, 383–385, 392–394, 401–402 (1970).

Yes, sovereign immunity must go. * * *

Sovereign immunity (1) often causes serious substantive injustice, (2) frequently results in final determinations without the safeguards that are necessary for procedural justice, and (3) causes gross inefficiency in the allocation of functions between officers and agencies, by preventing courts from resolving controversies they are especially qualified to solve.

Although the substantive injustice caused by sovereign immunity is widely recognized by thoughtful lawyers, the procedural injustice is usually overlooked. * * *

The allocation of functions that results from sovereign immunity is atrocious. Our normal system sensibly allocates functions between officers and courts on the basis of comparative qualifications so that controversies about governmental policies are decided primarily by officers and controversies about constitutionality or statutory interpretation or property law or commercial law are resolved primarily by judges. When the sovereign is held immune, courts are ousted from handling the very type of issues they are especially qualified to handle.

The strongest support for sovereign immunity is provided by that four-horse team so often encountered—historical accident, habit, a natural tendency to favor the familiar, and inertia. Nothing else supports sovereign immunity, despite the many recitations in judicial opinions that a court cannot "stop the government in its tracks" or interfere in public administration. What the courts should recite is largely the opposite—that courts should decide issues between government officers and private parties whenever the issues are appropriate for judicial determination, that courts do and should stop officers in their tracks when the officers are acting illegally and when the subject matter is within the competence of judges, and that courts should interfere in public administration * * * to the extent that the officers' action is found to be unconstitutional, in excess of statutory authority, an abuse of discretion, without procedure required by law, or based on findings unsupported by substantial evidence. Since courts are accustomed to stopping even Congress and the President in their tracks when programs are held unconstitutional, the many judicial recitations that courts cannot stop a single officer in his tracks even when a court finds that he is acting illegally and doing irreparable damage to the plaintiff are very much in need of reexamination.

To improve substantive justice, to enforce procedural justice, and to allocate functions efficiently, Congress should abolish nearly all of what is left of sovereign immunity.

Courts created sovereign immunity. Whether kings or others at one time could justify the doctrine seems unimportant in comparison with the needs of modern justice. The Supreme Court in 1882 acknowledged that sovereign immunity "has always been treated as an established doctrine" without judicial discussion of pros and cons.[3] Comparative research has demonstrated that the United States in retaining the doctrine is out of line with other parts of the world. Casuistry about the question whether a legal right can exist against the authority that makes the law on which the right depends has to yield to the practical fact that the federal government can and does often commit itself to obey judgments of courts in cases to which it is a party. * * *

Sovereign immunity often produces an uncivilized result, because what counts—what determines who gets the property, for instance—is not reason but force, not law but power, not orderly adjudication but physical taking by the stronger party, not refinements the sum of which we call civilization but crudities that are sometimes characteristic of primitive men.

The argument against sovereign immunity is on such an elementary plane that stating it is almost insulting to one's intelligence: Resolving controversies by adjudication before a qualified tribunal which tries to be impartial is better than the use of force because a just result is more likely.

What, then, is the argument *for* sovereign immunity?

3. United States v. Lee, 106 U.S. 196, 207 (1882).

One can read a hundred judicial opinions about sovereign immunity without ever encountering a reason in favor of it. Decisions based on sovereign immunity customarily rest on authority, the authority rests on history, and the history rests on medievalisms about monarchs.

A thoughtful district judge recently said that sovereign immunity "rests either on the theory that the United States is the institutional descendant of the Crown and enjoys its immunity or on a metaphysical doctrine that there can be no legal right as against the authority that makes the law."[30] Neither the history nor the metaphysics is a very satisfying basis on which to build modern law. The question worth asking is: From the standpoint of sound legal engineering, what reasons can be found for retaining sovereign immunity?

The most persuasive reason for sovereign immunity that has been found in reports of cases is a paragraph in the dissenting opinion of Mr. Justice Gray in United States v. Lee:

> The maxim is not limited to a monarchy, but is of equal force in a republic. In the one, as in the other, it is essential to the common defense and general welfare that the sovereign should not, without its consent, be dispossessed by judicial process of forts, arsenals, military posts, and ships of war, necessary to guard the national existence against insurrection and invasion; of customs-houses and revenue cutters, employed in the collection of the revenue; or of light-houses and light-ships, established for the security of commerce with foreign nations and among the different parts of the country.[31]

If the government were "dispossessed" of its military bases and equipment during an emergency, surely the judicial interference could be harmful.

The closest approach to a practical reason for sovereign immunity that has been found in the Supreme Court opinion of the twentieth century is a remark in the key case of Larson:

> There are the strongest reasons of public policy for the rule that such relief cannot be had against the sovereign. The Government, as representative of the community as a whole, cannot be stopped in its tracks by any plaintiff who presents a disputed question of property or contract right. As was early recognized, "The interference of the Courts with the performance of the ordinary duties of the executive departments of the government, would be productive of nothing but mischief...."[32]

The Court in Larson, except for the words quoted, did not identify "the strongest reasons of public policy." Even though all will agree that the government as a litigant differs from a private corporation or an individual in that it represents the community as a whole, and that the government clearly ought not to be stopped by "any plaintiff who presents a disputed

30. Martyniuk v. Pennsylvania, 282 F. Supp. 252, 255 (E.D.Pa.1968).

31. 106 U.S. 196, 226 (1882).

32. Larson v. Domestic & Foreign Corp., 337 U.S. 682, 704 (1949), quoting from Decatur v. Paulding, 14 Pet. 497, 516 (1840).

(This framing out the issue focuses on his rights, not gov't's expediency)

Larson's policy reason is in- applicable today

question," the crucial question is whether a private party who asserts that a government officer is wrongly interfering with his legal rights may have a judicial determination of the dispute between the private party and the officer. On that question the Larson opinion has nothing to offer except the 1840 statement that judicial interference in the ordinary duties of executive departments would be productive of nothing but mischief, and that statement was based on an assumption that was reasonable in 1840 but has turned out to be false during the ensuing century. The Court in 1840 assumed that it had to choose between performing executive tasks and refusing review; its choice was a good one. But later the Court learned that the assumption was mistaken; during the early part of the twentieth century, the Court invented a limited scope of review, so that the choice was no longer between judicial performance of executive tasks and refusal of review. By the time the Larson opinion was written in 1949, the usual practice was for courts to review the ordinary tasks of executive departments but to limit the review to such questions as constitutionality, statutory authority, proper procedure, abuse of discretion, and findings supported by substantial evidence.

Limited Rv. prevat

Closed- wheels

Instead of reciting in the Larson opinion the clearly false proposition that interference of the courts with ordinary duties of executive departments would produce nothing but mischief, the Supreme Court should have said that experience had proved overwhelmingly that a limited scope of judicial review of ordinary duties of executive departments produces better government, and that that is why the courts have developed such review and why the Congress had codified the judge-made law by embodying it in the Administrative Procedure Act.[33]

The Supreme Court's "strongest reasons of public policy" in favor of sovereign immunity turn out to embody nothing more than an 1840 assumption that experience has proved to be false and that is rejected by settled judge-made law, which in 1946 was codified by unanimous votes of both Houses of Congress.

'Arguments' for SI

But from the standpoint of sound legal engineering, do we not need a doctrine of sovereign immunity as a judicial tool, so that a court will not stop the government in its tracks whenever the court finds that a governmental program interferes with a plaintiffs legal rights, so that policies may be made by Congress and its delegates and not by courts, so that courts will be kept out of such areas as the execution of foreign policies and military policies where courts do not belong, and so that the representatives of the community as a whole will be free from judicial harassment in administering vital programs designed to benefit the whole society? These argumentative questions in defense of sovereign immunity may be about the best that

Author's Response

can be concocted, but they are easy to answer. The questions would be more effective if the courts were not limited by law about scope of review to issues appropriate for judicial determination (such as constitutionality, excess of authority, abuse of discretion), if courts did not restrict them-

---

33. 5 U.S.C § 706.

selves to subject matter within their competence, and if the substantive law administered by courts required governmental interests to be overridden by private rights in all circumstances. But each of the three *if's* is plainly contrary to prevailing judicial practices: The scope of review is limited to the kind of questions that judges are equipped to decide; courts are quite successful in staying out of areas into which they should not intrude; and the substantive law generally allows courts to balance the interests of opposing parties as equity requires.

The cts own scope of review will prevent it from deciding what is administratively efficient and what is not... ie. doctrine of judicial limits

What is needed is a much better balance between the public interest in the effectiveness of governmental programs and private interests. The present law, a mixture of medieval history and modern casuistry, does not even aim at creating such a balance, as shown in the next section.

Hardly any other branch of Supreme Court law is so permeated with sophistry as the law of sovereign immunity. Why is this so? Could it be that judges feel bound by the authority of the doctrine but are unable to discern a foundation for it in modern practicalities, so that they have nothing to guide them except application of refined logic to abstract concepts, many of which are almost devoid of meaning? * * *

* * * [I]n many opinions the Supreme Court in sovereign immunity contexts has asserted that courts cannot "interfere with the public administration." Another idea, or perhaps the same idea, is that "the Government cannot be stopped in its tracks."

The plain, clear, visible reality is, as no one knows better than Supreme Court Justices, that courts including the Supreme Court are constantly interfering with the public administration and constantly stopping the government in its tracks.

Yes.

Many of the great constitutional decisions throughout our history have stopped the government in its tracks and have interfered in public administration. * * *

courts.. 'Interfere' 'Stop in tracks'

Perhaps the most pervasive peacetime program of the federal government in American history was the National Industrial Recovery Act of the 1930's. It was overwhelmingly enacted and vigorously administered with the President's hearty support. But when the Schechter brothers took an appeal from a conviction for violating the Act, the Supreme Court stopped the whole government—both the Congress and the President in their tracks, in a most spectacular judicial interference in public administration.[49]

When President Truman seized most of the steel mills in order to avert a strike that he believed would jeopardize national defense, and the steel companies challenged the President's action in a suit against the Secretary of Commerce for declaratory judgment and injunction, the question was surely whether the courts would stop *the government* in its tracks. The Supreme Court in the Youngstown case held that the seizure was beyond the constitutional power of the President, affirming a decree against the

49. A.L.A. Schechter Poultry Corp. v. United States, 295 U.S 495 (1935).

Secretary.[50] The Court said nothing about stopping the government in its tracks or about interfering in public administration.

> How utterly incongruous for the courts to stop the President and Congress in their tracks and to interfere in the public administration of the most vital programs and at the same time to recite and hold that sovereign immunity prevents stopping the government in its tracks or interfering in public administration when a single officer is claiming a pile of coal or a piece of land and when the government has no special program with respect to the coal or the land!

Harold J. Krent, Reconceptualizing Sovereign Immunity

45 Vanderbilt Law Review 1529, 1529–1533 (1992).

The United States generally is immune from suit without its consent. Accordingly, neither Congress nor the executive branch need pay damages for any contract breached, any tort committed, or any constitutional right violated by the federal government. Although the doctrine of sovereign immunity persists, it persists subject to near unanimous condemnation from commentators. Many have rejected the underlying theory that the "King can do no wrong" as oddly out of place in our republican government[3] and many have noted as well that sovereign immunity was never applied as comprehensively in the past as it is today. Presently, there seems no justification for permitting government wrongdoing to go unremedied. Indeed, sovereign immunity confers upon the government an apparent advantage in the marketplace—unlike private individuals and entities, the government is liable only to the extent it deems appropriate.

Much of sovereign immunity, however, derives not from the infallibility of the state but from a desire to maintain a proper balance among the branches of the federal government, and from a proper commitment to majoritarian rule. For instance, Congress understandably might conclude that legislators would have too much incentive to conform their actions to the policy preferences of judges if the judiciary could second-guess whether congressional action or inaction were negligent. Furthermore, if the judiciary strictly enforced congressional contracts to the same extent as those of private parties, then succeeding generations might be bound excessively by the dead hand of Congresses past, preventing contemporary Congresses from pursuing current concerns as effectively.

Congress similarly could conclude that some damage actions against executive branch agencies or officials may distort public policy objectives.

---

50. Youngstown Sheet & Tube Co. v. Sawyer, 343 U.S. 579 (1952).

3. See, for example, Kenneth Culp Davis, 3 Administrative Law Treatise § 25.01 at 435–36 (West, 1958) (stating that "nearly every commentator who considers the subject vigorously asserts that the doctrine of sovereign immunity must go").

Although Congress is most concerned with safeguarding its own policy, Congress at times wishes to insulate its delegates in the executive branch who also formulate policy responsive to majoritarian politics. Judicial review could impede majoritarian policymaking if judges were empowered to review certain discretionary executive branch actions for their reasonableness or to force the executive branch to uphold contractual obligations that it believes are no longer in the nation's best interests. Moreover, the prospect of market damages in a tort or contract suit might deter even the most committed government officials or legislators from pursuing initiatives that they believe are in the public interest. Justification for continued sovereign immunity, therefore, may stem from concerns for preserving majoritarian policymaking and not from any need to honor hoary traditions.[5]

Immunity thus plays a vital role in our system; it is not so much a barrier to individual rights as it is a structural protection for democratic rule. The dominant justification for sovereign immunity must be that we trust Congress, unlike any other entity, to set the rules of the game. That insight derives from the general political accountability of Congress, both to the public and to the President. Congress may not always resolve the waiver issue wisely; nevertheless, the Constitution vests that decision in majoritarian hands, subject to the Takings and Due Process Clauses. In determining whether waiver is appropriate, Congress plausibly may conclude that the potential harm to majoritarian policymaking from damage actions outweighs the benefits in added deterrence of tortious conduct by the government, increased efficiency in contracting, and more equitable compensation of injured parties.

Those mistrusting Congress may find little comfort in a rule that authorizes Congress to shield itself from damage actions, and I by no means argue that the doctrine of sovereign immunity necessarily leads to better governance, although it may be of some benefit in the contract context. I argue, rather, that despite its bad press, sovereign immunity comports with our constitutional fabric and is at least normatively plausible.

Moreover, retained immunity does not result inevitably in insufficient deterrence of government misconduct or waste. Congressional policy, even if not subject to judicial review through a tort or contract action, is subject to the President's veto power and the electorate's displeasure. Actions by government officials may be checked by layers of internal debate, by the need to fashion policy prospectively, by the political necessity of placating constituents, and by the price that the government must pay to obtain services from the private sector. Congress also can subject executive branch actions to political checks, whether exercised by itself or by the courts. The

---

5. Maintaining government immunity risks substantial injustice by leaving those injured by government actions uncompensated when the same injury inflicted by a private party would be compensable. Although our private law system does not compensate all who are injured by tort or breach of contract, monetary relief is generally available for most claims.

Department of Defense may change procurement regulations, yet those regulations can be challenged directly under the Administrative Procedure ("APA") or indirectly through legislative oversight committees. The political and administrative processes may serve as substitutes for private lawsuits to deter arbitrary government action. The doctrine of sovereign immunity permits Congress to determine when to rely on the political process to safeguard majoritarian policy.

Concerns for safeguarding majoritarian policy, however, do not justify Congress's retention of blanket immunity. There are many instances of government negligence and breaches of contract that do not involve government policymaking. For example, government physicians may operate on the wrong patient, or government procurement officers may breach a contract to take advantage of a cheaper source of supply. Although all damage actions may affect government policy at some level, the less that a particular action jeopardizes purposeful policy, the less the concern from the separation-of-powers vantage point. At the same time, the further the government action is removed from purposeful policy, the more remote the possibility that the political process can act as an effective check upon government conduct. Government actions that are situation-specific, such as physician malpractice, rarely stem from previously set policy, and thus political forces have not molded the challenged action. Immunizing such acts from tort suits may not force the government to internalize the costs of its actions, which, in turn, may lead to inefficient governance in the future. Exempting the government from paying damages for breaches of contract when governmental policy is not threatened might permit opportunistic behavior and would likely increase the price that the government must pay for goods and services in the future. Without the deterrent of a tort or contract action, government officials may pursue shortsighted goals at the expense of long-range planning and efficiency.

Notes and Questions

1. Professors Kenneth Culp Davis and Harold Krent certainly differ on the legitimacy or defensibility of sovereign immunity. What does Davis see as the flaws in sovereign immunity as a concept and in practice? What of the concern that sovereign immunity protects the government from being "stopped in its tracks" or from having its war ships and military forts seized in time of war? How does Krent believe sovereign immunity can be justified in our constitutional system of government? In which branch of government does each—Davis and Krent—place greater trust with respect to the issues raised by claims against the government? Does this difference of confidence in different government institutions explain the contrasting answers that each reaches?

2. Interest in federal sovereign immunity as a concept has been reawakened among legal scholars in the past few years, leading to several significant works that look both back to the founding era and ahead to

application of the doctrine in the modern setting. *See generally* Gregory C. Sisk, *A Primer on the Doctrine of Federal Sovereign Immunity*, 58 Okla. L. Rev. 439 (2006). Below is a summary of a few leading examples of recent scholarly attention to this subject:

Professor Vicki C. Jackson has contributed a comprehensive history of federal sovereign immunity, together with an analysis of the principled or prudential reasons for the judicial recognition of the limitation on suits against the federal government, thereby providing both a detailed narrative of the dynamic evolution of the doctrine over time and raising questions about how it should be applied in the modern context. Vicki C. Jackson, *Suing the Federal Government: Sovereignty, Immunity, and Judicial Independence*, 35 Geo. Wash. Int'l. L. Rev. 521 (2003). She introduces her discussion by describing sovereign immunity as "a place of contest between important values of constitutionalism":

> On the one hand, constitutionalism entails a commitment that government should be limited by law and accountable under law for the protection of fundamental rights; if the "essence of civil liberty" is that the law provide remedies for violations of rights, immunizing government from ordinary remedies is in considerable tension with all but the most formalist understandings of law and rights. On the other hand, a commitment to democratic decisionmaking may underlie judicial hesitation about applying the ordinary law of remedies to afford access to the public fisc to satisfy private claims, in the absence of clear legislative authorization.

Id. at 521.

Jackson identifies three possible sources for "the remarkable staying power of the idea of federal sovereign immunity." *Id.* at 542. First, although perhaps misunderstood and too broadly read, English law, which had so profound an influence on early American law, did recognize some form of sovereign immunity. *Id.* at 542–43. Second, the Constitution commits the power to appropriate money to the Congress, thereby "lend[ing] force to the argument that money judgments against the United States cannot be *paid* without an appropriation from Congress." *Id.* at 543–46. Third, "Congress' control over the jurisdiction of the federal courts gives it considerable powers simply to refuse to authorize suits against the government." *Id.* at 546. And, indeed, in the First Judiciary Act of 1789, Congress gave jurisdiction to the lower federal courts over cases in which the United States was plaintiff or petitioner, thus implicitly prohibiting suits in which the federal government would be defendant. *Id.* at 546–48. Thus, Jackson suggests, "some aspects of the sovereign immunity doctrine—notably, those relating to judicially compelled payments from Treasury funds—are either required by, or consistent with, the U.S. Constitution at the federal level." *Id.* at 538. Moreover, she submits, "[w]hat we call the 'sovereign immunity' of the United States in many respects could be described instead as a particularized elaboration of Congress' control over the lower court's jurisdiction." *Id.* at 570.

Professor Susan Randall characterizes "[t]he history of sovereign immunity in the United States [a]s a history of mistakes." Susan Randall, *Sovereign Immunity and the Uses of History*, 81 Neb. L. Rev. 1, 2 (2002). She argues that, both expressly in the text of Constitution and as revealed through the ratification process, "the founding generation did not intend state sovereign immunity and instead viewed the ratification of the Constitution as consent to Article III suits by the states individually and collectively for the United States." *Id.* at 3. Looking at the language itself, Professor Randall reads Article III, Section 2 of the Constitution, which provides that the judicial power extends to "Controversies to which the United States shall be a party," as a clear grant of judicial authority to hear suits against the federal government. *Id.* at 38. Rather than merely bestowing jurisdiction, she contends, "[t]he term 'judicial power' is a broad and encompassing term" that "extends to the national judiciary a fundamental governmental authority" that supersedes sovereign immunity. *Id.* at 41. Looking at the state ratification process, Professor Randall asserts that the participants, both those Federalists who supported ratification and the Antifederalists who opposed it, well understood that the Constitution itself provided the necessary consent of the sovereign so that immunity had been waived, both for the individual states and the collectivity known as the United States. *Id.* at 30–31, 47–49.

As Professor Randall acknowledges, such prominent members of the founding generation as Alexander Hamilton, James Madison, and John Marshall did publicly endorse the concept of sovereign immunity during the ratification process. Hamilton, writing in *The Federalist 81*, wrote that "[i]t is inherent in the nature of sovereignty not to be amenable to the suit of an individual without its consent." James Madison who played a leading role in the drafting of the Constitution later told the Virginia ratification convention that Article III merely provided that a suit involving a state party, if initiated or permitted by the state, would be heard in federal court, but that an individual did not have the power to call any state into federal court. *Id.* at 11. John Marshall speaking at the Virginia convention made similar statements. *Id.* at 12. However, Professor Randall insists that "the interpretation advanced by Hamilton, Madison and Marshall is contradicted by the great weight of the historical evidence" including their own statements on other occasions, as well as the text of Article III, the reasons for the new national government and the creation of the judicial power, and the opinions of other leaders of the era. *Id.* at 13. Accordingly, she argues that "[a]gainst the weight of evidence, Madison's, Hamilton's, and Marshall's statements must be understood as part of the polemics of the ratification process rather than as the prevailing interpretation of the founding generation." *Id.* at 14.

Having contended that the historical justifications for sovereign immunity are invalid, Professor Randall concludes that sovereign immunity is supported "only by concerns about separation of powers," concerns that justify appropriate deference to the political branches but not broad immunity. *Id.* at 6; *see also id.* at 102, 104. She acknowledges that "[t]ime and tradition have * * * embedded the mistake of sovereign immunity in our legal culture," making its complete abolition "extraordinarily unlikely, and perhaps even impossible." *Id.* Nonetheless, she contends that sovereign immunity should henceforth be viewed as "a prudential rather than a jurisdictional doctrine," *id.*, under which "courts attempt to balance the needs of the political branches to govern effectively with the rights of the citizenry to redress governmental violations of the law," *id.* at 7.

For an interesting and iconoclastic argument that sovereign immunity is contrary to the intent of the framers of the Constitution, see James E. Pfander, *Sovereign Immunity and the Right to Petition: Toward a First Amendment Right to Pursue Judicial Claims Against the Government,* 91 Nw. U. L. Rev. 899 (1997). Professor Pfander argues that the trend among the states at the time of the adoption of the Constitution was toward eliminating the sovereign immunity of state governments from judicial claims and that the Petition Clause of the First Amendment of the Constitution (protecting the "right of the people * * * to petition the Government for a redress of grievances") should be interpreted "as a guaranteed right to pursue judicial remedies for unlawful government conduct." *Id.* at 899. He acknowledges that "[s]uch an understanding of the right to petition as a guarantee of government suability represents, to put the matter mildly, a departure from traditional accounts." *Id.* at 902. Nonetheless, he presents his thesis as a basis for "a frank reappraisal of standard accounts of the right to petition and the doctrine of sovereign immunity." *Id.* at 903. Under Pfander's thesis, sovereign immunity would be abandoned as a threshold barrier to suits against the federal government. Courts instead would exercise "remedial discretion" to determine when it is appropriate to uphold a cause of action against the federal government, the proper forum for such claims, and the appropriate relief, if any, in a particular case. *Id.* at 988 & n.336. For example, because the Constitution vests power over appropriations in Congress, a right to petition the government, including a right to pursue judicial redress of grievances, would still preserve the traditional deference of the courts to congressional primacy in fiscal matters. Thus, the availability of a monetary remedy would be limited. *Id.* at 985–86. *See also* James E. Pfander, *Restoring the Right to Petition,* 94 Nw. U. L. Rev. 219, 223 (1999) (reaffirming the argument that the Petition Clause affirms the right of individuals to petition the courts for redress and criticizing sovereign immunity "as a judge-made barrier to the assertion of claims against the government").

Professors Gary Lawson and Guy Seidman have filed a rebuttal to Pfander's scholarly brief; they conclude that the "right to petition the government for a redress of grievances is precisely—for want of a better phrase—the right to petition the government for a redress of grievances." Gary Lawson & Guy Seidman, *Downsizing the Right to Petition,* 93 Nw. U. L. Rev. 739, 740 (1999). "In particular," they argue, "we do not agree that the Petitions Clause imposes on Congress a general obligation to consider or respond in any fashion to petitions that it receives. Nor do we think that the clause either strengthens or weakens the case against federal sovereign immunity." *Id.* They contend that Pfander "confuse[s] the vehicle for enforcement of a right with the right itself." *Id.* at 765. The fact that one may have a right to file a petition with the courts, and that one may not be punished for doing so, does not translate into a right to prevail on the merits of a claim against the federal government. Lawson and Seidman conclude: "The existence of a right to petition * * * simply does not say anything about whether that right confers jurisdiction on the sovereign's courts to adjudicate claims against the sovereign." *Id.* Thus, the argument about the legitimacy of sovereign immunity must be debated on its own terms; "the right to petition does not contribute anything significant to that debate." *Id.* at 763.

SECTION C. JUDICIAL CONSTRUCTION OF STATUTORY WAIVERS OF SOVEREIGN IMMUNITY

In addition to understanding the basic concept of sovereign immunity, its historical origins, how it evolved as a doctrine in the Supreme Court, and the justifications for or critiques of the concept, one remaining aspect of federal sovereign immunity—the matter of statutory construction—should be addressed in this chapter, before we turn to the study of individual statutory waivers of sovereign immunity (a task that occupies most of the remaining chapters of this casebook). Even when Congress has waived sovereign immunity by enacting legislation granting express permission to seek judicial relief against the federal government, the doctrine exerts a pervasive influence upon the statutory analysis. With the underlying legal environment framed by sovereign immunity, the omnipresence of this foundational doctrine significantly affects the manner in which the courts approach the task of construing statutory waivers. Congress's consent to suit for a particular type of claim does not wholly deprive the federal government of the protective benefits of sovereign immunity. At the same time, as illustrated by the two Supreme Court decisions that follow— *Library of Congress v. Shaw* and *Irwin v. Department of Veterans Affairs*—a degree of tension in interpretive attitude persists in the Supreme Court caselaw regarding the proper mode of construction for statutory waivers of sovereign immunity.

Library of Congress v. Shaw   6-3

Supreme Court of the United States.
478 U.S. 310 (1986).

■ JUSTICE BLACKMUN delivered the opinion of the Court.

The no-interest rule is to the effect that interest cannot be recovered in a suit against the Government in the absence of an express waiver of sovereign immunity from an award of interest. In this case, attorney's fees as well as interest on those fees were awarded to a plaintiff who prevailed against petitioner Library of Congress in a suit brought under Title VII of the Civil Rights Act of 1964, as amended, 42 U.S.C. § 2000e *et seq.* We therefore must decide whether Congress, in enacting Title VII, expressly waived the Government's immunity from interest.

I

Respondent Tommy Shaw is an employee of the Library of Congress. He is black. During 1976 and 1977, he filed three complaints with the Library's Equal Employment Office alleging job-related racial discrimination. Following an investigation, Library officials rejected his complaints. Thereafter, respondent's counsel pursued administrative relief and settlement negotiations, and eventually reached a settlement with the Library. The latter agreed to promote Shaw retroactively with backpay provided that the Comptroller General first determined that the Library had authority to do so in the absence of a specific finding of racial discrimination. The Comptroller General ruled that the Library, under the Back Pay Act, 5 U.S.C. §§ 5595, 5596, lacked that power; he did not address whether such relief was authorized under Title VII.

Respondent then filed suit in the United States District Court for the District of Columbia, contending that Title VII authorized the Library to accord the relief specified in the settlement agreement. On cross-motions for summary judgment, the court agreed with respondent that the Library had the power under Title VII to settle his claim by awarding him a retroactive promotion with backpay without a formal finding of discrimination. 479 F.Supp. 945 (1979). The Library therefore was authorized to promote Shaw with backpay, and to pay a reasonable attorney's fee and costs pursuant to § 706(k) of the Civil Rights Act, 42 U.S.C. § 2000e–5(k). 479 F. Supp., at 949–950.

In a separate opinion calculating the attorney's fee, the District Court began with a lodestar of $8,435,[1] based on 99 hours of work at $85 per hour. The court then reduced the lodestar by 20 percent to reflect the quality of counsel's representation. Finally, and significantly for present purposes, the court increased the adjusted lodestar by 30 percent to compensate counsel for the delay in receiving payment for the legal services rendered. The District Court, relying on *Copeland v. Marshall*, 641 F.2d 880, 893 (1980) (en banc), indicated that increasing an attorney's fee award for delay is appropriate because the hourly rates used for the lodestar represent the prevailing rate for clients who typically pay their legal bills promptly, whereas court-awarded fees are normally received long after the legal services are rendered. An increase for delay is designed to compensate the attorney for the money he could have earned had he been paid earlier and invested the funds. The District Court concluded that the period of

---

1. The lodestar component of an attorney's fee is the product of "the number of hours reasonably expended on the litigation multiplied by a reasonable hourly rate." *Hensley v. Eckerhart*, 461 U.S. 424, 433 (1983).

delay ran from the time the case should have ended, which it viewed as the latter part of 1978, until just after judgment.

The Court of Appeals for the District of Columbia Circuit affirmed. 747 F.2d 1469 (1984). The court determined that, even though the adjustment was termed "compensation for delay" rather than "interest," the no-interest rule applied because the two adjustments were functionally equivalent. The court went on to examine whether the Government expressly had waived its immunity from interest in Title VII. Section 706(k) of Title VII, 42 U.S.C. § 2000e–5(k), provides in relevant part:

> "In any action or proceeding under this subchapter the court, in its discretion, may allow the prevailing party, other than the [EEOC] or the United States, a reasonable attorney's fee as part of the costs, and the [EEOC] and *the United States shall be liable for costs the same as a private person*." (Emphasis added.)

The Court of Appeals noted that in a Title VII suit against a private employer, interest on attorney's fees may be recovered. 747 F.2d, at 1475. Therefore, the Court of Appeals reasoned, in making the United States liable "the same as a private person," Congress waived the United States' immunity from interest. In the alternative, the Court of Appeals held that even if the "same as a private person" provision was not an express waiver, the District Court's adjustment was proper; when a statute measures the liability of the United States by that of a private person, the "traditional rigor of the sovereign-immunity doctrine" is relaxed. 747 F.2d, at 1479.

Judge Ginsburg dissented. *Id.,* at 1485. She found no express waiver of immunity from interest, and declined to join what she considered to be a judicial termination of the no-interest rule. She viewed the increase for delay in this case as an award of interest, based on the manner and timing of its computation. She indicated, however, that use of current rather than historical hourly rates in order to compensate for delay, or use of historical rates that were based on expected delay would not run afoul of the no-interest rule.

We granted certiorari to address the question whether the Court of Appeals' decision conflicts with this Court's repeated holdings that interest may not be awarded against the Government in the absence of express statutory or contractual consent.

II

In the absence of express congressional consent to the award of interest separate from a general waiver of immunity to suit, the United States is immune from an interest award. This requirement of a separate waiver reflects the historical view that interest is an element of damages separate from damages on the substantive claim. Because interest was generally presumed not to be within the contemplation of the parties, common-law courts in England allowed interest by way of damages only when founded upon agreement of the parties. In turn, the agreement-basis of interest was adopted by American courts. Gradually, in suits between private parties, the necessity of an agreement faded.

The agreement requirement assumed special force when applied to claims for interest against the United States. As sovereign, the United States, in the absence of its consent, is immune from suit. This basic rule of sovereign immunity, in conjunction with the requirement of an agreement to pay interest, gave rise to the rule that interest cannot be recovered unless the award of interest was affirmatively and separately contemplated by Congress. See, *e.g., United States ex rel. Angarica v. Bayard,* 127 U.S. 251, 260 (1888) ("The case, therefore, falls within the well-settled principle, that the United States are not liable to pay interest on claims against them, in the absence of express statutory provision to that effect"). The purpose of the rule is to permit the Government to "occupy an apparently favored position," *United States v. Verdier,* 164 U.S. 213, 219 (1896), by protecting it from claims for interest that would prevail against private parties.

For well over a century, this Court, executive agencies, and Congress itself consistently have recognized that federal statutes cannot be read to permit interest to run on a recovery against the United States unless Congress affirmatively mandates that result. * * *

III

Respondent acknowledges the longstanding no-interest rule, but argues that Congress, by § 706(k), waived the Government's immunity from interest in making the United States liable "the same as a private person" for "costs," including "a reasonable attorney's fee."

In analyzing whether Congress has waived the immunity of the United States, we must construe waivers strictly in favor of the sovereign, and not enlarge the waiver "beyond what the language requires," *Ruckelshaus v. Sierra Club,* 463 U.S. 680, 685–686 (1983). The no-interest rule provides an added gloss of strictness upon these usual rules.

"[T]here can be no consent by implication or by use of ambiguous language. Nor can an intent on the part of the framers of a statute or contract to permit the recovery of interest suffice where the intent is not translated into affirmative statutory or contractual terms. The consent necessary to waive the traditional immunity must be express, and it must be strictly construed." *United States v. N.Y. Rayon Importing Co.,* 329 U.S., at 659.

A

When Congress has intended to waive the United States' immunity with respect to interest, it has done so expressly; thus, waivers of sovereign immunity to suit must be read against the backdrop of the no-interest rule. Yet respondent contends that by equating the United States' liability to that of a private party, Congress waived the Government's immunity from interest. We do not agree.

Title VII's provision making the United States liable "the same as a private person" waives the Government's immunity from attorney's fees, but not interest. The statute, as well as its legislative history, contains no reference to interest. This congressional silence does not permit us to read the provision as the requisite waiver of the Government's immunity with respect to interest. * * *

Other statutes placing the United States in the same position as a private party also have been read narrowly to preserve certain immunities that the United States has enjoyed historically. In *Laird v. Nelms*, 406 U.S. 797 (1972), for example, the Court held that, although the Federal Tort Claims Act made the United States liable for the "negligent or wrongful act or omission of any employee of the Government ..., if a private person, would be liable to the claimant," 28 U.S.C. § 1346(b), the United States nonetheless was not liable for the entire range of conduct classified as tortious under state law. Cf. *Lehman v. Nakshian*, 453 U.S. 156 (1981) (jury trials are available to private, but not to Government, employees under the Age Discrimination in Employment Act).

B

Nor do we find the requisite waiver of immunity from interest in the statutory requirement of awarding "reasonable" attorney's fees. There is no basis for reading the term "reasonable" as the embodiment of a specific congressional choice to include interest as a component of attorney's fees, particularly where the legislative history is silent. The Court consistently has refused to impute an intent to waive immunity from interest into the ambiguous use of a particular word or phrase in a statute. For example, interest has been ruled unavailable under statutes or contracts directing the United States to pay the "amount equitably due." And the United States is not liable for interest under statutes and contracts requiring the payment of "just compensation," even though it long has been understood that the United States is required to pay interest where the Constitution mandates payment under the Just Compensation Clause.

Respondent argues, however, that the policy reasons that motivated Congress to permit recovery of a *reasonable* attorney's fee require reading the statute as a waiver of immunity from interest. But policy, no matter how compelling, is insufficient, standing alone, to waive this immunity:

> "[T]he immunity of the United States from liability for interest is not to be waived by policy arguments of this nature. Courts lack the power to award interest against the United States on the basis of what they think is or is not sound policy." *United States v. N.Y. Rayon Importing Co.*, 329 U.S., at 663.

C

Finally, we note that the provision makes the United States liable for "costs," and includes as an element of "costs" a reasonable attorney's fee. Prejudgment interest, however, is considered as damages, not a component of "costs." Indeed, the term "costs" has never been understood to include any interest component. A statute allowing costs, and within that category, attorney's fees, does not provide the clear affirmative intent of Congress to waive the sovereign's immunity.

IV

In the alternative, respondent argues that the no-interest rule does not prohibit the award of compensation for delay. But the force of the no-interest rule cannot be avoided simply by devising a new name for an old institution:

> "[T]he character or nature of 'interest' cannot be changed by calling it 'damages,' 'loss,' 'earned increment,' 'just compensation,' 'discount,' 'offset,' or 'penalty,' or any other term, because it is still interest and the no-interest rule applies to it." *United States v. Mescalero Apache Tribe*, 207 Ct. Cl. 369, 389, 518 F.2d 1309, 1322 (1975), cert. denied, 425 U.S. 911 (1976).

Respondent claims, however, that interest and delay represent more than mere semantic variations. Interest and a delay factor, according to respondent, have distinct purposes: the former compensates for loss in the use of money, while the latter compensates for loss in the value of money.

We are not persuaded. Interest and a delay factor share an identical function. They are designed to compensate for the belated receipt of money. The no-interest rule has been applied to prevent parties from holding the United States liable on claims grounded on the belated receipt of funds, even when characterized as compensation for delay. Thus, whether the loss to be compensated by an increase in a fee award stems from an opportunity cost or from the effects of inflation, the increase is prohibited by the no-interest rule.[7] * * *

V

In making the Government liable as a defendant under Title VII, Congress effected a waiver of the Government's immunity from suit, and from costs including reasonable attorney's fees. Congress did not waive the Government's traditional immunity from interest. Accordingly, the judgment of the Court of Appeals is reversed, and the case is remanded for further proceedings consistent with this opinion.

It is so ordered.

■ JUSTICE BRENNAN, with whom JUSTICE MARSHALL and JUSTICE STEVENS join, dissenting.

The Court today applies the rules for construing waivers of sovereign immunity in a wooden and archaic fashion to conclude that the United States has not waived its immunity to interest on attorney's fee awards.

---

7. When interest is awarded, as it was in this case, it is computed by multiplying a particular rate of interest by the amount of the award. An interest rate reflects not only the real opportunity cost of capital, but also the inflation rate. See R. Posner, Economic Analysis of Law 180 (3d ed. 1986). Thus, loss of value due to delay is an element of an interest adjustment.

Because the result reached by the Court frustrates the clear intention of Congress, I respectfully dissent.

The so-called "no-interest rule" is, as the Court suggests, one of considerable antiquity. It is a corollary of the ancient principle that the sovereign is immune from suit and from liability for damages in the absence of an express waiver of immunity. And, as a corollary of the general sovereign immunity doctrine, the no-interest rule logically should be governed by the same canons of construction we employ to interpret waivers of sovereign immunity for suits for damages. Just two Terms ago, we explained that "waiver of sovereign immunity is accomplished not by 'a ritualistic formula;' rather, intent to waive immunity and the scope of such a waiver can only be ascertained by reference to underlying congressional policy." *Franchise Tax Board of California v. United States Postal Service,* 467 U.S. 512, 521 (1984). Applying this standard here, I would hold that Congress has waived immunity from prejudgment interest on attorney's fees in all situations where a private individual would be liable for such interest.

I begin with the relevant language of § 706(k) of Title VII, 42 U.S.C. § 2000e–5(k): "[T]he court, in its discretion, may allow the prevailing party, other than the [EEOC] or the United States, a reasonable attorney's fee as a part of the costs, and the [EEOC] and the United States shall be liable for costs the same as a private person." By this language, Congress indisputably authorized the award of reasonable attorney's fees to prevailing parties against any losing party, including the United States. Since, in "appropriate circumstances," § 706(k) permits the award of prejudgment interest (or a delay adjustment) on attorney's fees awarded against losing parties other than the Federal Government, § 706(k) *by its terms* authorizes the award of prejudgment interest against the Federal Government under like circumstances and thus constitutes an express waiver of sovereign immunity.

The "underlying congressional policy," *Franchise Tax Board, supra,* at 521, also supports this conclusion. The Senate Report relevant to the Equal Employment Act of 1972—the legislation that amended Title VII, *inter alia,* to protect federal employees against employment discrimination—indicates that Congress intended that federal employees enjoy the same access to courts and the same judicial remedies that are available to other Title VII plaintiffs. S.Rep. No. 92–415 (1971). The Report states:

> "[T]he committee found that an aggrieved Federal employee does not have access to the courts. In many cases, the employee must overcome a U.S. Government defense of sovereign immunity or failure to exhaust administrative remedies.... Moreover, the remedial authority of the ... courts has also been in doubt. The provisions adopted by the committee will enable the Commission to grant full relief to aggrieved employees, or applicants.... *Aggrieved employees or applicants will also have the full rights available in the courts as are granted to individuals in the private sector under title VII.*" *Id.,* at 16 (emphasis added).

The legislative history of the 1972 amendments thus demonstrates that Congress intended that federal employees enjoy the same rights and remedies in the courts as private litigants. It therefore follows that Congress intended that in situations where private sector Title VII litigants may recover prejudgment interest on their attorney's fees awards, so may federal employees.

... same rights & remedies as private litigants.. like prejudgment interest

It is true, as the Court points out, that the legislative history of the 1972 amendments to Title VII seems devoid of explicit reference to the availability of prejudgment interest on attorney's fees awarded against the Federal Government. But, only under a highly formalistic, "ritualistic," *Franchise Tax Board, supra,* 467 U.S., at 521, canon of construction that ignores unmistakable congressional intent and that requires Congress to adhere to a talismanic formula in order to waive immunity can the absence of the words "interest on attorney's fees" from the congressional Committee Reports limit the waiver of sovereign immunity to the attorney's fees themselves and bar the award of interest on those fees. Such an antiquated canon of construction is unacceptable, both because it is unnecessary to protect the Government from liability to which it has not consented and because it frustrates the intention of Congress that federal employees enjoy the same rights and remedies in the courts as do individuals in the private sector.

'The Congressional silence w/ reference to "interest" doesn't mean that Congress didn't attempt to waive it'

difference in judgment attorney

In my view, the Court of Appeals correctly held that Congress, in stating that the Federal Government is liable for attorney's fees to the same extent as other losing parties, waived sovereign immunity for both fees and prejudgment interest thereon. I therefore dissent and would affirm the judgment below.

Civil Rights Act of 1991

Pub. L. No. 102–166, 105 Stat. 1079.

— example of clear Congressional waiver of immunity for award of interest

Sec. 114. Providing for Interest and Extending the Statute of Limitations in Actions Against the Federal Government.

Section 717 of the Civil Rights Act of 1964 (42 U.S.C. 2000e–16) is amended—

* * *

(2) in subsection (d), by inserting before the period ", and the same interest to compensate for delay in payment shall be available as in cases involving nonpublic parties."

Notes and Questions

1. In *Library of Congress v. Shaw,* the Supreme Court stated and applied a rule of strict construction of statutory waivers of sovereign

immunity. Thus, not only must Congress speak expressly before a waiver of sovereign immunity will be found, but the scope of such waivers will be narrowly read. Why does the Court adopt this rule? Is this an appropriate rule of statutory interpretation when sovereign immunity lies in the background?

Subsequent decisions appear to solidify that rule of strict construction by refusing to extend the scope of a waiver of sovereign immunity when the language of the statute leaves any ambiguity and by declining to look beyond the text to legislative history or statutory purpose. *See, e.g., Ardestani v. Immigration & Naturalization Service,* 502 U.S. 129 (1991); *United States v. Nordic Village, Inc.,* 503 U.S. 30 (1992); *United States Department of Energy v. Ohio,* 503 U.S. 607 (1992). Several commentators have described the Court's decisions as adopting a "clear statement" rule, that is, demanding a plain and unequivocal expression by Congress in the text of statute concerning the scope of a waiver of sovereign immunity. John Copeland Nagle, *Waiving Sovereign Immunity in an Age of Clear Statement Rules,* 1995 Wis. L. Rev. 771, 796–98; William N. Eskridge, Jr. & Philip P. Frickey, *Quasi–Constitutional Law: Clear Statement Rules as Constitutional Lawmaking,* 45 Vand. L. Rev. 593, 594 n.4, 643 (1992); Stephen M. Feldman, *The Supreme Court's New Sovereign Immunity Doctrine and the McCarran Amendment: Toward Ending State Adjudication of Indian Water Rights,* 18 Harv. Envtl. L. Rev. 433, 460–61 (1994). Under this rule, doubts about the textual meaning of a statute are resolved in favor of the preservation of sovereign immunity.

Professor John Copeland Nagle explains that the Supreme Court requires "specifically targeted statutory language and refuses to consider other indicia of legislative intent" in the construction of a statutory grant of judicial relief against the federal government. Nagle, *supra,* at 773. Nagle criticizes the requirement of a "clear statement," complaining that "while it is easy for Congress to write a provision that waives sovereign immunity generally, it is difficult for Congress to write a provision that specifies the *scope* of a waiver of sovereign immunity." *Id.* at 806. He argues that "a clear statement rule threatens legislative supremacy, especially because Congress does not share the same enthusiasm for sovereign immunity that the Court has demonstrated in its most recent decisions." *Id.*

Professor Vicki C. Jackson argues that, in an era of greater acceptance of the government's amenability to suit and of judicial independence, the "dynamic [should] move back towards more restrictive understandings of the doctrine's scope" so as to enhance the "courts' capacities to provide individual justice." Vicki C. Jackson, *Suing the Federal Government: Sovereignty, Immunity, and Judicial Independence,* 35 Geo. Wash. Int'l. L. Rev. 521, 607–09 (2003). Even though the doctrine may never actually be abolished, Jackson argues that the "abstract idea of sovereign immunity" should not be invoked to deny "remedies to address violations of legal rights" in cases in which "there is room for interpretation on questions of jurisdiction and remedies." *Id.* In sum, Jackson also would favor a more generous construction of scope and remedy when Congress grants permission to suit.

Do you share these critiques of the Court's interpretive approach? Should the Supreme Court address a statutory waiver of sovereign immunity in the same manner that it considers the meaning of other statutes? Or should the Court elevate sovereign immunity to a preferred value by strictly construing statutes that strip the government of immunity? What light is shed upon this question by the debate about the very concept of sovereign immunity that we explored earlier?

Does statutory waiver warrant a different rule of construction?

Nonetheless, commentators concede, under the Supreme Court's "clear statement" approach, doubts about the textual meaning of a statute are indeed resolved in favor of the preservation of sovereign immunity. Moreover, as the strict construction rule for waivers of sovereign immunity is not a recent innovation, Congress has legislated for many decades against this backdrop.

2. As shown above in the excerpt from the Civil Rights Act of 1991, five years after *Library of Congress v. Shaw,* Congress overturned the Supreme Court's holding in that particular case by amending Title VII to provide for compensation for delay in payment under that statute. Note that Congress used express language to achieve that result.

However, *Shaw* remains important as a statement of the general rule of construction of waivers of sovereign immunity. Moreover, the "no-interest rule" stated in *Shaw* remains the rule in other contexts where Congress has not enacted specific statutory provisions to the contrary. *See, e.g., Adams v. United States,* 350 F.3d 1216, 1229–30 (Fed. Cir. 2003) (holding that Border Patrol employees who were awarded overtime pay could not obtain prejudgment interest); *Smith v. Principi,* 281 F.3d 1384, 1387 (Fed. Cir. 2002) (holding that a veteran who had been awarded past-due compensation after successfully challenging disability rating could not recover interest because the statutes did not mention interest and thus did not expressly waive the no-interest rule); *Newton v. Capital Assurance Co.,* 245 F.3d 1306, 1310–12 (11th Cir. 2001) (holding that prejudgment interest could not be awarded to successful claimant for flood insurance benefits where insurer was subsidized by the Federal Emergency Management Agency and any interest payment would be a direct charge against the public treasury). *But see United States v. $277,000 U.S. Currency,* 69 F.3d 1491 (9th Cir. 1995) (holding in unsuccessful forfeiture case that requiring the government to "disgorge benefits that it has actually and calculably received from an asset that it has been holding improperly" did not run afoul of the no-interest rule).

Shaw's rule of construction still applies ✱

Irwin v. Veterans Affairs

Supreme Court of the United States.
498 U.S. 89 (1990).

■ CHIEF JUSTICE REHNQUIST delivered the opinion of the Court.

In April 1986, petitioner, Shirley Irwin, was fired from his job by respondent Veteran's Administration (VA). Irwin contacted an Equal Em-

Fed employee discharged from an executive dept.

ployment Opportunities Commission (EEOC) counselor and filed a complaint with the EEOC, alleging that the VA had unlawfully discharged him on the basis of his race and physical disability. The EEOC dismissed Irwin's complaint by a letter dated March 19, 1987. The letter, which was sent to both Irwin and his attorney, expressly informed them that Irwin had the right to file a civil action under Title VII, 42 U.S.C. § 2000e *et seq.,* within 30 days of receipt of the EEOC notice. According to Irwin, he did not receive the EEOC's letter until April 7, 1987, and the letter to his attorney arrived at the attorney's office on March 23, 1987, while the attorney was out of the country. The attorney did not learn of the EEOC's action until his return on April 10, 1987.

Irwin filed a complaint in the United States District Court for the Western District of Texas on May 6, 1987, 44 days after the EEOC notice was received at his attorney's office, but 29 days after the date on which he claimed he received the letter. The complaint alleged that the VA discriminated against him because of his race, age, and handicap, in violation of 42 U.S.C. § 2000e *et seq.,* 29 U.S.C. § 621 *et seq.,* 29 U.S.C. § 791 *et seq.,* and the First and Fifth Amendments. Respondent VA moved to dismiss, asserting, *inter alia,* that the District Court lacked jurisdiction because the complaint was not filed within 30 days of the EEOC's decision as specified in 42 U.S.C. § 2000e–16(c). The District Court granted the motion.

The Court of Appeals for the Fifth Circuit affirmed. 874 F.2d 1092 (1989). The court held that the 30–day period begins to run on the date that the EEOC right-to-sue letter is delivered to the offices of formally designated counsel or to the claimant, even if counsel himself did not actually receive notice until later. The Court of Appeals further determined that the 30–day span allotted under § 2000e–16(c) operates as an absolute jurisdictional limit. Accordingly, it reasoned that the District Court could not excuse Irwin's late filing because federal courts lacked jurisdiction over his untimely claim. That holding is in direct conflict with the decisions of four other Courts of Appeals.

We granted certiorari to determine when the 30–day period under § 2000e–16(c) begins to run and to resolve the Circuit conflict over whether late-filed claims are jurisdictionally barred.

Section 2000e–16(c) provides that an employment discrimination complaint against the Federal Government under Title VII must be filed "[w]ithin thirty days of receipt of notice of final action taken" by the EEOC. The Court of Appeals determined that a notice of final action is "received" when the EEOC delivers its notice to a claimant or the claimant's attorney, whichever comes first. Petitioner argues that the clock does not begin until the claimant himself has notice of his right to sue.

We conclude that Irwin's complaint filed in the District Court was untimely. As the Court of Appeals observed, § 2000e–16(c) requires only that the EEOC notification letter be "received"; it does not specify receipt by the claimant rather than by the claimant's designated representative.

- He files EEOC complaint
- EEOC dismisses – 3/19/1987 – letter
  - 30 day notice
- Atty receives 3/23 → 4/23
- Irwin receives – 4/7
- Atty returns 4/10
- 4/19 – expiration of suit window 4/22
- Irwin files it in fed. dist. ct – 5/6

Dist. ct. grants VA's M. to Dismiss

Ct. of Appeals HOLDINGS:
1. Ct. didn't have jd.
2. Ct. couldn't waive jd b/c 30 days is an absolute limit

Issue

(Argument)

(H)

There is no question but that petitioner appeared by his attorney in the EEOC proceeding. Under our system of representative litigation, "each party is deemed bound by the acts of his lawyer-agent and is considered to have notice of all facts, notice of which can be charged upon the attorney." *Link v. Wabash R. Co.,* 370 U.S. 626, 634. Congress has endorsed this sensible practice in the analogous provisions of the Federal Rules of Civil Procedure, which provide that "[w]henever under these rules service is required or permitted to be made upon a party represented by an attorney the service shall be made upon the attorney unless service upon the party is ordered by the court." Fed. Rule Civ. Proc. 5(b). To read the term "receipt" to mean only "actual receipt by the claimant" would render the practice of notification through counsel a meaningless exercise. If Congress intends to depart from the common and established practice of providing notification through counsel, it must do so expressly.

We also reject Irwin's contention that there is a material difference between receipt by an attorney and receipt by that attorney's office for purposes of § 2000e–16(c). The lower federal courts have consistently held that notice to an attorney's office which is acknowledged by a representative of that office qualifies as notice to the client. Federal Rule of Civil Procedure 5(b) also permits notice to a litigant to be made by delivery of papers to the litigant's attorney's office. The practical effect of a contrary rule would be to encourage factual disputes about when actual notice was received, and thereby create uncertainty in an area of the law where certainty is much to be desired.

The fact that petitioner did not strictly comply with § 2000e–16(c)'s filing deadline does not, however, end our inquiry. Petitioner contends that even if he failed to timely file, his error may be excused under equitable tolling principles. The Court of Appeals rejected this argument on the ground that the filing period contained in § 2000e–16(c) is jurisdictional, and therefore the District Court lacked authority to consider his equitable claims. The court reasoned that § 2000e–16(c) applies to suits against the Federal Government and thus is a condition of Congress' waiver of sovereign immunity. Since waivers of sovereign immunity are traditionally construed narrowly, the court determined that strict compliance with § 2000e–16(c) is a necessary predicate to a Title VII suit.

Respondent correctly observes that § 2000e–16(c) is a condition to its waiver of sovereign immunity and thus must be strictly construed. See *Library of Congress v. Shaw,* 478 U.S. 310 (1986). But our previous cases dealing with the effect of time limits in suits against the Government have not been entirely consistent, even though the cases may be distinguished on their facts. In *United States v. Locke,* 471 U.S. 84, 94, n. 10 (1985), we stated that we were leaving open the general question of whether principles of equitable tolling, waiver, and estoppel apply against the Government when it involves a statutory filing deadline. But, as Justice WHITE points out in his concurring opinion, nearly thirty years earlier in *Soriano v. United States,* 352 U.S. 270 (1957), we held the petitioner's claim to be jurisdictionally barred, saying that "Congress was entitled to assume that

Margin notes:

· Notification – through – counsel custom... of Congress

· To depart from this rule requires express intent

Atty's notice is deemed to be client's notice

Irwin's 2° Argument: Ct's power to waive untimely filing

... In *Soriano* we started to look at equitable tolling from a jurisdictional standpoint...

the limitation period it prescribed meant just that and no more." *Id.* at 276. More recently, in *Bowen v. City of New York,* 476 U.S. 467, 479 (1986), we explained that "we must be careful not to 'assume the authority to narrow the waiver that Congress intended,' or construe the waiver 'unduly restrictively' "(citation omitted).

Title 42 U.S.C. § 2000e–16(c) provides in relevant part:

"Within thirty days of receipt of notice of final action taken by ... the Equal Employment Opportunity Commission ... an employee or applicant for employment, if aggrieved by the final disposition of his complaint, or by the failure to take final action on his complaint, may file a civil action as provided in section 2000e–5 of this title...."

The phraseology of this particular statutory time limit is probably very similar to some other statutory limitations on suits against the Government, but probably not to all of them. In the present statute, Congress said that "within thirty days ... an employee ... may file a civil action...." In *Soriano, supra,* Congress provided that "every claim ... shall be barred unless the petition ... is filed ... within six years...." An argument can undoubtedly be made that the latter language is more stringent than the former, but we are not persuaded that the difference between them is enough to manifest a different congressional intent with respect to the availability of equitable tolling. Thus a continuing effort on our part to decide each case on an *ad hoc* basis, as we appear to have done in the past, would have the disadvantage of continuing unpredictability without the corresponding advantage of greater fidelity to the intent of Congress. We think that this case affords us an opportunity to adopt a more general rule to govern the applicability of equitable tolling in suits against the Government.

Time requirements in law suits between private litigants are customarily subject to "equitable tolling." Indeed, we have held that the statutory time limits applicable to lawsuits against private employers under Title VII are subject to equitable tolling.

A waiver of sovereign immunity "cannot be implied but must be unequivocally expressed." *United States v. Mitchell,* 445 U.S. 535, 538 (1980). Once Congress has made such a waiver, we think that making the rule of equitable tolling applicable to suits against the Government, in the same way that it is applicable to private suits, amounts to little, if any, broadening of the congressional waiver. Such a principle is likely to be a realistic assessment of legislative intent as well as a practically useful principle of interpretation. We therefore hold that the same rebuttable presumption of equitable tolling applicable to suits against private defendants should also apply to suits against the United States. Congress, of course, may provide otherwise if it wishes to do so.

But an examination of the cases in which we have applied the equitable tolling doctrine as between private litigants affords petitioner little help. Federal courts have typically extended equitable relief only sparingly. We have allowed equitable tolling in situations where the claimant has actively pursued his judicial remedies by filing a defective pleading during the statutory period, or where the complainant has been induced or tricked by his adversary's misconduct into allowing the filing deadline to pass. We have generally been much less forgiving in receiving late filings where the claimant failed to exercise due diligence in preserving his legal rights. Because the time limits imposed by Congress in a suit against the Government involve a waiver of sovereign immunity, it is evident that no more favorable tolling doctrine may be employed against the Government than is employed in suits between private litigants.

We don't apply equitable tolling here b/c Imm didn't exercise due diligence

Petitioner urges that his failure to file in a timely manner should be excused because his lawyer was absent from his office at the time that the EEOC notice was received, and that he thereafter filed within 30 days of the day on which he personally received notice. But the principles of equitable tolling described above do not extend to what is at best a garden variety claim of excusable neglect.

The judgment of the Court of Appeals is accordingly

Affirmed.

■ JUSTICE SOUTER took no part in the consideration or decision of this case.

■ JUSTICE WHITE, with whom JUSTICE MARSHALL joins, concurring in part and concurring in the judgment.

Although I agree with the Court that the 30–day period under 42 U.S.C. § 2000e–16(c) begins to run when the notice from the Equal Employment Opportunity Commission is delivered either to the claimant or the claimant's attorney, I do not join the portion of the opinion holding that the 30–day time period is subject to equitable tolling.

As the Court recognizes statutory deadlines for suits against the Government, such as the one in this case, are conditions on the Government's waiver of sovereign immunity. See, *e.g., United States v. Kubrick,* 444 U.S. 111, 117–118 (1979). As such, they must be "strictly observed and exceptions thereto are not to be implied." *Lehman v. Nakshian,* 453 U.S. 156, 161 (1981). In my view, the Court has failed to "strictly observe" the terms of the statute at issue in this case.

Statutory filing deadlines are conditions for the waiver!

Congress did not expressly provide for equitable tolling of the 30–day filing deadline in § 2000e–16(c). The Court, however, holds that like statutes of limitations for suits between private litigants, limitations periods for suits against the Government will now *presumptively* be subject to equitable tolling. That holding needlessly reverses at least one of this Court's prior decisions, and is in tension with several others.

The Ct's "presumption" is in conflict w/ holdings against waiver by implication...

Because of the existence of sovereign immunity, we have traditionally held that the Government's consent to be sued "cannot be implied but must be unequivocally expressed." *United States v. Mitchell,* 445 U.S. 535, 538 (1980). That rule applies even where there is a contrary presumption for suits against private defendants. Our decision in *Library of Congress v. Shaw,* 478 U.S. 310 (1986), is instructive on this point. There, we held that the Government was not liable under the federal provisions of Title VII for

See authority

interest. In reaching that conclusion, we reaffirmed the longstanding rule that despite consent to be sued, the Government will not be liable for interest unless there is a separate explicit waiver to that effect. Although the statute in that case provided that the Government was to be liable "the same as a private person" for "costs," including a "reasonable attorney's fee," we stated that "we must construe waivers strictly in favor of the sovereign ... and not enlarge the waiver 'beyond what the language requires.'" *Id.,* at 318. It seems to me that the Court in this case, by holding that the time limit in § 2000e–16(c) is subject to equitable tolling, has done exactly what *Shaw* proscribes—it has enlarged the waiver in § 2000e–16(c) beyond what the language of that section requires.

Not only is the Court's holding inconsistent with our traditional approach to cases involving sovereign immunity, it directly overrules a prior decision by this Court, *Soriano v. United States,* 352 U.S. 270 (1957). The question in *Soriano* was whether war tolled the statute of limitations for claims against the Government filed in the Court of Claims. In arguing for equitable tolling, the plaintiff there relied on a case in which this Court had held that war had tolled a limitations statute for purposes of private causes of action. The Court was not persuaded, stating that "[t]hat case involved private citizens, not the Government. It has no applicability to claims against the sovereign." *Id.,* at 275. The Court explained:

> "To permit the application of the doctrine urged by petitioner would impose the tolling of the statute in every time-limit-consent Act passed by the Congress.... Strangely enough, Congress would be required to provide expressly in each statute that the period of limitation was not to be extended by war. But Congress was entitled to assume that the limitation period it prescribed meant just that period and no more. With this intent in mind, Congress has passed specific legislation each time it has seen fit to toll such statutes of limitations because of war. And this Court has long decided that limitations and conditions upon which the Government consents to be sued must be strictly observed and exceptions thereto are not to be implied." *Id.,* at 275–276.

As in *Soriano,* here Congress "was entitled to assume that the limitation period it prescribed [in § 2000e–16(c)] meant just that period and no more."

The Court deviates from the above cases because it believes that our decisions concerning time requirements "have not been entirely consistent."[2] Even if that belief is well-founded, the doctrine of *stare decisis* demands that we attempt to reconcile our prior decisions rather than hastily overrule some of them. Such an attempt would reveal that *Bowen v.*

2. The Court also asserts that allowing equitable tolling against the Government "is likely to be a realistic assessment of legislative intent." It is unclear, however, why that likelihood, rather than the opposite, is true. The statute here, for example, was enacted in 1972 when the presumption was, as set forth in *Soriano v. United States,* 352 U.S. 270 (1957), that statutes of limitations for suits against the Government were not subject to equitable tolling. It is unlikely that the 1972 Congress had in mind the Court's present departure from that longstanding rule.

City of New York, 476 U.S. 467 (1986), cited by the Court for the alleged inconsistency is not irreconcilable with the cases discussed above. In *Bowen,* we allowed equitable tolling against the Government because, among other things, the statutory time period there, set forth in 42 U.S.C. § 405(g), expressly allowed tolling. Section 405(g) requires that a civil action be filed "within sixty days … *or within such further time as the Secretary may allow.*" See *id.,* at 472, n. 3 (emphasis added). We noted that the provision in that section allowing the Secretary to extend the filing deadline expressed Congress' "clear intention to allow tolling in some cases." *Id.,* at 480. Moreover, we observed that the regulations promulgated by the Secretary governing extensions of time under that provision were based on equitable concerns of fairness to claimants, further "support[ing] our application of equitable tolling." *Id.,* at 480, n. 12. The statute in this case, unlike the one in *Bowen,* does not manifest any "clear intention" by Congress to allow tolling and thus should be subject to the rule articulated in *Soriano, supra.*

Bowen — the statute expressly allowed tolling!

Accordingly, I concur in the judgment because I do not believe that equitable tolling is available as a defense to the 30–day filing requirement, and I would not reach the factual issue of whether equitable tolling is supported by the circumstances of this case.

■ JUSTICE STEVENS, concurring in part and dissenting in part.

(his concurrence is based only on Soriano & Bowen)

While I agree with the Court's conclusion that the filing deadline in 42 U.S.C. § 2000e–16(c) is subject to equitable tolling and that the petitioner has failed to establish a basis for tolling in this case, I do not agree that the 30–day limitations period began to run when petitioner's lawyer, rather than petitioner himself, received notice from the EEOC of petitioner's right to file a civil action. * * *

Notes and Questions

1. In *Library of Congress v. Shaw,* the Supreme Court held that the government was not liable for an award of interest (absent an express statutory provision) under a general waiver of sovereign immunity, even if a private person would be so liable. In *Irwin v. Veterans Affairs,* the Supreme Court held that a limitations period was subject to equitable tolling (even in the absence of an express statutory provision), because equitable tolling would be available in cases involving private parties. Can these two decisions be reconciled? How would you state the canons of statutory construction of waivers of sovereign immunity that describe each result? When a waiver of sovereign immunity exists, how should the courts approach questions of the scope of the waiver or exceptions to the waiver? Do *Shaw* and *Irwin* point in different directions? One possible distinction between the two is that *Shaw* involved the substantive question of the scope of liability in damages under a waiver of sovereign immunity, while *Irwin* involved the procedural question of time limitations for filing a suit under a waiver of sovereign immunity. Is this a principled distinction? For

further discussion of the tension between *Shaw* and *Irwin*, see generally Gregory C. Sisk, *A Primer on the Doctrine of Federal Sovereign Immunity*, 58 Okla. L. Rev. 439, 462–67 (2006).

2. For a period of time after *Irwin*, the Supreme Court appeared set on a course that limited *Irwin* as a precedent and seemed likely over time to confine it to its specific statutory context. In *United States v. Brockamp*, 519 U.S. 347 (1997), the Court refused to permit equitable tolling of the statutory limitations period on filing claims for tax refunds, notwithstanding that the taxpayers involved had suffered disabilities that arguably excused their delay. The Court distinguished *Irwin* by saying that the presumption that limitations periods for claims against the government may be equitably tolled applies to ordinary limitations statutes that "use fairly simple language." *Id.* at 350. By contrast, the Internal Revenue Code "sets forth its limitations in a highly detailed technical manner, that linguistically speaking, cannot easily be read as containing implicit exceptions." *Id.* at 350. The tax statute's "detail, its technical language, the iteration of the limitations in both procedural and substantive forms, and the explicit listing of exceptions, taken together indicate to [the Court] that Congress did not intend courts to read other unmentioned, open-ended 'equitable' exceptions into the statute that it wrote." *Id.* at 352. Similarly, in *United States v. Beggerly*, 524 U.S. 38 (1998), the Court held that equitable tolling is not available in a suit against the United States under the Quiet Title Act, 28 U.S.C. § 2409a. The Court observed that the Quiet Title Act provided an "unusually generous" 12–year limitations period and that the statute already incorporates a form of tolling by providing that the limitations period does not run until the plaintiff "knew or should have known of the claim of the United States" upon the property. *Id.* at 1868. Accordingly, the Court held that equitable tolling was inconsistent with the text of the statute. *Id.*

Thus, while the *Irwin* tolling rule continued to apply to ordinary and simple limitations provisions that did little more than announce a time deadline, the Court appeared increasingly reluctant to give an expansive interpretation to *Irwin* and seemed quick to distinguish it in each successive case. The *Brockamp* decision—particularly in its description of equitable tolling as embracing "unmentioned, open-ended 'equitable' exceptions"—suggested that the Court was becoming less hospitable to equitable or expansive interpretations of waivers of sovereign immunity than when the *Irwin* decision was rendered.

However, more recently, *Irwin*'s more generous approach toward a statutory waiver of sovereign immunity, at least in the context of a procedural time requirement, has received renewed vitality. In *Scarborough v. Principi*, 541 U.S. 401, 420–421 (2004), the Supreme Court relied upon *Irwin* as instructive in another context that also involved a time limitation contained in a waiver of sovereign immunity, although it did not raise the question of equitable estoppel of that limitation. In *Scarborough*, the Court held, over a dissent, that an otherwise-timely application for attorney's fees under the Equal Access to Justice Act, 28 U.S.C. § 2412 (which is ad-

[handwritten margin notes: "Synthesis of subsequent decisions" and "Court renewing Scarborough 2."]

dressed in Chapter VII.B.4 of this Casebook), that did not contain the statutorily-required allegation that the government's position was not "substantially justified" may be amended to cure this defect after the 30–day filing period had expired. In so holding, the Court found the *Irwin* decision to be "enlightening on this issue," because that precedent recognized that limitation principles should apply to the federal government in the same way as to private parties. The Court further said that "[o]nce Congress waives sovereign immunity, we observed [in *Irwin*], judicial application of a time prescription to suits against the Government, in the same way the prescription is applicable to private suits, 'amounts to little, if any, broadening of the congressional waiver.'" Justice Thomas, joined by Justice Scalia, in dissent, argued that the time limitation, including the requirement that the claimant timely set forth each of the required elements for the fee application, was "a condition on the United States' waiver of sovereign immunity," and thus was subject to the strict construction rule, citing *Library of Congress* and other precedents to that effect. *Scarborough*, 541 U.S. 401, 425–27 (Thomas, J., dissenting). Thus, the tension among Supreme Court rulings on the interpretation of waivers of sovereign immunity persists.

———

SECTION D. SUITS AGAINST THE SOVEREIGN AND GOVERNMENTAL IMMUNITY IN OTHER NATIONS

By looking at the concept of sovereign immunity and the circumstances under which a government allows suit against itself, we consider the legitimacy of governmental immunity in a modern society and the proper role of courts in resolving policy issues that may arise in suits against the government. We also learn much about a system of government by examining when and how that government responds (or fails to respond) to injuries inflicted by its agents or activities upon its own citizens and whether it permits litigation to uphold its own contracts.

We may also learn from the experiences of other nations and the choices they have made in terms of legal accountability in the courts for claims raised by people in those countries. In the pages that follow, excerpts of scholarly works examine the legal regime for government liability in three other nations: the United Kingdom (from which the American common law originally was drawn and which still bears many similarities—and also crucial differences—to the United States); France (which like other nations on the continent of Europe has adopted the civil law rather than the common-law approach); and the People's Republic of China (as an example of a government that is not democratically elected nor is structured by separation of powers among departments of government, but which has increasingly moved toward reforms designed to protect the individual interests of its citizens). Because much of our study in the next two chapters will focus on what are characterized as torts in the western legal system (see Chapter III.A) and on contracts (see Chapter IV.A.4), the excerpts that follow focus upon the arrangements made in these three nations with respect to lawsuits alleging tort and contract claims against the national government.

As you read these excerpts, consider these questions: Does that nation uphold a concept of sovereign immunity, either directly or indirectly, in whole or in part? How broadly has the national government made itself amenable to suits for torts or contracts? When there are exceptions to governmental liability, how are those exceptions defined and justified? How effective to you expect these various approaches are toward compensating those who have been injured or suffered an alleged breach of a government contractual responsibility? While perhaps expressed in different legal terms and in the context of different legal systems, do you find any parallels with the concept of federal sovereign immunity as it has evolved, or in how it is applied, in the United States? Your answer to this last question will be even more informed as we explore the limitations on federal government liability in tort and contract in the United States, which are prominent subjects of the next two chapters.

---

1. THE UNITED KINGDOM (GREAT BRITAIN)

James E. Pfander, Governmental Accountability in Europe: A Comparative Assessment

35 George Washington International Law Review 611, 611–617 (2003).
© 2003, The George Washington International Law Review.

A. England and the Rule of Law

As a parliamentary democracy, England relies upon a ministerial system of government that runs the country subject to the oversight of Parliament and the electorate. Although the Queen remains the country's titular monarch, executive power resides in the Prime Minister and the ministers who run the various departments of the government. The judicial system includes local magistrates and justices of the peace, a variety of specialized administrative tribunals, and the various departments of the Supreme Court of Judicature. These departments include the Court of Appeal and the High Court. The High Court acceded to much of the supervisory authority of King's Bench and now presides over the all-purpose action for judicial review that provides the framework within which individuals seek review of administrative action. The law lords, sitting as the House of Lords, act as the court of last resort and hear appeals from the Supreme Court as well as from the supreme courts of Northern Ireland and Scotland.

England continues to adhere to a robust principle of parliamentary supremacy. As a practical matter, parliamentary sovereignty helps to explain both the absence of judicially enforceable constitutional limits on Parliament and the country's dualist refusal to regard international treaties as binding in domestic law except to the extent specified in an incorporating act of Parliament. Courts still exercise a degree of control over the interpretation of legislation and typically presume an unwillingness on Parliament's part to invade certain cherished features of England's unwritten constitution. It remains true, nonetheless, that a clear statement by Parliament controls, even if it works a fundamental change in the structure of government or the rights of individuals.

The judicial role in securing government accountability in England thus consists less of limiting the authority of Parliament than of overseeing the functions of the executive branch. Here, the maxim that the "King (or Queen) can do no wrong" remains true,[12] but as a practical matter operates only in the narrow sphere of lawsuits brought against the Queen in her private capacity. In other realms, the government or Crown can clearly commit wrongs that the courts have the power to review and remedy. As a matter of history, England developed three principal mechanisms with which to control public authorities. First, the court of King's Bench developed the so-called prerogative writs of mandamus, certiorari, prohibition, quo warranto, and habeas corpus, all of which issued in the king's name and secured review of official action. Second, the courts entertained ordinary actions at common law—including trespass, negligence, nuisance, and false imprisonment—against Crown officers. Third, the common law petition of right gave individuals an opportunity to litigate property and contract claims with the government, provided the Crown permitted the action to go forward. As we shall see, these historical remedies continue to shape English notions of government accountability today.

* * *

2. Damages in Tort for Government Wrongs

England has long permitted individuals to file suit against government officials whose actions, unless justified in law, would have been tortious at common law. These officer suits often seek damages in accordance with common law precepts, and liability often turns on whether the official can statutorily justify the tortious conduct. Thus, one could say that a constable on the street corner committed the tort of trespass and false imprisonment if he entered onto private land to make an arrest without legal justification. Similarly, actions against government agents may allege simple negligence or the commission of a nuisance and resulting damages.

---

12. Although the "King could do no wrong" as a rhetorical matter in Blackstone's England, it seems quite clear that this truism meant something other than a complete immunity from government accountability. Indeed, the right of the subject to petition for redress, both to the Crown through the petition of right, and to the courts, through petitions for the issuance of prerogative writs, often provided relief. See James E. Pfander, Sovereign Immunity and the Right to Petition: Toward a First Amendment Right to Pursue Judicial Claims Against the Government, 91 Nw. L. Rev. 899, 926 (1997) (describing a fictionalized account of sovereign immunity in which Blackstone upheld both the ideal of royal prerogative and the rule of law).

For many years, English law imposed important restrictions on the scope of such remedies. First, the central government enjoyed sovereign immunity from suit in tort; plaintiffs could only sue government officers as natural persons and name local government entities as defendants in such actions. Second, vicarious liability followed the rules of sovereign immunity so courts could hold local, but not central governments vicariously liable for the torts. Under English law, the constable worked for the public as a whole, which meant that public funds were unavailable to compensate individuals for harm done by police officers. The constable, needless to say, often lacked funds to provide a complete remedy.

Parliament has in recent years set aside many of the rules that restrict liability in tort. The Crown Proceedings Act of 1947 abrogated the central government's sovereign immunity from suit in tort, making it clear that the Crown bore the same liability as a private party for damages resulting from its actions.[30] Since 1964, moreover, England has provided public funds to compensate victims of police misconduct. As a result, today one can, in principle, bring suit for damages resulting from the tortious acts of any public agent or officer, subject to a few remaining immunities.[32]

If the availability of suit now seems clear, the question of the scope of liability and the proper measure of damages remains in dispute. In general, England has been reluctant to recognize government liability for omissions. To the extent that a claim rests upon conduct that the common law recognizes as a trespass, the plaintiff may recover damages as a matter of course, even without a showing of pecuniary loss. The English courts have tightened the rules governing the availability of punitive damages in suits brought against public officers; however, since 1964, courts may only award such damages where the official in question abuses a public position or seeks to make a profit from his own wrong.

3.   Breach of Government Contracts

Claims against the government for the recovery of property and breach of contract were difficult to pursue at common law. In general, relying upon

---

30.   The Act provides as follows:

Subject to the provisions of this Act, the Crown shall be subject to all those liabilities in tort to which, if it were a private person of full age and capacity, it would be subject:

in respect of torts committed by its servants or agents;

in respect of any breach of those duties which a person owes to his servants or agents at common law by reason of being their employer; and

in respect of any breach of the duties attaching at common law to the ownership, occupation, possession or control of property. . . .

Crown Proceedings Act 1947, c. 44, § 2. Passage of the Act came in the wake of World War II, when the complexity of administrative life overwhelmed the Crown's practice of supplying the name of a "nominal" defendant in actions for personal injury.

32.   Some immunities derive from existing law and apply to all similarly situated defendants, including both Crown departments and private defendants. See, e.g., G.H. Teitel, Crown Proceedings: Some Recent Developments, [1957] Pub. L. 321, 322–26 (describing applicability of defamation defenses to both Crown and private defendants). Other immunities, such as the public interest immunity, may prevent the disclosure of sensitive documents during the discovery phase of a proceeding. See Conway v. Rimmer, [1968] A.C. 910, 920.

a suit against the responsible official did not work. Agents may commit tortious acts for which they bear personal liability in the course of government service, but they typically enter into contracts on behalf of their governmental principal and owe no personal liability for breach of the contract. Thus, the Crown's immunity from suit threatened to defeat liability in any case where the plaintiff sued the government as an entity rather suing its officers or agents.

English law overcame this immunity from suit with the petition of right. As the practice developed, plaintiffs had to submit a petition to the Crown seeking leave to proceed with a claim against money or property of which the Crown was the record owner. Following the issuance of the Crown's fiat or assent to "let right be done to the parties," an action proceeded pursuant to general common law rules. Over time, the consent became something of a formality, and plaintiffs could proceed in actions to test the Crown's title without a royal fiat. In 1860 the Petition of Right Act streamlined proceedings at the request of government contractors, and in 1947, the Crown Proceedings Act further simplified the practice, doing away with all vestiges of the requirement of royal assent.

———

2. FRANCE

James E. Pfander, Governmental Accountability in Europe: A Comparative Assessment

35 George Washington International Law Review 611, 618–619, 623–625, 649–650 (2003).
© 2003, The George Washington International Law Review.

The French Constitution of 1958 established the Fifth Republic, vesting legislative power in a national assembly, executive power in a president, and dividing judicial power among three different institutions. The Court of Cassation has jurisdiction to hear appeals in matters of civil and criminal law. The Constitutional Council has no appellate or reference jurisdiction with respect to the ordinary courts; rather, it performs the somewhat limited function of testing the constitutionality of legislation largely in the abstract, after passage but before promulgation of laws, at the instigation of the political branches of government. Finally, the Conseil d'Etat (Council of State) sits as the nation's highest administrative court, exercising original jurisdiction over certain matters and broader power to hear appeals from the usual first instance administrative courts, the Tribunaux Administratifs. A Court of Conflicts resolves jurisdictional disputes between the ordinary and administrative courts.

   * * *

3. Liability in Tort

French law distinguishes between suits against government officials who bear personal responsibility for the injury (faute personnelle) and suits against the government for actions taken in the scope of official duties (faute de service). Suits against officials in their personal capacity go forward in the ordinary civil courts, whereas actions against the government for course-of-employment torts go forward in the administrative courts. Often, litigants will strain, with some assistance from the Conseil d'Etat, to bring their claims within the bounds of faute de service in order to secure a recovery that the government, rather than a possibly impecunious official, must pay.

French law takes a relatively expansive view of the sorts of administrative faults that give rise to liability. For one thing, simple fault standing alone will often result in liability. Additionally, unlike its U.S. counterpart,[80] French law holds that gross fault or negligence will suffice for the imposition of liability even in the most sensitive areas of policy formation. Finally, and in some ways most interestingly, French administrative law imposes no-fault liability in cases where the state has engaged in conduct that creates a risk of injury; where the predictable injury occurs, the state must compensate the injured.

French liability without fault provides a striking example of the principle that the public must pay the cost of government conduct, and that an unequal burden should not fall upon any particular individual citizen of the nation. The same principle underlies the idea of even-handed taxation and the payment of compensation for governmental takings of private property, ideas that find an expression in Anglo–American public law, but French administrative law presses this notion of equality of burdens well beyond its English counterparts. Thus, the Conseil d'Etat (1) permitted a bank to recover compensation from the Minister of Justice for money lost as a result of a bank robbery conducted by three criminals on parole-like releases from a prison; (2) allowed an injured third party to recover against a local child care agency for injuries inflicted by a child in foster care; and (3) granted the child of a schoolteacher exposed in utero to German measles recovery for injuries from the public school. All of these instances of liability go well beyond what one could imagine in the United States.[84]

4. Liability in Contract

French law recognizes two broad categories of government contracts: concessions and procurement contracts. In a concession, a private firm contracts with the government to supply a particular service, such as water or gas, to local consumers. Although the firm contracts with consumers in such transactions, its concession contract with the government governs its relationship with consumers. In procurement contracts, by contrast, the

---

80. See United States v. Stanley, 483 U.S. 669 (1987) (holding that serviceman could not sue the U.S. government for injuries resulting from non-consensual LSD experiments).

84. Cf. DeShaney v. Winnebago County, 489 U.S. 189 (1998) (holding that the state owes no duty under the Constitution to protect its citizens against invasions by private actors). If the occasions for liability in France extend beyond those in England and the United States, however, the measure of damages may be somewhat less. Until comparatively recently, French law did not recognize public liability for resulting mental loss or anguish.

firm contracts to sell directly to the government. Procurement contracts thus cover the sale of supplies and durable goods to the government, such as cars and office supplies, as well as large-scale construction projects. The government can contract freely with concessionaires, but must generally provide for competitive bidding on procurement contracts. A detailed code of public contract law governs these matters.

Government liability for breach of contract follows as a matter of course from the principle of accountability in French administrative law. In general, French law tends to protect the rights of the contractor to some degree, and has developed a number of doctrines that set out to equalize the relationship. For example, in some cases, the Conseil d'Etat will modify the contract in light of changed circumstances to provide the contractor with protection. In other cases, the contractor may claim an intervening act of the government has interfered with its ability to perform, and necessitates compensation. Other doctrines address intervening changes in circumstances that render performance either uneconomical or impossible.

* * *

Despite its reputation for parliamentary primacy, in contrast, the French system of government accountability relies to a greater extent on judge-made rules. The Conseil d'Etat has long assumed the role of assuring government accountability and has defined such accountability to include both the invalidation of wrongful acts and the award of money damages to individuals who suffer losses. Neither one of these developments had to await the Parliamentary adoption of a supporting administrative code. The Conseil d'Etat has also developed a much more adventuresome set of rules to compensate individuals for the unequal burdens of government activity. Rather than a requirement that men turn square corners with the government, in Holmes's famous phrase,[201] one finds a solicitude in France for those who find themselves unwitting victims of a government program that was, after all, presumably adopted for the benefit of all and should not be permitted to burden the few disproportionately.

---

3. THE PEOPLE'S REPUBLIC OF CHINA

XiXin Wang, Suing the Sovereign Observed From the Chinese Perspective: The Idea and Practice of State Compensation in China

35 George Washington International Law Review 681, 681–82, 684–686, 689 (2003).
© 2003, The George Washington International Law Review.

I. Introduction

Unlike in the United States and other Western democratic societies, the Chinese Constitution of 1982 (Constitution) does not adopt separation

---

201. See Rock Island R. Co. v. United States, 254 U.S. 141, 143 (1920).

of powers as a fundamental principle of setting up the structure of state powers. Instead, the Chinese Constitution embraces the National People's Congress System, which looks like the British parliamentary system to some extent. Under the people's congress system, people's congresses at national level and sub-national levels are sources of state powers, which means both the executive and the judicial powers derive from the people's congress at corresponding levels and are subject to their control.

Because of the people's congress system, a constitutional provision guaranteeing judicial independence, such as Article III of the U.S. Constitution, does not exist. Although the Chinese Constitution declares that the courts shall be independent of any person, organization, or government agency, the courts lack independence for political, legal, personnel, institutional, and financial reasons. For example, the People's Congress or its standing Committee at corresponding levels shall select or approve all court judges, who are subject to removal by the standing committee of the People's Congress at that level. In addition, local people's governments designate—based on administrative regional divisions—and finance the local courts. Subsequently, local governments subject local courts to financial and political control. All of these institutional arrangements have resulted in serious problems in terms of judicial independence, particularly in the context of suing the government.

* * *

III. Suing the Government under the State Compensation System

The 1994 [State Compensation Law] established the state compensation system, requiring the state to compensate for damages caused by state organs——including administrative agencies and judicial organs—which resulted from infringements upon individuals' rights and interests. Article 2 of this law expressly provides that citizens, legal entities, or other organizations have the right to seek compensation from the state if state organs and officers abused their power, infringed upon their legal rights and interests, and caused damages. This provision makes the constitutional promise of state compensation more precise and practical, and lays down the cornerstone of the state compensation system.

A. Types of State Compensation: Administrative versus Criminal

The SCL specifies two kinds of compensation: administrative compensation and criminal compensation. Administrative compensation handles damages caused by administrative agencies or their officers in performing public functions. The state should assume responsibility if government agencies or their staffs abuse their power and infringe upon legal rights and interests of citizens, legal entities, or other organizations. Criminal compensation, sometimes called "judicial compensation," encompasses damages or wrongdoings, which resulted from activities by the police, prosecutor, or the courts in criminal proceedings. For example, unlawful detention of citizens or torture by the police may result in criminal compensation. In practice, administrative compensation is the primary component of state compensation. This is partly because administrative agencies have broad power, so administrators are more likely to infringe upon individuals' rights and partly because individuals believe that seeking criminal compensation is too difficult, if not impossible.

B.   Scope of Administrative Compensation

Not all administrative actions may result in state liability and compensation. In general, only when "concrete administrative actions" have caused damages to liberty or property of individuals can the aggrieved party claim compensation against the state. Individuals cannot challenge agency rules and claim compensation under the state compensation system. Articles 3 and 4 of the SCL specify the scope of compensation. According to the law, the following actions shall fall within the scope of state compensation:

a.   Administrative actions involving restriction or deprivation of citizen's liberty, or physical injuries to citizens. In particular, those actions include (1) to unlawfully detain citizens or adopt unlawful administrative, forceful measures to restrict citizens' liberty; (2) to unlawfully incarcerate citizens or adopt other measures depriving citizens of their corporal freedom; (3) to use violent means such as battering or induce others to use violent means such as battering that has caused physical injuries or death to citizens; (4) to abuse weapons or police devices and cause physical injuries or death to citizens; and (5) other unlawful acts that have caused physical injuries or death to citizens.

b.   Administrative actions involving punishment imposed on citizens or legal entities, such as imposing fines, revoking licenses or permits, ordering suspension of business or confiscation of property.

c.   Administrative compulsory measures involving infringement of property, such as sequestrating, freezing or expropriating of property and other unlawful actions that have caused damages to property.

The SCL also specifies a number of situations in which the state does not assume the liability of compensation, including: (1) personal acts by government employees unrelated to the exercise of official duties; (2) damages caused by acts committed by citizens, legal persons, or other organizations themselves; and (3) other situations as prescribed by law.[11]

* * *

IV.   Concluding Remarks: A Cry for Future Reforms

The legal principle of "suing the sovereign" in China, as summarized above, reveals the ambivalence of the government and contending social-political values in the context of state-individual relationship in this country. In the past two decades, the government initiated and manipulated all legal reforms, and the development of a state compensation system is no

---

11.   This "catch-all" clause is too broad, and potentially leaves great discretion to lawmakers to limit the scope of state compensation. Since there is no effective constitutional review under the current legal system, such catch-all provision may substantially endanger citizen's constitutional rights to state compensation.

exception. In this context, the establishment and improvement of state compensation system revealed the desire and efforts of the government to adapt itself to the changing social and political situations and to reinforce the legitimacy of its governance. At the same time, the current state compensation system also reveals the hesitation and anxiety of the government, as evident in the substantial limits of individuals' right to state compensation, including the scope of state compensation, unreasonably low standards for compensation, the problem of judicial independence, and the like. If we agree that the state compensation system must go beyond mere symbolism, those problems that are plaguing this system both in theory and in practice must be treated seriously.

CHAPTER III

SPECIFIC STATUTORY WAIVERS OF SOVEREIGN IMMUNITY

As introduced by the preceding chapter of this casebook, the concept of sovereign immunity underlies every aspect of litigation with the federal government. For any suit against the government, the plaintiff must find a particular statute that waives the government's sovereign immunity for that type of claim and then must follow the rules set down in that statute. Even when waived by congressional enactment, the power of sovereign immunity persists in the rule of strict construction that the courts generally apply when interpreting such statutes (see Chapter II.C).

To impose some structure for a methodical examination of the long and ever-growing list of statutes that authorize suits against the federal government, its officers, or its agencies, this casebook places statutory waivers of sovereign immunity into two broad collections: specific waivers (Chapter III) and general waivers (Chapter IV). Although this division is somewhat artificial, it is not without a principled basis and it serves to organize the multitude of pertinent statutes into understandable categories. By "Specific Statutory Waivers of Sovereign Immunity," your casebook author means those statutes that waive the government's immunity for particular types of substantive claims, such as the Federal Tort Claims Act for tort claims (Chapter III.A), the Suits in Admiralty Act for admiralty claims (Chapter III.B), Title VII of the Civil Rights Act of 1964 and related statutes for employment discrimination claims (Chapter III.C), etc. In other words, specific statutory waivers are those that are defined by the legal cause of action permitted under the particular statute.

"General Statutory Waivers of Sovereign Immunity" are those enactments that waive governmental immunity for claims seeking a particular type of relief, namely the Tucker Act for non-tort money claims (Chapter IV.A) and the Administrative Procedure Act for specific relief claims (Chapter IV.B). In other words, these statutes waive immunity based primarily upon the relief allowed rather than the substantive nature of the claim or the cause of action. (Of course, there is no true "general" waiver, that is, no statute that completely eliminates sovereign immunity, even for a particular type of claim or relief.)

As the materials in Chapters III and IV of this casebook will reveal, Congress has enacted statutory waivers of sovereign immunity that cover most substantive areas of law and apply to most situations in which a plaintiff would seek relief. (Indeed, the basic subjects that students typically study in the first-year of law school—torts, contracts, property—figure prominently in our study.) But the student should never lose sight of the fact that, because of the doctrine of sovereign immunity, the government always retains advantages and immunities not available to private parties. Moreover, while the statutory waivers of sovereign immunity do create something of a broad network or tapestry of authorized judicial actions against the government, they do not cover everything and each individual waiver is subject to significant exceptions. In addition, as we'll see in Chapter IV.C, some statutes overlap at the edges, which causes interpretive problems, particularly when one of those statutes directs claims to a specialized forum with exclusive jurisdiction.

SECTION A.   THE FEDERAL TORT CLAIMS ACT

1.   INTRODUCTION

Stanley Weintraub, The Last Great Victory: The End of World War II, July/August 1945

294 (1995).

What war might have been like to Americans had enemy technology a little more time to develop came home to New Yorkers when, at 9:49 A.M. on a misty Saturday morning [July 28, 1945], the equivalent of an unguided missile struck the Empire State Building, tallest in the world, 915 feet above street level. A B–25 "Mitchell" bomber, the type of twin-engine plane used for the Doolittle raid on Tokyo in April 1942, lost in blinding fog as it flew west from Squantum Army Air Force Base in Massachusetts, crashed into the seventy-ninth floor and engulfed two stricken floors in fire from its fuel tanks. Sheared off by the impact, its wings fell as fiery debris while the fuselage and motors ripped a hole eighteen feet wide and twenty feet high in the block wall, and the building swayed momentarily in a two-foot arc. One motor hurtled across the seventy-ninth floor, tore through the south wall, and fell to the roof of a twelve-story office building on Thirty-third Street, demolishing a penthouse apartment; the other, along with part of the landing gear, crashed into an elevator shaft, plummeting down a thousand feet to the subcellar.

The pilot, Lieutenant Colonel William F. Smith, Jr., had completed thirty-four bombing missions over Germany safely, but he and two others on board perished high over Manhattan, while ten people in the building, many fewer than would have been at risk on an ordinary working day, died. One man, panicked by the flames, leaped from a window, striking a ledge on the seventy-second floor. Empty elevators dropped eighty stories. Fire trucks materialized by the dozens, choking miles of streets.

Mayor Fiorello LaGuardia's car radio, always tuned to the police band, alerted him to the disaster. He rushed off, siren sounding, to Thirty-fourth Street, announced himself, and climbed to the nearest safe floor to supervise operations. It was almost like the old days, when he was Franklin Roosevelt's bumbling first Director of Civilian Defense—an appointment many took as reassurance to Americans that its cities would never be bombed. "If the pilot had been up there where he belonged," said the Mayor, "there would have been no trouble."

————

1 Lester S. Jayson & Robert C. Longstreth, Handling Federal Tort Claims

§ 2.01, at 2–3 to 2–4 (1999).*

On the morning of July 28, 1945, the nation was startled by radio news broadcasts reporting that an airplane had struck the Empire State Building, located in the heart of Manhattan, killing and seriously injuring a number of people in the building or on the streets, and causing extensive property damage. The aircraft was identified as a United States Army bomber piloted by a serviceman who was flying incredibly low over mid-New York. The victims of this frightful accident must have been shocked to learn later from their attorneys that there was no judicial remedy available to them through which they could recover damages from the United States Government. The doctrine of sovereign immunity from suit provided an insurmountable barrier.

Twelve months later, on August 2, 1946, the Federal Tort Claims Act became law. That Act constituted a broad waiver of the immunity of the United States from suit in tort. It conferred jurisdiction upon the United States District Courts on claims for damages "for injury or loss of property, or personal injury or death caused by the negligent or wrongful act or omission of any employee of the Government while acting within the scope of his office or employment, under circumstances where the United States, if a private person, would be liable to the claimant in accordance with the law of the place where the act or omission occurred."[2] Although the Act was, by its terms, made applicable to all claims accruing on and after January 1, 1945, thus providing a remedy to the victims of the Empire State Building crash,[4] it was not that accident which caused the Government to relinquish what had been described by the Supreme Court as its "exceptional freedom from legal responsibility" for the tortious acts of its employees. Rather, the enactment of the Federal Tort Claims Act in 1946

some text

2.   28 U.S.C. § 1346(b).

4.   Victims of this crash were among the first to bring suit against the United States under the FTCA. See Commissioners of the State Ins. Fund v. United States, 72 F. Supp. 549 (S.D.N.Y.1947).

had been preceded by "nearly thirty years of congressional consideration"[6] involving "drafting and redrafting, amendment and counter-amendment" of many legislative proposals.[7] Actually, * * * it had been preceded by more than a century of legislative deliberation accompanied by inequity and hardship suffered by other victims of the torts, misfeasance, or wrongful conduct of federal employees and representatives, whose only remedy against the Government was the desperate one of an appeal to Congress to enact a private relief measure.

---

2.   PREREQUISITES TO SUIT

28 United States Code § 2401(b)

(b) A tort claim against the United States shall be forever barred unless it is presented in writing to the appropriate Federal agency within two years after such claim accrues or unless action is begun within six months after the date of mailing, by certified or registered mail, of notice of final denial of the claim by the agency to which it was presented.

28 United States Code § 2675

(a) An action shall not be instituted upon a claim against the United States for money damages for injury or loss of property or personal injury or death caused by the negligent or wrongful act or omission of any employee of the Government while acting within the scope of his office or employment, unless the claimant shall have first presented the claim to the appropriate Federal agency and his claim shall have been finally denied by the agency in writing and sent by certified or registered mail. The failure of an agency to make final disposition of a claim within six months after it is filed shall, at the option of the claimant any time thereafter, be deemed a final denial of the claim for purposes of this section. The provisions of this subsection shall not apply to such claims as may be asserted under the Federal Rules of Civil Procedure by third party complaint, cross-claim, or counterclaim.

(b) Action under this section shall not be instituted for any sum in excess of the amount of the claim presented to the federal agency, except where the increased amount is based upon newly discovered evidence not reasonably discoverable at the time of presenting the claim to the federal agency, or upon allegation and proof of intervening facts, relating to the amount of the claim.

---

6. Dalehite v. United States, 346 US 15, 24 (1953).

7. United States v. Spelar, 338 US 217, 219–220 (1949).

(c) Disposition of any claim by the Attorney General or other head of a federal agency shall not be competent evidence of liability or amount of damages.

———

McNeil v. United States

United States Supreme Court.
508 U.S. 106 (1993).

— Strict interpretation
Timing of filing
— prior exhaustation

■ JUSTICE STEVENS delivered the opinion of the Court.

The Federal Torts Claims Act (FTCA) provides that an "action shall not be instituted upon a claim against the United States for money damages" unless the claimant has first exhausted his administrative remedies. The question presented is whether such an action may be maintained when the claimant failed to exhaust his administrative remedies prior to filing suit, but did so before substantial progress was made in the litigation.

I

On March 6, 1989, petitioner, proceeding without counsel, lodged a complaint in the United States District Court for the Northern District of Illinois, alleging that the United States Public Health Service had caused him serious injuries while "conducting human research and experimentation on prisoners" in the custody of the Illinois Department of Corrections. He invoked the federal court's jurisdiction under the FTCA and prayed for a judgment of $20 million.

— McNeil files under
FTCA on 3/6/1989

Four months later, on July 7, 1989, petitioner submitted a claim for damages to the Department of Health and Human Services.[2] The Department denied the claim on July 21, 1989. On August 7, 1989, petitioner sent a letter to the District Court enclosing a copy of the Department's denial of his administrative claim and an affidavit in support of an earlier motion for appointment of counsel. Petitioner asked that the court accept the letter "as a proper request, whereas plaintiff can properly commence his legal action accordingly."

— Files for admin. relief
7/7/1989
— 7/21/1989 —
fed. agency denies

For reasons that are not entirely clear, the United States was not served with a copy of petitioner's complaint until July 30, 1990. On September 19, 1990, the United States moved to dismiss the complaint on the ground that petitioner's action was barred by the 6–month statute of limitation. The motion was based on the assumption that the complaint had been filed on April 15, 1990, when petitioner paid the court filing fees, and that that date was more than six months after the denial of petitioner's

— 7/30/1990 —
U.S. is served
·M Dismiss
· SOL
28 USC 2401
(b)

---

2. Petitioner sought damages of $500,000 in his administrative claim, not the $20 million for which he prayed in his earlier federal court action. Pursuant to 28 U.S.C. § 2675(b), a claimant is barred from seeking in federal court "any sum in excess of the amount of the claim presented to the federal agency." That is, had petitioner properly filed an action in district court after his administrative claim was denied, he would have been limited in his recovery to $500,000.

administrative claim. In response to the motion, petitioner submitted that the complaint was timely because his action had been commenced on March 6, 1989, the date when he actually lodged his complaint and the Clerk assigned it a docket number.

The District Court accepted March 6, 1989 as the operative date of filing, but nonetheless granted the Government's motion to dismiss. Petitioner's suit was not out-of-time, the District Court reasoned, but, rather, premature. The Court concluded that it lacked jurisdiction to entertain an action "commenced before satisfaction of the administrative exhaustion requirement under § 2675(a)."

The Court of Appeals for the Seventh Circuit affirmed. The court explained:

> "According to 28 U.S.C. § 2401(b), a tort claim against the United States must be 'begun within six months after the date of mailing . . . of notice of final denial of the claim by the agency to which it was presented.' The administrative denial was mailed on July 21, 1989, so McNeil had between then and January 21, 1990, to begin his action. The complaint filed in March 1989 was too early. This left two options. Perhaps the document filed in March 1989 loitered on the docket, springing into force when the agency acted. Or perhaps the request for counsel in August 1989, during the six-month period, marks the real 'beginning' of the action. The district court rejected both options, and McNeil, with the assistance of counsel appointed by this court, renews the arguments here.
>
> . . .
>
> "March 1989 was too early. The suit did not linger, awaiting administrative action. Unless McNeil began a fresh suit within six months after July 21, 1989, he loses." 964 F.2d 647, 648–649 (1992).

The court reviewed the materials filed in August 1989 and concluded that the District Court had not committed plain error in refusing to construe them as having commenced a new action.[5]

Because decisions in other Circuits permit a prematurely filed FTCA action to proceed if no substantial progress has taken place in the litigation before the administrative remedies are exhausted, we granted certiorari to resolve the conflict.

II

As the case comes to us, we assume that the Court of Appeals correctly held that nothing done by petitioner after the denial of his administrative

---

5. In dissent, Judge Ripple expressed the opinion that petitioner had properly raised the issue in the District Court and on appeal, 964 F.2d, at 649, n. 1, and that in any event it was "clear that the plaintiff, a prisoner proceeding pro se, attempted to refile the action after the denial of the administrative claim." *Id.*, at 649. Our grant of certiorari did not encompass the question whether a new action had been filed in August and we therefore express no opinion as to the correctness of the Court of Appeals' ruling on that issue.

claim on July 21, 1989, constituted the commencement of a new action. The narrow question before us is whether his action was timely either because it was commenced when he lodged his complaint with the District Court on March 6, 1989, or because it should be viewed as having been "instituted" on the date when his administrative claim was denied.

The text of the statute requires rejection of the first possibility. The command that an "action shall not be instituted ... unless the claimant shall have first presented the claim to the appropriate Federal agency and his claim shall have been finally denied by the agency in writing and sent by certified or registered mail" is unambiguous. We are not free to rewrite the statutory text. As of March 6, 1989, petitioner had neither presented his claim to the Public Health Service, nor had his claim been "finally denied" by that agency. As the Court of Appeals held, petitioner's complaint was filed too early.

Ct: Petitioner filed claim too early

The statutory text does not speak with equal clarity to the argument that petitioner's subsequent receipt of a formal denial from the agency might be treated as the event that "instituted" his action. Petitioner argues the word "instituted" that is used in § 2675(a), is not synonymous with the word "begun" in § 2401(b), or with the word "commence" as used in certain other statutes and rules. He suggests that an action is not "instituted" until the occurrence of the events that are necessary predicates to the invocation of the court's jurisdiction—namely, the filing of his complaint and the formal denial of the administrative claim. This construction, he argues, is consistent with the underlying purpose of § 2675(a): As long as no substantial progress has been made in the litigation by the time the claimant has exhausted his administrative remedies, the federal agency will have had a fair opportunity to investigate and possibly settle the claim before the parties must assume the burden of costly and time-consuming litigation.[7]

Pet's Arg

We find this argument unpersuasive. In its statutory context, we think the normal interpretation of the word "institute" is synonymous with the words "begin" and "commence." The most natural reading of the statute indicates that Congress intended to require complete exhaustion of Execu-

Ct: Institution, filing, of the suit can only come after exhaustion

---

7. Prior to 1966, FTCA claimants had the option of filing suit in federal court without first presenting their claims to the appropriate federal agency. Moreover, federal agencies had only limited authority to settle claims. See Federal Tort Claims Act of 1946, ch. 753, §§ 403(a), 420, 60 Stat. 843, 845. Because the vast majority of claims ultimately were settled before trial, the Department of Justice proposed that Congress amend the FTCA to "requir[e] all claims to be presented to the appropriate agency for consideration and possible settlement before a court action could be instituted. This procedure would make it possible for the claim first to be considered by the agency whose employee's activity allegedly caused the damage. That agency would have the best information concerning the activity which gave rise to the claim. Since it is the one directly concerned, it can be expected that claims which are found to be meritorious can be settled more quickly without the need for filing suit and possible expensive and time-consuming litigation." S.Rep. No. 1327, 89th Cong., 2d Sess., 3 (1966).

The Senate Judiciary Committee further noted that "the improvements contemplated by [the 1966 amendments] would not only benefit private litigants, but would also be beneficial to the courts, the agencies, and the Department of Justice itself." *Id.*, at 2.

tive remedies before invocation of the judicial process. Every premature filing of an action under the FTCA imposes some burden on the judicial system and on the Department of Justice which must assume the defense of such actions. Although the burden may be slight in an individual case, the statute governs the processing of a vast multitude of claims. The interest in orderly administration of this body of litigation is best served by adherence to the straight-forward statutory command.

Moreover, given the clarity of the statutory text, it is certainly not a "trap for the unwary." It is no doubt true that there are cases in which a litigant proceeding without counsel may make a fatal procedural error, but the risk that a lawyer will be unable to understand the exhaustion requirement is virtually nonexistent. Our rules of procedure are based on the assumption that litigation is normally conducted by lawyers. While we have insisted that the pleadings prepared by prisoners who do not have access to counsel be liberally construed,[9] and have held that some procedural rules must give way because of the unique circumstance of incarceration, we have never suggested that procedural rules in ordinary civil litigation should be interpreted so as to excuse mistakes by those who proceed without counsel. As we have noted before, "in the long run, experience teaches that strict adherence to the procedural requirements specified by the legislature is the best guarantee of evenhanded administration of the law." *Mohasco Corp. v. Silver*, 447 U.S. 807, 826 (1980).

The FTCA bars claimants from bringing suit in federal court until they have exhausted their administrative remedies. Because petitioner failed to heed that clear statutory command, the District Court properly dismissed his suit.

The judgment of the Court of Appeals is

Affirmed.

Kokotis v. United States Postal Service

United States Court of Appeals for the Fourth Circuit.
223 F.3d 275 (4th Cir. 2000).

■ WILKINSON, CHIEF JUDGE.

Evelyn Mae Kokotis alleges injury due to the negligence of a United States Postal Service employee. Kokotis filed an administrative claim with the Postal Service within months of the accident, but failed to demand a sum certain until four months after the two-year statute of limitations had expired. The district court granted the Postal Service's motion to dismiss, holding that Kokotis' failure to provide a timely demand for a sum certain deprived the court of jurisdiction under the Federal Tort Claims Act, 28 U.S.C. § § 2671 et seq. (1994). In so doing, the district court also found that Kokotis' demand for a sum certain after the limitations period had

---

9. Again, the question whether the Court of Appeals should have liberally construed petitioner's letter of August 7, 1989, as instituting a new action is not before us. See n. 5, *supra*.

expired was not an amendment of a prior claim. Finding no error, we affirm.

I.

On October 29, 1995, Evelyn Kokotis was injured in an auto accident. The collision was allegedly due to the negligence of a Postal Service employee. Two days later, Kokotis was sent a Standard Form 95 (SF 95) to facilitate the filing of an administrative claim pursuant to the Federal Tort Claims Act (FTCA). A letter from the Postal Service accompanied the SF 95. The letter explained in multiple places, and in boldface and capitalized text, that Kokotis had two years to file a complete claim. The letter also stated, in boldface text, that for a claim to be considered complete an exact sum certain dollar amount must be included. Moreover, the SF 95 itself included numerous similar warnings. The form even indicated in italics above the entry for the total amount of the claim that *"[f]ailure to specify may cause forfeiture of your rights."* The box above the space for the claimant's signature on the SF 95 contained the following language in boldface capitals: *"I certify that the amount of claim covers only damages and injuries caused by the accident above and agree to accept said amount in full satisfaction and final settlement of this claim."*

In December 1995, approximately one month after the accident, Kokotis filed an SF 95 with the Postal Service without including a sum certain. Instead, the cover letter accompanying the form stated that Kokotis was still undergoing medical treatment and included an itemization of Kokotis' medical bills to date. Kokotis submitted supplemental letters to the Postal Service on February 27, 1996, March 25, 1996, December 12, 1996, August 21, 1997, and January 22, 1998. As of the August 21, 1997 letter (the last letter sent before the statute of limitations expired), the total damages claimed were $4,546.79. Kokotis finished the medical treatment for her accident on September 25, 1997, approximately one month before the statute of limitations expired.

On March 3, 1998, four months after the statute of limitations had expired but prior to final agency action, Kokotis submitted a revised SF 95 requesting a sum certain in the amount of $19,000. The Postal Service denied Kokotis' claim. The Postal Service explained that since the claim was not completed within the FTCA's two-year limitations period, it could not be considered. Kokotis' request for reconsideration of this decision was denied.

Kokotis filed suit for damages against the Postal Service on March 12, 1999. The Postal Service moved to dismiss the complaint for lack of subject matter jurisdiction. The district court granted the motion, holding that Kokotis' failure to identify a sum certain within the two-year statute of limitations deprived it of jurisdiction over her suit. The district court also declined to toll the statute of limitations on the grounds that there was no misleading conduct by the United States. Kokotis now appeals.

II.

Kokotis seeks to recover against the government under the limited waiver of sovereign immunity embodied in the FTCA. Sovereign immunity

Strict Const
of waiv. S.I.
under the FTCA

(R)

These procedural
requirements are
jurisdictional

can be waived only by the sovereign; the circumstances of its waiver must be scrupulously observed and not expanded by the courts. *See United States v. Kubrick,* 444 U.S. 111, 117–18 (1979). Precisely because the FTCA constitutes a waiver of sovereign immunity, plaintiffs like Kokotis must file an FTCA action in careful compliance with its terms. A key jurisdictional prerequisite to filing suit under the FTCA involves the presentation of an administrative claim to the government within two years of the incident. *See* 28 U.S.C. § 2401(b) (1994) (a tort claim "shall be forever barred unless it is presented in writing to the appropriate Federal agency within two years after such claim accrues...."). Moreover, "the requirement of filing an administrative claim is jurisdictional and may not be waived." *Henderson v. United States,* 785 F.2d 121, 123 (4th Cir.1986).

Req. of a
SF95 + Sum Cert.
a proper presentation

An administrative claim must be properly presented. The FTCA's implementing regulations consider a claim to be properly presented when the government receives a completed SF 95 (or other written notification of an incident), *and* "a claim for money damages *in a sum certain....*" 28 C.F.R. § 14.2(a) (1999) (emphasis added). Requesting a sum certain is a necessary element of any FTCA administrative claim. Failure to request a sum certain within the statute of limitations deprives a district court of jurisdiction over any subsequently filed FTCA suit.

Purpose of
the sum-
certain requirement

agency appropriations
vs.
other appropriations

The sum certain requirement is not a trap for the unwary. Rather, this requirement allows an agency to assess a claim's settlement value. Since the FTCA links both the authority to settle a claim and the source of settlement funds to the amount of the underlying claim, the Act's purpose is frustrated if the administrative claim does not indicate a specific amount of money. For example, claims of $2,500 or less can be settled on the authority of "[t]he head of each Federal agency or his designee" and are paid "out of appropriations available to that agency." 28 U.S.C. § 2672 (1994). Claims of between $2,500 and $25,000 can be settled on the same authority, but are paid out of a separate appropriation. Finally, claims in excess of $25,000 can only be settled "with the prior written approval of the Attorney General or his designee."

Jud.
- Economy

Rationale

If FTCA plaintiffs were allowed to pursue Kokotis' preferred route of not submitting a sum certain, the government's ability to determine a claim's value would be impaired. This, in turn, might push the government toward several unsatisfactory options: (1) channel all decisions to the highest levels in order to assure the decision to settle was made by someone authorized to do so; or (2) resist or postpone settlement so long as the amount of the claim could not be ascertained. Either way, the burden on the government would increase and the FTCA's goal of efficiently handling claims against the government would be undermined.

III.

A.

Notwithstanding the government's general interest in the sum certain requirement, Kokotis asserts that the requirement should not strictly be applied against her. She first contends she provided enough information to the Postal Service, in the form of periodic supplemental letters, for the agency to estimate the value of her claim. We disagree. Kokotis provides no explanation for how the Postal Service could have predicted a 418% increase in the size of her claim. Kokotis' last pre-statute of limitations supplemental letter of August 21, 1997 indicated total damages of $4,546.79; her post-statute of limitations request sought $19,000.* Moreover, even if Kokotis were correct that the Postal Service could somehow have estimated the value of her claim, she cannot escape the FTCA's unwavering requirement of submission of a sum certain within two years of the incident. No exception exists for cases where the agency might have been able to estimate the value of a claim, and courts cannot insert into the FTCA administrative process special provisions that the statute does not contain.

Kokotis next argues that she could not submit a sum certain before her treatment was complete and the extent of her injuries were known. While the record indicates that Kokotis' last medical treatment occurred one month before the filing period expired, that fact is beside the point. Every limitations period embodies the possibility that a complaint must be filed before the claimant's knowledge is complete. That possibility, however, affords no basis for disregarding the interest of finality embodied in a statute of limitations that a legislative body has chosen to enact.

Kokotis advances one further argument for why she should be excused from the sum certain requirement. She claims that she did not estimate her damages for fear that a low figure would be settled quickly and that a high figure would discourage settlement altogether. Such strategic calculations on the part of a claimant cannot be allowed to set aside the conditions attached to a sovereign immunity waiver. Standardized requirements promote the efficient resolution of large volumes of claims. The assessment of individual claimants of their own settlement prospects cannot be permitted to supersede the regulatory requirements to which all other claimants are expected to adhere.

B.

Kokotis next argues that because she presented a sum certain before final action on her claim, it is an amendment that relates back to her December 1995 filing. We disagree. An amendment of a claim can only occur if a complete claim, including a sum certain, is filed before the statute of limitations expires. The regulation states that "a claim shall be deemed to have been presented when the U.S. Postal Service receives ... *a claim for money damages in a sum certain....*" 39 C.F.R. § 912.5(a) (emphasis added). Since Kokotis' December 1995 filing did not include a sum certain, it was not "presented" within the meaning of § 912.5(a). The regulation further states that only a "claim *presented in compliance with [§ 912.5(a)]*"

---

* Kokotis does not claim that this letter was a submission of a sum certain. And the district court correctly noted that submitting information in "dribs and drabs" does not satisfy the sum certain requirement.

Amendment ≠ Complete the statement of a claim

can be amended before final agency action. 39 C.F.R. § 912.5(b) (emphasis added). Since Kokotis' original filing did not include a sum certain, it was not presented in compliance with § 912.5(a) and therefore not subject to amendment under § 912.5(b).

Moreover, the fact that there had been no final agency action is irrelevant given the absence of a sum certain in Kokotis' initial filing.

The Postal Service took no action on Kokotis' claim before March 3, 1998 because effectively there was no claim filed. Only when Kokotis finally submitted a sum certain could the Postal Service take action, and by that time Kokotis' claim was untimely. A rule allowing amendments to incomplete claims after the statute of limitations had expired would undermine Congress' intent to have FTCA claims presented within two years of the relevant incident.

C.

Q: Whether to Equitably toll it

• Requires π's diligence

• and presence of deception / concealment

Kokotis' final argument is that even if she failed to satisfy the sum certain requirement before the limitations period expired, the statute of limitations should be equitably tolled. Equitable tolling is not appropriate where, as was the case here, "the claimant failed to exercise due diligence in preserving his legal rights." *Irwin v. Dep't of Veterans Affairs,* 498 U.S. 89, 96 (1990). The SF 95 Kokotis signed contained several warnings on the consequences of failing to state a sum certain. The warnings appeared in multiple locations and in boldface. The same warnings also appeared separately in the letter that accompanied the SF 95. Kokotis' failure to heed these clear and repetitive warnings makes equitable tolling inappropriate.

Moreover, because of the importance of respecting limitations periods, equitable tolling is appropriate only "where the defendant has wrongfully deceived or misled the plaintiff in order to conceal the existence of a cause of action." *English v. Pabst Brewing Co.,* 828 F.2d 1047, 1049 (4th Cir.1987). Indeed, the doctrine of equitable tolling is based on the view that a defendant should not be encouraged to engage in "misconduct that prevents the plaintiff from filing his or her claim on time." *English,* 828 F.2d at 1049. In this case no evidence or allegation of misconduct by the Postal Service exists. The absence of a Postal Service objection to Kokotis' failure to submit a sum certain does not resemble the kind of misconduct required to equitably toll a limitations period.

IV.

For the foregoing reasons, the judgment of the district court is *AFFIRMED.*

Notes

1. Under Sections 2401(b) and 2675 of Title 28 of the United States Code, as a prerequisite to later institution of court action, a potential FTCA plaintiff must:

(1) present an administrative claim in writing, that is, provide written notice of the claim,

(2) to the appropriate agency, that is, the agency out of whose actions the claim arose,

(3) stating a sum certain request for damages,

(4) within two years of accrual of the claim.

2. To fully understand *McNeil v. United States*, chart out the chronology of procedural events. Where did the plaintiff go wrong? What term in the statute regarding the administrative claim requirement proves dispositive and how does the Court interpret that term? Why is the Supreme Court unwilling to excuse this procedural mistake? What difference does the order of events make as long as we get to the same point, a pending lawsuit after denial of an administrative claim, in the end? Does the plaintiff get any leniency from the Court based upon his pro se status? Why not? Is there a plausible argument that the pro se plaintiff should be understood to have instituted a new lawsuit after the denial of the administrative claim? Although the district court had rejected that argument, what do you think? In any event, if you were advising a client regarding a potential FTCA claim, what simple rule is clearly established by the statute as interpreted by the Court in *McNeil*?

3. In addition to the absolute requirement that an administrative claim be filed with the appropriate agency before any judicial proceedings, Section 2675 precludes a plaintiff from instituting a lawsuit for "any sum in excess of the amount of the claim presented to the federal agency." In *Kokotis v. United States Postal Service*, the court of appeals addressed this "sum-certain" requirement. What is the nature of the requirement? How did the plaintiff err? Why do you suppose the plaintiff failed to timely comply with the sum-certain requirement? Is there any indication that the plaintiff thought she was providing sufficient information to make the administrative claim viable? What justifications or excuses are asserted by the plaintiff for the delay in specifying the total sum certain amount? What should the plaintiff have done under the circumstances? Why does the court regard the sum certain requirement as so important? Beyond the textual statutory mandate, what purpose does it serve?

4. As the Supreme Court comments in footnote 7 in its *McNeil v. United States* opinion, the purpose of the administrative claim requirement is to allow the agency to consider possible settlement " 'without the need for filing suit and possible expensive and time-consuming litigation' " (quoting S. Rep. No. 1327, 89th Cong., 2d Sess. 3 (1966)). The Court further observes in *McNeil* that every filing "imposes some burden on the judicial system and on the Department of Justice which must assume the defense of such actions." Jeffrey Axelrad, the director of the Federal Tort Claims Act Staff of the Civil Division at the Department of Justice, argues that the administrative claim process has been a highly-successful alternative dispute resolution tool. Jeffrey Axelrad, *Federal Tort Claims Act Administrative Claims: Better Than Third–Party ADR for Resolving Feder-*

handwritten margin notes:
"not instituted.."
"unless first presented.
"unless... finally denied."
. Strict adherence to words
. Ct. not @ liberty to expand
   sov. imm.
Not prop. filed
until it is
filed w/ the
correct agency

Gives gov't idea
— of settlement prospects
— Procedural

al Tort Claims, 52 Admin. L. Rev. 1331 (2000). He reports that the vast majority of FTCA claims are resolved efficiently, through informal interaction between the claimant and the government, without the added time and delay of involving third-party neutrals, such as mediators or arbitrators, much less involving judicial actors and process through litigation. *Id.* at 1342–44.

5.   Substantial litigation also has focused upon the adequacy of the description of the "claim" in the submission to the appropriate agency or department. In general, the courts have held that the jurisdictional requirement is satisfied by merely providing notice of the nature of the claim, although more information and substantiation of the claim may be required by the agency as part of the settlement process. *Santiago–Ramirez v. Secretary of Defense,* 984 F.2d 16, 19 (1st Cir. 1993). To provide sufficient notice and preserve the right to file a later lawsuit, the courts have held that the claimant must file "(1) a written statement sufficiently describing the injury to enable the agency to begin its own investigation, and (2) a sum-certain damages claim." *GAF Corp. v. United States,* 818 F.2d 901, 919 (D.C.Cir. 1987); *see also Ahmed v. United States,* 30 F.3d 514, 517 (4th Cir. 1994); *Santiago-Ramirez,* 984 F.2d at 19; *Adkins v. United States,* 896 F.2d 1324, 1326 (11th Cir. 1990).

In many respects, this standard appears similar to the notice pleading requirement for complaints under Federal Rule of Civil Procedure 8. Sufficient information must be provided so that the government may reasonably begin investigation and determine whether to settle the claim. Indeed, some courts have viewed the standard as even more minimal than notice pleading. *See Burchfield v. United States,* 168 F.3d 1252, 1255 (11th Cir. 1999) (holding that the amount of information required in the administrative claim is "minimal," need only be enough "to allow the agency to 'begin its own investigation,'" and need not "provide the agency with a preview of his or her lawsuit by reciting every possible theory of recovery"). However, at least one other court of appeals has adopted a higher standard, saying that, while "resembl[ing] a civil complaint in not requiring a statement of legal theories," the administrative claim requirement is "more demanding" by requiring "a detailed statement of facts." *Murrey v. United States,* 73 F.3d 1448, 1452 (7th Cir. 1996).

In any event, the claimant plainly cannot present one claim based upon one set of facts and then seek to raise a second claim in court based upon a different set of facts, even if related and arising from the same general episode. For example, in *Roma v. United States,* 344 F.3d 352, 358–59 (3d Cir. 2003), a town firefighter filed a proper administrative claim alleging that he suffered smoke inhalation injuries when a Naval facility firefighter negligently ordered him to remove his breathing apparatus. However, the court of appeals refused to permit the plaintiff in his FTCA lawsuit to also pursue an allegation that the government was liable for his injuries because other government employees had contributed to the cause of the fire, reasoning that "[t]he facts concerning how the fire started and any negligence by federal employees in failing to prevent it are entirely distinct from the conduct involved in supervising the firefighting operations." *Id.* at 362–63. For further discussion of what constitutes proper notice in an FTCA administrative claim, and the division in the federal courts on some aspects of this question, see generally Gregory C. Sisk, *Litigation With the Federal Government* § 3.03(a)(3), at 108–11 (ALI–ABA, 4th ed. 2006).

6.   Under Department of Justice regulations, 28 C.F.R. § 14.2(a), a proper administrative claim must not only provide (1) notification of the incident, and (2) a demand for a sum certain, but also (3) the title or capacity of the person signing the claim, and (4) evidence of this person's authority to represent the claimant. Thus, the attorney should provide evidence, such as a power of attorney signed by the client, that he or she is authorized to represent the claimant. As the United States Court of Appeals for the Seventh Circuit noted, the courts of appeals are divided on the issue of whether the Department of Justice has authority to issue regulations establishing the claim requirements and whether an administrative claim must include evidence of the attorney's authority to represent the claimant. *Kanar v. United States,* 118 F.3d 527, 528–29 (7th Cir. 1997). The Seventh Circuit held that the Department of Justice regulation does establish the elements of a claim, but also explained that the court is willing to waive harmless noncompliance with the details of the regulations when the party's attorney promptly acts to correct those errors. *Id.* at 530–31.

7.   It is also important to note that the administrative claim must be presented to the proper agency within the statutory time period. 28 U.S.C. § 2401(b). Thus, the claimant must ascertain which agency's activities give rise to the claim. By regulation, 28 C.F.R. § 14.2(b)(1), an agency that receives a mistakenly delivered claim "shall transfer it forthwith to the appropriate agency if the proper agency can be identified from the claim." But the claim is regarded as presented to the proper agency only on the date it is actually received by the transferee agency.

On rare occasions involving inordinate governmental delay, a court will treat a claim as timely filed if it was sent to the wrong agency and transferred to the right one after the two-year statute of limitations had expired. Thus, when an agency fails to promptly effect a transfer, as required by the regulation, the claim may be treated as "constructively" filed even though it did not reach the proper agency until after the limitations period had expired. *See, e.g., Bukala v. United States,* 854 F.2d 201 (7th Cir. 1988); *Greene v. United States,* 872 F.2d 236, 237 (8th Cir. 1989). By contrast, when the failure to timely present the claim to the correct agency is not attributable to dilatory conduct on the part of the government, a claim will not be treated as timely when later transferred to the proper agency after the limitations period has passed. When "a claimant waits until the eleventh hour to file and, despite notification of the appropriate agency, the filing is misdirected, there is no compelling reason for allowing constructive filing." *Hart v. Department of Labor,* 116 F.3d 1338, 1341 (10th Cir. 1997).

[handwritten margin note: Gov't is subject to the procedural rules, too!]

8. Lest it be thought that the technical prerequisites governing a tort claim against the government apply only to claimants, the United States Court of Appeals for the Fifth Circuit in *Flory v. United States,* 138 F.3d 157 (5th Cir. 1998), reinstated a plaintiff's FTCA suit, which had been dismissed in the district court as untimely, because of the government's error. The government had failed to abide by the statutory requirement that its denial of the administrative claim be mailed to the claimant "by certified or registered mail." 28 U.S.C. § 2675(a). Instead, the government sent its denial letter by regular mail. For that reason, the plaintiff argued that the six-month period of limitations for filing suit after administrative denial had not been properly triggered. The government argued that it should be excused from the certified or registered mail requirement as it was undisputed that the plaintiff had received actual notice by regular mail. The court of appeals, however, noted that the government had previously obtained a dismissal of the same plaintiff's earlier timely FTCA suit because he had failed to serve the Attorney General as required by Federal Rule of Civil Procedure 4(i), even though the United States had received actual notice of the suit through service upon the United States Attorney. In other words, the government had regarded actual notice as insufficient when the plaintiff made a technical error in service of the complaint, but the government was now arguing that actual notice was sufficient when its own error was at issue. For this reason, the court found that the government did not come into court with "clean hands" and thus was not entitled to an actual-notice exception to the certified-and-registered-mail rule on the facts of this particular case. *Flory,* 138 F.3d at 160.

[handwritten margin note: - Knowledge of the injury - duty of π to follow up]

United States v. Kubrick

Supreme Court of the United States.
444 U.S. 111 (1979).

■ MR. JUSTICE WHITE delivered the opinion of the Court.

Under the Federal Tort Claims Act (Act), 28 U.S.C. § 2401(b), a tort claim against the United States is barred unless it is presented in writing to the appropriate federal agency "within two years after such claim accrues." The issue in this case is whether the claim "accrues" within the meaning of the Act when the plaintiff knows both the existence and the cause of his injury or at a later time when he also knows that the acts inflicting the injury may constitute medical malpractice.

[handwritten margin note: circled I]

I

Respondent Kubrick, a veteran, was admitted to the Veterans' Administration (VA) hospital in Wilkes–Barre, Pa., in April 1968, for treatment of an infection of the right femur. Following surgery, the infected area was irrigated with neomycin, an antibiotic, until the infection cleared. Approximately six weeks after discharge, Kubrick noticed a ringing sensation in his ears and some loss of hearing. An ear specialist in Scranton, Pa., Dr. Soma,

[handwritten margin note: 4/1968 - treatment w/ neomycin]

diagnosed the condition as bilateral nerve deafness. His diagnosis was confirmed by other specialists. One of them, Dr. Sataloff, secured Kubrick's VA hospital records and in January 1969, informed Kubrick that it was highly possible that the hearing loss was the result of the neomycin treatment administered at the hospital. Kubrick, who was already receiving disability benefits for a service-connected back injury, filed an application for an increase in benefits pursuant to 38 U.S.C. § 351,[2] alleging that the neomycin treatment had caused his deafness. The VA denied the claim in September 1969, and on resubmission again denied the claim, on the grounds that no causal relationship existed between the neomycin treatment and the hearing loss and that there was no evidence of "carelessness, accident, negligence, lack of proper skill, error in judgment or other fault on the part of the Government."

In the course of pursuing his administrative appeal, Kubrick was informed by the VA that Dr. Soma had suggested a connection between Kubrick's loss of hearing and his prior occupation as a machinist. When questioned by Kubrick on June 2, 1971, Dr. Soma not only denied making the statement attributed to him but also told respondent that the neomycin had caused his injury and should not have been administered. On Dr. Sataloff's advice, respondent then consulted an attorney and employed him to help with his appeal. In rendering its decision in August 1972, the VA Board of Appeals recognized that Kubrick's hearing loss "may have been caused by the neomycin irrigation" but rejected the appeal on the ground that the treatment was in accordance with acceptable medical practices and procedures and that the Government was therefore faultless.[3]

Kubrick then filed suit under the Act, alleging that he had been injured by negligent treatment in the VA hospital. After trial, the District Court rendered judgment for Kubrick, rejecting, among other defenses, the assertion by the United States that Kubrick's claim was barred by the 2–year statute of limitations because the claim had accrued in January 1969, when he learned from Dr. Sataloff that his hearing loss had probably resulted from the neomycin. The District Court conceded that the lower federal courts had held with considerable uniformity that a claim accrues within the meaning of the Act when "the claimant has discovered, or in the exercise of reasonable diligence should have discovered, the acts constituting the alleged malpractice," 435 F.Supp. 166, 180 (E.D.Pa.1977), and that

---

2. Title 38 U.S.C. § 351 provides that a veteran who suffers "an injury, or an aggravation of an injury, as the result of hospitalization, medical or surgical treatment" administered by the VA shall be awarded disability benefits "in the same manner as if such disability ... were service-connected." The regulations require the applicant for benefits to show that "the disability proximately resulted through carelessness, accident, negligence, lack of proper skill, error in judgment, or similar instances of indicat-

ed fault on the part of the Veterans Administration." 38 CFR § 3.358(c)(3).

3. In 1975, upon reconsideration of its decision, the VA Board of Appeals not only found, as it had before, that Kubrick's hearing loss may have been caused by neomycin irrigation but also concluded that there was fault on the part of the VA in administering that drug by irrigation. In the present litigation, the Government contested the allegation of malpractice despite the administrative finding of fault.

notice of the injury and its cause normally were sufficient to trigger the limitations period. As the District Court read the authorities, however, a plaintiff could avoid the usual rule by showing that he had exercised reasonable diligence and had no "reasonable suspicion" that there was negligence in his treatment. *Id.*, at 185. "[W]e do not believe it reasonable to start the statute running until the plaintiff had reason at least to suspect that a legal duty to him had been breached." *Ibid.* Here, the District Court found, Kubrick had no reason to suspect negligence until his conversation with Dr. Soma in June 1971, less than two years prior to presentation of his tort claim.

The District Court went on to hold, based on the expert testimony before it, that a reasonably competent orthopedic surgeon in the Wilkes–Barre community, which the VA doctor held himself out to be, should have known that irrigating Kubrick's wound with neomycin would cause deafness. It was therefore negligent to use that drug in that manner. Damages were determined and awarded.

* * * [T]he Court of Appeals for the Third Circuit affirmed. 581 F.2d 1092 (1978). It ruled that even though a plaintiff is aware of his injury and of the defendant's responsibility for it, the statute of limitations does not run where the plaintiff shows that "in the exercise of due diligence he did not know, nor should he have known, facts which would have alerted a reasonable person to the possibility that the treatment was improper." *Id.*, at 1097. We granted certiorari to resolve this important question of the administration of the statute, and we now reverse.

II

Statutes of limitations, which "are found and approved in all systems of enlightened jurisprudence," *Wood v. Carpenter,* 101 U.S. 135, 139 (1879), represent a pervasive legislative judgment that it is unjust to fail to put the adversary on notice to defend within a specified period of time and that "the right to be free of stale claims in time comes to prevail over the right to prosecute them." *Railroad Telegraphers v. Railway Express Agency,* 321 U.S. 342, 349 (1944). These enactments are statutes of repose; and although affording plaintiffs what the legislature deems a reasonable time to present their claims, they protect defendants and the courts from having to deal with cases in which the search for truth may be seriously impaired by the loss of evidence, whether by death or disappearance of witnesses, fading memories, disappearance of documents, or otherwise.

Section 2401(b), the limitations provision involved here, is the balance struck by Congress in the context of tort claims against the Government; and we are not free to construe it so as to defeat its obvious purpose, which is to encourage the prompt presentation of claims. We should regard the plea of limitations as a "meritorious defense, in itself serving a public interest." *Guaranty Trust Co. v. United States,* 304 U.S. 126, 136 (1938).

We should also have in mind that the Act waives the immunity of the United States and that in construing the statute of limitations, which is a condition of that waiver, we should not take it upon ourselves to extend the waiver beyond that which Congress intended. Neither, however, should we assume the authority to narrow the waiver that Congress intended.

It is in the light of these considerations that we review the judgment of the Court of Appeals.

III

It is undisputed in this case that in January 1969 Kubrick was aware of his injury and its probable cause. Despite this factual predicate for a claim against the VA at that time, the Court of Appeals held that Kubrick's claim had not yet accrued and did not accrue until he knew or could reasonably be expected to know that in the eyes of the law, the neomycin treatment constituted medical malpractice. The Court of Appeals thought that in "most" cases knowledge of the causal connection between treatment and injury, without more, will or should alert a reasonable person that there has been an actionable wrong. 581 F.2d, at 1096. But it is apparent, particularly in light of the facts in this record, that the Court of Appeals' rule would reach any case where an untutored plaintiff, without benefit of medical or legal advice and because of the "technical complexity" of the case, id., at 1097, would not himself suspect that his doctors had negligently treated him. As we understand the Court of Appeals, the plaintiff in such cases need not initiate a prompt inquiry and would be free to sue at any time within two years from the time he receives or perhaps forms for himself a reasonable opinion that he has been wronged. In this case, for example, Kubrick would have been free to sue if Dr. Soma had not told him until 1975, or even 1980, instead of 1971, that the neomycin treatment had been a negligent act.

There is nothing in the language or the legislative history of the Act that provides a substantial basis for the Court of Appeals' construction of the accrual language of § 2401(b). Nor did the prevailing case law at the time the Act was passed lend support for the notion that tort claims in general or malpractice claims in particular do not accrue until a plaintiff learns that his injury was negligently inflicted. Indeed, the Court of Appeals recognized that the general rule under the Act has been that a tort claim accrues at the time of the plaintiff's injury, although it thought that in medical malpractice cases the rule had come to be that the 2–year period did not begin to run until the plaintiff has discovered both his injury and its cause. But even so—and the United States was prepared to concede as much for present purposes—the latter rule would not save Kubrick's action since he was aware of these essential facts in January 1969. Reasoning, however, that if a claim does not accrue until a plaintiff is aware of his injury and its cause, neither should it accrue until he knows or should suspect that the doctor who caused his injury was legally blameworthy, the Court of Appeals went on to hold that the limitations period was not triggered until Dr. Soma indicated in June 1971 that the neomycin irrigation treatment had been improper.

We disagree. We are unconvinced that for statute of limitations purposes a plaintiff's ignorance of his legal rights and his ignorance of the fact

discovering harm & possible cause

of his injury or its cause should receive identical treatment. That he has been injured in fact may be unknown or unknowable until the injury manifests itself; and the facts about causation may be in the control of the putative defendant, unavailable to the plaintiff or at least very difficult to obtain. The prospect is not so bleak for a plaintiff in possession of the critical facts that he has been hurt and who has inflicted the injury. He is no longer at the mercy of the latter. There are others who can tell him if he has been wronged, and he need only ask. If he does ask and if the defendant has failed to live up to minimum standards of medical proficiency, the odds are that a competent doctor will so inform the plaintiff.

In this case, the trial court found, and the United States did not appeal its finding, that the treating physician at the VA hospital had failed to observe the standard of care governing doctors of his specialty in Wilkes–Barre, Pa., and that reasonably competent doctors in this branch of medicine would have known that Kubrick should not have been treated with neomycin. Crediting this finding, as we must, Kubrick need only have made inquiry among doctors with average training and experience in such matters to have discovered that he probably had a good cause of action. The difficulty is that it does not appear that Kubrick ever made any inquiry, although meanwhile he had consulted several specialists about his loss of hearing and had been in possession of all the facts about the cause of his injury since January 1969. Furthermore, there is no reason to doubt that Dr. Soma, who in 1971 volunteered his opinion that Kubrick's treatment had been improper, would have had the same opinion had the plaintiff sought his judgment in 1969.

Ⓗ

We thus cannot hold that Congress intended that "accrual" of a claim must await awareness by the plaintiff that his injury was negligently inflicted. A plaintiff such as Kubrick, armed with the facts about the harm done to him, can protect himself by seeking advice in the medical and legal community. To excuse him from promptly doing so by postponing the accrual of his claim would undermine the purpose of the limitations statute, which is to require the reasonably diligent presentation of tort claims against the Government.[10] If there exists in the community a generally applicable standard of care with respect to the treatment of his ailment, we see no reason to suppose that competent advice would not be available to the plaintiff as to whether his treatment conformed to that standard. If advised that he has been wronged, he may promptly bring suit. If competently advised to the contrary, he may be dissuaded, as he should be, from pressing a baseless claim. Of course, he may be incompetently advised or the medical community may be divided on the crucial issue of negligence, as the experts proved to be on the trial of this case. But however or even whether he is advised, the putative malpractice plaintiff

Ⓡ

Facts were all in Ps hands, could have found out

---

10. As the dissent suggests, we are thus in partial disagreement with the conclusion of the lower courts that Kubrick exercised all reasonable diligence. Although he diligently ascertained the cause of his injury, he sought no advice within two years thereafter as to whether he had been legally wronged. The dissent would excuse the omission. For statute of limitations purposes, we would not.

must determine within the period of limitations whether to sue or not, which is precisely the judgment that other tort claimants must make. If he fails to bring suit because he is incompetently or mistakenly told that he does not have a case, we discern no sound reason for visiting the consequences of such error on the defendant by delaying the accrual of the claim until the plaintiff is otherwise informed or himself determines to bring suit, even though more than two years have passed from the plaintiff's discovery of the relevant facts about injury.

The District Court, and apparently the Court of Appeals, thought its ruling justified because of the "technical complexity," of the negligence question in this case. But determining negligence or not is often complicated and hotly disputed, so much so that judge or jury must decide the issue after listening to a barrage of conflicting expert testimony. And if in this complicated malpractice case, the statute is not to run until the plaintiff is led to suspect negligence, it would be difficult indeed not to apply the same accrual rule to medical and health claims arising under other statutes and to a whole range of other negligence cases arising under the Act and other federal statutes, where the legal implications or complicated facts make it unreasonable to expect the injured plaintiff, who does not seek legal or other appropriate advice, to realize that his legal rights may have been invaded.

We also have difficulty ascertaining the precise standard proposed by the District Court and the Court of Appeals. On the one hand, the Court of Appeals seemed to hold that a Tort Claims Act malpractice claim would not accrue until the plaintiff knew or could reasonably be expected to know of the Government's breach of duty. On the other hand, it seemed to hold that the claim would accrue only when the plaintiff had reason to suspect or was aware of facts that would have alerted a reasonable person to the possibility that a legal duty to him had been breached. In any event, either of these standards would go far to eliminate the statute of limitations as a defense separate from the denial of breach of duty.

IV

It goes without saying that statutes of limitations often make it impossible to enforce what were otherwise perfectly valid claims. But that is their very purpose, and they remain as ubiquitous as the statutory rights or other rights to which they are attached or are applicable. We should give them effect in accordance with what we can ascertain the legislative intent to have been. We doubt that here we have misconceived the intent of Congress when § 2401(b) was first adopted or when it was amended to extend the limitations period to two years. But if we have, or even if we have not but Congress desires a different result, it may exercise its prerogative to amend the statute so as to effect its legislative will.

The judgment of the Court of Appeals is

Reversed.

■ MR. JUSTICE STEVENS, with whom MR. JUSTICE BRENNAN and MR. JUSTICE MARSHALL join, dissenting.

Normally a tort claim accrues at the time of the plaintiff's injury. In most cases that event provides adequate notice to the plaintiff of the possibility that his legal rights have been invaded. It is well settled, however, that the normal rule does not apply to medical malpractice claims under the Federal Tort Claims Act. The reason for this exception is essentially the same as the reason for the general rule itself. The victim of medical malpractice frequently has no reason to believe that his legal rights have been invaded simply because some misfortune has followed medical treatment. Sometimes he may not even be aware of the actual injury until years have passed; at other times, he may recognize the harm but not know its cause; or, as in this case, he may have knowledge of the injury and its cause, but have no reason to suspect that a physician has been guilty of any malpractice. In such cases—until today—the rule that has been applied in the federal courts is that the statute of limitations does not begin to run until after fair notice of the invasion of the plaintiff's legal rights.

Essentially, there are two possible approaches to construction of the word "accrues" in statutes of limitations: (1) a claim might be deemed to "accrue" at the moment of injury without regard to the potentially harsh consequence of barring a meritorious claim before the plaintiff has a reasonable chance to assert his legal rights, or (2) it might "accrue" when a diligent plaintiff has knowledge of facts sufficient to put him on notice of an invasion of his legal rights. The benefits that flow from certainty in the administration of our affairs favor the former approach in most commercial situations. But in medical malpractice cases the harsh consequences of that approach have generally been considered unacceptable. * * *

In my judgment, a fair application of this rule forecloses the Court's attempt to distinguish between a plaintiff's knowledge of the cause of his injury on the one hand and his knowledge of the doctor's failure to meet acceptable medical standards on the other. For in both situations the typical plaintiff will, and normally should, rely on his doctor's explanation of the situation.

The * * * rule would not, of course, prevent the statute from commencing to run if the plaintiff's knowledge of an injury, or its cause, would place a reasonably diligent person on notice that a doctor had been guilty of misconduct. But if he neither suspects, nor has any reason to suspect, malpractice, I see no reason to treat his claim differently than if he were not aware of the cause of the harm or, indeed, of the harm itself. In this case the District Court expressly found that "plaintiff's belief that there was no malpractice was reasonable in view of the technical complexity of the question whether his neomycin treatment involved excessive risks, the failure of any of his doctors to suggest prior to June 1971 the possibility of negligence, and the repeated unequivocal assertions by the Veterans Administration that there was no negligence on the part of the government." 435 F.Supp. 166, 174.

The Court is certainly correct in stating that one purpose of the statute of limitations is to require the "reasonably diligent presentation of tort claims against the Government." A plaintiff who remains ignorant through lack of diligence cannot be characterized as "blameless." But unless the Court is prepared to reverse the Court of Appeals' judgment that the District Court's findings were adequately supported by the evidence, the principle of requiring diligence does not justify the result the Court reaches today. The District Court found that "plaintiff exercised all kinds of reasonable diligence in attempting to establish a medical basis for increased disability benefits." 435 F.Supp., at 185. That diligence produced not only the Government's denials, but, worse, what may have been a fabrication. It was only after the Government told plaintiff that Dr. Soma had suggested that plaintiff's occupation as a machinist had caused his deafness that plaintiff, by confronting Dr. Soma, first became aware that neomycin irrigation may not have been an acceptable medical practice. Plaintiff was unquestionably diligent; moreover, his diligence ultimately bore fruit. There is no basis for assuming, as this Court holds, that plaintiff could have been more diligent and discovered his cause of action sooner.

The issue of diligence in a negligence case should be resolved by the factfinder—not by the Supreme Court of the United States—and its resolution should depend on the evidence in the record, rather than on speculation about what might constitute diligence in various other circumstances.[4]

The Maj. requires π to be "diligent"

Issue of π's diligence should have gone to the jury...

Notes and Questions

1. In *United States v. Kubrick,* the Court applied what is generally known as the "discovery rule" for accrual of a statute of limitations, under which a claim does not accrue until the plaintiff knows or reasonably should have known of both the injury and the cause (although not necessarily the wrongfulness) of the injury. Because *Kubrick* arose in a medical malpractice context, in which it may be difficult for a layperson to discover that a particular symptom or physical problem is attributable to a course of medical treatment, courts in the past debated whether the discovery rule is generally applicable in FTCA suits arising in non-medical malpractice contexts. At present, there is a consensus among the courts of appeals that the *Kubrick* discovery rule applies generally for accrual of claims in all tort cases under the FTCA. *See Diaz v. United States,* 165 F.3d 1337, 1339–40 (11th Cir. 1999); *Slaaten v. United States,* 990 F.2d 1038, 1041 (8th Cir. 1993); *Plaza Speedway Inc. v. United States,* 311 F.3d 1262, 1267–68 (10th

---

4. The factual predicate for the Court's speculation is its assumption that if a patient who has been mistreated by one doctor should ask another if the first "failed to live up to minimum standards of medical proficiency, the odds are that a competent doctor will so inform the plaintiff." I am not at all sure about those odds. But whatever the odds are generally, I would prefer to have the issue of the diligence in exploring the reason for the unfortunate condition of this deaf plaintiff decided on the basis of evidence relevant to his particular injury.

Cir. 2002) (holding that the circuit's general injury occurrence rule is not absolute and that the FTCA's two-year statute of limitations did not begin to accrue until the landowner was notified by a geologist that activities at the adjacent Army airfield had contaminated the groundwater and soil); *Garza v. United States Bureau of Prisons,* 284 F.3d 930, 934 (8th Cir. 2002) (holding that, although some precedent suggests that the diligence-discovery-accrual rule has been used primarily in medical malpractice cases, "based on authority addressing a diverse array of tort claims, [] its application is not so limited"); *Stoleson v. United States,* 629 F.2d 1265, 1268 (7th Cir. 1980).

2. The circuits remain in disagreement as to precisely *what* must be discovered for the claim to accrue. In *Zeleznik v. United States,* 770 F.2d 20, 23 (3d Cir. 1985), the Third Circuit ruled that "[d]iscovery of the cause of one's injury * * * does not mean knowing who is responsible for it. The 'cause' is known when the immediate physical cause of the injury is discovered." Similarly, in *Motley v. United States,* 295 F.3d 820, 822–24 (8th Cir. 2002), the Eighth Circuit held that the parents' claim accrued at the time of the child's stillbirth when they were aware of both the injury and the identity of the prenatal care provider. Even though they did not then know that the provider was a federal employee—because they had failed either during the care or during the two-year period after the stillbirth to inquire into the federal employment status—the initiation of the limitations period was not delayed.

By contrast, in *Skwira v. United States*, 344 F.3d 64, 77–78 (1st Cir. 2003), the First Circuit held that, at least outside of the medical malpractice context, "the proper subject of knowledge for accrual purposes under the FTCA is (1) the fact of injury and (2) the injury's causal connection with the government." The court further explained that "definitive knowledge" is not required, but rather that accrual is triggered when the plaintiff either knows, or "in the exercise of reasonable diligence should know, (1) of her injury and (2) sufficient facts to permit a reasonable person to believe that there is a causal connection between the government and her injury." Three other Courts of Appeals also have held that, for the claim to accrue under the FTCA, a plaintiff must have received some indication that, or reason to investigate whether, the government was a cause of that injury. *Garza,* 284 F.3d at 934–37 (holding that the limitations period does not begin to run until there is reasonable notice of the government cause, but that does not mean the plaintiff must have "actual knowledge" that the tortious actor was a government employee when the plaintiff was on "inquiry notice" and should have investigated the government affiliation); *Diaz,* 165 F.3d at 1340; *Drazan v. United States,* 762 F.2d 56, 59 (7th Cir. 1985) ("when there are two causes of an injury, and only one is the government, the knowledge that is required to set the statute of limitations running is knowledge of the government cause, not just of the other cause"). Does the Court in *Kubrick* say anything that suggests an answer to this problem?

3. In part II of the majority opinion in *United States v. Kubrick*, the Court, as part of its explanation of the statutory rule of construction, characterizes the statute of limitations as a "condition of [the] waiver" of sovereign immunity. This language could be understood to mean that compliance with the FTCA limitations period is an absolute prerequisite and cannot be waived, in the nature of a jurisdictional requirement. *See, e.g., Bradley v. United States ex rel. Veterans Admin.*, 951 F.2d 268, 270 (10th Cir. 1991); *Gould v. United States Dep't of Health & Human Servs.*, 905 F.2d 738, 741 (4th Cir. 1990). Thus, several courts in the past held that the statute of limitations under the FTCA is jurisdictional and is not subject to equitable tolling. *Dyniewicz v. United States*, 742 F.2d 484, 485 (9th Cir. 1984); *Rogers v. United States*, 675 F.2d 123, 124 (6th Cir. 1982) (per curiam).

However, subsequent to *Irwin v. Veterans Administration*, 498 U.S. 89 (1990) (set out in Chapter II.C)—which made available equitable tolling of the statute of limitations on Title VII employment discrimination claims against the federal government—several courts of appeals have held that equitable tolling is available for FTCA claims. For example, the Fifth Circuit ruled that the FTCA contains "a garden variety limitations provision," falling within the presumption of *Irwin* that the government is subject to equitable tolling. *Perez v. United States*, 167 F.3d 913, 917 (5th Cir. 1999) Similarly, the Ninth Circuit cited *Irwin* for the proposition that "[e]quitable tolling is available in suits against the United States absent evidence that Congress intended the contrary" and that "[n]othing in the FTCA indicates that Congress intended for equitable tolling not to apply." *Alvarez–Machain v. United States*, 107 F.3d 696, 701 (9th Cir. 1996). The Ninth Circuit found that the *Alvarez–Machain* case presented "that rare situation where equitable tolling is demanded by sound legal principles as well as the interests of justice." *Id.* The plaintiff (a Mexican national) brought FTCA claims based upon his abduction and transportation to the United States by federal agents. He had been incarcerated for over two years and charged with murder; he did not understand the language; his case involved numerous complex issues of first impression; and if he had filed an administrative claim before his acquittal in the criminal case, many of his claims would have been premature. *Id.* Other circuits also have upheld or suggested the availability of equitable tolling of the FTCA statute of limitations. *Gonzalez v. United States*, 284 F.3d 281, 288, 291 (1st Cir. 2002) (holding that limitations period is a "jurisdictional prerequisite," but nonetheless assuming that equitable tolling is available); *Hughes v. United States*, 263 F.3d 272, 278 (3d Cir. 2001) (although case actually involved accrual of the claim through discovery of the cause of the plaintiff's injury, the court spoke in terms of equitable tolling and held that the FTCA statute of limitations is not jurisdictional); *Glarner v. United States, Dept. of Veterans Admin.*, 30 F.3d 697, 701 (6th Cir. 1994); *Pipkin v. U.S. Postal Service*, 951 F.2d 272, 274–75 (10th Cir. 1991); *Schmidt v. U.S.*, 933 F.2d 639, 640 (8th Cir. 1991) (holding that strict compliance with FTCA statute of limitations is not a jurisdictional prerequisite).

Still, in *Wukawitz v. United States*, 170 F.Supp.2d 1165, 1169 (D. Utah 2001), one district court declined to fall into line and endorse the availability of equitable tolling in FTCA cases. Instead, the court cited scholarly commentary for the proposition that Congress did not intend to permit equitable tolling of the FTCA statute of limitations, based upon the language and legislative history of the FTCA. Richard Parker & Ugo Colella, *Revisiting Equitable Tolling and the Federal Tort Claims Act: The Impact of* Brockamp *and* Beggerly, 29 Seton Hall L. Rev. 885 (1999) (arguing that, in light of the Supreme Court's more recent decisions restricting the availability of equitable tolling against the federal government, the time limitations in the FTCA should be regarded as jurisdictional and not subject to tolling); Ugo Colella & Adam Bain, *Revisiting Equitable Tolling and the Federal Tort Claims Act: Putting the Legislative History in Proper Perspective,* 31 Seton Hall L. Rev. 174 (2000). The *Wukawitz* court highlighted the "unusually emphatic language," *Wukawitz,* 170 F.Supp.2d at 1169, in Section 2401(b) that untimely claims will be "forever barred."

Assuming its availability under the FTCA, consider the possible applicability of equitable tolling to the *Kubrick* facts: Kubrick might have argued that the government deceived him into allowing the limitations period to lapse, in light of the Veterans Administration's representation at one point that a physician "had suggested a connection between Kubrick's loss of hearing and his prior occupation as a machinist." Would this have been a plausible argument? If it had been made, should it have succeeded?

4. One of the other prerequisites to an FTCA suit is naming the proper defendant. The "United States" is the proper and sole defendant for a suit under the FTCA. *See* 28 U.S.C. § 2674. Thus, a tort suit directed against a federal officer (in his official capacity) or a federal agency is misdirected. However, an error in the naming of the proper defendant may be corrected by an amendment to the pleading, and the amendment will "relate back" under Federal Rule of Civil Procedure 15(c) to the date of the original complaint (assuming that the original complaint was timely filed and the United States received notice of the original suit within the limitations period or within the 120 days allowed for service of the complaint after filing). *McGuire v. Turnbo,* 137 F.3d 321, 324–26 (5th Cir. 1998). "Notice" of the original suit (with the misnamed defendant) means that the process was mailed or delivered either to the United States Attorney or the Attorney General. *Id.* at 325. However, the amended complaint must then be properly served upon the United States; that "service" requires *both* delivery to the U.S. Attorney and mailing of a copy to the Attorney General. Fed. R. Civ. P. 4(i). On service of process upon the United States generally , see Chapter I.D.

---

3.   Standards for Tort Liability

28 United States Code § 1346(b)(1)

(b)(1) Subject to the provisions of chapter 171 of this title, the district courts, together with the United States District Court for the District of the

Canal Zone and the District Court of the Virgin Islands, shall have exclusive jurisdiction of civil actions on claims against the United States, for money damages, accruing on and after January 1, 1945, for injury or loss of property, or personal injury or death caused by the negligent or wrongful act or omission of any employee of the Government while acting within the scope of his office or employment, under circumstances where the United States, if a private person, would be liable to the claimant in accordance with the law of the place where the act or omission occurred.

---

28 United States Code § 2674

The United States shall be liable, respecting the provisions of this title relating to tort claims, in the same manner and to the same extent as a private individual under like circumstances, but shall not be liable for interest prior to judgment or for punitive damages.

If, however, in any case wherein death was caused, the law of the place where the act or omission complained of occurred provides, or has been construed to provide, for damages only punitive in nature, the United States shall be liable for actual or compensatory damages, measured by the pecuniary injuries resulting from such death to the persons respectively, for whose benefit the action was brought, in lieu thereof.

With respect to any claim under this chapter, the United States shall be entitled to assert any defense based upon judicial or legislative immunity which otherwise would have been available to the employee of the United States whose act or omission gave rise to the claim, as well as any other defenses to which the United States is entitled.

With respect to any claim to which this section applies, the Tennessee Valley Authority shall be entitled to assert any defense which otherwise would have been available to the employee based upon judicial or legislative immunity, which otherwise would have been available to the employee of the Tennessee Valley Authority whose act or omission gave rise to the claim as well as any other defenses to which the Tennessee Valley Authority is entitled under this chapter.

* * *

Note

Sections 1346(b) and 2674 of the Federal Tort Claims Act (FTCA) set out basic parameters for the waiver of federal sovereign immunity for tort liability. (Subsequently, we will also examine several "exceptions" carved out by statute from the scope of liability otherwise established by the FTCA.) Section 1346(b) is primarily a jurisdictional statute, but it also includes language describing permissible claims and thus must be read together with Section 2674, which states the substantive waiver of sovereign immunity in the FTCA. From these two statutes, we can outline the following principal elements for substantive liability under the FTCA:

The United States is liable in tort

1) for personal injury, death, or property damage,

2) caused by negligent or wrongful acts or omissions,

3) by a government employee acting within the scope of his office or employment,

4) in the same manner and to the same extent as a private person under like circumstances,

5) in accordance with the law of the place (state) where the act or omission occurred, and

6) for money damages, but not for interest before judgment or for punitive damages.

---

a.   THE STATE LAW LIABILITY STANDARD

Richards v. United States

Supreme Court of the United States.
369 U.S. 1 (1962).

■ Mr. Chief Justice Warren delivered the opinion of the Court.

The question to be decided in this case is what law a Federal District Court should apply in an action brought under the Federal Tort Claims Act where an act of negligence occurs in one State and results in an injury and death in another State. The basic provision of the Tort Claims Act states that the Government shall be liable for tortious conduct committed by its employees acting within the scope of their employment "under circumstances where the United States, if a private person, would be liable to the claimant in accordance with the law of the place where the act or omission occurred."[2] The parties urge that the alternatives in selecting the law to determine liability under this statute are: (1) the internal law of the place where the negligence occurred, or (2) the whole law (including choice-of-law rules) of the place where the negligence occurred, or (3) the internal law of the place where the operative effect of the negligence took place.

Although the particular facts of this case are relatively unimportant in deciding the question before us, a brief recitation of them is necessary to set the context for our decision. The petitioners are the personal representatives of passengers killed when an airplane, owned by the respondent American Airlines, crashed in Missouri while en route from Tulsa, Oklahoma, to New York City. Suit was brought by the petitioners against the United States in the Federal District Court for the Northern District of

---

2.   28 U.S.C. § 1346(b).

Oklahoma, on the theory that the Government, through the Civil Aviation Agency, had "negligently failed to enforce the terms of the Civil Aeronautics Act and the regulations thereunder which prohibited the practices then being used by American Airlines, Inc., in the overhaul depot of Tulsa, Oklahoma." The petitioners in each case either had already received a $15,000 settlement from the Airlines, the maximum amount recoverable under the Missouri Wrongful Death Act, [or that amount had been tendered]. They sought additional amounts from the United States under the Oklahoma Wrongful Death Act which contains no limitation on the amount a single person may recover from a tortfeasor. The Government filed a third-party complaint against American Airlines, seeking reimbursement for any amount that the petitioners might recover against the United States.

After a pretrial hearing, the District Court ruled that the complaints failed to state claims upon which relief could be granted under the Oklahoma Act since that statute could not be applied extraterritorially "where an act or omission occurring in Oklahoma results in injury and death in the State of Missouri." Alternatively, the court noted that if Oklahoma law was applicable under the Federal Tort Claims Act, "then the general law of Oklahoma, including its conflicts of law rule, is applicable thereunder," thus precluding further recovery since the Oklahoma conflicts rule would refer the court to the law of Missouri, the place where the negligence had its operative effect. In dismissing the petitioners' complaints against the United States, the court found it unnecessary to pass upon the third-party complaint asserted by the Government against American. On appeal, the Court of Appeals for the Tenth Circuit affirmed the judgment by a divided vote, the majority agreeing with the lower court that the complaints failed to state a cause of action upon which relief could be based under either the Oklahoma or the Missouri Wrongful Death Act. In dissent, the chief judge, believing that Congress intended the internal law of the place where the act or omission occurred to control the rights and liabilities of the parties, stated that he thought it was error to apply the Oklahoma conflict-of-laws rule, and would have remanded the case for a determination of liability under the Oklahoma Act. * * *

I.

The principal provision of the Federal Tort Claims Act is Section 1346(b), reading in pertinent part:

"... the district courts ... shall have exclusive jurisdiction of civil actions on claims against the United States, for money damages ... for injury or loss of property, or personal injury or death caused by the negligent or wrongful act or omission of any employee of the Government while acting within the scope of his office or employment, under circumstances where the United States, if a private person, would be liable to the claimant in accordance with the law of the place where the act or omission occurred."

Section 2674, also relevant to our decision, provides:

"The United States shall be liable, respecting ... tort claims, in the same manner and to the same extent as a private individual under like circumstances, but shall not be liable for interest prior to judgment or for punitive damages."

The Tort Claims Act was designed primarily to remove the sovereign immunity of the United States from suits in tort and, with certain specific exceptions, to render the Government liable in tort as a private individual would be under like circumstances. It is evident that the Act was not patterned to operate with complete independence from the principles of law developed in the common law and refined by statute and judicial decision in the various States. Rather, it was designed to build upon the legal relationships formulated and characterized by the States, and, to that extent, the statutory scheme is exemplary of the generally interstitial character of federal law. If Congress had meant to alter or supplant the legal relationships developed by the States, it could specifically have done so to further the limited objectives of the Tort Claims Act. That is, notwithstanding the generally interstitial character of the law, Congress, in waiving the immunity of the Government for tortious conduct of its employees, could have imposed restrictions and conditions on the extent and substance of its liability. We must determine whether, and to what extent, Congress exercised this power in selecting a rule for the choice of laws to be applied in suits brought under the Act. And, because the issue of the applicable law is controlled by a formal expression of the will of Congress, we need not pause to consider the question whether the conflict-of-laws rule applied in suits where federal jurisdiction rests upon diversity of citizenship shall be extended to a case such as this, in which jurisdiction is based upon a federal statute.[13] In addition, and even though Congress has left to judicial implication the task of giving content to its will in selecting the controlling law, because of the formal expression found in the Act itself, we are presented with a situation wholly distinguishable from those cases in which our initial inquiry has been whether the appropriate rule should be the simple adoption of state law. Here, we must decide, first, to which State the words "where the act or omission occurred" direct us, and, second, whether application of the internal law or the whole law of that State would be most consistent with the legislative purpose in enacting the Tort Claims Act.

II.

The legislative history of the Act, although generally extensive, is not, except in a negative way, helpful in solving the problem of the law to be applied in a multistate tort action such as is presented by the facts of this case. It has been repeatedly observed that Congress did not consider choice-of-law problems during the long period that the legislation was being prepared for enactment. The concern of Congress, as illustrated by the legislative history, was the problem of a person injured by an employee operating a government vehicle or otherwise acting within the scope of his employment, situations rarely involving a conflict-of-laws question. In these

13. Klaxon Co. v. Stentor Electric Mfg. Co., 313 U.S. 487.

instances, where the negligence and the injury normally occur simultaneously and in a single jurisdiction, the law to be applied is clear, and no solution to the meaning of the words "the law of the place where the act or omission occurred" is required. Here, however, we are faced with events touching more than one "place"—a problem which Congress apparently did not explicitly consider—and, thus, we are compelled to give content to those critical words.

In the Tort Claims Act Congress has expressly stated that the Government's liability is to be determined by the application of a particular law, the law of the place where the act or omission occurred, and we must, of course, start with the assumption that the legislative purpose is expressed by the ordinary meaning of the words used. We believe that it would be difficult to conceive of any more precise language Congress could have used to command application of the law of the place where the negligence occurred than the words it did employ in the Tort Claims Act. Thus we first reject the alternative urged by American Airlines. The legislative materials cited to us by American not only lack probative force in a judicial sense, but they are completely unpersuasive to support the argument that Congress intended the words "act or omission" to refer to the place where the negligence had its operative effect. The ease of application inherent in the rule urged by American lends a certain attractiveness, but we are bound to operate within the framework of the words chosen by Congress and not to question the wisdom of the latter in the process of construction. We conclude that Congress has, in the Tort Claims Act, enacted a rule which requires federal courts, in multistate tort actions, to look in the first instance to "the law" of the place where the acts of negligence took place.

III.

However, our task is not completed. Having rejected the third alternative stated initially as inconsistent with the express terminology of the Act, we must now determine the reach of the words "law of the place." Do they embrace the whole law of the place where the negligence occurred, or only the internal law of that place? This problem, unlike the initial question discussed under II, supra, has not been dealt with by any formal expression of Congress and we must therefore establish the rule to be applied uniformly by lower federal courts, with due regard to the variant interests and policies expressed by the Tort Claims Act legislation.

We believe it fundamental that a section of a statute should not be read in isolation from the context of the whole Act, and that in fulfilling our responsibility in interpreting legislation, "we must not be guided by a single sentence or member of a sentence, but (should) look to the provisions of the whole law, and to its object and policy."[22] We should not assume that Congress intended to set the courts completely adrift from state law with regard to questions for which it has not provided a specific and definite answer in an act such as the one before us which, as we have indicated, is so intimately related to state law. Thus, we conclude that a reading of the

---

22. Mastro Plastics Corp. v. National Labor Relations Board, 350 U.S. 270, 285.

statute as a whole, with due regard to its purpose, requires application of the whole law of the State where the act or omission occurred.

We are led to our conclusion by other persuasive factors notwithstanding the fact that the very conflict among the lower federal courts that we must here resolve illustrates the also reasonable alternative view expressed by the petitioners. First, our interpretation enables the federal courts to treat the United States as a "private individual under like circumstances," and thus is consistent with the Act considered as a whole. The general conflict-of-laws rule, followed by a vast majority of the States, is to apply the law of the place of injury to the substantive rights of the parties. Therefore, where the forum State is the same as the one in which the act or omission occurred, our interpretation will enable the federal courts to treat the United States as an individual would be treated under like circumstances.[25] Moreover, this interpretation of the Act provides a degree of flexibility to the law to be applied in federal courts that would not be possible under the view advanced either by the petitioners or by American. Recently there has been a tendency on the part of some States to depart from the general conflicts rule in order to take into account the interests of the State having significant contact with the parties to the litigation. We can see no compelling reason to saddle the Act with an interpretation that would prevent the federal courts from implementing this policy in choice-of-law rules where the State in which the negligence occurred has adopted it. Should the States continue this rejection of the older rule in those situations where its application might appear inappropriate or inequitable, the flexibility inherent in our interpretation will also be more in step with that judicial approach, as well as with the character of the legislation and with the purpose of the Act considered as a whole.

In the absence of persuasive evidence to the contrary, we do not believe that Congress intended to adopt the inflexible rule urged upon us by the petitioners. Despite the power of Congress to enact for litigation of this type a federal conflict-of-laws rule independent of the States' development of such rules, we should not, particularly in the type of interstitial legislation involved here, assume that it has done so. Nor are we persuaded to require such an independent federal rule by the petitioners' argument that there are other instances, specifically set forth in the Act, where the liability of the United States is not coextensive with that of a private person under state law. It seems sufficient to note that Congress has been specific in those instances where it intended the federal courts to depart completely from state law and, also, that this list of exceptions contains no

25. For example, had the petitioners in the instant case brought suit against American as well as the United States, the petitioners' interpretation of the Act would have the District Court determine American's liability by the law of Missouri and the United States' by the law of Oklahoma. Under our construction of the Act, however, both defendants' liability would be determined by the law of Missouri. However, because of the venue provision in the statute, allowing suit to be brought where all the plaintiffs reside as well as where the act or omission occurred (28 U.S.C. § 1402(b)), a situation may arise where a District Court could not determine the Government's and a private individual's liability in exactly the same manner.

[Handwritten at top: Look to the law of where the neg. occurred → that state's choice of law, subst, etc.]

direct or indirect modification of the principles controlling application of choice-of-law rules. Certainly there is nothing in the legislative history that even remotely supports the argument that Congress did not intend state conflict rules to apply to multistate tort actions brought against the Government.

Under our interpretation of the Act we find it unnecessary to judge the effect of the Oklahoma courts' pronouncements that the Oklahoma Wrongful Death Act cannot be given extra-territorial effect.

IV.

Our view of a State's power to adopt an appropriate conflict-of-laws doctrine in a situation touching more than one place has been indicated by our discussion in Part III of this opinion. Where more than one State has sufficiently substantial contact with the activity in question, the forum State, by analysis of the interests possessed by the States involved, could constitutionally apply to the decision of the case the law of one or another state having such an interest in the multistate activity. Thus, an Oklahoma state court would be free to apply either its own law, the law of the place where the negligence occurred, or the law of Missouri, the law of the place where the injury occurred, to an action brought in its courts and involving this factual situation. Both the Federal District Court sitting in Oklahoma, and the Court of Appeals for the Tenth Circuit, have interpreted the pertinent Oklahoma decisions, which we have held are controlling, to declare that an action for wrongful death is based on the statute of the place where the injury occurred that caused the death. Therefore, Missouri's statute controls the case at bar. It is conceded that each petitioner has received $15,000, the maximum amount recoverable under the Missouri Act, and the petitioners thus have received full compensation for their claims. Accordingly, the courts below were correct in holding that, in accordance with Oklahoma law, petitioners had failed to state claims upon which relief could be granted. The judgment is affirmed.

Affirmed.

Notes and Questions

[Handwritten margin note: where π can file]

1. To test your understanding of the rule of *Richards v. United States,* consider the following hypothetical: Suppose that the plaintiff in the *Richards* case was a resident of New York (where the flight was headed). Under 28 U.S.C. § 1402(b) (which is included in the materials in Chapter I.C), venue for an FTCA suit lies in any "district where the plaintiff resides or wherein the act or omission complained of occurred." Thus, the New York resident could bring the suit in federal district court in either New York or Oklahoma. If the New York resident chooses to file suit in federal district court in New York against *both* the United States under the Federal Tort Claims Act and against American Airlines under state tort law

[Handwritten margin notes on right: the particular fed. dist. in NY where π resides; the particular fed. dist. in OK. where act/omission]

[Handwritten at bottom: any district w/in those states?] *[boxed: OK]* *[boxed: NY/ss]* *[boxed: NY]* *[note: Diversity]*

[handwritten margin notes:
- OK. law for claim vs. US
- But for claim ag. American, he could only sue in fed. ct is diverse... If so, NY law of multistate tort would apply
Fed. liability per se vs. State Fed. liability of 'state law', liability
requirement of state law analogues
Mere federal law cannot be evidence of duty — the what is evidence of a duty must come from STATE LAW]

in the same law suit,* how would the choice of law question be resolved for each defendant? Without knowing the particular choice of law rules for New York, we may not know exactly what the final resolution of the conflict would be, but would the process of deciding the choice of law question differ for American Airlines from that for the United States? Consider how the starting points of the choice of law analysis would differ with respect to the United States as opposed to American Airlines. Note the Supreme Court's anticipation of this type of situation in footnote 25 of the *Richards* opinion.

2.   As *Richards* explains, the FTCA does not create any new causes of action but instead turns on state law. The FTCA does not formulate federal rules of substantive tort law. As the Supreme Court confirmed in *Federal Deposit Insurance Corp. v. Meyer*, 510 U.S. 471, 478 (1994), state law is "the source of substantive liability under the FTCA" and the FTCA does not apply when "federal law, not state law, provides the source of liability for a claim." In *Chen v. United States*, 854 F.2d 622 (2d Cir. 1988), the Second Circuit summarized the state of the law:

> The FTCA's "law of the place" requirement is not satisfied by direct violations of the Federal Constitution, or of federal statutes or regulations standing alone. The alleged federal violations also must constitute violations of duties "analogous to those imposed under local law."

Id. at 628; *see also Pate v. Oakwood Mobile Homes, Inc.*, 374 F.3d 1081, 1084 (11th Cir. 2004); *Art Metal–U.S.A., Inc. v. United States*, 753 F.2d 1151, 1158 (D.C. Cir. 1985).

Nor may the exclusion of federal law as the source of the duty be evaded by invoking the doctrine of negligence per se when the underlying presumptive duty depends on federal statutory law. As the Fifth Circuit ruled in *Johnson v. Sawyer*, 47 F.3d 716 (5th Cir. 1995):

> Where a claim is wholly grounded on a duty imposed by an allegedly violated federal statute or regulation, to allow FTCA recovery merely on the basis of a general state doctrine of negligence *per se*,

---

* A plaintiff might join the non-federal defendant in the same tort lawsuit with the United States in federal district court either (1) by virtue of diversity of citizenship between the plaintiff and the non-federal defendant, thus conferring jurisdiction under 28 U.S.C. § 1332, or (2) under supplemental jurisdiction pursuant to 28 U.S.C. § 1367. Prior to the enactment of Section 1367, the Supreme Court had held that a non-diverse defendant could not be joined to an FTCA suit against the United States in federal court. In *Finley v. United States*, 490 U.S. 545 (1989), the Court held that pendent jurisdiction could not be asserted over additional parties, even if the claim against those additional parties arose out of the same occurrence as the FTCA suit against the United States. As you should recall from your first-year course in Civil Procedure, Congress subsequently enacted Section 1367 and overturned the *Finley* result. Under Section 1367(a), the federal district court may exercise jurisdiction over a supplemental claim—including a claim that involves joinder of additional parties—whenever it forms part of the same constitutional case or controversy as the claim that provides the basis for the court's original jurisdiction. Thus, a plaintiff may join non-diverse and non-federal parties to an FTCA suit against the United States if the state tort law claims against these supplemental parties and the tort claim against the United States both arise out of a common nucleus of operative fact.

without requiring that there be some specific basis for concluding that similar conduct by private persons or entities would be actionable under state law, is to in essence discriminate against the United States: recovery against it is allowed, although for similar conduct the private person or entity would not be subject to liability under state law.

Id. at 729; *see also* Myers v. United States, 17 F.3d 890, 899 (6th Cir. 1994). In sum, a negligence per se theory may not be applied to impose FTCA liability upon the government when the determination of whether governmental conduct was wrongful or negligent ultimately depends upon a duty defined by a federal statute or regulation.

————

b.   THE "PRIVATE PERSON" ANALOGY

United States v. Olson
Supreme Court of the United States.
546 U.S. 43 (2005).

■ JUSTICE BREYER delivered the opinion of the Court.

The Federal Tort Claims Act (FTCA or Act) authorizes private tort actions against the United States "under circumstances where the United States, if a private person, would be liable to the claimant in accordance with the law of the place where the act or omission occurred." 28 U.S.C. § 1346(b)(1). We here interpret these words to mean what they say, namely, that the United States waives sovereign immunity "under circumstances" where local law would make a *"private person"* liable in tort. (Emphasis added.) And we reverse a line of Ninth Circuit precedent permitting courts in certain circumstances to base a waiver simply upon a finding that local law would make a "state or municipal entit[y]" liable.

I

In this case, two injured mine workers (and a spouse) have sued the United States claiming that the negligence of federal mine inspectors helped bring about a serious accident at an Arizona mine. The Federal District Court dismissed the lawsuit in part upon the ground that their allegations were insufficient to show that Arizona law would impose liability upon a private person in similar circumstances. The Ninth Circuit, in a brief *per curiam* opinion, reversed this determination. It reasoned from two premises. First, where " 'unique governmental functions' " are at issue, the Act waives sovereign immunity if " 'a state or municipal entity would be [subject to liability] under the law [...] where the activity occurred.' " 362 F.3d 1236, 1240 (C.A.9 2004). Second, federal mine inspections being regulatory in nature are such " 'unique governmental functions,' " since "there is no private-sector analogue for mine inspections." The Circuit then held that Arizona law would make "state or municipal entities'' liable in the circumstances alleged; hence the FTCA waives the United States' sovereign immunity.

II

We disagree with both of the Ninth Circuit's legal premises.

A

The first premise is too broad, for it reads into the Act something that is not there. The Act says that it waives sovereign immunity ''under circumstances where the United States, if a *private person*,'' not ''the United States, if a state or municipal entity,'' would be liable. 28 U.S.C. § 1346(b)(1) (emphasis added). Our cases have consistently adhered to this ''private person'' standard. In *Indian Towing Co. v. United States,* 350 U.S. 61, 64 (1955), this Court rejected the Government's contention that there was ''no liability for negligent performance of 'uniquely governmental functions.' '' It held that the Act requires a court to look to the state-law liability of private entities, not to that of public entities, when assessing the Government's liability under the FTCA ''in the performance of activities which private persons do not perform.'' *Ibid.* In *Rayonier Inc. v. United States,* 352 U.S. 315, 318–319 (1957), the Court rejected a claim that the scope of FTCA liability for '' 'uniquely governmental' '' functions depends on whether state law ''imposes liability on municipal or other local governments for the negligence of their agents acting in'' similar circumstances. And even though both these cases involved Government efforts to *escape* liability by pointing to the *absence* of municipal entity liability, we are unaware of any reason for treating differently a plaintiff's effort to *base* liability solely upon the fact that a State would impose liability upon a municipal (or other state governmental) entity. Indeed, we have found nothing in the Act's context, history, or objectives or in the opinions of this Court suggesting a waiver of sovereign immunity solely upon that basis.

B

The Ninth Circuit's second premise rests upon a reading of the Act that is too narrow. The Act makes the United States liable ''in the same manner and to the same extent as a private individual under *like circumstances.*'' 28 U.S.C. § 2674 (emphasis added). As this Court said in *Indian Towing,* the words '' 'like circumstances' '' do not restrict a court's inquiry to the *same circumstances,* but require it to look further afield. 350 U.S., at 64; see also S.Rep. No. 1400, 79th Cong., 2d Sess., 32 (1946) (purpose of FTCA was to make the tort liability of the United States ''the same as that of a private person under like circumstance, in accordance with the local law''). The Court there considered a claim that the Coast Guard, responsible for operating a lighthouse, had failed ''to check'' the light's ''battery and sun relay system,'' had failed ''to make a proper examination'' of outside ''connections,'' had ''fail[ed] to check the light'' on a regular basis, and had failed to ''repair the light or give warning that the light was not operating.'' These allegations, the Court held, were analogous to allegations of negligence by a private person ''who undertakes to warn the public of danger and thereby induces reliance." It is "hornbook tort law," the Court added, that such a person "must perform his 'good Samaritan' task in a careful manner."

The Government in effect concedes that similar "good Samaritan" analogies exist for the conduct at issue here. It says that "there are private persons in 'like circumstances' " to federal mine inspectors, namely "private persons who conduct safety inspections." Reply Brief for United States 3. And other Courts of Appeals have found ready private person analogies for Government tasks of this kind in FTCA cases. *E.G., Dorking Genetics v. United States*, 76 F.3d 1261 (C.A.2 1996) (inspection of cattle); *Florida Auto Auction of Orlando, Inc. v. United States*, 74 F.3d 498 (C.A.4 1996) (inspection of automobile titles); *Ayala v. United States*, 49 F.3d 607 (C.A.10 1995) (mine inspections); *Myers v. United States*, 17 F.3d 890 (C.A.6 1994) (same); *Howell v. United States*, 932 F.2d 915 (C.A.11 1991) (inspection of airplanes). These cases all properly apply the logic of *Indian Towing*. Private individuals, who do not operate lighthouses, nonetheless may create a relationship with third parties that is similar to the relationship between a lighthouse operator and a ship dependent on the lighthouse's beacon. The Ninth Circuit should have looked for a similar analogy in this case.

III

Despite the Government's concession that a private person analogy exists in this case, the parties disagree about precisely which Arizona tort law doctrine applies here. We remand the case so that the lower courts can decide this matter in the first instance. The judgment of the Ninth Circuit is vacated, and the case is remanded for proceedings consistent with this opinion.

It is so ordered.

Notes and Questions

1. Under Section 2674 of Title 28 of the United States Code, the United States is liable in tort "in the same manner and to the same extent as a private individual under like circumstances." Subsection 1346(b)(1) of Title 28, which grants jurisdiction over FTCA suits to the District Court, reinforces the limitation of governmental amenability in tort to "circumstances where the United States, if a private person, would be liable to the claimant in accordance with the law of the place where the act or omission occurred."

In *United States v. Olson*, the government conceded that a private person analogy exists for holding the government liability for negligence by regulators in inspecting the safety of a mine. So what then is the government's complaint about the court of appeals decision? How did the court of appeals measure the liability of the government in *Olson*? Why does the

[handwritten margin note: whether a person would be liable under like circumstances]

[handwritten note above text: b/c thats what 1346(b)1 says!]

Supreme Court hold that a different standard of liability applies to the federal government under the FTCA and what is that standard?

2. While *Olson* confirms that the private person language in the FTCA directs application to the United States of state tort law in the same manner as it applies to a private entity, the courts have been less settled as to whether this language more affirmatively precludes imposition of liability when the federal government has acted in a manner that has no analogy in the private sector. As the Supreme Court affirmed again in *Olson*, the Court has rejected the argument that the government is immune from liability when exercising uniquely governmental functions. In language also reaffirmed in *Olson*, the Supreme Court in *Indian Towing Co. v. United States*, 350 U.S. 61, 64–69 (1955), observed that the language of the FTCA imposes liability upon the government when a private person would be liable under "*like* circumstances," as opposed to under the "*same*" circumstances." But in *Olson*, the Court emphatically insisted that the standard of liability under the FTCA requires comparison of the government's conduct to that of private parties, that is, a private person analogy. In *Olson*, the government conceded that a private person analogy existed for government safety inspections of mines. What then would be the result where the government's activities lack *any* private analogy, that is, where a private person would never find him or herself under circumstances even remotely similar to the government's activities in a particular context? The next case illustrates the answer that some, but not all, courts have reached on that question.

[handwritten margin notes left side: What if the government's action has no private analogy? "uniquely gov't'al functions"]

[handwritten margin note: Is there always a possibility of comparison?]

[handwritten margin note: We could argue over whether that would even happen; If you concede that there are some functions that don't have private analogues, you limit the reach of a state law to get the Gov't.]

[handwritten note under text: To what extent does the private person analogy divest the gov't of traditional functional immunities? actors]

Gelley v. Astra Pharmaceutical Products, Inc.   *[handwritten: 8th Cir.]*

United States District Court for the District of Minnesota.
466 F.Supp. 182 (D.Minn.), *aff'd*, 610 F.2d 558 (8th Cir. 1979).

ORDER

■ MacLaughlin, District Judge.

This matter comes before the Court on the defendants' renewed motions to dismiss for lack of subject matter jurisdiction and for failure to state a claim upon which relief can be granted pursuant to Federal Rule of Civil Procedure 12(b)(1) and (6). The defendant United States moves to dismiss on the grounds that no actionable tort duty was owed by Food and Drug Administration personnel to the plaintiff's decedent under the circumstances and that the government is immune from liability because of the "discretionary function" and "misrepresentation" exceptions of the Federal Tort Claims Act. 28 U.S.C. § 2680(a) and (h). * * *

Richard Gelley, plaintiff's decedent, died in 1973, allegedly as a result of an adverse reaction to lidocaine hydrochloride (trade name xylocaine), a local anesthetic drug manufactured by defendant Astra Pharmaceutical Products, Inc. [hereinafter Astra]. The xylocaine was administered to plaintiff's decedent by Dr. Jerry K. Brunsoman, who was associated with defendant MacKay & Fuller D.D.S. Professional Association. The United States Food and Drug Administration [hereinafter FDA], an agency of the Department of Health, Education and Welfare, had previously found xylocaine "safe for use" and approved the introduction of the drug into interstate commerce.

This wrongful death action was instituted by plaintiff Carol Gelley, as trustee for the heirs of Richard Gelley, in this Court in 1974. The plaintiff's complaint alleges that FDA personnel, as well as the other defendants, were negligent, that some defendants are liable on a strict liability theory, and that defendant Astra is independently liable because it violated the Food, Drug and Cosmetic Act, 21 U.S.C. § 301, *et seq.* Plaintiff has filed a "protective" action in the Ramsey County District Court against the same parties, except for the United States.

The United States' Motion to Dismiss

The plaintiff correctly concedes that any allegation that the government may be held liable for the FDA's approval of xylocaine as "safe for use" would come within the discretionary function exception of the Federal Tort Claims Act, and thus the government would be immune from liability. However, plaintiff has claimed that FDA personnel were negligent in other respects which primarily if not exclusively are premised on governmental nonfeasance. Generally, plaintiff's theory of liability against the government is that the FDA negligently failed to withdraw its prior approval of xylocaine and negligently failed to enforce the provisions of the Food, Drug and Cosmetic Act and its own regulations relating to information collection and labeling changes, thereby allowing xylocaine to remain in interstate commerce in a misbranded and/or adulterated condition. See 21 U.S.C. §§ 351, 352.

The Federal Tort Claims Act provides that the government shall be liable for death caused by the negligence of government employees "under circumstances where the United States, if a private person, would be liable to the claimant in accordance with the law of the place where the act or omission occurred." 28 U.S.C. § 1346(b). This particular language is the basis for the government's argument that no tort duty was owed by FDA personnel to plaintiff's decedent to withdraw the prior approval of xylocaine or enforce the provisions of the Food, Drug and Cosmetic Act or FDA regulations regarding labeling changes, reporting requirements or the maintenance of records with respect to xylocaine. As the law of the place where the act or omission occurred is the focal point with respect to whether liability may be imposed under the Act, the law of the District of Columbia[4] governs the immediate question of whether the government, if a private individual, would be liable under like circumstances.

---

4. As the bulk of the FDA activity complained of occurred in the District of Columbia during the relevant time period here, the acts or omissions giving rise to potential liability for the most part occurred in the District of Columbia, thus making its law applicable to the issue of whether the government owes an actionable tort duty under the circumstances.

The duties of FDA personnel are federally imposed, stemming either from the Food, Drug and Cosmetic Act or from regulations enacted by the FDA. However, as the Federal Tort Claims Act makes explicit, the law of the place where the act or omission occurred which gives rise to the claim is the foundation upon which federal governmental liability is predicated. Thus, if the law of the place where the act or omission occurred would not impose liability upon a private individual under similar circumstances, then the government cannot be held legally responsible for the acts of its negligent employees. The law of the District of Columbia does not impose a tort duty on private persons to perform activities required by the FDA regulatory scheme. Regulatory activity engaged in by FDA personnel simply has no counterpart in private activity and thus cannot give rise to liability under the common law of the District of Columbia or elsewhere. Therefore, as the law of the place where the act or omission occurred would not impose a duty upon a private person under these circumstances, FDA personnel similarly owed no actionable tort duty to the plaintiff's decedent. The result of the plaintiff's argument, if accepted, would be to impose liability on the federal government for the failure of its regulatory employees to protect the public in general against third party violations of federal law. This result would cast the federal government in the role of an insurer against violations of regulatory law, certainly a result not contemplated by Congress in enacting the Federal Tort Claims Act.

[The court also concluded that, even if the FDA owed a tort law duty to the plaintiff, the discretionary function exception to the FTCA, 28 U.S.C. § 2680(a), applied so as to render the United States immune from tort liability.]

[Following dismissal of the United States, the court dismissed the action as to the remaining private defendants for lack of complete diversity of citizenship among the parties.]

Notes and Questions

1. *Gelley v. Astra Pharmaceutical Products* is a classic example of a court decision concluding that the "private person under like circumstances" language in the FTCA *does* establish a limitation upon the government's liability, that it requires some private counterpart to the government's activities before tort liability may be imposed. Can the *Gelley* decision be reconciled with the Supreme Court's decisions in *United States*

Plaintiff argues that the law of Minnesota would ultimately apply to this issue because the application of conflict of laws principles of the state or district where the acts or omissions of the FDA occurred would require the application of the law of the place of injury, Minnesota. Even if this Court were to apply Minnesota law to this issue, the ultimate result reached by the Court would not change. This logically follows because the law of Minnesota would not impose liability upon a private person under these circumstances, as the duties imposed on FDA personnel by federal law have no "counterparts cognizable" under the law of Minnesota.

v. Olson and *Indian Towing Co. v. United States* that were discussed previously? On the one hand, those decisions ruled that the government may not escape liability by asserting that it had engaged in a "uniquely governmental function." On the other hand, those decisions recognized that the FTCA requires application of a private person standard for governmental liability. Indeed, the Court in *Olson* spoke about the need to find an analogy between the government's conduct and the conduct of private persons. The *Gelley* analysis and result might be reconciled with the Supreme Court's decisions by saying that while the government activity need not be identical to that engaged in by private entities before FTCA liability could lie, some persuasive private person analogy must be present. In *Gelley*, the court demanded only that some analogous form of private conduct be adduced for FTCA liability, but found that the government's licensing and regulatory conduct truly was without any counterpart in the private sector.

As a contrasting example, in *Wells v. United States*, 851 F.2d 1471, 1473–74 (D.C. Cir. 1988),* the United States Court of Appeals for the District of Columbia Circuit firmly resisted the argument that the FTCA "does not apply when the government is engaged in a 'core governmental function.'" In that case, families living near a lead smelter alleged that the Environmental Protection Agency negligently had failed to regulate against lead pollution, in particular by deciding to conduct a further study rather than taking immediate remedial action against the companies. Although the court held the government immune by reason of the discretionary function exception, the court said liability may be imposed on the United States "in many situations in which the government was engaged in activities that have no analogy in the private sector." *Id.* at 1474.

However, as illustrated by recent decisions in three courts of appeals, all within the past decade and all involving the Occupational Safety and Health Administration (OSHA), the debate on this issue is not yet closed and, indeed, the conception of the private person language as a meaningful limitation upon government liability may be enjoying a small revival. First, in *Irving v. United States*, 162 F.3d 154 (1st Cir. 1998) (en banc), an employee of a private manufacturer, who was injured when her hair became entangled in the shaft of a machine, filed an FTCA suit against the United States alleging negligent inspection of the plant by officers of the Occupational Safety and Health Administration (OSHA). She alleged that her injury was caused by OSHA's failure to identify the absence of a guard on the machine as an obvious violation of federal regulations. Among other defenses, the United States argued that the alleged failure of OSHA officers to follow OSHA directives in inspection of the plant was not analogous to any duty owed by a private person upon which liability could be based under §§ 1346(b) and 2674. *Irving v. United States,* 1998 WL 152941, at *20 (1st Cir. 1998) (this opinion was later withdrawn and overturned en banc). A majority of a three-judge panel of the First Circuit concluded

---

* In the interests of full disclosure, the author of this casebook was counsel for the United States in the *Wells* case before the court of appeals.

"that, standing alone, a tortfeasor's uniquely governmental purpose in undertaking to act is insufficient to remove the challenged conduct from the FTCA's waiver of sovereign immunity." *Id.* at *22. Thus, the panel upheld a judgment of liability in the plaintiff's favor. However, the panel said:

> We recognize that other courts have barred FTCA claims based upon conduct in the course of regulatory inspections where the statute that authorizes the inspection stipulates that the employer retains responsibility for complying with safety standards. We also recognize that, despite the Supreme Court's refusal to read either § 2680(a) or the analogous private liability requirement of §§ 1346(b) and 2674 as providing a blanket immunity for regulatory and other uniquely governmental functions, the interpretation of the FTCA's analogous private liability provision is not without conceptual difficulty in the context of a claim alleging negligence in the conduct of a federal regulatory enforcement inspection, for which there is no identical private analogue.

Id. at *25. One of the three judges on the panel dissented, expressing doubts about the majority's "rendition of both federal [FTCA] and state law," but focusing his attention primarily upon interpretation of the underlying state tort law. Subsequently, the First Circuit granted rehearing in the *Irving* case and withdrew the opinion. *Irving v. United States,* 146 F.3d 12 (1st Cir. 1998). The en banc First Circuit then reversed the outcome and dismissed the FTCA suit on the alternative ground of the discretionary function exception (see generally Chapter III.A.4). Because the en banc court's decision was based on this separate ground, the court found it unnecessary to address the private person limitation or state-law questions. *Irving v. United States,* 162 F.3d 154, 157 n. 1 (1st Cir. 1998) (en banc).

(Subsequently, the First Circuit emphatically reinvigorated the private person language as setting the parameters of FTCA liability in *Bolduc v. United States,* 402 F.3d 50, 55–59 (1st Cir. 2005). In *Bolduc,* the court held that a claim by an individual, who had been mistakenly convicted and imprisoned for armed robbery, that a federal agent negligently failed to give exculpatory evidence to the prosecutors, was outside of the jurisdictional grant of the FTCA. Rejecting the argument that liability should be imposed because the government is obliged to disclose exculpatory evidence, the First Circuit explained "the federal government does not yield its immunity with respect to obligations that are peculiar to governments or official-capacity state actors and which have no counterpart in private law." *Id.* at 57. The court further held that, even under the exceptionally broad definition of duty under the applicable state law, tort liability would not be imposed upon a private party who came into possession of exculpatory evidence in the course of an official investigation and carelessly, rather than with malice, failed to disclose it to prosecutors. *Id.* at 57–59.)

Second, the First Circuit panel's expressed uneasiness in *Irving* about imposing liability upon the government for OSHA regulatory conduct that had no private counterpart was followed by the Eleventh Circuit's forth-right refusal to do so in the similar FTCA case of *Pate v. Oakwood Mobile Homes, Inc.*, 374 F.3d 1081 (11th Cir. 2004). In *Pate*, an injured roofer sued the United States alleging that OSHA had negligently failed to abate safety violations for which his employer had been cited before the roofer's fall. The Eleventh Circuit observed that, "[o]f course, a private party would not ordinarily be engaged, as is OSHA, in enforcing compliance with workplace safety regulations." *Id.* at 1084. The court agreed that the FTCA does not deny a remedy for uniquely governmental activities simply "because there is no identical private activity for purposes of comparison," saying that the comparison need not be "exact" before FTCA liability may lie. *Id.* Nonethe-less, the Eleventh Circuit was unable to find any support for imposing liability, concluding that the "closest state analogy, the good samaritan doctrine" could not be stretched to cover the government's regulatory conduct at issue in the case.

Third, in *United States v. Agronics Inc.*, 164 F.3d 1343 (10th Cir. 1999), which yet again involved OSHA regulatory conduct, the Tenth Circuit expressly relied upon what it labeled as the "private analog" requirement to reject an FTCA suit against the United States. Moreover, the Tenth Circuit relied solely upon this ground, choosing not to decide whether the discretionary function exception applied. *Id.* at 1344–45. The FTCA claimant, Agronics, Inc., alleged that its mining business had suf-fered financially by reason of penalties and closure orders issued by the Occupational Safety and Health Administration, without proper authority, because the regulatory agency with legitimate jurisdiction over its activities was the Federal Mine Safety and Health Administration. *Id.* at 1344. The Tenth Circuit held that the FTCA did not apply to claimed negligence arising out of the failure of the federal government to carry out a federal statutory duty, saying that there was nothing remotely analogous in the private sphere to the question of a regulatory agency's determination of its jurisdiction. *Id.* at 1345–46. The court concluded:

> Not only would such liability constitute an impermissible state law encroachment upon the proper domain of the federal Administrative Procedures Act, it would place the government in a disadvantageous position compared to private entities or persons who bear no compara-ble duty. This, of course, exceeds the FTCA's waiver of sovereign immunity, which extends no farther than the limits of private tort liability[.]

Id. at 1347.

For further discussion of the private person analogy element of the FTCA, see generally Gregory C. Sisk, *Litigation With the Federal Govern-ment* § 3.05(c), at 129–38 (ALI–ABA, 4th ed. 2006).

2.   In cases involving governmental conduct, that does not neatly fit private law tort theories, plaintiffs generally allege liability based upon the "Good Samaritan" doctrine under state tort law. As the Supreme Court explained in *Indian Towing v. United States,* 350 U.S. 61, 64 (1955), the Good Samaritan doctrine provides that someone who voluntarily under-

takes a duty to warn or protect the public from danger, and thereby induces reliance, must perform those "Good Samaritan" tasks in a careful manner. *See also* Restatement (Second) of Torts §§ 323, 324A. Does the Good Samaritan doctrine fairly apply when the government's conduct involves mis-regulation of private conduct, as opposed to affirmative protection of the public (such as the maintenance of a government lighthouse in *Indian Towing*)? When the Food and Drug Administration regulates food, drug, and cosmetic manufacturers, or when the Environmental Protection Agency regulates private behavior involving pollution or hazardous waste, these agencies act pursuant to statutory direction. Can this be characterized as the type of gratuitous or voluntary undertaking necessary to find a Good Samaritan duty of care? Doesn't the *Gelley* court have a point that imposing liability in such a case places the government in the position of an insurer against the wrongdoing of any private actors subject to government regulation?

In *Irving v. United States, supra,* the three-judge panel had held that the United States was liable under the FTCA for negligent OSHA inspection of a workplace, based upon the New Hampshire common-law Good Samaritan doctrine which imposes a duty to use reasonable care when undertaking to act voluntarily for another's benefit. 1998 WL 152941, at *17–19, 28–35 (opinion withdrawn). The panel ruled that, if a private person would be obliged to exercise due care for undertaking the same inspection activities, "liability of the United States under the FTCA is not precluded as a matter of law simply because the tortfeasor is a government actor, carrying out a duty that devolves only upon agents of the federal government." *Id.* at *19. Judge Selya dissented from the panel's opinion, arguing that while the Good Samaritan doctrine may apply, for example, to a commercial entity that contracts to provide relatively comprehensive inspection services, it would not apply to unsolicited random and sporadic inspections, such as made by OSHA. *Id.* at *37–44. Judge Selya also contended that "[i]t is simply bad public policy to penalize the government for undertaking programs that augment workplace safety measures." *Id.* at *43. (As stated above, the First Circuit sitting en banc subsequently reversed the judgment in favor of the plaintiff on the alternative ground of the discretionary function exception and therefore found it unnecessary to again address the state-law question).

In *Pate v. Oakwood Mobile Homes, Inc.*, 374 F.3d 1081, 1084–87 (11th Cir. 2004), the Eleventh Circuit held that the Good Samaritan doctrine under Georgia law did not apply to OSHA's conduct in enforcing compliance by an employer with workplace safety regulations. The court found that the government by undertaking inspections and regulation had not thereby assumed a particular responsibility for employee safety, because the federal statutory responsibility for compliance with safety measures remained with the employer. Nor could reliance justifiably be placed upon OSHA's exercise of enforcement powers in identifying and abating any violations because, again, primary responsibility always remained with the employer.

Who do you think has the better of the argument on the application of the Good Samaritan doctrine to the federal government when it negligently inspects or regulates private actors?

————

c. THE EXCLUSION OF STRICT LIABILITY

[handwritten: Make point u/kant-out → combat necessarily implies risks (not the Stnd.-of-care)]

Laird v. Nelms

[handwritten: 6-2]

Supreme Court of the United States.
406 U.S. 797 (1972).

■ MR. JUSTICE REHNQUIST delivered the opinion of the Court.

Respondents brought this action in the United States District Court under the Federal Tort Claims Act, 28 U.S.C. §§ 1346(b), 2671–2680. They sought recovery for property damage allegedly resulting from a sonic boom caused by California-based United States military planes flying over North Carolina on a training mission. The District Court entered summary judgment for petitioners, but on respondents' appeal the United States Court of Appeals for the Fourth Circuit reversed. That court held that, although respondents had been unable to show negligence "either in the planning or operation of the flight," they were nonetheless entitled to proceed on a theory of strict or absolute liability for ultrahazardous activities conducted by petitioners in their official capacities. * * * We granted certiorari.

[handwritten margin notes: Sonic Boom damage; S.J. for P's; 4th Cir: Rev; based on Entitv. to proceed S.L]

Dalehite [*v. United States*, 346 U.S. 15 (1953)], held that the Government was not liable for the extensive damage resulting from the explosion of two cargo vessels in the harbor of Texas City, Texas, in 1947. The Court's opinion rejected various specifications of negligence on the part of Government employees that had been found by the District Court in that case, and then went on to treat petitioners' claim that the Government was absolutely or strictly liable because of its having engaged in a dangerous activity. The Court said with respect to this aspect of the plaintiffs' claim:

> "[T]he Act does not extend to such situations, though of course well known in tort law generally. It is to be invoked only on a 'negligent or wrongful act or omission' of an employee. Absolute liability, of course, arises irrespective of how the tortfeasor conducts himself; it is imposed automatically when any damages are sustained as a result of the decision to engage in the dangerous activity." 346 U.S., at 44.

This Court's resolution of the strict-liability issue in *Dalehite* did not turn on the question of whether the law of Texas or of some other State did or did not recognize strict liability for the conduct of ultrahazardous activities. It turned instead on the question of whether the language of the Federal Tort Claims Act permitted under any circumstances the imposition of liability upon the Government where there had been neither negligence nor wrongful act. The necessary consequence of the Court's holding in

[handwritten margin notes: (circled plus) regardless of vs. state law]

Dalehite is that the statutory language "negligent or wrongful act or omission of any employee of the Government," is a uniform federal limitation on the types of acts committed by its employees for which the United States has consented to be sued. Regardless of state law characterization, the Federal Tort Claims Act itself precludes the imposition of liability if there has been no negligence or other form of "misfeasance or nonfeasance," 346 U.S., at 45, on the part of the Government. * * *

* * * The legislative history [of the Act] indicates that Congress intended to permit liability essentially based on the intentionally wrongful or careless conduct of Government employees, for which the Government was to be made liable according to state law under the doctrine of *respondeat superior,* but to exclude liability based solely on the ultrahazardous nature of an activity undertaken by the Government.

A House Judiciary Committee memorandum explaining the "discretionary function" exemption from the bill when that exemption first appeared in the draft legislation in 1942 made the comment that "the cases covered by that subsection would probably have been exempted ... by judicial construction" in any event, but that the exemption was intended to preclude any possibility

> "that the act would be construed to authorize suit for damages against the Government growing out of a legally authorized activity, such as a floodcontrol or irrigation project, where no wrongful act or omission on the part of any Government agent is shown, and the only ground for suit is the contention that the same conduct by a private individual would be tortious...." Hearings on H.R. 5373 and H.R. 6463 before the House Committee on the Judiciary, 77th Cong., 2d Sess., ser. 13, pp. 65–66 (1942).

The same memorandum, after noting the erosion of the doctrine of sovereign immunity over the years, observed with respect to the bill generally:

> "Yet a large and highly important area remains in which no satisfactory remedy has been provided for the wrongs of Government officers or employees, the ordinary 'commonlaw' type of tort, such as personal injury or property damage caused by the negligent operation of an automobile." *Id.,* at 39. * * *

Our reaffirmation of the construction put on the Federal Tort Claims Act in *Dalehite,* makes it unnecessary to treat the scope of the discretionary-function exemption contained in the Act, or the other matters dealt with by the Court of Appeals.

Reversed.

■ MR. JUSTICE DOUGLAS, having heard the argument, withdrew from participation in the consideration or decision of this case.

■ MR. JUSTICE STEWART, with whom MR. JUSTICE BRENNAN joins, dissenting.

* * * The Court of Appeals in this case found that the law of North Carolina renders a person who creates a sonic boom absolutely liable for

any injuries caused thereby, and that finding is not challenged here. And while the petitioners argue that the conduct involved falls within one of the numerous express exceptions to the coverage of the Act contained in § 2680, the Court today does not reach that issue. Rather, the Court holds that the words "negligent or wrongful act or omission" preclude the application to the United States of any state law under which persons may be held absolutely liable for injuries caused by certain kinds of conduct. In my view, this conclusion is not justified by the language or the history of the Act, and is plainly contrary to the statutory purpose. I therefore dissent.

In the vast majority of cases in the law of torts, liability is predicated on a breach of some legal duty owed by the defendant to the plaintiff, whether that duty involves exercising reasonable care in one's activities or refraining from certain activities altogether. The law of most jurisdictions, however, imposes liability for harm caused by certain narrowly limited kinds of activities even though those activities are not prohibited and even though the actor may have exercised the utmost care. Such conduct is "tortious," not because the actor is necessarily blameworthy, but because society has made a judgment that while the conduct is so socially valuable that it should not be prohibited, it nevertheless carries such a high risk of harm to others, even in the absence of negligence, that one who engages in it should make good any harm caused to others thereby.

While the doctrine of absolute liability is not encountered in many situations even under modern tort law, it was nevertheless well established at the time the Tort Claims Act was enacted, and there is nothing in the language or the history of the Act to support the notion that this doctrine alone, among all the rules governing tort liability in the various States, was considered inapplicable in cases arising under the Act. The legislative history quoted by the Court relates solely to the "discretionary function" exception contained in § 2680, an exception upon which the Court specifically declines to rely. As I read the Act and the legislative history, the phrase "negligent or wrongful act or omission" was intended to include the entire range of conduct classified as tortious under state law.[4] The only intended exceptions to this sweeping waiver of governmental immunity were those expressly set forth and now collected in § 2680. This interpretation was put upon the Act by the legislative committees that recommended its passage in 1946: "The present bill would establish a uniform system . . . permitting suit to be brought on *any tort claim* . . . with the exception of certain classes of torts *expressly exempted* from the operation of the act."

---

4. A bill passed by the Senate in 1942 covered only actions based on the "negligence" of Government employees. S.2221, 77th Cong., 2d Sess. The House committee substituted the phrase "negligent or wrongful act or omission," saying that the "committee prefers its language as it would afford relief for certain acts or omissions which may be wrongful but not necessarily negligent." H.R.Rep. No. 2245, 77th Cong., 2d Sess., 11. The language used by the House committee was carried over into the bill finally enacted in 1946, without further mention in the committee reports of the intended scope of the words "wrongful act."

(Emphasis supplied.) H.R.Rep. No. 1287, 79th Cong., 1st Sess., 3; S.Rep.No. 1400, 79th Cong., 2d Sess., 31.

The Court rests its conclusion on language from *Dalehite v. United States*, 346 U.S. 15, where a four-man majority of the Court, in an opinion dealing primarily with the "discretionary function" exception, held the doctrine of absolute liability inapplicable in that extremely unusual case arising under the Federal Tort Claims Act. That language has been severely criticized; it has not since been relied upon in any decision of this Court; and it was rejected as a general principle by at least one Court of Appeals less than a year after *Dalehite* was decided. *United States v. Praylou*, 4 Cir., 208 F.2d 291, 295. Moreover, *Dalehite* represented an approach to interpretation of the Act that was abruptly changed only two years later in *Indian Towing Co. v. United States*, 350 U.S. 61. That decision rejected the proposition that the United States was immune from liability where the activity involved was "governmental" rather than "proprietary"—a proposition that seemingly had been established in *Dalehite*. And while the *Dalehite* opinion explicitly created a presumption in favor of sovereign immunity, to be overcome only where relinquishment by Congress was "clear," 346 U.S., at 30–31, the Court in *Indian Towing* recognized that the Tort Claims Act "cuts the ground from under" the doctrine of sovereign immunity, and cautioned that a court should not "as a self-constituted guardian of the Treasury import immunity back into a statute designed to limit it." 350 U.S., at 65, 69. These developments * * * have until today been generally understood to mean that the language in *Dalehite* rejecting the absolute-liability doctrine had been implicitly abandoned.

The rule announced by the Court today seems to me contrary to the whole policy of the Tort Claims Act. For the doctrine of absolute liability is applicable not only to sonic booms, but to other activities that the Government carries on in common with many private citizens. Absolute liability for injury caused by the concussion or debris from dynamite blasting, for example, is recognized by an overwhelming majority of state courts. A private person who detonates an explosion in the process of building a road is liable for injuries to others caused thereby under the law of most States even though he took all practicable precautions to prevent such injuries, on the sound principle that he who creates such a hazard should make good the harm that results. Yet if employees of the United States engage in exactly the same conduct with an identical result, the United States will not, under the principle announced by the Court today, be liable to the injured party. Nothing in the language or the legislative history of the Act compels such a result, and we should not lightly conclude that Congress intended to create a situation so much at odds with common sense and the basic rationale of the Act. We recognized that rationale in *Rayonier* [, *Inc. v. United States*, 352 U.S. 315], a case involving negligence by employees of the United States in controlling a forest fire:

"Congress was aware that when losses caused by such negligence are charged against the public treasury they are in effect spread among all those who contribute financially to the support of the Government and the resulting burden on each taxpayer is relatively slight. But when the entire burden falls on the injured party it may leave him destitute or grievously harmed. Congress could, and apparently did, decide that this would be unfair when the public as a whole benefits from the services performed by Government employees." 352 U.S., at 320.

For the reasons stated, I would hold that the doctrine of absolute liability is applicable to conduct of employees of the United States under the same circumstances as those in which it is applied to the conduct of private persons under the law of the State where the conduct occurs. * * *

[Justice Stewart also concluded that the discretionary function exception, 28 U.S.C. § 2680(a), was inapplicable to the case.]

———

Notes and Questions

In *Laird v. Nelms,* the Supreme Court defines what constitutes a "negligent or wrongful act or omission" that may give rise to governmental liability under the FTCA. How does the Court interpret this language? What is included? What is excluded? Why? How does the dissent interpret this phrase differently?

Consider the effect of the Court's decision: Suppose that a private citizen were injured when federal employees were blasting a ridge in Minnesota with dynamite to build a federal water reservoir. Assume further that Minnesota tort law provides for strict liability for the hazardous activity of using dynamite for blasting. How must the citizen proceed to establish liability under the FTCA? Notice how the focus shifts from the nature of the activity (strict liability) to the specific act or omission (negligence).

———

d.   THE SCOPE–OF–EMPLOYMENT REQUIREMENT

Piper v. United States

United States Court of Appeals for the Eighth Circuit.
887 F.2d 861 (8th Cir. 1989).

■ BRIGHT, SENIOR CIRCUIT JUDGE.

The United States appeals the district court's judgment awarding damages under the Federal Tort Claims Act, 28 U.S.C. §§ 1346(b), 2671–2680 (1982), for dog-bite wounds sustained by Matthew Durran, age eleven, while residing on a military base. The district court held the Government liable for the negligence of a servicemember, TSgt. Robert Williams, who permitted his dog to run free in violation of regulations promulgated by the

Little Rock (Arkansas) Air Force Base.[1] The district court ruled that Williams' responsibility to control his pet was within the scope of his employment in the military and rendered the United States liable on a respondeat superior theory. On appeal the United States asserts that TSgt. Williams did not act within the scope of his employment when he neglected to keep his dog under control at his personal residence. We agree with the Government's position and reverse and vacate the judgment, but remand for a determination of whether other grounds exist to support the award of damages.

I. BACKGROUND

At the time of the incident, Matthew Durran lived with his mother, June Piper, a National Guard enlisted person, at Little Rock Air Force Base (LRAFB). TSgt. Robert Williams, the owner of a large Airedale dog named Arby, lived nearby.

On the afternoon of January 18, 1986, Matthew returned from school on the bus and saw Arby in his backyard, sitting at the rear patio glass door and barking at the dogs in the house. Matthew called for the dog to follow him towards its own home. The dog attacked Matthew, knocked him to the ground and bit him on the forehead and around the scalp. The school bus driver, witnessing the incident, sounded her horn and the dog ran away. The bus driver then administered first aid to Matthew and called for an ambulance.

Matthew suffered considerable pain during and after the attack. He received several lacerations and puncture wounds on his head requiring treatment and approximately eight follow-up visits. The attack left scars on Matthew's head and resulted in some temporary emotional damage.

The attack on Matthew did not represent Arby's first attack upon a person nor the dog owner's first failure to control the dog. On January 11, 1985, one year prior to the attack on Matthew, airbase security police found Arby running at large and cited TSgt. Williams for failing to control his dog. As a result, the commanding officer verbally counseled TSgt. Williams on the need to control his pet.

On January 26, 1985, Arby bit three-year old LeChelle Stimson through the nose while she visited in TSgt. Williams' home. Although no one witnessed the incident, LeChelle's father told the security police that the dog bit the child when she pulled its whiskers. TSgt. Williams again received verbal counseling on the need to control his dog, but the security police did not report the incident as a nuisance, relying on the father's statement that LeChelle had provoked the dog.

On March 30, 1985, Arby bit one of Williams' sons at the Williams' home. Williams reported this incident to the base veterinarian who recorded it in a log book, but took no further action. The district court found that

1. The opinion of the district court is reported. *Piper v. United States,* 694 F.Supp. 614 (E.D.Ark.1988).

the veterinarian did not report the incident to security police because the veterinarian considered the incident a private matter.

Base regulations permit pets on the base as long as they do not become a nuisance, are not allowed to run free and are under the control of the owner at all times. LRAFB Regulation 125–2 (May 20, 1981). The base commander, security police and pet owner share responsibility for enforcing this regulation. The regulation further requires that any pet reported twice as a nuisance be removed from the base. Evidence in the record also suggests that emergency room personnel are required to report all dog-bite incidents to the security police, but the district court made no specific finding in this regard.

There are regs. in place to control animals & address incidents

The district court found that Arby did not habitually run free, but noted that the evidence conflicted on this point. The court also found that except for the three biting incidents, no evidence indicated that the dog had exhibited aggressive or vicious tendencies.

Matthew's mother, who brought the suit on behalf of Matthew, argued that the Government was liable under the FTCA, on either of two theories. First, Mrs. Piper contended that TSgt. Williams had acted negligently in the line of duty by failing to maintain control over Arby. Second, Mrs. Piper contended that airbase personnel responsible for maintaining order on the base had negligently permitted Arby to remain on the base when they knew or should have known of his dangerous propensities.

π Arg.

After a three-day bench trial, the district court found for Matthew and entered an award of damages in the amount of $9,600. As we have already mentioned, the court held TSgt. Williams acted in the line of duty because base regulations delegated to him the duty to control his dog. The district court relied on *Lutz v. United States,* 685 F.2d 1178 (9th Cir.1982), a factually similar case, for this proposition of law. The trial court determined that violation of LRAFB Regulation 125–2 (relating to control of pets) by Williams amounted to negligence in the line of duty and held the United States liable under the FTCA. The district court did not decide whether the United States could be liable for the negligence of other airbase personnel in duties relating to control of animals.

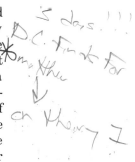

3 days!!! D.C. fmk for Om. the on theory I

II.   DISCUSSION

While this case factually resembles the *Lutz* case, we decline to follow it. Instead, we adopt the reasoning of another similar case, *Nelson v. United States,* 838 F.2d 1280 (D.C.Cir.1988), where the court held that an owner's failure to control his pet dog did not occur in the line of duty.

As a preliminary matter, we observe that the FTCA waives the Government's immunity to suit only for personal injuries caused by government employees acting within the scope of their employment. 28 U.S.C. § 1346(b). Military employees are within the scope of employment when they act in "the line of duty." 28 U.S.C. § 2671. "Line of duty" takes its meaning from the applicable state law of respondeat superior. *Williams v. United States,* 350 U.S. 857 (1955) (per curiam). Under Arkansas law an employee acts within the scope of employment or in the line of duty when he acts for his employer's benefit or furthers his employer's interest.

Borrowing the rationale from the *Lutz* case, the district court reasoned that TSgt. Williams had been delegated a duty to control his dog because of regulations relating to control of pets and because violation of these regulations subjects servicemembers to discipline. That court concluded that Williams' failure to control the dog therefore occurred in the line of duty.

This reasoning will not stand. Military bases regulate a wide variety of subjects, some of them trivial, such as housekeeping. It stretches the statute too far to say that any act or omission by a servicemember, if covered by a regulation, represents conduct in the line of duty. In this case and in many cases, connection between the duty imposed by the regulation and military service is far too tenuous to conclude that the FTCA applies. As the District of Columbia Circuit observed:

> Under *Lutz,* all duties imposed by military regulation, no matter how trivial, could fall within the serviceman's line of duty and thus within the employer-employee relationship. In the unique context of life on a military base, however, the government is much like an old-fashioned "company town." Within this multi-faceted relationship, the military imposes many duties on military personnel, not all of which are plausibly viewed as imposed by the government in its role as employer.

> Bolling Air Force Base regulations, for example, require base residents to use certain size pots and pans, to replace electrical fuses, and to refrain from smoking in bed. These duties are not imposed by the military in its role as an employer and they do not run to the employer's benefit. Rather, they are incidental regulations designed to ensure that the base functions under conditions of common consideration and orderliness that enhance community life; as such, they are designed to benefit all residents of the housing community. Because such duties, although established by military regulations, do not run to the benefit of the employer and are linked only incidentally with the employment relationship, they cannot be said to be discharged within the scope of employment.

Id. at 1283–84. We believe this analysis is sound and adopt it. Accordingly, the United States is not derivatively liable under the FTCA for negligence on the part of TSgt. Williams.

There is, however, another theory on which the Government might be liable. The district court heard evidence but did not decide whether other air base personnel negligently performed their duties. We cannot say from the record before us whether the commanding officer, security police or the veterinarian knew or should have known of the potential threat posed by Arby. On remand, however, the district court should decide this issue on the present record or it may permit the parties to introduce additional evidence on this issue.

III. CONCLUSION

Accordingly, we reverse the judgment of the district court and remand for a determination of whether there are other grounds to support the award of damages in favor of Matthew.

————

Notes

1. In holding that a military servicemember was not acting within the scope of employment when he violated a base "housekeeping" regulation in failing to control his pet dog who bit someone, the Eighth Circuit in *Piper v. United States* joins the District of Columbia Circuit in *Nelson v. United States*. Both courts reject the Ninth Circuit's contrary conclusion in *Lutz v. United States*. The Sixth Circuit in *Chancellor by Chancellor v. United States*, 1 F.3d 438 (6th Cir. 1993), has also joined the Eighth and District of Columbia Circuits in refusing to impose respondeat superior liability on the United States under similar circumstances. The Eleventh Circuit has rejected the *Lutz* analysis in the context of an FTCA suit brought by the victim of an accidental shooting in army barracks by an off-duty soldier, who violated base regulations requiring that privately owned firearms be registered. *Bennett v. United States*, 102 F.3d 486 (11th Cir. 1996). For a scholarly discussion of these cases, see Dianne Rosky, *Respondeat Inferior: Determining the United States' Liability for the Intentional Torts of Federal Law Enforcement Officials*, 36 U.C. Davis L. Rev. 895, 925–28 (2003).

2. Note that the question of whether a government employee was "acting within the scope of his office or employment," 28 U.S.C. § 1346(b)—so as to make the United States vicariously liable for the employee's wrongdoing—requires us to turn to the applicable state law on respondeat superior. *Bodin v. Vagshenian*, 462 F.3d 481, 484 (5th Cir. 2006); *Williams, v. United States*, 350 U.S. 857 (1955) (per curiam); *Palmer v. Flaggman*, 93 F.3d 196, 199 (5th Cir. 1996); *McHugh v. University of Vermont*, 966 F.2d 67, 75 n.9 (2d Cir. 1992). Thus, different conclusions may be reached in cases arising in different states on difficult questions regarding whether an employee was acting within the scope of employment. For a scholarly critique of the use of state law to determine the scope of employment for the FTCA, see Rosky, *supra*, at 897 (arguing that "[a]ppli-cation of varied state respondeat superior rules makes a mockery of meaningful federal accountability for official misconduct," especially in the context of federal law enforcement officers and military actors, given that state law rules developed in the private employment context fail to account for the unique nature and authority of federal law enforcement and the military, and accordingly proposing adoption of a uniform federal scope of employment rule).

3. Because the waiver of sovereign immunity applies only for acts committed by an "employee of the Government while acting within the scope of his office or employment," 28 U.S.C. § 1346(b)(1), the FTCA does not extend to acts of independent contractors engaged by the federal

government for a project. *United States v. Orleans,* 425 U.S. 807, 813–14 (1976). Moreover, the FTCA defines "employee of the government" as including "officers or employees of any federal agency," and then defines "federal agency" as "not includ[ing] any contractor with the United States." 28 U.S.C. § 2671. The critical factor in determining whether an individual is an employee of the government or an independent contractor is the power of the federal government to control the detailed physical performance of the individual. *Orleans,* 425 U.S. at 814; *see also Logue v. United States,* 412 U.S. 521, 527 (1973) ("[T]he distinction between the servant or agent relationship and that of independent contractor turn[s] on the absence of authority in the principal to control the physical conduct of the contractor in performance of the contract."). In addition to control of the detailed physical performance as the central factor, courts have looked to the factors stated in the Restatement (Second) of Agency § 220 to differentiate between an employee and an independent contractor under the FTCA, including the extent of control over the details of the work, whether the one employed is engaged in a distinct occupation or business, the skill required for the particular occupation, who supplies the instrumentalities and tools for the work, the length of time for which the person is employed, and the method of payment. *See, e.g., Linkous v. United States,* 142 F.3d 271, 276–77 (5th Cir. 1998) (finding that a physician who had contracted with an army hospital was an independent contractor, not an employee, because the government had no control over the day-to-day rendition of medical services, she was engaged in a distinct profession, and she was paid on a fee-for-service basis).

4. You should also be aware that when a government employee *is* determined to have been acting within the scope of employment at the time of an allegedly tortious incident, then by statute the United States is to be substituted as the defendant to an FTCA suit and the suit may no longer proceed against the government employee individually. Under the Federal Employees Liability Reform and Tort Compensation Act, 28 U.S.C. § 2679 (commonly known as the "Westfall Act"), the remedy against the United States under the FTCA "is exclusive of any other civil action or proceeding for money damages by reason of the same subject matter against the employee whose act or omission gave rise to the claim * * * ." *Id.* § 2679(b)(1). *See generally Gutierrez de Martinez v. Lamagno,* 515 U.S. 417 (1995). Thus, the Westfall Act grants personal immunity to government employees when acting within the scope of employment. A party seeking recovery for wrongful death, injuries, or property damage based upon an employee's tortious action while acting in the scope of employment is limited to a suit against the United States and may not recover from the individual employee, even if the FTCA suit fails because of special defenses available only to the federal government. *United States v. Smith,* 499 U.S. 160, 166–67 (1991). The Westfall Act is discussed in the context of suits against federal officers and immunity for federal officers in Chapter V.B.1.b.

4. THE DISCRETIONARY FUNCTION EXCEPTION

28 United States Code § 2680(a)

The provisions of this chapter and section 1346(b) of this title shall not apply to—

(a) Any claim based upon an act or omission of an employee of the Government, exercising due care, in the execution of a statute or regulation, whether or not such statute or regulation be valid, or based upon the exercise or performance or the failure to exercise or perform a discretionary function or duty on the part of a federal agency or an employee of the Government, whether or not the discretion involved be abused.

Dalehite v. United States

Supreme Court of the United States.
346 U.S. 15 (1953).

■ MR. JUSTICE REED delivered the opinion of the Court.

Petitioners seek damages from the United States for the death of Henry G. Dalehite in explosions of fertilizer with an ammonium nitrate base, at Texas City, Texas, on April 16 and 17, 1947. This is a test case, representing some 300 separate personal and property claims in the aggregate amount of two hundred million dollars. Consolidated trial was had in the District Court for the Southern District of Texas on the facts and the crucial question of federal liability generally. This was done under an arrangement that the result would be accepted as to those matters in the other suits. Judgment was rendered following separate proof of damages for these individual plaintiffs in the sum of $75,000. Damages in the other claims remain to be determined. The Court of Appeals for the Fifth Circuit unanimously reversed, however, *In re Texas City Disaster Litigation,* 197 F.2d 771, and we granted certiorari because the case presented an important problem of federal statutory interpretation.

The suits were filed under the Federal Tort Claims Act, 28 U.S.C. §§ 1346, 2671–2678, 2680. That Act waived sovereign immunity from suit for certain specified torts of federal employees. It did not assure injured persons damages for all injuries caused by such employees. * * *

There is an exception from the scope of this provision. Section 2680 reads:

"The provisions of this chapter and section 1346(b) of this title shall not apply to—

"(a) Any claim based upon an act or omission of an employee of the Government, exercising due care, in the execution of a statute or regulation, whether or not such statute or regulation be valid, or based upon the exercise or performance or the failure to exercise or perform a discretionary function or duty on the part of a federal agency or an employee of the Government, whether or not the discretion involved be abused."

Suing under this grant of jurisdiction, the plaintiffs claimed negligence, substantially on the part of the entire body of federal officials and employees involved in a program of production of the material—Fertilizer Grade Ammonium Nitrate (FGAN hereafter)—in which the original fire occurred and which exploded. This fertilizer had been produced and distributed at the instance, according to the specifications and under the control of the United States. * * *

The particular FGAN involved at Texas City came to be produced for foreign use for these reasons: Following the World War II hostilities, the United States' obligations as an occupying power, and the danger of internal unrest, forced this Government to deal with the problem of feeding the populations of Germany, Japan and Korea. Direct shipment of foodstuffs was impractical; available fertilizer was in short supply, and requirements from the United States were estimated at about 800,000 tons. However, some 15 ordnance plants had been deactivated and turned over to the War Assets Administration for disposal. Under–Secretary of War Royall suggested in May of 1946, and Secretary Patterson agreed, that these be used for production of fertilizer needed for export. The Director of the Office of War Mobilization and Reconversion acting under the power delegated by the President ordered the plants into operation. Cabinet approval followed. The War Department allocated funds from its appropriations for "Supplies" and "Military Posts" for 1946; direct appropriations for relief in the occupied areas were made by Congress in the following year. The Army's Chief of Ordnance was delegated the responsibility for carrying out the plan, and was authorized particularly to enter into cost-plus fixed fees contracts with private companies for the operation of the plants' facilities. He in turn appointed the Field Director of Ammunition Plants (FDAP) to administer the program. Thereafter the Department entered into a number of contracts with private firms—including the du Pont Co. and Hercules Powder Co.—to "operate the installations ... described herein for the graining of ammonium nitrate (fertilizer grade)," but subjecting "the work to be done by the Contractor ... to the general supervision, direction, control and approval of the Contracting Officer." A detailed set of specifications was drawn up and sent to each plant which included "FDAP Specifications for Products" and a similar TVA paper. Army personnel were appointed for each plant. These were responsible for the application of these specifications, liaison with supply officials, and satisfaction of production schedules, pursuant to an Army Standard Operating Procedure. Beyond this, operations were controlled by the administering corporation which supplied the personnel and production experience required.

FGAN's basic ingredient was ammonium nitrate, long used as a component in explosives. Its adaptability as a fertilizer stemmed from its high free nitrogen content. * * *

The particular FGAN transported to Texas City had been produced at three of the plants activated by the Government for the foreign fertilizer program * * *. * * * *

By April 15, 1947, following three weeks warehouse storage at Texas City * * * some 1,850 tons of the FGAN * * * had been loaded on the French Government-owned steamship *Grandcamp,* and some 1,000 tons on the privately-owned *High Flyer* by independent stevedores hired by the French. The *Grandcamp* carried in addition a substantial cargo of explosives, and the *High Flyer* 2,000 tons of sulphur at the time. At about 8:15 a.m. of the next day smoke was sighted in the *Grandcamp* hold and all efforts to halt the fire were unavailing.[7] Both ships exploded and much of the city was leveled and many people killed.

Since no individual acts of negligence could be shown, the suits for damages that resulted necessarily predicated government liability on the participation of the United States in the manufacture and the transportation of FGAN. Following the disaster of course, no one could fail to be impressed with the blunt fact that FGAN would explode. In sum petitioners charged that the Federal Government had brought liability on itself for the catastrophe by using a material in fertilizer which had been used as an ingredient of explosives for so long that industry knowledge gave notice that other combinations of ammonium nitrate with other material might explode. The negligence charged was that the United States, without definitive investigation of FGAN properties, shipped or permitted shipment to a congested area without warning of the possibility of explosion under certain conditions. The District Court accepted this theory. His judgment was based on a series of findings of causal negligence which, for our purposes, can be roughly divided into three kinds—those which held that the Government had been careless in drafting and adopting the fertilizer export plan as a whole, those which found specific negligence in various phases of the manufacturing process and those which emphasized official dereliction of duty in failing to police the shipboard loading. The Court of Appeals *en banc* unanimously reversed, but since only three of the six judges explicitly rejected the bulk of these findings, we shall consider the case as one in which they come to us unimpaired. Even assuming their correctness *arguendo*, though, it is our judgment that they do not establish a case within the Act. This is for the reason that as a matter of law the facts found cannot give the District Court jurisdiction of the cause under the Tort Claims Act.

I. The Federal Tort Claims Act was passed by the Seventy-ninth Congress in 1946 as Title IV of the Legislative Reorganization Act, 60 Stat. 842, after nearly thirty years of congressional consideration. It was the offspring of a feeling that the Government should assume the obligation to

---

7. The *Grandcamp* exploded about an hour after the fire was noticed. Meanwhile the captain of the ship had ordered all personnel off and the hatches closed. Steam was introduced into the holds. All admit that this is normal fire-fighting procedure aboard ships, but that it was less than effective in this case because of the oxidizing properties of the FGAN. Whether or not the captain was negligent this Court is not called upon to say.

pay damages for the misfeasance of employees in carrying out its work. And the private bill device was notoriously clumsy. Some simplified recovery procedure for the mass of claims was imperative. This Act was Congress' solution, affording instead easy and simple access to the federal courts for torts within its scope.

The meaning of the governmental regulatory function exception from suits shows most clearly in the history of the Tort Claims Bill in the Seventy-seventh Congress. The Seventy-ninth, which passed the Act, held no hearings on the Act. Instead, it integrated the language of the Seventy-seventh Congress, which had first considered the exception, into the Legislative Reorganization Act as Title IV.

Earlier tort claims bills considered by Congress contained reservations from the abdication of sovereign immunity. Prior to 1942 these exceptions were couched in terms of specific spheres of federal activity, such as postal service, the activities of the Securities and Exchange Commission, or the collection of taxes. In 1942, however, the Seventy-seventh Congress drafted a two-fold elimination of claims based on the execution of a regulation or statute or on the exercise of a discretionary function. The language of the bills then introduced in both the House and Senate in fact, was identical with that of § 2680(a) as adopted. The exception was drafted as a clarifying amendment to the House bill to assure protection for the Government against tort liability for errors in administration or in the exercise of discretionary functions. An Assistant Attorney General, appearing before the Committee especially for that purpose, explained it as avoiding "any possibility that the act may be construed to authorize damage suits against the Government growing out of a legally authorized activity," merely because "the same conduct by a private individual would be tortious." It was not "intended that the constitutionality of legislation, the legality of regulations, or the propriety of a discretionary administrative act should be tested through the medium of a damage suit for tort. The same holds true of other administrative action not of a regulatory nature, such as the expenditure of Federal Funds, the execution of a Federal project and the like." Referring to a prior bill which had not contained the "discretionary function" exemption, the House Committee on the Judiciary was advised that "the cases embraced within [the new] subsection would have been exempted from [the prior] bill by judicial construction. It is not probable that the courts would extend a Tort Claims Act into the realm of the validity of legislation or discretionary administrative action, but H.R. 6463 makes this specific."

The legislative history indicates that while Congress desired to waive the Government's immunity from actions for injuries to person and property occasioned by the tortious conduct of its agents acting within their scope of business, it was not contemplated that the Government should be subject to liability arising from acts of a governmental nature or function. Section 2680(a) draws this distinction. Uppermost in the collective mind of Congress were the ordinary common-law torts. Of these, the example which is reiterated in the course of the repeated proposals for submitting the United

States to tort liability, is "negligence in the operation of vehicles."[20] On the other hand the Committee's reports explain the boundaries of the sovereign immunity waived, as defined by this § 2680 exception, with one paragraph which appears time and again after 1942, and in the House Report of the Congress that adopted in § 2680(a) the limitation in the language proposed for the 77th Congress.[21] It was adopted by the Committee in almost the language of the Assistant Attorney General's explanation. This paragraph characterizes the general exemption as "a highly important exception, intended to preclude any possibility that the bill might be construed to authorize suit for damages against the Government growing out of authorized activity, such as a flood control or irrigation project, where no negligence on the part of any government agent is shown, and the only ground for the suit is the contention that the same conduct by a private individual would be tortious. . . . The bill is not intended to authorize a suit for damages to test the validity of or provide a remedy on account of such discretionary acts even though negligently performed and involving an abuse of discretion."

II. Turning to the interpretation of the Act, our reasoning as to its applicability to this disaster starts from the accepted jurisprudential principle that no action lies against the United States unless the legislature has authorized it. The language of the Act makes the United States liable "respecting the provisions of this title relating to tort claims, in the same manner and to the same extent as a private individual under like circumstances". 28 U.S.C. § 2674. This statute is another example of the progressive relaxation by legislative enactments of the rigor of the immunity rule. Through such statutes that change the law, organized government expresses the social purposes that motivate its legislation. Of course, these modifications are entitled to a construction that will accomplish their aim, that is, one that will carry out the legislative purpose of allowing suits against the Government for negligence with due regard for the statutory exceptions to that policy. In interpreting the exceptions to the generality of the grant, courts include only those circumstances which are within the words and reason of the exception. They cannot do less since petitioners obtain their "right to sue from Congress [and they] necessarily must take [that right] subject to such restrictions as have been imposed." *Federal Housing Administration v. Burr,* 309 U.S. 242, 251.

So, our decisions have interpreted the Act to require clear relinquishment of sovereign immunity to give jurisdiction for tort actions. Where jurisdiction was clear, though, we have allowed recovery despite arguable procedural objections.

---

20. H.R.Rep.No. 2428, 76th Cong., 1st Sess., p. 5; Hearings on H.R. 5373 and H.R. 6463, 77th Cong., 2d Sess., p. 66; Hearings on H.R. 7236, 76th Cong., 3d Sess., pp. 7, 16, 17; Hearings on S. 2690, 76th Cong., 3d Sess., p. 9. 69 Cong.Rec. 2192, 2193, 3118; 86 Cong. Rec. 12024.

21. See H.R.Rep.No. 2245, 77th Cong., 2d Sess., p. 10; S.Rep.No. 1196, 77th Cong., 2d Sess., p. 7; H.R.Rep.No. 1287, 79th Cong., 1st Sess., pp. 5–6; Hearings before H.Com. on Judiciary on H.R. 5373 and H.R. 6463, 77th Cong., 2d Sess., p. 33. * * *

One only need read § 2680 in its entirety to conclude that Congress exercised care to protect the Government from claims, however negligently caused, that affected the governmental functions. Negligence in administering the Alien Property Act, or establishing a quarantine, assault, libel, fiscal operations, etc., were barred. An analysis of § 2680(a), the exception with which we are concerned, emphasizes the congressional purpose to except the acts here charged as negligence from the authorization to sue. It will be noted from the form of the section that there are two phrases describing the excepted acts of government employees. The first deals with acts or omissions of government employees, exercising due care in carrying out statutes or regulations whether valid or not. It bars tests by tort action of the legality of statutes and regulations. The second is applicable in this case. It excepts acts of discretion in the performance of governmental functions or duty "whether or not the discretion involved be abused." Not only agencies of government are covered but all employees exercising discretion. It is clear that the just-quoted clause as to abuse connotes both negligence and wrongful acts in the exercise of the discretion because the Act itself covers only "negligent or wrongful act or omission of any employee", "within the scope of his office" "where the United States, if a private person, would be liable". 28 U.S.C. § 1346(b). The exercise of discretion could not be abused without negligence or a wrongful act. The Committee reports show this. They say § 2680(a) is to preclude action for "abuse of discretionary authority—whether or not negligence is alleged to have been involved." They speak of excepting a "remedy on account of such discretionary acts even though negligently performed and involving an abuse of discretion."

So we know that the draftsmen did not intend it to relieve the Government from liability for such common-law torts as an automobile collision caused by the negligence of an employee of the administering agency. We know it was intended to cover more than the administration of a statute or regulation because it appears disjunctively in the second phrase of the section. The "discretion" protected by the section is not that of the judge—a power to decide within the limits of positive rules of law subject to judicial review. It is the discretion of the executive or the administrator to act according to one's judgment of the best course, a concept of substantial historical ancestry in American law. * * *

It is unnecessary to define, apart from this case, precisely where discretion ends. It is enough to hold, as we do, that the "discretionary function or duty" that cannot form a basis for suit under the Tort Claims Act includes more than the initiation of programs and activities. It also includes determinations made by executives or administrators in establishing plans, specifications or schedules of operations. Where there is room for policy judgment and decision there is discretion. It necessarily follows that acts of subordinates in carrying out the operations of government in accordance with official directions cannot be actionable. If it were not so, the protection of § 2680(a) would fail at the time it would be needed, that is, when a subordinate performs or fails to perform a causal step, each action or nonaction being directed by the superior, exercising, perhaps abusing, discretion.

III.   That the cabinet-level decision to institute the fertilizer export program was a discretionary act is not seriously disputed. Nor do we think that there is any doubt that the need for further experimentation with FGAN to determine the possibility of its explosion, under conditions likely to be encountered in shipping, and its combustibility was a matter to be determined by the discretion of those in charge of the production. Obviously, having manufactured and shipped the commodity FGAN for more than three years without even minor accidents, the need for further experimentation was a matter of discretion. Reported instances of heating or bag damage were investigated and experiments, to the extent deemed necessary, were carried on. * * * It is, we think, just such matters of governmental duties that were excepted from the Act.

We turn, therefore, to the specific acts of negligence charged in the manufacture. Each was in accordance with, and done under, specifications and directions as to how the FGAN was produced at the plants. The basic "Plan" was drafted by the office of the Field Director of Ammunitions Plants in June, 1946, prior to beginning production. It was drawn up in the light of prior experience by private enterprise and the TVA. In fact it was, as we have pointed out, based on the latter agency's engineering techniques, and specifically adopted the TVA process description and specifications. This Plan was distributed to the various plants at the inception of the program.

Besides its general condemnation of the manufacture of FGAN, the District Court cited four specific acts of negligence in manufacture. Each of these acts looked upon as negligence was directed by this Plan. Applicable excerpts follow. Bagging temperature was fixed. The type of bagging and the labeling thereof were also established. The PRP coating, too, was included in the specifications. The acts found to have been negligence were thus performed under the direction of a plan developed at a high level under a direct delegation of plan-making authority from the apex of the Executive Department. The establishment of this Plan, delegated to the Field Director's Office clearly required the exercise of expert judgment.

This is to be seen, for instance, in the matter of the coating. The PRP was added in order to insure against water absorption. At stake was no mere matter of taste; ammonium nitrate when wet cakes and is difficult to spread on fields as a fertilizer. So the considerations that dictated the decisions were crucial ones, involving the feasibility of the program itself, balanced against present knowledge of the effect of such a coating and the general custom of similar private industries.

And, assuming that high bagging temperatures in fact obtained as the District Court found, the decision to bag at the temperature fixed was also within the exception. Maximum bagging temperatures were first established under the TVA specifications. That they were the product of an exercise of judgment, requiring consideration of a vast spectrum of factors, including some which touched directly the feasibility of the fertilizer export program, is clear. For instance, it appears several times in the record that the question of bagging temperatures was discussed by the Army plant officials, among others. * * * [It was,] however, recommended that reduced temperatures would be inadvisable. It would be possible to keep the product in graining kettles for a longer period or to install cooling equipment. But both methods would result in greatly increased production costs and/or greatly reduced production. This kind of decision is not one which the courts, under the Act, are empowered to cite as "negligence" * * *.

As well, serious judgment was involved in the specification of the bag labels and bills of lading. The importance of this rests on the fact that it is the latest point in time and geography when the Government did anything directly related to the fire, for after bagging the FGAN was of course physically in the hands of various non-governmental agents. So since there was serious room for speculation that the most direct operative fact causing the immediate fire on the *Grandcamp* arose from errors that the French Council, longshoremen or ship staff committed, it was and is important for the petitioners to emphasize the seriousness of the alleged labeling mistake.

This, too, though, falls within the exception for acts of discretion. The Plan had been prepared in this regard by the Transportation Officer of the Director's Office. His decision in the matter was dictated by the ICC regulations. These did not provide for a specific classification for the material other than as fertilizer. Labeling it as anything but "oxidizing material" was not required—indeed was probably forbidden—and even this requirement was waived for bags of less than 200 pounds. To the extent, then, that the Army had a choice in the matter, its decision not to seek to list its FGAN in any other fashion was within the exception. The immunity of a decision as to labeling, in fact, is quite clearly shown by the fact that the ICC's regulations, for instance, could not be attacked by claimants under the Act by virtue of the first phrase of § 2680(a).

In short, the alleged "negligence" does not subject the Government to liability. The decisions held culpable were all responsibly made at a planning rather than operational level and involved considerations more or less important to the practicability of the Government's fertilizer program.

"There must be knowledge of a danger, not merely possible, but probable", *MacPherson v. Buick Motor Co.*, 217 N.Y. 382, 389, 111 N.E. 1050, 1053. Here, nothing so startling was adduced. The entirety of the evidence compels the view that FGAN was a material that former experience showed could be handled safely in the manner it was handled here. Even now no one has suggested that the ignition of FGAN was anything but a complex result of the interacting factors of mass, heat, pressure and composition. * * *

V.   Though the findings of specific and general negligence do not support a judgment of government liability, there is yet to be disposed of some slight residue of theory of absolute liability without fault. This is reflected both in the District Court's finding that the FGAN constituted a nuisance, and in the contention of petitioner here. We agree with the six judges of the Court of Appeals, 197 F.2d 771, 776, 781, 786, that the Act does not extend to such situations, though of course well known in tort law generally. It is to be invoked only on a "negligent or wrongful act or omission" of an employee. Absolute liability, of course, arises irrespective of how the tortfeasor conducts himself; it is imposed automatically when any damages are sustained as a result of the decision to engage in the dangerous activity. The degree of care used in performing the activity is irrelevant to the application of that doctrine. But the statute requires a negligent act. So it is our judgment that liability does not arise by virtue either of United States ownership of an "inherently dangerous commodity" or property, or of engaging in an "extra hazardous" activity. *United States v. Hull,* 1 Cir., 195 F.2d 64, 67. * * *

S. L. under the FTCA.

Affirmed.

■ MR. JUSTICE DOUGLAS and MR. JUSTICE CLARK took no part in the consideration or decision of this case.

■ MR. JUSTICE JACKSON, joined by MR. JUSTICE BLACK and MR. JUSTICE FRANKFURTER, dissenting.

All day, April 15, 1947, longshoremen loaded bags of ammonium nitrate fertilizer aboard the S.S. *Grandcamp,* docked at Texas City, Texas. Shortly after 8 a.m. next morning, when work resumed, smoke was seen coming from the No. 4 hold and it was discovered that fire had broken out in the fertilizer. The ship's master ordered the hatch covered and battened down and steam was introduced into the hold. Local fire-fighting apparatus soon arrived, but the combined efforts to extinguish the fire were unavailing. Less than an hour after smoke was first seen, 880 tons of fertilizer in the No. 4 hold exploded and, in turn, detonated the fertilizer stored in the No. 2 hold. Fire spread to the dock area of Texas City and to the S.S. *High Flyer,* berthed at an adjoining pier and carrying a cargo of sulphur and ammonium nitrate fertilizer. Further efforts to extinguish or even contain the fire failed and, about 11 p.m., tugs unsuccessfully attempted to tow the *High Flyer* out to sea. Shortly after one o'clock on the morning of April 17, the sulphur and fertilizer aboard the *High Flyer* exploded, demolishing both that ship and the S. S. *Wilson B. Keene,* lying alongside. More than 560 persons perished in this holocaust, and some 3,000 were injured. The entire dock area of a thriving port was leveled and property damage ran into millions of dollars.

This was a man-made disaster; it was in no sense an "act of God." The fertilizer had been manufactured in Government-owned plants at the Government's order and to its specifications. It was being shipped at its direction as part of its program of foreign aid. The disaster was caused by forces set in motion by the Government, completely controlled or controllable by it. Its causative factors were far beyond the knowledge or control of the victims; they were not only incapable of contributing to it, but could not even take shelter or flight from it. * * *

This is one of those cases that a judge is likely to leave by the same door through which he enters. As we have been told by a master of our craft, "*Some* theory of liability, some philosophy of the end to be served by tightening or enlarging the circle of rights and remedies, is at the root of any decision in novel situations when analogies are equivocal and precedents are silent."[3] So, we begin by avowing a conception of the function of legal liability in cases such as this quite obviously at variance with the approach of the Court.

Congress has defined the tort liability of the Government as analogous to that of a private person. Traditionally, one function of civil liability for negligence is to supply a sanction to enforce the degree of care suitable to the conditions of contemporary society and appropriate to the circumstances of the case. The civil damage action, prosecuted and adjusted by private initiative, neither burdening our overworked criminal processes nor confined by the limits of criminal liability, is one of the law's most effective inducements to the watchfulness and prudence necessary to avoid calamity from hazardous operations in the midst of an unshielded populace.

Until recently, the influence of the Federal Government has been exerted in the field of tort law to tighten liability and liberalize remedies. Congress has even imposed criminal liability without regard to knowledge of danger or intent where potentially dangerous articles are introduced into interstate commerce. But, when the Government is brought into court as a tort defendant, the very proper zeal of its lawyers to win their case and the less commendable zeal of officials involved to conceal or minimize their carelessness militate against this trend. The Government, as a defendant, can exert an unctuous persuasiveness because it can clothe official carelessness with a public interest. Hence, one of the unanticipated consequences of the Tort Claims Act has been to throw the weight of government influence on the side of lax standards of care in the negligence cases which it defends.

It is our fear that the Court's adoption of the Government's view in this case may inaugurate an unfortunate trend toward relaxation of private as well as official responsibility in making, vending or transporting inherently dangerous products. For we are not considering here every-day commodities of commerce or products of nature but a complex compound not only proven by the event to be highly dangerous, but known from the beginning to lie somewhere within the range of the dangerous. Ammonium nitrate, as the Court points out, had been "long used as a component in explosives." * * *

Because of reliance on the reservation of governmental immunity for acts of discretion, the Court avoids direct pronouncement on the duty owing by the Government under these circumstances but does sound overtones and undertones with which we disagree. We who would hold the Government liable here cannot avoid consideration of the basic criteria by which courts determine liability in the conditions of modern life. This is a day of synthetic living, when to an ever-increasing extent our population is dependent upon mass producers for its food and drink, its cures and complexions, its apparel and gadgets. These no longer are natural or simple

---

3. Cardozo, The Growth of the Law, p. 102. (Emphasis his own.)

products but complex ones whose composition and qualities are often secret. Such a dependent society must exact greater care than in more simple days and must require from manufacturers or producers increased integrity and caution as the only protection of its safety and well-being. Purchasers cannot try out drugs to determine whether they kill or cure. Consumers cannot test the youngster's cowboy suit or the wife's sweater to see if they are apt to burst into fatal flames. Carriers, by land or by sea, cannot experiment with the combustibility of goods in transit. Where experiment or research is necessary to determine the presence or the degree of danger, the product must not be tried out on the public, nor must the public be expected to possess the facilities or the technical knowledge to learn for itself of inherent but latent dangers. The claim that a hazard was not foreseen is not available to one who did not use foresight appropriate to his enterprise.

Forward-looking courts, slowly but steadily, have been adapting the law of negligence to these conditions. The law which by statute determines the Government's liability is that of the place where the negligent act or omission occurred. This fertilizer was manufactured in Iowa and Nebraska, thence shipped to Texas. Speculation as to where the negligence occurred is unnecessary, since each of these jurisdictions recognizes the general proposition that a manufacturer is liable for defects in his product which could have been avoided by the exercise of due care. Where there are no specific state decisions on the point, federal judges may turn to the general doctrines of accepted tort law, whence state judges derive their governing principles in novel cases. We believe that whatever the source to which we look for the law of this case, if the source is as modern as the case itself, it supports the exaction of a higher degree of care than possibly can be found to have been exercised here.

We believe it is the better view that whoever puts into circulation in commerce a product that is known or even suspected of being potentially inflammable or explosive is under an obligation to know his own product and to ascertain what forces he is turning loose. If, as often will be the case, a dangerous product is also a useful one, he is under a strict duty to follow each step of its distribution with warning of its dangers and with information and directions to keep those dangers at a minimum.

It is obvious that the Court's only choice is to hold the Government's liability to be nothing or to be very heavy, indeed. But the magnitude of the potential liability is due to the enormity of the disaster and the multitude of its victims. The size of the catastrophe does not excuse liability but, on its face, eloquently pleads that it could not have resulted from any prudently operated Government project, and that injury so sudden and sweeping should not lie where it has fallen. It should at least raise immediate doubts whether this is one of those "discretionary" operations Congress sought to immunize from liability. With this statement of our general approach to the liability issue, we turn to its application to this case. * * *

The Government insists that each act or omission upon which the charge of negligence is predicated—the decisions as to discontinuing the investigation of hazards, bagging at high temperature, use of paperbagging material, absence of labeling and warning—involved a conscious weighing of expediency against caution and were therefore within the immunity for discretionary acts provided by the Tort Claims Act. It further argues, by way of showing that by such a construction the reservation would not completely swallow the waiver of immunity, that such discretionary decisions are to be distinguished from those made by a truck driver as to the speed at which he will travel so as to keep the latter within the realm of liability.

We do not predicate liability on any decision taken at "Cabinet level" or on any other high-altitude thinking. Of course, it is not a tort for government to govern, and the decision to aid foreign agriculture by making and delivering fertilizer is no actionable wrong. Nor do we find any indication that in these deliberations that any decision was made to take a calculated risk of doing what was done, in the way it was done, on the chance that what did happen might not happen. Therefore, we are not deterred by fear that governmental liability in this case would make the discretion of executives and administrators timid and restrained. However, if decisions are being made at Cabinet levels as to the temperature of bagging explosive fertilizers, whether paper is suitable for bagging hot fertilizer, and how the bags should be labeled, perhaps an increased sense of caution and responsibility even at that height would be wholesome. The common sense of this matter is that a policy adopted in the exercise of an immune discretion was carried out carelessly by those in charge of detail. We cannot agree that all the way down the line there is immunity for every balancing of care against cost, of safety against production, of warning against silence. * * *

* * * When an official exerts governmental authority in a manner which legally binds one or many, he is acting in a way in which no private person could. Such activities do and are designed to affect, often deleteriously, the affairs of individuals, but courts have long recognized the public policy that such official shall be controlled solely by the statutory or administrative mandate and not by the added threat of private damage suits. For example, the Attorney General will not be liable for false arrest in circumstances where a private person performing the same act would be liable, and such cases could be multiplied. The official's act might inflict just as great an injury and might be just as wrong as that of the private person, but the official is not answerable. The exception clause of the Tort Claims Act protects the public treasury where the common law would protect the purse of the acting public official.

But many acts of government officials deal only with the housekeeping side of federal activities. The Government, as landowner, as manufacturer, as shipper, as warehouseman, as shipowner and operator, is carrying on activities indistinguishable from those performed by private persons. In this area, there is no good reason to stretch the legislative text to immunize the Government or its officers from responsibility for their acts, if done without appropriate care for the safety of others. Many official decisions even in this area may involve a nice balancing of various considerations, but this is the same kind of balancing which citizens do at their peril and we think it is not within the exception of the statute.

The Government's negligence here was not in policy decisions of a regulatory or governmental nature, but involved actions akin to those of a private manufacturer, contractor, or shipper. Reading the discretionary exception as we do, in a way both workable and faithful to legislative intent, we would hold that the Government was liable under these circumstances. Surely a statute so long debated was meant to embrace more than traffic accidents. If not, the ancient and discredited doctrine that "The King can do no wrong" has not been uprooted; it has merely been amended to read, "The King can do only little wrongs."

———

Notes and Questions

1.   Section 2680(a) of Title 28 of the United States Code contains the first of a long list of exceptions (several more exceptions are also discussed in the succeeding parts of this casebook). Section 2680(a) is commonly known as the "discretionary function exception" and is probably the most often invoked and most important of the exceptions to the government's FTCA liability. Moreover, if too broadly applied, it may become the exception that swallows the rule.

Section 2680(a) actually has two parts or exceptions, both of which are implicated in the *Dalehite v. United States* case. First, Section 2680(a) provides that the United States may not be held liable based upon actions involving the non-negligent implementation of a statute or regulation, whether or not the statute or regulation is valid. Thus, claims of injury arising out of an allegedly invalid statute or regulation do not give rise to tort liability for the government. Challenges to the validity of a statute or regulation must be made through the political process or a court petition to strike down the statute or regulation through a constitutional attack or judicial review of administrative action—but not through the venue of a tort action. In *Dalehite,* the Supreme Court applied this first phrase of Section 2680(a) to hold that the labeling of the fertilizer according to Interstate Commerce Commission regulations could not be a basis for tort liability. The first phrase of Section 2680(a) has not presented difficult issues of interpretation or application.

The second phrase of Section 2680(a) immunizes the government from liability based upon an employee's exercise or failure to exercise a "discretionary function or duty * * * whether or not the discretion involved be abused." This second phrase, commonly known as the discretionary function exception, has been the subject of many and ongoing disputes as to what falls within its scope. The *Dalehite* Court considers its meaning and application in the context of the various phases of the fertilizer program and production, but deliberately chooses not to adopt a precise definition of the exception to decide this case. We will look at several more Supreme Court decisions in which this exception is further defined and refined.

2. If you were going to define the discretionary function exception by one word based upon the *Dalehite* analysis, what would that one word be? What is the essence of a discretionary function or duty that makes it different from other non-immunized choices, such as a government employee's choice between obeying or exceeding the speed limit when driving an automobile?

3. The *Dalehite* Court concludes that decisions involving production of the fertilizer were covered by the discretionary function exception because they affected the cost or effectiveness of the product. Thus, bagging the fertilizer at high temperatures may have increased the instability of the fertilizer, but reducing temperatures by holding the product in graining kettles for a longer period or installing cooling equipment would have raised costs or reduced production. Similarly, adding a special coating to prevent water absorption may have enhanced the explosive quality but was appropriate because fertilizer when wet "cakes" and is more difficult to spread. Note that these factors—increased cost, delays in production, reduced levels of production, and efficiency of the product—are no different than the factors weighed by private manufacturers. Yet the courts do not hesitate to second-guess those choices when determining whether the manufacturer was negligent. Why should the government be treated differently in this regard? Should the government always receive special treatment, or should it depend on the circumstances? What circumstances make the *Dalehite* situation special?

4. In one paragraph of the *Dalehite* opinion, the Supreme Court states that the decisions made cannot subject the government to liability because they "were all responsibly made at a planning rather than an operational level." After the *Dalehite* decision, several lower federal courts adopted a "planning level versus operational level" distinction for purposes of applying the discretionary function exception. *Estate of Gleason by Gleason v. United States,* 857 F.2d 1208, 1209 (8th Cir. 1988); *Wright v. United States,* 719 F.2d 1032, 1035 (9th Cir. 1983). Thus, if a decision were identified as having been made at a high policy-making level, it presumably would be immunized. By contrast, decisions made at an operational level in implementation of a general program would not be covered by the exception. Does this distinction adequately reflect the purposes underlying the exception? As you read the next few decisions, consider whether this distinction remains viable.

5. While the government argues in *Dalehite* that each decision "involved a conscious weighing of expediency against caution," the dissent protests that there in fact is no indication "that in these deliberations that any decision was made to take a calculated risk of doing what was done, in the way it was done, on the chance that what did happen might not happen." In other words, while we can imagine possible policy concerns that could have influenced the production choices, the record does not reflect that a conscious policy decision actually was made at the time. Is

such required, or should it be required, for application of the discretionary function exception? The United States Court of Appeals for the Third Circuit later suggested that, for the discretionary function exception, "the relevant question is not whether an explicit balancing of [policy factors] is proved, but whether the decision is susceptible to policy analysis." *United States Fidelity & Guaranty Co. v. United States*, 837 F.2d 116, 121 (3d Cir. 1988). Does this open the door to the government offering post hoc policy rationales for ordinary negligent misconduct? Consider whether this "susceptible to policy analysis" theory survives or is confirmed by the subsequent Supreme Court decisions we will read.

6. The *Dalehite* majority concludes by holding that "absolute liability without fault"—that is, strict liability based upon the ultra-hazardous (that is, highly explosive) nature of the fertilizer—does not apply against the government under the FTCA. As we saw earlier in *Laird v. Nelms*, 406 U.S. 797 (1972) (see Chapter III.A.3.c), the Supreme Court later reaffirmed this holding and requires a showing of blameworthy conduct for imposition of tort liability under the FTCA.

7. Even with the advent of consented government tort liability under the FTCA, a court remedy is not the only recourse for those injured by government activity. Indeed, when the claim is outside the scope of the FTCA or falls within an exception, litigation still may be foreclosed. The "private bill" in Congress remains available as an alternative, or in some cases the only, mechanism for compensating persons injured or suffering property damage by reason of a government decision or action. For example, following the *Dalehite* ruling immunizing the government from liability under the discretionary function exception, Congress passed a bill providing compensation to the victims of the Texas City disaster. *See Laird v. Nelms*, 406 U.S. 797, 802 (1972) (describing the congressional action).

United States v. Empresa de Viacao Aerea Rio Grandense (Varig Airlines)

Supreme Court of the United States.
467 U.S. 797 (1984).

■ CHIEF JUSTICE BURGER delivered the opinion of the Court.

We granted certiorari in these two cases to determine whether the United States may be held liable under the Federal Tort Claims Act, 28 U.S.C. § 2671 *et seq.*, for the negligence of the Federal Aviation Administration in certificating certain aircraft for use in commercial aviation.

I

A. *No. 82–1349*

On July 11, 1973, a commercial jet aircraft owned by respondent S.A. Empresa De Viacao Aerea Rio Grandense (Varig Airlines) was flying from Rio de Janeiro to Paris when a fire broke out in one of the aft lavatories.

The fire produced a thick black smoke, which quickly filled the cabin and cockpit. Despite the pilots' successful effort to land the plane, 124 of the 135 persons on board died from asphyxiation or the effects of toxic gases produced by the fire. Most of the plane's fuselage was consumed by a postimpact fire.

The aircraft involved in this accident was a Boeing 707, a product of the Boeing Co. In 1958 the Civil Aeronautics Agency, a predecessor of the FAA, had issued a type certificate for the Boeing 707, certifying that its designs, plans, specifications, and performance data had been shown to be in conformity with minimum safety standards. * * *

After the accident respondent Varig Airlines brought an action against the United States under the Federal Tort Claims Act seeking damages for the destroyed aircraft. The families and personal representatives of many of the passengers, also respondents here, brought a separate suit under the Act pressing claims for wrongful death. The two actions were consolidated in the United States District Court for the Central District of California.

Respondents asserted that the fire originated in the towel disposal area located below the sink unit in one of the lavatories and alleged that the towel disposal area was not capable of containing fire. In support of their argument, respondents pointed to an air safety regulation requiring that waste receptacles be made of fire-resistant materials and incorporate covers or other provisions for containing possible fires. Respondents claimed that the CAA had been negligent when it inspected the Boeing 707 and issued a type certificate to an aircraft that did not comply with CAA fire protection standards. The District Court granted summary judgment for the United States on the ground that California law does not recognize an actionable tort duty for inspection and certification activities. The District Court also found that, even if respondents had stated a cause of action in tort, recovery against the United States was barred by two exceptions to the Act: the discretionary function exception, 28 U.S.C. § 2680(a), and the misrepresentation exception, § 2680(h).

The United States Court of Appeals for the Ninth Circuit reversed. 692 F.2d 1205 (1982). The Court of Appeals reasoned that a private person inspecting and certificating aircraft for airworthiness would be liable for negligent inspection under the California "Good Samaritan" rule, see Restatement (Second) of Torts §§ 323 and 324A (1965), and concluded that the United States should be judged by the same rule. The Court of Appeals rejected the Government's argument that respondents' actions were barred by 28 U.S.C. § 2680(h), which provides that the United States is not subject to liability for any claim arising out of misrepresentation. Interpreting respondents' claims as arising from the negligence of the CAA inspection rather than from any implicit misrepresentation in the resultant certificate, the Court of Appeals held that the misrepresentation exception did not apply. Finally, the Court of Appeals addressed the Government's reliance upon the discretionary function exception to the Act, 28 U.S.C. § 2680(a), which exempts the United States from liability for claims "based upon the exercise or performance or the failure to exercise or perform a discretionary function or duty...." The Court of Appeals viewed the inspection of aircraft for compliance with air safety regulations as a function not entailing the sort of policymaking discretion contemplated by the discretionary function exception.

B.   *No. 82–1350*

On October 8, 1968, a DeHavilland Dove aircraft owned by respondent John Dowdle and used in the operation of an air taxi service caught fire in midair, crashed, and burned near Las Vegas, Nev. The pilot, copilot, and two passengers were killed. The cause of the crash was an in-flight fire in the forward baggage compartment of the aircraft.

The DeHavilland Dove airplane was manufactured in the United Kingdom in 1951 and then purchased by Air Wisconsin, another air taxi operator. In 1965 Air Wisconsin contracted with Aerodyne Engineering Corp. to install a gasoline-burning cabin heater in the airplane. Aerodyne applied for, and was granted, a supplemental type certificate from the FAA authorizing the installation of the heater. Aerodyne then installed the heater pursuant to its contract with Air Wisconsin. In 1966, relying in part upon the supplemental type certificate as an indication of the airplane's airworthiness, respondent Dowdle purchased the DeHavilland Dove from Air Wisconsin.

In the aftermath of the crash, respondent Dowdle filed this action for property damage against the United States under the Federal Tort Claims Act. Respondent insurance companies also filed suit under the Act, seeking reimbursement for moneys paid for liability coverage on behalf of Dowdle. The United States District Court for the Southern District of California found that the crash resulted from defects in the installation of the gasoline line leading to the cabin heater. The District Court concluded that the installation did not comply with the applicable FAA regulations and held that the Government was negligent in certifying an installation that did not comply with those safety requirements. Accordingly, the District Court entered judgment for respondents.

On appeal, the United States Court of Appeals for the Ninth Circuit reversed and remanded for the District Court to consider whether the California courts would impose a duty of due care upon the Government by applying the "Good Samaritan" doctrine of §§ 323 and 324A of the Restatement (Second) of Torts. The Court of Appeals also requested the District Court to determine whether, under the facts of this case, the California courts would find such a duty breached if a private person had issued the supplemental type certificate in question here. 614 F.2d 188 (1979). On remand, the District Court again entered judgment for respondents, finding that the California "Good Samaritan" rule would apply in this case and would give rise to liability on these facts.

On the Government's second appeal, the Ninth Circuit affirmed the judgment of the District Court. 692 F.2d 1209 (1982). In so holding, the Court of Appeals followed reasoning nearly identical to that employed in its decision in No. 82–1349, decided the same day.

We granted certiorari, and we now reverse.

II

[handwritten margin note: Lang. & purpose of FAA Act]

In the Federal Aviation Act of 1958, 49 U.S.C. § 1421(a)(1), Congress directed the Secretary of Transportation to promote the safety of flight of civil aircraft in air commerce by establishing minimum standards for aircraft design, materials, workmanship, construction, and performance. Congress also granted the Secretary the discretion to prescribe reasonable rules and regulations governing the inspection of aircraft, including the manner in which such inspections should be made. § 1421(a)(3). Congress emphasized, however, that air carriers themselves retained certain responsibilities to promote the public interest in air safety: the duty to perform their services with the highest possible degree of safety, § 1421(b), the duty to make or cause to be made every inspection required by the Secretary, § 1425(a), and the duty to observe and comply with all other administrative requirements established by the Secretary, § 1425(a).

[handwritten margin note: Certification process as prerequisite for mkting a private product]

Congress also established a multistep certification process to monitor the aviation industry's compliance with the requirements developed by the Secretary. Acting as the Secretary's designee, the FAA has promulgated a comprehensive set of regulations delineating the minimum safety standards with which the designers and manufacturers of aircraft must comply before marketing their products. See 14 CFR pts. 23, 25, 27, 29, 31, 33, and 35 (1983). At each step in the certification process, FAA employees or their representatives evaluate materials submitted by aircraft manufacturers to determine whether the manufacturer has satisfied these regulatory requirements. Upon a showing by the manufacturer that the prescribed safety standards have been met, the FAA issues an appropriate certificate permitting the manufacturer to continue with production and marketing. * * *

III

The Federal Tort Claims Act, 28 U.S.C. § 1346(b), authorizes suits against the United States for damages

> "for injury or loss of property, or personal injury or death caused by the negligent or wrongful act or omission of any employee of the Government while acting within the scope of his office or employment, under circumstances where the United States, if a private person, would be liable to the claimant in accordance with the law of the place where the act or omission occurred."

The Act further provides that the United States shall be liable with respect to tort claims "in the same manner and to the same extent as a private individual under like circumstances." § 2674.

The Act did not waive the sovereign immunity of the United States in all respects, however; Congress was careful to except from the Act's broad waiver of immunity several important classes of tort claims. Of particular relevance here, 28 U.S.C. § 2680(a) provides that the Act shall not apply to "[a]ny claim based upon an act or omission of an employee of the Government, exercising due care, in the execution of a statute or regulation, whether or not such statute or regulation be valid, *or based upon the exercise or performance or the failure to exercise or perform a discretionary function or duty on the part of a federal agency or an employee of the Government, whether or not the discretion involved be abused.*" (Emphasis added).

The discretionary function exception, embodied in the second clause of § 2680(a), marks the boundary between Congress' willingness to impose tort liability upon the United States and its desire to protect certain governmental activities from exposure to suit by private individuals. * * *

The nature and scope of § 2680(a) were carefully examined in *Dalehite v. United States, supra. Dalehite* involved vast claims for damages against the United States arising out of a disastrous explosion of ammonium nitrate fertilizer, which had been produced and distributed under the direction of the United States for export to devastated areas occupied by the Allied Armed Forces after World War II. Numerous acts of the Government were charged as negligent: the cabinet-level decision to institute the fertilizer export program, the failure to experiment with the fertilizer to determine the possibility of explosion, the drafting of the basic plan of manufacture, and the failure properly to police the storage and loading of the fertilizer.

The Court concluded that those allegedly negligent acts were governmental duties protected by the discretionary function exception and held the action barred by § 2680(a). Describing the discretion protected by § 2680(a) as "the discretion of the executive or the administrator to act according to one's judgment of the best course," *id.,* at 34, the Court stated:

> "It is unnecessary to define, apart from this case, precisely where discretion ends. It is enough to hold, as we do, that the 'discretionary function or duty' that cannot form a basis for suit under the Tort Claims Act includes more than the initiation of programs and activities. It also includes determinations made by executives or administrators in establishing plans, specifications or schedules of operations. Where there is room for policy judgment and decision there is discretion. It necessarily follows that acts of subordinates in carrying out the operations of government in accordance with official directions cannot be actionable." *Id.,* at 35–36.

Respondents here insist that the view of § 2680(a) expressed in *Dalehite* has been eroded, if not overruled, by subsequent cases construing the Act, particularly *Indian Towing Co. v. United States,* 350 U.S. 61 (1955) * * *. While the Court's reading of the Act admittedly has not followed a straight line, we do not accept the supposition that *Dalehite* no longer represents a valid interpretation of the discretionary function exception.

Indian Towing Co. v. United States, supra, involved a claim under the Act for damages to cargo aboard a vessel that ran aground, allegedly owing to the failure of the light in a lighthouse operated by the Coast Guard. The plaintiffs contended that the Coast Guard had been negligent in inspecting, maintaining, and repairing the light. Significantly, the Government conceded that the discretionary function exception was not implicated in *Indian Towing,* arguing instead that the Act contained an implied exception from liability for "uniquely governmental functions." *Id.,* at 64. The Court rejected the Government's assertion, reasoning that it would "push the courts into the 'non-governmental'-'governmental' quagmire that has long plagued the law of municipal corporations." *Id.,* at 65. * * *

As in *Dalehite,* it is unnecessary—and indeed impossible—to define with precision every contour of the discretionary function exception. From the legislative and judicial materials, however, it is possible to isolate several factors useful in determining when the acts of a Government employee are protected from liability by § 2680(a). First, it is the nature of the conduct, rather than the status of the actor, that governs whether the discretionary function exception applies in a given case. As the Court pointed out in *Dalehite,* the exception covers "[n]ot only agencies of government ... but all employees exercising discretion." 346 U.S., at 33. Thus, the basic inquiry concerning the application of the discretionary function exception is whether the challenged acts of a Government employee—whatever his or her rank—are of the nature and quality that Congress intended to shield from tort liability.

Second, whatever else the discretionary function exception may include, it plainly was intended to encompass the discretionary acts of the Government acting in its role as a regulator of the conduct of private individuals. Time and again the legislative history refers to the acts of regulatory agencies as examples of those covered by the exception, and it is significant that the early tort claims bills considered by Congress specifically exempted two major regulatory agencies by name. This emphasis upon protection for regulatory activities suggests an underlying basis for the inclusion of an exception for discretionary functions in the Act: Congress wished to prevent judicial "second-guessing" of legislative and administrative decisions grounded in social, economic, and political policy through the medium of an action in tort. By fashioning an exception for discretionary governmental functions, including regulatory activities, Congress took "steps to protect the Government from liability that would seriously handicap efficient government operations." *United States v. Muniz,* 374 U.S. 150, 163 (1963).

IV

We now consider whether the discretionary function exception immunizes from tort liability the FAA certification process involved in this case. Respondents in No. 82–1349 argue that the CAA was negligent in issuing a type certificate for the Boeing 707 aircraft in 1958 because the lavatory trash receptacle did not satisfy applicable safety regulations. Similarly, respondents in No. 82–1350 claim negligence in the FAA's issuance of a supplemental type certificate in 1965 for the DeHavilland Dove aircraft;

they assert that the installation of the fuel line leading to the cabin heater violated FAA airworthiness standards. From the records in these cases there is no indication that either the Boeing 707 trash receptacle or the DeHavilland Dove cabin heater was actually inspected or reviewed by an FAA inspector or representative. Respondents thus argue in effect that the negligent failure of the FAA to inspect certain aspects of aircraft type design in the process of certification gives rise to a cause of action against the United States under the Act.

The Government, on the other hand, urges that the basic responsibility for satisfying FAA air safety standards rests with the *manufacturer,* not with the FAA. The role of the FAA, the Government says, is merely to police the conduct of private individuals by monitoring their compliance with FAA regulations. According to the Government, the FAA accomplishes its monitoring function by means of a "spot-check" program designed to encourage manufacturers and operators to comply fully with minimum safety requirements. Such regulatory activity, the Government argues, is the sort of governmental conduct protected by the discretionary function exception to the Act.[12] We agree that the discretionary function exception precludes a tort action based upon the conduct of the FAA in certificating these aircraft for use in commercial aviation.

* * * [T]he Secretary of Transportation has the duty to promote safety in air transportation by promulgating reasonable rules and regulations governing the inspection, servicing, and overhaul of civil aircraft. 49 U.S.C. § 1421(a)(3)(A). In her discretion, the Secretary may also prescribe

> "the periods for, and *the manner in, which such inspection, servicing, and overhaul shall be made,* including provision for examinations and reports by properly qualified private persons whose examinations or reports the Secretary of Transportation may accept in lieu of those made by its officers and employees." § 1421(a)(3)(C) (emphasis added).

Thus, Congress specifically empowered the Secretary to establish and implement a mechanism for enforcing compliance with minimum safety standards according to her "judgment of the best course." *Dalehite v. United States,* 346 U.S., at 34.

In the exercise of this discretion, the FAA, as the Secretary's designee, has devised a system of compliance review that involves certification of aircraft design and manufacture at several stages of production. The FAA

---

12.   The Government presses two additional arguments in support of reversal. First, the Government asserts that the conduct of the FAA in certificating aircraft is a core governmental activity that is not actionable under the Act, because no private individual engages in analogous activity. See 28 U.S.C. §§ 1346(b) and 2674. Second, the Government interprets respondents' claims as based upon misrepresentations contained in the certificates and argues that they are barred by the misrepresentation exception to the Act. § 2680(h). Respondents urge that the first argument is precluded by *Indian Towing Co. v. United States, supra,* and the second by our decision last Term in *Block v. Neal,* 460 U.S. 289, 103 S.Ct. 1089, 75 L.Ed.2d 67 (1983). Because we rest our decision today upon the discretionary function exception, we find it unnecessary to address these additional issues. * * *

certification process is founded upon a relatively simple notion: the duty to ensure that an aircraft conforms to FAA safety regulations lies with the manufacturer and operator, while the FAA retains the responsibility for policing compliance. Thus, the manufacturer is required to develop the plans and specifications and perform the inspections and tests necessary to establish that an aircraft design comports with the applicable regulations; the FAA then reviews the data for conformity purposes by conducting a "spot check" of the manufacturer's work. * * *

Respondents' contention that the FAA was negligent in failing to inspect certain elements of aircraft design before certificating the Boeing 707 and DeHavilland Dove necessarily challenges two aspects of the certification procedure: the FAA's decision to implement the "spot-check" system of compliance review, and the application of that "spot-check" system to the particular aircraft involved in these cases. In our view, both components of respondents' claim are barred by the discretionary function exception to the Act.

The FAA's implementation of a mechanism for compliance review is plainly discretionary activity of the "nature and quality" protected by § 2680(a). When an agency determines the extent to which it will supervise the safety procedures of private individuals, it is exercising discretionary regulatory authority of the most basic kind. Decisions as to the manner of enforcing regulations directly affect the feasibility and practicality of the Government's regulatory program; such decisions require the agency to establish priorities for the accomplishment of its policy objectives by balancing the objectives sought to be obtained against such practical considerations as staffing and funding. Here, the FAA has determined that a program of "spot-checking" manufacturers' compliance with minimum safety standards best accommodates the goal of air transportation safety and the reality of finite agency resources. Judicial intervention in such decisionmaking through private tort suits would require the courts to "second-guess" the political, social, and economic judgments of an agency exercising its regulatory function. It was precisely this sort of judicial intervention in policymaking that the discretionary function exception was designed to prevent.

It follows that the acts of FAA employees in executing the "spot-check" program in accordance with agency directives are protected by the discretionary function exception as well. The FAA employees who conducted compliance reviews of the aircraft involved in this case were specifically empowered to make policy judgments regarding the degree of confidence that might reasonably be placed in a given manufacturer, the need to maximize compliance with FAA regulations, and the efficient allocation of agency resources. In administering the "spot-check" program, these FAA engineers and inspectors necessarily took certain calculated risks, but those risks were encountered for the advancement of a governmental purpose and pursuant to the specific grant of authority in the regulations and operating manuals. Under such circumstances, the FAA's alleged negligence in failing to check certain specific items in the course of certificating a particular aircraft falls squarely within the discretionary function exception of § 2680(a).

V

In rendering the United States amenable to some suits in tort, Congress could not have intended to impose liability for the regulatory enforcement activities of the FAA challenged in this case. The FAA has a statutory duty to *promote* safety in air transportation, not to insure it. We hold that these actions against the FAA for its alleged negligence in certificating aircraft for use in commercial aviation are barred by the discretionary function exception of the Federal Tort Claims Act. Accordingly, the judgments of the United States Court of Appeals for the Ninth Circuit are reversed.

It is so ordered.

Notes and Questions

1. What does the Supreme Court's decision in *Varig Airlines* add to the definition of the discretionary function exception? Beyond the vague statement in *Dalehite* that "[w]here there is room for policy judgment and decision there is discretion," what more do we know about the content of the exception from *Varig Airlines*? And with the emphasis on judicial deference to policymaking in the executive branch, are we seeing the return of the political question doctrine, discussed in Chapter I.C.2, in a different form? *See* Mark C. Niles, *"Nothing But Mischief": The Federal Tort Claims Act and the Scope of Discretionary Immunity*, 54 Admin. L. Rev. 1275, 1323 (2002) (saying that the *Varig Airlines* Court explained the purpose of the discretionary function exception in terms of "the basic principles that Congress intended to define the scope of the exception—separation of powers concerns").

2. As stated in the notes following the *Dalehite* decision, several lower courts had developed a "planning level v. operational level" test for the discretionary function exception. The exception applied only to the former and not to the latter. Does *Varig Airlines* say anything relevant to this subject? Identify the pertinent language in *Varig Airlines* and explain its effect upon this purported distinction.

3. At several points, the *Varig Airlines* opinion suggests a heightened level of immunity for the government's regulatory activities. For example, the Court says that "[w]hatever else the discretionary function exception may include, it plainly was intended to encompass the discretionary acts of the Government acting in its role as a regulator of the conduct of private individuals." The Court notes that Congress originally considered exempting all of the activities of certain regulatory agencies and then settled upon the discretionary function exception as a general protection of regulatory activities. Indeed, the Court concludes the opinion by stating that "[t]he

FAA has a statutory duty to *promote* safety in air transportation, not to insure it." (Although this case involves an exception to liability rather than the scope of liability, there are certain parallels with the "private person" analogy issue discussed earlier, Chapter III.A.3.b). Does this special protection for regulatory activities survive the very next case, *Berkovitz v. United States?*

Berkovitz v. United States

Supreme Court of the United States.
486 U.S. 531 (1988).

■ JUSTICE MARSHALL delivered the opinion of the Court.

The question in this case is whether the discretionary function exception of the Federal Tort Claims Act (FTCA or Act), 28 U.S.C. § 2680(a), bars a suit based on the Government's licensing of an oral polio vaccine and on its subsequent approval of the release of a specific lot of that vaccine to the public.

I

On May 10, 1979, Kevan Berkovitz, then a 2–month–old infant, ingested a dose of Orimune, an oral polio vaccine manufactured by Lederle Laboratories. Within one month, he contracted a severe case of polio. The disease left Berkovitz almost completely paralyzed and unable to breathe without the assistance of a respirator. The Communicable Disease Center, an agency of the Federal Government, determined that Berkovitz had contracted polio from the vaccine.

Berkovitz, joined by his parents as guardians, subsequently filed suit against the United States in Federal District Court. The complaint alleged that the United States was liable for his injuries under the FTCA, 28 U.S.C. §§ 1346(b), 2674, because the Division of Biologic Standards (DBS), then a part of the National Institutes of Health, had acted wrongfully in licensing Lederle Laboratories to produce Orimune and because the Bureau of Biologics of the Food and Drug Administration (FDA) had acted wrongfully in approving release to the public of the particular lot of vaccine containing Berkovitz's dose. According to petitioners, these actions violated federal law and policy regarding the inspection and approval of polio vaccines.

The Government moved to dismiss the suit for lack of subject-matter jurisdiction on the ground that the agency actions fell within the discretionary function exception of the FTCA. The District Court denied this motion, concluding that neither the licensing of Orimune nor the release of a specific lot of that vaccine to the public was a "discretionary function" within the meaning of the FTCA. At the Government's request, the District Court certified its decision for immediate appeal to the Third Circuit pursuant to 28 U.S.C. § 1292(b), and the Court of Appeals accepted jurisdiction.

A divided panel of the Court of Appeals reversed. 822 F.2d 1322 (1987).

* * *

We granted certiorari to resolve a conflict in the Circuits regarding the effect of the discretionary function exception on claims arising from the Government's regulation of polio vaccines. We now reverse the Third Circuit's judgment.

II

The FTCA, 28 U.S.C. § 1346(b), generally authorizes suits against the United States for damages

"for injury or loss of property, or personal injury or death caused by the negligent or wrongful act or omission of any employee of the Government while acting within the scope of his office or employment, under circumstances where the United States, if a private person, would be liable to the claimant in accordance with the law of the place where the act or omission occurred."[2]

The Act includes a number of exceptions to this broad waiver of sovereign immunity. The exception relevant to this case provides that no liability shall lie for

"[a]ny claim . . . based upon the exercise or performance or the failure to exercise or perform a discretionary function or duty on the part of a federal agency or an employee of the Government, whether or not the discretion involved be abused." 28 U.S.C. § 2680(a).

This exception, as we stated in our most recent opinion on the subject, "marks the boundary between Congress' willingness to impose tort liability upon the United States and its desire to protect certain governmental activities from exposure to suit by private individuals." *United States v. Varig Airlines,* 467 U.S., at 808.

The determination of whether the discretionary function exception bars a suit against the Government is guided by several established principles. This Court stated in *Varig* that "it is the nature of the conduct, rather than the status of the actor, that governs whether the discretionary function exception applies in a given case." *Id.,* at 813. In examining the nature of the challenged conduct, a court must first consider whether the action is a matter of choice for the acting employee. This inquiry is mandated by the language of the exception; conduct cannot be discretionary unless it involves an element of judgment or choice. See *Dalehite v. United States,* 346 U.S. 15, 34 (1953) (stating that the exception protects "the discretion of the executive or the administrator to act according to

---

2. There is currently no dispute in this case as to whether petitioners have stated a claim that falls within this general waiver of immunity. Although the Government raised this issue in its motion to dismiss petitioners' suit, the District Court found that the complaint stated a claim under the relevant state law, and the Government declined to request certification of this decision for immediate appeal.

one's judgment of the best course"). Thus, the discretionary function exception will not apply when a federal statute, regulation, or policy specifically prescribes a course of action for an employee to follow. In this event, the employee has no rightful option but to adhere to the directive. And if the employee's conduct cannot appropriately be the product of judgment or choice, then there is no discretion in the conduct for the discretionary function exception to protect.

Moreover, assuming the challenged conduct involves an element of judgment, a court must determine whether that judgment is of the kind that the discretionary function exception was designed to shield. The basis for the discretionary function exception was Congress' desire to "prevent judicial 'second-guessing' of legislative and administrative decisions grounded in social, economic, and political policy through the medium of an action in tort." *United States v. Varig Airlines, supra,* at 814. The exception, properly construed, therefore protects only governmental actions and decisions based on considerations of public policy. See *Dalehite v. United States, supra,* at 36 ("Where there is room for policy judgment and decision there is discretion"). In sum, the discretionary function exception insulates the Government from liability if the action challenged in the case involves the permissible exercise of policy judgment. * * *

In restating and clarifying the scope of the discretionary function exception, we intend specifically to reject the Government's argument, pressed both in this Court and the Court of Appeals, that the exception precludes liability for any and all acts arising out of the regulatory programs of federal agencies. That argument is rebutted first by the language of the exception, which protects "discretionary" functions, rather than "regulatory" functions. The significance of Congress' choice of language is supported by the legislative history. As this Court previously has indicated, the relevant legislative materials demonstrate that the exception was designed to cover not all acts of regulatory agencies and their employees, but only such acts as are "discretionary" in nature. See *Dalehite v. United States, supra,* at 33–34. This coverage accords with Congress' purpose in enacting the exception: to prevent "[j]udicial intervention in . . . the political, social, and economic judgments" of governmental—including regulatory—agencies. *United States v. Varig Airlines,* 467 U.S., at 820. Moreover, this Court twice before has rejected a variant of the Government's position. See *Indian Towing Co. v. United States,* 350 U.S. 61, 64–65 (1955) (disapproving argument that FTCA precludes liability for the performance of "uniquely governmental functions"); *Rayonier, Inc. v. United States,* 352 U.S. 315, 318–319 (1957) (same).[5] And in *Varig,* we ignored the precise argument the Government makes in this case, focusing instead on the particular nature of the regulatory conduct at issue. To the extent we have not already put the Government's argument to rest, we do so now.

---

5. The Government's position in this case at times appears to replicate precisely the position expressly rejected in *Indian Towing* and *Rayonier.* See Brief for United States 20 (arguing that Congress intended to preserve immunity for "core governmental function[s]"); *id.,* at 16.

The discretionary function exception applies only to conduct that involves the permissible exercise of policy judgment. The question in this case is whether the governmental activities challenged by petitioners are of this discretionary nature.

III

Petitioners' suit raises two broad claims. First, petitioners assert that the DBS violated a federal statute and accompanying regulations in issuing a license to Lederle Laboratories to produce Orimune. Second, petitioners argue that the Bureau of Biologics of the FDA violated federal regulations and policy in approving the release of the particular lot of Orimune that contained Kevan Berkovitz's dose. We examine each of these broad claims by reviewing the applicable regulatory scheme and petitioners' specific allegations of agency wrongdoing. Because the decision we review adjudicated a motion to dismiss, we accept all of the factual allegations in petitioners' complaint as true and ask whether, in these circumstances, dismissal of the complaint was appropriate.

A

* * * Petitioners' first allegation with regard to the licensing of Orimune is that the DBS issued a product license without first receiving data that the manufacturer must submit showing how the product, at the various stages of the manufacturing process, matched up against regulatory safety standards. The discretionary function exception does not bar a cause of action based on this allegation. The statute and regulations * * * require, as a precondition to licensing, that the DBS receive certain test data from the manufacturer relating to the product's compliance with regulatory standards. See § 351(d), 58 Stat. 702–703, as amended, 42 U.S.C. § 262(d) (providing that a license shall issue "only upon a showing" by the manufacturer); 42 CFR § 73.3 (Supp.1964); 21 CFR § 601.2 (1987) (providing that application for license shall be deemed as filed only upon receipt of relevant test data). The DBS has no discretion to issue a license without first receiving the required test data; to do so would violate a specific statutory and regulatory directive. Accordingly, to the extent that petitioners' licensing claim is based on a decision of the DBS to issue a license without having received the required test data, the discretionary function exception imposes no bar.

Petitioners' other allegation regarding the licensing of Orimune is difficult to describe with precision. Petitioners contend that the DBS licensed Orimune even though the vaccine did not comply with certain regulatory safety standards. This charge may be understood in any of three ways. First, petitioners may mean that the DBS licensed Orimune without first making a determination as to whether the vaccine complied with regulatory standards. Second, petitioners may intend to argue that the DBS specifically found that Orimune failed to comply with certain regulatory standards and nonetheless issued a license for the vaccine's manufacture. Third, petitioners may concede that the DBS made a determination of compliance, but allege that this determination was incorrect. Neither petitioners' complaint nor their briefs and argument before this Court make entirely clear their theory of the case.

If petitioners aver that the DBS licensed Orimune either without determining whether the vaccine complied with regulatory standards or after determining that the vaccine failed to comply, the discretionary function exception does not bar the claim. Under the scheme governing the DBS's regulation of polio vaccines, the DBS may not issue a license except upon an examination of the product and a determination that the product complies with all regulatory standards. See 42 CFR § 73.5(a) (Supp.1964); 21 CFR § 601.4 (1987). The agency has no discretion to deviate from this mandated procedure. Petitioners' claim, if interpreted as alleging that the DBS licensed Orimune in the absence of a determination that the vaccine complied with regulatory standards, therefore does not challenge a discretionary function. Rather, the claim charges a failure on the part of the agency to perform its clear duty under federal law. When a suit charges an agency with failing to act in accord with a specific mandatory directive, the discretionary function exception does not apply.

If petitioners' claim is that the DBS made a determination that Orimune complied with regulatory standards, but that the determination was incorrect, the question of the applicability of the discretionary function exception requires a somewhat different analysis. In that event, the question turns on whether the manner and method of determining compliance with the safety standards at issue involve agency judgment of the kind protected by the discretionary function exception. Petitioners contend that the determination involves the application of objective scientific whereas the Government asserts that the determination incorporates considerable "policy judgment." In making these assertions, the parties have framed the issue appropriately; application of the discretionary function exception to the claim that the determination of compliance was incorrect hinges on whether the agency officials making that determination permissibly exercise policy choice. The parties, however, have not addressed this question in detail, and they have given us no indication of the way in which the DBS interprets and applies the regulations setting forth the criteria for compliance. Given that these regulations are particularly abstruse, we hesitate to decide the question on the scanty record before us. We therefore leave it to the District Court to decide, if petitioners choose to press this claim, whether agency officials appropriately exercise policy judgment in determining that a vaccine product complies with the relevant safety standards.

B

The regulatory scheme governing release of vaccine lots is distinct from that governing the issuance of licenses. The former set of regulations places an obligation on manufacturers to examine all vaccine lots prior to distribution to ensure that they comply with regulatory standards. See 21 CFR § 610.1 (1978). These regulations, however, do not impose a corresponding duty on the Bureau of Biologics. Although the regulations empower the Bureau to examine any vaccine lot and prevent the distribution of a noncomplying lot, see 21 CFR § 610.2(a) (1978), they do not require the Bureau to take such action in all cases. The regulations generally allow the Bureau to determine the appropriate manner in which to regulate the release of vaccine lots, rather than mandating certain kinds of agency action. The regulatory scheme governing the release of vaccine lots is substantially similar in this respect to the scheme discussed in *United States v. Varig Airlines,* 467 U.S. 797 (1984).

This scheme involves permissible exercise of policy judgment

Given this regulatory context, the discretionary function exception bars any claims that challenge the Bureau's formulation of policy as to the appropriate way in which to regulate the release of vaccine lots. Cf. *id.,* at 819–820 (holding that discretionary function exception barred claim challenging FAA's decision to establish a spot-checking program). In addition, if the policies and programs formulated by the Bureau allow room for implementing officials to make independent policy judgments, the discretionary function exception protects the acts taken by those officials in the exercise of this discretion. Cf. *id.,* at 820 (holding that discretionary function exception barred claim that employees charged with executing the FAA's spot-checking program made negligent policy judgments respecting the proper inspection of airplanes). The discretionary function exception, however, does not apply if the acts complained of do not involve the permissible exercise of policy discretion. Thus, if the Bureau's policy leaves no room for an official to exercise policy judgment in performing a given act, or if the act simply does not involve the exercise of such judgment, the discretionary function exception does not bar a claim that the act was negligent or wrongful. Cf. *Indian Towing Co. v. United States,* 350 U.S., at 69 (holding that a negligent failure to maintain a lighthouse in good working order subjected the Government to suit under the FTCA even though the initial decision to undertake and maintain lighthouse service was a discretionary policy judgment).

Application
- Room for regulators to decide how they want to enforce the regs.

(But if they adopt a policy that leaves no room for exercise of judgment, then the disc. funct. exception ~ bar it)

Viewed in light of these principles, petitioners' claim regarding the release of the vaccine lot from which Kevan Berkovitz received his dose survives the Government's motion to dismiss. Petitioners allege that, under the authority granted by the regulations, the Bureau of Biologics has adopted a policy of testing all vaccine lots for compliance with safety standards and preventing the distribution to the public of any lots that fail to comply. Petitioners further allege that notwithstanding this policy, which allegedly leaves no room for implementing officials to exercise independent policy judgment, employees of the Bureau knowingly approved the release of a lot that did not comply with safety standards. Thus, petitioners' complaint is directed at a governmental action that allegedly involved no policy discretion. Petitioners, of course, have not proved their factual allegations, but they are not required to do so on a motion to dismiss. If those allegations are correct—that is, if the Bureau's policy did not allow the official who took the challenged action to release a noncomplying lot on the basis of policy considerations—the discretionary function exception does not bar the claim. Because petitioners may yet show, on the basis of materials obtained in discovery or otherwise, that the conduct challenged here did not involve the permissible exercise of policy discretion,

authority vs. requirement

TT's argument w/ respect to the release policy:
· The Bureau adopted a discretion-free policy -- and failed to follow it

Ct: If that is the case, the conduct complained of it outside the disc. function exception

the invocation of the discretionary function exception to dismiss petitioners' lot release claim was improper.

IV

For the foregoing reasons, the Court of Appeals erred in holding that the discretionary function exception required the dismissal of petitioners' claims respecting the licensing of Orimune and the release of a particular vaccine lot. The judgment of the Court of Appeals is accordingly reversed, and the case is remanded for further proceedings consistent with this opinion.

It is so ordered.

Notes and Questions

1. The *Berkovitz* decision has been understood to articulate a two-prong test for the discretionary function exception. Explain each of the two steps and appreciate how they are applied in the context of the *Berkovitz* case.

2. Note that the *Berkovitz* opinion specifically rejects the government's argument that the discretionary function exception precludes liability for acts arising out of regulatory programs. The Court makes this statement without even acknowledging the language in *Varig Airlines* that suggested a heightened level of protection for government actions in regulating private conduct. Is it appropriate to treat regulatory activities the same as other types of governmental activity?

As part of this analysis, the Court states in footnote 5 that the government's argument, suggesting immunity for certain "core governmental functions," appears to "replicate precisely" the position expressly rejected in *Indian Towing v. United States*. Is it fair to say that *Indian Towing* rejected the core or unique governmental function analysis? Is *Indian Towing* even relevant in this case? As the Court stated in *Varig Airlines* and will state again in the next case, *United States v. Gaubert*, the *Indian Towing* decision did not involve the discretionary function exception at all, as the government had conceded its inapplicability in that case. Moreover, while *Indian Towing* rejected the government's argument that the government could be liable under the FTCA only if private entities engaged in identical or the same conduct, the decision did not close the door to the argument that the "private person under like circumstances" language of Section 2674 required the existence of some analogy between the government's conduct and private activity. (For a general discussion of the "private person" analogy requirement, see Chapter III.A.3.b.) Thus, the argument that the government may not be held liable when performing a task for which no private counterpart exists at all was still at least plausible as an interpretation of the "private person" language which defines the scope of liability. However, the language in *Berkovitz*—although expressed in the context of an exception to liability (the discretionary function exception) rather than the scope of liability (including the "private person" language)—may well indicate the Court's hostility to the preservation of any area of governmental activity, however "unique" or "core," as per se immune under the FTCA.

3. The *Berkovitz* Court says that acts may be regarded as discretionary in nature, and thus within the exception, only when they "involve[] the permissible exercise of policy judgment." In the notes following the *Dalehite* decision, the issue was raised whether the government's conduct must involve a conscious weighing of policy factors/or merely be susceptible to policy analysis to fall within the exception. Does this *Berkovitz* language suggest an answer to that question? Ask the question again after reading *United States v. Gaubert,* which is next.

4. Because the *Berkovitz* case arose on review of a motion to dismiss, the Court states that it must accept all of the factual allegations in the complaint as true. Upon remand to the district court, what is the appropriate procedural step for the government to take next if it wishes to dispute that the FDA had licensed the vaccine before receiving the data that the manufacturer must submit under the regulation, or deny that the FDA had truly established a policy to test all vaccine lots for compliance rather than use a "spot-check" approach similar to that in *Varig Airlines?* If *Berkovitz* effectively introduces additional factual elements into a case, such as whether a statute, regulation or policy was violated or whether a particular decision implicated policy, the government would find it more difficult to achieve resolution of discretionary function exception cases on a motion to dismiss. Suppose the government believes there is no evidence to support a plaintiff's allegations of a failure to follow statutory or regulatory prescriptions. What other procedural mechanism, that you learned about in the first-year Civil Procedure course, might assure an early resolution short of trial?

United States v. Gaubert

Supreme Court of the United States.
499 U.S. 315 (1991).

■ JUSTICE WHITE delivered the opinion of the Court.

When the events in this case occurred, the Home Owners' Loan Act, 12 U.S.C. §§ 1461–1468c,[1] provided for the chartering and regulation of feder-

---

[1]. Subsequent to the events at issue here, and in response to the current crisis in the thrift industry, Congress enacted comprehensive changes to the statutory scheme concerning thrift regulation by means of the Financial Institutions Reform, Recovery, and Enforcement Act of 1989 (FIRREA), Pub.L. 101–73, 103 Stat. 183. FIRREA abolished the FHLBB and the Federal Savings and Loan Insurance Corporation (FSLIC), two of the agencies at issue here, and repealed the statutory provisions governing those agencies' conduct. §§ 401, 407, 103 Stat. 354–357, 363. At the same time, it granted to the Federal

al savings and loan associations (FSLA's). Section 1464(a) authorized the Federal Home Loan Bank Board (FHLBB) "under such rules and regulations as it may prescribe, to provide for the organization, incorporation, examination, operation, and regulation" of FSLA's, and to issue charters, "giving primary consideration to the best practices of thrift institutions in the United States." In this case the FHLBB and the Federal Home Loan Bank–Dallas (FHLB–D) undertook to advise about and oversee certain aspects of the operation of a thrift institution. Their conduct in this respect was challenged by a suit against the United States under the Federal Tort Claims Act, 28 U.S.C. §§ 1346(b), 2671 *et seq.* (FTCA), asserting that the FHLBB and FHLB–D had been negligent in carrying out their supervisory activities. The question before us is whether certain actions taken by the FHLBB and FHLB–D are within the "discretionary function" exception to the liability of the United States under the FTCA. The Court of Appeals for the Fifth Circuit answered this question in the negative. We have the contrary view and reverse.

I

This FTCA suit arises from the supervision by federal regulators of the activities of Independent American Savings Association (IASA), a Texas-chartered and federally insured savings and loan. Respondent Thomas A. Gaubert was IASA's chairman of the board and largest shareholder. In 1984, officials at the FHLBB sought to have IASA merge with Investex Savings, a failing Texas thrift. Because the FHLBB and FHLB–D were concerned about Gaubert's other financial dealings, they requested that he sign a "neutralization agreement" which effectively removed him from IASA's management. They also asked him to post a $25 million interest in real property as security for his personal guarantee that IASA's net worth would exceed regulatory minimums. Gaubert agreed to both conditions. Federal officials then provided regulatory and financial advice to enable IASA to consummate the merger with Investex. Throughout this period, the regulators instituted no formal action against IASA. Instead, they relied on the likelihood that IASA and Gaubert would follow their suggestions and advice.

In the spring of 1986, the regulators threatened to close IASA unless its management and board of directors were replaced; all of the directors agreed to resign. The new officers and directors, including the chief executive officer who was a former FHLB–D employee, were recommended by FHLB–D. After the new management took over, FHLB–D officials became more involved in IASA's day-to-day business. They recommended the hiring of a certain consultant to advise IASA on operational and financial matters; they advised IASA concerning whether, when, and how its subsidiaries should be placed into bankruptcy; they mediated salary disputes; they reviewed the draft of a complaint to be used in litigation;

Deposit Insurance Corporation (FDIC) and the newly established Office of Thrift Supervision discretionary enforcement authority similar to that enjoyed by the former agencies. §§ 201, 301, 103 Stat. 187–188, 277–343.

they urged IASA to convert from state to federal charter; and they actively intervened when the Texas Savings and Loan Department attempted to install a supervisory agent at IASA. In each instance, FHLB–D's advice was followed.

Although IASA was thought to be financially sound while Gaubert managed the thrift, the new directors soon announced that IASA had a substantial negative net worth. On May 20, 1987, Gaubert filed an administrative tort claim with the FHLBB, FHLB–D, and FSLIC, seeking $75 million in damages for the lost value of his shares and $25 million for the property he had forfeited under his personal guarantee. That same day, the FSLIC assumed the receivership of IASA. After Gaubert's administrative claim was denied six months later, he filed the instant FTCA suit in United States District Court for the Northern District of Texas, seeking $100 million in damages for the alleged negligence of federal officials in selecting the new officers and directors and in participating in the day-to-day management of IASA. The District Court granted the motion to dismiss filed by the United States, finding that all of the challenged actions of the regulators fell within the discretionary function exception to the FTCA, found in 28 U.S.C. § 2680(a).

The Court of Appeals for the Fifth Circuit affirmed in part and reversed in part. 885 F.2d 1284 (1989). Relying on this Court's decision in *Indian Towing Co. v. United States,* 350 U.S. 61 (1955), the court distinguished between "policy decisions," which fall within the exception, and "operational actions," which do not. 885 F.2d, at 1287. After claiming further support for this distinction in this Court's decisions in *United States v. S.A. Empresa de Viacao Aerea Rio Grandense (Varig Airlines),* 467 U.S. 797 (1984), and *Berkovitz v. United States,* 486 U.S. 531 (1988), the court explained:

> " * * * Only policy oriented decisions enjoy such immunity. Thus, the FHLBB and FHLB–Dallas officials were only protected by the discretionary function exception until their actions became operational in nature and thus crossed the line established in *Indian Towing.*" 885 F.2d, at 1289.

In the court's view, that line was crossed when the regulators "began to advise IASA management and participate in management decisions." *Id.,* at 1290. Consequently, the Court of Appeals affirmed the District Court's dismissal of the claims which concerned the merger, neutralization agreement, personal guarantee, and replacement of IASA management, but reversed the dismissal of the claims which concerned the regulators' activities after they assumed a supervisory role in IASA's day-to-day affairs. We granted certiorari and now reverse.

II

* * * The [discretionary function] exception covers only acts that are discretionary in nature, acts that "involv[e] an element of judgment or choice," *Berkovitz, supra,* at 536; see also *Dalehite v. United States,* 346 U.S. 15, 34; and "it is the nature of the conduct, rather than the status of

the actor," that governs whether the exception applies. *Varig Airlines, supra*, at 813. The requirement of judgment or choice is not satisfied if a "federal statute, regulation, or policy specifically prescribes a course of action for an employee to follow," because "the employee has no rightful option but to adhere to the directive." *Berkovitz*, 486 U.S., at 536.

Furthermore, even "assuming the challenged conduct involves an element of judgment," it remains to be decided "whether that judgment is of the kind that the discretionary function exception was designed to shield." *Ibid.* See *Varig Airlines*, 467 U.S., at 814. Because the purpose of the exception is to "prevent judicial 'second-guessing' of legislative and administrative decisions grounded in social, economic, and political policy through the medium of an action in tort," *id.*, at 814, when properly construed, the exception "protects only governmental actions and decisions based on considerations of public policy." *Berkovitz, supra*, at 537.

Where Congress has delegated the authority to an independent agency or to the executive branch to implement the general provisions of a regulatory statute and to issue regulations to that end, there is no doubt that planning-level decisions establishing programs are protected by the discretionary function exception, as is the promulgation of regulations by which the agencies are to carry out the programs. In addition, the actions of Government agents involving the necessary element of choice and grounded in the social, economic, or political goals of the statute and regulations are protected. * * *

* * * [I]f a regulation mandates particular conduct, and the employee obeys the direction, the Government will be protected because the action will be deemed in furtherance of the policies which led to the promulgation of the regulation. See *Dalehite, supra*, at 36. If the employee violates the mandatory regulation, there will be no shelter from liability because there is no room for choice and the action will be contrary to policy. On the other hand, if a regulation allows the employee discretion, the very existence of the regulation creates a strong presumption that a discretionary act authorized by the regulation involves consideration of the same policies which led to the promulgation of the regulations.

Not all agencies issue comprehensive regulations, however. Some establish policy on a case-by-case basis, whether through adjudicatory proceedings or through administration of agency programs. Others promulgate regulations on some topics, but not on others. In addition, an agency may rely on internal guidelines rather than on published regulations. In any event, it will most often be true that the general aims and policies of the controlling statute will be evident from its text.

When established governmental policy, as expressed or implied by statute, regulation, or agency guidelines, allows a Government agent to exercise discretion, it must be presumed that the agent's acts are grounded in policy when exercising that discretion. For a complaint to survive a motion to dismiss, it must allege facts which would support a finding that the challenged actions are not the kind of conduct that can be said to be grounded in the policy of the regulatory regime. The focus of the inquiry is not on the agent's subjective intent in exercising the discretion conferred by statute or regulation, but on the nature of the actions taken and on whether they are susceptible to policy analysis."[7]

III

In light of our cases and their interpretation of § 2680(a), it is clear that the Court of Appeals erred in holding that the exception does not reach decisions made at the operational or management level of the bank involved in this case. A discretionary act is one that involves choice or judgment; there is nothing in that description that refers exclusively to policymaking or planning functions. Day-to-day management of banking affairs, like the management of other businesses, regularly requires judgment as to which of a range of permissible courses is the wisest. Discretionary conduct is not confined to the policy or planning level. "[I]t is the nature of the conduct, rather than the status of the actor, that governs whether the discretionary function exception applies in a given case." *Varig Airlines, supra,* at 813.

In *Varig Airlines,* the Federal Aviation Administration had devised a system of "spot checking" airplanes. We held that not only was this act discretionary but so too were the acts of agency employees in executing the program since they had a range of discretion to exercise in deciding how to carry out the spot-check activity. 467 U.S., at 820. Likewise in *Berkovitz, supra,* although holding that some acts on the operational level were not discretionary and therefore were without the exception, we recognized that other acts, if held to be discretionary on remand would be protected. 486 U.S., at 545.

The Court's first use of the term "operational" in connection with the discretionary function exception occurred in *Dalehite,* where the Court noted that "[t]he decisions held culpable were all responsibly made at a planning rather than operational level and involved considerations more or less important to the practicability of the Government's fertilizer program." 346 U.S., at 42. Gaubert relies upon this statement as support for his argument that the Court of Appeals applied the appropriate analysis to the allegations of the Amended Complaint, but the distinction in *Dalehite* was merely description of the level at which the challenged conduct occurred. There was no suggestion that decisions made at an operational level could not also be based on policy.

Neither is the decision below supported by *Indian Towing.* There the Coast Guard had negligently failed to maintain a lighthouse by allowing the

7. There are obviously discretionary acts performed by a Government agent that are within the scope of his employment but not within the discretionary function exception because these acts cannot be said to be based on the purposes that the regulatory regime seeks to accomplish. If one of the officials involved in this case drove an auto-mobile on a mission connected with his official duties and negligently collided with another car, the exception would not apply. Although driving requires the constant exercise of discretion, the official's decisions in exercising that discretion can hardly be said to be grounded in regulatory policy.

[handwritten margin note: The U.S. did not have discretion/choice about whether to restore the light]

light to go out. The United States was held liable, not because the negligence occurred at the operational level but because making sure the light was operational "did not involve any permissible exercise of policy judgment." *Berkovitz, supra,* at 538, n. 3. Indeed, the Government did not even claim the benefit of the exception but unsuccessfully urged that maintaining the light was a governmental function for which it could not be liable. The Court of Appeals misinterpreted *Berkovitz*'s reference to *Indian Towing* as perpetuating a nonexistent dichotomy between discretionary functions and operational activities. Consequently, once the court determined that some of the actions challenged by Gaubert occurred at an operational level, it concluded, incorrectly, that those actions must necessarily have been outside the scope of the discretionary function exception.

[handwritten margin note: It is not the level @ which the decision is made that determines applicability of the exception, but the nature of the action, & whether it involves judgment]

IV

We now inquire whether the Court of Appeals was correct in holding that some of the acts alleged in Gaubert's Amended Complaint were not discretionary acts within the meaning of § 2680(a). The decision we review was entered on a motion to dismiss. We therefore "accept all of the factual allegations in [Gaubert's] complaint as true" and ask whether the allegations state a claim sufficient to survive a motion to dismiss. *Berkovitz, supra,* at 540.

The Court of Appeals dismissed several of the allegations in the Amended Complaint on the ground that the challenged activities fell within the discretionary function exception. These allegations concerned "the decision to merge IASA with Investex and seek a neutralization agreement from Gaubert," as well as "the decision to replace the IASA Board of Directors with FHLBB approved persons, and the actions taken to effectuate that decision." 885 F.2d, at 1290. Gaubert has not challenged this aspect of the court's ruling. Consequently, we review only those allegations in the Amended Complaint which the Court of Appeals viewed as surviving the Government's motion to dismiss.

[handwritten margin note: Challenges not the takeover, but the subs operations]

[handwritten margin note: Gaubert challenges these actions]

These claims asserted that the regulators had achieved "a constant federal presence" at IASA. In describing this presence, the Amended Complaint alleged that the regulators "consult[ed] as to day-to-day affairs and operations of IASA,"; "participated in management decisions" at IASA board meetings; "became involved in giving advice, making recommendations, urging, or directing action or procedures at IASA,"; and "advised their hand-picked directors and officers on a variety of subjects." * * * According to Gaubert, the losses he suffered were caused by the regulators' "assumption of the duty to participate in, and to make, the day-to-day decisions at IASA and [the] negligent discharge of that assumed duty." Moreover, he alleged that "[t]he involvement of the FHLB–Dallas in the affairs of IASA went beyond its normal regulatory activity, and the agency actually substituted its decisions for those of the directors and officers of the association."

We first inquire whether the challenged actions were discretionary, or whether they were instead controlled by mandatory statutes or regulations.

Berkovitz, 486 U.S., at 536. * * * The relevant statutory provisions were not mandatory, but left to the judgment of the agency the decision of when to institute proceedings against a financial institution and which mechanism to use. For example, the FSLIC had authority to terminate an institution's insured status, issue cease-and-desist orders, and suspend or remove an institution's officers, if "in the opinion of the Corporation" such action was warranted because the institution or its officers were engaging in an "unsafe or unsound practice" in connection with the business of the institution. 12 U.S.C. §§ 1730(b)(1), (e)(1), (g)(1). The FHLBB had parallel authority to issue cease-and-desist orders and suspend or remove an institution's officers. §§ 1464(d)(2)(A), (4)(A). Although the statute enumerated specific grounds warranting an appointment by the FHLBB of a conservator or receiver, the determination of whether any of these grounds existed depended upon "the opinion of the Board." § 1464(d)(6)(A). The agencies here were not bound to act in a particular way; the exercise of their authority involved a great "element of judgment or choice." *Berkovitz, supra,* at 536. * * *

Gaubert also argues that the challenged actions fall outside the discretionary function exception because they involved the mere application of technical skills and business expertise. But this is just another way of saying that the considerations involving the day-to-day management of a business concern such as IASA are so precisely formulated that decisions at the operational level never involve the exercise of discretion within the meaning of § 2680(a), a notion that we have already rejected in disapproving the rationale of the Court of Appeals' decision. It may be that certain decisions resting on mathematical calculations, for example, involve no choice or judgment in carrying out the calculations, but the regulatory acts alleged here are not of that genre. Rather, it is plain to us that each of the challenged actions involved the exercise of choice and judgment.

We are also convinced that each of the regulatory actions in question involved the kind of policy judgment that the discretionary function exception was designed to shield. The FHLBB Resolution quoted above, coupled with the relevant statutory provisions, established governmental policy which is presumed to have been furthered when the regulators exercised their discretion to choose from various courses of action in supervising IASA. Although Gaubert contends that day-to-day decisions concerning IASA's affairs did not implicate social, economic, or political policies, even the Court of Appeals recognized that these day-to-day "operational" decisions were undertaken for policy reasons of primary concern to the regulatory agencies:

> "[T]he federal regulators here had two discrete purposes in mind as they commenced day-to-day operations at IASA. First, they sought to protect the solvency of the savings and loan industry at large, and maintain the public's confidence in that industry. Second, they sought to preserve the assets of IASA for the benefit of depositors and shareholders, of which Gaubert was one." 885 F.2d, at 1290.

the Ct. looks at 'basis' for certain acts

Day-to-day involvement doesn't necessarily op outside discretion

Consequently, Gaubert's assertion that the day-to-day involvement of the regulators with IASA is actionable because it went beyond "normal regulatory activity" is insupportable.

We find nothing in Gaubert's Amended Complaint effectively alleging that the discretionary acts performed by the regulators were not entitled to the exemption. By Gaubert's own admission, the regulators replaced IASA's management in order to protect the FSLIC's insurance fund; thus it cannot be disputed that this action was based on public policy considerations. The regulators' actions in urging IASA to convert to federal charter and in intervening with the state agency were directly related to public policy considerations regarding federal oversight of the thrift industry. So were advising the hiring of a financial consultant, advising when to place IASA subsidiaries into bankruptcy, intervening on IASA's behalf with Texas officials, advising on litigation policy, and mediating salary disputes. There are no allegations that the regulators gave anything other than the kind of advice that was within the purview of the policies behind the statutes. * * *

Nature of act was the kind encouraged by the policies

In the end, Gaubert's Amended Complaint alleges nothing more than negligence on the part of the regulators. Indeed, the two substantive counts seek relief for "negligent selection of directors and officers" and "negligent involvement in day-to-day operations." Gaubert asserts that the discretionary function exception protects only those acts of negligence which occur in the course of establishing broad policies, rather than individual acts of negligence which occur in the course of day-to-day activities. But we have already disposed of that submission. If the routine or frequent nature of a decision were sufficient to remove an otherwise discretionary act from the scope of the exception, then countless policy-based decisions by regulators exercising day-to-day supervisory authority would be actionable. This is not the rule of our cases.

V

Because from the face of the Amended Complaint, it is apparent that all of the challenged actions of the federal regulators involved the exercise of discretion in furtherance of public policy goals, the Court of Appeals erred in failing to find the claims barred by the discretionary function exception of the Federal Tort Claims Act. We therefore reverse the decision of the Court of Appeals for the Fifth Circuit and remand for proceedings consistent with this opinion.

It is so ordered.

■ Justice Scalia, concurring in part and concurring in the judgment.

I concur in the judgment and in much of the opinion of the Court. I write separately because I do not think it necessary to analyze individually each of the particular actions challenged by Gaubert, nor do I think an individualized analysis necessarily leads to the results the Court obtains.

I

The so-called discretionary function exception to the Federal Tort Claims Act (FTCA) does not protect all governmental activities involving an element of choice. *Berkovitz v. United States,* 486 U.S. 531, 536–537 (1988). The choice must be "grounded in social, economic, [or] political policy," *United States v. Varig Airlines,* 467 U.S. 797, 814 (1984), or, more briefly, must represent a "policy judgment," *Berkovitz,* 486 U.S., at 537. Unfortunately, lower courts have had difficulty in applying this test.

The Court of Appeals in this case concluded that a choice involves policy judgment (in the relevant sense) if it is made at a planning rather than an operational level within the agency. 885 F.2d 1284, 1287 (1989). I agree with the Court that this is wrong. I think, however, that the level at which the decision is made is often *relevant* to the discretionary function inquiry, since the answer to that inquiry turns on *both* the subject matter and the *office* of the decisionmaker. In my view a choice is shielded from liability by the discretionary function exception if the choice is, under the particular circumstances, one that ought to be informed by considerations of social, economic, or political policy and is made by an officer whose official responsibilities include assessment of those considerations.

This test, by looking not only to the decision but also to the officer who made it, recognizes that there is something to the planning vs. operational dichotomy—though the "something" is not precisely what the Court of Appeals believed. Ordinarily, an employee working at the operational level is not responsible for policy decisions, even though policy considerations may be highly relevant to his actions. The dock foreman's decision to store bags of fertilizer in a highly compact fashion is not protected by this exception because, even if he carefully calculated considerations of cost to the government versus safety, it was not his responsibility to ponder such things; the Secretary of Agriculture's decision to the same effect *is* protected, because weighing those considerations is his task. Cf. *Dalehite v. United States,* 346 U.S. 15 (1953). In *Indian Towing Co. v. United States,* 350 U.S. 61 (1955), the United States was held liable for, among other things, the failure of Coast Guard maintenance personnel adequately to inspect electrical equipment in a lighthouse; though there could conceivably be policy reasons for conducting only superficial inspections, the decisions had been made by the maintenance personnel, and it was assuredly not their responsibility to ponder such things. This same factor explains why it is universally acknowledged that the discretionary function exception never protects against liability for the negligence of a vehicle driver. The need for expedition vs. the need for safety may well represent a policy choice, cf. *Dalehite, supra,* but the government does not expect its drivers to make that choice on a case-by-case basis.

Moreover, not only is it necessary for application of the discretionary function exception that the decisionmaker be an official who possesses the relevant policy responsibility, but also the decisionmaker's close identification with policymaking can be strong evidence that the other half of the test is met—*i.e.,* that the subject-matter of the decision is one that ought to

[margin note: relevant b/c it reflects whether the subject was a policy concern]

be informed by policy considerations. I am much more inclined to believe, for example, that the manner of storing fertilizer raises economic policy concerns if the decision on that subject has been reserved to the Secretary of Agriculture himself. That it is proper to take the level of the decision-maker into account is supported by the phrase of the FTCA immediately preceding the discretionary function exception, which excludes governmental liability for acts taken, "exercising due care, in the execution of a . . . regulation, whether or not such . . . regulation be valid." We have taken this to mean that regulations "[can] not be attacked by claimants under the Act." *Dalehite,* 346 U.S., at 42. This immunity represents an absolute statutory presumption, so to speak, that all regulations involve policy judgments that must not be interfered with. I think there is a similar presumption, though not an absolute one, that decisions reserved to policy-making levels involve such judgments—and the higher the policy-making level, the stronger the presumption.

II

[margin note: Q: what kind of choice?]

Turning to the facts of the present case, I find it difficult to say that the particular activities of which Gaubert complains are necessarily discretionary functions, so that a motion to dismiss could properly be granted on that ground. To take but one example, Gaubert alleges that the regulators acted negligently in selecting consultants to advise the bank. The Court argues that such a decision, even though taken in the course of "day-to-day" management, surely involves an element of choice. But that answers only the first half of the *Berkovitz* inquiry. It remains to be determined whether the choice is of a policymaking nature. Perhaps one can imagine a relatively high-level government official, authorized generally to manage the bank in such fashion as to further applicable government policies, who hires consultants and other employees with those policy objectives in mind. The discretionary function exception arguably *would* protect such a hiring choice. But one may also imagine a federal officer of relatively low level, authorized to hire a bank consultant by applying ordinary standards of business judgment, and not authorized to consider matters of government policy in the process. That hiring decision would not be protected by the discretionary function exception, even though some element of choice is involved.

[margin note: Re: "within the purview"]

I do not think it advances the argument to observe that "[t]here are no allegations that the regulators gave anything other than the kind of advice that was within the purview of the policies behind the statutes." An official may act "within the purview" of the relevant policy without himself making policy decisions—in which case, if the action is negligent (and was not specifically mandated by the relevant policy, see *Dalehite,* 346 U.S., at 36), the discretionary function exception does not bar United States liability. Contrariwise, action "outside the purview" of the relevant policy does not necessarily fail to qualify for the discretionary function defense. If the action involves policy discretion, and the officer is authorized to exercise that discretion, the defense applies even if the discretion has been exercised erroneously, so as to frustrate the relevant policy. See 28 U.S.C. § 2680(a) (discretionary function exception applies "whether or not the discretion involved be abused."). In other words, action "within the purview" of the relevant policy is neither a necessary nor a sufficient condition for invoking the discretionary function exception.

The present case comes to us on a motion to dismiss. Lacking any sort of factual record, we can do little more than speculate as to whether the officers here exercised policymaking responsibility with respect to the individual acts in question. Without more, the motion would have to be denied. I think, however, that the Court's conclusion to the contrary is properly reached under a slightly different approach. The alleged misdeeds complained of here were not actually committed by federal officers. Rather, federal officers "recommended" that such actions be taken, making it clear that if the recommendations were not followed the bank would be seized and operated directly by the regulators. In effect, the Federal Home Loan Bank Board (FHLBB) imposed the advice which Gaubert challenges as a condition of allowing the bank to remain independent. But surely the decision whether or not to take over a bank is a policy-based decision to which liability may not attach—a decision that ought to be influenced by considerations of "social, economic, [or] political policy," *Varig Airlines*, 467 U.S., at 814, and that in the nature of things can only be made by FHLBB officers responsible for weighing such considerations. I think a corollary is that setting the *conditions* under which the FHLBB will or will not take over a bank is an exercise of policymaking discretion. By establishing such a list of conditions, as was done here, the Board in effect announces guidelines pursuant to which it will exercise its discretionary function of taking over the bank. Establishing guidelines for the exercise of a discretionary function is unquestionably a discretionary function. Thus, without resort to item-by-item analysis, I would find each of Gaubert's challenges barred by the discretionary function exception.

whether to allow the bank to remain indy was a discret. choice

---

Notes and Questions

1.   If any doubt were left after *Varig Airlines* about the viability of the planning level versus operational level distinction as a test for applying the discretionary function exception, *Gaubert* lays it to rest. Justice Scalia in concurrence attempts to preserve the distinction, arguing that while it should not be dispositive, it can be relevant. He makes the common-sense assertion that a high level government official's decisions are more likely to be influenced by policy considerations than a lower level employee's, both because of the likelihood that policy factors will influence the choice and because of the different authority of individuals at different levels to consider policy concerns.

2.   Although *Berkovitz* opened the door to government liability in tort based upon regulation of private conduct, *Gaubert* makes clear that the door is not open very wide. To be sure, under the first prong of the *Berkovitz* test, which *Gaubert* confirms, the discretionary function excep-

Gaubert

analysis

tion will not apply when a government employee has failed to comply with a statute, regulation, or policy prescribing the specific course of action. A tort plaintiff who is able to point to a mandatory directive and demonstrate that the government employee failed to obey it will still be able to defeat the exception outright.

But *Gaubert* creates a strong presumption that regulatory activity will fall within the discretionary function exception under the second prong, which asks whether the conduct involved is of the nature that the exception was designed to protect. First, the Court now holds, when a statute, regulation, or policy does not mandate particular conduct and instead authorizes the employee to make a judgment, "the very existence of the regulation creates a strong presumption that a discretionary act authorized by the regulation involves consideration of the same policies which led to the promulgation of the regulations." Second, the *Gaubert* Court states that the "focus of the inquiry is not on the agent's subjective intent" in taking an action, but rather on "the nature of the actions taken and on whether they are susceptible to policy analysis." Thus, the government need not show that the acting employee consciously balanced policy considerations, but only that the type of decision is "susceptible to policy analysis."

Justice Scalia takes issue with this analysis and its attendant presumptions in favor of the government. By applying a somewhat holistic standard, he concludes that all of the government actions in this case are part of the single, plainly policy-oriented, decision on whether to take over the financial institution. However, if we were to consider the individual actions involved—selection of savings and loan management, hiring a consultant and other employees, etc.—Justice Scalia believes the choices may well have involved application of "ordinary standards of business judgment," rather than government policy. By suggesting that he would confine the exception to when a higher level official acted with "policy objectives in mind," he departs from the "susceptible to policy analysis" approach of the majority.

higher level of generality

In sum, the *Gaubert* decision appears to restore a higher level of protection from tort liability to the government's regulatory activities. Given that comprehensive statutory provisions, regulations, or policies are common in a regulatory context, it is likely that most decisions made by government regulators will come within the presumption that they are grounded in policy considerations. How closely related must an action be to the regulatory scheme before we would cease relying upon the presumption and demand some individualized showing of policy influence on the conduct before applying the exception? Outside of the context of government regulation of private conduct, such as when affirmative and active conduct by the government is the cause of a tortious injury, a government employee may be less readily able to point to a comprehensive statute, regulation, or policy that conferred policy judgment upon him or her.

3.   After *Berkovitz,* it appeared that the government would rarely be able to successfully invoke the discretionary function exception on a motion

to dismiss, instead having to resort to a motion for summary judgment or a request for a factual hearing. *Gaubert,* however, was decided in the government's favor on a motion to dismiss. Moreover, the Court stated that "[f]or a complaint to survive a motion to dismiss, it must allege facts which would support a finding that the challenged actions are not the kind of conduct that can be said to be grounded in the policy of the regulatory regime." Does this suggest that a heightened standard of pleading is required for plaintiffs seeking to hold the government liable in tort and to avoid dismissal on discretionary function exception grounds? *See also* Mark C. Niles, *"Nothing But Mischief": The Federal Tort Claims Act and the Scope of Discretionary Immunity,* 54 Admin. L. Rev. 1275, 1329–30 (2002) (saying, with disapproval, that "[a]fter *Gaubert,* the government can now argue, as a general matter, and without any factual development, that the decision or decisions at issue in an FTCA claim are susceptible to policy analysis regardless of whether any such analysis actually took place").

4.   Two commentators on the discretionary function exception contend that the "susceptible to policy analysis" standard from *Gaubert* "has greatly restricted the federal government's tort liability for all but the most mundane transgressions" and has allowed the government to more frequently win tort cases without going to trial. Bruce A. Peterson & Mark E. Van Der Weide, *Susceptible to Faulty Analysis:* United States v. Gaubert *and the Resurrection of Federal Sovereign Immunity,* 72 Notre Dame L. Rev. 447, 448 (1997). They report:

> One might have predicted after *Gaubert* that the now presumption and the shift of emphasis from actual to hypothetical policy considerations would significantly increase the proportion of government defendants able to satisfy the second prong of the *Berkovitz* test and obtain discretionary function immunity. The cases bear this out. Nearly three years passed between the Supreme Court's decisions in *Berkovitz*— June of 1988—and *Gaubert*—March of 1991. A comparative analysis of (1) discretionary function exception cases decided during the period between *Berkovitz* and *Gaubert* and (2) discretionary function cases decided in the three years following *Gaubert* illustrates the difference. In the period between *Berkovitz* and *Gaubert,* ninety-one relevant cases emerged. In thirty-nine of those cases, the plaintiff prevailed on at least one discretionary function claim, for a plaintiff success ratio of forty-three percent. We found ninety-five relevant cases in the three years following *Gaubert.* In only twenty-two of those cases did the plaintiff prevail on at least one discretionary function claim, for a plaintiff success ratio of twenty-three percent. Moreover, the twenty-three percent plaintiff success ratio in the three years following *Gaubert* understates the impact of susceptibility analysis. The plaintiff prevailed on twenty-six separate claims in the twenty-two cases containing at least one plaintiff discretionary function victory. In thirteen of these claims, the government lost at the first stage of the *Berkovitz* test; *i.e.,* the court found that the government actor deserved no immunity because he violated a mandatory directive—a statute, regulation, agency policy, or contract. The plaintiff in four more of the

twenty-six successful claims prevailed because the court, in apparent disregard of *Gaubert,* either required the government to produce specific evidence of policy consideration or found the government's evidence of policy consideration unpersuasive. Eight of the remaining nine claims challenged low-level, mundane decisions bordering on the ministerial: designing a metal grate; failing to maintain a bridge fender system; failing to inform overseas government employees about their health benefits, to transmit a crucial health-related message, and to conduct a test for meningitis; providing advice to mine operators on where to wire in safety lights; releasing a paranoid schizophrenic Vietnam veteran from a VA medical center; and selling hazardous materials in damaged containers. * * *

Gaubert has not only affected which cases the government wins; it has also affected how the government wins them. Since *Gaubert* permits government lawyers to invoke discretionary function immunity with presentation of hypothetical policy considerations rather than requiring evidence of actual policy considerations, one might expect more cases in the wake of *Gaubert* to be disposed of before proceeding to trial. The case law once again bears out this expectation in conclusive fashion. Fifty-one of the eighty-nine separate cases in our pre-*Gaubert* sample went to trial. Twenty-one of the eighty-eight separate cases in the post-*Gaubert* sample went to trial. Hypothesizing about what government decisionmakers might have done has largely replaced the presentation of evidence about what they actually did. While the reduction of procedural costs, such as trials, is a welcome incidental benefit of any rule of law, in the case of discretionary function analysis that benefit comes at the expense of permitting a wide range of injury-producing and possibly negligent state action to escape meaningful judicial scrutiny.

Id. at 465–68, 473 (footnotes omitted). Accordingly, these commentators argue that "discretionary function immunity ought to be reserved for (1) actual decisions (2) made by government officials possessing authority to direct policy (3) in consideration of legitimate policy factors." *Id.* at 486. Do you agree? Why or why not?

Cope v. Scott

United States Court of Appeals for the District of Columbia Circuit.
45 F.3d 445 (D.C.Cir. 1995).

■ TATEL, CIRCUIT JUDGE:

In this negligence case, John R. Cope appeals a grant of summary judgment against him in favor of the government. The District Court concluded that the government's allegedly negligent actions were "discretionary functions" immune from suit under the Federal Tort Claims Act ("FTCA"). 28 U.S.C. §§ 1346(b), 2671–2680. With respect to Cope's allegations of negligent road maintenance, we affirm the District Court's decision. We find, however, that any discretion exercised by the government with respect to where and how to post signs warning of dangerous road conditions did not implicate "political, social, or economic" policy choices of the sort that Congress intended to protect from suits under the FTCA. We therefore affirm in part, reverse in part, and remand so that the case may proceed to trial on the allegations of improper warnings.

I.

Beach Drive, a two-way, two-lane road, is the main north-south route through Rock Creek Park, an urban park in Washington, D.C. that is maintained by the National Park Service. The road was "originally designed for pleasure driving," as seems evident given what an engineering study described as its "poor alignment"—which we understand to refer to its many sharp curves. The Park Service alleges that the road is not "intended to provide fast and convenient transportation," but to "enhance visitor experience" in the park. Commuters in Washington appear to believe otherwise, however, and the Park Service has allowed Beach Drive to become an important commuter route connecting downtown Washington with its northern suburbs. As a result, the road carries heavy traffic throughout the day. National Park Service road standards recommend that a road like Beach Drive carry a maximum of 8,000 vehicles daily, but recent estimates indicate that the average daily traffic on the stretch of road involved in this case was between two and three times that load.

Public use & Traffic volume of the Road

On a rainy spring evening in 1987, Cope was driving north along Beach Drive. As a southbound vehicle driven by Roland Scott rounded a curve, it slid into the northbound lane and hit Cope's car. Cope alleges he suffered neck and back injuries. *(injury admission)* The Park Service officer who responded to the scene classified the pavement in his accident report as a "worn polished surface" that was "slick when wet." Cope sued Scott and the Park Service, alleging that the latter was negligent "in failing to appropriately and adequately maintain the roadway of Beach Drive ... and failing to place and maintain appropriate and adequate warning signs along the roadway."

Spring 1987 - cope's accident

While preparing for trial, Cope discovered an engineering study of roads in Rock Creek Park that was conducted between 1986 and 1988. The study identified this stretch of Beach Drive as one of nine "high accident areas" in the park, and noted that sections of Beach Drive, including, apparently, the location of the accident, fell below "acceptable skid-resistance levels" in a test conducted five months after the accident. The study recommended that future repaving use "polish-resistant coarse aggregate" as an overlay in the most dangerous curves. As for the stretch of road in question here, the study noted that "[t]he curves should be adequately signed and the skid resistance maintained with an opened graded friction course." Cope also offers an affidavit from a traffic engineer to the effect that over 50% of the accidents that occurred on that stretch of road over the last five years occurred during wet weather, while only 18% of accidents nationwide occur in wet conditions.

Evidence of Gov't's notice/knowledge & breach

Despite the less-than-perfect road surface, the 1988 study listed this stretch of Beach Drive as 33rd on a maintenance priority list of 80 sections of park road. Maintenance work on this section of road was preceded on the list by at least 15 other projects estimated to be of equal or less cost.

As for the presence of relevant warning signs, the record does not reflect precisely where such signs were located as of the date of the accident. A 1981 road sign inventory indicated that "slippery when wet" signs were located in two places on the half-mile stretch of road bracketing the curve where the accident occurred, and the Assistant Chief of Maintenance of the park stated that in 1990, a slippery road sign was posted in each direction on the same stretch of road, although there is no indication of how close such signs were to the curve where the accident occurred.

In the District Court, the government moved for summary judgment, arguing that its action (or inaction) with respect to the road was discretionary and therefore exempt from suit under the FTCA. The District Court agreed, ruling that it had no jurisdiction to hear the case. Cope settled with Scott and now appeals the District Court's immunity ruling.

II.

* * * [T]he "discretionary function" exception * * * lies at the heart of the dispute in this case. When an individual is injured by an act of the government or a government employee, section 1346(b) allows him or her to bring suit unless the action that allegedly caused the injuries is a discretionary function as defined under the FTCA. This exception was designed to prevent the courts from "second guessing," through decisions in tort actions, the way that government officials choose to balance economic, social, and political factors as they carry out their official duties. *See United States v. Varig Airlines,* 467 U.S. 797, 814, 820 (1984).

Discretionary function determinations are jurisdictional in nature. While we must review the complaint to determine what actions allegedly caused the injuries, we do so only to determine whether the district court has jurisdiction over those actions, not to prejudge the merits of the case. If the district court has jurisdiction over the suit, the plaintiff must still prove that the government's actions were negligent in order for him to prevail.

The Supreme Court has established a two-step test that we use to determine whether an action is exempt from suit under the discretionary function exemption. *See United States v. Gaubert,* 499 U.S. 315 (1991); *Berkovitz v. United States,* 486 U.S. 531 (1988). The two steps of the test largely track the two clauses of section 2680(a). In the first step, we determine whether it is appropriate to analyze the action under the first or the second clause of the exception. In other words, we ask whether any "federal statute, regulation, or policy specifically prescribes a course of action for an employee to follow." *Gaubert,* 499 U.S. at 322. If a specific directive exists, then the employee had no "choice." The only issue is whether the employee followed the directive, and is thus exempt under the first clause, or whether the employee did not follow the directive, thus opening the government to suit. *See* 28 U.S.C. § 2680(a). Because no choice is involved where a "specific prescription" exists, the discretionary function exception contained in the second clause is not applicable.

The discretionary function exception *may* be applicable where there is no specific prescription and the government employee has a "choice" regarding how to act in a particular circumstance. This is true more often than one might expect. Despite the pervasiveness of regulation, government policies will almost always leave some room for individual choice. If the choice led to the events being litigated, the exception may apply. But not all actions that require choice—actions that are, in one sense, "discretionary"—are protected as "discretionary functions" under the FTCA.

This brings us to the second step of the test, where the "basic inquiry" is whether the challenged discretionary acts of a government employee "are of the nature and quality that Congress intended to shield from tort liability." *Varig,* 467 U.S. at 813. Decisions that require choice are exempt from suit under the FTCA only if they are "susceptible to policy judgment" and involve an exercise of "political, social, [or] economic judgment." *Gaubert,* 499 U.S. at 325; *Varig,* 467 U.S. at 820. The Court recognized in *Gaubert,* for example, that daily decisions regarding the management of a troubled savings and loan "implicate[d] social, economic, or political policies," and were therefore exempt. *Gaubert,* 499 U.S. at 332. In contrast, the Court noted that a government employee may cause an automobile accident through the exercise of poor discretion, but that this type of "garden-variety" discretion is not protected. *See id.* at 325 n. 7. Only discretionary actions of greater significance—those grounded in "social, economic, or political goals"—fall within the protection of the statute. *See Gaubert,* 499 U.S. at 323.

Determining whether a decision is "essentially political, social, or economic," *Red Lake Band of Chippewa Indians v. United States,* 800 F.2d 1187, 1195 (D.C.Cir.1986), is admittedly difficult, since nearly every government action is, at least to some extent, subject to "policy analysis." "Budgetary constraints," for example, "underlie virtually all government activity." *ARA Leisure Services v. United States,* 831 F.2d 193, 196 (9th Cir.1987). At oral argument, counsel for the government asserted that these underlying fiscal constraints should therefore exempt "virtually all government activity." With the exception of discretion exercised by bad drivers, the government appears to argue that decisions that involve choice and the faintest hint of policy concerns are discretionary and subject to the exception. This approach, however, would not only eviscerate the second step of the analysis set out in *Berkovitz* and *Gaubert,* but it would allow the exception to swallow the FTCA's sweeping waiver of sovereign immunity. It was thus not surprising that, when pressed at oral argument, government counsel was unable to provide, under its theory, even one example of a discretionary decision that would not be exempt for failure to implicate policy concerns.

The government reads the exception far too broadly. The question is not whether there is any discretion at all, but whether the discretion is "grounded in the policy of the regulatory regime." *Gaubert,* 499 U.S. at 325 (emphasis added). The mere association of a decision with regulatory concerns is not enough; exempt decisions are those "fraught with ... public policy considerations." *Sami v. United States,* 617 F.2d 755, 767 (D.C.Cir.1979). The mere presence of choice—even if that choice involves whether money should be spent—does not trigger the exception.

Just as we reject the government's effort to expand the exception too far, we also reject Cope's efforts to restrict its application. Cope argues, first, that the government cannot claim the exemption unless it is able to demonstrate that there was an "actual, specific decision involving the balancing of competing policy considerations." The Supreme Court has emphasized, however, that the issue is not the decision as such, but whether the "nature" of the decision implicates policy analysis. *See Gaubert,* 499 U.S. at 325; *Varig,* 467 U.S. at 813. What matters is not what the decisionmaker was thinking, but whether the type of decision being challenged is grounded in social, economic, or political policy. Evidence of the actual decision may be helpful in understanding whether the "nature" of the decision implicated policy judgments, but the applicability of the exemption does not turn on whether the challenged decision involved such judgments.

For the same reasons, we reject Cope's argument that the government's acts are not discretionary since they involve the "implementation" of government policy. * * * *Gaubert* cautioned against this sort of shortcut when it rejected a lower court decision that relied upon a distinction between exempt "planning" decisions and non-exempt "operational" decisions. *See* 499 U.S. at 325–26. Recognizing that the focus is on the nature of the decision, not on the semantic pigeonhole into which the action can be put, we decline to follow Cope's reading of the case law, focusing instead, as we are required, on whether the decision is "fraught with" economic, political, or social judgments. No matter the level at which the decision was made, the nature of the decision, or the impact it had on others, we have consistently held that the discretionary function exception applies "only where 'the question is not negligence but social wisdom, not due care but political practicability, not reasonableness but economic expediency.' " *Sami,* 617 F.2d at 766 (citing *Blessing v. United States,* 447 F.Supp. 1160, 1170 (E.D.Pa.1978)). Using this approach as our touchstone, we proceed to an analysis of this case.

III.

* * * In his complaint, Cope makes two allegations regarding the conduct of the United States. He argues, first, that the government failed "to appropriately and adequately maintain the roadway of Beach Drive," and second, that the government failed "to place and maintain appropriate and adequate warning signs along the roadway." We address each of his points in turn, again emphasizing that we do not decide the merits of the case, but only whether Cope is entitled to an opportunity to prove his case at trial.

With respect to his allegation regarding the state of the road surface, Cope points to a manual entitled "Park Road Standards," and, applying step one of the analysis, argues that it sets forth "specific prescriptions" regarding skid resistance and surface type. We do not read the manual to set forth such requirements. The standards, which were adopted in 1984, apply only to "new construction and reconstruction" of park roads. But Beach Drive was neither constructed nor reconstructed after 1984. Even if the standards were relevant to the condition of Beach Drive, the manual notes that they are applicable only "to the extent practicable." To us, this caveat means that the standards are applicable only when no competing priorities exist. Such flexibility is the essence of discretion.

Nor are we persuaded by Cope's argument that statutes requiring the Park Service to work with other agencies to establish and implement highway safety programs create non-discretionary prescriptions. *See, e.g.,* 23 U.S.C. § 402. These statutes do not contain directives so precise that they constrain the Park Service's control over the surface of Beach Drive. Absent such directives, any action taken (or not taken) regarding the matter is an exercise of discretion.

We turn, then, to the second step of the analysis, in which we ask whether the discretion exercised over the maintenance and reconstruction of Beach Drive is "subject to policy analysis" and thus discretionary in the sense of the FTCA. The District Court ruled that Cope's complaint raised a "matter of roadway design and construction," concluding that "design" implicates policy judgments. As a result, the court held that the exception applied and that the government was immune from suit. The parties follow the lead of the District Court in their briefs before this court, and debate over whether the "failure to maintain adequate skid resistance" is a question of "design" or "maintenance." We decline to be drawn into this debate because it would divert us from the proper analysis—whether the "failure to maintain adequate skid resistance" is the kind of discretion that implicates "social, economic, or political" judgment.

As we understand the record and the facts as presented by the parties, no regular maintenance would have prevented the road from deteriorating in the way Cope alleges. This case is therefore different from a case involving mundane decisions to fill or not fill potholes, or even the cumulative effect of such decisions. In *ARA Leisure Services*, for example, the Ninth Circuit allowed plaintiffs to sue the government for the negligent maintenance of a "badly eroded stretch" of road in Denali National Park. 831 F.2d at 194–95. As we read the case, the Ninth Circuit appears to have believed that all the "decisions" that caused the road to deteriorate involved routine questions of maintenance not "grounded in social, economic, or political policies." *Id.* at 195. In this case, however, such decisions would not have prevented the alleged "inadequate skid resistance." The state of Beach Drive alleged by Cope could have been prevented only by reducing the traffic load, initially paving it with a different surface, resurfacing the curve entirely, or at least milling the curve to create grooves in the surface. Determining the appropriate course of action would require balancing factors such as Beach Drive's overall purpose, the allocation of funds among significant project demands, the safety of drivers and other park visitors, and the inconvenience of repairs as compared to the risk of safety hazards. These balances are apparent throughout the 1988 study that placed maintenance on this section of Beach Drive in the middle of a priority list of work that needed to be done on eighty different sections of park roads. Park Service decisions regarding the management of Beach Drive are therefore much like the decisions exempted by the Supreme Court in *Varig*: "[S]uch decisions require the agency to establish priorities for the accomplishment of its policy objectives by balancing the objectives sought to be obtained against such practical considerations as staffing and funding." 467 U.S. at 820. And, as in *Varig*, we decline to "second guess" those judgments here. *Id.*

IV.

We reach a different conclusion with respect to Cope's allegation that the government failed to post adequate warning signs about the nature of the road surface. His case rests on the argument that given the "very specific slippery road problem" on Beach Drive, a "permanently displayed static 'slippery when wet' road sign is inadequate to warn" of the hazard. Cope hints that the failure to post an adequate sign is nondiscretionary, but relies mostly on the second step argument that any discretion does not implicate policy concerns. The government argues that no specific prescriptions regarding the posting of signs exist, that the resulting discretion involves the exercise of "engineering and aesthetic factors" as well as economic considerations, and that the presence of those concerns in the decision making means that the decisions are exempt from suit under the FTCA.

The government admits that it "is the policy of the National Park Service to follow" the Manual on Uniform Traffic Control Devices when posting signs, but argues that the final decision depends on a variety of engineering and aesthetic considerations. Our own review of this manual reveals that it is more of a guidebook for the installation of signs than a "specific prescription" relied on by the Park Service. As the manual points out, it is "not a substitute for engineering judgment," and warning signs should be posted only "when it is deemed necessary." We conclude, then, that the posting of signs in Rock Creek Park involves the exercise of discretion.

In contrast to our decision regarding the road surface, however, we find that the discretion regarding where and what type of signs to post is not the kind of discretion protected by the discretionary function exception. While it may be true, as the government claims, that the placement of signs involves judgments because engineering and aesthetic concerns determine where they are placed, such judgments are not necessarily protected from suit; only if they are "fraught with public policy considerations" do they fall within the exception, and we do not think that is the case here. The "engineering judgment" the government relies on is no more a matter of policy than were the "objective scientific principles" that the *Berkovitz* court distinguished from exempt exercises of policy judgment.

With respect to the aesthetic considerations, while we acknowledge the Park Service's desire to maintain the park in as pristine a state as possible, the government has failed to demonstrate how such a desire affects the placement of traffic signs on Beach Drive. Indeed, the government's argument is difficult for us to accept in view of the fact that, including the "slippery when wet" signs, no less than "twenty-three traffic control, warning, and informational signs" already exist on the half-mile stretch of road bracketing the curve on which the accident occurred—a stretch of road that carries 20,000 vehicles daily. We agree that in certain circumstances, decisions will be exempt under the FTCA because they involve difficult policy judgments balancing the preservation of the environment against the blight of excess signs. But this is not one of those circumstances. Beach Drive is not the Grand Canyon's Rim Drive, nor Shenandoah's Skyline Drive. Here, the Park Service has chosen to manage the road in a manner more amenable to commuting through nature than communing with it. Having done so, and having taken steps to warn users of dangers inherent in that use, the Park Service cannot argue that its failure to ensure that those steps are effective involves protected "discretionary" decisions.

Other cases exempting the failure to post warning signs are thus easily distinguishable. In those cases, the decisions were based on a reasonable desire to protect the experience of the park visitor. In *Bowman v. United States*, 820 F.2d 1393, 1395 (4th Cir.1987), for example, the Fourth Circuit concluded that the failure to place a guardrail along the Blue Ridge Parkway was a decision that may have implicated policy considerations such as protecting the scenic vista. And in a case involving a fall at Pinnacles National Monument, the government was able to demonstrate that the decision not to post warning signs in the park, which was a wilderness area, was part of a policy decision to protect the wilderness experience in the park. *See Zumwalt v. United States*, 928 F.2d 951, 955 (10th Cir.1991).

* * * [W]e conclude that the failure to post adequate warning of dangers on the road does not implicate political, social, or economic decisions of the sort that the exception was designed to protect. Beach Drive is a commuter route through an urban park. The Park Service has already posted signs in an effort to alert drivers to safety hazards on the road. In light of these factors, the Park Service has understandably been unable to articulate how the placement of additional or different signs on Beach Drive implicates the type of economic, social, or political concerns that the discretionary function exception protects from suit under the FTCA.

We affirm the District Court's dismissal of Cope's claim regarding negligent maintenance of the road surface. We conclude, however, that the District Court had jurisdiction over the allegations that the Park Service failed adequately to warn of dangers on Beach Drive. To the extent the

Court ruled to the contrary, we vacate its order and remand for further proceedings. Cope is entitled to try to persuade a factfinder that the government acted negligently by failing adequately to sign the curve on Beach Drive.

So ordered.

I claim remains

————

Notes and Questions

The *Cope v. Scott* opinion provides a good summary of the Supreme Court's decisions on the discretionary function exception. It also illustrates again how a broad understanding of the exception could lead to immunization of virtually all governmental activity from tort liability. Indeed, the government counsel in the case contended that fiscal policy was implicated in nearly every governmental activity and then was unable to give an example of a single government act that would not fall within the exception. The court refuses to apply the exception whenever the "faintest hint of policy concerns" is present, instead demanding that activities be "fraught with public policy considerations" before the exception comes into play. The court is struggling to adhere to the Supreme Court's directive in *Gaubert* that activities "susceptible to policy analysis" are covered by the exception and yet ensure that at least some mundane or "garden-variety" conduct by the government remains a basis for a tort suit. *See also* Peter H. Schuck & James J. Park, *The Discretionary Function Exception in the Second Circuit,* 20 QLR 55, 65–66 (2000) (arguing against interpreting the discretionary function exception too broadly because (1) "even the most routine ministerial action by the lowest-level employee can be said to involve some judgment or choice" and if the exception encompasses "all actions as to which the actor had such choices, it would literally swallow the FTCA's general waiver of immunity;" and (2) "even the most routine agency action can always be linked to some general policy concern," but a general purpose, such as "using limited resources efficiently is too universal to constitute a policy judgment that triggers the" exception).

Notwithstanding the court's common-sense desire to prevent the exception from swallowing the rule, doesn't the court's decision come dangerously close to (or maybe even cross) the line? The court concludes that the claim of negligent signage is not within the exception because the government's asserted policy concern of aesthetics in the park is inapplicable to a road that has become a major commuter route. Does this amount to judicial second-guessing of a government policy choice? If the Park Service has determined that it remains a park road and that aesthetic considerations are crucial, may the court properly announce that it is not a park road but a commuter route without usurping the government's policy role to determine the nature of the road? And, yet, if the determination as to appropriate placement of signs on a manifestly busy road is protected by the exception, what is not? (For commentary on the *Cope v. Scott* decision, see

Kevin E. Lunday, Note, *Federal Tort Claims Act: Applying the Discretion-ary Function Exception,* 64 Geo. Wash. L. Rev. 1254 (1996)).

---

5. THE MISREPRESENTATION EXCEPTION

28 United States Code § 2680(h)

The provisions of this chapter and section 1346(b) of this title shall not apply to—

(h) Any claim arising out of * * * misrepresentation * * * .

Block v. Neal

Supreme Court of the United States.
460 U.S. 289 (1983).

■ JUSTICE MARSHALL delivered the opinion of the Court.

The Secretary of Agriculture is authorized by Title V of the Housing Act of 1949, 42 U.S.C. § 1471 *et seq.,* to extend financial and technical assistance through the Farmers Home Administration (FmHA) to low-income rural residents who seek to obtain housing. Respondent Onilea Neal, the recipient of an FmHA loan for the construction of a prefabricated house, brought this action under the Federal Tort Claims Act, 28 U.S.C. §§ 1346(b), 2671–2680. She alleged that defects discovered after she set up residence were partly attributable to the failure of FmHA employees properly to inspect and supervise construction of her house. This case presents the question whether respondent's action is barred by 28 U.S.C. § 2680(h), which precludes recovery under the Tort Claims Act for "[a]ny claim arising out of . . . misrepresentation."

I

A

The facts described in respondent's complaint may be summarized as follows. Unable to obtain credit from other sources, Neal applied for a Rural Housing Loan from FmHA pursuant to § 502(a) of the Housing Act of 1949, 42 U.S.C. § 1472(a). FmHA approved her application in June 1977. During the summer of that year, Neal received advice from S. Lain Parkison, the FmHA Supervisor for Roane County, Tennessee.

On August 8, 1977, Neal contracted with Home Marketing Associates, Inc. (Home Marketing), for the construction of a prefabricated house. The contract required that Home Marketing's work conform to plans approved by FmHA. It also granted FmHA the right to inspect and test all materials and workmanship and reject any that were defective. At the same time, Neal entered into a deed of trust with FmHA and signed a promissory note providing for repayment of the principal sum of $21,170, plus interest of 8% per annum on the unpaid principal.

Home Marketing commenced work on Neal's house in August 1977 and finished the following month. An FmHA official, Mary Wells, inspected the site on three occasions: soon after construction began, shortly before it was concluded, and after the house was completed. Her inspection reports contained no adverse comments on the construction work. After her third inspection, Wells issued a final report, signed by Neal, which indicated that the construction accorded with the drawings and specifications approved by FmHA. Home Marketing issued a one year builder's warranty covering workmanship, materials, and equipment.

Neal moved into the house in 1977. During the winter, she discovered that the heat pump in the house was not working properly. She notified FmHA and Home Marketing. An inspection by Parkison, the County FmHA Supervisor, revealed that the heat pump unit was either defective or undersized. On March 22, 1978, FmHA's State Director and other FmHA officials conducted a complete inspection and identified 13 additional defects in the construction of the house. These included deviations from plans approved by FmHA and from applicable Minimum Property Standards. The inadequacies in materials and workmanship included defects in caulking, bridging, sealing, and plumbing, and extended to all areas of the house, such as the porch, the rear door, the floor, the roof, the exterior paint, and the interior wall finish. Home Marketing refused to comply with FmHA's request to cure these defects in accordance with the builder's warranty.

In November 1978 respondent asked FmHA to pay for the correction of the heating system and other structural defects. It declined to do so.

B

The United States District Court for the Eastern District of Tennessee dismissed Neal's complaint for failure to state a claim on which relief can be granted. *Neal v. Bergland*, 489 F.Supp. 512 (1980). It found that no contractual duty to supervise the construction of respondent's home was created either by the Federal Housing Act of 1949 and the regulations promulgated thereunder or by the various agreements between respondent and FmHA. The court concluded that regulations requiring FmHA officials to ensure that the builder adhere to the terms of its construction contract were intended solely to protect the Government's security interest, and were not intended to make FmHA warrant the quality of construction for the benefit of those receiving rural assistance loans. The District Court also concluded that respondent failed to state a claim against FmHA under applicable tort law.

The Court of Appeals reversed. *Neal v. Bergland*, 646 F.2d 1178 (C.A.6 1981). It agreed with the District Court that FmHA had no contractual obligation to provide Neal with technical assistance or to inspect and supervise construction of her house. However, the Court of Appeals found that respondent's complaint stated a claim for negligence under the principle "that one who undertakes to act, even though gratuitously, is required to act carefully and with the exercise of due care and will be liable for injuries proximately caused by failure to use such care." *Id.*, at 1181–1182, citing Restatement (Second) of Torts § 323 (1965). It noted that, subject to express exceptions, the Tort Claims Act, 28 U.S.C. § 2674, authorizes suit against the Government for the negligence of a federal agency in performing a voluntary undertaking.

The Court of Appeals then considered the question now before us: whether respondent's claim "arise[s] out of . . . misrepresentation," 28 U.S.C. § 2680(h), and is therefore excluded from coverage by the Tort Claims Act. Distinguishing this case from others including *United States v. Neustadt*, 366 U.S. 696 (1961), the court concluded that respondent's negligence claim did not fall within this exception to the waiver of sovereign immunity. The Government petitioned for certiorari and suggested summary reversal on the ground that the decision below cannot be reconciled with this Court's decision in *Neustadt*. We granted the writ and we now affirm.

II

The question before us is a narrow one. The Government argues only that respondent's claim is a claim of "misrepresentation" within the meaning of § 2680(h). It does not seek review of the threshold determination that respondent's complaint states a claim for negligence under the Good Samaritan doctrine that is otherwise actionable under 28 U.S.C. § 2674. Thus, we need not decide precisely what Neal must prove in order to prevail on her negligence claim, nor even whether such a claim lies. Nor are we called on to consider whether recovery is barred by any other provision of the Tort Claims Act, including the exception for any action "based upon the exercise or performance or the failure to exercise or perform a discretionary function." § 2680(a). Finally, we are not asked to determine whether the administrative remedy created by the Housing Act of 1949, 42 U.S.C. § 1479(c), provides the exclusive remedy against the Government for damages attributable to the negligence of FmHA officials.

The scope of the "misrepresentation" exception to the Tort Claims Act was the focus of this Court's decision in *United States v. Neustadt, supra*. Neustadt purchased a house in reliance on an appraisal undertaken by the Federal Housing Administration (FHA) for mortgage insurance purposes. After he took up residence, cracks appeared in the ceilings and walls of his house. The cracks were caused by structural defects that had not been noticed by the FHA appraiser during the course of his inspection. Neustadt sued the Government under the Tort Claims Act to recover the difference between the fair market value of the property and the purchase price. He alleged that the FHA had negligently inspected and appraised the property, and that he had justifiably relied on the appraisal in paying a higher price for the house than he would otherwise have paid.

This Court held that the claim in *Neustadt* arose out of "misrepresentation" under § 2680(h). We determined initially that § 2680(h) applies to claims arising out of negligent, as well as intentional, misrepresentation. 366 U.S., at 703–706. This Court found that Neustadt's claim that the Government had breached its "duty to use due care in obtaining and communicating information upon which [the plaintiff] may reasonably be expected to rely in the conduct of his economic affairs," merely restated the traditional legal definition of "negligent misrepresentation" as would have been understood by Congress when the Tort Claims Act was enacted. *Id.*, at 706–707.[5] Finally, we examined the National Housing Act of 1934, as amended, under which the FHA had conducted its appraisal, and found nothing to indicate "that Congress intended, in a case such as this, to limit or suspend the application of the 'misrepresentation' exception of the Tort Claims Act." *Id.*, at 708–710.

We cannot agree with the Government that this case is controlled by *Neustadt.* As we recognized in that decision, the essence of an action for misrepresentation, whether negligent or intentional, is the communication of misinformation on which the recipient relies. The gravamen of the action against the Government in *Neustadt* was that the plaintiff was misled by a "Statement of FHA Appraisal" prepared by the Government. Neustadt alleged no injury that he would have suffered independently of his reliance on the erroneous appraisal. Because the alleged conduct that was the basis of his negligence claim was in essence a negligent misrepresentation, Neustadt's action was barred under the "misrepresentation" exception.

Section 2680(h) thus relieves the Government of tort liability for pecuniary injuries which are wholly attributable to reliance on the Government's negligent misstatements. As a result, the statutory exception undoubtedly preserves sovereign immunity with respect to a broad range of government actions. But it does not bar negligence actions which focus not on the Government's failure to use due care in communicating information, but rather on the Government's breach of a different duty.

In this case, unlike *Neustadt,* the Government's misstatements are not essential to plaintiff's negligence claim. The Court of Appeals found that to prevail under the Good Samaritan doctrine, Neal must show that FmHA officials voluntarily undertook to supervise construction of her house; that the officials failed to use due care in carrying out their supervisory activity; and that she suffered some pecuniary injury proximately caused by FmHA's failure to use due care. FmHA's duty to use due care to ensure that the builder adhere to previously approved plans and cure all defects before completing construction is distinct from any duty to use due care in communicating information to respondent. And it certainly does not "appea[r] beyond doubt" that the only damages alleged in the complaint to be caused by FmHA's conduct were those attributable to Neal's reliance on FmHA inspection reports. Neal's factual allegations would be consistent with proof at trial that Home Marketing would never have turned the

---

5. The Court distinguished negligent misrepresentation from the "many familiar forms of negligent misconduct [which] may be said to involve an element of 'misrepresentation,' [only] in the generic sense of that word." 366 U.S., at 711, n. 26. The "misrepresentation" exception applies only when the action itself falls within the commonly understood definition of a misrepresentation claim, which " 'has been identified with the common law action of deceit,' and has been confined 'very largely to the invasion of interests of a financial or commercial character, in the course of business dealings.' " *Ibid.,* quoting W. Prosser, Torts, § 85, at 702–703 (1941 ed.). * * *

house over to Neal in its defective condition if FmHA officials had pointed out defects to the builder while construction was still underway, rejected defective materials and workmanship, or withheld final payment until the builder corrected all defects.

Of course, in the absence of the "misrepresentation" exception to the Tort Claims Act, respondent could also have brought a claim for negligent misrepresentation to recover for any injury caused by her misplaced reliance on advice provided by FmHA officials and on the FmHA inspection reports. Common to both the misrepresentation and the negligence claim would be certain factual and legal questions, such as whether FmHA officials used due care in inspecting Neal's home while it was under construction. But the partial overlap between these two tort actions does not support the conclusion that if one is excepted under the Tort Claims Act, the other must be as well. Neither the language nor history of the Act suggest that when one aspect of the Government's conduct is not actionable under the "misrepresentation" exception, a claimant is barred from pursuing a distinct claim arising out of other aspects of the Government's conduct. "The exemption of the sovereign from suit involves hardship enough where consent has been withheld. We are not to add to its rigor by refinement of construction where consent has been announced." *United States v. Aetna Surety Co.*, 338 U.S. 366, 383 (1949). Any other interpretation would encourage the Government to shield itself completely from tort liability by adding misrepresentations to whatever otherwise actionable torts it commits.

We therefore hold that respondent's claim against the government for negligence by FmHA officials in supervising construction of her house does not "aris[e] out of . . . misrepresentation" within the meaning of 28 U.S.C. § 2680(h). The Court of Appeals properly concluded that Neal's claim is not barred by this provision of the Tort Claims Act because Neal does not seek to recover on the basis of misstatements made by FmHA officials. Although FmHA in this case may have undertaken both to supervise construction of Neal's house and to provide Neal information regarding the progress of construction, Neal's action is based solely on the former conduct. Accordingly, the judgment of the Court of Appeals is

Affirmed.

■ THE CHIEF JUSTICE concurs in the judgment.

Notes and Questions

1.   To fully understand the *Block v. Neal* decision, it may be helpful to think of the government as wearing two hats in the context of the case. Its first role is that of an inspector of the property advising the client as to the state of the property and any defects, for which the government is immunized from liability under the misrepresentation exception. Its second role is that of a general contractor or construction supervisor responsible for proper completion of the project, for which the misrepresentation exception does not apply.

2. Consider what might be the justification for an exception from governmental liability for the tort of misrepresentation. Why would Congress want to protect the government from being held liable on the basis of misinformation or miscommunication by its employees? As also illustrated in Chapter VI.A in the material on equitable estoppel, that is, whether unauthorized representations by government employees may bind the government, the exposure of the government might be enormously high given that there are hundreds of thousands of government employees, large numbers of whom disseminate information as part of their job. As the Supreme Court held in an early case, if equitable estoppel were applicable to the government based upon erroneous statements by government employees, even "the utmost vigilance would not save the public from the most serious losses" since the federal government's "operations are so various, and its agencies so numerous and scattered." *United States v. Kirkpatrick,* 22 U.S. (9 Wheat.) 720, 735 (1824). Moreover, in contrast with private commercial entities that supply information for profit and are subject to liability when errors are made, the government does not derive a "compensating financial benefit" from recipients of its information. Harold J. Krent, *Reconceptualizing Sovereign Immunity,* 45 Vanderbilt L.J. 1529, 1553 (1992). Thus, protecting the government from liability based upon errors in communication "preserv[es] the government's policy decision to communicate information in the first instance." *Id.* The alternative might be a significant curtailment of government information services to reduce the risk of liability, thus also reducing the average citizen's access to information or advice from his or her government.

---

6.   THE INTENTIONAL TORT EXCEPTION

28 United States Code § 2680(h)

The provisions of this chapter and section 1346(b) of this title shall not apply to—

     * * *

(h) Any claim arising out of assault, battery, false imprisonment, false arrest, malicious prosecution, abuse of process, libel, slander, misrepresentation, deceit, or interference with contract rights: Provided, That, with regard to acts or omissions of investigative or law enforcement officers of the United States Government, the provisions of this chapter and section 1346(b) of this title shall apply to any claim arising, on or after the date of the enactment of this proviso, out of assault, battery, false imprisonment, false arrest, abuse of process, or malicious prosecution. For the purpose of this subsection, "investigative or law enforcement officer" means any officer of the United States who is empowered by law to execute searches, to seize evidence, or to make arrests for violations of Federal law.

Sheridan v. United States   C ‑ 3

Supreme Court of the United States.
487 U.S. 392 (1988).

■ JUSTICE STEVENS delivered the opinion of the Court.

On February 6, 1982, an obviously intoxicated off-duty serviceman named Carr fired several rifle shots into an automobile being driven by petitioners on a public street near the Bethesda Naval Hospital. Petitioners brought suit against the United States alleging that their injuries were caused by the Government's negligence in allowing Carr to leave the hospital with a loaded rifle in his possession. The District Court dismissed the action—and the Court of Appeals affirmed—on the ground that the claim is barred by the intentional tort exception to the Federal Tort Claims Act (FTCA or Act). The question we granted certiorari to decide is whether petitioners' claim is one "arising out of" an assault or battery within the meaning of 28 U.S.C. § 2680(h).

I

When it granted the Government's motion to dismiss, the District Court accepted petitioners' version of the facts as alleged in their complaint and as supplemented by discovery. That version may be briefly stated. After finishing his shift as a naval medical aide at the hospital, Carr consumed a large quantity of wine, rum, and other alcoholic beverages. He then packed some of his belongings, including a rifle and ammunition, into a uniform bag and left his quarters. Some time later, three naval corpsmen found him lying face down in a drunken stupor on the concrete floor of a hospital building. They attempted to take him to the emergency room, but he broke away, grabbing the bag and revealing the barrel of the rifle. At the sight of the rifle barrel, the corpsmen fled. They neither took further action to subdue Carr, nor alerted the appropriate authorities that he was heavily intoxicated and brandishing a weapon. Later that evening, Carr fired the shots that caused physical injury to one of the petitioners and property damage to their car.

The District Court began its legal analysis by noting the general rule that the Government is not liable for the intentional torts of its employees. The petitioners argued that the general rule was inapplicable because they were relying, not on the fact that Carr was a Government employee when he assaulted them, but rather on the negligence of other Government employees who failed to prevent his use of the rifle. The District Court assumed that the alleged negligence would have made the defendant liable under the law of Maryland, and also assumed that the Government would have been liable if Carr had not been a Government employee. Nevertheless, although stating that it was "sympathetic" to petitioners' claim, it concluded that Fourth Circuit precedents required dismissal because Carr "happens to be a government employee rather than a private citizen."

The Court of Appeals affirmed. 823 F.2d 820 (C.A.4 1987). * * *

[handwritten margin notes:] Sheridan's claim : negligent failure to prevent intoxicated employee from doing such harm

Gov't: the harm claim arose from an intentional tort

II

The FTCA gives federal district courts jurisdiction over claims against the United States for money damages "for injury or loss of property, or personal injury or death caused by the negligent or wrongful act or omission of any employee of the Government while acting within the scope of his office or employment, under circumstances where the United States, if a private person, would be liable to the claimant in accordance with the law of the place where the act or omission occurred." 28 U.S.C. § 1346(b). However, among other limitations, the Act also provides that this broad grant of jurisdiction "shall not apply to . . . [a]ny claim arising out of assault, battery" or other specified intentional torts. 28 U.S.C. § 2680(h).

The words "any claim arising out of" an assault or battery are unquestionably broad enough to bar all claims based *entirely* on an assault or battery. The import of these words is less clear, however, when they are applied to a claim arising out of two tortious acts, one of which is an assault or battery and the other of which is a mere act of negligence. Nonetheless, it is both settled and undisputed that in at least some situations the fact that an injury was directly caused by an assault or battery will not preclude liability against the Government for negligently allowing the assault to occur. Thus, in *United States v. Muniz*, 374 U.S. 150 (1963), we held that a prisoner who was assaulted by other inmates could recover damages from the United States because prison officials were negligent in failing to prevent the assault that caused his injury.

Two quite different theories might explain why *Muniz*' claim did not "arise out of" the assault that caused his injuries. First, it might be assumed that since he alleged an independent basis for tort liability—namely, the negligence of the prison officials—the claim did not arise solely, or even predominantly, out of the assault. Rather, the attention of the trier of fact is focused on the Government's negligent act or omission; the intentional commission is simply considered as part of the causal link leading to the injury. Under this view, the assailant's individual involvement would not give rise to Government liability, but antecedent negligence by Government agents could, provided of course that similar negligent conduct would support recovery under the law of the State where the incident occurred.

In response to this theory, the Government argues that the "arising out of" language must be read broadly and that the Sheridans' negligence claim is accordingly barred, for in the absence of Carr's assault, there would be no claim. We need not resolve this dispute, however, because even accepting the Government's contention that when an intentional tort is a *sine qua non* of recovery the action "arises out of" that tort, we conclude that the exception does not bar recovery in this case. We thus rely exclusively on the second theory, which makes clear that the intentional tort exception is simply inapplicable to torts that fall outside the scope of § 1346(b)'s general waiver.

This second explanation for the *Muniz* holding, which is narrower but not necessarily inconsistent with the first, adopts Judge (later Justice)

Mustbe:
- Breach of duty of Care by Gov. (other than int. tort)
- Gov's Duty of Care ind. of actors

SECTION A   THE FEDERAL TORT CLAIMS ACT   **287**

USSC uses Panella

Harlan's reasoning in *Panella v. United States,* 216 F.2d 622 (C.A.2) 1954). In that case, as in *Muniz,* a prisoner claimed that an assault by another inmate had been caused by the negligence of federal employees. After recognizing that the "immunity against claims arising out of assault and battery can literally be read to apply to assaults committed by persons other than government employees," *id.,* at 624, his opinion concluded that § 2680(h) must be read against the rest of the Act. The exception should therefore be construed to apply only to claims that would otherwise be authorized by the basic waiver of sovereign immunity. Since an assault by a person who was not employed by the Government could not provide the basis for a claim under the FTCA, the exception could not apply to such an assault; rather, the exception only applies in cases arising out of assaults by federal employees.

The gov't can't be liable b/c it didn't waive immunity in 1346(b) for intentional torts committed by private parties in prison

In describing the coverage of the FTCA, Judge Harlan emphasized the statutory language that was critical to his analysis. As he explained, the Act covers actions for personal injuries "caused by the negligent or wrongful act or omission *of any employee of the Government* while acting within the scope of his office or employment ... (Italics supplied)." *Id.,* at 623. We need only move the emphasis to the next phrase—"while acting within the scope of his office or employment"—to apply his analysis to the assault and battery committed by the off-duty, inebriated enlisted man in this case. If nothing more was involved here than the conduct of Carr at the time he shot at petitioners, there would be no basis for imposing liability on the Government. The tortious conduct of an off-duty serviceman, not acting within the scope of his office or employment, does not in itself give rise to Government liability whether that conduct is intentional or merely negligent.

Language of 1346(b)

(This theory works b/c it's a claim of neg.)

As alleged in this case, however, the negligence of other Government employees who allowed a foreseeable assault and battery to occur may furnish a basis for Government liability that is entirely independent of Carr's employment status. By voluntarily adopting regulations that prohibit the possession of firearms on the naval base and that require all personnel to report the presence of any such firearm,[5] and by further voluntarily undertaking to provide care to a person who was visibly drunk and visibly armed, the Government assumed responsibility to "perform [its] 'good Samaritan' task in a careful manner." *Indian Towing Co. v. United States,* 350 U.S. 61, 65 (1955). The District Court and the Court of Appeals both assumed that petitioners' version of the facts would support recovery under Maryland law on a negligence theory if the naval hospital had been owned and operated by a private person. Although the Government now disputes this assumption, it is not our practice to reexamine a question of state law of that kind or, without good reason, to pass upon it in the first instance. On this assumption, it seems perfectly clear that the mere fact that Carr happened to be an off-duty federal employee should not

Status of man as gov't employee wouldn't matter under state law

---

5. Allegedly, Carr's roommate was aware that Carr improperly possessed a firearm prior to the shooting incident, yet failed to comply with Navy regulations requiring that he report this violation to the appropriate authorities.

But:

Q: Does state law provide imm. for fed. employees?

provide a basis for protecting the Government from liability that would attach if Carr had been an unemployed civilian patient or visitor in the hospital. Indeed, in a case in which the employment status of the assailant has nothing to do with the basis for imposing liability on the Government, it would seem perverse to exonerate the Government because of the happenstance that Carr was on a federal payroll.

In a case of this kind,[8] the fact that Carr's behavior is characterized as an intentional assault rather than a negligent act is also quite irrelevant. If the Government has a duty to prevent a foreseeably dangerous individual from wandering about unattended, it would be odd to assume that Congress intended a breach of that duty to give rise to liability when the dangerous human instrument was merely negligent but not when he or she was malicious. In fact, the human characteristics of the dangerous instrument are also beside the point. For the theory of liability in this case is analogous to cases in which a person assumes control of a vicious animal, or perhaps an explosive device. Cf. *Palsgraf v. Long Island R. Co.*, 248 N.Y. 339, 162 N.E. 99 (1928). Because neither Carr's employment status nor his state of mind has any bearing on the basis for petitioners' claim for money damages, the intentional tort exception to the FTCA is not applicable in this case.

The judgment of the Court of Appeals is reversed, and the case is remanded for further proceedings consistent with this opinion.

It is so ordered.

■ JUSTICE WHITE, concurring.

In *United States v. Shearer,* 473 U.S. 52 (1985), four Justices, including myself, were of the view that 28 U.S.C. § 2680(h) barred recovery for damage caused from an assault by a Government employee said to be the result of a negligent act by another employee. But we did not address whether the assaulter was acting within the scope of his employment or whether that factor made a difference in applying the § 2680(h) exclusion. In any event, to the extent the views I shared there are inconsistent with my present understanding, I think the Court's opinion, which I join, has the better of it.

■ JUSTICE KENNEDY, concurring in the judgment.

The question before us is how to interpret the intentional tort exception in the Federal Tort Claims Act, 28 U.S.C. §§ 1346(b) and 2671–2680, when a plaintiff's injury is caused both by an intentional tort and by negligence that precedes it. The intentional tort exception, 28 U.S.C. § 2680(h), provides, in pertinent part, that the United States shall not be liable for "[a]ny claim arising out of assault, battery...." Both the majority and the dissent provide persuasive reasons for their conclusions. I write separately to set forth the bases for my differences with those opinions, and

---

8. Because Carr's employment status is irrelevant to the outcome, it is not appropriate in this case to consider whether negligent hiring, negligent supervision, or negligent training may ever provide the basis for liability under the FTCA for a foreseeable assault or battery by a Government employee.

for my conclusion that the Court correctly decides that the judgment of the Court of Appeals must be reversed.

I

In an adaptation of Judge Harlan's analysis in *Panella v. United States,* 216 F.2d 622 (C.A.2 1954), the Court asks whether the tortfeasor's actions occurred "while acting within the scope of his office or employment." Since "[t]he tortious conduct of an off-duty serviceman, not acting within the scope of his office or employment, does not in itself give rise to Government liability whether that conduct is intentional or merely negligent," the Court concludes that the intentional tort exception is inapplicable to this case. In my view, this analysis is misdirected. Petitioners' claim here is that the Government acted negligently, quite apart from the intentional tort of its employee. The issue then is how to give effect to the Act's express authorization of suits grounded in negligence without eviscerating the Act's prohibition of claims "arising out of" intentional torts. Whether or not the intentional tortfeasor was on duty will not necessarily resolve this question. The proper inquiry must depend on an analysis of the Government's acts or omissions and of the theory on which the Government's negligence is predicated.

The Court seems to recognize as much when it states that it would allow a claim against the Government if based on negligence "of other Government employees ... entirely independent of [the intentional tortfeasor's] employment status." The Court, however, fails to clarify the meaning of "independent" negligence or to explain how the legal significance of antecedent negligence somehow changes with the employment status of the intentional tortfeasor. Although its opinion asserts that it avoids the question whether a negligent supervision claim may be pressed against the Government in such a case, that issue is unavoidable, both as an analytic matter and on the facts of this case. As I explain more fully below, our inquiry should address whether a finding of liability for negligent supervision would undermine substantially the intentional tort exception.

The dissenting opinion is correct to focus on the statutory language, but I submit, with all respect, that it reaches the wrong result. The dissent's fundamental premise seems to be that any injury in which an intentional act is a substantial cause necessarily arises only from that intentional act. This contradicts the basic rule that the same injury can arise from more than one wrongful act:

> "Where voluntary acts of responsible human beings intervene between defendant's conduct and plaintiff's injury, the problem of foreseeability is the same and courts generally are guided by the same test. If the likelihood of the intervening act was one of the hazards that made defendant's conduct negligent—that is, if it was sufficiently foreseeable to have this effect—then defendant will generally be liable for the consequences.... So far as scope of duty ... is concerned, it should make no difference whether the intervening actor is negligent or

intentional or criminal." 2 F. Harper & F. James, Law of Torts § 20.5, pp. 1143–1145 (1956).

The dissent's approach implies the converse: that an intentional act somehow obliterates the legal significance of any negligence that precedes or follows it. It must be noted that the phrase "arising out of" refers to claims, not suits. Congress did not bar any *suit* arising out of intentional torts; it barred only *claims* arising out of such wrongs. 28 U.S.C. § 2680(h) ("Any *claim* arising out of assault, battery . . .") (emphasis added). Whatever uncertainty surrounds the intentional tort exception, it is unlikely that Congress intended it, as the dissent suggests, to bar suits for "all injuries associated in any way with an assault or battery." It is standard tort doctrine that a reasonably foreseeable injury can arise from multiple causes, each arising from a breach of a different duty and each imposing liability accordingly. The dissent's position violates this basic principle by stating: "If we were to construe the words according to their ordinary meaning, we would say that a claim 'arises out of' a battery in any case in which the battery is essential to the claim."

II

I am in substantial agreement with the opinion of Chief Judge Winter, who wrote the dissenting opinion when this case was before the Court of Appeals. To determine whether a claim arises from an intentional assault or battery and is therefore barred by the exception, a court must ascertain whether the alleged negligence was the breach of a duty to select or supervise the employee-tortfeasor or the breach of some separate duty independent from the employment relation. See 823 F.2d 820, 824, 828 (C.A.4 1987). If the allegation is that the Government was negligent in the supervision or selection of the employee and that the intentional tort occurred as a result, the intentional tort exception of § 2680(h) bars the claim. Otherwise, litigants could avoid the substance of the exception because it is likely that many, if not all, intentional torts of Government employees plausibly could be ascribed to the negligence of the tortfeasor's supervisors. To allow such claims would frustrate the purposes of the exception.

The Court is wrong to imply that this issue is somehow removed from the facts of this case. It is squarely implicated here, and the trial court should be advised how to deal with it, not left to wonder. It is quite plausible to argue that Carr was missupervised by Government officers who had authority over him and had, we may assume, the duty to control his unauthorized behavior and enforce the Government regulations restricting the possession of firearms on the naval base. Absent the exception set forth in § 2680(h), the Government could be held negligent for failing to supervise Carr in a way such that the rifle would be discovered. We should state explicitly that this is not a theory that petitioners are free to pursue on remand.

An alternative theory of liability, however, is the Government's negligent performance of its Good Samaritan duty under the state law of

Maryland, which I assume, as the Court does, provides for such liability if Carr had been a private person. On this theory, the Government's negligence is independent of its employment relation with Carr. The Government's duty to control the behavior of individuals on the naval base extended to all individuals, employee and nonemployee alike. This theory of liability does not depend on the employment status of the intentional tortfeasor. When the Government would be liable even if the tortfeasor had been a private person, say an individual who wandered onto the naval base, there is little danger that § 2680(h) will be circumvented. The intentional tort exception does not preclude recovery under a theory of independent governmental negligence, despite the presence of a (barred) negligent supervision claim. Cf. *Block v. Neal,* 460 U.S. 289, 297–298 (1983) ("[T]he partial overlap between these two tort actions [of negligent misrepresentation and of negligent supervision regarding the construction of plaintiff's home] does not support the conclusion that if one is excepted under the Tort Claims Act, the other must be as well").

In sum, I would hold that where the plaintiff's tort claim is based on the mere fact of Government employment, a *respondeat superior* claim, or, a short step further, on the conduct of the employment relation between the intentional tortfeasor and the Government without more, a negligent supervision or negligent hiring claim, § 2680(h)'s exception applies and the United States is immune. I concur in the Court's judgment insofar as it finds that § 2680(h) does not bar tort claims based on the independent negligence of the Government. For these reasons, I agree that the judgment of the Court of Appeals must be reversed.

■ JUSTICE O'CONNOR, with whom THE CHIEF JUSTICE and JUSTICE SCALIA join, dissenting.

Petitioners seek to recover money damages under a section of the Federal Tort Claims Act (FTCA) that authorizes claims against the Government for personal injuries "caused by the negligent or wrongful act or omission of any employee of the Government while acting within the scope of his office or employment." 28 U.S.C. § 1346(b). That section is subject to an exception for any claim "arising out of" an assault or battery. 28 U.S.C. § 2680(h). Despite the unqualified language of this exception, the Court today holds that it does not protect the Government from liability for a battery committed by a Government employee who acted outside the scope of his employment, if other Government employees had a duty to prevent the battery.

If we were to construe the words according to their ordinary meaning, we would say that a claim "arises out of" a battery in any case in which the battery is essential to the claim. Thus when the Court construed another exception to the FTCA for claims "arising in respect of ... the detention of any goods" by customs or law enforcement officials, 28 U.S.C. § 2680(c), we equated "arising in respect of" with "arising out of" and decided that the phrase includes "all injuries associated in any way with the 'detention' of goods." See *Kosak v. United States,* 465 U.S. 848, 854 (1984). A parallel construction of the exception at issue here leads to the conclusion that it encompasses all injuries associated in any way with an assault or battery. Indeed, four Justices described the exception essentially in this way in *United States v. Shearer*, 473 U.S. 52 (1985). That case involved a claim against the Army for negligent supervision of a serviceman who kidnaped and murdered another serviceman. The plurality explained, in terms equally applicable here, why it thought the claim was barred.

> "Respondent cannot avoid the reach of § 2680(h) by framing her complaint in terms of negligent failure to prevent the assault and battery. Section 2680(h) does not merely bar claims *for* assault or battery; in sweeping language it excludes any claim *arising out of* assault or battery. We read this provision to cover claims like respondent's that sound in negligence but stem from a battery committed by a Government employee. Thus 'the express words of the statute' bar respondent's claim against the Government. *United States v. Spelar*, 338 U.S. 217, 219 (1949)." *Id.*, at 55 (emphasis in original).

The Court acknowledges that the exception for claims arising out of assault or battery is phrased in broad terms. The Court believes, however, that we recognized implicit limitations on that exception in *United States v. Muniz*, 374 U.S. 150 (1963). One of the cases consolidated for decision in *Muniz* was brought by a prisoner who alleged that negligent Government employees failed to prevent other inmates from assaulting and beating him. The Court rejected the Government's argument that Congress did not intend to allow prisoners to bring claims under the FTCA. The majority infers from this decision that the Government can be liable under the FTCA when Government employees fail to prevent nonemployees from committing assault or battery. But that inference is unnecessary, because the Court in *Muniz* expressly reserved judgment on whether one of the exceptions of § 2680 barred the prisoner's claim.

The Court's decision in this case extends its erroneous interpretation of *Muniz*. The Court develops a theory to explain why the assault and battery exception does not bar a claim based on the negligent failure of Government employees to prevent a battery by a nonemployee, and shows why that theory applies with equal force to a battery by a Government employee like Carr who was not acting within the scope of his employment. Because I reject the interpretation of *Muniz* on which the majority's argument is premised, I reject this extension as well.

There is no support in the legislative history for the limitation of the assault and battery exception that the Court adopts today. When Congress enacted the exception, it was concerned with a particular factual situation. Mr. Holtzoff, a Special Assistant to the Attorney General, told the Senate in general terms that the torts of assault and battery were excluded from the FTCA. Tort Claims Against the United States: Hearings on S. 2690 before a Subcommittee of the Senate Committee on the Judiciary, 76th Cong., 3d Sess., 39 (1940). At the House hearings, Mr. Holtzoff explained that "[t]he theory of these exemptions is that, since this bill is a radical innovation, perhaps we had better take it step by step and exempt certain torts and certain actions which might give rise to tort claims that would be difficult to defend, or in respect to which it would be unjust to make the Government liable." Tort Claims Against the United States: Hearings on H.R. 7236 before Subcommittee No. 1 of the House Committee on the Judiciary, 76th Cong., 3d Sess., 22 (1940). Interpreting this remark, the Government suggests that Congress reasonably might have concluded that it would be unjust to make the Government liable for claims arising out of an assault or battery merely because Government employees other than the tortfeasor were negligent, since the individual tortfeasor plainly is the more culpable party. Indeed, intentional torts sometimes are found to be superseding causes that relieve a negligent party of liability. This analysis applies whether the person committing the intentional tort is a Government employee, a nonemployee, or a Government employee acting outside the scope of his office.

The Court stops short of adopting petitioners' most ambitious argument, according to which the Government can be liable for negligently supervising a Government employee who commits an assault or battery while acting within the scope of his employment. I trust that the courts will preserve at least this core of the assault and battery exception. I dissent from the Court's decision to confine the exception to such a narrow scope.

Notes and Questions

1. This entire course is a study in statutory interpretation. The *Sheridan v. United States* case is a particularly good illustration of that aspect of the course. In the three separate opinions, there are three different interpretations of the assault and battery portion of the intentional tort exception, each of which is plausible. For each opinion, outline the analysis of the statute, tracking through each pertinent statutory provision and how the opinion construes them; articulate the opinion's definition of the intentional tort exception; and consider how the three opinions differ in theory and application. Justice Stevens's majority opinion is grounded in the scope of the FTCA and the function of an exception in a statute, which thus causes the opinion to focus upon whether the person committing the assault and battery was acting within the scope of employment and, concluding that he was not, looking to the nature of the cause of action alleged by the plaintiff. To fully understand this approach, outline each of these steps or elements in the analysis. Justice Kennedy places even greater weight on the theory of liability, although further insisting that the duty of the government be independent of the employment relationship. How does he build these factors into a theory of the intentional tort exception? Justice O'Connor's dissent reads the intentional tort exception in its literal and broadest sense. How does she read the statute and which language in the text does she emphasize to read this conclusion? How does she understand Congress's apparent purpose in adopting such a broad exception?

2.   The majority in *Sheridan* declined in footnote 8 to decide "whether negligent hiring, negligent supervision, or negligent training may ever provide the basis for liability under the FTCA for a foreseeable assault or battery by a Government employee." Justice Kennedy, of course, opined that it could not, and the dissent expressed the hope that "the courts will preserve at least this core of the assault and battery exception."

The lower courts have remained divided on this issue. In *Bennett v. United States,* 803 F.2d 1502, 1502–05 (9th Cir. 1986), the Ninth Circuit found the intentional tort exception inapplicable in the case of sexual abuse of children by a federal employee at a federally-run day care center. In a subsequent decision, the Ninth Circuit explained that this ruling meant that "the assault and battery exception does not immunize the Government from liability for negligently hiring and supervising an employee." *Brock v. United States,* 64 F.3d 1421, 1425 (9th Cir. 1995); *see also Senger v. United States,* 103 F.3d 1437, 1442 (9th Cir. 1996) (confirming holding of *Bennett* that claims for negligent hiring and supervision of federal employees are not barred by intentional tort exception). *See generally* Rebecca L. Andrews, Comment, *So the Army Hired an Ax–Murderer: The Assault and Battery Exception to the Federal Tort Claims Act Does Not Bar Suits for Negligent Hiring, Retention and Supervision,* 78 Wash. L. Rev. 161, 191–97 (2003) (approving of the Ninth Circuit approach and arguing that "[r]espondeat superior claims, which are based on vicarious liability and are barred by the assault and battery exception, are readily distinguishable from claims based on negligent hiring, retention and supervision," as the latter require proof of the employer's independent negligence).

By contrast, most courts that have addressed the question post-*Sheridan* have barred claims that are based on the employment relationship, such as negligent hiring or supervision. In *Billingsley v. United States,* 251 F.3d 696, 698 (8th Cir. 2001), involving an assault by a Job Corps enrollee who had the status of an employee by federal statute, the Eighth Circuit held that the government could not be held liable for negligent hiring and supervision of the enrollee because such a claim pertains to the government employment status, but that the government would be liable if the enrollee's supervisors knew of his dangerousness because of violent activity in public and outside the scope of his employment. *See also Leleux v. United States,* 178 F.3d 750, 756–58 & n.5 (5th Cir. 1999) (rejecting, among other claims under the FTCA, a claim for negligent training and supervision of a military recruitment officer who committed a form of sexual battery against the plaintiff, and expressly disagreeing with the Ninth Circuit's *Brock* decision); *Franklin v. United States,* 992 F.2d 1492, 1499 n.6 (10th Cir. 1993) (noting that "even after *Sheridan* it is doubtful * * * whether such a claim [for negligent hiring, training, or supervision], which would still ultimately derive from the government's employment relationship to the immediate tortfeasors, would escape the reach of § 2680(h)"); *Ryan v. United States,* 156 F.Supp.2d 900, 906–07 (N.D. Ill. 2001) (holding that claims for negligent hiring, supervision, or retention of letter carrier who sexually assaulted plaintiffs while on delivery route were barred by intentional tort exception and rejecting Ninth Circuit's interpretation as allowing "plaintiffs to circumvent the assault and battery exception altogether, providing them with relief against the government in most, if not all, cases," with citation to Justice Kennedy's concurrence in *Sheridan*); *Lilly v. United States*, 141 F.Supp.2d 626, 628–29 (S.D. W. Va. 2001) (holding that Fourth Circuit's pre-*Sheridan* ruling precluding claims for negligent supervision of government employees who commit assaults remained good law), *aff'd*, 22 Fed. Appx. 293 (4th Cir. 2001); *Pottle v. United States*, 918 F.Supp. 843, 847–48 (D. N.J. 1996) (ruling that the intentional tort exception barred suit by a military recruit who was assaulted by a Navy recruitment officer during a physical examination that was part of the recruitment process, including preclusion of negligence claims based on hiring, training, or supervision of a government employee who commits an intentional tort). *But see Bodin v. Vagshenian*, 462 F.3d 481, 491 (5th Cir. 2006) (Owens, J., concurring) (arguing that the "undeniable effect" of the majority's ruling was to impose liability on the federal government for failure to supervise a psychiatrist who committed sexual assault and further concluding that the government may be held liable for negligently supervising an employee who commits an assault). Speaking for a majority of the courts, one district court, in *Verran v. United States*, 305 F.Supp.2d 765, 776 (E.D. Mich. 2004), explained the line between exclusion under the intentional tort exception and permissibility as a viable claim under the FTCA as reflecting "the distinction between tort theories of liability that depend upon an employment relationship (*e.g.*, negligent hiring or supervision) and those that do not (*e.g.*, premises liability)."

3. The "intentional tort" exception in Subsection 2680(h) demonstrates that the Federal Tort Claims Act falls far short of a complete waiver of the government's sovereign immunity in tort. Note the breadth of the exception: "eleven familiar torts"—"a very considerable portion of the law torts"—are removed altogether from the government's consent to suit. 2 Lester S. Jayson & Robert C. Longstreth, *Handling Federal Tort Claims* § 13.06[1][a] (2005). However, not all intentional torts are so excluded, as trespass, conversion, and intentional infliction of emotional distress are not listed in Subsection 2680(h). *See Estate of Trentadue ex rel. Aguilar v. United States*, 397 F.3d 840, 858–59 (10th Cir. 2005) (holding that plaintiffs could recover for intentional infliction of emotional distress if they were ultimately able to prove each element of that tort).

4. There is an exception to the exception. The government *may* be held liable for certain intentional torts when committed by "investigative or law enforcement officers" of the federal government, as defined in Subsection 2680(h). This provision was added to the FTCA in 1974 in response to widespread publicity over abuse of search powers by federal law enforcement officers, in such sensational cases as a notorious "no-knock" drug raid without a warrant in Illinois, in which federal narcotics agents knocked down the door, shouted obscenities, and threatened the residents with drawn weapons, only to discover they were in the wrong house. S. Rep. No. 93–469, at 30–32 (1973). *See generally Orsay v. United States Depart. of Justice*, 289 F.3d 1125, 1132–36 (9th Cir. 2002) (discussing Congress's purpose for and the historical context behind the enactment of

the investigative or law enforcement officer proviso, concluding that Congress intended to provide a remedy to innocent victims for abuses of federal law enforcement powers, and holding, over a dissent, that the United States would be liable for an assault under this proviso only if the officer actually had been engaged at the time in investigative or law enforcement activities and not merely acting within the scope of employment).

Some commentators contend that the 1974 FTCA amendments were intended by Congress, and thus should have been construed by the courts, to provide a tort remedy against the United States for violation of constitutional rights, such as the protection against illegal search and seizure under the Fourth Amendment. Diana Hassel, *A Missed Opportunity: The Federal Tort Claims Act and Civil Rights Actions,* 49 Okla. L. Rev. 455 (1996). Instead, as with other claims under the FTCA, the courts have required that the plaintiff state a cause of action arising under state tort law. *Federal Deposit Ins. Corp. v. Meyer,* 510 U.S. 471, 478 (1994) (holding that "the United States simply has not rendered itself liable under § 1346(b) for constitutional tort claims") (the *Meyer* decision is set out in this casebook at Chapter V.B.2.d); *Carlson v. Green,* 446 U.S. 14, 23 (1980) (stating that the FTCA bases substantive liability on state law, not federal law, and thus does not apply to constitutional torts); *Brown v. United States,* 653 F.2d 196, 201 (5th Cir. 1981) (holding that the plaintiff's claims for violation of the Fourth and Fifth Amendments were not cognizable under the FTCA, unlike a state law tort claim for malicious prosecution). Thus, FTCA liability may not be premised upon a violation of a constitutional right as such; rather, the plaintiff must frame a cause of action against the United States, acting through federal investigative or law enforcement officers, under the applicable state's law for such traditional torts as assault, battery, false imprisonment, false arrest, or malicious prosecution. To maintain a claim for damages directly under the Constitution, a plaintiff must bring a judicially-created *Bivens* suit against the individual federal officer or employee for violation of constitutional rights. Common law and constitutional claims against federal officials and employees, and their qualified immunity from such actions, are discussed in Chapter V of this casebook.

---

7. MISCELLANEOUS EXCEPTIONS

28 United States Code § 2680(b)–(g), (i)–(n)

The provisions of this chapter and section 1346(b) of this title shall not apply to—

* * *

(b) Any claim arising out of the loss, miscarriage, or negligent transmission of letters or postal matter.

(c) Any claim arising in respect of the assessment or collection of any tax or customs duty, or the detention of any goods, merchandise, or other property by any officer of customs or excise or any other law enforcement officer, except that the provisions of this chapter and section 1346(b) of this title apply to any claim based on injury or loss of goods, merchandise, or other property, while in the possession of any officer of customs or excise or any other law enforcement officer, if—

(1) the property was seized for the purpose of forfeiture under any provision of Federal law providing for the forfeiture of property other than as a sentence imposed upon conviction of a criminal offense;

(2) the interest of the claimant was not forfeited;

(3) the interest of the claimant was not remitted or mitigated (if the property was subject to forfeiture); and

(4) the claimant was not convicted of a crime for which the interest of the claimant in the property was subject to forfeiture under a Federal criminal forfeiture law.

(d) Any claim for which a remedy is provided by chapter 309 or 311 of title 46 of Title 46, relating to claims or suits in admiralty against the United States.

(e) Any claim arising out of an act or omission of any employee of the Government in administering the provisions of sections 1–31 of Title 50, Appendix [the Trading With the Enemy Act].

(f) Any claim for damages caused by the imposition or establishment of a quarantine by the United States.

* * *

(i) Any claim for damages caused by the fiscal operations of the Treasury or by the regulation of the monetary system.

(j) Any claim arising out of the combatant activities of the military or naval forces, or the Coast Guard, during time of war.

(k) Any claim arising in a foreign country.

(*l*) Any claim arising from the activities of the Tennessee Valley Authority.

(m) Any claim arising from the activities of the Panama Canal Company.

(n) Any claim arising from the activities of a Federal land bank, a Federal intermediate credit bank, or a bank for cooperatives.

* * *

Note

The FTCA includes quite a number of exceptions to liability, in addition to the discretionary function, misrepresentation, and intentional tort exceptions that we have previously examined. Although in a survey course we cannot examine each of these exceptions in detail, these are further examples of the continuing power of sovereign immunity. In certain areas of government conduct—ranging from mail carriage and customs inspections to military combat and fiscal operations and monetary regulation—the sovereign immunity of the United States is fully preserved against tort liability. Moreover, while we will not pause to read illustrative cases, several of these exceptions have occasioned court review and interpretation. *See, e.g., Kosak v. United States,* 465 U.S. 848 (1984) (holding that the FTCA exception for "[a]ny claim arising in respect of * * * the detention of any goods or merchandise by an officer of customs," 28 U.S.C. § 2680(c), precluded recovery against the United States for damage to objects of art temporarily detained by the Customs Service upon entry into the country); *Dolan v. United States Postal Serv.,* 546 U.S. 481 (2006) (holding that the for "[a]ny claim arising out the loss, miscarriage, or negligent transmission of letters or postal matter," 28 U.S.C. § 2680(b), did not bar a resident's claim arising out of her alleged injury in tripping over letters, packages, and periodicals that had been negligently left on her porch by a mail carrier, but rather applied only to a failure to transmit mail or damage to its contents); *Sportique Fashions, Inc. v. Sullivan,* 597 F.2d 664 (9th Cir. 1979) (holding that the postal matter exception precluded a claim against postal service supervisors for business losses suffered when a clothing store's advertising mailers were not timely delivered); *Koohi v. United States,* 976 F.2d 1328 (9th Cir. 1992) (dismissing an FTCA claim by heirs of deceased passengers and crew of an Iranian civilian aircraft accidentally shot down by a United States warship, as barred by exception for claims "arising out of the combatant activities" of the armed forces "during time of war," even though there was no formal declaration of war in connection with "tanker war" during Iran–Iraq conflict); *Clark v. United States,* 974 F.Supp. 895, 898 (E.D.Tex.1996) (holding that an FTCA claim that a daughter suffered birth defects as a result of exposure of the father to toxic agents while serving in Saudi Arabia during the Persian Gulf War was barred by the exception for claims "arising out of the combatant activities" of the armed forces "during time of war").

In the following case, we look at one final exception—included among the miscellaneous exceptions excerpted above—that bars "[a]ny claim arising in a foreign country." 28 U.S.C. § 2680(k). In *Smith v. United States,* we find not only an explanation and application of yet another exception to the FTCA, but we also will observe an interesting exercise in statutory interpretation in which the members of the Court draw upon various provisions of the FTCA, which we have examined previously, to decipher the meaning of this particular exception in the fuller context of the entire statute.

Smith v. United States

United States Supreme Court.
507 U.S. 197 (1993).

■ CHIEF JUSTICE REHNQUIST delivered the opinion of the Court.

This case presents the question whether the Federal Tort Claims Act (FTCA), 28 U.S.C. §§ 1346(b), 1402(b), 2401(b), 2671–2680, applies to tortious acts or omissions occurring in Antarctica, a sovereignless region without civil tort law of its own.[1] We hold that it does not.

Petitioner Sandra Jean Smith is the widow of John Emmett Smith and the duly appointed representative of his estate. At the time of his death, Smith worked as a carpenter at McMurdo Station on Ross Island, Antarctica, for a construction company under contract to the National Science Foundation, an agency of the United States. Smith and two companions one day took a recreational hike to Castle Rock, located several miles outside of McMurdo Station. On their return, they departed from the marked route to walk across a snow field in the direction of Scott Base, a New Zealand outpost not far from McMurdo Station. After stopping for a snack, one of the three men took a step and suddenly dropped from sight. Smith followed, and he, too, disappeared. Both men had fallen into a crevasse. Despite search and rescue efforts, Smith died from exposure and internal injuries suffered as a result of the fall.

Petitioner filed this wrongful death action against the United States under the FTCA in the District Court for the District of Oregon, the district where she resides. Petitioner alleged that the United States was negligent in failing to provide adequate warning of the dangers posed by crevasses in areas beyond the marked paths. It is undisputed that petitioner's claim is based exclusively on acts or omissions occurring in Antarctica. Upon the motion of the United States, the District Court dismissed petitioner's complaint for lack of subject-matter jurisdiction, 702 F.Supp. 1480 (1989), holding that her claim was barred by 28 U.S.C. § 2680(k), the foreign-country exception. Section 2680(k) precludes the exercise of jurisdiction over "[a]ny claim arising in a foreign country."

The Court of Appeals affirmed, 953 F.2d 1116 (C.A.9 1991). It noted that the term "foreign country" admits of multiple interpretations, and thus looked to the language and structure of the FTCA as a whole to determine whether Antarctica is a "foreign country" within the meaning of the statute. Adopting the analysis and conclusion of then-Judge Scalia, see *Beattie v. United States*, 756 F.2d 91, 106–130 ([D.C.Cir.] 1984) (Scalia, J., dissenting), the Court of Appeals ruled that the FTCA does not apply to claims arising in Antarctica. To hold otherwise, the Court of Appeals

---

1. Without indigenous human population and containing roughly one-tenth of the world's land mass, Antarctica is best described as "an entire continent of disputed territory." F. Auburn, Antarctic Law and Politics 1 (1982). Seven nations—Argentina, Australia, Chile, France, New Zealand, Norway, and the United Kingdom—presently assert formal claims to pie-shaped portions of the continent that total about 85 percent of its expanse. The United States does not recognize other nations' claims and does not itself assert a sovereign interest in Antarctica, although it maintains a basis for such a claim. In any event, these sovereign claims have all been suspended by the terms of the Antarctic Treaty, concluded in 1959. Antarctic Treaty, Dec. 1, 1959 [1961] 12 U.S.T. 794, T.I.A.S. No. 4780. Article 4 of the Treaty states that no claim may be enforced, expanded, or compromised while the Treaty is in force, thus essentially freezing nations' sovereign claims as of the date of the Treaty's execution.

stated, would render two other provisions of the FTCA, 28 U.S.C. §§ 1402(b), 1346(b), nonsensical. The Court of Appeals held, in the alternative, that petitioner's suit would be barred even if Antarctica were not a "foreign country" for purposes of the FTCA. Because the FTCA was a limited relinquishment of the common-law immunity of the United States, the Court of Appeals concluded that the absence of any clear congressional intent to subject the United States to liability for claims arising in Antarctica precluded petitioner's suit. We granted certiorari to resolve a conflict between two Courts of Appeals and now affirm.

Petitioner argues that the scope of the foreign-country exception turns on whether the United States has recognized the legitimacy of another nation's sovereign claim over the foreign land. Otherwise, she contends, the land is not a "country" for purposes of the FTCA. Petitioner points out that the United States does not recognize the validity of other nations' claims to portions of Antarctica. She asserts, moreover, that this construction of the term "foreign country" is most consistent with the purpose underlying the foreign-country exception. According to petitioner, Congress enacted the foreign-country exception in order to insulate the United States from tort liability imposed pursuant to foreign law. Because Antarctica has no law of its own, petitioner claims that conventional choice-of-law rules control and require the application of Oregon law, the law of her domicile. Thus, petitioner concludes, the rationale for the foreign-country exception would not be compromised by the exercise of jurisdiction here, since the United States would not be subject to liability under the law of a foreign nation.

Petitioner's argument for governmental liability here faces significant obstacles in addition to the foreign-country exception, but we turn first to the language of that proviso. It states that the FTCA's waiver of sovereign immunity does not apply to "[a]ny claim arising in a foreign country." 28 U.S.C. § 2680(k). Though the FTCA offers no definition of "country," the commonsense meaning of the term undermines petitioner's attempt to equate it with "sovereign state." The first dictionary definition of "country" is simply "[a] region or tract of land." Webster's New International Dictionary 609 (2d ed. 1945). To be sure, this is not the only possible interpretation of the term, and it is therefore appropriate to examine other parts of the statute before making a final determination. But the ordinary meaning of the language itself, we think, includes Antarctica, even though it has no recognized government.

Our construction of the term "foreign country" draws support from the language of § 1346(b), "[t]he principal provision of the Federal Tort Claims Act." *Richards v. United States,* 369 U.S. 1, 6 (1962). That section waives the sovereign immunity of the United States for certain torts committed by federal employees "under circumstances where the United States, if a private person, would be liable to the claimant *in accordance with the law of the place where the act or omission occurred.*" 28 U.S.C. § 1346(b) (emphasis added). We have construed § 1346(b) in determining what law should apply in actions brought under the FTCA. But by its terms the section is more than a choice-of-law provision: it delineates the scope of the United States' waiver of sovereign immunity. If Antarctica were not a "foreign country," and for that reason included within the FTCA's coverage, § 1346(b) would instruct courts to look to the law of a place that has no law in order to determine the liability of the United States—surely a bizarre result.[3] Of course, if it were quite clear from the balance of the statute that governmental liability was intended for torts committed in Antarctica, then the failure of § 1346(b) to specify any governing law might be treated as a statutory gap that the courts could fill by decisional law. But coupled with what seems to us the most natural interpretation of the foreign-country exception, this portion of § 1346(b) reinforces the conclusion that Antarctica is excluded from the coverage of the FTCA.

Section 1346(b) is not, however, the only FTCA provision that contradicts petitioner's interpretation of the foreign-country exception. The statute's venue provision, § 1402(b), provides that claims under the FTCA may be brought "only in the judicial district where the plaintiff resides or wherein the act or omission complained of occurred." Because no federal judicial district encompasses Antarctica, petitioner's interpretation of the FTCA would lead to yet another anomalous result: the FTCA would establish jurisdiction for all tort claims against the United States arising in Antarctica, but no venue would exist unless the claimant happened to reside in the United States. As we observed in *Brunette Machine Works, Ltd. v. Kockum Industries, Inc.,* 406 U.S. 706, 710, n. 8 (1972), "Congress does not in general intend to create venue gaps, which take away with one hand what Congress has given by way of jurisdictional grant with the other." Thus, in construing the FTCA, it is "reasonable to prefer the construction that avoids leaving such a gap," *ibid.,* especially when that construction comports with the usual meaning of a disputed term.

Our decisions interpreting the FTCA contain varying statements as to how it should be construed. * * * A recent statement of this sort, and the one to which we now adhere, is found in *United States v. Kubrick,* 444 U.S. 111, 117–118 (1979): "We should also have in mind that the Act waives the immunity of the United States and that ... we should not take it upon ourselves to extend the waiver beyond that which Congress intended. Neither, however, should we assume the authority to narrow the waiver that Congress intended." Reading the foreign-country exception to the FTCA to exclude torts committed in Antarctica accords with this canon of construction.

Lastly, the presumption against extraterritorial application of United States statutes requires that any lingering doubt regarding the reach of the FTCA be resolved against its encompassing torts committed in Antarctica.

---

3. Nor can the law of the plaintiff's domicile, Oregon here, be substituted in FTCA actions based on torts committed in Antarctica. "Congress has expressly stated that the Government's liability is to be determined by the application of a particular law, the law of the place where the act or omission occurred...." *Richards v. United States,* 369 U.S. 1, 9 (1962). Petitioner does not contend that her cause of action is based on acts or omissions occurring in Oregon.

"It is a longstanding principle of American law 'that legislation of Congress, unless a contrary intent appears, is meant to apply only within the territorial jurisdiction of the United States.'" *EEOC v. Arabian American Oil Co.,* 499 U.S. 244, 248 (1991). In applying this principle, "[w]e assume that Congress legislates against the backdrop of the presumption against extraterritoriality." *Arabian American Oil Co., supra,* 499 U.S., at 248. The applicability of the presumption is not defeated here just because the FTCA specifically addresses the issue of extraterritorial application in the foreign-country exception. To the contrary, as we stated in *United States v. Spelar,* 338 U.S. 217, 222 (1949), "[t]hat presumption, far from being overcome here, is doubly fortified by the language of this statute and the legislative purpose underlying it." Petitioner does not assert, nor could she, that there is clear evidence of congressional intent to apply the FTCA to claims arising in Antarctica.

For all of these reasons, we hold that the FTCA's waiver of sovereign immunity does not apply to tort claims arising in Antarctica. Some of these reasons are based on the language and structure of the statute itself; others are based on presumptions as to extraterritorial application of Acts of Congress and as to waivers of sovereign immunity. We think these norms of statutory construction have quite likely led us to the same conclusion that the 79th Congress would have reached had it expressly considered the question we now decide: it would not have included a desolate and extraordinarily dangerous land such as Antarctica within the scope of the FTCA. The judgment of the Court of Appeals is therefore

Affirmed.

■ JUSTICE STEVENS, dissenting.

In my opinion the Court's decision to grant certiorari in this case was a wise exercise of its discretion. The question whether the United States should be held responsible for the tortious conduct of its agents in the vast "sovereignless region" of Antarctica is profoundly important, not only because its answer identifies the character of our concern about ordinary justice, but also because Antarctica is just one of three vast sovereignless places where the negligence of federal agents may cause death or physical injury. The negligence that is alleged in this case will surely have its parallels in outer space as our astronauts continue their explorations of ungoverned regions far beyond the jurisdictional boundaries that were familiar to the Congress that enacted the Federal Tort Claims Act (FTCA) in 1946. Moreover, our jurisprudence relating to negligence of federal agents on the sovereignless high seas points unerringly to the correct disposition of this case. Unfortunately, the Court has ignored that jurisprudence in its parsimonious construction of the FTCA's "sweeping" waiver of sovereign immunity.

In theory the territorial limits on the consent to sue the United States for the torts of its agents might be defined in four ways: (1) there is no such limit; (2) territory subject to the jurisdiction of a foreign country is the only exclusion; (3) it also excludes sovereignless land areas such as Antarctica, but it includes the high seas and outer space; or (4) it has an "exclusive domestic focus" that applies "only within the territorial jurisdiction of the United States." The "foreign country" exclusion in § 2680(k) unquestionably eliminates the first possibility. In my opinion, the second is compelled by the text of the Act. The third possibility is not expressly rejected by the Court, but the reasoning in its terse opinion seems more consistent with the Government's unambiguous adoption of the fourth, and narrowest, interpretation. I shall therefore first explain why the text of the FTCA unquestionably requires rejection of the Government's submission.

Foreign jure

I

The FTCA includes both a broad grant of jurisdiction to the federal courts in § 1346(b) and a broad waiver of sovereign immunity in § 2674. Neither of these sections identifies any territorial limit on the coverage of the Act. That Congress intended and understood the broad language of those two provisions to extend beyond the territory of the United States is demonstrated by its enactment of two express exceptions from that coverage that would have been unnecessary if the initial grant of jurisdiction and waiver of immunity had been as narrow as the Government contends. One of those, of course, is the "foreign country" exclusion in § 2680(k). The other is the exclusion in § 2680(d) for claims asserted under the Suits in Admiralty Act or the Public Vessels Act. Without that exclusion, a party with a claim against the United States cognizable under either of those venerable statutes would have had the right to elect the pre-existing remedy or the newly enacted FTCA remedy. Quite obviously that exclusion would have been unnecessary if the FTCA waiver did not extend to the sovereignless expanses of the high seas. * * *

In 1960, Congress amended the Suits in Admiralty Act so as to bring all maritime torts asserted against the United States * * * within the purview of the Suits in Admiralty Act and thus outside the waiver of sovereign immunity in the FTCA. See *United States v. United Continental Tuna Corp.,* 425 U.S. 164, 176, n. 14 (1976). There can be no disputing the fact, however, that at the time it was enacted, the FTCA waiver extended to the sovereignless reaches of the high seas. Since the geographic scope of that waiver has never been amended, the Government's submission that it is confined to territory under the jurisdiction of the United States is simply untenable.

That the 79th Congress intended the waiver of sovereign immunity in the FTCA to extend to the high seas does not, of course, answer the question whether that waiver extends to the sovereignless region of Antarctica. It does, however, undermine one premise of the Court's analysis: that the presumption against the extraterritorial application of federal statutes supports its narrow construction of the geographic reach of the FTCA. As the Court itself acknowledges, that presumption operates "unless a contrary intent appears." Here, the contrary intent is unmistakable. The same Congress that enacted the "foreign country" exception to the broad waiver of sovereign immunity in § 2674, subjected the United States to claims for wrongful death and injury arising well beyond the territorial jurisdiction of the United States. The presumption against extraterritorial application of federal statutes simply has no bearing on this case.

II

The Government, therefore, may not prevail unless Antarctica is a "foreign country" within the meaning of the exception in subsection (k). Properly, in my view, the Court inquires as to how we are to construe this exception to the FTCA's waiver of sovereign immunity. Instead of answering that question, however, the Court cites a nebulous statement in *United States v. Kubrick,* 444 U.S. 111, 117–118 (1979), and simply asserts that construing the foreign-country exception so as to deny recovery to this petitioner somehow accords with congressional intent.

I had thought that canons of statutory constructions were tools to be used to *divine* congressional intent, not empty phrases used to *ratify* whatever result is desired in a particular case. In any event, I would answer the question that the Court poses, but then ignores. And as I read our cases, the answer is clear: Exceptions to the "sweeping" waiver of sovereign immunity in the FTCA should be, and have been, "narrowly construed." *United States v. Nordic Village, Inc.,* 503 U.S. 30, 33 (1992). Accordingly, given a choice between two acceptable interpretations of the term "country"—it may designate either a sovereign nation or an expanse of land—it is our duty to adopt the former.

Even without that rule of construction, we should favor the interpretation of the term that the Court has previously endorsed. Referring specifically to the term as used in the FTCA, we stated: "We know of no more accurate phrase in common English usage than 'foreign country' to denote territory subject to the sovereignty of another nation." *United States v. Spelar,* 338 U.S. 217, 219 (1949). That interpretation is consistent with a statutory scheme that imposes tort liability on the Government "in the same manner and to the same extent as a private individual under like circumstances". As we explained in *Spelar:* "[T]hough Congress was ready to lay aside a great portion of the sovereign's ancient and unquestioned immunity from suit, it was unwilling to subject the United States to liabilities depending upon the laws of a foreign power." 338 U.S., at 221. Thus, the narrow interpretation of the term "foreign country" is precisely tailored to make the scope of the subsection (k) exception coextensive with its justification.

III

The Court seeks to buttress its interpretation of the "foreign country" exception by returning to the language of the jurisdictional grant in § 1346(b). As I have noted, federal courts have jurisdiction of civil claims against the United States "for injury or loss of property, or personal injury or death caused by the negligent or wrongful act or omission of any employee of the Government while acting within the scope of his office or employment, under circumstances where the United States, if a private person, would be liable to the claimant in accordance with the law of the place where the act or omission occurred." Emphasizing the last dozen words, the Court essentially argues that Antarctica is "a place that has no law" and therefore it would be "bizarre" to predicate federal liability on its governing law.[12]

Although the words the Court has italicized indicate that Congress may not have actually thought about sovereignless regions, they surely do not support the Court's conclusion. Those words, in conjunction with § 2674, require an answer to the question whether a private defendant, in like circumstances, would be liable to the complainant. The Court fails even to ask that question, possibly because it is so obvious that petitioner could maintain a cause of action against a private party whose negligence caused her husband's death in Antarctica. It is simply wrong to suggest, as the Court does, that Antarctica is "a place that has no law."[13]

The relevant substantive law in this case is the law of the State of Oregon, where petitioner resides. As was well settled at English common law before our Republic was founded, a nation's personal sovereignty over its own citizens may support the exercise of civil jurisdiction in transitory actions arising in places not subject to any sovereign. * * *

* * * Surely the State of Oregon, the forum State, has a substantial interest in applying its civil tort law to a case involving the allegedly wrongful death of the spouse of one of its residents. Certainly no other State has an interest in applying its law to these facts. Moreover, application of Oregon's substantive law would in no way conflict with an Act of Congress because Congress has expressly subjected the United States to the laws of the various States for torts committed by the United States and its agents. It is thus perfectly clear that were the defendant in this case a private party, there would be law to apply to determine that party's liability to petitioner. Given the plain language of § 2674, I see no basis for the Court's refusal to follow the statutory command and hold the United States "liable ... in the same manner and to the same extent as a private individual under like circumstances."

IV

Petitioner's action was filed "in the judicial district where the plaintiff resides", as § 1402(b) authorizes; there is, therefore, no objection to venue

---

12. Apparently the Court is assuming that private contracts made in Antarctica are unenforceable and that there is no redress for torts committed by private parties in sovereignless regions. Fortunately our legal system is not that primitive. The statutory reference to "the law of the place where the act or omission occurred" was unquestionably intended to identify the substantive law that would apply to a comparable act or omission by a private party at that place. As long as private conduct is constrained by rules of law, and it certainly is in Antarctica, there is a governing "law of the place" within the meaning of the FTCA.

13. Indeed, it borders on the absurd to suggest that Antarctica is governed by nothing more than the law of the jungle. The United States exercises both criminal jurisdiction, see 18 U.S.C. § 7(7), and taxing jurisdiction, see 26 U.S.C. § 863(d)(2)(A), over the approximately 2,500 Americans that live and work in and around Antarctica each year. The National Science Foundation operates three year-round stations in Antarctica, the largest of which is comprised of 85 buildings and has a harbor, landing strips on sea ice and shelf ice, and a helicopter pad. Transportation to and from New Zealand is frequent during the summer months.

in this case. Because that provision would not provide a forum for a comparable action brought by a nonresident alien, the statute contains an omission that is no stranger to our law. In our opinion in *Brunette Machine Works, Ltd. v. Kockum Industries, Inc.*, 406 U.S. 706, 710, n. 8 (1972), we identified examples of "cases in which the federal courts have jurisdiction but there is no district in which venue is proper" and stated that "in construing *venue statutes* it is reasonable to prefer the construction that avoids leaving such a gap." (emphasis added). Neither in that case nor in any other did we suggest that a venue gap should be avoided by adopting a narrow construction of either a jurisdictional grant or the scope of a federal cause of action. Yet that is the Court's perverse solution to the narrow venue gap in the FTCA.

Because a hypothetical handful of nonresident aliens may have no forum in which to seek relief for torts committed by federal agents in outer space or in Antarctica, the Court decides that the scope of the remedy itself should be narrowly construed. This anomalous conclusion surely derives no support whatsoever from the basic decision to include aliens as well as citizens within the protection of the statute, particularly since the overwhelming majority of aliens who may have occasion to invoke the FTCA are surely residents. As Judge Fletcher accurately observed in her dissenting opinion in the Court of Appeals:

> "Those who have no problem with venue should not be foreclosed from bringing suit simply because others cannot, particularly with respect to a statute such as the FTCA the primary purpose of which, as we have seen, was to expand the jurisdiction of the federal courts." 953 F.2d 1116, 1122 (C.A.9 1991).

At most, the imperfections in the statute indicate that in 1946 the 79th Congress did not specifically consider the likelihood of negligence actions arising in outer space or in a sovereignless territory such as Antarctica. In view of the fact that it did authorize actions against the United States arising out of negligence on the high seas, I am bewildered by the Court's speculation that if it had expressly considered the equally dangerous area at issue in this case, it would have distinguished between the two. The claim asserted in this case is entirely consistent with the central purpose of the entire Act. * * *

The wisdom that prompted the Court's grant of certiorari is not reflected in its interpretation of the 1946 Act. Rather, it reflects a vision that would exclude electronic eavesdropping from the coverage of the Fourth Amendment and satellites from the coverage of the Commerce Clause. The international community includes sovereignless places but no places where there is no rule of law. Majestic legislation like the Federal Tort Claims Act should be read with the vision of the judge, enlightened by an interest in justice, not through the opaque green eye-shade of the cloistered bookkeeper. As President Lincoln observed in his first State of the Union Message:

"It is as much the duty of Government to render prompt justice against itself, in favor of citizens, as it is to administer the same between private individuals."[17]

I respectfully dissent.

————

Notes and Questions

1. The *Smith v. United States* case presents another complex exercise in statutory interpretation. Outline the steps that the majority and dissent take to reach their competing conclusions about the application of the FTCA to alleged governmental negligence in Antarctica. Consider how each opinion marshals various provisions in the statute, including but beyond the "foreign country" exception of Section 2680(k), to support their contrasting constructions of the statute. Which do you find more persuasive? Can you describe the different attitudes or presumptions that each statutory interpretation approach reflects? Can the difference be explained by different attitudes toward the doctrine of sovereign immunity or how a waiver of sovereign immunity should be construed? If so, what is that difference in doctrinal approach?

2. In *Sosa v. Alvarez–Machain*, 542 U.S. 692 (2004), the Supreme Court unanimously, although somewhat divided on reasoning, agreed that the federal government's immunity from claims "arising in a foreign county" could not be overcome by alleging that an injury suffered overseas had been caused by tortious wrongdoing within the United States. The Court thereby rejected the so-called "headquarters doctrine" adopted by several courts of appeals, under which the federal government could be held liable for harms caused in other countries if the tortious activity could be connected to some planning or direction by government employees inside the United States. *Id.* at 700–12. Indeed, the Court found that the "potential effect of this sort of headquarters analysis flashes the yellow caution light," because nearly any negligence activity by a government employee causing injury in a foreign country could be "repackaged as headquarters claims based on a failure to train, a failure to warn, the offering of bad advice, or the adoption of a negligent policy." *Id.* at 702. Instead, because courts generally applied the *lex loci delicti* (place where the injury occurred) rule in choice of law analysis at the time that the FTCA was enacted, and because application of foreign substantive law was what Congress intended to avoid by the exception, Justice Souter for the majority concluded that Congress meant to exclude "all claims based on any injury suffered in a foreign country, regardless of where the tortious act or omission occurred." *Id.* at 704–12. Accordingly, the Court held that the plaintiffs' claim that his abduction in Mexico for criminal trial in the United States was barred under the FTCA foreign country exception, even

————

17. Cong. Globe, 37th Cong., 2d Sess., App. 2 (1861).

though the seizure in Mexico had been directed and planned by Drug Enforcement Administration employees in California. *Id.* at 697.

Justice Ginsburg, joined by Justice Breyer, agreed with the Court's result on the foreign-country exception, but would have eschewed reliance upon choice of law methodologies which she feared "risks giving undue prominence to a jurisdiction-selecting approach the vast majority of States have long abandoned." *Id.* at 751–52 (Ginsburg, J., concurring in part and concurring in the judgment). Indeed, she would read the words "arising in" to refer not to the place of injury but to the place where the act or omission occurred. *Id.* at 753–57. Nonetheless, Justice Ginsburg agreed that the "headquarters doctrine, which considers whether steps toward the commission of the tort occurred within the United States, risks swallowing up the foreign-country exception." *Id.* at 758. Justice Ginsburg would apply a "last significant act or omission" rule for the foreign-country exception, which "direct[s] attention to the place where the last significant act or omission occurred, rather than to a United States location where some authorization, support, or planning may have taken place." *Id.* at 759–60. Thus, Justice Ginsburg like the majority would "close the door to the headquarters doctrine," at least as applied in that case. *Id.* at 760.

---

8.   DAMAGES

28 United States Code § 2674

The United States shall be liable, respecting the provisions of this title relating to tort claims, in the same manner and to the same extent as a private individual under like circumstances, but shall not be liable for interest prior to judgment or for punitive damages.

If, however, in any case wherein death was caused, the law of the place where the act or omission complained of occurred provides, or has been construed to provide, for damages only punitive in nature, the United States shall be liable for actual or compensatory damages, measured by the pecuniary injuries resulting from such death to the persons respectively, for whose benefit the action was brought, in lieu thereof. * * *

Molzof v. United States

Supreme Court of the United States.
502 U.S. 301 (1992).

■ JUSTICE THOMAS delivered the opinion of the Court.

This case requires us to determine the scope of the statutory prohibition on awards of "punitive damages" in cases brought against the United States under the Federal Tort Claims Act, 28 U.S.C. §§ 2671–2680.

I

Petitioner Shirley Molzof is the personal representative of the estate of Robert Molzof, her late husband. On October 31, 1986, Mr. Molzof, a veteran, underwent lung surgery at a Veterans' Administration hospital in Madison, Wisconsin. After surgery, he was placed on a ventilator. For some undisclosed reason, the ventilator tube that was providing oxygen to him became disconnected. The ventilator's alarm system also was disconnected. As a result of this combination of events, Mr. Molzof was deprived of oxygen for approximately eight minutes before his predicament was discovered. Because of this unfortunate series of events, triggered by the hospital employees' conceded negligence, Mr. Molzof suffered irreversible brain damage, leaving him permanently comatose.

Mr. Molzof's guardian ad litem filed suit in District Court under the Federal Tort Claims Act (FTCA or Act) seeking damages for supplemental medical care, future medical expenses, and loss of enjoyment of life. Respondent (the Government) admitted liability, and the case proceeded to a bench trial on the issue of damages. The District Court determined that the free medical care being provided to Mr. Molzof by the veterans' hospital was reasonable and adequate, that Mrs. Molzof was satisfied with those services and had no intention of transferring Mr. Molzof to a private hospital, and that it was in Mr. Molzof's best interests to remain at the veterans' hospital because neighboring hospitals could not provide a comparable level of care. In addition to ordering the veterans' hospital to continue the same level of care, the court awarded Mr. Molzof damages for supplemental care—physical therapy, respiratory therapy, and weekly doctor's visits—not provided by the veterans' hospital.

The District Court refused, however, to award damages for medical care that would duplicate the free medical services already being provided by the veterans' hospital. Similarly, the court declined to award Mr. Molzof damages for loss of enjoyment of life. Mr. Molzof died after final judgment had been entered, and Mrs. Molzof was substituted as plaintiff in her capacity as personal representative of her late husband's estate.

The United States Court of Appeals for the Seventh Circuit affirmed the District Court's judgment. 911 F.2d 18 (1990). The Court of Appeals agreed with the District Court that, given the Government's provision of free medical care to Mr. Molzof and Mrs. Molzof's apparent satisfaction with that care, any award for future medical expenses would be punitive in effect and was therefore barred by the FTCA prohibition on "punitive damages." With respect to the claim for Mr. Molzof's loss of enjoyment of life, the Court of Appeals stated that Wisconsin law was unclear on the question whether a comatose plaintiff could recover such damages. The court decided, however, that "even if Wisconsin courts recognized the claim for loss of enjoyment of life, in this case it would be barred as punitive under the Federal Tort Claims Act," *ibid.*, because "an award of damages for loss of enjoyment of life can in no way recompense, reimburse or otherwise redress a comatose patient's uncognizable loss...." *Id.*, at 22.

We granted certiorari to consider the meaning of the term "punitive damages" as used in the FTCA.

II

Prior to 1946, the sovereign immunity of the United States prevented those injured by the negligent acts of federal employees from obtaining redress through lawsuits; compensation could be had only by passage of a private bill in Congress. See *Dalehite v. United States,* 346 U.S. 15, 24–25 (1953). The FTCA replaced that "notoriously clumsy," *id.,* at 25, system of compensation with a limited waiver of the United States' sovereign immunity. In this case, we must determine the scope of that waiver as it relates to awards of "punitive damages" against the United States. The FTCA provides in pertinent part as follows:

> "The United States shall be liable, respecting the provisions of this title relating to tort claims, in the same manner and to the same extent as a private individual under like circumstances, *but shall not be liable* for interest prior to judgment or *for punitive damages.*" 28 U.S.C. § 2674 (emphasis added).

As this provision makes clear, in conjunction with the jurisdictional grant over FTCA cases in 28 U.S.C. § 1346(b), the extent of the United States' liability under the FTCA is generally determined by reference to state law.

Nevertheless, the meaning of the term "punitive damages" as used in § 2674, a federal statute, is by definition a federal question. Petitioner argues that "§ 2674 must be interpreted so as to permit awards against the United States of those state-law damages which are intended by state law to act as compensation for injuries sustained as a result of the tort, and to preclude awards of damages which are intended to act as punishment for egregious conduct." We understand petitioner to be suggesting that the Court define the term "punitive damages" by reference to traditional common law, leaving plaintiffs free to recover any damages that cannot be characterized as "punitive" under that standard. The Government, on the other hand, suggests that we define "punitive damages" as "damages that are in excess of, or bear no relation to, compensation." In the Government's view, there is a strict dichotomy between compensatory and punitive damages; damages that are not strictly compensatory are necessarily "punitive damages" barred by the statute. Thus, the Government contends that any damages other than those awarded for a plaintiff's *actual* loss— which the Government narrowly construes to exclude damages that are excessive, duplicative, or for an inherently noncompensable loss—are "punitive damages" because they are punitive in *effect*.

We agree with petitioner's interpretation of the term "punitive damages," and conclude that the Government's reading of § 2674 is contrary to the statutory language. Section 2674 prohibits awards of "punitive damages," not "damage awards that may have a punitive effect." "Punitive damages" is a legal term of art that has a widely accepted common-law meaning; "[p]unitive damages have long been a part of traditional state tort law." *Silkwood v. Kerr–McGee Corp.,* 464 U.S. 238, 255 (1984).

Although the precise nature and use of punitive damages may have evolved over time, and the size and frequency of such awards may have increased, this Court's decisions make clear that the concept of "punitive damages" has a long pedigree in the law. "It is a well-established principle of the common law, that in actions of trespass and all actions on the case for torts, a jury may inflict what are called exemplary, punitive, or vindictive damages upon a defendant, having in view the enormity of his offense rather than the measure of compensation to the plaintiff." *Day v. Woodworth,* 13 How. 363, 371 (1851).

Legal dictionaries in existence when the FTCA was drafted and enacted indicate that "punitive damages" were commonly understood to be damages awarded to punish defendants for torts committed with fraud, actual malice, violence, or oppression. See, *e.g.,* Black's Law Dictionary 501 (3d ed. 1933); The Cyclopedic Law Dictionary 292 (3d ed. 1940). On more than one occasion, this Court has confirmed that general understanding. "By definition, punitive damages are based upon the degree of the defendant's culpability." *Massachusetts Bonding & Ins. Co. v. United States,* 352 U.S. 128, 133 (1956). The common law definition of "punitive damages" focuses on the nature of the defendant's conduct. As a general rule, the common law recognizes that damages intended to compensate the plaintiff are different in kind from "punitive damages."

> A cardinal rule of statutory construction holds that:
>
> "[W]here Congress borrows terms of art in which are accumulated the legal tradition and meaning of centuries of practice, it presumably knows and adopts the cluster of ideas that were attached to each borrowed word in the body of learning from which it was taken and the meaning its use will convey to the judicial mind unless otherwise instructed. In such case, absence of contrary direction may be taken as satisfaction with widely accepted definitions, not as a departure from them." *Morissette v. United States,* 342 U.S. 246, 263 (1952).

This rule carries particular force in interpreting the FTCA. "Certainly there is no warrant for assuming that Congress was unaware of established tort definitions when it enacted the Tort Claims Act in 1946, after spending some twenty-eight years of congressional drafting and redrafting, amendment and counter-amendment." *United States v. Neustadt,* 366 U.S. 696, 707 (1961).

The Government's interpretation of § 2674 appears to be premised on the assumption that the statute provides that the United States "shall be liable only for compensatory damages." But the first clause of § 2674, the provision we are interpreting, does not say that. What it clearly states is that the United States "shall not be liable ... for punitive damages." The difference is important. The statutory language suggests that to the extent a plaintiff may be entitled to damages that are not legally considered "punitive damages," but which are for some reason above and beyond ordinary notions of compensation, the United States is liable for them "in the same manner and to the same extent as a private individual." These damages in the "gray" zone are not by definition "punitive damages" barred under the Act. In the ordinary case in which an award of compensatory damages is subsequently reduced on appeal, one does not say that the jury or the lower court mistakenly awarded "punitive damages" above and beyond the actual compensatory damages. It is simply a matter of excessive or erroneous compensation. Excessiveness principles affect only the amount, and not the nature, of the damages that may be recovered. The term "punitive damages," on the other hand, embodies an element of the defendant's conduct that must be proved before such damages are awarded.

The Government argues that we must construe the prohibition on "punitive damages" *in pari materia* with the second clause of § 2674 which was added by Congress just one year after the FTCA was enacted. The amendment provides as follows:

> "If, however, in any case wherein death was caused, the law of the place where the act or omission complained of occurred provides, or has been construed to provide, for damages only punitive in nature, the United States shall be liable for actual or compensatory damages, measured by the pecuniary injuries resulting from such death to the persons respectively, for whose benefit the action was brought, in lieu thereof." 28 U.S.C. § 2674.

This provision was added to the statute to address the fact that two States, Alabama and Massachusetts, permitted only punitive damages in wrongful-death actions. The Government contends that the second clause of § 2674 "confirms the compensatory purpose of the statute and demonstrates that Congress intended to define 'punitive damages' by contrasting them with 'actual or compensatory damages.'" This argument is undermined, however, not only by the fact that "punitive damages" is a legal term of art with a well-established common law meaning, but also by the Government's own statement that, although the second clause defines "actual or compensatory damages" as "the pecuniary injuries resulting from such death," the "pecuniary injuries" standard does not apply in determining compensatory damages in any other kind of tort suit against the United States. Given this concession, which we agree to be a correct statement of the law, the second clause of § 2674 cannot be read as proving so much as the Government claims.

The Government's interpretation of "punitive damages" would be difficult and impractical to apply. Under the Government's reading, an argument could be made that Mr. Molzof's damages for future medical expenses would have to be reduced by the amount he saved on rent, meals, clothing, and other daily living expenses that he did not incur while hospitalized. Otherwise, these duplicative damages would be "punitive damages" because they have the effect of making the United States pay twice. The difficulties inherent in attempting to prove such offsets would be enormous. That the Government has refused to acknowledge the practical implications of its theory is evidenced by its representations at oral argument that, as a general matter, it is willing to accept state-law definitions of compensatory awards for purposes of the FTCA and that "there are very few circumstances" in which States have authorized damages awards that the Government would challenge as punitive.

The Government's reading of the statute also would create problems in liquidated damages cases and in other contexts in which certain kinds of injuries are compensated at fixed levels that may or may not correspond to a particular plaintiff's actual loss. At oral argument, however, the Government disclaimed that extension of its theory and instead asserted that its position was that state compensatory awards are recoverable under the Act so long as they are a "reasonable" approximation of the plaintiff's actual damages. We agree that § 2674 surely does not prohibit any compensatory award that departs from the actual damages in a particular case. But the Government's restrictive reading of the statute would involve the federal courts in the impractical business of determining the actual loss suffered in each case, and whether the damages awarded are a "reasonable" approximation of that loss. * * *

We conclude that § 2674 bars the recovery only of what are *legally* considered "punitive damages" under traditional common-law principles. This reading of the statute is consistent with the language of § 2674 and the structure of the Act, and it provides courts with a workable standard for determining when a plaintiff is improperly seeking "punitive damages" against the United States. Our interpretation of the term "punitive damages" requires us to reverse the Court of Appeals' decision that Mrs. Molzof is not permitted to recover damages for her husband's future medical expenses and his loss of enjoyment of life. It is undisputed that the claims in this case are based solely on a simple negligence theory of liability. Thus, the damages Mrs. Molzof seeks to recover are not punitive damages under the common law or the FTCA because their recoverability does not depend upon any proof that the defendant has engaged in intentional or egregious misconduct and their purpose is not to punish. We must remand, however, because we are in no position to evaluate the recoverability of those damages under Wisconsin law. It may be that under Wisconsin law the damages sought in this case are not recoverable as compensatory damages. This might be true because Wisconsin law does not recognize such damages, or because it requires a setoff when a defendant already has paid (or agreed to pay) expenses incurred by the plaintiff, or for some other reason. These questions were not resolved by the lower courts.

III

The judgment of the Court of Appeals is reversed, and the case is remanded for further proceedings consistent with this opinion.

It is so ordered.

———

Note

In *Molzof v. United States,* the Court considers the meaning of "punitive damages," which under Section 2674 may not be awarded against the

United States in FTCA actions. The reason for this limitation should be readily apparent. Given that punitive damages are commonly measured by reference to the net worth of the defendant in order to ensure that an award is sufficiently high to be severely felt as financial punishment, application of this theory against the United States would have obvious detrimental consequences for the public treasury. Moreover, unlike most scenarios in which punitive damages are imposed against a private defendant, an award of damages in an FTCA suit is not levied against the individual government agents responsible for the harm, or even the responsible agency, but in actuality is imposed against the United States as a whole and the taxpayers who fund it. Thus, the concept of punishment through an award of exemplary damages is inapposite in the federal government context.

----

9.   CLAIMANTS EXCLUDED FROM COVERAGE

As a general rule, anyone may bring an FTCA claim against the United States: aliens, executors of estates, infants represented by guardians, corporations, and state and local governments. *See generally* 1 Lester S. Jayson & Robert C. Longstreth, *Handling Federal Tort Claims* § 5.01, at 5–2 (2005) ("No person, natural or artificial, citizen or alien, is precluded as such from obtaining relief against the United States under the provisions of the Federal Tort Claims Act.").

Nonetheless, by operation of other statutes or by judicial implication, two key classes of people are excluded from seeking recovery under the FTCA. First, by express provision of 5 U.S.C. § 8116(c), a government employee within the scope of the Federal Employees Compensation Act (FECA)—a workers compensation program for federal employees—is exclusively limited to the remedy provided by that Act for personal injuries. Second, by judicial construction or implication, military service personnel are precluded from recovery under the FTCA for injuries incurred incident to service under the so-called *Feres* doctrine, which is discussed in the next subsection of this casebook.

----

a.   FEDERAL EMPLOYEES COMPENSATION ACT

Federal Employees Compensation Act, 5 United States Code § 8116(c)

(c) The liability of the United States or an instrumentality thereof under this subchapter [Federal Employees Compensation Act] or any extension thereof with respect to the injury or death of an employee is exclusive and instead of all other liability of the United States or the instrumentality to the employee, his legal representative, spouse, dependents, next of kin, and any other person otherwise entitled to recover damages from the United States or the instrumentality because of the injury or death in a direct judicial proceeding, in a civil action, or in admiralty, or by an administrative or judicial proceeding under a workmen's compensation statute or under a Federal tort liability statute. However, this subsection does not apply to a master or a member of a crew of a vessel.

Exception

Federal Employees Compensation Act, 5 United States Code § 8128(b)(1)–(2)

(b) The action of the Secretary of his designee in allowing or denying a payment under this subchapter is—

(1) final and conclusive for all purposes and with respect to all questions of law and fact; and

(2) not subject to review by another official of the United States or by a court by mandamus or otherwise.

United States v. Udy

United States Court of Appeals for the Tenth Circuit.
381 F.2d 455 (10th Cir. 1967).

■ DAVID T. LEWIS, CIRCUIT JUDGE.

The United States appeals from a judgment in the sum of $140,000 entered in the District of Utah in favor of appellees in an action considered by the court under the Federal Tort Claims Act, 28 U.S.C. § 1346(b). The plaintiff below, wife of a civilian employee of Hill Air Force Base, a large military installation located near Ogden, Utah, obtained such judgment on behalf of herself and children, as damages for the death of her husband who was killed in a motor vehicle accident occurring within the Base area. A single appellate question is presented: Did the district court err in refusing the request of the United States to stay or dismiss the suit so as to enable the United States Department of Labor to make an original determination of whether plaintiff's claim was covered by the Federal Employees' Compensation Act (FECA), 5 U.S.C. § 8101 et seq.

The question so presented is a recurring one within this circuit and the basic applicable principles of substantive and procedural law have been firmly established. The Federal Employees' Compensation Act constitutes the exclusive liability of the United States for the death of a federal employee sustained in the performance of his duty, and the actions of the Secretary in administering the Act are not reviewable and are final and conclusive for all purposes. 5 U.S.C. § 8102(a); 5 U.S.C. § 8116(c); 5 U.S.C. § 8128(b)(1)(2). Applicability of the FECA would thus be a complete bar to plaintiff's action herein. It is also fundamental that the provisions of the

FECA should be liberally construed to effectuate the humane purposes of the legislation in accord with judicial principles many times set forth in regard to other but comparable compensation acts. But the mere fact that an injury occurs upon government owned or controlled property does in no way impair the jurisdiction of the court under the Federal Tort Claims Act where it is clear that no proper administrative determination is interwoven with the tort claim. Thus, in United States v. Martinez, 10 Cir., 334 F.2d 728, this court held that the district court was free to adjudicate a tort claim arising from an injury occurring upon government property to a claimant not an employee of the United States. Our decision necessarily holds that the administrative remedy of the FECA is not applicable when the [status] of the injured party is not that of an "employee," a term used and a status necessary within the meaning and bounds of the FECA. So, too, this court has held that an employee injured while on government property is not, as a matter of law, unequivocally entitled to compensation and thus exclusively and automatically within the shelter of the FECA. United States v. Browning, 10 Cir., 359 F.2d 937. However, both in *Martinez* and *Browning* we recognized the persuasiveness of the holdings in Somma v. United States, 3 Cir., 283 F.2d 149, and Daniels–Lumley v. United States, 113 U.S.App.D.C. 162, 306 F.2d 769, to the effect that, upon request of the government, the district court should not proceed with the tort claim where a substantial question exists as to whether the claimant is covered under the FECA. In the case at bar, the parties presented their causes to the trial court in accord with these applicable principles and the trial court, and properly so, rendered judgment only after determination that there was no substantial question of coverage under the FECA and a finding that the decedent was not killed in the performance of his duties. In their appellate contentions the parties continue to agree to the stated legal principles and the government urges only that the court erred in determining that no substantial question of coverage under the FECA existed under the factual circumstances leading to Mr. Udy's death. We turn our consideration to this question.

Hill Air Force Base is a complex government facility of 6,664 acres containing 120.27 miles of roadway, Wherry Housing accommodations for 875 families, and many recreational facilities including a golf course, swimming pools and a theater. Parts of the Base are open to the public, many facilities are available only to employees, military personnel, guests and visitors and other parts are subject to restriction and varying security regulations of the Air Force. Verl N. Udy was employed at Hill Air Force Base as a civilian electrical-parts repairman and lived with his family off-Base. All duties of his employment were performed at a work bench in a building located within the restricted area of the Base. In order to get to and from work each day, Mr. Udy participated in a car pool with four fellow employees. Each day they would park the car being used in a public parking lot outside the restricted area and proceed to their respective work sites on the Base proper. On the day of the accident, Mr. Udy was the carpool driver. After finishing work, he passed out through the security fence and went to his car in the parking lot. Normally, he and the other car-pool members were not permitted to re-enter the restricted area of the Base and would drive home via the public access road and Utah State Highway 89. On this day and for several months prior thereto, however, portions of Highway 89 were under construction and the Air Force, for the convenience of its employees, was permitting them to drive into the restricted area and leave by an alternate route along the inside perimeter of the Base which would avoid the congestion in the areas of highway construction. There was no requirement that employees use this alternate route and the car pool had in fact come to work that morning by way of their regular route on Highway 89. For the trip home, however, Udy elected to take the alternate route through the Base. He displayed his security pass to the guard at the gate and proceeded into the restricted area along Perimeter Road. As he passed the area of the Base golf course about three miles from his employment site into the restricted area, Udy's car was struck by a trailer that had come loose from an oncoming government oil tank truck. Udy was killed in the collision and at least one of his passengers was severely injured.

Although presented with considerable elaboration, the legal argument of the government arises no higher than the simple summary that a substantial question of whether a person injured or killed "while in the performance of his duty" of employment as that term is contained in the FECA is presented in all instances whenever an employee is on the premises of his governmental employment. Reliance on the so-called "premises rule" when the employee was going to or from work would indeed have presumptive merit if consideration could be divorced from all other special circumstances surrounding the case. But the totality of circumstances must determine the right to compensation and, as we stated in *Browning,* the premises rule "must be treated as but one of a number of factors to be taken into consideration in reaching a decision as to whether or not the injury is compensable." 359 F.2d at 940. And the totality of circumstances must be similarly considered in reaching a decision as to whether or not there is even a substantial compensation question.

The occasion of Mr. Udy's death was remote in time, space and activity from the duties of his employment. He had checked out from his employment site, traveled three miles from that location, and was killed in an incident having no possible relationship to the usual and direct hazards of his employment as an electrical-parts repairman. He was driving his own car for his own purposes and the inherent risks of travel by automobile were not the risks incidental to his employment. His presence at the particular place of the fatal collision on the Base area was not dictated by his employment but by pure chance. The extraneous fact of state highway construction had apparently influenced him to forego his usual route home by way of public highway. Thus, contrary to the government's suggestion, it is quite clear that the "obligations or conditions" of employment had nothing to do with creating the "zone of special danger" out of which Mr. Udy's death arose. So, too, consideration must be given to the fact that Mr. Udy had *returned* to the restricted area with the permission of the government after having walked out through the security fence and into a public area. Because he was privileged to return for his own personal convenience and benefit and not for any duties of employment, Mr. Udy's status upon returning could well be characterized as that of a guest rather than an employee. Although the government characterizes his return as that to the "premises" we think it more accurate to term his return as one to the "property" of the government. "Premises," as generally construed under compensation acts, does not encompass all property of the employer but only that portion used in connection with the actual place of employment.

As indirect support for its position that there is a substantial question of Compensation Act coverage, the government places argumentative emphasis on the fact that "the premises rule is relatively easy to be applied by the administrative agencies responsible for administering the workmen's compensation laws, since it provides a tangible cutoff point between employment and non-employment associated risks." Sufficient it is to say, however, that ease of administration does not make an administrative determination any the less arbitrary when it otherwise had no substantial evidence to support it. And certain it is that the purpose of the FECA can never be well served by any strained interpretation that leads to the defeat of the equally important provisions of the Tort Claims Act.

We agree with the trial court's conclusion that there is no substantial question as to whether Mr. Udy's death occurred in the performance of his duties of employment and since liability under the Tort Claims Act is not otherwise questioned in any way the judgment is

Affirmed.

Cobia v. United States

United States Court of Appeals for the Tenth Circuit.
384 F.2d 711 (10th Cir. 1967), *cert. denied*, 390 U.S. 986 (1968).

■ Hickey, Circuit Judge.

Charles and Evelyn Cobia, husband and wife, appeal from a judgment in which the United States was given a non-suit in a Federal Tort Claims action. Recovery is sought under 28 U.S.C. §§ 1346(b), 2671 et seq. for injuries sustained by appellant Charles Cobia in a motor vehicle collision at Hill Air Force Base in which the United States confessed negligence as the proximate cause of the collision. Mr. Cobia made application for and continues to receive compensation for injuries under the Federal Employees Compensation Act, 5 U.S.C. § 8101 et seq.

The court found that application for and the continued acceptance of compensation under the FECA foreclosed the appellants from recovering under the Federal Tort Claims Act. We agree.

Appellants argue that United States v. Udy, 381 F.2d 455 (10th Cir.1967) determined that the collision out of which this claim arose was actionable under the Federal Tort Claims Act. It is true the claims grew out of the same collision and this court determined the remedy under the Federal Tort Claims Act was available to Udy; however, Udy did not elect to proceed under the FECA and proceeded only under the Tort Claims Act, thereby giving the court an opportunity to exercise its judgment regarding the remedy.

When application is made for FECA benefits, the determination of coverage is made by the Secretary of Labor or his designee and his finding is final and not subject to judicial review. 5 U.S.C. §§ 8145, 8128(b). Acceptance of benefits under the FECA is an injured employee's exclusive remedy. 5 U.S.C. § 8116(c). Therefore, we affirm the trial court's determination that the appellants have no claim under the Federal Tort Claims Act because they have exercised a choice of procedure which denies review by the courts.

Affirmed.

Lesson - File both FTCA / Admin Claim + FECA
— and hope there is no "yes" on FECA

Notes and Questions

1.   The Federal Employees Compensation Act (FECA), like workers compensation statutes in the various states, provides a generally certain payment of benefits for injuries suffered by a federal employee on the job without any showing of fault by the employer, in exchange for withdrawal of the ability to bring a tort suit against an employer for that injury. As the Supreme Court explained in *Lockheed Aircraft Corp. v. United States,* 400 U.S. 190, 193–94 (1983), the "FECA exclusive-liability provision" embodies "the principal compromise—the 'quid pro quo'—commonly found in workers' compensation legislation: employees are guaranteed the right to receive immediate, fixed benefits, regardless of fault and without need for legislation, but in return they lose the right to sue the Government."

2.   The Federal Tort Claims Act itself contains no limitation on suits being brought by federal employees. The exclusion instead is found in Section 8116(c) of FECA which provides that the liability of the United States under FECA "with respect to the injury or death of an employee is exclusive." When a physical injury falls within the coverage of FECA, its remedies are exclusive even though it may provide a smaller recovery than or fail to compensate for certain types of harm, such as pain and suffering or emotional distress, that might be obtained in a tort action. *See Saltsman v. United States,* 104 F.3d 787, 789–91 (6th Cir. 1997) (holding that FECA remedies were exclusive and therefore affirming dismissal of FTCA suit even though plaintiffs sought damages for pain and suffering and emotional distress that are not compensable under FECA).

FECA excludes FTCA recovery even if FECA provides less $

3.   FECA further provides that the determination of the Secretary of Labor with respect to FECA benefits is "final and conclusive" and is "not subject to review * * * by a court by mandamus or otherwise." 5 U.S.C. § 8128(b). Thus, the courts are ousted from reviewing a claim for FECA benefits or determining the scope of FECA.

In *Tarver v. United States,* 25 F.3d 900 (10th Cir. 1994), the court explained that "[t]wo questions are presented when the issue of FECA applicability arises." *Id.* at 903. The first, or jurisdictional, question, is whether FECA covers that particular type of injury, that is, the scope of FECA coverage. The second question is whether the employee is entitled to compensation under the particular facts of the case. "If the Secretary determines the employee was injured in the performance of duty, the Secretary's decision is binding on the court, regardless of whether compensation is actually awarded, and the [FTCA] action must be dismissed." *Id.*

What then should a court do when a government employee has filed an FTCA suit and the government contends that the suit is barred by the exclusive remedy provided under FECA? In other words, how much authority does a court have to go forward when there is some possibility of FECA coverage, which would then require dismissal of the FTCA suit? Since FECA determinations are within the exclusive authority of the Secretary of Labor to make, how can the court even decide whether the FTCA suit may be continued without intruding upon the prerogatives of the Secretary? Is there a procedural approach by which the court can navigate its way between these shoals, without either dismissing every FTCA suit whenever there is even the remotest possibility that the matter is within the scope of FECA *or* steaming ahead heedless to the Secretary's unreviewable jurisdiction to determine FECA matters? Is there a middle way that both preserves the court's need to decide whether it can proceed and maintains deference to the Secretary?

How do the decisions in *United States v. Udy* and *Cobia v. United States* suggest this dilemma should be resolved? There is certainly an inconsistency in result between *Udy* and *Cobia.* Where does this inconsistency come from? From the procedure followed by the court in *Udy*? Or from the conclusion that there was no substantial question of FECA coverage in *Udy*? *See also White v. United States,* 143 F.3d 232 (5th Cir. 1998) (holding that a substantial question of FECA coverage existed in the case of a civilian employee who was struck and injured by a government vehicle when he was driving home from work on a street within the military base where he worked, thus requiring the court to stay proceedings pending the Secretary's determination on the issue).

4. In light of the above, consider also how you would counsel a client who wished to pursue a tort claim against the United States but who might be covered by FECA. How would you advise that he or she proceed? Typically, the district court will stay an FTCA suit until FECA coverage has been determined by the Secretary. *See, e.g., Greathouse v. United States,* 961 F.Supp. 173, 175–76 (W.D.Ky.1997); *Daniels v. United States,* 916 F.Supp. 1125, 1126–27 (D.Kan.1996). If FECA coverage is found by the Secretary, the FTCA suit must be dismissed. If FECA coverage is denied, the FTCA suit may go forward. 1 Jayson & Longstreth, *supra,* § 5.05[2][g]. *See generally Noble v. United States,* 216 F.3d 1229, 1235 (11th Cir. 2000) (holding that when "a federal employee brings an action against the United States and there is a substantial question as to whether FECA provides the

employee's exclusive remedy for the alleged injury, the district court must do what the district court did in the instant case: hold the action in abeyance pending a coverage determination by the Secretary;" "[i]f the Secretary finds no FECA coverage of the alleged injury, the plaintiff is then free to proceed under the FTCA," but "[i]f the Secretary determines the injury falls within FECA's coverage, the federal courts generally lack jurisdiction to review the Secretary's decision to award or deny compensation for the injury"). Consider what risks would be entailed if you determined to proceed with the FTCA suit and allowed the time limitation (three years under 5 U.S.C. § 8122(a)) for filing a FECA benefit claim to pass? Could your client end up with neither remedy? Should he or she? What if, after the time period for filing a FECA claim has passed, a party files an FTCA suit and the district court concludes that there is a "substantial question" of FECA coverage (even if the court thinks the stronger argument is against coverage)? How should the court respond?

5.   For further discussion of the exclusion of federal civilian employees injured on the job from the FTCA and the exclusivity of FECA, see generally Gregory C. Sisk, *Litigation With the Federal Government* § 3.08(b), at 170–77 (ALI–ABA, 4th ed. 2006).

---

b.   THE FERES DOCTRINE

. △ were in military

Feres v. United States

Supreme Court of the United States.
340 U.S. 135 (1950).

■ Mr. Justice Jackson, delivered the opinion of the Court.

A common issue arising under the Tort Claims Act, as to which Courts of Appeals are in conflict, makes it appropriate to consider three cases in one opinion.

The *Feres* case: The District Court dismissed an action by the executrix of Feres against the United States to recover for death caused by negligence. Decedent perished by fire in the barracks at Pine Camp, New York, while on active duty in service of the United States. Negligence was alleged in quartering him in barracks known or which should have been known to be unsafe because of a defective heating plant, and in failing to maintain an adequate fire watch. The Court of Appeals, Second Circuit, affirmed.[1]

neg. case dismissed; 2nd Cir. aff'd.

The *Jefferson* case: Plaintiff, while in the Army, was required to undergo an abdominal operation. About eight months later, in the course of another operation after plaintiff was discharged, a towel 30 inches long by 18 inches wide, marked "Medical Department U.S. Army," was discovered and removed from his stomach. The complaint alleged that it was negli-

---

1.   177 F.2d 535.

gently left there by the army surgeon. The District Court, being doubtful of the law, refused without prejudice the Government's pretrial motion to dismiss the complaint.[2] After trial, finding negligence as a fact, Judge Chesnut carefully reexamined the issue of law and concluded that the Act does not charge the United States with liability in this type of case.[3] The Court of Appeals, Fourth Circuit, affirmed.[4]

The *Griggs* case: The District Court dismissed the complaint of Griggs' executrix, which alleged that while on active duty he met death because of negligent and unskillful medical treatment by army surgeons. The Court of Appeals, Tenth Circuit, reversed and, one judge dissenting, held that the complaint stated a cause of action under the Act.[5]

The common fact underlying the three cases is that each claimant, while on active duty and not on furlough, sustained injury due to negligence of others in the armed forces. The only issue of law raised is whether the Tort Claims Act extends its remedy to one sustaining "incident to the service" what under other circumstances would be an actionable wrong. * * *

There are few guiding materials for our task of statutory construction. No committee reports or floor debates disclose what effect the statute was designed to have on the problem before us, or that it even was in mind. Under these circumstances, no conclusion can be above challenge, but if we misinterpret the Act, at least Congress possesses a ready remedy.

We do not overlook considerations persuasive of liability in these cases. The Act does confer district court jurisdiction generally over claims for money damages against the United States founded on negligence. 28 U.S.C. § 1346(b). It does contemplate that the Government will sometimes respond for negligence of military personnel, for it defines "employee of the Government" to include "members of the military or naval forces of the United States," and provides that "acting within the scope of his office or employment" in the case of a member of the military or naval forces of the United States, means "acting in line of duty." 28 U.S.C. § 2671. Its exceptions might also imply inclusion of claims such as we have here. 28 U.S.C. § 2680(j) excepts "any claim arising out of the *combatant* activities of the military or naval forces, or the Coast Guard, *during time of war*" (emphasis supplied), from which it is said we should infer allowance of claims arising from non-combat activities in peace. Section 2680(k) excludes "any claim arising in a foreign country." Significance also has been attributed * * * to the fact that eighteen tort claims bills were introduced in Congress between 1925 and 1935 and all but two expressly denied recovery to members of the armed forces; but the bill enacted as the present Tort Claims Act from its introduction made no exception. * * * These considerations, it is said, should persuade us to cast upon Congress, as author of the confusion, the task of qualifying and clarifying its language

2. 74 F.Supp. 209.

3. D.C., 77 F.Supp. 706.

4. 178 F.2d 518.

5. 178 F.2d 1.

if the liability here asserted should prove so depleting of the public treasury as the Government fears.

This Act, however, should be construed to fit, so far as will comport with its words, into the entire statutory system of remedies against the Government to make a workable, consistent and equitable whole. The Tort Claims Act was not an isolated and spontaneous flash of congressional generosity. It marks the culmination of a long effort to mitigate unjust consequences of sovereign immunity from suit. While the political theory that the King could do no wrong was repudiated in America, a legal doctrine derived from it that the Crown is immune from any suit to which it has not consented was invoked on behalf of the Republic and applied by our courts as vigorously as it had been on behalf of the Crown. As the Federal Government expanded its activities, its agents caused a multiplying number of remediless wrongs—wrongs which would have been actionable if inflicted by an individual or a corporation but remediless solely because their perpetrator was an officer or employee of the Government. Relief was often sought and sometimes granted through private bills in Congress, the number of which steadily increased as Government activity increased. The volume of these private bills, the inadequacy of congressional machinery for determination of facts, the importunities to which claimants subjected members of Congress, and the capricious results, led to a strong demand that claims for tort wrongs be submitted to adjudication. Congress already had waived immunity and made the Government answerable for breaches of its contracts and certain other types of claims.[8] At last, in connection with the Reorganization Act, it waived immunity and transferred the burden of examining tort claims to the courts. The primary purpose of the Act was to extend a remedy to those who had been without; if it incidentally benefited those already well provided for, it appears to have been unintentional. Congress was suffering from no plague of private bills on the behalf of military and naval personnel, because a comprehensive system of relief had been authorized for them and their dependents by statute.

Looking to the detail of the Act, it is true that it provides, broadly, that the District Court "shall have exclusive jurisdiction of civil actions on claims against the United States, for money damages...."[9] This confers jurisdiction to render judgment upon all such claims. But it does not say that all claims must be allowed. Jurisdiction is necessary to deny a claim on its merits as matter of law as much as to adjudge that liability exists. We interpret this language to mean all it says, but no more. Jurisdiction of the defendant now exists where the defendant was immune from suit before; it remains for courts, in exercise of their jurisdiction, to determine whether any claim is recognizable in law.

For this purpose, the Act goes on to prescribe the test of allowable claims, which is, "The United States shall be liable ... in the same manner and to the same extent as a private individual under like circumstances ...," with certain exceptions not material here. 28 U.S.C. § 2674. It will be

8. 28 U.S.C. § 1491.   9. 28 U.S.C. § 1346(b). * * *

Not even doing an analogy

Is there analogous private liability?

Ct: No analogy

seen that this is not the creation of new causes of action but acceptance of liability under circumstances that would bring private liability into existence. * * * One obvious shortcoming in these claims is that plaintiffs can point to no liability of a "private individual" even remotely analogous to that which they are asserting against the United States. We know of no American law which ever has permitted a soldier to recover for negligence, against either his superior officers or the Government he is serving. Nor is there any liability "under like circumstances," for no private individual has power to conscript or mobilize a private army with such authorities over persons as the Government vests in echelons of command. The nearest parallel, even if we were to treat "private individual" as including a state,

what about soldiers in state militia?

would be the relationship between the states and their militia. But if we indulge plaintiffs the benefit of this comparison, claimants cite us no state, and we know of none, which has permitted members of its militia to maintain tort actions for injuries suffered in the service, and in at least one state the contrary has been held to be the case. It is true that if we consider relevant only a part of the circumstances and ignore the status of both the wronged and the wrongdoer in these cases we find analogous private liability. In the usual civilian doctor and patient relationship, there is of course a liability for malpractice. And a landlord would undoubtedly be held liable if an injury occurred to a tenant as the result of a negligently maintained heating plant. But the liability assumed by the Government here is that created by "all the circumstances," not that which a few of the circumstances might create. We find no parallel liability before, and we think no new one has been created by, this Act. Its effect is to waive immunity from recognized causes of action and was not to visit the Government with novel and unprecedented liabilities.

It is not without significance as to whether the Act should be construed to apply to service-connected injuries that it makes "... the law of the place where the act or omission occurred" govern any consequent liability. 28 U.S.C. § 1346(b). This provision recognizes and assimilates into federal law the rules of substantive law of the several states, among which divergencies are notorious. This perhaps is fair enough when the claimant is not on duty or is free to choose his own habitat and thereby limit the jurisdiction in which it will be possible for federal activities to cause him injury. That his tort claims should be governed by the law of the location where he has elected to be is just as fair when the defendant is the Government as when the defendant is a private individual. But a soldier on active duty has no such choice and must serve any place or, under modern conditions, any number of places in quick succession in the forty-eight states, the Canal Zone, or Alaska, or Hawaii, or any other territory of the

(But that's what Congress wanted)

United States. That the geography of an injury should select the law to be applied to his tort claims makes no sense. We cannot ignore the fact that most states have abolished the common-law action for damages between employer and employee and superseded it with workman's compensation statutes which provide, in most instances, the sole basis of liability. Absent this, or where such statutes are inapplicable, states have differing provisions as to limitations of liability and different doctrines as to assumption of risk, fellowservant rules and contributory or comparative negligence. It would hardly be a rational plan of providing for those disabled in service by others in service to leave them dependent upon geographic considerations over which they have no control and to laws which fluctuate in existence and value.

The relationship between the Government and members of its armed forces is "distinctively federal in character", as this Court recognized in *United States v. Standard Oil Co.*, 332 U.S. 301, wherein the Government unsuccessfully sought to recover for losses incurred by virtue of injuries to a soldier. The considerations which lead to that decision apply with even greater force to this case:

> " * * * To whatever extent state law may apply to govern the relations between soldiers or others in the armed forces and persons outside them or nonfederal governmental agencies, the scope, nature, legal incidents and consequence of the relation between persons in service and the Government are fundamentally derived from federal sources and governed by federal authority. * * *

This Court, in deciding claims for wrongs incident to service under the Tort Claims Act, cannot escape attributing some bearing upon it to enactments by Congress which provide systems of simple, certain, and uniform compensation for injuries or death of those in armed services. We might say that the claimant may (a) enjoy both types of recovery, or (b) elect which to pursue, thereby waiving the other, or (c) pursue both, crediting the larger liability with the proceeds of the smaller, or (d) that the compensation and pension remedy excludes the tort remedy. There is as much statutory authority for one as for another of these conclusions. If Congress had contemplated that this Tort Act would be held to apply in cases of this kind, it is difficult to see why it should have omitted any provision to adjust these two types of remedy to each other. The absence of any such adjustment is persuasive that there was no awareness that the Act might be interpreted to permit recovery for injuries incident to military service.

Congress has already passed statutes for soldier recovery & compensation

If it wanted the PTCA to be a part of these, it would have said so

A soldier is at peculiar disadvantage in litigation. Lack of time and money, the difficulty if not impossibility of procuring witnesses, are only a few of the factors working to his disadvantage. And the few cases charging superior officers or the Government with neglect or misconduct which have been brought since the Tort Claims Act, of which the present are typical, have either been suits by widows or surviving dependents, or have been brought after the individual was discharged. The compensation system, which normally requires no litigation, is not negligible or niggardly * * *. The recoveries compare extremely favorably with those provided by most workman's compensation statutes. * * *

The current compensation system is adequate

It is contended that all these considerations were before the Court in [*Brooks v. United States*, 337 U.S. 49,] and that allowance of recovery to Brooks requires a similar holding of liability here. The actual holding in the *Brooks* case can support liability here only by ignoring the vital distinction there stated. The injury to Brooks did not arise out of or in the course of military duty. Brooks was on furlough, driving along the highway, under

π: Brooks allows recovery

[handwritten margin note: CA: Brooks distinguished:
· JT was not in line of duty
· Gov't vehicle hit him
" JT wasn't acting as a soldier"]

compulsion of no orders or duty and on no military mission. A Government owned and operated vehicle collided with him. Brooks' father, riding in the same car, recovered for his injuries and the Government did not further contest the judgment but contended that there could be no liability to the sons, solely because they were in the Army. This Court rejected the contention, primarily because Brooks' relationship while on leave was not analogous to that of a soldier injured while performing duties under orders.

[handwritten margin note: The JT's senior, or the ∆'s (offi cers' soldiers') service]

We conclude that the Government is not liable under the Federal Tort Claims Act for injuries to servicemen where the injuries arise out of or are in the course of activity incident to service. Without exception, the relationship of military personnel to the Government has been governed exclusively by federal law. We do not think that Congress, in drafting this Act, created a new cause of action dependent on local law for service-connected injuries or death due to negligence. We cannot impute to Congress such a radical departure from established law in the absence of express congressional command. Accordingly, the judgments in the *Feres* and *Jefferson* cases are affirmed and that in the *Griggs* case is reversed. * * *

◼ MR. JUSTICE DOUGLAS concurs in the result.

————

Notes and Questions

1.   The Court in *Feres v. United States* begins its legal analysis with the candid admission that there are strong arguments in favor of liability, despite its ultimate conclusion that these claims by military personnel should be excluded from the FTCA. Outline the arguments "pro" and "con". How persuasive do you find the rationales for allowing FTCA liability here versus those for denying liability? Ask the question again after reading the next case, *United States v. Johnson*.

2.   At the end of its opinion in *Feres*, the Court distinguishes its earlier decision in *Brooks v. United States,* 337 U.S. 49 (1949), which also involved an FTCA suit by a serviceman, but in which recovery was allowed. Within the distinction between *Brooks* and *Feres* lies the essence of what has come to be known as the *Feres* doctrine. In one sentence, you should now be able to state the *Feres* doctrine.

————

United States v. Johnson

Supreme Court of the United States.
481 U.S. 681 (1987).

◼ JUSTICE POWELL delivered the opinion of the Court.

This case presents the question whether the doctrine established in *Feres v. United States,* 340 U.S. 135 (1950), bars an action under the Federal Tort Claims Act on behalf of a service member killed during the course of an activity incident to service, where the complaint alleges negligence on the part of civilian employees of the Federal Government.

I

Lieutenant Commander Horton Winfield Johnson was a helicopter pilot for the United States Coast Guard, stationed in Hawaii. In the early morning of January 7, 1982, Johnson's Coast Guard station received a distress call from a boat lost in the area. Johnson and a crew of several other Coast Guard members were dispatched to search for the vessel. Inclement weather decreased the visibility, and so Johnson requested radar assistance from the Federal Aviation Administration (FAA), a civilian agency of the Federal Government. The FAA controllers assumed positive radar control over the helicopter. Shortly thereafter, the helicopter crashed into the side of a mountain on the island of Molokai. All the crew members, including Johnson, were killed in the crash.

Respondent, Johnson's wife, applied for and received compensation for her husband's death pursuant to the Veterans' Benefits Act, 38 U.S.C. § 301 et seq.[1] In addition, she filed suit in the United States District Court for the Southern District of Florida under the Federal Tort Claims Act (FTCA), 28 U.S.C. §§ 1346, 2671–2680. Her complaint sought damages from the United States on the ground that the FAA flight controllers negligently caused her husband's death. The Government filed a motion to dismiss, asserting that because Johnson was killed during the course of his military duties, respondent could not recover damages from the United States. The District Court agreed and dismissed the complaint, relying exclusively on this Court's decision in *Feres.*

The Court of Appeals for the Eleventh Circuit reversed. 749 F.2d 1530 (C.A.11 1985). It noted the language of *Feres* that precludes suits by service members against the Government for injuries that "arise out of or are in the course of activity incident to service." 340 U.S., at 146. The court found, however, that the evolution of the doctrine since the *Feres* decision warranted a qualification of the original holding according to the status of the alleged tortfeasor. The court identified what it termed "the typical *Feres* factual paradigm" that exists when a service member alleges negligence on the part of another member of the military. 749 F.2d, at 1537. "[W]hen the *Feres* factual paradigm is present, the issue is whether the injury arose out of or during the course of an activity incident to service." *Ibid.* But when negligence is alleged on the part of a Federal Government employee who is not a member of the military, the court found that the propriety of a suit should be determined by examining the rationales that underlie the *Feres* doctrine. Although it noted that this Court has articulat-

---

1. Respondent has received $35,690.66 in life insurance and a $3,000 death gratuity, and receives approximately $868 per month in dependency and compensatory benefits. The dependency and compensatory benefits normally are payable for the life of the surviving spouse and include an extra monthly sum for any surviving child of the veteran below age 18. See 38 U.S.C. §§ 410, 411; 38 CFR § 3.461.

ed numerous rationales for the doctrine, it found the effect of a suit on military discipline to be the doctrine's primary justification.

Applying its new analysis to the facts of this case, the court found "absolutely no hint ... that the conduct of any alleged tortfeasor even remotely connected to the military will be scrutinized if this case proceeds to trial." 749 F.2d, at 1539. Accordingly, it found that *Feres* did not bar respondent's suit. * * *

The Court of Appeals granted the Government's suggestion for rehearing en banc. The en banc court found that this Court's recent decision in *United States v. Shearer*, 473 U.S. 52 (1985), "reinforc[ed] the analysis set forth in the panel opinion," 779 F.2d 1492, 1493 (C.A.11 1986) (*per curiam*), particularly the "[s]pecial emphasis ... upon military discipline and whether or not the claim being considered would require civilian courts to second-guess military decisions," *id.*, at 1493–1494. It concluded that the panel properly had evaluated the claim under *Feres* and therefore reinstated the panel opinion. Judge Johnson, joined by three other judges, strongly dissented. The dissent rejected the "*Feres* factual paradigm" as identified by the court, finding that because "Johnson's injury was undoubtedly sustained incident to service, ... under current law our decision ought to be a relatively straightforward affirmance." *Id.*, at 1494.

We granted certiorari to review the Court of Appeals' reformulation of the *Feres* doctrine and to resolve the conflict among the Circuits on the issue. We now reverse.

II

In *Feres,* this Court held that service members cannot bring tort suits against the Government for injuries that "arise out of or are in the course of activity incident to service." 340 U.S., at 146. This Court has never deviated from this characterization of the *Feres* bar. Nor has Congress changed this standard in the close to 40 years since it was articulated, even though, as the Court noted in *Feres,* Congress "possesses a ready remedy" to alter a misinterpretation of its intent. *Id.*, at 138. Although all of the cases decided by this Court under *Feres* have involved allegations of negligence on the part of members of the military, this Court has never suggested that the military status of the alleged tortfeasor is crucial to the application of the doctrine. Instead, the *Feres* doctrine has been applied consistently to bar all suits on behalf of service members against the Government based upon service-related injuries. We decline to modify the doctrine at this late date.

A

This Court has emphasized three broad rationales underlying the *Feres* decision. See *Stencel Aero Engineering Corp. v. United States,* 431 U.S. 666, 671–673 (1977), and n. 2, *supra*. An examination of these reasons for the doctrine demonstrates that the status of the alleged tortfeasor does not have the critical significance ascribed to it by the Court of Appeals in this case. First, "[t]he relationship between the Government and members of its armed forces is distinctively federal in character." *Feres,* 340 U.S., at 143. This federal relationship is implicated to the greatest degree when a service member is performing activities incident to his federal service. Performance of the military function in diverse parts of the country and the world entails a "[s]ignificant risk of accidents and injuries." *Stencel Aero Engineering Corp. v. United States, supra,* at 672. Where a service member is injured incident to service—that is, because of his military relationship with the Government—it "makes no sense to permit the fortuity of the situs of the alleged negligence to affect the liability of the Government to [the] serviceman." 431 U.S., at 672. Instead, application of the underlying federal remedy that provides "simple, certain, and uniform compensation for injuries or death of those in armed services," *Feres, supra,* at 144, is appropriate.

worldwide scope req
1
Fed remedy

Second, the existence of these generous statutory disability and death benefits is an independent reason why the *Feres* doctrine bars suit for service-related injuries. In *Feres,* the Court observed that the primary purpose of the FTCA "was to extend a remedy to those who had been without; if it incidentally benefited those already well provided for, it appears to have been unintentional." 340 U.S., at 140. Those injured during the course of activity incident to service not only receive benefits that "compare extremely favorably with those provided by most workmen's compensation statutes," *id.,* at 145, but the recovery of benefits is "swift [and] efficient," *Stencel Aero Engineering Corp. v. United States, supra,* at 673, "normally requir[ing] no litigation," *Feres, supra,* at 145. The Court in *Feres* found it difficult to believe that Congress would have provided such a comprehensive system of benefits while at the same time contemplating recovery for service-related injuries under the FTCA. Particularly persuasive was the fact that Congress "omitted any provision to adjust these two types of remedy to each other." 340 U.S., at 144. Congress still has not amended the Veterans' Benefits Act or the FTCA to make any such provision for injuries incurred during the course of activity incident to service. We thus find no reason to modify what the Court has previously found to be the law: the statutory veterans' benefits "provid[e] an upper limit of liability for the Government as to service-connected injuries." *Stencel Aero Engineering Corp. v. United States, supra,* at 673.

Purp. of FTCA is to prov a rem;
mil disabil[t] already prvd

Third, *Feres* and its progeny indicate that suits brought by service members against the Government for injuries incurred incident to service are barred by the *Feres* doctrine because they are the "*type[s]* of claims that, if generally permitted, would involve the judiciary in sensitive military affairs at the expense of military discipline and effectiveness." *United States v. Shearer,* 473 U.S., at 59 (emphasis in original). In every respect the military is, as this Court has recognized, "a specialized society." *Parker v. Levy,* 417 U.S. 733, 743 (1974). "[T]o accomplish its mission the military must foster instinctive obedience, unity, commitment, and esprit de corps." *Goldman v. Weinberger,* 475 U.S. 503, 507 (1986). Even if military negligence is not specifically alleged in a tort action, a suit based upon service-related activity necessarily implicates the military judgments and decisions

Keep cts out of Sovs v/o military matter & inhibit discipline

that are inextricably intertwined with the conduct of the military mission.[11] Moreover, military discipline involves not only obedience to orders, but more generally duty and loyalty to one's service and to one's country. Suits brought by service members against the Government for service-related injuries could undermine the commitment essential to effective service and thus have the potential to disrupt military discipline in the broadest sense of the word.

B

In this case, Lieutenant Commander Johnson was killed while performing a rescue mission on the high seas, a primary duty of the Coast Guard. See 14 U.S.C. §§ 2, 88(a)(1). There is no dispute that Johnson's injury arose directly out of the rescue mission, or that the mission was an activity incident to his military service. Johnson went on the rescue mission specifically because of his military status. His wife received and is continuing to receive statutory benefits on account of his death. Because Johnson was acting pursuant to standard operating procedures of the Coast Guard, the potential that this suit could implicate military discipline is substantial. The circumstances of this case thus fall within the heart of the *Feres* doctrine as it consistently has been articulated.

III

We reaffirm the holding of *Feres* that "the Government is not liable under the Federal Tort Claims Act for injuries to servicemen where the injuries arise out of or are in the course of activity incident to service." 340 U.S., at 146. Accordingly, we reverse the judgment of the Court of Appeals for the Eleventh Circuit and remand for proceedings consistent with this opinion.

It is so ordered.

Justice Scalia, with whom Justice Brennan, Justice Marshall and Justice Stevens join, dissenting.

As it did almost four decades ago in *Feres v. United States,* 340 U.S. 135 (1950), the Court today provides several reasons why Congress might have been wise to exempt from the Federal Tort Claims Act (FTCA), 28 U.S.C. §§ 1346(b), 2671–2680, certain claims brought by servicemen. The problem now, as then, is that Congress not only failed to provide such an exemption, but quite plainly excluded it. We have not been asked by respondent here to overrule *Feres;* but I can perceive no reason to accept petitioner's invitation to extend it as the Court does today.

I

Much of the sovereign immunity of the United States was swept away in 1946 with passage of the FTCA, which renders the Government liable

---

11. Civilian employees of the Government also may play an integral role in military activities. In this circumstance, an inquiry into the civilian activities would have the same effect on military discipline as a direct inquiry into military judgments. For example, the FAA and the United States Armed Services have an established working relationship that provides for FAA participation in numerous military activities.

"for money damages ... for injury or loss of property, or personal injury or death caused by the negligent or wrongful act or omission of any employee of the Government while acting within the scope of his office or employment, under circumstances where the United States, if a private person, would be liable to the claimant in accordance with the law of the place where the act or omission occurred." 28 U.S.C. § 1346(b).

Read as it is written, this language renders the United States liable to *all* persons, including servicemen, injured by the negligence of Government employees. Other provisions of the Act set forth a number of exceptions, but none generally precludes FTCA suits brought by servicemen. One, in fact, excludes "[a]ny claim arising out of the *combatant activities* of the military or naval forces, or the Coast Guard, *during time of war,*" § 2680(j) (emphasis added), demonstrating that Congress specifically considered, and provided what it thought needful for, the special requirements of the military. There was no proper basis for us to supplement—*i.e.*, revise—that congressional disposition. * * *

[I]n *Feres*, we held that servicemen could not recover under the FTCA for injuries that "arise out of or are in the course of activity incident to service," 340 U.S., at 146, and gave three reasons for our holding. First, the parallel private liability required by the FTCA was absent. Second, Congress could not have intended that local tort law govern the "distinctively federal" relationship between the Government and enlisted personnel. *Id.,* at 142 144. Third, Congress could not have intended to make FTCA suits available to servicemen who have already received veterans' benefits to compensate for injuries suffered incident to service. Several years after *Feres* we thought of a fourth rationale: Congress could not have intended to permit suits for service-related injuries because they would unduly interfere with military discipline. *United States v. Brown*, 348 U.S. 110, 112 (1954).

In my view, none of these rationales justifies the result. Only the first of them, the "parallel private liability" argument, purports to be textually based, as follows: The United States is liable under the FTCA "in the same manner and to the same extent as a private individual under like circumstances," 28 U.S.C. § 2674; since no "private individual" can raise an army, and since no State has consented to suits by members of its militia, § 2674 shields the Government from liability in the *Feres* situation. 340 U.S., at 141–142. Under this reasoning, of course, many of the Act's exceptions are superfluous, since private individuals typically do not, for example, transmit postal matter, 28 U.S.C. § 2680(b), collect taxes or customs duties, § 2680(c), impose quarantines, § 2680(f), or regulate the monetary system, § 2680(i). In any event, we subsequently recognized our error and rejected *Feres'* "parallel private liability" rationale. See *Rayonier, Inc. v. United States,* 352 U.S. 315, 319 (1957); *Indian Towing Co. v. United States,* 350 U.S. 61, 66–69 (1955).

Perhaps without that scant (and subsequently rejected) textual support, which could be pointed to as the embodiment of the legislative intent that its other two rationales speculated upon, the *Feres* Court would not as an original matter have reached the conclusion that it did. Be that as it may, the speculation outlived the textual support, and the *Feres* rule is now sustained only by three disembodied estimations of what Congress *must* (despite what it enacted) have intended. They are bad estimations at that. The first of them, *Feres'* second rationale, has barely escaped the fate of the "parallel private liability" argument, for though we have not yet acknowledged that it is erroneous we have described it as "no longer controlling." *United States v. Shearer,* 473 U.S. 52, 58, n. 4 (1985). The rationale runs as follows: Liability under the FTCA depends upon "the law of the place where the [negligent] act or omission occurred," 28 U.S.C. § 1346(b); but Congress could not have intended local, and therefore geographically diverse, tort law to control important aspects of the "distinctively federal" relationship between the United States and enlisted personnel. 340 U.S., at 142–144. *Feres* itself was concerned primarily with the unfairness to the soldier of making his recovery turn upon where he was injured, a matter outside of his control. Subsequent cases, however, have stressed the *military's need for uniformity* in its governing standards. See, *e.g., Stencel Aero Engineering Corp. v. United States,* 431 U.S. 666, 672 (1977). Regardless of how it is understood, this second rationale is not even a good excuse in policy, much less in principle, for ignoring the plain terms of the FTCA.

The unfairness to servicemen of geographically varied recovery is, to speak bluntly, an absurd justification, given that, as we have pointed out in another context, nonuniform recovery cannot possibly be worse than (what *Feres* provides) uniform nonrecovery. We have abandoned this peculiar rule of solicitude in allowing federal prisoners (who have no more control over their geographical location than servicemen) to recover under the FTCA for injuries caused by the negligence of prison authorities. There seems to me nothing "unfair" about a rule which says that, just as a serviceman injured by a negligent *civilian* must resort to state tort law, so must a serviceman injured by a negligent Government employee.

To the extent that the rationale rests upon the military's need for uniformity, it is equally unpersuasive. To begin with, that supposition of congressional intent is positively contradicted by the text. Several of the FTCA's exemptions show that Congress considered the uniformity problem, see, *e.g.,* 28 U.S.C. §§ 2680(b), 2680(i), 2680(k), yet it chose to retain sovereign immunity for only some claims affecting the military. § 2680(j). Moreover, we have effectively disavowed this "uniformity" justification—and rendered its benefits to military planning illusory—by permitting servicemen to recover under the FTCA for injuries suffered not incident to service, and permitting *civilians* to recover for injuries caused by military negligence. Finally, it is difficult to explain why uniformity (assuming our rule were achieving it) is indispensable for the military, but not for the many other federal departments and agencies that can be sued under the FTCA for the negligent performance of their "unique, nationwide function[s]," *Stencel Aero Engineering Corp. v. United States, supra,* at 675 (MARSHALL, J., dissenting), including, as we have noted, the federal prison system which may be sued under varying state laws by its inmates. In sum, the second *Feres* rationale, regardless of how it is understood, is not a plausible estimation of congressional intent, much less a justification for importing that estimation, unwritten, into the statute.

Feres's third basis has similarly been denominated "no longer controlling." *United States v. Shearer, supra,* at 58, n. 4. Servicemen injured or killed in the line of duty are compensated under the Veterans' Benefits Act (VBA), 38 U.S.C. §§ 101–8527 and the *Feres* Court thought it unlikely that Congress meant to permit additional recovery under the FTCA, 340 U.S., at 144–145. *Feres* described the absence of any provision to adjust dual recoveries under the FTCA and VBA as "persuasive [evidence] that there was no awareness that the Act might be interpreted to permit recovery for injuries incident to military service." *Id.,* at 144. Since Feres we have in dicta characterized recovery under the VBA as "the sole remedy for service-connected injuries," *Hatzlachh Supply Co. v. United States,* 444 U.S. 460, 464 (1980) (*per curiam*), and have said that the VBA "provides an upper limit of liability for the Government" for those injuries, *Stencel Aero Engineering Corp. v. United States, supra,* at 673.

The credibility of this rationale is undermined severely by the fact that both before and after *Feres* we permitted injured servicemen to bring FTCA suits, *even though they had been compensated under the VBA.* In *Brooks v. United States,* 337 U.S. 49 (1949), we held that two servicemen injured off duty by a civilian Army employee could sue the Government. The fact that they had already received VBA benefits troubled us little. We pointed out that "nothing in the Tort Claims Act or the veterans' laws . . . provides for exclusiveness of remedy" and we refused to "call either remedy . . . exclusive . . . when Congress has not done so." *Id.,* at 53. We noted further that Congress had included three exclusivity provisions in the FTCA, 28 U.S.C. §§ 2672, 2676, 2679, but had said nothing about servicemen plaintiffs, 337 U.S., at 53. We indicated, however, that VBA compensation could be taken into account in adjusting recovery under the FTCA. *Id.,* at 53–54. That *Brooks* remained valid after *Feres* was made clear in *United States v. Brown, supra,* in which we stressed again that because "Congress had given no indication that it made the right to compensation [under the VBA] the veteran's exclusive remedy, . . . the receipt of disability payments . . . did not preclude recovery under the Tort Claims Act." *Id.,* at 113.

Brooks and *Brown* (neither of which has ever been expressly disapproved) plainly hold that the VBA is *not* an "exclusive" remedy which places an "upper limit" on the Government's liability. Because of *Feres* and today's decision, however, the VBA will in fact be exclusive for service-connected injuries, but not for others. Such a result can no more be reconciled with the text of the VBA than with that of the FTCA, since the VBA compensates servicemen without regard to whether their injuries occur "incident to service" as *Feres* defines that term. See 38 U.S.C. § 105. Moreover, the VBA is not, as *Feres* assumed, identical to federal and state workers' compensation statutes in which exclusivity provisions almost invariably appear. See, *e.g.,* 5 U.S.C. § 8116(c). Recovery is possible under workers' compensation statutes more often than under the VBA, and VBA

*[handwritten margin notes: "Feres' Alternate Compensation rationale..."; "...BUT... We have always allowed dual compensation"; "off-duty?"; "Brown: Congress didn't say VBA comp. was exclusive"; "R *"]*

benefits can be terminated more easily than can workers' compensation. In sum, "the presence of an alternative compensation system [neither] explains [n]or justifies the *Feres* doctrine; it only makes the effect of the doctrine more palatable." *Hunt v. United States,* 636 F.2d 580, 598 ([D.C.Cir.] 1980).

The Feres
rationales are
weak

The foregoing three rationales—the only ones actually relied upon in *Feres*—are so frail that it is hardly surprising that we have repeatedly cited the later-conceived-of "military discipline" rationale as the "best" explanation for that decision. Applying the FTCA as written would lead, we have reasoned, to absurd results, because if suits could be brought on the basis of alleged negligence towards a serviceman by other servicemen, military discipline would be undermined and civilian courts would be required to second-guess military decisionmaking. See *Stencel Aero Engineering Corp. v. United States,* 431 U.S., at 671–672, 673. (Today the Court goes further and suggests that permitting enlisted men and women to sue their Government on the basis of negligence towards them *by any Government employee* seriously undermines "duty and loyalty to one's service and to one's country.") I cannot deny the possibility that some suits brought by servicemen will adversely affect military discipline, and if we were interpreting an ambiguous statute perhaps we could take that into account. But I do not think the effect upon military discipline is so certain, or so certainly substantial, that we are justified in holding (if we can ever be justified in holding) that Congress did not mean what it plainly said in the statute before us.

It is strange that Congress' "obvious" intention to preclude *Feres* suits because of their effect on military discipline was discerned neither by the *Feres* Court nor by the Congress that enacted the FTCA (which felt it necessary expressly to exclude recovery for combat injuries). Perhaps Congress recognized that the likely effect of *Feres* suits upon military discipline is not as clear as we have assumed, but in fact has long been disputed. Or perhaps Congress assumed that the FTCA's explicit exclusions would bar those suits most threatening to military discipline, such as claims based upon combat command decisions, 28 U.S.C. § 2680(j); claims based upon performance of "discretionary" functions, § 2680(a); claims arising in foreign countries, § 2680(k); intentional torts, § 2680(h); and claims based upon the execution of a statute or regulation, § 2680(a). Or perhaps Congress assumed that, since liability under the FTCA is imposed upon the Government, and not upon individual employees, military decisionmaking was unlikely to be affected greatly. Or perhaps—most fascinating of all to contemplate—Congress thought that *barring* recovery by servicemen might adversely affect military discipline. After all, the morale of Lieutenant Commander Johnson's comrades-in-arms will not likely be boosted by news that his widow and children will receive only a fraction of the amount they might have recovered had he been piloting a commercial helicopter at the time of his death.

To the extent that reading the FTCA as it is written will require civilian courts to examine military decisionmaking and thus influence military discipline, it is outlandish to consider that result "outlandish," *Brooks v. United States*, 337 U.S., at 53, since in fact it occurs frequently, even under the *Feres* dispensation. If Johnson's helicopter had crashed into a civilian's home, the homeowner could have brought an FTCA suit that would have invaded the sanctity of military decisionmaking no less than respondents'. If a soldier is injured *not* "incident to service," he can sue his Government regardless of whether the alleged negligence was military negligence. And if a soldier suffers service-connected injury because of the negligence of a civilian (such as the manufacturer of an airplane), he can sue that civilian, even if the civilian claims contributory negligence and subpoenas the serviceman's colleagues to testify against him.

In sum, neither the three original *Feres* reasons nor the *post hoc* rationalization of "military discipline" justifies our failure to apply the FTCA as written. *Feres* was wrongly decided and heartily deserves the "widespread, almost universal criticism" it has received. *In re "Agent Orange" Product Liability Litigation*, 580 F.Supp. 1242, 1246 (E.D.N.Y.), appeal dism'd, 745 F.2d 161 (C.A.2 1984).

II

The *Feres* Court claimed its decision was necessary to make "the entire statutory system of remedies against the Government ... a workable, consistent and equitable whole." 340 U.S., at 139. I am unable to find such beauty in what we have wrought. Consider the following hypothetical (similar to one presented by Judge Weinstein in *In re "Agent Orange" Product Liability Litigation, supra,* at 1252): A serviceman is told by his superior officer to deliver some papers to the local United States Courthouse. As he nears his destination, a wheel on his Government vehicle breaks, causing the vehicle to injure him, his daughter (whose class happens to be touring the courthouse that day), and a United States marshal on duty. Under our case law and federal statutes, the serviceman may not sue the Government (*Feres*); the guard may not sue the Government (because of the exclusivity provision of the Federal Employees' Compensation Act (FECA), 5 U.S.C. § 8116); the daughter may not sue the Government for the loss of her father's companionship (*Feres*), but may sue the Government for her own injuries (FTCA). The serviceman and the guard may sue the manufacturer of the vehicle, as may the daughter, both for her own injuries and for the loss of her father's companionship. The manufacturer may assert contributory negligence as a defense in any of the suits. Moreover, the manufacturer may implead the Government in the daughter's suit (*United States v. Yellow Cab Co.*, 340 U.S. 543 (1951)) and in the guard's suit (*Lockheed Aircraft Corp. v. United States*, 460 U.S. 190 (1983)), even though the guard was compensated under a statute that contains an exclusivity provision (FECA). But the manufacturer may *not* implead the Government in the serviceman's suit (*Stencel Aero Engineering Corp. v. United States*, 431 U.S. 666 (1977)), even though the serviceman was compensated under a statute that does not contain an exclusivity provision (VBA).

The point is not that all of these inconsistencies are attributable to *Feres* (though some of them assuredly are), but merely that bringing harmony to the law has hardly been the consequence of our ignoring what Congress wrote and imagining what it should have written. When confusion results from our applying the unambiguous text of a statute, it is at least a confusion validated by the free play of the democratic process, rather than what we have here: unauthorized rationalization gone wrong. We realized seven years too late that "[t]here is no justification for this Court to read exemptions into the Act beyond those provided by Congress. If the Act is to be altered that is a function for the same body that adopted it." *Rayonier, Inc. v. United States*, 352 U.S., at 320.

I cannot take comfort, as the Court does, from Congress' failure to amend the FTCA to overturn *Feres*. The unlegislated desires of later Congresses with regard to one thread in the fabric of the FTCA could hardly have any bearing upon the proper interpretation of the entire fabric of compromises that their predecessors enacted into law in 1946. And even if they could, intuiting those desires from congressional *failure* to act is an uncertain enterprise which takes as its starting point disregard of the checks and balances in the constitutional scheme of legislation designed to assure that not all desires of a majority of the Legislature find their way into law.

We have not been asked by respondent to overrule *Feres,* and so need not resolve whether considerations of *stare decisis* should induce us, despite the plain error of the case, to leave bad enough alone. As the majority acknowledges, however, "all of the cases decided by this Court under *Feres* have involved allegations of negligence on the part of members of the military." I would not extend *Feres* any further. I confess that the line between FTCA suits alleging military negligence and those alleging civilian negligence has nothing to recommend it except that it would limit our clearly wrong decision in *Feres* and confine the unfairness and irrationality that decision has bred. But that, I think, is justification enough.

Had Lieutenant Commander Johnson been piloting a commercial helicopter when he crashed into the side of a mountain, his widow and children could have sued and recovered for their loss. But because Johnson devoted his life to serving in his country's Armed Forces, the Court today limits his family to a fraction of the recovery they might otherwise have received. If our imposition of that sacrifice bore the legitimacy of having been prescribed by the people's elected representatives, it would (insofar as we are permitted to inquire into such things) be just. But it has not been, and it is not. I respectfully dissent.

Notes and Questions

1. Between the majority and the dissenting opinions in *United States v. Johnson*, the four basic rationales underlying the *Feres* doctrine are raised and critiqued. Describe each of the four rationales and the counter-

arguments made in the dissent. Which remain viable today? Which are the most important rationales and how, if at all, should those rationales influence the scope of the *Feres* exclusion?

2.   One of the key and continuing rationales for excluding military personnel injured incident to service from recovery under the FTCA is the analogy between Veterans' Benefits Act (VBA) benefits and Federal Employees Compensation Act (FECA) benefits, which as we've seen are the exclusive remedy for civilian federal employees injured within the scope of employment. One commentary makes the following point:

> Since the turn of the century, most tort remedies against employers for work-related injuries have been eliminated, with an administrative compensation scheme substituted in their place. As we have previously seen, this has been done with respect to federal civilian employees as well. The *Feres* doctrine, coupled with the provisions of the Veterans' Benefit Act, merely applies this same regime to members of the armed forces. It would certainly be strange to conclude that Congress intended that servicemen, virtually alone among American workers, be given free rein to sue their employer.

1 Lester S. Jayson & Robert C. Longstreth, *Handling Federal Tort Claims* § 5A.05 (2005). Do you find this analogy and the argument in support of it persuasive?

At the same, the VBA is not directly parallel to a workers compensation scheme such as that provided to civilian employees in FECA. To begin with, unlike FECA, the VA contains no express exclusivity provision. Moreover, VBA benefits are *not* awarded exactly the same as workers compensation benefits, as VBA benefits are not restricted to the context of a direct service-related injury in the sense of being incurred while on active duty conducting military activities. A member of the armed forces may receive VBA health or disability benefits for an injury that was *not* received incident to service. *See* Charles A. Shanor & L. Lynn Hogue, *Military Law in a Nutshell* 349 (2d ed. 1996) ("For example, a solider injured skiing while on leave is covered [under the VBA.]"). Thus, a servicemember whose injury was not received incident to service would be permitted to recover under the FTCA (assuming the government was the tortfeasor), in addition to receiving VBA benefits (although an off-set may be required).

Consider this hypothetical problem: Army Sgt. Linda is assigned by the base commander to drive a bus filled with service personnel who are on leave and their spouses to a nearby town. Linda's husband, Bob, who is neither a member of the service nor a federal civilian employee, rides along to go shopping in town. Col. Tom, who is on leave, is among those riding on the bus. As the bus nears the town, it is struck by a Postal Service truck, causing injury to all three. Under *Feres,* as reaffirmed by *Johnson,* who may maintain an FTCA suit? Certainly Bob may, and perhaps Col. Tom as well, given that he was off base and on leave and does not appear to have been under military orders at the time. Sgt. Linda who was on duty in driving the bus is plainly barred by *Feres* from an FTCA recovery. But consider who is eligible to receive VBA benefits? It may surprise you to learn that not only Sgt. Linda but also Col. Tom may well receive VBA benefits, as those benefits are not limited solely to injuries incident to service. Thus, Sgt. Linda obtains VBA benefits but is barred from an FTCA remedy. Col. Tom also may receive VBA benefits, but may file an FTCA suit. Is this appropriate? Is the *Feres* doctrine undermined by these inconsistent applications?

3. As the *Feres* doctrine operates to bar military service personnel from recovery under the FTCA for injuries "incident to military service," the meaning of "incident to military service" defines the scope of the exclusion. The "incident to service" determination is a question of fact, *Johnson v. United States*, 704 F.2d 1431, 1436 (9th Cir. 1983); *Parker v. United States*, 611 F.2d 1007 (5th Cir. 1980), but the factual determination must be made within the parameters of the legal definition of the crucial term.

The *Feres* Court itself offered the example in *Brooks v. United States*, 337 U.S. 49 (1949), of a serviceman receiving an injury that was *not* incident to military service. As the *Feres* Court described it, the serviceman "was on furlough," was driving on the highway, and was "under compulsion of no orders or duty and on no military mission." Reversing the order of this analysis, we then can derive three factual elements that define when an injury *would* be regarded as having occurred "incident to military position": (1) a servicemember was on active duty (not on leave or furlough), (2) the accident occurred on the military base, or (3) the servicemember was under compulsion of military orders, performing a military mission, or subject to military control. Traditionally, "the presence of any one of these mentioned factual elements will mandate application of the *Feres* doctrine." 1 Jayson & Longstreth *supra*, § 5A.02, at 5A–11 (citing cases); *see also* Shanor & Hogue, *supra*, at 324. Indeed, in *Feres* itself, off-duty servicemen—who were not on leave or furlough—were nonetheless held precluded from bringing an FTCA action for medical malpractice and a barracks fire, all of which occurred on the base. The traditional definition of "incident to service" continues to have force among some courts of appeals. *See, e.g., Whitley v. United States*, 170 F.3d 1061, 1068–75 (11th Cir. 1999) (applying *Brooks* factors to hold that a foreign serviceman was not acting "incident to service" while on furlough, off-duty, engaged in recreational activity, and injured far from the military base, and thus could bring FTCA suit); *Day v. Massachusetts Air National Guard*, 167 F.3d 678, 682–83 (1st Cir. 1999) (while suggesting that "possibly *Feres* itself deserves reexamination by the Supreme Court," holding that a serviceman's FTCA claims based upon injuries suffered through an assault by other servicemen while sleeping and off duty but on a military base was barred by the *Feres* doctrine).

However, the Second Circuit has held that the analysis "should proceed by considering the same question that would determine whether the plaintiff would be entitled to receive standard workers' compensation payments for his injury: was the plaintiff engaged in activities that fell within the scope of the plaintiff's military employment?" *Taber v. Maine,*

67 F.3d 1029, 1050 (2d Cir. 1995). Indeed, the court explained that "scope of employment" for application of the *Feres* doctrine should be defined in the same manner as for a federal civilian employee under the Federal Employees Compensation Act. *Id.* at 1050 n.21. *But see Skees v. United States,* 107 F.3d 421, 425 n. 3 (6th Cir. 1997) (declining to adopt the Second Circuit's approach in *Taber v. Maine*). Would application of the *Taber* test result in a different outcome for military medical malpractice cases? For a barracks fire injuring servicemen who were asleep? Is it consistent with *Feres*?

The Ninth Circuit adheres to a case-by-case analysis under which "the most relevant line of inquiry is whether or not the service member's activities at the time of injury are of the sort that could harm the disciplinary system if litigated in a civil action." *Dreier v. United States,* 106 F.3d 844, 853 (9th Cir. 1996). Can this approach be reconciled with *Johnson*? In *Johnson,* the Supreme Court did not appear to look at the specific disciplinary effects of the individual case and it is difficult to see how a suit based on negligence by civilian air traffic controllers would have impinged very directly on sensitive issues of military discipline. In addition, the Ninth Circuit has also held that the presence of the military serviceman on base at the time, while a factor, is not determinative of whether the *Feres* doctrine is a bar. *Dreier,* 106 F.3d at 852.

4.   Where then are we? While the Supreme Court has affirmed the continued validity of the *Feres* doctrine, at least for the moment, its contours and underlying rationale remain in a state of confusion. So, some 50 years later, how should we judge the work of the *Feres* Court? What lessons can we learn about the role or suitability of different institutions to resolve legal problems or about alternative approaches to statutory interpretation? What should a court do when it encounters a problem in applying a statute that the legislative drafters apparently did not anticipate? Should it try to determine what they would have done or what the present Congress would do if asked?

In recent years, legal scholars, and the courts, have given renewed attention to the problem of and approaches for statutory interpretation. One recently-formulated theory is that of "dynamic statutory interpretation," under which courts construe statutes in light of changing or unanticipated circumstances. As sketched by a leading advocate, Professor William Eskridge, statutory interpretation is "dynamic" in practice because "the meaning of a statute is not fixed until it is applied to concrete circumstances" and because "the gaps and ambiguities" in a statute "proliferate as society changes, adapts to the statute, and generates new variations on the problem initially targeted by the statute." William N. Eskridge, Jr., *Dynamic Statutory Interpretation* 9–10 (1994); *see also* Guido Calabresi, *A Common Law for the Age of Statutes* 2 (1982) (arguing that "the courts might begin a 'common law' process of renovation" of obsolete or anachronistic statutes, including "updat[ing] the statute directly by replacing it with new rules (derived either from the common law or from statutory sources)"). Moreover, Eskridge argues that a dynamic approach to establishing statutory meaning is justifiable and politically healthy, as it allows the interpreter to "reestablish the productivity of law" by conforming a statute to contemporary expectations, social practices, and public values and to pragmatically consider the consequences of different interpretive choices. Eskridge, *supra,* at 175–76, 201–02.

Does the Supreme Court's 1950 decision in *Feres v. United States* fit that dynamic model? Consider that, notwithstanding the absence of any express exclusionary language in the FTCA, the *Feres* Court was certain that Congress could not have intended to permit members of the armed forces, on active duty, to recover for injuries suffered incident to service: "We do not think that Congress, in drafting this Act, created a new cause of action dependent on local law for service-connected injuries or death due to negligence. We cannot impute to Congress such a radical departure from established law in the absence of express congressional command." Speaking 50 years ago, might not the *Feres* Court have been correct in divining the mood of the times, confirming the political and societal deference of that era toward military demands and the military command structure, and recognizing that Congress indeed likely would have excepted military personnel from the statute had it anticipated such claims? Isn't it arguable that the *Feres* Court did exactly what Congress would have done had it thought about the possibility of military personnel suing the government? *But see* Jonathan Turley, *Pax Militaris: The* Feres *Doctrine and the Retention of Sovereign Immunity in the Military System of Governance,* 71 Geo. Wash. L. Rev. 1, 4 (2003) (describing *Feres* as "a quintessential exercise of judicial activism).

And yet consider as well the continuing controversies concerning the reach and application, and even the legitimacy, of the so-called *Feres* doctrine. As discussed above, recall that application of the *Feres* rule may lead to inconsistent results among different people injured in the same incident. What about the confusion, uncertainties, unfairness, and anomalous results wrought by the *Feres* doctrine? And, as outlined immediately above, remember that the lower courts are deeply divided over the very definition of "incident to military service," which in turn defines the scope of the exclusion. In addition, Professor Jonathan Turley argues that, in addition to disenfranchising military servicemembers from recovery for injuries caused by governmental wrongdoing, the *Feres* doctrine has had "two systemic effects": (1) that with immunity from personal injury lawsuits, "the level of [medical] malpractice and negligence in the military appears much higher than in the private sector," and (2) "reduced liability has encouraged the expansion of the military into collateral areas of governance such as medicine, entertainment, and transportation," areas in which the military often "openly competes with private businesses for both military and civilian customers." Turley, *supra,* at 4.

In the end, however well the *Feres* Court may have identified the social and legal expectations of the period and however accurately it may have divined unstated congressional intent, would a solution to the problem of military service injuries have been better left to Congress? Could Congress, in its deliberative process, have produced a more carefully calibrated answer? Students should think about both the legal and practical consequences of alternative institutions—particularly the judicial and the legislative branches—for resolving different types of legal problems.

———

SECTION B.   THE SUITS IN ADMIRALTY ACT AND THE PUBLIC VESSELS ACT

In 2006, both the Suits in Admiralty Act and the Public Vessels Act were re-classified and revised by Congress, largely in non-substantive ways, as part of the completion of the re-codification of statutes and enactment of Title 46 of the United States Code as positive law. See Pub. L. No. 109–304, § 6(c), Oct. 6, 2006, 120 Stat. 1521. Accordingly, citations in the cases that follow to these two statutes are no longer current, but the legal principles articulated in those cases remain valid and unchanged by this statutory re-codification. *See* H.R. Rep. No. 109–170 (2006) (explaining that the reorganization and restatement of laws now to be codified in Title 45 "codifies existing law rather than creating new law").

Suits in Admiralty Act, 46 United States Code §§ 30901–30908

§ 30901.   Short title

This chapter may be cited as the "Suits in Admiralty Act".

§ 30902.   Definition

In this chapter, the term "federally-owned corporation" means a corporation in which the United States owns all the outstanding capital stock.

§ 30903.   Waiver of immunity

(a) **In general.**—In a case in which, if a vessel were privately owned or operated, or if cargo were privately owned or possessed, or if a private person or property were involved, a civil action in admiralty could be maintained, a civil action in admiralty in personam may be brought against the United States or a federally-owned corporation. In a civil action in admiralty brought by the United States or a federally-owned corporation, an admiralty claim in personam may be filed or a setoff claimed against the United States or corporation.

(b) **Non-jury.**—A claim against the United States or a federally-owned corporation under this section shall be tried without a jury.

§ 30904.   Exclusive remedy

If a remedy is provided by this chapter, it shall be exclusive of any other action arising out of the same subject matter against the officer, employee, or agent of the United States or the federally-owned corporation whose act or omission gave rise to the claim.

But can you file other statutory actions against the Gov't?

§ 30905.   Period for bringing action

A civil action under this chapter must be brought within 2 years after the cause of action arose.

§ 30906.   Venue

(a) In general.—A civil action under this chapter shall be brought in the district court of the United States for the district in which—

nerve test? muscle test??

(1) any plaintiff resides or has its principal place of business; or

(2) the vessel or cargo is found.

(b) Transfer.—On a motion by a party, the court may transfer the action to any other district court of the United States.

§ 30907.   Procedure for hearing and determination

(a) In general.—A civil action under this chapter shall proceed and be heard and determined according to the principles of law and the rules of practice applicable in like cases between private parties. *(maritime law)?*

Law

(b) In rem.—

(1) Requirements.—The action may proceed according to the principles of an action in rem if—

(A) the plaintiff elects in the complaint; and

(B) it appears that an action in rem could have been maintained had the vessel or cargo been privately owned and possessed.

(2) Effect on relief in personam.—An election under paragraph (1) does not prevent the plaintiff from seeking relief in personam in the same action.

§ 30908.   Period for bringing action

The following are not subject to arrest or seizure by judicial process in the United States:

(1) A vessel owned by, possessed by, or operated by or for the United States or a federally-owned corporation.

(2) Cargo owned or possessed by the United States or a federally-owned corporation.

———

Public Vessels Act, 46 United States Code §§ 31101–31104, 31111

§ 31101. Short title

This chapter may be cited as the "Public Vessels Act".

§ 31102. Waiver of immunity

(a) In general.—A civil action in personam in admiralty may be brought, or an impleader filed, against the United States for—

(1) damages caused by a public vessel of the United States; or

(2) compensation for towage and salvage services, including contract salvage, rendered to a public vessel of the United States.

(b) Counterclaim or setoff.—If the United States brings a civil action in admiralty for damages caused by a privately owned vessel, the owner of the vessel, or the successor in interest, may file a counterclaim in personam, or claim a setoff, against the United States for damages arising out of the same subject matter.

§ 31103. Applicable procedure

A civil action under this chapter is subject to the provisions of chapter 309 of this title except to the extent inconsistent with this chapter.

§ 31104. Venue

(a) In general.—A civil action under this chapter shall be brought in the district court of the United States for the district in which the vessel or cargo is found within the United States.

(b) Vessel or cargo outside territorial waters.—If the vessel or cargo is outside the territorial waters of the United States—

(1) the action shall be brought in the district court of the United States for any district in which any plaintiff resides or has an office for the transaction of business; or

(2) if no plaintiff resides or has an office for the transaction of business in the United States, the action may be brought in the district court of the United States for any district.

* * *

§ 31111. Claims by nationals of foreign countries

A national of a foreign country may not maintain a civil action under this chapter unless it appears to the satisfaction of the court in which the action is brought that the government of that country, in similar circumstances, allows nationals of the United States to sue in its courts.

Taghadomi v. United States

United States Court of Appeals for the Ninth Circuit.
401 F.3d 1080 (9th Cir. 2005).

■ O'Scannlain, Circuit Judge.

In this tort claim against the federal government arising out of an accident at sea, we explore whether suit can be brought under the Suits in Admiralty Act, the Public Vessels Act, or the Federal Tort Claims Act.

I

This case arises from an accident at sea. Manouchehr Monazzami Taghadomi (a U.S. citizen) and his wife Nahid Davoodabadi (a citizen of Iran) rented a kayak during their honeymoon in Maui. Their boat was buffeted by harsh wind and waves, and Nahid was tossed overboard, attacked by a shark, and died. Monazzami washed up on an island and was stranded for three days before he was rescued. He was hospitalized for several days.

While the couple was still in the foundering kayak, a witness on land noticed it through his binoculars. Concerned, he telephoned the Coast Guard's Maui office and gave a description of the kayak and its location. About twenty minutes after receiving the call, the Maui office contacted the Coast Guard Operations Center in Honolulu. The Operations Center, in turn, contacted a Coast Guard cutter—the Kiska—and directed it toward the kayak. The Kiska conducted a brief search, but darkness soon fell, and at about seven o'clock that evening the search was called off.

This lawsuit followed. Monazzami originally filed a complaint, individually and as special administrator of the estate of Nahid, against Extreme Sports Maui, the company that rented the kayak to Taghadomi. In subsequent amended complaints the estate and Nahid's parents were each added as separate plaintiffs and the United States was added as a defendant.[2] The plaintiffs (collectively, the "survivors") seek damages from the United States for wrongful death and emotional distress. They allege that the Coast Guard was negligent both in carrying out its rescue operation and in failing to contact local authorities who had access to better rescue equipment that might have been able to save the couple. The United States moved to dismiss or, in the alternative, for summary judgment. The survivors opposed the motion and also moved to amend their Complaint once again to clarify their claims against the United States. The district court granted the United States' motion for summary judgment, holding that the survivors' claims are not cognizable, and denied as futile the survivors' motion to amend. The court entered judgment for the United States and this appeal timely followed. We review the grant of summary judgment *de novo*.

---

2. The plaintiffs have settled their dispute with Extreme Sports Maui, and the United States is the only remaining defendant.

II

The United States, of course, is liable in court only when it has waived its sovereign immunity. Three immunity-waiving statutes are relevant here. The first is the Federal Tort Claims Act ("FTCA"), 28 U.S.C. § 2674 *et seq.*, which generally renders the United States liable for its torts to the same extent as a private actor. The FTCA includes an exception, however, for "[a]ny claim for which a remedy is provided" by either of the other two statutes relevant to this case. 28 U.S.C. § 2680. These are the Public Vessels Act ("PVA"), 46 U.S.C.App. § 781 *et seq.*, and the Suits in Admiralty Act ("SAA"), 46 U.S.C.App. § 741 *et seq.*

The PVA renders the United States liable in admiralty for "damages caused by a public vessel of the United States."[3] 46 U.S.C.App. § 781. The PVA, however, contains a special reciprocity requirement that permits foreign nationals to sue the U.S. government only if their country of nationality would permit a similar suit by a U.S. citizen. 46 U.S.C.App. § 785.

The SAA is broader: it renders the United States liable in admiralty in any case in which, "if a private person or property were involved, a proceeding in admiralty could be maintained." 46 U.S.C.App. § 742. It contains no reciprocity requirement. One might wonder why the PVA even exists, since the SAA appears to cover all admiralty claims, including those involving a public vessel. The answer lies in history. Until 1960 the SAA applied only to "merchant vessels," a category mutually exclusive of "public vessels." *See United States v. United Cont'l Tuna Corp.,* 425 U.S. 164, 167 n. 1 (1976). For this and other reasons, admiralty lawyers preparing to file a claim were often uncertain which statute to file under—the PVA, the SAA, or in some cases the FTCA or the Tucker Act.[4] Congress solved the problem by amending the SAA; one of the changes removed the reference to merchant vessels. *See United Cont'l Tuna,* 425 U.S. at 166–78.

The survivors cannot bring their claims under the PVA or the SAA, both because of the PVA's reciprocity requirement and because they failed to file within the applicable limitations periods under those statutes. They therefore seek, instead, to bring their claims under the FTCA.

A

The first question we must answer is whether the survivors' claims are maritime in nature—that is, whether they fall within federal admiralty

3. A "public vessel" is one owned or operated by the United States and used in a public capacity. *See In re United States and Mathiasen's Tanker Indus.,* 367 F.2d 505, 509 (3d Cir.1966) ("[G]overnment ownership and use as directed by the government exclusively for a public purpose suffice without more to make a ship a public vessel."); *United States v. United Cont'l Tuna Corp.,* 425 U.S. 164, 167 n. 1 (1976) (holding a naval destroyer is a "public vessel" under the PVA).

4. The Tucker Act applied to certain contract claims involving public vessels. The details of which statute applied in which situation are not relevant here. For a thorough explanation, see *Unifying Maritime Claims Against the United States,* 30 J. Mar. L. & Com. 41, 45–49 (1999).

jurisdiction. For the PVA and the SAA are relevant only to maritime claims and thus pose no obstacle to asserting non-maritime claims under the FTCA.

The survivors seek to bring two different claims against the United States. First, they claim that the Coast Guard cutter Kiska's search for the kayakers was negligently carried out (either by its crew or by land-based Coast Guard officers). We refer to this as the "negligent-search claim." Second, they claim that the two Coast Guard offices (in Maui and Honolulu) which knew about the kayak in distress negligently failed to contact the Maui Fire Department or any other local agency with access to a helicopter or other rescue vessels. We refer to this as the "failure-to-communicate claim."

No one disputes that the negligent-search claim is maritime in nature. The survivors argue, however, that the failure-to-communicate claim is not maritime and therefore not within the scope of the SAA or the PVA. Thus, they conclude, it is the proper subject of an action under the FTCA.

A tort claim falls within the admiralty jurisdiction of the federal courts when two conditions are met. First, the tort must occur on or over navigable waters; this is the "locality" or "situs" test. Second, the actions giving rise to the tort claim must "bear a significant relationship to traditional maritime activity." *Executive Jet Aviation, Inc. v. City of Cleveland,* 409 U.S. 249, 268 (1972). This is the "nexus" or "relationship" test. Admiralty jurisdiction exists only when both these requirements are satisfied. The survivors contend that neither test is met here.

1

With regard to the locality test, the survivors argue that because the Coast Guard's actions (or failure to act) took place entirely on land, the alleged negligence did not occur on navigable waters. This contention is unavailing, however, because it ignores the clear law of our circuit that the situs of a tort for the purpose of determining admiralty jurisdiction is the place where the injury occurs.[6]

* * *

2

We turn, then, to the nexus requirement. The survivors argue that the land-based Coast Guard's failure to communicate with the land-based Maui Fire Department is insufficiently related to maritime activity to support admiralty jurisdiction. The Supreme Court's opinion in [*Jerome B.*] *Grubar[t, Inc. v. Great Lakes Dredge & Dock Co.,* 513 U.S. 527 (1995)],describes the two relevant inquiries:

> The connection test raises two issues. A court first, must "assess the general features of the type of incident involved" to determine whether the incident has "a potentially disruptive impact on maritime com-

---

6. Indeed, we have occasionally characterized the first prong of the test for admiral-ty jurisdiction as simply requiring that "the *injury* occur on water."

merce." Second, a court must determine whether "the general character" of the "activity giving rise to the incident" shows a "substantial relationship to traditional maritime activity."

Grubart, 513 U.S. at 534. As to the first inquiry, the "type of incident involved" is to be considered at an "intermediate" level of generality. *Id.* at 538. In *Grubart,* for example, the Court described the incident (which specifically involved the faulty replacement of wooden pilings supporting bridges) as "damage by a vessel in navigable water to an underwater structure." *Id.* at 539. So described, the incident clearly posed a danger to maritime commerce.

A corresponding description of the "type of incident involved" in this case would thus be something such as "injury to boaters whose vessel capsizes at sea because of a potential rescuer's negligence in carrying out its rescue operation." One could quibble about precisely how to frame the question, but it is clear that at any reasonable level of generality the incident had a "potentially disruptive impact on maritime commerce." *See, e.g., Polly v. Estate of Carlson,* 859 F.Supp. 270, 272 (E.D.Mich.1994) ("That men were overboard in an emergency situation by itself is likely to disrupt commercial activity...."). The efficacy of search-and-rescue operations has a direct effect on the health and lives of seamen. While the kayakers in this case were engaged in recreational and not commercial activity, there is no reason to regard that fact as relevant to the nature of the Coast Guard's activity, which would presumably have been the same no matter the purpose of the kayakers' excursion at sea. Search-and-rescue operations also affect the vessels themselves: insofar as the rescuer can preserve the vessel, it prevents economic loss to the vessel's owner.

The second inquiry within the nexus test requires us to decide whether the "general character of the activity giving rise to the incident shows a substantial relationship to traditional maritime activity." *Grubart,* 513 U.S. at 534. A preliminary question arises: what constitutes the "activity giving rise to the incident"? The survivors ask us to follow the path carved out in *Delta Country Ventures, Inc. v. Magana,* 986 F.2d 1260 (9th Cir.1993). That case dealt with a claim against the owner of a houseboat by a guest who dove off the boat, hit an object in the water, and was paralyzed. The guest sued the owner for negligently situating the boat. The owner asserted admiralty jurisdiction so it could invoke the Limitation of Liability Act, 46 U.S.C.App. § 183, to limit its liability to the value of the boat. We held that there was no admiralty jurisdiction because the "activity giving rise to the incident" had no relationship to traditional maritime activity. We did so, however, because we conceived of the "activity" in question as the guest's diving into the water, and held that recreational diving has no relation to traditional maritime activity. *Id.* at 1262–63. It would be inappropriate, we held, to look past the immediate event surrounding the injury to a more remote cause such as the boat owner's negligent placement of the boat near an underwater object. *But see id.* at 1264 (Kozinski, J., dissenting).

Were we bound by the approach of the *Delta Country Ventures* majority, the survivors' argument might have some merit: the activity in question

[Handwritten margin notes:]
e.g.

- Application of first prong
- characterization

(1) Efficacy of search/rescues potentially disrupt maritime commerce
 - Recreational activity doesn't matter
 - Economic loss of the raft

(2) activity giving rise to the incident is substantially related to maritime activity?

Delta country immediate event surrounding the injury

could be defined as recreational kayaking, which (arguably, though not obviously) does not bear a sufficient relationship to traditional maritime activity. But the *Delta Country Ventures* approach is flatly inconsistent with the Supreme Court's subsequent decision in *Grubart* and hence is no longer good law. The Court held in *Grubart* that

> we need to look only to whether one of the arguably proximate causes of the incident originated in the maritime activity of a tortfeasor: as long as one of the putative tortfeasors was engaged in traditional maritime activity the allegedly wrongful activity will "involve" such traditional maritime activity and will meet the second nexus prong.

The activity giving rise to the incident is the behavior....→

513 U.S. at 541. The activity at issue, then, is not merely the event immediately surrounding the injury; it is the behavior of any "putative tortfeasor[ ]" (here, the Coast Guard) that is an "arguably proximate cause[]" of the injury. In this case, then, the relevant question is whether the Coast Guard's search-and-rescue operation shows a substantial relationship to traditional maritime activity.

Ct.:
Search & Rescue missions bear substantial relationship to maritime activity

It assuredly does. *See Berg v. Chevron U.S.A.*, 759 F.2d 1425, 1429 (9th Cir.1985) ("The law of admiralty has always sought to encourage and induce men of the sea to go to the aid of life and property in distress." (citations and internal quotation marks omitted)); *Kelly v. United States*, 531 F.2d 1144, 1147 (2d Cir.1976) ("[R]escue operations of the Coast Guard conducted on navigable waters do in fact bear a significant relationship to traditional maritime activities for purposes of admiralty jurisdiction."). The Supreme Court emphasized in *Grubart* that the nexus test is not meant to exclude broad swathes of activity; it wrote approvingly of the notion that "virtually every activity involving a vessel on navigable waters would be a traditional maritime activity sufficient to invoke maritime jurisdiction." 513 U.S. at 542.

Conc:

Thus, the locality test and both subprongs of the nexus test are satisfied in this case. It follows that all of the survivors' claims fall within federal admiralty jurisdiction.

① *Can the claims be brought under FTCA as well?*
B

#1 → PVA applies
#2 → SAA applies

We must next decide whether the survivors' claims can be brought under the FTCA despite their maritime nature. We consider their two claims separately. Because the negligent-search claim involves a public vessel within the meaning of the PVA, it must be analyzed under that statute. The failure-to-communicate claim, on the other hand, does not involve a public vessel, and so only the SAA will be relevant to its analysis.

1

The PVA provides:

A libel in personam in admiralty may be brought against the United States, or a petition impleading the United States, for damages caused by a public vessel of the United States. . . .

46 U.S.C.App. § 781. The reference to "damages caused by a public vessel" is not limited to damages physically caused by the ship itself. Rather, it includes "cases where the negligence of the personnel of a public vessel in the operation of the vessel causes damage." *Canadian Aviator, Ltd. v. United States,* 324 U.S. 215, 224–25 (1945).

The parties do not dispute that the Coast Guard cutter involved in the search for Nahid and Monazzami is a public vessel within the meaning of the Act.[8] The survivors' negligent-search claim thus falls within the scope of the PVA.[9] Two of the survivors are citizens of Iran, however. As the survivors allege and the United States does not dispute, Iran's courts would not permit U.S. citizens to bring suit under similar circumstances. Thus, because of the PVA's reciprocity provision, the two non-citizen survivors cannot bring suit under the PVA.

Nor may they bring the claim under the SAA. A literal reading of the SAA might permit such a suit, since the statute itself contains no reciprocity requirement and its language is broad:

> In cases where if [a vessel owned by the U.S.] were privately owned or operated, or if [cargo owned or possessed by the U.S.] were privately owned or possessed, or if a private person or property were involved, a proceeding in admiralty could be maintained, any appropriate nonjury proceeding in personam may be brought against the United States. . . .

46 U.S.C.App. § 742. The Supreme Court, however, held in *United States v. United Continental Tuna Corp.,* 425 U.S. 164 (1976), that a plaintiff whose claim falls within the scope of the PVA may not escape the PVA's reciprocity requirement by suing under the SAA. *Id.* at 181. The Court emphasized that to permit such a claim would "render nugatory the provisions of the Public Vessels Act." *Id.* at 178.

United Continental Tuna, however, did not involve the FTCA, and the survivors argue that they may still bring their claims under that statute. The FTCA provides:

> The United States shall be liable, respecting the provisions of this title relating to tort claims, in the same manner and to the same extent as a private individual under like circumstances. . . .

28 U.S.C. § 2674. The FTCA provides for several exceptions to this broad grant of liability, however, and one of them generally excludes claims remediable in admiralty:

> The provisions of this chapter . . . shall not apply to—

> . . .

---

8. Indeed, every reported opinion we have found that has considered the matter has concluded that Coast Guard vessels are public vessels. * * *

9. It is possible that the negligent-search claim falls outside the PVA to the extent that it involves the negligence of offi-

cials in the Coast Guard office on land rather than the crew of the Kiska. We need not limn the precise contours of the PVA, however, because the claims will turn out to be barred whether they arise under the PVA or not. *See infra.*

(d) Any claim for which a remedy is provided by sections 741–752 [the SAA], 781–790 [the PVA] of Title 46, relating to claims or suits in admiralty against the United States.

28 U.S.C. § 2680. The United States argues that this provision bars the non-citizen survivors' claim. The non-citizen survivors contend that it does not, because as foreign nationals who cannot show reciprocity they have no "remedy" under the PVA or SAA. They argue, not unreasonably, that a literal reading of the statute's language would not bar their suit. The parties thus address the question of the FTCA's applicability as if it were chiefly a matter of interpreting § 2680's admiralty exception. But it does not matter who is correct, because the survivors' claim is barred for reasons unrelated to the FTCA's admiralty exception. The PVA of its own force bars their claim.

The Supreme Court's decision in *United Continental Tuna* signaled that the PVA was not to be interpreted along purely textualist lines in its interaction with other statutes. The plain text of the PVA and the SAA, after all, would have allowed the plaintiffs in that case to avoid the PVA's reciprocity requirement by bringing their suit under the SAA. The Court did not permit such an evasion. Rather, it read the PVA to require that any claim within its scope (that is, involving a public vessel) meet the reciprocity requirement, *regardless* of whether some other statute seemed on its face to permit suit without reciprocity. In *United Continental Tuna*, the other statute in question was the SAA. In this case, the survivors seek to use the FTCA for the same purpose. To permit them to do so, however, would be entirely inconsistent with the *ratio decidendi* if not the letter of *United Continental Tuna*, because it would "effectively nullify specific policy judgments made by Congress when it enacted the Public Vessels Act, by enabling litigants to bring suits previously subject to the terms of the Public Vessels Act under" the Federal Tort Claims Act. *United Cont'l Tuna*, 425 U.S. at 181.

Thus, the survivors go astray in framing the issue as the interpretation of the FTCA's admiralty exception. In fact, *even if that exception to the FTCA did not exist*, the PVA would still prevent claims within its scope from being asserted under other statutes when the reciprocity requirement is not satisfied. Hence, those of the non-citizens survivors' claims which allege negligence relating to a Coast Guard vessel may not be brought under the FTCA or any other statute.[11]

---

11. The plaintiffs who are U.S. citizens—Monazzami and, we assume, Nahid's estate—cannot recover for the negligent-search claim under either the PVA or the SAA because that claim is time-barred by the statute of limitations for both statutes. The alleged negligence occurred on March 18, 1999, but Monazzami and Nahid's estate did not assert a claim against the United States until the second amended complaint was filed on January 29, 2002. *See* 46 U.S.C.App. § 745 (requiring claims under the SAA to be brought within two years); 46 U.S.C.App. § 782 (making the SAA's procedural provisions applicable to the PVA). Because the PVA or the SAA supplied a remedy, Monazzami and Nahid's estate may not bring the negligence claim under the FTCA. *See* 28 U.S.C. § 2680(d).

[handwritten margin notes:]
Ct: The PVA bars maritime claims under FTCA

The reason for the rule in United Continental is present here -- The purpose of PVA is to require claims w/in its scope to be brought solely under PVA -- can't evade the reciprocity decision

2

We turn now to the claim by the survivors (both citizen and non-citizen) that the Coast Guard negligently failed to communicate with local authorities who might have provided superior rescue equipment. The PVA does not apply to this claim—since it does not involve a public vessel—and therefore neither does the PVA's reciprocity requirement. The survivors thus had a remedy for their failure-to-communicate claim under the SAA. (That remedy is no longer available because the statute of limitations lapsed before they filed their claim against the United States. *See* 46 U.S.C.App. § 745 (requiring claims under the SAA to be brought within two years).) The failure-to-communicate claim thus falls squarely within the FTCA's exception for "claim [s] for which a remedy is provided by [the SAA]"—even on the literal reading of this clause for which the survivors argue—and the district court was correct to conclude that they cannot bring it under the FTCA. *See T.J. Falgout Boats, Inc. v. United States*, 508 F.2d 855, 858 (9th Cir.1974) (holding that a claim maintainable under the SAA but barred by the statute of limitations cannot be brought under the FTCA).

Since neither of the survivors' claims is cognizable under the FTCA, the district court was correct to grant summary judgment for the government.

AFFIRMED.

Notes and Questions

1. The Suits in Admiralty Act (SIAA) was the first waiver of federal sovereign immunity that included a remedy for tortious injuries. Although, as we will see in Chapter IV *infra,* the government waived its immunity for contract claims at a relatively early date, claims for tort-like harms were handled through private bills just 90 years ago. In 1920—more than two decades before enactment of the Federal Tort Claims Act—Congress enacted the SIAA (a predecessor statute had been enacted in 1916). In 1925, Congress enacted the Public Vessels Act (PVA) to make itself amenable to suit for injuries involving its "public" (generally meaning military) vessels.

The decision in *Taghadomi v. United States* provides an illustration of the jurisdictional issues that may arise concerning the SIAA, the PVA, and the Federal Tort Claims Act (which was the subject of preceding part of this casebook), a confusion that was settled in part by the Supreme Court's 1976 decision in *United States v. United Continental Tuna Corp.*, 425 U.S. 164 (1976), which is also discussed in the *Taghadomi* opinion. The determination as to which statute applies may well determine the outcome of the claim, as the procedural requirements and limitations differ among these statutes.

As noted in the *Taghadomi* decision, the SIAA as enacted in 1920 originally provided for liability of the United States only when the govern-

Handwritten margin notes:

Re: Failure-to-communicate claim

Ct: It's not w/in PVA b/c it doesn't involve a Pub. vessel, ...

... and ∏s can't bring it under FTCA b/c SOL has run ...

[margin: SIAA was originally for damage but merchant vessels.]

[margin: But . . .]

ment employed a vessel as a merchant vessel. However, admiralty claims may also arise against the government out of other activities, such as the crash of an airplane into the ocean. Thus, the question arose whether such an incident fell within the scope of the SIAA? Or was the Federal Tort Claims Act the proper remedy or at least available in the alternative? Moreover, did claims based upon admiralty contracts (that is, contracts related to maritime activities) fall outside of the SIAA given the statutory focus on the activities of government merchant vessels? As we will see in Chapter IV, contract claims against the United States for more than $10,000 must be heard in a specialized tribunal under the Tucker Act. Thus, uncertainty about which statute applied to admiralty contracts involving the government also created uncertainty about the forum in which the claim must be filed.

[margin: 1960 Amendment]

In 1960, the SIAA was amended to address these jurisdictional concerns. To clarify that all admiralty claims against the United States should be heard in admiralty under the SIAA, the phrase about employment of the vessel as a merchant ship was deleted and the government was generally made liable in admiralty as if "a private person or property were involved." 46 U.S.C. App. § 30903(a). Thus, if an aircraft crashes in navigable waters due to governmental wrongdoing, *see, e.g., Roberts v. United States,* 498 F.2d 520, 526 (9th Cir.), *cert. denied,* 419 U.S. 1070 (1974), or if the Coast Guard is negligent during a sea rescue mission, *see, e.g., Taghadomi, supra; Kelly v. United States,* 531 F.2d 1144, 1148–49 (2d Cir. 1976), the claim lies under the SIAA (or the PVA).

The 1960 amendment to the SIAA broadened that waiver of sovereign immunity to encompass all admiralty claims against the United States that otherwise would have been brought under the FTCA (and all admiralty contract claims that otherwise would be pursued under the Tucker Act).

[margin: Interplay b/t SIAA & PVA]

[margin: Does SIAA encompass claims arising by damage from public vessels?]

But there remains a further question to be resolved. Did the 1960 amendment expanding the scope of the SIAA also encompass claims involving government vessels previously covered by the Public Vessels Act (PVA)? The answer to that question may be crucial in some cases because the PVA includes certain limitations on suit, most notably, the reciprocity rule now codified in 46 U.S.C. 31111. Under the PVA's reciprocity requirement, a foreign national is barred from bringing suit unless it appears that the foreign national's country would permit United States nationals to sue for similar claims in its courts. (What do you think of this demand for reciprocity, which arguably denies justice to foreign nationals based upon the failure of their home nations to afford justice to Americans in like situation? Is that tit-for-tat rule justified as a matter of policy? Is it worthy of a great nation? Or is it a realistic assessment of governmental responsibilities in a world of troubled international relations?)

Other statutory waivers of sovereign immunity, notably the SIAA (and the FTCA), do not impose a reciprocity requirement—aliens are not excluded on the basis of their nationality from seeking recovery against the United States government. But if all admiralty claims may be pursued under the SIAA, then the PVA is largely eliminated, that is, effectively repealed, because any PVA claim could be brought under the SIAA. In sum, if the 1960 amendment to the SIAA includes claims involving public vessels, then any suit can be brought under the SIAA and the limitations of the PVA would be ineffectual in virtually every case.

How is this question answered in *Taghadomi* (following the Supreme Court's precedent in *United States v. United Continental Tuna Corp.*)? May the foreign national plaintiffs proceed under the SIAA rather than the PVA? Is *Taghadomi* a PVA case (at least in part)? Why? And what is the result?

2.   Admiralty law governs activities on the high seas and on navigable waters within the United States. *See generally* 1 Lester S. Jayson & Robert C. Longstreth, *Handling Federal Tort Claims* § 1.07[1] (2005). This is a special regime of law that governs tort and contract claims arising in this context. *See generally* Thomas J. Schoenbaum, *Admiralty and Maritime Law* (4th ed. 2004); Robert Force & Martin J. Norris, *The Law of Seamen* (3 vols., 5th ed. 2005); Frank L. Maraist & Thomas C. Galligan, Jr., *Admiralty in a Nutshell* (4th ed. 2001). Admiralty law is exclusively federal and jurisdictional authority to hear admiralty claims is vested in the federal courts. *See* 28 U.S.C. § 1333 (providing generally for jurisdiction in federal district court over admiralty or maritime claims); 46 U.S.C. § 30906 (providing for venue in federal district court over claims against the United States under the SIAA); 46 U.S.C. § 31104 (providing for venue in federal district courts over claims against the United States under the PVA).

The SIAA and the PVA do not create any new rights to recovery, but rather waive the sovereign immunity of the United States to impose the same liability that would be imposed by general admiralty law upon a private party. "[T]he Suits in Admiralty Act does not itself provide a cause of action against the United States. Instead, it only acts as a waiver of the sovereign immunity of the United States in admiralty suits. * * * Thus, the act merely provides a jurisdictional hook upon which to hang a traditional admiralty claim." *Trautman v. Buck Steber, Inc.,* 693 F.2d 440, 443–44 (5th Cir. 1982). The SIAA and PVA thus are parallel to the Federal Tort Claims Act, which also fails to create any cause of action, instead looking to the substantive tort law of the states. Moreover, the SIAA and PVA are mutually exclusive with the FTCA. In 1960, the FTCA was amended to exclude any claims that are covered by the SIAA or PVA. 28 U.S.C. § 2680(d).

Thus, in *Taghadomi*, the court was required to determine whether each of the claims raised by the plaintiffs fell on the admiralty side (covered exclusively by the SIAA/PVA) or the civil side (covered by the FTCA) of federal jurisdiction. How did the court analyze this question, that is, what test or set of factors did it apply to determine whether these were admiralty claims? What answers did the court reach and why? And why did the court then dismiss that claim which at least arguably could otherwise have been maintained under the FTCA?

3.   There is a crucial difference in procedure between admiralty claims against the United States and those against private parties. Admiralty

claims against private shipowners may be enforced by the seizure or arrest of the vessel—called a libel in rem. The purpose of an in rem proceeding is to guarantee a basis for recovery on the claim, that is, against the value of the ship. Moreover, because ships obviously are mobile, a libel in rem seizure may be necessary to ensure that the defendant does not abscond with the ship by leaving port and thereby make it difficult to enforce any judgment. This concern is not present when the United States government is the defendant, as it obviously is capable of paying any judgment. Moreover, if government-owned vessels were seized in port and thus removed from service, the public interest would be impaired. Under 46 U.S.C. 30908, Congress prohibited arrest or seizure of government vessels in the SIAA.

Can't proceed in rem against gov't vessels under SIAA

what is the exception & what is its scope?

Can you under PVA?

In rem?

In Re Joint Eastern and Southern Districts Asbestos Litigation (Robinson v. United States)

United States Court of Appeals for the Second Circuit.
891 F.2d 31 (2d Cir. 1989).

■ ALTIMARI, CIRCUIT JUDGE:

π appeals from E.D.N.Y. grant of U.S. M Diss for lack of SMJD

In this case, we consider the court's jurisdiction to entertain a personal injury claim against the United States for damages allegedly caused by exposure to asbestos on board ships of the United States' merchant fleet during World War II. Plaintiff-appellant Sally Robinson, as representative of the estate of her late husband Edward Robinson, appeals from a judgment of the United States District Court for the Eastern District of New York (Sifton, J.) which granted the United States' motion under Fed.R.Civ.P. 12(b)(1) to dismiss for lack of subject matter jurisdiction.

Edward Robinson had been employed on merchant ships operated by the United States through the War Shipping Administration during World War II. Plaintiff asserted wrongful death claims against a number of asbestos companies and against the United States under the Suits in Admiralty Act, 46 U.S.C.App. § 741 _et seq._ ("SAA"), and the War Shipping Administration Clarification Act of 1943, 50 U.S.C.App. § 1291 ("Clarification Act"). The district court determined that the United States' waiver of sovereign immunity embodied in the SAA and the Clarification Act is limited by the discretionary function exception. The court further found that the complained of governmental conduct was discretionary within the meaning of the exception. Accordingly, the district court granted the government's motion to dismiss and directed entry of final judgment pursuant to Fed.R.Civ.P. 54(b) as to all claims against the United States. Suit continues, however, against the asbestos companies.

Dist Ct:
· Lack of SMJD on claims which fell w/in discret. func. exception
· Summj for U.S. as to all others

On this appeal, plaintiff contends that the district court improperly implied the discretionary function exception to the SAA and the Clarification Act. Alternatively, she argues that the government conduct here at

Q: Is there an implied d.f. exception? in SAA? in Clarification Act?

issue is not covered by the exception. For the reasons that follow, we affirm the judgment of the district court.

BACKGROUND

"[I]n order to assure the most effective utilization of the shipping of the United States for the successful prosecution of [World War II]," President Franklin D. Roosevelt established the War Shipping Administration ("WSA") by executive order on February 7, 1942. Exec. Order No. 9054, 3 C.F.R. 1086 (1938–43), *reprinted in* 1942 U.S.Code Cong.Serv. 154. The WSA was empowered to "[c]ontrol the operation, purchase, charter, requisition, and use of all ocean vessels under the flag or control of the United States," with certain exceptions not relevant here. *Id.* at 1087. As a result, "substantially our entire merchant marine became part of a single vast shipping pool, said to have been the largest in history." *Hust v. Moore-McCormack Lines, Inc.*, 328 U.S. 707, 709 (1946), *overruled, Cosmopolitan Shipping Co. v. McAllister*, 337 U.S. 783, 794 (1949).

[margin note: Purpose of WSA]

The WSA obtained ships either through new construction or by transfer of existing vessels from private shipping interests. The transfer of vessels was effected by use of general agency agreements. Pursuant to these agreements, the vessels continued to be operated by their original owners, *Gordon v. Lykes Bros. S.S. Co.*, 835 F.2d 96, 97 (5th Cir.), *cert. denied*, 488 U.S. 825 (1988), "subject to the directions, orders, and regulations of the [WSA]" Note, *Remedies of Merchant Seamen Injured on Government Owned Vessels*, 55 Yale L.J. 584, 588 (1946).

[margin note: WSA obtained most vessels by agency agreements, in which private owners would operate them.]

Since the number of existing vessels was insufficient to satisfy the wartime needs of the United States, the majority of the WSA controlled fleet was obtained through new construction. *See* Report of the War Shipping Administrator to the President, *The United States Merchant Marine at War* 33 (Jan. 15, 1946). The United States' wartime shipbuilding effort was a "race between ship construction and sinkings by the enemy." *Id.* Thus, that "[e]fficient ship construction and operation was a very high priority of the United States government during World War II," *Gordon*, 835 F.2d at 97, is a vast understatement.

[margin note: · High need to build new ships to counteract loss in the war]

In response to the national emergency, the United States Maritime Commission Division of Emergency Ship Construction (the "Commission") was ordered to "get results fast, even at the sacrifice of some of the painstaking procedures which were part of the usual practice." F. Lane, *Ships for Victory: A History of Shipbuilding Under the U.S. Maritime Commission in World War II* 78 (1951). To achieve the desired efficiency, the Commission utilized nationwide standardization of design and materials. Standardized use of readily available materials ensured a steady flow from numerous suppliers to the many shipyards. Moreover, as voiced by the Commission's director of building operations, the Commission took a dim view of design improvements: " 'they are not only not desired, but are not to be accepted, unless it can be shown that they are essential to acceptable performance, and at the same time that they can be incorporated without prejudice to prompt procurement.' " *Id.* at 578.

[margin note: Judgment call WSA had to make]

[margin note: Efficient production vs. impeccability of design]

.. asbestos ...

As a consequence of the winning effort in the race between ship construction and sinkings, asbestos was used heavily in the construction of World War II merchant ships. *See Gordon,* 835 F.2d at 97.

DISCUSSION

A. *Applicability of the Discretionary Function Exception.*

Robinson contends that the district court improperly implied the discretionary function exception to the SAA and the Clarification Act. Specifically, she contends that the waiver of sovereign immunity expressed in those acts subjects the United States to liability on the same basis as private vessel owners and the court may not imply any exception not applicable in suits against private defendants. We disagree.

π: No implied d.f. exception exists in either SAA or C.A.

1. The Suits in Admiralty Act.

The SAA was one of "a series of statutes directed generally at affording private vessel owners an adequate and efficient remedy for damages arising from negligent operation of ships owned by the United States." *Canadian Aviator, Ltd. v. United States,* 324 U.S. 215, 218 (1945). Prior to 1916, persons injured by the negligent operation of vessels owned or operated by the United States could not recover against the United States due to the United States' sovereign immunity. In contrast, the United States could bring an action against private shipowners. Congress addressed this inequity by enacting the Shipping Act of 1916, ch. 451, 39 Stat. 728 (1916). The Shipping Act of 1916 subjected the United States' merchant fleet to "all laws, regulations, and liabilities governing merchant vessels." 39 Stat. 730–31.

Shipping Act of 1916

The Shipping Act of 1916 had broader reach than Congress intended. Application of the Act led to the seizure of a ship belonging to the United States incident to an admiralty proceeding *in rem. See The Lake Monroe,* 250 U.S. 246, 248 (1919). This occurrence embarrassed Congress and provided the impetus for the adoption of the SAA. The SAA declared that no vessel owned by or in the possession of the United States shall be subject to arrest or seizure by judicial process. Ch. 95, § 1 et seq., 41 Stat. 525 (1920). The SAA further stated that "in cases where if such vessel were privately owned or operated, ... a proceeding in admiralty could be maintained," a libel *in personam* for damages could be filed against the United States "provided that such vessel is employed as a merchant vessel or is a tugboat." *Id.* at § 2, 525–26.

SAA (1920)

. Congress limited liability/remedy somewhat

The SAA contains no express exception for discretionary functions. In contrast, Congress expressly included the discretionary function exception in the Federal Tort Claims Act, 28 U.S.C. § 2680(a) ("FTCA"), in order "to prevent judicial "second guessing" of legislative and administrative decisions grounded in social, economic, and political policy through the medium of an action in tort.'" *Berkovitz v. United States,* 486 U.S. 531 (1988) (quoting *United States v. Varig Airlines,* 467 U.S. 797, 814 (1984)).

FTCA has d.f. exception...

The inclusion of such an exception in the FTCA, on the one hand, and the omission of an express exception from the SAA, on the other, does not

Reason for the rule is to prevent judicial 2nd guessing of political policy decisions...

compel the conclusion that the SAA is not subject to the discretionary function exception. The exception was drafted merely as a "clarifying amendment" to the FTCA, *Dalehite v. United States,* 346 U.S. 15, 26 (1953), since Congress "believed that claims of the kind embraced by the discretionary function exception would have been exempted from the waiver of sovereign immunity by judicial construction." *Varig Airlines,* 467 U.S. at 810. This belief was well founded. * * *

this is based on S. O. P.

The wellspring of the discretionary function exception is the doctrine of separation of powers. Simply stated, principles of separation of powers mandate that the judiciary refrain from deciding questions consigned to the concurrent branches of the government. If substantial constitutional issues are not implicated, the wisdom of decisions made by the executive and legislative branches are not subject to judicial review.

The doctrine of separation of powers is "a doctrine to which the courts must adhere even in the absence of an explicit statutory command." *Canadian Transport [Co. v. United States],* 663 F.2d [1081,] 1086 [(D.C.Cir. 1980)]. Were we to find the discretionary function exception not to be applicable to the SAA, we would subject "all administrative and legislative decisions concerning the public interest in maritime matters ... to independent judicial review in the not unlikely event that the implementation of those policy judgments were to cause private injuries." *Bearce [v. United States],* 614 F.2d [556,] 559 [(7th Cir.), *cert. denied,* 449 U.S. 837 (1980)]. Such an outcome is intolerable under our constitutional system of separation of powers. Therefore, in accord with the great weight of authority, we find the SAA to be subject to the discretionary function exception. This result is compelled by our steadfast refusal to assume powers that are vested in the concurrent branches.

Result of judicial second-guessing of maritime executive/legls. decisions.

Conc: We imply a d.f. exception

2.   The Clarification Act.

The Clarification Act provides, *inter alia,* that seamen "employed on United States or foreign flag vessels as employees of the United States through the War Shipping Administration shall ... have all of the rights, benefits, exemptions, privileges, and liabilities, under law applicable to citizens of the United States employed as seamen on privately owned and operated American vessels." 50 U.S.C.App. § 1291(a).

(Must be able to distinguish b/t public & private vessels)

As previously discussed, Congress had enacted the SAA to provide private parties with a remedy for damages arising from the operation of ships owned by the United States. Following the WSA's assumption of control of the merchant fleet, however, it was often unclear whether an action would lie under the SAA.

who enjoy the SAA...

Operating conditions during World War II made it difficult to determine whether a particular vessel was a "merchant" ship or a "public vessel." S.Rep. No. 62, 78th Cong., 1st Sess. 5–6 (1943) (*"Senate Report"*). The significance of the distinction was that merchant ships fell within the coverage of the SAA, while public vessels were excluded. As noted in the legislative history of the Clarification Act:

but covered in Clarification Act

> [V]ital differences in ... rights are made to depend on whether the seaman happens to be employed aboard a vessel time-chartered to the [WSA] or owned by or bareboat-chartered to the [WSA]. Since seamen constantly change from one vessel to another, their rights ... also constantly change, depending upon the relationship of the [WSA] to the vessel. This fluctuation and lack of uniformity of rights leads to dependency of vital rights upon chance with a result of confusion and inequities. *The [Clarification Act] is designed to remove this confusion and these inequities.*

Id. (emphasis added). Thus, what the Clarification Act clarified was that seamen aboard WSA ships, "though technically Government employees, [could] have their rights determined" under the SAA, H.Rep. No. 107, 78th Cong., 1st Sess. 22 (1943), "regardless of the nature of the vessel on which [they served]." *Senate Report* at 14.

Since the Clarification Act employs the SAA to make its authorized claims enforceable, *Gordon,* 835 F.2d at 99, it would seem to follow that any exception applicable to the SAA must likewise be applicable to claims brought under the Clarification Act. Even if this is not the case, however, the court remains anchored by the doctrine of separation of powers regardless of whether a claim is launched pursuant to the SAA or the Clarification Act. Accordingly, we find the Clarification Act to be subject to the discretionary function exception.

B.   *Application of the Discretionary Function Exception*

Robinson contends that the United States' operation of ships upon which asbestos was present was not discretionary within the meaning of the discretionary function exception. In addition, she asserts that the exception does not shield the United States from liability arising from the failure to warn of dangers posed by asbestos on board the World War II merchant fleet. We disagree.

Although the precise contours of the discretionary function exception are hard to define, it is clear that the exception "insulates the Government from liability if the action challenged ... involves the permissible exercise of policy judgment." *Berkovitz,* 108 S. Ct. at 1959. To determine whether particular conduct falls within the exception, we employ the two-step analysis enunciated in *Berkovitz*. First, we consider whether the conduct is the product of choice, *Berkovitz,* 108 S. Ct. at 1958, and if so, whether the choice involves considerations of public policy. *Id.* at 1959. An action "cannot be discretionary unless it involves an element of judgment or choice." *Id.* at 1958 (citing *Dalehite,* 346 U.S. at 34). Thus, conduct is not the product of choice and "the discretionary function exception [does] not apply when a federal statute, regulation, or policy specifically prescribes a course of action for an employee to follow." *Id.* Likewise, the exception does not apply where no public policy is implicated because the exception is designed to shield only " 'legislative and administrative decisions grounded in social, economic, and political policy.' " *Id.* at 1959 (quoting *Varig Airlines,* 467 U.S. at 814).

[Handwritten margin notes:]

Result: employees of U.S., wherever boat they're on, are covered by SAA...

... t/f we imply a d.f. exception to the Clarification Act as well

Q: whether the gov't conduct falls w/in the exception

Berkovitz
1. Conduct is product of policy choice?
2. Is P.P. implicated?

There can be no doubt that each of the actions challenged by plaintiff were matters of choice for President Roosevelt and his administration. During the war, the government was faced with a desperate need to place merchant ships upon the seas. The decisions to operate existing ships, which contained asbestos, and to employ existing designs and materials, including asbestos, in the construction of new ships were not prescribed by any federal statute, regulation, or policy, save for the ultimate policy of defending the nation.

We are unpersuaded by Robinson's assertion that the government's decision to operate ships with asbestos on board was impermissible because the government had an absolute duty under the common law to provide "seaworthy" vessels. Under *Berkovitz*, a matter is removed from the realm of permissible choice by "federal statute, regulation, or policy." *Id.* at 1958 (emphasis added). The fact that the challenged actions were matters of choice "cannot be overcome by clothing the discretionary act[s] in the maritime uniform of a breach of a duty to provide a seaworthy vessel." *Gordon*, 835 F.2d at 100. We are unwilling to declare that during a world war, when ships were being sunk by the enemy as fast as they could be constructed, it was impermissible for the government to choose to deploy ships in less than "seaworthy" condition.

We need spend little time discussing whether the contested choices involved considerations of public policy. It is difficult to imagine a clearer example of a decision grounded in social, economic, and political policy than the choice of how to prosecute a world war

Finally, we do not accept plaintiff's contention that the discretionary function exception does not cover the government's failure to warn of the hazards of asbestos on board the merchant fleet. * * * Robinson asserts that the exception applies only to policy judgments which were actually made, and that the government made no such judgments with respect to the issuance of warnings. * * *

We believe that it is unimportant whether the government actually balanced economic, social, and political concerns in reaching its decision. The discretionary function exception applies " '[w]here there is room for policy judgment.' " *Berkovitz*, 108 S. Ct. at 1959 (quoting *Dalehite*, 346 U.S. at 36). Thus, "the relevant question is not whether an explicit balancing is proved, but whether the decision is susceptible to policy analysis." *United States Fidelity & Guar. Co. [v. United States]*, 837 F.2d [116,] 121 [(3d Cir.), *cert. denied*, 487 U.S. 1235 (1988)].

* * * We have no doubt that the record before us presents such circumstances. Accordingly, we find that the government's failure to adopt a safety program to warn of asbestos-related dangers on board ships in the midst of World War II is covered by the discretionary function exception.

CONCLUSION

For all of the foregoing reasons, the judgment of the district court is affirmed.

———

Notes and Questions

In contrast with Section 2680(a) of the Federal Tort Claims Act, 28 U.S.C. § 2680(a), the Suits in Admiralty Act contains no express provision protecting the government's discretionary functions. See Chapter III.A.4 (discussing the discretionary function exception under the FTCA). Nevertheless, as shown by the decision in *Robinson v. United States,** with only one exception that recently fell into line, every court of appeals to address the question has concluded that a discretionary function exception must be implicit in the SIAA. *See, e.g., Kristen M. Good v. Ohio Edison Co.*, 149 F.3d 413, 419 (6th Cir. 1998); *Tew v. United States*, 86 F.3d 1003, 1005 (10th Cir. 1996); *Earles v. United States*, 935 F.2d 1028, 1031–32 (9th Cir. 1991); *Sea-Land Serv., Inc. v. United States*, 919 F.2d 888, 891–93 (3d Cir. 1990); *Gordon v. United States*, 835 F.2d 96 (5th Cir. 1988); *United States Fire Ins. Co. v. United States*, 806 F.2d 1529, 1534–35 (11th Cir. 1986) (regarding both SIAA and PVA); *Brown v. United States*, 790 F.2d 199, 203–04 (1st Cir. 1986); *Bearce v. United States*, 614 F.2d 556, 559–60 (7th Cir. 1980); *Canadian Transport Co. v. United States*, 663 F.2d 1081, 1085–87 (D.C. Cir. 1980).

Until recently, the hold-out among the courts of appeals on this question was the Fourth Circuit. In *McMellon v. United States*, 338 F.3d 287, 291–92 (4th Cir. 2003) (panel opinion, later vacated), a three-judge panel of that court acknowledged that "[e]very other circuit to consider the question" had implied a discretionary function exception into the SIAA, but held over a dissent that the Fourth Circuit "has refused to read a discretionary function exception into the SIAA." Subsequently, the Fourth Circuit vacated the *McMellon* panel opinion and reheard the case en banc. Sitting en banc in *McMellon*, an eight-judge majority of the Fourth Circuit in an opinion by Judge Traxler overruled contrary circuit precedent and held that the SIAA implicitly contains a discretionary function exception to its waiver of sovereign immunity. *McMellon v. United States*, 387 F.3d 329, 338–49 (4th Cir. 2004) (en banc).

Although the *McMellon* en banc majority could "not conclude that Congress clearly intended for the SIAA's waiver of sovereign immunity to be subject to an exception for discretionary functions" nor could the court "reach that conclusion by resort to traditional tools of statutory construction," the court concluded the application of constitutional separation-of-powers principles compelled implication of the exception lest the executive branch's ability to faithfully execute the laws be substantially impaired and the judiciary "be called upon to decide issues it is not equipped to resolve." *Id.* at 340–43. Judge Wilkinson in a concurrence contended "any different result would not be supportable," because the courts otherwise would be set "on an aggressive course far afield of judicial competence and replete with matters of policy entrusted elsewhere." *Id.* at 349–53 (Wilkinson, J., concurring). Five judges refused to read a discretionary function exception into the SIAA that Congress had not expressly included, with Judge Luttig calling the majority decision "breathtaking" in "mistakenly equating liabil-

---

* In the interests of full disclosure, the author of this casebook was counsel for the   United States in the *Robinson* case before the court of appeals.

ity on behalf of the United States with infringement on the Executive's power to execute the laws" (although he acknowledged that the political question doctrine might require that the courts decline to hear some SIAA cases as nonjusticiable). *Id.* at 357–62 (Motz, J., joined by Michael, J., concurring in part and dissenting in part); *id.* at 362 (Widener, J., dissenting); *id.* at 362–82 (Luttig, J., dissenting); *id.* at 382–83 (Gregory, J., dissenting).

Who do you think has the better of the argument? The *Robinson* court and the *McMellon* majority? The dissenters in *McMellon*? Consider again the cases you studied concerning the discretionary function exception to the FTCA (see Chapter III.A.4). Indeed, the *Robinson* court (and the *McMellon* majority) elevates the discretionary function exception to a constitutional level, on the ground that judicial review of a discretionary function activity would violate the constitutional separation of powers. This should cause you to harken back as well to the earlier debate about the very foundation of sovereign immunity itself, see Chapter II, as well as the brief discussion of the political question doctrine, see Chapter I.C.2.

SECTION C.   EMPLOYMENT DISCRIMINATION CLAIMS

There is no single federal employment discrimination statute, but rather "a patchwork of statutes" covering different categories of people. *See* Mack A. Player, *Federal Law of Employment Discrimination in a Nutshell* 12 (1992). These statutes includes the Age Discrimination in Employment Act, 29 U.S.C. §§ 621–634, and the Americans With Disabilities Act. 42 U.S.C. §§ 12101–12213. Title VII of the Civil Rights Act of 1964, 42 U.S.C. §§ 2000e to 2000e–17, is undoubtedly "the centerpiece of employment discrimination law." Player, *supra*, at 12. As amended in 1972, Title VII proscribes discrimination by the federal government as an employer on the basis of race, color, religion, sex, and national origin. 42 U.S.C. § 2000e–16(a).

The detailed substance of employment discrimination law is well beyond the scope of this course. For purposes of this course, it is important to understand that the federal government is indeed subject to employment discrimination laws, but, as we see continually in so many areas, it is treated a little differently than other employers.

Civil Rights Act of 1964, Title VII, 42 United States Code § 2000e–16(a) to (d)

(a) Discriminatory practices prohibited; employees or applicants for employment subject to coverage

All personnel actions affecting employees or applicants for employment (except with regard to aliens employed outside the limits of the United

States) in military departments as defined in section 102 of Title 5, in executive agencies as defined in section 105 of Title 5 (including employees and applicants for employment who are paid from nonappropriated funds), in the United States Postal Service and the Postal Regulatory Commission, in those units of the Government of the District of Columbia having positions in the competitive service, and in those units of the judicial branch of the Federal Government having positions in the competitive service, in the Smithsonian Institution, and in the Government Printing Office, the Government Accountability Office, and the Library of Congress shall be made free from any discrimination based on race, color, religion, sex, or national origin.

(b) Equal Employment Opportunity Commission; enforcement powers, issuance of rules, regulations, etc.; annual review and approval of national and regional equal employment opportunity plans; review and evaluation of equal employment opportunity programs and publication of progress reports; consultations with interested parties; compliance with rules, regulations, etc.; contents of national and regional equal employment opportunity plans; authority of Librarian of Congress

Except as otherwise provided in this subsection, the Equal Employment Opportunity Commission shall have the authority to enforce the provisions of subsection (a) of this section through appropriate remedies, including reinstatement or hiring of employees with or without back pay, as will effectuate the policies of this section, and shall issue such rules, regulations, orders and instructions as it deems necessary and appropriate to carry out its responsibilities under this section. * * * The head of each such department, agency, or unit shall comply with such rules, regulations, orders, and instructions which shall include a provision that an employee or applicant for employment shall be advised of any final action taken on any complaint of discrimination filed by him thereunder. * * *

(c) Civil action by employee or applicant for employment for redress of grievances; time for bringing of action; head of department, agency, or unit as defendant

Within 90 days of receipt of notice of final action taken by a department, agency, or unit referred to in subsection (a) of this section, or by the Equal Employment Opportunity Commission upon an appeal from a decision or order of such department, agency, or unit on a complaint of discrimination based on race, color, religion, sex or national origin, brought pursuant to subsection (a) of this section, Executive Order 11478 or any succeeding Executive orders, or after one hundred and eighty days from the filing of the initial charge with the department, agency, or unit or with the Equal Employment Opportunity Commission on appeal from a decision or order of such department, agency, or unit until such time as final action may be taken by a department, agency, or unit, an employee or applicant for employment, if aggrieved by the final disposition of his complaint, or by the failure to take final action on his complaint, may file a civil action as provided in section 2000e–5 of this title, in which civil action the head of the department, agency, or unit, as appropriate, shall be the defendant.

(d) Section 2000e–5(f) through (k) of this title applicable to civil actions

The provisions of section 2000e–5(f) through (k) of this title, as applicable, shall govern civil actions brought hereunder, and the same interest to compensate for delay in payment shall be available as in cases involving nonpublic parties.

Brown v. General Services Administration

Supreme Court of the United States.
425 U.S. 820 (1976).

■ Mr. Justice Stewart delivered the opinion of the Court.

The principal question presented by this case is whether § 717 of the Civil Rights Act of 1964 provides the exclusive judicial remedy for claims of discrimination in federal employment.

The petitioner, Clarence Brown, is a Negro who has been employed by the General Services Administration since 1957. He is currently classified in grade GS–7 and has not been promoted since 1066. In December 1970 Brown was referred, along with two white colleagues, for promotion to grade GS–9 by his supervisors. All three were rated "highly qualified," and the promotion was given to one of the white candidates for the position. Brown filed a complaint with the GSA Equal Employment Opportunity Office alleging that racial discrimination had biased the selection process. That complaint was withdrawn when Brown was told that other GS–9 positions would soon be available.

Another GS–9 position did become vacant in June 1971, for which the petitioner along with two others was recommended as "highly qualified." Again a white applicant was chosen. Brown filed a second administrative complaint with the GSA Equal Employment Opportunity Office. After preparation and review of an investigative report, the GSA Regional Administrator notified the petitioner that there was no evidence that race had played a part in the promotion. Brown requested a hearing, and one was held before a complaints examiner of the Civil Service Commission. In February 1973, the examiner issued his findings and recommended decision. He found no evidence of racial discrimination; rather, he determined that Brown had not been advanced because he had not been *"fully cooperative."*

The GSA rendered its final decision in March 1973. The agency's Director of Civil Rights informed Brown by letter of his conclusion that considerations of race had not entered the promotional process. The Director's letter told Brown that if he chose, he might carry the administrative process further by lodging an appeal with the Board of Appeals and Review of the Civil Service Commission and that, alternatively, he could file suit within 30 days in federal district court.

Forty-two days later Brown filed suit in a Federal District Court. The complaint alleged jurisdiction under Title VII of the Civil Rights Act of 1964, 42 U.S.C. § 2000e *et seq.*, "with particular reference to" § 717; under 28 U.S.C. § 1331 (general federal-question jurisdiction); under the Declaratory Judgment Act, 28 U.S.C. §§ 2201, 2202; and under the Civil Rights Act of 1866, as amended, 42 U.S.C. § 1981.

The respondents moved to dismiss the complaint for lack of subject-matter jurisdiction, on the ground that Brown had not filed the complaint within 30 days of final agency action as required by § 717(c) of the Civil Rights Act of 1964, 42 U.S.C. § 2000e–16(c).* The District Court granted the motion.

The Court of Appeals for the Second Circuit affirmed the judgment of dismissal. 507 F.2d 1300 (1974). It held, first, that the § 717 remedy for federal employment discrimination was retroactively available to any employee, such as the petitioner, whose administrative complaint was pending at the time § 717 became effective on March 24, 1972. The appellate court held, second, that § 717 provides the exclusive judicial remedy for federal employment discrimination, and that the complaint had not been timely filed under that statute. Finally, the court ruled that if § 717 did not preempt other remedies, then the petitioner's complaint was still properly dismissed because of his failure to exhaust available administrative remedies. We granted certiorari to consider the important issues of federal law presented by this case.

The primary question in this litigation is not difficult to state: Is § 717 of the Civil Rights Act of 1964, as added by § 11 of the Equal Employment Opportunity Act of 1972, 42 U.S.C. § 2000e–16, the exclusive individual remedy available to a federal employee complaining of job-related racial discrimination? But the question is easier to state than it is to resolve. Congress simply failed explicitly to describe § 717's position in the constellation of antidiscrimination law. We must, therefore, infer congressional intent in less obvious ways. As Mr. Chief Justice Marshall once wrote for the Court: "Where the mind labours to discover the design of the legislature, it seizes everything from which aid can be derived...." *United States v. Fisher,* 2 Cranch 358, 386 (1805).

Title VII of the Civil Rights Act of 1964 forbids employment discrimination based on race, color, religion, sex, or national origin. 42 U.S.C. §§ 2000e–2, 2000e–3. Until it was amended in 1972 by the Equal Employment Opportunity Act, however, Title VII did not protect federal employees. 42 U.S.C. § 2000e(b). Although federal employment discrimination clearly violated both the Constitution and statutory law before passage of

---

* [As set out in the excerpt from Title VII at the beginning of this section, Section 717(c) now allows 90 days for filing of suit after final action by the agency or, if appealed, by the Equal Employment Opportunity Commission.]

the 1972 Act, the effective availability of either administrative or judicial relief was far from sure. Charges of racial discrimination were handled parochially within each federal agency. A hearing examiner might come from outside the agency, but he had no authority to conduct an independent examination, and his conclusions and findings were in the nature of recommendations that the agency was free to accept or reject.[5] Although review lay in the Board of Appeals and Review of the Civil Service Commission, Congress found "skepticism" among federal employees "regarding the Commission's record in obtaining just resolutions of complaints and adequate remedies. This has, in turn, discouraged persons from filing complaints with the Commission for fear that doing so will only result in antagonizing their supervisors and impairing any future hope of advancement."[6]

If administrative remedies were ineffective, judicial relief from federal employment discrimination was even more problematic before 1972. Although an action seeking to enjoin unconstitutional agency conduct would lie,[7] it was doubtful that backpay or other compensatory relief for employment discrimination was available at the time that Congress was considering the 1972 Act. For example, in *Gnotta v. United States,* 415 F.2d 1271, the Court of Appeals for the Eighth Circuit had held in 1969 that there was no jurisdictional basis to support the plaintiff's suit alleging that the Corps of Engineers had discriminatorily refused to promote him. Damages for alleged discrimination were held beyond the scope of the Tucker Act, 28 U.S.C. § 1346, since no express or implied contract was involved, 415 F.2d, at 1278. And the plaintiff's cause of action under the Administrative Procedure Act, 5 U.S.C. §§ 701–706, and the Mandamus Act, 28 U.S.C. § 1361, was held to be barred by sovereign immunity, since his claims for promotion would necessarily involve claims against the Treasury:

> "A suit against an officer of the United States is one against the United States itself if the decree would operate against the sovereign; or if the judgment sought would expend itself on the public treasury or domain, or interfere with the public administration; or if the effect of the judgment would be 'to restrain the Government from acting, or to compel it to act,' Larson v. Domestic & Foreign Commerce Corp., 337 U.S. 682, 704, . . . (1949)." 415 F.2d, at 1277.[8]

Concern was evinced during the hearings before the committees of both Houses over the apparent inability of federal employees to engage the judicial machinery in cases of alleged employment discrimination. Although there was considerable disagreement over whether a civil action would lie to remedy agency discrimination, the committees ultimately concluded that

5. S.Rep.No.92–415, p. 14 (1971).

6. *Ibid.;* see H.R.Rep.No.92–238, p. 24 (1971).

7. See, *e. g., Bolling v. Sharpe,* 347 U.S. 497 (1954); *Youngstown Sheet & Tube Co. v. Sawyer,* 343 U.S. 579 (1952).

8. By parity of reasoning, sovereign immunity would, of course, also bar claims against federal agencies for damages and promotion brought under the Civil Rights Act of 1866, as amended, 42 U.S.C. § 1981, and under the general federal-question jurisdictional grant of 28 U.S.C. § 1331.

judicial review was not available at all or, if available, that some forms of relief were foreclosed. * * *

The legislative history thus leaves little doubt that Congress was persuaded that federal employees who were treated discriminatorily had no effective judicial remedy. And the case law suggests that that conclusion was entirely reasonable. Whether that understanding of Congress was in some ultimate sense incorrect is not what is important in determining the legislative intent in amending the 1964 Civil Rights Act to cover federal employees. For the relevant inquiry is not whether Congress correctly perceived the then state of the law, but rather what its perception of the state of the law was.[10]

This unambiguous congressional perception seems to indicate that the congressional intent in 1972 was to create an exclusive, pre-emptive administrative and judicial scheme for the redress of federal employment discrimination. We need not, however, rest our decision upon this inference alone. For the structure of the 1972 amendment itself fully confirms the conclusion that Congress intended it to be exclusive and pre-emptive.

Section 717 of the Civil Rights Act of 1964, 42 U.S.C. § 2000e–16, proscribes federal employment discrimination and establishes an administrative and judicial enforcement system. Section 717(a) provides that all personnel actions affecting federal employees and applicants for federal employment "shall be made free from any discrimination based on race, color, religion, sex, or national origin."

Sections 717(b) and (c) establish complementary administrative and judicial enforcement mechanisms designed to eradicate federal employment discrimination. Subsection (b) delegates to the Civil Service Commission** full authority to enforce the provisions of subsection (a) "through appropriate remedies, including reinstatement or hiring of employees with or without back pay," to issue "rules, regulations, orders and instructions as it deems necessary and appropriate" to carry out its responsibilities under the Act, and to review equal employment opportunity plans that are annually submitted to it by each agency and department.

Section 717(c) permits an aggrieved employee to file a civil action in a federal district court to review his claim of employment discrimination. Attached to that right, however, are certain preconditions. Initially, the complainant must seek relief in the agency that has allegedly discriminated against him. He then may seek further administrative review with the Civil Service Commission or, alternatively, he may, within 30 days of receipt of notice of the agency's final decision, file suit in federal district court

---

10. The petitioner maintains that in 1972, despite adverse court decisions, 42 U.S.C. § 1981; the Mandamus Act, 28 U.S.C. § 1361; the Tucker Act, 28 U.S.C. § 1346; 28 U.S.C. § 1331 (general federal-question jurisdiction); and the Administrative Procedure Act, 5 U.S.C. § 702, all conferred jurisdiction on the federal courts in federal employment discrimination cases.

** [As set out in the excerpt from Title VII at the beginning of this section, Section 717(b) now delegates enforcement authority to the Equal Employment Opportunity Commission.]

without appealing to the Civil Service Commission. If he does appeal to the Commission, he may file suit within 30 days of the Commission's final decision.*** In any event, the complainant may file a civil action if, after 180 days from the filing of the charge or the appeal, the agency or Civil Service Commission has not taken final action.

Sections 706(f) through (k), 42 U.S.C. §§ 2000e–5(f) through 2000e–5(k), which are incorporated "as applicable" by § 717(d), govern such issues as venue, the appointment of attorneys, attorneys' fees, and the scope of relief. Section 717(e), finally, retains within each governmental agency "primary responsibility to assure nondiscrimination in employment...."

The balance, completeness, and structural integrity of § 717 are inconsistent with the petitioner's contention that the judicial remedy afforded by § 717(c) was designed merely to supplement other putative judicial relief. His view fails, in our estimation, to accord due weight to the fact that unlike these other supposed remedies, § 717 does not contemplate merely judicial relief. Rather, it provides for a careful blend of administrative and judicial enforcement powers. Under the petitioner's theory, by perverse operation of a type of Gresham's law, § 717, with its rigorous administrative exhaustion requirements and time limitations, would be driven out of currency were immediate access to the courts under other, less demanding statutes permissible. The crucial administrative role that each agency together with the Civil Service Commission was given by Congress in the eradication of employment discrimination would be eliminated "by the simple expedient of putting a different label on [the] pleadings." *Preiser v. Rodriguez,* 411 U.S. 475, 489–490 (1973). It would require the suspension of disbelief to ascribe to Congress the design to allow its careful and thorough remedial scheme to be circumvented by artful pleading.

The petitioner relies upon our decision in *Johnson v. Railway Express Agency,* 421 U.S. 454 (1975), for the proposition that Title VII did not repeal pre-existing remedies for employment discrimination. In *Johnson* the Court held that in the context of *private employment* Title VII did not pre-empt other remedies. But that decision is inapposite here. In the first place, there were no problems of sovereign immunity in the context of the *Johnson* case. Second, the holding in *Johnson* rested upon the explicit legislative history of the 1964 Act which "manifests a congressional intent to allow an individual to pursue independently his rights under both Title VII and other applicable state and federal statutes." 421 U.S., at 459. Congress made clear " 'that the remedies available to the individual under Title VII are co-extensive with the individual's right to sue under the provisions of the Civil Rights Act of 1866, 42 U.S.C. § 1981, and that the two procedures augment each other and are not mutually exclusive.' " 421 U.S., at 459, quoting H.R.Rep.No.92–238, p. 19 (1971). There is no such legislative history behind the 1972 amendments. Indeed, as indicated above, the congressional understanding was precisely to the contrary. * * *

*** [As noted, Section 717(c) now allows 90 days for filing of suit after final action by the agency or the Equal Employment Opportunity Commission.]

In the case at bar, * * * the established principle leads unerringly to the conclusion that § 717 of the Civil Rights Act of 1964, as amended, provides the exclusive judicial remedy for claims of discrimination in federal employment.

We hold, therefore, that since Brown failed to file a timely complaint under § 717(c), the District Court properly dismissed the case. Accordingly, the judgment is affirmed.

It is so ordered.

■ MR. JUSTICE MARSHALL took no part in the consideration or decision of this case.

■ MR. JUSTICE STEVENS, with whom MR. JUSTICE BRENNAN joins, dissenting.

Prior to the enactment of the Civil Rights Act of 1964 there was uncertainty as to what federal judicial remedies, if any, were available to persons injured by racially discriminatory employment practices in the private sector. Against that background of uncertainty, Congress enacted a comprehensive remedial statute which did not expressly state whether it was exclusive of, or supplementary to, whatever other remedies might exist.

In 1972 when Congress amended the statute to cover federal employees, there was similar uncertainty about what remedies were available to such employees. Since both the 1964 statute and the 1972 amendment were enacted in comparable settings, and since both pieces of legislation implement precisely the same important national interests, it is reasonable to infer that Congress intended to resolve the question of exclusivity in the same way at both times.

As the legislative history * * * demonstrates, Congress intended federal employees to have the same rights available to remedy racial discrimination as employees in the private sector. Since the law is now well settled that victims of racial discrimination in the private sector have a choice of remedies and are not limited to Title VII, federal employees should enjoy parallel rights. * * * There is no evidence, either in the statute itself or in its history, that Congress intended the 1972 amendment to be construed differently from the basic statute.

The fact that Congress incorrectly assumed that federal employees would have no judicial remedy if § 717 had not been enacted undermines rather than supports the Court's conclusion that Congress intended to repeal or amend laws that it did not think applicable. Indeed, the General Subcommittee on Labor of the House Committee on Education and Labor rejected an amendment which would have explicitly provided that § 717 would be the exclusive remedy for federal employees. In sum, the legislative history of § 717 discloses a clear intent to provide federal employees with rights that parallel those available to employees in the private sector, no evidence of an intention to make the remedy exclusive, and the rejection of an amendment which would have so provided.

The burden of persuading us that we should interpolate such an important provision into a complex, carefully drafted statute is a heavy one.

Since that burden has not been met, I would simply read the statute as Congress wrote it.

Notes and Questions

1. We have previously seen a couple of examples of the application of Title VII in the context of the federal employee. In *Library of Congress v. Shaw,* 478 U.S. 310 (1986) (see Chapter II.C), the Supreme Court held that the federal government is not subject to an award of interest absent an express waiver of sovereign immunity. In the Civil Rights Act of 1991, Congress waived the government's immunity for an award of interest under Title VII. 42 U.S.C. § 2000e–16(d). In *Irwin v. Veterans Affairs,* 498 U.S. 89 (see Chapter II.C), the Court held that the statute of limitations for bringing a Title VII suit against the federal government may be tolled for certain narrow equitable reasons, just as is the case against a private employer. (Subsequently, we'll study recovery of awards of attorney's fees in successful Title VII claims against the federal government. See Chapter VII.B.2.) Thus, in most respects, Title VII now applies to the federal government in the same manner as against a private employer.

However, as described by one commentator—

> [the] administrative process for federal employee discrimination claims * * * is far more elaborate than that governing other types of employment under Title VII. In sum, the statute contemplates filing an administrative complaint with the agency responsible for the discrimination. After that agency's final action on the complaint, the charging party has the option of appealing to the Equal Employment Opportunity Commission or filing action in district court. If appeal is taken to the EEOC, court suit may be brought after that agency's final decision.

I Charles A. Sullivan, et al., *Employment Discrimination* § 13.3 (2d ed. 1988). On the procedure and substance of federal employee claims under Title VII, the Rehabilitation Act of 1973, the Age Discrimination in Employment Act, and the Equal Pay Act, see generally Ernest C. Hadley, *A Guide to Federal Sector Equal Employment Law & Practice* (17th ed., 2004); *Federal Civil Service Law and Procedures: A Basic Guide* chs. 1, 2, & 5 (Ellen M. Bussey ed., 2d ed. 1990).

2. In *Brown v. General Services Administration,* the employee failed to initiate the court suit within the applicable time period after final agency action, which was then 30 days and now has been extended to 90 days. *See* 42 U.S.C. § 2000e–16(c). *Brown* further illustrates that in another important respect—the availability of alternative judicial remedies—Title VII is interpreted differently in the context of the federal sovereign than as against a private employer. Explain the majority's reasoning for concluding that Title VII is the exclusive remedy for federal employees alleging employment discrimination, notwithstanding the absence of any express provision to that effect in the statute. How does the dissent respond to each of these points?

3.   Despite the Supreme Court's ruling in *Brown* that Title VII is the exclusive remedy for federal employees suffering discriminatory treatment in employment, the United States Court of Appeals for the Ninth Circuit held in *Brock v. United States,* 64 F.3d 1421, 1423–24 (9th Cir. 1995) that Title VII did not preempt a suit for tortious wrongdoing against the government if the conduct alleged (there a rape of a Forest Service employee by her supervisor during overnight field outings) amounted to a "highly personal violation" beyond the meaning of workplace discrimination. Accordingly, the court allowed the plaintiff to pursue a claim against the federal government for negligent supervision under the Federal Tort Claims Act. *Id.* However, other courts of appeals have not followed the Ninth Circuit's lead. Both the Fifth and Eighth Circuits have precluded federal employees from pursuing outside of the Title VII process claims arising from alleged sexual harassment by supervisors outside. *Mathis v. Henderson,* 243 F.3d 446, 450–51 (8th Cir. 2001); *Pfau v. Reed,* 125 F.3d 927, 933 (5th Cir. 1997), *vacated and remanded on other grounds,* 525 U.S. 801 (1998). Both courts have held, in barring alternative state tort law claims against the supervisor individually or FTCA claims against the federal government, "[w]hen the same set of facts supports a Title VII claim and a non-Title VII claim against a federal employer, Title VII preempts the non-Title VII claim." *Mathis,* 243 F.3d at 451; *Pfau,* 125 F.3d at 933. More recently, the Ninth Circuit has narrowed, although not eliminated, this exception to the exclusivity of Title VII for discriminatory conduct by a federal employer. In *Sommatino v. United States,* 255 F.3d 704, 712 (9th Cir. 2001), the Ninth Circuit (over a dissent) held that a federal employee's allegations of "intentional touching" and "sexually suggestive and vulgar remarks" by a co-worker were "typical of the offensive workplace behavior giving rise to an action [under Title VII] to remedy a hostile work environment." The court majority held, this offensive conduct was "not of the order of magnitude of the personal violation of rape in *Brock,* the forced sexual assault [in another case] (forced kissing, fondling, and blocking the door), and the following and phone calling at home [in yet another case]." *Id.*

Library of Congress v. Shaw

Supreme Court of the United States.
478 U.S. 310 (1986).

[The opinion is set out in Chapter II(C).]

Civil Rights Act of 1991 Pub. L. No. 102–166, 105 Stat. 1079

[The statute is set out in Chapter II(C).]

Irwin v. Veterans Affairs

Supreme Court of the United States.
498 U.S. 89 (1990).

[The opinion is set out in Chapter II(C).]

SECTION D.   THE FREEDOM OF INFORMATION ACT

Freedom of Information Act, 5 United States Code § 552(a)(3)(A), (a)(4)(B)–(C), (b) to (d)

(a) Each agency shall make available to the public information as follows:

* * *

(3)(A) * * * [E]ach agency, upon any request for records which (i) reasonably describes such records and (ii) is made in accordance with published rules stating the time, place, fees (if any), and procedures to be followed, shall make the records promptly available to any person.

* * *

(4) * * *

(B) On complaint, the district court of the United States in the district in which the complainant resides, or has his principal place of business, or in which the agency records are situated, or in the District of Columbia, has jurisdiction to enjoin the agency from withholding agency records and to order the production of any agency records improperly withheld from the complainant. In such a case the court shall determine the matter de novo, and may examine the contents of such agency records in camera to determine whether such records or any part thereof shall be withheld under any of the exemptions set forth in subsection (b) of this section, and the burden is on the agency to sustain its action. In addition to any other matters to which a court accords substantial weight, a court shall accord substantial weight to an affidavit of an agency concerning the agency's determination as to technical feasibility under paragraph (2)(C) and subsection (b) and reproducibility under paragraph (3)(B).

(C) Notwithstanding any other provision of law, the defendant shall serve an answer or otherwise plead to any complaint made under this subsection within thirty days after service upon the defendant of the pleading in which such complaint is made, unless the court otherwise directs for good cause shown.

* * *

(b) This section does not apply to matters that are—

(1)(A) specifically authorized under criteria established by an Executive order to be kept secret in the interest of national defense or foreign policy and (B) are in fact properly classified pursuant to such Executive order;

(2) related solely to the internal personnel rules and practices of an agency;

(3) specifically exempted from disclosure by statute (other than section 552b of this title), provided that such statute (A) requires that the matters be withheld from the public in such a manner as to leave no discretion on the issue, or (B) establishes particular criteria for withholding or refers to particular types of matters to be withheld;

(4) trade secrets and commercial or financial information obtained from a person and privileged or confidential;

(5) inter-agency or intra-agency memorandums or letters which would not be available by law to a party other than an agency in litigation with the agency;

(6) personnel and medical files and similar files the disclosure of which would constitute a clearly unwarranted invasion of personal privacy;

(7) records or information compiled for law enforcement purposes, but only to the extent that the production of such law enforcement records or information (A) could reasonably be expected to interfere with enforcement proceedings, (B) would deprive a person of a right to a fair trial or an impartial adjudication, (C) could reasonably be expected to constitute an unwarranted invasion of personal privacy, (D) could reasonably be expected to disclose the identity of a confidential source, including a State, local, or foreign agency or authority or any private institution which furnished information on a confidential basis, and, in the case of a record or information compiled by criminal law enforcement authority in the course of a criminal investigation or by an agency conducting a lawful national security intelligence investigation, information furnished by a confidential source, (E) would disclose techniques and procedures for law enforcement investigations or prosecutions, or would disclose guidelines for law enforcement investigations or prosecutions if such disclosure could reasonably be expected to risk circumvention of the law, or (F) could reasonably be expected to endanger the life or physical safety of any individual;

(8) contained in or related to examination, operating, or condition reports prepared by, on behalf of, or for the use of an agency responsible for the regulation or supervision of financial institutions; or

(9) geological and geophysical information and data, including maps, concerning wells.

Any reasonably segregable portion of a record shall be provided to any person requesting such record after deletion of the portions which are exempt under this subsection. The amount of information deleted shall be indicated on the released portion of the record, unless including that indication would harm an interest protected by the exemption in this subsection under which the deletion is made. If technically feasible, the amount of the information shall be indicated at the place in the record where such deletion is made.

(c)(1) Whenever a request is made which involves access to records described in subsection (b)(7)(A) and—

> (A) the investigation or proceeding involves a possible violation of criminal law; and

> (B) there is reason to believe that (i) the subject of the investigation or proceeding is not aware of its pendency, and (ii) disclosure of the existence of the records could reasonably be expected to interfere with enforcement proceedings,

the agency may, during only such time as that circumstance continues, treat the records as not subject to the requirements of this section.

(2) Whenever informant records maintained by a criminal law enforcement agency under an informant's name or personal identifier are requested by a third party according to the informant's name or personal identifier, the agency may treat the records as not subject to the requirements of this section unless the informant's status as an informant has been officially confirmed.

(3) Whenever a request is made which involves access to records maintained by the Federal Bureau of Investigation pertaining to foreign intelligence or counterintelligence, or international terrorism, and the existence of the records is classified information as provided in subsection (b)(1), the Bureau may, as long as the existence of the records remains classified information, treat the records as not subject to the requirements of this section.

(d) This section does not authorize withholding of information or limit the availability of records to the public, except as specifically stated in this section. This section is not authority to withhold information from Congress.

National Archives and Records Administration v. Favish

Supreme Court of the United States.
541 U.S. 157 (2004).

■ JUSTICE KENNEDY delivered the opinion for a unanimous Court.

This case requires us to interpret the Freedom of Information Act (FOIA), 5 U.S.C. § 552. FOIA does not apply if the requested data fall within one or more exemptions. Exemption 7(C) excuses from disclosure "records or information compiled for law enforcement purposes" if their production "could reasonably be expected to constitute an unwarranted invasion of personal privacy." § 552(b)(7)(C).

In *Department of Justice v. Reporters Comm. for Freedom of Press,* 489 U.S. 749 (1989), we considered the scope of Exemption 7(C) and held that release of the document at issue would be a prohibited invasion of the personal privacy of the person to whom the document referred. The principal document involved was the criminal record, or rap sheet, of the person who himself objected to the disclosure. Here, the information pertains to an official investigation into the circumstances surrounding an apparent suicide. The initial question is whether the exemption extends to the decedent's family when the family objects to the release of photographs showing the condition of the body at the scene of death. If we find the decedent's family does have a personal privacy interest recognized by the statute, we must then consider whether that privacy claim is outweighed by the public interest in disclosure.

I

Vincent Foster, Jr., deputy counsel to President Clinton, was found dead in Fort Marcy Park, located just outside Washington, D.C. The United States Park Police conducted the initial investigation and took color photographs of the death scene, including 10 pictures of Foster's body. The investigation concluded that Foster committed suicide by shooting himself with a revolver. Subsequent investigations by the Federal Bureau of Investigation, committees of the Senate and the House of Representatives, and independent counsels Robert Fiske and Kenneth Starr reached the same conclusion. Despite the unanimous finding of these five investigations, a citizen interested in the matter, Allan Favish, remained skeptical. Favish is now a respondent in this proceeding. In an earlier proceeding, Favish was the associate counsel for Accuracy in Media (AIM), which applied under FOIA for Foster's death-scene photographs. After the National Park Service, which then maintained custody of the pictures, resisted disclosure, Favish filed suit on behalf of AIM in the District Court for the District of Columbia to compel production. The District Court granted summary judgment against AIM. The Court of Appeals for the District of Columbia unanimously affirmed.

Still convinced that the Government's investigations were " 'grossly incomplete and untrustworthy,' " Favish filed the present FOIA request in his own name, seeking, among other things, 11 pictures, 1 showing Foster's eyeglasses and 10 depicting various parts of Foster's body. Like the National Park Service, the Office of Independent Counsel (OIC) refused the request under Exemption 7(C).

Again, Favish sued to compel production, this time in the United States District Court for the Central District of California. As a preliminary matter, the District Court held that the decision of the Court of Appeals for the District of Columbia did not have collateral estoppel effect on Favish's California lawsuit brought in his personal capacity. On the merits, the court granted partial summary judgment to OIC. With the exception of the picture showing Foster's eyeglasses, the court upheld OIC's claim of exemption. Relying on the so-called *Vaughn* index provided by the Government—a narrative description of the withheld photos, see *Vaughn v. Rosen*, 484 F.2d 820 (C.A.D.C.1973)—the court held, first, that Foster's surviving family members enjoy personal privacy interests that could be infringed by disclosure of the photographs. It then found, with respect to the asserted public interest, that "[Favish] has not sufficiently explained how disclosure of these photographs will advance his investigation into Foster's death." Any purported public interest in disclosure, moreover, "is lessened because of the exhaustive investigation that has already occurred regarding Foster's death." Balancing the competing interests, the court concluded that "the privacy interests of the Foster family members outweigh the public interest in disclosure."

On the first appeal to the Court of Appeals for the Ninth Circuit, the majority reversed and remanded, over Judge Pregerson's dissent. 217 F.3d 1168 (C.A.9 2000). In the majority's view, although evidence or knowledge of misfeasance by the investigative agency may "enhanc[e] the urgency of the [FOIA] request," "[n]othing in the statutory command conditions [disclosure] on the requesting party showing that he has knowledge of misfeasance by the agency." Furthermore, because "Favish, in fact, tenders evidence and argument which, if believed, would justify his doubts," the FOIA request "is in complete conformity with the statutory purpose that the public know what its government is up to." This was so, the Court of Appeals held, even in the face of five previous investigations into Foster's death: "Nothing in the statutory command shields an agency from disclosing its records because other agencies have engaged in similar investigations.... [I]t is a feature of famous cases that they generate controversy, suspicion, and the desire to second guess the authorities." As the majority read the statute, there is "a right to look, a right to speculate and argue again, a right of public scrutiny."

The Court of Appeals, however, agreed with the District Court that the exemption recognizes the Foster family members' right to personal privacy. Although the pictures contain no information about Foster's relatives, the statute's protection "extends to the memory of the deceased held by those tied closely to the deceased by blood or love." Nevertheless, the majority held that the District Court erred in balancing the relevant interests based only on the *Vaughn* index. While "the [D]istrict [C]ourt has discretion to decide a FOIA case on the basis of affidavits, and affidavits are in some cases sufficient," "the agency affidavits are insufficiently detailed." It remanded the case to the District Court to examine the photos *in camera* and, "consistent with [the Court of Appeals'] opinion," "balance the effect of their release on the privacy of the Foster family against the public benefit to be obtained by their release."

On remand, the District Court ordered release of the following five photographs:

- "The photograph identified as '3–VF's [Vincent Foster's] body looking down from top of berm' must be released, as the photograph is not so explicit as to overcome the public interest.

- "The photograph entitled '5–VF's body-focusing on Rt. side of shoulder/arm' is again of such a nature as to be discoverable in that it is not focused in such a manner as to unnecessarily impact the privacy interests of the family.

- "The photograph entitled '1–Right hand showing gun & thumb in guard' is discoverable as it may be probative of the public's right to know.

- "The photograph entitled '4–VF's body focusing on right side and arm' is discoverable.

- "The photograph entitled '5–VF's body-focus on top of head thru heavy foliage' is discoverable."

On the second appeal to the same panel, the majority, again over Judge Pregerson's dissent, affirmed in part. 37 Fed.Appx. 863 (C.A.9 2002). Without providing any explanation, it upheld the release of all the pictures, "except that photo 3–VF's body looking down from top of berm is to be withheld."

We granted OIC's petition for a writ of certiorari to resolve a conflict in the Courts of Appeals over the proper interpretation of Exemption 7(C). The only documents at issue in this case are the four photographs the Court of Appeals ordered released in its 2002 unpublished opinion. We reverse.

The OIC terminated its operations on March 23, 2004, see 28 U.S.C. § 596(b)(2), and transferred all records-including the photographs that are the subject of Favish's FOIA request-to the National Archives and Records Administration, see § 594(k)(1). The National Archives and Records Administration has been substituted as petitioner in the caption of this case. As all the actions relevant to our disposition of the case took place before March 23, 2004, we continue to refer to petitioner as OIC in this opinion.

II

It is common ground among the parties that the death-scene photographs in OIC's possession are records or information "compiled for law enforcement purposes" as that phrase is used in Exemption 7(C). This leads to the question whether disclosure of the four photographs "could reasonably be expected to constitute an unwarranted invasion of personal privacy."

Favish contends the family has no personal privacy interest covered by Exemption 7(C). His argument rests on the proposition that the information is only about the decedent, not his family. FOIA's right to personal privacy, in his view, means only "the right to control information about oneself." He quotes from our decision in *Reporters Committee*, where, in holding that a person has a privacy interest sufficient to prevent disclosure of his own rap sheet, we said "the common law and the literal understandings of privacy encompass the individual's control of information concerning his or her person." 489 U.S., at 763. This means, Favish says, that the individual who is the subject of the information is the only one with a privacy interest.

We disagree. The right to personal privacy is not confined, as Favish argues, to the "right to control information about oneself." Favish misreads the quoted sentence in *Reporters Committee* and adopts too narrow an interpretation of the case's holding. To say that the concept of personal privacy must "encompass" the individual's control of information about himself does not mean it cannot encompass other personal privacy interests as well. *Reporters Committee* had no occasion to consider whether individuals whose personal data are not contained in the requested materials also have a recognized privacy interest under Exemption 7(C).

Reporters Committee explained, however, that the concept of personal privacy under Exemption 7(C) is not some limited or "cramped notion" of that idea. 489 U.S., at 763. Records or information are not to be released under FOIA if disclosure "could reasonably be expected to constitute an unwarranted invasion of personal privacy." 5 U.S.C. § 552(b)(7). This provision is in marked contrast to the language in Exemption 6, pertaining to "personnel and medical files," where withholding is required only if disclosure "would constitute a clearly unwarranted invasion of personal privacy." § 552(b)(6). The adverb "clearly," found in Exemption 6, is not used in Exemption 7(C). In addition, "whereas Exemption 6 refers to disclosures that 'would constitute' an invasion of privacy, Exemption 7(C) encompasses any disclosure that 'could reasonably be expected to constitute' such an invasion." *Reporters Committee*, 489 U.S., at 756. Exemption 7(C)'s comparative breadth is no mere accident in drafting. We know Congress gave special consideration to the language in Exemption 7(C) because it was the result of specific amendments to an existing statute.

Law enforcement documents obtained by Government investigators often contain information about persons interviewed as witnesses or initial suspects but whose link to the official inquiry may be the result of mere happenstance. There is special reason, therefore, to give protection to this intimate personal data, to which the public does not have a general right of access in the ordinary course. In this class of cases where the subject of the documents "is a private citizen," "the privacy interest . . . is at its apex." *Id.*, at 780.

Certain *amici* in support of Favish rely on the modifier "personal" before the word "privacy" to bolster their view that the family has no privacy interest in the pictures of the decedent. This, too, misapprehends the family's position and the scope of protection the exemption provides. The family does not invoke Exemption 7(C) on behalf of Vincent Foster in its capacity as his next friend for fear that the pictures may reveal private information about Foster to the detriment of his own posthumous reputation or some other interest personal to him. If that were the case, a different set of considerations would control. Foster's relatives instead invoke their own right and interest to personal privacy. They seek to be shielded by the exemption to secure their own refuge from a sensation-seeking culture for their own peace of mind and tranquility, not for the sake of the deceased.

In a sworn declaration filed with the District Court, Foster's sister, Sheila Foster Anthony, stated that the family had been harassed by, and deluged with requests from, "[p]olitical and commercial opportunists" who sought to profit from Foster's suicide. In particular, she was "horrified and devastated by [a] photograph [already] leaked to the press." "[E]very time I see it," Sheila Foster Anthony wrote, "I have nightmares and heart-pounding insomnia as I visualize how he must have spent his last few minutes and seconds of his life." She opposed the disclosure of the disputed pictures because "I fear that the release of [additional] photographs certainly would set off another round of intense scrutiny by the media. Undoubtedly, the photographs would be placed on the Internet for world consumption. Once again my family would be the focus of conceivably unsavory and distasteful media coverage." "[R]eleasing any photographs," Sheila Foster Anthony continued, "would constitute a painful unwarranted invasion of my privacy, my mother's privacy, my sister's privacy, and the privacy of Lisa Foster Moody (Vince's widow), her three children, and other members of the Foster family."

As we shall explain below, we think it proper to conclude from Congress' use of the term "personal privacy" that it intended to permit family members to assert their own privacy rights against public intrusions long deemed impermissible under the common law and in our cultural traditions. This does not mean that the family is in the same position as the individual who is the subject of the disclosure. We have little difficulty, however, in finding in our case law and traditions the right of family members to direct and control disposition of the body of the deceased and to limit attempts to exploit pictures of the deceased family member's remains for public purposes.

Burial rites or their counterparts have been respected in almost all civilizations from time immemorial. They are a sign of the respect a society shows for the deceased and for the surviving family members. The power of Sophocles' story in *Antigone* maintains its hold to this day because of the universal acceptance of the heroine's right to insist on respect for the body of her brother. The outrage at seeing the bodies of American soldiers mutilated and dragged through the streets is but a modern instance of the same understanding of the interests decent people have for those whom they have lost. Family members have a personal stake in honoring and mourning their dead and objecting to unwarranted public exploitation that, by intruding upon their own grief, tends to degrade the rites and respect they seek to accord to the deceased person who was once their own.

In addition this well-established cultural tradition acknowledging a family's control over the body and death images of the deceased has long been recognized at common law. Indeed, this right to privacy has much deeper roots in the common law than the rap sheets held to be protected from disclosure in *Reporters Committee*. * * *

We can assume Congress legislated against this background of law, scholarship, and history when it enacted FOIA and when it amended Exemption 7(C) to extend its terms. * * *

We have observed that the statutory privacy right protected by Exemption 7(C) goes beyond the common law and the Constitution. See *Reporters Committee*, 489 U.S., at 762, n. 13 (contrasting the scope of the privacy protection under FOIA with the analogous protection under the common law and the Constitution).

The statutory scheme must be understood, moreover, in light of the consequences that would follow were we to adopt Favish's position. As a general rule, withholding information under FOIA cannot be predicated on the identity of the requester. See *Reporters Committee, supra,* at 771. We are advised by the Government that child molesters, rapists, murderers, and other violent criminals often make FOIA requests for autopsies, photographs, and records of their deceased victims. Our holding ensures that the privacy interests of surviving family members would allow the Government to deny these gruesome requests in appropriate cases. We find it inconceivable that Congress could have intended a definition of "personal privacy" so narrow that it would allow convicted felons to obtain these materials without limitations at the expense of surviving family members' personal privacy.

For these reasons, * * * we hold that FOIA recognizes surviving family members' right to personal privacy with respect to their close relative's death-scene images. Our holding is consistent with the unanimous view of the Courts of Appeals and other lower courts that have addressed the question. Neither the deceased's former status as a public official, nor the fact that other pictures had been made public, detracts from the weighty privacy interests involved.

III

Our ruling that the personal privacy protected by Exemption 7(C) extends to family members who object to the disclosure of graphic details surrounding their relative's death does not end the case. Although this privacy interest is within the terms of the exemption, the statute directs nondisclosure only where the information "could reasonably be expected to constitute an unwarranted invasion" of the family's personal privacy. The term "unwarranted" requires us to balance the family's privacy interest against the public interest in disclosure. See *Reporters Committee*, 489 U.S., at 762.

FOIA is often explained as a means for citizens to know " 'what their Government is up to.' " *Id.*, at 773. This phrase should not be dismissed as a convenient formalism. It defines a structural necessity in a real democracy. The statement confirms that, as a general rule, when documents are within FOIA's disclosure provisions, citizens should not be required to explain why they seek the information. A person requesting the information needs no preconceived idea of the uses the data might serve. The information belongs to citizens to do with as they choose. Furthermore, as we have noted, the disclosure does not depend on the identity of the requester. As a general rule, if the information is subject to disclosure, it belongs to all.

When disclosure touches upon certain areas defined in the exemptions, however, the statute recognizes limitations that compete with the general interest in disclosure, and that, in appropriate cases, can overcome it. In the case of Exemption 7(C), the statute requires us to protect, in the proper degree, the personal privacy of citizens against the uncontrolled release of information compiled through the power of the State. The statutory direction that the information not be released if the invasion of personal privacy could reasonably be expected to be unwarranted requires the courts to balance the competing interests in privacy and disclosure. To effect this balance and to give practical meaning to the exemption, the usual rule that the citizen need not offer a reason for requesting the information must be inapplicable.

Where the privacy concerns addressed by Exemption 7(C) are present, the exemption requires the person requesting the information to establish a sufficient reason for the disclosure. First, the citizen must show that the public interest sought to be advanced is a significant one, an interest more specific than having the information for its own sake. Second, the citizen must show the information is likely to advance that interest. Otherwise, the invasion of privacy is unwarranted.

We do not in this single decision attempt to define the reasons that will suffice, or the necessary nexus between the requested information and the asserted public interest that would be advanced by disclosure. On the other hand, there must be some stability with respect to both the specific category of personal privacy interests protected by the statute and the specific category of public interests that could outweigh the privacy claim. Otherwise, courts will be left to balance in an ad hoc manner with little or no real guidance. In the case of photographic images and other data pertaining to an individual who died under mysterious circumstances, the justification most likely to satisfy Exemption 7(C)'s public interest requirement is that the information is necessary to show the investigative agency or other responsible officials acted negligently or otherwise improperly in the performance of their duties.

The Court of Appeals was correct to rule that the family has a privacy interest protected by the statute and to recognize as significant the asserted public interest in uncovering deficiencies or misfeasance in the Government's investigations into Foster's death. It erred, however, in defining the showing Favish must make to substantiate his public interest claim. It stated that "[n]othing in the statutory command conditions [disclosure] on the requesting party showing that he has knowledge of misfeasance by the agency" and that "[n]othing in the statutory command shields an agency from disclosing its records because other agencies have engaged in similar investigations." 217 F.3d, at 1172–1173. The court went on to hold that, because Favish has "tender[ed] evidence and argument which, if believed, would justify his doubts," the FOIA request "is in complete conformity with the statutory purpose that the public know what its government is up to." This was insufficient. The Court of Appeals required no particular showing that any evidence points with credibility to some actual misfeasance or other impropriety. The court's holding leaves Exemption 7(C) with little force or content. By requiring courts to engage in a state of suspended disbelief with regard to even the most incredible allegations, the panel transformed Exemption 7(C) into nothing more than a rule of pleading. The invasion of privacy under its rationale would be extensive. It must be remembered that once there is disclosure, the information belongs to the general public. There is no mechanism under FOIA for a protective order allowing only the requester to see whether the information bears out his theory, or for proscribing its general dissemination.

We hold that, where there is a privacy interest protected by Exemption 7(C) and the public interest being asserted is to show that responsible officials acted negligently or otherwise improperly in the performance of their duties, the requester must establish more than a bare suspicion in order to obtain disclosure. Rather, the requester must produce evidence that would warrant a belief by a reasonable person that the alleged Government impropriety might have occurred. In *Department of State v. Ray*, 502 U.S. 164 (1991), we held there is a presumption of legitimacy accorded to the Government's official conduct. The presumption perhaps is less a rule of evidence than a general working principle. However the rule is characterized, where the presumption is applicable, clear evidence is usually required to displace it. Given FOIA's prodisclosure purpose, however, the less stringent standard we adopt today is more faithful to the statutory scheme. Only when the FOIA requester has produced evidence sufficient to satisfy this standard will there exist a counterweight on the FOIA scale for the court to balance against the cognizable privacy interests in the requested records. Allegations of government misconduct are " 'easy to allege and hard to disprove,' " *Crawford–El v. Britton*, 523 U.S. 574, 585 (1998), so courts must insist on a meaningful evidentiary showing. It would be quite extraordinary to say we must ignore the fact that five different inquiries into the Foster matter reached the same conclusion. As we have noted, the balancing exercise in some other case might require us to make a somewhat more precise determination regarding the significance of the public interest and the historical importance of the events in question. We might need to consider the nexus required between the requested documents and the purported public interest served by disclosure. We need not do so here, however. Favish has not produced any evidence that would warrant a belief by a reasonable person that the alleged Government impropriety might have occurred to put the balance into play.

The Court of Appeals erred in its interpretation of Exemption 7(C). The District Court's first order in March 1998–before its decision was set aside by the Court of Appeals and superseded by the District Court's own order on remand-followed the correct approach. The judgment of the Court of Appeals is reversed, and the case is remanded with instructions to grant OIC's motion for summary judgment with respect to the four photographs in dispute.

It is so ordered.

———

United States v. Weber Aircraft Corporation

Supreme Court of the United States.
465 U.S. 792 (1984).

[The opinion is set out in Chapter I(D).]

———

Notes and Questions

1. The basic concept underlying the Freedom of Information Act, (FOIA) is simple: Any citizen for any reason may simply request information from the government and the government must provide it, unless it falls within the nine specified exemptions. The central purpose of the FOIA is also straightforward. The Senate Report on the FOIA legislation quoted James Madison: "Knowledge will forever govern ignorance, and a people who mean to be their own governors, must arm themselves with the power knowledge gives." S. Rep. No. 813, 89th Cong., 1st Sess. 2–3 (1965). The Supreme Court in *United States Department of Justice v. Reporters Committee for Freedom of the Press,* 489 U.S. 749, 774 (1989), identified the essential purpose of the FOIA as disclosing official information that sheds light on what the government is doing and how the agency is performing its statutory duties. In a democracy, shouldn't government be open to its citizens and provide information freely to the governed?

However, even in a democratic society, virtually everyone agrees that there are justifiable reasons for secrecy and confidentiality. Consider and evaluate possible justifications for government secrecy. (Note that we have encountered the FOIA previously in this course, in *United States v. Weber Aircraft Corp.,* 465 U.S. 792 (1984) (see Chapter I.E), where the Supreme Court held that Exemption 5—for certain inter-agency or intra-agency memorandum that would not otherwise be available by law—incorporated all of the privileges from discovery existing in civil litigation.)

The reasons for secrecy may include the interests of persons outside the government in privacy of information, as the *National Archives and Records Administration v. Favish* case illustrates. The nine exemptions in 5 U.S.C. § 552(b) set out what Congress believed were justifiable exceptions to a general duty of disclosure of government information. Which exception(s) are at issue in the *Favish* case? What interests are at stake on both sides of the issue, that is, those interests served by disclosure and those by non-disclosure? How does the Court weigh those interests in this case? For a scholarly critique suggesting that the *Favish* case creates an "obstacle that can stall journalistic efforts to expose corruption and waste, prevent historians from filling important historical gaps and correcting the historical record, and block the general public from scrutinizing and evaluating its

government," see Martin E. Halstuk, *When is an Invasion of Privacy Unwarranted Under the FOIA? An Analysis of the Supreme Court's "Sufficient Reason" and "Presumption of Legitimacy" Standards*, 16 U. Fla. J.L. & Pub. Pol'y 361, 400 (2005).

2.   Another question that arises in the FOIA context is whether the statute's benefits are worth the costs. Although the FOIA has been a gold mine for academic researchers and journalists, it may also be used by unsavory characters or for unanticipated purposes. The Drug Enforcement Administration claims that 60 percent of the FOIA requests it receives are from imprisoned or known drug traffickers. Alfred C. Aman, Jr. & William T. Mayton, *Administrative Law* 666 (1993). The Federal Bureau of Investigation says that 16 percent of the FOIA requests it receives are from known or suspected criminals. *Id.* at 666 n.21. Large numbers of FOIA requests are made by businesses seeking to obtain information gathered by the government about their competitors. *Id.* at 666. And, in any event, how much do we as taxpayers wish to pay so that academics and journalists and others can obtain access to government information? It costs money to pay people to dig through government files, examine each document to ensure that the information is not exempt or confidential, and to litigate disputes about whether information is protected from disclosure. By most estimates, the government spends more than $100 million each year complying with FOIA requests. *Id.* at 667. How much do we value and how much are we willing to pay for greater access to government records and information? Would we instead be willing to assume that the Congress will adequately monitor executive agencies? Or, in the context of a more than trillion-dollar budget, is $100 million a small price to pay for open government?

The coverage of the FOIA in this general course is necessarily limited. The study of the FOIA is typically more detailed in a course on administrative law. For more information about the FOIA, see generally Richard J. Pierce, Jr., Sidney A. Shapiro & Paul R. Verkuil, *Administrative Law and Process*, §§ 8.3 to 8.6, at 431–68 (4th ed. 2004); Alfred C. Aman, Jr. & William T. Mayton, *Administrative Law* §§ 17.1 to 19.1, at 630–739 (2d ed. 2001).

3.   In *Vaughn v. Rosen,* 484 F.2d 820 (D.C.Cir. 1973), which is cited repeatedly by the Supreme Court in *National Archives and Records Administration v. Favish,* a federal court of appeals addressed the difficult problem of how to preserve the advantages of the adversarial process in a FOIA lawsuit. The government possesses the documents but may seek to prevent disclosure. Thus, while the requester contends the documents should be disclosed, the requester obviously is prevented from seeing those documents. Under those circumstances, if the government withholds a document and asserts an exemption, how is the requester to formulate an argument for disclosure when he or she cannot view the document to evaluate whether it legitimately falls within an exemption? How can the requester challenge the government's characterization of the document and the applicability of an exemption to disclosure? Many disputes about disclosure of documents under FOIA turn on factual questions about

whether a document truly does fall within a defined exemption. The provision for in camera review of the document by the court provides only a partial answer. So what is the alternative? The alternative adopted by the courts is to require the government to prepare what has come to be known as a *Vaughn* index. The index must list each document, describe it generally, and correlate it to a claimed exemption. In this way, the government is forced to actually examine each document (and thus to disclose those documents or parts of documents for which no exemption is plausible). The requester receives at least some information about the nature of the documents so as to be able better to evaluate and challenge the government's claim of exemption (or perhaps to concede that at least some of the documents or parts of documents are plainly non-disclosable).

SECTION E.   SOCIAL SECURITY ACT

Social Security Act, 42 United States Code § 405(g)–(h)

(g) Judicial Review

Any individual, after any final decision of the Commissioner of Social Security made after a hearing to which he was a party, irrespective of the amount in controversy, may obtain a review of such decision by a civil action commenced within sixty days after the mailing to him of notice of such decision or within such further time as the Commissioner of Social Security may allow. Such action shall be brought in the district court of the United States for the judicial district in which the plaintiff resides, or has his principal place of business, or, if he does not reside or have his principal place of business within any such judicial district, in the United States District Court for the District of Columbia. As part of the Commissioner's answer the Commissioner of Social Security shall file a certified copy of the transcript of the record including the evidence upon which the findings and decision complained of are based. The court shall have power to enter, upon the pleadings and transcript of the record, a judgment affirming, modifying, or reversing the decision of the Commissioner of Social Security, with or without remanding the cause for a rehearing. The findings of the Commissioner of Social Security as to any fact, if supported by substantial evidence, shall be conclusive, and where a claim has been denied by the Commissioner of Social Security or a decision is rendered under subsection (b) of this section which is adverse to an individual who was a party to the hearing before the Commissioner of Social Security, because of failure of the claimant or such individual to submit proof in conformity with any regulation prescribed under subsection (a) of this section, the court shall review only the question of conformity with such regulations and the validity of such regulations. The court may, on motion of the Commissioner of Social Security made for good cause shown before the Commissioner files the Commissioner's answer, remand the case to the Commissioner of Social

Security for further action by the Commissioner of Social Security, and it may at any time order additional evidence to be taken before the Commissioner of Social Security, but only upon a showing that there is new evidence which is material and that there is good cause for the failure to incorporate such evidence into the record in a prior proceeding; and the Commissioner of Social Security shall, after the case is remanded, and after hearing such additional evidence if so ordered, modify or affirm the Commissioner's findings of fact or the Commissioner's decision, or both, and shall file with the court any such additional and modified findings of fact and decision, and, in any case in which the Commissioner has not made a decision fully favorable to the individual, a transcript of the additional record and testimony upon which the Commissioner's action in modifying or affirming was based. Such additional or modified findings of fact and decision shall be reviewable only to the extent provided for review of the original findings of fact and decision. The judgment of the court shall be final except that it shall be subject to review in the same manner as a judgment in other civil actions. Any action instituted in accordance with this subsection shall survive notwithstanding any change in the person occupying the office of Commissioner of Social Security or any vacancy in such office.

(h) Finality of Commissioner's Decision

The findings and decision of the Commissioner of Social Security after a hearing shall be binding upon all individuals who were parties to such hearing. No findings of fact or decision of the Commissioner of Social Security shall be reviewed by any person, tribunal, or governmental agency except as herein provided. No action against the United States, the Commissioner of Social Security, or any officer or employee thereof shall be brought under section 1331 or 1346 of Title 28 to recover on any claim arising under this subchapter.

[Note: In the Social Security Independence and Program Improvements Act of 1994, Pub. L. No. 103–296, § 101, 108 Stat. 1464, 1465, the Social Security Administration was removed from the Department of Health and Human Services and established as an independent agency in the Executive Branch. Accordingly, pertinent references in the Act to the Secretary of Health and Human Services have been changed to references to the Commissioner of Social Security.]

Barnhart v. Thomas

Supreme Court of the United States.
540 U.S. 20 (2003).

■ JUSTICE SCALIA delivered the opinion of the Court.

Under the Social Security Act, the Social Security Administration (SSA) is authorized to pay disability insurance benefits and Supplemental Security Income to persons who have a "disability." A person qualifies as disabled, and thereby eligible for such benefits, "only if his physical or mental impairment or impairments are of such severity that he is not only unable to do his previous work but cannot, considering his age, education, and work experience, engage in any other kind of substantial gainful work which exists in the national economy." 42 U.S.C. § § 423(d)(2)(A), 1382c(a)(3)(B). The issue we must decide is whether the SSA may determine that a claimant is not disabled because she remains physically and mentally able to do her previous work, without investigating whether that previous work exists in significant numbers in the national economy.

I

Pauline Thomas worked as an elevator operator for six years until her job was eliminated in August 1995. In June 1996, at age 53, Thomas applied for disability insurance benefits under Title II and Supplemental Security Income under Title XVI of the Social Security Act. See 49 Stat. 622, as amended, 42 U.S.C. § 401 *et seq.* (Title II); as added, 86 Stat. 1465, and as amended, § 1381 *et seq.* (Title XVI). She claimed that she suffered from, and was disabled by, heart disease and cervical and lumbar radiculo-pathy.

After the SSA denied Thomas's application initially and on reconsideration, she requested a hearing before an Administrative Law Judge (ALJ). The ALJ found that Thomas had "hypertension, cardiac arrythmia, [and] cervical and lumbar strain/sprain." He concluded, however, that Thomas was not under a "disability" because her "impairments do not prevent [her] from performing her past relevant work as an elevator operator." He rejected Thomas's argument that she is unable to do her previous work because that work no longer exists in significant numbers in the national economy. The SSA's Appeals Council denied Thomas's request for review.

Thomas then challenged the ALJ's ruling in the United States District Court for the District of New Jersey, renewing her argument that she is unable to do her previous work due to its scarcity. The District Court affirmed the ALJ, concluding that whether Thomas's old job exists is irrelevant under the SSA's regulations. The Court of Appeals for the Third Circuit, sitting en banc, reversed and remanded. Over the dissent of three of its members, it held that the statute unambiguously provides that the ability to perform prior work disqualifies from benefits only if it is "substantial gainful work which exists in the national economy." 294 F.3d 568, 572 (2002). That holding conflicts with the decisions of four other Courts of Appeals. We granted the SSA's petition for certiorari.

II

As relevant to the present case, Title II of the Act defines "disability" as the "inability to engage in any substantial gainful activity by reason of any medically determinable physical or mental impairment which can be expected to result in death or which has lasted or can be expected to last for a continuous period of not less than 12 months." 42 U.S.C. § 423(d)(1)(A). That definition is qualified, however, as follows:

"An individual shall be determined to be under a disability only if his physical or mental impairment or impairments are of such severity that *he is not only unable to do his previous work but cannot,* considering his age, education, and work experience, *engage in any other kind of substantial gainful work which exists in the national economy....*"
§ 423(d)(2)(A) (emphases added).

"[W]ork which exists in the national economy" is defined to mean "work which exists in significant numbers either in the region where such individual lives or in several regions of the country." *Ibid.* Title XVI of the Act, which governs Supplemental Security Income for disabled indigent persons, employs the same definition of "disability" used in Title II, including a qualification that is verbatim the same as § 423(d)(2)(A). For simplicity's sake, we will refer only to the Title II provisions, but our analysis applies equally to Title XVI.

Section 423(d)(2)(A) establishes two requirements for disability. First, an individual's physical or mental impairment must render him "unable to do his previous work." Second, the impairment must also preclude him from "engag[ing] in any other kind of substantial gainful work." The parties agree that the *latter* requirement is qualified by the clause that immediately follows it-"which exists in the national economy." The issue in this case is whether that clause also qualifies "previous work."

The SSA has answered this question in the negative. Acting pursuant to its statutory rulemaking authority, 42 U.S.C. §§ 405(a) (Title II), 1383(d)(1) (Title XVI), the agency has promulgated regulations establishing a five-step sequential evaluation process to determine disability. See 20 CFR § 404.1520 (2003) (governing claims for disability insurance benefits); § 416.920 (parallel regulation governing claims for Supplemental Security Income). If at any step a finding of disability or nondisability can be made, the SSA will not review the claim further. At the first step, the agency will find nondisability unless the claimant shows that he is not working at a "substantial gainful activity." At step two, the SSA will find nondisability unless the claimant shows that he has a "severe impairment," defined as "any impairment or combination of impairments which significantly limits [the claimant's] physical or mental ability to do basic work activities." At step three, the agency determines whether the impairment which enabled the claimant to survive step two is on the list of impairments presumed severe enough to render one disabled; if so, the claimant qualifies. If the claimant's impairment is not on the list, the inquiry proceeds to step four, at which the SSA assesses whether the claimant can do his previous work; unless he shows that he cannot, he is determined not to be disabled.[1] If the claimant survives the fourth stage, the fifth, and final, step requires the

---

1. The step-four instructions to the claimant read as follows: "If we cannot make a decision based on your current work activity or on medical facts alone, and you have a severe impairment(s), we then review your residual functional capacity and the physical and mental demands of the work you have done in the past. If you can still do this kind of work, we will find that you are not disabled." 20 CFR §§ 404.1520(e), 416.920(e) (2003).

SSA to consider so-called "vocational factors" (the claimant's age, education, and past work experience), and to determine whether the claimant is capable of performing other jobs existing in significant numbers in the national economy.

As the above description shows, step four can result in a determination of no disability without inquiry into whether the claimant's previous work exists in the national economy; the regulations explicitly reserve inquiry into the national economy for step five. Thus, the SSA has made it perfectly clear that it does not interpret the clause "which exists in the national economy" in § 423(d)(2)(A) as applying to "previous work." The issue presented is whether this agency interpretation must be accorded deference.

As we held in *Chevron U.S.A. Inc. v. Natural Resources Defense Council, Inc.*, 467 U.S. 837, 843 (1984), when a statute speaks clearly to the issue at hand we "must give effect to the unambiguously expressed intent of Congress," but when the statute "is silent or ambiguous" we must defer to a reasonable construction by the agency charged with its implementation. The Third Circuit held that, by referring first to "previous work" and then to "*any other* kind of substantial gainful work which exists in the national economy," 42 U.S.C. § 423(d)(2)(A) (emphasis added), the statute unambiguously indicates that the former is a species of the latter. "When," it said, "a sentence sets out one or more specific items followed by 'any other' and a description, the specific items must fall within the description." We disagree. For the reasons discussed below, the interpretation adopted by SSA is at least a reasonable construction of the text and must therefore be given effect.

The Third Circuit's reading disregards-indeed, is precisely contrary to-the grammatical "rule of the last antecedent," according to which a limiting clause or phrase (here, the relative clause "which exists in the national economy") should ordinarily be read as modifying only the noun or phrase that it immediately follows (here, "any other kind of substantial gainful work"). See 2A N. Singer, Sutherland on Statutory Construction § 47.33, p. 369 (6th rev. ed. 2000) ("Referential and qualifying words and phrases, where no contrary intention appears, refer solely to the last antecedent"). While this rule is not an absolute and can assuredly be overcome by other indicia of meaning, we have said that construing a statute in accord with the rule is "quite sensible as a matter of grammar." *Nobelman v. American Savings Bank,* 508 U.S. 324, 330 (1993). * * *

An example will illustrate the error of the Third Circuit's perception that the specifically enumerated "previous work" "must" be treated the same as the more general reference to "any other kind of substantial gainful work." Consider, for example, the case of parents who, before leaving their teenage son alone in the house for the weekend, warn him, "You will be punished if you throw a party or engage in any other activity that damages the house." If the son nevertheless throws a party and is caught, he should hardly be able to avoid punishment by arguing that the house was not damaged. The parents proscribed (1) a party, and (2) any other activity that damages the house. As far as appears from what they said, their reasons for prohibiting the home-alone party may have had nothing to do with damage to the house-for instance, the risk that under-age drinking or sexual activity would occur. And even if their only concern was to prevent damage, it does not follow from the fact that the same interest underlay both the specific and the general prohibition that proof of impairment of that interest is required for both. The parents, foreseeing that assessment of whether an activity had in fact "damaged" the house could be disputed by their son, might have wished to preclude all argument by specifying and categorically prohibiting the one activity-hosting a party-that was most likely to cause damage and most likely to occur.

The Third Circuit suggested that interpreting the statute as does the SSA would lead to "absurd results." The court could conceive of "no plausible reason why Congress might have wanted to deny benefits to an otherwise qualified person simply because that person, although unable to perform any job that actually exists in the national economy, could perform a previous job that no longer exists." But on the very next page the Third Circuit conceived of *just* such a plausible reason, namely, that "in the vast majority of cases, a claimant who is found to have the capacity to perform her past work also will have the capacity to perform other types of work." The conclusion which follows is that Congress could have determined that an analysis of a claimant's physical and mental capacity to do his previous work would "in the vast majority of cases" serve as an effective and efficient administrative proxy for the claimant's ability to do *some* work that does exist in the national economy. Such a proxy is useful because the step-five inquiry into whether the claimant's cumulative impairments pre-clude him from finding "other" work is very difficult, requiring consider-ation of "each of th[e] [vocational] factors and . . . an individual assessment of each claimant's abilities and limitations," *Heckler v. Campbell,* 461 U.S. 458, 460–461, n. 1. There is good reason to use a workable proxy that avoids the more expansive and individualized step-five analysis. As we have observed, "[t]he Social Security hearing system is 'probably the largest adjudicative agency in the western world.' . . . The need for efficiency is self-evident." 461 U.S., at 461, n. 2.

The Third Circuit rejected this proxy rationale because it would produce results that "may not always be true, and . . . may not be true in this case." That logic would invalidate a vast number of the procedures employed by the administrative state. To generalize is to be imprecise. Virtually *every* legal (or other) rule has imperfect applications in particular circumstances. Cf. *Bowen v. Yuckert,* 482 U.S. 137, 157, 107 S.Ct. 2287, 96 L.Ed.2d 119 (1987) (O'CONNOR, J., concurring) ("To be sure the Secre-tary faces an administrative task of staggering proportions in applying the disability benefits provisions of the Social Security Act. Perfection in processing millions of such claims annually is impossible"). It is true that, under the SSA's interpretation, a worker with severely limited capacity who has managed to find easy work in a declining industry could be penalized for his troubles if the job later disappears. It is also true, however, that under the Third Circuit's interpretation, impaired workers in declining or marginal industries who cannot do "other" work could simply refuse to return to their jobs—even though the jobs remain open and available—and nonetheless draw disability benefits. The proper *Chevron* inquiry is not whether the agency construction can give rise to undesirable results in some instances (as here *both* constructions can), but rather whether, in light of the alternatives, the agency construction is reasonable. In the present case, the SSA's authoritative interpretation certainly satisfies that test.

We have considered respondent's other arguments and find them to be without merit.

* * *

We need not decide today whether § 423(d)(2)(A) compels the interpretation given it by the SSA. It suffices to conclude, as we do, that § 423(d)(2)(A) does not unambiguously require a different interpretation, and that the SSA's regulation is an entirely reasonable interpretation of the text. The judgment of the Court of Appeals is reversed.

It is so ordered.

Notes and Questions

1.   There is no question about the immense size and great significance of the Social Security system. As one commentator states, Social Security has "expand[ed] to be the largest single piece of programmatic legislation in the nation—measured in terms of the federal budget outlay, staff, and recipients." Phyllis E. Bernard, *Social Security and Medicare Adjudications at HHS: Two Approaches to Administration Justice in an Ever–Expanding Bureaucracy,* 3 Health Matrix 339, 363 (1993). Although the retirement benefit part of the system tends to get the most public attention, the aspect of the system that generates the most litigation against the federal government is the disability benefit component. As noted in the *Barnhart v. Thomas* decision, the Supreme Court has described the administrative process for disability claims under the system as "probably the largest adjudicative agency in the western world," handling as many as two million claims each year. *Heckler v. Campbell,* 461 U.S. 458, 461 n. 2 (1983) (quoting Jerry L. Mashaw, et al., *Social Security Hearings and Appeals* ix (1978)). Under 42 U.S.C. § 405(g), the decisions of that agency adjudicative process are subject to judicial review in the courts.

2.   The Supreme Court's opinion in *Barnhart v. Thomas* is a good one for a quick dip into a complicated and rich area of law. The Court summarizes the two disability benefit programs—the Social Security Disability Insurance Program and the Supplemental Security Income Program—and how they operate largely parallel to one another. The Disability Insurance Program provides benefits to those who are covered by Social Security, that is, have adequate quarters of employment with payment into the system. Supplemental Security Income provides benefits for those who

are disabled and indigent. Both have the same definition of disability and apply the same standard and involve the same adjudicative process. The *Barnhart v. Thomas* opinion also addresses the meaning of "disability" and the five-step sequential evaluation process developed by regulation to determine whether a claimant qualifies for benefits. The Court's opinion also outlines the administrative adjudication process and demonstrates that a disappointed claimant may bring an action for judicial review of a final decision in federal district court. Thus, under 42 U.S.C. § 405(g), the government has waived its sovereign immunity for Social Security disability claims.

As also provided in Section 405(g) and (h), the Social Security Commissioner's findings regarding disability are conclusive if supported by "substantial evidence." Substantial evidence is a deferential standard of review of the agency's decision. It is a standard of reasonableness, even more circumscribed than the clearly erroneous standard for appellate review of district court factual findings. As the late-Professor Kenneth Culp Davis said, a finding can be clearly wrong without being unreasonable. 5 Kenneth Culp Davis, *Administrative Law Treatise* § 29:5 (1984). The "substantial evidence" standard bears great similarity to that applied in judicial evaluation of jury verdicts. Richard J. Pierce, Jr., *Administrative Law Treatise* § 11.2, at 768–69 (Aspen Law & Bus., 4th ed., 2002). However, despite the deferential nature of the "substantial evidence" standard, Professors Paul Verkuil and Jeffrey Lubbers report that "deference is not what the statistics show in SSA cases. District courts have long reversed and remanded disability cases on a greater than 50 percent basis." Paul R. Verkuil & Jeffrey S. Lubbers, *Alternative Approaches to Judicial Review of Social Security Disability Cases,* 55 Admin. L. Rev. 731, 741 (2003).

In recent years, a number of proposals have been made to create alternative mechanisms for judicial review of administrative disability decisions. As Verkuil and Lubbers explain, the two principal, and contrasting, legislative proposals have been either to create "a new Article I court (a Social Security Court) with Article III review limited to legal and constitutional issues," or to "maintain the current district court review structure but centralize court of appeals review in a special Article III court (a Social Security Court of Appeals." Verkuil & Lubbers, *supra,* at 733. In their study commissioned by the Social Security Administration, Verkuil and Lubbers recommend consideration of an Article I court, drawing upon the experiences of the Court of Appeals for Veterans Claims in addressing veterans disability cases. *Id.* at 778. (The Court of Appeals for Veterans Claims is described in Chapter III.G.4.)

For more information about Social Security claims, see generally Harvey J. McCormick, *Social Security Claims and Procedures* (2 vols., 5th ed., 1998).

———

SECTION F.   AGENCIES WITH "SUE AND BE SUED" CLAUSES AND GOVERNMENT CORPORATIONS

Certain federal agencies and instrumentalities, by statute, have been shed of most aspects of sovereign immunity and therefore are more amenable to liability for judgments. As the Supreme Court held in *Federal Housing Administration, Region No. 4 v. Burr*, 309 U.S. 242, 245 (1940), "[w]hen Congress launched a governmental agency into the commercial world and endowed it with authority to 'sue or be sued,' that agency is not less amenable to judicial process than a private enterprise under like circumstances would be." With these types of agencies and entities, sovereign immunity is at its lowest ebb. The traditionally strict and narrow interpretation of waivers of immunity gives way to a liberal construction.

Loeffler v. Frank

Supreme Court of the United States.
486 U.S. 549 (1988).

■ JUSTICE BLACKMUN delivered the opinion of the Court.

This case presents the question whether prejudgment interest may be awarded in a suit against the United States Postal Service brought under Title VII of the Civil Rights Act of 1964, 42 U.S.C. § 2000e *et seq.*

I

Petitioner Theodore J. Loeffler was discharged from his position as a rural letter carrier for the United States Postal Service. Petitioner appealed his termination to the Merit Systems Protection Board and, when his discharge was affirmed there, sought administrative relief from the Equal Employment Opportunity Commission. This, also, was without success. Contending that his discharge resulted from sex discrimination, petitioner subsequently brought this suit against the Postmaster General of the United States in his official capacity, pursuant to § 717 of Title VII, as amended, 42 U.S.C. § 2000e–16. After a bench trial, the United States District Court for the Eastern District of Missouri concluded that petitioner was a victim of discrimination and ordered his reinstatement with backpay. Relying on a decision of its controlling court, *Cross v. USPS*, 733 F.2d 1327, 1332 (C.A.8 1984) (en banc), cert. denied, 470 U.S. 1051 (1985), the District Court refused to award prejudgment interest. (In *Cross*, an equally divided Court of Appeals had affirmed the same District Judge's conclusion that sovereign immunity barred an award of prejudgment interest in a Title VII suit against the Postal Service.)

The United States Court of Appeals for the Eighth Circuit affirmed the denial of prejudgment interest. *Loeffler v. Carlin*, 780 F.2d 1365, 1370–1371

(1985). Concluding that the District Court's reliance on *Cross* was "understandable and proper," *id.*, at 1370, the court stated: "If the question of prejudgment interest is to be reconsidered, it should be reconsidered by the Court en banc." *Id.*, at 1371.

Subsequently, the Eighth Circuit undertook that en banc reconsideration, and, by a 6–to–5 vote, affirmed the judgment of the District Court. *Loeffler v. Tisch*, 806 F.2d 817 (1986). The majority adopted the reasoning of the majority of the original panel in *Cross*, 733 F.2d 1327, which concluded that Congress had not waived the sovereign immunity of the Postal Service with regard to prejudgment interest in a Title VII suit. The majority found its conclusion "strongly reinforced" by this Court's recent decision in *Library of Congress v. Shaw*, 478 U.S. 310 (1986), which the majority interpreted as "holding that Congress, in enacting Title VII, did not waive the Government's immunity from interest." 806 F.2d, at 818. In the majority's view, Congress' provision in the 1970 Postal Reorganization Act, 39 U.S.C. § 401(1), that the Postal Service may "sue and be sued" was irrelevant to the question before it, because "a sue-and-be-sued clause does not expand the obligations of a federal entity in a suit brought pursuant to another statute that is itself a waiver of immunity and which constitutes an exclusive remedy." 806 F.2d, at 819. * * *

Because of a conflict with the views of the Eleventh Circuit expressed in *Nagy v. USPS*, 773 F.2d 1190 (1985), we granted certiorari to decide whether, in a Title VII suit, prejudgment interest may be awarded against the Postal Service.

II

A

The question of statutory interpretation here presented, involving the interaction of the Postal Reorganization Act and Title VII, lends itself to straightforward resolution. Absent a waiver of sovereign immunity, the Federal Government is immune from suit. Congress, however, has waived the sovereign immunity of certain federal entities from the times of their inception by including in the enabling legislation provisions that they may sue and be sued. In *FHA v. Burr*, 309 U.S. 242 (1940), the Court explained:

> "[S]uch waivers by Congress of governmental immunity ... should be liberally construed.... Hence, when Congress establishes such an agency, authorizes it to engage in commercial and business transactions with the public, and permits it to 'sue and be sued,' it cannot be lightly assumed that restrictions on that authority are to be implied. Rather if the general authority to 'sue and be sued' is to be delimited by implied exceptions, it must be clearly shown that certain types of suits are not consistent with the statutory or constitutional scheme, that an implied restriction of the general authority is necessary to avoid grave interference with the performance of a governmental function, or that for other reasons it was plainly the purpose of Congress to use the 'sue and be sued' clause in a narrow sense. In the absence of such showing, it must be presumed that when Congress

launched a governmental agency into the commercial world and endowed it with authority to 'sue or be sued,' that agency is not less amenable to judicial process than a private enterprise under like circumstances would be."

Encompassed within this liberal-construction rule is the principle "that the words 'sue and be sued' normally include the natural and appropriate incidents of legal proceedings." [*Reconstruction Finance Corporation v.*] *J.G. Menihan Corp.,* 312 U.S., [81,] 85 [(1941)].

In accord with this approach, this Court has recognized that authorization of suits against federal entities engaged in commercial activities may amount to a waiver of sovereign immunity from awards of interest when such awards are an incident of suit. For example, in *Standard Oil Co. v. United States,* 267 U.S. 76 (1925), the Court reviewed a suit brought under § 5 of the Act of September 2, 1914, ch. 293, 38 Stat. 711, on insurance claims issued by the Bureau of War Risk Insurance. The Court concluded: "When the United States went into the insurance business, issued policies in familiar form and provided that in case of disagreement it might be sued, it must be assumed to have accepted the ordinary incidents of suits in such business." 267 U.S., at 79. Accordingly, interest was allowed.

When Congress created the Postal Service in 1970, it empowered the Service "to sue and be sued in its official name." 39 U.S.C. § 401(1). This sue-and-be-sued clause was a part of Congress' general design that the Postal Service "be run more like a business than had its predecessor, the Post Office Department." *Franchise Tax Board of California v. USPS,* 467 U.S., [512,] 520 [(1984)]. In *Franchise Tax Board,* this Court examined, in the context of an order issued by a state administrative agency, the extent to which Congress had waived the sovereign immunity of the Postal Service. After noting that "Congress has 'launched [the Postal Service] into the commercial world,'" *ibid.,* the Court held that the sue-and-be-sued clause must be liberally construed and that the Postal Service's liability must be presumed to be the same as that of any other business. Because the order to the Postal Service to withhold employees' wages had precisely the same effect on the Service's ability to operate efficiently as did such orders on other employers subject to the state statute that had been invoked, and because the burden of complying with the order would not impair the Service's ability to perform its functions, the Court concluded that there was no basis for overcoming the presumption that immunity from the state order had been waived.

Our unanimous view of the Postal Service expressed in *Franchise Tax Board* is controlling here. By launching "the Postal Service into the commercial world," and including a sue-and-be-sued clause in its charter, Congress has cast off the Service's "cloak of sovereignty" and given it the "status of a private commercial enterprise." *Shaw,* 478 U.S., at 317, n. 5. It follows that Congress is presumed to have waived any otherwise existing immunity of the Postal Service from interest awards.

None of the exceptions to the liberal-construction rule that guides our interpretation of the waiver of the Postal Service's immunity operates to overcome this presumption. Subjecting the Service to interest awards would not be inconsistent with the Postal Reorganization Act, 39 U.S.C. § 101 *et seq.,* the statutory scheme that created the Postal Service, nor would it pose a threat of "grave interference" with the Service's operation. *FHA v. Burr,* 309 U.S., at 245. Finally, we find nothing in the statute or its legislative history to suggest that "it was plainly the purpose of Congress to use the 'sue and be sued' clause in a narrow sense," *ibid.,* with regard to interest awards. To the contrary, since Congress expressly included several narrow and specific limitations on the operation of the sue-and-be-sued clause, see 39 U.S.C. § 409, none of which is applicable here, the natural inference is that it did not intend other limitations to be implied.

Accordingly, we conclude that, at the Postal Service's inception, Congress waived its immunity from interest awards, authorizing recovery of interest from the Postal Service to the extent that interest is recoverable against a private party as a normal incident of suit.

B

Respondent concedes, and apparently all the United States Courts of Appeals that have considered the question agree, that Title VII authorizes prejudgment interest as part of the backpay remedy in suits against private employers. This conclusion surely is correct. The backpay award authorized by § 706(g) of Title VII, as amended, 42 U.S.C. § 2000e–5(g), is a manifestation of Congress' intent to make "persons whole for injuries suffered through past discrimination." *Albemarle Paper Co. v. Moody,* 422 U.S. 405, 421 (1975). Prejudgment interest, of course, is "an element of complete compensation." *West Virginia v. United States,* 479 U.S. 305, 310 (1987). Thus, since Title VII authorizes interest awards as a normal incident of suits against private parties, and since Congress has waived the Postal Service's immunity from such awards, it follows that respondent may be subjected to an interest award in this case. * * *

III

* * * Respondent's view that *Shaw* stands for the proposition that § 717 implicitly states that prejudgment interest is unavailable in all suits brought under that section misunderstands the basis of our holding in that case. In *Shaw,* the Court faced the question whether § 706(k) of Title VII, 42 U.S.C. § 2000e–5(k), which provides that a party prevailing against the United States may recover attorney's fees from the United States, waived the sovereign immunity of the Library of Congress with respect to interest on an attorney's fees award. Unlike the Postal Service, the Library of Congress was not a "sue-and-be-sued" agency that Congress had " 'launched . . . into the commercial world,' " and thereby broadly waived sovereign immunity. *Franchise Tax Board of California v. USPS,* 467 U.S., at 520, quoting *FHA v. Burr,* 309 U.S., at 245. Thus, the starting point for our analysis was the "no-interest rule," which is to the effect that, absent express consent by Congress, the United States is immune from interest awards. See *Shaw,* 478 U.S., at 314. The dispositive question was not whether Title VII provided a cause of action that would allow recovery of

interest, but, rather, whether Title VII contained an express waiver of the Library of Congress' immunity from interest. Because no such waiver is contained within Title VII, the no-interest rule barred recovery of interest from the Library of Congress on the plaintiff's attorney's fees award. This conclusion had nothing to do with the scope of a § 717 cause of action.

The Court expressly noted in *Shaw:* "The no-interest rule is ... inapplicable where the Government has cast off the cloak of sovereignty and assumed the status of a private commercial enterprise." 478 U.S., at 317, n. 5. In creating the Postal Service, Congress did just that, and therefore, the no-interest rule does not apply to it. * * *

IV

Accordingly, we conclude that interest may be awarded against the Postal Service in a Title VII suit. The judgment of the Court of Appeals is reversed, and the case is remanded to that court for further proceedings consistent with this opinion.

It is so ordered.

■ Justice Kennedy took no part in the consideration or decision of this case.

■ Justice White, with whom The Chief Justice and Justice O'Connor join, dissenting.

Essentially for the reasons stated by the en banc Court of Appeals below, I believe that prejudgment interest is not available in Title VII suits against the Postal Service. Accordingly, I respectfully dissent.

Notes and Questions

1. With *Loeffler v. Frank,* we again encounter the persistent question of whether a governmental entity is subject to an award of prejudgment interest, under rules of sovereign immunity. Recall that in *Library of Congress v. Shaw,* 478 U.S. 310 (1986) (see Chapter II.C), the Supreme Court held that the federal government is not subject to an award of interest absent an express waiver of sovereign immunity. To be sure, in the Civil Rights Act of 1991, Congress waived the government's immunity for an award of interest under Title VII—making Title VII an exception to the general prohibition on prejudgment interest against the federal government. 42 U.S.C. § 2000e–16(d). However, while the *Loeffler* case does arise under Title VII, it was decided by the Supreme Court in 1988—before the amendment by Congress. And yet, notwithstanding *Library of Congress v. Shaw,* the Court permits an award of prejudgment interest against the United States Postal Service.

Why? What is different about the Postal Service from the types of governmental entities that we have explored previously? What about the Postal Service suggests that the rule of sovereign immunity applies differently in this context? Remember that the Court has generally held that waivers of sovereign immunity are to be strictly construed in favor of the government, but in *Loeffler,* the Court refers to a "liberal-construction rule." Explain under what circumstances this liberal construction rule, as opposed to the general strict construction rule, governs. Can you think of other governmentally-created entities to which the liberal construction rule should also apply, in terms of generously permitting litigation remedies?

2. While courts have suggested from time to time that the Postal Service retains no sovereign immunity, *see, e.g., Franchise Tax Bd. v. United States Postal Serv.,* 467 U.S. 512, 519–20 & n.12 (1984); *Harrison v. United States Postal Serv.,* 840 F.2d 1149, 1152 n.6 (4th Cir. 1988), this is an overstatement. The Postal Service remains by statute "an independent establishment of the executive branch of the Government of the United States," 39 U.S.C. § 201, and "operate[s] as a basic and fundamental service provided to the people by the Government of the United States," *id.* § 101(a). Thus, the Postal Service retains important incidents of sovereign immunity.

In *United States Postal Service v. Flamingo Industries (USA) Ltd.,* 540 U.S. 736 (2004), the Supreme Court emphasized that while the Postal Reorganization Act "gives the Postal Service a high degree of independence from the other offices of the Government, * * * it remains a part of the Government." *Id.* at 746. The Court observed that Congress "declined to create the Postal Service as a Government corporation, opting instead for an independent establishment." *Id.* Accordingly, the Court held, despite the sue-and-be-sued clause, the Postal Service, like the United States government of which it is a part, is not subject to antitrust liability under the Sherman Act. *Id.* at 738–48.

Similarly, in *Baker v. Runyon,* 114 F.3d 668 (7th Cir. 1997), the United States Court of Appeals for the Seventh Circuit reiterated that, while having considerable autonomy and being run in many ways *similar* to a private commercial entity, the United States Postal Service is *not* a private actor. *Id.* at 670–71. Under Title VII of the Civil Rights Act, as amended in 1991, a plaintiff may obtain punitive damages under certain circumstances—but not against a "government agency." For purposes of liability for punitive damages under Title VII, the court distinguished the Postal Service from actual government corporations, such as Amtrak and the Corporation for Public Broadcasting, which are not agencies or establishments of the federal government. *Id.* at 671. Accordingly, the court held that the Postal Service was a "government agency" for purposes of the statutory exemption from liability for punitive damages under Title VII. *Id.* at 670–72.

3. Despite the Supreme Court flourish in *Loeffler v. Frank* about "casting off the cloak of sovereign immunity," sue-and-be-sued clauses for certain agencies and government corporations are not completely open-ended nor do they encompass every possible cause of action. For example, most courts have held that suits that seek payment of funds from the public treasury (as contrasted with separate agency or corporation funds generated in other ways) should be seen as in reality against the United

States and framed under other statutes, usually the Tucker Act (see Chapter IV.A). Most importantly for our purposes, the Federal Tort Claims Act (FTCA) (see Chapter III.A) expressly modifies the sue-and-be-sued doctrine by making that Act the exclusive remedy for tort actions against federal agencies. 28 U.S.C. § 2679(a). For purposes of this exclusive remedy, the FTCA defines "federal agency" as including "corporations primarily acting as instrumentalities or agencies of the United States." 28 U.S.C. § 2671. The FTCA also covers the Postal Service, 28 U.S.C. § 2680(h), although tort judgments arising from Postal Service activities continue to be paid from Postal Service funds. This preemption by the FTCA of any claim for liability against a government agency or corporation directly through a sue-and-be-sued clause means that all such suits are subject to the limitations and exceptions in the FTCA. However, as the Supreme Court held in *Federal Deposit Insurance Corporation v. Meyer*, 510 U.S. 471, 475–86 (1994), the FTCA only supersedes an agency sue-and-be-sued clause if the tort claim is "cognizable" under that statute. For further discussion of the *Meyer* decision, see infra Chapter V.B.2.c).

On the amenability to suit of, and limitations on suits against, agencies with sue-and-be-sued clauses and government corporations, see generally Gregory C. Sisk, *Litigation With the Federal Government* §§ 3.22 to 3.24, at 216–24 (4th ed., 2006).

––––––

SECTION G.   OTHER STATUTORY WAIVERS OF SOVEREIGN IMMUNITY

The following are excerpts from a few additional statutes that waive the sovereign immunity of the federal government. Each of these statutes implicates often complex areas of law—tax, age discrimination, veterans benefits, environmental law, religious freedom, and copyright and intellectual property—that are beyond the scope of this course. Moreover, these statutes are only a few examples of a large number of statutes that authorize suit against the United States in a discrete area of law.

––––––

1.   TAX REFUND SUITS

28 United States Code § 1346(a)(1)

(a) The district courts shall have original jurisdiction, concurrent with the United States Court of Federal Claims, of:

(1) Any civil action against the United States for the recovery of any internal-revenue tax alleged to have been erroneously or illegally assessed or collected, or any penalty claimed to have been collected

without authority or any sum alleged to have been excessive or in any manner wrongfully collected under the internal-revenue laws * * *.

---

2.   ENVIRONMENTAL LIABILITY

Comprehensive Environmental Response, Compensation and Liability Act, 42 United States Code § 9620(a)(1)

Each department, agency, and instrumentality of the United States (including the executive, legislative, and judicial branches of government) shall be subject to, and comply with, this chapter in the same manner and to the same extent, both procedurally and substantively, as any nongovernmental entity, including liability under section 9607 of this title [which establishes liability for remediation costs resulting from the release of a hazardous substance].

On suits against the federal government under environmental protection statutes, see generally Gregory C. Sisk, *Litigation With the Federal Government* § 3.18, at 205–08 (4th ed., 2000). On enforcement of environmental laws against federal facilities, see Robert C. Yale, *Is There an Environmental Lawyer in the House?*, Fed. Lawyer, June 2006, at 35.

---

3.   VETERANS' BENEFITS DISPUTES

Veterans Judicial Review Act, 38 United States Code §§ 7251–7253(d), 7292

§ 7251.   Status

There is hereby established, under Article I of the Constitution of the United States, a court of record to be known as the United States Court of Appeals for Veterans Claims.

§ 7252.   Jurisdiction; finality of decisions

(a) The Court of Appeals for Veterans Claims shall have exclusive jurisdiction to review decisions of the Board of Veterans' Appeals. The Secretary may not seek review of any such decision. The Court shall have power to affirm, modify, or reverse a decision of the Board or to remand the matter, as appropriate.

(b) Review in the Court shall be on the record of proceedings before the Secretary and the Board. The extent of the review shall be limited to the scope provided in section 7261 of this title. The Court may not review the schedule of ratings for disabilities adopted under section 1155 of this title or any action of the Secretary in adopting or revising that schedule.

(c) Decisions by the Court are subject to review as provided in section 7292 of this title.

§ 7253. Composition

(a) COMPOSITION.—The Court of Appeals for Veterans Claims shall be composed of a chief judge and at least two and not more than six associate judges.

(b) APPOINTMENT.—The judges of the Court shall be appointed by the President, by and with the advice and consent of the Senate, solely on the grounds of fitness to perform the duties of the office. A person may not be appointed to the Court who is not a member in good standing of the bar of a Federal court or of the highest court of a State. Not more than the number equal to the next whole number greater than one-half of the number of judges of the Court may be members of the same political party.

(c) TERM OF OFFICE.—The term of office of the judges of the Court of Appeals for Veterans Claims shall be 15 years. * * *

(d) Chief judge.—(1) The chief judge of the Court is the head of the Court. * * *

* * *

§ 7292. Review by United States Court of Appeals for the Federal Circuit

(a) After a decision of the United States Court of Appeals for Veterans Claims is entered in a case, any party to the case may obtain a review of the decision with respect to the validity of a decision of the Court on a rule of law or of any statute or regulation (other than a refusal to review the schedule of ratings for disabilities adopted under section 1155 of this title) or any interpretation thereof (other than a determination as to a factual matter) that was relied on by the Court in making the decision. Such a review shall be obtained by filing a notice of appeal with the Court of Appeals for Veterans Claims within the time and in the manner prescribed for appeal to United States courts of appeals from United States district courts.

(b)(1) When a judge or panel of the Court of Appeals for Veterans Claims, in making an order not otherwise appealable under this section, determines that a controlling question of law is involved with respect to which there is a substantial ground for difference of opinion and that there is in fact a disagreement between the appellant and the Secretary with respect to that question of law and that the ultimate termination of the case may be materially advanced by the immediate consideration of that question, the judge or panel shall notify the chief judge of that determination. Upon receiving such a notification, the chief judge shall certify that such a question is presented, and any party to the case may then petition the Court of Appeals for the Federal Circuit to decide the question. That court may permit an interlocutory appeal to be taken on that question if such a petition is filed with it within 10 days after the certification by the chief judge of the Court of Appeals for Veterans Claims. Neither the application for, nor the granting of, an appeal under this paragraph shall stay proceedings in the Court of Appeals for Veterans Claims, unless a stay is ordered by a judge of the Court of Appeals for Veterans Claims or by the Court of Appeals for the Federal Circuit.

(2) For purposes of subsections (d) and (e) of this section, an order described in this paragraph shall be treated as a decision of the Court of Appeals for Veterans Claims.

(c) The United States Court of Appeals for the Federal Circuit shall have exclusive jurisdiction to review and decide any challenge to the validity of any statute or regulation or any interpretation thereof brought under this section, and to interpret constitutional and statutory provisions, to the extent presented and necessary to a decision. The judgment of such court shall be final subject to review by the Supreme Court upon certiorari, in the manner provided in section 1254 of title 28.

(d)(1) The Court of Appeals for the Federal Circuit shall decide all relevant questions of law, including interpreting constitutional and statutory provisions. The court shall hold unlawful and set aside any regulation or any interpretation thereof (other than a determination as to a factual matter) that was relied upon in the decision of the Court of Appeals for Veterans Claims that the Court of Appeals for the Federal Circuit finds to be—

(A) arbitrary, capricious, and abuse of discretion, or otherwise not in accordance with law;

(B) contrary to constitutional right, power, privilege, or immunity;

(C) in excess of statutory jurisdiction, authority, or limitations, or in violation of a statutory right; or

(D) without observance of procedure required by law.

(2) Except to the extent that an appeal under this chapter presents a constitutional issue, the Court of Appeals may not review (A) a challenge to a factual determination, or (B) a challenge to a law or regulation as applied to the facts of a particular case.

(e)(1) Upon such review, the Court of Appeals for the Federal Circuit shall have power to affirm or, if the decision of the Court of Appeals for Veterans Claims is not in accordance with law, to modify or reverse the decision of the Court of Appeals for Veterans Claims or to remand the matter, as appropriate.

(2) Rules for review of decisions of the Court of Appeals for Veterans Claims shall be those prescribed by the Supreme Court under section 2072 of title 28.

Gregory C. Sisk, The Trial Courts of the Federal Circuit: Diversity by Design

13 Federal Circuit Bar Journal 241, 259–63 (2003).

The United States Court of Appeals for Veterans Claims

While the United States Court of Appeals for Veterans Claims may be [one of] the youngest of the tribunals [among the federal courts], the matters that it addresses are among the oldest concerns for our Republic. The First Congress, meeting from 1789–1791, enacted a series of three statutes funding pensions for the veterans of the Revolutionary War. Today, Congress recognizes the nation's continuing obligations to those who have served their country in our armed forces by providing a variety of benefits to veterans and their dependents through the Department of Veterans Affairs. While those benefits include pensions, health care, educational benefits, vocational rehabilitation, home loan guaranties, life insurance, and burial benefits, the benefit that most frequently is the subject of dispute and potential litigation is entitlement to monthly compensation when a veteran establishes a service-connected disability.

If the story of litigation against the federal government is a tale of the gradual lowering of the shield of federal sovereign immunity, then the Court of Federal Claims is a crucial part of the beginning of that story and the Court of Appeals for Veterans Claims is an essential element of the ending.

The first significant statutory waiver of sovereign immunity came just before the Civil War with the authorization of contract claims in the newly-created Court of Claims. However, when Congress enacted the Tucker Act in 1887 to authorize statutory claims for money against the federal government to be pursued by citizens in the Court of Claims, Congress expressly exempted pension claims, which effectively excluded veterans' claims from the court. More than a century later, one of the last plates of that armor of sovereign immunity was shattered when Congress authorized judicial review of claims by veterans for statutory benefits and created a new forum for those claims—what is now denominated as the Court of Appeals for Veterans Claims.

Until very recently, the bar of sovereign immunity from veterans claims was most persistent and, as expressed in the text of the statute, rather absolute,[127] although as Chief Judge Kenneth Kramer noted, the courts in fact had created a number of exceptions so as to afford "Judicial Review of the Theoretically Non–Reviewable."[128] Indeed, the number of judicially-created exceptions to the statutory prohibition appeared to be rising inexorably, as the courts increasingly resisted the bar, most nota-

---

127. Steven W. Feldman, *United States Court of Appeals for Veterans Claims, in* 8 WEST'S FEDERAL FORMS § 13401, at 616–17 (perm. ed., rev. vol. 2002).

128. Kenneth B. Kramer, *Judicial Review of the Theoretically Non–Reviewable: An Overview of Pre–COVA Court Action on Claims for Veteran Benefits*, 17 OHIO N. U. L. REV. 99 (1990).

bly—but not only—when constitutional challenges were raised.[129] Nonetheless, the courthouse doors remained closed to the simple and ordinary claim by the veteran alleging basic error in the denial of an individual request for benefits.

The primary reason for resistance to court processes for veterans claims, asserted both by the government and by most organized veterans groups, was that the veterans benefits system was intended to be nonadversarial, thus supposedly obviating the need for lawyers.[131] The fear was that inserting a layer of judicial review would both add the expense of requiring lawyers and defeat the informal and accommodating administrative process to the ultimate detriment of veterans. The system was supposed to be pro-veteran. Indeed, the Department of Veterans Affairs by law is required to assist the veterans in "develop[ing] the claim to its optimum before deciding it on the merits,"[133] thus ideally alleviating the risk of erroneous denial of benefits.

In retrospect, however, the collapse of the wall of sovereign immunity for veterans benefits was inevitable. As Professor Robert Rabin noted, the Veterans Administration stood in "splendid isolation as the single federal administrative agency whose major functions [were] explicitly insulated from judicial review."[135] Given the general presumption today that the federal government both be held responsible for its obligations and be subject to judicial review to ensure that those obligations are legally satisfied, the area of veterans benefits was increasingly removed from the trends that had swept the field of federal government relations, along with the people subject to or affected by its authority. Whenever government officials are allowed to exercise judgment regarding a claim made by a citizen, judicial supervision has become a hallmark of our system of government, with exceptions being crafted only in those circumstances where a purported cause of action filed in court improperly asks a court to evaluate the wisdom rather than the legality of a policy decision by government officials. Accordingly, in 1988, leading members of Congress concluded that the time had come to establish "an avenue of independent review for [VA] claimants" victimized by egregious bureaucratic errors.[136]

In 1988, through the Veterans' Judicial Review Act, Congress dropped the sovereign immunity shield.[137] Not only did Congress reverse the prohi-

---

129. *See, e.g., id.* at 101–20 (discussing circumstances when courts have allowed judicial review of veteran claims); Johnson v. Robison, 415 U.S. 361, 366–74 (1974) (concluding that challenges to the constitutionality of veteran benefit laws are subject to judicial review).

131. Bill Russo, *Ten Years After the Battle for Veterans Judicial Review: An Assessment*, 46 FED. LAW., June 1999, at 26, 26–27.

133. Feldman, *supra* note 127, § 13401, at 619.

135. Robert L. Rabin, *Preclusion of Judicial Review in the Processing of Claims for Veterans' Benefits: A Preliminary Analysis*, 27 STAN. L. REV. 905, 905 (1975); *see also* H.R. REP. NO. 100–963, at 10 (1988), *reprinted in* 1988 U.S.C.C.A.N. 5782, 5791 (quoting Rabin, *supra*, at 905).

136. 134 CONG. REC. S9188–89 (daily ed. July 11, 1988) (statement of Sen. Cranston).

137. *See* Veterans' Benefits Improvement Act of 1988, Pub. L. No. 100–687, 102 Stat. 4105.

bition on judicial review, but it created a new forum denominated as the United States Court of Veterans Appeals. Effective in 1999, Congress changed the name to the United States Court of Appeals for Veterans Claims (CAVC).[139] As with the [Court of Federal Claims], the CAVC was established under Congress's Article I powers, with judges appointed by the President and confirmed by the Senate for terms of 15 years.[140]

[In contrast, however, with the Court of Federal Claims], the CAVC is *not* a trial court. Rather, the CAVC provides a judicial forum for appellate review of final decisions by the Board of Veterans' Appeals (BVA), which is a non-judicial agency tribunal within the Department of Veterans Affairs.[141]

Congress granted the CAVC the necessary authority to resolve all legal questions, whether involving a rule of law, a constitutional command, or a statutory provision, raised in veterans' benefits disputes.[142] At the same time, given that it is an appellate court, one would expect institution of a deferential standard of review to the factual findings made at a lower level. This, indeed, is the case under 38 U.S.C. § 7261, which empowers the CAVC to set aside or reverse the factual findings made by the BVA only if "clearly erroneous" and further provides that those findings of fact are not subject to trial *de novo* by the court.[143] However, the CAVC is the first stage of judicial adjudication and is intended to be an important safeguard against error at the administrative level, so persistent questions have been raised as to just how deferential the court should be toward the resolution of factual disputes by the BVA, at least insofar as those factual findings do not favor the petitioning veteran.

* * * [I]n the Veterans Benefits Act of 2002,[144] Congress signaled that it wished to see somewhat less deference accorded by the court to the BVA, although the legislation as enacted is more in the nature of a subtle rewording of the existing standards than a radical substitution of new rules, and the CAVC has not yet had an opportunity to construe the recent amendments. Although earlier legislative proposals would have eliminated the clearly erroneous standard in favor of the substantial evidence standard commonly applied in judicial review of administrative rulings, the compromise bill eventually passed by Congress retained the clearly erroneous standard. Congress, however, added statutory language requiring that the CAVC in each case "review the record of proceedings before the Secretary and Board of Veterans' Appeals," giving due account to the pro-veteran "benefit of the doubt" rule.[147] Congress further clarified that only findings

---

139. Veterans' Programs Enhancement Act of 1998, Pub. L. No. 105–368 § 511, 112 Stat. 3315, 3341 (codified at 38 U.S.C. 7251 (2000)).

140. 38 U.S.C. § 7253 (2000).

141. *See id.* § 7104.

142. H.R. REP. No. 100–963, at 5 (1988), *reprinted in* 1988 U.S.C.C.A.N. 5782, 5786.

143. 38 U.S.C.A. § 7261(a)(4), (c) (West Supp. 2003).

144. Pub. L. No. 107–330, 2002 U.S.C.C.A.N. (116 Stat.) 2820.

147. 38 U.S.C.A. § 7261(b) (West Supp. 2003); *see also* 148 CONG. REC. S11337.

of fact "adverse to the claimant" are reviewable (meaning that those adverse to the government cannot be challenged before the CAVC.)[148] * * *

After initial judicial oversight by the CAVC as an appellate tribunal, further review by the [United States Court of Appeals for the] Federal Circuit is more circumscribed, so as to prevent undue duplication of appellate efforts. Accordingly, under 38 U.S.C. § 7292, the Federal Circuit's appellate review primarily is limited to questions involving statutes, regulations, and rules of law, but generally does not include review of factual matters or the application of a statute or regulation to the facts of a particular case.[150]

---

4. RELIGIOUS FREEDOM CLAIMS

The Religious Freedom Restoration Act, 42 U.S.C. § 2000bb

Section 2000bb: Congressional Findings and Declaration of Purpose

(a) Findings

The Congress finds that—

(1) the framers of the Constitution, recognizing free exercise of religion as an unalienable right, secured its protection in the First Amendment to the Constitution;

(2) laws "neutral" toward religion may burden religious exercise as surely as laws intended to interfere with religious exercise;

(3) governments should not substantially burden religious exercise without compelling justification;

(4) in Employment Division v. Smith, 494 U.S. 872 (1990) the Supreme Court virtually eliminated the requirement that the government justify burdens on religious exercise imposed by laws neutral toward religion; and

(5) the compelling interest test as set forth in prior Federal court rulings is a workable test for striking sensible balances between religious liberty and competing prior governmental interests.

(b) Purposes

The purposes of this chapter are—

(1) to restore the compelling interest test as set forth in Sherbert v. Verner, 374 U.S. 398 (1963) and Wisconsin v. Yoder, 406 U.S. 205 (1972) and to guarantee its application in all cases where free exercise of religion is substantially burdened; and

---

148. 38 U.S.C.A. § 7261(a)(4) (West Supp. 2003).

150. 38 U.S.C. § 7292(a) (2000); *see generally* Feldman, *supra* note 127, § 13402.

(2) to provide a claim or defense to persons whose religious exercise is substantially burdened by government.

Section 2000bb–1: Free Exercise of Religion Protected

(a) In general

Government shall not substantially burden a person's exercise of religion even if the burden results from a rule of general applicability, except as provided in subsection (b) of this section.

(b) Exception

Government may substantially burden a person's exercise of religion only if it demonstrates that application of the burden to the person—

(1) is in furtherance of a compelling governmental interest; and

(2) is the least restrictive means of furthering that compelling governmental interest.

(c) Judicial relief

A person whose religious exercise has been burdened in violation of this section may assert that violation as a claim or defense in a judicial proceeding and obtain appropriate relief against a government. Standing to assert a claim or defense under this section shall be governed by the general rules of standing under article III of the Constitution.

Section 2000bb–2: Definitions

As used in this chapter—

(1) the term "government" includes a branch, department, agency, instrumentality, and official (or other person acting under color of law) of the United States, or of a covered entity;

(2) the term "covered entity" means the District of Columbia, the Commonwealth of Puerto Rico, and each territory and possession of the United States;

(3) the term "demonstrates" means meets the burdens of going forward with the evidence and of persuasion; and

(4) the term "exercise of religion" means religious exercise, as defined in section 2000cc–5 of this title.

Section 2000bb–3: Applicability

(a) In general

This chapter applies to all Federal law, and the implementation of that law, whether statutory or otherwise, and whether adopted before or after November 16, 1993.

(b) Rule of construction

Federal statutory law adopted after November 16, 1993 is subject to this chapter unless such law explicitly excludes such application by reference to this chapter.

(c) Religious belief unaffected

Nothing in this chapter shall be construed to authorize any government to burden any religious belief.

Section 2000bb–4: Establishment Clause unaffected

Nothing in this chapter shall be construed to affect, interpret, or in any way address that portion of the First Amendment prohibiting laws respecting the establishment of religion (referred to in this section as the "Establishment Clause"). Granting government funding, benefits, or exemptions, to the extent permissible under the Establishment Clause, shall not constitute a violation of this chapter. As used in this section, the term "granting", used with respect to government funding, benefits, or exemptions, does not include the denial of government funding, benefits, or exemptions.

Note

Congress enacted the Religious Freedom Restoration Act (RFRA) in response to a particular Supreme Court ruling narrowly interpreting religious freedom rights under the Constitution. For that reason, the statute has occasioned constitutional controversy from its inception. Indeed, the Supreme Court has ruled the statute unconstitutional as applied to state and local governments. However, as outlined below, the weight of judicial authority is that the statute continues to apply to the federal government.

The prelude to the enactment of RFRA was the 1990 decision by the Supreme Court in *Employment Division v. Smith,* 494 U.S. 872 (1990). In that case, the Court held that the Free Exercise of Religion Clause of the First Amendment did not prohibit enforcement of Oregon drug laws against sacramental use of peyote by Native Americans. *Id.* at 874–90. More broadly, the Court ruled that the state did not need to establish any compelling governmental interest to justify application of these laws in a manner that burdened a religious practice. *Id.* at 882–89. Enforcement of a law of general application that is formally neutral toward religion, the Court ruled, does not infringe upon the free exercise of religion, notwithstanding that application of such a general law may significantly burden the exercise of religious faith through religious practice. *Id.* at 878–82. Thus, a general law does not implicate the First Amendment and is not subject to any constitutional scrutiny. In sum, the *Smith* Court ruled that the Free Exercise Clause protects "the right to believe and profess whatever religious doctrine one desires," *id.* at 877, but does not extend protection to religious practices that contradict generally applicable law, *id.* at 878.

In the Religious Freedom Restoration Act (RFRA), Pub. L. No. 103–141, 107 Stat. 1488 (1993) (codified at 42 U.S.C. §§ 2000bb et seq.), Congress by legislative enactment intended to enhance protection for exercise of religious practices by establishing a "compelling government interest" standard for evaluating any government regulation that burdens religious exercise, whether or not intentionally and whether the statute applies generally or singles out religious practices for different treatment. Under RFRA, governments through laws and regulations were permitted to burden religious liberty only if that burden were the least restrictive means to serve a compelling government interest. On the Religious Freedom Restoration Act, see generally *James R. Browning Symposium for 1994: the Religious Freedom Restoration Act,* 56 Mont. L. Rev. 5 et seq. (1995); *Symposium: The Religious Freedom Restoration Act,* 1993 B.Y.U. L. Rev. 7 et seq.

As originally enacted, RFRA defined the term "government," for purposes of its commands, as including departments and agencies of the "United States, a State, or a subdivision of a State." 42 U.S.C. § 2000bb–2(1). (In 2000, in response to *City of Boerne v. Flores,* 521 U.S. 507 (1997), discussed in the next paragraph, Congress amended RFRA to strike references to state and local governments and thus to re-define "government" for purposes of the statute to cover only the United States government and its territories and possessions. Pub. L. No. 106–274, § 7 (2000).) The statute further provides that "[a] person whose religious exercise has been burdened in violation of this section may assert that violation as a claim or defense in a judicial proceeding and obtain appropriate relief against a government." *Id.* § 2000bb–1(c). Thus, RFRA not only defines a standard for governmental behavior, it plainly waives the sovereign immunity of the United States for lawsuits asserting a violation of that standard.

In *City of Boerne v. Flores,* 521 U.S. 507 (1997), the Supreme Court invalidated RFRA as applied to state and local governments, holding that Congress exceeded its power under the Fourteenth Amendment to enforce constitutional rights by enacting a law that purported to change the substance of a constitutional provision. *Id.* at 515–36. On the *City of Boerne* decision, see generally *Symposium: Reflection on* City of Boerne v. Flores, 39 Wm. & Mary L. Rev. 601 et seq. (1998); *Symposium,* 20 U. Ark. Little Rock L.J. 555 et seq. (1998).

However, the constitutionality of RFRA as applied to the federal government and as it implicates federal law is a very different question. The trend among the lower federal courts strongly is in the direction of reading *City of Boerne* narrowly and regarding the federal government itself, through RFRA, as having validly accepted additional obligations to protect religious exercise—even if it may not impose those burdens upon the states. As the United States Court of Appeals for the Seventh Circuit has observed, "[e]very appellate court that has squarely addressed the question has held that the RFRA governs the activities of federal officers and agencies." *O'Bryan v. Bureau of Prisons,* 349 F.3d 399, 401 (7th Cir. 2003). The Seventh Circuit in *O'Bryan* then joined the other circuits in holding that the RFRA constitutionally "may be applied to the internal operations of the national government." *See, e.g., Hankins v. Lyght,* 441 F.3d 96, 106 (2d Cir. 2006); *Guam v. Guerrero,* 290 F.3d 1210, 1220–21 (9th Cir. 2002); *Kikumura v. Hurley,* 242 F.3d 950, 958–59 (10th Cir. 2001); *Alamo v. Clay,* 137 F.3d 1366 (D.C. Cir. 1998) (assuming without deciding that RFRA is constitutional as applied to federal law); *In re Young,* 141 F.3d 854, 854 (8th Cir. 1998). *See also Cutter v. Wilkinson,* 544 U.S. 709, 715 n.2 (2005) (noting that the courts of appeals have held that RFRA "remains operative" against the federal government, but that the Supreme Court has not yet had occasion to address the issue). *But see United States v. Grant,* 117 F.3d 788, 792 n. 6 (5th Cir. 1997) (noting that *City of Boerne* "arguably casts some doubt on the continued viability of RFRA" to the federal government, while declining to address the issue). Moreover, the Department of Justice has taken the position that RFRA does indeed bind the federal government, which may have the practical effect of reducing the occasions on which courts may be called upon to consider its constitutionality as so applied. For contrasting scholarly discussion on the question of the continued application of RFRA to the federal government, see Gregory P. Magarian, *How to Apply the Religious Freedom Restoration Act to Federal Law Without Violating the Constitution,* 99 Mich. L. Rev. 1903 (2001); Thomas C. Berg, *The Constitutional Future of Religious Freedom Legislation,* 20 Ark.–Little Rock L.J. 715 (1998); Marci A. Hamilton, *The Religious Freedom Restoration Act is Unconstitutional, Period,* 1 U. Pa. J. Const. L. 1 (1998); Edward J.W. Blatnik, Note, *No RFRAF Allowed: The Statute of the Religious Freedom Restoration Act's Federal Application in the Wake of City of Boerne v. Flores,* 98 Colum. L. Rev. 1410 (1998).

––––––

5. PATENT AND COPYRIGHT INFRINGEMENT CLAIMS

Patent and Copyright Infringement Act, 28 United States Code § 1498(a)–(b)

(a) Whenever an invention described in and covered by a patent of the United States is used or manufactured by or for the United States without license of the owner thereof or lawful right to use or manufacture the same, the owner's remedy shall be by action against the United States in the United States Court of Federal Claims for the recovery of his reasonable and entire compensation for such use and manufacture. * * *

For the purposes of this section, the use or manufacture of an invention described in and covered by a patent of the United States by a contractor, a subcontractor, or any person, firm, or corporation for the Government and with the authorization or consent of the Government, shall be construed as use or manufacture for the United States.

The court shall not award compensation under this section if the claim is based on the use or manufacture by or for the United States of any article owned, leased, used by, or in the possession of the United States prior to July 1, 1918.

A Government employee shall have the right to bring suit against the Government under this section except where he was in a position to order, influence, or induce use of the invention by the Government. This section shall not confer a right of action on any patentee or any assignee of such patentee with respect to any invention discovered or invented by a person while in the employment or service of the United States, where the invention was related to the official functions of the employee, in cases in which such functions included research and development, or in the making of which Government time, materials or facilities were used.

(b) Hereafter, whenever the copyright in any work protected under the copyright laws of the United States shall be infringed by the United States, by a corporation owned or controlled by the United States, or by a contractor, subcontractor, or any person, firm, or corporation acting for the Government and with the authorization or consent of the Government, the exclusive action which may be brought for such infringement shall be an action by the copyright owner against the United States in the Court of Federal Claims for the recovery of his reasonable and entire compensation as damages for such infringement, including the minimum statutory damages as set forth in section 504(c), of title 17, United States Code: *Provided,* That a Government employee shall have a right of action against the Government under this subsection except where he was in a position to order, influence, or induce use of the copyrighted work by the Government: *Provided, however,* That this subsection shall not confer a right of action on any copyright owner or any assignee of such owner with respect to any copyrighted work prepared by a person while in the employment or service of the United States, where the copyrighted work was prepared as a part of the official functions of the employee, or in the preparation of which Government time, material, or facilities were used: *And provided further,* That before such action against the United States has been instituted the appropriate corporation owned or controlled by the United States or the head of the appropriate department or agency of the Government, as the case may be, is authorized to enter into an agreement with the copyright owner in full settlement and compromise for the damages accruing to him by reason of such infringement and to settle the claim administratively out of available appropriations.

Except as otherwise provided by law, no recovery shall be had for any infringement of a copyright covered by this subsection committed more than three years prior to the filing of the complaint or counterclaim for infringement in the action, except that the period between the date of receipt of a written claim for compensation by the Department or agency of the Government or corporation owned or controlled by the United States, as the case may be, having authority to settle such claim and the date of mailing by the Government of a notice to the claimant that his claim has been denied shall not be counted as a part of the three years, unless suit is brought before the last-mentioned date.

———

Note

Because patented technology is regularly used throughout the federal government, one commentary suggests that "[t]he United States Government * * * undoubtedly is one of the most frequent 'infringers' in the United States." David M. Schlitz & Richard J. McGrath, *Patent Infringement Claims Against the United States Government*, 9 Fed. Cir. Bar J. 351, 351 (1999). For a discussion of the basics of patent infringement claims against the federal government and the waiver of sovereign immunity for patent infringement claims for money damages under 28 U.S.C. § 1498, see generally *id. See also* Richard T. Ruzich, *Government Patent and Copyright Infringement Overseas Under 28 U.S.C. § 1498 (In the Shadow of the RIM Decisions)*, 15 Fed. Cir. B. J. 401, 403–10 (2006); Dana H. Schultz, *Patents, Copyrights, Government*, Cal. Bar J., April 2005, at 14.

CHAPTER IV

GENERAL STATUTORY WAIVERS OF SOVEREIGN IMMUNITY

As discussed at the beginning of Chapter III, this casebook divides statutory waivers of sovereign immunity into two broad categories: specific waivers (Chapter III) and general waivers (Chapter IV). Although this division is somewhat artificial, it has a principled basis and serves the purpose of organizing the multitude of statutes into understandable categories (at least for the author of this casebook). As used in this casebook, "Specific Statutory Waivers of Sovereign Immunity" (the focus of the previous chapter) denotes those statutes that waive the government's immunity for particular types of substantive claims, defined by the type of cause of action cognizable under the particular statute. "General Statutory Waivers of Sovereign Immunity" (the focus of this present chapter) includes those statutes that waive governmental immunity for general claims seeking a particular type of relief. In other words, the statutes addressed in this chapter waive immunity based primarily upon the form of relief allowed rather than the substantive nature of the claim.

Two major statutes form the framework for this chapter, namely (1) the Tucker Act, 28 U.S.C. §§ 1346(a)(2), 1491, which authorizes non-tort money claims against the United States (see Chapter IV.A); and (2) the Administrative Procedure Act, 5 U.S.C. §§ 701–706, which authorizes claims for specific relief against the federal government (see Chapter IV.B). The century-old Tucker Act has been superseded in recent decades for certain types of claims that formerly fell within its purview, by such subsequent enactments as the Contract Disputes Act, 41 U.S.C. §§ 601–613 (see Chapter IV.A.4.b) and the Civil Service Reform Act., codified in scattered sections of 5 U.S.C. (see Chapter IV.A.2.b). Nonetheless, the discussion of contract claims and civilian employment claims in this treatise proceeds under the Tucker Act topic heading for practical organizational reasons and because the preexisting Tucker Act structure influenced Congress in developing the current statutory form for resolution of these claims.

There are, of course, no true "general" waivers, that is, no statute that completely eliminates all incidents of sovereign immunity, even in a particular field of law or for a type of relief. Both the Tucker Act and the Administrative Procedure Act contain important limitations that will be highlighted in this chapter. At the close of this chapter (Chapter IV.C), we examine the intersection of these two statutes, with attendant problems (or

Spec → type based
ble → Relief based

opportunities, depending on one's perspective) for forum-shopping between separately-created courts.

SECTION A.   THE TUCKER ACT

1.   JURISDICTION

a.   TRIAL JURISDICTION—THE UNITED STATES COURT OF FEDERAL CLAIMS AND THE DISTRICT COURTS

Tucker Act, 28 United States Code § 1491(a)(1)   *→ Big*

(a)(1) The United States Court of Federal Claims shall have jurisdiction to render judgment upon any claim against the United States founded either upon the Constitution, or any Act of Congress or any regulation of an executive department, or upon any express or implied contract with the United States, or for liquidated or unliquidated damages in cases not sounding in tort. * * *

→ Monetary Claims
w/ limited eq relief
+ assoc.

Little Tucker Act, 28 United States Code § 1346(a)(2)

(a) The district courts shall have original jurisdiction, concurrent with the United States Court of Federal Claims, of:

* * *   *↳ Pub Claims only*

(2) Any other civil action or claim against the United States, not exceeding $10,000 in amount, founded either upon the Constitution, or any Act of Congress, or any regulation of an executive department, or upon any express or implied contract with the United States, or for liquidated or unliquidated damages in cases not sounding in tort[.]
* * *

Primarily Bench trials ⇓ exception: tax claims

6-year SoL

28 United States Code § 1500

The United States Court of Federal Claims shall not have jurisdiction of any claim for or in respect to which the plaintiff or his assignee has pending in any other court any suit or process against the United States or any person who, at the time when the cause of action alleged in such suit or process arose, was, in respect thereto, acting or professing to act, directly or indirectly under the authority of the United States.

Gregory C. Sisk, The Tapestry Unravels: Statutory Waivers of Sovereign Immunity and Money Claims Against the United States

71 George Washington Law Review 602, 606–11 (2003).

* * * What today is the Court of Federal Claims shared its birth with that of the first significant grant of permission by the sovereign United States to its citizens to seek relief against it in the courts.

The United States Court of Claims ("Court of Claims") was created by Congress in 1855 and given authority to hear claims against the United States founded upon federal statutes, regulations, and contracts.[37] Prior to 1855, individuals with contract or other monetary claims against the federal government were barred by sovereign immunity from seeking redress in court and thus were left to petition Congress to enact legislation—in the form of "private bills"—appropriating funds to pay those claims. As originally conceived, the Court of Claims had authority only to make recommendations to Congress to pay claims, thereby serving as an advisor to Congress regarding the merits of such claims. President Lincoln urged Congress to give the "power of making judgments final" to the Court of Claims, arguing that "[i]t is as much the duty of Government to render prompt justice against itself, in favor of its citizens, as it is to administer the same between private individuals." As President Lincoln requested, and "under the deluge of Civil War claims,"[41] Congress acted in 1863 to grant the Court of Claims power to make binding and final judgments with appellate review by the Supreme Court.[42]

From a historical and a practice perspective, it is not at all surprising that the very first congressional waiver of the United States' immunity from legal action and liability was focused primarily upon disputes involving government contractors. Professor Harold J. Krent explains that "[t]he [pre–Civil War waiver of immunity from contract suit] was viewed as indispensable to the efficient operation of government, for without it, qualified private contractors might not undertake government projects and the government could not obtain the goods and services it needed at affordable prices."[43] Professor Gillian Hadfield writes that the waiver of sovereign immunity in contract cases served not only practical ends but promoted democratic theory:

> The ability of the sovereign to bind itself in contract has been an important step in the evolution of the modern democratic state. Through the use of contracts, government has been able to perform its functions more effectively by drawing on private resources to deliver governmental goods and services. Politically, by honoring its contracts,

---

37. Act of February 24, 1855, ch. 122, 10 Stat. 612.

41. C. Stanley Dees, *The Future of the Contract Disputes Act: Is It Time to Roll Back Sovereign Immunity?*, 28 PUB. CONT. L.J. 545, 546 (1999).

42. Act of March 3, 1863, ch. 92, 12 Stat. 766 * * *.

43. Harold J. Krent, *Reconceptualizing Sovereign Immunity*, 45 VAND. L.J. 1529, 1565 (1992).

government has reinforced its democratic legitimacy as a government subject to the rule of law.[44]

In 1886, Representative John Randolph Tucker introduced a bill in Congress to revise the jurisdiction and procedures of the Court of Claims and to replace the earlier 1855 and 1863 statutes. The Tucker Act,[46] enacted in 1887, remains the "foundation stone" in the adjudication of money claims against the United States.[47] This statute confirmed the powers and nationwide jurisdiction of the Court of Claims over money claims (other than in tort) based upon federal statutes, executive regulations, and contract, and also expanded that court's authority to hear suits based upon the Constitution. Moreover, the Tucker Act granted the then–circuit courts (today the District Courts) concurrent jurisdiction with the Court of Claims over monetary claims not exceeding $10,000 in amount. In 1972, Congress enacted the Remand Act[50] as an amendment to the Tucker Act, which permits the court to grant certain types of equitable relief "incident of and collateral to" a money judgment, such as reinstatement of an employee to a position or correction of records. In 1996, the Tucker Act was amended to grant the Court of Federal Claims jurisdiction, including the power to issue declaratory and injunctive relief as well as money damages, over protests arising from solicitations of bids for government contracts, a field of litigation that has become a sizable part of the court's docket.[52] With these and other minor exceptions, the substance of the Tucker Act has been remarkably stable during the past century.

During the past quarter century, however, the Tucker Act has been revised in two important structural ways, and the former Court of Claims has been reconstituted once and renamed twice. First, prior to 1978, contract disputes with the government generally fell under the provision of the Tucker Act covering claims founded on contract. Since 1978, the now–Court of Federal Claims has original court jurisdiction, shared only with the agency boards of contract appeals, over all contract claims covered by the Contract Disputes Act of 1978 ("CDA").[56] The CDA governs all contracts entered into by the government for the procurement of property, other than real property; the procurement of services; the procurement of construction, alteration, repair or maintenance of real property; or the disposal of personal property. The vast majority of contracts with federal government departments and agencies fall within the coverage of the CDA. Pursuant to the CDA, a government contractor has two alternatives avenues for review of an adverse decision by a government agency contracting officer: (1) a "direct access" suit in the Court of Federal Claims under

44. Gillian Hadfield, *Of Sovereignty and Contract: Damages for Breach of Contract by Government*, 8 S. CAL. INTERDISC. L.J. 467, 467 (1999).

46. Tucker Act, ch. 359, 24 Stat. 505 (1887) * * *.

47. Dees, *supra* note 41, at 546.

50. Remand Act of 1972, Pub. L. No. 92–415, 86 Stat. 652 (codified at 28 U.S.C. § 1491(a)(2)).

52. Pub. L. No. 104–320, § 12, 110 Stat. 3870, 3874–76 (1996) (codified at 28 U.S.C. § 1941(b)).

56. Contract Disputes Act of 1978, Pub. L. No. 95–563, 92 Stat. 2383 (codified at 41 U.S.C. §§ 601–613).

the Tucker Act as amended by the CDA, or (2) review by the Board of Contract Appeals for the agency. Whether the case is heard by the Court of Federal Claims or the Board of Contract Appeals, either the contractor or the government may seek appellate review in the Federal Circuit.[62]

Second, the Federal Courts Improvement Act of 1982 ("FCIA")[63] bifurcated the original Court of Claims into two separate but related judicial entities. The Court of Claims was an Article III court, with its judges being appointed for life tenure as with judges on other federal courts. As part of the FCIA, Congress established the slightly renamed Claims Court as the trial court for Tucker Act and CDA claims and, then, created the Federal Circuit to hear appeals involving these and other claims. Congress designated the Claims Court as an "Article I court,"— that is, a court created by Congress pursuant to its legislative powers under Article I of the Constitution and whose judges do not have the life-tenure protection guaranteed to members of the regular federal judiciary by Article III of the Constitution. The creation of the Federal Circuit, however, preserved appellate review by an Article III court.

In 1992, the Claims Court was renamed the "United States Court of Federal Claims,"[69] the denomination that it retains today. By statute, the court consists of sixteen judges, appointed for fifteen-year terms by the president, with the advice and consent of the Senate. Congress, however, has provided that judges who are not reappointed following expiration of their terms may, under certain circumstances, become "senior judges," perform judicial duties as requested by the chief judge, and continue to receive an annuity equal to the salary payable to active judges.

Notes

1. A comprehensive history of the Federal Courts Improvement Act of 1982, Pub. L. No. 97–164, 96 Stat. 25, which produced the Court of Federal Claims (then denominated the Claims Court) may be found in Richard H. Seamon, *The Provenance of the Federal Courts Improvement Act of 1982,* 71 Geo. Wash. L. Rev. 543, 554–84 (2003). Professor Seamon explains, and Professor Daniel Meador (who should be appreciated as the father of the court due to his essential work on court reform legislation while serving in the Department of Justice under Attorney General Griffin Bell) confirms, that this "creation of a new trial court * * * was incidental to the creation of the [United States Court of Appeals for the] Federal Circuit" as the new appellate court with authority over patent appeals as well as appeal from

---

62.   28 U.S.C. § 1295(a)(3), (a)(10), (b).

63.   Federal Courts Improvement Act of 1982, Pub. L. No. 97–164, 96 Stat. 39 (codified as amended in scattered sections of 28 U.S.C.).

69.   Federal Courts Administration Act of 1992, Pub. L. No. 102–572, § 902, 106

Stat. 4506, 4516 (codified in scattered sections of 18 and 28 U.S.C.). On the jurisdictional and structural reforms that accompanied the name change in 1992, see generally Loren A. Smith, *The Renovation of an Old Court,* 40 Fed. B. News & J. 530 (1993).

the Court of Federal Claims. *Id.* at 545, 585–87; *see also* Daniel J. Meador, *Origin of the "Claims" Court*, 71 Geo. Wash. L. Rev. 599, 599 (2003) (explaining that the creation of the court was "incidental, not unimportant, but incidental in the sense that the primary concern [of the Congress] was with appellate matters"). Nonetheless, by advancing from the prior system of court commissioners who handled trial matters in government claims cases to Article I judges with final-judgment authority "upgraded the trial forum for government claims and made it more efficient." Seamon, *supra*, at 545.

2. Building upon the model of the United States Tax Court, another federal trial court that had nationwide jurisdiction over particular categories of claims, the Court of Federal Claims was designed by Congress in 1982 as an Article I court, that is, a court whose judges were appointed not for life but for a term of years. Meador, *supra*, at 599. As Seamon reports, witnesses testified at congressional hearings preceding the 1982 legislation that the judges of what would become the Court of Federal Claims should have Article III status, but that matter was not discussed in any committee report or floor debate, indicating that, "[o]n balance, it does not appear that Congress really considered this issue, and it may well merit further congressional attention." Seamon, *supra*, at 586. The author of this casebook has said the following on this topic:

> [T]he simple answer is to integrate the Court of Federal Claims more fully into the judicial branch by giving it Article III status. Given that a judge of the Court of Federal Claims upon expiration of his or her fifteen-year term may assume "senior" status and thereby continue to act in a judicial capacity and receive a full salary, the court already has been given *de facto* Article III status by Congress.[697] For Congress now to acknowledge that the Court of Federal Claims in practice is indistinguishable from other federal courts and to enhance the standing of the court and its judges among their judicial brethren would be but a small step.

Gregory C. Sisk, *The Tapestry Unravels: Statutory Waivers of Sovereign Immunity and Money Claims Against the United States*, 71 Geo. Wash. L. Rev. 601, 706 (2003). As an insightful alternative perspective, Professor Judith Resnick places the Court of Federal Claims in the context of the growth of a multitude of innovative in venues for adjudication in recent decades, making it no longer an oddity or anomaly within the federal adjudicatory system. Judith Resnick, *Of Courts, Agencies, and the Court of Federal Claims: Fortunately Outliving One's Anomalous Character*, 71 Geo.

---

697. *See* [Eric] Bruggink, [*A Model Proposal*, 28 Pub. Cont. L.J. 529, 531 (1999)] ("In 1992 Congress changed the tenure provisions of [Court of Federal Claims] judges to give them *de facto* salaries for life."); [Robert] Meltz, *"Property Rights" Bills Take a Process Approach: H.R. 992 and H.R. 1534*, 9 n.26, Congressional Research Service Report for Congress (1998) at (reporting the testimony of Court of Federal Claims Chief Judge Loren Smith on proposed legislation, in which he "asserted that since each [Court of Federal Claims] active-status judge has the option of taking lifetime senior status at the end of his or her fifteen-year term (if not reappointed), [Court of Federal Claims] judges are likely to have the same independence of judgment as Article III judges").

Wash. L. Rev. 798 (2003). Thus, she explains, while the Court of Federal Claims, or its predecessor the Court of Claims, "once marked a frontier, in hindsight, it anticipated structural developments of the twentieth century, both in terms of devolving adjudication to agencies and in terms of staffing federal adjudication with non-life-tenured-judges" such as magistrate and bankruptcy judges. *Id.* at 798.

3.   The docket of the Court of Federal Claims is varied, although all of the claims that it hears are, in one form or another, claims against the sovereign United States:

> About one-third of the COFC's cases involve contract claims against the government. Another one-quarter or so of its cases are tax refund suits against the government. Yet another major portion of the COFC's docket consists of cases in which civilian employees or members of the military sue the government over pay. Also large in number, as well as doctrinal importance, are cases involving claims that the government has taken the plaintiff's property without paying the "just compensation" required by the Fifth Amendment of the Constitution. Smaller in number, but of historical and political importance, are claims brought against the government by Native Americans and disputes referred to the COFC by Congress. The COFC also hears claims against the United States for patent infringement and copyright infringement and for rights in protected plant varieties.

Seamon, *supra*, at 548.

Smith v. Orr

United States Court of Appeals for the Federal Circuit.
855 F.2d 1544 (Fed.Cir. 1988).

■ Edward S. Smith, Circuit Judge.

In this military separation/discharge case, the United States District Court for the Southern District of Mississippi, in an order dated February 19, 1987, granted the Secretary of the Air Force's (Government) motion to dismiss and/or for summary judgment and dismissed with prejudice Capt. James H. Smith's (Captain Smith) complaint seeking both reinstatement and back pay as a result of his alleged illegal separation from active duty in the United States Air Force. We vacate the district court's order and remand this case to that court with instructions to transfer the case in its entirety to the United States Claims Court.

I.   *Issues*

In reviewing the order of the district court, dismissing with prejudice Captain Smith's complaint, we address the following two issues.

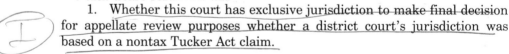

1.   Whether this court has exclusive jurisdiction to make final decision for appellate review purposes whether a district court's jurisdiction was based on a nontax Tucker Act claim.

2.   Whether, under the Tucker Act, the district court loses jurisdiction over a nontax Little Tucker Act claim if the claim, when first filed, did not exceed $10,000, but over the course of the litigation accrued to exceed this amount.

II.   *Background*

Captain Smith, on January 31, 1984, involuntarily received an honorable discharge from the United States Air Force on grounds that he twice had been nonselected for promotion and retention on active duty. Prior to his discharge, Captain Smith determined that his military records were incomplete as a result of the entrance of a wrong social security number with his name in the Air Force's Automated Personnel System. Consequently, Captain Smith's records not only failed to contain all of his data but included erroneous data.

On April 7, 1981, Captain Smith applied to the Air Force Board for Correction of Military Records (AFBCMR) for correction of his military records and for supplemental consideration for promotion based upon the erroneous personal records. * * * [T]he AFBCMR concluded that Captain Smith's nonselection was not caused by the deficiencies in his military record. * * *

In an attempt to prevent his discharge, Captain Smith, on October 25, 1983, filed an action in the United States District Court for the Southern District of Mississippi. * * *

As well as pursuing his administrative remedies, Captain Smith sought relief in the district court seeking both reinstatement and back pay. Captain Smith's claim for back pay began to accrue on his separation from the Air Force. At the time Captain Smith filed in the district court his claim for back pay, the accrued amount of his back pay did not exceed $10,000. Once the accrued amount exceeded $10,000, the Government moved to dismiss Captain Smith's complaint on the ground that the district court no longer had jurisdiction under the Little Tucker Act.[2] The district court denied that motion holding that it had jurisdiction.

On February 19, 1987, the district court reached the merits of Captain Smith's case and granted the Government's motion to dismiss and/or for summary judgment. Captain Smith's complaint was dismissed with prejudice. The district court held that Captain Smith's claims were not subject to judicial review by that court and, even if they were, that Captain Smith's discharge was lawful. Subsequently, Captain Smith appealed that judgment to the United States Court of Appeals for the Fifth Circuit. The Fifth Circuit, without explanation, transferred the case to this court.

III.   *Analysis*

A.   *Inherent Jurisdiction To Determine Jurisdiction*

[With respect to jurisdiction over the appeal, the court ruled that the Federal Circuit has *exclusive* appellate jurisdiction over appeals from cases

---

2.   28 U.S.C. § 1346(a)(2).

involving monetary claims against the United States cognizable under the Tucker Act *only* if the district court itself had proper jurisdiction. The district courts are without proper jurisdiction under the Tucker Act over claims against the United States in excess of $10,000 which instead must be brought in the Claims Act. 28 U.S.C. §§ 1346(a)(2), 1491(a)(1). In cases where claims for more than $10,000 are filed in a district court, the regional courts of appeals have concurrent appellate jurisdiction with the Federal Circuit to determine whether the case states a monetary claim cognizable under the Tucker Act and whether the amount in controversy exceeds $10,000 so as to mandate that the claim be pursued in the Claims Court.]

B. *Jurisdiction of the District Court*

The Government, on two different occasions, argued to the district court that it lacked jurisdiction under the Little Tucker Act over Captain Smith's case. The Government contended that although Captain Smith's back pay, at the time he filed his claim, did not exceed $10,000, Captain Smith's back pay had subsequently accrued to an amount exceeding $10,000. Because Captain Smith had not waived his right to the amount exceeding $10,000, the Government argued that the district court lost jurisdiction when the back pay accrued to more than $10,000. The district court rejected these assertions and continued with the case, ultimately reaching the merits and granting the Government's motion to dismiss and/or for summary judgment. Because we hold that the district court lacked Little Tucker Act jurisdiction over Captain Smith's case, we vacate the district court's order and remand this case to that court with instructions to transfer the case to the Claims Court.

Our analysis of this issue begins with the Little Tucker Act itself, which act operates both as a grant of jurisdiction as well as a waiver of sovereign immunity:

§ 1346. **United States as defendant**

(a) The district courts shall have original jurisdiction, concurrent with the United States Claims Court, of:

* * *

(2) Any other civil action or claim against the United States, not exceeding $10,000 in amount, founded either upon the Constitution, or any act of Congress, or any regulation of an executive department, or upon any express or implied contract with the United States, or for liquidated or unliquidated damages in cases not sounding in tort * * *.

It is clear from the language of the Little Tucker Act that the district courts are without jurisdiction over a nontax claim against the United States on which claim plaintiff's request for recovery exceeds $10,000. Such an action is proper only in the Claims Court.[41]

41. 28 U.S.C. § 1491.

The Tucker Act operates as a waiver of sovereignty by the United States and we are obliged to construe such waivers strictly. Accordingly, we * * * hold that, within the ambit of section 1346(a)(2), the amount of a claim against the United States for back pay is the total amount of back pay the plaintiff stands ultimately to recover in the suit and is not the amount of back pay accrued at the time the claim is filed. Any other interpretation would circumvent congressional intent in limiting the Tucker Act jurisdiction of the district courts to claims not exceeding $10,000. Our holding does not preclude a plaintiff from bringing in a district court a claim against the United States worth more than $10,000. Rather, our holding is entirely consistent with the well-established principle that a plaintiff may pursue such a claim in a district court if the plaintiff waives his right to recover the amount exceeding $10,000. The amount of a claim under the Little Tucker Act, for jurisdictional purposes, is based on the actual recovery sought by a plaintiff pursuant to that claim and is not based on the potential worth of the claim.

Here, Captain Smith filed a claim with the district court for back pay. Although at the time he filed his complaint the accrued amount of his claim did not exceed $10,000, Captain Smith's claim for back pay did accrue to greater than $10,000 during the district court's consideration of his claim. Because Captain Smith did not waive his right to recover the amount exceeding $10,000, the district court lost jurisdiction over his claim when it exceeded this amount.

Typically, when a back pay claim exceeds $10,000, district courts transfer it, along with any associated equitable claim, to the Claims Court. This is true unless the type of equitable relief sought is outside that available in the Claims Court. In that instance, the claim for money damages would be transferred to the Claims Court, and the district court would retain jurisdiction over the equitable claim.[49] Such was not the case here. Captain Smith's equitable claim for reinstatement was within the Claims Court's jurisdiction.[50] Therefore, the district court had no basis to refuse transferring both the monetary and equitable claims to the Claims Court.

IV.   CONCLUSION

In view of the foregoing, we hold that the district court lacked jurisdiction over Captain Smith's case. Accordingly, we vacate the district court's order and remand this case to that court with instructions to transfer the case in its entirety to the United States Claims Court.

VACATED AND REMANDED.

[The concurring opinion of BISSELL, CIRCUIT JUDGE is omitted.]

---

49. *See Gower v. Lehman,* 799 F.2d 925, 928–29 (4th Cir.1986).

50. 28 U.S.C. § 1491(a)(2).

Notes and Questions

1.   The *Smith v. Orr** decision nicely illustrates and explains (1) the division of Tucker Act jurisdiction between the federal district courts and the Court of Federal Claims and (2) the significance of the $10,000 dividing line. The substance of military employment claims against the federal government will be addressed later in this chapter (see Chapter IV.A.2.b).

The *Smith* court concludes that, even if subject matter jurisdiction in the district court was valid at the time of filing of the claim, the district court may subsequently lose jurisdiction when the amount in controversy accrues beyond $10,000. After reading the next decision, *Keene Corp. v. United States,* you might return to the *Smith* court's treatment of this subsequent accrual issue in light of the general principle that subject matter jurisdiction is determined at the time of the filing of a lawsuit. Is this accrual of backpay an appropriate exception to that general rule?

2.   As the *Smith* court properly states in its conclusion to the opinion, and contrary to the government's apparent argument in the district court when it moved for dismissal, the proper disposition of a case that is improperly filed in the district court because of Tucker Act jurisdictional limitations is a transfer under 28 U.S.C. § 1631 to the Court of Federal Claims—not a dismissal of the lawsuit. Thus, rather than requiring the plaintiff to re-file the lawsuit in the Court of Federal Claims, which might be impossible if the general six-year statute of limitations on Tucker Act claims (28 U.S.C. § 2501) has passed in the interim, the lawsuit is simply moved to the proper court and continues to proceed unabated in the new forum.

3.   You should also be aware of a procedure available to obtain early and final resolution of Tucker Act subject matter jurisdiction disputes, which was enacted by Congress subsequent to the *Smith* decision. As explained in detail later in this chapter (see Chapter IV.A.1.b), Section 1292(d)(4) of Title 28 authorizes an interlocutory appeal to the United States Court of Appeals for the Federal Circuit from district court orders granting or denying motions to transfer a case to the Court of Federal Claims. (An "interlocutory" appeal is one taken before final judgment in the trial court, such as to challenge rulings on jurisdiction, discovery motions, etc. Interlocutory appeals are generally disfavored, but Section 1292(d)(4) allows an early appeal of the Tucker Act jurisdiction issue.) Had that procedure been available at the time of the *Smith* case, the government would have been able to immediately appeal the district court's denial of its jurisdictional motion, rather than waiting until after disposition of the case by the district court on the merits. The plaintiff Smith would also have benefited from such a procedure as well, because the jurisdictional issue would have been resolved early. The case would have been transferred

---

* In the interests of full disclosure, the author of this casebook was counsel for the Secretary of Health and Human Services as amicus curiae on the appellate jurisdiction issue in *Smith v. Orr* before the United States Court of Appeals for the Federal Circuit.

immediately for hearing on the merits to the Court of Federal Claims, without unnecessary loss of time and the expense to the plaintiff of trial proceedings in the district court, only to later be returned to the starting line in another forum.

———

Keene Corporation v. United States

United States Supreme Court.
508 U.S. 200 (1993).

■ JUSTICE SOUTER delivered the opinion of the Court.

Keene Corporation has been sued by thousands of plaintiffs alleging injury from exposure to asbestos fibers and dust released from products made by Keene and by a company it acquired. In trying to recoup some of the money it was paying to litigate and settle the cases, Keene filed two complaints against the United States in the Court of Federal Claims.[1] When it filed each complaint, however, Keene had a similar claim pending against the Government in another court. We hold that 28 U.S.C. § 1500 consequently precludes Court of Federal Claims jurisdiction over Keene's actions and affirm the dismissal of its complaints.

I

* * * Keene manufactured and sold thermal insulation and acoustical products containing asbestos * * *. In the mid–1970's, plaintiffs began suing Keene in tort, alleging injury or death from exposure to asbestos fibers. In a typical case filed against Keene and other defendants in the District Court for the Western District of Pennsylvania, *Miller v. Johns–Manville Products Corp.*, No. 78–1283E, the plaintiff alleged, on behalf of the estate of one Dzon, that the decedent had died of lung cancer caused by asbestos fibers and dust inhaled during employment in 1943 and 1944. In June 1979, Keene filed a third-party complaint against the United States, alleging that any asbestos products to which Dzon was exposed had been supplied to the Government in accordance with specifications set out in Government contracts, and seeking indemnification or contribution from the Government for any damages Keene might have to pay the plaintiff. This third-party action ended, however, in May 1980, when the District Court granted Keene's motion for voluntary dismissal of its complaint.

In the meantime, in December 1979, with the *Miller* third-party action still pending, Keene filed the first of its two complaints in issue here, seeking damages from the United States in the Court of Federal Claims

---

1. Keene actually filed its complaints in the old Court of Claims. Soon thereafter, Congress transferred the trial functions of the Court of Claims to a newly created "United States Claims Court." Federal Courts Improvement Act of 1982, § 133, 96 Stat. 39–41. The Claims Court has just been renamed the "United States Court of Federal Claims." See Court of Federal Claims Technical and Procedural Improvements Act of 1992, § 902, 106 Stat. 4516. To avoid confusion, we will refer to the trial court in this case by its latest name.

"for any amounts which have been, or which may be recovered from Keene by the claimants, by settlement or judgment." *Keene Corp. v. United States,* No. 579–79C (*Keene I*). The "claimants" are defined as the plaintiffs in the more than 2,500 lawsuits filed against Keene "by persons alleging personal injury or death from inhalation of asbestos fibers contained in thermal insulation products" manufactured or sold by Keene or its subsidiaries. Keene alleges conformance with Government specifications in the inclusion of asbestos within the thermal insulation products Keene supplied to Government shipyards and other projects funded or controlled by the Government, and Keene further claims that the Government even sold it some of the asbestos fiber used in its products. Keene's theory of recovery is breach by the United States of implied warranties in contracts between the Government and Keene, a theory only the Court of Federal Claims may entertain, given the amount of damages requested, under the Tucker Act, 28 U.S.C. § 1491(a)(1).

Keene's next move against the Government came the following month when it filed a 23–count complaint in the District Court for the Southern District of New York. *Keene Corp. v. United States,* No. 80–CIV–0401(GLG). The pleadings tracked, almost verbatim, the lengthy factual allegations of *Keene I,* but the action was recast in terms of various tort theories, again seeking damages for any amounts paid by Keene to asbestos claimants. Keene also added a takings claim for the Government's allegedly improper recoupment, under the Federal Employees' Compensation Act (FECA), 5 U.S.C. § 8132, of money paid by Keene to claimants covered by the Act. For this, Keene sought restitution of "the amounts of money which have been, or which may be, recouped by [the United States] from claimants from judgments and settlements paid by Keene," as well as an injunction against the Government's collection of FECA refunds thereafter. This suit suffered dismissal in September 1981, on the basis of sovereign immunity, which the court held unaffected by any waiver found in the Federal Tort Claims Act, the Suits in Admiralty Act, and the Public Vessels Act. The Court of Appeals affirmed, *Keene Corp. v. United States,* 700 F.2d 836 (C.A.2 1983), and we denied certiorari, 464 U.S. 864 (1983).

Only five days before the Southern District's dismissal of that omnibus action, Keene returned to the Court of Federal Claims with the second of the complaints in issue here. *Keene Corp. v. United States,* No. 585–81C (*Keene II*). Although this one, too, repeats many of the factual allegations of *Keene I,* it adopts one of the theories raised in the Southern District case, seeking payment for "the amounts of money that [the United States] has recouped" under FECA from asbestos claimants paid by Keene. Again, the recoupments are said to be takings of Keene's property without due process and just compensation, contrary to the Fifth Amendment. See 28 U.S.C. § 1491(a)(1) (covering, *inter alia,* certain claims "founded ... upon the Constitution").

After the Court of Federal Claims raised the present jurisdictional issue *sua sponte* in similar actions brought by Johns–Manville, the Government invoked 28 U.S.C. § 1500 in moving to dismiss both *Keene I* and

Keene II, as well as like actions by five other asbestos product manufacturers. * * * [T]he Court of Federal Claims ... entered dismissals in *Keene I* and *Keene II,* among other cases, finding that when Keene had filed both *Keene I* and *Keene II,* it had the same claims pending in other courts. 17 Cl.Ct. 146 (1989). While a panel of the Court of Appeals for the Federal Circuit reversed on the ground that § 1500 was inapplicable because no other claim had been pending elsewhere when the Court of Federal Claims entertained and acted upon the Government's motion to dismiss, *UNR Industries, Inc. v. United States,* 911 F.2d 654 (1990), the Court of Appeals, en banc, subsequently vacated the panel opinion, 926 F.2d 1109 (1990), and affirmed the trial court's dismissals, 962 F.2d 1013 (1992). We granted certiorari.

II

The authority cited for dismissing Keene's complaints for want of jurisdiction was 28 U.S.C.A. § 1500:

> "The United States Court of Federal Claims shall not have jurisdiction of any claim for or in respect to which the plaintiff or his assignee has pending in any other court any suit or process against the United States or any person who, at the time when the cause of action alleged in such suit or process arose, was, in respect thereto, acting or professing to act, directly or indirectly under the authority of the United States."

The lineage of this text runs back more than a century to the aftermath of the Civil War, when residents of the Confederacy who had involuntarily parted with property (usually cotton) during the war sued the United States for compensation in the Court of Claims, under the Abandoned Property Collection Act, ch. 120, 12 Stat. 820 (1863). When these cotton claimants had difficulty meeting the statutory condition that they must have given no aid or comfort to participants in the rebellion, they resorted to separate suits in other courts seeking compensation not from the Government as such but from federal officials, and not under the statutory cause of action but on tort theories such as conversion. It was these duplicative lawsuits that induced Congress to prohibit anyone from filing or prosecuting in the Court of Claims "any claim ... for or in respect to which he ... shall have commenced and has pending" an action in any other court against an officer or agent of the United States. Act of June 25, 1868, ch. 71, § 8, 15 Stat. 77. The statute has long outlived the cotton claimants * * *.

Keene argues it was error for the courts below to apply the statute by focusing on facts as of the time Keene filed its complaints (instead of the time of the trial court's ruling on the motion to dismiss) and to ignore differences said to exist between the Court of Federal Claims actions and those filed in the District Courts. Neither assignment of error will stand.

A

Congress has the constitutional authority to define the jurisdiction of the lower federal courts, see *Finley v. United States,* 490 U.S. 545, 548

(1989), and, once the lines are drawn, "limits upon federal jurisdiction . . . must be neither disregarded nor evaded." *Owen Equipment & Erection Co. v. Kroger,* 437 U.S. 365, 374 (1978). In § 1500, Congress has employed its power to provide that the Court of Federal Claims "shall not have jurisdiction" over a claim, "for or in respect to which" the plaintiff "has [a suit or process] pending" in any other court. In applying the jurisdictional bar here by looking to the facts existing when Keene filed each of its complaints, the Court of Federal Claims followed the longstanding principle that "the jurisdiction of the Court depends upon the state of things at the time of the action brought." *Mollan v. Torrance,* 9 Wheat. 537, 539 (1824) (Marshall, C.J.).

While acknowledging what it calls this "general rule" that subject-matter jurisdiction turns on the facts upon filing, Keene would have us dispense with the rule here. Assuming that we could, however, Keene gives us nothing to convince us that we should. Keene argues that if § 1500 spoke of "jurisdiction to render judgment" instead of "jurisdiction" pure and simple, the phrase would "all but preclude" application of the time-of-filing rule. But, without deciding whether such a change of terms would carry such significance, we have only to say that § 1500 speaks of "jurisdiction," without more, whereas some nearby sections of title 28 use the longer phrase. This fact only underscores our duty to refrain from reading a phrase into the statute when Congress has left it out. "[W]here Congress includes particular language in one section of a statute but omits it in another . . . , it is generally presumed that Congress acts intentionally and purposely in the disparate inclusion or exclusion." *Russello v. United States,* 464 U.S. 16, 23 (1983). * * *

* * * [W]e read the statute as continuing to bar jurisdiction over the claim of a plaintiff who, upon filing, has an action pending in any other court "for or in respect to" the same claim.[4]

B

The statutory notion of comparable claims is more elusive. By precluding jurisdiction over the claim of a plaintiff with a suit pending in another court "for or in respect to" the same claim, § 1500 requires a comparison between the claims raised in the Court of Federal Claims and in the other lawsuit. The exact nature of the things to be compared is not illuminated, however, by the awkward formulation of § 1500. * * *

Fortunately, though, we can turn to earlier readings of the word "claim" as it appears in this statute. The phrase "any claim . . . for or in respect to which" has remained unchanged since the statute was first adopted in 1868, and prior encounters with § 154 of the Judicial Code of

---

4. We do not decide whether the statute also continues to bar a plaintiff from prosecuting a claim in the Court of Federal Claims while he has pending a later-filed suit in another court "for or in respect to" the same claim. Cf. *Tecon Engineers, Inc. v. Unit-* *ed States,* 170 Ct.Cl. 389, 343 F.2d 943 (1965), cert. denied, 382 U.S. 976 (1966). As the dissenting judge noted below, this case does not raise that issue. *UNR Industries, Inc. v. United States,* 962 F.2d 1013, 1030, n. 5 (C.A.Fed.1992) (Plager, J., dissenting).

1911, the immediate predecessor to § 1500, shed some light on the issue. *Corona Coal Co. v. United States,* 263 U.S. 537 (1924), was an action brought against the United States in the Court of Claims, seeking compensation for coal requisitioned by the Government. Before bringing its appeal to this Court, the plaintiff sued the President's agent in Federal District Court, "the causes of action therein set forth being the same as that set forth in the [Court of Claims] case." *Id.,* at 539. After noting that the causes of action "arose out of" the same factual setting, we applied § 154 and dismissed the appeal. *Id.,* at 539–540. * * *

A few years later, the Court of Claims settled a key question * * *: whether § 154 applied when the Court of Claims action and the "other" suit proceeded under different legal theories. In *British American Tobacco Co. v. United States,* 89 Ct.Cl. 438 (1939) (*per curiam*), after the plaintiff had surrendered his gold bullion to the Government (in compliance with executive orders and regulations that took this country off the gold standard), he sued in the Court of Claims on allegations that he had been underpaid by more than $4.3 million. Earlier the same day, the plaintiff had filed a suit in Federal District Court "for the recovery of the same amount for the same gold bullion surrendered." *Id.,* at 439. The Court of Claims observed that "[t]he only distinction between the two suits instituted in the District Court and in this court is that the action in the District Court was made to sound in tort and the action in this court was alleged on contract." *Id.,* at 440. Because the two actions were based on the same operative facts, the court dismissed the Court of Claims action for lack of jurisdiction, finding it to be "clear that the word 'claim,' as used in section 154, ... has no reference to the legal theory upon which a claimant seeks to enforce his demand." *Ibid.*

These precedents demonstrate that under the immediate predecessor of § 1500, the comparison of the two cases for purposes of possible dismissal would turn on whether the plaintiff's other suit was based on substantially the same operative facts as the Court of Claims action, at least if there was some overlap in the relief requested.[6] That the two actions were based on different legal theories did not matter. Since Keene has given us no reason to doubt that these cases represented settled law when Congress reenacted the "claim for or in respect to which" language in 1948, see 62 Stat. 942, we apply the presumption that Congress was aware of these earlier judicial interpretations and, in effect, adopted them. The decision in *British American Tobacco* strikes us, moreover, as a sensible reading of the statute, for it honors Congress's decision to limit Court of Federal Claims jurisdiction not only as to claims "for ... which" the plaintiff has sued in another court, but as to those "in respect to which" he has sued elsewhere as well. While the latter language does not set the limits of claim identity with any precision, it does make it clear that

6. Because the issue is not presented on the facts of this case, we need not decide whether two actions based on the same operative facts, but seeking completely different relief, would implicate § 1500. Cf. *Casman v. United States,* 135 Ct.Cl. 647 (1956); *Boston Five Cents Savings Bank, FSB v. United States,* 864 F.2d 137 (C.A.Fed.1988).

Congress did not intend the statute to be rendered useless by a narrow concept of identity providing a correspondingly liberal opportunity to maintain two suits arising from the same factual foundation.

Keene nonetheless argues, for the first time in its merits brief, that "[a] claim brought outside the [Court of Federal Claims] is 'for or in respect to' a claim in the [Court of Federal Claims only] when claim-splitting law would treat them as the same—*i.e.*, require them to be joined in a single suit—if the two claims were both brought against the United States." Under this theory, § 1500 would not apply to a Court of Federal Claims plaintiff unless his suit pending in the other court rested on a legal theory that could have been pleaded (as Keene's could not have been) in the Court of Federal Claims. But this reinterpretation of § 1500 is bound to fail, not because novelty is always fatal in the construction of an old statute, but because the novel proposition in Keene's suggested reading would have rendered the statute useless, in all or nearly all instances, to effect the very object it was originally enacted to accomplish. Keene fails to explain how the original statute would have applied to the cotton claimants, whose tort actions brought in other courts were beyond the jurisdiction of the Court of Claims, just as tort cases are outside the jurisdiction of the Court of Federal Claims today. Keene's theory was squarely rejected in *British American Tobacco,* and it must be rejected again this time.

III

* * * In applying § 1500 to the facts of this case, we find it unnecessary to consider, much less repudiate, the "judicially created exceptions" to § 1500 found in *Tecon Engineers,* [*Inc. v. United States,* 170 Ct.Cl. 389, 343 F.2d 943 (1965), cert. denied, 382 U.S. 976 (1966)], *Casman* [*v. United States,* 135 Ct.Cl. 647 (1956)], and *Boston Five* [*Cents Savings Bank, FSB v. United States,* 864 F.2d 137 (C.A.Fed.1988)]. *Tecon Engineers* held that a later-filed action in another court does not oust the Court of Federal Claims of jurisdiction over an earlier-filed complaint; our decision turns on Keene's earlier-filed District Court actions, and even Keene now concedes it to be "unnecessary for the Court to address the *Tecon* question" in ruling on the dismissal of Keene's claims. The *Casman* court recognized an exception (followed in *Boston Five*) for plaintiffs who seek distinctly different types of relief in the two courts; here, Keene had sought monetary relief in each of the cases pending when it filed the complaints seeking monetary relief in *Keene I* and *Keene II.* * * *

IV

We have said nothing until now about Keene's several policy arguments, and now can only answer that Keene addresses the wrong forum. It may well be, as Keene argues, that § 1500 operates in some circumstances to deprive plaintiffs of an opportunity to assert rights that Congress has generally made available to them "under the complex legal and jurisdictional schemes that govern claims against the Government." The trial judge in this case was not the first to call this statute anachronistic, and there is a good argument that, even when first enacted, the statute did not actually perform the preclusion function emphasized by its sponsor. But the "proper theater" for such arguments, as we told another disappointed claimant many years ago, "is the halls of Congress, for that branch of the government has limited the jurisdiction of the Court of Claims."[14] *Smoot's Case*, 15 Wall. 36 (1872). We enjoy no "liberty to add an exception ... to remove apparent hardship," *Corona Coal*, 263 U.S., at 540, and therefore enforce the statute.

The judgment of the Court of Appeals is

Affirmed.

■ JUSTICE STEVENS, dissenting.

In my opinion, 28 U.S.C. § 1500 does not require the Court of Federal Claims to dismiss an action against the United States simply because another suit on the same claim was once, but is no longer, pending in district court. Rather, the plaintiff may continue to pursue his claim so long as there is no other suit pending when the Court of Federal Claims decides the motion to dismiss. Neither the text nor the history of the statute demands more of the plaintiff than that he make an "election either to leave the Court of Claims or to leave the other courts" at that time.[1]

Section 1500 is not itself a grant of jurisdiction to the Court of Federal Claims. That function is performed by other sections of the Judicial Code immediately preceding § 1500, which give the court "jurisdiction *to render judgment* upon any claim against the United States founded either upon the Constitution, or any Act of Congress or any regulation of an executive department, or upon any express or implied contract with the United States," 28 U.S.C. § 1491(a)(1), and "jurisdiction *to render judgment* upon any claim by a disbursing officer of the United States ...," 28 U.S.C. § 1496 (emphases added). See also 28 U.S.C. § 1497; 28 U.S.C. § 1499 (granting jurisdiction to "render judgment" over other claims). Section 1500, by contrast, "takes away jurisdiction even though the subject matter of the suit may appropriately be before the Claims Court." *UNR Industries, Inc. v. United States,* 962 F.2d 1013, 1028 (C.A.Fed.1992) (Plager, J., dissenting). It is only reasonable to assume that the "jurisdiction" § 1500

---

14. A recent attempt to repeal § 1500 failed in Congress. See S. 2521, 102d Cong., 2d Sess., § 10(c) (1992); 138 Cong.Rec. S4830–S4832 (Apr. 2, 1992).

1. Senator Edmunds explained the purpose of the provision that is now § 1500, as follows:

" 'The object of this amendment is to put to their election that large class of persons having cotton claims particularly, who have sued the Secretary of the Treasury and the other agents of the Government in more than a hundred suits that are now pending, scattered over the country here and there, and who are here at the same time endeavoring

to prosecute their claims, and have filed them in the Court of Claims, so that after they put the Government to the expense of beating them once in a court of law they can turn around and try the whole question in the Court of Claims. The object is to put that class of persons to their election either to leave the Court of Claims or to leave the other courts. I am sure everybody will agree to that.' "

UNR Industries, Inc. v. United States, 962 F.2d 1013, 1018 (C.A.Fed.1992) (quoting 81 Cong. Globe, 40th Cong., 2d Sess., 2769 (1868)).

takes away is the same as the "jurisdiction" surrounding Code provisions bestow: the jurisdiction to enter judgment.

The text of § 1500 simply provides that the Court of Federal Claims "shall not have jurisdiction" over a claim "which" the plaintiff "has pending" in any other court. Accordingly, so long as a plaintiff has pending another suit in another court, the Court of Federal Claims may not adjudicate the plaintiff's claim, even though its subject matter would otherwise bring it within the court's jurisdiction. The Government may invoke this exception by putting such a plaintiff to his choice: either "leave the other courts," or forgo further proceedings in the Court of Federal Claims. If the plaintiff declines to leave the other courts, then the Court of Federal Claims is without jurisdiction to proceed with the case before it, though it may retain the case on its docket pending disposition of the other action. But if the plaintiff does dismiss his other action, then the Court of Federal Claims is free to decide his case. Section 1500 was so construed over a quarter of a century ago, see *Brown v. United States,* 175 Ct.Cl. 343, 358 F.2d 1002 (1966), and I see no reason to interpret it now as a broader prohibition on pretrial proceedings. * * *

Admittedly, this is a badly drafted statute. Viewed against a legal landscape that has changed dramatically since the days of the cotton claimants, it does not lend itself easily to sensible construction. Moreover, the Court's interpretation of § 1500 today may have the salutary effect of hastening its repeal or amendment. Nevertheless, a reading that is faithful not only to the statutory text but also to the statute's stated purpose is surely preferable to the harsh result the Court endorses here. Accordingly, I respectfully dissent.

Notes and Questions

1. With the introduction of the Tucker Act into our discussion, we have the addition not only of another statutory waiver of sovereign immunity but also of a problem of forum. The existence of specialized tribunals (such as the Court of Federal Claims), which have exclusive authority to hear certain types of claims, adds the complication of making sure that those claims are properly routed to the right forum. However, many cases may be formulated in more than one way. What are we to do with a case against the United States that could be plead alternatively (1) as a contract claim within the exclusive jurisdiction of the Court of Federal Claims or (2) as a tort claim that falls within the jurisdiction of the district courts and is excluded from the purview of the Court of Federal Claims?

Before turning to the particular answer given in the governing statute here, consider the theoretical possible alternatives. First, we could allow a party to bring both suits in the two different forums and allow each to proceed simultaneously. Second, we could permit the party to pursue only one suit at a time, although allowing both suits to be brought seriatim. If we do so, do we permit both actions to be filed simultaneously and hold one in abeyance, sitting on the docket, until the other is completed? If we instead permit only one suit to be filed at a time, there is the risk that the statute of limitations might run on the unfiled suit before the filed action is completed. And does it matter which suit in which court is filed or goes forward first? Third, we could force the party to elect which action to pursue and hold the party to that choice by barring any subsequent suit on the same claim but on a different legal theory. (A fourth alternative would be to eliminate specialized tribunals with exclusive jurisdiction, which would resolve the problem by eliminating the issue.) What are the pros and cons of each of these alternatives?

Which alternative does the Supreme Court determine is required by 28 U.S.C. § 1500?

2. In *Keene,* the Federal Tort Claims Act suit was filed in district court first and thus was actually pending at the time that the Court of Federal Claims suit was filed. What if the plaintiff reversed the order of filing? If the plaintiff filed the Tucker Act claim in the Court of Federal Claims first and then, a month or so later, filed the FTCA suit in district court? The Supreme Court expressly declined to decide this "later-filed suit" issue as it was not presented on the facts of the *Keene* decision. *See* footnote 4 of the Court's opinion. Under the Court's reasoning, which at least in part is based on the idea that jurisdiction is determined as of the time of filing, isn't it plausible that the order of filing would make all the difference, because then the FTCA suit would not be "pending" at the time the Court of Federal Claims suit was filed? And yet should such a clever device change the outcome? The problem of multiple suits on the same claim proceeding simultaneously would remain.

In *Tecon Engineers v. United States,* 170 Ct.Cl. 389, 343 F.2d 943 (1965), the Court of Claims held that a later-filed district court suit did *not* oust the Court of Claims of jurisdiction to hear a prior-filed Tucker Act claim. In *UNR Industries, Inc. v. United States,* 962 F.2d 1013 (Fed.Cir. 1992) (in banc), the Federal Circuit, sitting in banc, purported to overrule the *Tecon Engineers* "later-filed suit" exception to Section 1500. The *UNR Industries* court said that Section 1500 does preclude jurisdiction in the Court of Federal Claims over the "later-filed suit," reasoning that "Congress wanted not to dictate the order in which a claimant files suits in the [Court of Federal Claims] and another court on the same claim, but to discourage [duplicative filings] altogether." *Id.* at 1022. The *UNR Industries* decision was reviewed by the Supreme Court in the *Keene* decision that you have just read. In *Keene,* the Supreme Court regarded the lower court's discussion of the "later-filed suit" issue as unnecessary dicta because the issue was not raised on the facts of case. *See* footnote 4 of the *Keene* opinion. Subsequent to *Keene,* the Federal Circuit has reaffirmed the *Tecon Engineers* "later-filed suit" exception to Section 1500. In *Hardwick Bros. Co. II v. United States,* 72 F.3d 883 (Fed.Cir. 1995), the court held that a Federal Tort Claims Act action filed later in district court did not divest the Court of Federal Claims of its earlier-established jurisdiction over a contract action involving the same claims.

Does this outcome make any sense? Should the order of filing determine whether the Court of Federal Claims may hear the case? Isn't this just an end-run around *Keene*? And yet, Section 1500 by its terms limits Court of Federal Claims jurisdiction only when another suit on the same claim is "pending" in another court, and the Supreme Court in *Keene* relied on the traditional rule that this determination is to be made at the time of filing and not later. Perhaps the problem lies with Section 1500 and the attempt to give meaning to this statute in a modern context.

3.   The next question, of course, is what constitutes the same "claim". If simultaneous lawsuits raising the same claim may not be filed in separate forums, we must identify what makes one claim identical to another. What test does the Supreme Court adopt for defining "claim" in the *Keene* decision? The next case, *Loveladies Harbor, Inc. v. United States,* addresses this issue as well in a different context.

4.   Section 1500 was adopted to address a particular situation arising in a particular historical context, as explained by the *Keene* court. The Congress that enacted Section 1500's original predecessor statute could not have had in mind coordination of Tucker Act and FTCA claims, as neither the Tucker Act nor the FTCA yet existed in 1863. Thus, this presents the not uncommon statutory interpretation problem of applying an old statute enacted for an outdated purpose to a new situation. How should a court approach such a problem? By applying strictly the plain language of the statute? Dynamically re-construing the statute to accomplish a different modern purpose?

Commentators have suggested that Section 1500 is an historical anachronism and should be repealed. *See* Payson R. Peabody, Thomas K. Gump & Michael S. Weinstein, *A Confederate Ghost That Haunts the Federal Courts: The Case for Repeal of 28 U.S.C. § 1500,* 4 Fed. Circuit B.J. 95 (1994). The Supreme Court in *Keene* states that such arguments must be directed to Congress. A proposal to repeal Section 1500 passed the House of Representatives in 1998. See the discussion of the proposed Tucker Act Shuffle Relief Act of 1997 (H.R. 992), which also included a repealer of Section 1500, in the note material following the next case. If Section 1500 is to be repealed, what, if anything, should be substituted in its place?

————

Loveladies Harbor, Inc. v. United States

United States Court of Appeals for the Federal Circuit.
27 F.3d 1545 (Fed.Cir. 1994) (in Banc).

■ PLAGER, CIRCUIT JUDGE.

This case first came before the court as a regulatory takings case. The United States Government (Government) appealed from the merits of a decision of the Court of Federal Claims, which had granted monetary relief to a property owner, Loveladies Harbor, Inc. and Loveladies Harbor, Unit

D, Inc. (collectively, Loveladies), as a consequence of the Government's denial of a wetlands development permit. In light of an intervening decision by this court on an unrelated matter, the Government moved to dismiss for lack of jurisdiction. The court has taken the jurisdictional dispute *in banc*. We hold that this court has jurisdiction over the matter. The panel decision on the merits of the dispute will be issued in a separate opinion.

BACKGROUND

The facts of the case, insofar as they are relevant to the jurisdictional question, may be summarized as follows. Plaintiffs Loveladies own a wetlands tract located on Long Beach Island, Ocean County, New Jersey. Loveladies sought a fill permit, pursuant to § 404 of the Clean Water Act, from the Army Corps of Engineers (Corps). The Corps denied the permit. Loveladies challenged the validity of that permit denial in a proceeding in federal district court under § 554 of the Administrative Procedure Act (APA). The challenge proved unsuccessful.

Loveladies appealed the decision of the trial court to the Court of Appeals for the Third Circuit, which affirmed the judgment for the Government. Loveladies then proceeded with a suit in the Court of Federal Claims which they had filed the year before. (By consent of the parties, prosecution of the suit had been stayed pending the outcome of the district court litigation.) In their Court of Federal Claims suit, Loveladies maintained that the permit denial constituted a taking of private property, and that the Fifth Amendment of the Constitution required the Government to compensate Loveladies. The Court of Federal Claims agreed, and awarded Loveladies compensation of $2,658,000 plus interest.[7] The Government appealed the award to this court.

After a panel of the court heard oral argument in this case, but before an opinion was issued, the full court sitting *in banc* decided *UNR Industries, Inc. v. United States*, 962 F.2d 1013 (Fed.Cir.1992) (*UNR*). That case was taken on certiorari by the Supreme Court and affirmed. *Keene Corp. v. United States*, 508 U.S. 200 (1993) (*UNR/Keene*). In *UNR* this court undertook a comprehensive review of the jurisprudence surrounding 28 U.S.C. § 1500, which in pertinent part states:

> The United States [Court of Federal Claims] shall not have jurisdiction of any claims for or in respect to which the plaintiff or his assignee has pending in any other court any suit or process against the United States. . . .

Based on our decision in *UNR*, but prior to the decision of the Supreme Court in *UNR/Keene*, the Government moved in this court to vacate the judgment in favor of Loveladies. The Government in its motion argued that *UNR* compelled the conclusion that, since the suit in the Court of Federal Claims had been filed while the appeal in the earlier district court suit was still pending, § 1500 bars the jurisdiction of the Court of Federal Claims over the cause.

7. *Loveladies Harbor, Inc. v. United States*, 21 Cl. Ct. 153 (1990).

In opposition to the Government's motion, Loveladies argued that *UNR* did not compel that conclusion for several reasons, including that the same claims were not involved and that *Casman v. United States,* 135 Ct. Cl. 647 (1956) and like cases, distinguishing claims on the basis of the relief sought, supported jurisdiction. * * *

DISCUSSION

I.

As a preliminary matter, we observe that our decision in *UNR* does not constrain our decision today. Appellants in *UNR,* asbestos manufacturers, filed suit against the United States in the district court seeking money damages based on tort claims. They then filed in the Court of Federal Claims for money damages based on certain contracts they had with the Government. Both suits arose out of the same underlying events. Appellants challenged the longstanding rule that suits involving the same operative facts and seeking the same relief were the same "claims" for purposes of § 1500, even if based on different legal theories.

Appellants in *UNR* raised another issue. Appellants' contractual claims had been filed, but not acted upon, when their district court claims were dismissed. Thus, when the Government moved to dismiss their claims in the Court of Federal Claims pursuant to § 1500, appellants had no pending claims. Appellants hence argued that jurisdiction in the Court of Federal Claims was barred only if a claim was pending when the Government moved to dismiss under § 1500. In *UNR,* this court rejected both of appellants' contentions.

The Supreme Court on *certiorari* agreed. In *UNR/Keene,* the Supreme Court held that § 1500 precluded the Court of Federal Claims from exercising jurisdiction over the manufacturers' contract-based claims against the United States, because the manufacturers' tort claims were still pending in district court when suit in the Court of Federal Claims was filed. The question of whether another claim is "pending" for purposes of § 1500 is determined at the time at which the suit in the Court of Federal Claims is filed, not the time at which the Government moves to dismiss the action.

When this court decided *UNR,* we chose "to revisit the jurisprudence encumbering this statute." *Id.,* 962 F.2d at 1021. In so doing, we declared "overruled" a number of cases, including *Casman. UNR,* 962 F.2d at 1022 n. 3. The Supreme Court took exception to our efforts. "Because the issue is not presented on the facts of this case, we need not decide whether two actions based on the same operative facts, but seeking completely different relief, would implicate § 1500." *UNR/Keene,* 508 U.S. at 212 n. 6. * * *

* * * The issue the Government raises, and which is now properly before us on the facts of this case, is whether § 1500 denies jurisdiction to the Court of Federal Claims if, at the time a complaint for money damages is filed, there is a pending action in another court that seeks distinctly different relief. Our precedent, *Casman* and cases like it, tells us the

answer is no. As we are unwilling to give *stare decisis* effect to a matter that we did not fully consider and that was not before us in the prior case, we do not consider today's case as a 'resurrection' of *Casman* (*see* dissent), but as an opportunity for the Government to persuade us why we should abandon *Casman*.

II.

The precise issue in this case is the meaning of the term "claims" as it is used in § 1500, which states that the Court of Federal Claims shall not have jurisdiction "of ***any claims*** for or in respect to which the plaintiff ... has pending in any other court any suit or process against the United States ..." (Emphasis added.) Specifically, the question is whether the "claims" which Loveladies brought to the Court of Federal Claims are the same as the "claims" which Loveladies had already sued upon in the district court. If the claims are the same, the jurisdiction of the Court of Federal Claims over the same claims, still pending before the district court when the second suit was filed, was barred by § 1500. If the claims are distinctly different, Loveladies are excused from the jurisdictional dance required by § 1500.

Deciding if the claims are the same or distinctly different "requires a comparison between the claims raised in the Court of Federal Claims and in the other lawsuit." *UNR/Keene,* 508 U.S. at 210. It also requires a definition of "claims" that the statute does not provide. * * *

Viewing claims as related to the nature of the relief sought is unremarkable. And using differing relief as a characteristic for distinguishing claims was especially appropriate here, because the Court of Federal Claims and its predecessors have been courts with limited authority to grant relief. These courts could not grant the kinds of general equitable relief the district courts could, even in cases over which they otherwise have had subject-matter jurisdiction. Although the powers of the Court of Federal Claims have been increased in recent years, so that in some instances it can grant complete relief in cases over which it has subject matter jurisdiction, the Court of Federal Claims remains a court with limited remedial powers.

The *Casman* case * * * arose when a government employee sued in district court for reinstatement to his position with the Government, and while that suit was pending, sued in the Court of Claims for back pay denied him as a result of the allegedly unlawful removal.[15] When the Government moved to dismiss under § 1500 the monetary claim in the Court of Claims, that court denied the motion. The court held that the two suits alleged different "claims"—although the two suits involved the same conflict between the same parties, the claims were distinguished by the different form of relief each sought. * * *

---

15. Under the jurisdictional rules then in effect, the district court could not grant the monetary damages alleged, and the Court of Claims did not have authority to order reinstatement. Now, under 28 U.S.C. § 1491(a)(2), the Court of Federal Claims can order reinstatement.

Litigation can serve public interests as well as the particular interests of the parties. The nation is served by private litigation which accomplishes public ends, for example, by checking the power of the Government through suits brought under the APA or under the takings clause of the Fifth Amendment. Because this nation relies in significant degree on litigation to control the excesses to which Government may from time to time be prone, it would not be sound policy to force plaintiffs to forego monetary claims in order to challenge the validity of Government action, or to preclude challenges to the validity of Government action in order to protect a Constitutional claim for compensation. Section 1500 was enacted to preclude duplicate cotton claims—claims for money damages—at a time when *res judicata* principles did not provide the Government with protection against such "duplicative lawsuits." Whatever viability remains in § 1500, absent a clear expression of Congressional intent we ought not extend the statute to allow the Government to foreclose non-duplicative suits, and to deny remedies the Constitution and statutes otherwise provide.

CONCLUSION

The motion of the Government that the judgment of the Court of Federal Claims be vacated and the complaint dismissed is denied. The case is returned to the panel for decision on the merits.

MOTION DENIED.

■ MAYER, CIRCUIT JUDGE, with whom NIES and RADER, CIRCUIT JUDGES, join, dissenting.

Because I see no reason to reconsider our recent in banc decision in *UNR v. United States*, 962 F.2d 1013 (Fed.Cir.1992), *aff'd sub nom. Keene Corp. v. United States*, 508 U.S. 200 (1993), I dissent.

I.

* * * In *UNR* we addressed the meaning of "claim" under section 1500. The claims heard by the Court of Federal Claims generally involve requests for monetary relief. But it does not follow that only suits brought in other courts for money damages can give rise to section 1500's jurisdictional bar. Section 1500 divests the Court of Federal Claims of jurisdiction over such a claim where the plaintiff has a suit for the claim pending in another court or where the one in the Court of Federal Claims relates to— is "in respect to"—another suit. The jurisdictional question raised by section 1500 is thus not simply whether the claims are the "same," but whether they are sufficiently related to invoke the bar. In *UNR*, the in banc court reaffirmed that the answer lies in a comparison of the operative facts from which the suits arise. "[C]orrectly construed, section 1500 applies to all claims on whatever theories that 'arise from the same operative facts.' " 962 F.2d at 1023. * * *

* * * We also considered the exception to this rule set out in *Casman v. United States*, 135 Ct. Cl. 647 (1956), which excused adherence to section

1500 where the claims in question seek different forms of relief. We all knew a factual predicate for a *Casman* exception was not before us in *UNR,* but during the course of our consideration of the statute, it was plain that we could not square that and like cases with the clear meaning of the jurisdictional statute. That statute, as a whole, was before us in *UNR;* there is no requirement that a factual predicate underlay every jot and tittle of it before a court can explain what it means.

The history of section 1500 is replete with instances where courts sought to temper perceived inequity by inventing exceptions to the rule. In *Casman,* the injustice was thought to arise because no court was able to simultaneously grant complete relief to the petitioner: he sought restoration to his position, available only in the district court, and back pay, which he could only recover in the Court of Claims. *Casman* held section 1500 inapplicable because it was thought unfair to force the plaintiff to choose between the two courts.

But it is axiomatic that courts cannot extend their jurisdiction in the interest of equity. Faced with a jurisdictional statute riddled with judicially created loopholes, in *UNR* we concluded that section 1500 should be applied according to its plain words, and that instrumental to such application was a single, coherent definition of the word "claim" as referring only to the facts underlying the petitioner's action against the government. * * * We overruled *Casman* because it was in conflict with this interpretation.

The Supreme Court agreed that "the comparison of the two cases for purposes of possible dismissal would turn on whether the plaintiff's other suit was based on substantially the same operative facts as the Court of Claims action, at least if there was some overlap in the relief requested." [*Keene,*] 508 U.S. at 212. Finding that the *Casman* exception was not implicated by the facts of the case before it, the Court chose not to decide whether two actions seeking different relief would require dismissal under the statute. *Id.* 213 n. 6. The Court said nothing by way of disapproval of our ruling on *Casman.* But nine of the ten judges hearing that case here said that *Casman* was unsound and inconsistent with section 1500. One wonders why six of them now think otherwise. * * *

I agree that plaintiffs should have access to the full range of remedies which the Constitution and statutes provide, especially in light of the important public interest in controlling government excesses. Indeed, the claims of these property owners might well be valid on the merits, if only it were appropriate to reach them. When the government takes private property it must pay just compensation. But Congress set out just how such plaintiffs may bring their suits; we have no right to second guess in the absence of congressional transgression of the Constitution.

It cannot seriously be doubted that Congress has the power to order that the government need not defend claims arising from the same operative facts simultaneously in several forums. That a commonly based suit is pending in the district court does not necessarily forever divest the Court of Federal Claims of jurisdiction over a claim; section 1500 decrees only that a party cannot maintain actions in both courts at the same time. It may sometimes happen that the district court challenge is not finished within six years, after which any Court of Federal Claims action would be barred. *See* 28 U.S.C. § 2501 (1988 & Supp. IV 1992). But statutes limiting courts' jurisdiction will always work injustice in particular cases. This is not such a case, however, for Loveladies' district court action, including its appeal to the Court of Appeals for the Third Circuit, was resolved within three years. Loveladies still would have had three years in which to file its claim in the Court of Federal Claims for compensation after the resolution of its challenge to the permit denial.

As we said in *UNR*, "[i]t may have seemed unfair 'to deprive plaintiffs of the only forum they [had] in which to test their demand,' but that does not justify rewriting the statute." 962 F.2d at 1022. * * * In *Keene,* the Supreme Court suggested that efforts to reform section 1500 should be addressed to Congress. 508 U.S. at 217. That was the point of *UNR,* and I still think so. In fact, a bill to do just that has been introduced. S. 1355, 103d Cong., 1st Sess. (1993). * * *

Notes and Questions

1. The United States Court of Appeals for the Federal Circuit in *Loveladies Harbor* addresses an issue that the Supreme Court in *Keene* expressly chose not to decide: the application of Section 1500 to claims arising out of the same set of facts but seeking different relief. The Federal Circuit determines that the *Loveladies* case is distinguishable from *Keene* because the two claims brought in different forums involve not merely different legal theories to the same end but requests for different relief. Is this a legitimate distinction?

Although Keene Corporation in *Keene Corp. v. United States* sought money damages in both claims, it nevertheless could assert a tort claim only in district court and a contract claim only in the Court of Federal Claims. If the tort claim were to fail in district court (as in fact it ultimately did in the second district court action brought by *Keene*), Keene Corporation could be left without the alternative remedy of a contract action if the six-year statute of limitations for filing a Court of Federal Claims suit had since expired. Thus, the Supreme Court in *Keene* well understood that ordering dismissal of the Court of Federal Claims suit, because an FTCA suit was pending in district court, could leave *Keene* without a remedy, notwithstanding whether there was any merit to its contract claim. Is it any more harsh to require a party seeking different relief on the same set of operative facts to choose the claim upon which to stake the outcome?

On the other hand, while the *Keene* decision might (depending upon whether the statute of limitations expired during the pendency of the first suit) force an election of a particular legal theory, application of the same outcome to the *Loveladies* situation would preclude full recovery notwithstanding the merits of the case. If the *Keene* party made the right choice of legal theory, it would obtain a full recovery. By contrast, the *Loveladies* party cannot obtain monetary relief in the district court under the Administrative Procedure Act and cannot obtain equitable relief in the Court of Federal Claims under the Tucker Act (for reasons further explained shortly, see Chapter IV.1.c). If the *Loveladies* plaintiffs are barred from maintaining two suits, there is no strategy by which they can obtain full equitable and monetary relief. Should this make the difference?

2. During the 1998 session of Congress, the House of Representatives passed a bill that would have allowed property owners alleging takings of their property by the federal government to seek both equitable and monetary relief in either federal district court or the Court of Federal Claims. 144 Cong. Rec. H1135–40 (daily ed. Mar. 12, 1998). (The bill also provided for repeal of Section 1500.) The proposed legislation was designed to avoid the "Tucker Act shuffle" that may result under present law, by which property owners find themselves bounced between district court and the Court of Federal Claims depending upon the type of relief sought. A property owner seeking monetary compensation above $10,000 for a taking is required to bring suit in the Court of Federal Claims, while a plaintiff seeking equitable relief (such as an injunction against future government encroachments upon the land or a challenge to the validity of a regulatory action) must file in district court because the Court of Federal Claims lacks the power to grant that equitable relief. (The limitation on relief available in the Court of Federal Claims is discussed at Chapter IV.A.1.c.) Neither court may offer both damages and equitable relief for this type of claim.

The proposed "Tucker Act Shuffle Relief Act of 1997" (H.R. 992) would have authorized the district courts to award monetary compensation for a taking, even if more than $10,000 was sought, and also would have conferred upon the Court of Federal Claims the power to grant equitable relief in takings cases, thus allowing a plaintiff the choice of either forum for complete relief. (The Democratic minority in the House proposed an amendment to the bill that would have granted jurisdiction to the district court to address all issues, including both damages and equitable relief, in takings cases, but which would not have expanded the equitable powers of the Court of Federal Claims. This proposed amendment was defeated on a close vote. 144 Cong. Rec. at 1138.) However, parallel legislation in the Senate encountered a filibuster on the floor by the Democratic minority— primarily based on concerns about other provisions in the Senate bill that would have made it easier for property owners to file takings claims against state and local governments in federal court and bypass state court and administrative proceedings. The Republican leadership failed to win enough votes to close debate and bring the bill to a floor vote. 144 Cong. Rec. S8048–49 (daily ed. July 13, 1998). The bill also was opposed by President Clinton—who threatened a veto if the bill passed by Congress—and by the United States Judicial Conference which represents the federal judiciary.

Should such legislation be enacted? Or would this proposal simply promote forum-shopping between the district court and the Court of Federal Claims? Alternatively, should the Court of Federal Claims be maintained as the sole forum to grant monetary compensation above $10,000 but also be given authority to grant full relief, including equitable remedies? Consider also that claims for equitable relief in takings cases have not been common,* as the government ordinarily is not prohibited from taking property but is only required to pay just compensation when it has done so. As a consequence, in cases alleging a taking of property without just compensation in violation of the Fifth Amendment, a plaintiff is generally relegated to an action for recovery of the compensation. See Chapter IV.A.5.a. Does this suggest that one or the other forum is best suited for resolution of takings disputes?

---

b. APPELLATE JURISDICTION—THE UNITED STATES COURT OF APPEALS FOR THE FEDERAL CIRCUIT

Federal Courts Improvement Act, 28 United States Code § 1295(a)(2)–(3)

(a) The United States Court of Appeals for the Federal Circuit shall have exclusive jurisdiction—

* * *

(2) of an appeal from a final decision of a district court of the United States, the United States District Court for the District of the Canal Zone, the District Court of Guam, the District Court of the Virgin Islands, or the District Court for the Northern Mariana Islands, if the jurisdiction of that court was based, in whole or in part, on section 1346 of this title, except that jurisdiction of an appeal in a case brought in a district court under section 1346(a)(1), 1346(b), 1346(e), or 1346(f) of this title or under section 1346(a)(2) when the claim is founded upon an Act of Congress or a regulation of an executive department providing for internal revenue shall be governed by sections 1291, 1292, and 1294 of this title; [and]

(3) of an appeal from a final decision of the United States Court of Federal Claims * * *.

---

* However, the number of cases is growing in which equitable relief in sought in addition to or instead of monetary relief for an alleged taking. The ordinary takings case involves expropriation of or physical invasion by the government with one's real or personal property. But in recent years, plaintiffs have increasingly alleged that the government's regulatory activities have interfered with property rights in a manner that constitutes a taking. The *Loveladies* case is such an example. In such a case, the plaintiff may challenge the validity of the regulatory program and seek to have it enjoined (usually under the Administrative Procedure Act, in federal district court), before seeking compensation for the past (or continuing) interference with property rights (which, if in excess of $10,000, may only be pursued in the Court of Federal Claims).

28 United States Code § 1346

(a) The district courts shall have original jurisdiction, concurrent with the United States Court of Federal Claims, of:

(1) Any civil action against the United States for the recovery of any internal-revenue tax alleged to have been erroneously or illegally assessed or collected, or any penalty claimed to have been collected without authority or any sum alleged to have been excessive or in any manner wrongfully collected under the internal-revenue laws;

(2) Any other civil action or claim against the United States, not exceeding $10,000 in amount, founded either upon the Constitution, or any Act of Congress, or any regulation of an executive department, or upon any express or implied contract with the United States, or for liquidated or unliquidated damages in cases not sounding in tort * * *;

(b)(1) Subject to the provisions of chapter 171 of this title, the district courts, together with the United States District Court for the District of the Canal Zone and the District Court of the Virgin Islands, shall have exclusive jurisdiction of civil actions on claims against the United States, for money damages, accruing on and after January 1, 1945, for injury or loss of property, or personal injury or death caused by the negligent or wrongful act or omission of any employee of the Government while acting within the scope of his office or employment, under circumstances where the United States, if a private person, would be liable to the claimant in accordance with the law of the place where the act or omission occurred.

* * *

(e) The district courts shall have original jurisdiction of any civil action against the United States provided in section 6226, 6228(a), 7426, or 7428 (in the case of the United States district court for the District of Columbia) or section 7429 of the Internal Revenue Code of 1986.

(f) The district courts shall have exclusive original jurisdiction of civil actions under section 2409a to quiet title to an estate or interest in real property in which an interest is claimed by the United States. * * *

---

28 United States Code § 1292(d)(2), (4)

(d)(2) When the chief judge of the United States Court of Federal Claims issues an order under section 798(b) of this title, or when a judge of the United States Court of Federal Claims, in issuing an interlocutory order, includes in the order a statement that a controlling question of law is involved with respect to which there is a substantial ground for difference of opinion and that an immediate appeal from that order may materially advance the ultimate termination of the litigation, the United States Court of Appeals for the Federal Circuit may, in its discretion, permit an appeal to be taken from such order, if application is made to that Court within ten days after the entry of such order.

* * *

(4)(A) The United States Court of Appeals for the Federal Circuit shall have exclusive jurisdiction of an appeal from an interlocutory order of a district court of the United States, the District Court of Guam, the District Court of the Virgin Islands, or the District Court for the Northern Mariana Islands, granting or denying, in whole or in part, a motion to transfer an action to the United States Court of Federal Claims under section 1631 of this title.

(B) When a motion to transfer an action to the Court of Federal Claims is filed in a district court, no further proceedings shall be taken in the district court until 60 days after the court has ruled upon the motion. If an appeal is taken from the district court's grant or denial of the motion, proceedings shall be further stayed until the appeal has been decided by the Court of Appeals for the Federal Circuit. The stay of proceedings in the district court shall not bar the granting of preliminary or injunctive relief, where appropriate and where expedition is reasonably necessary. However, during the period in which proceedings are stayed as provided in this subparagraph, no transfer to the Court of Federal Claims pursuant to the motion shall be carried out.

Richard H. Seamon, The Provenance of the Federal Courts Improvement Act of 1982

71 George Washington Law Review 543, 551–54 (2003).

The United States Court of Appeals for the Federal Circuit

The Federal Circuit consists of twelve Article III judges appointed by the president with the advice and consent of the Senate. It occupies the same tier of the federal court system as the regional courts of appeals. Thus, as discussed below, the Federal Circuit hears appeals in certain cases from the federal district courts (among other entities), and its decisions are subject to discretionary review by the Supreme Court. * * *

As already mentioned, the Federal Circuit reviews cases from all over the country. These cases come not just from the [United States Court of Federal Claims] but from many other tribunals, including numerous federal agencies and officials and two types of Article III courts: the Court of International Trade and the federal district courts. All told, the cases from these courts and other entities are of two types: (1) cases involving claims against the federal government (including intellectual property claims) and (2) patent cases.

Most of the first type of cases—disputes involving the federal government—fall into one of eight categories: (1) federal taxes; (2) alleged federal "takings" of private property for which just compensation is due; (3)

alleged federal infringement of intellectual property rights such as copyright and patent rights; (4) Native Americans; (5) vaccine-related injuries; (6) federal employment; (7) international trade; and (8) federal contracts. Cases in the first six categories come to the Federal Circuit from the [Court of Federal Claims]. Additional sources of cases in the sixth category, cases involving federal employment, are the Merit Systems Protection Board and the United States Court of Appeals for Veterans Claims. Many cases in the seventh category, cases about international trade, come to the Federal Circuit from the Court of International Trade. Other international trade cases come to the Federal Circuit from agencies such as the International Trade Commission ("ITC") and from officials such as the Secretary of Commerce. Cases in the eighth category, contract claims against the government, can come to the Federal Circuit from the COFC, the federal district courts, or agency boards of contract appeals. Because of its authority to review this wide variety of cases involving the federal government, the Federal Circuit serves as a federal court of appeals for disputes involving the federal government.

It would be wrong, however, to label the Federal Circuit solely a federal appellate court for disputes involving the government. That is because, in addition to those disputes, the Federal Circuit hears the great majority of appeals in patent cases, regardless whether or not those cases involve claims against the federal government. The primary source of that appellate authority is 28 U.S.C. § 1295(a)(1). With certain exceptions, § 1295(a)(1) gives the Federal Circuit exclusive jurisdiction over final decisions of the district courts in cases in which the jurisdiction of the district court "was based, in whole or in part, on section 1338 of this title." Section 1338, in turn, gives the district courts exclusive jurisdiction over cases arising under the patent laws. This means that, whereas most appeals from federal district court decisions go to the regional courts of appeals, appeals in patent cases go from federal district courts throughout the country to the Federal Circuit. Patent cases make up about 25 to 30% of the Federal Circuit's caseload.

Besides possessing nationwide jurisdiction defined by subject matter, the Federal Circuit differs from the regional courts of appeals in one other important way: all of the cases in the Federal Circuit's jurisdiction arise under federal civil law. The Federal Circuit has no diversity jurisdiction or criminal jurisdiction.

———

United States v. Hohri

Supreme Court of the United States.
482 U.S. 64 (1987).

■ JUSTICE POWELL delivered the opinion of the Court.

In this case we must decide which court—the Court of Appeals for the Federal Circuit or the appropriate regional Court of Appeals—has jurisdiction over an appeal from a Federal District Court's decision of a case raising both a nontax claim under the Little Tucker Act and a claim under the Federal Tort Claims Act (FTCA).

I

During World War II, the Government of the United States removed approximately 120,000 Japanese–Americans from their homes and placed them in internment camps. Respondents are an organization of Japanese–Americans and 19 individuals—former internees and their representatives. They filed this action in the United States District Court for the District of Columbia, seeking damages and declaratory relief for the tangible and intangible injuries suffered because of this incident. Jurisdiction was based on, *inter alia*, the Little Tucker Act, 28 U.S.C. § 1346(a)(2),[1] and the FTCA, 28 U.S.C. § 1346(b). The District Court concluded that all claims were barred either by sovereign immunity or the applicable statute of limitations. 586 F.Supp. 769 (1984).

Respondents appealed to the Court of Appeals for the District of Columbia Circuit. That court reversed the District Court's dismissal of certain claims under the Little Tucker Act. 782 F.2d 227 ([D.C.Cir.] 1986). First, the court concluded that it, rather than the Court of Appeals for the Federal Circuit, had jurisdiction over the appeal. It noted that 28 U.S.C. § 1295(a)(2) generally grants the Federal Circuit exclusive jurisdiction of appeals in cases involving nontax claims under the Little Tucker Act. But it concluded that Congress did not intend the Federal Circuit to hear appeals of such cases when they also included FTCA claims. 782 F.2d, at 239–241. On the merits, the court concluded that the statute of limitations did not begin to run on certain of respondents' Little Tucker Act claims until 1980, when Congress created the Commission on Wartime Relocation and Internment of Civilians. 782 F.2d, at 253. Chief Judge Markey, sitting by designation pursuant to 28 U.S.C. § 291(b), filed a dissent, disagreeing with the court's jurisdictional analysis as well as its decision as to the statute of limitations. 782 F.2d, at 256–263. * * *

Because of the potentially broad impact of the Court of Appeals' decision and because of the importance of the jurisdictional question, we granted the Government's petition for a writ of certiorari. We conclude that the Court of Appeals did not have jurisdiction and therefore do not address the merits of its decision.

---

1. Jurisdiction in district courts under the Little Tucker Act is limited to nontort claims not exceeding $10,000. 28 U.S.C. § 1346(a)(2). See 14 C. Wright, A. Miller, & E. Cooper, Federal Practice and Procedure § 3657, pp. 284–288 (2d ed. 1985). This decentralized jurisdiction was designed to "give all persons having claims for comparatively small amounts the right to bring suits in the districts where they and their witnesses reside without subjecting them to the expense and annoyance of litigating in Washington." *Id.*, at 274. With minor exceptions, the Tucker Act grants the United States Claims Court jurisdiction of similar claims without regard to the amount of the claim. 28 U.S.C. § 1491(a)(1). Thus, Tucker Act claims for more than $10,000 can be brought only in the United States Claims Court. Claims for less than $10,000 generally can be brought either in a federal district court or in the United States Claims Court.

II

In 1982, Congress passed the Federal Courts Improvement Act, creating the United States Court of Appeals for the Federal Circuit. Among other things, the Act grants the Federal Circuit exclusive appellate jurisdiction over a variety of cases involving the Federal Government. 28 U.S.C. § 1295(a)(2). Specifically, the Act provides:

"The United States Court of Appeals for the Federal Circuit shall have exclusive jurisdiction—

. . .

"(2) of an appeal from a final decision of a district court of the United States ... if the jurisdiction of that court was based, in whole or in part, on section 1346 of this title, except that jurisdiction of an appeal in a case brought in a district court under section 1346(a)(1), 1346(b), 1346(e), or 1346(f) of this title or under section 1346(a)(2) when the claim is [related to federal taxes] shall be governed by sections 1291, 1292, and 1294 of this title."

This section establishes two undisputed propositions relevant to this case. First, the Federal Circuit has exclusive appellate jurisdiction of a case raising *only* a nontax claim under the Little Tucker Act, § 1346(a)(2). Second, the appropriate regional Court of Appeals—in this case, the Court of Appeals for the District of Columbia Circuit—has exclusive appellate jurisdiction under §§ 1291, 1292, and 1294 of a case raising only a claim under the FTCA, § 1346(b).

This case presents claims under both the Little Tucker Act and the FTCA, a situation not specifically addressed by § 1295(a)(2). Resolution of this problem turns on interpretation of the second clause of this subsection, the so-called "except clause." The Solicitor General contends that the except clause merely describes claims that do not suffice to create jurisdiction in the Federal Circuit. Thus, he argues, appeals of FTCA claims must be heard in the Federal Circuit if, as in this case, they are joined with claims that fall within its exclusive jurisdiction. By contrast, respondents contend that the except clause indicates not only that FTCA claims fail to create jurisdiction in the Federal Circuit, but also that the presence of an FTCA claim renders inapplicable the Federal Circuit's otherwise exclusive jurisdiction over nontax Little Tucker Act claims.[3]

A

As always, the "starting point in every case involving construction of a statute is the language itself." *Kelly v. Robinson*, 479 U.S. 36, 43 (1986).

---

3. Neither the parties nor any judge of the Court of Appeals suggested bifurcating the case so that the Little Tucker Act claims would be transferred to the Federal Circuit and the FTCA claims would remain in the Court of Appeals for the District of Columbia Circuit. We agree that bifurcation is inappropriate. The language of § 1295(a)(2) discusses jurisdiction over an appeal "in a case," not over an appeal from decision of "a claim." This strongly suggests that appeals of different parts of a single case should not go to different courts. Also, at least when a case has not been bifurcated in the district court, a bifurcated appeal of the different legal claims raised in any one case would result in an inefficient commitment of the limited resources of the federal appellate courts.

Unfortunately, as we have noted, the language of this statute does not clearly address a "mixed" case that presents both nontax Little Tucker Act claims and FTCA claims. Congress could have expressed the Solicitor General's interpretation more clearly by adding the word "solely" to the except clause, and thus provided that an appeal from a case brought *solely* under § 1346(b) should be to the regional court of appeals. Or, if Congress had intended the broader meaning of the except clause urged by respondents, it could have added a phrase akin to "in whole or in part" to the except clause, thus providing that an appeal of a case brought *in whole or in part* under § 1346(b) should be to the regional court of appeals. Because Congress employed neither of these alternatives, we are left with the task of determining the more plausible interpretation of the language Congress did include in § 1295(a)(2).

In our view, the Solicitor General's reading of the statute is more natural. Although Congress included the phrase "in whole or in part" in the granting clause at the beginning of § 1295(a)(2), it did not repeat this phrase in the except clause later in the same paragraph. The proximity of the clauses suggests that the variation in wording was not accidental. Also, in one instance the statute describes the excepted cases by reference to the basis of "the claim." See § 1295(a)(2) (providing for appeals to regional courts of appeals "in a case brought in a district court ... under section 1346(a)(2) when *the claim* is [related to federal taxes]" (emphasis added)). This suggests that the except clause was directed at cases raising only one claim; it strains the language to apply the except clause to cases raising multiple claims, some within and some not within the except clause. * * *

B

Because the statute is ambiguous, congressional intent is particularly relevant to our decision. A motivating concern of Congress in creating the Federal Circuit was the "special need for nationwide uniformity" in certain areas of the law. S.Rep. No. 97–275, p. 2 (1981) (hereinafter 1981 Senate Report), U.S.Code Cong. & Admin.News 1982, pp. 11, 12; S.Rep. No. 96–304, p. 8 (1979) (hereinafter 1979 Senate Report). The Senate Reports explained: "[T]here are areas of the law in which the appellate courts reach inconsistent decisions on the same issue, or in which—although the rule of law may be fairly clear—courts apply the law unevenly when faced with the facts of individual cases." 1981 Senate Report, at 3; 1979 Senate Report, at 9. The Federal Circuit was designed to provide "a prompt, definitive answer to legal questions" in these areas. 1981 Senate Report, at 1; 1979 Senate Report, at 1. Nontort claims against the Federal Government present one of the principal areas in which Congress sought such uniformity. Thus, Congress decided to confer jurisdiction on the Federal Circuit in "all federal contract appeals in which the United States is a defendant." H.R.Rep. No. 97–312, p. 18 (1981) (hereinafter 1981 House Report); H.R.Rep. No. 96–1300, p. 16 (1980) (hereinafter 1980 House Report).[4]

---

4. The Little Tucker Act, of course, covers not only contract claims, but also other claims for money damages "founded either upon the Constitution, or any Act of Con-

For the most part, the statute unambiguously effectuates this goal. Tucker Act claims for more than $10,000 may be brought only in the United States Claims Court. 28 U.S.C. § 1491(a)(1). Decisions of the United States Claims Court are appealable only to the Federal Circuit, not the regional courts of appeals. § 1295(a)(3). Claims for less than $10,000 (*i.e.*, Little Tucker Act claims) may be brought either in a federal district court or in the United States Claims Court. § 1346(a)(2). These claims, so long as they are not related to federal taxes, also are appealable only to the Federal Circuit. §§ 1295(a)(2), (3). A conspicuous feature of these judicial arrangements is the creation of exclusive Federal Circuit jurisdiction over *every appeal* from a Tucker Act or nontax Little Tucker Act claim. Given this comprehensive framework and the strong expressions of the need for uniformity in the area, one would expect any exception intended by Congress to have been made explicit, rather than left to inferences drawn from loose language.

C

Despite the language of the statute and the evident congressional desire for uniform adjudication of Little Tucker Act claims, the Court of Appeals inferred an exception to exclusive Federal Circuit jurisdiction in cases that include FTCA claims. In supporting the Court of Appeals' judgment, respondents rely on the statement, thrice repeated in the congressional Reports, that "[b]ecause cases brought under the Federal Tort Claims Act frequently involve the application of State law, those appeals will continue to be brought to the regional courts of appeals." 1981 Senate Report, at 20; 1981 House Report, at 42; 1980 House Report, at 34. Respondents argue that this statement evidences a congressional intent to deprive the Federal Circuit of its otherwise exclusive appellate jurisdiction over nontax Little Tucker Act claims whenever an FTCA claim is presented in the same case. We find this argument unpersuasive when viewed in the context of the legislative history as a whole.

First, the congressional Reports indicate only that Congress saw no affirmative need for national uniformity in FTCA cases, not that the perceived need for regional adjudication of FTCA claims outweighed the strong and oft-noted intent of Congress that only the Federal Circuit should have jurisdiction of appeals in nontax Little Tucker Act cases. Second, Congress specifically rejected the idea that patent and Tucker Act appeals should be decided by a "specialized court" incapable of deciding more general legal issues. The Federal Circuit decides questions arising under the Federal Constitution and statutes whenever such questions arise in cases within the Federal Circuit's jurisdiction. There is no reason to believe that Congress intended to exempt the relatively common tort questions presented by the average FTCA cases from the Federal Circuit's already-broad docket. Third, if Congress thought the presence of state-law issues was sufficient to override the need for centralization of nontax Little

gress, or any regulation of an executive department, . . . or for liquidated or unliquidat-

ed damages in cases not sounding in tort." 28 U.S.C. § 1346(a)(2).

Tucker Act claims, the except clause logically should have included all cases raising state-law issues, not just cases under the FTCA. * * *

For these reasons, we conclude that Congress intended for centralized determination of nontax Little Tucker Act claims to predominate over regional adjudication of FTCA claims. We hold that a mixed case, presenting both a nontax Little Tucker Act claim and an FTCA claim, may be appealed only to the Federal Circuit.

III

We vacate the judgment of the Court of Appeals, and remand the case to that court, with instructions to transfer the case to the Federal Circuit. See 28 U.S.C. § 1631.

It is so ordered.

■ JUSTICE SCALIA took no part in the consideration or decision of this case.

■ JUSTICE BLACKMUN, concurring.

I join the Court's opinion and its judgment. I do so, however, with less than full assurance and satisfaction.

[First, I have concern for] the consequent element of further delay in the decision on the merits in a case that has roots already more than four decades old. The issue on the merits probably will be back in this Court once again months or years hence. [Second,] the statute the Court is forced to construe in this case is not a model of legislative craftsmanship. Surely, Congress is able to make its intent more evident than in the language it has utilized here. It is to be hoped that Congress will look at the problem it has created and will set forth in precise terms its conclusion as to jurisdiction of federal appellate courts in mixed-claims cases of this kind. * * *

Notes and Questions

1. As we saw in the previous cases addressing trial jurisdiction over Tucker Act claims, the United States Court of Appeals for the Federal Circuit plays a prominent role in deciding claims involving the Tucker Act. The old Court of Claims was abolished in 1982 and two new courts were created in its place. The Claims Court (now Court of Federal Claims) was given trial responsibility for Tucker Act claims, while the Federal Circuit was given appellate jurisdiction over these claims. Pub. L. No. 97–164, 96 Stat. 25 (1982).

The appellate jurisdiction of the Federal Circuit is set out primarily in 28 U.S.C. § 1295. Subsection 1295(a)(2) gives this court exclusive appellate jurisdiction over Little Tucker Act claims, that is, Tucker Claims for not more than $10,000, brought in the federal district courts under 28 U.S.C. § 1346(a)(2). Subsection 1295(a)(3) gives the Federal Circuit appellate jurisdiction over appeals from the Court of Federal Claims. Thus, between these two subsections of Section 1295, the Federal Circuit is the forum for appeals in both "Little" and "Big" Tucker Act claims.

2. The question in *United States v. Hohri* is the proper home for appeals in a "mixed" case that involves both a Little Tucker Act claim and a Federal Tort Claims Act claim brought together in district court. It is undisputed that the Federal Circuit has exclusive appellate jurisdiction over Tucker Act claims when brought alone, including Little Tucker Act claims filed in district court. It is likewise clear that an FTCA claim, by itself, would be heard on appeal in the regional circuit court covering that district. But what is to be done when these two claims are combined together in the same suit? Should the Little Tucker Act claim follow the FTCA claim on appeal to the regional circuit? Or instead should the FTCA claim tag along with the Little Tucker Act claim on appeal to the Federal Circuit? Which claim takes priority for assigning appellate jurisdiction?

The Supreme Court answers this question by looking both to the language of Subsection 1295(a)(2) and to the congressional purpose behind the statute creating the Federal Circuit and granting it appellate jurisdiction over Tucker Act claims. The interpretation problem lies in an oddly worded statute. As the primary purpose of Subsection 1295(a)(2) is to direct appeals in Little Tucker Act cases to the Federal Circuit, one would have expected the statute to provide directly that the Federal Circuit has appellate jurisdiction over claims based, in whole or in part, upon Subsection 1346(a)(2) (which is the statutory subsection known as the Little Tucker Act). Instead, Subsection 1295(a)(2) approaches the issue backwards: First, the statute generally grants the Federal Circuit jurisdiction over claims "based, in whole or in part, on Section 1346"—thus referring to the entire statutory section which authorizes federal court jurisdiction not only over the Little Tucker Act (Subsection 1346(a)(2)) but also other claims arising under other statutes such as the Federal Tort Claims Act (Subsection 1346(b)). Second, the statute then adds an exception that lists nearly all of these other causes of action created by Section 1346, leaving only the Little Tucker Act *outside* of the exception and thus *within* Federal Circuit appellate jurisdiction.

How does the Supreme Court make sense of this verbose and indirect language? How does the Court suggest Congress could have made its intent clearer? What does the Court believe was the congressional purpose? From this, what would you say is the presumption in terms of appellate jurisdiction when a Tucker Act claim is part of a case?

3. In *Smith v. Orr*, 855 F.2d 1544, 1547 (Fed. Cir. 1988) (the trial jurisdiction discussion in this opinion was set out previously in this casebook at Chapter III.A.1.a) the Federal Circuit disclaimed exclusive authority over an appeal from a final District Court judgment in what your casebook author calls the "disguised Big Tucker Act" case. In such a case, what is effectively a Tucker Act claim seeking more than $10,000 has been wrongly filed by the plaintiff in District Court rather than the Court of Federal Claims. Relying upon the literal language of 28 U.S.C. § 1295(a)(2), the Federal Circuit held that it had been granted exclusive appellate jurisdiction over appeals from money judgments against the United States *only* where the district court itself had proper jurisdiction. In other words,

Smith v. Orr

Federal Circuit Jd
as derivative of
Fed. district ct's
jd

the Federal Circuit read its exclusive appellate jurisdiction as derivative of the trial court's jurisdiction; if the district court lacked proper Tucker Act jurisdiction to enter the judgment, then the Federal Circuit lacks exclusive appellate jurisdiction to review the judgment.

In 1988, as a partial response to *Smith v. Orr*, Congress enacted legislation permitting an interlocutory appeal to the Federal Circuit from district court rulings on motions to transfer actions to the Court of Federal Claims.* Pub. L. No. 100–702, Title V, § 501, 102 Stat. 4642 (1988) (codified at 28 U.S.C. § 1292(d)(4)). In the interests of resolving jurisdictional questions at the outset of litigation, and thereby avoiding wasteful and duplicative litigation on the merits in the wrong trial court, 28 U.S.C. § 1292(d)(4) permits an immediate appeal by either the plaintiff or the government from an adverse district court ruling on a motion to transfer the action to the Court of Federal Claims. Thus, if either a plaintiff or the government seeks interlocutory review in an arguable "disguised Big Tucker Act case," the jurisdictional issue may be resolved promptly and surely before the district court hears the case on the merits.

To "ensure uniform adjudication of Tucker Act issues in a single forum," H.R. Rep. No. 100–889, at 52 (1988), *reprinted in* 1988 U.S.C.C.A.N. 5982, 6012, the interlocutory appeal is within the exclusive jurisdiction of the Federal Circuit. Unless there is Supreme Court review, the Federal Circuit's disposition of the interlocutory appeal is binding upon the parties as law of the case in any subsequent proceedings in the litigation.

---

c. LIMITATIONS ON RELIEF   *of   Court of Claims*

United States v. King
Supreme Court of the United States.
395 U.S. 1 (1969).

■ MR. JUSTICE BLACK delivered the opinion of the Court.

Colonel John P. King, respondent, was retired from the Army for longevity (length of service) over his objection that he should have been retired for physical disability. Had his retirement been based on disability, Colonel King would have been entitled to an exemption from income taxation allowed by § 104(a)(4) of the Internal Revenue Code of 1954, 26 U.S.C. § 104(a)(4). He brought this action in the Court of Claims alleging

---

* In your casebook author's former life as an attorney with the Department of Justice, he drafted this legislation providing for interlocutory appeal to the Federal Circuit from district court decisions on motions to transfer to the then-Claims Court. *See generally* Gregory C. Sisk, *Tucker Act Appeals to the Federal Circuit*, 36 Fed. Bar News & J. 41 (1989). Although my Justice Department colleagues honored (teased) me by referring for a time within the office to such interlocutory appeals to the Federal Circuit as "Sisk appeals," that appellation perhaps sadly but understandably has not come into general usage.

that the Secretary of the Army's action in rejecting his disability retirement was arbitrary, capricious, not supported by evidence, and therefore unlawful, and asked for a judgment against the United States for an amount of excess taxes he had been compelled to pay because he had been retired for longevity instead of disability. The Court of Claims agreed with the United States that the claim as filed was basically one for a refund of taxes and was therefore barred by King's failure to allege that he had filed a timely claim for refund as required by 26 U.S.C. § 7422(a). In this situation, the court suggested to counsel that it might have jurisdiction under the Declaratory Judgment Act and requested that briefs and arguments on this point be submitted to the court. This was done. The Court of Claims, in an illuminating and interesting opinion by Judge Davis, reached the conclusion that the court could exercise jurisdiction under the Declaratory Judgment Act, 28 U.S.C. § 2201. In so holding, the court thereby rejected the Government's contentions that the Declaratory Judgment Act does not apply to the Court of Claims and that the court's jurisdiction is limited to actions asking for money judgments. * * * As the opinion of Judge Davis showed, the question of whether the Court of Claims has jurisdiction to issue declaratory judgments is both substantial and important. We granted certiorari to decide that question.

The Court of Claims was established by Congress in 1855. Throughout its entire history up until the time that this case was filed, its jurisdiction has been limited to money claims against the United States Government. In 1868 this Court held that "the only judgments which the Court of Claims [is] authorized to render against the government . . . are judgments for money found due from the government to the petitioner." *United States v. Alire*, 6 Wall. 573, 575. In *United States v. Jones*, 131 U.S. 1 this Court reaffirmed this view of the limited jurisdiction of the Court of Claims, and held that the passage of the Tucker Act in 1887 had not expanded that jurisdiction to equitable matters. More recently, in 1962, it was said in the prevailing opinion in *Glidden Co. v. Zdanok*, 370 U.S. 530, 557, on a point not disputed by any of the other members of the Court that "[f]rom the beginning [the Court of Claims] has been given jurisdiction only to award damages. . . ." * * *

The foregoing cases decided by this Court therefore clearly show that neither the Act creating the Court of Claims nor any amendment to it grants that court jurisdiction of this present case. That is true because Colonel King's claim is not limited to actual, presently due money damages from the United States. Before he is entitled to such a judgment he must establish in some court that his retirement by the Secretary of the Army for longevity was legally wrong and that he is entitled to a declaration of his right to have his military records changed to show that he was retired for disability. This is essentially equitable relief of a kind that the Court of Claims has held throughout its history, up to the time this present case was decided, that it does not have the power to grant.

It is argued, however, that even if the Court of Claims Act with its amendments did not grant that court the authority to issue declaratory judgments, it was given that authority by the Declaratory Judgment Act of 1934. Support for this proposition is drawn from the language in the

Cases seeking other than actual money damages are outside its j.d.

Proof of Court of Claims' jd to render the relief sought (by way of any other statute) requires affirmative & unequivocal indication

Declaratory Judgment Act that "[i]n a case of actual controversy within its jurisdiction * * * any court of the United States ... may declare the rights and other legal relations of any interested party seeking such declaration." The first answer to this contention is that, as we have pointed out, cases seeking relief other than money damages from the Court of Claims have never been "within its jurisdiction." And we agree with the opinion of the Court of Claims in this case that the legislative history materials concerning the application of this Act to the Court of Claims "are, at best, ambiguous." For the court below, it was sufficient that there was no clear indication that Congress affirmatively intended to exclude the Court of Claims from the scope of the Declaratory Judgment Act. We think that this approach runs counter to the settled propositions that the Court of Claims' jurisdiction to grant relief depends wholly upon the extent to which the United States has waived its sovereign immunity to suit and that such a waiver cannot be implied but must be unequivocally expressed. * * * There is not a single indication in the Declaratory Judgment Act or its history that Congress, in passing that Act, intended to give the Court of Claims an expanded jurisdiction that had been denied to it for nearly a century. In the absence of an express grant of jurisdiction from Congress, we decline to assume that the Court of Claims has been given the authority to issue declaratory judgments.

Reversed.

Note

The Supreme Court in *United States v. King* states the general rule that the Court of Claims—and its present-day successor, the Court of Federal Claims—is limited to awarding monetary relief and is precluded from granting equitable remedies, such as injunctions or specific performance in contract. *See generally* Richard H. Seamon, *Separation of Powers and the Separate Treatment of Contract Claims Against the Federal Government for Specific Performance*, 43 Vill. L. Rev. 155 (1998) (discussing the history and continued validity of the traditional rule barring the remedy of specific performance in contract claims against the federal government and allowing only damages as a remedy for contract breach). Since the date of the *King* decision, the powers of the Court of Federal Claims have been expanded in certain defined circumstances, but the court still does not possess general equitable powers of the scope that district courts have. (Among the more significant expansions of the court's remedial powers are the Remand Act of 1972, which is discussed and applied in *United States v. Testan*, 424 U.S. 392 (1976), presented in the next subpart of this casebook, and a 1992 amendment to the Tucker Act that authorizes the court to resolve nonmonetary disputes arising under the Contract Disputes Act, 28 U.S.C. § 1491(b).)

When the legislation establishing the Court of Federal Claims was before Congress, Senator Robert Dole proposed granting the court authority to grant declaratory and equitable relief in all matters within its jurisdiction. However, as Professor Richard Seamon reports, "[t]his provision did not survive enactment, apparently because of opposition from the [Department of Justice]." Richard H. Seamon, *The Provenance of the Federal Courts Improvement Act of 1982,* 71 Geo. Wash. L. Rev. 543, 581 (2003). In addition to Seamon, other scholars on the court (including the author of this casebook) have suggested renewed congressional attention to the scope of its remedial powers:

> Although expanding the equitable authority of the Court of Federal Claims to cover all cases within its bailiwick might appear to be a dramatic enlargement of the powers of a court traditionally limited to monetary relief, it actually is a modest and incremental step justified by experience. To begin with, as with its current limited equitable powers under the Remand Act of 1972 (such as the power to order an agency to restore an employee to a position or correct personnel records), the court under this proposal would not gain general equitable powers nor the authority to grant equitable relief detached from a monetary claim. The court only would be authorized to grant equitable relief that is collateral to a cognizable Tucker Act claim for monetary relief. Moreover, because the Court of Federal Claims has national jurisdiction over the cases that fall within its purview and because a money judgment has future effect by reason of rules of preclusion and precedent ..., the practical effect of enlarging the court's equitable powers would be negligible in most cases. In the few cases in which these enhanced remedial powers would be implicated so as to provide meaningful relief beyond those consequences that flow from a money judgment, the new authority conferred on the Court of Federal Claims would make it possible to efficiently resolve all matters relating to a claim in a single forum. This injunctive power could be exercised only as appropriate under the circumstances, under basic principles of equity, and subject to limitations imposed by other statutory laws. In sum, the Court of Federal Claims would not be granted power over any new category of case or any new field of law but rather would be empowered to grant a complete remedy in a single forum in all cases within its jurisdiction.

Gregory C. Sisk, *The Tapestry Unravels: Statutory Waivers of Sovereign Immunity and Money Claims Against the United States,* 71 Geo. Wash. L. Rev. 601, 704–05 (2003).

---

2.   TUCKER ACT CLAIMS FOUNDED UPON STATUTES

a.   THE REQUIREMENT OF A MONEY–MANDATING STATUTE

Eastport Steamship Corp. v. United States

United States Court of Claims.
178 Ct.Cl. 599, 372 F.2d 1002 (1967).

■ DAVIS, JUDGE.

In 1946, in the train of World War II, the United States was offered some former German merchant vessels as part of reparations. Despite some initial misgivings that the Maritime Commission already had enough American-built surplus vessels to dispose of, the Commission ultimately agreed with the Department of State to accept thirteen of these ex-German ships on the understanding that they would be used by American operators under the American flag and would not be sold on the world market. Eleven vessels were offered for sale, including the *Empire Roding* (which came to plaintiff and was renamed the *Eastport*). The Commission's invitation for bids, as modified, provided that the purchasers would be barred from selling the ships or operating them prior to documentation under the American flag. Plaintiff's president specifically inquired whether there would be any restriction on a later sale foreign. The Commissions's reply was that any application for such a sale would have to be considered under Sections 9 and 37 of the Shipping Act and that no prior assurance could be given.

Five bids were received for the *Empire Roding*. The high bidder (offering $425,000) conditioned its bid on the Commission's agreeing to a transfer to the Danish flag immediately after American documentation. This qualification was unacceptable and the bid was rejected. The next highest bidder, which did not wish to accept more than two of the four vessels on which it bid, was allocated two other ships and its proffer of $190,300 for the *Empire Roding* was set aside. Plaintiff then became the higher offeror and received the vessel in April 1947 for $130,750 in cash.

At considerable cost the ship was altered and converted to meet the requirements of American documentation. She was then put to sea and pursued a disastrous career until plaintiff finally gave up in June 1949 and placed her in lay-up awaiting sale. From May 1948, when it realized she was a "lemon", plaintiff made strenuous but unsuccessful efforts to sell her domestically. In June 1948 the company turned to the foreign market.

Sale alien, plaintiff knew, would require the Commission's permission, and preliminary conferences were held with the agency's staff to sound out the possibilities. Other purchasers of the ex-German vessels were having comparable difficulties, and the problem of this group of ships had been mooted before the Commission. In the first part of 1948 it had denied some applications to transfer formerly German ships to Panamanian registry and flag without change in American ownership. In October 1948, the Commission rejected a similar recommendation of its staff as to three other such ships. On February 18, 1949, at the request of some of the owners, the Commission held an open hearing on the subject of whether to permit the foreign sale of this ex-German group.

One week before this hearing (i.e. on February 11, 1949), plaintiff concluded a contract for the sale of the *Eastport* to a Danish buyer for $560,000, conditioned upon the seller's obtaining Commission approval within three months. The application for approval was filed on February 24, 1949. When the three-month period neared its close without Commission action, plaintiff made efforts to have its request disposed of within the time limit, and also obtained, as a last resort, a two-week extension from the Danish purchaser (from May 11 to May 25, 1949). The extended deadline passed without affirmative action by the Commission and the Danish firm canceled the contract.

Months later, at the end of December 1949, after a sharp fall in the world market price, plaintiff contracted to sell the *Eastport* to an Israeli corporation for the lower price of $375,000 (and also subject to Commission approval of the foreign transfer). In March 1950 the Commission approved this application upon payment by plaintiff of "the sum of $10,000 as consideration for the release of the * * * *Eastport* from United States flag operation." This condition was imposed under a policy, first formally adopted by the Commission in June 1949, of requiring owners of ex-German vessels to pay a monetary sum (differing with the individual ship) for the release the vessels from the requirement of restricted operation.

In a series of cases this court has held that monetary conditions, such as these, for permission to transfer a vessel are unlawful and beyond the Commission's authority under Section 9 of the Shipping Act. Those claimants were allowed to recover the amounts illegally exacted.

Plaintiff's petition in this court sought (in count II) return of the $10,000 it was required to pay upon the approval of its sale to the Israeli company. In count I plaintiff sought damages for the Commission's earlier failure to approve the potential sale to the Danish buyer. * * * We are now concerned, after a trial, with the claim for damages, as set forth in count I.

The gist of that grievance is that in the spring of 1949 the Commission deliberately withheld its consent to the foreign sale and transfer of the *Eastport* to the Danish buyer while the agency was secretly formulating an illegal policy of selling such approvals for money, and that this conduct gives rise to an action for damages, cognizable in this court, for loss of the Danish contract which expired for lack of Commission consent in May 1949.

The trial commissioner examined at length the factual underpinning of this claim and made several findings favorable to plaintiff (although he ultimately decided against recovery). These findings are vigorously contested by defendant all along the line. We do not determine these factual issues because we believe that, even if the facts are [determined] for present purposes to be with plaintiff, it does not state a cause of action upon which this court can grant any further relief.

I

Section 1491 of Title 28 of the United States Code allows the Court of Claims to entertain claims against the United States "founded either upon the Constitution, or any Act of Congress, or any regulation of an executive department, or upon any express or implied contract with the United States, or for liquidated or unliquidated damages in cases not sounding in tort". But it is not every claim involving or invoking the Constitution, a federal statute, or a regulation which is cognizable here. The claim must, of course, be for money. Within that sphere, the non-contractual claims we consider under Section 1491 can be divided into two somewhat overlapping classes—those in which the plaintiff has paid money over to the Government, directly or in effect, and seeks return of all or part of that sum; and those demands in which money has not been paid but the plaintiff asserts that he is nevertheless entitled to a payment from the treasury. In the first group (where money or property has been paid or taken), the claim must assert that the value sued for was improperly paid, exacted, or taken from the claimant in contravention of the Constitution, a statute, or a regulation. In the second group, where no such payment has been made, the allegation must be that the particular provision of law relied upon grants the claimant, expressly or by implication, a right to be paid a certain sum.

In the former class fall, among many others, tax refund suits and the claims by purchasers of ex-German vessels for the sums exacted by the Maritime Commission * * * . We have referred to these cases as those in which "the Government has the citizen's money in its pocket" and the claim is "to recover an illegal exaction made by officials of the Government, which exaction is based upon a power supposedly conferred by a statute" (Clapp v. United States, 117 F.Supp. [576,] 580, 127 Ct.Cl. [505,] 512, 513 [(1954)]); and we have held that "suit can be brought in this court to recover [such] exactions said to have been illegally imposed by federal officials (except where Congress has expressly placed jurisdiction elsewhere)." South Puerto Rico Sugar Trading Corp. v. United States, 334 F.2d [622,] 626, 167 Ct.Cl. [236,] 244 [(1964), cert. denied, 379 U.S. 964 (1965)].

The second category includes the varied litigations in which we are urged to hold that some specific provision of law embodies a command to the United States to pay the plaintiff some money, upon proof of conditions which he is said to meet. Familiar examples are inverse eminent domain by a taking without formal proceedings; a suit by a separated reserve officer for disability retired pay; an action for back pay occasioned by a wrongful dismissal from the civil service; or a claim for compensation for flood damage authorized by statute. In this type of case, we have held, "a claimant who says that he is entitled to money from the United States because a statute or a regulation (or the Constitution) grants him that right, in terms or by implication, can properly come to the Court of Claims, at least if his claim is not frivolous but arguable." Ralston Steel Corp. v. United States, 340 F.2d 663, 667, 169 Ct.Cl. 119, 125 (1965), cert. denied, 381 U.S. 950.

Monetary claims which cannot be brought within these limits[7] are beyond this court's jurisdiction, even though they may intimately involve the Constitution, an Act of Congress, or an executive regulation. This is the reverse of saying that this court is not concerned with any and all pecuniary claims against the Federal Government, simply because they rely upon (and in that sense are "founded upon") an aspect of federal, constitu-

---

7. And which do not fall under another head of jurisdiction, such as a contract with the United States.

tional, statutory or regulatory law. Where the claimant is not suing for money improperly exacted or retained (the first class defined above), the historical boundaries of our competence have excluded those instances in which the basis of the federal claim—be it the Constitution, a statute, or a regulation—cannot be held to command, in itself and as correctly interpreted, the payment of money to the claimant, but in which some other principle of damages has to be invoked for recovery. A federal criminal defendant, for instance, who has been invalidly convicted or deprived of his liberty because of a violation of the Constitution or an Act of Congress cannot obtain compensation under 28 U.S.C. § 1491 for his loss (although remedies may occasionally be available under the unjust conviction sections (28 U.S.C. §§ 1495, 2513) or some parts of the civil rights legislation). The provisions which void the conviction do not direct the payment of damages for the consequences of the illegality. Under Section 1491 what one must always ask is whether the constitutional clause or the legislation which the claimant cites can fairly be interpreted as mandating compensation by the Federal Government for the damage sustained. If not, this court cannot give relief under Section 1491, although some separate general principle— arising, for example, from tort law—might lead to a remedy in another forum or under some special relief provision.

Since plaintiff has already recovered the money (i.e., $10,000) illegally exacted, its present claim must be that Section 9 of the Shipping Act, on which it primarily rests its case, grants it compensation for the business loss it incurred. On its face the section is simply a regulatory measure (comparable to many another permission or license-granting statute) forbidding foreign sale of a vessel purchased from the Maritime Commission— unless the Commission sanctions the sale—and requiring Commission authorization for any foreign transfer. There is not a word in the test suggesting that the United States will compensate an applicant who suffers a business loss because of the Commission's improper failure to grant the request. Nor are we pointed to anything in the Act's legislative history hinting at that result. There is no decision of this or any other federal court holding or intimating that the United States will be liable under the Tucker Act for such a commercial injury resulting from a failure or wrong done in the course of the regulatory process. We would have to break entirely new and treacherous ground to find in Section 9 an implied directive to allow such compensation.

We decline to take that giant step. In its relevant aspects Section 9 does not differ from the licensing or permission-granting authority of numerous other federal agencies—the Atomic Energy Commission, Civil Aeronautics Board, Civil Service Commission, Comptroller of the Currency, Federal Aviation Agency, Federal Communications Commission, Federal Home Loan Bank Board, Federal Power Commission, Federal Reserve Board, Interstate Commerce Commission, Securities and Exchange Commission and the Tariff Commission. If we were to infer from Section 9 an unexpressed summons to compensate plaintiff for its business loss, we would necessarily have to open the doors to similar claims by other applicants who suffer commercial damage from a wrongful denial of a license or permission by these other agencies (or as a result of the agency's improper refusal to act). More than that, we would be hard put to give a preferential reading to these license-authorizing statutes—implying compensation for this particular type of business injury—over the mass of other regulatory and prohibitory activities of the Federal Government (including criminal prosecutions) which can and do cause pecuniary loss if improperly conducted—personal, property, and business loss which up to now has not been redressed through this or the district courts. The same principles to which the present claimant appeals would also call for a drastic extension of federal liability to all of these fields. A wholly new ground of obligation would be summarily created by mere implication from statutes which say nothing to suggest such pecuniary responsibility.

Yet Congress has thus far been very careful, whenever it has dealt with the regulatory area, not to go that far. Not only is the mass of regulatory legislation (including Section 9) entirely silent on the subject of compensation for loss due to erroneous or wrongful regulation. Congress has always withheld from this court and from the Tucker Act original jurisdiction over tort claims against the Government; and liability for damages occasioned by wrongful regulatory action[10] smacks more of tort than of non-tortious obligation.

Above all, when the Federal Tort Claims Act (now 28 U.S.C. §§ 1346, 2680) was passed, Congress specifically exempted injuries traceable to performance of a "discretionary function". * * * Dalehite v. United States, 346 U.S. 15, 26–30, 32–34, 35–38 (1953), makes it absolutely plain that the Maritime Commission's function in acting under Section 9 was discretionary and that there would be no liability under the Tort Claims Act even if the agency abused its discretion (as plaintiff asserts). The discretion protected by § 2680(a) "is the discretion of the executive or the administrator to act according to one's judgment of the best course, a concept of substantial historical ancestry in American law." Id. at 34. "Where there is room for policy judgment and decision there is discretion." Id. at 36. And "it is clear that the * * * clause as to abuse connotes both negligence and wrongful acts in the exercise of the discretion * * *. The exercise of discretion could not be abused without negligence or a wrongful act." Id. at 33. The legislative history of the Tort Claims Act fully and specifically supports these holdings. The House Committee, for example, said over and over again that the "discretionary function" exception was "also designed to preclude application of the bill to a claim against a regulatory agency, such as the Federal Trade Commission or the Securities and Exchange Commission, based upon an alleged abuse of discretionary authority by an officer or employee, whether or not negligence is alleged to have been involved." Id. at 29.

In the face of this persistent refusal by the federal legislature to permit damage claims against the United States resulting from wrongful regulatory activity, we cannot read into Section 9 of the Shipping Act any implied

---

10. I.e., damages other than recovery from the Government of the claimant's mon- ey or property which has been improperly taken or retained.

direction to compensate plaintiff. To do so, we would be supported neither by the text of the section, nor by its context, legislative background, or past-enactment history. At the same time we would be ignoring the uniformly stony face Congress has turned toward a judicial remedy for this kind of business injury. If plaintiff had sued under the Tort Claims Act, its action would undoubtedly have fallen afoul of Section 2680(a), the "discretionary function" exception. If the suit in this court had asserted, without relying directly on Section 9 as the basis of the claim, a wrongful refusal by the Maritime Commission to approve the transfer, the petition would clearly have to be dismissed as a demand, founded in tort, for business damages due to misconduct. We cannot evade these barriers by incorporating into Section 9 something which is not there, either in terms or by fair implication—a mandate for compensation. Rather, we must follow the admonition of the Supreme Court, almost a century ago, "to be cautious that we do not permit the decisions of this court to become authority for the righting, in the Court of Claims, of all wrongs done to individuals by the officers of the General Government, though they may have been committed while serving that government, and in the belief that it was for its interest. In such cases, where it is proper for the nation to furnish a remedy, Congress has wisely reserved the matter for its own determination. It certainly has not conferred it on the Court of Claims." Gibbons v. United States, supra, 75 U.S. (8 Wall.) at 275–276.[14]

II

Secondarily, plaintiff bases its claim on the Constitution, on the existence of an actual contract to consider its application for foreign transfer, on a novel variant of the doctrine of "pendent jurisdiction", and on the clause of 28 U.S.C. § 1491 referring to damages not sounding in tort. We find these grounds equally without merit.

There was no taking requiring compensation under the Fifth Amendment. Neither the plaintiff's ship nor its contract with the Danish buyer was appropriated. The Commission's role was simply part of a pre-existing regulatory process known to plaintiff from the time it purchased the *Eastport,* and the Commission's failure to give its approval within the necessary time took no property from plaintiff any more than a comparable failure by the Federal Trade Commission, the Securities and Exchange Commission, or the Federal Power Commission, in their administrative processes, would amount to a taking.

Nor has plaintiff proved the breach of a contract with the United States * * *. We agree with the trial commissioner when he said: "Plaintiff, it will be recalled, inquired of Maritime, before submitting its bid, whether the sale would carry a restriction against foreign transfer or sale at some later time, and Maritime replied, in effect, that there would be no restriction other than the consideration normally applied to section 9

---

14. Since plaintiff's claim that Section 9 grants it the right to compensation is not frivolous, we hold, not that the court is without jurisdiction, but that on the merits the statutory argument is erroneous.

applications. Plaintiff would ascribe to this exchange of telegrams a significant role in the negotiation of the contract of sale. It is not so entitled, in my opinion, since the essence of Maritime's reply was only that it would obey the law in relation to applications for section 9 approvals. Whatever may have been plaintiff's need for reassurance on this point, the assurance when given was only what plaintiff had a right to assume in the first place and was not a part of the contract negotiations." There was no contract with the Commission with respect to a sale alien, but merely an ordinary declaration by the agency that it would consider such an application under the law, as it had to do.

Plaintiff also invokes Hurn v. Oursler, 289 U.S. 238 (1933), and the uncertain doctrine of "pendent jurisdiction". See, also, United Mine Workers of America v. Gibbs, 383 U.S. 715, 722 (1966). The argument is that, since the court has already entertained and granted the claim for the return of the $10,000 exaction, we ought also to consider and decide the present claim (even though we would not otherwise consider it) because it stems, in plaintiff's view, from the same illegal determination of the Commission to exact a money payment as a condition to any foreign sale of the *Eastport*. Whatever the role "pendent jurisdiction" may play for this court, it is clear that the two separate counts in the plaintiff's petition did not involve "the violation of a single right" (289 U.S. at 246) or "arise out of the same transaction". The $10,000 payment was connected with the sale to the Israeli buyer in late 1949 and early 1950, while the present claim stems from the aborted contract with the Danish firm in the spring of 1949. These were "two separate and distinct causes of action" (289 U.S. at 246), and did not have to be resolved in the same proceeding. Moreover, it is hard to see how "pendent jurisdiction" could lead this court to decide a case which no court, state or federal, could entertain. On this phase of its argument plaintiff must assume that its claim is founded in tort; but Congress has withheld this kind of tort action from all federal courts, and state courts would obviously be powerless. For us to consider the cause of action would not be to save time or trouble, or to eliminate duplicate litigation, but to decide a claim, under the camouflage of "pendent jurisdiction", which no court has the right to decide.

It is also said, finally, that this is a claim "for liquidated or unliquidated damages in cases not sounding in tort" (28 U.S.C. § 1491). We need not now explore the full shape of that still-amorphous and unfamiliar part of our jurisdiction, for plaintiff's present claim—if it is not validated by a statute, the Constitution, or a contract (as we have already held in this opinion)—must be tortious. What is asserted is wrongful conduct by the Maritime Commission, breaching its legal duty to plaintiff, which led to a business loss through failure of the Danish contract. This could be called interference with plaintiff's rights under the Danish contract, or a breach of legal duty independent of any agreement between plaintiff and the Commission, or unjustified conduct (negligent or intentional) causing injury under the *prima facie* theory. Whatever the characterization, the gravamen of the cause of action, under normal legal theory, would be tortious as between private parties. We must apply the same standards. The whole history of federal consent-to-sue on tort claims, as well as the structure of the Tort Claims Act (especially the exceptions (28 U.S.C. § 2680(a)–(n))), demonstrates that Congress has thought of cases "sounding in tort" as those which would be tort-grounded as between private persons.

III

Even if we were to decide (contrary to our holdings in Parts I and II, supra) that plaintiff could maintain in this court a claim for loss due to the Commission's withholding of approval under Section 9 while it was formulating an illegal policy of exacting money as a condition of approval, we could not grant judgment to plaintiff on this record. One reason is that the Commission was under no obligation to pass upon plaintiff's application within the three months allowed by the Danish contract. In the realm of administrative determination, that is a relatively short period; it would not be unreasonable or unprecedented for the Commission to take more time. We cannot say, no matter what the considerations flowing through the Commission's collective mind, that it breached any duty to plaintiff when it failed to act upon the application within the short time allowed by the Danish contract. Even if, as the trial commissioner thought, the delay here was founded upon a determination to consummate an illegal exaction from the shipowners, the agency would not commit an abuse of discretion, or violate a duty owed to plaintiff, until it sustained its refusal to act for a period which could objectively be deemed unusually long and three months would not be such. It is the length of the delay, not the Commission's secret motivation alone, which makes the difference.

A separate ground for refusing recovery—the basis on which the trial commissioner ultimately rested—is that we cannot say that the Commission would have granted approval even if it had not been improperly motivated. The Commission had not obtained the views of the other interested departments and agencies as to the effect of the pending Danish sale upon the national defense, the foreign policy, or the commerce of the United States, nor had the Commission made any determination as to the need for the *Eastport* in the United States merchant marine. Not even a preliminary survey had been made; the whole matter still lay within the agency's broad discretion. The trial commissioner was unable to say that approval would have been granted if the illegal factor had been excised— and we agree. It may be that approval would have been denied outright, or the Commission might have imposed legal conditions which would be unacceptable to plaintiff or its customer. These were not mere theoretical possibilities, but live alternatives. There is too much speculation and conjecture in making the necessary judgment that approval would have been given flatly or on tolerable terms.

For these reasons, plaintiff is not entitled to prevail on count I of its petition and that count is dismissed.

Notes and Questions

1.   What is the substantive nature of a Tucker Act claim? The Tucker Act is a jurisdictional statute, specifying the proper federal forum for non-tort money claims; it also provides a waiver of the government's sovereign immunity for such money claims. But it does not create substantive law or a cause of action in and of itself. Nor, like the Federal Tort Claims (see Chapter III.A.3a) does it refer us to state law for a cause of action against the federal government. Instead, by its terms, the Tucker Act refers us to the Constitution, to statutes or regulations, or to contract law as sources of law for a claim encompassed by the Tucker Act. Thus, we must look outside of the Tucker Act itself—to the Constitution, statutes or regulations, or to federal contract law—to find a substantive legal theory allowing recovery against the United States.

In this part of the casebook, we look first at Tucker Act claims founded upon statutes, where the substantive nature of Tucker Act claims has been well-developed by the courts. What does it mean to say that a Tucker Act claim is "founded upon" a statute?

Not every violation of a statute or non-fulfillment of a statutory duty by the federal government gives rise to a Tucker Act claim. For example, a military base might be closed in violation of a statutory procedure or even of a directive by Congress that facilities of a certain nature not be closed. But that statutory violation by itself would not support a Tucker Act claim by businesses in the community surrounding the base for damages in the form of lost business profits. Similarly, if the Federal Communications Commission unlawfully denied a radio license, that statutory violation likely would not permit a Tucker Act claim by the radio station for lost economic opportunities. As we'll see later (see Chapter IV.B), both cases might give rise to a claim under the Administrative Procedure Act to require that the base be reopened or the radio license be given. But, in all likelihood (depending upon the specific language of the underlying base-closing and radio-licensing statutes), no claim against the government for money damages under the Tucker Act would be allowed.

So how do we identify those statutes that *do* allow a private claim for money under the Tucker Act for the violation of the statutory duty? What is the essence of a statutory provision that gives rise to a Tucker Act claim?

2.   In the classic and oft-cited decision of *Eastport Steamship,* the plaintiff presents two claims for money, one which is accepted by the court as a proper Tucker Act claim founded upon statute, and the other which is rejected. What is the nature of each claim and why is one successful and the other not? For purposes of the Tucker Act, what does the court hold that it means to say that a claim is "founded" upon a statute? The court in this case sets forth a test for Tucker Act claims founded upon statute that is later quoted and adopted by the Supreme Court in the next case, *Testan.* What is that test and how it is applied here?

———

United States v. Testan

Supreme Court of the United States.
424 U.S. 392 (1976).

■ MR. JUSTICE BLACKMUN delivered the opinion of the Court.

This is a suit for reclassification of federal civil service positions and for backpay. It presents a substantial issue concerning the jurisdiction of the Court of Claims and the relief available in that tribunal.

I

The plaintiff-respondents, Herman R. Testan and Francis L. Zarrilli, are trial attorneys employed in the Office of Counsel, Defense Personnel Support Center, Defense Supply Agency, in Philadelphia. They represent the Government in certain matters that come before the Armed Services Board of Contract Appeals of the Department of Defense. Their positions are subject to the Classification Act, 5 U.S.C. § 5101 *et seq.*, and they are presently classified at civil service grade GS–13.

In December 1969 respondents, through their Chief Attorney, requested their employing agency to reclassify their positions to grade GS–14. The asserted ground was that their duties and responsibilities met the requirements for the higher grade under standards promulgated by the Civil Service Commission * * * In addition, they contended that their duties were identical to those of other trial attorneys in positions classified as GS–14 in the Contract Appeals Division, Office of the Staff Judge Advocate, Headquarters, Air Force Logistics Command, Wright–Patterson Air Force Base, Dayton, Ohio, and that under the principle of "equal pay for substantially equal work," prescribed in § 5101(1)(A), they were entitled to the higher classification.

The agency, after an audit by a position classification specialist, concluded that the respondents' assigned duties were properly classified at the GS–13 level under the Commission's classification standards. On appeal, the Commission reached the same conclusion and denied reclassification. The Commission also ruled that comparison of the positions held by the respondents with those of attorneys employed by the referenced Logistics Command was not a proper method of classification.

The two respondents then instituted this suit in the Court of Claims. Each sought an order directing reclassification of his position as of the date (May 8, 1970) of the first administrative denial of his request, and backpay, computed at the difference between his salary and grade GS–14 (and the claimed appropriate within-grade step), from that date. The trial judge, in a long opinion, concluded that the respondents were not entitled to backpay due to their allegedly wrongful classification. But he also concluded that the Commission's refusal to reclassify respondents to GS–14 was arbitrary, discriminatory, and not supported by substantial evidence, and that as a matter of law the respondents were entitled to an order remanding the case to the Commission with direction so to reclassify the respondents.

The Court of Claims considered the case en banc and divided 4–3. The majority disapproved the trial judge's recommendation that the court was empowered to direct the reclassification of respondents to GS–14, for the Court of Claims is not authorized to create an entitlement to a governmental position. "If entitlement depends on the exercise of discretion by someone else we cannot substitute our own discretion." 205 Ct.Cl. 330, 332, 499 F.2d 690, 691 (1974). The majority felt, however, that if the Commission were to determine that it had made an erroneous classification, that determination "could create a legal right which we could then enforce by a money judgment." *Id.*, at 333, 499 F.2d, at 691.

The majority agreed with the trial judge that the Commission's failure to compare respondents' positions with those of the Logistics Command attorneys was arbitrary and capricious. * * * The court ruled that it had the power under the remand statute, 86 Stat. 652, now codified as part of 28 U.S.C. § 1491, to order the Commission to reconsider its classification decision "under proper directions." Accordingly, and pursuant to its Rule 149(b), the court remanded the case to the Commission to make the comparison and to report the result to the court.

The dissent argued that the jurisdiction of the Court of Claims is limited to money judgments and, since none had been or could be ordered in this case, the court was without jurisdiction even to remand the case to the Civil Service Commission. In addition, the respondents had not stated a claim upon which relief could be granted, for they were asking for positions, and pay, to which they had never been appointed. * * * It asserted that the decision of the majority was but a declaratory judgment, a legal function not within the court's jurisdiction. Finally, the dissent argued that the classification decision of the Commission was neither arbitrary nor capricious and was supported by substantial evidence.

We granted certiorari because of the importance of the issue in the measure of the Court of Claims' statutory jurisdiction, and because of the significance of the court's decision upon the Commission's administration of the civil service classification system.

II

We turn to the respective statutes that are advanced as support for the action taken by the Court of Claims.

A.   The Tucker Act. The central provision establishing the jurisdiction of the court is that part of the Tucker Act now codified as 28 U.S.C. § 1491:

> "The Court of Claims shall have jurisdiction to render judgment upon any claim against the United States founded either upon the Constitution, or any Act of Congress, or any regulation of an executive department, or upon any express or implied contract with the United States, or for liquidated or unliquidated damages in cases not sounding in tort." * * *

The Tucker Act, of course, is itself only a jurisdictional statute; it does not create any substantive right enforceable against the United States for money damages. The Court of Claims has recognized that the Act merely confers jurisdiction upon it whenever the substantive right exists. *Eastport S.S. Corp. v. United States,* 178 Ct.Cl. 599, 605–607, 372 F.2d 1002, 1007–1009 (1967). We therefore must determine whether the two other federal statutes that are invoked by the respondents confer a substantive right to recover money damages from the United States for the period of their allegedly wrongful civil service classifications.

B. The Classification Act. Inasmuch as the trial judge proposed, that the respondents were not entitled to backpay under the Back Pay Act, 5 U.S.C. § 5596, and the Court of Claims held that there was no need for it to reach and construe that Act, 205 Ct.Cl., at 333, 499 F.2d, at 691, it is implicit in the court's decision in favor of respondents that a violation of the Classification Act gives rise to a claim for money damages for pay lost by reason of the allegedly wrongful classifications. * * *

We find no provision in the Classification Act that expressly makes the United States liable for pay lost through allegedly improper classifications. To be sure, in the "purpose" section of the Act, 5 U.S.C. § 5101(1)(A), Congress stated that it was "to provide a plan for classification of positions whereby ... the principle of equal pay for substantially equal work will be followed." And in subsequent sections, there are set forth substantive standards for grading particular positions, and provisions for procedures to ensure that those standards are met. But none of these several sections contains an express provision for an award of backpay to a person who has been erroneously classified.

In answer to this fact, the respondents and the *amici* make two observations. They first argue that the Tucker Act fundamentally waives sovereign immunity with respect to any claim invoking a constitutional provision or a federal statute or regulation, and makes available any and all generally accepted and important forms of redress, including money damages. It is said that the Government has confused two very different issues, namely, whether there has been a waiver of sovereignty, and whether a substantive right has been created, and it is claimed that where there has been a violation of a substantive right, the Tucker Act waives sovereign immunity as to all measures necessary to redress that violation.

The argument does not persuade us. As stated above, the Tucker Act is merely jurisdictional, and grant of a right of action must be made with specificity. The respondents do not rest their claims upon a contract; neither do they seek the return of money paid by them to the Government. It follows that the asserted entitlement to money damages depends upon whether any federal statute "can fairly be interpreted as mandating compensation by the Federal Government for the damage sustained." *Eastport S.S. Corp. v. United States,* 178 Ct.Cl., at 607, 372 F.2d, at 1009. We are not ready to tamper with these established principles because it might be thought that they should be responsive to a particular conception of enlightened governmental policy. In a suit against the United States, there cannot be a right to money damages without a waiver of sovereign immunity, and we regard as unsound the argument of amici that all substantive rights of necessity create a waiver of sovereign immunity such that money damages are available to redress their violation.

* * * The respondents and the *amici* next argue that the violation of any statute or regulation relating to federal employment automatically creates a cause of action against the United States for money damages because, if this were not so, the employee would then have a right without a remedy, inasmuch as he is denied access to the one forum where he may seek redress.

Here again we are not persuaded. Where the United States is the defendant and the plaintiff is not suing for money improperly exacted or retained, the basis of the federal claim whether it be the Constitution, a statute, or a regulation does not create a cause of action for money damages unless as the Court of Claims has stated, that basis "in itself . . . can fairly be interpreted as mandating compensation by the Federal Government for the damage sustained." *Eastport S.S. Corp. v. United States,* 178 Ct.Cl., at 607, 372 F.2d, at 1008, 1009. We see nothing akin to this in the Classification Act or in the context of a suit seeking reclassification.

The present action, of course, is not one concerning a wrongful discharge or a wrongful suspension. In that situation, at least since the Civil Service Act of 1883, the employee is entitled to the emoluments of his position until he has been legally disqualified. There is no claim here that either respondent has been denied the benefit of the position to which he was appointed. The claim, instead, is that each has been denied the benefit of a position to which he should have been, but was not, appointed. The established rule is that one is not entitled to the benefit of a position until he has been duly appointed to it. The Classification Act does not purport by its terms to change that rule, and we see no suggestion in it or in its legislative history that Congress intended to alter it. * * *

The situation, as we see it, is not that Congress has left the respondents remediless, as they assert, for their allegedly wrongful civil service classification, but that Congress has not made available to a party wrongfully classified the remedy of money damages through retroactive classification. There is a difference between prospective reclassification, on the one hand, and retroactive reclassification resulting in money damages, on the other. See *Edelman v. Jordan,* 415 U.S. 651 (1974). Respondents, of course, have an administrative avenue of prospective relief available to them under the elaborate and structured provisions of the Classification Act, 5 U.S.C. §§ 5101–5115. * * * A second possible avenue of relief and it, too, seemingly, is only prospective is by way of mandamus, under 28 U.S.C. § 1361, in a proper federal district court. In this way, also, the respondents have asserted their claims.

The respondents, thus, are not entirely without remedy. They are without the remedies in the Court of Claims of retroactive classification and money damages to which they assert they are entitled. Additional remedies of this kind are for the Congress to provide and not for the courts to construct.

Finally, we note that if the respondents were correct in their claims to retroactive classification and money damages, many of the federal statutes such as the Back Pay Act that expressly provide money damages as a remedy against the United States in carefully limited circumstances would be rendered superfluous.

The Court of Claims, in the present case, sought to avoid all this by its remand to the Civil Service Commission for further proceedings. If, then, the Commission were to find that the respondents were entitled to a higher grade, the Court of Claims announced that it would be prepared on appropriate motion to enter an award of money damages for the respondents for whatever backpay they lost during the period of their wrongful classifications. The remand statute, now codified as part of 28 U.S.C. § 1491, authorizes the Court of Claims to "issue orders directing restoration to . . . position, placement in appropriate duty . . . status, and correction of applicable records" in order to complement the relief afforded by a money judgment, and also to "remand appropriate matters to any administrative . . . body" in a case "within its jurisdiction." The remand statute, thus, applies only to cases already within the court's jurisdiction. The present litigation is not such a case. * * *

C   The Back Pay Act. This statute, which the Court of Claims found unnecessary to evaluate in arriving at its decision, does not apply, in our view, to wrongful-classification claims. The Act does authorize retroactive recovery of wages whenever a federal employee has "undergone an unjustified or unwarranted personnel action that has resulted in the withdrawal or reduction of all or a part of" the compensation to which the employee is otherwise entitled. 5 U.S.C. § 5596(b). The statute's language was intended to provide a monetary remedy for wrongful reductions in grade, removals, suspensions, and "other unwarranted or unjustified actions affecting pay or allowances [that] could occur in the course of reassignments and change from full-time to part-time work." S.Rep.No.1062, 89th Cong., 2d Sess., 3 (1966), U.S.Code Cong. & Admin.News 1966, pp. 2097, 2099. The Commission consistently has so construed the Back Pay Act. So has the Court of Claims.

For many years federal personnel actions were viewed as entirely discretionary and therefore not subject to any judicial review, and in the absence of a statute eliminating that discretion, courts refused to intervene where an employee claimed that he had been wrongfully discharged. Relief was invariably denied where the claim was that the employee had been denied a promotion on improper grounds.

Congress, of course, now has provided specifically in the Lloyd–LaFollette Act, 5 U.S.C. § 7501, for administrative review of a claim of wrongful adverse action, and in the Back Pay Act for the award of money damages for a wrongful deprivation of pay. But federal agencies continue to have discretion in determining most matters relating to the terms and conditions of federal employment. One continuing aspect of this is the rule, mentioned above, that the federal employee is entitled to receive only the salary of the position to which he was appointed, even though he may have performed the duties of another position or claims that he should have been placed in a higher grade. Congress did not override this rule, or depart from it, with its enactment of the Back Pay Act. It could easily have so provided had that been its intention. * * *

* * * [T]he Back Pay Act, as its words so clearly indicate, was intended to grant a monetary cause of action only to those who were subjected to a reduction in their duly appointed emoluments or position.

III

We therefore conclude that neither the Classification Act nor the Back Pay Act creates a substantive right in the respondents to backpay for the period of their claimed wrongful classifications. This makes it unnecessary for us to consider the additional argument advanced by the United States that the Classification Act does not require that positions held by employees of one agency be compared with those of employees in another agency.

The Court of Claims was in error when it remanded the case to the Civil Service Commission for further proceedings. That court's judgment is therefore reversed, and the case is remanded with directions to dismiss the respondents' suit.

It is so ordered.

■ Mr. Justice Stevens took no part in the consideration or decision of this case.

Notes and Questions

1. The Supreme Court in *United States v. Testan* adopts the "money-mandating" test for identifying the type of statute that gives rise to a Tucker Act claim. How is that test applied in this case to the Classification Act? To the Back Pay Act? What is missing in the Classification Act that is required to successfully assert a Tucker Act statute-founded claim? By contrast, the Back Pay Act is plainly a money-mandating statute, but the plaintiffs lose because it doesn't apply to this type of situation. Why doesn't it apply?

2. The *Testan* opinion must be corrected on one significant point. The Court states that the Tucker Act "is itself only a jurisdictional statute," and later suggests that it does not waive the government's sovereign immunity. As Professor Mary Christina Wood aptly labels it, this judicial nullification of the statutory waiver of sovereign immunity was "a bizarre lapse from standard Tucker Act analysis." Mary Christina Wood, *Indian Land and the Promise of Native Sovereignty: The Trust Doctrine Revisited,* 1994 Utah L. Rev. 1471, 1518 n. 218. In the subsequent decision of *United States v. Mitchell,* 463 U.S. 206 (1983), the Supreme Court explained that the Tucker Act is *both* a jurisdictional statute and a waiver of sovereign

immunity. Because few statutes contain express language waiving the sovereign immunity of the government, if the Tucker Act were not deemed to achieve this purpose, then viable Tucker Act claims founded upon statute would be rare. Indeed, if another statute itself provides an express waiver of sovereign immunity, then the suit could be brought directly pursuant to that statute with no need for recourse to the Tucker Act. Given the correction made by the Court in *Mitchell,* we now are instructed to look to the substance of the other statute as a source of law, but we need not demand that the statute expressly provide for judicial action. The Tucker Act itself provides the government's consent to suit; the other statute upon which the Tucker Act claim is founded need only supply the cause of action. It remains true, as the *Testan* opinion states, that the Tucker Act itself "does not create any substantive right enforceable against the United States for money damages." Rather, the substantive right must be found in another source of law, hence the requirement that the claimant demonstrate that the statute relied upon may be interpreted as mandating compensation.

In its more recent decision in *United States v. White Mountain Apache Tribe,* 537 U.S. 465 (2003) (which is set out in Chapter IV.A.3 of this casebook), the Supreme Court confirmed that, although an unequivocal waiver of sovereign immunity is a predicate to any suit against the United States, the Tucker Act (and a companion statute pertinent in that case, the Indian Tucker Act) provide such a consent, *Id.* at 472. To be sure, the Tucker Act does not create a cause of action, meaning that the plaintiff must premise the substantive right upon a statute that "can fairly be interpreted as mandating compensation by the Federal Government for the damage sustained." *Id.* (quoting *Mitchell,* 463 U.S. at 217). However, because the Tucker Act itself provides the necessary sovereign immunity waiver, a strict construction rule does not apply to this stage of the analysis. Thus, the Court explained, the pertinent statute need only "be reasonably amenable to the reading that it mandates a right of recovery in damages"; that is, "a fair inference will do." *Id.* at 473.

The author of this casebook reads the Supreme Court's decision in *White Mountain Apache* as a confirmation and clarification of the requirements for presenting a Tucker Act claim. The Court quoted and reaffirmed the "fair interpretation" rule, while giving it further definition. *White Mountain Apache,* 537 U.S. at 472. Rather than altering or relaxing the standard for statutory analysis of a substantive claim founded upon a statute or other source of law, the Court was rejecting the suggestion that the kind of strict construction analysis should apply that would govern the inquiry into whether a statute waives sovereign immunity. Given that the Tucker Act itself accomplishes the waiver of sovereign immunity, the Court said, the " 'fair interpretation' rule demands a showing demonstrably lower than the standard for the initial waiver of sovereign immunity." *Id.* Thus, the Court's statement that the underlying statutory source of law need only be "reasonably amenable to the reading that it mandates a right of recovery in damages," *id.* at 473, was designed to contrast ordinary rules of statutory interpretation with the demand for a explicit statement applicable to the sovereign immunity waiver stage. Accordingly, on the merits, your author understands the required analysis in this way:

> If a plaintiff pursues a "regular" Tucker Act claim, the substantive right adduced from a statute must be one that entails the payment of money; that is, one that mandates compensation. Thus, while the statute need not authorize judicial action or even contemplate the prospect of litigation—the Tucker Act expressly creates the right to file suit—the statute must speak in the dialect of lucre. Without some reference to money or financial consequences in the statute relied upon for the cause of action, the statute cannot be fairly interpreted as conveying a right to monetary compensation within the meaning of the Tucker Act.

Gregory C. Sisk, *Yesterday and Today: Of Indians, Breach of Trust, Money, and Sovereign Immunity*, 39 Tulsa L. Rev. 313, 340 (2003). Accordingly, Tucker Act claims founded upon statute traditionally have included federal civilian and military employment claims, which are the subjects of the next two subparts of this casebook, as well as other government benefit and spending program statutes.

3.   As you will recall, the Supreme Court in *United States v. King,* 395 U.S. 1 (1969) (see Chapter IV.A.1.c), stated the general presumption that the Court of Federal Claims is limited to awarding monetary relief and is precluded from granting equitable remedies. One of the most significant expansions of the Court of Federal Claims' remedial powers came in the Remand Act of 1972, which is codified as part of the Tucker Act, 28 U.S.C. § 1491(a)(2). The Remand Act authorizes the court to order an agency to restore an employee of the federal government to an office or position, place him or her in the appropriate duty or retirement status, and correct employment records. *Id.* However, the statute makes this limited equitable power incidental and collateral to a Tucker Act claim for monetary relief. *Id.* Thus, a federal employee may not bring an independent suit that seeks purely equitable relief from the Court of Federal Claims, but rather must request this additional relief in conjunction with a valid underlying claim for monetary relief under the Tucker Act. The *Testan* opinion applies the Remand Act in precisely this way and with this limitation. (The Remand Act is explored further in the context of military employment claims. See Chapter IV.A.2.c.)

b.   CIVILIAN EMPLOYMENT CLAIMS

Back Pay Act, 5 United States Code § 5596(b)(1)(A)

(b)(1) An employee of an agency who, on the basis of a timely appeal or an administrative determination (including a decision relating to an unfair labor practice or a grievance) is found by appropriate authority under applicable law, rule, regulation, or collective bargaining agreement, to have been affected by an unjustified or unwarranted personnel action which has resulted in the withdrawal or reduction of all or part of the pay, allowances, or differentials of the employee—

(A) is entitled, on correction of the personnel action, to receive for the period for which the personnel action was in effect—

(i) an amount equal to all or any part of the pay, allowances, or differentials, as applicable which the employee normally would have earned or received during the period if the personnel action had not occurred, less any amounts earned by the employee through other employment during that period; and

(ii) reasonable attorney fees related to the personnel action which, with respect to any decision relating to an unfair labor practice or a grievance processed under a procedure negotiated in accordance with chapter 71 of this title, or under chapter 11 of title I of the Foreign Service Act of 1980, shall be awarded in accordance with standards established under section 7701(g) of this title * * * .

* * *

Civil Service Reform Act, 5 United States Code
§ 7701(a), 7703(a)–(c)

§ 7701.   Appellate procedures

(a) An employee, or applicant for employment, may submit an appeal to the Merit Systems Protection Board from any action which is appealable to the Board under any law, rule, or regulation. * * *

* * *

§ 7703.   Judicial review of decisions of the Merit Systems Protection Board

(a)(1) Any employee or applicant for employment adversely affected or aggrieved by a final order or decision of the Merit Systems Protection Board may obtain judicial review of the order or decision.

(2) The Board shall be named respondent in any proceeding brought pursuant to this subsection, unless the employee or applicant for employment seeks review of a final order or decision on the merits on the underlying personnel action or on a request for attorney fees, in which case the agency responsible for taking the personnel action shall be the respondent.

(b)(1) Except as provided in paragraph (2) of this subsection, a petition to review a final order or final decision of the Board shall be filed in the United States Court of Appeals for the Federal Circuit. Notwithstanding any other provision of law, any petition for review must be filed within 60 days after the date the petitioner received notice of the final order or decision of the Board.

(2) Cases of discrimination subject to the provisions of section 7702 of this title shall be filed under section 717(c) of the Civil Rights Act of 1964

(42 U.S.C. 2000e–16(c)), section 15(c) of the Age Discrimination in Employment Act of 1967 (29 U.S.C. 633a(c)), and section 16(b) of the Fair Labor
Standards Act of 1938, as amended (29 U.S.C. 216(b)), as applicable.
Notwithstanding any other provision of law, any such case filed under any
such section must be filed within 30 days after the date the individual filing
the case received notice of the judicially reviewable action under such
section 7702.

(c) In any case filed in the United States Court of Appeals for the
Federal Circuit, the court shall review the record and hold unlawful and set
aside any agency action, findings, or conclusions found to be—

(1) arbitrary, capricious, an abuse of discretion, or otherwise not in
accordance with law;

(2) obtained without procedures required by law, rule, or regulation
having been followed; or

(3) unsupported by substantial evidence;

except that in the case of discrimination brought under any section referred
to in subsection (b)(2) of this section, the employee or applicant shall have
the right to have the facts subject to trial de novo by the reviewing court.

* * *

Federal Courts Improvement Act, 28 United States Code § 1295(a)(9)

(a) The United States Court of Appeals for the Federal Circuit shall
have exclusive jurisdiction—

* * *

(9) of an appeal from a final order or final decision of the Merit
Systems Protection Board, pursuant to sections 7703(b)(1) and 7703(d)
of title 5;

* * *

United States v. Fausto

Supreme Court of the United States.
484 U.S. 439 (1988).

■ JUSTICE SCALIA delivered the opinion of the Court.

Respondent Joseph A. Fausto, an employee of the Department of the
Interior Fish and Wildlife Service (FWS), was suspended from his job for 30
days because of unauthorized use of a Government vehicle. The United
States Court of Appeals for the Federal Circuit held that he could maintain
a suit for backpay in the United States Claims Court alleging that his

suspension was in violation of Department of the Interior regulations. We granted certiorari to decide whether the Civil Service Reform Act of 1978 (CSRA or Act), Pub.L. 95–454, 92 Stat. 1111 *et seq.* (codified, as amended, in various sections of 5 U.S.C.), which affords an employee in respondent's situation no review of the agency's decision, precludes such a Claims Court suit.

I

Respondent was hired by FWS in January 1978, as an administrative officer for the Young Adult Conservation Corps camp in Virginia Beach, Virginia. His position was in the excepted service,[1] and was to last for the duration of the Conservation Corps program at Virginia Beach, but not beyond September 30, 1982.

In November 1980, FWS advised respondent that it intended to dismiss him for a number of reasons, including unauthorized use of a Government vehicle. After respondent replied to the charges, he received a memorandum from FWS informing him that he would be removed effective January 16, 1981. * * *

Respondent sought review of his removal with the Merit Systems Protection Board (MSPB), which dismissed his appeal in August 1981, on the ground that under the CSRA a nonpreference eligible in the excepted service has no right to appeal to the MSPB. *Fausto v. Department of Interior,* No. PH 075281102271 (M.S.P.B. Aug. 27, 1981), aff'd, 790 F.2d 454 (CA Fed.1984) (judgment order). On September 18, 1981, FWS permanently closed the camp at Virginia Beach. In March 1982, in response to an inquiry initiated on behalf of respondent, FWS admitted that respondent had not been informed of his grievance rights, and offered him the opportunity to challenge his removal. Respondent filed a formal grievance, and on June 30, 1982, FWS concluded, based on the administrative file and without a hearing, that respondent should not have been removed. FWS found that most of the charges against respondent were *de minimis* and warranted no penalty, but imposed a 30–day suspension for misuse of a Government vehicle. FWS offered respondent backpay from February 15,

---

1. The CSRA divides civil service employees into three main classifications that can be generally described as follows: "Senior Executive Service" employees are those who occupy high-level positions in the Executive Department, but for whom appointment by the President and confirmation by the Senate is not required. 5 U.S.C. § 3132(a)(2). "Competitive service" employees are all other employees for whom nomination by the President and confirmation by the Senate is not required, and who are not specifically excepted from the competitive service by statute or by statutorily authorized regulation. § 2102. "Excepted service" personnel are the remainder—those who are in neither the competitive service nor the Senior Executive Service. § 2103. Respondent's position was in the excepted service because it had been excluded from the competitive service by authorized Civil Service Commission (now Office of Personnel Management) regulation.

Within each of the three classifications of employment, the Act accords preferential treatment to certain veterans and their close relatives—so-called "preference eligibles." § 2108. Respondent, who is not a preference eligible, is referred to as a nonpreference member of the excepted service.

1981, the date his 30–day suspension would have ended, through September 18, 1981, the date the camp was closed.

Respondent filed an appeal with the Department of the Interior * * * . The Secretary of the Interior upheld FWS's decision.

In February 1983, respondent filed the present action under the Back Pay Act, 5 U.S.C. § 5596, in the Claims Court. The Claims Court dismissed, holding that the CSRA comprised the exclusive catalog of remedies for civil servants affected by adverse personnel action. 7 Cl.Ct. 459, 461 (1985). The Federal Circuit reversed and remanded, 783 F.2d 1020 (1986), holding that although the CSRA did not afford nonpreference excepted service employees a right of appeal to the MSPB, it did not preclude them from seeking the Claims Court review traditionally available under the Tucker Act, 28 U.S.C. § 1491, based on the Back Pay Act. On the merits it found Fausto's suspension wrongful and awarded backpay for the period of the suspension. The Court of Appeals denied the Government's petition for rehearing of the case en banc, but issued a second panel opinion reaffirming its decision. 791 F.2d 1554 (1986).

The Government petitioned for certiorari on the question whether a nonveteran member of the excepted service may obtain, under the Tucker Act, judicial review of adverse personnel action for which the CSRA does not provide him a right of review.

II

We have recognized that the CSRA "comprehensively overhauled the civil service system," *Lindahl v. OPM,* 470 U.S. 768, 773 (1985), creating an elaborate "new framework for evaluating adverse personnel actions against [federal employees]," *id.,* at 774. It prescribes in great detail the protections and remedies applicable to such action, including the availability of administrative and judicial review. No provision of the CSRA gives nonpreference members of the excepted service the right to administrative or judicial review of suspension for misconduct. The question we face is whether that withholding of remedy was meant to preclude judicial review for those employees, or rather merely to leave them free to pursue the remedies that had been available before enactment of the CSRA. The answer is to be found by examining the purpose of the CSRA, the entirety of its text, and the structure of review that it establishes.

A leading purpose of the CSRA was to replace the haphazard arrangements for administrative and judicial review of personnel action, part of the "outdated patchwork of statutes and rules built up over almost a century" that was the civil service system, S.Rep. No. 95–969, p. 3 (1978). Under that pre-existing system, only veterans enjoyed a statutory right to appeal adverse personnel action to the Civil Service Commission (CSC), the predecessor of the MSPB. Other employees were afforded this type of administrative review by Executive Order. Still others, like employees in respondent's classification, had no right to such review. As for appeal to the courts: Since there was no special statutory review proceeding relevant to personnel action, employees sought to appeal the decisions of the CSC, or the agency decision unreviewed by the CSC, to the district courts through the various forms of action traditionally used for so-called nonstatutory review of agency action, including suits for mandamus, injunction, and declaratory judgment. For certain kinds of personnel decisions, federal employees could maintain an action in the Court of Claims of the sort respondent seeks to maintain here.

Criticism of this "system" of administrative and judicial review was widespread. The general perception was that "appeals processes [were] so lengthy and complicated that managers [in the civil service] often avoid[ed] taking disciplinary action" against employees even when it was clearly warranted. S.Rep. No. 95–969, at 9. With respect to judicial review in particular, there was dissatisfaction with the "wide variations in the kinds of decisions ... issued on the same or similar matters," *id.*, at 63, which were the product of concurrent jurisdiction, under various bases of jurisdiction, of the district courts in all Circuits and the Court of Claims. Moreover, as the Court of Appeals for the District of Columbia Circuit repeatedly noted, beginning the judicial process at the district court level, with repetition of essentially the same review on appeal in the court of appeals, was wasteful and irrational.

Congress responded to this situation by enacting the CSRA, which replaced the patchwork system with an integrated scheme of administrative and judicial review, designed to balance the legitimate interests of the various categories of federal employees with the needs of sound and efficient administration. Three main sections of the CSRA govern personnel action taken against members of the civil service. In each of these sections, Congress deals explicitly with the situation of nonpreference members of the excepted service, granting them limited, and in some cases conditional, rights.

Chapter 43 of the CSRA governs personnel actions based on unacceptable job performance. It applies to both competitive service employees and members of the excepted service. 5 U.S.C. § 4301. It provides that before an employee can be removed or reduced in grade for unacceptable job performance certain procedural protections must be afforded, including 30 days' advance written notice of the proposed action, the right to be represented by an attorney or other representative, a reasonable period of time in which to respond to the charges, and a written decision specifying the instances of unacceptable performance. § 4303(b)(1). Although Congress extended these protections to nonpreference members of the excepted service, it denied them the right to seek either administrative or judicial review of the agency's final action. Chapter 43 gives only competitive service employees and preference eligible members of the excepted service the right to appeal the agency's decision to the MSPB and then to the Federal Circuit. § 4303(e).

Chapter 23 of the CSRA establishes the principles of the merit system of employment, § 2301, and forbids an agency to engage in certain "prohibited personnel practices," including unlawful discrimination, coercion of political activity, nepotism, and reprisal against so-called whistleblowers.

§ 2302. Nonpreference excepted service employees who are not in positions of a confidential or policymaking nature are protected by this chapter, § 2302(a)(2)(B), and are given the right to file charges of "prohibited personnel practices" with the Office of Special Counsel of the MSPB, whose responsibility it is to investigate the charges and, where appropriate, to seek remedial action from the agency and the MSPB. § 1206.

Chapter 75 of the Act governs adverse action taken against employees for the "efficiency of the service," which includes action of the type taken here, based on misconduct. Subchapter I governs minor adverse action (suspension for 14 days or less), §§ 7501–7504, and Subchapter II governs major adverse action (removal, suspension for more than 14 days, reduction in grade or pay, or furlough for 30 days or less), §§ 7511–7514. In each subchapter, covered employees are given procedural protections similar to those contained in Chapter 43, §§ 7503(b), 7513(b), and in Subchapter II covered employees are accorded administrative review by the MSPB, followed by judicial review in the Federal Circuit. §§ 7513(d), 7703. The definition of "employee[s]" covered by Subchapter II (major adverse action) specifically includes preference eligibles in the excepted service, § 7511(a)(1)(B), but does not include other members of the excepted service. The Office of Personnel Management is, however, given authority to extend coverage of Subchapter II to positions in the excepted service that have that status because they have been excluded from the competitive service by OPM regulation. § 7511(c).

The Court of Appeals viewed the exclusion of nonpreference members of the excepted service from the definitional sections of Chapter 75 as congressional silence on the issue of what review these employees should receive for the categories of personnel action covered by that chapter, including a suspension of the duration at issue here, which would come within Subchapter II. The court therefore found respondent free to pursue whatever judicial remedies he would have had before enactment of the CSRA. We view the exclusion quite differently. In the context of the entire statutory scheme, we think it displays a clear congressional intent to deny the excluded employees the protections of Chapter 75—including judicial review—for personnel action covered by that chapter.

* * * The comprehensive nature of the CSRA, the attention that it gives throughout to the rights of nonpreference excepted service employees, and the fact that it does not include them in provisions for administrative and judicial review contained in Chapter 75, combine to establish a congressional judgment that those employees should not be able to demand judicial review for the type of personnel action covered by that chapter. Their exclusion from the scope of those protections can hardly be explained on the theory that Congress simply did not have them in mind, since, as noted earlier, Congress specifically included in Chapter 75 *preference eligible* excepted service employees, § 7511(a)(1)(B), and specifically provided for optional inclusion (at the election of OPM) of *certain* nonpreference excepted service employees with respect to *certain* protections of the chapter, including MSPB and judicial review, § 7511(c). (Respondent, inci-

dentally, falls within the category eligible for that optional inclusion, which OPM has chosen not to invoke.) It seems to us evident that the absence of provision for these employees to obtain judicial review is not an uninformative consequence of the limited scope of the statute, but rather manifestation of a considered congressional judgment that they should not have statutory entitlement to review for adverse action of the type governed by Chapter 75.

This conclusion emerges not only from the statutory language, but also from what we have elsewhere found to be an indicator of nonreviewability, the structure of the statutory scheme. Two structural elements important for present purposes are clear in the framework of the CSRA: First, the preferred position of certain categories of employees—competitive service employees and "preference eligibles" (veterans). This is of course not an innovation of the CSRA, but continuation of a traditional feature of the civil service system. The second structural element is the primacy of the MSPB for administrative resolution of disputes over adverse personnel action, 5 U.S.C. §§ 1205, 4303(e), 7513(d), 7701, and the primacy of the United States Court of Appeals for the Federal Circuit for judicial review, § 7703. This enables the development, through the MSPB, of a unitary and consistent Executive Branch position on matters involving personnel action, avoids an "unnecessary layer of judicial review" in lower federal courts, and "[e]ncourages more consistent judicial decisions...." S.Rep. No. 95–969, at 52; see *Lindahl v. OPM,* 470 U.S., at 797–798.

Interpreting the exclusion of nonpreference excepted service personnel from Chapter 75 as leaving them free to pursue other avenues of review would turn the first structural element upside down, and would seriously undermine the second. As to the former: Under respondent's view, he would be able to obtain judicial review of a 10–day suspension for misconduct, even though a competitive service employee would not, since Chapter 75 makes MSPB review, and hence judicial review, generally unavailable for minor adverse personnel action, including suspensions of less than 14 days. Moreover, this inverted preference shown to nonpreference excepted service employees would be shown as well to probationary employees, another disfavored class. See 5 U.S.C. § 4303(f)(2) (expressly excluding probationary employees from review under Chapter 43); § 7511(a)(1)(A) (expressly excluding probationary employees from Chapter 75); S.Rep. No. 95–969, at 45 ("It is inappropriate to restrict an agency's authority to separate an employee who does not perform acceptably during the [probationary period]"). Since probationary employees, like nonpreference excepted service employees, are excluded from the definition of "employee" for purposes of Chapter 75, respondent's theory that persons so excluded retain their pre-CSRA remedies must apply to them as well. * * *

The manner in which respondent's interpretation would undermine the second structural element of the Act is obvious. First, for random categories of employees, legally enforceable employment entitlements will exist that are not subject to the unifying authority, in consistency of fact-finding as well as interpretation of law, of the MSPB. Second, for these same employees, the second layer of judicial review, which Congress meant to eliminate, would persist, since pre-CSRA causes of action had to be commenced in the federal courts of first instance rather than in the courts of appeals. Finally, for certain kinds of actions, these employees would be able to obtain review in the district courts and the regional courts of appeals throughout the country, undermining the consistency of interpretation by the Federal Circuit envisioned by § 7703 of the Act. Although a Tucker Act suit is appealable only to the Federal Circuit, regardless of whether it is brought in the Claims Court or in district court, see 28 U.S.C. §§ 1295(a)(2), 1295(a)(3), 1346(a)(2), actions brought under the other statutes used to obtain judicial review before the CSRA, would be appealable to the various regional Circuits. When, as would often be the case, particular agency action could be challenged under either the Tucker Act or one of the other bases of jurisdiction, an agency office would not know whether to follow the law of its geographical Circuit or the conflicting law of the Federal Circuit. This, and the other consequences of respondent's theory that the pre-CSRA remedies of nonpreference excepted service employees were not meant to be affected by the Act, are inherently implausible. * * *

[An]other principle of statutory construction to which *amicus* appeals is the doctrine that repeals by implication are strongly disfavored, so that a later statute will not be held to have implicitly repealed an earlier one unless there is a clear repugnancy between the two. This means, amicus asserts, that absent an express statement to the contrary, the CSRA cannot be interpreted to deprive respondent of the statutory remedy he possessed under the Back Pay Act. * * *

* * * By reason of the interpretation we adopt today, the Back Pay Act does not stand repealed, but remains an operative part of the integrated statutory scheme set up by Congress to protect civil servants. All that we find to have been "repealed" by the SCRA is the judicial interpretation of the Back Pay Act—or, if you will, the Back Pay Act's implication—allowing review in the Court of Claims of the underlying personnel decision giving rise to the claim for backpay.

To be more explicit: The Back Pay Act provides in pertinent part:

"An employee of an agency who, on the basis of a timely appeal or an administrative determination ... is found *by appropriate authority under applicable law,* rule, regulation, or collective bargaining agreement, to have been affected by an unjustified or unwarranted personnel action ... [is entitled to back pay]." 5 U.S.C. § 5596(b)(1) (emphasis added).

Before enactment of the CSRA, regulations promulgated by the Civil Service Commission provided that a court authorized to correct, or to direct the correction of, an unjustified personnel action was an "appropriate authority" within the meaning of the Back Pay Act. And the Court of Claims had held (with some circularity of reasoning) that it was such a court because it had jurisdiction to award backpay. Without disagreeing with that determination made in the context of the pre-existing patchwork scheme, we find that under the comprehensive and integrated review scheme of the CSRA, the Claims Court (and any other court relying on Tucker Act jurisdiction) is not an "appropriate authority" to review an agency's personnel determination. This does not mean that the statutory remedy provided in the Back Pay Act is eliminated, or even that the conditions for invoking it are in any way altered. Now, as previously, if an employee is found by an "appropriate authority" to have undergone an unwarranted personnel action a suit for backpay will lie. Post–CSRA, such an authority would include the agency itself, or the MSPB or the Federal Circuit where those entities have the authority to review the agency's determination. * * *

The CSRA established a comprehensive system for reviewing personnel action taken against federal employees. Its deliberate exclusion of employees in respondent's service category from the provisions establishing administrative and judicial review for personnel action of the sort at issue here prevents respondent from seeking review in the Claims Court under the Back Pay Act. Accordingly, the judgment of the Court of Appeals is

Reversed.

[The concurring opinion of JUSTICE BLACKMUN and the dissenting opinion of JUSTICE STEVENS, with whom JUSTICE BRENNAN and JUSTICE MARSHALL joined, are omitted.]

Notes and Questions

1. In the private sector, employee claims for wrongful discharge ordinarily constitute a contractual claim. In the federal public sector, employment is regulated by statute. Accordingly, a federal employment dispute traditionally implicated that branch of the Tucker Act for claims founded upon a statute. Indeed, before 1978, the Tucker Act was the primary vehicle for resolution of federal employment disputes, both civilian and military. A suit alleging an illegal discharge or reduction in rank typically would be pursued under the Tucker Act, with the Back Pay Act, 5 U.S.C. § 5596 (excerpts of which are set out in the materials above) providing the substantive right or money-mandating basis for the claim. In addition, the Remand Act, 28 U.S.C. § 1491(a)(2), which was discussed in the notes following the previous case, authorized the then-Court of Claims not only to award a money judgment for backpay but also to order the agency to restore the individual to a position or employment status. Civilian and military pay claims made up a substantial portion of the Tucker Act docket of what was then the Court of Claims.

In 1978, Congress enacted the Civil Service Reform Act (CSRA), excerpts of which are set out above in the materials and which is well surveyed in *United States v. Fausto*. In general the CSRA provides that individuals within most categories of federal civilian employment who have suffered an adverse employment action may seek administrative review before the Merit Systems Protection Board (MSPB) and then judicial review in the United States Court of Appeals for the Federal Circuit:

> Generally, MSPB appeals are initiated by federal civil service employees who seek to challenge actions by their employing agencies. For the MSPB to have jurisdiction, the action must be appealable to the board by some law, rule, or regulation. With the exception of certain cases within the board's original jurisdiction, most appeals to the MSPB are first heard by an administrative judge ("AJ"). * * * Within 35 days after the AJ has issued an initial decision, any party may file a petition for review with the three-member, bipartisan board. * * *

> In most MSPB cases, the agency has taken an action that adversely affected the appealing employee. Generally, the board will sustain the agency's action if it is supported by a preponderance of the evidence. The board will not sustain the agency's action, even in the face of preponderant evidence, if the appellant shows that the agency's action was based on a prohibited personnel practice or was not in accordance with law, or that the agency committed harmful error in applying its procedures. * * *

> An appellant who does not prevail before the board may obtain judicial review. Unless the case includes certain discrimination claims or is a Hatch Act case involving state or local government employees, the reviewing court is the U.S. Court of Appeals for the Federal Circuit. The Federal Circuit will set aside an MSPB decision if it finds it to be (1) arbitrary, capricious, an abuse of discretion, or otherwise not in accordance with law; (2) obtained without procedures required by law, rule or regulation having been followed; or (3) unsupported by substantial evidence.

Jeffrey Gauger, Bosley v. Merit Systems Protection Board: *Reviving the Waiver Test,* 8 Fed. Cir. Bar J. 9, 10–12 (1999). *See also* Daniel R. Levinson, *The Federal Circuit and Federal Personnel Law,* 14 Geo. Mason U. L. Rev. 537 (1992). On federal civil service, see generally Peter B. Broida, *A Guide to Merit Systems Protection Board Law and Practice* (21st ed., 2004).

The uniformity of the federal civil service system has been somewhat fragmented by the congressional creation in 2002 of the Department of Homeland Security, which was granted authority to establish its own human resources management system, Homeland Security Act of 2002, Pub. L. No. 107–296, Title VIII, § 841, 116 Stat. 2135, 2229 (codified at 6 U.S.C. § 411), and by the subsequent authorization by Congress in 2003 for the Department of Defense likewise to develop its own personnel system for its civilian employees, National Defense Authorization Act for Fiscal Year 2004, Pub. L. No. 108–135, Title XI, § 1101(a)(1), 117 Stat. 1392, 1621–31 (codified at 5 U.S.C. § 9902). These two statutes collectively removed some 30 percent of the federal workforce from the direct parameters of the CSRA. Sarah T. Zaffina, Note, *For Whom the Bell Tolls: The New Human Resources Management System at the Department of Homeland Security Sounds the Death Knell for a Uniform Civil Service,* 14 Fed. Cir. Bar J. 705, 710, 739 (2005). However, while the Department of Homeland Security has established an internal appeals board for cases in which an employee is removed for certain serious offenses having "a direct and substantial adverse impact" on the department's security mission, 5 C.F.R. § 9701.607, most personnel matters in that department remain subject to administrative appeal to the MSPB. Moreover, judicial review of adverse personnel actions by the Federal Circuit under the CSRA has not been displaced. 5 C.F.R. § 9701.707(e). Accordingly, in terms of court litigation, the judicial review process under the CSRA, and its exclusivity as discussed below, remains largely unaltered.

2.   The question presented in *United States v. Fausto* is whether there remains any room under the Tucker Act for civilian employment disputes after the enactment of the CSRA. As you read *Fausto,* consider how such an employment dispute would have been procedurally handled for most federal employees. Why was Fausto excluded from this process? To fully understand the statutory background, you should outline the categories of federal civilian employees. Because Fausto was not covered by CSRA procedures for administrative appeal to the Merit Systems Protection Board and judicial review by the Federal Circuit, what other remedies, if any, were available? Is a backpay claim in the Court of Federal Claims—the traditional Tucker Act remedy for federal employment disputes—permissible for Fausto? What harm does the Court believe would result to the CSRA scheme if Fausto and others similarly situated were allowed to seek judicial review under other statutes?

3.   The Civil Service Reform Act is the sole avenue for judicial review of adverse personnel decisions for federal civilian employees—with three key exceptions:

a.   *Employment Discrimination.* Employment discrimination claims raise complex questions of alternative remedies, which may be pursued both within and outside the CSRA scheme. *See generally* Ernest C. Hadley, *A Guide to Federal Sector Equal Employment Law and Practice* (17th ed., 2005). As discussed previously in this casebook (see Chapter III.C), federal employees are protected against employment discrimination and have an alternative right to judicial review under various employment discrimination statutes.

b.   *Federal Labor Relations Law.* For federal employees in a labor union-represented bargaining unit, alternative procedures for employment disputes—negotiated grievance or unfair labor practice procedures—may be available, under the administrative purview of the Federal Labor Relations Authority (FLRA), 5 U.S.C. §§ 7101–7135. Grievance arbitration decisions by the FLRA ordinarily are not reviewable by the courts; unfair labor practice decisions by the FLRA may be appealed to the appropriate federal court of appeals.

c.   *Overtime Compensation.* Claims for overtime compensation or calculation of pay unrelated to an adverse personnel action may be heard in the Court of Federal Claims under the Tucker Act (or in the district court under the Little Tucker Act). Because the Merit Systems Protection Board does not have jurisdiction over cases involving calculation of pay for federal employees who have not suffered an underlying adverse personnel action, overtime compensation cases ordinarily fall outside of the CSRA. The Federal Circuit and the Court of Federal Claims have held that the Tucker Act remains as the jurisdictional statute when another statute provides the right to employee compensation and the underlying personnel action is not one related to individual performance as is exclusively covered by the CSRA. *See, e.g., Bosco v. United States*, 976 F.2d 710, 714 (Fed. Cir. 1992); *Hannon v. United States*, 48 Fed. Cl. 15, 24–25 (2000); *Worthington v. United States*, 41 Fed. Cl. 181, 185 (1998), *rev'd on other grounds*, 168 F.3d 24 (Fed. Cir. 1999). Thus, for example, the Court of Federal Claims hears claims by civilian government employees for overtime compensation and benefits in accordance with such statutes as the Fair Labor Standards Act, 29 U.S.C. §§ 201–219, the Federal Employees Pay Act, 5 U.S.C. §§ 5542, 5543, and the Federal Law Enforcement Pay Reform Act, Pub. L. No. 101–509, §§ 401–412, 104 Stat. 1389, 1465–69 (1990) (codified as amended in scattered sections of 5 U.S.C.).

As a particularly pertinent example for this course of an overtime compensation case, in late 1998, a class action suit was filed in the Court of Federal Claims on behalf of some 12,000 current and former Department of Justice attorneys alleging that the department had failed to provide over-time pay as required by the Federal Employees Pay Act (FEPA), and seeking $500 million in damages. David E. Rovella, *Overtime Suit Roils DOJ*, Nat'l L.J., May 24, 1999, at A4. Given that FEPA contemplates payment to employees for overtime hours, it constitutes a money-mandat-ing statute for purposes of a Tucker Act claim. *Doe v. United States,* 47 Fed. Cl. 594 (Fed. Cl. 2000) (denying motion to dismiss and holding that FEPA is a money-mandating statute giving rise to Tucker Act jurisdiction). The Department of Justice contended that it was obliged to pay overtime compensation only when excess hours were worked by attorneys at the specific request of superiors. The plaintiffs claimed that overtime work was performed by Department of Justice attorneys with the knowledge and at the encouragement (even inducement) of their superiors. Rovella, *supra.*

This litigation is of particular interest to us in this course for several reasons. First, it is an example of the limited availability of the Tucker Act for employment-related claims. The specific provisions of FEPA provided a basis for seeking judicial relief outside of the CSRA process. Second, the plaintiffs suing the government in this case are themselves attorneys within the Department of Justice and thus include those who ordinarily defend the government against suit (and whose role was a primary focus of Chapter II of this casebook). Indeed, Department of Justice attorneys were on both sides of the lawsuit, as attorneys from the Civil Division have to defend the government in the Court of Federal Claims suit. Third, the suit prompted many government attorneys to reconsider how they think of themselves and their work. The Department of Justice traditionally has taken the position that paying overtime is "at odds with a culture of professionalism," and, indeed, at least some department attorneys appar-ently resent the idea of being seen as "clock-punchers." Rovella, *supra.* Before the Court of Federal Claims, the government argued that "treating lawyers professionally, rather than as hourly workers, is consistent with the way the attorneys see themselves," and that allowing attorneys discretion in determining how to arrange the work day is one of the factors that "makes the Department so attractive to its highly qualified lawyers in the first place." *Doe v. United States*, 54 Fed. Cl. 404, 417 (Fed. Cl. 2002) (quoting government brief). However, evidence was presented that Department supervisors well understood that overtime work was necessary and expected. *Id.* at 414. The plaintiffs argued that the Department has exploited their attorney-employees' sense of duty, exacted unduly long work hours for no monetary reward, and come to expect every attorney regularly to work overtime. Rovella, *supra*.

In 2003, the Court of Federal Claims ruled that the Department had ordered or approved overtime and thus that the attorneys were owed overtime pay. *Doe*, 54 Fed. Cl. at 405. However, in 2004, the Federal Circuit reversed, citing an Office of Personnel Management regulation that provided that overtime work must be formally authorized and approved in writing to qualify for compensation and rejecting the plaintiffs' argument that Department of Justice manuals stating that overtime work by attorneys is expected should be treated as providing the requisite written approval. *Doe v. United States*, 372 F.3d 1347, 1357–62 (Fed. Cir. 2004). In the interim, Congress enacted legislation prohibiting the payment of overtime compensation to Department of Justice attorneys, thus apparently adopting the Department's policy position with respect to the subject. *See* Department of Justice Appropriations Act, Pub. L. No. 106–113, § 1000(a)(1), 113 Stat. 1501, 1535, 1501A–21 (1999).

————

c. MILITARY EMPLOYMENT CLAIMS

Military Pay Act, 37 United States Code § 204(a)

(a) The following persons are entitled to the basic pay of the pay grade to which assigned or distributed, in accordance with their years of service computed under section 205 of this title—

(1) a member of a uniformed service who is on active duty; and

(2) a member of a uniformed service, or a member of the National Guard who is not a Reserve of the Army or the Air Force, who is participating in full-time training, training duty with pay, or other full-time duty, provided by law, including participation in exercises or the performance of duty * * *.

————

Tucker Act (Remand Act), 28 United States Code § 1491(a)(2)

(2) To provide an entire remedy and to complete the relief afforded by the judgment, the [United States Court of Federal Claims] may, as an

incident of and collateral to any such judgment, issue orders directing restoration to office or position, placement in appropriate duty or retirement status, and correction of applicable records, and such orders may be issued to any appropriate official of the United States. In any case within its jurisdiction, the court shall have the power to remand appropriate matters to any administrative or executive body or official with such direction as it may deem proper and just. * * *

Richey v. United States

United States Court of Appeals for the Federal Circuit.
322 F.3d 1317 (Fed.Cir. 2003).

■ DYK, CIRCUIT JUDGE.

The United States ("the government") appeals from the United States Court of Federal Claims' grant of summary judgment in favor of the appellee, Stephen W. Richey ("Richey").

Richey, a former Army officer, sought reinstatement to active duty, alleging that he was denied promotion due to two erroneous Officer Evaluation Reports ("OERs"). The court ordered the reinstatement to active duty of Richey, because the Army Board for the Correction of Military Records ("the Corrections Board") failed to comply with that court's earlier order to make specific findings of fact and conclusions of law regarding, *inter alia*, the alleged nexus between an erroneous 1989 OER and the Army's failure to promote Richey. *Richey v. United States,* 50 Fed.Cl. 3, 17 (Fed.Cl.2001) (*"Richey II"*). We hold that the Court of Federal Claims was without authority to require the Corrections Board to make such findings; that the court failed to comply with this court's decision in *Porter v. United States,* 163 F.3d 1304 (Fed.Cir.1998), *cert. denied,* 528 U.S. 809 (1999); that the Corrections Board properly referred the matter of Richey's promotion to a series of Special Selection Boards ("SSBs"); and that Richey has not shown that the SSB decisions were arbitrary and capricious or contrary to law. We accordingly reverse, and remand with instructions to dismiss the complaint with prejudice.

BACKGROUND

This case has a tortuous history. * * * We simply summarize here the relevant facts.

Richey, a former captain in the Regular Army, received two adverse OERs while in the service. The first OER covered the period from December 3, 1988, through September 15, 1989 ("1989 OER"), during which time Richey was a Squadron Maintenance Officer stationed at Fort Bliss, Texas. One of Richey's raters, Major Stephen M. Speakes ("Speakes"), stated in the 1989 OER that Richey "was just not the man for the job and it showed. He would be better utilized in a concepts and doctrinal line of work where his intellect could be better utilized." The second OER covered the period from January 29, 1991, through April 18, 1991 ("1991 OER"), during which time Richey was serving in Southwest Asia in Operation Desert Storm. In the 1991 OER, Richey was rated below the average of his contemporaries.

While still in the service, Richey unsuccessfully petitioned the Officer Special Review Board ("OSRB") for the removal of both OERs. Richey alleged that the 1989 OER was erroneous due to a hostile relationship between Richey and his rater, Speakes, and because he was not responsible for the inefficiency and incompetence of the regiment. With regard to the 1991 OER, Richey contended that the senior rater had incorrectly evaluated the comparison of Richey with other officers of the same grade under Army Reg. 623–105 ¶ 4–16(b), because the senior rater had generally rated other officers too high, such that the rated scores did not fall along a bell curve. The OSRB denied Richey's petitions for removal of the OERs.

Richey then appealed the OSRB's denials to the Corrections Board, which denied relief. On April 1, 1996, after twice being passed over for promotion to the rank of major by selection boards that considered the adverse OERs, Richey received an involuntary honorable discharge, pursuant to the Army's "up or out" policy.

Richey filed suit in the Court of Federal Claims on July 15, 1997, claiming that the discharge was improper because it was the result of the two allegedly erroneous OERs. *Id.* at 4. While the case was pending, on November 9, 1998, we issued our decision in *Porter,* 163 F.3d at 1323–24. Before *Porter,* as discussed in greater detail below, this court's precedent required that, in a suit claiming relief on account of wrongful separation or relief from active duty, two elements had to be established in order for the plaintiff to prevail: "(a) there was a material legal error or an injustice in the proceedings of the correction board, or other entity within the military department, which led to the adverse action against [the plaintiff], and also (b) that there is an adequate nexus or link between the error or injustice and the adverse action." *Hary v. United States,* 223 Ct.Cl. 10, 618 F.2d 704, 706 (1980), *superseded by statute as stated in Porter,* 163 F.3d at 1323–24; *see also Sanders v. United States,* 219 Ct.Cl. 285, 594 F.2d 804, 815 (1979) (*en banc*). In *Porter* we held that the enactment of 10 U.S.C. § 628 superseded this precedent, insofar as that precedent required proof of lack of causation in all cases. We held that under section 628, once it is determined that the initial promotion board's decision involved administrative error, the matter should be referred to a Special Selection Board ("SSB") for a determination of whether to promote the officer based on a military record purged of the error, and that an SSB determination not to promote is dispositive.

On cross-motions for summary judgment on the administrative record, over ten months after our decision in *Porter,* the Court of Federal Claims remanded the case to the Corrections Board. In its opinion, the court failed to rely on or even cite to our controlling opinion in *Porter.* Instead, the court concluded that in order to determine whether Richey's removal was improper, it was required to apply the two-part test of *Hary,* the decision effectively overruled by section 628. The court determined that it could not apply the *Hary* test with regard to the 1989 OER, because the Board's opinion was "vague and conclusory." The court found that "the administrative record is deficient in that this court cannot properly determine from said record the merits of Mr. Richey's contentions." The court, therefore, remanded to the Corrections Board with instructions to make specific, numbered findings of fact and conclusions of law regarding "external circumstances that could have affected Mr. Richey's job performance," "the degree to which the rater was biased against Mr. Richey," and the nexus between the 1989 OER and Richey's non-promotion.

The court found that the 1991 OER was tainted with error. Following *Hary,* the court ordered the Corrections Board "to make findings regarding the nexus between the 1991 OER, which we find to be in error, and Mr. Richey's nonpromotion." The court retained jurisdiction over the case and deferred ruling on the motions for summary judgment "until the Corrections Board's factual findings and legal conclusions on remand are presented to this court." The court also ordered the government "to file with the court every 30 days a status report regarding the proceedings on remand."

On remand, after holding an evidentiary hearing, the Corrections Board determined that the 1991 OER was "substantially inaccurate because of procedural error on the part of the senior rater" in comparing Richey with officers of the same grade. Therefore, the Corrections Board ordered that the 1991 OER be corrected to award Richey a " 'top block' or highest rating for the period." The Corrections Board initially determined that the 1989 OER "was not substantially inaccurate," but the Assistant Secretary of Army Review Boards ("the Secretary") overruled this determination and ordered that the 1989 OER be deleted from Richey's record. Thus, both OERs were determined to be erroneous. However, rather than determining whether there was a nexus between the erroneous OERs and Richey's non-promotion, the Corrections Board submitted Richey's military record to four separate SSBs, pursuant to 10 U.S.C. § 628(b), for a decision as to whether Richey should be promoted to the rank of Major.

The first two SSBs considered Richey's military record with the correction of the 1991 OER as ordered by the Board, but without the deletion of the 1989 OER, and denied Richey's application for promotion. The second two SSBs considered Richey's military record with both the 1989 OER deleted and the 1991 OER corrected, but also declined to promote Richey. Pursuant to section 628, the SSBs submitted written reports to the Secretary that were signed by each member of the Board and certified that "[t]he board, acting under oath and having in view the special fitness of an officer and the efficiency of the Army, has carefully considered the record of every officer whose name was furnished to it under Section 628, Title 10."

Throughout the period of time between the Court of Federal Claims' first remand of August 26, 1999, and the decision on appeal of July 18, 2001, the court required the government to file monthly status reports regarding the progress of the remand proceedings. During this period the court remanded the case back to the Corrections Board an additional three times, on November 21, 2000, February 21, 2001, and June 26, 2001, in order to "request[ ] certain specific findings which were either not made by the [Board] or not submitted to the court." On June 29, 2001, the government submitted to the court the SSB decisions denying Richey promotion on his corrected military record. The government also filed with the court copies of Richey's complete military record as it appeared before each of the four SSBs.

On this record, the Court of Federal Claims considered anew the cross motions for judgment on the administrative record. Once again, despite our decision in *Porter,* the court stated its conclusion that it was bound to apply the two-part test articulated in *Hary.* With regard to the 1991 OER, the court determined that although the government "has not, as per our previous orders, submitted to the court any document clearly indicating what standards the SSBs applied in rendering their decisions," it would "defer to [the SSBs'] ultimate conclusion that Capt. Richey would still not have been promoted in 1994 and 1995 [absent the erroneous 1991 OER]."

With regard to the 1989 OER, however, the court came to a different conclusion. The court found that the Corrections Board had failed to address the second (nexus) element of *Hary,* as the court had directed in its remand order. The court noted, "[t]his question regarding the 'nexus' between the erroneous and adverse 1989 OER and Capt. Richey's nonpromotion ('the harmless error' test) was responded to by the [Corrections Board] in a conclusory fashion." Because of this omission, the court found, "we are unable to properly determine if the clear legal error committed by defendant was 'harmless error' to Capt. Richey under the *Hary* test enunciated by our first opinion in this case." The court further found that it could not determine if the non-promotion decisions of the SSBs were proper, because "the text of the four (4) SSBs' decisions do[es] not show what standards they used and how they justified making their determination denying Capt. Richey's application for promotion." The court stated that "the SSBs' decisions submitted to us were wholly conclusory and, apparently, a 'rubber stamping' of the [Board's] ultimate conclusion to deny Capt. Richey Relief." The court expressed doubt that an additional remand would "likely generate answers to our questions previously posed to [the government]."

Therefore, the court decided, "we will render a decision herein with what we have before us." The court then concluded that because the 1989 OER was tainted with legal error and because of the failure of the Board to address the "nexus" question, it would grant Richey the following relief:

> [Richey] shall be reinstated to his former position of Captain in the Regular Army from the date of this invalid honorable discharge until such time as his record is properly passed upon by a Special Selection Board, or other duly authorized body, with a reasoned and fully expressed decision indicating that his application for promotion or permanent rank was evaluated fairly as required by law. Additionally, we order that any subsequent decision by the Army regarding any

prospective request by Capt. Richey for promotion is not to be applied retroactively to a date prior to this opinion.

The court also awarded Richey all attendant back pay and benefits from the date of his discharge to the date of the court's opinion, an after-tax payment in the amount of $113,638.18, and "all additional relief as determined by the Secretary of the Army and to which plaintiff is entitled.".

For the first time the court addressed the conflict between its approach and our decision in *Porter*. The court recognized that "[o]ur ruling here, however, is in some conflict with a portion of the *Porter* decision." But the court evidently disagreed with *Porter*'s reading of the statute. After summarizing the holding of *Porter*, the court stated that the rule of *Porter* constituted "a position we reject because of the plain language of 10 U.S.C. § 628 and the distinguishing facts of this case." Specifically the court took issue with *Porter*'s holding that SSB decisions relate back to and stand in the place of original promotion board decisions, stating, "we do not believe 10 U.S.C. § 628 requires a relation back in all instances." The court attempted to distinguish *Porter* on the grounds that in *Porter*, the court "apparently, had a complete record before it," whereas, in contrast, "[w]e have no such decision; we have only naked conclusions made by the SSBs involved, stated to us as four (4), nearly identical, one-page decisions." The court therefore held that in the present case, the failure of the Corrections Board to demonstrate harmless error would result in the reinstatement of Richey.

The government timely appealed. We have jurisdiction pursuant to 28 U.S.C. § 1295(a)(3). "We review the grant or denial of motions for summary judgment upon the administrative record without deference." *Info. Tech. & Applications Corp. v. United States*, 316 F.3d 1312, 1318 (Fed.Cir. 2003).

DISCUSSION

I

There is no longer any issue here concerning the erroneous nature of the 1989 and 1991 OERs, and there is no question but that these OERs were improperly considered by the original selection boards that declined to promote Richey. The first question in this case is whether the Court of Federal Claims had authority to require the Corrections Board to make findings regarding the nexus between Richey's erroneous OERs and Richey's non-promotion. We hold that under our decision in *Porter*, it did not.

Congress has given the military secretaries the power to correct military records using civilian Corrections Boards. 10 U.S.C. § 1552(a)(1). An officer seeking correction of military records may either apply as an initial matter to a Corrections Board, or file suit under the Tucker Act in the Court of Federal Claims. If an officer elects to pursue a remedy before the Corrections Board, after the Board renders a final decision, the officer may effectively obtain review of that decision in the Court of Federal

Claims by filing suit under the Tucker Act. Typically, if suit is filed just in the Court of Federal Claims, that court will require resort to a Corrections Board while the matter remains pending in that court.

The Tucker Act, as amended, gives the Court of Federal Claims the authority "to remand appropriate matters to any administrative or executive body or official with such direction as it may deem proper and just." 28 U.S.C. § 1491(a)(2). But this provision does not give the Court of Federal Claims unlimited authority to require subordinate bodies to conduct investigations and find facts. Any remand must be consistent with the statutory scheme under which the agency has taken action. In the present case, the Court of Federal Claims' remand to the agency requiring it to make a nexus finding went beyond its authority, because under 10 U.S.C. § 628(b), in cases such as this, the Corrections Board should not make a nexus finding, but rather should refer the officer's military record, purged of its errors, to an SSB for a determination of whether the officer should be promoted.

Before the enactment of section 628 in 1980, our decisions in *Sanders* [and] *Hary* would have supported the action taken by the Court of Federal Claims in this case. In *Sanders,* we held that, where an officer demonstrates that his military record contains defective OERs, the ultimate burden is on the government to show that the officer would not have been promoted had his record contained no error. In *Hary,* we further refined the test of *Sanders,* holding that in order for a claimant to prevail, it must be shown that:

> (a) there was a material legal error or an injustice in the proceedings of the correction board, or other entity within the military department, which led to the adverse action against him, and also (b) that there is an adequate nexus or link between the error or injustice and the adverse action.

618 F.2d at 706.

In *Porter,* however, we held that the enactment of section 628, at least in large part,[1] had overruled those decisions, insofar as they required the government to prove harmless error. Section 628(b)(1) provides:

> If the Secretary of the military department concerned determines, in the case of a person who was considered for selection for promotion by a promotion board but was not selected, that there was material unfairness with respect to that person, the Secretary may convene a special selection board under this subsection to determine whether that person (whether or not then on active duty) should be recommended for promotion. In order to determine that there was material unfairness, the Secretary must determine that

---

1. The court in *Porter* noted, without deciding, that some types of egregious error, "such as impermissible consideration of race, sex or religion, or instances of an illegally composed selection board," might justify the Board in voiding the non-promotion decision and the discharge without referring the matter to a Special Selection Board. 163 F.3d at 1321. The present case does not involve these types of error.

(A) the action of the promotion board that considered the person was contrary to law or involved material administrative error; or

(B) the board did not have before it for its consideration material information.

10 U.S.C. § 628(b)(1). The statute prescribes how an SSB should make the promotion decision:

A special selection board convened under paragraph (1) shall consider the record of the person whose name was referred to it for consideration as that record, if corrected, would have appeared to the board that considered him. That record shall be compared with the records of a sampling of those officers of the same competitive category who were recommended for promotion, and those officers who were not recommended for promotion, by the board that considered him.

10 U.S.C. § 628(b)(2). Upon reaching a decision, the statute requires that the SSB submit a written report to the "Secretary of the military department concerned," which is "signed by each member of the board, containing the name of each person it recommends for promotion and certifying that the board has carefully considered the record of each person whose name was referred to it." 10 U.S.C. § 628(c).

In *Porter* we held that once it is determined that the initial selection board's decision "involved material administrative error," nothing in this statute requires the Secretary, acting through the Corrections Board, to make a harmless error determination. Instead, under the statute, as interpreted in *Porter,* the Corrections Board should refer the matter to an SSB, which decides whether to promote the officer based on his corrected military record, and, therefore, "the harmless error rule has no application."

Once the SSB renders a decision, review of that decision is available by the Corrections Board and, thereafter under section 628, by the Court of Federal Claims under essentially an Administrative Procedure Act standard of review:

A court of the United States may review the action of a special selection board convened under this section or an action of the Secretary of the military department concerned on the report of such a board. In any such case, a court may set aside the action only if the court finds that the action was—

(A) arbitrary or capricious;

(B) not based on substantial evidence;

(C) a result of material error of fact or material administrative error; or

(D) otherwise contrary to law.

10 U.S.C.A. § 628(g)(2).

On the Court of Federal Claims' remand in this case, the Corrections Board exactly followed the procedure provided for in the statute and described in *Porter*. The Corrections Board determined that the 1991 OER was erroneous and that the 1989 OER was not erroneous. The Corrections Board then convened two SSBs to review Richey's military record as corrected. Neither SSB selected Richey for promotion. After the Secretary determined that the 1989 OER was also substantially erroneous, the Corrections Board convened two additional SSBs to consider Richey for promotion based on a completely purged military record. Neither of these SSBs selected Richey for promotion. The Court of Federal Claims had no authority to order the Corrections Board to make a finding on the issue of causation and then to grant Richey summary judgment, based on the Corrections Board's failure to make a causation finding. The Corrections Board was not required to make a causation finding and was entitled to refer the matter to the SSBs under section 628 and our decision in *Porter*.[2]

II

The question remains whether the decisions of the SSBs not to promote Richey were erroneous. Richey claims that they were. However, Richey fails to raise a substantial issue for two separate reasons.

First, Richey, by his own admission, failed to request review of the SSB decisions at the Corrections Board, before returning to the Court of Federal Claims. There is no question that such a remedy is available. We observed in *Porter* that "[i]f an officer meets an SSB unsuccessfully and can point to a material flaw in the SSB's procedures arguably undermining the SSB's nonselection judgment, he may petition the corrections board to alter or void the SSB's decision." 163 F.3d at 1325. Generally in military discharge cases, there is no requirement that a claimant exhaust his remedies before the Corrections Board before seeking relief in the Court of Federal Claims under the Tucker Act. As we stated in *Heisig*, "although relief has usually been first sought from military correction boards since their creation in 1946, there is here no requirement of exhaustion of administrative remedies *prior to pursuit of judicial review*." [*Heisig v. United States*,] 719 F.2d [1153,] 1155 [(Fed.Cir.1983)] (emphasis added). However, where, as here, the administrative process is initiated after judicial relief has been sought and is still pending, a claimant must exhaust the Corrections Board process before returning to the Court of Federal Claims. * * * Exhaustion of the agency procedures in such circumstances serves "the twin purposes ... of protecting administrative agency authority and promoting judicial efficiency." *Sandvik Steel Co. v. United States*, 164 F.3d 596, 600 (Fed.Cir.1998) (citation omitted).

2. The Court of Federal Claims attempted to distinguish *Porter* on the grounds that in *Porter*, the court had before it "a complete, if not procedurally correct, SSB decision." The court held that in contrast, "[w]e have no such decision; we have only naked conclusions made by the SSBs involved." This is factually incorrect. The SSB decisions at issue in *Porter* apparently were no more elaborate in stating the bases for their decisions than the SSB decisions here. In any event, the Court of Federal Claims was obligated to follow *Porter*'s interpretation of the statute even if it believed that the facts of *Porter* itself were distinguishable.

Second, the record before the Court of Federal Claims here does not contain evidence to overcome the presumption of regularity that attaches to all administrative decisions. The Court of Federal Claims, in ordering Richey's reinstatement, noted that "the[ ] written decisions [of the SSBs] still do not fully answer the court's questions posed to defendants in [its] three prior remand orders." The court further observed that "the SSBs' decisions submitted to [it] were wholly conclusory and, apparently, a 'rubber stamping' of the [Corrections Board's] ultimate conclusion to deny Capt. Richey relief." In particular, the court determined that the SSB reports were deficient, because:

> we do not even know if the SSBs followed the dictates of 10 U.S.C. § 628(b), which requires all Special Selection Boards to specifically indicate: "that [the] record [of plaintiff's employment history] shall be compared with the records of a sampling of those officers of the same competitive category who were recommended for promotion, and those officers who were not recommended for promotion by the board that considered him."

[*Richey II,* 50 Fed.Cl. at 18] (emphasis in original) (quoting 10 U.S.C. § 628(b)).

But the statute imposes no requirement on the SSBs to provide detailed findings, and the SSB reports here complied with the statutory requirements. Section 628 provides:

> Each special selection board convened under this section shall submit to the Secretary of the military department concerned a written report, signed by each member of the board, containing the name of each person it recommends for promotion and certifying that the board has carefully considered the record of each person whose name was referred to it.

10 U.S.C. § 628(c)(1) (2000). The SSBs that declined to promote Richey on his corrected military record submitted reports to the Secretary that met these certification requirements. The SSB reports certified that "[t]he board, acting under oath and having in view the special fitness of an officer and the efficiency of the Army, has carefully considered the record of every officer whose name was furnished to it *under Section 628, Title 10.*" The court could not require the SSBs to meet additional reporting requirements beyond those that were mandated by the statute. * * *[4]

This limitation on the Court of Federal Claims' authority has particular force in cases involving the military. As we observed in *Porter:*

---

4. It is also worth noting that even if the Court of Federal claims had properly found error in the decisions of the SSBs, the remedy would not have been reinstatement. Rather, the required remedy is provided by statute:

> If a court finds that the action of a special selection board which considers an officer or former officer was contrary to law or involved material error of fact or material administrative error, it shall remand the case to the Secretary concerned, who shall provide the officer or former officer reconsideration by a new special selection board.

10 U.S.C. § 14502.

The reluctance of the judiciary to review promotion actions of selection boards is rooted not only in the court's incurable lack of knowledge of the total grist which the boards sift, but also in a preference not to meddle with the internal workings of the military. . . . The promotion of an officer in the military service is a highly specialized function involving military requirements of the service and the qualifications of the officer in comparison with his contemporaries, plus expertise and judgment possessed only by the military. No court is in a position to resolve and pass upon the highly complicated questions and problems involved in the promotion procedure.

Porter, 163 F.3d at 1316–17.

III

Finally, under *Porter,* the existence of error in the original promotion board decisions does not entitle the appellant to any relief. Contrary to the Court of Federal Claims' view, section 628, as interpreted in *Porter,* requires retroactivity. In *Porter,* we made clear that the decision of a Special Selection Board "relate[s] back to the date of the original selection board's decision" and "stand[s] in place of the earlier selection board decision." *Id.* at 1315. The court based this conclusion on a construction of the statutory language. First, section 628(b)(2) provides that the SSB "shall consider the record of the person . . . as that record, if corrected, would have appeared to the board that considered him." 10 U.S.C. § 628(b)(2). Second, section (d)(2) states that a person who is selected for promotion by an SSB,

shall, upon that appointment, have the same date of rank, the same effective date for the pay and allowances of that that grade, and the same position on the active-duty list as he would have had if he had been recommended for promotion to that grade by the board which should have considered, or which did consider, him.

10 U.S.C. § 628(d)(2). In *Porter,* we read these statutory provisions as clearly requiring that the decision of an SSB be retroactive and stand in the place of the earlier promotion board decision. In this case, Richey won the relief of review for promotion by two SSBs examining a record purged of error. The decisions of those SSBs replaced the decisions of the original promotion boards that passed Richey over for promotion when he was in the service. The SSB decisions cannot, therefore, be challenged on the basis of errors in the earlier promotion decisions that have now been purged from Richey's military record.

CONCLUSION

Accordingly, we reverse the decision of the Court of Federal Claims and remand with directions that the complaint be dismissed with prejudice.

REVERSED AND REMANDED.

Notes and Questions

1. As with civilian employment claims against the federal government, military employment claims are governed by statute, not by contract. *Schism v. United States*, 316 F.3d 1259, 1271 (Fed. Cir. 2002) (en banc). Although the Civil Service Reform Act now occupies most of the field for civilian employment claims, as we saw in the preceding part of this casebook, the Tucker Act continues to be the primary vehicle for military employment claims. While the Back Pay Act, 5 U.S.C. § 5596(b)(1), does not apply to members of the armed forces, a parallel statutory provision, often called the Military Pay Act, 37 U.S.C. § 204(a), plays a similar role for military servicemembers who are involuntarily separated from service. Like the civilian service Back Pay Act, the Military Pay Act is a money-mandating statute triggering Tucker Act jurisdiction and providing that members of the service are entitled to the basic compensation for their pay grade. As the United States Court of Appeals for the Federal Circuit sitting en banc held in *Martinez v. United States*, 333 F.3d 1295, 1315 (Fed. Cir. 2003) (en banc), "the source of the right to back pay" in military employment cases brought in the Court of Federal Claims under the Tucker Act comes from a money-mandating statute such as the Military Pay Act.

2. To fully understand the opinion in *Richey v. United States*, you need to recognize that two different, but interrelated, military boards were at work in the case and that the court's review of the actions of each board differs:

> *Selection Board*. Decisions concerning promotion in rank are made by Selection Boards in each of the branches of the armed forces. (As discussed further below, a variation on the Selection Board comes into play when it is determined that an initial consideration of a promotion was based on erroneous records, thus resulting in submission of the matter to a Special Selection Board.) However, the courts generally disclaim any authority to directly review the denial of a promotion by the Selection Board. Thus, rather than or in addition to challenging the promotion decision directly, a typical military pay claim may allege that the decision was made based upon an inaccurate evidentiary record, an issue that the courts are somewhat more comfortable addressing, and which implicates the work of the other board.

> *Board for Correction of Military Records*. A military service member who is discharged or dismissed ordinarily will first seek relief in the form of correction of his or her service evaluation records before the Board for Correction of Military Records for that branch of the armed services. "This is a civilian body within the military service, with broad-ranging authority to review a servicemember's 'discharge or dismissal (other than a discharge or dismissal by sentence of a general court-martial),' 10 U.S.C. § 1553(a), or 'to correct an error or remove an injustice' in a military record, § 1552(a)(1)." *Clinton v. Goldsmith*, 526 U.S. 529, 538 (1999). On the administrative process for correction of military records, see generally Mark L. Waple, *Is There Adequate Due Process for Military Personnel*, 42 Fed. Lawyer 22, 24–25 (1995);

Charles A. Shanor & L. Lynn Hogue, *Military Law in a Nutshell* 314–15 (2d ed. 1996). When the service member is separated from the military upon failure to be promoted, a claim for backpay and restoration to position is then combined with a collateral request for correction of the military records, thus asking the court to review the underlying failure of the Board for Correction of Military Records to change the record information.

Much of the complexity that arises in military pay cases which involve a promotion denial, such as the *Richey* case, flows from the efforts of the courts to walk a tight-rope between exercising the power to review the procedural requirements while carefully not intruding upon the ultimate discretion of the military services in deciding whether or not to promote a particular individual. The court generally lacks the authority to directly review the merits of the denial of a promotion. Yet for Tucker Act jurisdiction to lie, the claim must be one for money and thus must be grounded upon the discharge from the military. Moreover, the court's power to review and potentially order correction of military records under the Remand Act is dependent upon the validity of the underlying claim for backpay under the Military Pay Act. However, the servicemember was separated from the service precisely because he or she was not promoted. For that reason, the court's review of the separation decision necessarily, albeit indirectly, is a review of the promotion decision. Thus, the courts tend to approach the problem indirectly, focusing upon procedural errors and problems with the military records, while stepping back from the ultimate promotion decision itself and at most ensuring that the process be repeated. A good part of the controversy in the *Richey* case is whether the Court of Federal Claims intruded too far into the process, although even that court did not go so far as to order a promotion.

In *Richey*, what did the Court of Federal Claims demand from the Correction Board? What showing did the Court of Federal Claims expect from the government with respect to the reconsideration of the promotion decisions and with respect to the now-admitted erroneous military records? Do you see that the Court of Federal Claims essentially is trying to return the process to "square one" by ordering that erroneous records be purged and demanding that a new Selection Board review the promotion on a cleansed record (that is, without knowledge of the earlier mistakes in the record)? Why does the Federal Circuit reverse the Court of Federal Claims? What statutory change has altered the process and how? Notice as well the relief that the Court of Federal Claims granted (reinstatement to prior military rank). Why does the Federal Circuit reverse that part of the judgment as well?

The approach followed by and the relief granted by the Court of Federal Claims in *Richey* is that which was followed for many years by the courts. As the Federal Circuit explains in *Richey*, however, Congress in 2000 established a special process to evaluate promotion prospects in the specific context where an individual was passed-over for promotion in the ordinary process but the Correction Board later determines that there were errors in the record upon which the Selection Board made its decision. Under 10 U.S.C. § 628, the Correction Board, upon determining that a servicemember's record was faulty, may recommend to the Secretary of the pertinent branch of the armed forces that a Special Selection Board (SSB) be convened to review the matter. The SSB participates in the records correction process itself and is charged with reviewing the original promotion prospects of the officer, that is, determining whether the officer would have been promoted by the original Selection Board absent the error in the record. *Porter v. United States,* 163 F.3d 1304, 1325 (Fed.Cir. 1998). In other words, the SSB framework makes it unnecessary to repeat the process and instead allows the special body to evaluate what has gone before and either confirm the original decision to deny promotion or grant promotion. As affirmed by the Federal Circuit's *Porter* decision, if "the officer is not promoted by the special selection board, but is instead nonselected for promotion again, the [military department] presumes the SSB's action ratifies and retroactively cures the earlier defective nonselection." Russell O. Wheeler, *The Secretary of the Air Force, Correction of Military Records and the Limits of Discretion,* 7 Fed. Cir. Bar J. 193, 196 (1997) (describing and criticizing the military's understanding of the SSB process).

Because of the existence of the SSB procedure and because it is designed to retroactively correct any historical error, the Federal Circuit also has explained that reinstatement of a discharged servicemember and automatic voidance of prior passovers generally should not be granted. *Roth v. United States,* 378 F.3d 1371, 1393–95 (Fed.Cir. 2004). First, as noted, if the SSB determines that the original denial of promotion was appropriate, even in light of the errors in the record, then the servicemember's proper separation from service is confirmed; of course, if the SSB grants promotion, then the servicemember will be reinstated to active military service, promoted, and granted backpay. Second, because the SSB acts as part of the correction process, it need not always be shielded from knowledge of prior passovers for promotion, although the Correction Board has the flexibility to void prior passovers if it deems it necessary in a particular case. *Porter,* 163 F.3d at 1305–26. Thus, the extraordinary remedies of reinstatement and voiding of previous passovers are not necessarily required when a Special Selection Board enters into the picture under this new statutory procedure.

3. In *Richey,* the serviceman was discharged for failure to obtain a promotion (the "up or out" aspect of military service). However, servicemembers may be discharged or separated from the service for other reasons. *See generally* Shanor & Hoge, *supra,* ch. 6. Under most other circumstances, the administrative body reviewing military discharges is the Discharge Review Board. *Id.* at 313–14. The Board for Correction of Military Records may continue to be a vital part of this process as well, with power to review and correct errors in military records and erroneous discharges. *Id.* at 314–15. Judicial review may occur here as well, with the same attitude of deference toward military decisions. *Id.* at 315–17.

4. Although boards for correction of military records generally labor in obscurity to the general public, the Army Board for Correction of Military Records drew public attention for attempting to intervene in the historical controversy concerning Samuel Mudd, the physician who set John Wilkes Booth's broken leg after he shot President Abraham Lincoln. Mudd was convicted by a military court as a conspirator or an accessory after the fact to the assassination, but his descendants have always maintained his innocence and requested that the corrections board review the matter. The late-Chief Justice William H. Rehnquist, in a book on civil liberties during wartime, deprecatingly described what followed: "The board, apparently having no pressing current business, decided to look into the Mudd descendants' claim that a military commission could not have lawfully tried the physician in 1865." William H. Rehnquist, *All the Laws But One* 168 (1998). The board granted the requested relief, ruling that Mudd had been entitled to trial in a civilian court. However, that recommendation was overruled by the Assistant Secretary for the Army who, in Rehnquist's tart words, "brought the proceedings down to earth by observing that it was not the function of the board to settle historical disputes." *Id.* at 169.

5. A military servicemember who has not been separated from the service (or who has not yet suffered any loss of pay) or a veteran who was voluntarily discharged (or otherwise is not entitled to any past-due compensation) may seek correction of inaccurate service records through an action in federal district court under the Administrative Procedure Act (APA), 5 U.S.C. §§ 701–706. Without an underlying and cognizable money claim, the action may not be pursued under the Tucker Act in the Court of Federal Claims. In *Clinton v. Goldsmith*, 526 U.S. 529 (1999), the Supreme Court explained the options available to such a servicemember:

> A servicemember claiming something other than monetary relief may challenge a BCMR's decision to sustain a decision to drop him from the rolls (or otherwise dismissing him) as final agency action under the Administrative Procedure Act (APA), 5 U.S.C. § 551 et seq.; see §§ 704, 706. * * * In the instances in which a claim for monetary relief may be framed, a servicemember may enter the Court of Federal Claims with a challenge to dropping from the rolls (or other discharge) under the Tucker Act, 28 U.S.C. § 1491. * * * Or he may enter a district court under the "Little Tucker Act," 28 U.S.C. § 1346(a)(2) [for claims of $10,000 or less].

Id. at 539–40.

Consider if a servicemember were first to seek equitable or specific relief, in the form of correction of military records, in federal district court, and further assume that the court in fact ordered correction of the records. Then, with that order in hand, suppose he or she files a second suit in the Court of Federal Claims under the Tucker Act seeking backpay, asserting that the district court's order for correction of records has already established that the discharge was improperly based on erroneous records (a claim of issue preclusion). May a plaintiff split the equitable claims from the monetary claims and pursue two successive suits in this manner? What about Section 1500's prohibition of duplicative claims between the Court of Federal Claims and another court? Review the discussion of Section 1500 and the pertinent caselaw in Chapter IV.A.1.a.

In *Kidwell v. Department of the Army,* 56 F.3d 279, 284 (D.C. Cir. 1995), the United States Court of Appeals for the District of Columbia Circuit held that "[e]ven where a monetary claim may be waiting on the sidelines, so long as the plaintiff's complaint only requests non-monetary relief that has 'considerable value' independent of any future potential for monetary relief—that is, as long as the sole remedy requested is declaratory or injunctive relief that is not 'negligible in comparison' with the potential monetary recovery—we respect the plaintiff's choice of remedies and treat the complaint as something more than an artfully drafted effort to circumvent the jurisdiction of the Court of Federal Claims."

However, in *Burkins v. United States,* 112 F.3d 444 (10th Cir. 1997), the Eleventh Circuit held that the Court of Federal Claims had exclusive jurisdiction under the Tucker Act over a suit by a veteran for correction of military records to reflect a disability, rather than honorable, discharge. Even though the veteran's complaint did not seek monetary relief, the court concluded that his "prime objective" in obtaining a correction of the records was to be able to claim retroactive disability benefits (in excess of $10,000). *Id.* at 449. The Eleventh Circuit distinguished the D.C. Circuit's *Kidwell* decision, saying the veteran there had a significant non-monetary purpose in seeking a change from a general to disability-related discharge because this change " 'would lift some of the shame associated with failing to receive an honorable discharge.' " *Id.* at 450 n.5 (quoting *Kidwell,* 56 F.3d at 285).

As with the Eleventh Circuit, the Federal Circuit in *Mitchell v. United States,* 930 F.2d 893, 894–96 (Fed. Cir. 1991), affirmed the expertise and authority of the then-Claims Court to handle military employment claims, both correcting military records and affording monetary relief. In *Mitchell,* a discharged military reserve officer filed suit in district court seeking an order restoring him retroactively to active duty for an additional two years, which then would have qualified him for retirement with twenty years of service. After the district court denied the government's motion to dismiss or transfer the case to the Claims Court, the government filed an interlocutory appeal to the Federal Circuit. The Federal Circuit in *Mitchell* concluded that this was "specifically the kind of claim for which the Claims Court can provide 'special and adequate review procedures' " and thus for which the APA "direct[s] litigation away from the district courts." *Id.* at 896 (quoting Bowen v. Massachusetts, 487 U.S. 879, 900–01 n.31 (1988)). The Federal Circuit explained that the "Claims Court has explicit statutory authority, which it has exercised, to provide all relief" that the plaintiff sought, namely backpay, reinstatement, and correction of records. *Id.*

On the availability of an APA suit as an alternative to the Tucker Act for relief in military employment cases, see generally Gregory C. Sisk,

Litigation With the Federal Government § 4.06(b), at 273–79 (ALI–ABA, 4th ed., 2006).

––––––––

3.   INDIAN CLAIMS AND THE INDIAN TUCKER ACT

Indian Tucker Act, 28 United States Code § 1505

The United States Court of Federal Claims shall have jurisdiction of any claim against the United States accruing after August 13, 1946, in favor of any tribe, band, or other identifiable group of American Indians residing within the territorial limits of the United States or Alaska whenever such claim is one arising under the Constitution, laws or treaties of the United States, or Executive orders of the President, or is one which otherwise would be cognizable in the Court of Federal Claims if the claimant were not an Indian tribe, band or group.

––––––––

United States v. White Mountain Apache Tribe

Supreme Court of the United States.
537 U.S. 465 (2003).

■ JUSTICE SOUTER delivered the opinion of the Court.

The question in this case arises under the Indian Tucker Act: does the Court of Federal Claims have jurisdiction over the White Mountain Apache Tribe's suit against the United States for breach of fiduciary duty to manage land and improvements held in trust for the Tribe but occupied by the Government. We hold that it does.

I

The former military post of Fort Apache dates back to 1870 when the United States established the fort within territory that became the Tribe's reservation in 1877. In 1922, Congress transferred control of the fort to the Secretary of the Interior (Secretary) and, in 1923, set aside about 400 acres, out of some 7,000, for use as the Theodore Roosevelt Indian School. Congress attended to the fort again in 1960, when it provided by statute that "former Fort Apache Military Reservation" would be "held by the United States in trust for the White Mountain Apache Tribe, subject to the right of the Secretary of the Interior to use any part of the land and improvements for administrative or school purposes for as long as they are needed for the purpose." Pub. L. 86–392, 74 Stat. 8 (1960 Act). The Secretary exercised that right, and although the record does not catalog the uses made by the Department of the Interior, they extended to about 30 of the post's buildings and appurtenances, a few of which had been built when the Government first occupied the land. Although the National Park Service listed the fort as a national historical site in 1976, the recognition was no augury of fortune, for just over 20 years later the World Monuments Watch placed the fort on its 1998 List of 100 Most Endangered Monuments.

In 1993, the Tribe commissioned an engineering assessment of the property, resulting in a finding that as of 1998 it would cost about $14 million to rehabilitate the property occupied by the Government in accordance with standards for historic preservation. This is the amount the Tribe sought in 1999, when it sued the United States in the Court of Federal Claims, citing the terms of the 1960 Act, among others and alleging breach of fiduciary duty to "maintain, protect, repair and preserve" the trust property.

The United States moved to dismiss for failure to state a claim upon which relief might be granted and for lack of subject-matter jurisdiction. While the Government acknowledged that the Indian Tucker Act, 28 U.S.C. § 1505, invested the Court of Federal Claims with jurisdiction to render judgments in certain claims by Indian tribes against the United States, including claims based on an Act of Congress, it stressed that the waiver operated only when underlying substantive law could fairly be interpreted as giving rise to a particular duty, breach of which should be compensable in money damages. The Government contended that jurisdiction was lacking here because no statute or regulation cited by the Tribe could fairly be read as imposing a legal obligation on the Government to maintain or restore the trust property, let alone authorizing compensation for breach.

The Court of Federal Claims agreed with the United States and dismissed the complaint for lack of jurisdiction, relying primarily on the two seminal cases of tribal trust claims for damages, *United States v. Mitchell,* 445 U.S. 535 (1980) *(Mitchell I),* and *United States v. Mitchell,* 463 U.S. 206 (1983) *(Mitchell II). Mitchell I* held that the Indian General Allotment Act (Allotment Act), 24 Stat. 388, as amended, 25 U.S.C. § 331 *et seq.* (1976 ed.) (§§ 331–333 repealed 2000), providing that "the United States does and will hold the land thus allotted . . . in trust for the sole use and benefit of the Indian," established nothing more than a "bare trust" for the benefit of tribal members. The general trust provision established no duty of the United States to manage timber resources, tribal members, rather, being "responsible for using the land," "occupy[ing] the land," and "manag[ing] the land." The opposite result obtained in *Mitchell II,* however, based on timber management statutes, 25 U.S.C. §§ 406–407, 466, and regulations, under which the United States assumed "elaborate control" over the tribal forests. *Mitchell II* identified a specific trust relationship enforceable by award of damages for breach.

Here, the Court of Federal Claims compared the 1960 Act to the Allotment Act in *Mitchell I,* as creating nothing more than a "bare trust." It saw in the 1960 Act no mandate that the United States manage the site on behalf of the Tribe, and thus no predicate in the statutes and regulations identified by the Tribe for finding a fiduciary obligation enforceable by monetary relief.

The Court of Appeals for the Federal Circuit reversed and remanded, on the understanding that the United States's use of property under the proviso of the 1960 Act triggered the duty of a common law trustee to act reasonably to preserve any property the Secretary had chosen to utilize, an obligation fairly interpreted as supporting a claim for money damages. The Court of Appeals held that the provision for the Government's exclusive control over the building actually occupied raised the trust to the level of *Mitchell II,* in which the trust relationship together with Government's control over the property triggered a specific responsibility. * * *

We granted certiorari to decide whether the 1960 Act gives rise to jurisdiction over suits for money damages against the United States, and now affirm.

II

A

Jurisdiction over any suit against the Government requires a clear statement from the United States waiving sovereign immunity, *Mitchell I, supra,* at 538–539, together with a claim falling within the terms of the waiver, *Mitchell II, supra,* at 216–217. The terms of consent to be sued may not be inferred, but must be "unequivocally expressed," *Mitchell I, supra,* in order to "define [a] court's jurisdiction," *Mitchell I, supra.* The Tucker Act contains such a waiver, giving the Court of Federal Claims jurisdiction to award damages upon proof of "any claim against the United States founded either upon the Constitution, or any Act of Congress," 28 U.S.C. § 1491(a)(1), and its companion statute, the Indian Tucker Act, confers a like waiver for Indian tribal claims that "otherwise would be cognizable in the Court of Federal Claims if the claimant were not an Indian tribe," § 1505.

Neither Act, however, creates a substantive right enforceable against the Government by a claim for money damages. As we said in *Mitchell II,* a statute creates a right capable of grounding a claim within the waiver of sovereign immunity if, but only if, it "can fairly be interpreted as mandating compensation by the Federal Government for the damage sustained." 463 U.S., at 217 (quoting *United States v. Testan,* 424 U.S. 392, 400 (1976)).

This "fair interpretation" rule demands a showing demonstrably lower than the standard for the initial waiver of sovereign immunity. "Because the Tucker Act supplies a waiver of immunity for claims of this nature, the separate statutes and regulations need not provide a second waiver of sovereign immunity, nor need they be construed in the manner appropriate to waivers of sovereign immunity." *Mitchell II, supra,* at 218–219. It is enough, then, that a statute creating a Tucker Act right be reasonably amenable to the reading that it mandates a right of recovery in damages. While the premise to a Tucker Act claim will not be "lightly inferred," a fair inference will do.

B

The two *Mitchell* cases give a sense of when it is fair to infer a fiduciary duty qualifying under the Indian Tucker Act and when it is not. The characterizations of the trust as "limited," or "bare," distinguish the Allotment Act's trust-in-name from one with hallmarks of a more conventional fiduciary relationship. Although in form the United States "h[e]ld the land ... in trust for the sole use and benefit of the Indian," 25 U.S.C. § 348, the statute gave the United States no functional obligations to manage timber; on the contrary, it established that "the Indian allottee, and not a representative of the United States, is responsible for using the land," that "the allottee would occupy the land," and that "the allottee, and not the United States, was to manage the land." *Mitchell I,* 445 U.S., at 542–543. Thus, we found that Congress did not intend to "impose any duty" on the Government to manage resources * * *.

The subsequent case of *Mitchell II* arose on a claim that did look beyond the Allotment Act, and we found that statutes and regulations specifically addressing the management of timber on allotted lands raised the fair implication that the substantive obligations imposed on the United States by those statutes and regulations were enforceable by damages. The Department of the Interior possessed "comprehensive control over the harvesting of Indian timber" and "exercise[d] literally daily supervision over [its] harvesting and management," *Mitchell II, supra,* at 209, 222, giving it a "pervasive" role in the sale of timber from Indian lands under regulations addressing "virtually every aspect of forest management," *Mitchell II, supra,* at 219, 220. As the statutes and regulations gave the United States "full responsibility to manage Indian resources and land for the benefit of the Indians," we held that they "define[d] ... contours of the United States' fiduciary responsibilities" beyond the "bare" or minimal level, and thus could "fairly be interpreted as mandating compensation" through money damages if the Government faltered in its responsibility. 463 U.S., at 224–226.

III

A

The 1960 Act goes beyond a bare trust and permits a fair inference that the Government is subject to duties as a trustee and liable in damages for breach. The statutory language, of course, expressly defines a fiduciary relationship in the provision that Fort Apache be "held by the United States in trust for the White Mountain Apache Tribe." 74 Stat. 8. Unlike the Allotment Act, however, the statute proceeds to invest the United States with discretionary authority to make direct use of portions of the trust corpus. The trust property is "subject to the right of the Secretary of the Interior to use any part of the land and improvements for administrative or school purposes for as long as they are needed for the purpose," *ibid.,* and it is undisputed that the Government has to this day availed itself of its option. As to the property subject to the Government's actual use, then, the United States has not merely exercised daily supervision but has enjoyed daily occupation, and so has obtained control at least as plenary as its authority over the timber in *Mitchell II*. While it is true that the 1960 Act does not, like the statutes cited in that case, expressly subject the Government to duties of management and conservation, the fact that the property occupied by the United States is expressly subject to a trust supports a fair inference that an obligation to preserve the property improvements was incumbent on the United States as trustee. This is so because elementary trust law, after all, confirms the commonsense assumption that a fiduciary actually administering trust property may not allow it to fall into ruin on his watch. "One of the fundamental common-law duties of a trustee is to preserve and maintain trust assets," *Central States, Southeast & Southwest Areas Pension Fund v. Central Transport, Inc.,* 472 U.S. 559, 572 (1985); Restatement (Second) of Trusts § 176 (1957) ("The trustee is under a duty to the beneficiary to use reasonable care and skill to preserve the trust property"). Given this duty on the part of the trustee to preserve corpus, "it naturally follows that the Government should be liable in damages for the breach of its fiduciary duties." *Mitchell II, supra,* at 226.

B

The United States raises three defenses against this conclusion, the first being that the property occupied by the Government is not trust corpus at all. It asserts that in the 1960 Act Congress specifically "carve[d] out of the trust" the right of the Federal Government to use the property for the Government's own purposes. Brief for United States 24–25. According to the United States, this carve-out means that the 1960 Act created even less than the "bare trust" in *Mitchell I*. But this position is at odds with a natural reading of the 1960 Act. It provided that "Fort Apache" was subject to the trust; it did not read that the trust consisted of only the property not used by the Secretary. Nor is there any apparent reason to strain to avoid the straightforward reading; it makes sense to treat even the property used by the Government as trust property, since any use the Secretary would make of it would presumably be intended to redound to the benefit of the Tribe in some way.

Next, the Government contends that no intent to provide a damages remedy is fairly inferable, for the reason that "[t]here is not a word in the 1960 Act—the only substantive source of law on which the Tribe relies—that suggests the existence of such a mandate." Brief for United States 28. The argument rests, however, on a failure to appreciate either the role of trust law in drawing a fair inference * * *.

To the extent that the Government would demand an explicit provision for money damages to support every claim that might be brought under the Tucker Act, it would substitute a plain and explicit statement standard for the less demanding requirement of fair inference that the law was meant to provide a damages remedy for breach of a duty. To begin with, this would leave *Mitchell II* a wrongly decided case, for one would look in vain for a statute explicitly providing that inadequate timber management would be compensated through a suit for damages. But the more fundamental objection to the Government's position is that, if carried to its conclusion, it would read the trust relation out of Indian Tucker Act analysis; if a specific provision for damages is needed, a trust obligation and trust law are not. * * * To find a specific duty, a further source of law was needed to provide focus for the trust relationship. But once that focus was provided, general trust law was considered in drawing the inference that Congress intended damages to remedy a breach of obligation. * * *

Finally, the Government argues that the inference of a damages remedy is unsound simply because damages are inappropriate as a remedy for failures of maintenance, prospective injunctive relief being the sole relief tailored to the situation. We think this is clearly wrong. If the Government is suggesting that the recompense for run-down buildings should be an affirmative order to repair them, it is merely proposing the economic (but perhaps cumbersome) equivalent of damages. But if it is suggesting that relief must be limited to an injunction to toe the fiduciary mark in the future, it would bar the courts from making the Tribe whole for deterioration already suffered, and shield the Government against the remedy whose very availability would deter it from wasting trust property in the period before a Tribe has gone to court for injunctive relief. *Mitchell II*, 463 U.S., at 227 ("Absent a retrospective damages remedy, there would be little to deter federal officials from violating their trust duties, at least until the allottees managed to obtain a judicial decree against future breaches of trust").

IV

The judgment of the Court of Appeals for the Federal Circuit is affirmed, and the case is remanded to the Court of Federal Claims for further proceedings consistent with this opinion.

It is so ordered.

[The concurring opinion of JUSTICE GINSBURG, with whom JUSTICE BREYER joins, is omitted].

■ JUSTICE THOMAS, with whom THE CHIEF JUSTICE, JUSTICE SCALIA, and JUSTICE KENNEDY join, dissenting.

The majority's conclusion that the Court of Federal Claims has jurisdiction over this matter finds support in neither the text of the 1960 Act, nor our case law. As the Court has repeatedly held, the test to determine if Congress has conferred a substantive right enforceable against the Government in a suit for money damages is whether an Act "can fairly be *interpreted* as mandating compensation by the Federal Government for the damage sustained." *United States v. Testan*, 424 U.S. 392, 400 (1976) (quoting *Eastport S.S. Corp. v. United States*, 178 Ct.Cl. 599, 607, 372 F.2d 1002, 1009 (1967)) (emphasis added). Instead of faithfully applying this test, however, the Court engages in a new inquiry, asking whether common-law trust principles permit a "fair inference" that money damages are available, that finds no support in existing law. But even under the majority's newly devised approach, there is no basis for finding that

Congress intended to create anything other than a "bare trust," which we have found insufficient to confer jurisdiction on the Court of Federal Claims in *United States v. Mitchell,* 445 U.S. 535 *(Mitchell I).* Because the 1960 Act "can[not] fairly be interpreted as mandating compensation by the Federal Government for damage sustained" by the White Mountain Apache Tribe (Tribe), *Testan, supra,* at 400, I respectfully dissent.

I

In *United States v. Testan, supra,* at 400, the Court stated that a "grant of a right of action [for money damages against the United States] must be made with specificity." The majority agrees that the 1960 Act does not specifically authorize the award of money damages; indeed, the Act does not even "spea[k] in terms of money damages or of a money claim against the United States." *Gnotta v. United States,* 415 F.2d 1271, 1278 (C.A.8 1969) (Blackmun, J.). Instead, the Court holds that the use of the word "trust" in the 1960 Act creates a "fair inference" that there is a cause of action for money damages in favor of the Tribe.

But the Court made clear in *Mitchell I* that the existence of a trust relationship does not itself create a claim for money damages. The General Allotment Act, the statute at issue in *Mitchell I,* expressly placed responsibility on the United States to hold lands "in trust for the sole use and benefit of the Indian...." Despite this language, the Court concluded that the congressional intent necessary to render the United States liable for money damages was lacking. The Court reasoned that the General Allotment Act created only a "bare trust" because Congress did "not *unambiguously* provide that the United States ha[d] undertaken full fiduciary responsibilities as to the management of allotted lands." 445 U.S., at 542.

The statute under review here provides no more evidence of congressional intent to authorize a suit for money damages than the General Allotment Act did in *Mitchell I.* The Tribe itself acknowledges that the 1960 Act is "silen[t]" not only with respect to money damages, but also with regard to any underlying "maintenance and protection duties" that can fairly be construed as creating a fiduciary relationship. Brief for Respondent 11. Indeed, unlike the statutes and regulations at issue in *United States v. Mitchell,* 463 U.S. 206 (1983) *(Mitchell II),* the 1960 Act does not "establish ... 'comprehensive' responsibilities of the Federal Government in managing the" Fort Apache property. *Id.,* at 222. Because there is nothing in the statute that "clearly establish[es] fiduciary obligations of the Government in the management and operation of Indian lands," the 1960 Act creates only a "bare trust." *Id.,* at 226.

In addition, unlike the statutes and regulations at issue in *Mitchell I* and *Mitchell II,* "[n]othing in the 1960 Act imposes a fiduciary responsibility to manage the fort for the benefit of the Tribe and, in fact, it specifically carves the government's right to unrestricted use for the specified purposes out of the trust." 249 F.3d, at 1384 (Mayer, C. J., dissenting). The 1960 Act authorizes the "Secretary of the Interior to use any part of the land and improvements for administrative or school purposes for as long as they are needed for that purpose." 74 Stat. 8. The Government's use of the land does not have to inure to the benefit of the Indians. Nor is there any requirement that the United States cede control over the property now or in the future. Thus, if anything, there is less evidence of a fiduciary relationship in the 1960 Act than there was in the General Allotment Act at issue in *Mitchell I*.

If Congress intended to create a compensable trust relationship between the United States and the Tribe with respect to the Fort Apache property, it provided no indication to this effect in the text of the 1960 Act. Accordingly, I would hold that the 1960 Act created only a "bare trust" between the United States and the Tribe.

II

In concluding otherwise, the majority gives far too much weight to the Government's factual "control" over the Fort Apache property, which is all that distinguishes this case from *Mitchell I*. The majority holds that the United States "has obtained control at least as plenary as its authority over the timber in *Mitchell II*." This analysis, however, "misconstrues ... *Mitchell II* by focusing on the extent rather than the nature of control necessary to establish a fiduciary relationship." 46 Fed.Cl. 20, 27 (1999). The "timber management *statutes* and the *regulations* promulgated thereunder," *Mitchell II*, 463 U.S., at 222 (emphasis added), are what led the Court to conclude that there was "pervasive federal control" in the "area of timber sales and timber management," *id.*, at 225, n. 29. But, until now, the Court has never held the United States liable for money damages under the Tucker Act or Indian Tucker Act based on notions of factual control that have no foundation in the actual text of the relevant statutes.

Respondent argues that *Mitchell II* raised control to talismanic significance in our Indian Tucker Act jurisprudence. To be sure, the Court did state:

> "[A] fiduciary relationship necessarily arises when the Government assumes such elaborate control over forests and properties belonging to the Indians.... '[W]here the Federal Government takes on or has control or supervision over tribal monies or properties ... (unless Congress has provided otherwise) even though nothing is said expressly in the authorizing or underlying statute (or other fundamental document) about a trust fund, or a trust or fiduciary connection.'" *Id.*, at 225

However, this case does not involve the level of "*elaborate* control over" the Tribe's property that the Court found sufficient to create a compensable trust duty in *Mitchell II*. *Mitchell II* involved a "comprehensive" regulatory scheme that "addressed virtually every aspect of forest management," and under which the United States assumed "*full* responsibility to manage Indian resources and land for the benefit of the Indians." 463 U.S., at 220, 222, 224 (emphasis added). Here, by contrast, there are no management duties set forth in any "fundamental document," and thus the United States has the barest degree of control over the Tribe's property. And, unlike *Mitchell II,* the bare control that *is* exercised by the United States over the property does not inure to the benefit of the Indians. In my view, this is more than sufficient to distinguish this case from *Mitchell II.*

Moreover, even assuming that *Mitchell II* can be read to support the proposition that mere factual control over property is sufficient to create compensable trust duties (which it cannot), the Court has never provided any guidance on the nature and scope of such duties. And, in any event, the Court has never before held that "control" alone can give rise to, as the majority puts it, the specific duty to "preserve the property." Indeed, had Congress wished to create such a duty, it could have done so expressly in the 1960 Act. Its failure to follow that course strongly suggests that Congress did not intend to create a compensable trust relationship between the United States and the Tribe.

In addition, the Court's focus on control has now rendered the inquiry open-ended, with questions of jurisdiction determined by murky principles of the common law of trusts, and a parcel-by-parcel determination whether "portions of the property were under United States control," 249 F.3d, at 1383. Such an approach provides little certainty to guide Congress in fashioning legislation that insulates the United States from damages for breach of trust. Instead, to the ultimate detriment of the Tribe, Congress might refrain from creating trust relationships out of apprehension that the use of the word "trust" will subject the United States to liability for money damages.

* * *

The Court today fashions a new test to determine whether Congress has conferred a substantive right enforceable against the United States in a suit for money damages. In doing so, the Court radically alters the relevant inquiry from one focused on the actual fiduciary duties created by statute or regulation to one divining fiduciary duties out of the use of the word "trust" and notions of factual control. Because I find no basis for this approach in our case law or in the language of the Indian Tucker Act, I respectfully dissent.

———

Notes and Questions

1.   As with so many of the subjects that we lightly pass over during this survey course, our brief glance into Indian law necessarily fails to even begin to uncover the richness of this area of law. Moreover, we can offer but a taste of the controversy and ideological implications flowing from the nation's uneasy and historically turbulent relationship with indigenous tribal peoples, who are treated sometimes as sovereign nations and at other times as dependent wards of a federal government guardian.

One prominent commentator, Professor Robert A. Williams, Jr., summarizes Indian law in this manner:

Practitioners and students of United States Federal Indian Law are all intimately familiar with the three core, fundamental principles in the field from which all Supreme Court Indian law jurisprudence extends: the Congressional Plenary Power doctrine, which holds that Congress exercises a plenary authority in Indian affairs; the Diminished Tribal Sovereignty doctrine, which holds that Indian tribes still retain those aspects of their inherent sovereignty not expressly divested by treaty or statute, or implicitly divested by virtue of their status; and the Trust doctrine, which holds that in exercising its broad discretionary authority in Indian affairs, Congress and the Executive are charged with the responsibilities of a guardian acting on behalf of its dependent Indian wards.

Robert A. Williams, Jr., *Columbus's Legacy: Law as an Instrument of Racial Discrimination Against Indigenous Peoples' Rights of Self–Determination,* 8 Ariz. J. Int'l & Comp. L. 51, 67 (1991); *see also* William C. Canby, *American Indian Law in a Nutshell* 1–2 (2d ed. 1988); L. Scott Gould, *The Consent Paradigm: Tribal Sovereignty at the Millennium,* 96 Colum. L. Rev. 809, 810–11 & n.6 (1996). For a comprehensive treatment of Indian law, see generally *Cohen's Handbook of Federal Indian Law* (Nell Jessup Newton, et al., eds., 2005). The third of these core doctrines of Indian law— the Trust doctrine—may give rise to a cognizable money claim against the United States.

2. When the Court of Claims was originally created 150 years ago, claims by Indian tribes were excluded from the purview of the court. Act of March 3, 1863, ch. 92, § 9, 12 Stat. 765, 767 (1863) (excepting claims "dependent on any treaty stipulation entered into with foreign nations or with the Indian tribes"). As Dean Nell Jessup Newton has noted, the plain language of the 1863 statute suggested that it excluded only treaty-based claims and did not deny access by tribes to the Court of Claims for other types of claims. Nell Jessup Newton, *Indian Claims in the Courts of the Conqueror,* 41 Am. U. L. Rev. 753, 770 (1992). Nonetheless, she explains, for the next eight decades, "all assumed that the clause excepted any claim brought by an Indian tribe against the Government." *Id.* Accordingly, Indian tribes could seek redress in money damages in court only if Congress enacted special jurisdictional statutes, forcing the various tribes to regularly petition Congress for such extraordinary legislation.

To avoid the "vast and growing burden" of responding to such requests, *United States v. Mitchell,* 463 U.S. 206, 214 (1983) (quoting H.R. No. 79–1466 (1945)), Congress in 1946 enacted the Indian Tucker Act, which is set forth above. Tribal claimants through the Indian Tucker Act thus have access to the Court of Federal Claims in the same manner and under the same general terms as individual claimants have through what might be called the "regular" Tucker Act. Accordingly, the Tucker Act and the Indian Tucker Act, are congruous, differing only in the identity of the eligible claimant.

However, the presence of a Native American claimant potentially implicates a source of substantive law beyond that available to the ordinary claimant. As addressed frequently in this part of the casebook, a claimant seeking a monetary remedy against the United States must identify a money-mandating source of law outside of the Tucker Act itself. The same is true under the Indian Tucker Act. While individual Native American and tribal claimants may pursue constitutional and statutory claims in the same manner as ordinary claimants for money against the federal government, the historical guardian-ward relationship between the federal government and indigenous peoples also may give rise to a special "breach of trust" cause of action, which is presumptively redressable in money damages. (In addition, tribes also may maintain direct actions against the United States under the Indian Tucker Act alleging violation of governmental obligations in treaties with the various tribes.) 28 U.S.C. § 1505 (referring to claims arising under "treaties of the United States").

3.   And with that background, we come to the *White Mountain Apache* case set out above, which is important both for Tucker Act jurisdictional/waiver of sovereign immunity purposes and in defining what constitutes a governmental trust duty to an Indian tribe that is enforceable through the remedy of a Tucker Act action for damages.

a.   *Tucker Act Jurisdiction/Waiver of Sovereign Immunity.* While the Supreme Court has clearly established that the Tucker Act itself accomplishes the requisite waiver of sovereign immunity as well as provides federal court jurisdiction, the plaintiff still must identify a right to monetary relief from another source of law. For ordinary litigants, as discussed in Chapter IV.A.2.a, while they have been relieved of the requirement of making the rigorous showing that another statute also includes consent to suit (because the Tucker Act serves that purpose), they still must demonstrate that the substantive right found in that other statute is a right to money, that is, money-mandating in nature. However, when the grievances of Native Americans against the government for neglect of trust responsibilities are at issue, the trust doctrine comes into play.

What does the Court majority say in *White Mountain Apache* say about the role of trust law in finding an inference that money damages are available for breach? Is an express statutory reference to money damages required in Indian trust doctrine cases? Why not? How and why does the dissent parts ways with the majority on this crucial point?

The *White Mountain Apache* ruling thus provides a significant advantage (assuming an actionable trust relationship is established) to Native American claimants over the ordinary Tucker Act litigant. Although relieved of the burden of demonstrating a waiver of sovereign immunity, the ordinary Tucker Act litigant must adduce a substantive right to compensation from a statute (that is, find a money-mandating statute). While the statute need not authorize judicial action or even contemplate the prospect of litigation—the Tucker Act expressly creates the right to file suit—there must be some reference to money or financial consequences in the statute relied upon for the cause of action. For the Native American claimant, liberation from the requirement that the underlying statutory right be defined in terms of money becomes a further advantage in litigation. When the case is one for breach of the government's fiduciary responsibilities to indigenous peoples, the monetary nature of the remedy is implicit in the trust doctrine. By contrast, the permissive inference that breach of the governmental duty necessarily justifies a monetary remedy simply is not available to the ordinary litigant seeking to hold the federal government amenable to damages, when there is not "any trust relationship in the mix of relevant fact." *White Mountain Apache*, 537 U.S. at 477. On sovereign immunity and substantive rights under the Tucker Act and the Indian Tucker Act, see generally Gregory C. Sisk, *Yesterday and Today: Of Indians, Breach of Trust, Money, and Sovereign Immunity*, 39 Tulsa L. Rev. 313, 334–40 (2003).

b. *Actionable Trust Relationship*. The next question in *White Mountain Apache* is whether the relevant statute clearly provides that the United States has undertaken a full fiduciary relationship and its attendant responsibilities. How does the Court analyze that issue in the *White Mountain Apache* case? What are the crucial elements that the Court identifies in the pertinent statute (and the government's conduct under the statute) that gives rise to an enforceable trust obligation? What more would the dissent demand, that is, what is missing in the dissent's view? What factors or elements can be derived from *White Mountain Apache* that strengthen or weaken a claim of an actionable Indian trust relationship?

During the same term in which the Supreme Court decided *White Mountain Apache* and found an actionable trust relationship in that case, the Court also decided *United States v. Navajo Nation*, 537 U.S. 488 (2003), in which case the trust claim was rejected. In *Navajo Nation*, the tribe claimed that the Secretary of the Interior had breached the government's trust obligations by failing to insist upon a higher rate of return when approving leases between the tribe and private companies for extracting coal from reservation lands. The Supreme Court ruled that the pertinent statute did not impose "detailed fiduciary responsibilities" sufficient to support a claim for monetary relief. *Id.* at 507. Instead, the Court found, the statute "simply requires Secretarial approval before coal mining leases negotiated between Tribes and third parties become effective and [further] authorizes the Secretary generally to promulgate regulations governing mining operations." *Id.* Thus, far from being a case where the government had been "assigned a comprehensive managerial role" over the mineral resources or given the "responsibility to secure 'the needs and best interests of the Indian[s]' " that would characterize a full fiduciary responsibility, the statute, by failing to introduce any managerial role for the government, did not "even establish the 'limited trust relationship' " found inadequate to support a claim for relief in *Mitchell. Id.* at 507–08. The Court further ruled that "imposing fiduciary duties on the Government here would be out of line with one of the statute's principal purposes." *Id.* at 508. Because the statute "aims to enhance tribal self-determination by giving Tribes, not the Government, the lead role in negotiating mining leases with third parties," the congressional purpose would be defeated by "[i]mposing upon the Government a fiduciary duty to oversee the management of allotted lands." *Id.*

How can we distinguish the *White Mountain Apache* and *Navajo Nation* cases? What factors were present in the former that were missing in the latter? What additional element in *Navajo Nation* worked against the finding of an actionable fiduciary relationship?

On the factors that support and undermine an actionable Indian trust claim for money, see generally *Cohen's Handbook of Federal Indian Law, supra,* § 5.05[1], [2], at 426–34; Sisk, *supra,* at 340–52.

4.   The federal government's persistent dereliction of duty as steward of resources held in trust for American Indians is both a century-old saga and as fresh as today's newspaper. Indeed, the continuing legal wrangling about the government's trust obligations to Indians recently produced an extraordinary event, one of the historically rare occasions on which a federal judge has held a member of the President's Cabinet in contempt of court. *Lamberth Lambastes the State—Again,* Legal Times, Mar. 1, 1999, at 12. And before the case was concluded, the trial judge himself was removed from the case by the court of appeals as having regularly exceeded the bounds of judicial authority and become so extremely hostile to the government as to be unable to render fair judgment.

In 1996, a class action lawsuit on behalf of more than 300,000 Indians was filed as *Cobell v. Babbitt* in the United States District Court for the District of Columbia alleging that the United States had failed to account for billions of dollars earned on oil and logging leases of millions of acres of land allotted to Indians in the last century but held in trust for them by the federal government. The lawsuit has been described as the most significant Indian case and one of the largest lawsuits ever brought against the United States. John Gibeaut, *Another Broken Trust,* A.B.A. J., Sept. 1999, at 40; Robert L. Jackson, *Suit Stands to Repay Billions to Indians,* L.A. Times, Aug. 21, 1999, at A1.

According to the district court's ultimate findings, the government has kept such poor records that it is incapable of determining what it owes each individual Indian, or for that matter even which individuals own which allotments, and has lost perhaps billions of dollars in earnings over the past century. *Cobell v. Norton,* 240 F.3d 1081, 1088–90 (D.C. Cir. 2001); *Cobell v. Babbitt,* 91 F.Supp.2d 1, 6–12 (D.D.C. 1999). As one newspaper editorial described the situation: "Picture a bank keeping records so poorly that it didn't know who deposited or withdrew funds and what the balance was in individual accounts. Picture that going on for a century. Unimaginable, but that's exactly what the government did with funds belonging to Native American tribes." *Finally Tribes Are Heard,* L.A. Times, Dec. 23, 1999, at B10.

When the government during discovery in *Cobell* failed to turn over records for Indian trust accounts promised by Department of Justice lawyers, District Judge Royce C. Lamberth took the extraordinary step of holding several leading officials, including the Secretary of the Interior, in contempt. The judge said that the government had "abused the rights of the plaintiffs to obtain these trust documents, and [] engaged in a shocking pattern of deception of the court," such that the judge had "never seen more egregious conduct by the federal government." *Cobell,* 37 F.Supp.2d at 38. The court explained that misconduct by the federal government in litigation is especially troubling; "[t]he institutions of our federal government cannot continue to exist if they cannot be trusted." *Id.*

Ultimately the government had to admit that it was unable to produce the records, many of which had been lost or destroyed or stored in wooden sheds exposed to the weather. Government attorneys and officials began pointing fingers at one another, with Interior Department officers contending that the Department of Justice attorneys had bungled the case because of their unfamiliarity with the complexities of Indian law, while the attorneys blamed the Interior Department, as the client agency, for failing to provide necessary information, assist their counsel in understanding the problem, and diligently search the records. In the meantime, of course, generations of Indians have been cheated out of the income generated on their allotments of land. The only point of consensus, at long last, is the government's belated admission that it had breached its fiduciary duty to the Indians. Gibeaut, *supra.*

At the end of 1999, Judge Lamberth entered judgment on most of the claims in *Cobell v. Babbitt* after a bench trial, finding that the United States is incapable of providing an accurate accounting and therefore had violated its fiduciary responsibility to these Indians. *Cobell v. Babbitt,* 91 F.Supp.2d 1, 6–7 (D.D.C. 1999). He concluded:

> The United States' mismanagement of the [Individual Indian Money] trust is far more inexcusable than garden-variety trust mismanagement of a typical donative trust. For the beneficiaries of this trust did not voluntarily choose to have their lands taken from them; they did not willingly relinquish pervasive control of their money to the United States. The United States imposed this trust on the Indian people.

Id. at 6. Judge Lamberth retained continuing jurisdiction over the matter, including periodic review of the government's ongoing efforts to prepare a full accounting of the trust. *Id.* at 58–59. (The Court of Appeals affirmed the order on appeal in 2001. *Cobell v. Norton,* 240 F.3d 1081 (D.C. Cir. 2001).)

More than two years later, in 2002, still dissatisfied with the progress of the Department of Interior in performing an historical accounting of allotment accounts, Judge Lamberth issued a new contempt citation to another cabinet secretary, Interior Secretary Gale A. Norton of the succeeding administration, based upon findings of deception and abject failure in continuing efforts to reform the trust system. *Cobell v. Norton,* 226 F.Supp.2d 1, 19–20 (D.D.C. 2002); *see also* Helen Rumbelow & Neely Tucker, *Interior's Norton Cited for Contempt in Trust Suit,* Wash. Post., Sept. 18, 2002, at A1 (reporting citation of Interior secretary for contempt because court found that government officials "deceived [Judge Lamberth] about the agency's failure to reform a trust fund for Native Americans"). However, on this occasion, the D.C. Circuit held that Judge Lamberth had overstepped his authority, reversing the contempt citation against Secretary Norton as improperly holding her responsible for the conduct of her predecessor in office and rejecting the district court's finding that the Secretary had committed fraud on the court through deceptive status reports. *Cobell v. Norton*, 334 F.3d 1128, 1148–50 (D.C. Cir. 2003). Moreover, the court of appeals ruled that the district court had clearly erred in reappointing a monitor who had been invested "with wide-ranging extrajudicial duties over the Government's objections." *Id.* at 1142.

More than six years after the trial and judgment, the parties and the courts remain at work attempting to create order out of the chaos caused by the government's mismanagement of the Indian land allotment program, although the effectiveness of the continuing litigation in achieving such reform has attracted increasing criticism and appellate intervention. Professor Richard Pierce argued that Judge Lamberth's propensity for threatening contempt citations against government employees that the judge regards as misbehaving has initiated a "reign of terror" by a runaway federal judge, creating chaos within the Department of Interior, destroying morale throughout the agency, costing the government huge sums of money, abusing scores of federal employees, and inhibiting effective reform of the Indian trust system. Richard J. Pierce, Jr., *Judge Lamberth's Reign of Terror at the Department of Interior*, 56 Admin. L. Rev. 235 (2004). In 2006, the United States Court of Appeals for the D.C. Circuit reversed yet additional orders by Judge Lamberth as exceeding judicial authority and then punctuated its ruling by ordering the action assigned to a different judge. *Cobell v. Kempthorne*, 455 F.3d 317 (D.C. Cir. 2006), *cert. denied*, 127 S.Ct. 1876 (2007). The court ruled that Judge Lamberth had "exceeded the role of an impartial arbiter," leveled serious charges against Interior and its officials unrelated to the issue before the court, and become so extreme in "professed hostility to Interior" as to display a clear inability to render a fair judgment. *Id.* at 335. (The plaintiffs bemoaned the appellate court's removal of a person they characterize as "a dedicated and fair jurist." http://www.indiantrust.com).

Some observers believe that what might have begun as a salutary legal effort to highlight government mismanagement and spur reform of the Indian trust accounts had degenerated into bitter series of collateral disputes that threatened progress on the main subject at hand. Even other Native American groups cautiously began to express concern that the dominating attention given to this litigation is drawing government resources away from and resulting in neglect of other Indian matters. Greg Gordon, *Indian Tribes Say Reorganization of Trust Fund Left Them Out of Loop*, STAR TRIBUNE., May 13, 2004, at A16 (reporting that leaders of Indian tribes that receive little royalties on leases of trust lands fear they will be hurt by cuts in Bureau of Indian Affairs funding for education and other programs necessary to fund new office for trust fund management). As this edition of the casebook was being completed, the new judge had ordered a trial on the continuing efforts to make an accounting for October of 2007, the parties were making some noises about settlement in terms of a sum of money to be paid by the government, and Congress was considering legislation that would direct a settlement of the dispute.

Interestingly, particularly for the purposes of this course on civil litigation with the federal government, the jurisdiction of the district court to even hear this matter was by no means certain (and, in your casebook author's view, was lacking). Because the plaintiffs ultimately are hoping to recover a large sum of money, at least in part based upon past conduct (retrospective relief), the case might appear to more appropriately framed as a Tucker Act or Indian Tucker Act claim within the exclusive jurisdiction of the Court of Federal Claims (unless individual claims were limited to $10,000). (For the immediate purposes of this case, the plaintiffs disavowed any request for an actual award of money, but the request for a retrospective accounting, and thus a determination or estimate of the money owed, confirms that the case in essence is about money and the eventual payment of money.) However, the Department of Justice failed to raise the jurisdictional argument until late in the game. Gibeaut, *supra,* at 44, 46–47. The belated motion to transfer the case to the Court of Federal Claims was denied, and Judge Lamberth repeatedly asserted district court authority to grant both prospective and retrospective relief under the Administrative Procedure Act. *Cobell v. Babbitt,* 91 F.Supp.2d 1, 24–28 (D.D.C. 1999); *Cobell v. Babbitt,* 52 F.Supp.2d 11, 20–22 (D.D.C. 1999); *Cobell v. Babbitt,* 30 F.Supp.2d 24, 30–35, 38–42 (D.D.C. 1998).

As we'll later discover in Chapter IV.C, the Supreme Court has not strictly adhered to a money/non-money jurisdictional line between Tucker Act claims belonging in the Court of Federal Claims and Administrative Procedure Act claims brought in the district court. Thus, the conclusion that an accounting of the records is a form of specific relief that may be pursued outside of a Tucker Act claim for money in the Court of Federal Claims—even if the practical effect of the lawsuit is to set the stage for the payment of money for the government's past failures—may be plausible under current Supreme Court doctrine. But it is not without question either. *See generally* Gregory C. Sisk, *The Tapestry Unravels: Statutory Waivers of Sovereign Immunity and Money Claims Against the United States,* 71 Geo. Wash. L. Rev. 601, 658–66 (2003) (arguing that jurisdiction over the *Cobell* case properly lay exclusively in the Court of Federal Claims, saying that the "plaintiffs did not seek an accounting from the government because they value book-keeping exactitude in the abstract or appreciate the intrinsic beauty of a well-prepared financial statement," but rather "for the practical purpose of hastening the day that the government will be called to account for—that is, required to *pay*—the money that it has wrongfully withheld").

———

4.   CONTRACT CLAIMS AND THE TUCKER ACT

We now turn our attention to another category of Tucker Act claims and, with that, to another category of substantive law—contract law. The economic importance and breadth of governmental contractual activity is manifest. As Allan J. Joseph notes:

[T]he federal government, along with its major contractors, buys a wide range of products and services. Yes, some of the those government needs do involve rocket science, as well as aircraft carriers, jet planes, armored vehicles and sophisticated electronic communications systems. But increasingly, the government is turning to the commercial marketplace to buy commonplace things, such as food, clothing, office supplies and information technology.

Allan J. Joseph, *Look Before You Leap*, 90 A.B.A. J. 58 (Oct. 2004).

Government procurement contracts alone amount to hundreds of billions of dollars each year. The Federal Procurement Data System reports that the federal government contracted for more than $376 billion in procurements in fiscal year 2005, of which more than $268 billion was by the Department of Defense. Federal Procurement Data Center, 2005 Federal Procurement Report at 19–20, http://www.fpdsng.com/fpr_reports_fy_05.html. Accordingly, the government purchases nearly $700,000 in goods and services every minute of every day of the year. Many private enterprises, as well as many lawyers and law firms, are substantially or wholly dependent upon federal government contract activity.

Congress waived the government's immunity from claims arising in contract very early, even before the enactment of the Tucker Act and almost a century before the Federal Tort Claims Act. Since the creation of the Court of Claims in 1855, the government has been subject to at least some type of litigation based upon contract disputes. Why do you suppose that this was one of the first statutory waivers of sovereign immunity? What incentive would the government have to consent to suit in contract disputes? *See* Harold J. Krent, *Reconceptualizing Sovereign Immunity,* 45 Vand. L.J. 1529, 1565 (1992) ("The [pre-Civil War waiver of immunity from contract suit] was viewed as indispensable to the efficient operation of government, for without it, qualified private contractors might not undertake government projects and the government could not obtain the goods and services it needed at affordable prices."). Professor Gillian Hadfield writes

The ability of the sovereign to bind itself in contract has been an important step in the evolution of the modern democratic state. Through the use of contracts, government has been able to perform its functions more effectively by drawing on private resources to deliver governmental goods and services. Politically, by honoring its contracts, government has reinforced its democratic legitimacy as a government subject to the rule of contract.

Gillian Hadfield, *Of Sovereignty and Contract: Damages for Breach of Contract by Government,* 8 S. Cal. Interdisciplinary L.J. 467, 467 (1999).

However, as we will see and have seen previously in other areas of the law of federal government litigation, sovereign immunity has not been wholly abandoned and the government retains special privileges, rules, and limitations on liability in contract disputes. To again quote Professor Hadfield, "[w]hen sovereign immunity is waived and the sovereign enters the world of contract, it assumes the position of a private person for juridical purposes and yet, in fact, it never leaves behind its sovereign status and its overriding power." Hadfield, *supra,* at 472. As one example, and we will see others, the remedies available in a contract claim against the federal government are limited. In particular, the remedy of specific performance on a contract is barred against the United States. This restriction has been justified as "prevent[ing] judicial interference with the discretion of officials in the political branches. In particular, the rule gives officials flexibility to get out of contracts that, they determine, no longer serve the public interest." Richard H. Seamon, *Separation of Powers and the Separate Treatment of Contract Claims Against the Federal Government for Specific Performance,* 43 Vill. L. Rev. 155, 199 (1998); *see also* Krent, *supra,* at 1566 ("Specific performance would afford private contractors a weapon to gain relief based upon their expectancy interest, and more importantly, to force the government to expend funds for work it no longer believes to be in the nation's interests."). Note, however, that this rule "does not immunize the government from liability for violations of contractual rules; it merely limits the remedy for such violations." Seamon, *supra,* at 202.

Prior to 1978, contract disputes with the government generally fell under the provision of the Tucker Act covering claims founded on contract. Since 1978, procurement contracts—that is, contracts to purchase supplies, for construction, and for services, which are the vast majority of government contracts—are governed by another statute, the Contract Disputes Act, 41 U.S.C. § 601 et seq. See Chapter IV.4.b. Before we turn to the Contract Disputes Act, we need to look at contract claims under the Tucker Act, because non-procurement contracts remain covered by that statute and because the Tucker Act process influenced the drafters of the Contract Disputes Act.

------

a.   IMPLIED CONTRACTS

Tucker Act, 28 United States Code § 1491(a)(1)

(a)(1) The United States Court of Federal Claims shall have jurisdiction to render judgment upon any claim against the United States founded either upon the Constitution, or any Act of Congress or any regulation of an executive department, or upon any express or implied contract with the United States, or for liquidated or unliquidated damages in cases not sounding in tort. For the purpose of this paragraph, an express or implied contract with the Army and Air Force Exchange Service, Navy Exchanges, Marine Corps Exchanges, Coast Guard Exchanges, or Exchange Councils of the National Aeronautics and Space Administration shall be considered an express or implied contract with the United States.

Schwartz v. United States

United States Claims Court.
16 Cl. Ct. 182 (1989).

■ NAPIER, JUDGE:

This case is brought under 28 U.S.C. § 1491(a)(1) by an attorney seeking recovery from the Government of attorney fees he was unable to collect from his client. He alleges that the Government's refusal to pay his client's claim in the form of a joint-payee check, payable to the attorney and his client, constitutes a breach of an agreement between himself and the Government. Furthermore, the complaint alleges that the Government violated applicable federal regulations. The complaint asserts that both causes of action render the Government liable for the uncollected contingent fee from plaintiff's client.

Defendant has filed a motion to dismiss for lack of subject-matter jurisdiction or, in the alternative, a motion for summary judgment * * *.
* * *

I. *Facts*

Plaintiff is a duly licensed attorney admitted to practice in the State of Oregon and before the Department of Interior's (DOI) Bureau of Indian Affairs (BIA). In August 1985 he was retained by Mrs. Linda Slockish to represent her before the BIA.

A brief description of Mrs. Slockish's underlying claim is necessary to fully understand plaintiff's complaint. In 1975 a BIA probate judge issued an order by which Mrs. Slockish received a sum of money as the beneficiary of the estate of Mr. Harvey K. Phillips. This money was deposited into Mrs. Slockish's Individual Indian Account and subsequently withdrawn by Mrs. Slockish. In 1978 the Bureau believed that it had erroneously overpaid Mrs. Slockish in regard to the Phillips estate. However, Mrs. Slockish had no funds in her account to recover for overpayment. In 1981 Mrs. Slockish became the beneficiary of funds from a separate estate also administered under BIA jurisdiction. The BIA withheld $19,000 of these funds, representing the alleged overpayment, plus $6,000 interest. Mrs. Slockish then hired plaintiff in August 1985, claiming that the Government erred in withholding the funds.

In exchange for legal services to be rendered by the plaintiff, a contingent fee agreement and an assignment were executed by plaintiff and Mrs. Slockish. The contingent fee agreement stated that plaintiff would receive 33.3 percent of Mrs. Slockish's award if the case were settled without filing suit or a demand for arbitration.

On April 29, 1986, the Comptroller General of the United States issued an opinion on the matter, and BIA repaid Mrs. Slockish $19,457.26. Thereafter, a warrant for repayment was issued and the BIA transferred the amount from the general Bureau account to Mrs. Slockish's Individual Indian Account. The day after the money was deposited Mrs. Slockish withdrew the entire amount.

The dispute between plaintiff and defendant arises out of an alleged promise made by Mr. Don Gray of the BIA to plaintiff to issue a joint-payee check in the amount of Mrs. Slockish's award. In an effort to ensure payment for legal services rendered to Mrs. Slockish, plaintiff had requested that Mr. Gray issue such joint-payee check. According to plaintiff, on or before January 6, 1986, Mr. Gray stated to plaintiff that a joint-payee check would be issued if the Bureau received notarized authorization from Mrs. Slockish. Plaintiff then sent Mr. Gray a copy of the notarized assignment and the contingent fee agreement. BIA thereafter sent plaintiff a letter dated May 8, 1987, which stated that Mrs. Slockish's award was transferred to her account in lieu of issuing a joint-payee check. Plaintiff's complaint asserts that defendant owes him $6,485.42, representing one-third of Mrs. Slockish's $19,457.26 award, because it breached its promise to issue a joint-payee check.

II.   *Discussion*

A.   *Rule 12(b)(1) Motion to Dismiss*

Defendant moves for dismissal pursuant to Rule 12(b)(1), asserting that plaintiff's claim does not satisfy the requirements of the Tucker Act, 28 U.S.C. § 1491(a)(1), necessary to invoke this Court's jurisdiction.

This section of the Tucker Act confers jurisdiction upon the Court as follows:

> The United States Claims Court shall have jurisdiction to render judgment upon any claim against the United States founded either upon the Constitution, or any act of Congress, or any regulation of an executive department, or upon any express or implied contract with the United States, or for liquidated or unliquidated damages in cases not sounding in tort * * *.

28 U.S.C. § 1491(a)(1).

In a case such as this, where a party moves to dismiss for lack of subject-matter jurisdiction, the Court must consider the facts alleged in the complaint to be true and correct.

In his complaint plaintiff states facts allegedly supporting two legal theories under the Tucker Act.

It appears to the Court that the first legal theory upon which plaintiff seeks to recover is that of breach of contract by defendant. Secondly, through its recitation of the facts, plaintiff alleges the violation of an express federal regulation by a Government official. In this latter claim, plaintiff asserts that Mr. Don Gray, a Government official in the New Mexico office of the BIA, acting with statutory authorization and in the course of his employment, expressly promised that a joint-payee check would be issued to plaintiff, which, after reliance thereon by plaintiff, the Government refused to do. * * *

Privity of contract between a claimant and the United States is a necessary element of a breach of contract action brought under 28 U.S.C.

§ 1491. Defendant claims that the only privity of contract in this case was between plaintiff and his client, Linda Slockish, which cannot bind the United States to claimant in a contractual capacity. Plaintiff asserts that he entered into a contract with the United States through Mr. Don Gray, acting as an agent of the Government.

Whether Mr. Gray was in fact an agent representing the United States is not a material issue to this claim. Nor is it material to the contract claim whether Mr. Gray in fact promised plaintiff to issue a joint-payee check. Assuming plaintiff's alleged facts to be true, i.e., that Mr. Gray was serving as an official representative of the Government when he promised plaintiff a joint-payee check, plaintiff does not allege nor otherwise demonstrate that he provided any consideration to support a contract between the parties, other than detrimental reliance.

In his amended complaint, plaintiff states that "[p]laintiff relied on Gray's statement [to issue a check made payable to both plaintiff and Ms. Slockish] and did not otherwise secure his right to a share of the Slockishes' funds." Nowhere does plaintiff state or imply that anything other than detrimental reliance was afforded defendant in return for Mr. Gray's promise.

Detrimental reliance upon a statement made by one opposing the existence of a contract is controlled by the law of contracts, specifically promissory estoppel. Promissory estoppel operates in an equitable sense to bind one party to a promise made by him to another when the latter has reasonably relied on that promise to his detriment. Such a contract is one implied-in-law. Although the Tucker Act confers jurisdiction upon this Court over "express and implied contracts", the cases have uniformly interpreted the term "implied contracts" to mean only contracts implied-in-fact. Therefore, since plaintiff has not alleged purported consideration to the Government other than that of detrimental reliance, a contract of the nature requisite to this Court's jurisdictional authority does not exist. Plaintiff's claim for breach of contract must therefore be dismissed under defendant's motion for lack of subject-matter jurisdiction pursuant to [Rule] 12(b)(1).

B.   *Rule 56 Motion for Summary Judgment*

Plaintiff's second claim, i.e., that Mr. Gray acted pursuant to statutory authority in promising to issue a joint-payee check, is disposed of pursuant to Rule 56. * * *

[The court ruled that the beneficiary's action to recover funds erroneously held by the BIA qualified as a "claim against the government," subject to the requirements of the Anti–Assignment Act, 31 U.S.C. § 3727. The purpose of the Act is to safeguard governmental interests whenever a demand is made upon it to make payment or deliver property. The government will pay a claim only to the party making the claim unless the strict requirements of the Act are satisfied. Under the Anti–Assignment Act, before an assignment can be deemed valid, the claim must be allowed and the amount ascertained; a warrant for payment must be issued; the assignment must be made freely and attested to by two witnesses; and the one making the assignment must acknowledge it before an official authorized to acknowledge a deed and the official must certify that he or she fully explained the assignment.

Assuming that Don Gray of the BIA was authorized to waive the requirements of the Anti–Assignment Act, there was insufficient evidence in the record to support a factual finding that he did so. Plaintiff simply alleged that he was "told by Don Gray that a joint payee check would be made if a notarized authorization was received by the BIA." Since the purported assignment signed by Mrs. Slockish was dated more than one month before the claim was allowed, the assignment was not executed in accordance with the Act's requirements. Therefore, Mrs. Slockish's assignment of her claim to the plaintiff was not valid to bind the Government.]

Conclusion

* * * The Court has allowed plaintiff all favorable inferences and concludes that the law, as applied to the facts alleged in plaintiff's complaint, requires that defendant's 12(b)(1) motion on plaintiff's breach of contract action, and its Rule 56(c) motion on statutory violation must be granted. The Clerk is directed to dismiss the complaint. No costs.

[The Appendix to the opinion is omitted.]

Notes and Questions

1. The Tucker Act applies to claims founded on "express or implied contract." We know what an "express" contract is, but what does the statute mean by an "implied" contract? In the *Schwartz v. United States* case, the court refers to "implied-in-fact" contracts as contrasted with "implied-in-law" contracts. What is the difference? Why does the difference matter? If the court is not clear on the complete definition of "implied-in-fact" contract, what at least must exist to create such a contract under the court's reasoning? In a lawsuit between private parties, if one party makes a promise and the other relies upon that promise, what is the result? Why is detrimental reliance insufficient to bind the federal government? Why would the government be reluctant to waive immunity for claims involving an equitable substitute for certain contractual elements? What are the risks to the government, government operations, and the integrity of statutory and regulatory rules if promissory estoppel is permitted against the United States? See generally Chapter VI.A (discussing attempts to bind the federal government by equitable estoppel based upon unauthorized representations by government employees).

2. In addition to requiring actual consideration for an implied contract to be enforceable against the federal government, and thus excluding equitable substitutes or implied-in-law contracts, a cognizable implied-in-fact contract must satisfy the other elements for a valid contract. In *Pacific*

Gas & Electric Co. v. United States, 3 Cl. Ct. 329 (1983), *aff'd*, 738 F.2d 452 (Fed. Cir. 1984) (table), the then-Claims Court explained the requirements for an implied-in-fact contract that may be the basis for a Tucker Act claim:

> A contract implied-in-fact requires a showing of the same mutual intent to contract as that required for an express contract. The fact that an instrument was not executed is not essential to consummation of the agreement. It is essential, however, that the acceptance of an offer be manifested by conduct that indicates assent to the proposed bargain. The requirements of mutuality of intent, and the lack of ambiguity in offer and acceptance, are the same for an implied-in-fact contract as for an express contract; only the nature of the evidence differs. The officer whose conduct is relied upon must have had actual authority to bind the Government in contract.

Id. at 338–39. In sum, an implied-in-fact contract is one that involves the same mutual consent as in an express contract; indeed, the principal difference between an express and implied contract lies in the absence of a signed instrument for the latter.

3.   In *Hercules Inc. v. United States,* 516 U.S. 417 (1996), the Supreme Court confirmed a restrictive understanding of what constitutes an implied-in-fact contract under the Tucker Act. In an opinion by Chief Justice Rehnquist, the Court stated that "[w]e have repeatedly held that [Tucker Act] jurisdiction extends only to contracts either express or implied in fact, and not to claims on contracts implied in law." *Id.* at 423. The Court further explained:

> The distinction between "implied in fact" and "implied in law," and the consequent limitation, is well established in our cases. An agreement implied in fact is "founded upon a meeting of minds, which, although not embodied in an express contract, is inferred, as a fact, from conduct of the parties showing, in the light of the surrounding circumstances, their tacit understanding."

Id. at 423–24 (quoting *Baltimore & Ohio Railway Co. v. United States,* 261 U.S. 592, 597 (1923)).

In *Hercules,* chemical manufacturers had produced the plant defoliant Agent Orange, which was extensively used by the military during the Vietnam war to eliminate the enemy's hiding places and destroy its food supplies. Subsequently, these manufacturers were sued by Vietnam veterans and their families alleging health problems due to exposure to Agent Orange. After settling those claims with the veterans, the manufacturers in turn sought indemnification from the government, for whom it had produced the defoliant, by bringing a contract claim under the Tucker Act. *Id.* at 419–22. Because their contracts with the government to produce the chemical did not contain express indemnification provisions, they argued, based upon the circumstances at the time of contracting, that there was an implied agreement by the government to reimburse them for liabilities. The manufacturers noted that the government had effectively required them to produce the chemical, imposed detailed specifications, and even seized production facilities. *Id.* at 423–26. Nonetheless, the Supreme Court held that these circumstances did not establish that the government, in fact, had agreed to provide indemnification. Indeed, the Court questioned whether a government contracting officer would have had the authority to enter into such an open-ended indemnification agreement. Because a limitation upon government contracting authority is as applicable to contracts by implication as those expressly made, the Court denied the contract claim. *Id.* at 426–30. Justice Breyer, joined by Justice O'Connor, dissented, saying that "the companies argue factual circumstances—compelled production, superior knowledge, detailed specifications, and significant defect—which, if true, suggest that a government, dealing in good faith with its contractors, would have agreed to the 'implied promise' [to indemnity]." *Id.* at 440 (Breyer, J., dissenting).

----

b.   THE CONTRACT DISPUTES ACT

Contract Disputes Act, 41 United States Code §§ 438; 605(a)–(d); 606; 607(a), (c)–(d), (g)(1); 609(a)–(c); 612(a)–(c)

§ 438.   Civilian Board of Contract Appeals

(a) Board Established.

There is established in the General Services Administration a board of contract appeals to be known as the Civilian Board of Contract Appeals (in this section referred to as the "Civilian Board").

(b) Membership.

(1) Appointment.

(A) The Civilian Board shall consist of members appointed by the Administrator of General Services (in consultation with the Administrator for Federal Procurement Policy) from a register of applicants maintained by the Administrator of General Services, in accordance with rules issued by the Administrator of General Services (in consultation with the Administrator for Federal Procurement Policy) for establishing and maintaining a register of eligible applicants and selecting Civilian Board members. The Administrator of General Services shall appoint a member without regard to political affiliation and solely on the basis of the professional qualifications required to perform the duties and responsibilities of a Civilian Board member.

(B) The members of the Civilian Board shall be selected and appointed to serve in the same manner as administrative law judges appointed pursuant to section 3105 of title 5, United States Code, with an additional requirement that such members shall have had not fewer than five years of experience in public contract law.

(C) Notwithstanding subparagraph (B) and subject to paragraph (2), the following persons shall serve as Civilian Board members: any full-time member of any agency board of contract appeals other than the Armed Services Board of Contract Appeals, the Postal Service Board of Contract Appeals, and the board of contract appeals of the Tennessee Valley Authority serving as such on the day before the effective date of this section.

(2) Removal.

Members of the Civilian Board shall be subject to removal in the same manner as administrative law judges, as provided in section 7521 of title 5, United States Code.

(3) Compensation.

Compensation for members of the Civilian Board shall be determined under section 5372a of title 5, United States Code.

(c) Functions.

(1) In general.

The Civilian Board shall have jurisdiction as provided by section 8(d) of the Contract Disputes Act of 1978 (41 U.S.C. 607(b)).

(2) Additional Jurisdiction.

The Civilian Board may, with the concurrence of the Federal agency or agencies affected—

(A) assume jurisdiction over any additional category of laws or disputes over which an agency board of contract appeals established pursuant to section 8 of the Contract Disputes Act exercised jurisdiction before the effective date of this section; and

(B) assume any other functions performed by such a board before such effective date on behalf of such agencies.

§ 605. Decision by contracting officer

(a) Contractor claims

All claims by a contractor against the government relating to a contract shall be in writing and shall be submitted to the contracting officer for a decision. All claims by the government against a contractor relating to a contract shall be the subject of a decision by the contracting officer. Each claim by a contractor against the government relating to a contract and each claim by the government against a contractor relating to a contract shall be submitted within 6 years after the accrual of the claim. The preceding sentence does not apply to a claim by the government against a contractor that is based on a claim by the contractor involving fraud. The contracting officer shall issue his decisions in writing, and shall mail or otherwise furnish a copy of the decision to the contractor. The decision shall state the reasons for the decision reached, and shall inform the contractor of his rights as provided in this chapter. Specific findings of fact are not required, but, if made, shall not be binding in any subsequent proceeding. The authority of this subsection shall not extend to a claim or dispute for penalties or forfeitures prescribed by statute or regulation which another Federal agency is specifically authorized to administer, settle, or determine. This section shall not authorize any agency head to settle, compromise, pay, or otherwise adjust any claim involving fraud.

(b) Review; performance of contract pending appeal

The contracting officer's decision on the claim shall be final and conclusive and not subject to review by any forum, tribunal, or Government agency, unless an appeal or suit is timely commenced as authorized by this chapter. Nothing in this chapter shall prohibit executive agencies from including a clause in government contracts requiring that pending final decision of an appeal, action, or final settlement, a contractor shall proceed diligently with performance of the contract in accordance with the contracting officer's decision.

(c) Amount of claim; certification; notification; time of issuance; presumption; authorization of certifier

(1) A contracting officer shall issue a decision on any submitted claim of $100,000 or less within sixty days from his receipt of a written request from the contractor that a decision be rendered within that period. For claims of more than $100,000, the contractor shall certify that the claim is made in good faith, that the supporting data are accurate and complete to the best of his knowledge and belief, that the amount requested accurately reflects the contract adjustment for which the contractor believes the government is liable, and that the certifier is duly authorized to certify the claim on behalf of the contractor.

(2) A contracting officer shall, within sixty days of receipt of a submitted certified claim over $100,000—

(A) issue a decision; or

(B) notify the contractor of the time within which a decision will be issued.

(3) The decision of a contracting officer on submitted claims shall be issued within a reasonable time, in accordance with regulations promulgated by the agency, taking into account such factors as the size and complexity of the claim and the adequacy of the information in support of the claim provided by the contractor.

(4) A contractor may request the tribunal concerned to direct a contracting officer to issue a decision in a specified period of time, as determined by the tribunal concerned, in the event of undue delay on the part of the contracting officer.

(5) Any failure by the contracting officer to issue a decision on a contract claim within the period required will be deemed to be a decision by the contracting officer denying the claim and will authorize the commencement of the appeal or suit on the claim as otherwise provided in this chapter. However, in the event an appeal or suit is so commenced in the

absence of a prior decision by the contracting officer, the tribunal concerned may, at its option, stay the proceedings to obtain a decision on the claim by the contracting officer.

(6) The contracting officer shall have no obligation to render a final decision on any claim of more than $100,000 that is not certified in accordance with paragraph (1) if, within 60 days after receipt of the claim, the contracting officer notifies the contractor in writing of the reasons why any attempted certification was found to be defective. A defect in the certification of a claim shall not deprive a court or an agency board of contract appeals of jurisdiction over the claim. Prior to the entry of a final judgment by a court or a decision by an agency board of contract appeals, the court or agency board shall require a defective certification to be corrected.

(7) The certification required by paragraph (1) may be executed by any person duly authorized to bind the contractor with respect to the claim.

(d) Alternative means of dispute resolution

Notwithstanding any other provision of this chapter, a contractor and a contracting officer may use alternative means of dispute resolution under subchapter IV of chapter 5 of Title 5, or other mutually agreeable procedures, for resolving claims. The contractor shall certify the claim when required to do so as provided under subsection (c)(1) of this section or as otherwise required by law. All provisions of subchapter IV of chapter 5 of Title 5 shall apply to such alternative means of dispute resolution.

* * *

§ 606. Contractor's right of appeal to board of contract appeals

Within ninety days from the date of receipt of a contracting officer's decision under section 605 of this title, the contractor may appeal such decision to an agency board of contract appeals, as provided in section 607 of this title.

§ 607. Agency boards of contracts appeals

(a) Establishment; consultation; Tennessee Valley Authority

(1) An Armed Services Board of Contract Appeals may be established within the Department of Defense when the Secretary of Defense, after consultation with the Administrator, determines from a workload study that the volume of contract claims justifies the establishment of a full-time agency board of at least three members who shall have no other inconsistent duties. Workload studies will be updated at least once every three years and submitted to the Administrator.

(2) The Board of Directors of the Tennessee Valley Authority may establish a board of contract appeals for the Authority of an indeterminate number of members.

* * *

(c) Appeals; inter-agency arrangements

There is established an agency board of contract appeals to be known as the "Postal Service Board of Contract Appeals". Such board shall have jurisdiction to decide any appeal from a decision of a contracting officer of the United States Postal Service or the Postal Regulatory Commission relative to a contract made by either agency. Such board shall consist of judges appointed by the Postmaster General who shall meet the qualifications of and serve in the same manner as members of the Civilian Board of Contract Appeals. This chapter shall apply to contract disputes before the Postal Service Board of Contract Appeals in the same manner as they apply to contract disputes before the Civilian Board.

(d) Jurisdiction

The Armed Services Board shall have jurisdiction to decide any appeal from a decision of a contracting officer of the Department of Defense, the Department of the Army, the Department of the Navy, the Department of the Air Force, or the National Aeronautics and Space Administration relative to a contract made by that department or agency. The Civilian Board shall have jurisdiction to decide any appeal from a decision of a contracting officer of any executive agency (other than the Department of Defense, the Department of the Army, the Department of the Navy, the Department of the Air Force, the National Aeronautics and Space Administration, the United States Postal Service, the Postal Regulatory Commission, or the Tennessee Valley Authority) relative to a contract made by that agency. Each other agency board shall have jurisdiction to decide any appeal from a decision of a contracting officer relative to a contract made by its agency. In exercising this jurisdiction, the agency board is authorized to grant any relief that would be available to a litigant asserting a contract claim in the United States Court of Federal Claims.

* * *

(g) Review

(1) The decision of an agency board of contract appeals shall be final, except that—

(A) a contractor may appeal such a decision to the United States Court of Appeals for the Federal Circuit within one hundred twenty days after the date of receipt of a copy of such decision, or

(B) the agency head, if he determines that an appeal should be taken, and with the prior approval of the Attorney General, transmits the decision of the board of contract appeals to the Court of Appeals for the Federal Circuit for judicial review under section 1295 of Title 28, within one hundred and twenty days from the date of the agency's receipt of a copy of the board's decision.

* * *

§ 609.   Judicial review of board decisions

(a)   Actions in United States Court of Federal Claims; district court actions; time for filing

(1) Except as provided in paragraph (2), and in lieu of appealing the decision of the contracting officer under section 605 of this title to an agency board, a contractor may bring an action directly on the claim in the United States Court of Federal Claims, notwithstanding any contract provision, regulation, or rule of law to the contrary.

(2) In the case of an action against the Tennessee Valley Authority, the contractor may only bring an action directly on the claim in a United States district court pursuant to section 1337 of title 28, notwithstanding any contract provision, regulation, or rule of law to the contrary.

(3) Any action under paragraph (1) or (2) shall be filed within twelve months from the date of the receipt by the contractor of the decision of the contracting officer concerning the claim, and shall proceed de novo in accordance with the rules of the appropriate court.

(b)   Finality of board decision

In the event of an appeal by a contractor or the Government from a decision of any agency board pursuant to section 607 of this title, notwithstanding any contract provision, regulation, or rules of law to the contrary, the decision of the agency board on any question of law shall not be final or conclusive, but the decision on any question of fact shall be final and conclusive and shall not be set aside unless the decision is fraudulent, or arbitrary, or capricious, or so grossly erroneous as to necessarily imply bad faith, or if such decision is not supported by substantial evidence.

(c)   Remand or retention of case

In any appeal by a contractor or the Government from a decision of an agency board pursuant to section 607 of this title, the court may render an opinion and judgment and remand the case for further action by the agency board or by the executive agency as appropriate, with such direction as the court considers just and proper.

* * *

§ 612.   Payment of claims

(a)   Judgments

Any judgment against the United States on a claim under this chapter shall be paid promptly in accordance with the procedures provided by section 1304 of Title 31.

(b)   Monetary awards

Any monetary award to a contractor by an agency board of contract appeals shall be paid promptly in accordance with the procedures contained in subsection (a) of this section.

(c) Reimbursement

Payments made pursuant to subsections (a) and (b) of this section shall be reimbursed to the fund provided by section 1304 of Title 31 by the agency whose appropriations were used for the contract out of available funds or by obtaining additional appropriations for such purposes.

Tucker Act, 28 United States Code § 1491(a)(2)

(a)(2) * * * The Court of Federal Claims shall have jurisdiction to render judgment upon any claim by or against, or dispute with, a contractor arising under section 10(a)(1) of the Contract Disputes Act of 1978 (41 U.S.C. § 609(a)(1)), including a dispute concerning termination of a contract, rights in tangible or intangible property, compliance with cost accounting standards, and other nonmonetary disputes on which a decision of the contracting officer has been issued under section 6 of that Act.

Little Tucker Act, 28 United States Code § 1346(a)(2)

(a) The district courts shall have original jurisdiction, concurrent with the United States Court of Federal Claims, of:

(2) Any other civil action or claim against the United States, not exceeding $10,000 in amount, founded either upon the Constitution, or any Act of Congress, or any regulation of an executive department, or upon any express or implied contract with the United States, or for liquidated or unliquidated damages in cases not sounding in tort, except that the district courts shall not have jurisdiction of any civil action or claim against the United States founded upon any express or implied contract with the United States or for liquidated or unliquidated damages in cases not sounding in tort which are subject to sections 8(g) (1) and 10(a)(1) of the Contract Disputes Act of 1978. * * *

Federal Courts Improvement Act, 28 United States Code § 1295(a)(10), (b)–(c)

(a) The United States Court of Appeals for the Federal Circuit shall have exclusive jurisdiction—* * *

(10) of an appeal from a final decision of an agency board of contract appeals pursuant to section 8(g)(1) of the Contract Disputes Act of 1978 (41 U.S.C. 607(g) (1)).

(b) The head of any executive department or agency may, with the approval of the Attorney General, refer to the Court of Appeals for the Federal Circuit for judicial review any final decision rendered by a board of contract appeals pursuant to the terms of any contract with the United States awarded by that department or agency which the head of such department or agency has concluded is not entitled to finality pursuant to the review standards specified in section 10(b) of the Contract Disputes Act of 1978 (41 U.S.C. 609(b)). The head of each executive department or agency shall make any referral under this section within one hundred and twenty days after the receipt of a copy of the final appeal decision.

(c) The Court of Appeals for the Federal Circuit shall review the matter referred in accordance with the standards specified in section 10(b) of the Contract Disputes Act of 1978. The court shall proceed with judicial review on the administrative record made before the board of contract appeals on matters so referred as in other cases pending in such court, shall determine the issue of finality of the appeal decision, and shall, if appropriate, render judgment thereon, or remand the matter to any administrative or executive body or official with such direction as it may deem proper and just.

———

Seaboard Lumber Co. v. United States

United States Court of Appeals for the Federal Circuit.
903 F.2d 1560 (Fed.Cir. 1990), cert. denied, 499 U.S. 919 (1991).

■ NIES, CIRCUIT JUDGE.

This appeal is from a certified interlocutory order of the United States Claims Court denying appellants' motion to dismiss the government's counterclaims for breach by the contractors of particular government contracts. Our jurisdiction rests on 28 U.S.C. § 1292(d)(2) (1988). Appellants urged dismissal of the government's counterclaims on the grounds that the appellants have a right to defend against the government's claims in an Article III court. Appellants also assert a right to a jury trial. The Claims Court rejected these constitutional arguments. *See Seaboard Lumber Co. v. United States,* 15 Cl.Ct. 366 (1988) (Smith, C.J.). We affirm on narrower grounds.

BACKGROUND

Appellants are timber companies that individually contracted with the United States to purchase timber from National Forests. With respect to each contract, the government asserted its breach claim against the contractor by means of an appropriate contracting officer's decision. In each case, the contracting officer issued a decision that the contractor failed to cut, remove and pay for timber as required by the contract and assessed a specific dollar amount of damages in each instance. *See* 41 U.S.C. § 605(a) (1982).

Each timber purchasing contract, as originally executed or later amended, contained a standard disputes clause which provides in pertinent part:

C9.2 (disputes).

(a) This contract is subject to the Contract Disputes Act of 1978 (Pub.L. 95–563).

(b) Except as provided in the Act, all disputes arising under or relating to this contract shall be resolved in accordance with this provision.

. . .

(c) iii ... A claim by the government against the contractor shall be subject to a decision by the contracting officer.

. . .

(f) The contracting officer's decision shall be final unless the contractor appeals or files a suit as provided in the Act.

By the Contract Disputes Act, 41 U.S.C. §§ 601–613, Congress mandated that these provisions be included in government contracts generally. *See* 41 U.S.C. § 602.

Under the above clause, once the decision of the contracting officer becomes final on a government claim against the contractor, the merits of that decision cannot be judicially challenged. To prevent that preclusive effect, the contractor has two options under the contract provisions which incorporate the CDA. The contractor may either appeal within 90 days to the appropriate Board of Contract Appeals as provided in 41 U.S.C. § 606 or within twelve months file a direct access suit in the United States Claims Court, an Article I court, under 41 U.S.C. § 609(a)(3). In these proceedings, the facts, as well as the law, are decided *de novo* by the board or the court. *See id.;* 41 U.S.C. § 605(a). At the time the CDA became effective, and at the time all but four of the contracts at issue were executed, a direct access suit would have been filed in the United States Court of Claims, an Article III court. That was changed, effective October 1, 1982, by the Federal Courts Improvement Act of 1982 (FCIA), which placed jurisdiction over direct access suits in a new Article I court, the United States Claims Court. FCIA also provided that an appeal from either the appropriate Board of Contract Appeals or from the United States Claims Court may only be taken to the United States Court of Appeals for the Federal Circuit, an Article III court. The jurisdiction over such appeals is exclusive. 28 U.S.C. §§ 1295(a)(3), (10).

Each appellant filed suit in the Claims Court seeking review of the contracting officer's decision in favor of the government as provided in 41 U.S.C. § 609(a). Had they failed to seek review, the contracting officer's decisions under the contracts (and CDA) would have become final and could not thereafter be judicially challenged on the merits. In each suit, the government filed a counterclaim asserting the breach of contract claim which was the subject of the contracting officer's decision. Thus, the government's breach of contract claim underlies both the complaint and the counterclaim. Each appellant then filed a motion to dismiss the government's counterclaim urging that adjudication of the counterclaim must occur in an Article III court and that, under the Seventh Amendment, the contractor was entitled to a jury trial.

Appellants' suits were consolidated in the Claims Court for consideration of the constitutional issues. In denying the appellants' motion to dismiss the government's counterclaims, the Claims Court held that: (1) a government contract claim was not an action at common law and therefore did not require resolution by an Article III court; (2) such claim fell within the "public rights" exception to Article III and Congress could thus constitutionally provide for adjudication by a non-Article III tribunal; and (3) the Seventh Amendment did not entitle the contractors to a jury trial of the government's claims. The Claims Court dealt summarily with the government's alternative defense that the contractors had waived the asserted rights, if any existed. Recognizing that controlling questions of law were at issue, the questions of appellants' right to trial in an Article III court and right to jury trial, the Claims Court certified the interlocutory order for immediate appeal pursuant to 28 U.S.C. § 1292(d)(2). This court granted appellants permission to appeal.

ISSUE

Whether the CDA, as originally enacted or as amended by FCIA, unconstitutionally deprives appellants of either a right to an Article III court or a jury trial on the government counterclaims for breach of contract?

OPINION

The Seventh Amendment provides:

In Suits at common law, where the value in controversy shall exceed twenty dollars, the right of trial by jury shall be preserved, and no fact tried by a jury shall be otherwise reexamined in any Court of the United States, than according to the rules of the common law.

Seaboard and all other contractors (hereinafter Seaboard) assert that the government's breach of contract claim should be deemed comparable to a private contract claim which, historically must be litigated in an Article III court with a right to a jury. In support of this analogy, it asserts that prior to the CDA, the government had to litigate a breach claim against a contractor in an Article III court (although it cites no authority for this proposition). It maintains further that waiver of sovereign immunity and the authority of an Article I court to adjudicate claims against the government are not involved here. These premises lead Seaboard to its ultimate conclusion that the CDA's review procedures are unconstitutional. We disagree. The premises of Seaboard's syllogism are fatally flawed in a number of respects.

I

Seaboard correctly states that the Seventh Amendment preserves a right to a jury trial on issues of fact in suits for breach of contract damages between private party litigants, *see Northern Pipeline Constr. Co. v. Mara-*

thon Pipe Line, 458 U.S. 50 (1982), but Seaboard fails to carry its analogy through to its logical conclusion. The Supreme Court has long recognized that a private litigant may waive its right to a jury and to an Article III court in civil cases. Waiver can be either express or implied. Waiver requires only that the party waiving such right do so "voluntarily" and "knowingly" based on the facts of the case. The acceptance of contract provisions providing for dispute resolution in a forum where there is no entitlement to a jury trial may satisfy the "voluntary" and "knowing" standard.

Contrary to Seaboard's view, Congress has not taken away the contractor's right to have the government establish its breach claim in an Article III court before a jury. By contractual agreement, the government had regularly provided (until curbed by Congress) that the decision of a contracting officer was final and not subject to review in *any judicial* forum. *United States v. Moorman*, 338 U.S. 457 (1950) (and cases cited therein). Moreover, these contractual provisions denying judicial review were specifically upheld by the Supreme Court, except for fraud on the government's part. *Wunderlich v. United States*, 342 U.S. 98, 99 (1951). Government contractors long have been held to be bound by a provision vesting dispute resolution in a nonjury/non-Article III forum. *United States v. Moorman*, 338 U.S. at 460–62. In *Wunderlich*, the Supreme Court upheld the enforceability of the "finality clause" of a standard form government contract which provided that disputes between the parties "shall be decided by the contracting officer with a right of appeal to the head of the department 'whose decision shall be final and conclusive upon the parties thereto.' " As stated in *Wunderlich*, 342 U.S. at 99–100:

> The same Article 15 of a government contract was before this Court recently, and we held, after a review of the authorities, that such Article was valid. *United States v. Moorman*, 338 U.S. 457. Nor was the *Moorman* case one of first impression. Contracts, both governmental and private, have been before this Court in several cases in which provisions equivalent to Article 15 have been approved and enforced "in the absence of fraud or such gross mistake as would necessarily imply bad faith, or a failure to exercise an honest judgment...."

Thus, voluntary waiver of both Article III and Seventh Amendment rights, as a matter of both private or government contract law, suffers from no inherent constitutional or legal infirmity. Contrary to Seaboard's premise, by the permissible terms in its contracts, the government did not have to litigate the merits of such claim against a contractor, either as to entitlement or amount, in an Article III court before a jury.

Seaboard argues that any waiver was not "voluntary" because government contracts are inherently adhesion contracts, and cites to precedent invalidating contractual provisions where the provision for a waiver resulted from the unfair bargaining positions between the parties. The bare fact that the contracts in question are "take it or leave it" offers by the government is not controlling on the dispute resolution provision's validity, as we read the precedent. The Supreme Court in *Wunderlich,* 342 U.S. at 100, addressed the nature of the government-contractor relationship:

> Respondents were not compelled or coerced into making the contract [with the government]. It was a voluntary undertaking on their part. As competent parties they have contracted for the settlement of disputes in an arbitral manner. This, we have said in *Moorman,* Congress has left them free to do. *United States v. Moorman, supra,* 338 U.S. at 462. The limitation upon this arbitral process is fraud, placed there by this Court.

With respect to the voluntariness of agreeing to the dispute resolution provision in this contract, *Wunderlich* is controlling.

After the *Wunderlich* decision, Congress, as a matter of grace, provided for narrow judicial review of a contracting officer's decision, limiting by statute (the Wunderlich Act) the contractual options previously available to the government. *See* 41 U.S.C. §§ 321, 322. However, absent a contractor's invoking the allowed procedures, a contracting officer's decision became the final adjudication of the government's claim by reason of the disputes clause in the contract.

The CDA, which followed the Wunderlich Act, further restricted the government's options on dispute resolution. Congress mandated that the government had to include in its contracts the broader review provisions set out in the CDA, that is, the dual avenues of review either by appeal to a Board of Contract Appeals or by a direct access suit in the Court of Claims. However, Congress confirmed the use of a finality clause in the contract with respect to a contracting officer's decision in favor of the government, absent the contractor's resort to these review procedures. *See* 41 U.S.C. § 605. Otherwise, the government is not required to litigate the merits of its breach claim.

As in *Moorman* and *Wunderlich,* Seaboard agreed to the contract provisions spelling out the specific procedures for dispute resolution, none of which entail a jury trial in an Article III court. The effect of such agreement is that at least Seaboard *prima facie* voluntarily and knowingly waived any right to dispute resolution except in accordance with the contract.

Finally, Seaboard asserts that the contractors who entered contracts prior to the FCIA cannot be held to have waived trial level adjudication by Article III judges. As indicated, FCIA amended the CDA so that direct access suits could no longer be brought in the Article III Court of Claims but would be brought in the Article I Claims Court with appeal to this Article III court. However, under the prior procedure, a trial commissioner was statutorily authorized to conduct the trial and to file a report of factual findings. *See* 28 U.S.C. § 2503 (1976). The Article III judges of the Court of Claims reviewed reported findings for error under a "presumption of correctness" standard. Thus, the split of trial and review functions under both systems is substantially similar. Moreover, the disputes clause of the subject contracts referenced the CDA, not specific procedures. In such circumstances, where a contract incorporates procedures under a statute, an expectation that the statute will remain unchanged would not be reasonable. Congress, having enacted the CDA procedures, clearly had the power to change them. By referencing the CDA procedures generally, the parties can be held to the CDA procedures in effect at the time the dispute arises. In view of these circumstances, we conclude that Seaboard has demonstrated no change so material or drastic with respect to fact-finding by Article III judges that the revised system cannot be deemed reasonably within the scope of the subject waiver.

II

Another fallacy of Seaboard's position is that its challenge to the government's claim before the Claims Court does not implicate sovereign immunity, and therefore Congress' power to place litigation involving the sovereign in an Article I court cannot be relied on in these cases. Since the venerable case of *Murray v. Hoboken Land and Improvement Co.,* 59 U.S. (18 How.) 272 (1855), it has been established that the authorization by Congress of a suit to challenge a government claim against the plaintiff can be brought only because of the consent of the sovereign. In *Murray's Lessee,* Congress enacted a statute which permitted the Treasury Department to audit and assess customs officials' accounts, to issue a warrant of indebtedness for any delinquency, and to levy against that delinquency. Thereafter the customs collector was allowed to contest the determination of indebtedness in district court. In upholding the constitutionality of these procedures, the Supreme Court expressly noted that they implicated sovereign immunity, stating:

> When ... after the levy of the distress warrant has been begun, the collector may bring before a district court the question, whether he is indebted as recited in the warrant, it simply waives a privilege which belongs to the government, and consents to make the legality of its future proceedings dependent on the judgment of the court.... The United States consents that this fact of indebtedness may be drawn in question by a suit against them.

Murray's Lessee, 59 U.S. (18 How.) at 284. Similarly, the complaints in this appeal are pursuant to a structural system set up by the CDA, which is dependent on waiver of sovereign immunity. Indeed, the CDA review procedures attacked here provide a more expansive waiver than the prior procedures provided in the Wunderlich Act. It is not disputed that the government may condition its consent to suit upon a plaintiff suing only in an Article I court, on waiving a jury trial, or on other conditions including provision for counterclaims to be asserted by the government. *See United States v. Mitchell,* 463 U.S. 206 (1983) (Tucker Act, 28 U.S.C. § 1491, constitutes waiver of sovereign immunity, conditioned on conferring jurisdiction in Claims Court, an Article I tribunal); *Lehman v. Nakshian,* 453 U.S. 156 (1981) (Age Discrimination in Employment Act, 29 U.S.C. § 633a, constitutes waiver of sovereign immunity conditioned on relinquishing right to jury trial).

It has also long been the law that an Article I court without a jury may adjudicate fact issues related to a counterclaim by the government against the plaintiff. In *McElrath v. United States,* 102 U.S. 426, 440 (1880), the Supreme Court held that counterclaims by the government in a suit brought in the Court of Claims (then deemed to be an Article I court) is not controlled by the Seventh Amendment due to conditions placed on the waiver of sovereign immunity:

> The government cannot be sued, except with its own consent. It can declare in what court it may be sued, and prescribe the forms of pleading and the rules of practice to be observed in such suits. It may restrict the jurisdiction of the court to a consideration of only certain classes of claims against the United States. Congress, by the act in question, informs the claimant that *if he avails himself of the privilege of suing the government in* the special court organized for that purpose, he may be met with a set-off, *counter-claim,* or other demand of the government, upon which judgment may go against him, *without the intervention of a jury,* if the court, upon the whole case, is of [the] opinion that the government is entitled to such judgment. *If the claimant avails himself of the privilege thus granted [to sue the sovereign],* he must do so subject to the conditions annexed by the government to the exercise of the privilege. Nothing more need be said on this subject. [Emphasis added.]

Seaboard has invoked the privilege of suing the government by filing its complaint in the Claims Court for review of the contracting officer's decision. Absent the waiver of sovereign immunity provided by the CDA, Seaboard could not have filed that complaint. Having invoked that privilege, Seaboard is subject to the conditions of such waiver, one of which is that it subjects itself to the possibility of a government counterclaim to be tried in a non-jury/Article I tribunal, conditions which Congress may impose. The Supreme Court has spoken unequivocally on this point in *McElrath.* * * *

In sum, it is only as a matter of legislative grace that Seaboard has access to any Article I or III forum. Before Congress' restriction of the government's contract options, the government, by contract provisions, could and did avoid litigation of the merits of its contract claims in any tribunal. Thus, the basis for Seaboard's suit in the Claims Court is a statutory right, which involves a waiver of sovereign immunity. That review is *de novo,* rather than limited, is also a matter of legislative grace. Seaboard is not, as it would have it, merely facilitating the government's obligation to litigate a contract claim for a determination of the government's rights. Seaboard is asserting its own right, a right to review that is given to Seaboard by the contract provisions incorporating the CDA which waives sovereign immunity to that extent.

Conclusion

In conclusion, we agree with the government that under the lawful terms of the contract, Seaboard has agreed to only limited rights of review of the government's counterclaim. Under these circumstances, assuming it has the rights it asserts in the absence of its contract, Seaboard has waived any right to have the government counterclaim litigated in an Article III court before a jury. Moreover, the CDA's non-Article III/non-jury review procedures, enacted to restrict the government's dispute resolution options, are, under controlling precedent, constitutionally permissible as a condition on the waiver of sovereign immunity. The order of the Claims Court denying Seaboard's motion to dismiss is

AFFIRMED.

————

Notes and Questions

1.   Federal government contract law justifies, and at some law schools is offered as, a complete and separate course in itself. *See, e.g.,* John W. Whelan, *Federal Government Contracts: Cases and Materials* (1985 & Supp. 1989). While by the nature of this survey course we can look at only a couple of cases that involve litigation of contract disputes, federal government contract law also raises issues involving the federal acquisition regulation system, competition requirements, contractor qualifications, bidding, contract negotiation, standard contract clauses, contract financing, contract administration, contract modification, subcontracting, and contract termination. For more detailed explication of government contract law, including but going well beyond the litigation of claims that is the focus of this treatise, essential sources include Margaret M. Worthington & Louis P. Goldsman, *Contracting with the Federal Government* (4th ed. 1998); Ralph C. Nash, Jr., Steven L. Schooner & Karen R. O'Brien, *The Government Contracts Reference Book: A Comprehensive Guide to the Language of Procurement* (2d ed., 1998); Robert T. Peacock & Peter D. Ting, *Contract Disputes Act: Annotated* (1998); John Cibinic, Jr. & Ralph C. Nash, Jr., *Administration of Government Contracts* (4th ed., 2006); Eugene W. Massengale, *Fundamentals of Federal Contract Law* (1991). For a comprehensive history of government contracting, see generally James F. Nagle, *A History of Government Contracting* (2d ed., 1999).

2.   The Contract Disputes Act (CDA) governs all contracts entered into by the government for the procurement of property, other than real property; the procurement of services; the procurement of construction, alteration, repair or maintenance of real property; or the disposal of personal property. 41 U.S.C. § 602(a). Accordingly, the vast majority of contracts with federal government departments and agencies fall within the scope of the CDA.

There are exceptions, however, to the CDA, most notably including non-procurement contracts and implied contracts. Contracts in which the government supplies a service are not covered by the CDA. Thus, for example, when companies that contracted with the government to place satellites into space sought recovery for delays in launches carrying commercial payloads following the Challenger spaceshuttle explosion, those actions were brought under the Tucker Act rather than the CDA. *See, e.g., Hughes Communications Galaxy, Inc. v. United States,* 38 Fed. Cl. 578 (1997), *aff'd,* 271 F.3d 1060 (Fed.Cir. 2001); *New Valley Corp. v. United States,* 34 Fed. Cl. 703 (1996), *rev'd,* 119 F.3d 1576 (Fed.Cir. 1997); *American Satellite Co. v. United States,* 26 Cl. Ct. 146 (1992), *rev'd in part, vacated in part,* 998 F.2d 950 (Fed.Cir. 1993). Similarly, agreements by the government arising out of its regulatory activities are not created under the CDA process. For an example of such an agreement, in the context of regulation of financial institutions, see the discussion of the Supreme Court's decision in *United States v. Winstar Corp.,* 518 U.S. 839 (1996), in Chapter IV.A.4.d. In the immediately preceding section of this casebook, we looked at implied in fact contracts. Although the CDA purports to apply to "any express or implied contract," 41 U.S.C. § 602(a), it actually does not apply to most implied-in-fact contracts which by their nature do not have a contracting officer to make the decision that initiates proceedings under the Act. The next case in this casebook, *Reflectone v. Dalton,* illustrates the importance of the contracting officer decision to the CDA scheme.

3.   The Contract Disputes Act governs contractual disputes with the designated contractor during performance of the contract. Disputes also may arise regarding the formation of a contract—in particular when disappointed contract bidders challenge the validity of a contract award to another party—which may lead to litigation against the federal government. As Professor Stephen L. Schooner explains, bid "[p]rotests are challenges concerning the formation or award of government contracts ...; [b]y contrast, contract disputes involve controversies or claims arising during performance of a contract." Steven L. Schooner, *Fear of Oversight: The Fundamental Failure of Businesslike Government,* 50 Am. U. L. Rev. 627, 638–39 (2001).

Until fairly recently, the Court of Federal Claims and the district courts shared authority to hear "bid protests." In the Administrative Dispute Resolution Act of 1996, Pub. L. No. 104–320, § 12, 110 Stat. 3870, 3874–76 (1996), Congress conferred concurrent jurisdiction upon the district courts and the Court of Federal Claims over bid protests, whether made before or after the contract is awarded, with the power to grant declaratory and injunctive relief, as well as monetary relief that is limited to the cost of bid preparation (and therefore does not include lost anticipated profits). Tucker Act, 28 U.S.C. § 1941(b). Under the Administrative Dispute Resolution Act, the bid protest jurisdiction of the district courts was subject to a sunset provision and terminated on January 1, 2001, thereby making the Court of Federal Claims henceforth the exclusive *judicial* forum for bid disputes. Pub. L. No. 104–320, § 12(d), 110 Stat. at 3875. However, the Court of Federal Claims continues to share authority over bid disputes with the Government Accountability Office, 31 U.S.C. § 3553, which receives a much larger volume of bid protests. On the history of government procurement contract review, *see generally Impresa Construzioni Geom. Domenico Garufi v. United States,* 238 F.3d 1324, 1331–32 (Fed.Cir. 2001). On the developing law of bid protests, see generally Jennifer Wittmeyer, Note, *Conflicts in the Court of Federal Claims: The*

Federal Circuit's Key Decisions and Resolutions Over Bid Protest Practice,
13 Fed. Cir. B.J. 507 (2004).

   4.   Before turning to the specific issues in *Seaboard Lumber Co. v.
United States,* it is essential to understand the basic procedures involved in
litigation of a contract claim under the Contract Disputes Act. From the
excerpts of the statute included in the materials and the description of the
statutory scheme in *Seaboard,* you should be able to outline each of the
steps, identify the forum choices (if any) at each step, and the time
limitations for taking the next step. The flowchart below, reprinted from
the Judge Advocate General's School, U.S. Army, Contract Attorney's
Course, 1995,* should assist in understanding the process:

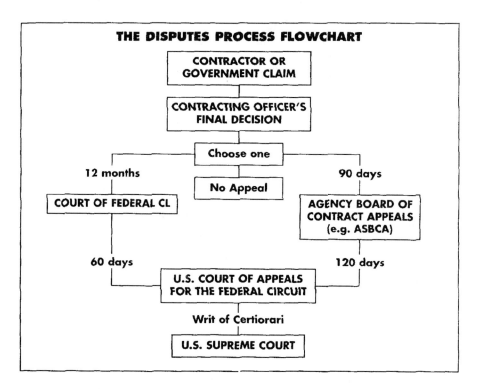

THE DISPUTES PROCESS FLOWCHART

CONTRACTOR OR GOVERNMENT CLAIM

CONTRACTING OFFICER'S FINAL DECISION

Choose one

12 months — No Appeal — 90 days

COURT OF FEDERAL CL

AGENCY BOARD OF CONTRACT APPEALS (e.g. ASBCA)

60 days   120 days

U.S. COURT OF APPEALS FOR THE FEDERAL CIRCUIT

Writ of Certiorari

U.S. SUPREME COURT

   In this regard, you might wonder what factors would influence a
contractor's choice between the Court of Federal Claims and the Board of
Contract Appeals when seeking review of a contracting officer's decision.**

---

   * The Judge Advocate General's School's
materials have been reproduced for private
practitioners by the Section of Public Contract Law of the American Bar Association,
in *Government Contract Law—The Deskbook
for Procurement Professionals* (1995).

   ** Until recently, many different agencies created their own Board of Contract Appeals. Beginning in 2007, most of these bod-

ies have been consolidated into two major
boards: the Armed Services Board of Contract Appeals and the Civilian Board of Contract Appeals (with only the Postal Service
and the Tennessee Valley Authority continuing to have separate boards). *See* National
Defense Authorization Act for Fiscal Year
2006, Pub. L. No. 109–163, § 847, 119 Stat.
3136, 3145.

The procedures in both forums are similar; discovery is available in both. In both forums, the contracting officer's decision is subject to de novo review on both facts and law. The governing law in both is the same. Appellate review from both lies in the Court of Appeals for the Federal Circuit. Thus, such basic considerations are not implicated by a choice of one or the other forum. Instead, the choice involves a more sophisticated election. Practical concerns, such as the backlog in one or the other forum and the attendant delay in decision may be a factor.

Lawyers who specialize in government contract law overwhelmingly choose to pursue claims in the Boards—a ratio of ten board proceedings to one 'direct access' Court of Federal Claims case. An American Bar Association study found that specialists tend to choose the Court of Federal Claims only when certain special factors are present, such as the belief that the court's judges are more likely to respond favorably to novel arguments. By contrast, non-specialists tend to sue in the Court of Federal Claims because they feel more comfortable in a judicial forum than in an unfamiliar administrative tribunal. For further information regarding the choice between these two forums, see generally Michael J. Schaengold, Robert S. Brams & Christopher Lerner, *Choice of Forum for Contract Claims: Court vs. Board,* 3 Fed. Circuit B.J. 35 (1993).

In terms of appellate review by the Federal Circuit, there is a subtle difference in the standards of review applied to factual questions raised in appeals from the boards as opposed to the Court of Federal Claims. (Of course, the Federal Circuit, like any appellate court, reviews questions of law de novo.) Under the CDA, 41 U.S.C. § 609(b), the decision of a board "on any question of fact shall be final and conclusive and shall not be set aside unless the decision is fraudulent, or arbitrary, or capricious, or so grossly erroneous as to necessarily imply bad faith, or if such decision is not supported by substantial evidence." The standard of review for factual findings by the Court of Federal Claims, like the typical standard for appellate review of district court factual findings, is whether the decision is "clearly erroneous." *See Scott Timber Co. v. United States*, 333 F.3d 1358, 1365 (Fed.Cir. 2003). Because a decision may be reasonable, and thus supported by substantial evidence, even if it is clearly mistaken, the "substantial evidence" standard of review is slightly more deferential to the fact-finder than the "clearly erroneous" standard. Thus, as Professor W. Noel Keyes suggested, "it is conceivable that a board decision could be upheld because it met the [substantial evidence standard], but a [Court of Federal Claims] decision could be reversed on substantially the same facts on the ground that a majority of the Court of Appeals for the Federal Circuit felt that the [Court of Federal Claims] decision was 'clearly erroneous.' " W. Noel Keyes, *Government Contracts in a Nutshell* 338–39 (2d ed. 1990). However, since both standards of review are extremely deferential toward the fact-finder, differences in outcome should be rare.

5. Turning then at last to the *Seaboard* decision, what are the constitutional claims raised by the contractor here in opposition to application of the CDA scheme? How did the CDA procedure change, at least in form, in 1982? How did the Claims Court (now Court of Federal Claims) answer these challenges? How does the Federal Circuit rule on these same questions? The contractor argues that its claimed rights to an Article III forum and a jury trial are strengthened by the fact that the case involves not only a suit by the contractor against the government pursuant to a permissive waiver of sovereign immunity but also a counterclaim by the government against the contractor. What is the basis for this argument? How does the court of appeals address it?

Reflectone, Inc. v. Dalton, Secretary of the Navy

United States Court of Appeals for the Federal Circuit.
60 F.3d 1572 (Fed.Cir. 1995) (en banc).

■ MICHEL, CIRCUIT JUDGE.

Reflectone, Inc. (Reflectone) appeals from the decision of the Armed Services Board of Contract Appeals (Board) dismissing Reflectone's appeal for lack of subject matter jurisdiction. The Board held that Reflectone had not submitted a "claim" within the meaning of the Contract Disputes Act of 1978 (CDA), 41 U.S.C. § § 601–13 , as interpreted in the Federal Acquisition Regulation (FAR), because a dispute over the amount of money Reflectone asserted it was owed did not predate Reflectone's June 1, 1990 Request for Equitable Adjustment (REA), the purported claim. Board jurisdiction is grounded in the CDA which authorizes Board review only of a contracting officer's final decision on a "claim." The CDA, however, does not define "claim." Because we conclude that FAR 33.201, which alone defines "claim" for purposes of the CDA, does not require a pre-existing dispute as to either amount or liability when, as here, a contractor submits a non-routine "written demand ... seeking, as a matter of right, the payment of money in a sum certain," FAR 33.201, we hold that Reflectone's REA was a CDA "claim" and, therefore, the Board has jurisdiction. Accordingly, we reverse the dismissal and remand for adjudication of Reflectone's appeal from the contracting officer's decision on its merits.

BACKGROUND

On April 15, 1988, Reflectone entered into a $4,573,559 fixed price contract with the Naval Training Systems Center in Orlando, Florida, requiring Reflectone to update helicopter weapon system trainers. The contract called for delivery of the first trainer on February 15, 1989, with the other three trainers to follow at three-month intervals. In a letter dated December 14, 1988, Reflectone advised the contracting officer (CO) that delivery of certain equipment was being delayed by late, unavailable or defective government-furnished property. In response, the Navy denied responsibility for the delay and issued a cure notice warning Reflectone that unless the condition endangering timely delivery of the equipment was eliminated within thirty days, the Navy might terminate the contract for default.

On January 17, 1989, Reflectone again wrote the CO that the delays were the fault of the government and requested an extension of the contract delivery schedule. Subsequently, the Navy modified two of the original four delivery dates but reserved its right to seek additional compensation for delay. After Reflectone advised the Navy that it would be unable to meet even the extended delivery dates due to faulty government-furnished property, the CO indicated on May 5, 1989, that Reflectone was delinquent on the contract and that the Navy would seek compensation for the delay. Between May 1989 and April 1990, the contract delivery schedule was modified at least three more times and each time the Navy reserved the right to make a claim against Reflectone for delay. In response, Reflectone continued to inform the Navy that it considered the government to have caused all delays and that it would claim relief once the full economic impact of the delay was known.

On June 1, 1990, Reflectone submitted an REA [Request for Equitable Adjustment] to the CO demanding $266,840 for costs related to government-caused delay with respect to twenty-one enumerated items. Reflectone's President and CEO certified the REA and requested a decision from the CO. In the initial review of the REA, completed on January 15, 1991, the CO denied sixteen of the twenty-one items in their entirety, estimated entitlement in the remaining five items at $17,662, and advised Reflectone that a counterclaim and set-off, exceeding the amount requested by Reflectone, was being prepared.[1] On March 19, 1991, the CO rendered a final decision indicating that the government's position remained the same and advising Reflectone of its right to appeal to the Board.

Reflectone appealed the CO's final decision to the Board, which held that the REA was not a "claim" within the meaning of the Contract Disputes Act and, therefore, it did not have jurisdiction over the appeal. The Board relied on language from *Dawco Constr., Inc. v. United States,* 930 F.2d 872, 878 (Fed.Cir.1991), stating, "A contractor and the government contracting agency must already be in dispute over the amount requested." *Dawco* also states "The [CDA] and its implementing regulation require that a 'claim' arise from a request for payment that is 'in dispute.'" *Id.* The Board interpreted *Dawco* as holding that no demand for payment could be a claim unless the *amount* of the payment had been put in dispute. The Board reasoned that because Reflectone first requested a specific amount from the government in the REA, no dispute over the amount existed prior to the REA and, therefore, the REA could not be a claim according to its interpretation of *Dawco.* * * *

On appeal to this court, a divided, three-judge panel affirmed the Board's dismissal decision, accepting its interpretation of *Dawco* and its

---

1. The CO forwarded a counterclaim to Reflectone for late and deficient contractor performance totaling $657,388 on November 8, 1991.

rationale, in an opinion dated September 1, 1994, now vacated. Due to the exceptional public importance of the issue of first impression presented by this case concerning the proper definition of a CDA "claim," we granted Reflectone's Suggestion for Rehearing In Banc.Fed.Cir.R. 35.

We have jurisdiction pursuant to 28 U.S.C. § 1295(a)(10) and Section 8 of the Contract Disputes Act, 41 U.S.C. § 607(g)(1).

STANDARD OF REVIEW

The CDA dictates the standards this court applies in reviewing decisions of agency contract appeal boards. 41 U.S.C. § 609(b). A determination of CDA jurisdiction and interpretation of applicable procurement regulations present questions of law which we review *de novo*

ANALYSIS

I

A. *FAR 33.201 Does Not Require That A Payment Demanded In A Non–Routine Submission Be In Dispute Before The Submission To A Contracting Officer Can Be A "Claim"*

Under the CDA, a final decision by a CO on a "claim" is a prerequisite for Board jurisdiction. Because the CDA itself does not define the term "claim,"[2] we must assess whether a particular demand for payment constitutes a claim, based on the FAR [Federal Acquisition Regulation] implementing the CDA, the language of the contract in dispute, and the facts of the case. The FAR defines "claim" as:

> [1]   a written demand or written assertion by one of the contracting parties seeking, as a matter of right, the payment of money in a sum certain, the adjustment or interpretation of contract terms, or other relief arising under or relating to the contract.... [2] A voucher, invoice, or other *routine request for payment that is not in dispute when submitted is not a claim.* [3] The submission may be converted to a claim, by written notice to the contracting officer as provided in 33.206(a), if it is disputed either as to liability or amount or is not acted upon in a reasonable time.

FAR (48 C.F.R. §) 33.201 (emphasis added). The issue is whether sentence [2] adds a requirement to those stated in sentence [1] that applies to all submissions.

The government and the Board would require that before Reflectone's REA can qualify as a claim, it be preceded by a dispute over entitlement to and the amount of a demand for payment. According to the government, this requirement is mandated by the language of FAR 33.201. In order to

---

2. The CDA, 41 U.S.C. § 605(a), states in relevant part:

> All claims by a contractor against the government relating to a contract shall be in writing and shall be submitted to the contracting officer for a decision. All claims by the government against a contractor relating to a contract shall be the subject of a decision by the contracting officer.

explore whether a CDA "claim" requires a dispute which pre-dates the submission to the CO, we requested that the following question be addressed by the *in banc* briefs.

> Did *Dawco Constr., Inc. v. United States,* 930 F.2d 872 (Fed.Cir.1991), properly conclude that a Contract Disputes Act (CDA) "claim" as defined in FAR 33.201 requires a pre-existing dispute between a contractor and the government when the claim is in the form of a "written assertion ... seeking, as a matter of right, the payment of money in a sum certain" or other contract relief per the first sentence of the FAR definition, or does that requirement only apply when the claim initially is in the form of a "routine request for payment"?

We answer the first half of this question in the negative and the second half in the affirmative. We hold that sentence [1] of FAR 33.201 sets forth the only three requirements of a non-routine "claim" for money: that it be (1) a written demand, (2) seeking, as a matter of right, (3) the payment of money in a sum certain. That sentence simply does not require that entitlement to the amount asserted in the claim or the amount itself already be in dispute when the document is submitted. The subsequent sentence does not add another requirement to a non-routine submission.

FAR 33.201 does not mention a dispute until the fourth sentence, sentence [2], which provides, "[a] voucher, invoice, or other routine request for payment that is not in dispute when submitted is not a claim." Routine requests for payment, too, are "written demand[s] ... seeking, as a matter of right, payment of money in a sum certain" and, therefore, appear to fall within the definition of claim recited in sentence [1] of FAR 33.201. However, the FAR explicitly excludes from the definition of "claim" those "routine request[s] for payment" that are not in dispute when submitted to the CO.[6] Nevertheless, nothing in the definition suggests that *other* written demands seeking payment of a sum certain as a matter of right, i.e., those demands that are not "routine request[s] for payment," also must be already in dispute to constitute a "claim." Moreover, that the regulation specifically excludes only undisputed *routine* requests for payment from the category of written demands for payment that satisfy the definition of "claim" implies that all other written demands seeking payment as a matter of right are "claims," whether already in dispute or not. The inclusion of only one exception to the definition of "claim"—undisputed, routine requests—implies the exclusion of any others.

* * *

Moreover, as Reflectone points out, it is illogical to require a dispute before a demand for payment rightfully due can be a "claim" because to have a dispute the contractor first must make a demand as a matter of

---

6. The distinction excluding routine requests for payment from the definition of "claim" relieves COs from the requirement of issuing a CDA final decision on each and every voucher that the government is obligated to pay under the express terms of the contract during its ordinary progression, including "progress payments." The process for converting such routine requests, if disputed, into claims assures that only those submissions that need final decisions will require them.

right, i.e., a claim, that is then refused. Furthermore, neither the CDA, its legislative history, nor the FAR, nor its history, suggests that a dispute must pre-date the contractor's submission of the claim to the CO when the claim is in the form of a non-routine demand as of right.

The government argues, nevertheless, that a close reading of the regulation demonstrates that a "claim" always requires a pre-existing dispute. The government's analysis begins correctly by acknowledging that sentence [1] of the FAR, defining "claim" as "a written demand ... seeking, as a matter of right, the payment of money in a sum certain" appears to include vouchers, invoices and other routine requests for payment. According to the government, because the regulation later makes clear that the drafters intended to exclude routine requests for payment from the definition of "claim" unless they are in dispute, the question becomes one of distinguishing between non-routine written demands seeking the payment of a sum certain as a matter of right and "routine request[s] for payment." The government next asserts, incorrectly, that it is the existence of a dispute which distinguishes a non-routine "claim" from a routine request for payment and, therefore, every "claim" must involve a pre-existing dispute.

The government's interpretation of the FAR must fail, as a matter of logic, because it recognizes only two categories of potential claims, undisputed routine requests for payment, which do not satisfy the definition, and disputed non-routine written demands seeking payment as a matter of right, which do. This interpretation ignores a third category, undisputed, non-routine written demands seeking payment as a matter of right. Under the literal language of the FAR, however, the critical distinction in identifying a "claim" is not between undisputed and disputed submissions, but between routine and non-routine submissions.

To read the dispute requirement of sentence [2] of FAR 33.201 as applying to all submissions for payment, as the government suggests, one would have to construe *every* demand for payment as a matter of right as a "routine request for payment." However, this is clearly not so. For instance, an REA [Request for Equitable Adjustment] is anything but a "routine request for payment." It is a remedy payable only when unforeseen or unintended circumstances, such as government modification of the contract, differing site conditions, defective or late-delivered government property or issuance of a stop work order, cause an increase in contract performance costs. A demand for compensation for unforeseen or unintended circumstances cannot be characterized as "routine." The Supreme Court has confirmed the non-routine nature of an REA by equating it with assertion of a breach of contract. *Crown Coat Front Co. v. United States*, 386 U.S. 503, 511 (1967) ("With respect to claims arising under the typical government contract, the contractor has agreed in effect to convert what otherwise might be claims for breach of contract into claims for equitable adjustment."). Thus, an REA provides an example of a written demand for payment as a matter of right which is not "a routine request for payment" and, therefore, it satisfies the FAR definition of "claim" whether or not the government's liability for or the amount of the REA was already disputed before submission of the REA to the CO.[7]

A routine request for payment, on the other hand, is made under the contract, not outside it. For example, a voucher or invoice is submitted for work done or equipment delivered by the contractor in accordance with the expected or scheduled progression of contract performance. Similarly, progress payments are made by the government when the contractor completes predetermined stages of the contract. An REA can hardly be compared to an invoice, voucher or progress payment.

Thus, we hold that FAR 33.201 does not require that "a written demand . . . seeking, as a matter of right, the payment of money in a sum certain" must already be in dispute when submitted to the CO to satisfy the definition of "claim," *except* where that demand or request is a "voucher, invoice or other routine request for payment." This interpretation, based on the plain language of the FAR, examines and reconciles the text of the entire regulation, not simply isolated sentences. FAR 33.201, viewed as a whole, establishes a framework in which written demands seeking a sum certain as a matter of right are CDA "claims" with the only exception of "routine request[s] for payment" which may be converted to claims by the existence of a dispute and compliance with other require ments of conversion in FAR 33.206(a). Routine requests are a subset of all written demands for payment. Special requirements apply to the subset, but not to the rest of the set.

Reflectone's REA is clearly "a written demand or written assertion by one of the contracting parties seeking, as a matter of right, the payment of money in a sum certain." Reflectone, a contracting party, submitted a written document to the CO demanding the payment of $266,840 which it asserted the government owed for delaying performance of the contract by furnishing defective goods. The submission was certified and requested a CO decision. Consequently, Reflectone's REA satisfies all the requirements listed for a CDA "claim" according to the plain language of the first sentence of FAR 33.201. The REA is not a "routine request for payment" and, therefore, the fourth sentence of the FAR definition does not apply here to require, *inter alia,* a pre-existing dispute as to either liability or amount. Because we conclude that Reflectone's REA is a "claim" according to the FAR, we further conclude that the Board has jurisdiction to review the CO's denial of Reflectone's REA.

---

7. We do not hold, however, that every non-routine submission constitutes a "claim" under the FAR. Those submissions which do not seek payment as a matter of right are not claims, a definition which excludes, for example, cost proposals for work the government later decides it would like performed. *See Essex Electro Eng'rs,* 960 F.2d at 1581–82 (excluding cost proposals and inspection reports from the FAR definition of a CDA "claim").

B.   *Dawco's Holding Is Overruled*

The Board and the government relied on language in *Dawco* to support the conclusion that a dispute as to amount is required before *any* demand for payment can be a CDA "claim." * * *

* * *

* * * To the extent that *Dawco* and its progeny have been read to also hold that, based on FAR 33.201, a "claim" (other than a routine request for payment) must already be in dispute when submitted to the CO, they are hereby overruled. * * *

* * *

C.   *The Effect Of Dawco's Holding That The FAR Always Requires A Dispute Is Contrary To The Goals Of The CDA*

The *Dawco* dispute requirement has proven to be inimical to at least two goals of the CDA: providing for the efficient and fair resolution of contract claims.

Even where the parties proceed in a shared belief that they are in dispute, and the CO issues a final decision on a contractor's claim, as happened here, the issue of whether the payment demand was actually in dispute when the purported claim was submitted can be raised anytime, before the Board or the Court of Federal Claims or on appeal to us. Since the court's ruling in *Dawco* in 1991, nearly two hundred Board, Court of Federal Claims, and Federal Circuit decisions have addressed whether a particular contractor's demand for payment was "in dispute" before it filed its claim, according to Donald P. Arnavas, *To Claim or Not to Claim,* 8 Nash & Cibinic Rep. ¶ 63 (1994). According to one Armed Services Board of Contract Appeals Judge, one-half of all cases considered by the agency boards that concerned *Dawco*'s dispute requirement resulted in dismissal for lack of jurisdiction. *Half of All Dawco Cases at Agency Boards Result in Dismissal,* 61 Fed.Cont.Rep. (BNA) 18 (1994).

These judicial inquiries into whether a dispute pre-dated a submission are at best an inefficient use of limited resources, given that before the Board or court reaches this question there will necessarily have been a final CO's decision denying the contractor's submission or at least a deemed denial based on the CO's failure to respond. Moreover, in each case, the government continues to dispute the claim, because otherwise it would have settled the matter and no appeal would be necessary. Because a dispute clearly exists at the time an appeal is dismissed for lack of a dispute pre-dating submission of the demand for payment to the CO, after dismissal the contractor need only resubmit the identical demand to the CO. The resubmitted demand would now indisputedly satisfy the pre-existing dispute requirement and, therefore, be a CDA claim. The process of final decision and appeal would begin all over again, but at great cost to the parties, the boards and the courts, and often with no benefit because the disputed issues on the merits have already been well defined by the course of litigation. Clearly, this repetitive and needlessly drawn-out process can hardly be said to promote the "efficient" resolution of claims. Nor is it "fair." Requiring contractors to submit the identical claim twice, as the government would have them do, is a waste of the contractor's time and money. The taxpayers' money is likewise wasted when the agency boards or the Court of Federal Claims must hear the same case on two different occasions. Nor has the government shown how this process is not seriously inefficient, unfair and wasteful.

* * *

CONCLUSION

We hold that properly construed for its plain meaning, the language of FAR 33.201 does not require that a payment demand contained in a purported CDA claim be in dispute before being submitted for decision to the CO unless that demand is a "voucher, invoice or other routine request for payment." To the extent that *Dawco* and cases relying on *Dawco* can be read to suggest otherwise, they are overruled. We further hold that Reflectone's REA satisfies the definition of "claim," and, therefore, we reverse the Board's dismissal for lack of jurisdiction and remand this case to the Board for further proceedings on Reflectone's appeal consistent with this opinion.[17]

REVERSED AND REMANDED

■ NIES, CIRCUIT JUDGE, concurring.

I concur in holding that the Armed Services Board of Contract Appeals has jurisdiction in this case. I conclude that there is no requirement for a preexisting dispute as to the *amount* of a demand for an equitable adjustment where the government has denied *any* liability. This conclusion is sufficient to dispose of this appeal and I would reverse and remand for this reason.

Notes and Questions

The "linchpin" of court jurisdiction under the CDA is a final decision by the contracting officer regarding a certified claim. *See generally* C. Stanley Dees & David A. Churchill, *Government Contract Cases in the United States Court of Appeals for the Federal Circuit: 1996 in Review,* 46 Am. U. L. Rev. 1807, 1816 (1997). In order to trigger the CDA procedures and lead to a judicially-reviewable decision, the submission to the contracting officer must be a "claim." As two leading practitioners in public contract law have observed, "[t]he definition of what constitutes a 'claim' has, in recent years, been the subject of more wasteful and confusing government contract litigation than any other aspect of the CDA." Dees & Churchill, *supra,* at 1810. The Federal Circuit's en banc decision in

---

17. We, or course, take no position on whether there is any merit to Reflectone's appeal.

Reflectone v. Dalton was intended to resolve that question, at least in general terms.

The controversy about the meaning of "claim" for purposes of the CDA arose in this way: A contractor submits a voucher or request for payment for work performed, and the contracting officer refuses payment. At that point, has the contractor submitted a "claim" within the meaning of the CDA, such that the denial of payment by the agency constitutes a final contracting officer decision that is now immediately subject to court or board review? Or must the contractor take some further action at the contracting officer stage before proceeding to the next stage? What if the contractor submits a request for a different kind of relief from the contracting officer, that is, something that is not routine? Must the contractor wait until the contracting officer grants or denies the request and then re-new it yet again to constitute a "claim"? That is, must there be a pre-existing dispute before the non-routine request is made? Or does the very non-routine nature of the request suffice to fit it into the category of a "claim" to the contracting officer that starts the CDA ball rolling?

What answers does the Federal Circuit give to these questions in *Reflectone* and why? If the contractor was merely making "a routine request for payment" for work performed in the expected progression of the contract, then is the contractor's submission to be regarded as a "claim"? Why not? Why should routine requests for payment be excluded from the definition of a "claim"? What practical purpose is promoted by that understanding? If the "routine" submission for payment is refused is refused, and thus a dispute is confirmed by the very denial, what now must the contractor do to initiate the CDA dispute resolution process that ultimately leads to the possibility of judicial review? Are there any circumstances under which a "routine" request for payment may qualify as a "claim" under the CDA? What if the matter was already "in dispute"—as evidenced by conflicts between the contractor and the agency or an impasse in negotiations—before the request for payment was made? By contrast, if the contractor makes a "non-routine" request for payment, is anything more required to make it a "claim"? Must the contractor demonstrate that the matter was already in dispute before a non-routine request will be treated as the submission of a "claim"? And into what category does the submission in *Reflectone* fall? Was it a routine or non-routine request? Was there a preexisting dispute or not and did it matter in this case for purposes of triggering the CDA process?

---

c.   GOVERNING LAW IN FEDERAL GOVERNMENT CONTRACTS

United States v. Kimbell Foods, Inc.

Supreme Court of the United States.
440 U.S. 715 (1979).

■ MR. JUSTICE MARSHALL delivered the opinion of the Court.

We granted certiorari in these cases to determine whether contractual liens arising from certain federal loan programs take precedence over private liens, in the absence of a federal statute setting priorities. To resolve this question, we must decide first whether federal or state law governs the controversies; and second, if federal law applies, whether this Court should fashion a uniform priority rule or incorporate state commercial law. We conclude that the source of law is federal, but that a national rule is unnecessary to protect the federal interests underlying the loan programs. Accordingly, we adopt state law as the appropriate federal rule for establishing the relative priority of these competing federal and private liens.

I

A

No. 77–1359 involves two contractual security interests in the personal property of O. K. Super Markets, Inc. Both interests were perfected pursuant to Texas' Uniform Commercial Code (UCC). The United States' lien secures a loan guaranteed by the Small Business Administration (SBA). The private lien, which arises from security agreements that preceded the federal guarantee, secures advances respondent made after the federal guarantee.

In 1968, O. K. Super Markets borrowed $27,000 from Kimbell Foods, Inc. (Kimbell), a grocery wholesaler. Two security agreements identified the supermarket's equipment and merchandise as collateral. The agreements also contained a standard "dragnet" clause providing that this collateral would secure future advances from Kimbell to O. K. Super Markets. Kimbell properly perfected its security interests by filing financing statements with the Texas Secretary of State according to Texas law.

In February 1969, O. K. Super Markets obtained a $300,000 loan from Republic National Bank of Dallas (Republic). The bank accepted as security the same property specified in Kimbell's 1968 agreements, and filed a financing statement with the Texas Secretary of State to perfect its security interest. The SBA guaranteed 90% of this loan under the Small Business Act, which authorizes such assistance but, with one exception, does not specify priority rules to govern the SBA's security interests.

* * * Kimbell continued credit sales to O. K. Super Markets until the balance due reached $18,258.57 on January 15, 1971. Thereupon, Kimbell initiated state proceedings against O. K. Super Markets to recover this inventory debt.

Shortly before Kimbell filed suit, O. K. Super Markets had defaulted on the SBA-guaranteed loan. Republic assigned its security interest to the SBA in late December 1970 * * *. The United States then honored its guarantee and paid Republic $252,331.93 (90% of the outstanding indebtedness) on February 3, 1971. * * * Approximately one year later, the state court entered judgment against O. K. Super Markets, and awarded Kimbell

$24,445.37, representing the inventory debt, plus interest and attorney's fees.

Kimbell thereafter brought the instant action to foreclose on its lien, claiming that its security interest in the escrow fund was superior to the SBA's. The District Court held for the Government. On determining that federal law controlled the controversy, the court applied principles developed by this Court to afford federal statutory tax liens special priority over state and private liens where the governing statute does not specify priorities. *Kimbell Foods, Inc. v. Republic Nat. Bank of Dallas,* 401 F.Supp. 316, 321–322 (N.D.Tex.1975). Under these rules, the lien "first in time" is "first in right." However, to be considered first in time, the nonfederal lien must be "choate," that is, sufficiently specific, when the federal lien arises. A state-created lien is not choate until the "identity of the lienor, the property subject to the lien, and the amount of the lien are established." *United States v. New Britain,* 347 U.S. 81, 84 (1954). Failure to meet any one of these conditions forecloses priority over the federal lien, even if under state law the nonfederal lien was enforceable for all purposes when the federal lien arose.

Because Kimbell did not reduce its lien to judgment until February 1972, and the federal lien had been created either in 1969, when Republic filed its financing statement, or in 1971, when Republic recorded its assignment, the District Court concluded that respondent's lien was inchoate when the federal lien arose. * * *

The Court of Appeals reversed. *Kimbell Foods, Inc. v. Republic Nat. Bank of Dallas,* 557 F.2d 491 (C.A.5 1977). It agreed that federal law governs the rights of the United States under its SBA loan program, and that the "first in time, first in right" priority principle should control the competing claims. However, the court refused to extend the choateness rule to situations in which the Federal Government was not an involuntary creditor of tax delinquents, but rather a voluntary commercial lender. Instead, it fashioned a new federal rule for determining which lien was first in time, and concluded that "in the context of competing state security interests arising under the U. C. C.," the first to meet UCC perfection requirements achieved priority.

The Court of Appeals then considered which lien qualified as first perfected. * * * [T]he court determined that, under Texas law, the 1968 security agreements covered Kimbell's future advances, and that the liens securing those advances dated from the filing of the security agreements before the federal lien arose. But the Court of Appeals did not adopt Texas law. Rather, it proceeded to decide whether the future advances should receive the same treatment under federal common law. * * * [T]he court held that Kimbell's future advances dated back to the 1968 agreements, and therefore took precedence over Republic's 1969 loan.

B

At issue in No. 77–1644 is whether a federal contractual security interest in a tractor is superior to a subsequent repairman's lien in the same property. From 1970 to 1972, Ralph Bridges obtained several loans from the Farmers Home Administration (FHA), under the Consolidated Farmers Home Administration Act of 1961. Like the Small Business Act, this statute does not establish rules of priority. To secure the FHA loans, the agency obtained a security interest in Bridges' crops and farm equipment, which it perfected by filing a standard FHA financing statement with Georgia officials on February 2, 1972. Bridges subsequently took his tractor to respondent Crittenden for repairs on numerous occasions, accumulating unpaid repair bills * * *. * * * When Bridges could not pay the balance of $2,151.28, respondent retained the tractor and acquired a lien therein under Georgia law.

On May 1, 1975, after Bridges had filed for bankruptcy and had been discharged from his debts, the United States instituted this action against Crittenden to obtain possession of the tractor. The District Court rejected the Government's claim that the FHA's security interest was superior to respondent's, and granted summary judgment for respondent on alternative grounds. First, it held that the agency had not properly perfected its security interest because the financing statement inadequately described the collateral. Second, it found that even if the description were sufficient, both federal and state law accorded priority to respondent's lien.

The Court of Appeals affirmed in part and reversed in part. It first ruled that "the rights and liabilities of the parties to a suit arising from FHA loan transactions must, under the rationale of the *Clearfield Trust* doctrine, be determined with reference to federal law." 563 F.2d 678, 680–681 (C.A.5 1977) (footnotes omitted). See *Clearfield Trust Co. v. United States*, 318 U.S. 363 (1943). In fashioning a federal rule for assessing the sufficiency of the FHA's financing statement, the court elected to follow the Model UCC rather than to incorporate Georgia law. And, it determined that the description of the collateral was adequate under the Model UCC to perfect the FHA's security interest.

The Court of Appeals then addressed the priority question and concluded that neither state law nor the first-in-time, first-in-right and choateness doctrines were appropriate to resolve the conflicting claims. In their place, the court devised a special "federal commercial law rule," using the Model UCC and the Tax Lien Act of 1966 as guides. *Id.,* at 679, 688–690. This rule would give priority to repairman's liens over the Government's previously perfected consensual security interests when the repairman continuously possesses the property from the time his lien arises. Applying its rule, the Court of Appeals concluded that Crittenden's lien for only the final $543.81 repair bill took precedence over the FHA's security interest.

II

This Court has consistently held that federal law governs questions involving the rights of the United States arising under nationwide federal programs. As the Court explained in *Clearfield Trust Co. v. United States, supra,* at 366–367:

"When the United States disburses its funds or pays its debts, it is exercising a constitutional function or power. . . . The authority [to do so] had its origin in the Constitution and the statutes of the United States and was in no way dependent on the laws [of any State]. The duties imposed upon the United States and the rights acquired by it . . . find their roots in the same federal sources. In absence of an applicable Act of Congress it is for the federal courts to fashion the governing rule of law according to their own standards."

Guided by these principles, we think it clear that the priority of liens stemming from federal lending programs must be determined with reference to federal law. The SBA and FHA unquestionably perform federal functions within the meaning of *Clearfield*. Since the agencies derive their authority to effectuate loan transactions from specific Acts of Congress passed in the exercise of a "constitutional function or power," *Clearfield Trust Co. v. United States, supra,* at 366, their rights, as well, should derive from a federal source. When Government activities "aris[e] from and bea[r] heavily upon a federal . . . program," the Constitution and Acts of Congress " 'require' otherwise than that state law govern of its own force." *United States v. Little Lake Misere Land Co.,* 412 U.S. 580, 592, 593 (1973). In such contexts, federal interests are sufficiently implicated to warrant the protection of federal law.

That the statutes authorizing these federal lending programs do not specify the appropriate rule of decision in no way limits the reach of federal law. It is precisely when Congress has not spoken "in an area comprising issues substantially related to an established program of government operation," *id.,* at 593, that *Clearfield* directs federal courts to fill the interstices of federal legislation "according to their own standards." *Clearfield Trust Co. v. United States,* 318 U.S., at 367.

Federal law therefore controls the Government's priority rights. The more difficult task, to which we turn, is giving content to this federal rule.

III

Controversies directly affecting the operations of federal programs, although governed by federal law, do not inevitably require resort to uniform federal rules. Whether to adopt state law or to fashion a nationwide federal rule is a matter of judicial policy "dependent upon a variety of considerations always relevant to the nature of the specific governmental interests and to the effects upon them of applying state law." *United States v. Standard Oil Co.,* 332 U.S. 301, 310 (1947).

Undoubtedly, federal programs that "by their nature are and must be uniform in character throughout the Nation" necessitate formulation of controlling federal rules. *United States v. Yazell,* 382 U.S. 341, 354 (1966). Conversely, when there is little need for a nationally uniform body of law, state law may be incorporated as the federal rule of decision. Apart from considerations of uniformity, we must also determine whether application of state law would frustrate specific objectives of the federal programs. If so, we must fashion special rules solicitous of those federal interests.

Finally, our choice-of-inquiry must consider the extent to which application of a federal rule would disrupt commercial relationships predicated on state law.

The Government argues that effective administration of its lending programs requires uniform federal rules of priority. It contends further that resort to any rules other than first in time, first in right and choateness would conflict with protectionist fiscal policies underlying the programs. We are unpersuaded that, in the circumstances presented here, nationwide standards favoring claims of the United States are necessary to ease program administration or to safeguard the Federal Treasury from defaulting debtors. Because the state commercial codes "furnish convenient solutions in no way inconsistent with adequate protection of the federal interest[s]," *United States v. Standard Oil Co., supra,* at 309, we decline to override intricate state laws of general applicability on which private creditors base their daily commercial transactions.

A

Incorporating state law to determine the rights of the United States as against private creditors would in no way hinder administration of the SBA and FHA loan programs. * * *

* * * [T]he Government maintains that requiring the agencies to assess security arrangements under local law would dictate close scrutiny of each transaction and thereby impede expeditious processing of loans. We disagree. Choosing responsible debtors necessarily requires individualized selection procedures, which the agencies have already implemented in considerable detail. Each applicant's financial condition is evaluated under rigorous standards in a lengthy process. Agency employees negotiate personally with borrowers, investigate property offered as collateral for encumbrances, and obtain local legal advice on the adequacy of proposed security arrangements. In addition, they adapt the terms of every loan to the parties' needs and capabilities. Because each application currently receives individual scrutiny, the agencies can readily adjust loan transactions to reflect state priority rules, just as they consider other factual and legal matters before disbursing Government funds. * * * Since there is no indication that variant state priority schemes would burden current methods of loan processing, we conclude that considerations of administrative convenience do not warrant adoption of a uniform federal law.

B

The Government argues that applying state law to these lending programs would undermine its ability to recover funds disbursed and therefore would conflict with program objectives. In the Government's view, it is difficult "to identify a material distinction between a dollar received from the collection of taxes and a dollar returned to the Treasury on repayment of a federal loan." Therefore, the agencies conclude, just as "the purpose of the federal tax lien statute to insure prompt and certain collection of taxes" justified our imposition of the first-in-time and choateness doctrines in the tax lien context, the federal interest in recovering on loans compels similar legal protection of the agencies' consensual liens. However, we believe significant differences between federal tax liens and consensual liens counsel against unreflective extension of rules that immunize the United States from the commercial law governing all other voluntary secured creditors. These differences persuade us that deference to customary commercial practices would not frustrate the objectives of the lending programs.

That collection of taxes is vital to the functioning, indeed existence, of government cannot be denied. Congress recognized as much over 100 years ago when it authorized creation of federal tax liens. The importance of securing adequate revenues to discharge national obligations justifies the extraordinary priority accorded federal tax liens through the choateness and first-in-time doctrines. By contrast, when the United States operates as a moneylending institution under carefully circumscribed programs, its interest in recouping the limited sums advanced is of a different order. Thus, there is less need here than in the tax lien area to invoke protective measures against defaulting debtors in a manner disruptive of existing credit markets.

To equate tax liens with these consensual liens also misperceives the principal congressional concerns underlying the respective statutes. The overriding purpose of the tax lien statute obviously is to ensure prompt revenue collection. The same cannot be said of the SBA and FHA lending programs. They are a form of social welfare legislation, primarily designed to assist farmers and businesses that cannot obtain funds from private lenders on reasonable terms. We believe that had Congress intended the private commercial sector, rather than taxpayers in general, to bear the risks of default entailed by these public welfare programs, it would have established a priority scheme displacing state law. * * *

The Government's ability to safeguard its interests in commercial dealings further reveals that the rules developed in the tax lien area are unnecessary here, and that state priority rules would not conflict with federal lending objectives.[37] The United States is an involuntary creditor of delinquent taxpayers, unable to control the factors that make tax collection likely. In contrast, when the United States acts as a lender or guarantor, it does so voluntarily, with detailed knowledge of the borrower's financial status. The agencies evaluate the risks associated with each loan, examine the interests of other creditors, choose the security believed necessary to assure repayment, and set the terms of every agreement. By carefully selecting loan recipients and tailoring each transaction with state law in

---

37. We reject the Government's suggestion that the choateness and first-in-time doctrines are needed to prevent States from "undercutting" the agencies' liens by creating "arbitrary" rules. Adopting state law as an appropriate federal rule does not preclude federal courts from excepting local laws that prejudice federal interests. The issue here, however, involves commercial rules of general applicability, based on codes that are remarkably uniform throughout the Nation.

mind, the agencies are fully capable of establishing terms that will secure repayment.[39] * * *

C

In structuring financial transactions, businessmen depend on state commercial law to provide the stability essential for reliable evaluation of the risks involved. However, subjecting federal contractual liens to the doctrines developed in the tax lien area could undermine that stability. Creditors who justifiably rely on state law to obtain superior liens would have their expectations thwarted whenever a federal contractual security interest suddenly appeared and took precedence.[42]

Because the ultimate consequences of altering settled commercial practices are so difficult to foresee,[43] we hesitate to create new uncertainties, in the absence of careful legislative deliberation. Of course, formulating special rules to govern the priority of the federal consensual liens in issue here would be justified if necessary to vindicate important national interests. But neither the Government nor the Court of Appeals advanced any concrete reasons for rejecting well-established commercial rules which have proven workable over time. Thus, the prudent course is to adopt the readymade body of state law as the federal rule of decision until Congress strikes a different accommodation.

IV

Accordingly, we hold that, absent a congressional directive, the relative priority of private liens and consensual liens arising from these Government lending programs is to be determined under nondiscriminatory state laws. * * *

So ordered.

39. The facts presented here demonstrate the ease with which the agencies could have protected themselves. O. K. Super Markets informed the SBA of Kimbell's security interests in the inventory. Had the agency followed its guidelines and checked local records, it would have discovered the 1968 security agreements Kimbell filed with its financing statements. Thus, the agency should have known that the agreements secured future advances. * * *

42. The cases under consideration illustrate the substantial new risks that creditors would encounter. Neither the financing statement filed by Republic nor its security agreement mentioned the SBA. To give the federal lien priority in this situation would undercut the reliability of the notice filing system, which plays a crucial role in commercial dealings. Subsequent creditors such as Crittenden and prior creditors such as Kimbell would have no trustworthy means of discovering the undisclosed security interest. Even

those creditors aware of a federal agency's lien would have to adjust their lending arrangements to protect against the stringent choateness requirements. In recognition of these burdens, commentators have criticized the doctrine for frustrating private creditors' expectations as well as generating inconsistencies in application.

Considerable uncertainty would also result from the approach used in the opinions below. Developing priority rules on a case-by-case basis, depending on the types of competing private liens involved, leaves creditors without the definite body of law they require in structuring sound business transactions.

43. For example, the decision below in No. 77–1359 noted that priority rules favoring the Government could inhibit private lenders' extension of credit to the very people for whom Congress created these programs. 557 F.2d, at 500.

———

Notes and Questions

1.   When Congress waives sovereign immunity and authorizes a cause of action against the United States, it may or may not specify the source of law that provides the basis for the claim. Under the Federal Tort Claims Act, 28 U.S.C. § 1346(b), the rule of decision is provided by the "law of the place where the act or omission occurs," which is a reference to state law. See Chapter III.A.3.a. Thus, by direct statutory command, the courts are directed to apply state substantive tort law to decide FTCA suits against the federal government. By contrast, however, the Tucker Act and the subsequently-enacted Contract Disputes Act do not identify the substantive law that governs the merits. When a Tucker Act claim is founded upon a money-mandating statute or constitutional provision, the particular statute or constitutional provision giving rise to the claim obviously provides the governing substantive law. But what is the law that applies in the context of contract disputes with the federal government?

2.   Before answering that question directly, it is appropriate to ask the prior question of how the problem should be addressed, how the issue should be analyzed. The case of *United States v. Kimbell Foods, Inc.,* although not itself a government contracts decision, is the classic precedent on the basic issue of how to determine the substance of a rule of decision to apply in a case where the claim is created by federal statute but Congress has not specified the source of law for the resolution of a dispute. What alternative sources of law exist? Can and should the federal courts exercise common law-making powers? What are the benefits and disadvantages of choosing a uniform federal law or deferring to state law as the rule of decision? What factors or considerations should be weighed in reaching the decision? How do those factors apply in the context of the government lien priority issues raised in *Kimbell Foods*?

Subsequent to the *Kimbell Foods* decision, the Supreme Court has manifested a rather strong presumption against judicial creation of federal common-law rules. As students may remember from their first-year civil procedure course, in the classic case of *Erie Railroad v. Tompkins,* 304 U.S. 64 (1938), the Court overturned a century of federal court experimentation in common law-making and ruled that a federal district court sitting in diversity of citizenship jurisdiction must apply both the statutory and common law rules of the state in which it sits. In so ruling, the *Erie* Court stated that "there is no federal general common law." *Id.* at 78. In two later decisions, the Supreme Court has quoted this line from *Erie* and reiterated the Court's reluctance to engage in policymaking through creation of federal common law rules. *O'Melveny & Myers v. Federal Deposit Ins. Corp.,* 512 U.S. 79, 83 (1994); *Atherton v. Federal Deposit Ins. Corp.,* 519 U.S. 213, 218 (1997).

The case of *O'Melveny & Myers* arose from the Federal Deposit Insurance Corporation's (FDIC) takeover of a failed savings and loan corporation and subsequent prosecution of a professional malpractice suit against the corporation's former legal counsel. The FDIC argued that, because it was acting as receiver of a federally insured financial institution, the defenses available to the former legal counsel should be determined by federal common law—particularly the defense that the FDIC as successor to the corporation was estopped because the corporate directors had been aware of the law firm's conduct and that knowledge was imputed to the corporation itself. The Supreme Court rejected that argument, admonishing that resort to federal common law is warranted only in "extraordinary cases." *O'Melveny & Myers,* 512 U.S. at 89. Before judicial formulation of a federal rule will be contemplated, there must be a "significant conflict between some federal policy or interest and the use of state law." *Id.* at 87. The Court stated that when a matter is left unaddressed in a statutory scheme, such as the detailed statutory system establishing the FDIC and granting it regulatory power, that matter is "presumably left subject to the disposition provided by state law." *Id.* at 85. The Court explained that policymaking should be reserved to the branches of government that enact the laws, rather than the courts, and expressed concern about "the runaway tendencies of 'federal common law' untethered to a genuinely identifiable (as opposed to judicially constructed) federal policy." *Id.* at 89. For scholarly examinations of the concept and legitimacy of federal common law, see Bradford R. Clark, *Federal Common Law: A Structural Reinterpretation,* 144 U. Pa. L. Rev. 1245, 1368 (1996) ("The Supreme Court's unanimous decision in *O'Melveny & Myers* may signal heightened sensitivity to the constitutional concerns raised by federal common law."); Paul Lund, *The Decline of Federal Common Law,* 76 B.U. L. Rev. 895, 915 (1996) (acknowledging that recent Supreme Court decisions have "signalled a substantial decline in the common law making powers of the federal courts," although criticizing this development as threatening federal power and leaving federal interests unprotected); Gregory C. Sisk & Jerry L. Anderson, *The Sun Sets on Federal Common Law: Corporate Successor Liability Under CERCLA After* O'Melveny & Myers, 16 Va. Env'tl L.J. 505, 551–60 (1997) (arguing that, just as the Rules of Decision Act establishes a positive presumption in favor of state law as the rule of decision when a federal statute is silent on a matter, *O'Melveny & Myers* erects a negative presumption against federal common law absent a compelling showing that state law conflicts with a federal policy or interest).

3. After studying *Kimbell Foods,* and considering the strong presumption in favor of adopting state law as the rule of decision as stated in *O'Melveny & Myers,* consider how those same considerations apply in the context of federal government contract law. How important is achievement of national uniformity in the law to be applied? Would application of state law impair the objectives of the government contracting program? Would adoption of federal law disrupt the expectations of contractors choosing to enter into government contractors? How does this situation differ from that presented in *Kimbell Foods*? Does judicial creation of federal contract law

place too much policy making power in the hands of the judges? *See generally* W. Noel Keyes, *Government Contracts in a Nutshell* 285–91 (2d ed. 1990) (criticizing the federal common law of federal contracts as unfairly applying different law than would apply to private contractual disputes).

Whether one agrees or disagrees, and whether or not the answer can be directly reconciled with *Kimbell Foods* and *O'Melveny & Myers,* the federal courts have long since arrived at the answer with respect to government contract law (at least in the ordinary kind of procurement contract case under the CDA). That answer is laid out in the brief, one paragraph excerpt from *Seaboard Lumber Co. v. United States* set out immediately below. What is the source of law for government contracts? How do the courts formulate that law? Other than judicial creation of rules, how is the substance of federal contract law developed?

Seaboard Lumber Co. v. United States

United States Claims Court.
15 Cl. Ct. 366 (1988), aff'd, 903 F.2d 1560 (Fed.Cir. 1990).

[T]he law to be applied in cases related to federal contracts is federal and not state law. *United States v. Allegheny County,* 322 U.S. 174, 183 (1944); *Forman v. United States,* 767 F.2d 875, 879–80 (Fed.Cir.1985). The federal law applied in breach of contract claims is not, however, created by statute but rather for the most part has been developed by the Court of Appeals for the Federal Circuit and the Court of Claims, with the Claims Court, or the Boards of Contract Appeals applying the law in the first instance. This federal contract law also reflects the various contract clauses developed over time for the benefit of both the sovereign and the contractor through the practice of agencies and the bargaining leverage of contractors. It has drawn as well upon traditional private contract law for analogies and concepts. However, it is a separate and distinct body of law.

[The opinion of the United States Court of Appeals for the Federal Circuit, affirming the Claims Court decision on other grounds, is set out above in Chapter IV(A)(4)(b).]

Note

1.   As mentioned in the brief excerpt from the *Seaboard Lumber Co. v. United States* decision above, the federal law of contracts has developed primarily around standard contract clauses that the government includes in every procurement contract. These standard contract clauses are set out in the Federal Acquisition Regulations at 48 C.F.R. part 52. *See generally* W. Noel Keyes, *Government Contracts in a Nutshell* ch. 21 (1990) (government contract clauses). Indeed, because the Federal Acquisition Regula-

tions have the force of law and government contractors are presumed to be familiar with it, the standard clauses are treated as included in every contract, even if inadvertently omitted by the government contracting officer. In *G.L. Christian & Associates v. United States,* 160 Ct.Cl. 1, 312 F.2d 418, 424 (1963), the then-Court of Claims, in what has come to be known as the *Christian* doctrine, held that standard clauses established by regulation must be read into every federal contract. (Subsequently, the Federal Circuit has ameliorated the *Christian* doctrine somewhat, holding that it only "applies to mandatory contract clauses which express a significant or deeply ingrained strand of public procurement policy." *General Engineering & Machine Works v. O'Keefe,* 991 F.2d 775, 779 (Fed.Cir. 1993); *see also S.J. Amoroso Constr. Co. v. United States,* 12 F.3d 1072, 1075 (Fed.Cir. 1993).)

2.   With respect to contracts not governed by the CDA and the FAR, the federal courts have common-law authority to determine the content of law for interpretation of federal contracts. In *Mobil Oil Exploration & Producing Southeast, Inc. v. United States,* 530 U.S. 604 (2000), the Supreme Court found that when oil companies had paid $158 million to obtain lease rights to explore for and develop oil off the coast of North Carolina and the contract incorporated the terms of pre-existing statutes and regulations regarding obtaining permission for off-shore oil drilling, the subsequent enactment of a new statute that created new requirements for off-shore drilling and that therefore prevented the federal government from keeping its promise amounted to a repudiation of those contracts. In analyzing whether the government's conduct constituted a repudiation of the contracts and whether the oil companies were entitled to restitution, the Supreme Court applied general principles of contract law and drew upon the articulation of those principles in the Restatement (Second) of Contracts. *Mobil Oil,* 530 U.S. at 608, 621–22. As a general proposition, the Court reiterated that " '[w]hen the United States enters into contract relations, its rights and duties therein are governed generally by the law applicable to contracts between private individuals.' " *Id.* at 607–08 (quoting *United States v. Winstar Corp.,* 518 U.S. 839, 895 (1996) (plurality opinion)); *see also Franconia Associates, Inc. v. United States,* 536 U.S. 129 (2002) (same).

————

d.   THE "SOVEREIGN ACTS" DOCTRINE OR DEFENSE

Before leaving the subject of contract claims against the federal government, a special defense against claims for breach of contract potentially available to the government should be mentioned: When the United States government enters into a contract, it remains both contractor and sovereign. When the United States subsequently acts in its capacity as a sovereign in a manner that undermines or even prevent performance of a contract, the government ordinarily cannot be held liable on that account for breach of the existing contract. If a private party entered into a contract, and then by its own actions made completion of the contract impossible, that party could not excuse the breach by reference to its own detrimental conduct. But when the United States, acting not as a contractor but independently in its capacity as a sovereign government, takes an action that frustrates completion of a federal contract, it remains immune from liability. For example, if the government sets up an embargo of a hostile foreign country that prevents necessary supplies from being imported by a federal contractor, or adopts new regulations of business that increase the contractor's costs of performing the contract, these governmental actions may not give rise to a claim of breach of contract. As the Supreme Court has explained:

> The two characters which the government possesses as a contractor and as a sovereign cannot be * * * fused; nor can the United States while sued in the one character be made liable in damages for their acts done in the other. Whatever acts the government may do, be they legislative or executive, so long as they be public and general cannot be deemed specially to * * * violate the particular contracts into which it enters with private persons. * * * Though their sovereign acts performed for the general good may work injury to some private contractors, such parties gain nothing by having the United States as their defendants.

Horowitz v. United States, 267 U.S. 458, 461 (1925).

Thus, once again, as has been a theme throughout this casebook, the United States stands in a special position as a party to a judicial action. Its sovereign role as the government of the national community prevents the courts from treating it the same as an ordinary litigant. Professor Harold Krent contends that—

> [c]oncerns for majoritarian governance support this result. If courts could impose liability on the government for its sovereign acts, the costs of compensating private parties for the increased expenses of performing government contracts might deter the government from effectuating public policy. Just as Congress and government agencies generally are immune from any damage caused by their exercises of regulatory authority, whether through zoning, food regulation, or banking oversight, so government agencies are immune from the additional costs imposed on private contractors by sovereign acts of government.

Harold J. Krent, *Reconceptualizing Sovereign Immunity,* 45 Vand. L. Rev. 1529, 1569–70 (1992).

However, the "Sovereign Acts Doctrine" is not absolute and does not always confer immunity upon the government from a claim of breach of contract based upon its legislative or regulatory behavior, as demonstrated in a recent landmark Supreme Court case. During the savings and loan crisis of the 1980's, the Federal Home Loan Bank Board encouraged healthy financial institutions and investors to take over ailing thrifts. As an inducement, the Board agreed to permit the acquiring entities to designate a portion of the purchase price as an intangible "goodwill" asset that could be counted toward the capital reserve requirements set for financial institutions by federal regulation. Subsequently, in the Financial Institutions Reform, Recovery, and Enforcement Act of 1989 (FIRREA), Congress strengthened regulation of financial institutions, including specifically forbidding counting such goodwill toward the required reserves. Entities which had acquired thrifts on the basis of the Board's promise filed suit in the Court of Federal Claims under the Tucker Act alleging breach of contract.* The government raised several defenses, including the Sovereign Acts Doctrine. When the case reached the Supreme Court in *United States v. Winstar Corp.,* 518 U.S. 839 (1996), the Court, with badly divided reasoning, rejected the government's position and held that the United States was contractually obliged to permit these financial institutions to use the special accounting methods (and thus pay damages for breach of that obligation), despite the intervening regulatory change.

In *Winstar,* Justice Souter, speaking for a plurality of four justices, concluded that, while nothing in the contracts between the Board and the entities acquiring ailing thrifts restricted the government's ability to change its regulation of the thrift industry, the government had agreed to indemnify these particular acquiring entities for any losses resulting from future regulatory change. *Id.* at 866–91. This plurality did not find that awarding damages for a breach of the contracts was tantamount to a limitation on the government's sovereign power to modify banking regulations. *Id.* at 881–89. Justice Souter also rejected the government's "sovereign acts doctrine" defense, holding that FIRREA was not a "public and general act" adopted by the government in its capacity as a sovereign and distinct from its capacity as a contractor. *Id.* at 891–96. Justice Souter, speaking for only three members of the Court on this point, explained that, because the legislation had the "substantial effect of releasing the Govern-

---

* Because these contracts arose out of the government's regulation of financial institutions, and did not involve procurement of goods or services, they were not covered by the Contract Disputes Act (CDA). See Chapter IV.A.4.b (Contract Disputes Act). With respect to contracts reached under the CDA, regulations direct inclusion of a contract clause allowing the government to terminate any contract for convenience. When the government terminates a contract under such a clause, a determination is made of appropriate restitution to the contractor, generally measured as the cost of the work performed thus far together with a profit for that completed work, but not including anticipated but unearned profits. W. Noel Keyes, *Contract Law in a Nutshell* 502–03 (2d ed. 1990). On the *Winstar* contracts falling outside of the CDA, and thus not including a standard termination for convenience clause, see Joshua I. Schwartz, *Liability for Sovereign Acts:*

Congruence and Exceptionalism in Government Contracts Law, 64 Geo. Wash. L. Rev. 633, 651–52 n.103, 695 & n.359 (1996); Gillian Hadfield, *Of Sovereignty and Contract: Damages for Breach of Contract by Government,* 8 S. Cal. Interdisciplinary L.J. 467, 492–94 (1999). Thus, had the *Winstar* situation arisen under the CDA, termination for the government's convenience would have been permissible by express contract provision, a remedy for the contractors would have been provided, and the Sovereign Acts Doctrine issue would not have been offered in defense. Accordingly, the only instances in which the "Sovereign Acts" Doctrine is likely to arise are those less common contractual arrangements that fall outside of the CDA. *See* Joshua I. Schwartz, *Assembling* Winstar: *Triumph of the Ideal of Congruence in Government Contracts Law?,* 26 Pub. Cont. L.J. 481, 509–10 & n.127 (1997).

ment from its contractual obligations," "it is impossible to attribute the exculpatory 'public and general' character to FIRREA." *Id.* at 896–900. In sum, Justice Souter believed, government acts "tainted by a governmental object of self-relief" from its contractual obligations are not entitled to immunity. *Id.* at 896. Moreover, Justice Souter maintained, writing once again for a plurality of four justices on these points, that the Sovereign Acts Doctrine could not excuse the government's breach here, because the doctrine applies only when (1) an intervening change of governmental policy was an event contrary to the basic assumptions upon which the parties agreed, and (2) that the language of the contract or circumstances do not indicate that the government was to be liable. *Id.* at 904–05. Here, Justice Souter concluded, some changes in regulatory structure were foreseeable and likely when the parties contracted, and the government's express assumption of any risk of loss indicates "that the parties' agreement was not meant to be rendered nugatory by a change in the regulatory law." *Id.* at 905–07.

In a separate opinion in *Winstar*, Justice Scalia, speaking for three justices, stated that the enactment of FIRREA "was an unquestionably sovereign act of government," but nonetheless also upheld the government's liability for depriving the parties of the benefit of their contracts. *Id.* at 920. He would have held that the Sovereign Acts Doctrine is unavailable whenever the government had attempted "to abrogate the *essential bargain*" of an agreement. *Id.* at 923–24. He concluded that, while there is a general presumption that "[g]overnments do not ordinarily agree to curtail their sovereign or legislative powers," the government here had unmistakably agreed to regulate these entities in a particular fashion into the future. *Id.* at 920–22. When the government by contract does assume the risk of a change in the laws, Justice Scalia saw the Sovereign Acts Doctrine as having no force. *Id.* at 923–24.

Chief Justice Rehnquist dissented,** contending that the plurality "render[s] the [sovereign acts] doctrine a shell," such "that it will have virtually no future application." *Id.* at 924, 931. He argued that whenever the government enacts general regulations, the Sovereign Acts Doctrine abrogates any inconsistent contractual obligations, without consideration of the government's "motive" or whether or not the government acted to avoid the contract. *Id.* at 931–34. *See also* Krent, *supra,* at 1570 (arguing that subsequent events demonstrated that the government's relaxing of capital requirements for thrifts was "a fiasco that fueled the collapse of the industry" and that, under the Sovereign Acts Doctrine, Congress should be permitted to change its regulation "in light of the critical crisis in the industry" without becoming liable to contractual damages).

Because the *Winstar* Court was so splintered in reasoning, it is difficult to ascertain the current status or meaning of the Sovereign Acts Doctrine as a defense by the government to a claim of breach of contract. The *Winstar* scenario may prove to be a relatively unique one, given that the

---

** Justice Ginsburg joined Chief Justice Rehnquist in dissent but did not join that part of his dissent addressing the Sovereign Acts Doctrine.

Court found the government had entered into a contract by which it agreed to assume the risk of loss from any modification of regulatory policy (to which the government will rarely agree) and that the legislative history of the statute indicates that Congress was concerned with and expected the legislation to abrogate the government's contractual obligations. *Winstar,* 518 U.S. at 900–03. Justice Souter cautioned that "the sun is not, in fact, likely to set on the sovereign acts doctrine," and foresaw its continued application whenever governmental action is directed at a "broader governmental objective" with only an incidental impact upon public contracts. *Id.* at 898 & n.45. However, the fact that only one justice in dissent adhered to the traditional and broadest understanding of the doctrine as preserving the government's authority to adopt new legislation regardless of, and immune from, effects on existing contracts, suggests that this is a legal doctrine in transition. *See also* Joshua I. Schwartz, *Assembling* Winstar: *Triumph of the Ideal of Congruence in Government Contracts Law?,* 26 Pub. Cont. L.J. 481, 483, 552–65 (1997) (concluding that "Justice Scalia's analysis, rather than Justice Souter's, provides the key to formulating * * * a consensus approach" on the Supreme Court regarding the sovereign acts doctrine, an approach that is something akin to a presumption that the government would not agree to limit its sovereign powers which is rebuttable by evidence that the government agreed to indemnify contractors for losses attributable to changes in law).

Professor Joshua Schwartz finds that the confusion and controversy surrounding the "sovereign acts doctrine," and related rules, reflects a fundamental tension that runs through the law of federal contracts. Joshua I. Schwartz, *Liability for Sovereign Acts: Congruence and Exceptionalism in Government Contracts Law,* 64 Geo. Wash. L. Rev. 633 (1996):

> On the one hand, there is a tradition of "exceptionalism," which emphasizes that, because of its sovereign status, unique functions, and special responsibilities, the government as a contracting party is not subject to all of the legal obligations and liabilities of private contracting parties. * * * Yet the law of government contracts also reflects an opposing tradition of "congruence," the thrust of which is [that] "[w]hen the United States enters into contract relations, its rights and duties therein are governed generally by the law applicable to contracts between private individuals."

Id. at 637–38 (quoting *Lynch v. United States,* 292 U.S. 571, 579 (1934)); *but see* Gillian Hadfield, *Of Sovereignty and Contract: Damages for Breach of Contract by Government,* 8 S. Cal. Interdisciplinary L.J. 467, 536–37 (1999) (arguing that any attempt to determine "whether government has acted as contractor or as sovereign" is a misleading distraction, that the government always acts as the government, and that the government therefore should be liable only for reliance, but not expectation, damages when it changes course and repudiates a contractual obligation). Although Professor Schwartz suggests several factors to be considered in applying the Sovereign Acts Doctrine in an attempt to synthesize the opposing traditions, he concludes that the tension cannot be entirely avoided "[b]ecause the law of government contracts occupies an intersection between private contract law and the special principles of law applicable to the [federal] government." *See* Schwartz, *Liability for Sovereign Acts, supra,* at 638.

That is a good note upon which to end our discussion of federal contract law, as it returns us to a continuing theme of this course on litigation with the federal government. As we have seen repeatedly through this course, that same fundamental tension—between treating the government as a private party for imposing liability and yet preserving special prerogatives and limitations to protect the sovereign United States—runs throughout the entire law of litigation with the federal government.

5. TUCKER ACT CLAIMS FOUNDED UPON THE CONSTITUTION

The Tucker Act waives the government's sovereign immunity for claims "founded either upon the Constitution, or any Act of Congress or any regulation of an executive department, or upon any express or implied contract with the United States." 28 U.S.C. § 1491(a)(1); *see also* 28 U.S.C. § 1346(a)(2). We've looked at claims founded upon statutes or regulations, and at litigation of contract disputes. We now turn to the branch of Tucker Act claims that is listed first in the statute—those founded upon the Constitution. As with claims founded upon statute or regulation, the question arises as to the requisite nature or substance of a constitutional provision to give rise to a Tucker Act claim. Does every constitutional violation that has monetary consequences give rise to a Tucker Act claim under the Constitution?

a. FIFTH AMENDMENT TAKING CLAIMS

Preseault v. Interstate Commerce Commission

Supreme Court of the United States.
494 U.S. 1 (1990).

■ JUSTICE BRENNAN delivered the opinion of the Court.

The question presented is the constitutionality of a federal "rails-to-trails" statute under which unused railroad rights-of-way are converted into recreational trails notwithstanding whatever reversionary property interests may exist under state law. Petitioners contend that the statute violates both the Fifth Amendment Takings Clause and the Commerce Clause, Art. I, § 8. We find it unnecessary to evaluate the merits of the taking claim because we hold that even if the rails-to-trails statute gives rise to a taking, compensation is available to petitioners under the Tucker Act, 28 U.S.C. § 1491(a)(1), and the requirements of the Fifth Amendment are satisfied. We also hold that the statute is a valid exercise of congressional power under the Commerce Clause.

I

A

The statute at issue in this case, the National Trails System Act Amendments of 1983 (Amendments), Pub.L. 98–11, 97 Stat. 48, to the National Trails System Act (Trails Act), Pub.L. 90–543, 82 Stat. 919 (codified, as amended, 16 U.S.C. § 1241 *et seq.*), is the culmination of congressional efforts to preserve shrinking rail trackage by converting unused rights-of-way to recreational trails. In 1920, the Nation's railway system reached its peak of 272,000 miles; today only about 141,000 miles are in use, and experts predict that 3,000 miles will be abandoned every year through the end of this century. * * *

* * * Congress enacted the Amendments to the Trails Act, which authorize the Interstate Commerce Commission (ICC or Commission) to preserve for possible future railroad use rights-of-way not currently in service and to allow interim use of the land as recreational trails. Section 8(d) provides that a railroad wishing to cease operations along a particular route may negotiate with a State, municipality, or private group that is prepared to assume financial and managerial responsibility for the right-of-way. If the parties reach agreement, the land may be transferred to the trail operator for interim trail use, subject to ICC-imposed terms and conditions; if no agreement is reached, the railroad may abandon the line entirely and liquidate its interest.

Section 8(d) of the amended Trails Act provides that interim trail use "shall not be treated, for any purposes of any law or rule of law, as an abandonment of the use of such rights-of-way for railroad purposes." 16 U.S.C. § 1247(d). This language gives rise to a taking question in the typical rails-to-trails case because many railroads do not own their rights-of-way outright but rather hold them under easements or similar property interests. While the terms of these easements and applicable state law vary, frequently the easements provide that the property reverts to the abutting landowner upon abandonment of rail operations. State law generally governs the disposition of reversionary interests, subject of course to the ICC's "exclusive and plenary" jurisdiction to regulate abandonments, *Chicago & North Western Transp. Co. v. Kalo Brick & Tile Co.*, 450 U.S. 311, 321 (1981), and to impose conditions affecting post-abandonment use of the property. By deeming interim trail use to be like discontinuance rather than abandonment, Congress prevented property interests from reverting under state law * * * . The primary issue in this case is whether Congress has violated the Fifth Amendment by precluding reversion of state property interests.

B

Petitioners claim a reversionary interest in a railroad right-of-way adjacent to their land in Vermont. In 1962, the State of Vermont acquired the Rutland–Canadian Railway Company's interest in the right-of-way and then leased the right-of-way to Vermont Railway, Inc. Vermont Railway stopped using the route more than a decade ago and has since removed all railroad equipment, including switches, bridges, and track, from the portion of the right-of-way claimed by petitioners. In 1981, petitioners brought a quiet-title action in the Superior Court of Chittenden County, alleging that the easement had been abandoned and was thus extinguished, and that the right-of-way had reverted to them by operation of state property law. In August 1983, the Superior Court dismissed the action, holding that it lacked jurisdiction because the ICC had not authorized abandonment of the route and therefore still exercised exclusive jurisdiction over it. The Vermont Supreme Court affirmed. *Trustees of the Diocese of Vermont v. State*, 145 Vt. 510, 496 A.2d 151 (1985).

Petitioners then sought a certificate of abandonment of the rail line from the ICC. The State of Vermont intervened, claiming title in fee simple to the right-of-way and arguing in the alternative that, even if the State's interest were an easement, the land could not revert while it was still being used for a public purpose. Vermont Railway and the State then petitioned the ICC to permit the railroad to discontinue rail service and transfer the right-of-way to the City of Burlington for interim use as a public trail under § 8(d) of the Trails Act. * * * [T]he ICC allowed the railroad to discontinue service and approved the agreement between the State and the City for interim trail use. * * *

Petitioners sought review of the ICC's order in the Court of Appeals for the Second Circuit, arguing that § 8(d) of the Trails Act is unconstitutional on its face because it takes private property without just compensation and because it is not a valid exercise of Congress' Commerce Clause power. The Court of Appeals rejected both arguments. 853 F.2d 145 (1988). It reasoned that the ICC has "plenary and exclusive authority" over abandonments, *id.*, at 151, and that federal law must be considered in determining the property right held by petitioners. "For as long as it determines that the land will serve a 'railroad purpose,' the ICC retains jurisdiction over railroad rights-of-way; it does not matter whether that purpose is immediate or in the future." *Ibid.* Because the court believed that no reversionary interest could vest until the ICC determined that abandonment was appropriate, the court concluded that the Trails Act did not result in a taking. Next, the court found that the Trails Act was reasonably adapted to two legitimate congressional purposes under the Commerce Clause: "preserving rail corridors for future railroad use" and "permitting public recreational use of trails." *Id.*, at 150. The Court of Appeals therefore dismissed petitioners' Commerce Clause challenge. We granted certiorari.

II

The Fifth Amendment provides in relevant part that "private property [shall not] be taken for public use, without just compensation." The Amendment "does not prohibit the taking of private property, but instead places a condition on the exercise of that power." *First English Evangelical Lutheran Church v. County of Los Angeles,* 482 U.S. 304, 314 (1987). It is designed "not to limit the governmental interference with property rights per se, but rather to secure compensation in the event of otherwise proper interference amounting to a taking." *Id.,* at 315 (emphasis in original). Furthermore, the Fifth Amendment does not require that just compensation be paid in advance of or even contemporaneously with the taking. All that is required is the existence of a "reasonable, certain and adequate provision for obtaining compensation" at the time of the taking. *Regional Rail Reorganization Act Cases,* 419 U.S. 102, 124–125 (1974). "If the government has provided an adequate process for obtaining compensation, and if resort to that process 'yield[s] just compensation,' then the property owner 'has no claim against the Government' for a taking." *Williamson County Regional Planning Comm'n [v. Hamilton Bank of Johnson City],* 473 U.S. [172,] 195 [(1985)].

For this reason, "taking claims against the Federal Government are premature until the property owner has availed itself of the process provided by the Tucker Act." *Williamson County Regional Planning Comm'n,* 473 U.S., at 195. The Tucker Act provides jurisdiction in the United States Claims Court for any claim against the Federal Government to recover damages founded on the Constitution, a statute, a regulation, or an express or implied-in-fact contract. See 28 U.S.C. § 1491(a)(1); see also § 1346(a)(2) (Little Tucker Act, which creates concurrent jurisdiction in the district courts for such claims not exceeding $10,000 in amount). "If there is a taking, the claim is 'founded upon the Constitution' and within the jurisdiction of the [Claims Court] to hear and determine." *United States v. Causby,* 328 U.S. 256, 267 (1946).

The critical question in this case, therefore, is whether a Tucker Act remedy is available for claims arising out of takings pursuant to the Amendments. The proper inquiry is not whether the statute "expresses an affirmative showing of congressional intent to permit recourse to a Tucker Act remedy," but rather "whether Congress has in the [statute] *withdrawn* the Tucker Act grant of jurisdiction to the [Claims Court] to hear a suit involving the [statute] 'founded . . . upon the Constitution.' " *Regional Rail Reorganization Act Cases,* 419 U.S., at 126 (emphasis in original). Under this standard, we conclude that the Amendments did not withdraw the Tucker Act remedy. Congress did not exhibit the type of "unambiguous intention to withdraw the Tucker Act remedy," *[Ruckelshaus v.] Monsanto [Co.],* 467 U.S. [1013,] 1019 [(1984)], that is necessary to preclude a Tucker Act claim.

Neither the statute nor its legislative history mentions the Tucker Act. As indirect evidence of Congress' intent to prevent recourse to the Tucker Act, petitioners point to § 101 of the Amendments which, although it was not codified into law, provides in relevant part that:

"Notwithstanding any other provision of this Act, authority to enter into contracts, and to make payments, under this Act shall be effective only to such extent or in such amounts as are provided in advance in appropriation Acts." 97 Stat. 42, note following 16 U.S.C. § 1249.

Petitioners contend that this section limits the ICC's authority for conversions to those not requiring the expenditure of any funds and to those others for which funds had been appropriated in advance. Thus, any conversion that could result in Claims Court litigation was not authorized by Congress, since payment for such an acquisition would not have been approved by Congress in advance. Petitioners insist that such *unauthorized* government actions cannot create Tucker Act liability * * * .

We need not decide what types of official authorization, if any, are necessary to create federal liability under the Fifth Amendment, because we find that rail-to-trail conversions giving rise to just compensation claims are clearly authorized by § 8(d). That section speaks in capacious terms of trail "interim use of *any* established railroad rights-of-way" (emphasis added) and does not support petitioners' proposed distinction between conversions that might result in a taking and those that do not. Although Congress did not explicitly promise to pay for any takings, we have always assumed that the Tucker Act is an "implie[d] promis[e]" to pay just compensation which individual laws need not reiterate. *Yearsley v. W.A. Ross Construction Co.,* 309 U.S. 18, 21 (1940). Petitioners' argument that specific congressional authorization is required for those conversions that might result in takings is a thinly veiled attempt to circumvent the established method for determining whether Tucker Act relief is available for claims arising out of takings pursuant to a federal statute. We reaffirm that a Tucker Act remedy exists unless there are unambiguous indications to the contrary.

Section 101, moreover, speaks only to appropriations under the Amendments themselves and not to relief available under the Tucker Act, as evidenced by § 101's opening clause—"[n]otwithstanding any other provision of *this* Act" (emphasis added)—which refers to the 1983 Amendments. The section means simply that payments made pursuant to the Amendments, such as funding for scenic trails, markers, and similar purposes, are effective only "in such amounts as are provided in advance in appropriation Acts," a concept that mirrors Art. I, § 9, of the Constitution ("No Money shall be drawn from the Treasury, but in Consequence of Appropriations made by Law"). Payments for takings claims are not affected by this language, because such claims "arise" under the Fifth Amendment. Payments for takings would be made "under" the Tucker Act, not the Trails Act, and would be drawn from the Judgment Fund, which is a separate appropriated account, see 31 U.S.C. § 1304(a). Section 101 does not manifest the type of clear and unmistakable congressional intent necessary to withdraw Tucker Act coverage.

Petitioners next assert that Congress' desire that the Amendments operate at "low cost," somehow indicates that Congress withdrew the Tucker Act remedy. There is no doubt that Congress meant to keep the costs of the Amendments to a minimum. This intent, however, has little bearing on the Tucker Act question. We have previously rejected the argument that a generalized desire to protect the public fisc is sufficient to withdraw relief under the Tucker Act. * * * Similar logic applies to the instant case. The statements made in Congress during the passage of the Trails Act Amendments might reflect merely the decision not to create a program of direct federal purchase, construction, and maintenance of trails, and instead to allow state and local governments and private groups to establish and manage trails. The alternative chosen by Congress is less costly than a program of direct federal trail acquisition because, under any view of takings law, only some rail-to-trail conversions will amount to takings. Some rights-of-way are held in fee simple. Others are held as easements that do not even as a matter of state law revert upon interim use as nature trails. In addition, under § 8(d) the Federal Government neither incurs the costs of constructing and maintaining the trails nor assumes legal liability for the transfer or use of the right-of-way. In contrast, the costs of acquiring and administering National Scenic and National Historic Trails are borne directly by the Federal Government. Thus, the "low cost" language might reflect Congress' rejection of a more ambitious program of federally owned and managed trails, rather than withdrawal of a Tucker Act remedy. The language does not amount to the "unambiguous intention" required by our prior cases.

In sum, petitioners' failure to make use of the available Tucker Act remedy renders their taking challenge to the ICC's order premature. We need not decide whether a taking occurred in this case.

III

[The property owners also contended that the amendments to the Trails Act were not a valid exercise of congressional power under the Commerce Clause, Art. I, § 8. The Court held that the amendments were a valid exercise of congressional power because they are reasonably adapted to the goals of encouraging the development of additional recreational trails, and to preserve established railroad rights-of-way for future reactivation of rail service.]

IV

For the reasons stated, the judgment of the Court of Appeals is affirmed.

It is so ordered.

■ JUSTICE O'CONNOR, with whom JUSTICE SCALIA and JUSTICE KENNEDY join, concurring.

Petitioners assert that the Interstate Commerce Commission's (ICC) actions prevent them from enjoying property rights secured by Vermont law and thereby have effected a compensable taking. The Court of Appeals for the Second Circuit determined that, no matter what Vermont law might provide, the ICC's actions forestalled petitioners from possessing the asserted reversionary interest, and thus that no takings claim could arise. Today the Court affirms the Second Circuit's judgment on quite different grounds. I join the Court's opinion, but write separately to express my view that state law determines what property interest petitioners possess and that traditional takings doctrine will determine whether the Government must compensate petitioners for the burden imposed on any property interest they possess.

As the Court acknowledges, state law creates and defines the scope of the reversionary or other real property interests affected by the ICC's actions pursuant to Section 208 of the National Trails System Act Amendments of 1983, 16 U.S.C. § 1247(d). In determining whether a taking has occurred, "we are mindful of the basic axiom that property interests ... are not created by the Constitution. Rather, they are created and their dimensions are defined by existing rules or understandings that stem from an independent source such as state law." *Ruckelshaus v. Monsanto Co.,* 467 U.S. 986, 1001 (1984). * * * Determining what interest petitioners would have enjoyed under Vermont law, in the absence of the ICC's recent actions, will establish whether petitioners possess the predicate property interest that must underlie any takings claim. We do not attempt to resolve that issue.

It is also clear that the Interstate Commerce Act, and the ICC's actions pursuant to it, pre-empt the operation and effect of certain state laws that "conflict with or interfere with federal authority over the same activity." *Chicago & North Western Transp. Co. v. Kalo Brick & Tile Co.,* 450 U.S. 311, 319 (1981). * * * As the Vermont Supreme Court recognized, state courts cannot enforce or give effect to asserted reversionary interests when enforcement would interfere with the Commission's administration of the Interstate Commerce Act. See *Trustees of the Diocese of Vermont v. State,* 145 Vt. 510, 496 A.2d 151 (1985). These results are simply routine and well-established consequences of the Supremacy Clause, U.S. Const., Art. VI, cl. 2.

The scope of the Commission's authority to regulate abandonments, thereby delimiting the ambit of federal power, is an issue quite distinct from whether the Commission's exercise of power over matters within its jurisdiction effected a taking of petitioners' property. Although the Commission's actions may pre-empt the operation and effect of certain state laws, those actions do not displace state law as the traditional source of the real property interests. The Commission's actions may delay property owners' enjoyment of their reversionary interests, but that delay burdens and defeats the property interest rather than suspends or defers the vesting of those property rights. Any other conclusion would convert the ICC's power to pre-empt conflicting state regulation of interstate commerce into the power to pre-empt the rights guaranteed by state property law, a result incompatible with the Fifth Amendment.

The Court of Appeals for the Second Circuit adopted just this unjustified interpretation of the effect of the ICC's exercise of federal power. The court concluded that even if petitioners held the reversionary interest they claim, no taking occurred because "no reversionary interest can or would vest" until the ICC determines that abandonment is appropriate. See 853 F.2d 145, 151 (1988). This view conflates the scope of the ICC's power with the existence of a compensable taking and threatens to read the Just Compensation Clause out of the Constitution. The ICC may possess the power to postpone enjoyment of reversionary interests, but the Fifth Amendment and well-established doctrine indicate that in certain circumstances the Government must compensate owners of those property interests when it exercises that power. Nothing in the Court's opinion disavows these principles. * * *

Well-established principles will govern analysis of whether the burden the ICC's actions impose upon state-defined real property interests amounts to a compensable taking. We recently concluded in *Nollan v. California Coastal Comm'n,* 483 U.S. 825, 831–832 (1987), that a taking would occur if the Government appropriated a public easement. In such a case, a "permanent physical occupation" of the underlying property "has occurred . . . where individuals are given a permanent and continuous right to pass to and fro, so that the real property may continuously be traversed, even though no particular individual is permitted to station himself permanently upon the premises." *Nollan, supra,* at 832. The Government's appropriation of other, lesser servitudes may also impose a burden requiring payment of just compensation. And the Court recently concluded that the Government's burdening of property for a distinct period, short of a permanent taking, may nevertheless mandate compensation. See *First English Evangelical Lutheran Church, supra,* 482 U.S., at 318–319. Of course, a party may gain the benefit of these principles only after establishing possession of a property interest that has been burdened. As today's decision indicates, petitioners and persons similarly situated will have ample opportunity to make that showing.

With this understanding, and for the reasons set forth in the Court's opinion, I agree that the judgment below should be affirmed.

————

Notes and Questions

1.   In considering what constitutes a cognizable constitutional claim under the Tucker Act, we begin by looking at claims founded upon a constitutional provision that plainly and most clearly does contemplate payment of money by the government to individual claimants—the Fifth Amendment takings clause. The Fifth Amendment states, in pertinent part, that no "private property shall be taken for public use, without just compensation." U.S. Const., amend. V.

When the Tucker Act was originally enacted in 1887, the provision of a judicial review mechanism for takings claims was most clearly within the contemplation of Congress. Nevertheless, for more than 60 years, the scope of the Tucker Act was read narrowly in this context to apply only to condemnation cases, that is, when the government affirmatively sought to obtain title to property and thus was effectively purchasing the property (albeit involuntarily from the seller's standpoint). Indeed, even under these circumstances, the Supreme Court treated the claim—not as one founded upon the Constitution—but rather as a contract action. When the government took private property for public use, the Court implied a contractual promise by the government to pay just compensation. *United States v. Great Falls Manufacturing Co.,* 112 U.S. 645, 656–57 (1884). *See generally* Paul Frederic Kirgis, *Section 1500 and the Jurisdictional Pitfalls of Federal Government Litigation,* 47 Am. U. L. Rev. 301, 309 (1997).

By contrast, if the government seized property and contested another's title to it, or took actions that deprived individuals of the use of their property—what is commonly referred to today as "inverse condemnation"—the Supreme Court regarded the government's action as a tort. *Hill v. United States,* 149 U.S. 593 (1893). Because the Tucker Act expressly excludes actions "sounding in tort," 28 U.S.C. §§ 1346(a)(2), 1491(a)(1), these claims could not be pursued in the then-Court of Claims. Moreover, no waiver of sovereign immunity for claims in tort existed until the enactment of the Federal Tort Claims Act in 1946 (see Chapter III.A.1). Thus, claimants who had suffered a deprivation of property by the government (other than through a formal condemnation process) generally were left in the awkward position of trying to file suits for specific relief, such as ejectment, against the government official in possession of the property, while contending that sovereign immunity did not bar the suit because the government officer was acting unconstitutionally. The classic example of this—and a decision which indulged the fiction that such suits were against the government officer rather than the government itself—was *United States v. Lee,* 106 U.S. 196 (1882), which was included earlier in this casebook (see Chapter II.A).

Finally, in 1946, the Supreme Court reexamined its rigid approach to the Tucker Act and held that seizures of property were indeed takings under the Fifth Amendment and thus compensable under the Tucker Act, even if they alternatively could also be characterized as torts. The doctrinal change came in the first of the major airplane overflight cases in which landowners adjoining airports make claims for the damage caused by the noise and vibration of overflight by aircraft. *United States v. Causby,* 328 U.S. 256 (1946). The case involved a chicken farm at which chickens were literally being frightened to death by the noise of heavy bombers overflying at 65 feet. The Government conceded at oral argument that overflights rendering the property uninhabitable would be a taking compensable under the Fifth Amendment. Overturning more than a half-century of doctrine, the Supreme Court held the jurisdiction of the Court of Claims to be "clear" because "[i]f there is a taking the claim is founded upon the Constitution" within the meaning of the Tucker Act. *Id.* at 267.

Today, the primary question in the taking area is no longer whether there is a waiver of sovereign immunity for inverse condemnation takings claims or a forum to hear them. Rather, the controversy is one of the merits—when does an infringement upon property rights rise to the level of a "taking," thereby requiring compensation by the government. The detailed substantive law of the Fifth Amendment is beyond the scope of this survey course. *See generally* David F. Coursen, *The Takings Jurisprudence of the Court of Federal Claims and the Federal Circuit,* 29 Envtl. L. 821 (1999).

2.   The *Preseault v. Interstate Commerce Commission* case well illustrates the remedy available under the Tucker Act and how that affects the resolution of takings disputes. What does the Fifth Amendment takings clause require of the government? Does it prohibit a taking of property? What do the plaintiffs in this case ask for, that is, what relief do they seek? Why can't they get it? May a party sue to set aside a seizure or is he or she instead limited to a claim for compensation? In a statute that effects a seizure of property, must Congress expressly refer to the remedy of the Tucker Act to ensure that this compensation scheme is available? What presumption does the Court make concerning the availability of the Tucker Act as a remedy? And, finally, what is the nature of a property right? Under what law are property rights defined for purposes of determining whether a taking has occurred? What is the point of the concurrence?

The property owners in the *Preseault* case accepted the Supreme Court's advice concerning the remedy available under the Tucker Act and pursued a claim for just compensation in the Court of Federal Claims. The Court of Federal Claims found in favor of the government, *Preseault v. United States,* 24 Cl. Ct. 818 (1992); 27 Fed. Cl. 69 (1992), and, on appeal, a three-judge panel of the Federal Circuit affirmed, in an opinion later vacated. Then, the Federal Circuit, sitting en banc, ruled in favor of the property owners. *Preseault v. United States,* 100 F.3d 1525 (Fed.Cir.1996) (en banc). Four judges (the plurality) held that under state property law the railroads had possessed only an easement, with the fee estate remaining in the original property owners; that the scope of the easement for railroad use could not be read to include public recreational hiking and biking trails; that, in any event, the railroad easements had been abandoned many years before creation of the trails; and thus that the conversion of the railroad right-of-ways to trails under the Rails-to-Trails Act constituted a taking of property for which compensation must be paid. *Id.* at 1532–52. The plurality rejected the government's contention that federal legislation on interstate railroads had redefined the nature of the private property rights, instead relying on Justice O'Connor's *Preseault* concurrence to hold that state law creates and gives content to property rights. *Id.* at 1537–40. Two judges concurred, agreeing that the question of whether just compensation is due for deprivation of property rights turns on the nature of the property rights under state law. *Id.* at 1552–54. Three judges dissented, arguing that the railroad rights-of-way had not been abandoned and that the current use of the land for recreational trails was permissible under state property law. *Id.* at 1554–76. For a good summation of the complexity of the issues and the convoluted history of the *Preseault* case, from start before the Interstate Commerce Commission to finish in the Federal Circuit, see Robert L. Bronston, *Federal Circuit Sitting In Banc Finds a Taking Under the "Rails-to-Trails" Act,* 7 Fed. Cir. Bar. J. 100 (1997).

b.   OTHER CONSTITUTIONAL CLAIMS

United States v. Connolly

United States Court of Appeals for the Federal Circuit.
716 F.2d 882 (Fed.Cir. 1983) (en banc), *cert. denied,* 465 U.S. 1065 (1984).

■ DAVIS, CIRCUIT JUDGE.

This case comes to us on interlocutory appeal from a decision of the United States Claims Court pursuant to 28 U.S.C. § 1292(d)(2). The trial judge granted the government's motion to dismiss appellee's wrongful removal action in part, but denied the government's full motion for judgment. The court held that it possessed jurisdiction "over that portion of [appellee's] claim ... based upon allegations that the dismissal was taken in retaliation for the exercise of first amendment rights." *Connolly v. United States,* 1 Cl.Ct. 312, 323, 554 F.Supp. 1250, 1262 (1982). Finding the first amendment claim "ripe for consideration" by this court, the Claims Court certified the question of its jurisdiction over the first amendment claim to us. This court has granted interlocutory review. Because we now conclude that the Claims Court is without jurisdiction to entertain wrongful removal actions by probationary employees of the Postal Service—whether or not such claims involve first amendment allegations—we affirm in part and reverse in part.

I

Appellee Connolly commenced employment as a probationary employee of the United States Postal Service (USPS) on April 4, 1981, at the Flagstaff, Arizona, post office. Serving as a postal clerk, his tasks included, among other things, mail sorting and the lifting of heavy cages containing parcel post packages. One month after Connolly began his service at USPS, he received an initial performance evaluation from his supervisor. That evaluation assessed appellee's productivity as "unsatisfactory," and it characterized him as an individual who did not accept criticism gracefully. The supervisor noted, however, that appellee's attitude toward criticism had improved somewhat since his hiring.

In the meantime, Connolly began to experience severe pain in his forearms and a numbness in his fingers. He consulted a neurologist, who diagnosed his malady as bilateral carpal tunnel syndrome, a condition which the doctor attributed to appellee's duties. Connolly, at the specialist's recommendation, began to wear braces on his arms. He also filed a compensation claim with the Department of Labor. The next day—May 13, 1981—Connolly received a second performance evaluation; it characterized his attitude as unsatisfactory with respect to "productivity and work habits," "safety," and "acceptance of criticism."

On the following day, Connolly submitted a letter to the postmaster at the Flagstaff office, explaining the nature of his injury and recommending safety procedures for lifting and carrying mail. The postmaster returned the letter to him without comment. Later that day, Connolly received a removal notice, separating him for unsatisfactory performance.

Connolly filed a wrongful removal suit in the Court of Claims, seeking reinstatement, back pay, damages, and various other forms of relief. He alleged that his poor performance evaluations and resulting dismissal were motivated by his injury, his compensation claim, and his grievances about the lack of proper safety procedures. The government filed a motion for summary judgment, contending that the Civil Service Reform Act of 1978 precluded probationary employees such as appellee from filing wrongful removal actions in the then Court of Claims. Treating the government's motion as a motion to dismiss the complaint, the trial court dismissed that part of plaintiff's complaint based upon statutory and regulatory provisions. The court held that it had no jurisdiction over appellee's claims because alleged violations of Postal Service regulations "cannot form the basis for jurisdiction in [the Claims Court]," and because the Civil Service Reform Act of 1978 effectively bars judicial review of an agency's dismissal of a probationary employee. *Connolly v. United States, supra,* 1 Cl.Ct. at 314–21, 554 F.Supp. at 1254–60.

However, the trial judge denied the government's motion insofar as it suggested that the first amendment[3] did not provide the court with jurisdiction over appellee's claim. The court concluded that it possessed "jurisdiction over that portion of [appellee's] claim which is based upon the first amendment," *Connolly, supra,* 1 Cl.Ct. at 323, 554 F.Supp. at 1261, and certified that issue to this court for review.

II

* * * We hold * * * that the nature and scope of our review are not limited to the certified question but that we are free to consider all questions material to the trial court's order sustaining its jurisdiction. We therefore proceed to consider whether the Claims Court may entertain appellee's wrongful removal action on any jurisdictional basis.

III

The trial court correctly held that it was without jurisdiction to review appellee's dismissal based upon allegations of regulatory or statutory violations. It is now settled that the Tucker Act does not itself confer a substantive right of recovery; rather, the prospective claimant must invoke substantive rights grounded expressly or by implication in a contract, an act of Congress or a regulation of an executive department.

Appellee, as a probationary employee of the Postal Service, cannot rely on alleged violations of Postal Service regulations and the Civil Service Reform Act of 1978, Pub.L. No. 95–454, 92 Stat. 1111 (1978), as the

---

3. U.S. Const. amend. I provides:

Congress shall make no law respecting an establishment of religion, or prohibiting the free exercise thereof; or abridging the freedom of speech, or of the press; or the right of the people peaceably to assemble, and to petition the Government for a redress of grievances.

substantive bases for his suit. Even if we assume *arguendo* that the Postal Service failed to comply with its own regulations in ordering appellee's dismissal, that would not support jurisdiction in the Claims Court. Since the enactment of the Postal Reorganization Act of 1970, Pub.L. No. 91–375, 84 Stat. 719 (1970), the Postal Service has not been considered one of the "executive departments" within the meaning of 5 U.S.C. § 101 (1982). Only the regulations of an "executive department" can form the basis for a regulatory claim cognizable under Tucker Act jurisdiction. *See* 28 U.S.C. § 1491.

We also agree with the trial judge's conclusion that Connolly, as a probationary employee, has no right under the Civil Service Reform Act to seek review of his dismissal in the Claims Court. The Reform Act established a comprehensive scheme for judicial review of adverse actions but at the same time deliberately precluded such review under that Act for probationary employees. Civil service employees, as defined by the Act, do not include those serving "probationary or trial" terms of employment. 5 U.S.C. § 7511(a)(1)(A). The statutory definition of "employee" denotes the only class of civil service workers entitled to procedural and appeal rights provided by the Act. *See* 5 U.S.C. § 7513(b), (d), (e). On the basis of this explicit legislative exclusion of probationary workers, courts have concluded that probationary employees may not appeal adverse actions under the Act.

We think that the legislative history of the Reform Act entirely forecloses the possibility that probationary employees have some sort of unspecified private right of action in the Claims Court under the Act to seek judicial review of their removals. The policy of denying probationary employees the right to challenge such terminations was explicitly outlined in the Senate Report accompanying the Act:

> The probationary or trial period . . . is an extension of the examining process to determine an employee's ability to actually perform the duties of the position. It is inappropriate to restrict an agency's authority to separate an employee who does not perform acceptably during this period.

S.Rep. No. 969, 95th Cong., 2d Sess. 45 (1978), *reprinted in* 1978 U.S.Code Cong. & Ad.News 2723, 2767. * * *

IV

The trial court wrongly concluded, however, that it possessed jurisdiction over that portion of Connolly's claim which was predicated upon the first amendment. Although we recognize that if "a claim falls within the terms of the Tucker Act, the United States has presumptively consented to suit," *see United States v. Mitchell*, 463 U.S. 206, 215 (1983), the basic issue is whether the first amendment "can fairly be interpreted as mandating compensation for the damages sustained." *See id.; United States v. Testan*, 424 U.S. 392, 400 (1976); *Eastport Steamship Co. v. United States*, 178 Ct.Cl. 599, 607, 372 F.2d 1002, 1009 (1967).

* * * [T]he first amendment, standing alone, cannot be so interpreted to command the payment of money. Like the due process clause of the fifth amendment, the literal terms of the first amendment neither explicitly nor implicitly obligate the federal government to pay damages. That amendment merely forbids Congress from enacting certain types of laws; it does not provide persons aggrieved by governmental action with an action for damages in the absence of some other jurisdictional basis. In construing the contours of Tucker Act jurisdiction, it would be, of course, impertinent for us to consider whether appellee may make such a first amendment claim within the non-monetary jurisdiction of a district court, or in a district court suit against the Postal Service. * * *

Nor can we accept Connolly's contention that the Back Pay Act, 5 U.S.C. § 5596, provides jurisdiction to hear his first amendment claim. Even assuming that the Back Pay Act is applicable to Postal Service employees—an issue which we do not decide—Connolly has failed to show that his separation from the Postal Service violated any relevant statute or regulation covered by the Tucker Act. The Back Pay Act is merely derivative in application; it is not itself a jurisdictional statute. We must conclude that, on any theory, the Claims Court lacks jurisdiction over appellee's first amendment claim.[7]

V

For these reasons, we affirm the trial court's determination that it lacks jurisdiction over appellee's claim to the extent that it is based upon statutes and regulations. We reverse the trial court's ruling that it possessed jurisdiction over appellee's first amendment claim. The case is remanded to the Claims Court with instructions to grant judgment in favor of the government by dismissing appellee's petition for lack of jurisdiction.

AFFIRMED IN PART, REVERSED IN PART, AND REMANDED.

Notes and Questions

1.   The Fifth Amendment takings clause is the classic constitutional provision upon which a Tucker Act may be founded. What if the government violates another constitutional requirement and a person suffers monetary consequences? Does the Tucker Act provide a remedy? What is the analysis? The Federal Circuit's decision in *United States v. Connolly* addresses and answers this question. What is the constitutional provision involved here and how does it differ from the Fifth Amendment takings clause for purposes of the Tucker Act remedy?

7.   "[O]rdinary dismissals from government service which violate no fixed tenure or applicable statute or regulation are not subject to judicial review even if the reasons for the dismissal are alleged to be mistaken or unreasonable." *Connick v. Myers,* 461 U.S. 138, 146 (1983).

If the Tucker Act is unavailable as a remedy, is another remedy available for a First Amendment freedom of speech constitutional claim? What would it be and what relief would be available?

2.   In addition to the constitutional claim, Connolly asserts a *statutory* Tucker Act claim, that is, a Tucker Act claim founded upon a statute. However, for reasons we explored earlier in the context of civilian employment claims (see Chapter IV.A.2.b), the Civil Service Reform Act is the exclusive remedy for employment claims raised by federal employees. If the CSRA does not authorize judicial review for a class of employee (such as probationary or excepted service employees), then no judicial review right exists and the Tucker Act is not available as an alternative. *See United States v. Fausto,* 484 U.S. 439 (1988). Thus, Connolly's claim stands, or in this case falls, on the constitutional foundation.

3.   Is there any constitutional provision other than the Fifth Amendment takings clause upon which a Tucker Act claim can be founded? The Court of Federal Claims and the United States Court of Appeals for the Federal Circuit have excluded the possibility of Tucker Act claims for money based on the First Amendment free speech clause (in the *Connolly* case set out above); the Fourth Amendment search and seizure clause, *Smith v. United States,* 51 Fed. Cl. 36, 38 (2001), *aff'd,* 36 Fed. Appx. 444 (Fed.Cir. 2002), *LaChance v. United States,* 15 Cl. Ct. 127, 129–30 (1988); the Fifth Amendment due process clause, *Smith, supra, LaChance, supra;* the assistance of counsel requirement of the Sixth Amendment, *Smith, supra;* the excessive fines clause of the Eighth Amendment, *Fireman v. United States,* 49 Fed. Cl. 290, 292–94 (2001); and the involuntary servitude prohibition of the Thirteenth Amendment, *Smith, supra.* In each instance, the court reasoned that these constitutional provisions are not money-mandating in nature.

Can you conceive of another constitutional provision that can be characterized as "money mandating" in nature? The Federal Circuit has found that the "Compensation Clause" of Article III—which guarantees that the compensation of federal judges "shall not be diminished during their Continuance in Office" (Art. III, § 1)—to be money-mandating and thus permitting federal judges to challenge deduction of social security taxes from salary in the Court of Federal Claims under the Tucker Act. *Hatter v. United States,* 953 F.2d 626 (Fed.Cir. 1992), *aff'd by lack of quorum,* 519 U.S. 801 (1996). (Subsequently the Supreme Court heard the *Hatter* case on the merits, and while mentioning the earlier jurisdictional ruling in the Federal Circuit, did not question the availability of Tucker Act jurisdiction over the matter. *United States v. Hatter,* 532 U.S. 557, 564 (2001).) In *Cyprus Amax Coal Co. v. United States,* 205 F.3d 1369, 1373–74 (Fed.Cir. 2000), the Federal Circuit held that the "Export Clause" of Article I, which states that "[n]o Tax or Duty shall be laid on Articles exported from any state," U.S. Const., art. I, § 9, cl. 5, also provides an independent, self-executing basis for a Tucker remedy because the necessary implication is that Congress must refund any taxes unlawfully exacted in contravention of the clause.

_____

SECTION B.   THE ADMINISTRATIVE PROCEDURE ACT

Administrative Procedure Act, 5 United States Code §§ 701(a), 702–706

§ 701.   Application; definitions

(a) This chapter applies, according to the provisions thereof, except to the extent that—

(1) statutes preclude judicial review; or

(2) agency action is committed to agency discretion by law.

* * *

§ 702.   Right of review

A person suffering legal wrong because of agency action, or adversely affected or aggrieved by agency action within the meaning of a relevant statute, is entitled to judicial review thereof. An action in a court of the United States seeking relief other than money damages and stating a claim that an agency or an officer or employee thereof acted or failed to act in an official capacity or under color of legal authority shall not be dismissed nor relief therein be denied on the ground that it is against the United States or that the United States is an indispensable party. The United States may be named as a defendant in any such action, and a judgment or decree may be entered against the United States: *Provided,* That any mandatory or injunctive decree shall specify the Federal officer or officers (by name or by title), and their successors in office, personally responsible for compliance. Nothing herein (1) affects other limitations on judicial review or the power or duty of the court to dismiss any action or deny relief on any other appropriate legal or equitable ground; or (2) confers authority to grant relief if any other statute that grants consent to suit expressly or impliedly forbids the relief which is sought.

§ 703.   Form and venue of proceeding

The form of proceeding for judicial review is the special statutory review proceeding relevant to the subject matter in a court specified by statute or, in the absence or inadequacy thereof, any applicable form of legal action, including actions for declaratory judgments or writs of prohibitory or mandatory injunction or habeas corpus, in a court of competent jurisdiction. If no special statutory review proceeding is applicable, the action for judicial review may be brought against the United States, the agency by its official title, or the appropriate officer. Except to the extent that prior, adequate, and exclusive opportunity for judicial review is provided by law, agency action is subject to judicial review in civil or criminal proceedings for judicial enforcement.

§ 704. Actions reviewable

Agency action made reviewable by statute and final agency action for which there is no other adequate remedy in a court are subject to judicial review. A preliminary, procedural, or intermediate agency action or ruling not directly reviewable is subject to review on the review of the final agency action. Except as otherwise expressly required by statute, agency action otherwise final is final for the purposes of this section whether or not there has been presented or determined an application for a declaratory order, for any form of reconsideration, or, unless the agency otherwise requires by rule and provides that the action meanwhile is inoperative, for an appeal to superior agency authority.

§ 705. Relief pending review

When an agency finds that justice so requires, it may postpone the effective date of action taken by it, pending judicial review. On such conditions as may be required and to the extent necessary to prevent irreparable injury, the reviewing court, including the court to which a case may be taken on appeal from or on application for certiorari or other writ to a reviewing court, may issue all necessary and appropriate process to postpone the effective date of an agency action or to preserve status or rights pending conclusion of the review proceedings.

§ 706. Scope of review

To the extent necessary to decision and when presented, the reviewing court shall decide all relevant questions of law, interpret constitutional and statutory provisions, and determine the meaning or applicability of the terms of an agency action. The reviewing court shall—

(1) compel agency action unlawfully withheld or unreasonably delayed; and

(2) hold unlawful and set aside agency action, findings, and conclusions found to be—

(A) arbitrary, capricious, an abuse of discretion, or otherwise not in accordance with law;

(B) contrary to constitutional right, power, privilege, or immunity;

(C) in excess of statutory jurisdiction, authority, or limitations, or short of statutory right;

(D) without observance of procedure required by law;

(E) unsupported by substantial evidence in a case subject to sections 556 and 557 of this title or otherwise reviewed on the record of an agency hearing provided by statute; or

(F) unwarranted by the facts to the extent that the facts are subject to trial de novo by the reviewing court.

In making the foregoing determinations, the court shall review the whole record or those parts of it cited by a party, and due account shall be taken of the rule of prejudicial error.

———

Citizens to Preserve Overton Park, Inc. v. Volpe

Supreme Court of the United States.
401 U.S. 402 (1971).

■ Opinion of the Court by MR. JUSTICE MARSHALL, announced by MR. JUSTICE STEWART.

The growing public concern about the quality of our natural environment has prompted Congress in recent years to enact legislation designed to curb the accelerating destruction of our country's natural beauty. We are concerned in this case with § 4(f) of the Department of Transportation Act of 1966, as amended, and § 18(a) of the Federal–Aid Highway Act of 1968, 23 U.S.C. § 138 (hereafter § 138). These statutes prohibit the Secretary of Transportation from authorizing the use of federal funds to finance the construction of highways through public parks if a "feasible and prudent"[4] alternative route exists. If no such route is available, the statutes allow him to approve construction through parks only if there has been "all possible planning to minimize harm"[5] to the park.

Petitioners, private citizens as well as local and national conservation organizations, contend that the Secretary has violated these statutes by authorizing the expenditure of federal funds for the construction of a six-lane interstate highway through a public park in Memphis, Tennessee. Their claim was rejected by the District Court, which granted the Secretary's motion for summary judgment, and the Court of Appeals for the Sixth Circuit affirmed. After oral argument, this Court granted a stay that halted construction and, treating the application for the stay as a petition for certiorari, granted review. We now reverse the judgment below and remand for further proceedings in the District Court.

Overton Park is 342–acre city park located near the center of Memphis. The park contains a zoo, a nine-hole municipal golf course, an outdoor theater, nature trails, a bridle path, an art academy, picnic areas, and 170 acres of forest. The proposed highway, which is to be a sixlane, high-speed, expressway, will sever the zoo from the rest of the park. Although the roadway will be depressed below ground level except where it crosses a small creek, 26 acres of the park will be destroyed. The highway is to be a segment of Interstate Highway I–40, part of the National System of Interstate and Defense Highways. I–40 will provide Memphis with a major

---

4. 49 U.S.C. § 1653(f); 23 U.S.C. § 138. **5.** *Ibid.*

east-west expressway which will allow easier access to downtown Memphis from the residential areas on the eastern edge of the city.

Although the route through the park was approved by the Bureau of Public Roads in 1956 and by the Federal Highway Administrator in 1966, the enactment of § 4(f) of the Department of Transportation Act prevented distribution of federal funds for the section of the highway designated to go through Overton Park until the Secretary of Transportation determined whether the requirements of § 4(f) had been met. * * * In April 1968, the Secretary announced that he concurred in the judgment of local officials that I–40 should be built through the park. And in September 1969 the State acquired the right-of-way inside Overton Park from the city. Final approval for the project—the route as well as the design—was not announced until November 1969, after Congress had reiterated in § 138 of the Federal–Aid Highway Act that highway construction through public parks was to be restricted. Neither announcement approving the route and design of I–40 was accompanied by a statement of the Secretary's factual findings. He did not indicate why he believed there were no feasible and prudent alternative routes or why design changes could not be made to reduce the harm to the park.

Petitioners contend that the Secretary's action is invalid without such formal findings and that the Secretary did not make an independent determination but merely relied on the judgment of the Memphis City Council. They also contend that it would be "feasible and prudent" to route I–40 around Overton Park either to the north or to the south. And they argue that if these alternative routes are not "feasible and prudent," the present plan does not include "all possible" methods for reducing harm to the park. Petitioners claim that I–40 could be built under the park by using either of two possible tunneling methods, and they claim that, at a minimum, by using advanced drainage techniques the expressway could be depressed below ground level along the entire route through the park including the section that crosses the small creek.

Respondents argue that it was unnecessary for the Secretary to make formal findings, and that he did, in fact, exercise his own independent judgment which was supported by the facts. In the District Court, respondents introduced affidavits, prepared specifically for this litigation, which indicated that the Secretary had made the decision and that the decision was supportable. These affidavits were contradicted by affidavits introduced by petitioners, who also sought to take the deposition of a former Federal Highway Administrator who had participated in the decision to route I–40 through Overton Park.

The District Court and the Court of Appeals found that formal findings by the Secretary were not necessary and refused to order the deposition of the former Federal Highway Administrator because those courts believed that probing of the mental processes of an administrative decisionmaker was prohibited. And, believing that the Secretary's authority was wide and reviewing courts' authority narrow in the approval of highway routes, the lower courts held that the affidavits contained no basis for a determination that the Secretary had exceeded his authority.

We agree that formal findings were not required. But we do not believe that in this case judicial review based solely on litigation affidavits was adequate.

A threshold question—whether petitioners are entitled to any judicial review—is easily answered. Section 701 of the Administrative Procedure Act, 5 U.S.C. § 701, provides that the action of "each authority of the Government of the United States," which includes the Department of Transportation, is subject to judicial review except where there is a statutory prohibition on review or where "agency action is committed to agency discretion by law." In this case, there is no indication that Congress sought to prohibit judicial review and there is most certainly no "showing of 'clear and convincing evidence' of a ... legislative intent" to restrict access to judicial review. *Abbott Laboratories v. Gardner,* 387 U.S. 136, 141 (1967).

Similarly, the Secretary's decision here does not fall within the exception for action "committed to agency discretion." This is a very narrow exception. The legislative history of the Administrative Procedure Act indicates that it is applicable in those rare instances where "statutes are drawn in such broad terms that in a given case there is no law to apply." S.Rep. No. 752, 79th Cong., 1st Sess., 26 (1945).

Section 4(f) of the Department of Transportation Act and § 138 of the Federal–Aid Highway Act are clear and specific directives. Both the Department of Transportation Act and the Federal–Aid to Highway Act provide that the Secretary "shall not approve any program or project" that requires the use of any public parkland "unless (1) there is no feasible and prudent alternative to the use of such land, and (2) such program includes all possible planning to minimize harm to such park...." 23 U.S.C. § 138; 49 U.S.C. § 1653(f). This language is a plain and explicit bar to the use of federal funds for construction of highways through parks—only the most unusual situations are exempted.

Despite the clarity of the statutory language, respondents argue that the Secretary has wide discretion. They recognize that the requirement that there be no "feasible" alternative route admits of little administrative discretion. For this exemption to apply the Secretary must find that as a matter of sound engineering it would not be feasible to build the highway along any other route. Respondents argue, however, that the requirement that there be no other "prudent" route requires the Secretary to engage in a wide-ranging balancing of competing interests. They contend that the Secretary should weigh the detriment resulting from the destruction of parkland against the cost of other routes, safety considerations, and other factors, and determine on the basis of the importance that he attaches to these other factors whether, on balance, alternative feasible routes would be "prudent."

But no such wide-ranging endeavor was intended. It is obvious that in most cases considerations of cost, directness of route, and community disruption will indicate that parkland should be used for highway construction whenever possible. Although it may be necessary to transfer funds from one jurisdiction to another, there will always be a smaller outlay required from the public purse when parkland is used since the public already owns the land and there will be no need to pay for right-of-way. And since people do not live or work in parks, if a highway is built on parkland no one will have to leave his home or give up his business. Such factors are common to substantially all highway construction. Thus, if Congress intended these factors to be on an equal footing with preservation of parkland there would have been no need for the statutes.

Congress clearly did not intend that cost and disruption of the community were to be ignored by the Secretary. But the very existence of the statutes indicates that protection of parkland was to be given paramount importance. The few green havens that are public parks were not to be lost unless there were truly unusual factors present in a particular case or the cost or community disruption resulting from alternative routes reached extraordinary magnitudes. If the statutes are to have any meaning, the Secretary cannot approve the destruction of parkland unless he finds that alternative routes present unique problems.

Plainly, there is "law to apply" and thus the exemption for action "committed to agency discretion" is inapplicable. But the existence of judicial review is only the start: the standard for review must also be determined. For that we must look to § 706 of the Administrative Procedure Act, 5 U.S.C. § 706, which provides that a "reviewing court shall . . . hold unlawful and set aside agency action, findings, and conclusions found" not to meet six separate standards. In all cases agency action must be set aside if the action was "arbitrary, capricious, an abuse of discretion, or otherwise not in accordance with law" or if the action failed to meet statutory, procedural, or constitutional requirements. 5 U.S.C. §§ 706(2) (A), (B), (C), (D). In certain narrow, specifically limited situations, the agency action is to be set aside if the action was not supported by "substantial evidence." And in other equally narrow circumstances the reviewing court is to engage in a de novo review of the action and set it aside if it was "unwarranted by the facts." 5 U.S.C. §§ 706(2)(E), (F).

Petitioners argue that the Secretary's approval of the construction of I–40 through Overton Park is subject to one or the other of these latter two standards of limited applicability. First, they contend that the "substantial evidence" standard of § 706(2)(E) must be applied. In the alternative, they claim that § 706(2)(F) applies and that there must be a de novo review to determine if the Secretary's action was "unwarranted by the facts." Neither of these standards is, however, applicable.

Review under the substantial-evidence test is authorized only when the agency action is taken pursuant to a rulemaking provision of the Administrative Procedure Act itself, 5 U.S.C. § 553, or when the agency action is based on a public adjudicatory hearing. See 5 U.S.C. §§ 556, 557. The Secretary's decision to allow the expenditure of federal funds to build I–40 through Overton Park was plainly not an exercise of a rulemaking function. And the only hearing that is required by either the Administrative Procedure Act or the statutes regulating the distribution of federal funds for highway construction is a public hearing conducted by local officials for the purpose of informing the community about the proposed project and eliciting community views on the design and route. 23 U.S.C. § 128. The hearing is nonadjudicatory, quasi-legislative in nature. It is not designed to produce a record that is to be the basis of agency action—the basic requirement for substantial-evidence review.

Petitioners' alternative argument also fails. *De novo* review of whether the Secretary's decision was "unwarranted by the facts" is authorized by § 706(2)(F) in only two circumstances. First, such *de novo* review is authorized when the action is adjudicatory in nature and the agency factfinding procedures are inadequate. And, there may be independent judicial factfinding when issues that were not before the agency are raised in a proceeding to enforce nonadjudicatory agency action. Neither situation exists here.

Even though there is no *de novo* review in this case and the Secretary's approval of the route of I–40 does not have ultimately to meet the substantial-evidence test, the generally applicable standards of § 706 require the reviewing court to engage in a substantial inquiry. Certainly, the Secretary's decision is entitled to a presumption of regularity. But that presumption is not to shield his action from a thorough, probing, in-depth review.

The court is first required to decide whether the Secretary acted within the scope of his authority. This determination naturally begins with a delineation of the scope of the Secretary's authority and discretion. As has been shown, Congress has specified only a small range of choices that the Secretary can make. Also involved in this initial inquiry is a determination of whether on the facts the Secretary's decision can reasonably be said to be within that range. The reviewing court must consider whether the Secretary properly construed his authority to approve the use of parkland as limited to situations where there are no feasible alternative routes or where feasible alternative routes involve uniquely difficult problems. And the reviewing court must be able to find that the Secretary could have reasonably believed that in this case there are no feasible alternatives or that alternatives do involve unique problems.

Scrutiny of the facts does not end, however, with the determination that the Secretary has acted within the scope of his statutory authority. Section 706(2)(A) requires a finding that the actual choice made was not "arbitrary, capricious, an abuse of discretion, or otherwise not in accordance with law." 5 U.S.C. § 706(2)(A). To make this finding the court must consider whether the decision was based on a consideration of the relevant factors and whether there has been a clear error of judgment. Although this inquiry into the facts is to be searching and careful, the ultimate standard of review is a narrow one. The court is not empowered to substitute its judgment for that of the agency.

The final inquiry is whether the Secretary's action followed the necessary procedural requirements. Here the only procedural error alleged is the failure of the Secretary to make formal findings and state his reason for allowing the highway to be built through the park.

Undoubtedly, review of the Secretary's action is hampered by his failure to make such findings, but the absence of formal findings does not necessarily require that the case be remanded to the Secretary. Neither the Department of Transportation Act nor the Federal–Aid Highway Act requires such formal findings. Moreover, the Administrative Procedure Act requirements that there be formal findings in certain rulemaking and adjudicatory proceedings do not apply to the Secretary's action here. See 5 U.S.C. §§ 553(a)(2), 554(a). And, although formal findings may be required in some cases in the absence of statutory directives when the nature of the agency action is ambiguous, those situations are rare. Plainly, there is no ambiguity here; the Secretary has approved the construction of I–40 through Overton Park and has approved a specific design for the project.
* * *

* * * [The] administrative record is not, however, before us. The lower courts based their review on the litigation affidavits that were presented. These affidavits were merely *"post hoc"* rationalizations, which have traditionally been found to be an inadequate basis for review. And they clearly do not constitute the "whole record" compiled by the agency: the basis for review required by § 706 of the Administrative Procedure Act.

Thus it is necessary to remand this case to the District Court for plenary review of the Secretary's decision. That review is to be based on the full administrative record that was before the Secretary at the time he made his decision. But since the bare record may not disclose the factors that were considered or the Secretary's construction of the evidence it may be necessary for the District Court to require some explanation in order to determine if the Secretary acted within the scope of his authority and if the Secretary's action was justifiable under the applicable standard.

The court may require the administrative officials who participated in the decision to give testimony explaining their action. Of course, such inquiry into the mental processes of administrative decisionmakers is usually to be avoided. *United States v. Morgan,* 313 U.S. 409, 422 (1941). And where there are administrative findings that were made at the same time as the decision, as was the case in *Morgan,* there must be a strong showing of bad faith or improper behavior before such inquiry may be made. But here there are no such formal findings and it may be that the only way there can be effective judicial review is by examining the decisionmakers themselves.

The District Court is not, however, required to make such an inquiry. It may be that the Secretary can prepare formal findings * * * that will provide an adequate explanation for his action. Such an explanation will, to some extent, be a *"post hoc* rationalization"* and thus must be viewed critically. If the District Court decides that additional explanation is necessary, that court should consider which method will prove the most expeditious so that full review may be had as soon as possible.

Reversed and remanded.

■ MR. JUSTICE DOUGLAS took no part in the consideration or decision of this case.

■ Separate opinion of MR. JUSTICE BLACK, with whom MR. JUSTICE BRENNAN joins.

I agree with the Court that the judgment of the Court of Appeals is wrong and that its action should be reversed. I do not agree that the whole matter should be remanded to the District Court. I think the case should be sent back to the Secretary of Transportation. It is apparent from the Court's opinion today that the Secretary of Transportation completely failed to comply with the duty imposed upon him by Congress not to permit a federally financed public highway to run through a public park "unless (1) there is no feasible and prudent alternative to the use of such land, and (2) such program includes all possible planning to minimize harm to such park...." 23 U.S.C. § 138; 49 U.S.C. § 1653(f). That congressional command should not be taken lightly by the Secretary or by this Court. It represents a solemn determination of the highest law-making body of this Nation that the beauty and health-giving facilities of our parks are not to be taken away for public roads without hearings, factfindings, and policy determinations under the supervision of a Cabinet officer—the Secretary of Transportation. The Act of Congress in connection with other federal highway aid legislation, it seems to me, calls for hearings—hearings that a court can review, hearings that demonstrate more than mere arbitrary defiance by the Secretary. Whether the findings growing out of such hearings are labeled "formal" or "informal" appears to me to be no more than an exercise in semantics. Whatever the hearing requirements might be, the Department of Transportation failed to meet them in this case. I regret that I am compelled to conclude for myself that, except for some too-late formulations, apparently coming from the Solicitor General's office, this record contains not one word to indicate that the Secretary raised even a finger to comply with the command of Congress. It is our duty, I believe, to remand this whole matter back to the Secretary of Transportation for him to give this matter the hearing it deserves in full good-faith obedience to the Act of Congress. That Act was obviously passed to protect our public parks from forays by road builders except in the most extraordinary and imperative circumstances. This record does not demonstrate the existence of such circumstances. I dissent from the Court's failure to send the case back to the Secretary, whose duty has not yet been performed.

■ MR. JUSTICE BLACKMUN.

I fully join the Court in its opinion and in its judgment. I merely wish to state the obvious: (1) The case comes to this Court as the end product of more than a decade of endeavor to solve the interstate highway problem at Memphis. (2) The administrative decisions under attack here are not those of a single Secretary; some were made by the present Secretary's predecessor and, before him, by the Department of Commerce's Bureau of Public Roads. (3) The 1966 Act and the 1968 Act have cut across former methods and here have imposed new standards and conditions upon a situation that already was largely developed.

This undoubtedly is why the record is sketchy and less than one would expect if the project were one which had been instituted after the passage of the 1966 Act.

Notes and Questions

1. For purposes of general classification, this casebook divides statutory waivers of sovereign immunity into two general categories: specific and general. Under this descriptive dichotomy, specific waivers are those statutory grants of suit that are limited to a particular subject matter, such as the Federal Tort Claims Act that authorizes only suits sounding in tort and seeking traditional tort relief, that is, money damages (see generally Chapter III.A). By contrast, a general waiver of sovereign immunity is one that covers several broad subject areas, although it may be limited in terms of relief available. Thus, the author of this casebook classifies the Tucker Act as a general waiver of sovereign immunity because it authorizes suits founded upon the Constitution, federal statutes, and contracts—essentially all claims for money judgments other than those sounding in tort—although, as we've seen, the Tucker Act is subject to significant limitations.

Similarly, the Administrative Procedure Act (APA) is a general waiver of sovereign immunity, broadly authorizing suits to challenge or demand agency action and seeking specific forms of relief. As with the Tucker Act, classification as a general waiver of sovereign immunity does not mean the APA does not impose limitations on the government's consent to suit. For example, the APA does not permit a suit seeking money damages. 5 U.S.C. § 702. Moreover, the APA does not apply when there is another adequate remedy in another court. *Id.* § 704. These two limitations on the APA are both studied in the next section of the casebook. See Chapter IV.C.

Professor Edward Rubin helpfully summarizes the basic nature of the APA in this way:

> The APA imposes three types of requirements on the administrative process. First, it requires that various governmental actions be publicized, or made available to public scrutiny. This requirement, the least developed of the three in the original statute, has been the subject of its most extensive amendments, which include the Freedom of Information Act and the Government in the Sunshine Act. Second, the APA imposes various procedural requirements on rulemaking and adjudication. To make a rule, an agency must publish a proposed version of the rule or a statement of the rule's subject matter, allow a period of time for private parties to file written comments with the agency and, after the comments have been received, publish a final

version of the rule with a statement of basis and purpose. To adjudicate an issue, the agency must provide interested parties with notice of the subject matter to be decided, conduct a hearing, and then issue a decision based upon the record of the hearing. Third, the APA grants aggrieved parties the opportunity to challenge agency action in court on the grounds that it violates the Constitution or federal statutory law, including, of course, the procedural requirements of the APA.

Edward Rubin, *It's Time to Make the Administrative Procedure Act Administrative*, 89 Cornell L. Rev. 95, 100–01 (2003).

Thus, the APA is much more than a waiver of sovereign immunity for suits seeking judicial review of agency action. And it is important for reasons other than litigation, although that will be our focus given the nature of this course. The APA creates a framework for administrative agency activity. By this point in your law school career, you are undoubtedly familiar with administrative agencies and the importance such entities play in regulation and achievement of statutory objectives. In enforcement and implementation of statutes, administrative agencies promulgate regulations that are binding upon the public. Agencies also conduct administrative adjudications of disputes under such statutes, such as whether to impose penalties for violation of the law. The APA establishes the procedural requirements for agency promulgation of regulations (rule-making) and for agency adversarial proceedings (adjudications). 5 U.S.C. §§ 551–559. On the APA and administrative law, see generally Richard J. Pierce, Jr., Sidney A. Shapiro & Paul R. Verkuil, *Administrative Law and Process* (4th ed. 2004); Richard J. Pierce, Jr., *Administrative Law Treatise* (3 vols., 4th ed. 2002 & Supp. 2005); Alfred C. Aman, Jr. & William T. Mayton, *Administrative Law* (2d ed. 2001). Our primary concern is with the judicial review provisions of the APA, which are excerpted in the casebook above.

2. Before 1976, a lawsuit asserting unlawful action by a federal agency had to be framed as a suit against the individual government official, because the United States had not waived its sovereign immunity to be sued directly. Thus, parties aggrieved by agency action had to fit the lawsuit within the rule of *Larson v. Domestic & Foreign Commerce Corp.*, 337 U.S. 682 (1949). Under *Larson*, which interpreted and applied the Supreme Court's earlier ruling in *United States v. Lee*, 106 U.S. 196 (1882), a suit could go forward against the official only if (1) the official had acted outside of his statutorily delegated authority, or (2) the official had acted contrary to constitutional command. In the first instance, the lawsuit was regarded as one directed against the government official individually because he or she was regarded as having abdicated his or her role as a government agent by acting in an unauthorized manner. The *Larson* Court described the second instance variously as (a) another example of a government agent acting *ultra vires* by violating the command of the Constitution or (b) as a constitutional exception to the doctrine of sovereign immunity. Under these two narrow circumstances, a suit against a government official would be treated as something other than a regular suit against the government itself, which would be barred by sovereign immunity. However,

if a government official was acting within the scope of his or her general authority and the claim was that he or she abused discretion, reached an arbitrary and capricious decision, or made a procedural error—but did not act unconstitutionally—the *Larson* rule would treat any suit as one challenging the actions of the government itself and thus as barred by sovereign immunity. This subject is treated at length in Chapter II.A.

In 1976, Congress amended the APA to bypass the *Larson* limitations and expressly waive the sovereign immunity of the government, thereby allowing suits seeking judicial review of an agency's action to be brought directly against the government itself. Pub. L. No. 94–574, 90 Stat. 2721 (1976). Section 702 of the APA now reads: "An action in a court of the United States * * * stating a claim that an agency or an officer or employee thereof acted or failed to act in an official capacity or under color of legal authority shall not be dismissed nor relief therein be denied on the ground that it is against the United States or that the United States is an indispensable party. The United States may be named as a defendant in any such action, and a judgment or decree may be entered against the United States."

3. Because this is a vital area of law in and of itself, a law student would be well advised to take a course on administrative law. An examination of a single APA case in a litigation course cannot begin to do justice to the subject. Nevertheless, if only one case were to be studied, the Supreme Court's decision in *Citizens to Preserve Overton Park, Inc. v. Volpe* is a good illustration, as it surveys so many of the judicial review provisions of the APA in a single setting.*

In studying the *Overton Park* decision, consider first the threshold question of whether judicial review of the agency decision is available at all. Look at the exceptions to the general presumption in favor of judicial review stated in Section 701. What are the exceptions? How are these exceptions explained and applied by the Court? (Note there are also certain prerequisites to seeking judicial review, which are not addressed in *Overton Park* because they are apparently present or undisputed, such as standing of the party to raise the issue, exhaustion of administrative remedies, and ripeness for review, issues that would be addressed in detail in a typical course on administrative law. *See generally* Aman & Mayton, *supra,* §§ 12.7, 12.9, 12.10. Justiciability is briefly outlined in Chapter I.C.2 of this casebook.)

---

* *But see* 2 Kenneth C. Davis & Richard J. Pierce, Jr., *Administrative Law Treatise* § 11.4, at 201 (3d ed. 1994) ("*Overton Park* was a hastily drafted opinion that includes considerable misleading and excessive dicta."). In particular, this treatise argues that the *Overton Park* decision "overstated the requirements of the arbitrary and capricious test when it referred to a 'searching and careful' inquiry into the facts that support an agency's decision." *Id.* The treatise observes, quite correctly, that the Supreme Court "has said many times that the arbitrary and capricious test is *less* demanding than the substantial evidence test." *Id.* Notwithstanding this sharp criticism of the opinion, the author of this casebook remains convinced it is valuable as an illustration in a short survey of the APA.

Next, assuming judicial review is available, what is the appropriate standard of judicial review? Read Section 706(2). The *Overton Park* Court directly or indirectly appears to address five of the six standards. List each one, determine what it means, and when it is applicable. Which are applicable in *Overton Park*? Which are not? Why? On which standard or standards of review does the Secretary of Transportation's decision in this case run aground?

(For the curious, on remand, the Secretary of Transportation reversed position and disapproved construction of the highway through the park, a decision that was upheld by the lower courts. *Citizens to Preserve Overton Park, Inc. v. Brinegar,* 494 F.2d 1212, 1216 (6th Cir. 1974). On the *Overton Park* decision and its aftermath, see Daniel A. Farber, *Saving Overton Park: A Comment on Environmental Values,* 146 U. Pa. L. Rev. 1671, 1672–73 (1998).)

Finally, although the *Overton Park* Court did not directly address it since the case was remanded on the merits, the last question in a typical APA suit would be the relief available against the agency. Section 702 authorizes actions "seeking relief other than money damages" and further refers to mandatory or injunctive relief. In sum, the relief contemplated under the APA judicial review provisions tends to be equitable in nature (although the statute does not adopt that particular term). May an APA claim for specific relief ever include a monetary award? Or is monetary relief barred by the exception for "money damages"? Moreover, does the general availability of monetary relief under the Tucker Act preclude the alternative of an APA suit seeking such relief? That leads us into the next section of the materials and the next case.

———

SECTION C.   THE RELATIONSHIP BETWEEN THE APA AND THE TUCKER ACT

Although statutory waivers of federal sovereign immunity have been enacted piecemeal by Congress over the course of 150 years, they nevertheless fit together into a reasonably well-woven tapestry of causes of action covering most subjects of dispute between the government and its citizens. *See* Gregory C. Sisk, *The Tapestry Unravels: Statutory Waivers of Sovereign Immunity and Money Claims Against the United States,* 71 Geo. Wash. L. Rev. 601, 603 (2003). Congress has contributed to this cohesion, intentionally or unintentionally, by generally limiting the sweep of one statute and thereby avoiding conflict with another. For example, the Tucker Act was enacted in 1887 to authorize money claims against the federal government for "cases not sounding in tort," 28 U.S.C. §§ 1346(a)(2), 1491. Thus, when the Federal Tort Claims Act (FTCA), 28 U.S.C. §§ 1346(b), 2671–2680, was subsequently enacted in 1946, it filled an empty niche and operates independently from the Tucker Act in most respects. Similarly, by its terms, the Administrative Procedure Act (APA) excludes actions for "money damages," 5 U.S.C. § 702, thereby directing most money claimants to frame an action under other statutes designed for money judgments, such as the Tucker Act and the FTCA—although, as will be seen in the next case, this particular design arguably became somewhat muddled in the wake of a leading Supreme Court decision.

When Congress was considering amendments to the APA in 1976, proponents of a waiver of sovereign immunity for judicial review of agency action also desired to pull together the "patchwork" of various statutory waivers of immunity in the hopes of regularizing this area of law and reducing confusion. *See Massachusetts v. Departmental Grant Appeals Bd.*, 815 F.2d 778, 782–83 & n.3 (1st Cir. 1987); *see also* H.R. Rep. No. 94–1656, at 11 (1976), *reprinted in* 1976 U.S.C.C.A.N. 6121, 6131 (the "explicit exclusion of monetary relief [from the amendment to the APA leaves] limitations on the recovery of money damages contained in * * * the Tucker Act * * * unaffected"); *New Mexico v. Regan*, 745 F.2d 1318, 1321–22 (10th Cir. 1984). In other words, Congress apparently wished to ensure that a remedy existed for wrongs that are appropriately addressed in a court, but simultaneously wanted to avoid confusing intersecting jurisdiction between different statutes. Richard H. Fallon, Jr., *Claims Court at the Crossroads*, 40 Cath. U. L. Rev. 517, 527 (1991) ("Congress clearly seems to have contemplated that there can be no suit in federal district court if the suit can instead be brought in the Claims Court under the Tucker Act.").

Before 1988, the APA and the Tucker Act were regarded by the federal courts as complementary but separate provisions addressing different types of judicial review, not as overlapping or conflicting statutes. Lawsuits challenging administrative actions and seeking nonmonetary relief could properly be brought in federal district court under the APA. If the plaintiff sought relief, other than in tort, in the form of a money judgment, or the practical equivalent of a money judgment, that legal action could be maintained only under the Tucker Act, in the absence of a specific jurisdictional statute encompassing a claim for monetary relief under a particular statutory scheme, such as Title VII of the Civil Rights Act of 1964, 42 U.S.C. §§ 2000e to 2000e–17 (see Chapter III.C), or the Social Security Act, 42 U.S.C. § 405(g) (see Chapter III.E). Accordingly, during this period, the courts of appeals almost uniformly recognized that actions seeking monetary relief from the federal government were cognizable, if at all, only under the Tucker Act. *See, e.g., Chula Vista City Sch. Dist. v. Bennett*, 824 F.2d 1573, 1579 (Fed.Cir. 1987); *Amoco Prod. Co. v. Hodel*, 815 F.2d 352, 361–68 (5th Cir. 1987); *Hahn v. United States*, 757 F.2d 581, 586–88 (3d Cir. 1985); *Portsmouth Redevelopment & Hous. Auth. v. Pierce*, 706 F.2d 471, 473–75 (4th Cir. 1983); *Bakersfield City Sch. Dist. of Kern County v. Boyer*, 610 F.2d 621, 627–28 (9th Cir. 1979). *But see Maryland Dep't of Human Res. v. Department of Health & Human Servs.*, 763 F.2d 1441 (D.C. Cir. 1985) (holding that certain claims for specific relief in money were cognizable under the APA).

Then, in 1988, in *Bowen v. Massachusetts*, 487 U.S. 879 (1988)—the next case in this casebook—the Supreme Court addressed the distinction between a proper claim under the APA for specific relief (routed to the federal district courts) and a Tucker Act claim for money damages (falling within the exclusive jurisdiction of the United States Court of Federal Claims). Instead of drawing a bright line between money and nonmoney claims, the Supreme Court adopted a case-by-case approach, allowing plaintiffs to frame some claims for monetary relief as falling within the APA framework rather than under the purview of the Tucker Act. The Court thereby blurred the lines between the APA and the Tucker Act, which is also the jurisdictional border between the District Courts and the Court of Federal Claims. More recently, however, and as discussed near the end of this chapter, the Supreme Court has resisted extension of *Bowen v. Massachusetts* to new contexts, and the United States Court of Appeals for the Federal Circuit has attempted to establish jurisdictional clarity and renew stability in assignment of claims between these judicial institutions.

Bowen v. Massachusetts

Supreme Court of the United States.
487 U.S. 879 (1988).

■ Justice Stevens delivered the opinion of the Court.

The principal question presented by these cases is whether a federal district court has jurisdiction to review a final order of the Secretary of Health and Human Services refusing to reimburse a State for a category of expenditures under its Medicaid program. All of the Courts of Appeals that have confronted this precise question have agreed that district courts do have jurisdiction in such cases. * * * Moreover, although the Medicaid program was established in 1965, the novel proposition that the Claims Court is the exclusive forum for judicial review of this type of agency action does not appear to have been advocated by the Secretary until this case reached the Court of Appeals. As we shall explain, the conclusion that the District Court had jurisdiction in these cases is supported by the plain language of the relevant statutes, their legislative history, and a practical understanding of their efficient administration. Before turning to the legal arguments, however, it is appropriate to say a few words about the mechanics of the federal financial participation (FFP) in the States' Medicaid programs and the character of the issue decided by the District Court.

I

In 1965 Congress authorized the Medicaid program by adding Title XIX to the Social Security Act, 79 Stat. 343. The program is "a cooperative endeavor in which the Federal Government provides financial assistance to participating States to aid them in furnishing health care to needy persons." *Harris v. McRae,* 448 U.S. 297, 308 (1980). Subject to the federal standards incorporated in the statute and the Secretary's regulations, each participating State must develop its own program describing conditions of eligibility and covered services. At present, 18 different categories of medical assistance are authorized.

Although the federal contribution to a State's Medicaid program is referred to as a "reimbursement," the stream of revenue is actually a series of huge quarterly advance payments that are based on the State's estimate of its anticipated future expenditures. The estimates are periodically adjusted to reflect actual experience. Overpayments may be withheld from future advances or, in the event of a dispute over a disallowance, may be retained by the State at its option pending resolution of the dispute.

Two procedures are available to the Secretary if he believes that a State's expenditures do not comply with either the Act or his regulations. First: If he concludes that the State's administration of its plan is in "substantial noncompliance" with federal requirements, he may initiate a compliance proceeding pursuant to 42 U.S.C. § 1316(a); in such a proceeding he may order termination of FFP for entire categories of state assistance, or even (theoretically) the entire state program. * * * A final order in a compliance proceeding is reviewable in the "United States court of appeals for the circuit in which such State is located." § 1316(a)(3). Second: The Secretary may "disallow" reimbursement for "any item or class of items." § 1316(d). "In general, ... a disallowance represents an isolated and highly focused inquiry into a State's operation of the assistance program." The statute does not expressly provide for judicial review of a disallowance order. In several cases a State has sought direct review of a disallowance order in a Court of Appeals, but in each such case the court has concluded that the State should proceed in the district court.

Massachusetts has participated in the Medicaid program continuously since 1966. One of the categories of assistance covered by the Massachusetts program is the provision of medical and rehabilitative services to patients in intermediate care facilities for the mentally retarded (ICF1 MR services). These services include such matters as "training in" the activities of daily living "(such as dressing and feeding oneself)," *Massachusetts v. Heckler,* 616 F.Supp. 687, 691 (Mass.1985) (case below), and are performed jointly by personnel from the State Departments of Mental Health and Education, working pursuant to state mental health and "special education" laws. See *Massachusetts v. Secretary of Health and Human Services,* 816 F.2d 796, 798 (C.A.1 1987) (case below). Although the Secretary apparently would have regarded these services as covered had they been performed solely by the Massachusetts Department of Mental Health, his auditors classified them as uncovered educational services because they were performed in part by employees of the State Department of Education. On August 23, 1982, the Regional Administrator of the Department's Health Care Financing Administration (HCFA) notified the State that he had disallowed $6,414,964 in FFP for the period July 1, 1978, to December 31, 1980. The Departmental Grant Appeals Board affirmed this decision on May 31, 1983.

On August 26, 1983, the State filed a complaint in the Federal District Court for the District of Massachusetts. The State's complaint invoked federal jurisdiction pursuant to 28 U.S.C. § 1331 and alleged that the United States had waived its sovereign immunity through 5 U.S.C. § 702. The complaint requested declaratory and injunctive relief and specifically asked the District Court to "set aside" the Board's order. * * *

On August 27, 1985, the District Court issued an opinion * * *. It did not discuss the jurisdictional issue. On the merits, it held that the services in question were in fact rehabilitative, and that this classification was not barred by the fact that the Department of Education had played a role in their provision. *Massachusetts v. Heckler,* 616 F.Supp. 687 (Mass.1985) (case below). Its judgment, dated October 7, 1985, simply "reversed" the Board's decision disallowing reimbursement of the sum of $6,414,964 in FFP under the Medicaid program. * * * It entered an appropriate judgment on December 2, 1985. That judgment did not purport to state what amount of money, if any, was owed by the United States to Massachusetts, nor did it order that any payment be made.

The Secretary at first had challenged the District Court's subject-matter jurisdiction, but later filed a memorandum stating that as "a matter of policy, HHS has decided not to press the defense of lack of jurisdiction in this action." In his consolidated appeal to the First Circuit, the Secretary reexamined this policy decision and decided to argue that the District Court did not have jurisdiction. The Court of Appeals accepted the Secretary's argument that the District Court could not order him to pay money to the State, but held that the District Court had jurisdiction to review the Board's disallowance decision and to grant declaratory and injunctive relief. * * *

On the merits, the Court of Appeals agreed with the District Court that the Secretary could not lawfully exclude the rehabilitative services provided to the mentally retarded just because the State had labeled them (in part) "educational" services and had used Department of Education personnel to help provide them. It therefore affirmed the District Court's holding that the decisions of the Grant Appeals Board must be reversed because the Secretary's "special education exclusion" violated the statute. It held, however, that it could not rule that the services in dispute were reimbursable because it had "no evidentiary basis for doing so." *Id.,* at 804. In sum, the Court of Appeals affirmed the District Court's declaratory judgment, vacated the "money judgment" against the Secretary, and remanded to the Secretary for further determinations regarding whether the services are reimbursable.[13]

---

13. The Court of Appeals explained:

"On remand the district court should send the case back to the Secretary for action consistent with the Medicaid Act as interpreted in this decision. Should the Secretary persist in withholding reimbursement for reasons inconsistent with our decision, the Commonwealth's remedy would be a suit for money past due under the Tucker Act in the Claims Court. In that subsequent suit we assume that the Secretary would be collaterally estopped from raising issues decided here."

816 F.2d, at 800.

In his petition for certiorari, the Secretary asked us to decide that the United States Claims Court had exclusive jurisdiction over the State's claim. In its cross-petition, the State asked us to decide that the District Court had jurisdiction to grant complete relief. We granted both petitions. The basic jurisdictional dispute is over the meaning of the Administrative Procedure Act (APA), 5 U.S.C. §§ 702, 704. The Secretary argues that § 702, as amended in 1976, does not authorize review because this is not an action "seeking relief other than money damages" within the meaning of the 1976 amendment to that section; he also argues that even if § 702 is satisfied, § 704 bars relief because the State has an adequate remedy in the Claims Court. The State must overcome both arguments in order to prevail; we shall discuss them separately.

II

[I]t is undisputed that the 1976 amendment to § 702 was intended to broaden the avenues for judicial review of agency action by eliminating the defense of sovereign immunity in cases covered by the amendment * * *. * * *

* * * [The 1976 amendment to the APA] added the following sentence to the already broad coverage of § 702:

> "An action in a court of the United States seeking relief other than money damages and stating a claim that an agency or an officer or employee thereof acted or failed to act in an official capacity or under color of legal authority shall not be dismissed nor relief therein be denied on the ground that it is against the United States or that the United States is an indispensable party."

There are two reasons why the plain language of this amendment does not foreclose judicial review of the actions brought by the State challenging the Secretary's disallowance decisions. First, insofar as the complaints sought declaratory and injunctive relief, they were certainly not actions for money damages. Second, and more importantly, even the monetary aspects of the relief that the State sought are not "money damages" as that term is used in the law.

Neither a disallowance decision, nor the reversal of a disallowance decision, is properly characterized as an award of "damages." Either decision is an adjustment—and, indeed, usually a relatively minor one—in the size of the federal grant to the State that is payable in huge quarterly installments. * * *

Our cases have long recognized the distinction between an action at law for damages—which are intended to provide a victim with monetary compensation for an injury to his person, property, or reputation—and an equitable action for specific relief—which may include an order providing for the reinstatement of an employee with backpay, or for "the recovery of specific property *or monies,* ejectment from land, or injunction either directing or restraining the defendant officer's actions." *Larson v. Domestic & Foreign Commerce Corp.,* 337 U.S. 682, 688 (1949) (emphasis added).

The fact that a judicial remedy may require one party to pay money to another is not a sufficient reason to characterize the relief as "money damages." * * *

Judge Bork's explanation of the plain meaning of the critical language in this statute merits quotation in full. In his opinion for the Court of Appeals for the *District of Columbia Circuit in Maryland Dept. of Human Resources v. Department of Health and Human Services,* 763 F.2d 1441 ([D.C.Cir.] 1985), he wrote:

"We turn first to the question whether the relief Maryland seeks is equivalent to money damages. Maryland asked the district court for a declaratory judgment and for injunctive relief 'enjoin[ing] defendants from reducing funds otherwise due to plaintiffs, or imposing any sanctions on such funds for alleged Title XX violations.' ... We are satisfied that the relief Maryland seeks here is not a claim for money damages, although it is a claim that would require the payment of money by the federal government.

"We begin with the ordinary meaning of the words Congress employed. The term 'money damages,' 5 U.S.C. § 702, we think, normally refers to a sum of money used as compensatory relief. Damages are given to the plaintiff to *substitute* for a suffered loss, whereas specific remedies 'are not substitute remedies at all, but attempt to give the plaintiff the very thing to which he was entitled.' D. Dobbs, *Handbook on the Law of Remedies* 135 (1973). Thus, while in many instances an award of money is an award of damages, '[o]ccasionally a money award is also a specie remedy.' *Id.*" * * * 763 F.2d, at 1446.

In arguing for a narrow construction of the 1976 amendment—which was unquestionably intended to broaden the coverage of § 702—the Secretary asks us to substitute the words "monetary relief" for the words "money damages" actually selected by Congress. Given the obvious difference in meaning between the two terms and the well-settled presumption that Congress understands the state of existing law when it legislates, only the most compelling reasons could justify a revision of a statutory text that is this unambiguous. Nevertheless, we have considered the Secretary's argument that the legislative history of § 702 supports his reading of the amendment.

The 1976 amendment to § 702 was an important part of a major piece of legislation designed to remove "technical" obstacles to access to the federal courts.[22] The statute was the culmination of an effort generated by scholarly writing and bar association work in the early 1960's. Although the Department of Justice initially opposed the proposal, it eventually reversed course and offered its support. We shall comment first on the legislative materials that relate directly to the bill that passed in 1976, and then refer to the 1970 Hearing on which the Government places its principal reliance.

---

22.   See H.R.Rep. No. 94–1656, pp. 3, 23 (1976) (H.R.Rep.); S.Rep., at 2, 22 (same).

Two propositions are perfectly clear. The first concerns the text of the amendment. There is no evidence that any legislator in 1976 understood the words "money damages" to have any meaning other than the ordinary understanding of the term as used in the common law for centuries. No one suggested that the term was the functional equivalent of a broader concept such as "monetary relief" and no one proposed that the broader term be substituted for the familiar one. Each of the Committee Reports repeatedly used the term "money damages"; the phrase "monetary relief" was used in each Report once, and only in intentional juxtaposition and distinction to "specific relief," indicating that the drafters had in mind the time-honored distinction between damages and specific relief. There is no support in that history for a departure from the plain meaning of the text that Congress enacted.

Second, both the House and Senate Committee Reports indicate that Congress understood that § 702, as amended, would authorize judicial review of the "administration of Federal grant-in-aid programs."[28] The fact that grant-in-aid programs were expressly included in the list of proceedings in which the Committees wanted to be sure the sovereign-immunity defense was waived is surely strong affirmative evidence that the members did not regard judicial review of an agency's disallowance decision as an action for damages.

If we turn to the 1970 Hearing and the earlier scholarly writings, we find that the terms "monetary relief" and "money damages" were sometimes used interchangeably. That fact is of only minimal significance, however, for several reasons. First, given the high caliber of the scholars who testified, it seems obvious that if they had intended the exclusion for proceedings seeking "money damages" to encompass all proceedings seeking any form of monetary relief, they would have drafted their proposal differently. Second, they cited cases involving challenges to federal grant-in-aid programs as examples of the Government's reliance on a sovereign-immunity defense that should be covered by the proposed legislation. Third, the case that they discussed at the greatest length in the 1970 Hearing was *Larson v. Domestic & Foreign Commerce Corp.*, 337 U.S. 682 (1949). Although they criticized the reliance on sovereign immunity in that opinion, they made no objection to its recognition of the classic distinction between the recovery of money damages and "the recovery of specific property or monies." * * *

Thus, the combined effect of the 1970 Hearing and the 1976 legislative materials is to demonstrate conclusively that the exception for an action seeking "money damages" should not be broadened beyond the meaning of its plain language. The State's suit to enforce § 1396b(a) of the Medicaid Act, which provides that the Secretary "shall pay" certain amounts for appropriate Medicaid services, is not a suit seeking money in *compensation* for the damage sustained by the failure of the Federal Government to pay as mandated; rather, it is a suit seeking to enforce the statutory mandate

---

28. H.R.Rep., at 9; S. Rep., at 8 (same).

itself, which happens to be one for the payment of money.[31] The fact that the mandate is one for the payment of money must not be confused with the question whether such payment, in these circumstances, is a payment of money as damages or as specific relief. Judge Bork's explanation bears repeating:

"[The State] is seeking funds to which a statute allegedly entitles it, rather than money in compensation for the losses, whatever they may be, that [the State] will suffer or has suffered by virtue of the withholding of those funds. * * *" 763 F.2d, at 1446.

III

The Secretary's novel submission that the entire action is barred by § 704 must be rejected because the doubtful and limited relief available in the Claims Court is not an adequate substitute for review in the District Court. A brief review of the principal purpose of § 704 buttresses this conclusion.

Section 704 was enacted in 1946 as § 10(c) of the APA. In pertinent part, it provided:

"Every agency action made reviewable by statute and every final agency action for which there is no other adequate remedy in any court shall be subject to judicial review." 60 Stat. 243.[32]

Earlier drafts of what became § 704 provided that "only final actions, rules, or orders, *or* those for which there is no other adequate judicial remedy ... shall be subject to such review," or that "[e]very final agency action, *or* agency action for which there is no other adequate remedy in any court, shall be subject to judicial review." Professor Davis, a widely respected administrative law scholar, has written that § 704 "has been almost completely ignored in judicial opinions,"[34] and has discussed § 704's bar to judicial review of agency action when there is an "adequate remedy" elsewhere as merely a restatement of the proposition that "[o]ne need not exhaust administrative remedies that are inadequate."

---

31. There are, of course, many statutory actions over which the Claims Court has jurisdiction that enforce a statutory mandate for the payment of money rather than obtain compensation for the Government's failure to so pay. The jurisdiction of the Claims Court, however, is not expressly limited to actions for "money damages," whereas that term does define the limits of the exception to § 702. Moreover, such statutes, unlike a complex scheme such as the Medicaid Act that governs a set of intricate, ongoing relationships between the States and the Federal Government, are all statutes that provide compensation for specific instances of past injuries or labors; suits brought under these statutes do not require the type of injunctive and declaratory powers that the district courts can bring to bear in suits under the Medicaid Act. Thus, to the extent that suits to enforce these statutes can be considered suits for specific relief, suits under the Tucker Act in the Claims Court offer precisely the sort of "special and adequate review procedures" that § 704 requires to direct litigation away from the district courts.

32. The provision now reads "[a]gency action made reviewable by statute and final agency action for which there is no other adequate remedy in a court are subject to judicial review." 5 U.S.C. § 704.

34. K. Davis, Administrative Law, § 26:12, p. 468 (2d ed. 1983).

However, although the primary thrust of § 704 was to codify the exhaustion requirement, the provision as enacted also makes it clear that Congress did not intend the general grant of review in the APA to duplicate existing procedures for review of agency action. As Attorney General Clark put it the following year, § 704 "does not provide additional judicial remedies in situations where the Congress has provided special and adequate review procedures." At the time the APA was enacted, a number of statutes creating administrative agencies defined the specific procedures to be followed in reviewing a particular agency's action; for example, Federal Trade Commission and National Labor Relations Board orders were directly reviewable in the regional courts of appeals, and Interstate Commerce Commission orders were subject to review in specially constituted three-judge district courts. When Congress enacted the APA to provide a general authorization for review of agency action in the district courts, it did not intend that general grant of jurisdiction to duplicate the previously established special statutory procedures relating to specific agencies.

The exception that was intended to avoid such duplication should not be construed to defeat the central purpose of providing a broad spectrum of judicial review of agency action. * * * A restrictive interpretation of § 704 would unquestionably, in the words of Justice Black, "run counter to § 10 and § 12 of the Administrative Procedure Act. Their purpose was to remove obstacles to judicial review of agency action under subsequently enacted statutes...." *Shaughnessy v. Pedreiro,* 349 U.S. 48, 51 (1955).

The Secretary argues that § 704 should be construed to bar review of the agency action in the District Court because monetary relief against the United States is available in the Claims Court under the Tucker Act. This restrictive—and unprecedented—interpretation of § 704 should be rejected because the remedy available to the State in the Claims Court is plainly not the kind of "special and adequate review procedure" that will oust a district court of its normal jurisdiction under the APA.[39] Moreover, the availability of any review of a disallowance decision in the Claims Court is doubtful.

The Claims Court does not have the general equitable powers of a district court to grant prospective relief. Indeed, we have stated categorically that "the Court of Claims has no power to grant equitable relief."[40] As

---

39. As noted above, litigation in the Claims Court can offer precisely the kind of "special and adequate review procedures" that are needed to remedy particular categories of past injuries or labors for which various federal statutes provide compensation. Managing the relationships between States and the Federal Government that occur over time and that involve constantly shifting balance sheets requires a different sort of review and relief process. The APA is tailored to fit the latter situation; the Tucker Act, the former.

40. *Richardson v. Morris,* 409 U.S. 464, 465 (1973) (*per curiam*); see also, *e.g., Glidden Co. v. Zdanok,* 370 U.S. 530, 557 (1962) (opinion of Harlan, J.) ("From the beginning [the Court of Claims] has been given jurisdiction only to award damages, not specific relief"). Although Congress has subsequently given the Claims Court certain equitable powers in specific kinds of litigation, see 28 U.S.C. §§ 1491(a)(2)-(3), the statements from *Richardson* and *Glidden* are still applicable to actions involving review of an agency's administration of a grant-in-aid program.

the facts of these cases illustrate, the interaction between the State's administration of its responsibilities under an approved Medicaid plan and the Secretary's interpretation of his regulations may make it appropriate for judicial review to culminate in the entry of declaratory or injunctive relief that requires the Secretary to modify future practices. We are not willing to assume, categorically, that a naked money judgment against the United States will always be an adequate substitute for prospective relief fashioned in the light of the rather complex ongoing relationship between the parties.

Moreover, in some cases the jurisdiction of the Claims Court to entertain the action, or perhaps even to enter a specific money judgment against the United States, would be at least doubtful.[42] Regarding the former dilemma: If a State elects to retain the amount covered by a disallowance until completion of review by the Grant Appeals Board, see 42 U.S.C. § 1396b(d)(5); it will not be able to file suit in the Claims Court until after the disallowance is recouped from a future quarterly payment. It is no answer to suggest that a State will not be harmed as long as it retains the money, because its interest in planning future programs for groups such as the mentally retarded who must be trained in ICF's may be more pressing than the monetary amount in dispute. Such planning may make it important to seek judicial review—perhaps in the form of a motion for a preliminary injunction—as promptly as possible after the agency action becomes final. A district court has jurisdiction both to grant such relief and to do so while the funds are still on the State's side of the ledger (assuming administrative remedies have been exhausted); the Claims Court can nei-

---

42. As a threshold matter, it is not altogether clear that the Claims Court would have jurisdiction under the Tucker Act, 28 U.S.C. § 1491(a)(1), to review a disallowance claim. To determine whether one may bring, pursuant to Tucker Act jurisdiction, a "claim against the United States founded . . . upon . . . any Act of Congress," *ibid.*, "one must always ask . . . whether the . . . legislation which the claimant cites can fairly be interpreted as mandating compensation by the Federal Government for the damage sustained." *Eastport S.S. Corp. v. United States*, 372 F.2d 1002, 1009, 178 Ct.Cl. 599 (1967) (cited with approval in *United States v. Testan*, 424 U.S. 392, 398, 400 (1976)). Statutes that have been "interpreted as mandating compensation by the Federal Government for the damage sustained," 372 F.2d, at 1009, generally are provisions such as the Back Pay Act, 5 U.S.C. § 5596(b), and 37 U.S.C. § 242 (1958 ed.) (repealed, see 76 Stat. 498 (1962)), which provided compensation to prisoners of war. These laws attempt to compensate a particular class of persons for past injuries or labors. In contrast, the statutory mandate of a federal grant-in-aid program directs the Secretary to pay money to the State, not as compensation for a past wrong, but to subsidize future state expenditures.

Moreover, Congress has not created an express cause of action providing for the review of disallowance decisions in the Claims Court. To construe statutes such as the Back Pay Act and the old 37 U.S.C. § 242, as "mandating compensation by the Federal Government for the damage sustained," 372 F.2d, at 1009, one must imply from the language of such statutes a cause of action. The touchstone here, of course, is whether Congress intended a cause of action that it did not expressly provide. See, *e.g., Thompson v. Thompson*, 484 U.S. 174 (1988); *Cort v. Ash*, 422 U.S. 66 (1975). It seems likely that while Congress intended "shall pay" language in statutes such as the Back Pay Act to be self-enforcing—*i.e.*, to create both a right and a remedy—it intended similar language in § 1396b(a) of the Medicaid Act to provide merely a right, knowing that the APA provided for review of this sort of agency action.

ther grant equitable relief, nor act in any fashion so long as the Federal Government has not yet offset the disallowed amount from a future payment. Regarding the latter problem: Given the fact that the quarterly payments of federal money are actually advances against expenses that have not yet been incurred by the State, it is arguable that a dispute concerning the status of the open account is not one in which the State can claim an entitlement to a specific sum of money that the Federal Government owes to it.

Further, the nature of the controversies that give rise to disallowance decisions typically involve state governmental activities that a district court would be in a better position to understand and evaluate than a single tribunal headquartered in Washington. We have a settled and firm policy of deferring to regional courts of appeals in matters that involve the construction of state law. That policy applies with special force in this context because neither the Claims Court nor the Court of Appeals for the Federal Circuit has any special expertise in considering the state-law aspects of the controversies that give rise to disallowances under grant-in-aid programs. It would be nothing less than remarkable to conclude that Congress intended judicial review of these complex questions of federal-state interaction to be reviewed in a specialized forum such as the Court of Claims. More specifically, it is anomalous to assume that Congress would channel the review of compliance decisions to the regional courts of appeals, see 42 U.S.C. § 1316(a)(3); and yet intend that the same type of questions arising in the disallowance context should be resolved by the Claims Court or the Federal Circuit.

IV

We agree with the position advanced by the State in its cross-petition— that the judgments of the District Court should have been affirmed in their entirety—for two independent reasons. First, neither of the District Court's orders in these cases was a "money judgment," as the Court of Appeals held. The first order (followed in the second) simply "reversed" the "decision of the Department Grant Appeals Board of the United States Department of Health and Human Services in Decision No. 438 (May 31, 1983)." It is true that it describes Decision No. 438 as one that had disallowed reimbursement of $6,414,964 to the State, but it did not order that amount to be paid, and it did not purport to be based on a finding that the Federal Government owed Massachusetts that amount, or indeed, any amount of money. Granted, the judgment tells the United States that it may not disallow the reimbursement on the grounds given, and thus it is likely that the Government will abide by this declaration and reimburse Massachusetts the requested sum. But to the extent that the District Court's judgment engenders this result, this outcome is a mere by-product of that court's primary function of reviewing the Secretary's interpretation of federal law.

Second, even if the District Court's orders are construed in part as orders for the payment of money by the Federal Government to the State, such payments are not "money damages," and the orders are not excepted from § 702's grant of power by § 704. That is, since the orders are for specific relief (they undo the Secretary's refusal to reimburse the State) rather than for money damages (they do not provide relief that substitutes for that which ought to have been done) they are within the District Court's jurisdiction under § 702's waiver of sovereign immunity. The District Court's jurisdiction to award complete relief in these cases is not barred by the possibility that a purely monetary judgment may be entered in the Claims Court.[48]

The question whether the District Court had the power to enter the orders it did is governed by the plain language of 5 U.S.C. § 706. It seems perfectly clear that, as "the reviewing court," the District Court had the authority to "hold unlawful and set aside agency action" that it found to be "not in accordance with law." As long as it had jurisdiction under § 702 to review the disallowance orders of the Secretary, it also had the authority to grant the complete relief authorized by § 706. Neither the APA nor any of our decisions required the Court of Appeals to split either of these cases into two parts.

In his explanation to Congress of the basic purpose of what became the 1976 amendment to the APA, Dean Cramton endorsed the view that " 'today the doctrine [of sovereign immunity] may be satisfactory to technicians but not at all to persons whose main concern is with justice.... The trouble with the sovereign immunity doctrine is that it interferes with consideration of practical matters, and transforms everything into a play on words.' "[51] In our judgment a fair consideration of "practical matters" supports the conclusion that the district courts and the regional courts of appeals have jurisdiction to review agency action of the kind involved in these cases and to grant the complete relief authorized by § 706. Accordingly, the Court of Appeals should have affirmed the judgments of the District Court in their entirety.

Thus, we affirm in part, reverse in part, and remand to the Court of Appeals for further proceedings consistent with this opinion.

It is so ordered.

48. It is often assumed that the Claims Court has exclusive jurisdiction of Tucker Act claims for more than $10,000. (Title 28 U.S.C. § 1346(a)(2) expressly authorizes concurrent jurisdiction in the district courts and the Claims Court for claims under $10,000.) That assumption is not based on any language in the Tucker Act granting such exclusive jurisdiction to the Claims Court. Rather, that court's jurisdiction is "exclusive" only to the extent that Congress has not granted any other court authority to hear the claims that may be decided by the Claims Court. If, however, § 702 of the APA is construed to authorize a district court to grant monetary relief—other than traditional "money damages"—as an incident to the complete relief that is appropriate in the review of agency action, the fact that the purely monetary aspects of the case could have been decided in the Claims Court is not a sufficient reason to bar that aspect of the relief available in a district court.

51. 1970 Hearing, at 115 (quoting Carrow, Sovereign Immunity in Administrative Law—A New Diagnosis, 9 J.Pub.L. 1, 22 (1960) (in turn quoting letter written by Professor Walter Gellhorn)).

■ Justice White, concurring in the judgment.

The Court construes the District Court's orders as not having entered a judgment for money damages within the meaning of 5 U.S.C. § 702. I am prepared to accept that view of what the District Court did, although the Court of Appeals had a different view.

The Court's opinion, as I understand it, also concludes that the District Court, in the circumstances present here, would have had jurisdiction to entertain and expressly grant a prayer for a money judgment against the United States. I am unprepared to agree with this aspect of the opinion and hence concur only in the result the Court reaches with respect to the construction of § 702.

The Court is correct in holding that § 704 does not bar District Court review of the challenged orders, the reason being that the Claims Court could not entertain and grant the claims presented to and granted by the District Court. I thus agree with the result reached in Part III of the Court's opinion.

■ Justice Scalia, with whom The Chief Justice and Justice Kennedy join, dissenting.

The Court holds for the State because it finds that these suits do not seek money damages, and involve claims for which there is no "adequate remedy" in the Claims Court. I disagree with both propositions, and therefore respectfully dissent.

I

"The States of the Union, like all other entities, are barred by federal sovereign immunity from suing the United States in the absence of an express waiver of this immunity by Congress." *Block v. North Dakota ex rel. Bd. of Univ. and School Lands,* 461 U.S. 273, 280 (1983). For this waiver, the Commonwealth of Massachusetts (hereafter respondent) relies on a provision added to § 10 of the Administrative Procedure Act (APA) in 1976:

> "An action in a court of the United States *seeking relief other than money damages* and stating a claim that an agency or an officer or employee thereof acted or failed to act in an official capacity or under color of legal authority shall not be dismissed nor relief therein be denied on the ground that it is against the United States or that the United States is an indispensable party." 5 U.S.C. § 702 (emphasis added).

The Government contends that respondent's lawsuits seek "money damages" and therefore § 702 is unavailing.

In legal parlance, the term "damages" refers to money awarded as reparation for injury resulting from breach of legal duty. Webster's Third New International Dictionary 571 (1981); Black's Law Dictionary 351–352 (5th ed. 1979); D. Dobbs, Law of Remedies § 3.1, p. 135 (1973); W. Hale, Law of Damages 1 (Cooley 2d ed. 1912). Thus the phrase "money damages" is something of a redundancy, but it is, nonetheless, a common usage and refers to one of the two broad categories of judicial relief in the common-law system. The other, of course, is denominated "specific relief." Whereas damages compensate the plaintiff for a loss, specific relief prevents or undoes the loss—for example, by ordering return to the plaintiff of the precise property that has been wrongfully taken, or by enjoining acts that would damage the plaintiff's person or property. See 5A A. Corbin, Contracts § 1141, p. 113 (1964); Dobbs, *supra,* at 135.

The use of the term "damages" (or "money damages") in a context dealing with legal remedies would naturally be thought to advert to this classic distinction. This interpretation is reinforced by the desirability of reading § 702 *in pari materia* with the Tucker Act, 28 U.S.C. § 1491, which grants the Claims Court jurisdiction over certain suits against the Government. Although the Tucker Act is not expressly limited to claims for money damages, it "has long been construed as authorizing only actions for money judgments and not suits for equitable relief against the United States. The reason for the distinction flows from the fact that the Court of Claims has no power to grant equitable relief. . . ." *Richardson v. Morris,* 409 U.S. 464, 465 (1973) (per curiam). Since under the Tucker Act the *absence* of Claims Court jurisdiction generally turns upon the distinction between money damages and specific relief,[1] it is sensible, if possible (and here it is not only possible but most natural), to interpret § 702 so that the *presence* of district court jurisdiction will turn upon the same distinction. Otherwise, there would be a gap in the scheme of relief—an utterly irrational gap, which we have no reason to believe was intended.

The Court agrees that "the words 'money damages' [were not intended to] have any meaning other than the ordinary understanding of the term as used in the common law for centuries," and that § 702 encompasses "the time-honored distinction between damages and specific relief." It concludes, however, that respondent's suits seek the latter and not the former. The first theory the Court puts forward to support this conclusion is that, "insofar as [respondent's] complaints sought declaratory and injunctive relief, they were certainly not actions for money damages," and since the District Court simply reversed the decision of the Departmental Grant Appeals Board, "neither of [its] orders in this case was a 'money judgment.' " I cannot agree (nor do I think the Court really agrees) with this reasoning. If the jurisdictional division established by Congress is not to be reduced to an absurdity, the line between damages and specific relief must surely be drawn on the basis of the substance of the claim, and not its mere form. It does not take much lawyerly inventiveness to convert a claim for

---

1.   In 1972 the Tucker Act was amended to give the Claims Court jurisdiction to issue "orders directing restoration to office or position, placement in appropriate duty or retirement status, and correction of applicable records," and "[i]n any case within its jurisdiction, . . . to remand appropriate matters to any administrative or executive body or official with such direction as it may deem proper and just." 28 U.S.C. § 1491(a)(2). In 1982 the Tucker Act was again amended to give the Claims Court exclusive jurisdiction to grant declaratory and equitable relief "on any contract claim brought before the contract is awarded." 28 U.S.C. § 1491(a)(3).

payment of a past due sum (damages) into a prayer for an injunction against refusing to pay the sum, or for a declaration that the sum must be paid, or for an order reversing the agency's decision not to pay. It is not surprising, therefore, that "in the 'murky' area of Tucker Act jurisprudence . . . one of the few clearly established principles is that the substance of the pleadings must prevail over their form," *Amoco Production Co. v. Hodel,* 815 F.2d 352, 361 (C.A.5 1987), cert. pending, No. 87–372. All the Courts of Appeals that to my knowledge have addressed the issue, 12 out of 13, are unanimous that district court jurisdiction is not established merely because a suit fails to pray for a money judgment. The Court cannot intend to stand by a theory that obliterates § 702's jurisdictional requirements, that permits every Claims Court suit to be brought in district court merely because the complaint prays for injunctive relief, and that is contrary to the law of all 12 Circuits that have addressed the issue. Therefore, although the Court describes this first theory as an "independent reaso[n]" for its conclusion, I must believe that its decision actually rests on different grounds.

The Court's second theory is that "the monetary aspects of the relief that the State sought are not 'money damages' as that term is used in the law." This at least focuses on the right question: whether the claim is in substance one for money damages. But the reason the Court gives for answering the question negatively, that respondent's suits are not "seeking money in *compensation* for the damage sustained by the failure of the Federal Government to pay as mandated," is simply wrong. Respondent sought money to compensate for the monetary loss (damage) it sustained by expending resources to provide services to the mentally retarded in reliance on the Government's statutory duty to reimburse, just as a Government contractor's suit seeks compensation for the loss the contractor sustains by expending resources to provide services to the Government in reliance on the Government's contractual duty to pay. Respondent's lawsuits thus precisely fit the classic definition of suits for money damages. It is true, of course, that they also fit a general description of a suit for specific relief, since the award of money undoes a loss by giving respondent the very thing (money) to which it was legally entitled. As the Court recognizes, however, the terms "damages" and "specific relief" have been "used in the common law for centuries," and have meanings well established by tradition. Part of that tradition was that a suit seeking to recover a past due sum of money that does no more than compensate a plaintiff's loss is a suit for damages, not specific relief; a successful plaintiff thus obtains not a decree of specific performance requiring the defendant to pay the sum due on threat of punishment for contempt, but rather a money judgment permitting the plaintiff to order "the sheriff to seize and sell so much of the defendant's property as was required to pay the plaintiff." Farnsworth, Legal Remedies for Breach of Contract, 70 Colum.L.Rev. 1145, 1152 (1970). Those rare suits for a sum of money that were not suits for money damages (and that resulted at common law in an order to the defendant rather than a judgment executable by the sheriff) did not seek to compensate the plaintiff for a past loss in the amount awarded, but rather to prevent future losses that were either incalculable or would be greater than the sum awarded. Specific relief was available, for example, to enforce a promise to loan a sum of money when the unavailability of alternative financing would leave the plaintiff with injuries that are difficult to value; or to enforce an obligor's duty to make future monthly payments, after the obligor had consistently refused to make past payments concededly due, and thus threatened the obligee with the burden of bringing multiple damages actions. Almost invariably, however, suits seeking (whether by judgment, injunction, or declaration) to compel the defendant to pay a sum of money[3] to the plaintiff are suits for "money damages," as that phrase has traditionally been applied, since they seek no more than compensation for loss resulting from the defendant's breach of legal duty. The present cases are quite clearly of this usual sort.

The Court's second theory, that "the monetary aspects of the relief that the State sought are not 'money damages,'" is not only wrong, but it produces the same disastrous consequences as the first theory. As discussed above, and as the Court recognizes, the Claims Court has jurisdiction only to award damages, not specific relief. But if actions seeking past due sums are actions for specific relief, since "they undo the [Government's] refusal" to pay the plaintiff, then the Claims Court is out of business. Almost its entire docket fits this description. In the past, typical actions have included suits by Government employees to obtain money allegedly due by statute which the Government refused to pay. Another large category of the Claims Court's former jurisdiction consisted of suits for money allegedly due under Government grant programs that the Government refused to pay. All these suits, and even actions for tax refunds, are now disclosed to be actions for specific relief and beyond the Claims Court's jurisdiction, since they merely seek "to enforce the statutory mandate . . . which happens to be one for the payment of money."

Most of these suits will now have to be brought in the district courts, as suits for specific relief "to undo the Government's refusal to pay." Alas, however, not all can be. The most regrettable consequence of the Court's analysis is its effect upon suits for a sum owed under a contract with the Government. In the past, the Claims Court has routinely exercised jurisdiction over a seller's action for the price. But since, on the Court's theory, such a suit is not a suit for money damages but rather for specific relief, that jurisdiction will have to be abandoned. Unfortunately, however, those suits will not lie in district court either. It is settled that sovereign immunity bars a suit against the United States for specific performance of a contract, and that this bar was not disturbed by the 1976 amendment to § 702. * * * But since the Claims Court is also barred from granting

---

3. Suit for a sum of money is to be distinguished from suit for specific currency or coins in which the plaintiff claims a present possessory interest. Specific relief is available for that, through a suit at law for replevin or detinue, or through a suit in equity for injunctive relief, if the currency or coins in question (for example, a collection of rare coins) are "unique" or have an incalculable value. That is obviously not the case here. Respondent seeks fungible funds, not any particular notes in the United States Treasury.

specific performance, the Court's theory, in addition to leaving the Claims Court without a docket, leaves the contractor without a forum.

I am sure, however, that neither the judges of the Claims Court nor Government contractors need worry. The Court cannot possibly mean what it says today—except, of course, the judgment. What that leaves, unfortunately, is a judgment without a reason.

II

I agree with the Court that sovereign immunity does not bar respondent's actions insofar as they seek injunctive or declaratory relief with prospective effect. An action seeking an order that will prevent the wrongful disallowance of future claims is an action seeking specific relief and not damages, since no damage has yet occurred. Cf. *United States v. Testan*, 424 U.S. 392, 403 (1976) (distinguishing "between prospective reclassification, on the one hand, and retroactive reclassification resulting in money damages, on the other").

I do not agree, however, that respondent can pursue these suits in district court, as it has sought to, under the provisions of the APA, since in my view they are barred by 5 U.S.C. § 704, which is entitled "Actions reviewable," and which reads in relevant part:

> "Agency action made reviewable by statute and final agency action for which there is *no other adequate remedy in a court* are subject to judicial review."

The purpose and effect of this provision is to establish that the APA "does not provide additional judicial remedies in situations where the Congress has provided special and adequate review procedures." Attorney General's Manual on the Administrative Procedure Act § 10(c), p. 101 (1947). Respondent has an adequate remedy in a court and may not proceed under the APA in the District Court because (1) an action for reimbursement may be brought in the Claims Court pursuant to the Tucker Act, and (2) that action provides all the relief respondent seeks.

The Tucker Act grants the Claims Court

> "jurisdiction to render judgment upon any claim against the United States founded either upon the Constitution, or any Act of Congress or any regulation of an executive department, or upon any express or implied contract with the United States, or for liquidated or unliquidated damages in cases not sounding in tort." 28 U.S.C. § 1491(a)(1).

The Claims Court has not always clearly identified which of the several branches of jurisdiction recited in this provision it is proceeding under. It has held that Government grant instruments, although not formal contracts, give rise to enforceable obligations analogous to contracts. The Medicaid Act itself can be analogized to a unilateral offer for contract— offering to pay specified sums in return for the performance of specified services and inviting the States to accept the offer by performance. But regardless of the propriety of invoking the Claims Court's contractual jurisdiction, I agree with the Secretary that respondent can assert a claim "founded ... upon [an] Act of Congress," to wit, the Medicaid provision mandating that "the Secretary (except as otherwise provided in this section) *shall pay* to each State which has a plan approved under this subchapter" the amounts specified by statutory formula. 42 U.S.C. § 1396b(a) (emphasis added).

We have held that a statute does not create a cause of action for money damages unless it " 'can fairly be interpreted as mandating compensation by the Federal Government for the damage sustained.' " *United States v. Testan, supra*, at 400, quoting *Eastport S.S. Corp. v. United States*, 178 Ct.Cl. 599, 607, 372 F.2d 1002, 1009 (1967). Although § 1396b(a) does not, in so many words, mandate damages, a statute commanding the payment of a specified amount of money by the United States impliedly authorizes (absent other indication) a claim for damages in the defaulted amount.

I conclude, therefore, that respondent may bring an action in the Claims Court based on § 1396b(a). The Court does not disagree with this conclusion but does comment that "[i]t seems likely that while Congress intended 'shall pay' language in statutes such as the Back Pay Act to be self-enforcing—*i.e.*, to create both a right and a remedy—it intended similar language in § 1396b(a) of the Medicaid Act to provide merely a right, knowing that the APA provided for review of this sort of agency action." (n. 42) I fail to understand this reasoning, if it is intended as reasoning rather than as an unsupported conclusion. * * *

There remains to be considered whether the relief available in the Claims Court, damages for failure to pay a past due allocation, is an "adequate remedy" within the meaning of § 704. Like the term "damages," the phrase "adequate remedy" is not of recent coinage. It has an established, centuries old, common-law meaning in the context of specific relief—to wit, that specific relief will be denied when damages are available and are sufficient to make the plaintiff whole. Thus, even though a plaintiff may often prefer a judicial order enjoining a harmful act or omission before it occurs, damages after the fact are considered an "adequate remedy" in all but the most extraordinary cases. There may be circumstances in which damages relief in the Claims Court is available, but is not an adequate remedy. For example, if a State could prove that the Secretary intended in the future to deny Medicaid reimbursement in bad faith, forcing the State to commence a new suit for each disputed period, an action for injunctive relief in district court would lie. Or if a State wished to set up a new program providing certain services that the Secretary had made clear his intention to disallow for reimbursement, an action seeking a declaration as to the correct interpretation of the statute would lie, since it would be necessary to prevent the irreparable injury of either forgoing a reimbursable program or mistakenly expending state funds that will not be reimbursed. But absent such unusual circumstances, the availability of damages in the Claims Court precludes suit in district court under the provision of the APA permitting review of "agency action for which there is no other adequate remedy."[4]

The Court does not dispute that in the present cases an action in Claims Court would provide respondent complete relief. Respondent can assert immediately a claim for money damages in Claims Court, which if successful will as effectively establish its rights as would a declaratory judgment in district court. Since there is no allegation that the Secretary will not honor in the future a Claims Court judgment that would have not only precedential but collateral-estoppel effect, the ability to bring an action in Claims Court with regard to disallowance decisions already made provides effective prospective relief as well.

Rather than trying to argue that the Claims Court remedy is inadequate in this case, the Court declares in a footnote that "[s]ince, as a *category of case*, alleged 'improper Medicaid disallowances' cannot always be adequately remedied in the Claims Court, as a jurisdictional, or threshold matter, these actions should proceed in the district court." This novel approach completely ignores the well-established meaning of "adequate remedy," which refers to the adequacy of a remedy for a particular plaintiff in a particular case rather than the adequacy of a remedy for the average plaintiff in the average case of the sort at issue. * * * [W]ere the Court's rationale taken seriously, it would (like the Court's novel analysis of "money damages" in § 702) divest the Claims Court of the bulk of its docket. It is difficult to think of a category of case that can "always be adequately remedied in the Claims Court." Nor is a categorical rule for challenges to Medicaid disallowance decisions justifiable on the basis that in *most* (not just some) such cases prospective or injunctive relief is required, and therefore it is efficient to have a bright-line rule. The traditional legal presumption (and the common-sense presumption) with respect to all other statutes that obligate the Government to pay money is that money damages are ordinarily an adequate remedy. I am aware of no empirical evidence to rebut that presumption with respect to Medicaid. Among the reported disallowance decisions, there appear to be none where a State has asserted a basis for prospective injunctive relief.

Nor can Medicaid disallowance cases be singled out for special treatment as a group because, as the Court declares, "[m]anaging the relationships between States and the Federal Government that occur over time and that involve constantly shifting balance sheets requires a different sort of review and relief process" than is provided in Claims Court, since the Medicaid Act is a "complex scheme ... that governs a set of intricate, ongoing relationships between the States and the Federal Government."

---

4. Of course, many suits, both for specific relief and for damages, reach district court under the APA because they come within the more specific rubric of § 704, "[a]gency action made reviewable by statute." See, *e.g.* 42 U.S.C. § 405(g) (Social Security benefits); 42 U.S.C. § 1395oo(f) (reimbursement of Medicare providers). And even where no special review statute exists, the vast majority of specific-relief suits challenging agency action will reach district court because they are unaffected by the "other adequate remedy" provision of § 704, since they challenge the application of statutes or regulations that cannot be regarded as providing for damages. See, *e.g.*, *Abbott Laboratories v. Gardner*, 387 U.S. 136 (1967) (suit challenging drug-labeling regulations).

All aspects of this assertion are without foundation. The area of law involved here, Medicaid, is indistinguishable for all relevant purposes from many other areas of law the Claims Court routinely handles. Medicaid statutes and regulations are not more complex than, for example, the federal statutes and regulations governing income taxation or Government procurement, and the Government's relationship with the States is neither more intricate and ongoing nor uses a different kind of balance sheet than its relationship with many defense contractors or with large corporate taxpayers subject to perpetual audit. And I cannot imagine in what way district courts adjudicating Medicaid disallowance claims would apply "a different sort of review and relief process" so as to "manag[e] the relationships between States and Federal Governments." Just like the Claims Court, district courts adjudicate concrete cases, one at a time, that present discrete factual and legal disputes.

Finally, the Court suggests that Medicaid disallowance suits are more suitably heard in district court with appeal to the regional courts of appeals than in the Claims Court with appeal to the Court of Appeals for the Federal Circuit, because (1) disallowance decisions have "state-law aspects" over which the regional courts of appeals have a better grasp, (2) it is anomalous to have Medicaid compliance decisions reviewed in the regional courts of appeals while reviewing disallowance decisions in Claims Court, and (3) it is "highly unlikely that Congress intended to designate an Article I court as the primary forum for judicial review of agency action that may involve questions of policy." I do not see how these points have anything to do with the question before us (whether the Claims Court can provide an adequate remedy in these cases), but even if relevant they seem to me wrong. (1) Adjudicating a disallowance decision does not directly implicate state law. As the present cases illustrate, the typical dispute involves only the interpretation of federal statutes and regulations. * * * (2) It is not at all anomalous for the Claims Court to share jurisdiction over controversies arising from Medicaid. In fact, quite to the contrary, the Claims Court *never* exercises exclusive jurisdiction over any body of law, but only over particular types of claims. (3) It is not more likely that Congress intended disputes involving "questions of policy" to be heard in district court before appeal to an Article III court, since it is the business neither of district courts nor of Article III appellate courts to determine questions of policy. It is the norm for Congress to designate an Article I judge, usually an administrative law judge, as the initial forum for resolving policy disputes (to the extent they are to be resolved in adjudication rather than by rulemaking), with the first stop in an Article III court being a court of appeals such as the Federal Circuit—where, of course, the policy itself would not be reviewed but merely its legality and the procedures by which it was pronounced. Ordinarily, when Congress creates a special judicial review mechanism using district courts, it is to get an independent adjudication of the facts, not an unconstitutional judicial determination of policy. See, *e.g.*, 42 U.S.C. § 405(g). * * *

Nothing is more wasteful than litigation about where to litigate, particularly when the options are all courts within the same legal system that will apply the same law. Today's decision is a potential cornucopia of waste. Since its reasoning cannot possibly be followed where it leads, the jurisdiction of the Claims Court has been thrown into chaos. On the other hand, perhaps this is the opinion's greatest strength. Since it cannot possibly be followed where it leads, the lower courts may have the sense to conclude that it leads nowhere, and to limit it to the single type of suit before us. Even so, because I think there is no justification in law for treating this single type of suit differently, I dissent.

Notes and Questions

1.   The problem of overlapping coverage and the attendant possibility of forum-shopping may be unavoidable, as long as there are separate statutory waivers of sovereign immunity—instead of one overarching government consent to suit—and particularly as long as some of these waivers direct claims to special forums. We were exposed to this problem previously in the context of the intersection between the Federal Tort Claims Act and the Tucker Act, that is, when a claim could be characterized alternatively as a tort or as a contractual or statutory claim for money, and thus might be pursued either in the district court under the FTCA or in the Court of Federal Claims under Tucker Act, or perhaps both. This problem implicated 28 U.S.C. § 1500 which precludes the Court of Federal Claims from adjudicating a claim that is pending simultaneously in another court (see Chapter IV.A.1.a).

The same problem may arise when the Tucker Act and the Administrative Procedure Act meet at the edges of their authority. Arguably, Congress anticipated this very problem when it excluded "money damages" from the APA in 5 U.S.C. § 702. And Congress further precluded resort to the APA whenever another "adequate remedy" is available in court. Both of these limitations in the APA could be read to direct all claims that can be remedied by monetary relief to the Tucker Act forum. However, as *Bowen v. Massachusetts* demonstrates, these statutory provisions are subject to differing interpretations.

2.   After coming to an understanding of the underlying dispute on the merits that gives rise to the lawsuit in *Bowen v. Massachusetts*, outline the jurisdictional arguments made by the United States and the State of Massachusetts. Compare the majority and dissenting opinions on each of these issues. For analysis, divide each opinion between its discussion of (1) the "money damages" limitation in Section 702, and (2) the preclusion of APA relief when there is another "adequate remedy" within the meaning of Section 704.

a.   *Section 702 and "Money Damages"*: With respect to Section 702, what does the term "money damages" mean? Can money ever be the subject of a claim for specific relief? If so, under what circumstances? How broad does such a interpretation sweep in terms of the types of claims that would be brought within the APA? What are the consequences of the alternative understandings of "money damages" by the majority and dissent for APA and Tucker Act coverage? Would the Court of Federal Claims have jurisdiction over the type of claim brought in *Bowen v. Massachusetts* (see footnote 31 in the majority opinion)? Is the district court forum also available?

The majority distinguishes between monetary relief that is compensation for a loss ("money damages" excepted from Section 702) and specific relief to enforce a statutory mandate for the payment of money (which is not excepted from the APA). How far might this expand the reach of the APA? Consider the case of *United States v. Connolly*, 716 F.2d 882 (Fed.Cir. 1983) (en banc), which you read earlier in Chapter IV.A.5.b. In *Connolly*, the Federal Circuit held that a probationary federal employee who asserted he had been discharged in violation of the First Amendment free speech clause could not seek backpay, because the free speech clause was not a "money-mandating" provision within the meaning of the Tucker Act. Could that employee bring an action under the APA for review of the discharge as in violation of the Constitution and seek, in addition to reinstatement, backpay on the grounds that he is not seeking money damages but rather specific relief for the very thing to which he is entitled under the statute? Could the plaintiff argue that the payment of wages for the wrongly lost employment position is the very thing to which he is entitled? Doesn't this argument plausibly fit under the *Bowen v. Massachusetts* Court's reasoning? And, yet, federal employee claims for backpay have long been traditional grist for the Court of Federal Claims mill, such that inclusion of such claims under the APA would be a rather surprising change in understanding of the governing law. On the real and potential disruptive effect of the *Bowen v. Massachusetts* holding to areas of settled Tucker Act jurisprudence, including civilian employment claims, military employment claims, Indian money claims, and even contract claims, see generally Gregory C. Sisk, *The Tapestry Unravels: Statutory Waivers of Sovereign Immunity and Money Claims Against the United States*, 71 Geo. Wash. L. Rev. 601, 627–66 (2003).

Consider the prospects for forum-shopping occasioned by the majority opinion versus the dissent in *Bowen v. Massachusetts*. Doesn't the majority's drawing a distinction between compensatory "money damages" and specific monetary relief encourage artful pleading of money claims against the government in a manner that will ensure the plaintiff that he or she desires? If the plaintiff wishes to pursue a cognizable claim for money in the Court of Federal Claims under the Tucker Act, the complaint would be framed forthrightly as one seeking money damages. If, instead, the plaintiff wished to avoid the Court of Federal Claims and litigate in a federal district court, many plaintiffs could frame the request for monetary relief as something other than "damages" as defined by the *Bowen v. Massachusetts* majority. Couldn't nearly any complaint seeking the recovery of money be framed as a request for an injunction against nonpayment of that money or for specific relief requiring a federal official to pay money?

Critics of *Bowen v. Massachusetts* (including your casebook author) have contended that this blurring of the jurisdictional lines generates pointless and distracting litigation over the threshold question of the forum for a claim and further depreciates the jurisdictional authority and substantive expertise of the Court of Federal Claims over certain fields of law. *See, e.g.*, Sisk, *supra*; Michael F. Noone, Jr. & Urban A. Lester, *Defining Tucker Act Jurisdiction After* Bowen v. Massachusetts, 40 Cath. U. L. Rev. 571, 593–603 (1991); *see also* H.R. Rep. No. 100–889, at 52, 54 (1988), reprinted in 1988 U.S.C.C.A.N. 5982, 6014 (House committee report saying that *Bowen v. Massachusetts* created "an uncertain exception to the general principle that monetary claims against the United States must proceed under the Tucker Act"). Others have argued that the "multiplicity of fora for and forms of relief against the government" is simply an element of the "contemporary functional character" of federal courts, *see* Judith Resnik, *Of Courts, Agencies, and the Court of Federal Claims: Fortunately Outliving One's Anomalous Character*, 71 Geo. Wash. L. Rev. 798, 810–17 (2003), or that the "most likely interpretation" of *Bowen v. Massachusetts* is that it does not "transfer matters traditionally within the exclusive jurisdiction of the Claims Court" to district courts, but more narrowly applies to grant-in-aid cases involving "equitable 'reimbursement'" in which a party has "expended funds in reliance upon the federal government's statutory obligation to reimburse" the party for those expenditures, *see* Cynthia Grant Bowman, Bowen v. Massachusetts: *The "Money Damages Exception" to the Administrative Procedure Act and Grant-in-Aid Litigation*, 21 Urb. Law. 557, 577–78 (1989).

b.   *Section 704 and Another Adequate Remedy*: With respect to Section 704, how do the majority and dissent in *Bowen v. Massachusetts* differ in their view of what constitutes an "other adequate remedy in court," the presence of which would make resort to the APA impermissible? Why is the Tucker Act remedy for money in the Court of Federal Claims regarded as inadequate in the majority's view? The majority notes that the Court of Federal Claims lacks the power to issue injunctive relief in cases such as this. Why does the dissent believe that the monetary remedy that is available in that court nonetheless remains adequate? Even when a dispute concerns an ongoing relationship between the parties, a money judgment based upon past liability has future effect, both as a matter of preclusion law (collateral estoppel or issue preclusion) as to those particular litigants and as a matter of precedent as to other concerned entities. How does this affect the majority's and dissent's analysis?

3.   More than ten years after *Bowen v. Massachusetts*, the Supreme Court returned to the question of the APA and claims involving money in *Department of Army v. Blue Fox*, 525 U.S. 255 (1999). A subcontractor on a federal project who had not been paid by the prime contractor attempted to impose an "equitable lien" upon funds held by the United States, asserting that the federal government had wrongly failed to ensure that the prime contractor posted a payment bond. The appeals court, relying upon *Bowen v. Massachusetts*, had approved this clever gambit as an action under the APA for equitable relief. *Blue Fox Inc. v. Small Business Admin.*, 121 F.3d 1357, 1360–63 (9th Cir. 1997). The Supreme Court reversed, finding that

liens "are merely a means to the end of satisfying a claim for the recovery of money" and thus fall within the exclusion under the APA of actions for "money damages." *Blue Fox*, 525 U.S. at 263. Because a lien's "goal is to seize or attach money in the hands of the Government as compensation for the loss," and thus does not constitute a true form of specific relief, the Court declared that the action fell outside of Section 702's waiver of sovereign immunity. *Id.*

Does *Blue Fox* signal a retreat by the Court or a recognition that *Bowen v. Massachusetts* had engendered confusion? To be sure, the *Blue Fox Court* did reaffirm *Bowen v. Massachusetts* in the course of its discussion. *Id.* at 261–62. However, *Bowen v. Massachusetts* was not further extended and the Court made clear that artful framing of money claims as requests for specific relief can go only so far. The actual holding in *Blue Fox*—that assertions of liens are claims for money damages—may be narrow and involve an atypical scenario. Attempts to levy a lien against the United States have been routinely rebuffed in the past—indeed there is something faintly absurd about the idea of attaching or executing a claim against federal property (it evokes such humorous prospects as the execution of a judgment against a post office building). And after *Blue Fox*, such attempts are unlikely to be repeated. However, the decision still may have larger significance by indicating that the types of lawsuits or litigation devices that traditionally have been designed to recover money will be recognized for what they are in substance—money claims. Thus traditional monetary claims may be declared off-limits for the APA. In sum, a path may have been shown out of the jurisdictional quagmire created by *Bowen v. Massachusetts*, but whether it can guide the courts all of the way out remains to be seen. This is unlikely to be the last word on the subject.

4.   At the end of his dissenting opinion, Justice Scalia contends that the decision in *Bowen v. Massachusetts* creates "chaos" and expresses the hope that the lower courts will confine it to the type of suit involved in that case. *See also* David A. Webster, *Choice of Forum in Claims Litigation—A Written Response to Two Proposals Presented to Clarify the Tucker Act Jurisdiction of the Claims Court*, 37 Fed. B. News & J. 534, 536 (1990) (suggesting that the Supreme Court might "simply see the light and reverse" its decision in *Bowen v. Massachusetts* if "enough lower courts send appropriate signals of distress"). Is the next case such a "signal of distress"? Is the United States Court of Federal Circuit appropriately "confin[ing]" *Bowen v. Massachusetts* to the particular type of suit involved or instead failing to fully uphold and apply the Court's precedent? Has the Federal Circuit restored order to the jurisdictional lines?

———

Suburban Mortgage Associates, Inc. v. United States Department of Housing and Urban Development

United States Court of Appeals for the Federal Circuit.
480 F.3d 1116 (Fed.Cir. 2007).

■ PLAGER, SENIOR CIRCUIT JUDGE.

This case requires us to reexamine the jurisdictional boundary between the Tucker Act and the Administrative Procedure Act, as that boundary is understood in the light of the Supreme Court's decision in *Bowen v. Massachusetts.*[1] The case began as a dispute between plaintiff Suburban Mortgage Associates, Inc. ("Suburban"), and defendants, the United States Department of Housing and Urban Development ("HUD") et al. ("Government"), with regard to a contract for insurance. Plaintiff sued the Government in the United States District Court for the District of Columbia. The suit was cast in part as an action for specific performance of the contract and in part as a declaratory judgment action. The relief sought was to require the Government to perform its contract obligations so that Suburban Mortgage could get the money allegedly due it under the insurance agreement.

The action quickly morphed into a dispute over what court had been authorized by Congress to hear the case: was it the district court (the plaintiff's choice) or was it the United States Court of Federal Claims (the Government's choice)? The Government forced the issue by moving in the district court to have that court either dismiss the entire case or transfer it from the district court to the Court of Federal Claims. The district court denied the Government's motion.

Litigation over where to litigate is the unfortunate consequence of the complex of statutes and courts that comprise the federal system. "Nothing is more wasteful than litigation about where to litigate, particularly when the options are all courts within the same legal system that will apply the same law." *Bowen,* 487 U.S. at 930 (Scalia, J., dissenting). This court plays a role in such litigation. When a district court denies a motion to transfer an action to the Court of Federal Claims as provided by 28 U.S.C. § 1631, an interlocutory appeal from such a denial may be taken to the United States Court of Appeals for the Federal Circuit. 28 U.S.C. § 1292(d)(4)(A). The Government has exercised that right in this case.

For the reasons we shall explain, and despite Suburban's valiant effort to frame the suit as one for declaratory or injunctive relief, this kind of litigation should be understood for what it is. At bottom it is a suit for money for which the Court of Federal Claims can provide an adequate remedy, and it therefore belongs in that court. The district court's determination to the contrary is reversed, and the matter is remanded to that court with instructions to either dismiss the suit in its entirety or transfer it to the Court of Federal Claims.

BACKGROUND

Suburban is a commercial mortgage lender based in Maryland. In 1998 Suburban made a loan, secured by a mortgage on the subject property, to Hillside Nursing Home ("Hillside"), a now defunct nursing home and assisted living facility in Rhode Island. To encourage development of such facilities for the elderly, Congress has authorized HUD to underwrite such

---

1.   487 U.S. 879 (1988).

loans, that is, to guarantee payment of the mortgage loan. *See* National Housing Act ("NHA") § 232, 12 U.S.C. § 1715w. In effect, the Government insures the loan. At Suburban's request, HUD, in exchange for premiums paid by Suburban, undertook that obligation with regard to the Hillside loan.

The agreement with HUD means that, should the borrower (Hillside) default on the underlying loan and the lender (Suburban) consequently incur loses, HUD will reimburse the lender pursuant to the terms of the insurance agreement. In order to collect the insurance proceeds when there has been a default by the borrower, the lender must first transfer its interest in the mortgage and mortgaged property to HUD. The lender has the option of foreclosing and taking title to the property, then transferring the property to HUD, or directly assigning the defaulted note and mortgage to HUD. In either case, HUD pays the lender the outstanding debt the borrower owed, less certain charges.

In this case, the nursing home (Hillside) defaulted on its mortgage loan. Thereafter, Suburban notified HUD that it wished to exercise its contractual right * * * to assign the defaulted Hillside mortgage to HUD. HUD, however, declined to accept assignment. Under HUD's statutory authority for these insurance agreements, there is an incontestability clause that generally precludes HUD from challenging its duty to pay. However, an exception to that clause exists when the agreement involves "fraud or misrepresentation on the part of [the lender]." In this case, HUD thought it had sufficient reason to believe that Suburban had committed fraud or made material misrepresentations to HUD.[6]

An extensive period of negotiation between the parties proved fruitless. Suburban then sued HUD in the District Court for the District of Columbia, asserting jurisdiction under 28 U.S.C. § 1331 as well as the Administrative Procedure Act ("APA"), 5 U.S.C. §§ 701–06; the Declaratory Judgment Act, 28 U.S.C. §§ 2201–02, and the Fifth Amendment to the United States Constitution. The complaint contained two counts.

The first count, entitled "Declaratory Judgment: for HUD to comply with its [contractual] obligations * * *," asked the district court to declare HUD's actions unlawful and to order HUD to perform its duties under the agreement, specifically, to accept assignment of the loan with ultimate

---

6. The Government's concern related to the actions of one Antonio L. Giordano, whom the Government believed owned or controlled both Suburban Mortgage and the Hillside Nursing Home, and that fraudulent conduct by him caused Hillside's failure. Subsequent to the argument in this case, * * * both the Government and Suburban Mortgage have advised this court regarding the guilty plea of Mr. Giordano to a charge of equity-skimming and his indictment on other charges, relating to the Hillside Nursing Home among other properties. Suburban alleges that Mr. Giordano never "owned or controlled" Suburban Mortgage, and though at one time he owned 50% of the company he was not its president or chair of its board, and his conduct cannot be imputed to Suburban Mortgage. The trial court in its opinion detailed other Suburban Mortgage business activities that had alerted HUD to a problem. The truth of these matters is not directly relevant to the jurisdiction question before us, and remains to be determined on the merits by a court of competent jurisdiction.

reimbursement of the loan balance to Suburban. Echoing the language of the APA, Suburban alleged that the Government, by denying its assignment, acted arbitrarily, capriciously, and in violation of Suburban's due process rights under the Fifth Amendment. The second count, entitled "Breach of Contract: Request for Specific Relief under § 702 of the APA," asked the court for "specific relief in the form of payment of the insured loan amount" and reimbursement of certain taxes and fees as losses plaintiff suffered because the Government allegedly did not perform its duties under the insurance contract.

The Government moved in the district court to dismiss the suit for lack of subject matter jurisdiction on the grounds that the suit was basically a contract action, and therefore can only be heard in the Court of Federal Claims under the Tucker Act, 28 U.S.C. § 1491(a)(1). As an alternative to dismissal, the Government requested that the district court transfer the case to the Court of Federal Claims pursuant to 28 U.S.C. § 1631.

In ruling on the motion, the district court looked for guidance to the precedent of its regional circuit, the United States Court of Appeals for the District of Columbia Circuit. The district court recognized that it could exercise subject matter jurisdiction over claims against the Government only if a plaintiff identifies an explicit waiver of sovereign immunity. Citing *Transohio Savings Bank v. Office of Thrift Supervision*, 967 F.2d 598, 607 (D.C. Cir. 1992), the court noted that the APA provides the necessary waiver of sovereign immunity for challenges to agency action, subject to three exceptions found in 5 U.S.C. §§ 702 and 704: "the APA excludes from its waiver of sovereign immunity (1) claims for money damages, (2) claims for which an adequate remedy is available elsewhere, and (3) claims seeking relief expressly or impliedly forbidden by another statute." *Suburban Mortgage Assocs., Inc. v. U.S. Dep't of Hous. & Urban Dev.*, No. 05–00856, 2005 WL 3211563, at *6 (D.D.C. Nov.14, 2005). The court then examined Suburban's claims in light of these exceptions.

With regard to Count II of the complaint, the district court viewed that as a contract claim asking for "essentially 'the classic contractual remedy of specific performance.'" The court read the relevant precedent as precluding it from hearing contract claims against the Government, whether for money damages or specific relief, because the Tucker Act "impliedly forbids" (as that term is used in the APA) any such relief by district courts. Applying this case law, the district court concluded that the APA did not waive sovereign immunity for Count II, and accordingly that Count II was outside of its jurisdiction.

The district court viewed Count I differently. With regard to the first exception limiting the APA's waiver of sovereign immunity, the district court cited *Bowen v. Massachusetts* for the proposition that a claim for money is not necessarily a claim for "money damages" as that term is used in the APA. Citing *Maryland Department of Human Resources v. Department of Health and Human Services*, 763 F.2d 1441, 1446 (D.C. Cir. 1985), the court drew a distinction based on the *purpose* behind the payment sought: is the plaintiff seeking money damages "to substitute for a suffered loss," or is the plaintiff seeking specific relief in the form of money, i.e., "the very thing to which he was entitled"? Although Suburban characterized its requested relief in injunctive terms, the court recognized that Suburban would recover money from HUD if it prevailed. Nevertheless, the court concluded that any such recovery would be money that HUD was obligated to pay under the agreement. Suburban therefore was seeking specific relief in the form of money to which it was entitled, rather than money damages.

Turning to the second exception, the district court determined that Suburban Mortgage did not have an adequate remedy in the Court of Federal Claims. While some of plaintiff's claimed losses could be reduced to a monetary sum, the district court concluded that concerns about possible bankruptcy, loss of reputation, and lost future profits could only be addressed through injunctive relief.

Finally, the district court held that Count I did not seek relief expressly or impliedly forbidden by the Tucker Act. The Government had argued that the claim was a disguised contract claim and therefore, like Count II, could not be adjudicated in district court. But the court concluded that plaintiff's allegations regarding HUD's arbitrary refusal to accept assignment because of unproven fraud suspicions found their source in the statutes and constitutional provisions cited by Suburban, and not the underlying contract for Insurance that it had with HUD. The district court therefore granted the Government's motion to dismiss Count II, and denied the motion to dismiss Count I or to transfer the remaining case to the Court of Federal Claims.

In the same order, the district court granted Suburban's motion to require HUD to file with the court a copy of the administrative record on which it relied in making its determination with respect to the election of assignment. Since an APA suit basically challenges an agency's actions, the agency's administrative record of what it has done is the record on which the court bases its decision. The effect of filing the agency's administrative record in the matter would be to provide Suburban with what amounts to discovery of the Government's case, i.e., whatever information the Government may have for suspecting fraud. The Government, however, would not have an equal opportunity for discovery of the facts known to Suburban, the kind of discovery that could be had in a normal civil suit, including a contract dispute in the Court of Federal Claims.

The Government resisted producing the administrative record under the circumstances and promptly took an interlocutory appeal of the Count I jurisdictional issue to this court, as it is entitled to do pursuant to 28 U.S.C. § 1292(d)(4)(A).

DISCUSSION

A.

Sovereign immunity—the notion cherished by the medieval English Kings and Queens that they could do no wrong, at least no wrong correctable in their own courts—is a privilege still granted by the federal courts to the Royals' successor, the United States Government. One consequence of this doctrine is that, absent a Constitutional grant of authority, if one wishes to sue the United States for a wrong committed by one of its agents (and agencies), one must find an appropriate Act of Congress that waives the Government's immunity from suit for that particular wrong.

If the suit is a civil action, other than in tort, there are two general statutes that waive sovereign immunity. One is the Tucker Act, the origins of which go back to the late 1800s. In the Tucker Act, Congress recognized that for a variety of reasons it was in the Government's interest to waive immunity and to allow people to bring suit against the Government for money they believed was owed to them. For one thing, it relieved Congress of the hassle of having to enact special bills to resolve run-of-the-mill disputes. For another, in the absence of such a waiver, the Government's cost of doing business would be greater since parties contracting with the Government would understand that they had to factor in the costs of arbitrary bureaucratic behavior for which, absent the waiver, no judicial remedy would be available. The Tucker Act both waives sovereign immunity for, and grants the Court of Federal Claims exclusive jurisdiction over, actions for money damages of more than $10,000. 28 U.S.C. § 1491(a)(1).

The other general statute is the Administrative Procedure Act ("APA"). Enacted to provide for judicial review in the federal district courts of certain agency actions, the Act was amended in 1976 to expressly waive sovereign immunity for actions against the Government. 5 U.S.C. §§ 701–06, *amended by* Pub.L. No. 94–574, 90 Stat. 2721 (1976). Though the APA itself does not provide an independent grant of subject matter jurisdiction, the general federal question jurisdictional statute, 28 U.S.C. § 1331, confers authority on the district courts to hear APA cases.

Congress reconciled these two general statutory waivers by providing in the APA the three specific limitations noted by the trial court: (1) a suit under the APA can only seek relief other than "money damages," 5 U.S.C. § 702; (2) the suit would lie under the APA only if there were "no other adequate remedy" in a court, 5 U.S.C. § 704; and (3) the suit could not be maintained if "any other statute that grants consent to suit expressly or impliedly forbids the relief which is sought," 5 U.S.C. § 702. With these limitations, the APA and the Tucker Act were understood to cover quite different challenges to Government action. A plaintiff seeking relief, other than monetary relief, from a disputed government agency action could challenge that action in district court under the APA. In contrast, a suit requesting relief in the form of a money judgment against the Government could be brought in the Court of Federal Claims under the Tucker Act, but not in a district court.[10] For jurisdictional purposes between the district courts under the APA and the Court of Federal Claims under the Tucker Act, the money distinction seemed to provide a relatively watertight barrier.

---

10. [Noting the] Little Tucker Act exception for claims not exceeding $10,000.

In 1988 the barrier sprang a leak, a leak that has threatened to become a gusher. *Bowen v. Massachusetts*, 487 U.S. 879 (1988), is the source of the leak. In that case, the Commonwealth of Massachusetts brought suit challenging a decision by the Secretary of Health and Human Services refusing to reimburse the state for certain Medicaid expenditures. Under the Medicaid program, the Government makes quarterly advance payments to the state in anticipation of future reimbursable costs. When the Secretary disallowed costs as not covered by the program, the result was a withholding of funds from future advances to compensate for past overpayments and to preclude future overpayments.

Massachusetts filed suit in federal district court requesting declaratory and injunctive relief setting aside the Secretary's decision. The state invoked federal question jurisdiction pursuant to 28 U.S.C. § 1331 and alleged that the APA waived the Government's immunity. The Government challenged the district court's authority to hear the case, arguing that the Claims Court had exclusive jurisdiction over the state's claim because it was one for money in excess of $10,000.

The Supreme Court agreed with the district court and the First Circuit that the APA provided a waiver of sovereign immunity for the state's claim and that the case was properly before the district court. In its opinion, the Court first analyzed whether the claim was one for "money damages," which would take it outside the purview of the APA under 5 U.S.C. § 702. Although the ultimate relief sought by the state was monetary, that did not necessarily mean it could be described as "money damages." *Bowen*, 487 U.S. at 893. The Court understood the term "money damages" to mean "*compensation* for the damage sustained by the failure of the Federal Government to pay as mandated." *Id.* at 900. In contrast, the state was seeking to "enforce the statutory mandate itself, which happens to be one for the payment of money." *Id.* Because the state sought to recover money it thought it was entitled to under the relevant statutes, the state's claim was for "specific relief" rather than "money damages." *Id.* at 900–01. The dissent found this distinction unconvincing. *Id.* at 917–21 (Scalia, J., dissenting).

The Court next addressed the Government's argument that the state's APA claim was barred under 5 U.S.C. § 704 because there was an "adequate remedy" in the Claims Court. The Court rejected the Government's position on the ground that the Claims Court had no power to grant equitable relief. *Id.* at 905. The state sought declaratory and injunctive relief requiring the Secretary to modify future Medicaid practices. Since the Medicaid program was ongoing and a judgment in the case would require future cooperation between the parties, the Court was "not willing to assume, categorically, that a naked money judgment against the United States will always be an adequate substitute for prospective relief fashioned in the light of the rather complex ongoing relationship between the parties." *Id.* The dissent disagreed with the majority on this issue as well, stating that a successful claim for money damages in the Claims Court would have precedential as well as collateral estoppel effect and therefore would be as effective in establishing the state's future rights as would a declaratory judgment in district court. *Id.* at 926–27 (Scalia, J., dissenting). In the dissent's view, "[s]ince [the majority's] reasoning cannot possibly be followed where it leads, the jurisdiction of the Claims Court has been thrown into chaos." *Id.* at 929 (Scalia, J., dissenting).

B.

As the dissent predicted, the *Bowen* case has generated much confusion regarding the jurisdiction of the courts, as well as adverse commentary.[12] In 1988, the same year *Bowen* was decided, Congress attempted to bring some order to the process. It enacted a statute providing that, when a district court order grants or denies a motion to transfer a suit against the Government to the Court of Federal Claims, an interlocutory appeal can be taken by either plaintiff or the Government. Pub.L. No. 100–702, Title V, § 501, 102 Stat. 4652 (1988) (codified at 28 U.S.C. § 1292(d)(4)). Prior to then, parties could not obtain appellate review of the jurisdictional question until the case had been tried on the merits, possibly in the wrong trial court. To ensure uniform adjudication of all Tucker Act issues in a single forum, when Congress established interlocutory review of these jurisdictional disputes it assigned the Federal Circuit exclusive jurisdiction over such appeals.

One consequence of the *Bowen* case has been to create a sort of cottage industry among lawyers attempting to craft suits, ultimately seeking money from the Government, as suits for declaratory or injunctive relief without mentioning the money. If successful, a plaintiff could have the case heard under the APA in one or another district court, with appeal to a regional circuit, rather than in the Court of Federal Claims, where money claims against the Government are routinely heard and decided, with appeal in the Federal Circuit. This court has had several opportunities to deal with such attempts, and to interpret and apply *Bowen.*

To thwart such attempted forum shopping, our cases have emphasized that in determining whether a plaintiff's suit is to be heard in district court or the Court of Federal Claims, we must look beyond the form of the pleadings to the substance of the claim. We have cautioned litigants that dressing up a claim for money as one for equitable relief will not remove the claim from Tucker Act jurisdiction and make it an APA case. *See, e.g., Christopher Vill., L.P. v. United States,* 360 F.3d 1319, 1328 (Fed.Cir.2004) ("A party may not circumvent the Claims Court's exclusive jurisdiction by framing a complaint in the district court as one seeking injunctive, declaratory or mandatory relief where the thrust of the suit is to obtain money from the United States."); *Consol. Edison Co. of N.Y., Inc. v. United States,*

---

12. For a thorough review of the *Bowen* case and its consequences, with extensive citation, see Gregory C. Sisk, *The Tapestry Unravels: Statutory Waivers of Sovereign Immunity and Money Claims Against the United States,* 71 Geo. Wash. L.Rev. 602, 707 (2003)

("The Supreme Court by overruling *Bowen v. Massachusetts,* the Federal Circuit by limiting it, or the Congress by modest legislative intervention should act to restore clarity and stability to jurisdictional lines.").

247 F.3d 1378, 1385 (Fed.Cir.2001) ("This court and its sister circuits will not tolerate a litigant's attempt to artfully recast its complaint to circumvent the jurisdiction of the Court of Federal Claims.").

Once we discern the true nature of a plaintiff's claim as a claim for money, because of *Bowen* we still must determine whether the claim is excluded from APA jurisdiction by the limitations in 5 U.S.C. §§ 702 and 704. *Bowen* and several cases following *Bowen* begin their analysis by asking first whether the claim is for other than "money damages," as that term is used in 5 U.S.C. § 702, and thus whether the suit meets this requirement for district court jurisdiction. The problem with that approach is that it turns on a linguistic distinction between 'money damages' and a claim that happens to be for money, a distinction that is at best murky, and at worst without a difference.

Our cases, and Congress's purpose in giving this court jurisdiction over these interlocutory appeals, dictate that the better course is to ask first whether the cause is one over which the Court of Federal Claims has jurisdiction under the Tucker Act. The analysis begins, then, with the question raised by 5 U.S.C. § 704—is there an "adequate remedy" in a court other than the district court, that is, can the Court of Federal Claims provide an adequate remedy under the Tucker Act for the alleged wrong?

One reason for beginning the analysis with the "adequate remedy" issue is that its resolution often will be dispositive. If the suit is at base a claim for money, and the relief available through the Court of Federal Claims under the Tucker Act—a money judgment—will provide an adequate remedy, the inquiry is at an end. There is no need to address the § 702 "money damages" limitation because § 704 precludes adjudication under the APA. A number of cases have recognized the value in this approach. *See Christopher Vill.,* 360 F.3d at 1327–29 (determining there was an adequate remedy in the Court of Federal Claims without analyzing the "money damages" limitation); *Consol. Edison,* 247 F.3d at 1382–83 (declining to address the "money damages" issue because the Court of Federal Claims would provide an adequate remedy).

Another reason it is preferable to start with the § 704 "adequate remedy" limitation rather than the "money damages" limitation found in § 702 is the way the Supreme Court has read the § 702 limitation. As earlier noted, the Supreme Court in *Bowen* interpreted the § 702 term "money damages" to mean that not all monetary relief is "money damages," an interpretation that opened the way to linguistic manipulation and the consequent opportunity for forum shopping. As the Court explained, if the plaintiff requests funds to which a statute allegedly entitles it, rather than money in compensation for sustained losses, the relief sought is something other than "money damages." *Bowen,* 487 U.S. at 900. Thus if a plaintiff seeks a money judgment but a court concludes that the relief sought is other than "money damages," the § 702 limitation is not an impediment to APA review by the district court.

However, even if the plaintiff escapes the § 702 limitation in this manner, the inquiry cannot end there because a claim seeking monetary relief, however defined, may nevertheless be within the jurisdictional scope of the Tucker Act.[13] A court must therefore undertake the second analytical step-determining whether there is an adequate remedy available under the Tucker Act in the Court of Federal Claims for the sought-after monetary relief. If the jurisdictional requirements of the Tucker Act are satisfied, i.e., the claim is for more than $10,000 and is based on a money-mandating statute, regulation, or constitutional provision, or an express or implied contract with the Government, and if the Court of Federal Claims through a money judgment can provide an adequate remedy under the Tucker Act, § 704 bars the district court from hearing the case because it belongs in another court—the Court of Federal Claims. Again, the same conclusion could have been reached without first addressing the "money damages" limitation of § 702. *See Consol. Edison,* 247 F.3d at 1382–83 (acknowledging that plaintiff might satisfy § 702 by seeking monetary relief other than "money damages," but declining to address the issue because the Court of Federal Claims would provide an adequate remedy).

In sum, when the plaintiff's claims, regardless of the form in which the complaint is drafted, are understood to be seeking a monetary reward from the Government, then, for the reasons explained, a straightforward analysis calls for determining whether the case falls within the jurisdiction of the Court of Federal Claims. If that court can provide an adequate remedy—if a money judgment will give the plaintiff essentially the remedy he seeks—then the proper forum for resolution of the dispute is not a district court under the APA but the Court of Federal Claims under the Tucker Act. There is no need at that point to even address the other APA limitations, the "money damages" and the "expressly or impliedly forbids" provisions. The three limitations function in the disjunctive; the application of any one is enough to deny a district court jurisdiction under the APA.

C.

Applying these concepts to the case before us, it is clear that the proper forum for Suburban's claim is the Court of Federal Claims. In Count I of the complaint, Suburban seeks a declaration that HUD acted unlawfully when it refused to accept assignment of the mortgage and defaulted loan. Though the claim is styled as one for declaratory relief, Suburban in essence is seeking to obtain the financial benefit of a prior contract-based obligation that allegedly has not been honored by the Government. Suburban contracted with HUD for mortgage insurance. Suburban filed a claim under the insurance policy; HUD refused to pay the claim. Suburban's ultimate goal now is to recover the insurance proceeds. We therefore agree with the Government that despite the form of the complaint, Suburban's claim is in substance a contract-based action asking for monetary relief from the Government.

---

13. "The jurisdiction of the Claims Court, however, is not expressly limited to actions for 'money damages,' ... whereas that term does define the limits of the exception to § 702." *Bowen,* 487 U.S. at 900 n. 31.

With that in mind, we must decide whether the Court of Federal Claims can provide Suburban with an "adequate remedy" within the meaning of § 704. We begin with the proposition that "[t]he availability of an action for money damages under the Tucker Act or Little Tucker Act is presumptively an 'adequate remedy' for § 704 purposes." *Telecare Corp. v. Leavitt,* 409 F.3d 1345, 1349 (Fed. Cir. 2005) (citing *Christopher Vill.,* 360 F.3d at 1327–29; *Consol. Edison,* 247 F.3d at 1382–84). The Government asserts, and Suburban does not dispute, that Suburban could have brought an action for breach of contract in the Court of Federal Claims. As the Government suggests, if Suburban were to obtain a judgment for breach of contract, the Court of Federal Claims could order payment of the insurance proceeds as a form of expectation damages, giving Suburban the benefits it expected to receive had the Government not breached the insurance contract. An adequate remedy is therefore presumptively available in the Court of Federal Claims.

Suburban relies on *Bowen* to support its contention that a money judgment from the Court of Federal Claims will not be adequate. But, as we have noted elsewhere, *Bowen* turned on the "complexity of the continuous relationship between the federal and state governments administering the Medicaid program," *Consol. Edison,* 247 F.3d at 1383, and the Court "linked its judgment to a specific set of circumstances" that are not present in most cases, *Id.* at 1384. These circumstances include: *Bowen* was a dispute between two sovereigns—a state government and the federal government-implicating federalism issues; the dispute centered on the administration of a major federal grant, the Medicaid program, involving enormous sums of money and complex interactions between the governments and the beneficiaries; at issue were the institutional arrangements between these two governments; the governments were locked into a fabric of long-term administration of the program; and the money involved in the uncovered education services was a small fraction of the total reimbursement the state received each year for its Medicaid costs under the program. In addition, the Court's focus was on the statutory requirements set forth in this complex grant program—nowhere in *Bowen* did the Court make reference to the existence of any specific contract or express agreement defining the relationship between the parties.

Furthermore, unlike *Bowen,* this case does not involve a complex, ongoing relationship between plaintiff and the Government in which the plaintiff seeks declaratory or injunctive relief to modify the Government's *future* obligations under the program. Suburban does not seek to change any long-term future conduct by the Government. Even if we were to discount the point made by the dissent in *Bowen,* that a money judgment against the Government can impact on its future behavior through doctrines such as collateral estoppel, a judgment ordering prospective relief would not be necessary or appropriate.

The thrust of Suburban's claim is that HUD breached the insurance contract when it refused to accept assignment of the mortgage and pay Suburban the insurance proceeds. Accordingly, "[e]very legal issue that

[Suburban] seeks to resolve in the district court could be ... decided in a suit before the Court of Federal Claims." *Consol. Edison,* 247 F.3d at 1385. Nor are Suburban's concerns about possible bankruptcy, loss of reputation, and lost future profits a basis for saying that there is not an adequate remedy in the Court of Federal Claims. Those concerns can be alleged by any claimant seeking money from the Government for an allegedly wrongful failure to pay a claim; to the extent they have merit in a given case, money usually can assuage the wrong.

We have considered the other arguments raised by Suburban, including its argument that it has been denied due process and that that alone entitles it to APA review in the district court. We agree with the Government that a claim that a government agency has violated a party's right to due process by refusing performance under a contract is substantively indistinguishable from a breach of contract claim. The process to which plaintiff is due on these facts is a post-deprivation suit for breach of the contract. We find these further arguments without merit. Because an adequate remedy is available under the Tucker Act in the Court of Federal Claims, this case cannot proceed in the district court under the APA.

D.

The district court in making its determination in this case sought guidance from and relied heavily on decisions from its regional circuit. The Government seemed to shape its case for dismissal on the same basis, arguing that because Suburban's claim arose out of a contract, there was no APA jurisdiction. The source for that argument is a line of cases in other courts of appeals, including the Court of Appeals for the District of Columbia, holding that claims based on contracts can only be brought in the Court of Federal Claims. The basis for this rule is the third limitation on the APA's waiver of sovereign immunity—waiver is not available "if any other statute that grants consent to suit expressly or impliedly forbids the relief which is sought." 5 U.S.C. § 702. Since the Tucker Act grants consent for suits based on contract, this has been interpreted by these other courts to preclude under the APA contract claims of any kind, either for damages or specific performance. This court has acknowledged the issue but not squarely addressed it. Since we conclude the case is better decided under the limitation in § 704 of the APA, we need not address the argument further.[15]

Finally, the regional circuits are of course free to provide such guidance as they choose to the district courts in their circuits, and when the question of jurisdiction comes up outside of these interlocutory appeals, the district courts properly may look to the law of their circuit for guidance. But guidance from and reliance upon regional circuit law must take into account two considerations. First, since 1988 and the *Bowen* decision, there has been considerable development regarding this jurisdictional issue. The

---

15. For a full discussion of the issue, see Richard H. Seamon, *Separation of Powers and the Separate Treatment of Contract* *Claims Against the Federal Government for Specific Performance,* 43 Vill. L.Rev. 155 (1998).

regional circuit court cases may be older cases, and indeed, as was the case here, some may have been decided before *Bowen*.

Second, and of equal if not greater importance, for almost twenty years this court has been tasked by Congress to be the exclusive arbiter of the issue when it is brought to us in these interlocutory appeals. We of course are bound to follow our own circuit law. District courts, as well as counsel for the parties, would be better able to predict the outcome of such appeals if they follow the same law.

CONCLUSION

The judgment of the district court is reversed. The matter is remanded with instructions to either dismiss Count I of the complaint or transfer it to the Court of Federal Claims.

REVERSED and REMANDED.

––––––––

Notes and Questions

1. As we return to the intersection between the Administrative Procedure Act and the Tucker Act in *Suburban Mortgage Associates, Inc. v. United States Department of Housing and Urban Development*, remind yourself of the special role of the United States Court of Appeals for the Federal Circuit when it comes to the Tucker Act and defining its jurisdiction and scope (see Chapter IV.A.1.b). Review the nature (exclusive) and scope (nationwide) of the Federal Circuit's appellate jurisdiction over Tucker Act appeals. 28 U.S.C. § 1295(a)(2), (3). Remember also that the Federal Circuit is granted authority to hear interlocutory appeals (that is, appeals before final judgment) of district court order granting or denying motions to transfer a case to the Court of Federal Claims. 28 U.S.C. § 1292(d)(4). Now you should better appreciate how the Federal Circuit is in a unique position to stabilize Tucker Act jurisdiction doctrine nationally and to clarify the scope of *Bowen v. Massachusetts*. And, as the case you've just read demonstrates, the Federal Circuit appears to have done just that.

2. In *Suburban Mortgage Associates*, identify the cause of action(s) or claim(s) made by the plaintiff, as well as the true gravamen of the plaintiff's complaint. Given that the dispute revolves around a contract and its terms, isn't this precisely the kind of dispute that ordinarily would be heard in the Court of Federal Claims? Wouldn't allowing district court jurisdiction over what is essentially a breach of contract claim truly invade the exclusive authority of the Court of Federal Claims over one of its primary subjects for adjudication?

Note also the remedy that the plaintiff sought in the district court under the APA: specific performance of the contract with the federal government. But as has been mentioned twice earlier in this chapter (see Chapter IV.A.1.c and IV.A.4), one of the most enduring limitations on government liability has been the rule barring specific performance in contract actions against the federal government and thereby generally limiting contract claimants to a damage remedy. *See generally* Richard H. Seamon, *Separation of Powers and the Separate Treatment of Contract Claims Against the Federal Government for Specific Performance,* 43 Vill. L. Rev. 155 (1998). In the dissent in *Bowen v. Massachusetts* which was set out earlier, Justice Scalia argued that it is "settled that sovereign immunity bars a suit against the United States for specific performance of a contract, and that this bar was not disturbed by the 1976 amendment to § 702." Although scholarly commentators have identified one court of appeals decision that appears to depart from this basic understanding, *Hamilton Stores, Inc. v. Hodel,* 925 F.2d 1272, 1276–79 (10th Cir. 1991) (citing *Bowen v. Massachusetts*), most federal courts continue to adhere firmly to the traditional understanding that the Tucker Act impliedly forbids specific performance in contract actions against the federal government whether brought in the Court of Federal Claims or in the district court. *See, e.g., Presidential Gardens Assocs. v. United States,* 175 F.3d 132, 143 (2d Cir. 1999); *North Star Alaska v. United States,* 14 F.3d 36, 38 (9th Cir. 1994); *Transohio Sav. Bank v. Director, Office of Thrift Supervision,* 967 F.2d 598, 613 (D.C. Cir. 1992); *Coggeshall Dev. Corp. v. Diamond,* 884 F.2d 1, 3 (1st Cir. 1989). For scholarly analyses that, notwithstanding *Bowen v. Massachusetts* and the waiver of sovereign immunity in the APA, the Tucker Act still does impliedly forbid specific performance on a contract claim against the government, see Gregory C. Sisk, *The Tapestry Unravels: Statutory Waivers of Sovereign Immunity and Money Claims Against the United States,* 71 Geo. Wash. L. Rev. 601, 627–36 (2003); Seamon, *supra,* at 191–97. In *Suburban Mortgage Associates,* given the Federal Circuit's ruling on the adequacy of a remedy in the Court of Federal Claims as precluding district court jurisdiction under Section 704 of the APA, the Federal Circuit found it unnecessary to decide whether the Tucker Act impliedly forbids contract claims, whether for specific performance or otherwise, in other courts. Nonetheless, the very fact that the plaintiff attempted to pursue such a non-traditional remedy in district court illustrates how the APA, if construed broadly in scope with a very generous reading of *Bowen v. Massachusetts,* could become the basis for an end-run around the Tucker Act, the Court of Federal Claims, and the limitations on relief attendant to such claims in that court.

3. In *Bowen v. Massachusetts,* the Supreme Court addressed both whether the monetary relief sought there constituted "money damages" within the exception to the APA in Section 702 and whether resort to the APA was precluded under Section 704 because another "adequate remedy in court" was available under the Tucker Act. How does the Federal Circuit in *Suburban Mortgage Associates* approach these questions in the context of the claim in this case? Which limitation on the APA does the Federal Circuit find dispositive in this case? And why does the Federal Circuit suggest that addressing this limitation ordinarily will be sufficient—and ordinarily will be preferable—for resolving these kinds of cases without considering the other limitation?

In the course of determining that a monetary remedy under the Tucker Act in the Court of Federal Claims will be adequate, and thus precludes the plaintiff's request for other forms of relief under the APA in the district court, the Federal Circuit must distinguish the Supreme Court's opposite conclusion in the context of the grant-in-aid dispute in *Bowen v. Massachusetts*. In effect, the Federal Circuit has narrowly confined *Bowen v. Massachusetts* to its specific context. What is that context? How is *Bowen v. Massachusetts* distinguished? Does the Federal Circuit respectfully account for *Bowen v. Massachusetts* or is this an evasion of the Supreme Court's precedent? And what are the practical reasons why the Federal Circuit concludes that the kind of claim raised in *Suburban Mortgage* should be reserved to the Tucker Act and the Court of Federal Claims? How has the Federal Circuit attempted through this case and others to establish jurisdictional clarify and stability in assigning of claims between the district court and the Court of Federal Claims? Will its efforts to set a national standard succeed (and what advice does the Federal Circuit offer to the lower federal courts, including the district courts around the country, toward that end)?

4.   The Federal Circuit's decision in *Suburban Mortgage* is (as of the date of this casebook) the latest in a series of decisions attempting to apply *Bowen v. Massachusetts* in a sensible manner consistent with traditional understandings of money claims and statutory waivers of sovereign immunity. Indeed, the Federal Circuit in *Suburban Mortgage* cited to two of its earlier decisions that set the stage, each of which deserves some further explanation here:

First, in *Consolidated Edison Company v. United States Department of Energy*, 247 F.3d 1378 (Fed.Cir. 2001), nuclear utilities brought suit in district court against the federal government, challenging the constitutionality of provisions of the Energy Policy Act that assessed payments from utilities for the government's costs in decontaminating and decommissioning uranium processing facilities. *Id.* at 1380–81. Instead of directly seeking refunds of prior assessments, the utilities sought a declaratory judgment that the statute was unconstitutional and an injunction against enforcement of the assessments. The government moved to transfer the case to the Court of Federal Claims, asserting that (assuming success on the merits) adequate relief in the form of a refund would be available through the Tucker Act. After the district court denied transfer and asserted authority under the APA, with citation to *Bowen v. Massachusetts,* the government took an interlocutory appeal to the Federal Circuit. *Id.* at 1382.

A divided three-judge panel of the Federal Circuit initially affirmed the district court's denial of the motion to transfer. *Consolidated Edison Co. v. United States Dept. of Energy*, 234 F.3d 642 (Fed.Cir. 2000). In an unusual step, the Federal Circuit, acting en banc, vacated the first panel decision in the *Consolidated Edison* case and then reassigned the opinion to the panel for revision, which produced a reversal of the outcome. In the new opinion, the court held that, although the nuclear utilities may have avoided the "money damages" exclusion in Section 702 of the APA by seeking only prospective relief, the district court nonetheless was ousted from jurisdiction under Section 704 of the APA because the Court of Federal Claims was empowered to provide an effective remedy. *Id.* at 1382–85. If the utilities were successful in a suit for refund of previously paid assessments under the Tucker Act in the Court of Federal Claims, that judgment would operate by principles of res judicata to preclude the government from continuing unlawful assessments in the future. *Id.* at 1384–85. Thus, because "[r]elief from its retrospective obligations will also relieve it from the same obligations prospectively," the Court of Federal Claims through a money judgment "can supply an adequate remedy even without an explicit grant of prospective relief." *Id.* For that reason, the court now rejected the utilities "blatant forum shopping to avoid adequate remedies in an alternative forum." *Id.* at 1385.

As for the precedential effect of *Bowen v. Massachusetts,* the Federal Circuit in *Consolidated Edison* noted that the Supreme Court there had "emphasized the complexity of the continuous relationship between the federal and state governments administering the Medicaid program." *Id.* at 1383. Unlike *Bowen v. Massachusetts,* the suit by the nuclear utilities challenging the assessments did not involve a state party and did "not involve the complexities of government-to-government relationships." *Id.* at 1384. In sum, the Federal Circuit reasoned, the Supreme Court's decision in *Bowen v. Massachusetts* was linked to "a specific set of circumstances" that defines the scope of its reach. *Id.*

Judge Plager of the Federal Circuit (who later authored the *Suburban Mortgage* decision included in this casebook) offered a concurring remark to the *Consolidated Edison* opinion:

> This case confronts the court with a choice between a seemingly illogical Supreme Court rule, calling for a less-than-sensible result, on the one hand, or underrruling the Supreme Court decision, here *Bowen v. Massachusetts,* on the other. This time the court has chosen the latter course. I cannot disagree; it remains to be seen whether the Supreme Court will.

Id. at 1386 (Plager, J., concurring) (citation omitted). The Supreme Court subsequently denied a petition for certiorari filed by nuclear utilities, thus acquiescing at least for the moment in the Federal Circuit's restrictive reading of the *Bowen v. Massachusetts* precedent. 534 U.S. 1054 (2001).

Second, in *Christopher Village, L.P. v. United States,* 360 F.3d 1319 (Fed.Cir. 2004), the Federal Circuit confirmed its *Consolidated Edison* precedent and gave it further emphasis by declaring as void a ruling by another circuit in the same case as having been issued without proper jurisdiction. Owners of federally-subsidized low-income housing challenged the government's foreclosure as a breach of contracts with the Department of Housing and Urban Development. The plaintiffs initially filed suit in federal district court under the APA seeking a declaratory judgment that the government was liable for breach of contract (as well as asking the court to enjoin foreclosure, although the injunctive relief request became moot after the foreclosure occurred and the property was razed). Although the district court ruled in favor of the government, the United States Court of Appeals for the Fifth Circuit held that the district court on remand should issue the declaratory judgment (although no formal judgment apparently was ever issued). The plaintiffs then filed suit for damages in the Court of Federal Claims, arguing that the Fifth Circuit's ruling barred the government from relitigating the issue of breach of contract under res judicata. *Id.* at 1323–24. After the Court of Federal Claims granted summary judgment to the government, the Federal Circuit ruled based upon *Consolidated Edison* that "a litigant's ability to sue the government for money damages in the Court of Federal Claims is an 'adequate remedy' that precludes an APA waiver of sovereign immunity in other courts." *Id.* at 1327.

In *Christopher Village*, the Federal Circuit reiterated its understanding that the Supreme Court majority's reasoning in *Bowen v. Massachusetts* was tied to the specific circumstances in that case of an ongoing matter with potential for prospective relief and involving state governmental activities. *Id.* at 1328 n.2. By contrast, the Federal Circuit ruled, a district court does not have jurisdiction "to issue a declaratory judgment as to the government's liability for breach of contract solely in order to create a 'predicate' for suit to recover damages in the Court of Federal Claims." *Id.* at 1321. Because the district court's exercise of jurisdiction in the related case (and thus that of the United States Court of Appeals for the Fifth Circuit on appeal from that district court) infringed upon the authority of another tribunal, the Federal Circuit ruled in *Christopher Village* that neither it nor the Court of Federal Claims were bound to follow the earlier judgment in any respect. *Id.* at 1329–33. Accordingly, in *Christopher Village*, the Federal Circuit affirmed its "[r]espect for the exclusive authority of the Court of Federal Claims" over monetary claims, even to the extent of refusing to recognize a judgment of a sister circuit that had been issued without proper jurisdiction (and even though the jurisdictional obstacle had not been raised directly in the earlier phase of the litigation). *Id.* at 1333.

For more on the Federal Circuit's response to *Bowen v. Massachusetts*, see Gregory C. Sisk, *Litigation With the Federal Government* § 4.13(4), at 346–51 (ALI–ABA, 4th ed., 2006).

CHAPTER V

SUITS AGAINST FEDERAL OFFICERS

Although our primary focus in this course is upon litigation against the federal government itself, the question of whether and when a federal officer individually is amenable to suit in his or her official capacity often has been intertwined with the subject of the liability of the government as a collective entity. Indeed, as we saw in Chapter II, the concept of sovereign immunity in the United States evolved in tandem with rules governing suits against government officers. The controversy continues today, as courts, legislators, and scholars continue to debate whether official wrongdoing, including infringement of constitutional rights, is best addressed and compensated by imposing personal liability upon individual officers or by holding the government directly responsible for the acts of its agents.

In Chapter V, we look in greater detail and with sharper focus at suits that name a federal government official or employee as defendant, rather than an agency or the United States. We begin in Chapter V.A with suits that do not seek monetary relief from the government officer, but rather seek to compel the officer to do or not to do something that is legally required or prohibited, that is, suits for specific or equitable-type relief. In Chapter V.B, we examine suits for money damages against government officers, both those grounded in the common law and those alleging constitutional violations. Throughout the chapter, but particularly in the last section, we consider the question of whether it is more appropriate to hold government officers individually liable for their wrongful acts or, instead, whether the government itself should pay compensation for official wrongs committed against its citizens, in terms of assessment of fault, full compensation to victims, fairness to government employees, moral responsibility, and deterrence of future wrongdoing.

SECTION A. SUITS FOR SPECIFIC OR EQUITABLE RELIEF

1. NON-STATUTORY SUITS AGAINST OFFICERS

In Chapter II of this casebook, as part of a survey on the evolution of federal sovereign immunity, we examined *non-statutory suits* against government officers acting in their official capacities, that is, claims made against government officers based upon common-law causes of action rather than any statutory authorization for such litigation.

In Chapter II.A, we studied the Supreme Court's 1882 decision in *United States v. Lee*, 106 U.S. 196 (1882), in which a landowner sought to eject a government officer who held the property for the United States. In that decision, the Court resorted to a legal fiction to allow relief to a citizen harmed by governmental action, without congressional authority and notwithstanding sovereign immunity. The Court apparently was willing to pretend that a suit for affirmative relief against a government agent was not the equivalent of an action against the government itself, regardless of the effect on governmental operations, and thus was not barred by sovereign immunity. However, in 1949, the Supreme Court abandoned that fiction in *Larson v. Domestic & Foreign Commerce Corp.*, 337 U.S. 682 (1949). In *Larson*, a plaintiff similarly sought non-monetary relief, on that occasion in the form of a common-law claim for specific performance of a contract with a government agency, framed as a suit against the agency head. When the relief sought in a lawsuit is directed against the federal government (that is, implicates governmental rights or duties or directly will affect government operations), the Court held that such an action must be recognized as one against the government itself, even if nominally framed as against an individual officer. And unless the government officer was acting beyond the general scope of statutory duties or in violation of constitutional standards, the constraints of sovereign immunity are fully applicable. The Court confirmed this modern approach to sovereign immunity and direct officer suits in *Malone v. Bowdoin*, 369 U.S. 643 (1962).

Congress by legislation largely has superseded the *ultra vires* basis for non-statutory officer suits by providing remedies directly against the government itself, as discussed previously in Chapters III and IV of this casebook. Actions against federal government officers, in their official capacity, to compel compliance with statutory and regulatory obligations also have received legislative approval, through an action under the Administrative Procedure Act, 5 U.S.C. §§ 701–06, or for a writ of mandamus, 28 U.S.C. § 1361. Accordingly, non-statutory or common-law suits against government officers for non-monetary or equitable-type relief largely have been superseded by legislative developments.

————

2.   THE ADMINISTRATIVE PROCEDURE ACT

As we studied in Chapter IV.B of this casebook, the Administrative Procedure Act (APA), 5 U.S.C. §§ 701–06, authorizes claims for specific relief against the federal government. In 1976, Congress amended the APA to expressly waive the sovereign immunity of the government, thereby allowing suits "stating a claim that an agency or an officer or employee thereof acted or failed to act in an official capacity or under color of legal authority" to proceed, whether framed as a suit against the officer or the federal government itself. Pub. L. No. 94–574, 90 Stat. 2721 (1976) (codified in 5 U.S.C. § 702); *see also* 5 U.S.C. § 703 (permitting action for judicial review to be "brought against the United States, the agency by its official title, or the appropriate officer"). When a plaintiff seeks specific relief against the federal government, this expansion of the waiver of sovereign immunity in the APA means that the availability of this relief no longer turns upon whether the suit is viewed as one brought against the officer or instead directly against the United States.

Accordingly, as was illustrated through the decision of *Citizens to Preserve Overton Park, Inc. v. Volpe*, 401 U.S. 402 (1971), actions for judicial review of agency action, seeking such specific or equitable-type relief as an injunction to prevent or compel action by government officers, may be pursued under the APA. (However, as addressed previously in Chapter IV.C, the APA does not authorize claims for "money damages," 5 U.S.C. § 702, and is not available when an alternative adequate remedy is available in a court, *id.* § 704.)

---

3.   MANDAMUS

28 United States Code § 1361

The district courts shall have original jurisdiction of any action in the nature of mandamus to compel an officer or employee of the United States or any agency thereof to perform a duty owed to the plaintiff.

Fallini v. Hodel

United States Court of Appeals for the Ninth Circuit.
783 F.2d 1343 (9th Cir. 1986).

■ SKOPIL, CIRCUIT JUDGE:

The Secretary of the Interior and officials of the Bureau of Land Management appeal from the district court's grant of mandamus and a mandatory injunction compelling them to prevent wild, free-roaming horses from straying off public lands onto private lands. Appellees ("Fallini") were granted their requested relief under section 4 of the Wild Free–Roaming Horses and Burros Act ("Act"), 16 U.S.C. §§ 1331–40. The requested relief was not available under section 4 of the Act. We reverse and remand.

FACTS AND PROCEEDINGS BELOW

Appellees are private landowners who maintain a ranching operation in Nye County, Nevada. Appellants ("the BLM") are responsible for administering the public lands in Nevada. Fallini owns approximately 1,800 acres of private land in the Reveille Allotment of the Tonopah Resource Area. The allotment contains an additional 657,520 acres of public land. Fallini owns water rights to all known waters within the allotment.

Since Congress passed the Act in 1971, the population of wild horses in the Tonopah Resource Area has steadily increased. Although the Act contemplates that wild horses and burros will be managed on public lands, the animals often stray onto private lands. Because of the growth of the herd and the availability of water on Fallini's land, many wild horses stray onto his land. The horses trample fences, destroy watering tanks and troughs, consume large quantities of water and range forage, and pose a threat to the safety of ranch hands.

On several occasions Fallini requested the BLM to remove wild horses from his property. The BLM failed to respond to the requests. Pursuant to section 4 of the Act, Fallini sought mandamus to compel the BLM to remove wild horses from his land. Fallini also requested the BLM to take "all steps necessary" to prevent wild horses from straying onto his land in the future.

The district court granted Fallini's motion for summary judgment and issued a writ of mandamus compelling the BLM to remove the stray wild horses from Fallini's land. The BLM does not appeal this ruling. The district court also issued a writ of mandamus and continuing mandatory injunction compelling the BLM to take all necessary steps to prevent a recurrence of the straying of wild horses onto Fallini's land. The BLM appeals this ruling.

DISCUSSION

A. The Remedy Granted by the District Court.

The district court granted Fallini's request for mandamus to compel the BLM to "take all steps necessary to prevent" wild horses from entering his land in the future and, "continually enjoined and restrained [the BLM] from suffering or permitting the presence of wild free-roaming horses and burros to hereafter be upon [Fallini's] lands...." *Fallini v. Watt*, No. LV 81–536 RDF, Writ of Mandamus and Preliminary Injunction (D.Nev. Oct. 3, 1984). The injunction is mandatory in nature. It places an affirmative duty upon the BLM to keep wild horses off Fallini's land. In effect, the injunction is no different than the mandamus. When the effect of a mandatory injunction is equivalent to the issuance of mandamus it is governed by similar considerations.

The federal mandamus statute provides: "The district courts shall have original jurisdiction of any action in the nature of mandamus to compel an officer or employee of the United States or any agency thereof to perform a duty owed to the plaintiff." 28 U.S.C. § 1361 (1982). Mandamus relief is only available to compel an officer of the United States to perform a duty if (1) the plaintiff's claim is clear and certain; (2) the duty of the officer "is ministerial and so plainly prescribed as to be free from doubt," *Tagupa v. East–West Center, Inc.*, 642 F.2d 1127, 1129 (9th Cir.1981); and (3) no other adequate remedy is available.

B. Standard of Review.

The extraordinary remedy of mandamus traditionally lies within the trial court's discretion. A trial court abuses its discretion when its decision is based on clearly erroneous factual findings or an incorrect legal standard.

Whether each element of the three-part mandamus test is satisfied is a question of law. We review *de novo*. Fallini's claim fails the second and third prongs of the mandamus test. The district court therefore erred in granting mandamus and a mandatory injunction.

1.   No Plainly Prescribed Duty

Section 4 of the Act provides, in pertinent part:

> If wild free-roaming horses or burros stray from public lands onto privately owned land, *the owners of such land may inform the nearest Federal marshal or agent of the Secretary, who shall arrange to have the animals removed.* In no event shall such wild free-roaming horses and burros be destroyed except by agents of the Secretary. . . .

16 U.S.C.A. § 1334 (emphasis added).

Section 4 is the only provision of the Act that pertains to wild horses straying onto private lands. Under section 4 a landowner may, *inter alia*, notify the BLM when wild horses stray onto his or her land. Upon notification, the BLM has a plainly prescribed, ministerial duty to remove the horses. Section 4 does not require the BLM to prevent straying in the first instance.

Whether the Act impliedly imposes a ministerial duty to prevent wild horses from straying onto private land is a question of first impression. To determine if such a duty exists, we must analyze the language of the entire Act. "[T]he fact that a statute requires construction by ... the court in order to determine what duties it creates does not mean that mandamus is not proper to compel the officer to perform the duty, once it is determined." *Knuckles v. Weinberger,* 511 F.2d 1221, 1222 (9th Cir.1975). However, where the statute prescribes an exclusive remedy, we should be cautious in extending it.

The BLM argues that upon notification it need only remove stray wild horses and burros from private land. It insists its duty is limited to viewing the complainant's land, surveying it for wild horses, and removing the horses. It contends that the district court, in requiring the prevention of wild horses from straying onto private lands, is imposing a duty not contemplated by Congress under section 4 of the Act.

Because of the general duty imposed upon the BLM to manage wild horses and burros on public lands, Fallini contends that requesting removal is not the only remedy. Implied in the general duty is the ministerial duty to keep wild horses off private lands. Because section 4 specifically deals with strays, Fallini insists it is proper to invoke this implied duty.

We accept the BLM's interpretation of its statutory duty. The Act does not charge the BLM with the duty to "prevent" wild horses from straying. We are unable to imply such a duty. Although the BLM is charged with broad duties in managing the animals on public lands, *see* 16 U.S.C. §§ 1331, 1333, the Act fails to charge the BLM with a duty to prevent straying that is "so plainly prescribed as to be free from doubt." *See Tagupa,* 642 F.2d at 1129.

Section 4 of the Act clearly contemplates the possibility that wild horses may stray onto private lands. The legislative history of the Act indicates that Congress was aware of this possibility. Congress declined to authorize the BLM to fence the wild horses or to use intensive management techniques. The Senate Report discussing the Act states: "The Committee wishes to emphasize that the management of the wild free-roaming horses and burros be kept to a minimum ... to deter the possibility of 'zoolike' developments." S.Rep. No. 92–242, 97th Cong., 1st Sess., *reprinted in* 1971 U.S.Code Cong. & Ad.News 2149, 2151–52. * * *

Even assuming the BLM has a general duty under section 4 to manage wild horses solely on public lands, we cannot imply a duty to prevent straying of wild horses onto private lands. We fail to find any suggestion by Congress or otherwise that the BLM had a duty, ministerial or prescribed, to prevent straying of wild horses onto private land.

2. The Remedy Under the Act is Adequate

The district court found that mandamus and mandatory injunction were the only remedies available to adequately protect Fallini from harm caused by straying wild horses. The district court relied on uncontroverted evidence that the BLM delayed for three and five months in responding to two prior requests to have wild horses removed from Fallini's land. We reverse the grant of these remedies because the remedy prescribed by section 4 of the Act provides adequate relief.

The BLM has a plainly prescribed, ministerial duty to remove wild horses and burros from private land upon notification. The duty is nondiscretionary. It was imposed by Congress to benefit the public by keeping the animals on public lands. Private landowners are benefited by having wild horses removed from their land without cost.

A meaningful removal remedy under section 4 requires the BLM to remove the horses within a reasonable time. Although Congress did not provide a time limit within which the animals must be removed, an unreasonable delay would violate the spirit and purpose of the Act.

A reasonable time for removal of the animals must be determined by the particular facts and circumstances of each case. Because of the variety of facts and circumstances, it would be imprudent for this court to establish a universal standard. In some cases twenty-four hours may be unreasonable and in other cases a period of several weeks may be entirely reasonable. The reasonable time for removal must be determined by the trier of fact on the particular circumstance of each landowner's request.

CONCLUSION

We remand to allow the district court to modify its mandatory injunction to require removal of wild horses from the Fallini property within reasonable time of notice that the wild horses have strayed onto their property. The district court should make a determination of what shall constitute a reasonable time for such removal.

Notes and Questions

In this chapter, we turn from a focus upon suits maintained directly against the sovereign United States, or one of its agencies or entities, to suits naming a federal government official or employee as defendant. We begin with suits that do not seek monetary relief from the government officer, but rather seek to compel the officer to do or not to do something, that is, equitable or specific relief. In the next section of this chapter, Chapter V.B, we examine suits for money damages against government officers, both those grounded in the common law and those alleging constitutional violations.

With respect to specific, equitable, or non-monetary relief against government officials or employees, we have examined two of the three primary causes of action previously. First, in Chapter II.A, as part of the survey of the evolution of sovereign immunity, we studied *non-statutory suits* against government officers acting in their official capacities. Second, even when a suit against a government officer seeks specific or affirmative relief from the government, Congress may of course waive sovereign immunity and consent to suit. As we studied in Chapter IV.B, Congress has generally waived the sovereign immunity of the government to authorize suits against government officers for specific relief under the Administrative Procedure Act, 5 U.S.C. § 701–06.

The third basic avenue for non-monetary relief against a government officer is the remedy of mandamus. *Mandamus* has a long history as a writ specifically designed to control legal action by government officers. Indeed, the seminal decision of *Marbury v. Madison,* 5 U.S. (1 Cranch.) 137 (1803)—with which the constitutional law course in law school traditionally begins—was framed as a suit by a judicial appointee for a writ of mandamus to the secretary of state to deliver his commission of office. In that famous case, the Court established its power of judicial review by holding constitutionally invalid a federal statute that authorized the Supreme Court to issue a writ of mandamus as a matter of original, rather than appellate, jurisdiction. Mandamus relief in the district courts is now expressly contemplated by statute. 28 U.S.C. § 1361.

Although little used today, given the breadth of matters subject to judicial review under the APA, *mandamus* survives as a class of cases in which mandatory relief may be sought against a government officer. The *Fallini v. Hodel* decision above well illustrates the nature and limitations of mandamus relief. What does it mean to say that mandamus may be used only to compel a government officer to perform a "ministerial" duty? How does the court analyze the question? How strict is the standard for granting mandamus relief? Why does the court reverse the remedy granted by the district court? Is any mandamus relief available in this case? State the mandamus relief that might still be granted consistent with the court's opinion.

SECTION B.   SUITS FOR DAMAGES

Suits against federal officers for specific or equitable-type relief may differ from a suit against the federal government itself in form only. But when monetary relief is sought, if the suit against a federal employee is permitted to proceed, the employee may be left to pay any judgment for damages out of his or her own pocket (although indemnification by the government is not uncommon). Because holding individual federal officers or employees personally liable might discourage them from diligently performing their jobs, the courts and more recently the Congress have granted a level of immunity from suit to federal officers and employees.

Thus, the story of suits for damages against federal officers involves two elements: First, we must determine whether there is a substantive basis for imposing liability, based either upon the common law or a constitutional standard. Second, even if substantive liability otherwise would lie, we must inquire whether the officer has been granted immunity, absolute or qualified, to protect governmental interests.

1.   COMMON-LAW CLAIMS

a.   IMMUNITY CREATED BY COURT DECISION

Barr v. Matteo

Supreme Court of the United States.
360 U.S. 564 (1959)

■ MR. JUSTICE HARLAN announced the judgment of the Court, and delivered an opinion, in which MR. JUSTICE FRANKFURTER, MR. JUSTICE CLARK, and MR. JUSTICE WHITTAKER join.

We are called upon in this case to weigh in a particular context two considerations of high importance which now and again come into sharp conflict—on the one hand, the protection of the individual citizen against pecuniary damage caused by oppressive or malicious action on the part of officials of the Federal Government; and on the other, the protection of the public interest by shielding responsible governmental officers against the harassment and inevitable hazards of vindictive or ill-founded damage suits brought on account of action taken in the exercise of their official responsibilities.

This is a libel suit, brought in the District Court of the District of Columbia by respondents, former employees of the Office of Rent Stabilization. The alleged libel was contained in a press release issued by the office on February 5, 1953, at the direction of petitioner, then its Acting Director. The circumstances which gave rise to the issuance of the release follow.

In 1950 the statutory existence of the Office of Housing Expediter, the predecessor agency of the Office of Rent Stabilization, was about to expire. Respondent Madigan, then Deputy Director in charge of personnel and fiscal matters, and respondent Matteo, chief of the personnel branch, suggested to the Housing Expediter a plan designed to utilize some $2,600,000 of agency funds earmarked in the agency's appropriation for the fiscal year 1950 exclusively for terminal-leave payments. The effect of the plan would have been to obviate the possibility that the agency might have to make large terminal-leave payments during the next fiscal year out of general agency funds, should the life of the agency be extended by Congress. In essence, the mechanics of the plan were that agency employees would be discharged, paid accrued annual leave out of the $2,600,000 earmarked for terminal-leave payments, rehired immediately as temporary employees, and restored to permanent status should the agency's life in fact be extended.

Petitioner, at the time General Manager of the agency, opposed respondents' plan on the ground that it violated the spirit of the Thomas Amendment, 64 Stat. 768, and expressed his opposition to the Housing Expediter. The Expediter decided against general adoption of the plan, but at respondent Matteo's request gave permission for its use in connection with approximately fifty employees, including both respondents, on a voluntary basis. Thereafter the life of the agency was in face extended.

Some two and a half years later, on January 28, 1953, the Office of Rent Stabilization received a letter from Senator John J. Williams of Delaware, inquiring about the terminal-leave payments made under the plan in 1950. Respondent Madigan drafted a reply to the letter, which he did not attempt to bring to the attention of petitioner, and then prepared a reply which he sent to petitioner's office for his signature as Acting Director of the agency. Petitioner was out of the office, and a secretary signed the submitted letter, which was then delivered by Madigan to Senator Williams on the morning of February 3, 1953.

On February 4, 1953, Senator Williams delivered a speech on the floor of the Senate strongly criticizing the plan, stating that "to say the least it is an unjustifiable raid on the Federal Treasury, and heads of every agency in the Government who have condoned this practice should be called to task." The letter above referred to was ordered printed in the Congressional Record. Other Senators joined in the attack on the plan. Their comments were widely reported in the press on February 5, 1953, and petitioner, in his capacity as Acting Director of the agency, received a large number of inquiries from newspapers and other news media as to the agency's position on the matter.

On that day petitioner served upon respondents letters expressing his intention to suspend them from duty, and at the same time ordered issuance by the office of the press release which is the subject of this litigation, and the text of which appears in the margin.[5]

---

5. "William G. Barr, Acting Director of Rent Stabilization today served notice of sus-   pension on the two officials of the agency who in June 1950 were responsible for the

Respondents sued, charging that the press release, in itself and as coupled with the contemporaneous news reports of senatorial reaction to the plan, defamed them to their injury, and alleging that its publication and terms had been actuated by malice on the part of petitioner. Petitioner defended, *inter alia*, on the ground that the issuance of the press release was protected by either a qualified or an absolute privilege. The trial court overruled these contentions, and instructed the jury to return a verdict for respondents if it found the release defamatory. The jury found for respondents.

Petitioner appealed, raising only the issue of absolute privilege. The judgment of the trial court was affirmed by the Court of Appeals, which held that "in explaining his decision [to suspend respondents] to the general public [petitioner] ... went entirely outside his line of duty" and that thus the absolute privilege, assumed otherwise to be available, did not attach. 100 U.S.App.D.C. 319, 244 F.2d 767, 768. We granted certiorari, vacated the Court of Appeals' judgment, and remanded the case "with directions to pass upon petitioner's claim of a qualified privilege." 355 U.S. 171, 173. On remand the Court of Appeals held that the press release was protected by a qualified privilege, but that there was evidence from which a jury could reasonably conclude that petitioner had acted maliciously, or had spoken with lack of reasonable grounds for believing that his statement was true, and that either conclusion would defeat the qualified privilege. Accordingly it remanded the case to the District Court for retrial. 103 U.S.App.D.C. 176, 256 F.2d 890. At this point petitioner again sought, and we again granted certiorari, to determine whether in the circumstances of this case petitioner's claim of absolute privilege should have stood as a bar

plan which allowed 53 of the agency's 2,681 employees to take their accumulated annual leave in cash.

"Mr. Barr's appointment as Acting Director becomes effective Monday, February 9, 1953, and the suspension of these employees will be his first act of duty. The employees are John J. Madigan, Deputy Director for Administration, and Linda Matteo, Director of Personnel.

" 'In June 1950,' Mr. Barr stated, 'my position in the agency was not one of authority which would have permitted me to stop the action. Furthermore, I did not know about it until it was almost completed.

" 'When I did learn that certain employees were receiving cash annual leave settlements and being returned to agency employment on a temporary basis, I specifically notified the employees under my supervision that if they applied for such cash

settlements I would demand their resignations and the record will show that my immediate employees complied with my request.

" 'While I was advised that the action was legal, I took the position that it violated the spirit of the Thomas Amendment and I violently opposed it. Monday, February 9th, when my appointment as Acting Director becomes effective, will be the first time my position in the agency has permitted me to take any action on this matter, and the suspension of these employees will be the first official act I shall take.'

"Mr. Barr also revealed that he has written to Senator Joseph McCarthy, Chairman of the Committee on Government Operations, and to Representative John Phillips, Chairman of the House Subcommittee on Independent Offices Appropriations, requesting an opportunity to be heard on the entire matter."

to maintenance of the suit despite the allegations of malice made in the complaint.

The law of privilege as a defense by officers of government to civil damage suits for defamation and kindred torts has in large part been of judicial making, although the Constitution itself gives an absolute privilege to members of both Houses of Congress in respect to any speech, debate, vote, report, or action done in session.[6] This Court early held that judges of courts of superior or general authority are absolutely privileged as respects civil suits to recover for actions taken by them in the exercise of their judicial functions, irrespective of the motives with which those acts are alleged to have been performed, and that a like immunity extends to other officers of government whose duties are elated to the judicial process. Nor has the privilege been confined to officers of the legislative and judicial branches of the Government and executive officers [whose duties are related to the judicial process.] * * *

The reasons for the recognition of the privilege have been often stated. It has been thought important that officials of government should be free to exercise their duties unembarrassed by the fear of damage suits in respect of acts done in the course of those duties—suits which would consume time and energies which would otherwise be devoted to governmental service and the threat of which might appreciably inhibit the fearless, vigorous, and effective administration of policies of government. The matter has been admirably expressed by Judge Learned Hand:

> "It does indeed go without saying that an official, who is in fact guilty of using his powers to vent his spleen upon others, or for any other personal motive not connected with the public good, should not escape liability for the injuries he may so cause; and, if it were possible in practice to confine such complaints to the guilty, it would be monstrous to deny recovery. The justification for doing so is that it is impossible to know whether the claim is well founded until the case has been tried, and that to submit all officials, the innocent as well as the guilty, to the burden of a trial and to the inevitable danger of its outcome would dampen the ardor of all but the most resolute, or the most irresponsible, in the unflinching discharge of their duties. Again and again the public interest calls for action which may turn out to be founded on a mistake, in the face of which an official may later find himself hard put to it to satisfy a jury of his good faith. There must indeed be means of punishing public officers who have been truant to their duties; but that is quite another matter from exposing such as have been honestly mistaken to suit by anyone who has suffered from their errors. As is so often the case, the answer must be found in a balance between the evils inevitable in either alternative. In this instance it has been thought in the end better to leave unredressed the wrongs done by dishonest officers than to subject those who try to do their duty to the constant dread of retaliation. . . . * * * "

6. U.S.Const. Art. I, § 6.

We do not think that the principle * * * can properly be restricted to executive officers of cabinet rank, and in fact it never has been so restricted by the lower federal courts. The privilege is not a badge or emolument of exalted office, but an expression of a policy designed to aid in the effective functioning of government. The complexities and magnitude of governmental activity have become so great that there must of necessity be a delegation and redelegation of authority as to many functions, and we cannot say that these functions become less important simply because they are exercised by officers of lower rank in the executive hierarchy.

To be sure, the occasions upon which the acts of the head of an executive department will be protected by the privilege are doubtless far broader than in the case of an officer with less sweeping functions. But that is because the higher the post, the broader the range of responsibilities and duties, and the wider the scope of discretion, it entails. It is not the title of his office but the duties with which the particular officer sought to be made to respond in damages is entrusted—the relation of the act complained of to "matters committed by law to his control or supervision," *Spalding v. Vilas,* [161 U.S. 483,] 498 [(1896)]—which must provide the guide in delineating the scope of the rule which clothes the official acts of the executive officer with immunity from civil defamation suits.

Judged by these standards, we hold that petitioner's plea of absolute privilege in defense of the alleged libel published at his direction must be sustained. The question is a close one, but we cannot say that it was not an appropriate exercise of the discretion with which an executive officer of petitioner's rank is necessarily clothed to publish the press release here at issue in the circumstances disclosed by this record. Petitioner was the Acting Director of an important agency of government, and was clothed by redelegation with "all powers, duties, and functions conferred on the President by Title II of the Housing and Rent Act of 1947...."[12] The integrity of the internal operations of the agency which he headed, and thus his own integrity in his public capacity, had been directly and severely challenged in charges made on the floor of the Senate and given wide publicity; and without his knowledge correspondence which could reasonably be read as impliedly defending a position very different from that which he had from the beginning taken in the matter had been sent to a Senator over his signature and incorporated in the Congressional Record. The issuance of press releases was standard agency practice, as it has become with many governmental agencies in these times. We think that under these circumstances a publicly expressed statement of the position of the agency head, announcing personnel action which he planned to take in reference to the charges so widely disseminated to the public, was an appropriate exercise of the discretion which an officer of that rank must possess if the public service is to function effectively. It would be an unduly restrictive view of the scope of the duties of a policy-making executive official to hold that a public statement of agency policy in respect to matters of wide public interest and concern is not action in the line of duty.

---

12. 61 Stat. 193.

That petitioner was not *required* by law or by direction of his superiors to speak out cannot be controlling in the case of an official of policy-making rank, for the same considerations which underlie the recognition of the privilege as to acts done in connection with a mandatory duty apply with equal force to discretionary acts at those levels of government where the concept of duty encompasses the sound exercise of discretionary authority. * * *

We are told that we should forbear from sanctioning any such rule of absolute privilege lest it open the door to wholesale oppression and abuses on the part of unscrupulous government officials. It is perhaps enough to say that fears of this sort have not been realized within the wide area of government where a judicially formulated absolute privilege of broad scope has long existed. It seems to us wholly chimerical to suggest that what hangs in the balance here is the maintenance of high standards of conduct among those in the public service. To be sure, as with any rule of law which attempts to reconcile fundamentally antagonistic social policies, there may be occasional instances of actual injustice which will go unredressed, but we think that price a necessary one to pay for the greater good. And there are of course other sanctions than civil tort suits available to deter the executive official who may be prone to exercise his functions in an unworthy and irresponsible manner. We think that we should not be deterred from establishing the rule which we announce today by any such remote forebodings.

Reversed.

■ MR. JUSTICE BLACK, concurring.

I concur in the reversal of this judgment but briefly summarize my reasons because they are not altogether the same as those stated in the opinion of MR. JUSTICE HARLAN.

The petitioner Barr, while acting as Director of the Office of Rent Stabilization, a United States Government Agency, issued a press release in which he gave reasons why he intended to suspend the respondents Matteo and Madigan, who were also officers of the Agency. There is some indication in the record that there was an affirmative duty on Mr. Barr to give press releases like this, but however that may be it is clear that his action was forbidden neither by an Act of Congress nor by any governmental rule duly promulgated and in force. It is also clear that the subject matter discussed in the release was germane to the proper functioning of the Rent Stabilization Agency and Mr. Barr's duties in relation to it. In fact, at the time the release was issued congressional inquiries were being made into the operations of the Agency and the controversy upon which the threatened suspensions were based, and the press release revealed that Barr had requested an opportunity to testify before a Congressional Committee with respect to the whole dispute.

The effective functioning of a free government like ours depends largely on the force of an informed public opinion. This calls for the widest possible understanding of the quality of government service rendered by all elective or appointed public officials or employees. Such an informed understanding depends, of course, on the freedom people have to applaud or to criticize the way public employees do their jobs, from the least to the most important.

Mr. Barr was peculiarly well qualified to inform Congress and the public about the Rent Stabilization Agency. Subjecting him to libel suits for criticizing the way the Agency or its employees perform their duties would certainly act as a restraint upon him. So far as I am concerned, if federal employees are to be subjected to such restraints in reporting their views about how to run the government better, the restraint will have to be imposed expressly by Congress and not by the general libel laws of the States or of the District of Columbia. How far the Congress itself could go in barring federal officials and employees from discussing public matters consistently with the First Amendment is a question we need not reach in this case. It is enough for me here that the press release was neither unauthorized nor plainly beyond the scope of Mr. Barr's official business, but instead related more or less to general matters committed by law to his control and supervision.

■ Mr. Chief Justice Warren, with whom Mr. Justice Douglas joins, dissenting.

The principal opinion in this case purports to launch the Court on a balancing process in order to reconcile the interest of the public in obtaining fearless executive performance and the interest of the individual in having redress for defamation. Even accepting for the moment that these are the proper interests to be balanced, the ultimate disposition is not the result of a balance. On the one hand, the principal opinion sets up a vague standard under which no government employee can tell with any certainty whether he will receive absolute immunity for his acts. On the other hand, it has not given even the slightest consideration to the interest of the individual who is defamed. It is a complete annihilation of his interest. * * *

I.

The history of the privileges conferred upon the three branches of Government is a story of uneven development. Absolute legislative privilege dates back to at least 1399. This privilege is given to Congress in the United States Constitution and to State Legislatures in the Constitutions of almost all of the States of the Union. The absolute immunity arising out of judicial proceedings existed at least as early as 1608 in England.

But what of the executive privilege? * * *

In *Chatterton v. Secretary of State for India,* [1895] 2 Q.B. 189, the defendant had been apprised that his action with respect to the plaintiff would be made the subject of a parliamentary inquiry. In the communication alleged to be libelous, the defendant told his Under Secretary what answer should be made if the question were asked him in Parliament. The court affirmed dismissal of the complaint relying on Fraser on The Law of Libel and Slander (1st ed.), p. 95, where the author, * * * observed * * * :

> "For reasons of public policy the same protection would, no doubt, be given to anything in the nature of an act of state, e.g., to every communication relating to state matters made by one minister to another, or to the Crown."

This was the actual birth of executive privilege in England.

Such was the state of English law when, the next year, this Court decided *Spalding v. Vilas, supra.* In granting the Postmaster General absolute immunity for "matters committed by law to his control or supervision," this Court relied exclusively on the judicial privilege cases and the English military cases. Thus, leaving aside the military cases, which are unique, the executive privilege in defamation actions would appear to be a judicial creature of less than 65 years' existence. Yet, without statute, this relatively new privilege is being extended to open the possibility of absolute privilege for innumerable government officials.

It may be assumed, *arguendo,* that a government employee should have absolute immunity when according to his duty he makes internal reports to his superior or to another upon his superior's order. This might be a practical necessity of government that would find its justification in the need for a free flow of information within every executive department. * * *

I would not extend *Spalding v. Vilas* to cover public statements of lesser officials. Releases to the public from the executive branch of government imply far greater dangers to the individual claiming to have been defamed than do internal libels. First, of course, a public statement— especially one arguably libelous—is normally intended for and reaches a larger audience than an internally communicated report. Even if the release can later be shown libelous, it is most unusual for a libeled person to obtain the same hearing that was available for the original press release. Second, a release is communicated to a public in no position to evaluate its accuracy; where the report is made internally, the superior is usually in a position to do so. If the report is false, the superior can undo much of the harm of the report by countermanding it or halting its spread.

Giving officials below cabinet or equivalent rank qualified privilege for statements to the public would in no way hamper the internal operation of the executive department of government, nor would it unduly subordinate the interest of the individual in obtaining redress for the public defamation uttered against him.

II.

The foregoing discussion accepted for the purpose of argument the majority's statement of the interest involved here. But as so often happens in balancing cases, the wrong interests are being balanced. This is not a case where the only interest is in plaintiff's obtaining redress of a wrong. The public interest in limiting libel suits against officers in order that the public might be adequately informed is paralleled by another interest of equal importance: that of preserving the opportunity to criticize the administration of our Government and the action of its officials without being subjected to unfair—and absolutely privileged—retorts. If it is important to permit government officials absolute freedom to say anything they wish in the name of public information, it is at least as important to preserve and foster public discussion concerning our Government and its operation.

* * * [H]ere the Court has given some amorphous group of officials—who have the most direct and personal contact with the public—an absolute privilege when their agency or their action is criticized. In this situation, it will take a brave person to criticize government officials knowing that in reply they may libel him with immunity in the name of defending the agency and their own position. This extension of *Spalding v. Vilas* can only have the added effect of deterring the desirable public discussion of all aspects of our Government and the conduct of its officials. It will sanctify the powerful and silence debate. This is a much more serious danger than the possibility that a government official might occasionally be called upon to defend his actions and to respond in damages for a malicious defamation.

III.

The principal opinion, while attempting to balance what it thinks are the factors to be weighed, has not effectuated the goal for which it originally strove. Rather, its result has been an uncertain standard whose effect can unfold only on a case-to-case basis, and which does not provide a guide for executive conduct. But more important, the opinion has set out the wrong interests and by its extension of absolute privilege in this case has seriously weakened another great public interest—honest and open discussion and criticism of our Government.

I would affirm.

■ Mr. Justice Brennan, dissenting.

I think it is demonstrable that the solution of Mr. Justice Harlan's opinion to the question whether an absolute privilege should be allowed in these cases is not justified by the considerations offered to support it, and unnecessarily deprives the individual citizen of all redress against malicious defamation. Surely the opinion must recognize the existence of the deep-rooted policy of the common law generally to provide redress against defamation. But the opinion in sweeping terms extinguishes that remedy, if the defamation is committed by a federal official, by erecting the barrier of an absolute privilege. In my view, only a qualified privilege is necessary here, and that is all I would afford the officials. A qualified privilege would be the most the law would allow private citizens under comparable circumstances. It would protect the government officer unless it appeared on trial that his communication was (a) defamatory, (b) untrue, and (c) "malicious."[2]

2. Actual "malice" is required to vitiate a qualified privilege, not simply the "constructive" malice that is inferred from the publication.

A qualified privilege, as I have described, would, in giving the official protection against the consequences of his honest mistakes, give him all the protection he could properly claim. As is quoted, if that were all that there were to the matter, it would be indeed "monstrous" to grant the absolute defense and preclude all examination of the matter at the suit of a citizen claiming legal injury. But what more is involved? The opinion's position is simply that there are certain societal interests in relieving federal officials from judicial inquiry into their motives that outweigh all interest in affording relief. There is adopted Judge Learned Hand's statement of this added factor that is said to make an absolute privilege imperative: "it is impossible to know whether the claim is well founded until the case has been tried, and that to submit all officials, the innocent as well as the guilty, to the burden of a trial and to the inevitable danger of its outcome, would dampen the ardor of all but the most resolute, or the most irresponsible, in the unflinching discharge of their duties." *Gregoire v. Biddle,* 177 F.2d 579, 581. In the first place, Professors Harper and James have, I think, squarely met and refuted that argument on its own terms: "Where the charge is one of honest mistake we exempt the officer because we deem that an *actual holding of liability* would have worse consequences than *the possibility of an actual mistake* (which under the circumstances we are willing to condone). But it is stretching the argument pretty far to say that the *mere inquiry into malice* would have worse consequences than the *possibility of actual malice* (which we would not, for a minute, condone). Since the danger that official power will be abused is greatest where motives are improper, the balance here may well swing the other way." Harper and James, Torts (1956), p. 1645. And in the second place, the courts should be wary of any argument based on the fear that subjecting government officers to the nuisance of litigation and the uncertainties of its outcome may put an undue burden on the conduct of the public business. Such a burden is hardly one peculiar to public officers; citizens generally go through life subject to the risk that they may, though in the right, be subject to litigation and the possibility of a miscarriage of justice. It is one of the goals of a well-operating legal system to keep the burden of litigation and the risks of such miscarriages to a minimum; in this area, which is governed by federal law, proof of malice outside of the bare fact of the making of the statement should be forthcoming, and summary judgment practice offers protection to the defendant; but the way to minimizing the burdens of litigation does not generally lie through the abolition of a right of redress for an admitted wrong. The method has too much of the flavor of throwing out the baby with the bath—today's sweeping solution insures that government officials of high and low rank will not be involved in litigation over their allegedly defamatory statements, but it achieves this at the cost of letting the citizen who is defamed even with the worst motives go without remedy. * * *

■ MR. JUSTICE STEWART, dissenting.

My brother HARLAN'S opinion contains, it seems to me, a lucid and persuasive analysis of the principles that should guide decision in this troublesome area of law. Where I part company is in the application of these principles to the facts of the present case.

I cannot agree that the issuance by the petitioner of this press release was "action in the line of duty." The statement to the press (set out in note 5 of MR. JUSTICE HARLAN'S opinion) did not serve to further any agency function. Instead, it represented a personally motivated effort on the petitioner's part to disassociate himself from the alleged chicanery with which the agency had been charged.

By publicizing the action which he intended to take when he became permanent Acting Director, and his past attitude as a lesser functionary, the petitioner was seeking only to defend his own individual reputation. This was not within, but beyond "the outer perimeter of petitioner's line of duty."

Notes and Questions

1. The subject of this subset of materials is claims for money damages against government officials or employees acting in their official capacity. We begin with claims that are founded upon ordinary common-law causes of action, such as state tort claims. Consider the breadth of government activities that could give rise to ordinary tort claims against a government officer: an Assistant United States Attorney seeking to convict and imprison a criminal defendant; a prison official or guard controlling the behavior of inmates; an employee of the Environmental Protection Agency charging a manufacturer with disposal of hazardous wastes; a Social Security Administration adjudicator denying or revoking disability benefits; etc. When a government officer while acting as an agent of the federal government commits an allegedly tortious act that harms the plaintiff, should he or she be subject to liability? Ever? Under certain circumstances? What are the interests of the injured party? Fairness? What about the effect on government employees who have to defend themselves against lawsuits, with or without merit, that place them at risk of personal liability? What are the risks to the public if government employees are too easily subjected to personal liability?

In *Barr v. Matteo*, the Supreme Court considered a claim of common law libel arising out of the issuance of a press release by the defendant government officer (the petitioner before the Court) that allegedly defamed the plaintiffs (the respondents before the Court). Justice Harlan wrote an opinion for a plurality of four justices, with Justice Black's concurrence providing a majority in favor of immunity for the government officer. In the first paragraph of Justice Harlan's plurality opinion, he describes the conflicting interests of the injured citizen and the public. What are these? How does the majority of the Court strike that balance? Why do the dissenters disagree?

Note that nearly every member of the Court (except Justice Stewart) agrees that some form of immunity should be extended here, but they disagree on the strength of that immunity. The various opinions discuss "absolute" and "qualified" immunity. Define each and explain the difference between them (refer to the dissenting opinions for a fuller explanation of qualified immunity). How does that difference between the two types of immunity also affect the different results the majority and the dissents would reach?

2.   The concept of privilege for the purpose of protecting government operations comes into the picture only when government officers are *acting* as government officers. If a government employee engages in tortious or otherwise wrongful behavior in his or her private affairs, the interests of the federal government are not implicated and questions of privilege do not arise. Thus, if a federal employee is involved in an automobile accident while off work or on vacation, the matter falls entirely outside of the scope of this course and raises no issues of sovereign immunity, privilege, etc. The individual would be liable in the same manner as anyone else under such circumstances. Indeed, the Supreme Court held that even the President is not absolutely immune from suit, during his term of office, based upon allegations unrelated to his official duties. *See Clinton v. Jones,* 520 U.S. 681 (1997) (holding that President Clinton was not temporarily immune from a civil suit alleging sexual harassment that occurred prior to his election). (The President, however, "is entitled to absolute immunity from damage liability predicated upon his official acts." *Nixon v. Fitzgerald,* 457 U.S. 731, 749 (1982).)

However, it remains necessary to determine when a government officer is or is not acting within the line of duty, and how the line should be drawn. The plurality attempts to define that point in its opinion. Under its analysis, when does an employee act in an official capacity so as to allow him or her to invoke immunity? Justice Stewart dissented separately on this issue. What is his argument?

3.   The decision in *Barr v. Matteo* suggests that federal government officials and employees are generally and broadly entitled to absolute immunity as a defense against common-law tort actions. (As will be addressed in Chapter V.B.2.b, *qualified* immunity for federal officers is the general rule for *constitutional* tort claims.) However, the Supreme Court revisited federal employee liability for common-law torts in the next case of *Westfall v. Erwin,* which in turn set the stage for legislative intervention by Congress.

Westfall v. Erwin

Supreme Court of the United States.
484 U.S. 292 (1988).

■ JUSTICE MARSHALL delivered the opinion of the Court.

Respondent William Erwin and his wife respondent Emely Erwin brought a state-law tort suit against petitioners, federal employees in the

Executive Branch, alleging that he had suffered injuries as a result of petitioners' negligence in performing official acts. The issue presented is whether these federal officials are absolutely immune from liability under state tort law for conduct within the scope of their employment without regard to whether the challenged conduct was discretionary in nature.

I

Respondents William and Emely Erwin commenced this tort action in state court. At the time of the alleged tort, William Erwin was employed by the Federal Government as a civilian warehouseman at the Anniston Army Depot in Anniston, Alabama. Petitioners were supervisors at the Depot. Respondents' complaint alleged that while working at the Depot William Erwin came into contact with bags of toxic soda ash that "were improperly and negligently stored." The complaint stated that William Erwin suffered chemical burns to his eyes and throat when he inhaled soda ash dust that had spilled from its bag. William Erwin also asserted that the soda ash "should not have been routed to the warehouse where [he] was working," and that "someone should have known that it was there and provided [him] with some warning as to its presence and danger before [he] inhaled it." The complaint charged petitioners with negligence "in proximately causing, permitting, or allowing [him] to inhale the . . . soda ash."

Petitioners removed the action to the United States District Court for the Northern District of Alabama pursuant to 28 U.S.C. § 1442(a)(1). The District Court held that petitioners were absolutely immune from suit and granted summary judgment in their favor. After finding that the alleged tort was committed while petitioners were acting within the scope of their employment, the court held that "any federal employee is entitled to absolute immunity for ordinary torts committed within the scope of their jobs." Civ. Action No. CV85–H–874–S, p. 2 (June 5, 1985). The Court of Appeals reversed, reasoning that a federal employee enjoys immunity "only if the challenged conduct is a discretionary act *and* is within the outer perimeter of the actor's line of duty." 785 F.2d 1551, 1552 (C.A.11 1986). The court held that the District Court erred in failing to consider whether the challenged conduct was discretionary, in addition to being within the scope of petitioners' duties, before finding that petitioners were absolutely immune from suit. Summary judgment was inappropriate, the court concluded, because respondents had "alleged undisputed facts sufficient to create a material question of whether or not [petitioners'] complained-of acts were discretionary." 785 F.2d, at 1553.

We granted certiorari to resolve the dispute among the Courts of Appeals as to whether conduct by federal officials must be discretionary in nature, as well as being within the scope of their employment, before the conduct is absolutely immune from state-law tort liability. We affirm.

II

In *Barr v. Matteo,* 360 U.S. 564 (1959), and *Howard v. Lyons,* 360 U.S. 593 (1959), this Court held that the scope of absolute official immunity afforded federal employees is a matter of federal law, "to be formulated by the courts in the absence of legislative action by Congress." *Id.,* at 597. The purpose of such official immunity is not to protect an erring official, but to insulate the decisionmaking process from the harassment of prospective litigation. The provision of immunity rests on the view that the threat of liability will make federal officials unduly timid in carrying out their official duties, and that effective government will be promoted if officials are freed of the costs of vexatious and often frivolous damages suits. This Court always has recognized, however, that official immunity comes at a great cost. An injured party with an otherwise meritorious tort claim is denied compensation simply because he had the misfortune to be injured by a federal official. Moreover, absolute immunity contravenes the basic tenet that individuals be held accountable for their wrongful conduct. We therefore have held that absolute immunity for federal officials is justified only when "the contributions of immunity to effective government in particular contexts outweigh the perhaps recurring harm to individual citizens." *Doe v. McMillan,* [412 U.S. 306,] 320 [(1973)]. * * *

The central purpose of official immunity, promoting effective government, would not be furthered by shielding an official from state-law tort liability without regard to whether the alleged tortious conduct is discretionary in nature. When an official's conduct is not the product of independent judgment, the threat of liability cannot detrimentally inhibit that conduct. It is only when officials exercise decisionmaking discretion that potential liability may shackle "the fearless, vigorous, and effective administration of policies of government." *Barr v. Matteo, supra,* 360 U.S., at 571. Because it would not further effective governance, absolute immunity for nondiscretionary functions finds no support in the traditional justification for official immunity. * * *

As an alternative position, petitioners contend that even if discretion is required before absolute immunity attaches, the requirement is satisfied as long as the official exercises "minimal discretion." If the precise conduct is not mandated by law, petitioners argue, then the act is "discretionary" and the official is entitled to absolute immunity from state-law tort liability. We reject such a wooden interpretation of the discretionary function requirement. Because virtually all official acts involve some modicum of choice, petitioners' reading of the requirement would render it essentially meaningless. Furthermore, by focusing entirely on the question whether a federal official's precise conduct is controlled by law or regulation, petitioners' approach ignores the balance of potential benefits and costs of absolute immunity under the circumstances and thus loses sight of the underlying purpose of official immunity doctrine. Conduct by federal officials will often involve the exercise of a modicum of choice and yet be largely unaffected by the prospect of tort liability, making the provision of absolute immunity unnecessary and unwise.

* * * Applying the foregoing reasoning to this case, it is clear that the court was correct in reversing the District Court's grant of summary judgment. Petitioners have the burden of proving that they are entitled to absolute immunity from the tort suit. Respondent William Erwin asserted that petitioners' "duties only require them to follow established procedures and guidelines," and that they "are not involved in any policy-making work for the United States Government." In response, petitioners have not presented any evidence relating to their official duties or to the level of discretion they exercise. Petitioners aver merely that the alleged tortious conduct was "within the scope of their official duties." As we stated above, federal officials are not absolutely immune from state-law tort liability for all actions committed within the outer perimeter of their duties. A material issue of fact thus exists as to whether petitioners exercised sufficient discretion in connection with the alleged tort to warrant the shield of absolute immunity.

Because this case comes to us on summary judgment and the relevant factual background is undeveloped, we are not called on to define the precise boundaries of official immunity or to determine the level of discretion required before immunity may attach. In deciding whether particular governmental functions properly fall within the scope of absolute official immunity, however, courts should be careful to heed the Court's admonition in *Doe* to consider whether the contribution to effective government in particular contexts outweighs the potential harm to individual citizens. Courts must not lose sight of the purposes of the official immunity doctrine when resolving individual claims of immunity or formulating general guidelines. We are also of the view, however, that Congress is in the best position to provide guidance for the complex and often highly empirical inquiry into whether absolute immunity is warranted in a particular context. Legislated standards governing the immunity of federal employees involved in state-law tort actions would be useful.

III

The Court of Appeals was correct in holding that absolute immunity does not shield official functions from state-law tort liability unless the challenged conduct is within the outer perimeter of an official's duties and is discretionary in nature. Moreover, absolute immunity does not attach simply because the precise conduct of the federal official is not prescribed by law. There is thus a genuine issue of material fact as to whether petitioners' conduct is entitled to absolute immunity. Accordingly, the judgment of the Court of Appeals is affirmed.

It is so ordered.

Notes and Questions

1. Does the decision in *Westfall v. Erwin* constitute a retreat from the rule set down in *Barr v. Matteo*? What additional requirement or require-

ments does the *Westfall* decision prescribe before a government employee may invoke absolute immunity from liability for an ordinary tort? And what does "discretionary" mean in this context? Note that the Court makes offhand references to "function" and to "policy." Does this suggest that "discretionary" here means the same thing as it does for purposes of the discretionary function exception under the Federal Tort Claims Act, 28 U.S.C. § 2680(a), as discussed previously in Chapter III.A.4?

2.   The *Westfall* decision is largely of historical interest, as it has been superseded by statute. The Court in *Westfall* candidly says that Congress is in a better position to evaluate when immunity for federal employees is warranted and even pleads for legislated standards. Congress responded by enacting a statute that substitutes the United States as the defendant whenever a federal employee is sued for ordinary torts based on conduct within the scope of his or her employment. 28 U.S.C. § 2679. Thus, with the significant exception of constitutional torts (which are excepted from the statute), suits for damages against federal employees acting within the scope of their official duties are now barred. This statute, which for obvious reasons is commonly known as the "Westfall Act," is the subject of the next subset of materials.

————

b.   IMMUNITY CREATED BY STATUTE

Federal Employees Liability Reform and Tort Compensation Act (Westfall Act), 28 United States Code § 2679(b)–(e)

(b)(1) The remedy against the United States provided by sections 1346(b) and 2672 of this title for injury or loss of property, or personal injury or death arising or resulting from the negligent or wrongful act or omission of any employee of the Government while acting within the scope of his office or employment is exclusive of any other civil action or proceeding for money damages by reason of the same subject matter against the employee whose act or omission gave rise to the claim or against the estate of such employee. Any other civil action or proceeding for money damages arising out of or relating to the same subject matter against the employee or the employee's estate is precluded without regard to when the act or omission occurred.

(2) Paragraph (1) does not extend or apply to a civil action against an employee of the Government—

(A) which is brought for a violation of the Constitution of the United States, or

(B) which is brought for a violation of a statute of the United States under which such action against an individual is otherwise authorized.

(c) The Attorney General shall defend any civil action or proceeding brought in any court against any employee of the Government or his estate for any such damage or injury. The employee against whom such civil action or proceeding is brought shall deliver within such time after date of service or knowledge of service as determined by the Attorney General, all process served upon him or an attested true copy thereof to his immediate superior or to whomever was designated by the head of his department to receive such papers and such person shall promptly furnish copies of the pleadings and process therein to the United States attorney for the district embracing the place wherein the proceeding is brought, to the Attorney General, and to the head of his employing Federal agency.

(d)(1) Upon certification by the Attorney General that the defendant employee was acting within the scope of his office or employment at the time of the incident out of which the claim arose, any civil action or proceeding commenced upon such claim in a United States district court shall be deemed an action against the United States under the provisions of this title and all references thereto, and the United States shall be substituted as the party defendant.

(2) Upon certification by the Attorney General that the defendant employee was acting within the scope of his office or employment at the time of the incident out of which the claim arose, any civil action or proceeding commenced upon such claim in a State court shall be removed without bond at any time before trial by the Attorney General to the district court of the United States for the district and division embracing the place in which the action or proceeding is pending. Such action or proceeding shall be deemed to be an action or proceeding brought against the United States under the provisions of this title and all references thereto, and the United States shall be substituted as the party defendant. This certification of the Attorney General shall conclusively establish scope of office or employment for purposes of removal.

(3) In the event that the Attorney General has refused to certify scope of office or employment under this section, the employee may at any time before trial petition the court to find and certify that the employee was acting within the scope of his office or employment. Upon such certification by the court, such action or proceeding shall be deemed to be an action or proceeding brought against the United States under the provisions of this title and all references thereto, and the United States shall be substituted as the party defendant. A copy of the petition shall be served upon the United States in accordance with the provisions of Rule 4(d)(4) of the Federal Rules of Civil Procedure. In the event the petition is filed in a civil action or proceeding pending in a State court, the action or proceeding may be removed without bond by the Attorney General to the district court of the United States for the district and division embracing the place in which it is pending. If, in considering the petition, the district court determines that the employee was not acting within the scope of his office or employment, the action or proceeding shall be remanded to the State court.

(4) Upon certification, any action or proceeding subject to paragraph (1), (2), or (3) shall proceed in the same manner as any action against the

United States filed pursuant to section 1346(b) of this title and shall be subject to the limitations and exceptions applicable to those actions.

(5) Whenever an action or proceeding in which the United States is substituted as the party defendant under this subsection is dismissed for failure first to present a claim pursuant to section 2675(a) of this title, such a claim shall be deemed to be timely presented under section 2401(b) of this title if—

(A) the claim would have been timely had it been filed on the date the underlying civil action was commenced, and

(B) the claim is presented to the appropriate Federal agency within 60 days after dismissal of the civil action.

(e) The Attorney General may compromise or settle any claim asserted in such civil action or proceeding in the manner provided in section 2677, and with the same effect.

Gutierrez de Martinez v. Lamagno

Supreme Court of the United States.
515 U.S. 417 (1995).

■ JUSTICE GINSBURG delivered the opinion of the Court, except as to Part IV.

When a federal employee is sued for a wrongful or negligent act, the Federal Employees Liability Reform and Tort Compensation Act of 1988 (commonly known as the Westfall Act) empowers the Attorney General to certify that the employee "was acting within the scope of his office or employment at the time of the incident out of which the claim arose...." 28 U.S.C. § 2679(d)(1). Upon certification, the employee is dismissed from the action and the United States is substituted as defendant. The case then falls under the governance of the Federal Tort Claims Act (FTCA). Generally, such cases unfold much as cases do against other employers who concede respondeat superior liability. If, however, an exception to the FTCA shields the United States from suit, the plaintiff may be left without a tort action against any party.

This case is illustrative. The Attorney General certified that an allegedly negligent employee "was acting within the scope of his ... employment" at the time of the episode in suit. Once brought into the case as a defendant, however, the United States asserted immunity, because the incident giving rise to the claim occurred abroad and the FTCA excepts "[a]ny claim arising in a foreign country." 28 U.S.C. § 2680(k). Endeavoring to redeem their lawsuit, plaintiffs (petitioners here) sought court review of the Attorney General's scope-of-employment certification, for if the employee was acting outside the scope of his employment, the plaintiffs' tort action could proceed against him. The lower courts held the certification unreviewable. We reverse that determination and hold that the scope-of-employment certification is reviewable in court.

I

Shortly before midnight on January 18, 1991, in Barranquilla, Colombia, a car driven by respondent Dirk A. Lamagno, a special agent of the United States Drug Enforcement Administration (DEA), collided with petitioners' car. Petitioners, who are citizens of Colombia, allege that Lamagno was intoxicated and that his passenger, an unidentified woman, was not a federal employee.

Informed that diplomatic immunity shielded Lamagno from suit in Colombia, petitioners filed a diversity action against him in the United States District Court for the Eastern District of Virginia, the district where Lamagno resided. Alleging that Lamagno's negligent driving caused the accident, petitioners sought compensation for physical injuries and property damage. In response, the local United States Attorney, acting pursuant to the Westfall Act, certified on behalf of the Attorney General that Lamagno was acting within the scope of his employment at the time of the accident. The certification, as is customary, stated no reasons for the U.S. Attorney's scope-of-employment determination.

In the Westfall Act, Congress instructed:

"Upon certification by the Attorney General that the defendant employee was acting within the scope of his office or employment at the time of the incident out of which the claim arose, any civil action or proceeding commenced upon such claim in a United States district court shall be deemed an action against the United States under the provisions of this title and all references thereto, and the United States shall be substituted as the party defendant." § 2679(d)(1).

Thus, absent judicial review and court rejection of the certification, Lamagno would be released from the litigation; furthermore, he could not again be pursued in any damages action arising from the "same subject matter." § 2679(b)(1). Replacing Lamagno, the United States would become sole defendant.

Ordinarily, scope-of-employment certifications occasion no contest. While the certification relieves the employee of responsibility, plaintiffs will confront instead a financially reliable defendant. But in this case, substitution of the United States would cause the demise of the action: petitioners' claims "ar[ose] in a foreign country," FTCA, 28 U.S.C. § 2680(k), and thus fell within an exception to the FTCA's waiver of the United States' sovereign immunity. See § 2679(d)(4) (upon certification, the action "shall proceed in the same manner as any action against the United States ... and shall be subject to the limitations and exceptions applicable to those actions"). Nor would the immunity of the United States allow petitioners to bring Lamagno back into the action. See *United States v. Smith*, 499 U.S. 160 (1991).

To keep their action against Lamagno alive, and to avoid the fatal consequences of unrecallable substitution of the United States as the party defendant, petitioners asked the District Court to review the certification. Petitioners maintained that Lamagno was acting outside the scope of his employment at the time of the accident; certification to the contrary, they argued, was groundless and untrustworthy. Following Circuit precedent, the District Court held the certification unreviewable, substituted the United States for Lamagno, and dismissed petitioners' suit. In an unadorned order, the Fourth Circuit affirmed. 23 F.3d 402 (1994).

The Circuits divide sharply on this issue. Parting from the Fourth Circuit, most of the Courts of Appeals have held certification by the Attorney General or her delegate amenable to court review. We granted certiorari to resolve the conflict,[4] and we now reverse the Fourth Circuit's judgment.

II

A

We encounter in this case the familiar questions: where is the line to be drawn; and who decides. Congress has firmly answered the first question. "Scope of employment" sets the line. See § 2679(b)(1); *United States v. Smith*, 499 U.S. 160 (1991). If Lamagno is inside that line, he is not subject to petitioners' suit; if he is outside the line, he is personally answerable. The sole question, then, is *who decides* on which side of the line the case falls: the local U.S. Attorney, unreviewably or, when that official's decision is contested, the court. Congress did not address this precise issue unambiguously, if at all. As the division in the lower courts and in this Court shows, the Westfall Act is, on the "who decides" question we confront, open to divergent interpretation.

Two considerations weigh heavily in our analysis, and we state them at the outset. First, the Attorney General herself urges review, mindful that in cases of the kind petitioners present, the incentive of her delegate to certify is marked. Second, when a government official's determination of a fact or circumstance—for example, "scope of employment"—is dispositive of a court controversy, federal courts generally do not hold the determination unreviewable. Instead, federal judges traditionally proceed from the "strong presumption that Congress intends judicial review." *Bowen v. Michigan Academy of Family Physicians*, 476 U.S. 667, 670 (1986). Chief Justice Marshall long ago captured the essential idea:

> "It would excite some surprise if, in a government of laws and of principle, furnished with a department whose appropriate duty it is to decide questions of right, not only between individuals, but between the government and individuals; a ministerial officer might, at his discretion, issue this powerful process . . . leaving to [the claimant] no remedy, no appeal to the laws of his country, if he should believe the claim to be unjust. But this anomaly does not exist; this imputation

---

4. The United States, in accord with petitioners, reads the Westfall Act to allow a plaintiff to challenge the Attorney General's scope-of-employment certification. We therefore invited Michael K. Kellogg to brief and argue this case, as amicus curiae, in support of the judgment below. Mr. Kellogg accepted the appointment and has well fulfilled his assigned responsibility.

cannot be cast on the legislature of the United States." *United States v. Nourse,* 34 U.S. (9 Pet.) 8, 28–29 (1835).

Accordingly, we have stated time and again that judicial review of executive action "will not be cut off unless there is persuasive reason to believe that such was the purpose of Congress." *Abbott Laboratories [v. Gardner],* 387 U.S., [136,] 140 [(1967)]. No persuasive reason for restricting access to judicial review is discernible from the statutory fog we confront here.

B

Congress, when it composed the Westfall Act, legislated against a backdrop of judicial review. Courts routinely reviewed the local U.S. Attorney's scope-of-employment certification under the Westfall Act's statutory predecessor, the Federal Drivers Act, Pub.L. 87–258, § 1, 75 Stat. 539 (previously codified as 28 U.S.C. § 2679(d)). Similar to the Westfall Act but narrower in scope, the Drivers Act made the FTCA the exclusive remedy for motor vehicle accidents involving federal employees acting within the scope of their employment. The Drivers Act, like the Westfall Act, had a certification scheme, though it applied only to cases brought in state court. Once the Attorney General or her delegate certified that the defendant driver was acting within the scope of employment, the case was removed to federal court and the United States was substituted as defendant. But the removal and substitution were subject to the federal court's control; a court determination that the driver was acting outside the scope of his employment would restore the case to its original status.

When Congress wrote the Westfall Act, which covers federal employees generally and not just federal drivers, the legislators had one purpose firmly in mind. That purpose surely was not to make the Attorney General's delegate the final arbiter of "scope-of-employment" contests. Instead, Congress sought to override *Westfall v. Erwin,* 484 U.S. 292 (1988). In *Westfall,* we held that, to gain immunity from suit for a common law tort, a federal employee would have to show (1) that he was acting within the scope of his employment, and (2) that he was performing a discretionary function. Congress reacted quickly to delete the "discretionary function" requirement, finding it an unwarranted judicial imposition, one that had "created an immediate crisis involving the prospect of personal liability and the threat of protracted personal tort litigation for the entire Federal workforce." § 2(a)(5), 102 Stat. 4563.

The Westfall Act trained on this objective: to "return Federal employees to the status they held prior to the *Westfall* decision." H.R.Rep. No. 100–700, p. 4 (1988). Congress was notably concerned with the *significance* of the scope-of-employment inquiry—that is, it wanted the employee's personal immunity to turn on that question alone. But nothing tied to the purpose of the legislation shows that Congress meant the Westfall Act to commit the critical "scope-of-employment" inquiry to the unreviewable judgment of the Attorney General or her delegate, and thus to alter fundamentally the answer to the "who decides" question.

C

Construction of the Westfall Act as Lamagno urges—to deny to federal courts authority to review the Attorney General's scope-of-employment certification—would oblige us to attribute to Congress two highly anomalous commands. Not only would we have to accept that Congress, by its silence, authorized the Attorney General's delegate to make determinations of the kind at issue without any judicial check. At least equally perplexing, the proposed reading would cast Article III judges in the role of petty functionaries, persons required to enter as a court judgment an executive officer's decision, but stripped of capacity to evaluate independently whether the executive's decision is correct.

1

In the typical case, by certifying that an employee was acting within the scope of his employment, the Attorney General enables the tort plaintiff to maintain a claim for relief under the FTCA, a claim against the financially reliable United States. In such a case, the United States, by certifying, is acting *against* its financial interest, exposing itself to liability as would any other employer at common law who admits that an employee acted within the scope of his employment. See Restatement (Second) of Agency § 219 (1958).

The situation alters radically, however, in the unusual case—like the one before us—that involves an exception to the FTCA. When the United States retains immunity from suit, certification disarms plaintiffs. They may not proceed against the United States, nor may they pursue the employee shielded by the certification. *Smith,* 499 U.S., at 166–167. In such a case, the certification surely does not qualify as a declaration against the Government's interest: it does not expose the United States to liability, and it shields a federal employee from liability.

But that is not all. The impetus to certify becomes overwhelming in a case like this one, as the Attorney General, in siding with petitioners, no doubt comprehends. If the local U.S. Attorney, to whom the Attorney General has delegated responsibility, refuses certification, the employee can make a federal case of the matter by alleging a wrongful failure to certify. See § 2679(d)(3). The federal employee's claim is one the U.S. Attorney has no incentive to oppose for the very reason the dissent suggests: win or lose, the United States retains its immunity; hence, were the United States to litigate "scope of employment" against its own employee—thereby consuming the local U.S. Attorney's precious litigation resources—it would be litigating solely for the benefit of the plaintiff. Inevitably, the U.S. Attorney will feel a strong tug to certify, even when the merits are cloudy, and thereby "do a favor," both for the employee and for the United States as well, at a cost borne solely, and perhaps quite unfairly, by the plaintiff.

The argument for unreviewability in such an instance runs up against a mainstay of our system of government. Madison spoke precisely to the point in The Federalist No. 10:

"No man is allowed to be a judge in his own cause, because his interest would certainly bias his judgment, and, not improbably, corrupt his integrity. With equal, nay with greater reason, a body of men are unfit to be both judges and parties at the same time...." The Federalist No. 10, p. 79 (C. Rossiter ed. 1961) (J. Madison).

In sum, under Lamagno's reading of the congressional product at issue, whenever the case falls within an exception to the FTCA, the Attorney General sits as an unreviewable "judge in her own cause"; she can block petitioners' way to a tort action in court, at no cost to the federal treasury, while avoiding litigation in which the United States has no incentive to engage, and incidentally enhancing the morale—or at least sparing the purse—of federal employees. The United States, as we have noted, disavows this extraordinary, conspicuously self-serving interpretation. Recognizing that a U.S. Attorney, in cases of this order, is hardly positioned to act impartially, the Attorney General reads the law to allow judicial review.

2

If Congress made the Attorney General's delegate sole judge, despite the apparent conflict of interest, then Congress correspondingly assigned to the federal court only rubber-stamp work. Upon certification in a case such as this one, the United States would automatically become the defendant and, just as automatically, the case would be dismissed. The key question presented—scope of employment—however contestable in fact, would receive no judicial audience. The Court could do no more, and no less, than convert the executive's scarcely disinterested decision into a court judgment. This strange course becomes all the more surreal when one adds to the scene the absence of an obligation on the part of the Attorney General's delegate to conduct a fair proceeding, indeed, any proceeding. She need not give the plaintiff an opportunity to speak to the "scope" question, or even notice that she is considering the question. Nor need she give any explanation for her action.

Congress may be free to establish a compensation scheme that operates without court participation. But that is a matter quite different from instructing a court automatically to enter a judgment pursuant to a decision the court has no authority to evaluate. We resist ascribing to Congress an intention to place courts in this untenable position.

III

We return now, in more detail, to the statutory language, to determine whether it overcomes the presumption favoring judicial review, the tradition of court review of scope certifications, and the anomalies attending foreclosure of review.

The certification, removal, and substitution provisions of the Westfall Act, 28 U.S.C. § 2679(d)(1)-(3), work together to assure that, when scope of employment is in controversy, that matter, key to the application of the FTCA, may be resolved in federal court. To that end, the Act specifically allows employees whose certification requests have been denied by the Attorney General, to contest the denial in court. § 2679(d)(3). If the action was initiated by the tort plaintiff in state court, the Attorney General, on the defendant-employee's petition, is to enter the case and may remove it to the federal court so that the scope determination can be made in the federal forum. *Ibid.*

When the Attorney General has granted certification, if the case is already in federal court (as is this case, because of the parties' diverse citizenship), the United States will be substituted as the party defendant. § 2679(d)(1). If the case was initiated by the tort plaintiff in state court, the Attorney General is to remove it to the federal court, where, as in a case that originated in the federal forum, the United States will be substituted as the party defendant. § 2679(d)(2).

The statute next instructs that the "certification of the Attorney General shall conclusively establish scope of office or employment *for purposes of removal.*" *Ibid.* (emphasis added). The meaning of that instruction, in the view of petitioners and the Attorney General, is just what the emphasized words import. Congress spoke in discrete sentences in § 2679(d)(2) first of removal, then of substitution. Next, Congress made the Attorney General's certificate conclusive solely for purposes of removal, and notably not for purposes of substitution. It follows, petitioners and the Attorney General conclude, that the scope-of-employment judgment determinative of substitution can and properly should be checked by the court, *i.e.,* the Attorney General's scarcely disinterested certification on that matter is by statute made the first, but not the final word.

Lamagno's construction does not draw on the "certification . . . shall [be conclusive] . . . for purposes of removal" language of § 2679(d)(2). Instead, Lamagno emphasizes the word "shall" in the statement: "Upon certification by the Attorney General . . . any civil action or proceeding . . . *shall* be deemed an action against the United States . . . , and the United States shall be substituted as the party defendant." § 2679(d)(1) (emphasis added). Any doubt as to the commanding force of the word "shall," Lamagno urges, is dispelled by this further feature: the Westfall Act's predecessor, the Federal Drivers Act, provided for court review of "scope-of-employment" certifications at the tort plaintiff's behest. Not only does the Westfall Act fail to provide for certification challenges by tort plaintiffs, Lamagno underscores, but the Act prominently provides for court review of refusals to certify at the behest of defending employees. See § 2679(d)(3). Congress, in Lamagno's view, thus plainly intended the one-sided review, *i.e.,* a court check at the call of the defending employee, but no check at the tort plaintiff's call.

We recognize that both sides have tendered plausible constructions of a text most interpreters have found far from clear. Indeed, the United States initially took the position that the local U.S. Attorney's scope-of-employment certifications are conclusive and unreviewable but, on further consideration, changed its position. Because the statute is reasonably susceptible to divergent interpretation, we adopt the reading that accords with traditional understandings and basic principles: that executive determinations generally are subject to judicial review and that mechanical judgments are not the kind federal courts are set up to render. Under our reading, the Attorney General's certification that a federal employee was acting within the scope of his employment—a certification the executive official, in cases of the kind at issue, has a compelling interest to grant—does not conclusively establish as correct the substitution of the United States as defendant in place of the employee.

IV

Treating the Attorney General's certification as conclusive for purposes of removal but not for purposes of substitution, *amicus* ultimately argues, "raise[s] a potentially serious Article III problem." If the certification is rejected, because the federal court concludes that the employee acted outside the scope of his employment, and if the tort plaintiff and the employee resubstituted as defendant are not of diverse citizenship, *amicus* urges, then the federal court will be left with a case without a federal question to support the court's subject matter jurisdiction. This last-pressed argument by *amicus* largely drives the dissent.

This case itself, we note, presents not even the specter of an Article III problem. The case was initially instituted in federal court; it was not removed from a state court. The parties' diverse citizenship gave petitioners an entirely secure basis for filing in federal court.

In any event, we do not think the Article III problem *amicus* describes is a grave one. There may no longer be a federal question once the federal employee is resubstituted as defendant, but in the category of cases *amicus* hypothesizes, there was a nonfrivolous federal question, certified by the local U.S. Attorney, when the case was removed to federal court. At that time, the United States was the defendant, and the action was thus under the FTCA. Whether the employee was acting within the scope of his federal employment is a significant federal question—and the Westfall Act was designed to assure that this question could be aired in a federal forum. Because a case under the Westfall Act thus "raises [a] questio[n] of substantive federal law at the very outset," it "clearly 'arises under' federal law, as that term is used in Art. III." *Verlinden B.V. v. Central Bank of Nigeria,* 461 U.S. 480, 493 (1983).

In adjudicating the scope-of-federal-employment question "at the very outset," the court inevitably will confront facts relevant to the alleged misconduct, matters that bear on the state tort claims against the employee. Cf. *Mine Workers v. Gibbs,* 383 U.S. 715, 725 (1966) (approving exercise of pendent jurisdiction when federal and state claims have "a common nucleus of operative fact" and would "ordinarily be expected to [be tried] all in one judicial proceeding"). "[C]onsiderations of judicial economy, convenience and fairness to litigants," *id.,* at 726, make it reasonable and proper for the federal forum to proceed beyond the federal question to final judgment once it has invested time and resources on the initial scope-of-employment contest.

If, in preserving judicial review of scope-of-employment certifications, Congress "approach[ed] the limit" of federal court jurisdiction—and we do not believe it did—we find the exercise of federal court authority involved here less ominous than the consequences of declaring certifications of the kind at issue uncontestable: The local U.S. Attorney, whose conflict of interest is apparent, would be authorized to make final and binding decisions insulating both the United States and federal employees like Lamagno from liability while depriving plaintiffs of potentially meritorious tort claims. The Attorney General, having weighed the competing considerations, does not read the statute to confer on her such extraordinary authority. Nor should we assume that Congress meant federal courts to accept cases only to stamp them "Dismissed" on an interested executive official's unchallengeable representation. The statute is fairly construed to allow petitioners to present to the District Court their objections to the Attorney General's scope-of-employment certification, and we hold that construction the more persuasive one.

* * *

For the reasons stated, the judgment of the United States Court of Appeals for the Fourth Circuit is reversed, and the case is remanded for proceedings consistent with this opinion.

It is so ordered.

■ JUSTICE O'CONNER, concurring in part and concurring in the judgment.

For the reasons given in Parts I–III of the Court's opinion, which I join, I agree with the Court (and the Attorney General) that the Attorney General's scope-of-employment certifications in Westfall Act cases should be judicially reviewable. I do not join Part IV of the Court's opinion, however. That discussion all but conclusively resolves a difficult question of federal jurisdiction that, as the Court notes, is not presented in this case. In my view, we should not resolve that question until it is necessary for us to do so.

Of course, I agree with the dissent, that we ordinarily should construe statutes to avoid serious constitutional questions, such as that discussed in Part IV of the Court's opinion, when it is fairly possible to do so. And I recognize that reversing the Court of Appeals' judgment in this case may make it impossible to avoid deciding that question in a future case. But even such an important canon of statutory construction as that favoring the avoidance of serious constitutional questions does not *always* carry the day. In this case, as described in detail by the Court, several other important legal principles, including the presumption in favor of judicial review of executive action, the prohibition against allowing anyone "to be a judge in his own cause," the peculiarity inherent in concluding that Congress has "assigned to the federal court only rubber-stamp work," and the "sound general rule that Congress is deemed to avoid redundant drafting," point in the other direction. The highly unusual confluence of those principles in this case persuades me that, despite the fact that the dissent's reading has the virtue of avoiding the possibility that a difficult constitutional question will arise in a future case, reversal is nonetheless the proper course.

■ JUSTICE SOUTER, with whom THE CHIEF JUSTICE, JUSTICE SCALIA and JUSTICE THOMAS join, dissenting.

One does not instinctively except to a statutory construction that opens the door of judicial review to an individual who complains of a decision of the Attorney General, when the Attorney General herself is ready to open the door. But however much the Court and the Attorney General may claim their reading of the Westfall Act to be within the bounds of reasonable policy, the great weight of interpretive evidence shows that they misread Congress's policy. And so I respectfully dissent.

The two principal textual statements under examination today are perfectly straightforward. "Upon certification by the Attorney General . . . any civil action or proceeding . . . shall be deemed an action against the United States . . . and the United States shall be substituted as the party defendant." 28 U.S.C. § 2679(d)(1). Notwithstanding the Court's observation that some contexts can leave the word "shall" a bit slippery, we have repeatedly recognized the normally uncompromising directive that it carries. There is no hint of wobbling in the quoted language, and the normal meaning of its plain provisions that substitution is mandatory on certification is the best evidence of the congressional intent that the Court finds elusive. That normal meaning and manifest intent is confirmed by additional textual evidence and by its consonance with normal jurisdictional assumptions.

We would not, of course, read "shall" as so uncompromising if the Act also included some express provision for review at the behest of the tort plaintiff when the Attorney General certifies that the acts charged were inside the scope of a defendant employee's official duties. But the Westfall Act has no provision to that effect, and the very fact that its predecessor, the Federal Drivers Act, combined "shall" with just such authorization for review at the will of a disappointed tort plaintiff, makes the absence of a like provision from the Westfall Act especially good evidence that Congress meant to drop this feature from the system, leaving "shall" to carry its usual unconditional message. That conclusion gains further force from the presence in the Westfall Act of an express provision for judicial review at the behest of a defending employee, when the Attorney General refuses to certify that the acts fell within the scope of government employment. Providing authority in one circumstance but not another implies an absence of authority in the statute's silence.

Even if these textually grounded implications were not enough to confirm a plain reading of the text and decide the case, an anomalous jurisdictional consequence of the Court's position should be enough to warn us away from treating the Attorney General's certification as reviewable. The Court recognizes that there is nothing equivocal about the Act's provision that once a state tort action has been removed to a federal court after a certification by the Attorney General, it may never be remanded to the state system: "certification of the Attorney General shall conclusively establish scope of office or employment for purposes of removal," 28 U.S.C. § 2679(d)(2). As the Court concedes, its reading supposes that Congress intended federal courts to retain jurisdiction over state-law tort claims between nondiverse parties even after determining that the Attorney General's certification (and thus the United States's presence as the defendant) was improper. But there is a serious problem, on the Court's reasoning, in requiring a federal district court, after rejecting the Attorney General's certification, to retain jurisdiction over a claim that does not implicate federal law in any way. Although we have declined recent invitations to define the outermost limit of federal court jurisdiction authorized by the "Arising Under" Clause of Article III of the Constitution, on the Court's reading this statute must at the very least approach the limit, if it does not cross the line. This, then, is just the case for adhering to the Court's practice of declining to construe a statute as testing this limit when presented with a sound alternative.

The Court departs from this practice, however. Instead, it looks for jurisdictional solace in the theory that once the Attorney General has issued a scope-of-employment certification, the United States's (temporary) appearance as the sole defendant suffices forever to support jurisdiction in federal court, even if the district court later rejects the Attorney General's certification and resubstitutes as defendant the federal employee first sued in state court. Whether the employee was within the scope of his federal employment, the Court reasons, is itself a sufficient federal question to bring the case into federal court, and " 'considerations of judicial economy, convenience and fairness to litigate,' " quoting *Mine Workers v. Gibbs*, 383 U.S. 715, 726 (1966), are sufficient to keep it there even after a judicial determination that the United States is not the proper defendant.

But the fallacy of this conclusion appears as soon as one recalls the fact that substitution of the United States as defendant (which establishes federal-question jurisdiction) is exclusively dependant on the scope-of-employment certification. The challenge to the certification is thus the equivalent of a challenge to the essential jurisdictional fact that the United States is a party, and the federal court's jurisdiction to review scope of employment (on the Court's theory) is merely an example of any court's necessary authority to rule on a challenge to its own jurisdiction to try a particular action. To argue, as the Court does, that authority to determine scope of employment justifies retention of jurisdiction whenever evidence bearing on jurisdiction and liability overlaps, is therefore tantamount to saying the authority to determine whether a Court has jurisdiction over the cause of action supplies the very jurisdiction that is subject to challenge. It simply obliterates the distinction between the authority to determine jurisdiction and the jurisdiction that is the subject of the challenge, and the party whose jurisdictional claim was challenged will never lose: litigating the question whether an employee's allegedly tortious acts fall within the scope of employment will, of course, always require some evidence to show what the acts were. * * *

It would never be sound to attribute such an aberrant concept of federal question jurisdiction to Congress; it is impossible to do so when we realize that Congress expressly provided that when a federal court considers a challenge to the Attorney General's refusal to certify (raised by an employee-defendant) and finds the act outside the scope of employment, a case that originated in a state court must be remanded back to the state court. See 28 U.S.C. § 2679(d)(3). In such a case, there will have been just as much overlap of jurisdictional evidence and liability evidence as there will be when the jurisdictional issue is litigated at the behest of a plaintiff (as here) who contests a scope-of-employment certification. If Congress thought the federal court should retain jurisdiction when it is revealed that none exists in this latter case, it should have thought so in the former. But it did not, and the reason it did not is obvious beyond any doubt. It assumed a federal court would never be in the position to retain jurisdiction over an action for which a tort plaintiff has shown there is no federal-question basis, and Congress was entitled to assume this, because it had provided that a certification was conclusive.

In sum, the congressional decision to make the Attorney General's certification conclusive was couched in plain terms, whose plain meaning is confirmed by contrasting the absence of any provision for review with just such a provision in the predecessor statute, and with an express provision for review of a refusal to certify, contained in the Westfall Act itself. The Court's contrary view implies a jurisdictional tenacity that Congress expressly declined to assert elsewhere in the Act, and invites a difficult and wholly unnecessary constitutional adjudication about the limits of Article III jurisdiction. These are powerful reasons to recognize the unreviewability of certification, and the Court's contrary arguments fail to measure up to them.

The Court raises three counterpoints to a straightforward reading of the Act. First, it suggests that language in § 2679(d)(2) negatively implies that Congress intended to authorize judicial review of scope-of-employment certifications, and that, in fact, the straightforward reading of the statute results in a drafting redundancy. Second, the Court claims that the straightforward reading creates an oddity by limiting the role of federal courts in certain cases. Finally, the Court invokes the presumption against judging one's self.

The redundancy argument, it must be said, is facially plausible. It begins with the sound general rule that Congress is deemed to avoid redundant drafting, from which it follows that a statutory interpretation that would render an express provision redundant was probably unintended and should be rejected. Applying that rule here, the argument is that if certification by the Attorney General conclusively establishes scope of employment for substitution purposes, then there is no need for the final sentence in § 2679(d)(2), that certification "shall conclusively establish scope of office or employment for purposes of removal" in cases brought against federal employees in state court. If certification is conclusive as to substitution it will be equally conclusive as to removal, since the federal defendant will necessarily be entitled to claim jurisdiction of a federal court under 28 U.S.C. § 1346(b). Accordingly, the Court suggests the provision making certification conclusive for purposes of removal must have greater meaning; it must carry the negative implication that certification is not conclusive for purposes of substitution.

Sometimes, however, there is an explanation for redundancy, rendering any asserted inference from it too shaky to be trusted. That is the case with the provision that certification is conclusive on the issue of removal from state to federal court. The explanation takes us back to the Westfall Act's predecessor, the Federal Drivers Act, which was superseded upon passage of the current statute. The Drivers Act made the FTCA the exclusive source of remedies for injuries resulting from the operation of any motor vehicle by a federal employee acting within the scope of his employment. Like the Westfall Act, the Drivers Act authorized the Attorney General to certify that a federal employee sued in state court was acting within the scope of employment during the incident allegedly giving rise to the claim, and it provided in that event for removal to the federal system, as well as for substitution of the United States as the defendant. Unlike the Westfall Act, however, the Drivers Act explicitly directed district courts to review, "on a motion to remand held before a trial on the merits," whether any such case was "one in which a remedy by suit ... is not available against the United States." The district courts and the courts of appeals routinely read this language to permit district courts to hear motions to remand challenging the Attorney General's scope-of-employment determination. Given the express permissibility of a motion to remand in order to raise a post-removal challenge to certification under the Drivers Act, when the old Act was superseded, and challenges to certification were eliminated, Congress could sensibly have seen some practical value in the redundancy of making it clear beyond question that the old practice of considering scope of employment on motions to remand was over.

How then does one assess the force of the redundancy? On my plain reading of the statute, one may take it as an understandable inelegance of drafting. One could, in the alternative, take it as some confirmation for the Court's view, even though the Court's view brings with it both a jurisdictional anomaly and the consequent certainty of a serious constitutional question. Is it not more likely that Congress would have indulged in a little redundancy, than have meant to foist such a pointless need for constitutional litigation onto the federal courts? Given the choice, inelegance may be forgiven.

The Court's second counterpoint is that we should be reluctant to read the Westfall Act in a way that leaves a district court without any real work to do. The Court suggests that my reading does just that in cases like this one, because the district court's sole function after the Attorney General has issued a scope-of-employment certification is to enter an order of dismissal. Of course, in the bulk of cases with an Attorney General's certification, the sequence envisioned by the Court will never materialize. Even though a district court may not review the scope-of-employment determination, it will still have plenty of work to do in the likely event that either liability or amount of damages is disputed, or the United States's claim to immunity under 28 U.S.C. § 2680 turns on disputed facts. Only in those rare cases presenting a claim to federal immunity too air-tight for the plaintiff to challenge will the circumstance identified by the Court even occur. It is hard to find any significance in the fact that now and then a certification will relieve a federal court of further work, given the straight-forward and amply confirmed provision for conclusiveness.

The Court's final counterpoint to plain reading relies heavily on "the strong presumption that Congress intends judicial review of administrative action," citing a line of cases involving judicial challenges to regulations claimed to be outside the statutory authority of the administrative agencies that promulgated them. It is, however, a fair question whether this presumption, usually applied to permit review of agency regulations carrying the force and effect of law, should apply with equal force to a Westfall Act certification. The very narrow factual determination committed to the Attorney General's discretion is related only tangentially, if at all, to her primary executive duties; she determines only whether a federal employee, who will probably not even be affiliated with the Justice Department, acted within the scope of his employment on a particular occasion. * * *

The Court's answer that the presumption of reviewability should control this case rests on the invocation of a different, but powerful principle, that no person may be a judge in his own cause. But this principle is not apt here. The Attorney General (who has delegated her Westfall Act responsibilities to the United States Attorneys, 28 CFR § 15.3(a)) is authorized to determine when any one of nearly three million federal employees was acting within the scope of authority at an allegedly tortious moment. She will characteristically have no perceptible interest in the effect of her certification decision, except in the work it may visit on her employees or the liability it may ultimately place on the National Government (each of which considerations could only influence her to deny certification subject to the employee's right to challenge her). And even where she certifies under circumstances of the Government's immunity, as here, she does not save her employer, the United States, from any liability it would face in the absence of certification; if she refused to certify, the Government would remain as free of exposure as if she issued a certification. The most that can be claimed is that when the Government would enjoy immunity it would be easy to do a favor for a federal employee by issuing a certification. But at this point the possibility of institutional self interest has simply become *de minimis,* and the likelihood of improper influence has become too attenuated to analogize to the case in which the interested party would protect himself by judging his own cause or otherwise take the law into his own hands in disregard of established legal process. Although the Court quotes at length from the traditional condemnations of self-interested judgments, its citations would be on point here only if the employee were issuing the certification. But of course, the employee is not the one who does it, and the Attorney General plainly lacks the kind of self-interest that " 'would certainly bias [her] judgment, and, not improbably, corrupt [her] integrity....'" Quoting The Federalist No. 10, p. 79 (C. Rossiter ed. 1961) (J. Madison).

In any event, even when this presumption is applicable, it is still no more than a presumption, to be given controlling effect only if reference to "specific language or specific legislative history" and "inferences of intent drawn from the statutory scheme as a whole," *Block v. Community Nutrition Institute,* 467 U.S. 340, 349 (1984), leave the Court with "substantial doubt" as to Congress's design, *id.,* at 351. There is no substantial doubt here. The presumption has no work to do.

I would affirm.

———

Notes and Questions

1. In studying the decision in *Gutierrez de Martinez v. Lamagno,* review first the statute itself, 28 U.S.C. § 2679(b)–(e), as set out in these materials and establish a firm understanding of the basics of the Westfall Act and its significance for lawsuits framed against individual government officers. In response to the Supreme Court's decision in *Westfall v. Erwin,* which we read earlier, Congress enacted this statute—commonly known as the Westfall Act—that generally grants immunity from suit to federal government employees acting within the scope of employment, by requiring that the United States be substituted as the sole defendant. In sum, the Westfall Act converts a lawsuit for money damages against a federal employee into a suit under the Federal Tort Claims Act (FTCA) against the United States. Moreover, if such a suit is filed in state court, it will be removed to federal district court. Thus, the Westfall Act eliminates ordinary common-law suits against federal employees when acting within the scope of employment, but does provide the plaintiff with a substitute defendant (the United States) against whom to maintain the action.

However, as Professors Kenneth Culp Davis and Richard Pierce pointed out in an earlier edition of the administrative law treatise, the Westfall Act's transfer of liability from the individual government employee to the government "is seriously incomplete because federal employees remain potentially liable for constitutional torts, and victims of some intentional torts continue to have no remedy against the government." 3 Kenneth C. Davis & Richard J. Pierce, Jr., *Administrative Law Treatise* § 19.3, at 227 (3d ed. 1994).

First, as addressed next in Chapter V.B, the Supreme Court under certain circumstances has implied private actions against federal employees for money damages for violations of constitutional rights. The Westfall Act expressly excludes civil actions against government employees "brought for a violation of the Constitution of the United States." 28 U.S.C. § 2679(b)(2)(A). Thus, such suits would continue to proceed under pre-existing caselaw, as we shall survey in the next subsection of this casebook.

Second, as Justice Ginsburg observes in the very first paragraph of the *Gutierrez de Martinez* decision, although the Westfall Act substitutes the United States as the defendant, "[i]f * * * an exception to the FTCA shields the United States from suit, the plaintiff may be left without a tort action against any party." In the comment quoted above, Professors Davis and Pierce were referring to the intentional tort exception to the FTCA. Other exceptions might bar such suits as well. See Chapter III.A.4 to 7 (discussing exceptions to the FTCA). Indeed, the *Gutierrez de Martinez* case illustrates this consequence in potential operation. If the suit is reformulated as against the United States, what exception to the FTCA precludes recovery by the plaintiff in this case?

2. In *Barr v. Matteo,* 360 U.S. 564 (1959), which we read in the previous subset of case materials, one of the issues was whether a government official was acting within the line of duty when issuing an allegedly libelous press release. (Compare the majority opinion and Justice Stewart's dissent in *Barr v. Matteo.*) The same issue arises and is indeed central to the application of the Westfall Act. The statute immunizes the individual employee and substitutes the United States as a defendant only when the employee committed the negligent or wrongful act or omission "while acting within the scope of his office or employment." 28 U.S.C. § 2679(b)(1). However, while the issue of scope of duty is not new, the Westfall Act introduces a new procedural question: *Who decides* whether the employee was acting within the scope of employment? Who makes the initial decision and is that decision reviewable by anyone else?

The Westfall Act provides for certification by the Attorney General (or her delegate, usually a United States Attorney) "that the defendant employee was acting within the scope of his office or employment at the time of the incident out of which the claim arose." 28 U.S.C. § 2679(d)(1).* This certification has two consequences: First, upon certification by the Attorney General, any suit filed in state court may be removed to federal district court. The statute expressly provides that the Attorney General's certification is conclusive (that is, may not be reviewed in court) for purposes of removal.

Second, as the central point of the Westfall Act, the Attorney General's certification has the effect of dropping the employee from the lawsuit and converting it into an FTCA suit against the federal government. In many circumstances, the plaintiff's claim will simply go forward on the issue of liability against a new defendant. As Justice Ginsburg says in *Gutierrez de Martinez,* "[w]hile the certification relieves the employee of responsibility, plaintiffs will confront a financially reliable defendant." However, if the

---

* If the Attorney General refuses to certify that the employee was acting within the scope of employment (which thus leaves the suit pending against the individual employee), the Westfall Act allows the employee to petition the court to find that he or she was acting within the scope of employment. 28 U.S.C. § 2679(d)(3). The case may be removed to federal court to decide this certification question. *Id.* If the federal court grants the employee's petition for certification, the employee will then be dismissed from the suit and it will proceed in federal court against the United States under the FTCA. *See id.*

plaintiff faces the insurmountable obstacle of an exception to the FTCA that immunizes the United States from liability, the plaintiff would be left without a remedy against any defendant. In such a case, the plaintiff understandably would wish to challenge the Attorney General's certification, and instead contend that the employee was *not* acting within the scope of employment and should remain as the defendant to the suit.

Thus, the question arises: Is the Attorney General's certification on the scope of employment issue (for purposes of substituting the United States as the sole defendant) conclusive or instead is it subject to court review? That is the question before the Supreme Court in *Gutierrez de Martinez*. In deciding the question, the majority and dissenting opinions (1) consider the proper framework within which to approach this statutory interpretation question, (2) give close and careful attention to the text of the Westfall Act, and (3) address potential constitutional concerns raised by the alternative interpretations. As has been emphasized repeatedly in this casebook, a course in Litigation With the Federal Government is largely a study in statutory interpretation. A student and future practitioner in this area, or in any complex area of federal statutory or administrative law, must develop the ability to fully appreciate, and engage in discussion and debate about, the precision type of statutory interpretation issue raised in *Gutierrez de Martinez*.

As confirmed by the sharp division among the justices (five-to-four), this is a close question of statutory interpretation. Compare the majority and dissenting opinions. With what general rules or canons of statutory interpretation do the contrasting opinions approach the question? Justice Ginsburg's majority opinion addresses these considerations at length before turning in detail to the statutory text, while Justice Souter's dissent begins almost immediately with the language of the statute. Why? What does that reveal about the premises or presumptions with which each justice begins?

With respect to the text of the statute, what specific language in the Westfall Act is deemed most important by Justice Ginsburg for the majority? And by Justice Souter for the dissent? Indeed, what word is thought most important by the dissent in answering the question of reviewability of the Attorney General's certification? How does the majority respond to that point? How does each opinion view the statutory provision for Attorney General certification to substitute the United States as defendant within the larger context of the statute and surrounding provisions? Why do the majority and dissent reach different conclusions based on the plain language of the statute?

What about concerns of policy or fairness (or due process)? *Should* the Attorney General be permitted to make a conclusive and unreviewable determination of whether an employee was acting within the scope of employment? Does she have a conflict of interest in such cases? Is it a significant conflict?

3. Depending upon how one answers the question of whether the Attorney General's certification is reviewable, the justices reviewing *Gutierrez de Martinez* recognize that a constitutional question about permissible

federal court jurisdiction may be raised. What exactly is that issue? What happens if the Attorney General's certification is deemed conclusive for purposes of removing a case from state to federal court, but is held reviewable (and thereby potentially reversible) for purposes of determining whether to substitute the United States as defendant in the lawsuit and dismiss the individual employee from the suit? To fully appreciate the problem, consider the following scenario: Suppose the reviewing federal court overturns the Attorney General's certification on the substitution question, thereby reinstating the individual employee as the proper defendant and dismissing the United States as a party to the suit. In that event, the case would then, once again, be a simple state-law tort case. If there is no diversity of citizenship between the plaintiff and the defendant employee, may the case remain in federal court as a matter of jurisdiction under Article III of the Constitution? Without the United States as a continuing party (after reversal of the Attorney General's certification), is there a federal question allowing federal court jurisdiction? (Review the basic principles of federal subject matter jurisdiction from your first-year Civil Procedure course.) And yet doesn't the Westfall Act plainly state that the Attorney General's certification is conclusive for purposes of removal to federal court? Could that mean that this part of the Westfall Act is unconstitutional?

How does Justice Souter's dissent in *Gutierrez de Martinez* view this constitutional dilemma? How does the emergence of this jurisdictional issue influence the dissent's analysis of the reviewability of the certification? Why? And how does Justice Ginsburg for the majority respond? (Note that Justice Ginsburg speaks for only four justices on the Article III question, as Justice O'Connor in concurrence noted that the issue was not plainly raised in *Gutierrez de Martinez* because there was diversity of citizenship between the parties and thus wished to reserve disposition of this question for a future case that more squarely presents it.)

After *Gutierrez de Martinez,* the courts of appeals were divided on the question of whether a case could be retained in federal court when the Attorney General's certification is reversed or instead should be remanded to state court as a tort action against the individual defendant. *Compare Garcia v. United States,* 88 F.3d 318, 324 (5th Cir. 1996) (holding that the case could not be remanded to state court under the Westfall Act, notwithstanding reversal of the Attorney General's scope of employment certification, and adopting the analysis of Justice Ginsburg's plurality opinion in *Gutierrez de Martinez* on the constitutionality question), and *Borneman v. United States,* 213 F.3d 819, 826–29 & n.2 (4th Cir. 2000) (holding that federal court may not remand to state court even if the scope of employment certification is erroneous and stating that "federal jurisdiction is based on the fact that at the time of removal, a federal employee ostensibly in the scope of his employment with the United States was a party"), *with Haddon v. United States,* 68 F.3d 1420, 1426–27 (D.C. Cir. 1995) (holding that the case must be remanded to state court after reversal of the Attorney General's certification under the Westfall Act to avoid a serious constitutional question, citing Justice Souter's dissent in *Gutierrez de Martinez*).

In *Osborn v. Haley*, ___ U.S. ___, 127 S.Ct. 881 (2007), the Supreme Court resolved this question in a case where, if the certification were reversed and the United States was removed from the case, the parties were not of diverse citizenship and no federal law was at issue. The Court held that "on the jurisdictional issues, we hold that the Attorney General's certification is conclusive for purposes of removal, *i.e.*, once certification and removal are effected, exclusive competence to adjudicate the case resides in the federal court, and that court may not remand the suit to the state court." *Id.* at 888–89. In sum, for "purposes of establishing a forum to adjudicate the case," Section 2679(d)(2) makes the Attorney General's certification conclusive and dispositive. *Id.* at 894. Nor does this retention of jurisdiction to adjudicate the merits of the tort suit between the two private parties exceed the constitutional boundaries of federal jurisdiction. The Court explained that "[b]ecause a significant federal question (whether [the individual defendant] has Westfall Act immunity) would have been raised at the outset, the case would 'aris[e] under' federal law, as that term is used in Article III." *Id.* at 896.

4.   Under *Gutierrez de Martinez,* the Attorney General's certification of the scope of employment is reviewable in court. By what rule of law? As with the determination of scope of employment under the Federal Tort Claims Act for purposes of alleging respondeat superior liability by the United States (see Chapter III.A.3.d), state law provides the general principles for determining whether the employee acted within the scope of the federal office or position. The First Circuit has explained:

> Federal law determines whether a person is a federal employee and defines the nature and contours of his official responsibilities; but the law of the state in which the tortious act allegedly occurred determines whether the employee was acting within the scope of those responsibilities.

Lyons v. Brown, 158 F.3d 605, 609 (1st Cir. 1998); *see also Gutierrez de Martinez v. Drug Enforcement Admin.,* 111 F.3d 1148, 1156 (4th Cir. 1997) (on remand from Supreme Court); *RMI Titanium Co. v. Westinghouse Elec. Co.,* 78 F.3d 1125, 1143 (6th Cir. 1996).

While the question of whether the employee's conduct in a particular case was within the scope of his or her federal duties may be largely a factual one, state legal precedent may establish a framework for evaluating a set of facts, such as presumptions based upon certain factors or the weight to be given to the presence of a particular fact or element. Thus, state law may be important on such questions as the importance of the act taking place on the employment premises, *e.g., McLachlan v. Bell,* 261 F.3d 908, 911–12 (9th Cir. 2001) (applying California law to determine that federal employees acted within scope of employment when engaging in harassing conduct where the entire affair took place at work, in ways relating to work, and on issues arising out of work); whether conduct occurring after hours at a remote or recreational site falls within the scope of employment, *e.g., Snodgrass v. Jones,* 957 F.2d 482, 485 (7th Cir. 1992) (holding that, under Illinois law, a federal employee could not be determined to have been acting in scope of his employment while "hanging out" at a bar, simply because part of his duty was to act as liaison with other law enforcement agencies and he was talking with a former FBI agent); or the significance of whether the employee was acting with a private purpose or with an intent to serve employer's interest, *e.g., Davric Maine Corp. v. U.S. Postal Service,* 238 F.3d 58, 66–67 (1st Cir. 2001) (holding that, under Maine law, seemingly work-related acts taken by federal employee would fall outside of scope of employment if done with a private purpose, but would be within scope of employment if done in good faith to serve the employer's interest, even if the federal employee's judgment was mistaken); *Maron v. United States,* 126 F.3d 317, 326–27 (4th Cir. 1997) (under Maryland law, acts of harassment were done within scope of employment if the employee was motivated at least partially by the desire to perform duties properly even if the employee also had personal and improper motives).

State legal standards regarding the scope of employment have evolved in the course of determining when the employer is appropriately held responsible under the respondeat superior doctrine for the wrongdoing of an employee. Accordingly, over time, state law rules have tended to broaden the scope of employment concept so as to expand employer accountability to others for the misdeeds of employees. Ironically—or some might say, perversely—application of these state law expectations to the peculiar Westfall Act context occasionally may have precisely the opposite effect. If the federal employee is found to have acted within the scope of employment, he or she individually will be immune from liability. And if the federal government, as the substituted sole defendant, successfully invokes an exception to FTCA liability, it too will enjoy immunity from liability. Thus, rather than expanding tort liability and enhancing the opportunity for plaintiffs to sue a financially responsible defendant—as generally was the intent behind state court decisions broadening the reach of respondeat superior in recent decades—application of liberal state scope-of-employment rules sometimes may operate to narrow tort liability in the federal employee/federal government context. Of course, in the typical case involving garden-variety negligence occurring inside the nation's borders, substituting the United States as the defendant under the FTCA leaves the plaintiff with a legally-amenable and financially-responsible defendant comfortably in place.

5. Under the Westfall Act, "the limitations and exceptions of the FTCA apply to an action after the United States substitutes itself for the individual defendants," including the requirement that an administrative claim be filed and the FTCA lawsuit be filed within six months of denial of the administrative claim. *Roman v. Townsend,* 224 F.3d 24, 28 (1st Cir. 2000) (holding that "transformation" of lawsuit into one against the federal government does not "excuse" compliance with requirements of the FTCA); *see also Singleton v. United States,* 277 F.3d 864, 872–73 (6th Cir. 2002) (upholding substitution of United States as defendant in tort suit

against federal employee and then affirming dismissal of plaintiff's lawsuit for failure to have presented an administrative claim to the agency under the FTCA). Still, "Congress recognized that plaintiffs might suppose their claims to be against an individual government employee (as indeed they would still be if the employee had not been acting within the scope of his employment), and thus might fail to timely present their claims to the agency, so it fashioned special rules to account for the possibility." *Mittleman v. United States*, 104 F.3d 410, 412 (D.C. Cir. 1997). Accordingly, pursuant to a savings clause codified at 28 U.S.C. § 2679(d)(5), Congress provided that if the United States is substituted as the party defendant and the action is dismissed for failure to present an administrative claim under the FTCA, the plaintiff may then file an administrative claim, which will be deemed timely filed if (1) the administrative claim "would have been timely had it been filed on the date the underlying civil action was commenced," that is, if the underlying lawsuit against the government employee was filed within two years of the accrual of the tort cause of action, and (2) "the claim is presented to the appropriate Federal agency within 60 days after dismissal of the civil action."

6. Finally, to follow the story through to its conclusion, the lower courts on remand in *Gutierrez de Martinez* upheld the scope-of-employment certification, dismissed Kirk Lamagno from the action, substituted the United States as the defendant, and dismissed the suit based upon the foreign country exception to the Federal Tort Claims Act. *Gutierrez de Martinez v. Drug Enforcement Admin.*, 111 F.3d 1148 (4th Cir. 1997), *cert. denied*, 522 U.S. 931 (1997). As the Fourth Circuit explained, the undisputed facts were that "Lamagno had a female passenger; that the restaurant was only two blocks from the hotel where Lamagno was staying; that the accident occurred more than 20 blocks from either the hotel or the restaurant; that at the time of the accident, Lamagno was driving in the opposite direction from the hotel; and that Lamagno had been drinking." *Id.* at 1151. However, the government offered an explanation of these facts consistent with the certification. Contrary to the plaintiffs' allegation, which was recited in the Supreme Court's opinion, Lamagno's female passenger *was* a federal employee, an analyst with the Drug Enforcement Administration. Lamagno claimed that, pursuant to DEA policy that female agents not travel alone after dark due to a high crime rate in that Colombian city, he had been assigned to drive her to the hotel, but that they had become lost in the streets of the city due to his unfamiliarity with the area. He acknowledged that he had been drinking, but denied that he was intoxicated. *Id.* Holding that the burden of proof is upon a plaintiff challenging the Attorney General's certification, the district court found and the court of appeals affirmed that the plaintiffs had failed to meet their burden of coming forward with specific evidence, beyond mere speculation, that contradicted the government's explanation. *Id.* at 1153–56. The courts concluded that, applying Virginia law, these events did not fall outside of the scope of employment. *Id.* at 1156–58.

2. CONSTITUTIONAL CLAIMS

a. CAUSE OF ACTION FOR CONSTITUTIONAL CLAIMS

That individuals would bring common-law suits for ordinary torts against individuals who happened to be government employees, even when those employees were acting within the scope of their government duties, was inevitable and unremarkable. Indeed, as we saw in Chapter II.A, such actions have been attempted since the early days of the Republic. With respect to ordinary tort suits, the common law already supplied the cause of action; the only issue has been whether the defendant's status as a federal employee afforded a degree of immunity. In the previous set of materials, we examined common-law actions against government officers or employees, including the issue of absolute or qualified privilege, the determination of scope of duty for immunity purposes, and, ultimately, the legislative determination of these questions through the Westfall Act.

However, it was *not* inevitable that an employee's violation of a constitutional provision would be recognized as the equivalent of a tort that gives rise to a private remedy in court for damages against the individual employee. Indeed, the Constitution does not expressly speak to the availability of a private cause of action for those suffering an infringement of constitutional rights, and further does not indicate that individual officers, rather than the government itself, bear personal responsibility at the risk of private liability for upholding constitutional standards. Not until some 180 years after ratification of the United States Constitution did the Supreme Court first recognize a private judicial action against a federal government employee premised upon a constitutional transgression.

Bivens v. Six Unknown Named Agents of Federal Bureau of Narcotics

Supreme Court of the United States.
403 U.S. 388 (1971).

■ MR. JUSTICE BRENNAN delivered the opinion of the Court.

The Fourth Amendment provides that:

"The right of the people to be secure in their persons, houses, papers, and effects, against unreasonable searches and seizures, shall not be violated...."

In *Bell v. Hood,* 327 U.S. 678 (1946), we reserved the question whether violation of that command by a federal agent acting under color of his authority gives rise to a cause of action for damages consequent upon his unconstitutional conduct. Today we hold that it does.

This case has its origin in an arrest and search carried out on the morning of November 26, 1965. Petitioner's complaint alleged that on that day respondents, agents of the Federal Bureau of Narcotics acting under claim of federal authority, entered his apartment and arrested him for alleged narcotics violations. The agents manacled petitioner in front of his wife and children, and threatened to arrest the entire family. They searched the apartment from stem to stern. Thereafter, petitioner was taken to the federal courthouse in Brooklyn, where he was interrogated, booked, and subjected to a visual strip search.

On July 7, 1967, petitioner brought suit in Federal District Court. In addition to the allegations above, his complaint asserted that the arrest and search were effected without a warrant, and that unreasonable force was employed in making the arrest; fairly read, it alleges as well that the arrest was made without probable cause. Petitioner claimed to have suffered great humiliation, embarrassment, and mental suffering as a result of the agents' unlawful conduct, and sought $15,000 damages from each of them. The District Court, on respondents' motion, dismissed the complaint on the ground, *inter alia,* that it failed to state a cause of action.[2] 276 F.Supp. 12 (E.D.N.Y.1967). The Court of Appeals, one judge concurring specially, affirmed on that basis. 409 F.2d 718 (C.A.2 1969). We granted certiorari. We reverse.

I

Respondents do not argue that petitioner should be entirely without remedy for an unconstitutional invasion of his rights by federal agents. In respondents' view, however, the rights that petitioner asserts—primarily rights of privacy—are creations of state and not of federal law. Accordingly, they argue, petitioner may obtain money damages to redress invasion of these rights only by an action in tort, under state law, in the state courts. In this scheme the Fourth Amendment would serve merely to limit the extent to which the agents could defend the state law tort suit by asserting that their actions were a valid exercise of federal power: if the agents were shown to have violated the Fourth Amendment, such a defense would be lost to them and they would stand before the state law merely as private individuals. * * *

We think that respondents' thesis rests upon an unduly restrictive view of the Fourth Amendment's protection against unreasonable searches and seizures by federal agents, a view that has consistently been rejected by this Court. Respondents seek to treat the relationship between a citizen and a federal agent unconstitutionally exercising his authority as no different from the relationship between two private citizens. In so doing, they ignore the fact that power, once granted, does not disappear like a magic gift when it is wrongfully used. An agent acting—albeit unconstitutionally—in the name of the United States possesses a far greater capacity for harm than an individual trespasser exercising no authority other than his own. Accordingly, as our cases make clear, the Fourth Amendment operates as a limitation upon the exercise of federal power regardless of whether the State in whose jurisdiction that power is exercised would

---

2. The agents were not named in petitioner's complaint, and the District Court ordered that the complaint be served upon "those federal agents who it is indicated by the records of the United States Attorney participated in the November 25, 1965, arrest of the (petitioner)." Five agents were ultimately served.

prohibit or penalize the identical act if engaged in by a private citizen. It guarantees to citizens of the United States the absolute right to be free from unreasonable searches and seizures carried out by virtue of federal authority. And "where federally protected rights have been invaded, it has been the rule from the beginning that courts will be alert to adjust their remedies so as to grant the necessary relief." *Bell v. Hood,* 327 U.S., at 684 (footnote omitted).

First. Our cases have long since rejected the notion that the Fourth Amendment proscribes only such conduct as would, if engaged in by private persons, be condemned by state law. * * *

Second. The interests protected by state laws regulating trespass and the invasion of privacy, and those protected by the Fourth Amendment's guarantee against unreasonable searches and seizures, may be inconsistent or even hostile. Thus, we may bar the door against an unwelcome private intruder, or call the police if he persists in seeking entrance. The availability of such alternative means for the protection of privacy may lead the State to restrict imposition of liability for any consequent trespass. A private citizen, asserting no authority other than his own, will not normally be liable in trespass if he demands, and is granted, admission to another's house. But one who demands admission under a claim of federal authority stands in a far different position. The mere invocation of federal power by a federal law enforcement official will normally render futile any attempt to resist an unlawful entry or arrest by resort to the local police; and a claim of authority to enter is likely to unlock the door as well. * * *

Third. That damages may be obtained for injuries consequent upon a violation of the Fourth Amendment by federal officials should hardly seem a surprising proposition. Historically, damages have been regarded as the ordinary remedy for an invasion of personal interests in liberty. Of course, the Fourth Amendment does not in so many words provide for its enforcement by an award of money damages for the consequences of its violation. But "it is ... well settled that where legal rights have been invaded, and a federal statute provides for a general right to sue for such invasion, federal courts may use any available remedy to make good the wrong done." *Bell v. Hood,* 327 U.S., at 684 (footnote omitted.) The present case involves no special factors counseling hesitation in the absence of affirmative action by Congress. * * * Finally, we cannot accept respondents' formulation of the question as whether the availability of money damages is necessary to enforce the Fourth Amendment. For we have here no explicit congressional declaration that persons injured by a federal officer's violation of the Fourth Amendment may not recover money damages from the agents, but must instead be remitted to another remedy, equally effective in the view of Congress. The question is merely whether petitioner, if he can demonstrate an injury consequent upon the violation by federal agents of his Fourth Amendment rights, is entitled to redress his injury through a particular remedial mechanism normally available in the federal courts. "The very essence of civil liberty certainly consists in the right of every individual to claim the protection of the laws, whenever he receives an injury." *Marbury* *v. Madison,* 1 Cranch 137, 163 (1803). Having concluded that petitioner's complaint states a cause of action under the Fourth Amendment, we hold that petitioner is entitled to recover money damages for any injuries he has suffered as a result of the agents' violation of the Amendment.

II

In addition to holding that petitioner's complaint had failed to state facts making out a cause of action, the District Court ruled that in any event respondents were immune from liability by virtue of their official position. 276 F.Supp., at 15. This question was not passed upon by the Court of Appeals, and accordingly we do not consider it here. The judgment of the Court of Appeals is reversed and the case is remanded for further proceedings consistent with this opinion.

So ordered.

■ Mr. JUSTICE HARLAN, concurring in the judgment.

My initial view of this case was that the Court of Appeals was correct in dismissing the complaint, but for reasons stated in this opinion I am now persuaded to the contrary. Accordingly, I join in the judgment of reversal. * * *

For the reasons set forth below, I am of the opinion that federal courts do have the power to award damages for violation of "constitutionally protected interests" and I agree with the Court that a traditional judicial remedy such as damages is appropriate to the vindication of the personal interests protected by the Fourth Amendment.

I

* * * [T]he interest which Bivens claims—to be free from official conduct in contravention of the Fourth Amendment—is a federally protected interest. Therefore, the question of judicial *power* to grant Bivens damages is not a problem of the "source" of the "right"; instead, the question is whether the power to authorize damages as a judicial remedy for the vindication of a federal constitutional right is placed by the Constitution itself exclusively in Congress' hands.

II

The contention that the federal courts are powerless to afford a litigant damages for a claimed invasion of his federal constitutional rights until Congress explicitly authorizes the remedy cannot rest on the notion that the decision to grant compensatory relief involves a resolution of policy considerations not susceptible of judicial discernment. * * *

More importantly, the presumed availability of federal equitable relief against threatened invasions of constitutional interests appears entirely to negate the contention that the status of an interest as constitutionally protected divests federal courts of the power to grant damages absent express congressional authorization. * * *

If explicit congressional authorization is an absolute prerequisite to the power of a federal court to accord compensatory relief regardless of the necessity or appropriateness of damages as a remedy simply because of the status of a legal interest as constitutionally protected, then it seems to me that explicit congressional authorization is similarly prerequisite to the exercise of equitable remedial discretion in favor of constitutionally protected interests. Conversely, if a general grant of jurisdiction to the federal courts by Congress is thought adequate to empower a federal court to grant equitable relief for all areas of subject-matter jurisdiction enumerated therein, see 28 U.S.C. § 1331(a), then it seems to me that the same statute is sufficient to empower a federal court to grant a traditional remedy at law. Of course, the special historical traditions governing the federal equity system might still bear on the comparative appropriateness of granting equitable relief as opposed to money damages. That possibility, however, relates, not to whether the federal courts have the power to afford one type of remedy as opposed to the other, but rather to the criteria which should govern the exercise of our power. To that question, I now pass.

III

The major thrust of the Government's position is that, where Congress has not expressly authorized a particular remedy, a federal court should exercise its power to accord a traditional form of judicial relief at the behest of a litigant, who claims a constitutionally protected interest has been invaded, only where the remedy is "essential," or "indispensable for vindicating constitutional rights." While this "essentially" test is most clearly articulated with respect to damage remedies, apparently the Government believes the same test explains the exercise of equitable remedial powers. It is argued that historically the Court has rarely exercised the power to accord such relief in the absence of an express congressional authorization and that "[i]f Congress had thought that federal officers should be subject to a law different than state law, it would have had no difficulty in saying so, as it did with respect to state officers...." Although conceding that the standard of determining whether a damage remedy should be utilized to effectuate statutory policies is one of "necessity" or "appropriateness," see *J. I. Case Co. v. Borak,* 377 U.S. 426, 432 (1964); *United States v. Standard Oil Co.,* 332 U.S. 301, 307 (1947), the Government contends that questions concerning congressional discretion to modify judicial remedies relating to constitutionally protected interests warrant a more stringent constraint on the exercise of judicial power with respect to this class of legally protected interests.

These arguments for a more stringent test to govern the grant of damages in constitutional cases[7] seem to be adequately answered by the point that the judiciary has a particular responsibility to assure the vindication of constitutional interests such as those embraced by the

---

7. I express no view on the Government's suggestion that congressional authority to simply discard the remedy the Court today authorizes might be in doubt; nor do I understand the Court's opinion today to express any view on that particular question.

Fourth Amendment. To be sure, "it must be remembered that legislatures are ultimate guardians of the liberties and welfare of the people in quite as great a degree as the courts." *Missouri, Kansas & Texas R. Co. of Texas v. May,* 194 U.S. 267, 270 (1904). But it must also be recognized that the Bill of Rights is particularly intended to vindicate the interests of the individual in the face of the popular will as expressed in legislative majorities; at the very least, it strikes me as no more appropriate to await express congressional authorization of traditional judicial relief with regard to these legal interests than with respect to interests protected by federal statutes.

The question then, is, as I see it, whether compensatory relief is "necessary" or "appropriate" to the vindication of the interest asserted. In resolving that question, it seems to me that the range of policy considerations we may take into account is at least as broad as the range of a legislature would consider with respect to an express statutory authorization of a traditional remedy. In this regard I agree with the Court that the appropriateness of according Bivens compensatory relief does not turn simply on the deterrent effect liability will have on federal official conduct. Damages as a traditional form of compensation for invasion of a legally protected interest may be entirely appropriate even if no substantial deterrent effects on future official lawlessness might be thought to result. Bivens, after all, has invoked judicial processes claiming entitlement to compensation for injuries resulting from allegedly lawless official behavior, if those injuries are properly compensable in money damages. I do not think a court of law—vested with the power to accord a remedy—should deny him his relief simply because he cannot show that future lawless conduct will thereby be deterred.

And I think it is clear that Bivens advances a claim of the sort that, if proved, would be properly compensable in damages. The personal interests protected by the Fourth Amendment are those we attempt to capture by the notion of "privacy"; while the Court today properly points out that the type of harm which officials can inflict when they invade protected zones of an individual's life are different from the types of harm private citizens inflict on one another, the experience of judges in dealing with private trespass and false imprisonment claims supports the conclusion that courts of law are capable of making the types of judgment concerning causation and magnitude of injury necessary to accord meaningful compensation for invasion of Fourth Amendment rights.[9]

On the other hand, the limitations on state remedies for violation of common-law rights by private citizens argue in favor of a federal damages remedy. The injuries inflicted by officials acting under color of law, while no less compensable in damages than those inflicted by private parties, are substantially different in kind, as the Court's opinion today discusses in detail. It seems to me entirely proper that these injuries be compensable according to uniform rules of federal law, especially in light of the very

---

9. The same, of course, may not be true with respect to other types of constitutionally protected interests, and therefore the appropriateness of money damages may well vary with the nature of the personal interest asserted.

large element of federal law which must in any event control the scope of official defenses to liability. Certainly, there is very little to be gained from the standpoint of federalism by preserving different rules of liability for federal officers dependent on the State where the injury occurs.

Putting aside the desirability of leaving the problem of federal official liability to the vagaries of common-law actions, it is apparent that some form of damages is the only possible remedy for someone in Bivens' alleged position. It will be a rare case indeed in which an individual in Bivens' position will be able to obviate the harm by securing injunctive relief from any court. However desirable a direct remedy against the Government might be as a substitute for individual official liability, the sovereign still remains immune to suit. Finally, assuming Bivens' innocence of the crime charged, the "exclusionary rule" is simply irrelevant. For people in Bivens' shoes, it is damages or nothing. * * *

For these reasons, I concur in the judgment of the Court.

■ MR. CHIEF JUSTICE BURGER, dissenting.

I dissent from today's holding which judicially creates a damage remedy not provided for by the Constitution and not enacted by Congress. We would more surely preserve the important values of the doctrine of separation of powers—and perhaps get a better result—by recommending a solution to the Congress as the branch of government in which the Constitution has vested the legislative power. Legislation is the business of the Congress, and it has the facilities and competence for that task—as we do not. * * *

■ MR. JUSTICE BLACK, dissenting.

In my opinion for the Court in *Bell v. Hood,* 327 U.S. 678 (1946), we did as the Court states, reserve the question whether an unreasonable search made by a federal officer in violation of the Fourth Amendment gives the subject of the search a federal cause of action for damages against the officers making the search. There can be no doubt that Congress could create a federal cause of action for damages for an unreasonable search in violation of the Fourth Amendment. Although Congress has created such a federal cause of action against *state* officials acting under color of state law, it has never created such a cause of action against federal officials. If it wanted to do so, Congress could, of course, create a remedy against federal officials who violate the Fourth Amendment in the performance of their duties. But the point of this case and the fatal weakness in the Court's judgment is that neither Congress nor the State of New York has enacted legislation creating such a right of action. For us to do so is, in my judgment, an exercise of power that the Constitution does not give us.

Even if we had the legislative power to create a remedy, there are many reasons why we should decline to create a cause of action where none has existed since the formation of our Government. The courts of the United States as well as those of the States are choked with lawsuits. * * *

We sit at the top of a judicial system accused by some of nearing the point of collapse. Many criminal defendants do not receive speedy trials and neither society nor the accused are assured of justice when inordinate delays occur. Citizens must wait years to litigate their private civil suits. Substantial changes in correctional and parole systems demand the attention of the lawmakers and the judiciary. If I were a legislator I might well find these and other needs so pressing as to make me believe that the resources of lawyers and judges should be devoted to them rather than to civil damage actions against officers who generally strive to perform within constitutional bounds. There is also a real danger that such suits might deter officials from the *proper* and honest performance of their duties.

All of these considerations make imperative careful study and weighing of the arguments both for and against the creation of such a remedy under the Fourth Amendment. I would have great difficulty for myself in resolving the competing policies, goals, and priorities in the use of resources, if I thought it were my job to resolve those questions. But that is not my task. The task of evaluating the pros and cons of creating judicial remedies for particular wrongs is a matter for Congress and the legislatures of the States. Congress has not provided that any federal court can entertain a suit against a federal officer for violations of Fourth Amendment rights occurring in the performance of his duties. A strong inference can be drawn from creation of such actions against state officials that Congress does not desire to permit such suits against federal officials. Should the time come when Congress desires such lawsuits, it has before it a model of valid legislation, 42 U.S.C. § 1983, to create a damage remedy against federal officers. Cases could be cited to support the legal proposition which I assert, but it seems to me to be a matter of common understanding that the business of the judiciary is to interpret the laws and not to make them.

I dissent.

■ MR. JUSTICE BLACKMUN, dissenting.

I, too, dissent. * * * [T]he judicial legislation, which the Court by its opinion today concededly is effectuating, opens the door for another avalanche of new federal cases. Whenever a suspect imagines, or chooses to assert, that a Fourth Amendment right has been violated, he will now immediately sue the federal officer in federal court. This will tend to stultify proper law enforcement and to make the day's labor for the honest and conscientious officer even more onerous and more critical. Why the Court moves in this direction at this time of our history, I do not know. The Fourth Amendment was adopted in 1791, and in all the intervening years neither the Congress nor the Court has seen fit to take this step. I had thought that for the truly aggrieved person other quite adequate remedies have always been available. If not, it is the Congress and not this Court that should act.

Notes and Questions

1.   Empowering a private individual who has suffered a constitutional deprivation at the hands of a government official to file a civil suit for

damages was not unprecedented, even before *Bivens v. Six Unknown Named Agents of the Federal Bureau of Narcotics.* Through a civil rights act passed by Congress after the Civil War, 42 U.S.C. § 1983, an individual who is deprived of federal rights, including constitutional guarantees, by a person acting under color of state law is entitled to recover damages from that person. However, Section 1983 by its express color-of-state-law provision is limited in application to state government officials and employees.

By contrast, recognition of a parallel right to recovery against a federal employee was accomplished by judicial implication in *Bivens.* Therein, of course, lies the controversy. Was this a proper exercise of judicial power or was it improper judicial legislation? Should the Supreme Court have created a private right of action based upon the Constitution? Is the Court or Congress better suited to create a damages remedy for a constitutional violation? On these questions, compare Justice Brennan's opinion for the majority, Justice Harlan's opinion concurring in the judgment, and the dissenting opinions of Chief Justice Burger, Justice Black, and Justice Blackmun. Who do you believe has the stronger argument on the validity of judicial creation of this right to a damage remedy and on the consequences of this new cause of action for both the courts and government administration?

What about an ordinary tort suit as an alternative remedy? Actions by federal officers or employees that violate the Constitution might often be characterized instead as ordinary torts, such as assault and battery, false arrest, or false imprisonment. Indeed, in *Bivens,* the defendant federal agents argued that the alleged constitutional violations would remain relevant even if plaintiffs were precluded from framing a suit directly upon the Constitution. If official conduct offends constitutional limitations, they acknowledged, the government officers would be precluded from defending the tort suit by arguing that their actions were a valid exercise of federal law enforcement power. But Justice Brennan finds the alternative of a state tort law suit inadequate. Why? Would every violation of a constitutional provision comfortably fit within the elements of a state tort cause of action? Is there a difference in the harm suffered by an unconstitutional exercise of official power from that occasioned by wrongful acts committed by a private individual?

2. As discussed earlier in Chapter V.B.1.b, the availability of a damages remedy for constitutional wrongdoing by individual government officers remains unaffected by the Westfall Act. In extending immunity from suit to government employees acting within the scope of employment, the Westfall Act expressly excludes civil actions against government employees "brought for a violation of the Constitution of the United States." 28 U.S.C. § 2679(b)(2)(A). Thus, *Bivens* suits, as they are commonly called, continue to be viable notwithstanding the Westfall Act and are governed by caselaw, not statutory, standards.

As also addressed earlier in Chapter III.A.6, the government itself may be liable today under the Federal Tort Claims Act (FTCA) for the type of wrongdoing alleged in *Bivens,* that is, improper conduct by law enforcement officers in conducting searches and arrests. Subsequent to *Bivens,* and in response to congressional concerns about abuse of search powers by federal law enforcement agents, particularly in "no-knock" drug raids, Congress partially lifted the general immunity of the federal government against suits for intentional torts. Under Subsection 2680(h) of the FTCA—the "Intentional Tort Exception"—the United States generally is not liable for the intentional torts of "assault, battery, false imprisonment, false arrest, malicious prosecution, abuse of process, libel, slander, misrepresentation, deceit, or interference with contract rights." 28 U.S.C. § 2680(h). In 1974, Congress created an exception to the exception—now the government *is* liable for the torts of assault, battery, false imprisonment, false arrest, abuse of process, or malicious prosecution when committed by "investigative or law enforcement officers" of the federal government, as defined in Subsection 2680(h).

However, the 1974 amendment to the FTCA does not directly address or cover the *Bivens* scenario, because it makes the government liable only on the basis of the specified common-law torts. It has *not* been construed to provide a tort remedy against the United States for violation of *constitutional* rights, such as the protection against unreasonable search and seizure under the Fourth Amendment. Instead, as with other claims under the FTCA, the courts have required that the plaintiff plead a cause of action arising under state tort law. *Federal Deposit Ins. Corp. v. Meyer,* 510 U.S. 471, 478 (1994) (holding that "the United States simply has not rendered itself liable under § 1346(b) for constitutional tort claims") (the *Meyer* decision is set out in this casebook at Chapter V.B.2.d). Thus, to maintain a claim for damages directly under the Constitution, a plaintiff must bring a judicially-created *Bivens* suit against the individual federal officer or employee for violation of constitutional rights. *See Carlson v. Green,* 446 U.S. 14, 19–20 (1980) (holding that the 1974 amendments to the FTCA are not an exclusive remedy against the United States substituting for a *Bivens* action against the federal employee).

3. In his dissent in *Bivens,* Justice Black raises the concern about whether the *Bivens*-type suit "might deter officials from the *proper* and honest performance of their duties." This is the same question that was raised earlier in the context of common law suits for damages against federal employees (see Chapter V.B.1.a). Even if a cause of action is created, as it was in *Bivens,* might it not be appropriate to confer some form of qualified immunity upon a federal employee who inadvertently, in good faith, or by reasonable mistake violates a constitutional standard? How should immunity be defined or qualified in this context? The Court in *Bivens* remands the case to the lower courts to address the question of immunity from liability and thus left that issue for another day. We will turn to that question shortly in Chapter V.B.2.b.

4. Justice Brennan states (1) that the *Bivens* case "involves no special factors counseling hesitation in the absence of affirmative action by Congress" and (2) that "we have here no explicit congressional declaration that persons injured by a federal officer's violation [of the constitutional provi-

sion] may not recover money damages from the [government employees], but must instead be remitted to another remedy, equally effective in the view of Congress." When would there be "special factors counseling hesitation"? What would constitute "special factors"? When would a congressionally-established alternative be an adequate substitute for a *Bivens* action? The next case in these materials picks up these questions.

5. As a practice note, you should be aware that although a *Bivens* action proceeds against the federal employee individually—and not the government itself—the federal employee will frequently be represented by government attorneys in his or her defense:

> [F]ederal employees, if determined to have been acting within the course and scope of their employment, may request and be provided representation by the Department of Justice. In such cases, the federal employee is required to sign a representation agreement acknowledging that, although representation is provided by the Department, the possibility of a conflict between the employee's interests and those of the United States is recognized. If a conflict arises, Department of Justice attorneys may withdraw as attorneys of record. Moreover, the employee is advised that, should an adverse judgment be entered, it will be satisfied solely out of the employee's assets and not out of public funds. The employee may request indemnification of the adverse judgment by the government. Although the procedures for effecting indemnification vary among the agencies, the decision to indemnify is, in all cases, discretionary and subject to a determination that such indemnification would be in the best interests of the United States. [*See* 28 C.F.R. § 50.15 (1993).]

John E. Nordin II, *The Constitutional Liability of Federal Employees:* Bivens *Claims,* 41 Fed. Bar News & J. 342, 343 & n.25 (1994). Mr. Nordin's article provides a useful and practical discussion of the litigation of *Bivens* actions, including the proper defendant, pleading with specificity, statute of limitations, discovery, available remedies, immunity, and particular types of claims. *Id.*

Bush v. Lucas

Supreme Court of the United States.
462 U.S. 367 (1983).

■ JUSTICE STEVENS delivered the opinion of the Court.

Petitioner asks us to authorize a new nonstatutory damages remedy for federal employees whose First Amendment rights are violated by their superiors. Because such claims arise out of an employment relationship that is governed by comprehensive procedural and substantive provisions giving meaningful remedies against the United States, we conclude that it would be inappropriate for us to supplement that regulatory scheme with a new judicial remedy.

Petitioner Bush is an aerospace engineer employed at the George C. Marshall Space Flight Center, a major facility operated by the National Aeronautics and Space Administration in Alabama. Respondent Lucas is the Director of the Center. In 1974 the facility was reorganized and petitioner was twice reassigned to new positions. He objected to both reassignments and sought formal review by the Civil Service Commission. In May and June 1975, while some of his administrative appeals were pending, he made a number of public statements, including two televised interviews, that were highly critical of the agency. The news media quoted him as saying that he did not have enough meaningful work to keep him busy, that his job was "a travesty and worthless," and that the taxpayers' money was being spent fraudulently and wastefully at the Center. His statements were reported on local television, in the local newspaper, and in a national press release that appeared in newspapers in at least three other States.

In June 1975 respondent, in response to a reporter's inquiry, stated that he had conducted an investigation and that petitioner's statements regarding his job had "no basis in fact." In August 1975 an adverse personnel action was initiated to remove petitioner from his position. Petitioner was charged with "publicly mak[ing] intemperate remarks which were misleading and often false, evidencing a malicious attitude towards Management and generating an environment of sensationalism demeaning to the Government, the National Aeronautics and Space Administration and the personnel of the George C. Marshall Space Flight Center, thereby impeding Government efficiency and economy and adversely affecting public confidence in the Government service." He was also informed that his conduct had undermined morale at the Center and caused disharmony and disaffection among his fellow employees. Petitioner had the opportunity to file a written response and to make an oral presentation to agency officials. Respondent then determined that petitioner's statements were false and misleading and that his conduct would justify removal, but that the lesser penalty of demotion was appropriate for a "first offense." He approved a reduction in grade from GS–14 to GS–12, which decreased petitioner's annual salary by approximately $9,716.

Petitioner exercised his right to appeal to the Federal Employee Appeals Authority. After a three-day public hearing, the Authority upheld some of the charges and concluded that the demotion was justified. It specifically determined that a number of petitioner's public statements were misleading and that, for three reasons, they "exceeded the bounds of expression protected by the First Amendment." First, petitioner's statements did not stem from public interest, but from his desire to have his position abolished so that he could take early retirement and go to law school. Second, the statements conveyed the erroneous impression that the agency was deliberately wasting public funds, thus discrediting the agency and its employees. Third, there was no legitimate public interest to be served by abolishing petitioner's position.[4]

---

4. Petitioner could have obtained judicial review of the Authority's determination by filing suit in a federal district court or in the U.S. Court of Claims, but did not do so.

Two years after the Appeals Authority's decision, petitioner requested the Civil Service Commission's Appeals Review Board to reopen the proceeding. The Board reexamined petitioner's First Amendment claim and, after making a detailed review of the record and the applicable authorities, applied the balancing test articulated in *Pickering v. Board of Education,* 391 U.S. 563 (1968). On the one hand, it acknowledged the evidence tending to show that petitioner's motive might have been personal gain, and the evidence that his statements caused some disruption of the agency's day-to-day routine. On the other hand, it noted that society as well as the individual had an interest in free speech, including "a right to disclosure of information about how tax dollars are spent and about the functioning of government apparatus, an interest in the promotion of the efficiency of the government, and in the maintenance of an atmosphere of freedom of expression by the scientists and engineers who are responsible for the planning and implementation of the nation's space program." Because petitioner's statements, though somewhat exaggerated, "were not wholly without truth, they properly stimulated public debate." Thus the nature and extent of proven disruption to the agency's operations did not "justify abrogation of the exercise of free speech." The Board recommended that petitioner be restored to his former position, retroactively to November 30, 1975, and that he receive back pay. That recommendation was accepted. Petitioner received approximately $30,000 in back pay.

While his administrative appeal was pending, petitioner filed an action against respondent in state court in Alabama seeking to recover damages for defamation and violation of his constitutional rights. Respondent removed the lawsuit to the United States District Court for the Northern District of Alabama, which granted respondent's motion for summary judgment. It held, first, that the defamation claim could not be maintained because, under *Barr v. Matteo,* 360 U.S. 564 (1959), respondent was absolutely immune from liability for damages for defamation; and second, that petitioner's demotion was not a constitutional deprivation for which a damages action could be maintained. The United States Court of Appeals for the Fifth Circuit affirmed. 598 F.2d 958 (1979). We vacated that court's judgment, 446 U.S. 914 (1980), and directed that it reconsider the case in the light of our intervening decision in *Carlson v. Green,* 446 U.S. 14 (1980). The Court of Appeals again affirmed the judgment against petitioner. It adhered to its previous conclusion "that plaintiff had no cause of action for damages under the First Amendment for retaliatory demotion in view of the available remedies under the Civil Service Commission regulations." 647 F.2d 573, 574 (1981). It explained that the relationship between the Federal Government and its civil service employees was a special factor counselling against the judicial recognition of a damages remedy under the Constitution in this context.

We assume for purposes of decision that petitioner's First Amendment rights were violated by the adverse personnel action.[7] We also assume that,

---

7. Competent decisionmakers may reasonably disagree about the merits of petitioner's First Amendment claim. This question is not before us.

as petitioner asserts, civil service remedies were not as effective as an individual damages remedy[8] and did not fully compensate him for the harm he suffered.[9] Two further propositions are undisputed. Congress has not expressly authorized the damages remedy that petitioner asks us to provide. On the other hand, Congress has not expressly precluded the creation of such a remedy by declaring that existing statutes provide the exclusive mode of redress.

Thus, we assume, a federal right has been violated and Congress has provided a less than complete remedy for the wrong. If we were writing on a clean slate, we might answer the question whether to supplement the statutory scheme in either of two quite simple ways. We might adopt the common-law approach to the judicial recognition of new causes of action and hold that it is the province of the judiciary to fashion an adequate remedy for every wrong that can be proved in a case over which a court has jurisdiction.[10] Or we might start from the premise that federal courts are courts of limited jurisdiction whose remedial powers do not extend beyond the granting of relief expressly authorized by Congress.[11] Under the former approach, petitioner would obviously prevail; under the latter, it would be equally clear that he would lose.

Our prior cases, although sometimes emphasizing one approach and sometimes the other, have unequivocally rejected both extremes. They establish our power to grant relief that is not expressly authorized by statute, but they also remind us that such power is to be exercised in the light of relevant policy determinations made by the Congress. We therefore first review some of the cases establishing our power to remedy violations of the Constitution and then consider the bearing of the existing statutory scheme on the precise issue presented by this case.

I

The federal courts' power to grant relief not expressly authorized by Congress is firmly established. Under 28 U.S.C. § 1331 (1976), the federal courts have jurisdiction to decide all cases "aris[ing] under the Constitu-

---

8. Petitioner contends that, unlike a damages remedy against respondent individually, civil service remedies against the Government do not provide for punitive damages or a jury trial and do not adequately deter the unconstitutional exercise of authority by supervisors.

9. His attorney's fees were not paid by the Government, and he claims to have suffered uncompensated emotional and dignitary harms. In light of our disposition of this case, we do not need to decide whether such costs could be recovered as compensation in an action brought directly under the Constitution.

10. In *Marbury v. Madison,* 1 Cranch 137, 162–163 (1803), Chief Justice Marshall invoked the authority of Blackstone's Commentaries in support of this proposition. Blackstone had written, "it is a general and indisputable rule, that where there is a legal right, there is also a legal remedy by suit, or action at law, whenever that right is invaded.... [I]t is a settled and invariable principle in the laws of England, that every right, when withheld, must have a remedy, and every injury its proper redress." 3 Commentaries *23, *109.

11. See *Bivens v. Six Unknown Fed. Narcotics Agents,* 403 U.S. 388, 428 (1971) (Black, J., dissenting).

tion, laws, or treaties of the United States." This jurisdictional grant provides not only the authority to decide whether a cause of action is stated by a plaintiff's claim that he has been injured by a violation of the Constitution, but also the authority to choose among available judicial remedies in order to vindicate constitutional rights. This Court has fashioned a wide variety of nonstatutory remedies for violations of the Constitution by federal and state officials. The cases most relevant to the problem before us are those in which the Court has held that the Constitution itself supports a private cause of action for damages against a federal official. *Bivens v. Six Unknown Fed. Narcotics Agents,* 403 U.S. 388 (1971).

In *Bivens* the plaintiff alleged that federal agents, without a warrant or probable cause, had arrested him and searched his home in a manner causing him great humiliation, embarrassment, and mental suffering. He claimed damages on the theory that the alleged violation of the Fourth Amendment provided an independent basis for relief. The Court upheld the sufficiency of his complaint, rejecting the argument that a state tort action in trespass provided the only appropriate judicial remedy. The Court explained why the absence of a federal statutory basis for the cause of action was not an obstacle to the award of damages:

> "That damages may be obtained for injuries consequent upon a violation of the Fourth Amendment by federal officials should hardly seem a surprising proposition. Historically, damages have been regarded as the ordinary remedy for an invasion of personal interests in liberty. Of course, the Fourth Amendment does not in so many words provide for its enforcement by an award of money damages for the consequences of its violation. But 'it is ... well settled that where legal rights have been invaded, and a federal statute provides for a general right to sue for such invasion, federal courts may use any available remedy to make good the wrong done.' * * *" 403 U.S., at 395–396. * * *

In *Davis v. Passman,* [442 U.S. 228 (1979)], the petitioner, former deputy administrative assistant to a Member of Congress, alleged that she had been discharged because of her sex, in violation of her constitutional right to the equal protection of the laws. We held that the Due Process Clause of the Fifth Amendment gave her a federal constitutional right to be free from official discrimination and that she had alleged a federal cause of action. In reaching the conclusion that an award of damages would be an appropriate remedy, we emphasized the fact that no other alternative form of judicial relief was available. * * *

Carlson v. Green, 446 U.S. 14 (1980), involved a claim that a federal prisoner's Eighth Amendment rights had been violated. The prisoner's mother brought suit on behalf of her son's estate, alleging that federal prison officials were responsible for his death because they had violated their constitutional duty to provide him with proper medical care after he suffered a severe asthmatic attack. Unlike *Bivens* and *Davis,* the *Green* case was one in which Congress had provided a remedy, under the Federal Tort Claims Act, against the United States for the alleged wrong. 28 U.S.C. § 2671 *et seq.* (1976). As is true in this case, that remedy was not as completely effective as a *Bivens*-type action based directly on the Constitution.

The Court acknowledged that a *Bivens* action could be defeated in two situations, but found that neither was present. First, the Court could discern "no special factors counselling hesitation in the absence of affirmative action by Congress." 446 U.S., at 18–19. Second, there was no congressional determination foreclosing the damages claim and making the Federal Tort Claims Act exclusive. 446 U.S., at 19, and n. 5. No statute expressly declared the FTCA remedy to be a substitute for a *Bivens* action; indeed, the legislative history of the 1974 amendments to the FTCA "made it crystal clear that Congress views FTCA and *Bivens* as parallel, complementary causes of action." *Id.,* at 19–20.

This much is established by our prior cases. The federal courts' statutory jurisdiction to decide federal questions confers adequate power to award damages to the victim of a constitutional violation. When Congress provides an alternative remedy, it may, of course, indicate its intent, by statutory language, by clear legislative history, or perhaps even by the statutory remedy itself, that the Court's power should not be exercised. In the absence of such a congressional directive, the federal courts must make the kind of remedial determination that is appropriate for a common-law tribunal, paying particular heed, however, to any special factors counselling hesitation before authorizing a new kind of federal litigation.

Congress has not resolved the question presented by this case by expressly denying petitioner the judicial remedy he seeks or by providing him with an equally effective substitute. There is, however, a good deal of history that is relevant to the question whether a federal employee's attempt to recover damages from his superior for violation of his First Amendment rights involves any "special factors counselling hesitation." * * *

* * * We should * * * begin by considering whether there are reasons for allowing Congress to prescribe the scope of relief that is made available to federal employees whose First Amendment rights have been violated by their supervisors.

II

* * * [T]his case concerns a claim that a constitutional right has been violated. Nevertheless, * * * the ultimate question on the merits in this case may appropriately be characterized as one of "federal personnel policy." When a federal civil servant is the victim of a retaliatory demotion or discharge because he has exercised his First Amendment rights, what legal remedies are available to him?

The answer to that question has changed dramatically over the years. Originally the answer was entirely a matter of Executive discretion. During the era of the patronage system that prevailed in the federal government prior to the enactment of the Pendleton Act in 1883, 22 Stat. 403, the federal employee had no legal protection against political retaliation. * * *

In the Pendleton Act Congress created the Civil Service Commission and provided for the selection of federal civil servants on a merit basis by competitive examination. Although the statute did not address the question of removals in general, it provided that no employee in the public service could be required to contribute to any political fund or fired for refusing to do so, and it prohibited officers from attempting to influence or coerce the political actions of others. * * *

In the ensuing years, repeated consideration of the conflicting interests involved in providing job security, protecting the right to speak freely, and maintaining discipline and efficiency in the federal workforce gave rise to additional legislation, various executive orders, and the promulgation of detailed regulations by the Civil Service Commission. Federal civil servants are now protected by an elaborate, comprehensive scheme that encompasses substantive provisions forbidding arbitrary action by supervisors and procedures—administrative and judicial—by which improper action may be redressed. They apply to a multitude of personnel decisions that are made daily by federal agencies.[28] Constitutional challenges to agency action, such as the First Amendment claims raised by petitioner, are fully cognizable within this system. As the record in this case demonstrates, the Government's comprehensive scheme is costly to administer, but it provides meaningful remedies for employees who may have been unfairly disciplined for making critical comments about their agencies.

A federal employee in the competitive service may be removed or demoted "only for such cause as will promote the efficiency of the service." * * * The regulations required that the final agency decision be made by an official higher in rank than the official who proposed the adverse action. * * *

The next step was a right to appeal to the Civil Service Commission's Federal Employee Appeals Authority.[33] The Appeals Authority was required to hold a trial-type hearing at which the employee could present witnesses, cross-examine the agency's witnesses, and secure the attendance of agency officials, and then to render a written decision. An adverse decision by the FEAA was judicially reviewable in either federal district court or the Court of Claims.[35] In addition, the employee had the right to ask the Commission's Appeals Review Board to reopen an adverse decision by the FEAA.

---

28. Not all personnel actions are covered by this system. For example, there are no provisions for appeal of either suspensions for 14 days or less, 5 U.S.C. § 7503, or adverse actions against probationary employees, § 7511. In addition, certain actions by supervisors against federal employees, such as wiretapping, warrantless searches, or uncompensated takings, would not be defined as "personnel actions" within the statutory scheme.

33. The 1978 Civil Service Reform Act gave the Commission's adjudicative functions to the Merit Systems Protection Board (MSPB). 5 U.S.C. §§ 1205, 7543(d), 7701.

35. Under the law now in effect, the United States Court of Appeals for the Federal Circuit has exclusive jurisdiction over appeals from the MSPB. 5 U.S.C. § 7703; 28 U.S.C. § 1295.

If the employee prevailed in the administrative process or upon judicial review, he was entitled to reinstatement with retroactive seniority. He also had a right to full back pay * * * . Congress intended that these remedies would put the employee "in the same position he would have been in had the unjustified or erroneous personnel action not taken place."[36]

Given the history of the development of civil service remedies and the comprehensive nature of the remedies currently available, it is clear that the question we confront today is quite different from the typical remedial issue confronted by a common-law court. The question is not what remedy the court should provide for a wrong that would otherwise go unredressed. It is whether an elaborate remedial system that has been constructed step by step, with careful attention to conflicting policy considerations, should be augmented by the creation of a new judicial remedy for the constitutional violation at issue. That question obviously cannot be answered simply by noting that existing remedies do not provide complete relief for the plaintiff. The policy judgment should be informed by a thorough understanding of the existing regulatory structure and the respective costs and benefits that would result from the addition of another remedy for violations of employees' First Amendment rights.

The costs associated with the review of disciplinary decisions are already significant—not only in monetary terms, but also in the time and energy of managerial personnel who must defend their decisions. The Government argues that supervisory personnel are already more hesitant than they should be in administering discipline, because the review that ensues inevitably makes the performance of their regular duties more difficult. Whether or not this assessment is accurate, it is quite probable that if management personnel face the added risk of personal liability for decisions that they believe to be a correct response to improper criticism of the agency, they would be deterred from imposing discipline in future cases. In all events, Congress is in a far better position than a court to evaluate the impact of a new species of litigation between federal employees on the efficiency of the civil service. Not only has Congress developed considerable familiarity with balancing governmental efficiency and the rights of employees, but it also may inform itself through factfinding procedures such as hearings that are not available to the courts.

Nor is there any reason to discount Congress' ability to make an evenhanded assessment of the desirability of creating a new remedy for federal employees who have been demoted or discharged for expressing controversial views. Congress has a special interest in informing itself about the efficiency and morale of the Executive Branch. In the past it has demonstrated its awareness that lower-level government employees are a valuable source of information, and that supervisors might improperly attempt to curtail their subordinates' freedom of expression.

Thus, we do not decide whether or not it would be good policy to permit a federal employee to recover damages from a supervisor who has

---

36. S.Rep. No. 1062, 89th Cong., 2d Sess. 1 (1966).

improperly disciplined him for exercising his First Amendment rights. * * * [W]e decline "to create a new substantive legal liability without legislative aid and as at the common law," [*United States v. Standard Oil Co.,* 332 U.S. [301,] 302 [(1947)], because we are convinced that Congress is in a better position to decide whether or not the public interest would be served by creating it.

The judgment of the Court of Appeals is

Affirmed.

■ JUSTICE MARSHALL, with whom JUSTICE BLACKMUN joins, concurring.

I join the Court's opinion because I agree that there are "special factors counselling hesitation in the absence of affirmative action by Congress." *Bivens v. Six Unknown Fed. Narcotics Agents,* 403 U.S. 388, 396 (1971). I write separately only to emphasize that in my view a different case would be presented if Congress had not created a comprehensive scheme that was specifically designed to provide full compensation to civil service employees who are discharged or disciplined in violation of their First Amendment rights, and that affords a remedy that is substantially as effective as a damage action. * * *

Notes and Questions

1. In the course of Justice Stevens's opinion for the Court in *Bush v. Lucas,* he mentions other Supreme Court decisions that have recognized *Bivens* remedies in additional contexts and based upon constitutional provisions beyond the Fourth Amendment that was at issue in *Bivens.* In *Davis v. Passman,* 442 U.S. 228 (1979), the Court implied a right to a damages remedy for employment discrimination against a federal employer under the Due Process Clause of the Fifth Amendment. In *Carlson v. Green,* 446 U.S. 14 (1980), the Court authorized a *Bivens* suit by a federal prison inmate against prison officials for violation of the prescription against cruel and unusual punishment in the Eighth Amendment.

2. In *Bush v. Lucas,* the Court declines to extend *Bivens* to a claim by a federal employee that his First Amendment free speech rights were violated by his superior. Why? Does the Court question whether the employee has truly suffered a constitutional infringement? Has Congress expressly prohibited such a suit by an employee against a supervisor? If not, what "special factors counseling hesitation" are present here? Are the ordinary civil service remedies available to all (or nearly all) federal employees for adverse personnel actions adequate to protect First Amendment rights? Note that the employee here has already regained his prior position and obtained backpay. What more does he seek through a *Bivens* action? (See footnotes 8 and 9 to the opinion.) The Court acknowledges that the civil service procedures provide a less than complete remedy for the constitutional violation alleged here, and yet the Court still declines to allow a constitutional damages suit. Why? How does the *Bush* decision

suggest the Court will approach the question of whether alternative remedies to *Bivens* actions are adequate in the future?

Most recently, in *Wilkie v. Robbins*, 127 S.Ct. 2588 (2007), a majority
of the Court declined to recognize a *Bivens* remedy for a rancher who
complained about the use of extortionate tactics by Bureau of Land
Management employees to coerce the granting of an easement to the
government. The rancher alleged that the government's conduct violated
the Fifth Amendment by retaliating against him for the exercise of his
property right to exclude the government from his property and to refuse
to grant an easement without compensation. Writing for a seven-justice
majority, Justice Souter observed that most of the rancher's complaints—
including trespass by government employees, civil and criminal fines and
charges, and cancellation of a right-of-way across government land and
revocation of grazing permits—were redressable by other administrative
and judicial remedies. *Id*. at 2598–2600. As for the rancher's aggregate
complaint that the campaign of harassment and intimidation against him
to extract the easement violated his constitutionally-protected property
rights, the Court held that it was difficult "to defin[e] a workable cause of
action." *Id*. at 2601. "[C]onsidering the more abstract concept of liability
for retaliatory or undue pressure on a property owner for standing firm on
property rights," the Court concluded that "[a] judicial standard to identify
illegitimate pressure going beyond legitimately hard bargaining would be
endlessly knotty to work out, and a general provision for tortlike liability
when Government employees are unduly zealous in pressing a governmental interest affecting property would invite an onslaught of *Bivens* actions."
Id. at 2604–05. Justice Thomas, joined by Justice Scalia, concurred, writing
that " '*Bivens* a relic of the heady days in which this Court assumed
common-law powers to create causes of action,' " and thus should be
confined to its precise circumstances. *Id*. at 2608 (Thomas, J., concurring)
(quoting *Correctional Services Corp. v. Malesko*, 534 U.S. 61, 75 (2001)
(Scalia, J., concurring)). Justice Ginsburg, joined by Justice Stevens, dissented from the refusal to recognize a *Bivens* remedy. She wrote that, in
contrast with other instances in which *Bivens* was not extended because
there was "a carefully calibrated administrative scheme" to provide some
remedy, the rancher "has no alternative remedy for the relentless torment
he alleges." *Id*. at 2613 (Ginsburg, J., concurring in part and dissenting in
part). Insisting that "this is no ordinary case of 'hard bargaining' or
bureaucratic arrogance," Justice Ginsburg argued that the Fifth Amendment should be held to "provide an effective check on federal officers who
abuse their regulatory powers by harassing and punishing property owners
who refuse to surrender their property to the United States without fair
compensation." *Id*. at 2609.

3. Do the *Bush* and *Wilkie* decisions indicate that the Court has
changed its attitude toward damages suits against federal officers for
constitutional wrongs from that which was evident in the earlier *Bivens*
decision? Is the Court becoming more protective of the interests of the
government and government administrators than it was in *Bivens*? In 1983,
Professor Peter Schuck described the *Bivens* remedy as "a powerful new

string in the victim's bow." Peter H. Schuck, *Suing Government* 42 (1983). But by 1995, Professor Susan Bandes lamented that that the guarantee of adequate remediation for constitutional violations had been eroded and that "there is little left of the *Bivens* principle." Susan Bandes, *Reinventing* Bivens: *The Self-Executing Constitution,* 68 S. Cal. L. Rev. 289, 293–94 (1995). What happened in the interim? Following *Bush v. Lucas,* the Supreme Court in a string of other decisions, including those discussed below, has been more cautious about extending the *Bivens* approach to new contexts. Professor Richard J. Pierce, Jr. says that the Supreme Court's opinions since the mid–1980s "seem to reflect waning enthusiasm for the *Bivens* doctrine and increasing willingness to conclude that available alternative remedies displace the *Bivens* remedy in specific contexts." 3 Richard J. Pierce, Jr., *Administrative Law Treatise* § 19.5, at 1467 (4th ed., 2002).

For example, in *Schweiker v. Chilicky,* 487 U.S. 412 (1988), the Court refused to authorize a *Bivens* action for Social Security beneficiaries who alleged that federal administrators had violated the Due Process Clause of the Fifth Amendment by establishing continuing administrative reviews of claimants' entitlement to disability benefits. Although these beneficiaries had obtained reinstatement of their disability benefits, including back benefits, they sought compensation for mental anguish suffered during the time that benefits were discontinued. In an opinion by Justice O'Connor, the Court noted that Congress had provided an elaborate system for judicial review of Social Security disability determinations, but had not allowed compensation for emotional distress. The Court also stated that "[t]he prospect of personal liability for official acts * * * would undoubtedly lead to new difficulties and expense in recruiting administrators for the programs Congress has established." *Id.* at 425. Assume a government administrator knew that he or she might be exposed to personal liability if a new procedure or administrative reform for a government program were instituted and then was later found by a court to offer inadequate due process protections. What would be the impact upon creativity in government administration or initiatives for reforms in efficiency?

4. The Supreme Court has been especially averse to implying a *Bivens* remedy for military service personnel against superior officers, expressing a strong deference to the special needs of the military for discipline. In *Chappell v. Wallace,* 462 U.S. 296 (1983) (which was decided by the Court on the same day as *Bush v. Lucas*), the Court unanimously rejected a *Bivens* action for enlisted military personnel who alleged that they had been injured by the unconstitutional actions of their superior officers and had no remedy against the government itself. The Court stated that "[t]he special nature of military life, the need for unhesitating and decisive action by military officers and equally disciplined responses by enlisted personnel, would be undermined by a judicially created remedy exposing officers to personal liability at the hands of those they are charged to command." *Id.* at 304. Accordingly, the Court held that "the unique disciplinary structure of the military establishment" and Congress's failure to provide a damages remedy for such claims constituted "special factors" that precluded creation of a *Bivens* remedy. *Id.*

The Court's powerful deference to the military is particularly illustrated by the decision in *United States v. Stanley,* 483 U.S. 669 (1987). In *Stanley,* a former serviceman claimed that the Army in 1958 had conducted medical experiments upon him without his knowledge, by secretly supplying him with the hallucinogenic drug LSD and evaluating the effects upon him. As Justice Brennan characterized the facts in his dissenting opinion, "[t]he Government of the United States treated thousands of its citizens as though they were laboratory animals, dosing them with this dangerous drug without their consent." *Id.* at 686 (Brennan, J., concurring in part and dissenting in part). By a five-to-four vote, the Court broadly applied its earlier decision in *Chappell* and refused to allow a *Bivens* suit against the allegedly responsible government officers. Justice Scalia, writing for the majority, stated that "the insistence (evident from the number of Clauses devoted to the subject) with which the Constitution confers authority over the Army, Navy, and militia upon the political branches" counsels hesitation in judicial intrusion into this distinctive area. *Id.* at 682. Accordingly, the Court held that a *Bivens* action is unavailable "whenever the injury arises out of activity 'incident to service.'" *Id.* at 681. (Note that this "incident to service" rule is the same standard that defines the scope of the government's immunity from Federal Tort Claims liability to service members under the *Feres* doctrine (see Chapter III.A.9.b).) Justice Brennan dissented in an opinion joined by two other justices. Justice O'Connor wrote a separate dissent, accepting the "incident to service" rule of *Chappell,* but concluding that "conduct of the type alleged in this case is so far beyond the bounds of human decency as a matter of law it simply cannot be considered a part of the military mission." *Id.* at 709 (O'Connor, J., concurring in part and dissenting in part). Observing that involuntary human experimentation was condemned as a war crime in the prosecution of Nazi officials at Nuremberg following World War II, Justice O'Connor argued that "the very least that society can do is to see that the victims are compensated, as best they can be, by the perpetrators." *Id.* at 710. Subsequently, through a private relief bill, Congress authorized payment of $400,577 in compensation to Stanley, subject to determination of the facts and damages through independent arbitration. *See* 141 Cong. Rec. H1115 (1995) (announcing President's signature on bill); 140 Cong. Rec. S15020 (1994) (final passage and floor discussion of arbitration procedures).

---

b.   IMMUNITY

Harlow v. Fitzgerald
Supreme Court of the United States.
457 U.S. 800 (1982).

■ JUSTICE POWELL delivered the opinion of the Court.

The issue in this case is the scope of the immunity available to the senior aides and advisers of the President of the United States in a suit for damages based upon their official acts.

I

[The underlying facts of the case are set out in the Court's accompanying opinion in *Nixon v. Fitzgerald,* 457 U.S. 731 (1982). In 1970, A. Ernest Fitzgerald lost his job as a management analyst with the Department of the Air Force. Fitzgerald's dismissal occurred in the context of a departmental reorganization and reduction-in-force, in which his job was eliminated. In 1968, Fitzgerald had attained national prominence for his testimony before a congressional subcommittee in which he revealed cost-overruns on a military transport plane. It was not disputed that officials in the Department of Defense were both embarrassed and angered by Fitzgerald's testimony.

President Nixon initially directed White House officials to arrange for Fitzgerald's assignment to another job within the administration. However, Fitzgerald's proposed reassignment encountered resistance within the administration. In an internal memorandum, White House aide Alexander Butterfield reported that "Fitzgerald is no doubt a top-notch cost expert, but he must be given very low marks in loyalty; and, after all, loyalty is the name of the game." Butterfield recommended that "[W]e should let him bleed, for a while at least." Subsequent to Butterfield's memorandum, there was no indication of White House efforts to reemploy Fitzgerald.

Absent any offer of alternative federal employment, Fitzgerald complained to the Civil Service Commission. Fitzgerald alleged that he had been dismissed in retaliation for his testimony before the congressional subcommittee. After a public hearing, the Civil Service Commission ruled that, although the evidence did not support a conclusion of retaliation for his congressional testimony, Fitzgerald's dismissal was motivated by reasons personal to him and thus offended civil service regulations.

Following the Civil Service Commission's decision in 1973, Fitzgerald then filed a suit for damages in United States District Court, naming several Department of Defense and White House officials, including White House aides Alexander Butterfield and Bryce Harlow. In an amended complaint filed in 1978, Fitzgerald named former President Richard Nixon as an additional defendant. Fitzgerald alleged a conspiracy to remove him from his position in retaliation for his congressional testimony.]

In this suit for civil damages petitioners Bryce Harlow and Alexander Butterfield are alleged to have participated in a conspiracy to violate the constitutional and statutory rights of the respondent A. Ernest Fitzgerald. Respondent avers that petitioners entered the conspiracy in their capacities as senior White House aides to former President Richard M. Nixon. * * *

Respondent claims that Harlow joined the conspiracy in his role as the Presidential aide principally responsible for congressional relations. At the conclusion of discovery the supporting evidence remained inferential. As evidence of Harlow's conspiratorial activity respondent relies heavily on a series of conversations in which Harlow discussed Fitzgerald's dismissal with Air Force Secretary Robert Seamans. The other evidence most supportive of Fitzgerald's claims consists of a recorded conversation in which the President later voiced a tentative recollection that Harlow was "all for canning" Fitzgerald.

Disputing Fitzgerald's contentions, Harlow argues that exhaustive discovery has adduced no direct evidence of his involvement in any wrongful activity. He avers that Secretary Seamans advised him that considerations of efficiency required Fitzgerald's removal by a reduction in force, despite anticipated adverse congressional reaction. Harlow asserts he had no reason to believe that a conspiracy existed. He contends that he took all his actions in good faith.[5]

Petitioner Butterfield also is alleged to have entered the conspiracy not later than May 1969. Employed as Deputy Assistant to the President and Deputy Chief of Staff to H. R. Haldeman, Butterfield circulated a White House memorandum in that month in which he claimed to have learned that Fitzgerald planned to "blow the whistle" on some "shoddy purchasing practices" by exposing these practices to public view. * * * Fitzgerald [also] cites communications between Butterfield and Haldeman in December 1969 and January 1970. After the President had promised at a press conference to inquire into Fitzgerald's dismissal, Haldeman solicited Butterfield's recommendations. In a subsequent memorandum emphasizing the importance of "loyalty," Butterfield counseled against offering Fitzgerald another job in the administration at that time.

For his part, Butterfield denies that he was involved in any decision concerning Fitzgerald's employment status until Haldeman sought his advice in December 1969—more than a month after Fitzgerald's termination had been scheduled and announced publicly by the Air Force. Butterfield states that he never communicated his views about Fitzgerald to any official of the Defense Department. He argues generally that nearly eight years of discovery have failed to turn up any evidence that he caused injury to Fitzgerald.

Together with their codefendant Richard Nixon, petitioners Harlow and Butterfield moved for summary judgment on February 12, 1980. In denying the motion the District Court upheld the legal sufficiency of Fitzgerald's *Bivens* (*Bivens v. Six Unknown Fed. Narcotics Agents,* 403 U.S. 388 (1971)) claim under the First Amendment * * * . The court found that

---

5. In support of his version of events Harlow relies particularly on the deposition testimony of Air Force Secretary Seamans, who stated that he regarded abolition of Fitzgerald's position as necessary "to improve the efficiency" of the Financial Management Office of the Air Force and that he never received any White House instruction regarding the Fitzgerald case. Harlow also disputes the probative value of Richard Nixon's recorded remark that Harlow had supported Fitzgerald's firing. Harlow emphasizes the tentativeness of the President's statement. To the President's query whether Harlow was "all for canning [Fitzgerald], wasn't he?", White House Press Secretary Ronald Ziegler in fact gave a negative reply: "No, I think Bryce may have been the other way." The President did not respond to Ziegler's comment.

genuine issues of disputed fact remained for resolution at trial. It also ruled that petitioners were not entitled to absolute immunity.

Independently of former President Nixon, petitioners invoked the collateral order doctrine and appealed the denial of their immunity defense to the Court of Appeals for the District of Columbia Circuit. The Court of Appeals dismissed the appeal without opinion. Never having determined the immunity available to the senior aides and advisers of the President of the United States, we granted certiorari.

[In the companion case of *Nixon v. Fitzgerald,* 457 U.S. 731 (1982), the Court held that the President of the United States is absolutely immune from damages liability predicated upon his official acts. The Court held that the President's absolute immunity is a functionally mandated incident of his unique office, rooted in the constitutional tradition of the separation of powers and supported by the Nation's history. Because of the singular importance of the President's duties, diversion of his energies by concern with private lawsuits would raise unique risks to the effective functioning of the government.]

II

* * * [O]ur decisions consistently have held that government officials are entitled to some form of immunity from suits for damages. As recognized at common law, public officers require this protection to shield them from undue interference with their duties and from potentially disabling threats of liability.

Our decisions have recognized immunity defenses of two kinds. For officials whose special functions or constitutional status requires complete protection from suit, we have recognized the defense of "absolute immunity." The absolute immunity of legislators, in their legislative functions, and of judges, in their judicial functions, now is well settled. Our decisions also have extended absolute immunity to certain officials of the Executive Branch. These include prosecutors and similar officials, executive officers engaged in adjudicative functions, and the President of the United States.

For executive officials in general, however, our cases make plain that qualified immunity represents the norm. * * * In *Butz v. Economou,* [438 U.S. 478 (1978)], * * * we explained that the recognition of a qualified immunity defense for high executives reflected an attempt to balance competing values: not only the importance of a damages remedy to protect the rights of citizens, 438 U.S., at 504–505, but also "the need to protect officials who are required to exercise their discretion and the related public interest in encouraging the vigorous exercise of official authority." *Id.,* at 506. * * * [W]e emphasized our expectation that insubstantial suits need not proceed to trial:

"Insubstantial lawsuits can be quickly terminated by federal courts alert to the possibilities of artful pleading. Unless the complaint states a compensable claim for relief ..., it should not survive a motion to dismiss. Moreover, * * * damages suits concerning constitutional violations need not proceed to trial, but can be terminated on a properly supported motion for summary judgment based on the defense of immunity.... In responding to such a motion, plaintiffs may not play dog in the manger; and firm application of the Federal Rules of Civil Procedure will ensure that federal officials are not harassed by frivolous lawsuits." 438 U.S., at 507–508 (citations omitted). * * *

III

A

Petitioners argue that they are entitled to a blanket protection of absolute immunity as an incident of their offices as Presidential aides. In deciding this claim we do not write on an empty page. In *Butz v. Economou, supra,* the Secretary of Agriculture—a Cabinet official directly accountable to the President—asserted a defense of absolute official immunity from suit for civil damages. We rejected his claim. In so doing we did not question the power or the importance of the Secretary's office. Nor did we doubt the importance to the President of loyal and efficient subordinates in executing his duties of office. Yet we found these factors, alone, to be insufficient to justify absolute immunity. "[T]he greater power of [high] officials," we reasoned, "affords a greater potential for a regime of lawless conduct." 438 U.S., at 506. Damages actions against high officials were therefore "an important means of vindicating constitutional guarantees." *Ibid.* * * *

Having decided in *Butz* that Members of the Cabinet ordinarily enjoy only qualified immunity from suit, we conclude today that it would be equally untenable to hold absolute immunity an incident of the office of every Presidential subordinate based in the White House. Members of the Cabinet are direct subordinates of the President, frequently with greater responsibilities, both to the President and to the Nation, than White House staff. The considerations that supported our decision in *Butz* apply with equal force to this case. It is no disparagement of the offices held by petitioners to hold that Presidential aides, like Members of the Cabinet, generally are entitled only to a qualified immunity. * * *

IV

Even if they cannot establish that their official functions require absolute immunity, petitioners assert that public policy at least mandates an application of the qualified immunity standard that would permit the defeat of insubstantial claims without resort to trial. We agree.

A

The resolution of immunity questions inherently requires a balance between the evils inevitable in any available alternative. In situations of abuse of office, an action for damages may offer the only realistic avenue for vindication of constitutional guarantees. It is this recognition that has required the denial of absolute immunity to most public officers. At the same time, however, it cannot be disputed seriously that claims frequently run against the innocent as well as the guilty—at a cost not only to the defendant officials, but to society as a whole. These social costs include the expenses of litigation, the diversion of official energy from pressing public issues, and the deterrence of able citizens from acceptance of public office. Finally, there is the danger that fear of being sued will "dampen the ardor of all but the most resolute, or the most irresponsible [public officials], in the unflinching discharge of their duties." *Gregoire v. Biddle,* 177 F.2d 579, 581 (C.A.2 1949), cert. denied, 339 U.S. 949 (1950). * * *

B

Qualified or "good faith" immunity is an affirmative defense that must be pleaded by a defendant official. Decisions of this Court have established that the "good faith" defense has both an "objective" and a "subjective" aspect. The objective element involves a presumptive knowledge of and respect for "basic, unquestioned constitutional rights." *Wood v. Strickland,* 420 U.S. 308, 322 (1975). The subjective component refers to "permissible intentions." *Ibid.* Characteristically the Court has defined these elements by identifying the circumstances in which qualified immunity would *not* be available. Referring both to the objective and subjective elements, we have held that qualified immunity would be defeated if an official *"knew or reasonably should have known* that the action he took within his sphere of official responsibility would violate the constitutional rights of the [plaintiff], *or* if he took the action *with the malicious intention* to cause a deprivation of constitutional rights or other injury . . . ." *Ibid.* (emphasis added).

The subjective element of the good-faith defense frequently has proved incompatible with our admonition in *Butz* that insubstantial claims should not proceed to trial. Rule 56 of the Federal Rules of Civil Procedure provides that disputed questions of fact ordinarily may not be decided on motions for summary judgment. And an official's subjective good faith has been considered to be a question of fact that some courts have regarded as inherently requiring resolution by a jury.

In the context of *Butz'* attempted balancing of competing values, it now is clear that substantial costs attend the litigation of the subjective good faith of government officials. Not only are there the general costs of subjecting officials to the risks of trial—distraction of officials from their governmental duties, inhibition of discretionary action, and deterrence of able people from public service. There are special costs to "subjective" inquiries of this kind. Immunity generally is available only to officials performing discretionary functions. In contrast with the thought processes accompanying "ministerial" tasks, the judgments surrounding discretionary action almost inevitably are influenced by the decisionmaker's experiences, values, and emotions. These variables explain in part why questions of subjective intent so rarely can be decided by summary judgment. Yet they also frame a background in which there often is no clear end to the relevant evidence. Judicial inquiry into subjective motivation therefore may entail broad-ranging discovery and the deposing of numerous persons, including an official's professional colleagues. Inquiries of this kind can be peculiarly disruptive of effective government.

Consistently with the balance at which we aimed in *Butz,* we conclude today that bare allegations of malice should not suffice to subject government officials either to the costs of trial or to the burdens of broad-reaching discovery. We therefore hold that government officials performing discretionary functions generally are shielded from liability for civil damages insofar as their conduct does not violate clearly established statutory or constitutional rights of which a reasonable person would have known.

Reliance on the objective reasonableness of an official's conduct, as measured by reference to clearly established law, should avoid excessive disruption of government and permit the resolution of many insubstantial claims on summary judgment. On summary judgment, the judge appropriately may determine, not only the currently applicable law, but whether that law was clearly established at the time an action occurred. If the law at that time was not clearly established, an official could not reasonably be expected to anticipate subsequent legal developments, nor could he fairly be said to "know" that the law forbade conduct not previously identified as unlawful. Until this threshold immunity question is resolved, discovery should not be allowed. If the law was clearly established, the immunity defense ordinarily should fail, since a reasonably competent public official should know the law governing his conduct. Nevertheless, if the official pleading the defense claims extraordinary circumstances and can prove that he neither knew nor should have known of the relevant legal standard, the defense should be sustained. But again, the defense would turn primarily on objective factors.

By defining the limits of qualified immunity essentially in objective terms, we provide no license to lawless conduct. The public interest in deterrence of unlawful conduct and in compensation of victims remains protected by a test that focuses on the objective legal reasonableness of an official's acts. Where an official could be expected to know that certain conduct would violate statutory or constitutional rights, he should be made to hesitate; and a person who suffers injury caused by such conduct may have a cause of action. But where an official's duties legitimately require action in which clearly established rights are not implicated, the public interest may be better served by action taken "with independence and without fear of consequences." *Pierson v. Ray,* 386 U.S. 547, 554 (1967).[34]

C

In this case petitioners have asked us to hold that the respondent's pretrial showings were insufficient to survive their motion for summary judgment. We think it appropriate, however, to remand the case to the District Court for its reconsideration of this issue in light of this opinion.

---

34. We emphasize that our decision applies only to suits for civil damages arising from actions within the scope of an official's duties and in "objective" good faith. We express no view as to the conditions in which injunctive or declaratory relief might be available.

The trial court is more familiar with the record so far developed and also is better situated to make any such further findings as may be necessary.

V

The judgment of the Court of Appeals is vacated, and the case is remanded for further action consistent with this opinion.

So ordered.

■ JUSTICE BRENNAN, with whom JUSTICE MARSHALL, and JUSTICE BLACKMUN join, concurring.

I agree with the substantive standard announced by the Court today, imposing liability when a public-official defendant "knew or should have known" of the constitutionally violative effect of his actions. This standard would not allow the official who *actually knows* that he was violating the law to escape liability for his actions, even if he could not "reasonably have been expected" to know what he actually did know. Thus the clever and unusually well-informed violator of constitutional rights will not evade just punishment for his crimes. * * * I write separately only to note that given this standard, it seems inescapable to me that some measure of discovery may sometimes be required to determine exactly what a public-official defendant did "know" at the time of his actions. * * *

■ JUSTICE BRENNAN, JUSTICE WHITE, JUSTICE MARSHALL and JUSTICE BLACKMUN, concurring.

We join the Court's opinion but, having dissented in *Nixon v. Fitzgerald,* [457 U.S. 731 (1982)], we disassociate ourselves from any implication in the Court's opinion in the present case that *Nixon v. Fitzgerald* was correctly decided.

■ JUSTICE REHNQUIST, concurring.

At such time as a majority of the Court is willing to re-examine our holding in *Butz v. Economou,* 438 U.S. 478 (1978), I shall join in that undertaking with alacrity. But until that time comes, I agree that the Court's opinion in this case properly disposes of the issues presented, and I therefore join it.

[The dissenting opinion of CHIEF JUSTICE BURGER is omitted.]

———

Notes and Questions

1. On the subject of official immunity raised in *Harlow v. Fitzgerald,* the first question that should be asked is why any form of immunity should be granted to any official who is accused of infringing a citizen's constitutional right? Shouldn't an official engaging in such wrongful conduct pay the penalty without being allowed any excuse? Yet the Court is unanimous in *Harlow* in agreeing that at least some level of immunity should be available to defendants in *Bivens* actions. Why? What compelling need for some form of immunity is perceived by the Court?

The second question then is what level of immunity is appropriate? In the companion decision of *Nixon v. Fitzgerald,* 457 U.S. 731 (1982), a divided Court held that the President is entitled to *absolute immunity* for actions taken in his official capacity. (As the Court notes, prior decisions had also conferred absolute immunity upon legislators in their legislative functions, to judges in their judicial functions, and to prosecutors engaged in prosecutorial activities.)* Why does Justice Powell writing for the Court in *Harlow v. Fitzgerald* decline to extend absolute immunity to senior executive officials, such as White House aides? What interests are being balanced here and how does the Court strike that balance?

2. What is *qualified immunity*? In what way is this form of immunity "qualified" and not absolute? The *Harlow* Court changes the criteria for qualified immunity from that set out in prior decisions. In what way? How is it made more "objective"? Why is the Court uncomfortable with an inquiry into the "subjective" motivation of government officials? Why does it believe an "objective" test will be better?

In *Brosseau v. Haugen,* 543 U.S. 194 (2004), which involved a suit under 42 U.S.C. § 1983 against a police officer for allegedly using excessive force to effectuate an arrest, the Court reaffirmed the objective reasonableness test:

> Qualified immunity shields an officer from suit when she makes a decision that, even if constitutionally deficient, reasonably misapprehends the law governing the circumstances she confronted. Because the focus is on whether the officer had fair notice that her conduct was unlawful, reasonableness is judged against the backdrop of the law at the time of the conduct. If the law at that time did not clearly establish that the officer's conduct would violate the Constitution, the officer should not be subject to liability or, indeed, even the burdens of litigation.

Id. at 198.

3. How should the "objective" inquiry into whether the official knew or should have known that his actions violated a clearly established right be applied in a particular case? At what level of generality or specificity? For example, if a federal law enforcement officer is accused of conducting an "unreasonable search" in violation of the Fourth Amendment, is qualified immunity defeated if the court concludes that the search was in fact unreasonable and thus a violation of the Fourth Amendment? Or may the defendant officer still plead immunity by arguing that he *reasonably* believed that the search was *reasonable* under the Fourth Amendment, even if the court concludes the search was *unreasonable* as a matter of law? (See how confusing this can get!)

---

* Legislators, judges, and prosecutors are granted absolute immunity from damages claims only when engaged in those particular functions. Thus, a judge is entitled only to qualified—not absolute—immunity when acting in an administrative capacity, such as hiring and firing subordinates. *Forrester v. White,* 484 U.S. 219 (1988).

The Supreme Court regularly has grappled with, and just as regularly divided over, how to determine whether an official accused of constitutional misconduct should have known that his or her actions violated a clearly established right in a particular instance. The primary difficulty lies in determining at what level of specificity the law on the point must be established before the cover of qualified immunity may be stripped away.

In *Anderson v. Creighton,* 483 U.S. 635 (1987), the Court recognized that the Fourth Amendment sometimes raises difficult questions of interpretation that have divided the Court itself, and thus on which law enforcement officers could understandably be confused. (*See also Wood v. Strickland,* 420 U.S. 308, 329 (1975) (Powell, J., concurring in part and dissenting in part) ("[O]ne need only look to the decisions of this Court—to our reversals, our recognition of evolving concepts, and our five-to-four splits—to recognize the hazard of even informed prophecy as to what are 'unquestioned constitutional rights.' ").) Thus, Justice Scalia said for a majority of the Court, even if a search is later held to be unreasonable as a matter of law under the Fourth Amendment, the officer may still be entitled to qualified immunity if he reasonably believed that the search was valid under the state of the law that existed at the time. Before qualified immunity may be withdrawn, "[t]he contours of the right must be sufficiently clear that a reasonable official would understand that what he is doing violates the right." *Anderson,* 483 U.S. at 640.

Subsequently, the Court extended the holding in *Anderson v. Creighton,* which involved qualified immunity in the context of the reasonableness of a search under the Fourth Amendment, to what the majority viewed as the analogous context of a charge of excessive use of force in making an arrest. In *Saucier v. Katz,* 533 U.S. 194 (2001), in a *Bivens* suit against the arresting federal law enforcement officer for alleged violation of the Fourth Amendment by the use of excessive force, a six-Justice majority held that the qualified immunity question analysis was "not susceptible of fusion with the question whether unreasonable force was used in making the arrest." *Id.* at 197. The Court therefore reversed the holding of the court of appeals which had denied summary judgment and held the qualified immunity issue over for trial, reasoning that the qualified immunity inquiry and the merits were "identical, since both concern the objective reasonableness of the officer's conduct in light of the circumstances the officer faced on the scene." *Id.* at 199–200 (describing court of appeals ruling).

The Court agreed with the "general proposition that the use of force is contrary to the Fourth Amendment if it is excessive under objective standards of reasonableness." *Id.* at 201–02. But the Court held that the qualified immunity inquiry requires considering whether the right against excessive use of force was clearly established on a more specific level. *Id.* at 200. Writing for the majority, Justice Kennedy explained that, while the constitutional question on the merits is whether an officer reasonably believed that the force necessary was justified—

The qualified immunity inquiry * * * has a further dimension. The concern of the immunity inquiry is to acknowledge that reasonable mistakes can be made as to the legal constraints on particular police conduct. It is sometimes difficult for an officer to determine how the relevant legal doctrine, here excessive force, will apply to the factual situation the officer confronts. An officer might correctly perceive all of the relevant facts but have a mistaken understanding as to whether a particular amount of force is legal in those circumstances. If the officer's mistake as to what the law requires is reasonable, however, the officer is entitled to the immunity defense.

Id. at 205. With respect to the area of search and seizure addressed in *Anderson* and the area of excessive force addressed here, "in both spheres the law must be elaborated from case to case." *Id.* at 206.

The concurring justices in *Saucier,* while agreeing that qualified immunity should have been afforded the officer in that case, argued that a single and simple "objective reasonableness standard is both necessary, under currently governing precedent, and * * * sufficient to resolve cases of this genre." Justice Ginsburg, joined by two other members of the Court, found it unnecessary "to tack[] on * * * a second, overlapping reasonableness inquiry," and feared that the "two-part test" of reasonableness for qualified immunity determinations in excessive force cases "holds large potential to confuse." *Id.* at 210 (Ginsburg, J., concurring in the judgment). The concurrence distinguished *Anderson v. Creighton* and the Fourth Amendment search and seizure context, saying that the "[l]aw in that area is constantly evolving and, correspondingly, variously interpreted." *Id.* at 214. By contrast, Justice Ginsburg believed, whether the use of force was reasonable in given circumstances ordinarily can be answered simply. By asking the question on the merits, "whether an officer's use of force was within a range of reasonable options, the decisionmaker is also (and necessarily) answering the [qualified immunity] question whether a reasonable officer 'could have believed' his use of force 'to be lawful.'" *Id.* at 215 (quoting *Anderson,* 482 U.S. at 638).

However, while the specific contours of some constitutional provisions may need to be fleshed out in certain circumstances, the Court recently held that what is demanded by other constitutional provisions may be plain on their face at least some of the time, both for purposes of determining whether there was a constitutional violation and for purposes of qualified immunity. In *Groh v. Ramirez,* 540 U.S. 551 (2004), Justice Stevens writing for a five-justice majority held that "[g]iven that the particularity requirement [of the Fourth Amendment] is set forth in the text of the Constitution, no reasonable officer could believe that a warrant that plainly did not comply with that requirement was valid." *Id.* at 563. In that case, while the application for a warrant submitted by a special agent for the Bureau of Alcohol, Tobacco and Firearms to the federal magistrate did particularly describe the place to be searched and the illegal weapons to be seized, the warrant itself failed to identify any of the items intended to be seized at the plaintiffs' home. *Id.* at 554–55. The search of the plaintiffs' house uncovered no illegal firearms or explosives and no charges were ever filed against them. *Id.* The plaintiffs later filed a *Bivens* suit against the executing officers alleging a violation of the Fourth Amendment. *Id.* at 555.

For the majority, Justice Stevens in *Groh* first confirmed that "[t]he warrant was plainly invalid" as "[t]he Fourth Amendment states unambiguously that 'no Warrants shall issue, but upon probable cause, supported by Oath or affirmation, and *particularly describing* the place to be searched, and *the persons or things to be seized*." *Id.* at 557 (emphasis in original). The Court explained that the particular warrant requirement " 'assures the individual whose property is searched or seized of the lawful authority of the executing officer, his need to search, and the limits of his power to search.' " *Id.* at 561 (quoting *United States v. Chadwick*, 433 U.S. 1, 9 (1977)). (Justice Thomas, joined on this point only by Justice Scalia, dissented from the threshold finding that a Fourth Amendment violation had occurred in the case, arguing that because the underlying application had detailed the items to be seized, and a neutral magistrate had approved the warrant, the accidental defect in the warrant did not render the search warrantless or unreasonable. *Id.* at 571–76 (Thomas, J., dissenting).)

On the qualified immunity question, Justice Stevens for the Court in *Groh* then stated that "even a cursory reading of the warrant in this case—perhaps just a simple glance—would have revealed a glaring defect that any reasonable police officer would have known was constitutionally fatal." *Id.* at 564. Accordingly, the Court majority held, the federal officers involved could not claim qualified immunity from liability in the *Bivens* suit. *Id.* at 563–65. Four justices dissented, contending that qualified immunity should not be withdrawn when "the officer simply made a clerical error when he filled out the proposed warrant," but had properly complied with all other duties including providing a particularized description in the application submitted to the magistrate. *Id.* at 566–69 (Kennedy, J., dissenting); *see also id.* at 579–80 (Thomas, J., dissenting) (arguing that the executing officer was entitled to qualified immunity because he reasonably believed the warrant was valid, despite his good faith error, and that the majority's rule effectively imposes a new "proofreading requirement" upon officers executing warrants). Justice Kennedy further observed that the *Bivens* plaintiffs in that case could not present the usual claim that "they were injured by a defect that led to an improper search," but rather asserted they were harmed because the warrant form did not properly describe the items to be seized, even though no items in fact were seized. *Id.* at 570–71.

4. In *Harlow*, Justice Powell quotes the Court's earlier statement in *Butz v. Economou*, 438 U.S. 478, 507–08 (1978), encouraging termination of insubstantial *Bivens* suits on motions to dismiss or for summary judgment. Indeed, the *Harlow* Court's revision of the qualified immunity criteria is substantially influenced by the Court's desire to allow immunity questions to be answered at an early procedural stage in litigation and without extensive factual discovery. How does the *Harlow* Court's modification of the qualified immunity standard make disposition on summary judgment more likely in such cases? Why is this desirable? Or is it? Justice Brennan

in his first concurring opinion notes that some measure of discovery may sometimes still be necessary even under the modified standard. What would that be?

In the subsequent decision of *Mitchell v. Forsyth,* 472 U.S. 511 (1985), the Court further attempted to ensure that immunity claims would be resolved at the earliest possible stage of litigation, by authorizing a defendant to immediately appeal a district court's denial of immunity. (Ordinarily, a party may take an appeal only from a final judgment in the trial court, that is, after completion of all proceedings—including any trial on the merits—in the lower court.) The *Mitchell* Court stated that "[t]he entitlement is an *immunity from suit* rather than a mere defense to liability; and like an absolute immunity, it is effectively lost if a case is erroneously permitted to go to trial." *Id.* at 526 (emphasis in original). The Court explained that qualified immunity provides "an entitlement not to stand trial or face the other burdens of litigation, conditioned on the resolution of the essentially legal question of whether the conduct of which the plaintiff complains violated clearly established law." *Id.*

In light of subsequent cases, such as *Anderson v. Creighton,* the Court may have been unduly hopeful in *Harlow* that qualified immunity invariably would be a purely legal issue that could be decided by the trial court at the beginning stages of the litigation. Commentators have observed that the Court's refined standard for qualified immunity may be on a collision course with its stated desire to allow for early resolution of qualified immunity issues:

> [P]rotecting officers who may be innocent of wrongdoing from the necessity of trial or exposure to extensive discovery is difficult, perhaps even more difficult than even [the Supreme Court's decisions] acknowledge. For, while the question of whether a constitutional right exists and is clearly established easily may be characterized as a question of law, it is difficult to untangle from the facts of particular cases. Moreover, the question whether an official could reasonably have believed that his or her acts were constitutional necessarily implicates the underlying facts—facts that are often hotly contested.

Jerry L. Mashaw, Richard A. Merrill & Peter M. Shane, *Administrative Law: Cases and Materials* 1176 (5th ed. 2003); *see also* Alan K. Chen, *The Facts About Qualified Immunity,* 55 Emory L.J. 229, 232 (2006) (contending that the Court's treatment of qualified immunity as a legal question, and its failure to acknowledge the factual complexity of many cases, reflects the Court's discomfort with the qualified nature of immunity and has the effect of "transferring the adjudication of civil rights claims toward judges and away from juries").

5. In a sharply-divided decision, the Supreme Court clarified that, even after *Harlow,* a government officer's intent in acting may remain relevant in claims of certain constitutional violations, thereby requiring discovery concerning and inquiry into the defendant's subjective motivation and also raising issues not as easily amenable to resolution short of trial. In *Crawford–El v. Britton,* 523 U.S. 574 (1998), an inmate sued a correctional

official under 42 U.S.C. § 1983 asserting that, during the inmate's transfer from one prison to another, the official had intentionally misdelivered boxes of the inmate's legal papers and personal possessions and had done so for the purpose of retaliating against the inmate's exercise of First Amendment free speech rights about prison conditions. (As noted earlier, a Section 1983 suit against state officers for violation of federal and constitutional rights is parallel in many respects, including the definition of the constitutional right and the qualified immunity analysis, to *Bivens* claims.) Writing for a five-justice majority, Justice Stevens explained that there remains "a wide array of different federal law claims for which an official's motive is a necessary element, such as claims of race and gender discrimination in violation of the Equal Protection Clause, cruel and unusual punishment in violation of the Eighth Amendment, and termination of employment based on political affiliation in violation of the First Amendment, as well as retaliation for the exercise of free speech or other constitutional rights." *Id.* at 585. He distinguished the Court's rejection of a subjective inquiry in *Harlow* as limited to the qualified immunity analysis and not implicating the necessary elements of the plaintiff's initial burden of proving a constitutional violation: "Thus, although evidence of improper motive is irrelevant on the issue of qualified immunity, it may be an essential component of the plaintiff's affirmative case." *Id.* at 589. Accordingly, to carry a constitutional case requiring proof of improper intent beyond summary judgment, the plaintiff need only come forward with specific and affirmative evidence from which a jury could reasonably find that it is more likely than not that the defendant acted with an unconstitutional motivation; the plaintiff is not obliged to make a showing of clear and convincing evidence. *See id.* at 594–600. However, notwithstanding the presence of substantial issues surrounding the constitutional claim, a case still may be dismissed before trial on the separate and objective ground of immunity and, per *Harlow,* discovery may not be permitted until the threshold question of qualified immunity is resolved. *Id.* at 597–600.

Four justices dissented, regarding *Harlow* as more broadly purging Section 1983 and *Bivens* cases of subjective components. Chief Justice Rehnquist, joined by Justice O'Connor, argued that plaintiffs should not be permitted "to strip defendants of *Harlow*'s protections by a simple act of pleading—any minimally competent attorney (or pro se litigant) can convert any adverse decision into a motive-based tort, and thereby subject government officials to some measure of intrusion into their subjective worlds." *Id.* at 604–05 (Rehnquist, C.J., dissenting). Thus, he preferred strengthening the objective qualified immunity defense by the following test: "When a plaintiff alleges that an official's action was taken with an unconstitutional or otherwise unlawful motive, the defendant will be entitled to immunity and immediate dismissal of the suit if he can offer a lawful reason for his action and the plaintiff cannot establish, through objective evidence, that the offered reason is actually a pretext." *Id.* at 605. Justice Scalia, joined by Justice Thomas, would have further ensured a "subjective-less" inquiry and not permitted evidence of pretext (such as remarks revealing that the defendant had a partisan-political animus against the plaintiff) when a constitutionally-valid reason is offered by the government official for the action: "[O]nce the trial court finds that the asserted grounds for the official action were objectively valid (*e.g.,* the person fired for alleged incompetence was indeed incompetent), it would not admit any proof that something other than those reasonable grounds were the genuine motive (*e.g.,* the incompetent person fired was a Republican)." *Id.* at 612 (Scalia, J., dissenting).

————

c. IMPLYING A BIVENS CLAIM AGAINST THE UNITED STATES

Federal Deposit Insurance Corp. v. Meyer

Supreme Court of the United States.
510 U.S. 471 (1994).

■ JUSTICE THOMAS delivered the opinion of the Court.

In *Bivens v. Six Unknown Fed. Narcotics Agents,* 403 U.S. 388 (1971), we implied a cause of action for damages against federal agents who allegedly violated the Constitution. Today we are asked to imply a similar cause of action directly against an agency of the Federal Government. Because the logic of *Bivens* itself does not support such an extension, we decline to take this step.

I

On April 13, 1982, the California Savings and Loan Commissioner seized Fidelity Savings and Loan Association (Fidelity), a California-chartered thrift institution, and appointed the Federal Savings and Loan Insurance Corporation (FSLIC) to serve as Fidelity's receiver under state law. That same day, the Federal Home Loan Bank Board appointed FSLIC to serve as Fidelity's receiver under federal law. In its capacity as receiver, FSLIC had broad authority to "take such action as may be necessary to put [the thrift] in a sound solvent condition." 48 Stat. 1259, as amended, 12 U.S.C. § 1729(b)(1)(A)(ii) (repealed 1989). Pursuant to its general policy of terminating the employment of a failed thrift's senior management, FSLIC, through its special representative Robert L. Pattullo, terminated respondent John H. Meyer, a senior Fidelity officer.

Approximately one year later, Meyer filed this lawsuit against a number of defendants, including FSLIC and Pattullo, in the United States District Court for the Northern District of California. At the time of trial, Meyer's sole claim against FSLIC and Pattullo was that his summary discharge deprived him of a property right (his right to continued employment under California law) without due process of law in violation of the Fifth Amendment. In making this claim, Meyer relied upon *Bivens v. Six Unknown Fed. Narcotics Agents, supra,* which implied a cause of action for damages against federal agents who allegedly violated the Fourth Amendment. The jury returned a $130,000 verdict against FSLIC, but found in favor of Pattullo on qualified immunity grounds.

Petitioner Federal Deposit Insurance Corporation (FDIC), FSLIC's statutory successor,[1] appealed to the Court of Appeals for the Ninth Circuit, which affirmed. 944 F.2d 562 (1991). First, the Court of Appeals determined that the Federal Tort Claims Act (FTCA or Act), 28 U.S.C. §§ 1346(b), 2671–2680, did not provide Meyer's exclusive remedy. Although the FTCA remedy is "exclusive" for all "claims which are cognizable under section 1346(b)" of the Act, 28 U.S.C. § 2679(a), the Court of Appeals decided that Meyer's claim was not cognizable under § 1346(b). The court then concluded that the "sue-and-be-sued" clause contained in FSLIC's organic statute, 12 U.S.C. § 1725(c)(4) (repealed 1989), constituted a waiver of sovereign immunity for Meyer's claim and entitled him to maintain an action against the agency. Finally, on the merits, the court affirmed the jury's conclusion that Meyer had been deprived of due process when he was summarily discharged without notice and a hearing. We granted certiorari to consider the validity of the damages award against FSLIC.

II

Absent a waiver, sovereign immunity shields the Federal Government and its agencies from suit. Sovereign immunity is jurisdictional in nature. Indeed, the "terms of [the United States'] consent to be sued in any court define that court's jurisdiction to entertain the suit." *United States v. Sherwood,* 312 U.S. 584, 586 (1941). Therefore, we must first decide whether FSLIC's immunity has been waived.

A

When Congress created FSLIC in 1934, it empowered the agency "[t]o sue and be sued, complain and defend, in any court of competent jurisdiction." 12 U.S.C. § 1725(c)(4) (repealed 1989).[3] By permitting FSLIC to sue and be sued, Congress effected a "broad" waiver of FSLIC's immunity from suit. *United States v. Nordic Village, Inc.,* 503 U.S. 30 (1992). In 1946, Congress passed the FTCA, which waived the sovereign immunity of the United States for certain torts committed by federal employees. 28 U.S.C. § 1346(b). In order to "place torts of 'suable' agencies ... upon precisely the same footing as torts of 'nonsuable' agencies," *Loeffler [v. Frank],* 486 U.S., [549,] 562 [(1988)] (internal quotation marks omitted), Congress, through the FTCA, limited the scope of sue-and-be-sued waivers such as that contained in FSLIC's organic statute. The FTCA limitation provides:

"The authority of any federal agency to sue and be sued in its own name shall not be construed to authorize suits against such federal

---

1. See 12 U.S.C. § 1821(d). After FSLIC was abolished by the Financial Institutions Reform, Recovery, and Enforcement Act of 1989 (FIRREA), Pub.L. 101–73, 103 Stat. 183, FDIC was substituted for FSLIC in this suit.

3. The statute governing FDIC contains a nearly identical sue-and-be-sued clause. See 12 U.S.C. § 1819(a) Fourth (FDIC "shall have power ... [t]o sue and be sued, and complain and defend, in any court of law or equity, State or Federal").

agency on claims which are cognizable under section 1346(b) of this title, and the remedies provided by this title in such cases shall be exclusive." 28 U.S.C. § 2679(a).

Thus, if a suit is "cognizable" under § 1346(b) of the FTCA, the FTCA remedy is "exclusive" and the federal agency cannot be sued "in its own name," despite the existence of a sue-and-be-sued clause.

The first question, then, is whether Meyer's claim is "cognizable" under § 1346(b). The term "cognizable" is not defined in the Act. In the absence of such a definition, we construe a statutory term in accordance with its ordinary or natural meaning. Cognizable ordinarily means "[c]apable of being tried or examined before a designated tribunal; within [the] jurisdiction of [a] court or power given to [a] court to adjudicate [a] controversy." Black's Law Dictionary 259 (6th ed. 1990). Under this definition, the inquiry focuses on the jurisdictional grant provided by § 1346(b).

Section 1346(b) grants the federal district courts jurisdiction over a certain category of claims for which the United States has waived its sovereign immunity and "render[ed]" itself liable. *Richards v. United States,* 369 U.S. 1, 6 (1962). This category includes claims that are:

> "[1] against the United States, [2] for money damages, ... [3] for injury or loss of property, or personal injury or death [4] caused by the negligent or wrongful act or omission of any employee of the Government [5] while acting within the scope of his office or employment, [6] under circumstances where the United States, if a private person, would be liable to the claimant in accordance with the law of the place where the act or omission occurred." 28 U.S.C. § 1346(b).

A claim comes within this jurisdictional grant—and thus is "cognizable" under § 1346(b)—if it is actionable under § 1346(b). And a claim is actionable under § 1346(b) if it alleges the six elements outlined above.

Applying these principles to this case, we conclude that Meyer's constitutional tort claim is not "cognizable" under § 1346(b) because it is not actionable under § 1346(b)—that is, § 1346(b) does not provide a cause of action for such a claim. As noted above, to be actionable under § 1346(b), a claim must allege, *inter alia,* that the United States "would be liable to the claimant" as "a private person" "in accordance with the law of the place where the act or omission occurred." A constitutional tort claim such as Meyer's could not contain such an allegation. Indeed, we have consistently held that § 1346(b)'s reference to the "law of the place" means law of the State—the source of substantive liability under the FTCA. By definition, federal law, not state law, provides the source of liability for a claim alleging the deprivation of a federal constitutional right. To use the terminology of *Richards,* the United States simply has not rendered itself liable under § 1346(b) for constitutional tort claims. Thus, because Meyer's constitutional tort claim is not cognizable under § 1346(b), the FTCA does not constitute his "exclusive" remedy. His claim was therefore properly brought against FSLIC "in its own name." 28 U.S.C. § 2679(a). * * *

B

Because Meyer's claim is not cognizable under § 1346(b), we must determine whether FSLIC's sue-and-be-sued clause waives sovereign immunity for the claim. FDIC argues that the scope of the sue-and-be-sued waiver should be limited to cases in which FSLIC would be subjected to liability as a private entity. A constitutional tort claim such as Meyer's, FDIC argues, would fall outside the sue-and-be-sued waiver because the Constitution generally does not restrict the conduct of private entities. In essence, FDIC asks us to engraft a portion of the sixth element of § 1346(b)—liability "under circumstances where the United States, if a private person, would be liable to the claimant"—onto the sue-and-be-sued clause.

On its face, the sue-and-be-sued clause contains no such limitation. To the contrary, its terms are simple and broad: FSLIC "shall have power . . . [t]o sue and be sued, complain and defend, in any court of competent jurisdiction in the United States." 12 U.S.C. § 1725(c)(4) (repealed 1989). In the past, we have recognized that such sue-and-be-sued waivers are to be "liberally construed," *Federal Housing Admin. v. Burr*, 309 U.S. [242,] 245 [(1940)], notwithstanding the general rule that waivers of sovereign immunity are to be read narrowly in favor of the sovereign. *Burr* makes it clear that sue-and-be-sued clauses cannot be limited by implication unless there has been a

> "clea[r] show[ing] that certain types of suits are not consistent with the statutory or constitutional scheme, that an implied restriction of the general authority is necessary to avoid grave interference with the performance of a governmental function, or that for other reasons it was plainly the purpose of Congress to use the 'sue and be sued' clause in a narrow sense." 309 U.S., at 245.

Absent such a showing, agencies "authorized to 'sue and be sued' are presumed to have fully waived immunity." *International Primate Protection League v. Administrators of Tulane Ed. Fund*, 500 U.S. 72, 86, n. 8 (1991) (describing the holding in *Burr*). * * *

* * * [W]e hesitate to engraft language from § 1346(b) onto the sue-and-be-sued clause when Congress, in § 2679(a), expressly set out how the former provision would limit the latter. As provided in § 2679(a), § 1346(b) limits sue-and-be-sued waivers for claims that are "cognizable" under § 1346(b). Thus, § 2679(a) contemplates that a sue-and-be-sued waiver could encompass claims not cognizable under § 1346(b) and render an agency subject to suit unconstrained by the express limitations of the FTCA. FDIC's construction—taken to its logical conclusion—would not permit this result because it would render coextensive the scope of the waivers contained in § 1346(b) and sue-and-be-sued clauses generally. Had Congress wished to achieve that outcome, it surely would not have employed the language it did in § 2679(a). Because "[n]o showing has been made to overcome [the] presumption" that the sue-and-be-sued clause "fully waived" FSLIC's immunity in this instance, *Franchise Tax Board, supra*, 467 U.S., at 520, 104 S. Ct., at 2554; *International Primate Protec-*

tion League, 500 U.S., at 86, we hold that FSLIC's sue-and-be-sued clause waives the agency's sovereign immunity for Meyer's constitutional tort claim.

III

Although we have determined that Meyer's claim falls within the sue-and-be-sued waiver, our inquiry does not end at this point. Here we part ways with the Ninth Circuit, which determined that Meyer had a cause of action for damages against FSLIC *because* there had been a waiver of sovereign immunity. The Ninth Circuit's reasoning conflates two "analytically distinct" inquiries. *United States v. Mitchell,* 463 U.S. [206,] 218 [(1983)]. The first inquiry is whether there has been a waiver of sovereign immunity. If there has been such a waiver, as in this case, the second inquiry comes into play—that is, whether the source of substantive law upon which the claimant relies provides an avenue for relief. It is to this second inquiry that we now turn.

Meyer bases his due process claim on our decision in *Bivens,* which held that an individual injured by a federal agent's alleged violation of the Fourth Amendment may bring an action for damages against the agent. In our most recent decisions, we have "responded cautiously to suggestions that *Bivens* remedies be extended into new contexts." *Schweiker v. Chilicky,* 487 U.S. 412, 421 (1988). In this case, Meyer seeks a significant extension of *Bivens*: he asks us to expand the category of defendants against whom *Bivens*-type actions may be brought to include not only federal agents, but federal agencies as well.

We know of no Court of Appeals decision, other than the Ninth Circuit's below, that has implied a *Bivens*-type cause of action directly against a federal agency. Meyer recognizes the absence of authority supporting his position, but argues that the "logic" of *Bivens* would support such a remedy. We disagree. In *Bivens,* the petitioner sued the agents of the Federal Bureau of Narcotics who allegedly violated his rights, not the Bureau itself. Here, Meyer brought precisely the claim that the logic of *Bivens* supports—a *Bivens* claim for damages against Pattullo, the FSLIC employee who terminated him.

An additional problem with Meyer's "logic" argument is the fact that we implied a cause of action against federal officials in *Bivens* in part because a direct action against the Government was not available. *Id.,* at 410 (Harlan, J., concurring in judgment). In essence, Meyer asks us to imply a damages action based on a decision that presumed the *absence* of that very action.

Meyer's real complaint is that Pattullo, like many *Bivens* defendants, invoked the protection of qualified immunity. But *Bivens* clearly contemplated that official immunity would be raised. More importantly, Meyer's proposed "solution"—essentially the circumvention of qualified immunity—would mean the evisceration of the *Bivens* remedy, rather than its extension. It must be remembered that the purpose of *Bivens* is to deter the officer. See *Carlson v. Green,* 446 U.S. 14, 21(1980) ("Because the *Bivens* remedy is recoverable against individuals, it is a more effective deterrent than the FTCA remedy against the United States"). If we were to imply a damages action directly against federal agencies, thereby permitting claimants to bypass qualified immunity, there would be no reason for aggrieved parties to bring damages actions against individual officers. Under Meyer's regime, the deterrent effects of the *Bivens* remedy would be lost.

Finally, a damages remedy against federal agencies would be inappropriate even if such a remedy were consistent with *Bivens*. Here, unlike in *Bivens,* there are "special factors counselling hesitation" in the creation of a damages remedy. *Bivens,* 403 U.S., at 396. If we were to recognize a direct action for damages against federal agencies, we would be creating a potentially enormous financial burden for the Federal Government. Meyer disputes this reasoning and argues that the Federal Government already expends significant resources indemnifying its employees who are sued under *Bivens*. Meyer's argument implicitly suggests that the funds used for indemnification could be shifted to cover the direct liability of federal agencies. That may or may not be true, but decisions involving " 'federal fiscal policy' " are not ours to make. *Ibid.* We leave it to Congress to weigh the implications of such a significant expansion of Government liability.[11]

IV

An extension of *Bivens* to agencies of the Federal Government is not supported by the logic of *Bivens* itself. We therefore hold that Meyer had no *Bivens* cause of action for damages against FSLIC. Accordingly, the judgment below is reversed.

So ordered.

––––––––

Notes and Questions

1. *Federal Deposit Insurance Corporation v. Meyer* brings together the subjects of suits against government officers and suits against the government itself. Moreover, it reprises some matters we have covered previously, such as the Federal Tort Claims Act (see Chapter III.A) and actions involving so-called "sue-and-be-sued" agencies or government corporations that have broadly waived sovereign immunity (see Chapter III.F). Most importantly, however, the *Meyer* case provides another occasion to ask whether it is more appropriate to hold the government itself directly liable for wrongdoing by government agents rather than relegate injured parties to suits against government officers. When a government official has infringed a constitutional protection to the harm of a citizen—the so-called "constitutional tort"—should the government itself compensate the citizen

––––––––

11. In this regard, we note that Congress has considered several proposals that would have created a *Bivens*-type remedy directly against the Federal Government. See, *e.g.,* H.R. 440, 99th Cong., 1st Sess. (1985); H.R. 595, 98th Cong., 1st Sess. (1983); S. 1775, 97th Cong., 1st Sess. (1981); H.R. 2659, 96th Cong., 1st Sess. (1979).

for the injury (assuming a monetary remedy should be allowed at all)? Or should we continue to impose the liability upon the government employee through the *Bivens*-type action?

2.   The *Meyer* case begins by asking whether: (1) the Federal Tort Claims Act (FTCA) (with the United States as the proper defendant) is the exclusive remedy for a tort-style lawsuit involving a government agency, or (2) whether the action may be maintained directly against an agency whose sovereign immunity has been waived through a statutory clause allowing the agency to "sue and be sued." In general, the FTCA is the exclusive provision for tort suits against the federal government—but that exclusivity is not unlimited. Under 28 U.S.C. § 2679(a), the FTCA exclusively governs suits against even agencies that are authorized to sue and be sued in their own name *if* the claim is "cognizable" under Section 1346(b) of the FTCA, 28 U.S.C. § 1346(b). What does it mean to say that a claim must be "cognizable" under Section 1346(b) of the FTCA? What are the elements of a "cognizable" FTCA action? Why does the Court conclude that a "constitutional tort" is *not* "cognizable" under the FTCA?

If the FTCA is not the exclusive remedy in a case because a constitutional tort claim is not cognizable under that statute, then the agency's "sue-and-be-sued" clause has not been superseded and remains available as a hook upon which to hang a cause of action. Indeed, the Court here agrees that the "sue-and-be-sued" clause does waive the agency's sovereign immunity for a constitutional tort claim. But a waiver of sovereign immunity only gets a plaintiff part of the way to recovery. What more is required? Why does the *Meyer* Court conclude that the plaintiff may not recover under the "sue-and-be-sued" clause? The complete answer to that question requires analysis of the *Bivens* cause of action and its scope and limitations.

3.   In the final step of the analysis, the *Meyer* Court concludes that "the 'logic' of *Bivens*" does not support extending a cause of action in damages for a constitutional violation to the government itself. What then *is* "the logic of *Bivens*"? Why in the Court's view would it not make sense to hold the government directly liable for the constitutional wrongs of its agents? The Court says that the premise of *Bivens* is that the agents of the government agency violated the plaintiff's constitutional rights, not the agency itself. Isn't that simply a resurrection of the fictional dichotomy between government officers and the government they serve? The government officer acts as an agent of the government, and the government can only act through its agents. Why should they not be seen as one and the same? What benefits does the Court perceive in preserving the *Bivens* remedy as one against the government employee personally rather than adding or substituting the government as the defendant?

A number of commentators have argued that there would be substantial advantages in shifting liability for both ordinary and constitutional torts from public employees to the government itself. Professor Peter Schuck lists a variety of defects flowing from imposing liability directly upon officials rather than upon the government: "its propensity to chill vigorous decisionmaking; to leave deserving victims uncompensated and losses concentrated; to weaken deterrence; to obscure the morality of the law; and to generate high system costs." Peter H. Schuck, *Suing Government* 100 (1983). Professor Richard Pierce contends that "[e]xposing individual government employees to potential tort liability is particularly likely to produce socially undesirable decisionmaking incentives." 3 Richard J. Pierce, Jr., *Administrative Law Treatise* § 19.2, at 1390 (4th ed., 2002). Because individuals are most likely to fear substantial personal liability, holding government employees personally liable for ordinary or constitutional torts may discourage them from undertaking new initiatives or reforms. Pierce notes that "many public officials routinely act in areas in which the legal constraints on their actions are both dynamic and murky." *Id.* (The doctrine of qualified immunity is designed to address this concern. Does it fully succeed?) Even when the conduct is plainly wrongful, Professor Schuck argues that "the costs of wrongdoing [should be] imposed upon the entity responsible for recruiting, training, guiding, constraining, managing, and disciplining" government employees, rather than visiting liability upon individual officials who may be merely "instrument[s] of impersonal bureaucratic, political, and social processes over which they have little or no effective control." Schuck, *supra,* at 101–02.

In addition to the effect on government interests and the injustice to public officials, these commentators argue that focusing liability upon government officials, rather than the government, weakens the claims of those who have been wronged by government agents:

> Allowing tort actions against government employees, rather than government, has three other adverse effects. First, sympathy for the plight of the public employee defendant often induces courts to adopt unduly narrow interpretations of constitutional and statutory rights. * * * Second, sympathy for the plight of the public servant employee often induces juries to resolve close factual disputes in favor of the defendant and to award lower damages than would otherwise be warranted. Third, plaintiffs who are seriously injured by unlawful government conduct rarely can recover their full damages from a government employee defendant because government employees rarely have unencumbered assets sufficient to satisfy a large judgment.

Pierce, *supra,* § 19.2, at 1391–92; *see also* Schuck, *supra,* at 101; Cornelia T.L. Pillard, *Taking Fiction Seriously: The Strange Results of Public Officials' Individual Liability Under* Bivens, 88 Geo. L.J. 65, 66 (1998) (arguing that the "low rate of successful claims indicates that, notwithstanding *Bivens,* federal constitutional violations are almost never remedied by damages"). For these reasons, Professor Pierce concludes that "[t]ort law would provide a more appropriate constraint on government action and a more secure source of compensation for victims of torts committed by government if all potential exposure to tort liability were transferred from public employees to government." Pierce, *supra,* at 1392. *Cf.* Richard H. Fallon, Jr. & Daniel J. Meltzer, *New Law, Non–Retroactivity, and Constitutional Remedies,* 104 Harv. L. Rev. 1731, 1822–23 (1991) (observing that, if suits against officers are seen as "functionally necessary surrogates for governmental liability" and the government is understood to be the real party in interest—although formally protected from suit by sovereign immunity—then the logical course would be to narrow the scope of official immunity and thus expand the occasions upon which officers would be held liable, which in turn "would pressure government to provide indemnification and thereby internalize the costs of government, which in turn would permit victims to obtain relief even if the official tortfeasors themselves were judgment-proof").

By contrast, Professor Barbara Armacost generally defends the Supreme Court's resistance to respondeat superior liability by governmental entities and its focus upon the individual conduct of government officials. Barbara E. Armacost, *Qualified Immunity: Ignorance Excused,* 51 Vand. L. Rev. 583, 663–76 (1998). In partial response to the concern that the risk of personal liability deters government officials not only from wrongdoing but also from initiative and creativity in governance, she notes that (at least in the parallel context of state government employee liability for violations of constitutional rights under Section 1983) "governmental employers routinely indemnify their employees for the costs of liability, creating a de facto (if not de jure) entity liability in which the blameworthy individual rarely bears the monetary burden." *Id.* at 591. Even though the government itself generally covers the officer's liability through indemnification, Professor Armacost contends that "fault-based, individual liability—in which a particular official is identified as a 'constitutional wrongdoer'—serves a moral blaming function that has independent value regardless of who ultimately bears the financial cost of liability." *Id.* at 592. She concludes:

> Entities don't engage in malfeasance, the people who run them do. Something would be lost in a regime in which impersonal entities were the identified perpetrators of the constitutional harm rather than the blameworthy individuals. The label "wrongdoer" simply does not have the same moral significance as applied to governmental entities or institutions as it does when applied to individuals. Notions of fault and blameworthiness are understood to be personal, and individual liability attaches the label "malefactor" to officials with names and faces. Thus, important moral and societal interests are vindicated by a regime that makes blameworthy officials personally liable for their unconstitutional behavior, even if they do not ultimately pay the judgment.

Id. at 670.

You've now seen which side the Supreme Court has taken in this debate between individual officer versus governmental liability. Note that the *Meyer* decision was unanimous, thus suggesting the Court is unlikely to change its mind on the proper nature and scope of the *Bivens* remedy for constitutional torts.* Of course, Congress would be free to adopt a legisla-

---

* In *Correction Services Corporation v. Malesko,* 534 U.S. 61 (2001), the Supreme Court extended the *Meyer* rationale to a *Bi-* vens suit brought against a private corporate entity by a federal prisoner who suffered a heart attack and fell when made to take the

tive alternative and authorize constitutional tort suits against the federal government, while simultaneously eliminating individual officer liability under *Bivens*. Do you think it is likely to do so? Should it? Unless and until Congress acts (or the Court reconsiders its rulings), the *Bivens* remedy, limited though it may be in scope to certain circumstances and qualified as it is by immunity for defendants acting with objective reasonableness, remains a prominent landmark of the jurisprudential landscape.

stairs by employees of the private operator of a halfway house. Writing for the Court, Chief Justice Rehnquist emphasized that the *Bivens* cause of action applies only against individual officers alleged to have acted unconstitutionally and cited *Meyer* for the proposition that "the threat of suit against an individual's employer was not the kind of deterrence contemplated by *Bivens*." *Id.* at 519–21. Accordingly, the Court refused to imply a private right of action pursuant to *Bivens* for damages against private entities that engaged in allegedly unconstitutional deprivations while acting under color of federal law. *Id.* at 521–22. However, in contrast with the unanimous *Meyer* Court, the *Correction Services* Court was divided by a 5–4 vote. The dissenting Justices argued that *Meyer* had concluded only that federal agencies are not suable under *Bivens,* but did not preclude suit against government agents who violated constitutional rights, whether those agents are individual humans or private corporate entities. *Id.* at 524–25 (Stevens, J., dissenting).

CHAPTER VI

Binding The Federal Government

Section A. Unauthorized Representations by Government Employees—Equitable Estoppel

Justice Oliver Wendell Holmes admonished nearly a hundred years ago that "[m]en must turn square corners when they deal with the Government." *Rock Island, Ark. & La. R.R. Co. v. United States*, 254 U.S. 141, 143 (1920) (Holmes, J.). But it is impossible to turn squarely unless one learns where those corners are. And when a government agent purports to offer a map to negotiate those curves, that turns out to be false because the agent lacked authority and was speaking out of bounds, the sharp edges of those corners hurt all the more. Yet if a court were to afford a plaintiff a means to escape erroneous governmental advice, especially when the agent's advice exceeded statutory or regulatory boundaries, the result might undermine the rule of law, transgress the constitutional boundaries between the branches of the federal government, or discourage the government from offering informational services. The courts continue to struggle with those competing interests.

Office of Personnel Management v. Richmond

Supreme Court of the United States.
496 U.S. 414 (1990).

■ Justice Kennedy delivered the opinion of the Court.

This case presents the question whether erroneous oral and written advice given by a Government employee to a benefit claimant may give rise to estoppel against the Government, and so entitle the claimant to a monetary payment not otherwise permitted by law. We hold that payments of money from the Federal Treasury are limited to those authorized by statute, and we reverse the contrary holding of the Court of Appeals.

I

Not wishing to exceed a statutory limit on earnings that would disqualify him from a disability annuity, respondent Charles Richmond sought advice from a federal employee and received erroneous information. As a result he earned more than permitted by the eligibility requirements of the relevant statute and lost six months of benefits. Respondent now claims that the erroneous and unauthorized advice should give rise to equitable estoppel against the Government, and that we should order payment of the benefits contrary to the statutory terms. Even on the assumption that much equity subsists in respondent's claim, we cannot agree with him or the Court of Appeals that we have authority to order the payment he seeks.

Respondent was a welder at the Navy Public Works Center in San Diego, California. He left this position in 1981 after petitioner, the Office of Personnel Management (OPM), approved his application for a disability retirement. OPM determined that respondent's impaired eyesight prevented him from performing his job and made him eligible for a disability annuity under 5 U.S.C. § 8337(a). Section 8337(a) provides this benefit for disabled federal employees who have completed five years of service. The statute directs, however, that the entitlement to disability payments will end if the retired employee is "restored to an earning capacity fairly comparable to the current rate of pay of the position occupied at the time of retirement." 5 U.S.C. § 8337(d).

The statutory rules for restoration of earning capacity are central to this case. Prior to 1982, an individual was deemed restored to earning capacity, and so rendered ineligible for a disability annuity, if

"in *each of 2 succeeding calendar years* the income of the annuitant from wages or self-employment ... equals at least 80 percent of the current rate of pay of the position occupied immediately before retirement." 5 U.S.C. § 8337(d) (1976 ed.) (emphasis added).

The provision was amended in 1982 by the Omnibus Budget Reconciliation Act, Pub.L. 97–253, 96 Stat. 792, to change the measuring period for restoration of earning capacity from two years to one:

"Earning capacity is deemed restored if *in any calendar year* the income of the annuitant from wages or self-employment or both equals at least 80 percent of the current rate of pay of the position occupied immediately before retirement." 5 U.S.C. § 8337(d) (emphasis added).

After taking disability retirement for his vision impairment, respondent undertook part-time employment as a school bus driver. From 1982 to 1985, respondent earned an average of $12,494 in this job, leaving him under the 80% limit for entitlement to continued annuity payments. In 1986, however, he had an opportunity to earn extra money by working overtime. Respondent asked an Employee Relations Specialist at the Navy Public Works Center's Civilian Personnel Department for information about how much he could earn without exceeding the 80% eligibility limit. Relying upon the terms of the repealed pre–1982 statute, under which respondent could retain the annuity unless his income exceeded the 80% limit in two consecutive years, the specialist gave respondent incorrect advice. * * *

After receiving the erroneous information, respondent concluded that he could take on the extra work as a school bus driver in 1986 while still receiving full disability benefits for impaired vision so long as he kept his income for the previous and following years below the statutory level. He earned $19,936 during 1986, exceeding the statutory eligibility limit. OPM discontinued respondent's disability annuity on June 30, 1987. The annuity was restored on January 1, 1988, since respondent did not earn more than allowed by the statute in 1987. Respondent thus lost his disability payments for a 6–month period, for a total amount of $3,993.

Respondent appealed the denial of benefits to the Merit Systems Protection Board (MSPB). He argued that the erroneous advice given him by the Navy personnel should estop OPM and bar its finding him ineligible for benefits under the statute. * * * The MSPB held that "OPM cannot be estopped from enforcing a statutorily imposed requirement for retirement eligibility." The MSPB denied respondent's petition for review, and respondent appealed to the Court of Appeals for the Federal Circuit.

A divided panel of the Court of Appeals reversed * * *. * * * The Court of Appeals acknowledged the longstanding rule that "ordinarily the government may not be estopped because of erroneous or unauthorized statements of government employees when the asserted estoppel would nullify a requirement prescribed by Congress." 862 F.2d 294, 296 (C.A.Fed. 1988). Nonetheless, the Court of Appeals focused on this Court's statement in an earlier case that "we are hesitant ... to say that there are *no cases*" where the Government might be estopped. *Heckler v. Community Health Services of Crawford County, Inc.,* 467 U.S. 51, 60 (1984). * * *

* * * The Court reasoned that the provision of the out-of-date OPM form was "affirmative misconduct" that should estop the Government from denying respondent benefits in accordance with the statute. The facts of this case, it held, are "sufficiently unusual and extreme that no concern is warranted about exposing the public treasury to estoppel in broad or numerous categories of cases." *Id.,* at 301. Judge Mayer dissented, stating that the majority opinion made "a chasm out of the crack the Supreme Court left open in *Community Health Services,*" and that the award of benefits to respondent "contravenes the express mandate of Congress in 5 U.S.C. § 8337(d) ... and Supreme Court precedent." *Id.,* at 301, 303.

We granted certiorari.

II

From our earliest cases, we have recognized that equitable estoppel will not lie against the Government as against private litigants. * * *

The principles of these and many other cases were reiterated in *Federal Crop Insurance Corporation v. Merrill,* 332 U.S. 380 (1947), the leading case in our modern line of estoppel decisions. In *Merrill,* a farmer applied for insurance under the Federal Crop Insurance Act to cover his wheat farming operations. An agent of the Federal Crop Insurance Corporation advised the farmer that his entire crop qualified for insurance, and the farmer obtained insurance through the Corporation. After the crop was lost, it was discovered that the agent's advice had been in error, and that part of the farmer's crop was reseeded wheat, not eligible for federal insurance under the applicable regulation. While we recognized the serious hardship caused by the agent's misinformation, we nonetheless rejected the argument that his representations estopped the Government to deny insurance benefits. We recognized that "not even the temptations of a hard case" will provide a basis for ordering recovery contrary to the terms of the regulation, for to do so would disregard "the duty of all courts to observe the conditions defined by Congress for charging the public treasury." *Id.*, at 385–386.

Despite the clarity of these earlier decisions, dicta in our more recent cases have suggested the possibility that there might be some situation in which estoppel against the Government could be appropriate. The genesis of this idea appears to be an observation found at the end of our opinion in *Montana v. Kennedy,* 366 U.S. 308 (1961). In that case, the petitioner brought a declaratory judgment action seeking to establish his American citizenship. After discussing the petitioner's two statutory claims at length, we rejected the final argument that a consular official's erroneous advice to petitioner's mother that she could not return to the United States while pregnant prevented petitioner from having been born in the United States and thus deprived him of United States citizenship. Our discussion was limited to the observation that in light of the fact that no legal obstacle prevented petitioner's mother from returning to the United States,

> "what may have been only the consular official's well-meant advice—'I am sorry, Mrs., you cannot [return to the United States] in that condition'—falls far short of misconduct such as might prevent the United States from relying on petitioner's foreign birth. In this situation, we need not stop to inquire whether, as some lower courts have held, there may be circumstances in which the United States is estopped to deny citizenship because of the conduct of its officials." *Id.,* at 314–315.

The proposition about which we did not "stop to inquire" in *Kennedy* has since taken on something of a life of its own. Our own opinions have continued to mention the possibility, in the course of rejecting estoppel arguments, that some type of "affirmative misconduct" might give rise to estoppel against the Government.

The language in our decisions has spawned numerous claims for equitable estoppel in the lower courts. As JUSTICE MARSHALL stated in dissent in [*Schweiker v.*] *Hansen,* [450 U.S. 785 (1981) (*per curiam*)], "[t]he question of when the Government may be equitably estopped has divided the distinguished panel of the Court of Appeals in this case, has received inconsistent treatment from other Courts of Appeals, and has been the subject of considerable ferment." 450 U.S., at 791 (citing cases). Since that observation was made, federal courts have continued to accept estoppel claims under a variety of rationales and analyses. In sum, courts of appeals have taken our statements as an invitation to search for an appropriate case in which to apply estoppel against the Government, yet we have reversed every finding of estoppel that we have reviewed. Indeed, no less than three of our most recent decisions in this area have been summary reversals of decisions upholding estoppel claims. Summary reversals of courts of appeals are unusual under any circumstances. The extraordinary number of such dispositions in this single area of the law provides a good indication that our approach to these cases has provided inadequate guidance for the federal courts and served only to invite and prolong needless litigation.

The Solicitor General proposes to remedy the present confusion in this area of the law with a sweeping rule. As it has in the past, the Government asks us to adopt "a flat rule that estoppel may not in any circumstances run against the Government." The Government bases its broad rule first upon the doctrine of sovereign immunity. Noting that the "United States, as sovereign, is immune from suit save as it consents to be sued," *United States v. Mitchell,* 445 U.S. 535, 538 (1980), the Government asserts that the courts are without jurisdiction to entertain a suit to compel the Government to act contrary to a statute, no matter what the context or circumstances. The Government advances as a second basis for this rule the doctrine of separation of powers. The Government contends that to recognize estoppel based on the misrepresentations of Executive Branch officials would give those misrepresentations the force of law, and thereby invade the legislative province reserved to Congress. This rationale, too, supports the Government's contention that estoppel may never justify an order requiring executive action contrary to a relevant statute, no matter what statute or what facts are involved.

We have recognized before that the "arguments the Government advances for the rule are substantial." *Community Health Services, supra,* 467 U.S., at 60. And we agree that this case should be decided under a clearer form of analysis than "we will know an estoppel when we see one." *Hansen, supra,* at 792 (MARSHALL, J., dissenting). But it remains true that we need not embrace a rule that no estoppel will lie against the Government in any case in order to decide this case. We leave for another day whether an estoppel claim could ever succeed against the Government. A narrower ground of decision is sufficient to address the type of suit presented here, a claim for payment of money from the Public Treasury contrary to a statutory appropriation.

III

The Appropriations Clause of the Constitution, Art. I, § 9, cl. 7, provides that: "No Money shall be drawn from the Treasury, but in Consequence of Appropriations made by Law." For the particular type of claim at issue here, a claim for money from the Federal Treasury, the Clause provides an explicit rule of decision. Money may be paid out only through an appropriation made by law; in other words, the payment of money from the Treasury must be authorized by a statute. All parties here agree that the award respondent seeks would be in direct contravention of the federal statute upon which his ultimate claim to the funds must rest, 5 U.S.C. § 8337. * * * It follows that Congress has appropriated no money for the payment of the benefits respondent seeks, and the Constitution prohibits that any money "be drawn from the Treasury" to pay them.

Our cases underscore the straightforward and explicit command of the Appropriations Clause. "It means simply that no money can be paid out of the Treasury unless it has been appropriated by an act of Congress." *Cincinnati Soap Co. v. United States,* 301 U.S. 308, 321 (1937). * * *

We have not had occasion in past cases presenting claims of estoppel against the Government to discuss the Appropriations Clause, for reasons that are apparent. Given the strict rule against estoppel applied as early as 1813 in *Lee v. Munroe & Thornton,* 7 Cranch 366 (1813), claims of estoppel could be dismissed on that ground without more. In our cases reserving the possibility that estoppel might lie on some facts, we have held only that the particular facts presented were insufficient. As discussed above, we decline today to accept the Solicitor General's argument for an across-the-board no-estoppel rule. But this makes it all the more important to state the law and to settle the matter of estoppel as a basis for money claims against the Government.

Our decision is consistent with both the holdings and the rationale expressed in our estoppel precedents. Even our recent cases evince a most strict approach to estoppel claims involving public funds. See *Community Health Services,* 467 U.S., at 63 ("Protection of the public fisc requires that those who seek public funds act with scrupulous regard for the requirements of law"). The course of our jurisprudence shows why: Opinions have differed on whether this Court has ever accepted an estoppel claim in other contexts, but not a single case has upheld an estoppel claim against the Government for the payment of money. And our cases denying estoppel are animated by the same concerns that prompted the Framers to include the Appropriations Clause in the Constitution. As Justice Story described the Clause,

> "The object is apparent upon the slightest examination. It is to secure regularity, punctuality, and fidelity, in the disbursements of the public money. As all the taxes raised from the people, as well as revenues arising from other sources, are to be applied to the discharge of the expenses, and debts, and other engagements of the government, it is highly proper, that congress should possess the power to decide how and when any money should be applied for these purposes. If it were otherwise, the executive would possess an unbounded power over the public purse of the nation; and might apply all its moneyed resources at his pleasure. The power to control and direct the appropriations, constitutes a most useful and salutary check upon profusion and extravagance, as well as upon corrupt influence and public peculation.... § 2 J. Story, Commentaries on the Constitution of the United States § 1348 (3d ed. 1858).

The obvious practical consideration cited by Justice Story for adherence to the requirement of the Clause is the necessity, existing now as much as at the time the Constitution was ratified, of preventing fraud and corruption. We have long ago accepted this ground as a reason that claims for estoppel cannot be entertained where public money is at stake, refusing to "introduce a rule against an abuse, of which, by improper collusions, it would be very difficult for the public to protect itself." *Lee,* 7 Cranch, at 370. But the Clause has a more fundamental and comprehensive purpose, of direct relevance to the case before us. It is to assure that public funds will be spent according to the letter of the difficult judgments reached by Congress as to the common good, and not according to the individual favor of Government agents or the individual pleas of litigants.

Extended to its logical conclusion, operation of estoppel against the Government in the context of payment of money from the Treasury could in fact render the Appropriations Clause a nullity. If agents of the Executive were able, by their unauthorized oral or written statements to citizens, to obligate the Treasury for the payment of funds, the control over public funds that the Clause reposes in Congress in effect could be transferred to the Executive. If, for example, the President or Executive Branch officials were displeased with a new restriction on benefits imposed by Congress to ease burdens on the fisc (such as the restriction imposed by the statutory change in this case) and sought to evade them, agency officials could advise citizens that the restrictions were inapplicable. Estoppel would give this advice the practical force of law, in violation of the Constitution.

It may be argued that a rule against estoppel could have the opposite result, that the Executive might frustrate congressional intent to appropriate benefits by instructing its agents to give claimants erroneous advice that would deprive them of the benefits. But Congress may always exercise its power to expand recoveries for those who rely on mistaken advice should it choose to do so. * * *

The provisions of the Federal Torts Claims Act (FTCA), 28 U.S.C. §§ 1346(b), 2671 *et seq.,* also provide a strong indication of Congress' general approach to claims based on governmental misconduct, and suggest that it has considered and rejected the possibility of an additional exercise of its appropriation power to fund claims similar to those advanced here. The FTCA provides authorization in certain circumstances for suits by citizens against the Federal Government for torts committed by Government agents. Yet the FTCA by its terms excludes both negligent and intentional misrepresentation claims from its coverage. See 28 U.S.C. § 2680(h). The claim brought by respondent is in practical effect one for misrepresentation, despite the application of the "estoppel" label. We would be most hesitant to create a judicial doctrine of estoppel that would nullify a congressional decision against authorization of the same class of claims.

Indeed, it would be most anomalous for a judicial order to require a Government official, such as the officers of petitioner OPM, to make an extrastatutory payment of federal funds. It is a federal crime, punishable by fine and imprisonment, for any Government officer or employee to knowingly spend money in excess of that appropriated by Congress. See 31 U.S.C. §§ 1341, 1350. If an executive officer on his own initiative had decided that, in fairness, respondent should receive benefits despite the statutory bar, the official would risk prosecution. That respondent now seeks a court order to effect the same result serves to highlight the weakness and novelty of his claim.

The whole history and practice with respect to claims against the United States reveals the impossibility of an estoppel claim for money in violation of a statute. Congress' early practice was to adjudicate each individual money claim against the United States, on the ground that the Appropriations Clause forbade even a delegation of individual adjudicatory functions where payment of funds from the treasury was involved. As the business of the federal legislature has grown, Congress has placed the individual adjudication of claims based on the Constitution, statutes, or contracts, or on specific authorizations of suit against the Government, with the Judiciary. See, *e.g.*, the Tucker Act, 28 U.S.C. §§ 1346, 1491. But Congress has always reserved to itself the power to address claims of the very type presented by respondent, those founded not on any statutory authority, but upon the claim that "the equities and circumstances of a case create a moral obligation on the part of the Government to extend relief to an individual." Subcommittee on Administrative Law and Governmental Relations of the House Committee on the Judiciary, Supplemental Rules of Procedure for Private Claims Bills, 101st Cong., 1st Sess., 2 (Comm. Print 1989).

In so-called "congressional reference" cases, Congress refers proposed private bills to the United States Claims Court for an initial determination of the merits of the claim, but retains final authority over the ultimate appropriation. See 28 U.S.C. §§ 1492, 2509(c). Congress continues to employ private legislation to provide remedies in individual cases of hardship. Where sympathetic facts arise, these examples show the means by which they can be addressed. In short, respondent asks us to create by judicial innovation an authority over funds that is assigned by the Constitution to Congress alone, and that Congress has not seen fit to delegate.

Congress has, of course, made a general appropriation of funds to pay judgments against the United States rendered under its various authorizations for suits against the Government, such as the Tucker Act and the FTCA. See 31 U.S.C. § 1304. But respondent's claim for relief does not arise under any of these provisions. Rather, he sought and obtained an order of enrollment in the disability annuity plan, 5 U.S.C. § 8337, in direct violation of that plan's requirements.

The general appropriation for payment of judgments, in any event, does not create an all-purpose fund for judicial disbursement. A law that identifies the source of funds is not to be confused with the conditions prescribed for their payment. Rather, funds may be paid out only on the basis of a judgment based on a substantive right to compensation based on the express terms of a specific statute. This principle is set forth in our leading case on jurisdiction over claims against the Government, *United States v. Testan*, 424 U.S. 392 (1976). As stated in JUSTICE BLACKMUN's opinion for the Court,

"Where the United States is the defendant and the plaintiff is not suing for money improperly exacted or retained, the basis of the federal claim—whether it be the Constitution, a statute, or a regulation—does not create a cause of action for money damages unless . . . that basis 'in itself . . . can fairly be interpreted as mandating compensation by the Federal Government for the damage sustained.' " *Id.,* at 401–402.

Given this rule, as well as our many precedents establishing that authorizations for suits against the Government must be strictly construed in its favor, see, *e.g., Library of Congress v. Shaw,* 478 U.S. 310, 318 (1986), we cannot accept the suggestion that the terms of a statute should be ignored based on the facts of individual cases. Here the relevant statute by its terms excludes respondent's claim, and his remedy must lie with Congress.

Respondent would have us ignore these obstacles on the ground that estoppel against the Government would have beneficial effects. But we are unwilling to "tamper with these established principles because it might be thought that they should be responsive to a particular conception of enlightened governmental policy." *Testan, supra,* 424 U.S., at 400. And respondent's attempts to justify estoppel on grounds of public policy are suspect on their own terms. Even short of collusion by individual officers or improper Executive attempts to frustrate legislative policy, acceptance of estoppel claims for Government funds could have pernicious effects. It ignores reality to expect that the Government will be able to "secure perfect performance from its hundreds of thousands of employees scattered throughout the continent." *Hansen v. Harris,* 619 F.2d 942, 954 (C.A.2 1980) (Friendly, J., dissenting), rev'd *sub nom., Schweiker v. Hansen,* 450 U.S. 785 (1981). To open the door to estoppel claims would only invite endless litigation over both real and imagined claims of misinformation by disgruntled citizens, imposing an unpredictable drain on the public fisc. Even if most claims were rejected in the end, the burden of defending such estoppel claims would itself be substantial.

Also questionable is the suggestion that if the Government is not bound by its agents' statements, then citizens will not trust them, and will instead seek private advice from lawyers, accountants, and others, creating wasteful expenses. Although mistakes occur, we may assume with confidence that Government agents attempt conscientious performance of their duties, and in most cases provide free and valuable information to those who seek advice about Government programs. A rule of estoppel might create not more reliable advice, but less advice. The natural consequence of a rule that made the Government liable for the statements of its agents would be a decision to cut back and impose strict controls upon Government provision of information in order to limit liability. Not only would valuable informational programs be lost to the public, but the greatest impact of this loss would fall on those of limited means, who can least afford the alternative of private advice. See Braunstein, In Defense of a Traditional Immunity—Toward an Economic Rationale for Not Estopping the Government, 14 Rutgers L.J. 1 (1982). The inevitable fact of occasional individual hardship cannot undermine the interest of the citizenry as a whole in the ready availability of Government information. The rationale of the Appropriations Clause is that if individual hardships are to be remedied by payment of Government funds, it must be at the instance of Congress.

Respondent points to no authority in precedent or history for the type of claim he advances today. Whether there are any extreme circumstances that might support estoppel in a case not involving payment from the Treasury is a matter we need not address. As for monetary claims, it is enough to say that this Court has never upheld an assertion of estoppel against the Government by a claimant seeking public funds. In this context there can be no estoppel, for courts cannot estop the Constitution. The judgment of the Court of Appeals is

Reversed.

■ [The concurring opinions of JUSTICE WHITE and JUSTICE STEVENS are omitted.]

■ JUSTICE MARSHALL, with whom JUSTICE BRENNAN joins, dissenting.

Respondent, a recipient of a federal disability annuity, was unsure whether he could accept limited overtime work without forfeiting his right to disability payments. He went to his former Government employer seeking an answer, asked the right questions, received an answer in the form of both oral advice and an official Government publication, and relied on that answer. Unfortunately, the publication the Government gave Richmond was years out of date, and the oral information was similarly erroneous. In this case, we must decide who should bear the burden of the Government's error.

The majority hints that it is unsympathetic to Richmond's claim that he was treated unfairly, but it does not rule on that basis. Rather, the majority resolves the issue by holding as a general rule that a litigant may not succeed on a claim for payment of money from the Treasury in the absence of a statutory appropriation. Although the Constitution generally forbids payments from the Treasury without a congressional appropriation, that proposition does not resolve this case. Most fundamentally, Richmond's collection of disability benefits would be fully consistent with the relevant appropriation. And even if the majority is correct that the statute cannot be construed to appropriate funds for claimants in Richmond's position, the Government may nonetheless be estopped, on the basis of its prelitigation conduct, from arguing that the Appropriations Clause bars his recovery. Both the statutory construction and the estoppel arguments turn on the equities, and the equities favor Richmond. I therefore dissent.

I

As the majority notes, the Appropriations Clause generally bars recovery from the Treasury unless the money sought "has been appropriated by an Act of Congress." The majority acknowledges that Congress *has* appropriated funds to pay disability annuities in 5 U.S.C. § 8348(a), but holds that the fund created is intended for the payment of benefits only "as provided by" law. Section 8337(d) provides that a disability annuity terminates when the annuitant's earning capacity is restored and that such capacity is "deemed restored" if in any calendar year the annuitant makes more than 80% of the current rate of pay of the position he left. The majority contends on the basis of this provision that paying benefits to an annuitant who has exceeded the 80% limit would violate the Appropriations Clause because such benefits are not "provided by" the statute.

The Court need not read the statute so inflexibly, however. When Congress passes a law to provide a benefit to a class of people, it intends and assumes that the executive will fairly implement that law. Where necessary to effectuate Congress' intent that its statutory schemes be fully implemented, this Court therefore often interprets the apparently plain words of a statute to allow a claimant to obtain relief where the statute on its face would bar recovery. * * *

Respect for Congress' purposes in creating the federal disability annuity system and principles of elementary fairness require that we read the statute in this case as not barring Richmond's claim. Perhaps "[t]he equities do not weigh in favor of modifying statutory requirements when the procedural default is caused by petitioners' 'failure to take the minimal steps necessary' to preserve their claims." *Hallstrom [v. Tillamook County]*, 493 U.S., 20, 27 (1989)]. But the equities surely *do* weigh in favor of reading the disability annuity statute to authorize payment of the claim of an annuitant rendered ineligible for benefits by his reliance on misinformation from the responsible federal authorities.

II

Even if the majority is correct that the statute does not itself require an exception where the executive has misled a claimant, Richmond should still prevail. Although the Government has an Appropriations Clause argument against any claim for money not authorized by a statutory appropriation, a court is not invariably required to entertain that argument. A number of circumstances may operate to estop the Government from invoking the Appropriations Clause in a particular case. For example, this Court's normal practice is to refuse to consider arguments not presented in the petition for certiorari. This Court customarily applies a similar rule to questions that were not raised in the Court of Appeals. These rules apply to *all* arguments, even those of constitutional dimension. Thus, had the Government failed to raise the argument on which it now prevails either in its petition for certiorari or in the Court of Appeals, we likely would have refused to consider it. Of course, we would have had the power to consider the claim. We would not, however, have been obligated to do so.

The grounds on which a court may refuse to entertain an argument are many, but most have an equitable dimension. The courts' general refusal to consider arguments not raised by the parties, for example, is founded in part on the need to ensure that each party has fair notice of the arguments to which he must respond. Thus, the Appropriations Clause's bar against litigants' collection of money from the Treasury where payment is not authorized by statute may not be enforced in a particular case if a court determines that the equities counsel against entertaining the Government's Appropriations Clause argument.

The question here is thus similar to ones that we have posed and answered in any number of recent cases: should the Government *in this case* be barred from invoking the statutory eligibility requirement (and through it, the Appropriations Clause) because Richmond's ineligibility for benefits was due entirely to the Government's own error? The majority refuses to answer this question. The Court of Appeals addressed it directly, concluding that the facts in this case were so "unusual and extreme" that the Government should be estopped from applying the statutory restrictions to bar Richmond's recovery. I agree with the Court of Appeals' ruling.

III

The majority argues that policy concerns justify its general refusal to apply estoppel against the Government in cases in which a claimant seeks unappropriated funds from the Treasury. Such a rule is necessary, says the majority, to protect against "fraud and corruption" by executive branch officials. If such officials are "displeased" with a statute, the argument goes, they may misinform the public as to the statute's meaning, thereby binding the Government to the officials' representations. The majority's concern with such dangers is undercut, however, by its observation that "Government agents attempt conscientious performance of their duties." The majority also contends that even if most claims of equitable estoppel are rejected in the end, "open[ing] the door" to such claims would impose "an unpredictable drain on the public fisc." The door has been open for almost 30 years, with an apparently unnoticeable drain on the public fisc. This reality is persuasive evidence that the majority's fears are overblown.

Significant policy concerns would of course be implicated by an indiscriminate use of estoppel against the Government. But estoppel is an equitable doctrine. As such, it can be tailored to the circumstances of particular cases, ensuring that fundamental injustices are avoided without seriously endangering the smooth operation of statutory schemes. In this case, the Federal Circuit undertook a thorough examination of the circumstances and concluded that denying Richmond his pension simply because he followed the Government's advice would be fundamentally unjust.

The majority does not reject the court's findings on the facts but rejects Richmond's claim on the theory that, except where the Constitution requires otherwise, equitable estoppel may not be applied against the Government where the claimant seeks unappropriated funds from the Treasury. This Court has never so much as mentioned the Appropriations Clause in the context of a discussion of equitable estoppel, nor has the majority's theory ever before been discussed, much less adopted, by any court. This lack of precedent for the majority's position is not surprising because the Appropriations Clause does not speak either to the proper interpretation of any statute or to the question whether the Government should be estopped from invoking the Clause in a particular case. I dissent.

Notes and Questions

1. Before asking whether the government may be subject to equitable estoppel in the same manner as a private party, we first should understand the basic nature of the doctrine. A leading administrative law treatise explains the elements of the private law of equitable estoppel in this way:

> When Jones makes a representation to Smith, who reasonably relies to his detriment on that representation, Jones is then estopped to deny the truth of that representation. In this general form, estoppel includes elements of reasonable reliance on a representation and detrimental change in position caused by this reliance.

Alfred C. Aman, Jr. & William T. Mayton, *Administrative Law* § 11.2.1, at 324–25 (2d ed., 2001).

The classic government equitable estoppel case involves an alleged misstatement by a government employee about the rules establishing the process to apply for or the rules governing eligibility for a government benefit or program. The claimant or putative beneficiary relies upon this statement, but then discovers it is mistaken, to his or her detriment. For example, the person may decide not to apply for the program, based upon mistaken advice by a government employee that he or she was not eligible, thereby forgoing valuable benefits for a period of time. Or an individual may rely upon program coverage to which he or she has been assured by a government employee, only to later find that the coverage is not there when he or she really needs it, owing to mistaken advice about eligibility or the scope of the program. The archetypal scenario is that which framed the background to the Supreme Court's 1947 decision in *Federal Crop Insurance Corp. v. Merrill,* 332 U.S. 380 (1947), which is described in part II of the majority's opinion in *Office of Personnel Management v. Richmond.* And the *Richmond* case itself falls into that same basic category of cases, as it involves mistaken advice given by a government employee to the plaintiff regarding the amount of income he could earn without losing his federal disability benefits.

2. While both *Merrill* and *Richmond* fall into that typical pattern of a citizen's reliance on a government agent's misrepresentation, the outcome in these cases departs sharply from that which would pertain to a private defendant. In the non-governmental context, a person who reasonably relied upon a statement would be able to estop the person making the representation from denying the benefit. In the governmental cases of *Merrill* and *Richmond,* however, the Supreme Court acknowledges that the plaintiff may have suffered a hardship because of the government agent's erroneous communication, but refuses to estop the government from denying insurance coverage in the *Merrill* case and disability benefits in the *Richmond* case. Before we turn to the dispositive point upon which the *Richmond* decision turned (the Appropriations Clause), consider the general question of the applicability of equitable estoppel against the government. Should it so apply? Isn't holding the government bound by the representations of its agents only fair and just?

In *Richmond,* the Court says that the government's arguments for a flat rule that estoppel may never bind the government are substantial. What are those arguments? Do you find them persuasive? The United States Court of Appeals for the Seventh Circuit, in rejecting an estoppel claim against the government, stated that " '[e]stoppel' is just a way to describe a decision of a subordinate official that prevails over a decision of the political branches expressed in a law or regulation." *United States v. Medico Industries, Inc.,* 784 F.2d 840, 845 (7th Cir. 1986). What does the Seventh Circuit mean by that? Is that a valid description of what would be the effect of estoppel against the government? Does such a concern justify an absolute no-estoppel rule when it comes to the sovereign? A leading treatise says that application of equitable estoppel against the government, as contrasted with a private person, raises additional "considerations, such as rule of law, separation of powers, sovereign immunity, and an appropriate regard for the fiscal and administrative integrity of public programs." Aman & Mayton, *supra,* § 11.2.2, at 326. Outline how each consideration could be marshaled to support the "no-estoppel" position advanced by the government.

Consider also the potential practical consequences if the government could be easily estopped based upon the careless statements of one of its tens of thousands of employees? How likely is it that the government would continue to regularly provide information? Professor Michael Braunstein contends that a rule imposing liability based upon erroneous informal advice by government employees "could be expected to reduce the occasions on which advice is given and thereby reduce the total amount of information available to those who either desire or are forced to deal with the Government," which he suggests would disproportionately harm the poor who, unlike wealthier members of society, do not have access to alternative sources of information. Michael Braunstein, *In Defense of a Traditional Immunity—Toward an Economic Rationale for Not Estopping the Government,* 14 Rutgers L. J. 1, 32–33, 37 (1982). Toward the end of the majority opinion, the *Richmond* Court echoes this analysis. In this regard, note also that the Court in part III of the *Richmond* opinion cites the misrepresentation exception to the Federal Tort Claims Act (FTCA), 28 U.S.C. § 2680(h), in support of its conclusion that estoppel should not be applied. What is the Court's point in mentioning this FTCA provision? Review the discussion of misrepresentation exception of the FTCA and its purpose in Chapter III.A.5.

On the other hand, the plaintiff in *Richmond* diligently sought information from the government concerning the permissible amount of outside income that he could earn without jeopardizing his disability retirement benefits. The government employee whose job was to know and provide the correct answer instead provided him with outdated information, and the plaintiff relied upon this erroneous information in deciding to work additional hours at his part-time job.* Is it fair to penalize him with a

---

* Although not relevant to the legal issues in the case, it is curious to note that the plaintiff had been granted a disability retirement by reason of impaired eyesight and yet still was able to secure part-time work transporting school children as a bus driver!

withdrawal of benefits under these circumstances? Justice Marshall in dissent argues that the equities favor the plaintiff. Should fairness and equity be a factor here or are basic concerns of fairness outweighed by the government's countervailing public interests? In another decision, *Heckler v. Community Health Services, Inc.*, 467 U.S. 51, 60–61 (1984), the Supreme Court said that there is a legitimate interest of "citizens in some minimum standard of decency, honor and reliability in their dealings with their Government." *See also* Kenneth D. Dean, *Equitable Estoppel Against the Government—The Missouri Experience: Time to Rethink the Concept,* 37 St. Louis U. L.J. 63, 106 (1992) (arguing that "if citizens are to retain faith and trust in government," then some remedy should be available when individuals unjustly suffer by reasons of governmental mistakes). Does fairness or a "standard of decency, honor, and reliability" demand application of estoppel in an appropriate case? Is the *Richmond* case one of those appropriate cases?

Professor Joshua Schwartz argues that estoppel relief should be granted against the federal government when a citizen reasonably relies upon a misrepresentation by a government employee, and either (1) the agency has the discretionary authority to waive the legal requirements involved, or (2) denial of relief to the citizen would violate fundamental notions of fairness under the Due Process Clause of the Fifth Amendment to the Constitution. Joshua I. Schwartz, *The Irresistible Force Meets the Immovable Object: Estoppel Remedies for an Agency's Violation of Its Own Regulations or Other Misconduct,* 44 Admin. L. Rev. 653, 659–60, 743–44 (1992). In his view, "[d]rawing on both substantive and procedural due process elements, remedial due process makes available an estoppel-like remedy when the government violates a requirement of fair warning, working a substantial injury to an important private interest, and no other form of remedy can meaningfully redress the harm done." *Id.* at 660. He contends that, in cases like *Richmond,* "the argument can credibly be made that the government's actions and misrepresentations caused the affected individual to lose [the right to benefits] without due process of law." *Id.* at 738.

Consider also those Supreme Court decisions that allow equitable tolling of statutes of limitations against the federal government in at least some cases, such as *Irwin v. Veterans Affairs,* 498 U.S. 89 (1990) (Title VII statute of limitations), discussed in Chapter II.C. Professor Schwartz argues that the tolling cases are simply examples of equitable estoppel by another label. Schwartz, *supra,* at 658 (citing "the Court's proclivity for inventing other doctrinal labels whenever it wishes to estop a federal government agency"). Or is tolling of statutory time periods different in a meaningful way from waiver of the substantive rules governing eligibility for government benefits or government action? In what practical ways might equitable adjustment of procedural rules be less significant and intrude less upon the public interest than equitable excusing of substantive requirements?

In the end, the general question of the availability of equitable estoppel against the federal government is left unresolved in *Richmond*. The Court observes that it has rejected every claim for estoppel against the government that has come before it; expresses concern that equitable estoppel cases have taken on a life of their own; criticizes the courts of appeals as mistakenly searching for the opportunity to apply estoppel against the government; acknowledges there is confusion in this area of law; and describes the government's argument for an absolute no-estoppel rule as substantial. Nonetheless, and somewhat frustratingly, the Court leaves the question about general application of equitable estoppel against the government for another day.

3.   Instead of developing a general rule on estoppel of the government, the *Richmond* Court states that "[a] narrower ground of decision is sufficient to address the type of suit presented here, a claim for payment of money from the Public Treasury contrary to a statutory appropriation." The Court cites the Appropriations Clause of the Constitution, Art. I, § 9, cl. 7, as precluding waiver of the statutory limitations on disability benefits in this case. In the majority's view, what is the purpose of the Appropriations Clause? How does the clause apply to this case? How does the dissent respond?

Justice Stevens, in a separate concurring opinion in *Richmond* that is omitted from the excerpt in this casebook, argued that the Appropriations Clause is not relevant to the case: "The Constitution contemplates appropriations that cover programs—not individual appropriations for individual payments." A distinction is commonly drawn (at least in theory) between *authorization* and *appropriation* legislation passed by Congress. The particular rules governing eligibility for government benefits or directing how an agency is to implement a program are established through permanent authorization statutes, enacted separately from the annual appropriations process. By contrast, the annual appropriations bills allocate certain sums of money for departments and programs and generally do not include detailed programmatic rules. Expanding upon Justice Stevens's point, Professor Schwartz argues that the *Richmond* case is the exception rather than the rule, even with respect to equitable estoppel in money cases against the federal government. In *Richmond,* the appropriations legislation for the disability benefits arguably incorporated the substantive terms of the statutory authorization, and thereby directly imposed a programmatic restriction through an appropriations statute. In most instances, however, an appropriations bill will not include programmatic directives. Thus, he argues, in the ordinary monetary case, application of equitable estoppel to force the government to pay benefits contrary to an authorization statute— as opposed to a general appropriations bill—would not implicate the Appropriations Clause relied upon by the Court in the *Richmond* case. Schwartz, *supra,* at 720–22.

However, Professor Schwartz acknowledges that the *Richmond* majority does not appear to contemplate its holding so narrowly: "*Richmond* appears to create an absolute bar to the operation of estoppel in any case where the remedy would require the payment of funds out of the Treasury." Schwartz, *supra,* at 658. Indeed, the fact that the Court thought that it was generally clarifying the state of equitable estoppel law indicates that it viewed its holding as broadly governing all cases in which monetary relief is sought. *See id.* at 718.

4. Even with an expansive understanding of *Richmond* as applying to all claims for payment of money contrary to a statutory rule, two categories of cases are left open for possible estoppel assertions against the federal government:

First, "*Richmond* leaves open the narrower but important question of whether monetary relief sought in violation of agency regulations (as opposed to statutory restrictions) is barred by the Appropriations Clause rationale." Schwartz, *supra,* at 724. The Appropriations Clause, at least in its most direct application, precludes only expenditure of money contrary to a congressional appropriation and thus arguably may not apply to a restriction on payment adopted by an agency through administrative regulations. On the other hand, given that agencies are delegated authority to implement programs and ensure that benefits are provided in accordance with general statutory guidelines, the courts may determine that a regulatory limitation on expenditure of funds may implicate the Appropriations Clause, or other separation of powers concerns, as well.

Second, and even more clearly, *Richmond* and its Appropriations Clause rationale have no application to cases in which a plaintiff asserts equitable estoppel but does not seek monetary relief. Thus, for example, if a federal employee asserts equitable estoppel to prevent discharge from government employment or if an immigrant interposes equitable estoppel to prevent deportation or denial of citizenship, the *Richmond* Court's "narrower ground" of the Appropriations Clause is inapposite to the situation. *See generally* Schwartz, *supra,* at 725–26. The Army discharge case discussed below in note 5, although arising prior to *Richmond,* is a case that falls outside of the *Richmond* monetary claim rule.

Thus, in cases that do not involve monetary claims and perhaps those involving regulatory rather than statutory limitations on payments, estoppel *may* remain a possibility. The possibility of an "affirmative misconduct" basis for estoppel against the government—which the Supreme Court alluded to in dicta in the past and again in *Richmond*—has not been laid to rest. Of course, the *Richmond* decision reflects a generally negative attitude toward equitable estoppel in government cases, and the Court neither endorses nor rejects the "affirmative misconduct" exception. Nor has the Court *ever* found a case that involved the kind of "affirmative misconduct" that could justify estoppel. In the future, the Court may well finally accept what it calls the government's "substantial" case for a flat no-estoppel rule. But it has not yet.

5. Prior to *Richmond,* the United States Court of Appeals for the Ninth Circuit was perhaps the boldest in applying equitable estoppel to the government through the purported "affirmative misconduct" exception, although even that court found the occasions for doing so to be exceptional.

Under the Ninth Circuit's caselaw, the doctrine of equitable estoppel could be asserted against the United States only if the party establishes (1) "affirmative misconduct going beyond mere negligence," and (2) "the government's wrongful act will cause a serious injustice, and the public's interest will not suffer undue damage." *Morgan v. Heckler,* 779 F.2d 544, 545 (9th Cir. 1985).

The leading, and most controversial, Ninth Circuit equitable estoppel decision was its en banc ruling in *Watkins v. United States Army,* 875 F.2d 699 (9th Cir. 1989) (en banc). In *Watkins,* the plaintiff relied upon equitable estoppel to prevent the Army from discharging him because of his homosexuality. A slim majority of six judges on the 11–judge en banc panel ruled that the government was estopped from relying on a regulation expressly barring enlistment of homosexuals, because the Army, with full knowledge of the plaintiff's homosexuality, had repeatedly permitted him to reenlist in the past. *Id.* at 701–11. One judge concurred in the judgment, concluding that equitable estoppel could not be applied to the government on these circumstances, but believing that the regulation prohibiting enlistment of homosexuals was unconstitutional. *Id.* at 711–31 (Norris, J., concurring in the judgment). Four judges dissented. *Id.* at 731–39 (Hall, J., dissenting). All four judges in dissent agreed that a common law claim like equitable estoppel was not justiciable against the military given its unique position within the government. Two judges further opined that the majority's holding on the merits of the equitable estoppel claim was "entirely unpersuasive." *Id.* at 737 (Hall, J., dissenting). These judges concluded that the mere fact that the Army had failed to apply the regulation against the plaintiff in the past fell far short of "affirmative misconduct." *Id.* at 737–39.

In the years following the Supreme Court's *Richmond* decision, only one court of appeals on a single occasion has forthrightly** relied upon equitable estoppel to bind the government, and that court not surprisingly was the Ninth Circuit. Having previously declared the continuing validity of its "affirmative misconduct" caselaw, *Pauly v. U.S. Dept. of Agriculture,* 348 F.3d 1143, 1149–50 (9th Cir. 2003), the Ninth Circuit in *Salgado–Diaz v. Gonzales,* 395 F.3d 1158, 1165–67 (9th Cir. 2005), found the necessary affirmative misconduct by border patrol agents in allegedly arresting and forcing the petitioner from the country to support application of equitable estoppel to prevent the government from relying upon post-misconduct events to justify exclusion of an alien from the country. In *Salgado–Diaz,* the petitioner alleged that while immigration proceedings were pending, he was unlawfully stopped by border agents and expelled from the country,

---

** In *Nixon v. Office of Personal Management,* 452 F.3d 1361, 1370–71 (Fed.Cir. 2006) (Michel, Chief Judge, dissenting), a dissenting judge contended that the majority opinion by directing that survivor spouse benefits be paid despite the employee's failure to formally elect survivor benefits for her due to misleading agency communications constituted the improper use of equitable estoppel to grant monetary benefits contrary to *Richmond.* The majority, however, did not characterize its ruling as equitable estoppel, responded that it had not acted contrary to *Richmond,* and emphasized that the employee had wished to elect a spousal annuity. *Id.* at 1367–68.

thus aborting his request for suspension of deportation. If this governmental misconduct were established at an evidentiary hearing on remand, the government would be estopped from relying upon the petitioner's attempted re-entry into the United States without legal status and using false documentation as an independent and adequate basis for ordering his removal from the country. *Id.*

SECTION B.   PRIOR ADJUDICATION—RES JUDICATA, COLLATERAL ESTOPPEL, AND STARE DECISIS

If you managed to escape your basic or advanced civil procedure course without being confronted by res judicata (claim preclusion) and collateral estoppel (issue preclusion), a basic understanding of these concepts is necessary before reading the next case. As a nutshell summary, a party who had a full opportunity to litigate a controverted issue in a prior case, even involving a different cause of action or claim, that ended in a final judgment on the merits is said to be collaterally estopped or precluded from re-litigating that issue again in future litigation. When both parties to the future litigation are the same, the collateral estoppel or issue preclusion is "mutual;" when the party asserting estoppel was not a party to the prior lawsuit, it is "nonmutual."

Both claim preclusion (res judicata) and issue preclusion (collateral estoppel) arise from the common-sense notion that a party in litigation should get only "one bite at the apple." Professors Jay Tidmarsh and Roger H. Trangsrud explain the difference between the two doctrines, and the crucial differences in elements, in their *Complex Litigation* casebook:

> [C]laim preclusion [res judicata] and issue preclusion [collateral estoppel] are distinct doctrines with distinct elements. Claim preclusion bars the subsequent assertion of any claims or defenses that were *actually* presented, or that *should have been* presented, in a prior lawsuit whose judgment has become final. Issue preclusion prevents re-litigation of any issues that were *actually* presented in a prior lawsuit and that were *necessary* to the final judgment in that prior suit. There are some significant differences in the doctrines. Most obviously, claim preclusion precludes the relitigation of entire claims or defenses, while issue preclusion precludes the re-litigation of certain issues. Next, claim preclusion bars the re-litigation of matters that either were or should have been presented in the first case, while issue preclusion bars the re-litigation only of those issues that actually were litigated in the first case. Finally, * * * claim preclusion operates only between the two parties to the first litigation. Although the same "mutuality of estoppel" idea used to operate with respect to issue preclusion, * * * with the advent of the concept of defense and offensive collateral estoppel, the requirement of mutuality has significantly eroded.

Jay Tidmarsh & Roger H. Trangsrud, *Complex Litigation and the Adversary System* 166–67 (Foundation Press, 1998).

In the first part of this chapter (Chapter VI.A), we asked whether the federal government should be bound by the unauthorized representations of its agents, that is, whether the government may be equitably estopped from denying a benefit or applying a rule when a citizen has reasonably relied upon the mistaken advice of a government agent. In this part of the chapter, we explore estoppel by judgment. The question in this part of Chapter VI is whether the United States is subject on the same terms to the rules precluding relitigation of matters resolved, or that could have been resolved, in prior litigation that ended in a final judgment. As with equitable estoppel, concerns about justifiable reliance by citizens upon official declarations (here in the form of court judgments) collide with purported public interests in the nature (and here the development and evolution) of public law.

United States v. Mendoza

Supreme Court of the United States.
464 U.S. 154 (1984).

■ JUSTICE REHNQUIST delivered the opinion of the Court.

In 1978 respondent Sergio Mendoza, a Filipino national, filed a petition for naturalization under a statute which by its terms had expired 32 years earlier. Respondent's claim for naturalization was based on the assertion that the government's administration of the Nationality Act denied him due process of law. Neither the District Court nor the Court of Appeals for the Ninth Circuit ever reached the merits of his claim, because they held that the government was collaterally estopped from litigating that constitutional issue because of an earlier decision against the government in a case brought by other Filipino nationals in the United States District Court for the Northern District of California. We hold that the United States may not be collaterally estopped on an issue such as this, adjudicated against it in an earlier lawsuit brought by a different party. We therefore reverse the judgment of the Court of Appeals.

The facts bearing on respondent's claim to naturalization are not in dispute. In 1942 Congress passed the Nationality Act, § 701 of which provided that non-citizens who served honorably in the Armed Forces of the United States during World War II were exempt from some of the usual requirements for nationality. In particular, such veterans were exempt from the requirement of residency within the United States and literacy in the English language. Congress later provided by amendment that all naturalization petitions seeking to come under § 701 must be filed by December 31, 1946. * * * In order to implement that provision, the Immigration and Naturalization Service from 1943 to 1946 sent representatives abroad to naturalize eligible alien servicemen.

Respondent Mendoza served as a doctor in the Philippine Common-wealth Army from 1941 until his discharge in 1946. Because Japanese occupation of the Philippines had made naturalization of alien servicemen there impossible before the liberation of the Islands, the INS did not designate a representative to naturalize eligible servicemen there until 1945. Because of concerns expressed by the Philippine government to the United States, however, to the effect that large numbers of Filipinos would be naturalized and would immigrate to the United States just as the Philippines gained their independence, the Attorney General subsequently revoked the naturalization authority of the INS representative. Thus all naturalizations in the Philippines were halted for a nine-month period from late October 1945 until a new INS representative was appointed in August of 1946.

Respondent's claim for naturalization is based on the contention that that conduct of the government deprived him of due process of law in violation of the Fifth Amendment to the United States Constitution, because he was present in the Philippines during part, but not all, of the nine-month period during which there was no authorized INS representa-tive there. The naturalization examiner recommended denial of Mendoza's petition, but the District Court granted the petition without reaching the merits of Mendoza's constitutional claim. The District Court concluded that the government could not relitigate the due process issue because that issue had already been decided against the government in *In re Naturaliza-tion of 68 Filipino War Veterans,* 406 F.Supp. 931 (N.D.Cal.1975) (hereinaf-ter *68 Filipinos*), a decision which the government had not appealed.

Noting that the doctrine of nonmutual offensive collateral estoppel has been conditionally approved by this Court in *Parklane Hosiery Co. v. Shore,* 439 U.S. 322 (1979), the Court of Appeals concluded that the District Court had not abused its discretion in applying that doctrine against the United States in this case. 672 F.2d 1320, 1322 (C.A.9 1982). The Court of Appeals rejected the government's argument that *Parklane Hosiery* should be limited to private litigants. Although it acknowledged that the government is often involved in litigating issues of national significance where conserva-tion of judicial resources is less important than "getting a second opinion," it concluded that litigation concerning the rights of Filipino war veterans was not such a case. 672 F.2d, at 1329–1330. For the reasons which follow, we agree with the government that *Parklane Hosiery*'s approval of nonmu-tual offensive collateral estoppel is not to be extended to the United States.

Under the judicially-developed doctrine of collateral estoppel, once a court has decided an issue of fact or law necessary to its judgment, that decision is conclusive in a subsequent suit based on a different cause of action involving a party to the prior litigation. *Montana v. United States,* 440 U.S. 147, 153 (1979). Collateral estoppel, like the related doctrine of res judicata,[3] serves to "relieve parties of the cost and vexation of multiple

---

3. Under res judicata, a final judgment on the merits bars further claims by parties or their privies on the same cause of action. The Restatement of Judgments speaks of res

lawsuits, conserve judicial resources, and, by preventing inconsistent decisions, encourage reliance on adjudication." *Allen v. McCurry,* 449 U.S. 90 (1980). In furtherance of those policies, this Court in recent years has broadened the scope of the doctrine of collateral estoppel beyond its common law limits. It has done so by abandoning the requirement of mutuality of parties, and by conditionally approving the "offensive" use of collateral estoppel by a non-party to a prior lawsuit. *Parklane Hosiery, supra.*[4]

In *Standefer v. United States,* 447 U.S. 10, 24 (1980), however, we emphasized the fact that * * * *Parklane Hosiery* involved disputes over private rights between private litigants. We noted that "[i]n such cases, no significant harm flows from enforcing a rule that affords a litigant only one full and fair opportunity to litigate an issue, and [that] there is no sound reason for burdening the courts with repetitive litigation." *Ibid.* Here, as in *Montana v. United States, supra,* the party against whom the estoppel is sought is the United States; but here, unlike in *Montana,* the party who seeks to preclude the government from relitigating the issue was not a party to the earlier litigation.[5]

We have long recognized that "the Government is not in a position identical to that of a private litigant," *INS v. Hibi,* 414 U.S. 5, 8 (1973) (*per curiam*), both because of the geographic breadth of government litigation and also, most importantly, because of the nature of the issues the government litigates. It is not open to serious dispute that the government is a party to a far greater number of cases on a nationwide basis than even the most litigious private entity; in 1982, the United States was a party to more than 75,000 of the 206,193 filings in the United States District Courts. In the same year the United States was a party to just under 30% of the civil cases appealed from the District Courts to the Court of Appeals. Government litigation frequently involves legal questions of substantial public importance; indeed, because the proscriptions of the United States Constitution are so generally directed at governmental action, many constitutional questions can arise only in the context of litigation to which the government is a party. Because of those facts the government is more likely than any private party to be involved in lawsuits against different parties which nonetheless involve the same legal issues.

---

judicata as "claim preclusion" and of collateral estoppel as "issue preclusion." Restatement (Second) of Judgments § 27 (1982).

4. Offensive use of collateral estoppel occurs when a plaintiff seeks to foreclose a defendant from relitigating an issue the defendant has previously litigated unsuccessfully in another action against the same or a different party. Defensive use of collateral estoppel occurs when a defendant seeks to prevent a plaintiff from relitigating an issue the plaintiff has previously litigated unsuccessfully in another action against the same or a different party.

5. In *Montana* we held that the government was estopped from relitigating in federal court the constitutionality of Montana's gross receipts tax on contractors of public construction firms. That issue had previously been litigated in state court by an individual contractor whose litigation had been totally financed and controlled by the federal government.

A rule allowing nonmutual collateral estoppel against the government in such cases would substantially thwart the development of important questions of law by freezing the first final decision rendered on a particular legal issue. Allowing only one final adjudication would deprive this Court of the benefit it receives from permitting several courts of appeals to explore a difficult question before this Court grants certiorari. Indeed, if nonmutual estoppel were routinely applied against the government, this Court would have to revise its practice of waiting for a conflict to develop before granting the government's petitions for certiorari.

The Solicitor General's policy for determining when to appeal an adverse decision would also require substantial revision. The Court of Appeals faulted the government in this case for failing to appeal a decision that it now contends is erroneous. But the government's litigation conduct in a case is apt to differ from that of a private litigant. Unlike a private litigant who generally does not forego an appeal if he believes that he can prevail, the Solicitor General considers a variety of factors, such as the limited resources of the government and the crowded dockets of the courts, before authorizing an appeal. The application of nonmutual estoppel against the government would force the Solicitor General to abandon those prudential concerns and to appeal every adverse decision in order to avoid foreclosing further review.

In addition to those institutional concerns traditionally considered by the Solicitor General, the panoply of important public issues raised in governmental litigation may quite properly lead successive Administrations of the Executive Branch to take differing positions with respect to the resolution of a particular issue. While the Executive Branch must of course defer to the Judicial Branch for final resolution of questions of constitutional law, the former nonetheless controls the progress of government litigation through the federal courts. It would be idle to pretend that the conduct of government litigation in all its myriad features, from the decision to file a complaint in the United States District Court to the decision to petition for certiorari to review a judgment of the Court of Appeals, is a wholly mechanical procedure which involves no policy choices whatever.

For example, in recommending to the Solicitor General in 1977 that the government's appeal in *68 Filipinos* be withdrawn, newly appointed INS Commissioner Castillo commented that such a course "would be in keeping with the policy of the [new] Administration," described as "a course of compassion and amnesty." But for the very reason that such policy choices are made by one Administration, and often reevaluated by another Administration, courts should be careful when they seek to apply expanding rules of collateral estoppel to government litigation. The government of course may not now undo the consequences of its decision not to appeal the District Court judgment in the *68 Filipinos* case; it is bound by that judgment under the principles of res judicata. But we now hold that it is not further bound in a case involving a litigant who was not a party to the earlier litigation.

The Court of Appeals did not endorse a routine application of nonmutual collateral estoppel against the government, because it recognized that the government does litigate issues of far-reaching national significance which in some cases, it concluded, might warrant relitigation. But in this case it found no "record evidence" indicating that there was a "crucial need" in the administration of the immigration laws for a redetermination of the due process question decided in *68 Filipinos* and presented again in this case. 672 F.2d, at 1329–1330. The Court of Appeals did not make clear what sort of "record evidence" would have satisfied it that there *was* a "crucial need" for redetermination of the question in this case, but we pretermit further discussion of that approach; we believe that the standard announced by the Court of Appeals for determining when relitigation of a legal issue is to be permitted is so wholly subjective that it affords no guidance to the courts or to the government. Such a standard leaves the government at sea because it can not possibly anticipate, in determining whether or not to appeal an adverse decision, whether a court will bar relitigation of the issue in a later case. By the time a court makes its subjective determination that an issue cannot be relitigated, the government's appeal of the prior ruling of course would be untimely.

We hold, therefore, that nonmutual offensive collateral estoppel simply does not apply against the government in such a way as to preclude relitigation of issues such as those involved in this case. The conduct of government litigation in the courts of the United States is sufficiently different from the conduct of private civil litigation in those courts so that what might otherwise be economy interests underlying a broad application of collateral estoppel are outweighed by the constraints which peculiarly affect the government. We think that our conclusion will better allow thorough development of legal doctrine by allowing litigation in multiple forums. Indeed, a contrary result might disserve the economy interests in whose name estoppel is advanced by requiring the government to abandon virtually any exercise of discretion in seeking to review judgments unfavorable to it. The doctrine of res judicata, of course, prevents the government from relitigating the same cause of action against the parties to a prior decision, but beyond that point principles of nonmutual collateral estoppel give way to the policies just stated.

Our holding in this case is consistent with each of our prior holdings to which the parties have called our attention, and which we reaffirm. Today in a companion case we hold that the government may be estopped under certain circumstances from relitigating a question when the parties to the two lawsuits are the same. *United States v. Stauffer Chemical Co.,* [464 U.S.] 165 [(1984)]. None of those cases, however, involve the effort of a party to estop the government in the absence of mutuality.

The concerns underlying our disapproval of collateral estoppel against the government are for the most part inapplicable where mutuality is present, as in *Stauffer Chemical,* [and] *Montana* * * *.[9] The application of

---

9. In *Montana* an individual contractor brought an initial action to challenge Montana's gross receipts tax in state court, and the federal government brought a second acan estoppel when the government is litigating the same issue with the same party avoids the problem of freezing the development of the law because the government is still free to litigate that issue in the future with some other party. And, where the parties are the same, estopping the government spares a party that has already prevailed once from having to relitigate—a function it would not serve in the present circumstances. We accordingly hold that the Court of Appeals was wrong in applying nonmutual collateral estoppel against the government in this case. Its judgment is therefore

Reversed.

Notes and Questions

1. Should the United States be exempted from the general principle of collateral estoppel or issue preclusion, whether or not it is mutual? If the government has had a "full and fair opportunity to litigate an issue" involving interpretation of a federal statute or application of a federal regulation in a prior case, even though against a different party, why should it not be bound by the ruling in that prior case in all subsequent lawsuits? What consequences attaching to such a course lead the Supreme Court to reject application of nonmutual collateral estoppel against the federal government?

In *Mendoza,* the Court refers to its earlier decision in *Parklane Hosiery Co. v. Shore,* 439 U.S. 322 (1979). In *Parklane Hosiery,* the Court described the issue as "whether a party who has had issues of fact adjudicated adversely to it in [a prior action] may be collaterally estopped from relitigating the same issues * * * in a subsequent legal action brought against it by a new party." *Id.* at 324. Or "[s]pecifically, * * * whether a litigant who was not a party to a prior judgment may nevertheless use that judgment 'offensively' to prevent a defendant from relitigating issues resolved in the earlier proceeding." *Id.* at 326. The *Parklane Hosiery* Court ruled that this "nonmutual offensive collateral estoppel" could be applied in the discretion of the trial court when the party against whom it is asserted had a "full and fair" opportunity to litigate the issue in the prior proceeding. *Id.* at 326–32. The issue in *Mendoza* is whether nonmutual offensive collateral estoppel may also apply against the federal government.

2. You should understand that the Court is *not* saying that the principles of res judicata (claim preclusion) and collateral estoppel (issue preclusion) have no application to the United States. The Court holds only that the government is not bound by *nonmutual* collateral estoppel. Thus,

---

tion in federal court raising the same challenge. The government totally controlled and financed the state-court action; thus for all practical purposes, there was mutuality of parties in the two cases. "The United States had a sufficient 'laboring oar' in the conduct of the state-court litigation," *Montana v. United States,* 440 U.S., at 155, to be constituted a "party" in all but a technical sense.

for example, the *Mendoza* Court emphasizes that by virtue of res judicata, the government is bound by the final and unappealed judgment in the *68 Filipinos* case. What does this mean in practical terms? Moreover, the Court endorses application of *mutual* collateral estoppel against the United States, giving the example of its earlier decision *Montana v. United States,* 440 U.S. 147 (1979) (the Court outlines and explains the prior *Montana* decision in footnotes 5 and 9 of the *Mendoza* opinion). What is different about the *Montana* case? Why does collateral estoppel apply there but not in *Mendoza*? Why are the Court's concerns about applying nonmutual collateral estoppel in *Mendoza* not presented in the *Montana*-type case?

3. Even when there is mutuality between the United States and the party who is asserting preclusion based on former adjudication, there is authority for the proposition that the United States is not bound by an earlier judgment which was entered without the government's waiver of sovereign immunity, at least when the sovereign immunity defense was not passed upon in the earlier lawsuit.

In *United States v. United States Fidelity & Guaranty Company,* 309 U.S. 506 (1940), the United States previously had filed a claim on behalf of Indian tribes against a debtor in a bankruptcy reorganization. The debtor in turn filed a cross-claim (what we would call a counterclaim today) seeking an amount greater than the amount of the tribe's claim. (As we will see in Chapter VIII.C, while a party generally may defend against a claim by the government by asserting a counterclaim in the form of a "set off" against the amount sought by the government, sovereign immunity bars use of a counterclaim to obtain an affirmative recovery greater than the amount of the government's claim, absent a specific statutory waiver of sovereign immunity for that claim. *United States v. Shaw,* 309 U.S. 495 (1940) (decided the same day as *United States Fidelity & Guaranty*).) However, in *United States Fidelity & Guaranty,* the United States for whatever reason failed to assert sovereign immunity as a defense to the cross-claim (and the Indian tribes would have shared in that immunity). The bankruptcy court approved the government's claim against the debtor for $2,000, but also allowed the cross-claim by the debtor against the government for more than $11,000. Subsequently, the United States filed suit against the debtor's surety asserting the very same claim on behalf of the Indian tribes. The surety, standing in the shoes of the debtor (thus establishing mutuality for preclusion purposes), argued that the bankruptcy judgment stood as res judicata and barred the claim.

The Supreme Court ultimately held that the earlier judgment on the cross-claim against the United States acting on behalf of the tribes was void for lack of jurisdiction by reason of sovereign immunity. *United States Fidelity & Guaranty Co.,* 309 U.S. at 512–15. Now ordinarily, a judgment may not be collaterally attacked in subsequent litigation as having been entered without subject matter jurisdiction. *See* Restatement (Second) of Judgments, § 12. Does an exceptional rule hold when sovereign immunity is at issue? In *United States Fidelity & Guaranty,* the Court held that, if a judgment entered contrary to immunity could be binding in subsequent litigation because the government's lawyers had failed to assert sovereign immunity in the first lawsuit, "it would subject the Government to suit in any court in the discretion of its responsible officers." *United States Fidelity & Guaranty Co.,* 309 U.S. at 513. Commentators have understood the decision in this way: "The question of sovereign immunity (at least where it was not put in issue in the earlier case) is recognized as an exception to the rule that a court's determination that it has jurisdiction to decide the case is itself res judicata." William T. Plumb, *The Tax Recommendations of the Commission on the Bankruptcy Laws—Tax Procedures,* 88 Harv. L. Rev. 1360, 1448 n.493 (1975).

How broadly should the Supreme Court's decision in *United States Fidelity & Guaranty* be understood? Does it really stand for the general proposition that an earlier judgment does not have preclusive effect if the United States was immune from that claim but immunity had not been raised in the preceding action? What would be the consequences of such a "sovereign-immunity exception" to res judicata or collateral estoppel, applied even in cases where the parties to the second lawsuit are the same? In the following case, the United States Court of Appeals for the Seventh Circuit construes *United States Fidelity & Guaranty* narrowly and imposes res judicata against the federal government under what appear to be similar circumstances:

United States v. County of Cook, Illinois

United States Court of Appeals for the Seventh Circuit.
167 F.3d 381 (7th Cir. 1999).

■ EASTERBROOK, CIRCUIT JUDGE.

This long-running dispute about real estate taxation of two buildings in which the United States was a tenant was resolved by *United States v. Hynes,* 20 F.3d 1437 (7th Cir.1994) (en banc). Or so we thought. But the United States now contends that because its lawyers neglected to invoke sovereign immunity it is entitled to a fresh adjudication. Needless to say, the taxing authorities reply that claim preclusion (res judicata) cannot be avoided by raising new arguments; judgments are conclusive not only with respect to arguments actually made, but also with respect to arguments that could have been made. We must decide whether there is a sovereign-immunity exception to this rule.

Hynes explains the essential facts, so we can be brief. Although state and local governments usually cannot tax transactions or entities in which the United States has a beneficial interest, see *McCulloch v. Maryland,* 17 U.S. (4 Wheat.) 316 (1819), Congress has consented to the taxation of real estate when the United States has entered into a financing lease. 40 U.S.C. § 602a(d). Two federal buildings in Chicago were constructed under this program. Construction funds were advanced, and title was held, by private investors until the United States exercised its option to purchase outright.

Cook County sought to collect real estate taxes based on the value of each building, and despite § 602a(d) the United States invoked intergovernmental tax immunity. A panel of this court sustained that defense, *United States v. County of Cook*, 725 F.2d 1128 (7th Cir.1984), but after a change in the local tax statutes the full court overruled the panel's decision and held that § 602a(d) relinquishes any immunity the United States otherwise would enjoy. After our decision the United States prepaid the leases for the remaining years and took title to both buildings, which stopped the accrual of taxes (and avoided any possibility that the buildings would be sold to satisfy unpaid tax bills). When title changed hands, the United States owed more than $65 million in taxes, interest, and penalties for 1985–93. Cook County has not sought to collect for earlier years, but the United States insists that despite our opinion it need not pay the balance. It has tendered the principal amount of taxes but refuses to pay more, observing that sovereign immunity bars interest and penalties against the United States unless Congress has authorized these remedies explicitly. *Department of Energy v. Ohio,* 503 U.S. 607 (1992) (penalties); *Library of Congress v. Shaw,* 478 U.S. 310 (1986) (interest).

Section 602a(d) refers only to "taxes" and therefore, the United States insists, does not encompass interest and penalties for delayed payment of taxes. This argument could have been made in prior proceedings but was not. By the time the United States brought its action substantial interest and penalties had accrued, and more were in prospect. * * * Objections to all penalties available under state and local law could have been asserted in the prior litigation. Every legal theory pertaining to one transaction is part of a single claim. * * * All of the financial consequences of nonpayment were, or could have been, addressed in the earlier litigation, and all are therefore part of the same claim. The arguments the United States now advances are foreclosed by normal principles of preclusion unless these have a sovereign-immunity exception. The district court held, 1997 WL 639049, that they do. Reaching the merits, the court concluded that * * * interest and penalties are not comprehended in the authorization of "taxes." * * *

For a long time it has been understood that the United States, like a private litigant, cannot relitigate claims that have reached final judgment. *United States v. Stauffer Chemical Co.,* 464 U.S. 165 (1984); *United States v. Moser,* 266 U.S. 236 (1924). (The special treatment of offensive nonmutual issue preclusion, see *United States v. Mendoza,* 464 U.S. 154 (1984), does not qualify this rule when identical parties contest the sequential suits.) Likewise it is settled that a "claim" for purposes of this rule means all legal theories bearing on a set of facts; an omitted argument cannot be raised later. *Nevada v. United States,* 463 U.S. [110], 129–30 [(1983)]. To create a sovereign-immunity exception to these principles would be to abolish them, for *every* suit involving the interests of the United States potentially involves sovereign immunity. What it means to say that the United States possesses sovereign immunity is that there is no common-law or equitable liability. Relief depends on statutes, which should not be read to expose the United States to liability unless Congress makes a remedy available explicitly. *United States v. King,* 395 U.S. 1, 4 (1969); *United States v. Testan,* 424 U.S. 392, 399–403 (1976). Thus *every* statute authorizing the courts to adjudicate claims to property or funds of the United States is a waiver of sovereign immunity, and *every* argument that the United States makes (or omits) in defense is in the end an argument about sovereign immunity. Even prospective relief depends on the waiver of sovereign immunity in 5 U.S.C. § 702. Compare *Bowen v. Massachusetts,* 487 U.S. 879 (1988), with *Department of the Army v. Blue Fox, Inc.,* 119 S. Ct. 687 (1999).

Consider a suit under the Federal Tort Claims Act, 28 U.S.C. §§ 2671–80. The plaintiff says that he received negligent medical treatment in a veterans' hospital; the United States denies that the treatment was negligent; after a trial the judge rules in the plaintiff's favor and awards damages. Must the United States pay? One would suppose so; but if there is a sovereign-immunity exception to the law of judgments then it need not. Instead the United States could balk, force the plaintiff to sue to enforce the judgment, and assert some additional defense-say, that the administrative claim or suit was untimely under 28 U.S.C. §§ 2401(a) and 2675(a). Because the FTCA waives sovereign immunity, each limitation presents a question about the extent of the waiver. See *United States v. Kubrick,* 444 U.S. 111, 117–18 (1979). If there is a sovereign-immunity exception to claim preclusion, then the United States could make its timeliness defense in a second suit. And if it lost that suit, it *still* could refuse to pay and insist that the plaintiff file a third suit in order to address the discretionary-function exception to liability, 28 U.S.C. § 2680(a), a fourth to overcome the intentional-tort exception, § 2680(h), and so on *ad infinitum.* At oral argument counsel for the United States candidly conceded that this is a logical consequence of the position the government advances.

It is a most unpalatable consequence—likely an unconstitutional one. For it would reduce to advisory status all decisions adverse to the financial interests of the United States. If the United States thinks that it has a new and better argument, it would be free to ignore the judgment and go on as before. That prospect led the Supreme Court to hold that federal courts may not decide veterans' claims under a statute that left their decisions subject to administrative approval. *Hayburn's Case,* 2 U.S. (2 Dall.) 409 (1792). Justice Kennedy worried last spring that permitting a government to raise sovereign immunity for the first time on appeal would allow it "to proceed to judgment without facing any real risk of adverse consequences." *Wisconsin Department of Corrections v. Schacht,* 118 S. Ct. 2047, 2055 (1998) (concurring opinion). How much worse if the governmental body *never* had to raise the defense in the first litigation, but could simply ignore the judgment and insist that its adversary try again! That approach is not compatible with the Constitution, for Article III courts exercise the "judicial Power of the United States"—which is to say, a power to enter judgments that are conclusive between the parties. Although the raw power of Congress to withhold appropriations means that a given judgment requiring the United States to pay money may be unenforceable, this remote possibility does not render all judgments advisory. *Glidden Co. v. Zdanok,* 370 U.S. 530, 571 (1962) (plurality opinion). But the position taken by the United States in this case would make judgments contingent on the inability of federal lawyers to think up a new theory. Many a lawyer comes to believe, after a case is over, that a better line of argument was available. If the United States is right, then it is entitled to as many bites at the apple as it finds necessary, until it has prevailed or exhausted all available lines of argument. * * *

The foundation of the United States' current position is that agents of the Executive Branch, including its lawyers, cannot waive the sovereign immunity of the United States. Only Congress and the President, acting together through legislation, may do so. See also Art. I § 9 cl. 7: "No Money shall be drawn from the Treasury, but in Consequence of Appropriations made by Law". Giving legal effect to an attorney's failure to make a sovereign-immunity argument would permit that attorney to waive the immunity of the United States, the argument concludes. The problem with this argument lies not in its premises but in the expression of its conclusion—for a court does not "give effect" to attorneys' arguments (or silence). It is the judgment of the court, and not of the attorneys, that has legal effect. A court with authority to consider and reject an invocation of sovereign immunity also has authority to enter judgment adverse to the interests of the United States without "waiving" (or violating) that immunity.

To see this consider a close parallel: rulings that concern (or suppose the existence of) subject-matter jurisdiction. No court may decide a case without subject-matter jurisdiction, and neither the parties nor their lawyers may stipulate to jurisdiction or waive arguments that the court lacks jurisdiction. If the parties neglect the subject, a court must raise jurisdictional questions itself. But if the court decides a case on the merits after an adversarial presentation, the judgment cannot be collaterally attacked on the ground that the court lacked subject-matter jurisdiction. The parties' failure to address jurisdiction fully or cogently does not deprive the judgment of force. *Durfee v. Duke,* 375 U.S. 106 (1963). Indeed, the parties' failure to address a jurisdictional issue at *all* does not diminish the authority of the judgment. * * * There is [a] commonly used[] exception to the principle that a court's jurisdiction may not be collaterally attacked. A party that simply refuses to appear may contend in a later case that the first tribunal lacked jurisdiction—though jurisdiction is the *only* issue thus preserved, and if the first court had jurisdiction then the judgment must be enforced. The exception is necessary because otherwise a court that lacked jurisdiction could strong-arm a party to litigate the subject, decide in favor of its own power, and thus block any review of its adjudicatory competence. Notice, however, [such exceptions have nothing] to do with the rule that parties may not waive jurisdictional shortcomings or stipulate to jurisdiction. A final judgment is the work of the court, not of the parties, and as a court has jurisdiction to determine its own jurisdiction it may decide the subject; whether it does so expressly or by implication the decision ordinarily is conclusive. This approach is essential if judgments are to resolve the parties' disputes, rather than just set the stage for the next act. * * *

Despite all of this, the district judge wrote that a sovereign-immunity "exception to res judicata has a long, unbroken history." * * * [T]he district court cited only two decisions of the Supreme Court. One is *Durfee,* which holds that questions of subject-matter jurisdiction litigated and resolved adversely to a party are covered by res judicata. This hardly establishes a sovereign-immunity exception to claim preclusion (not only because the Court rejected an argument for an exception, but also because sovereign immunity had not been invoked in *Durfee*), but on the way to decision the Court made this remark:

> To be sure, the general rule of finality of jurisdictional determinations is not without exceptions. Doctrines of federal pre-emption or sovereign immunity may in some contexts be controlling. But no such overriding considerations are present here.

375 U.S. at 114 (footnote omitted). "[M]ay in some contexts" poses but does not answer the question "in which contexts?" For the answer one must turn to *United States v. United States Fidelity & Guaranty Co.,* 309 U.S. 506 (1940) (*USF & G*), the second case on which the district judge relied. * * *

In *USF & G* the United States, as trustee for the Choctaw and Chickasaw Nations, filed a claim for $2,000 in the bankruptcy of the Central Coal & Coke Company. The coal company responded with a cross-claim for some $11,000, which the United States ignored—for claims against Indian tribes had to be filed in a "United States court in the Indian Territory", a category to which the bankruptcy court did not belong. Nonetheless the referee in bankruptcy allowed the coal company's claim, leaving it the Tribes' judgment creditor to the tune of $9,000. When the coal company attempted to enforce this judgment, the United States resisted on immunity grounds. After assimilating the sovereign immunity of Indian tribes to that of the United States the Court observed: "No statutory authority granted jurisdiction to the Missouri Court [i.e., the referee in bankruptcy] to adjudicate a cross-claim against the United States." 309 U.S. at 512. After additional exposition the Court declared the referee's decision "void" to the extent it awarded the coal company relief in excess of setting off the original $2,000 claim. The Court's analysis has two strands. One emphasizes the referee's lack of subject-matter jurisdiction and the other the Tribes' sovereign immunity, neither of which attorneys could waive. This second strand is the peg on which the United States now hangs its hat. Some language in *USF & G* supports that understanding. Other language supports the view that the Court thought of the case as one combining the absence of subject-matter jurisdiction with a litigant's disdain of the tribunal—a combination that traditionally permits a collateral attack (though one limited to the jurisdictional issue).

Which is the right way to understand the case? One clue is the Court's thoroughgoing equation of sovereign immunity to a jurisdictional shortcoming—for this suggests that the rule giving effect to a court's determination of its own jurisdiction carries over to potential sovereign immunity defenses. A second clue is the Court's statement of the questions presented:

This certiorari brings two questions here for review: (1) Is a former judgment against the United States on a cross-claim, which was entered without statutory authority, fixing a balance of indebtedness to be collected as provided by law, res judicata in this litigation for collection of the balance; and (2) as the controverted former judgment was entered against the Choctaw and Chickasaw Nations, appearing by the United States, does the jurisdictional act of April 26, 1906, authorizing adjudication of cross demands by defendants in suits on behalf of these Nations, permit the former credit, obtained by the principal in a bond guaranteed by the sole original defendant here, to be set up in the present suit.

309 U.S. at 509. This puts the case squarely in the jurisdictional camp and supports a reading that it was the referee's lack of subject-matter jurisdiction, rather than counsel's failure to advance a sovereign-immunity defense before the referee, that made the judgment void. On that understanding *USF & G* offers the United States no aid, for the subject-matter jurisdiction of the district court (and this court) in *Hynes* is beyond doubt. Still a third reason for thinking that *USF & G* is about subject-matter jurisdiction rather than a sovereign-immunity exception to the enforcement of judgments is the dire effect of the latter reading, which would make res judicata all but disappear for claims against the United States and make many judgments advisory in the process. The Court did not suggest that its decision had such a sweeping effect, and no later case imputes that consequence to *USF & G*. Indeed, the opinion in *USF & G* vanished from the law of judgments as soon as the ink dried on volume 309 of the United States Reports. Other than the elliptical reference in *Durfee,* the case has been cited by the Supreme Court only for the proposition that Indian tribes possess sovereign immunity. Opinions such as *Montana, Nevada,* and *Stauffer Chemical* do not cite or distinguish *USF & G,* though it would have been a major stumbling block to those decisions if it had the effect that the United States now attributes to it.

USF & G is the beginning and end of the Supreme Court cases on which the United States relies. We conclude that *USF & G* does not protect the United States from the risk of losing a case it brought on its own behalf in the proper court. *USF & G* permits the United States to ignore proceedings instituted against it in the wrong court. * * * None of the other cases that the district court cited holds that the United States may initiate a case in a court that possesses subject-matter jurisdiction, vigorously contest the merits, and then refuse to accept defeat on the ground that its lawyers did not adequately argue sovereign immunity. * * *

REVERSED.

■ ILANA DIAMOND ROVNER, CIRCUIT JUDGE, dissenting.

The majority holds that a claim of sovereign immunity litigated in a prior action cannot be relitigated in a later action. That is not, however, what happened here. The claims before us today were never litigated in *United States v. Hynes,* 20 F.3d 1437 (7th Cir.1994) (en banc), and in fact some arguably arose only after *Hynes.* The majority employs the legal fiction that all claims arising from a single transaction are one claim to assert that the government has already argued immunity and cannot do so again. Because I do not think *United States v. United States Fidelity & Guaranty Co.*, 309 U.S. 506 (1940) (*"USF & G"*), supports that holding, I respectfully dissent.

A very brief recitation of the facts is necessary. In *Hynes,* the U.S. Government ("Government") brought a declaratory judgment action seeking to preclude Cook County from imposing, assessing, or collecting taxes on real property owned by the Government. The complaint acknowledged that interest and penalties were being imposed as well as taxes, but requested relief only from taxes. Cook County did not file a counterclaim seeking the taxes, interest, or penalties, choosing instead to pursue such judgments in the state court. We rejected the Government's claim of immunity in *Hynes* in an *en banc* decision. Cook County obtained judgments in state court against the Government for interest and penalties and orders of tax sale for those properties. The Government did not appear in those state court actions and did not consent to jurisdiction. The Government subsequently filed the declaratory judgment action which underlies this appeal, seeking injunctive and declaratory relief from interest, penalties and tax sales based on principles of sovereign immunity.

At issue before this Court today is whether the failure of the Government to challenge the interest, penalties and tax sales in *Hynes* precludes it from raising the defense of sovereign immunity now. Generally, under the doctrine of res judicata, a prior judgment has preclusive effect over claims that were actually raised or could have been raised in the prior proceeding. Claims that "could have been raised" include those that arose out of the same transaction as the claims that were raised. Although some of the claims in the instant case possibly could not have been raised in *Hynes,* I will assume for purposes of this dissent that all claims raised here could have been raised in *Hynes.* None of the claims in the present case, however, were actually litigated in *Hynes.* The general rule of preclusion is subject to exceptions, one of which is set forth in *USF & G* and which applies in this case.

In *USF & G,* the Supreme Court held that collateral estoppel did not preclude the Government from raising a sovereign immunity defense to a royalties claim that had been actually decided in a prior case brought by the Government. 309 U.S. 506. In the earlier action, the Government had not presented any sovereign immunity defense, and the court had decided the royalties claim adversely to the Government. The Government subsequently brought another action, and a party argued that the Government was collaterally estopped from challenging the first decision. The Court held, however, that the immunity of the United States cannot be waived by the action of government officials—specifically, by the failure of those officials to raise the sovereign immunity defense in the preceding action. That was because consent to be sued could only be granted by Congress. The Court further held that "[t]he reasons for the conclusion that this immunity may not be waived govern likewise the question of res judicata.... Consent alone gives jurisdiction to adjudge against a sovereign. Absent that consent, the attempted exercise of judicial power is void." *Id.* at 514. When faced with the "collision between the desirable principle that rights may be adequately vindicated through a single trial of an issue and the sovereign right of immunity from suit ... [w]e are of the opinion ... the doctrine of immunity should prevail." *Id.* at 514–15. The Court explicitly stated that the "desirability for complete settlement of all issues between parties must ... yield to the principle of immunity." *Id.* at 513.[2]

We are presented with a similar situation in this case. The Government in this case failed to raise any challenge regarding interest, penalties, and tax sales in *Hynes*. As in *USF & G,* however, the failure of the Government to raise a sovereign immunity claim cannot waive the Government's immunity. The principles of res judicata that would prevent the Government from raising immunity now cannot control where there is a clash between the immunity interest and the desire for finality of judgments. Arguably, this case is even stronger than *USF & G,* because there the royalties claim was actually decided by the Court while the government stood mute regarding its immunity rights. In this case, no court has addressed the claims regarding interest, penalties, and tax sales,[3] and the interest in finality of judgments is presumably weaker.

Ultimately, the majority refuses to distinguish between claims actually litigated and those that could have been raised, holding that they are all one claim. Because they are considered one claim, the majority asserts that the government cannot litigate an immunity claim and then bring a subsequent action asserting a second immunity claim. Moreover, from this premise the majority expresses the fear that the Government could raise its attacks on a judgment piecemeal. This is not, however, a challenge to the obligation to pay taxes, which was decided in *Hynes*. If the Government unveiled a "new" immunity challenge to the taxes, such as is envisioned in the majority opinion, then a different result might be required. *USF & G* does not necessarily require that the Government be allowed to argue its immunity defense multiple times. The Supreme Court hinted as much in *Durfee v. Duke,* 375 U.S. 106 (1963):

> To be sure, the general rule of finality of jurisdictional determinations is not without exceptions. Doctrines of federal pre-emption or sovereign immunity may in some contexts be controlling.[12]

---

2. The majority dismisses *USF & G* by characterizing the holding as based on principles of subject matter jurisdiction rather than sovereign immunity. A plain reading of that case suggests otherwise. *See, e.g.,* Wright and Miller, FEDERAL PRACTICE AND PROCEDURES § 4429 (stating that *USF & G* was not based on jurisdiction but rather "[t]he decision rested solely on the ground of sovereign immunity and the doctrine that sovereign immunity cannot be waived."). The principle of sovereign immunity has been afforded much more protection—and respect—by the courts than the majority would afford it here.

3. And in fact, the government often retains immunity from interest even if it consents to waive immunity regarding the underlying judgment. *See Library of Congress v. Shaw,* 478 U.S. 310 (1986). As in this case, the immunity analysis may be very different regarding the two.

12. It is to be noted, however, that in neither of these cases had the jurisdictional issues been *actually litigated* in the first forum....

375 U.S. at 114 (emphasis added).

The claims in the present case, however, were not actually argued in *Hynes.* We are instead presented with an immunity challenge regarding claims that arguably could (and should) have been presented in *Hynes* but were not. This is not a second bite at the tax decision. It is a first bite at penalties, interest, and tax sales. The only question is whether the failure of the Government attorneys to raise it in the prior case can preclude the Government from now asserting immunity to those subsequent state court judgments. *USF & G* establishes that the failure of a government official to assert an immunity claim that could have been made does not preclude the Government's later assertion of that claim. The right of immunity supersedes the interest in adjudication of all related issues in a single case. Just as the Government officials could not consent to waive immunity by failing to raise the immunity defense in *USF & G,* they could not consent to waive immunity by failing to raise the interest, penalties and tax sales claims in this case. Although I am dismayed by the protracted approach taken by the Government, I am constrained by *USF & G* to conclude that the Government is not precluded from pursuing the claims in this case. If *USF & G* is to be reconsidered or limited, that remains the province of the Supreme Court. Because I agree with the district court's conclusions on the merits, I would affirm the decision of the district court.

Notes and Questions

1. In *United States v. Cook County,* the United States Court of Appeals for the Seventh Circuit emphasizes that the government's objections on sovereign immunity grounds to payment of interest and penalties could have been asserted in the prior litigation. The court further rules that the prior lawsuit involves the same claim or transaction, that is, the dispute concerning local taxation of federal office buildings. Nor does this case fall under the exception of *United States v. Mendoza* for nonmutual collateral estoppel, as the identical parties are involved in this subsequent lawsuit. Thus, the court holds, res judicata plainly is triggered. But is that enough? What about the fact that the government is asserting sovereign immunity and that the objection had not been raised and decided in the prior lawsuit? What about the Supreme Court's decision in *United States v. United States Fidelity & Guaranty Co.,* 309 U.S. 506 (1940)?

Note that the district court ruled in favor of the government in this case, relying upon what it called the "seminal case" of *United States Fidelity & Guaranty* and saying that the Supreme Court there had refused "to find that the government's failure in the prior cause of action to raise sovereign immunity or to appeal the final judgment led to either waiver of sovereign immunity or res judicata." *United States v. Cook County,* 1997

WL 639049, at *9 (N.D.Ill.1997). Likewise, Judge Rovner, the dissenting judge on the court of appeals, concludes that *United States Fidelity & Guaranty* plainly permits the government to assert an objection of sovereign immunity, which was not raised in a prior action, notwithstanding res judicata. Because consent to suit can only be granted by Congress, she says that the failure of the government's lawyers to raise a sovereign immunity objection in the preceding action cannot operate to waive that immunity in the subsequent action. What is the response given by Judge Easterbrook in his opinion for the majority? How does he distinguish *United States Fidelity & Guaranty*? If that decision does not reflect a sovereign-immunity exception to res judicata, into what category of exceptions from preclusion should it be placed? Do you find his limiting interpretation of that decision persuasive? What unacceptable consequence does Judge Easterbrook foresee if a "sovereign-immunity exception" is carved into the basic principles of preclusion? What does he fear might occur if the government is afforded this special opportunity to evade the outcome of prior adjudication? How does Judge Rovner respond to these concerns?

2.   Dean Mary Kay Kane explains the principles underlying the preclusion rules of res judicata and collateral estoppel in this way:

> Res judicata and collateral estoppel both operate with almost total disregard for what the truth is. They are premised on the beliefs that the judicial system cannot tolerate constant relitigation or it will be overburdened; that judgments must be stable and final so that persons will be able to rely on them and plan for the future; and that the judicial system must prevent itself from being used as a tool of harassment.

Mary Kay Kane, *Civil Procedure in a Nutshell* 217 (5th ed. 2003). If the government is allowed to relitigate a legal question that was resolved in a prior lawsuit involving a different party and before a different court, aren't these principles undermined? In the case that follows, does concern with stability in the rule of law and the entitlement of citizens to rely upon judicial rulings explain the court's vehement insistence that the government was bound to obey an earlier court decision, even one by another court and involving a different claimant?

_____

Johnson v. United States Railroad Retirement Board

United States Court of Appeals for the District of Columbia Circuit.
969 F.2d 1082 (D.C.Cir. 1992).

■ MIKVA, CHIEF JUDGE:

In a bold challenge to judicial authority, the United States Railroad Retirement Board argues that it is free, when it chooses, to ignore the decisions of United States courts of appeals. Since 1981, the Board has cut off benefits for the spouses and widows of railroad workers after their dependent children turn sixteen, even though the Railroad Retirement Act of 1974, 45 U.S.C. §§ 231–231v, says that they are entitled to benefits until the children turn eighteen. In 1985, the Court of Appeals for the Eighth Circuit rejected the Board's position that an amendment to the Social Security Act required the change. *Costello v. United States R.R. Retirement Bd.*, 780 F.2d 1352 (8th Cir.1985). The Board, however, refused to apply the *Costello* decision, even within the Eighth Circuit, and continued to deny benefits at the administrative level. In March 1991, the Court of Appeals for the Eleventh Circuit rejected the Board's position for the same reasons as the Eighth Circuit. *Johnson v. United States R.R. Retirement Bd.*, 925 F.2d 1374 (11th Cir.1991). The Board still refuses to acquiesce. Since individual challenges have been ineffective, Nancy Johnson, whose spousal benefits were denied, tried to bring a class action in district court challenging the Board's interpretation of the Railroad Act and its policy of intracircuit nonacquiescence.

Because we think that Mrs. Johnson has not been denied "meaningful" access to judicial review, we uphold the district court's conclusion that the Railroad Act vests exclusive jurisdiction in the courts of appeals. But we join the Eighth and Eleventh Circuits and reject the Board's interpretation of the Railroad Act for the third time. We also think that the Board's unapologetic policy of nonacquiescence is inconsistent with the Board's own jurisdictional arguments and troubling on statutory and constitutional grounds. If the Board continues to deny benefits after our decision today, we expect that the policy itself can be directly challenged in an appropriate action before this court.

I. BACKGROUND

Nancy Johnson is the wife of Edward Johnson, a former railroad employee. As the mother and stepmother of his five children, the Board found her eligible for a spousal annuity effective September 10, 1976. In late 1986, the Board notified her that the Tier I component of her annuity would be cut off on April 1, 1987, when her youngest child turned sixteen. (The Railroad Act divides the benefit into two tiers, with separate eligibility criteria). On reconsideration, Mrs. Johnson's claim was denied, and her monthly payment was reduced from $391.11 to $84.11. She filed an administrative appeal, and was told that the issue presented "was solely a matter of law," and did not require a hearing. The first appeals referee denied Mrs. Johnson's claim, and came to the remarkable conclusion that the *Costello* case requires her benefits to be terminated, even though the case explicitly requires the opposite result. A second appeals referee reopened the decision and again rejected her argument, noting that "*Costello* was not a class action case and the Board did not pursue it further." Mrs. Johnson appealed again, and on May 16, 1989, a three-member panel of the Board issued its final decision, affirming the decision of the second appeals referee in a one-sentence order. The third panel member dissented vigorously, calling the Board's policy of nonacquiescence "grossly unjust" and urging payment of Tier I benefits to all widows and spouses with children between sixteen and eighteen.

Having exhausted her administrative remedies, Mrs. Johnson filed a class action in district court, suing individually and on behalf of similarly situated beneficiaries under the Act. She claimed that the Board's denial of full benefits to those in her circumstances violated the Act and the Fifth Amendment's Due Process clause. She also claimed that the Board's policy of intracircuit nonacquiescence violated the statutory and constitutional rights of her class.

The district court decided that the Railroad Act gives the federal courts of appeals exclusive jurisdiction to review the Board's decisions. Concluding, accordingly, that it lacked subject matter jurisdiction over Mrs. Johnson's complaint, it transferred her case to this court pursuant to 28 U.S.C. § 1631 on July 12, 1990. This presented Mrs. Johnson with a dilemma: although an appeals court can adjudicate her individual claim, it cannot adjudicate the class action; and if she chose to pursue the transfer, she would have to abandon the class action challenge. She chose instead to move for reconsideration, requesting that the district court dismiss her complaint, or that it certify its order finding no jurisdiction for interlocutory review under 28 U.S.C. § 129[2](b). While her complaint was pending in the district court, Mrs. Johnson petitioned this court for review, to protect her individual claim for benefits. The district court, in turn, granted reconsideration, vacated the transfer, and on October 4, 1990, dismissed Johnson's case for lack of jurisdiction.

This appeal followed.

II. ANALYSIS

A. *District Court Jurisdiction*

[The court held that the district court lacked subject matter jurisdiction to entertain a class action concerning the determination of benefits under the Railroad Retirement Act. Under the Act, decisions of the Railroad Retirement Board may be reviewed by the United States court of appeals for the circuit in which the claimant lives or in the Courts of Appeals for the District of Columbia Circuit or the Seventh Circuit. 45 U.S.C. § 355(f). The court also concluded that no exception to jurisdiction in the court of appeals was justified on the ground that such review was inadequate or less than meaningful. The relevant parties could be joined in a single proceeding in the court of appeals, the administrative record was adequate for review, and there was no penalty that would be imposed by seeking judicial review in the appellate court.]

B. *Mrs. Johnson's Entitlement*

[The court held that the Railroad Retirement Board was not entitled to deference under *Chevron U.S.A. Inc. v. Natural Resources Defense Council, Inc.,* 467 U.S. 837 (1984), in its interpretation of the statutory provisions at issue in the case. In *Chevron*, the Supreme Court held that when Congress has not directly determined the precise question at issue by the terms of the statute, the agency's construction of the statute it administers is entitled to deference if it is a reasonable interpretation of the statute. The court here ruled that *Chevron* deference did not apply because the Board was not interpreting its governing statute alone, but rather the relationship between the Railroad Retirement Act and the Social Security Act for purposes of determining eligibility for benefits. Since the Social Security Act is outside the Board's area of expertise, the court concluded it was not necessary to defer even to a reasonable Board interpretation of the statutory relationship.

In any event, the court ruled that the Board's interpretation of the statute was not reasonable. Although the railroad retirement benefit is measured under the Social Security Act, which provides for an age 16 cut off, 42 U.S.C. § 402(s)(1), the court held that the Railroad Retirement Act refers to the Social Security Act only to determine the amount of benefits, not eligibility. Accordingly, benefits for spouses and widows of railroad workers under the Railroad Retirement Act are cut off only when the youngest dependent child has turned 18 rather than 16. The court stated that explicit authorization in the Railroad Retirement Act is necessary to reduce those benefits.]

For all these reasons, we reverse the Board's order and remand with directions to award to Mrs. Johnson a Tier I spouse's annuity for the period that began with the termination of her annuity and which ended when her youngest child turned eighteen.

C. *Nonacquiescence*

"We have been grossly unjust," the dissenting Board member wrote, in refusing to follow the *Costello* case, even within the Eighth Circuit. "Moreover," he added, "the Court may severely criticize us for our handling of these cases." He was correct.

In response to the *Costello* case, the Board refused to pay Tier I benefits even within the Eighth Circuit, unless claimants complete the administrative process, which includes an initial decision, reconsideration, a hearing before a referee, and a final decision by the three-member Board itself. At oral argument before this court, furthermore, the Board repeated its extraordinary position that an agency is not bound to respect the pronouncements of a U.S. Court of Appeals, even within its own circuit. Mrs. Johnson challenged the constitutionality of the nonacquiescence policy in her complaint, and asked for, among other things, mandamus relief. We think such a dramatic step would be premature, since the Board has not announced definitively that it will refuse to acquiesce in our decision today; and in the interest of judicial restraint, we will give the Board a chance to reconsider its position in light of our opinion. To inform the Board's response, however, we think it useful to suggest why the Board's policy is inconsistent with the Board's jurisdictional arguments and troubling on statutory and constitutional grounds.

First, the Board's entire jurisdictional argument is based on the claim that Congress put great stock on the efficiency and expertise of appellate review. But the same legislative history the Board quotes to suggest that

Congress intended to preclude district court jurisdiction also suggests that Congress expected the Board to respect circuit court decisions rather than to defy them. The Board put particular emphasis on the testimony of Mr. Schoene, the labor representative, who showed a special concern for avoiding the "further expense" of additional appeals that would be forced on a claimant if she lost in the district court. [*Hearings on H.R. 1362 Before the House Comm. on Interstate and Foreign Commerce*, 79th Cong., 1st Sess., pt. 3,] at 1083–93 (1946). Yet the Board itself has put claimants to further expense and meaningless appeals by forcing them to exhaust their administrative remedies before they can receive benefits. Mr. Schoene also noted that "more careful consideration will be given to the entire case ... in the circuit court of appeals," *id.;* and the Board took great pains to argue that Congress intended appellate judges to apply their expertise to legal challenges to the Board's policies. Now, however, the Board refuses to respect the "expert" judgments of appellate courts.

The Board's refusal to acquiesce, in short, undermines all of the advantages of appellate review that the Board insists Congress intended to recognize. To the degree that the Board's policy clashes with the intent of the framers of the Railroad Act, it cannot be sustained. More generally, defenders of nonacquiescence rely heavily on the premise that the "current administrative landscape" suggests an "implicit authorization of nonacquiescence," Estreicher & Revesz, *Nonacquiescence by Federal Administrative Agencies*, 98 Yale L.J. 679, 729 (1989). Evidence that Congress intended the opposite in this case leaves the argument without a foundation.

The Board's position also ignores basic rules of legal precedent, which are governed not by an inherent judicial hierarchy, but by the mechanisms of review provided by Congress. State courts, for example, are bound to follow Supreme Court precedent because if they do not, they can be reversed. Federal courts of appeals, by contrast, do not review state decisions, so their decisions are not generally considered binding precedent in state courts. In the current tax court, similarly, identical cases on the merits may receive different dispositions, because they are appealable to different federal circuits. The Board's refusal to acquiesce even in cases it knows will be appealed to the Eighth Circuit defies Congress's plan in making decisions under the Railroad Act reviewable by the courts of appeals in which the injury arose.

On the broadest level, the Board's position raises serious statutory and constitutional questions. Intracircuit nonacquiescence has been condemned by almost every circuit court of appeals that has confronted it. * * *

Several courts have questioned the constitutionality of intracircuit nonacquiescence with broad references to *Cooper v. Aaron*, 358 U.S. 1 (1958), and *Marbury v. Madison*, 5 U.S. (1 Cranch) 137, 177 (1803). But it is not necessary to accept the *Cooper* analogy to criticize the Board's policy in this case. In *Cooper*, the Supreme Court said that its interpretations of the Constitution are binding on state officials, even on those who were not parties to the case or bound by a court order. *Marbury*, according to the *Cooper* Court, "declared the basic principle that the federal judiciary is supreme in the exposition of the law of the Constitution"; therefore, the Court concluded, judicial interpretations of the Constitution are the 'supreme law of the land,? and state officials are bound by oath to follow them. 358 U.S. at 18. Circuit courts, for their part, have compared the nonacquiescence of federal agencies to the defiance of Governor Faubus at Little Rock, noting that "[w]hat the *[Cooper]* Court said with regard to the Constitution applies with full force with regard to federal statutory law." *Lopez [v. Heckler],* 725 F.2d [1498,] 1497 n. 5 [(9th Cir. 1984), *vacated on other grounds and remanded,* 469 U.S. 1082 (1984) (mem.).

Defenders of nonacquiescence argue that the *Cooper* analogy is inexact. Although *Cooper* speaks not of the Supreme Court but of *"the federal judiciary* [as] supreme in the exposition of the law of the Constitution," 358 U.S. at 18 (emphasis added), the decision seems to assume that "the law forming the basis for the obligation to acquiesce is no longer in flux." Estreicher & Revesz, 98 YALE L.J. at 725. Supreme Court decisions, the argument goes, should be followed in the interests of national uniformity; but until the Supreme Court has spoken, agencies have argued that their responsibility to formulate "uniform and orderly national policy in adjudications" allows them to refuse to acquiescence in the conflicting views of U.S. Courts of Appeals. At oral argument before this court, similarly, the Railroad Board emphasized its responsibilities as a "nationwide authority." This Board offered no other arguments to defend its policy.

But even if we assume, for the sake of argument, that an interest in national uniformity might justify nonacquiescence in some cases, the sincerity of the Railroad Board's interest in uniformity is open to question. When an agency honestly believes a circuit court has misinterpreted the law, there are two places it can go to correct the error: Congress or the Supreme Court. The Railroad Retirement Board has done neither. It has not asked Congress to clarify its intentions, even after two circuits said it had misunderstood Congress's intentions. More remarkably, it has failed to petition the Supreme Court for certiorari, even in the decisions it claims to believe were wrongly decided. The Board appears, as a result, to be less interested in national uniformity than in denying benefits one way or another.

The Board, in the end, can hardly defend its policy of selective nonacquiescence by invoking national uniformity. The policy has precisely the opposite effect, since it results in very different treatment for those who seek and who do not seek judicial review. If a Railroad spouse, like a social security claimant,

> has the determination and the financial and physical strength and lives long enough to make it through the administrative process, he can turn to the courts and ultimately expect them to apply the law as announced [by the Circuit]. If exhaustion overtakes him and he falls somewhere along the road leading to such ultimate relief, the nonacquiescence and the resulting termination stand. Particularly with respect to the types of individuals here concerned, whose resources ...

are by definition, relatively limited, such a dual system of law is prejudicial and unfair.

Lopez v. Heckler, 572 F.Supp. 26, 28 (C.D.Cal.1983).

Conceding the lack of vertical uniformity—similar treatment of all claimants in the same circuit—defenders of nonacquiescence have tried to point to the benefits of what they call horizontal uniformity—similar treatment of all national claimants in initial agency proceedings. At the same time, they acknowledge that horizontal uniformity is not an end in itself, but a means to other values, such as fairness. It is a peculiar view of fairness, however, that treats all claimants equally poorly by depriving them of benefits they will eventually receive if they have the fortitude to run an administrative gauntlet. This looks uncomfortably like the frivolous and obstructionistic litigation that the Supreme Court has severely criticized in the context of habeas corpus.

Because of the venue provisions of the Railroad Act, furthermore, *any* claimant who is denied Tier I benefits in the future can eventually receive benefits by seeking review in our circuit. *See* 45 U.S.C. § 355(f) (1988). It is hard to see the fairness of a policy that guarantees benefits to those who can afford to appeal in the District of Columbia and denies benefits to those who cannot. Under these circumstances, the interests of both fairness and national uniformity suggest that the Board should consider reinstating Tier I benefits in all jurisdictions.

Ordinarily, of course, the arguments against *inter*circuit nonacquiescence (which occurs when an agency refuses to apply the decision of one circuit to claims that will be reviewed by another circuit) are much less compelling than the arguments against *intra*circuit nonacquiescence. Although the decision of one circuit deserves respect, we have recognized that "it need not be taken by the Board as the law of the land." *Givens v. United States R.R. Retirement Bd.,* 720 F.2d 196, 200 (D.C.Cir.1983). When the Board's position is rejected in one circuit, after all, it should have a reasonable opportunity to persuade other circuits to reach a contrary conclusion. And there is an additional value to letting important legal issues "percolate" throughout the judicial system, so the Supreme Court can have the benefit of different circuit court opinions on the same subject. *See, e.g., United States v. Mendoza,* 464 U.S. 154, 160 (1984). But now that three circuits have rejected the Board's position, and not one has accepted it, further resistance would show contempt for the rule of law. After ten years of percolation, it is time for the Board to smell the coffee.

In light of our decision today, we hope that the Board will choose to abandon its policy of intracircuit nonacquiescence, as the Social Security Administration did after being severely criticized by the Courts and by Congress. But if the Board persists, we expect that the policy of nonacquiescence itself could be considered a "final decision of the Board" under 45 U.S.C. § 355(f) that could be challenged by a spouse or widow in an appropriate action before this court.

III. CONCLUSION

We affirm the district court's dismissal of the complaint for lack of jurisdiction. We reverse the Board's order and remand with directions to award Mrs. Johnson a Tier I spouse's annuity for the period which began with the termination of her annuity and which ended when her youngest child turned eighteen.

It is so ordered.

■ BUCKLEY, CIRCUIT JUDGE, concurring in part and dissenting in part:

I concur in the majority's conclusion that the district court lacked jurisdiction over the class action. I dissent, however, from its rejection of the Railroad Retirement Board's denial of Tier I benefits for Mrs. Johnson. As I find 45 U.S.C. § 231c(a)(1) ambiguous and the Board's interpretation of it permissible, I believe we are obliged to accede to the Board's disposition of her claim. *See Chevron U.S.A. Inc. v. NRDC, Inc.,* 467 U.S. 837, 843 (1984). I also write separately to comment on the majority's discussion of nonacquiescence by federal agencies in circuit court decisions. * * *

II. APPLICABILITY OF *CHEVRON*

[Judge Buckley argued that the Railroad Retirement Board was owed deference under the *Chevron* doctrine because the nature of the relationship between the Railroad Retirement Act and the Social Security Act is defined entirely by the former. Because the benefit decision was based therefore on an interpretation of the Railroad Retirement Act, the case raises a matter within the Board's area of expertise for which it is entitled to deference. Judge Buckley further concluded that the Board was reasonable in its interpretation of the eligibility requirement in the Railroad Retirement Act as resulting in a cut off of benefits when a spouse or widow's youngest dependent child turns age 16.]

III. NONACQUIESCENCE

Although dicta, the majority's discussion of agency nonacquiescence suggests that we may be prepared to draw some rather hard lines on the matter. While I share the majority's exasperation with the Board's refusal to apply the *Costello* ruling to claims arising within the Eighth Circuit, there are circumstances where intracircuit nonacquiescence may be justified. *See* Estreicher & Revesz, *Nonacquiescence by Federal Administrative Agencies,* 98 Yale L.J. 679, 743–53 (1989). In this instance, I can see no extenuating circumstances, especially in light of the bureaucratic obstacles a claimant must overcome before she can petition for judicial review. Nevertheless, I would not want us to leave the impression that this court will find intracircuit nonacquiescence unacceptable under any and every circumstance.

Nor should we suggest a rigid rule of "three strikes and out," as the majority does in the case of intercircuit nonacquiescence. It is easy enough to say that when an agency is reversed on an important issue, its proper course is to appeal to Congress or the Supreme Court. Catching Congress's ear, however, is more easily said than done; and given the huge volume of petitions for certiorari that flood the Supreme Court, it is often necessary to establish a split among the circuits before the Court will examine an issue. If an agency is confident enough of its own position, I would be reluctant to establish an arbitrary limit on the intercircuit waters it would be allowed to test.

———

Notes and Questions

1.   Not surprisingly, government positions persistently taken directly in the teeth of adverse precedent have not received a favorable reception by the courts, as illustrated by Chief Judge Mikva's majority ruling for the United States Court of Appeals for the District of Columbia Circuit in *Johnson v. United States Railroad Retirement Board.* Nonetheless, is this vehement rejection of the government's "nonacquiescence"—that is, refusal to follow previous circuit rulings involving different claimants—consistent with the Supreme Court's refusal to apply nonmutual collateral estoppel against the federal government in *United States v. Mendoza,* 464 U.S. 154 (1984)? The D.C. Circuit purports to reach this conclusion based upon stare decisis as entailing a duty to comply with circuit precedent, not by direct application of principles of collateral estoppel or preclusion. But does that eliminate the tension between *Johnson* and *Mendoza?* If the United States is bound to follow a prior ruling in a circuit as a matter of precedent, doesn't that have the same effect of preventing the government from preserving its position in a different case for potential Supreme Court review? The D.C. Circuit in *Johnson* chastises the government for failing to comply with a prior ruling when the issue arises again in the same circuit or when substantial time has passed with no effort by the government to seek Supreme Court review. Is the D.C. Circuit essentially imposing limits upon the flexibility afforded to the government in conducting litigation by the Supreme Court in *Mendoza?* Is this narrowing of *Mendoza*'s application legitimate?

Commentators differ on the significance and meaning of the *Mendoza* decision to the nonacquiescence question, at least in the context of an agency's refusal to follow the law of the very circuit that will review its decision. Professors Samuel Estreicher and Richard Revesz acknowledge that *Mendoza* is not dispositive on the question of nonacquiescence, but state that "a rigid insistence that administrative proceedings adhere to a circuit court's rulings may produce some of the same undesirable consequences for process of national law development that led to the rejection of nonmutual collateral estoppel in *Mendoza.*" Samuel Estreicher & Richard L. Revesz, *Nonacquiescence by Federal Administrative Agencies,* 98 Yale L.J. 679, 686 (1989). Professor Rebecca Hanner White likewise contends that, while not directly "immuniz[ing] nonacquiescence at the circuit court level," the reasoning of *Mendoza*—with its concern about thwarting or freezing the development of the law—"suggests that commanding acquiescence is improper." Rebecca Hanner White, *Time for New Approach: Why the Judiciary Should Disregard the "Law of the Circuit" when Confronting Nonacquiescence by the National Labor Relations Board,* 69 N.C. L. Rev. 639, 670 (1991).

By contrast, Professor Joshua Schwartz argues that "it is stare decisis rather than collateral estoppel that compels acquiescence" by agencies in circuit precedent. Joshua I. Schwartz, *Nonacquiescence,* Crowell v. Benson, *and Administrative Adjudication,* 77 Geo. L.J. 1815, 1880 (1989). Schwartz agrees that the Supreme Court likely did not intend to limit the privilege created in *Mendoza* for government relitigation through "an intracircuit relitigation exception," and that the policy considerations reflected in *Mendoza,* while diminished, are not eliminated in the intracircuit context. *Id.* at 1879. Nonetheless, he concludes that when an agency is exercising "adjudicatory authority to determine the rights and obligations of private parties"—such as awarding benefits or imposing penalties—rather than merely acting as "an advocate in litigation before the courts," that distinctive role carries an obligation to adhere to judicial precedent that constrains and directs the agency's exercise of judgment. *Id.* at 1880. Professor Dan Coenen, contending that agency nonacquiescence is unconstitutional, distinguishes *Mendoza* as not involving a constitutional challenge to an agency's refusal to follow precedent and notes that *Mendoza* involved the binding effect of an earlier ruling by a district court rather than a circuit court. Dan T. Coenen, *The Constitutional Case Against Intracircuit Nonacquiescence,* 75 Minn. L. Rev. 1339, 1370–71 (1991). Coenen concludes that "the agency—even if required to comply with local circuit court precedent—may pursue its own policies in other circuits, defend those policies in those circuits when challenged, seek Supreme Court review when it so desires, and thus avoid the nationwide 'freezing ... of the law' that the Court in *Mendoza* eschewed." *Id.* at 1372.

Doesn't the *Johnson* decision and its vehement disapproval of intracircuit nonacquiescence mean that an agency must *either* (1) surrender to the first adverse court of appeals decision and bring its national policy into compliance with the opinion of a single court of appeals—unless the government seeks immediate Supreme Court review after an initial loss, *or* (2) adopt a practice of *inter*circuit (as opposed to *intra*circuit) nonacquiescence, in which "the agency accepts the decisions of a circuit for the geographic area of that circuit but applies its own understanding of the law to other circuits." *See* Frank B. Cross, *Shattering the Fragile Case for Judicial Review of Rulemaking,* 85 Va. L. Rev. 1243, 1253 (1999). With respect to the first option, the Supreme Court's opinion in *United States v. Mendoza* spoke approvingly of the Solicitor General's exercise of prudential discretion to allow an issue to percolate among the lower courts before seeking high Court review, as well as allowing successive political administrations to review and revise administrative policy. With respect to the second option, if the agency applies different administrative rules from circuit-to-circuit to avoid transgressing precedent within a particular circuit while preserving its policy elsewhere, doesn't that lack of national uniformity also impair fair administration and undermine the rule of law? *Id.* at

1253–54 (arguing that, if an agency chooses "to tailor its enforcement to the idiosyncratic law of a given circuit," resulting in varying legal rules in different regions, the agency's statutory duty to apply the law is violated); Estreicher & Revesz, *supra,* 98 Yale L.J. at 748 ("Whether the agency acts as regulator of private sector activity or administers a benefit program, Congress intended, by enacting federal law to promote horizontal uniformity—equal treatment of regulatees or claimants regardless of where in this country the dispute or claim arose.").

Moreover, as one commentator notes, the *Johnson* court "never even attempted to identify the type of nonacquiescence at issue." Samuel Figler, *Executive Agency Nonacquiescence to Judicial Opinions,* 61 Geo. Wash. L. Rev. 1664, 1680 (1993). In fact, because the Railroad Retirement Act allows the choice of appeal to the circuit where the claimant resides (Johnson resided in the Sixth Circuit), to the circuit where the Railroad Retirement Board is located (in the Seventh Circuit), or to the D.C. Circuit, 45 U.S.C. § 355(g), the Board's refusal in the *Johnson* case to follow adverse precedents in the Eighth and Eleventh Circuits amounted to *inter*circuit nonacquiescence. Figler, *supra,* at 1678, 1684–85 & n.182. Indeed, Judge Mikva in *Johnson* boldly suggests doubts about *inter*circuit nonacquiescence as well, saying that the fact that three circuits (out of 12 regional circuits) had now rejected the government's position means that "further resistance would show contempt for the rule of law." Judge Buckley, in dissent, criticizes this as a "rigid rule of 'three strikes and out' "for intercircuit nonacquiescence. On the other hand, how many times must the courts shoot down a government legal position before citizens can safely rely upon that precedent in their relationships with their government?

2. The *Johnson* court makes a brief reference to the most controversial episode of a federal government agency's determination not to follow circuit precedent—the policy of "nonacquiescence" adopted during the 1980's by the Social Security Administration (SSA) toward court of appeals rulings on disability claims that conflicted with the agency's preferred interpretation of the statute. Essentially, if the SSA disagreed with a particular circuit's determination of when Social Security disability benefits were available or how to evaluate claims, it refused to apply that circuit's precedent. The SSA argued that it was entitled to apply uniform rules nationwide and was not obliged to make exceptions for individual circuits that had a different approach. Among the cases criticizing the SSA's "non-acquiescence" policy were *Hyatt v. Sullivan,* 899 F.2d 329, 331–34 (4th Cir. 1990); *Stieberger v. Bowen,* 801 F.2d 29, 32–33 (2d Cir. 1986); *Layton v. Heckler,* 726 F.2d 440, 442 (8th Cir. 1984); and *Lopez v. Heckler,* 725 F.2d 1489, 1497, 1503 (9th Cir.), *vacated and remanded on other grounds,* 469 U.S. 1082 (1984). For contrasting views on the Social Security Administration's "non-acquiescence" policy, see generally Estreicher & Revesz, *supra,* 98 Yale L.J. at 692–704; Carolyn A. Kubitschek, *Social Security Administration Nonacquiescence: The Need for Legislative Curbs on Agency Discretion,* 50 U. Pitt. L. Rev. 399 (1989); Angela M. Johnson, Note, *The Social Security Administration's Policy of Nonacquiescence,* 62 Ind. L.J. 1101

(1987); and Carolyn B. Kuhl, *The Social Security Administration's Nonacquiescence Policy,* 1984 Det. C.L. Rev. 913.

One consequence of the SSA's nonacquiescence policy was the imposition of attorney's fee awards against the federal government in disability cases under the Equal Access to Justice Act, 28 U.S.C. § 2412. (The Equal Access to Justice Act is explored at length in Chapter VII.B.5.) Under the statutory standard that fees are to be awarded when the government's position in the lawsuit is not "substantially justified" (which has been interpreted to mean that the government's position was unreasonable), the courts regularly concluded that the government was liable for fees in nonacquiescence cases. *See, e.g., Thompson v. Sullivan,* 980 F.2d 280, 283 (4th Cir. 1992) ("A policy of 'non-acquiescence' cannot be 'substantially justified' in law."); *Hyatt v. Heckler,* 807 F.2d 376, 382 (4th Cir. 1986) ("[T]he Secretary's policy of nonacquiescence entitle[s] the claimant to attorney's fees."). Attorney's fees, including awards of fees against the federal government, is the subject of the next chapter.

———

ATTORNEY'S FEES—LIMITATIONS AND AWARDS

Chapter VII introduces students to the subject of attorney's fees in litigation, both as charged against a client and as recovered from an opponent in litigation. While the ethical standards for charging and collecting legal fees may be addressed in the Professional Responsibility course, additional restrictions are imposed upon an attorney by statute when representing a party making certain types of claims against the federal government. Moreover, given the exponential proliferation of statutes that authorize awards of attorney's fees—that is, shifting of legal fees from the prevailing party to the losing party in litigation—and the accompanying increase in contentious fee disputes in court, this is a topic of vital importance in the practice of law today. "To the old adage that death and taxes share a certain inevitable character, federal judges may be excused for adding attorneys' fees cases." *Kennedy v. Whitehurst*, 690 F.2d 951, 952 (D.C.Cir. 1982). Yet it is a subject that often is not covered elsewhere in the law school curriculum. The majority of law students graduate with little exposure to attorney's fee-shifting and minimal awareness that the so-called American Rule (that each party bears it own legal fees) has been eroded by a multitude of exceptions.

A study of attorney's fees is also an integral part of a course on the federal government as a litigant, owing both to the special limitations on charging a fee against one's own client for certain types of claims against the government and to the many statutory provisions allowing fee awards against the sovereign. Accordingly, the subject of attorney's fees in federal government litigation deserves special attention and separate treatment. Much of the law of attorney's fees is the same in this context, but much also is different.

———

SECTION A.   LIMITATIONS ON PRIVATE ATTORNEY'S FEES CONTRACTS

1.   FEDERAL TORT CLAIMS ACT

28 United States Code § 2678

No attorney shall charge, demand, receive, or collect for services rendered, fees in excess of 25 per centum of any judgment rendered pursuant to section 1346(b) of this title or any settlement made pursuant to section 2677 of this title, or in excess of 20 per centum of any award, compromise, or settlement made pursuant to section 2672 of this title.

Any attorney who charges, demands, receives, or collects for services rendered in connection with such claim any amount in excess of that allowed under this section, if recovery be had, shall be fined not more than $2,000 or imprisoned not more than one year, or both.

———

Wyatt v. United States

United States Court of Appeals for the Sixth Circuit.
783 F.2d 45 (6th Cir. 1986).

■ WELLFORD, CIRCUIT JUDGE.

In 1981, Floyd Wyatt, a federal employee on a military base, filed a Federal Tort Claims Act suit after losing four fingers during operation of a forklift. Following extensive discovery, the parties agreed to a structured settlement in February 1983.[1] The structured settlement, which was acceptable to Wyatt, provided for an initial cash payment of $153,626, and for deferred payments in future years. As a part of the settlement, the government was to purchase two annuities at a total cost of $119,702. One of the annuities would yield monthly payments of $800 to Wyatt for twenty years or during his lifetime, whichever was the longer period. This would bring about a guaranty of at least $192,000 over this period of time. The second annuity would pay Wyatt periodic lump sums totalling $200,000 and be distributed as follows: $25,000 after five years, $25,000 after ten years, $50,000 after fifteen years, $100,000 after twenty years.

Plaintiffs' attorney, who is the real party in interest in this appeal, submitted a proposed judgment providing for payment of $95,626 in attorney's fees and $25,000 in litigation costs. Wyatt and his wife, who was also a party in the proceeding, acknowledged that they understood that these amounts would be deducted from the initial cash settlement,[2] and made no objection to their attorneys' calculation of and request for fees and costs.

---

1. Plaintiff Wyatt, after consulting with his counsel, rejected the government's offer to make a lump sum settlement in the amount of $280,000.

2. The Wyatts would receive nothing from the initial payment proceeds since the balance of approximately $33,000 would represent sums due the workmen's compensa-

The government objected to the amount of attorneys' fees, claiming that the award violated the 25% limitation imposed by the Federal Tort Claims Act. The government has standing to challenge the amount of attorneys' fees to be paid to plaintiffs' attorney. The government argued before the district court that the Act requires that attorneys' fees be calculated on the basis of the cost of the settlement package to the government, the equivalent of the actual present value of the total settlement to the plaintiff in this case. The total settlement cost to the government was $273,328 (the initial cash settlement of $153,626 and the cost of purchasing the annuities, $119,702). Based on this calculation of the total costs of the settlement, the government contends that the maximum allowable attorney fee should therefore be $68,332.

The district court ruled that in a structured settlement, the base figure upon which an attorney fee award is to be determined under the Act in question is the "present value of the settlement to the plaintiff" and not the cost to the government. He denied, however, the government's request for an evidentiary hearing as to the actual present value of the structured settlement, and instead relied on the representations of plaintiffs' counsel to conclude that the package had "conservatively" a value of $385,000. After deducting the court litigation costs of approximately $25,000, the district court awarded attorney fees of $89,870, which he calculated to be the 25% maximum fee amount allowable.[4]

The sole question in this appeal is whether the district court used a proper legal standard in determining the amount of plaintiffs' attorneys' fees allowable under the Federal Tort Claims Act. * * *

The trial judge found unpersuasive the government's argument that 25% of "the amount appropriated" for the settlement to be an equivalent base representing the cost of the settlement to the government. The "amount appropriated" equivalence came from the government's reference to the legislative history of 28 U.S.C. § 2678. Prior to enactment of the present Federal Tort Claims Act, limitations on fee awards were made with reference to appropriations on private relief bills. Attorney fees were allowed based on the "amount appropriated for a particular settlement." The trial judge, although unpersuaded, acknowledged that the argument of

---

tion carrier which had previously made these payments to Floyd Wyatt or for his benefit.

There is no indication that the workmen's compensation insurance company which received this subrogation benefit from the structured settlement was called upon to share any part of the fees or costs charged the Wyatts. Thus, as consequence of this settlement which the Wyatts' counsel argued was of great advantage to them, it would have taken them almost ten years, if Wyatt lived that long, to receive an amount equiva- lent to fees and expenses proposed to be paid to their attorney immediately upon approval of this structured arrangement. We have some doubt as to the benefit of this particular settlement over the $280,000 cash settlement proposed by the government.

4. Attorney for plaintiffs apparently does not contest for purposes of this appeal the deduction of litigation expenses before applying the 25% for the attorney's fee. We therefore do not have occasion to address this matter.

the government "has force." We are persuaded by the government's argument, and we therefore reverse.

We are not in disagreement with the district court that the Federal Tort Claims Act is "remedial and must be liberally construed." *See United States v. Alexander*, 238 F.2d 314 (5th Cir.1956). It is to be liberally construed, however, in favor of the claimant, not the claimant's attorney. In our view, the construction placed on the Act by the district court in this case was inappropriate, liberal to the attorney, not to the claimants whom he represented.

While we disagree with the result reached by the district court, we do not take issue with the trial judge's reference to "the present value of the settlement" to be the "proper base amount for determining an attorney fee in this structured settlement." Unlike the district court in this case, it is clear to us that absent the submission of any contrary evidence the present value of the structured settlement in this case was, in fact, the *cost* of that settlement, namely, what it took in money to produce the agreed settlement payments over the entire period involved. No evidence was presented to show that the "present value" of this settlement was anything more than its actual cost of $273,328. The district judge merely indicated that he was "persuaded by the argument in plaintiff's brief that the present value to plaintiffs of this settlement is conservatively $385,000."

The basis of the argument made by plaintiffs' attorney and accepted by the district court was that the court should look to "unique" benefits to the plaintiff in this type of settlement, involving payments spread over future installments with supposed beneficial tax consequences. Plaintiffs' attorney admits that "this benefit to the injured plaintiff is intangible, yet very real and important to the plaintiff as well as his attorney...." Evidently, supposed tax and other intangible benefits are speculative at best. Plaintiffs' attorney does not address other alternatives available to an injured plaintiff such as investment of lump sum settlement proceeds in government or municipal bonds, or in other types of secured investments and/or annuities that would produce favorable tax consequences. The plaintiffs' attorney also argues that a provision for assured payments in the future in the form of a structured settlement would "prevent plaintiffs from squandering a recovery and ending up with nothing." We are not impressed by these arguments about some added value to the plaintiffs through the device of deferring payments in the future. * * *

Another appellate court, albeit in a somewhat different context, has considered the problem inherent in this case involving a 25% fee award in an FTCA case to the injured plaintiff's attorney. That case involved an action by the district court in a structured settlement limiting the attorney to 25% of the cash amount paid, omitting any fee for future "lifetime medical care and treatment." We agree with that court's general discussion and description of the type of settlement involved in that case and in the instant case:

> Generally, a structured settlement entails a cash payment made on settlement, sufficient to cover at least special damages such as medical

bills incurred and past lost wages, and guaranteed periodic payments in the future. Such payments are commonly funded by an annuity policy. This settlement technique has been both applauded and criticized. Its proponents point to the tax free status of the payments if certain requirements are observed and the "spendthrift preventative nature" of periodic payments. Critics stress that the defendant's insurance company might not pass on to the plaintiff some of the cost savings achieved through this form of settlement, and that the possibility of carrier insolvency is also a significant drawback. All agree that the manner in which contingent fees are to be computed in a structured settlement with periodic payments, particularly when there is a reversion in the event of death, poses a dilemma.

Since the use of a structured settlement as a vehicle for resolving major tort litigation is "still in its embryonic stages," *see* Hyland & Keeley, *Using the Structured Settlement*, Nat'l L.J., Dec. 19, 1983, at 15, it is unlikely that Congress contemplated how such benefits were to be calculated in the 1966 revision of section 2678 of the Federal Tort Claims Act.

Godwin v. Schramm, 731 F.2d [153,] 157–58 [(3d Cir.), *cert. denied*, 469 U.S. 882 (1984)].

The *Godwin* court noted the case of *Johnson v. Sears, Roebuck & Co.*, 291 Pa.Super. 625, 436 A.2d 675 (1981) which held, (according to Judge Sloviter) "that where the future payments [in a structured settlement] were funded by an annuity policy, the cost of the annuity represented the base on which attorney's fees were due.["] 291 Pa.Super. at 630, 436 A.2d at 678. The dissenting judge would have used the present value of the future benefits as determined by actuarial tables . . ." 731 F.2d at 158. The *Godwin* court then went on to observe:

> It may be, as appellant suggests, that contingent services are susceptible of determination by experts and reducible to present value. If so, computation of counsel fee on such a basis may not violate the literal terms of the statutory maximum fixed by section 2678, provided there are adequate findings by the district court as to present value supported by the record.

731 F.2d at 158.

We share the concern of the court in *Godwin* that payment in full on the front end of a 25% attorney fee allowed under § 2678 where substantial payments are to be made to the claimant-plaintiff in the future may work a serious hardship on the very person intended to be benefited by FTCA, and "such matters are not always settled amicably between counsel and the client." 731 F.2d at 159. *Godwin* is distinguishable from this case in that it involved the difficult matter of assessing and placing a present monetary value to future lifetime medical services and care; but we have cited at length from what is essentially dicta in that case, because it addresses the concerns that we share in determining a proper standard to apply to attorney fees in this type of FTCA settlement.[7] In any event we agree fully with the observation

> the lawyer's share would not be more than s/he bargained for at the outset of the litigation.

731 F.2d at 159. * * *

In the case at bar apparently plaintiffs were amenable to payment of attorney fees to their attorney (assuming they understood fully the import and impact of such agreement) upon approval of the settlement and the amount of the fees. Absent any such pre-existing arrangement or agreement about how and when fees were to be disbursed, we would see no objection to allowing the plaintiffs' attorney to receive 25% of each payment made to plaintiffs under the structured settlement. We do not interpret any of the cases heretofore cited as necessarily precluding this type of determination and payment of attorney fees under the Federal Tort Claims Act. * * * This, of course, could involve practical difficulties for the attorney but the latter may always protect his or her interest by agreement with the client.

> There is no indication that Congress intended to prohibit a litigant and attorney from agreeing, for example, to forgo a large cash award in favor of a substantial package of benefits, to assign a present value to the benefits and to allot the lawyer a share of that figure.

Godwin, 731 F.2d at 159.

Any such agreement reached as to "present value" and amount of attorney fees, however, must be subject to the approval of the district court so that it may ascertain, based on adequate proof, that the fee does not exceed the limitation of 28 U.S.C. § 2678. In this case, had the district judge entertained any doubt that the cost of the settlement did not reflect the reasonable present cash value of the entire structured settlement, he should have conducted a hearing with adequate opportunity for development of proof of such value by the plaintiff's attorney, the government, and the plaintiffs themselves. Thus, if the district court were "unpersuaded" by what the government demonstrated as cost, which it properly argued in this case to be equivalent to the actual present cash value of the settlement, then the court must require proof to establish the present value base upon which the 25% maximum fee is to be calculated. We emphasize that it is within the reasonable discretion of the trial court, absent an agreement which is fair and equitable to the FTCA claimant, to determine the manner and amount of attorney fee payment, within the parameters of 28 U.S.C. § 2678. The 25% limitation set out in the statute may not, of course, be exceeded, and it is to be based upon the present value of the total settlement, excluding any speculative and intangible benefits to the plaintiff.

---

7. The language cited from *Godwin* is dicta * * * because *Godwin* disposed of the lawyer fee dispute on appeal without applying 28 U.S.C. § 2678.

In reaching this decision, we have not in any way intended to discourage, where helpful or beneficial, a structured settlement in a Federal Tort Claims Act (or any other) context. We appreciate that lawyers may render their clients in appropriate circumstances a special service by devising deferred payments or arranged settlements to serve particular purposes that a cash settlement could not reach. In some instances a structured settlement might be reached when an all cash arrangement would not be acceptable to one party or the other.

We reverse and remand for an award to counsel for the plaintiffs in the amount of $68,332 consistent with the views herein expressed. Each party will bear its own costs, but those properly assessed to plaintiffs-appellees will be borne by their counsel, the real party in interest.

――――――

Notes and Questions

1. With respect to compensation for legal services, an attorney ordinarily has a contract with his or her client under which the client agrees to pay the attorney a fee, either at a specified rate by the hour or as a percentage of the amount recovered. In the private sector, the limitations on fee arrangements come as a matter of contract law governing the validity of agreements and the rules of professional ethics. As you have or will study in a course on legal ethics or professional responsibility, both the Model Rules of Professional Conduct (Rule 1.5) and the Model Code of Professional Responsibility (Disciplinary Rule 2–106) set forth standards for determining a reasonable fee, limitations on when a fee may be made contingent upon an outcome, and other requirements or expectations concerning fee arrangements between attorneys and clients.

For the most part, these same rules apply when attorneys are hired to represent clients in litigation against the federal government. However, in some circumstances, the federal government itself takes an interest in the fee arrangement between an attorney and a client. To ensure that the party who has suffered an injury or who has an entitlement to a government benefit enjoys the primary welfare of the public funds paid to that party, Congress has enacted limitations on the amount that an attorney may collect and thus effectively subtract from the client's recovery on certain claims (as the fee typically is paid out of the funds recovered from the government in settlement or by judgment). The Federal Tort Claims Act provides one example of these restrictions. *See generally* 2 Lester S. Jayson & Robert C. Longstreth, *Handling Federal Tort Claims* §§ 10.01, 16.10[3] (2005). The next section on attorney's fees in the context of Social Security Act claims offers another.

2. In *Wyatt v. United States*, the court begins by describing the plaintiff as a "federal employee on a military base." However, if that description is accurate, then as we've seen previously the plaintiff would be barred from seeking recovery under the Federal Tort Claims Act for any injury incurred during the performance of his duties because of the exclu-

sive alternative remedy available under the Federal Employees Compensation Act (FECA). By the express provision of 5 U.S.C. § 8116(c), a government employee within the scope of FECA—the workers compensation program for federal employees—is exclusively limited to the remedy provided by that Act (see Chapter III.A.9.a). However, from other evidence in the *Wyatt* opinion, it appears that the reference to the plaintiff as a "federal employee" is a misnomer. In footnote 2, the court refers to a "workmen's compensation carrier" as having paid benefits to the plaintiff; a federal employee would never receive workers compensation benefits from an insurance carrier but would instead be covered by FECA. In all likelihood, the plaintiff here was actually an employee of an independent contractor hired by the federal government to perform work on the base, and thus was not a federal employee covered by FECA.

3.   Turning to the point of the *Wyatt* case, first outline the nature of the fee arrangement between the attorney and his client. Is this arrangement equitable? Is the attorney taking unfair advantage of this client? What standing does the government have to object to this fee payment— that is, why should the government be heard to complain, when it is the client (not the government) that is paying the attorney? What is the statutory limitation on the recovery of attorney's fees that applies in this case? What is the problem in calculation that arises here? What are the arguments for different methods of calculation? Consider whether the choice between these methods is a false one. What possibly could be the measure of the present value of a structured settlement other than its actual cost in implementation?

The *Wyatt* case illustrates the difficulties that can arise in applying a 25 percent limitation on contingent fee recovery, a rule that at first glance seems simple. A similar problem in calculation might arise if a settlement or award included non-monetary benefits, such as a government agreement to provide future medical services at no cost. (*See, e.g., Molzof v. United States,* 502 U.S. 301 (1992); see Chapter III.A.8.) How would you calculate a fee in such a case? Should any fee be permitted, for example, on an award of future medical services?

————

2.   SOCIAL SECURITY ACT

42 United States Code § 406(a), (b), (c)

(a) Recognition of representatives; fees for representation before Commissioner of Social Security

(1) The Commissioner of Social Security may prescribe rules and regulations governing the recognition of agents or other persons, other than attorneys as hereinafter provided, representing claimants before the Commissioner of Social Security, and may require of such agents or other persons, before being recognized as representatives of claimants that they

shall show that they are of good character and in good repute, possessed of the necessary qualifications to enable them to render such claimants valuable service, and otherwise competent to advise and assist such claimants in the presentation of their cases. An attorney in good standing who is admitted to practice before the highest court of the State, Territory, District, or insular possession of his residence or before the Supreme Court of the United States or the inferior Federal courts, shall be entitled to represent claimants before the Commissioner of Social Security. Notwithstanding the preceding sentences, the Commissioner, after due notice and opportunity for hearing, (A) may refuse to recognize as a representative, and may disqualify a representative already recognized, any attorney who has been disbarred or suspended from any court or bar to which he or she was previously admitted to practice or who has been disqualified from participating in or appearing before any Federal program or agency, and (B) may refuse to recognize, and may disqualify, as a non-attorney representative any attorney who has been disbarred or suspended from any court or bar to which he or she was previously admitted to practice. A representative who has been disqualified or suspended pursuant to this section from appearing before the Social Security Administration as a result of collecting or receiving a fee in excess of the amount authorized shall be barred from appearing before the Social Security Administration as a representative until full restitution is made to the claimant and, thereafter, may be considered for reinstatement only under such rules as the Commissioner may prescribe. The Commissioner of Social Security may, after due notice and opportunity for hearing, suspend or prohibit from further practice before the Commissioner any such person, agent, or attorney who refuses to comply with the Commissioner's rules and regulations or who violates any provision of this section for which a penalty is prescribed. The Commissioner of Social Security may, by rule and regulation, prescribe the maximum fees which may be charged for services performed in connection with any claim before the Commissioner of Social Security under this subchapter, and any agreement in violation of such rules and regulations shall be void. Except as provided in paragraph (2)(A), whenever the Commissioner of Social Security, in any claim before the Commissioner for benefits under this subchapter, makes a determination favorable to the claimant, the Commissioner shall, if the claimant was represented by an attorney in connection with such claim, fix (in accordance with the regulations prescribed pursuant to the preceding sentence) a reasonable fee to compensate such attorney for the services performed by him in connection with such claim.

(2)(A) In the case of a claim of entitlement to past-due benefits under this subchapter, if—

(i) an agreement between the claimant and another person regarding any fee to be recovered by such person to compensate such person for services with respect to the claim is presented in writing to the Commissioner of Social Security prior to the time of the Commissioner's determination regarding the claim,

(ii) the fee specified in the agreement does not exceed the lesser of—

(I) 25 percent of the total amount of such past-due benefits * * *, or

(II) $4,000, and

(iii) the determination is favorable to the claimant,

then the Commissioner of Social Security shall approve that agreement at the time of the favorable determination, and (subject to paragraph (3)) the fee specified in the agreement shall be the maximum fee. The Commissioner of Social Security may from time to time increase the dollar amount under clause (ii)(II) to the extent that the rate of increase in such amount, as determined over the period since January 1, 1991, does not at any time exceed the rate of increase in primary insurance amounts under section 415(i) of this title since such date. The Commissioner of Social Security shall publish any such increased amount in the Federal Register.

* * *

(D) In the case of a claim with respect to which the Commissioner of Social Security has approved an agreement pursuant to subparagraph (A), the Commissioner of Social Security shall provide the claimant and the person representing the claimant a written notice of—

(i) the dollar amount of the past-due benefits * * * and the dollar amount of the past-due benefits payable to the claimant,

(ii) the dollar amount of the maximum fee which may be charged or recovered as determined under this paragraph, and

(iii) a description of the procedures for review under paragraph (3).

(3)(A) The Commissioner of Social Security shall provide by regulation for review of the amount which would otherwise be the maximum fee as determined under paragraph (2) if, within 15 days after receipt of the notice provided pursuant to paragraph (2)(D)—

(i) the claimant, or the administrative law judge or other adjudicator who made the favorable determination, submits a written request to the Commissioner of Social Security to reduce the maximum fee, or

(ii) the person representing the claimant submits a written request to the Commissioner of Social Security to increase the maximum fee.

Any such review shall be conducted after providing the claimant, the person representing the claimant, and the adjudicator with reasonable notice of such request and an opportunity to submit written information in favor of or in opposition to such request. The adjudicator may request the Commissioner of Social Security to reduce the maximum fee only on the basis of evidence of the failure of the person representing the claimant to represent adequately the claimant's interest or on the basis of evidence that the fee is clearly excessive for services rendered.

(B)(i) In the case of a request for review under subparagraph (A) by the claimant or by the person representing the claimant, such review shall be conducted by the administrative law judge who made the favorable determination or, if the Commissioner of Social Security determines that such administrative law judge is unavailable or if the determination was not made by an administrative law judge, such review shall be conducted by another person designated by the Commissioner of Social Security for such purpose.

(ii) In the case of a request by the adjudicator for review under subparagraph (A), the review shall be conducted by the Commissioner of Social Security or by an administrative law judge or other person (other than such adjudicator) who is designated by the Commissioner of Social Security.

(C) Upon completion of the review, the administrative law judge or other person conducting the review shall affirm or modify the amount which would otherwise be the maximum fee. Any such amount so affirmed or modified shall be considered the amount of the maximum fee which may be recovered under paragraph (2). The decision of the administrative law judge or other person conducting the review shall not be subject to further review.

(4) Subject to subsection (d), if the claimant is determined to be entitled to past-due benefits under this subchapter and the person representing the claimant is an attorney, the Commissioner of Social Security shall, notwithstanding section 405(i) of this title, certify for payment out of such past due benefits (as determined before any applicable reduction under section 1320a–6(a) of this title) to such attorney an amount equal to so much of the maximum fee as does not exceed 25 percent of such past-due benefits (as determined before any applicable reduction under section 1320a–6(a) of this title).

(5) Any person who shall, with intent to defraud, in any manner willfully and knowingly deceive, mislead, or threaten any claimant or prospective claimant or beneficiary under this subchapter by word, circular, letter or advertisement, or who shall knowingly charge or collect directly or indirectly any fee in excess of the maximum fee, or make any agreement directly or indirectly to charge or collect any fee in excess of the maximum fee, prescribed by the Commissioner of Social Security shall be deemed guilty of a misdemeanor and, upon conviction thereof, shall for each offense be punished by a fine not exceeding $500 or by imprisonment not exceeding one year, or both.

(b) Attorney fees

(1)(A) Whenever a court renders a judgment favorable to a claimant under this subchapter who was represented before the court by an attorney, the court may determine and allow as part of its judgment a reasonable fee for such representation, not in excess of 25 percent of the total of the past-due benefits to which the claimant is entitled by reason of such judgment, and the Commissioner of Social Security may * * * certify the amount of such fee for payment to such attorney out of, and not in addition to, the amount of such past-due benefits. In case of any such judgment, no other fee may be payable or certified for payment for such representation except as provided in this paragraph.

     * * *

(2) Any attorney who charges, demands, receives, or collects for services rendered in connection with proceedings before a court to which paragraph (1) of this subsection is applicable any amount in excess of that allowed by the court thereunder shall be guilty of a misdemeanor and upon conviction thereof shall be subject to a fine of not more than $500, or imprisonment for not more than one year, or both.

(c) Notification of options for obtaining attorneys

The Commissioner of Social Security shall notify each claimant in writing, together with the notice to such claimant of an adverse determination, of the options for obtaining attorneys to represent individuals in presenting their cases before the Commissioner of Social Security. Such notification shall also advise the claimant of the availability to qualifying claimants of legal services organizations which provide legal services free of charge.

Gisbrecht v. Barnhart

United States Supreme Court.
535 U.S. 789 (2002).

■ JUSTICE GINSBURG delivered the opinion of the Court.

This case concerns the fees that may be awarded attorneys who successfully represent Social Security benefits claimants in court. Under 42 U.S.C. § 406(b) (1994 ed. and Supp. V), a prevailing claimant's fees are payable only out of the benefits recovered; in amount, such fees may not exceed 25 percent of past-due benefits. At issue is a question that has sharply divided the Federal Courts of Appeals: What is the appropriate starting point for judicial determinations of "a reasonable fee for [representation before the court]"? See *ibid.* Is the contingent-fee agreement between claimant and counsel, if not in excess of 25 percent of past-due benefits, presumptively reasonable? Or should courts begin with a lodestar calculation (hours reasonably spent on the case times reasonable hourly rate) of the kind we have approved under statutes that shift the obligation to pay to the loser in the litigation?

Congress, we conclude, designed § 406(b) to control, not to displace, fee agreements between Social Security benefits claimants and their counsel. Because the decision before us for review rests on lodestar calculations and rejects the primacy of lawful attorney-client fee agreements, we reverse the judgment below and remand for recalculation of counsel fees payable from the claimants' past-due benefits.

I

A

Fees for representation of individuals claiming Social Security old-age, survivor, or disability benefits, both at the administrative level and in court, are governed by prescriptions Congress originated in 1965. The statute deals with the administrative and judicial review stages discretely: § 406(a) governs fees for representation in administrative proceedings; § 406(b) controls fees for representation in court.

For representation of a benefits claimant at the administrative level, an attorney may file a fee petition or a fee agreement. 42 U.S.C. § 406(a). In response to a petition, the agency may allow fees "for services performed in connection with any claim before" it; if a determination favorable to the benefits claimant has been made, however, the Commissioner of Social Security "*shall* ... fix ... a reasonable fee" for an attorney's services. § 406(a)(1) (emphasis added). In setting fees under this method, the agency takes into account, in addition to any benefits award, several other factors. Fees may be authorized, on petition, even if the benefits claimant was unsuccessful.

As an alternative to fee petitions, the Social Security Act, as amended in 1990, accommodates contingent-fee agreements filed with the agency in advance of a ruling on the claim for benefits. If the ruling on the benefits claim is favorable to the claimant, the agency will generally approve the fee agreement, subject to this limitation: Fees may not exceed the lesser of 25 percent of past-due benefits or $4,000 (increased to $5,300 effective February 2002). §§ 406(a)(2)(A)(ii), (iii).

For proceedings in court, Congress provided for fees on rendition of "a judgment favorable to a claimant." 42 U.S.C. § 406(b)(1)(A). The Commissioner has interpreted § 406(b) to "prohibi[t] a lawyer from charging fees when there is no award of back benefits."

As part of its judgment, a court may allow "a reasonable fee ... not in excess of 25 percent of the ... past-due benefits" awarded to the claimant. § 406(b)(1)(A). The fee is payable "out of, and not in addition to, the amount of [the] past-due benefits." *Ibid.* Because benefits amounts figuring in the fee calculation are limited to those past due, attorneys may not gain additional fees based on a claimant's continuing entitlement to benefits.

The prescriptions set out in §§ 406(a) and (b) establish the exclusive regime for obtaining fees for successful representation of Social Security benefits claimants. Collecting or even demanding from the client anything more than the authorized allocation of past-due benefits is a criminal offense. §§ 406(a)(5), (b)(2).

In many cases, as in the instant case, the Equal Access to Justice Act (EAJA), enacted in 1980, effectively increases the portion of past-due benefits the successful Social Security claimant may pocket. 28 U.S.C. § 2412. Under EAJA, a party prevailing against the United States in court, including a successful Social Security benefits claimant, may be awarded fees payable by the United States if the Government's position in the litigation was not "substantially justified." § 2412(d)(1)(A). EAJA fees are determined not by a percent of the amount recovered, but by the "time expended" and the attorney's "[hourly] rate," § 2412(d)(1)(B), capped in the mine run of cases at $125 per hour, § 2412(d)(2)(A).

Congress harmonized fees payable by the Government under EAJA with fees payable under § 406(b) out of the claimant's past-due Social Security benefits in this manner: Fee awards may be made under both prescriptions, but the claimant's attorney must "refun[d] to the claimant the amount of the smaller fee." Act of Aug. 5, 1985, Pub.L. 99–80, i 3, 99 Stat. 186. "Thus, an EAJA award offsets an award under Section 406(b), so that the [amount of the total past-due benefits the claimant actually receives] will be increased by the ... EAJA award up to the point the claimant receives 100 percent of the past-due benefits." Brief for United States 3.

B

Petitioners Gary Gisbrecht, Barbara Miller, and Nancy Sandine brought three separate actions in the District Court for the District of Oregon under 42 U.S.C. § 405(g)[5] seeking Social Security disability benefits under Title II of the Social Security Act. All three petitioners were represented by the same attorneys, and all three prevailed on the merits of their claims. Gisbrecht was awarded $28,366 in past-due benefits; Miller, $30,056; and Sandine, $55,952. Each petitioner then successfully sought attorneys' fees payable by the United States under EAJA: Gisbrecht was awarded $3,339.11, Miller, $5,164.75, and Sandine, $6,836.10.

Pursuant to contingent-fee agreements standard for Social Security claimant representation, see 1 B. Samuels, Social Security Disability Claims i 21:10 (2d ed.1994), Gisbrecht, Miller, and Sandine had each agreed to pay counsel 25 percent of all past-due benefits recovered. Their attorneys accordingly requested § 406(b) fees of $7,091.50 from Gisbrecht's recovery, $7,514 from Miller's, and $13,988 from Sandine's. Given the EAJA offsets, the amounts in fact payable from each client's past-due benefits recovery would have been $3,752.39 from Gisbrecht's recovery, $2,349.25 from Miller's, and $7,151.90 from Sandine's.

Following Circuit precedent, the District Court in each case declined to give effect to the attorney-client fee agreement. Instead, the court employed for the § 406(b) fee calculation a "lodestar" method, under which the number of hours reasonably devoted to each case was multiplied by a reasonable hourly fee. This method yielded as § 406(b) fees $3,135 from Gisbrecht's recovery, $5,461.50 from Miller's, and $6,550 from Sandine's. Offsetting the EAJA awards, the court determined that no portion of Gisbrecht's or Sandine's past-due benefits was payable to counsel, and that

---

5. Section 405(g) authorizes judicial review of administrative denials of applications for Social Security benefits.

only $296.75 of Miller's recovery was payable to her counsel as a § 406(b) fee. The three claimants appealed.[6]

Adhering to Circuit precedent applying the lodestar method to calculate fees under § 406(b), the Court of Appeals for the Ninth Circuit consolidated the cases and affirmed the District Court's fee dispositions. *Gisbrecht v. Apfel,* 238 F.3d 1196 (2000). The Appeals Court noted that fees determined under the lodestar method could be adjusted by applying 12 further factors, one of them, "whether the fee is fixed or contingent." While "a district court must *consider* a plaintiff's request to increase a fee [based on a contingent-fee agreement]," the Ninth Circuit stated, "a court 'is not required to articulate its reasons' for accepting or rejecting such a request." (emphasis in original).

We granted certiorari, ,in view of the division among the Circuits on the appropriate method of calculating fees under § 406(b). We now reverse the Ninth Circuit's judgment.

II

Beginning with the text, § 406(b)'s words, "a reasonable fee ... not in excess of 25 percent of ... the past-due benefits," read in isolation, could be construed to allow either the Ninth Circuit's lodestar approach or petitioners' position that the attorney-client fee agreement ordinarily should control, if not "in excess of 25 percent." The provision instructs "a reasonable fee," which could be measured by a lodestar calculation. But § 406(b)'s language does not exclude contingent-fee contracts that produce fees no higher than the 25 percent ceiling. Such contracts are the most common fee arrangement between attorneys and Social Security claimants. Looking outside the statute's inconclusive text, we next take into account, as interpretive guides, the origin and standard application of the proffered approaches.

The lodestar method has its roots in accounting practices adopted in the 1940's to allow attorneys and firms to determine whether fees charged were sufficient to cover overhead and generate suitable profits. * * *

Hourly records initially provided only an internal accounting check. * * * As it became standard accounting practice to record hours spent on a client's matter, attorneys increasingly realized that billing by hours devoted to a case was administratively convenient; moreover, as an objective measure of a lawyer's labor, hourly billing was readily impartable to the client. By the early 1970's, the practice of hourly billing had become widespread.

The federal courts did not swiftly settle on hourly rates as the overriding criterion for attorney's fee awards. In 1974, for example, the

---

6. Although the claimants were named as the appellants below, and are named as petitioners here, the real parties in interest are their attorneys, who seek to obtain higher fee awards under § 406(b). For convenience, we nonetheless refer to claimants as petitioners. We also note that the Commissioner of Social Security here, as in the Ninth Circuit, has no direct financial stake in the answer to the § 406(b) question; instead, she plays a part in the fee determination resembling that of a trustee for the claimants.

Fifth Circuit issued an influential opinion holding that, in setting fees under Title VII of the Civil Rights Act of 1964, 42 U.S.C. § 2000e–5(k), courts should consider not only the number of hours devoted to a case but also 11 other factors. *Johnson v. Georgia Highway Express, Inc.*, 488 F.2d 714, 717–719 (C.A.5 1974). The lodestar method did not gain a firm foothold until the mid–1970's, see *Lindy Bros. Builders, Inc. of Philadelphia v. American Radiator & Standard Sanitary Corp.*, 487 F.2d 161 (C.A.3 1973), appeal after remand, 540 F.2d 102 (1976), and achieved dominance in the federal courts only after this Court's decisions in *Hensley v. Eckerhart*, 461 U.S. 424 (1983), *Blum v. Stenson*, 465 U.S. 886 (1984), and *Pennsylvania v. Delaware Valley Citizens' Council for Clean Air*, 478 U.S. 546 (1986).

Since that time, "[t]he 'lodestar' figure has, as its name suggests, become the guiding light of our fee-shifting jurisprudence." *Burlington v. Dague*, 505 U.S. 557, 562 (1992). As we recognized in *Hensley*, "[i]deally, . . . litigants will settle the amount of a fee." 461 U.S., at 437. But where settlement between the parties is not possible, "[t]he most useful starting point for [court determination of] the amount of a reasonable fee [payable by the loser] is the number of hours reasonably expended on the litigation multiplied by a reasonable hourly rate." *Id.*, at 433. Thus, the lodestar method today holds sway in federal-court adjudication of disputes over the amount of fees properly shifted to the loser in the litigation.

Fees shifted to the losing party, however, are not at issue here. Unlike 42 U.S.C. § 1988 and EAJA, 42 U.S.C. § 406(b) does not authorize the prevailing party to recover fees from the losing party. Section 406(b) is of another genre: It authorizes fees payable from the successful party's recovery. Several statutes governing suits against the United States similarly provide that fees may be paid from the plaintiff's recovery. See, *e.g.,* Federal Tort Claims Act (FTCA), 28 U.S.C. § 2678 ("No attorney shall charge, demand, receive, or collect for services rendered, fees in excess of 25 per centum of any [court] judgment rendered [in an FTCA suit], or in excess of 20 per centum of any award, compromise, or settlement made [by a federal agency to settle an FTCA claim]."); Veterans' Benefits Act, 38 U.S.C. § 5904(d)(1) ("When a claimant [for veterans' benefits] and an attorney have entered into a [contingent-]fee agreement [under which fees are paid by withholding from the claimant's benefits award], the total fee payable to the attorney may not exceed 20 percent of the total amount of any past-due benefits awarded on the basis of the claim."). Characteristically in cases of the kind we confront, attorneys and clients enter into contingent-fee agreements "specifying that the fee will be 25 percent of any past-due benefits to which the claimant becomes entitled." Brief for National Organization of Social Security Claimants' Representatives as *Amicus Curiae* 2; see Brief for Washington Legal Foundation et al. as *Amici Curiae* 9, n. 6 ("There is no serious dispute among the parties that virtually every attorney representing Title II disability claimants includes in his/her retainer agreement a provision calling for a fee equal to 25% of the past-due benefits awarded by the courts.").

Contingent fees, though problematic, particularly when not exposed to court review, are common in the United States in many settings. Such fees, perhaps most visible in tort litigation, are also used in, *e.g.,* patent litigation, real estate tax appeals, mergers and acquisitions, and public offerings. Traditionally and today, "the marketplace for Social Security representation operates largely on a contingency fee basis." SSA Report 3.

Before 1965, the Social Security Act imposed no limits on contingent-fee agreements drawn by counsel and signed by benefits claimants. In formulating the 1965 Social Security Act amendments that included § 406(b), Congress recognized that "attorneys have upon occasion charged ... inordinately large fees for representing claimants [in court]." S.Rep. No. 404, 89th Cong., 1st Sess., pt. 1, p. 122 (1965), U.S.Code Cong. & Admin.News 1965, pp. 1943, 2062. Arrangements yielding exorbitant fees, the Senate Report observed, reserved for the lawyer one-third to one-half of the accrued benefits. Congress was mindful, too, that the longer the litigation persisted, the greater the buildup of past-due benefits and, correspondingly, of legal fees awardable from those benefits if the claimant prevailed.

Attending to these realities, Congress provided for "a reasonable fee, not in excess of 25 percent of accrued benefits," as part of the court's judgment, and further specified that "no other fee would be payable." *Ibid.* Violation of the "reasonable fee" or "25 percent of accrued benefits" limitation was made subject to the same penalties as those applicable for charging a fee larger than the amount approved by the Commissioner for services at the administrative level—a fine of up to $500, one year's imprisonment, or both. *Ibid.* "[T]o assure the payment of the fee allowed by the court," Congress authorized the agency "to certify the amount of the fee to the attorney out of the amount of the accrued benefits." *Ibid.*

Congress thus sought to protect claimants against "inordinately large fees" and also to ensure that attorneys representing successful claimants would not risk "nonpayment of [appropriate] fees." SSA Report 66 (internal quotation marks omitted). But nothing in the text or history of § 406(b) reveals a "desig[n] to prohibit or discourage attorneys and claimants from entering into contingent fee agreements." *Ibid.* Given the prevalence of contingent-fee agreements between attorneys and Social Security claimants, it is unlikely that Congress, simply by prescribing "reasonable fees," meant to outlaw, rather than to contain, such agreements.

This conclusion is bolstered by Congress' 1990 authorization of contingent-fee agreements under § 406(a), the provision governing fees for agency-level representation. Before enacting this express authorization, Congress instructed the Social Security Administration to prepare a report on attorney's fees under Title II of the Social Security Act.–295. The report, presented to Congress in 1988, reviewed several methods of determining attorney's fees, including the lodestar method. See SSA Report 10–11. This review led the agency to inform Congress that, although the contingency method was hardly flawless, the agency could "identify no more effective means of ensuring claimant access to attorney representation." *Id.,* at 25.

* * *

Most plausibly read, we conclude, § 406(b) does not displace contingent-fee agreements as the primary means by which fees are set for successfully representing Social Security benefits claimants in court. Rather, § 406(b) calls for court review of such arrangements as an independent check, to assure that they yield reasonable results in particular cases. Congress has provided one boundary line: Agreements are unenforceable to the extent that they provide for fees exceeding 25 percent of the past-due benefits. Within the 25 percent boundary, as petitioners in this case acknowledge, the attorney for the successful claimant must show that the fee sought is reasonable for the services rendered.

Courts that approach fee determinations by looking first to the contingent-fee agreement, then testing it for reasonableness, have appropriately reduced the attorney's recovery based on the character of the representation and the results the representative achieved. If the attorney is responsible for delay, for example, a reduction is in order so that the attorney will not profit from the accumulation of benefits during the pendency of the case in court. If the benefits are large in comparison to the amount of time counsel spent on the case, a downward adjustment is similarly in order. In this regard, the court may require the claimant's attorney to submit, not as a basis for satellite litigation, but as an aid to the court's assessment of the reasonableness of the fee yielded by the fee agreement, a record of the hours spent representing the claimant and a statement of the lawyer's normal hourly billing charge for noncontingent-fee cases. Judges of our district courts are accustomed to making reasonableness determinations in a wide variety of contexts, and their assessments in such matters, in the event of an appeal, ordinarily qualify for highly respectful review.

* * *

The courts below erroneously read § 406(b) to override customary attorney-client contingent-fee agreements. We hold that § 406(b) does not displace contingent-fee agreements within the statutory ceiling; instead, § 406(b) instructs courts to review for reasonableness fees yielded by those agreements. Accordingly, we reverse the judgment of the Court of Appeals for the Ninth Circuit and remand the case for further proceedings consistent with this opinion.

It is so ordered.

■ JUSTICE SCALIA, dissenting.

I do not know what the judges of our district courts and courts of appeals are to make of today's opinion. I have no idea what the trial judge is to do if he finds the fee produced by the ("presumptively reasonable") contingent-fee agreement to be 25% above the lodestar amount; or 40%; or 65%. Or what the appellate court is to do in an appeal from a district judge's reduction of the contingent fee to 300% of the lodestar amount; or 200%; or to the lodestar amount itself. While today's opinion gets this case out of our "in" box, it does nothing whatever to subject these fees to anything approximating a uniform rule of law. That is, I think, the inevitable consequence of trying to combine the incompatible. The Court tells the judge to commence his analysis with the contingent-fee agreement, but then to adjust the figure that agreement produces on the basis of factors (most notably, the actual time spent multiplied by a reasonable hourly rate) that are, in a sense, the precise antithesis of the contingent-fee agreement, since it was the very *purpose* of that agreement to eliminate them from the fee calculation. In my view, the only possible way to give uniform meaning to the statute's "reasonable fee" provision is to understand it as referring to the fair value of the work actually performed, which we have held is best reflected by the lodestar.

I think it obvious that the reasonableness of a contingent-fee arrangement *has to be* determined by viewing the matter *ex ante,* before the outcome of the lawsuit and the hours of work expended on the outcome are definitively known. For it is in the nature of a contingent-fee agreement to *gamble* on outcome and hours of work—assigning the risk of an unsuccessful outcome to the attorney, in exchange for a percentage of the recovery from a successful outcome that will (because of the risk of loss the attorney has borne) be higher, and perhaps much higher, than what the attorney would receive in hourly billing for the same case. That is why, in days when obtaining justice in the law courts was thought to be less of a sporting enterprise, contingent fees were unlawful.

It is one thing to say that a contingent-fee arrangement is, *ex ante,* unreasonable because it gives the attorney a percentage of the recovery so high that no self-respecting legal system can tolerate it; the statute itself has made this determination for Social–Security-benefit cases, prescribing a maximum contingent fee of 25%. And one can also say that a contingent-fee arrangement is, *ex ante,* unreasonable because the chances of success in the particular case are so high, and the anticipated legal work so negligible, that the percentage of the recovery assured to the lawyer is exorbitant; but neither I nor the Court thinks that the "reasonable fee" provision of the statute anticipates such a case-by-case *ex post* assessment of *ex ante* predictions in the thousands of (mostly small recovery) Social-Security-benefit cases. It is something quite different, however—and something quite irrational—to look at the *consequences* of a contingent-fee agreement *after the contingencies have been resolved,* and proclaim those consequences unreasonable because the attorney has received too much money for too little work. That is rather like declaring the purchase of the winning lottery ticket void because of the gross disparity between the $2 ticket price and the million-dollar payout.[2]

2. There is one *ex post* element prominent in Social-Security-benefit cases that assuredly should reduce the amount of an otherwise reasonable (that is to say, an *ex ante* reasonable) contingent-fee award: Since the award is based upon past-due benefits, and since the amount of those benefits increases with the duration of the litigation, a lawyer can increase his contingent-fee award by dragging his feet. It is unreasonable to be rewarded for dilatoriness. But *that* element need not be made part of an overall *ex post*

I think, in other words, that the "reasonable fee" provision must require *either* an assessment of the reasonableness of the contingent-fee agreement when it was concluded, *or* an assessment of the reasonableness of the fee charged after the outcome and work committed to it are known; it cannot combine the two. And since an *ex post* assessment of the *ex ante* reasonableness of the contingent-fee agreement (already limited by statute to a maximum 25% of the recovery) is not what the statute could conceivably have contemplated, I conclude that a "reasonable fee" means not the reasonableness of the agreed-upon contingent fee, but a reasonable recompense for the work actually done. We have held that this is best calculated by applying the lodestar, which focuses on the quality and amount of the legal work performed, and "provides an objective basis on which to ... estimate ... the value of a lawyer's services." *Hensley*, 461 U.S., at 433.

This is less of a departure than the Court suggests from the normal practice of enforcing privately negotiated fee agreements. The fee agreements in these Social–Security cases are hardly negotiated; they are akin to adherence contracts. It is uncontested that the specialized Social–Security bar charges uniform contingent fees (the statutory maximum of 25%), which are presumably presented to the typically unsophisticated client on a take-it-or-leave-it basis. * * *

> * * *

Because I think there is no middle course between, on the one hand, determining the reasonableness of a contingent-fee agreement and, on the other hand, determining the reasonableness of the actual fee; because I think the statute's reference to a "reasonable fee" must connote the latter; and because I think the Court's hybrid approach establishes no clear criteria and hence will generate needless satellite litigation; I respectfully dissent.

Notes and Questions

1. The statutory provisions governing collection by an attorney of fees from a Social Security claimant are set out above before the *Gisbrecht v. Barnhardt* opinion. Section 406(a) of Title 42 covers fees for legal work done at the administrative level, providing for approval of fees by the Social Security Administration. Section 406(b) covers fees for legal services in court proceedings, providing for approval by the district court. Similar to the Federal Tort Claims Act fees provision we looked at earlier, the Social Security Act authorizes a fee of up to 25 percent of any recovery. However, "unlike the Social Security Act, the FTCA does not direct courts to

reasonableness assessment, as the Court would do. For it is not only unreasonable; it is a breach of contract. Surely the representation agreement contains as an implicit term that the lawyer will bring the matter to a conclusion as quickly as practicable—or at least will not intentionally delay its conclusion. Any breach of that condition justifies a reduction of the contracted contingent-fee award.

'determine and allow' a 'reasonable fee' up to 25 percent of a plaintiff's recovery; that is, the FTCA, on its face anticipates a more passive judicial role in fee determinations." Alison M. MacDonald & Victor Williams, *In Whose Interests? Evaluating Attorneys' Fee Awards and Contingent–Fee Agreements in Social Security Disability Benefits Cases,* 47 Admin. L. Rev. 115, 147 (1995). Thus, by contrast, the Social Security Act provision suggests an active role for the court in evaluating and approving a fee award to the claimant's attorney. Why? If the claimant and his or her attorney entered into a contract for a contingent fee, what concern is it to the court or the government, as long as the 25 percent ceiling is not exceeded? Why might the government oppose an award at the maximum level? Why is court approval mandated by the statute? Why might courts be more aggressive in policing fee awards in Social Security disability cases than in FTCA tort cases?

2.   Before 2002, the federal courts of appeals were divided on the manner in which attorney's fees should be measured in Social Security benefits cases. A minority of the circuits adopted the 25 percent statutory figure as the "benchmark" for attorney's fees in Social Security cases, thus granting the 25 percent contingency fee the weight of a rebuttable presumption. Thus, under the minority approach, the 25 percent contingent figure was the starting point and would be adjusted only when shown to be unreasonably high. By contrast, a majority of the circuits instead endorsed a lodestar approach, by which the attorney's fee was measured by the number of hours worked by the attorney for the claimant multiplied by the attorney's reasonable hourly rate. The court would carefully evaluate the amount of the fee and not confer presumptive reasonableness upon a contingency fee arrangement between a claimant and counsel.

Commentators Alison MacDonald and Victor Williams criticized both approaches. Because "past-due benefits accrue principally due to factors beyond the control of counsel (administrative and judicial delays), attorneys have the potential to reap fees that bear little relation to the effort expended litigating their clients' claims," resulting in a significant deprivation of disability benefits to the claimant. MacDonald & Williams, *supra,* at 118. For this reason, they criticized the approach that presumptively allows a 25 percent contingency fee. However, they believed the lodestar method "is burdensome for courts, litigants, and counsel," and failed to "sufficiently consider the unique nature of Social Security litigation: the benefits' relevant worth to the claimant is not weighed at all in the fee equation." *Id.* at 159–60. Accordingly, they suggested a simpler, bright-line alternative rule that would first establish a floor on recoverable fees; limited enhancements would then be allowed, but only upon a showing of good cause by the attorney and after allowing the claimant an opportunity to be heard. *Id.* at 168–69. They urged that this approach be adopted by court rule or legislation.

In 2002, the Supreme Court resolved the inter-circuit split in *Gisbrecht v. Barnhart.* How did the majority and dissent define the method by which a court should evaluate what is a reasonable fee in the Social Security context? How much weight did the majority give to the contract entered into by the attorney and the client? Why does the dissent disagree on this point? Under what circumstances should the 25 percent contingency fee amount be reduced in the majority's view? What important factor is identified by both the majority and dissent as requiring a reduction in the fee when it is present?

3. Section 406 "establishes a fee payment arrangement by ensuring the payment of a claimant's attorney out of the benefit award; it is not a fee-shifting statute authorizing the exaction of a fee award from the government." Gregory C. Sisk, *The Essentials of the Equal Access to Justice Act: Court Awards of Attorney's Fees for Unreasonable Government Conduct (Part One),* 55 La. L. Rev. 217, 251–52 (1994). But in addition to payment of the attorney's fee out of the claimant's past-due benefits, a Social Security claimant may be able to obtain an award of attorney's fees from the government—that is, a shifting of the fees to the government—under the Equal Access to Justice Act (EAJA), 28 U.S.C. § 2412. The EAJA is discussed later in Chapter VII.B.5. In general, fee awards are available under the EAJA only if the government's position in the case is found to have been without "substantial justification," that is, without a reasonable basis. Despite this presumably high threshold, studies have found that the overwhelming majority of Social Security claimants who have sought EAJA fee awards have been successful. Harold J. Krent, *Fee Shifting Under the Equal Access to Justice Act—A Qualified Success,* 11 Yale L. & Pol'y Rev. 458, 487–88 (1993); Susan G. Mezey & Susan M. Olson, *Fee Shifting and Public Policy: The Equal Access to Justice Act,* 77 Judicature 13, 18 (1993). On the question of EAJA fee awards in Social Security cases, see also Gregory C. Sisk, *The Essentials of the Equal Access to Justice Act: Court Awards of Attorney's Fees for Unreasonable Government Conduct (Part Two),* 56 La. L. Rev. 1, 30–34 (1995).

As the Supreme Court explained in *Gisbrecht v. Barnhart,* an uncodified provision of the EAJA provides that if the attorney obtains fees for the same work under both the Social Security Act (from past-due benefits) and the EAJA (from the government), the attorney must refund to the claimant the amount of the smaller fee. Pub. L. No. 99–80, § 3(b), 99 Stat. 183, 186 (1985).

---

3. VETERANS' BENEFITS

38 United States Code § 5904(c), (d)

(c)(1) Except as provided in paragraph (4), in connection with a proceeding before the Department with respect to benefits under laws administered by the Secretary, a fee may not be charged, allowed, or paid for services of agents and attorneys with respect to services provided before the date a notice of disagreement is filed with respect to the case. The limitation in the preceding sentence does not apply to fees charged, allowed, or paid for services provided with respect to proceedings before a court.

(2) A person who, acting as agent or attorney in a case referred to in paragraph (1) of this subsection, represents a person before the Department or the Board of Veterans' Appeals after a notice of disagreement is filed with respect to the case shall file a copy of any fee agreement between them with the Secretary pursuant to regulations prescribed by the Secretary.

(3)(A) The Secretary may, upon the Secretary's own motion or at the request of the claimant, review a fee agreement filed pursuant to paragraph (2) and may order a reduction in the fee called for in the agreement if the Secretary finds that the fee is excessive or unreasonable.

(B) A finding or order of the Secretary under subparagraph (A) may be reviewed by the Board of Veterans' Appeals under section 7104 of this title.

(C) If the Secretary under subsection (b) suspends or excludes from further practice before the Department any agent or attorney who collects or receives a fee in excess of the amount authorized under this section, the suspension shall continue until the agent or attorney makes full restitution to each claimant from whom the agent or attorney collected or received an excessive fee. If the agent or attorney makes such restitution, the Secretary may reinstate such agent or attorney under such rules as the Secretary may prescribe.

(4) A reasonable fee may be charged or paid in connection with any proceeding before the Department in a case arising out of a loan made, guaranteed, or insured under chapter 37 of this title. A person who charges a fee under this paragraph shall enter into a written agreement with the person represented and shall file a copy of the fee agreement with the Secretary at such time, and in such manner, as may be specified by the Secretary.

(d) Payment of fees out of past-due benefits.—

(1) When a claimant and an agent or attorney have entered into a fee agreement described in paragraph (2), the total fee payable to the agent or attorney may not exceed 20 percent of the total amount of any past-due benefits awarded on the basis of the claim.

(2)(A) A fee agreement referred to in paragraph (1) is one under which the total amount of the fee payable to the agent or attorney—

(i) is to be paid to the agent or attorney by the Secretary directly from any past-due benefits awarded on the basis of the claim; and

(ii) is contingent on whether or not the matter is resolved in a manner favorable to the claimant.

(B) For purposes of subparagraph (A), a claim shall be considered to have been resolved in a manner favorable to the claimant if all or any part of the relief sought is granted.

(3) To the extent that past-due benefits are awarded in any proceeding before the Secretary, the Board of Veterans' Appeals, or the United States Court of Appeals for Veterans Claims, the Secretary may direct that payment of any fee to an agent or attorney under a fee arrangement described in paragraph (1) be made out of such past-due benefits. In no event may the Secretary withhold for the purpose of such payment any portion of benefits payable for a period after the date of the final decision of the Secretary, the Board of Veterans' Appeals, or Court of Appeals for Veterans Claims making (or ordering the making of) the award.

———

Veterans' Judicial Review Act, 38 United States Code § 7263

(a) The Secretary shall be represented before the Court of Appeals for Veterans Claims by the General Counsel of the Department.

(b) Representation of appellants shall be in accordance with the rules of practice prescribed by the Court under section 7264 of this title. In addition to members of the bar admitted to practice before the Court in accordance with such rules of practice, the Court may allow other persons to practice before the Court who meet standards of proficiency prescribed in such rules of practice.

(c) A person who represents an appellant before the Court shall file a copy of any fee agreement between the appellant and that person with the Court at the time the appeal is filed. The Court, on its own motion or the motion of any party, may review such a fee agreement.

(d) In reviewing a fee agreement under subsection (c) of this section or under section 5904(c)(2) of this title, the Court may affirm the finding or order of the Board and may order a reduction in the fee called for in the agreement if it finds that the fee is excessive or unreasonable. An order of the Court under this subsection is final and may not be reviewed in any other court.

———

SECTION B.   AWARDS OF ATTORNEY'S FEES

Gregory C. Sisk, A Primer on Awards of Attorney's Fees Against the Federal Government

25 Arizona State Law Journal 733, 735–736 (1993).

To the old adage that death and taxes share a certain inevitable character, federal judges may be excused for adding attorneys' fees cases.[1]

---

1. Kennedy v. Whitehurst, 690 F.2d 951, 952 (D.C.Cir. 1982).

Over the past twenty years, the federal government has gradually lowered the shield of sovereign immunity and made itself increasingly amenable to awards of attorney's fees to those who succeed in litigation against the government. Congress began cautiously, waiving federal sovereign immunity for attorney's fees only with respect to claims made under selected statutes that protect fundamental rights. For example, in 1972, Congress amended the fee-shifting provision in Title VII of the Civil Rights Act of 1964 to expressly authorize awards against the United States government.[2] As time passed, Congress further enlarged the federal government's exposure to fee liability by extending fee-shifting provisions in other statutes to the United States, including other civil rights statutes[3] and environmental statutes.[4] At the same time, Congress created statutory causes of action unique to the federal government, such as the Freedom of Information Act,[5] that carried their own provisions for awards of attorney's fees. The trend against immunity from fee awards reached its crescendo with the enactment of the Equal Access to Justice Act, which puts the government on equal footing with private defendants in terms of fee-shifting and further makes the government liable in fees whenever its position is not substantially justified.[6]

In general, the curtain of federal sovereign immunity against awards of attorney's fees has been lifted. Because the federal government is a party to as many as one-third of the civil cases filed in federal court,[7] the inevitability of attorney's fees cases necessarily includes fee litigation against the sovereign United States government. However, because of the particular requirements of certain statutes and because even the broad waiver of immunity in the Equal Access to Justice Act imposes special limitations on that new basis for fee-shifting, the federal government cannot be regarded as just another litigant. Moreover, while Congress has exposed the government to liability under many circumstances, the doctrine of sovereign immunity lingers in the form of narrow rules of statutory construction that favor the government in the application of fee award provisions. Accordingly, the subject of awards of attorney's fees against the federal government continues to deserve special attention and separate treatment. Much of the law of attorney's fees is the same with respect to both the federal government and other defendants, but much also is different.

---

2. 42 U.S.C. § 2000e–5(k).

3. *See, e.g.,* Fair Housing Act, 42 U.S.C. § 3613(c)(2) (attorney's fee provision).

4. *See, e.g.,* Clean Water Act, 33 U.S.C. §§ 1365(d), 1369(b)(3) (attorney's fee provision); Clean Air Act, 42 U.S.C. §§ 7604(d), 7607(f) (attorney's fee provision).

5. 5 U.S.C. § 552(a)(4)(E).

6. 28 U.S.C. § 2412.

7. Urban A. Lester Et Al., Litigation With The Federal Government ix (1989 Supp.).

1.   The American Rule

Palmer v. General Services Administration

United States Court of Appeals for the Eighth Circuit.
787 F.2d 300 (8th Cir. 1986).

■ Fagg, Circuit Judge.

Alfred Palmer appeals the dismissal of his civil complaint brought under the Age Discrimination in Employment Act of 1967 (ADEA), 29 U.S.C. § 621 *et seq.* We affirm.

Palmer is a former employee of the General Services Administration (GSA). In 1980, Palmer filed an administrative complaint against GSA claiming it had discriminated against him because of his age in violation of the ADEA. Palmer eventually prevailed on that complaint and was awarded both a retroactive promotion and back pay. GSA, however, refused to award Palmer attorneys' fees and costs (collectively attorneys' fees or fees).

Palmer then instituted the present judicial action seeking an award of fees against GSA. The district court rejected Palmer's claim and dismissed his action after concluding that the ADEA did not authorize it to award fees to someone in Palmer's position. This appeal followed.

A single issue is presented by Palmer's appeal. Specifically, is this court authorized to award attorneys' fees to a federal employee who prevails at the administrative level on a claim of age discrimination brought under the ADEA? * * *

Because any liability imposed in this case will run against the federal government, the doctrine of sovereign immunity imposes an initial barrier to Palmer's claim. Under that doctrine, this court is without authority to impose any type of liability on the government, unless an "unequivocally expressed" congressional waiver is present. Additionally, even if Congress has waived the government's immunity in a particular case, the terms and conditions of that waiver must be strictly and narrowly construed and all doubts must be resolved in favor of the government.

Underscoring the overriding principle of sovereign immunity in this case is the American Rule of attorneys' fees. Under that rule, absent express statutory authorization to the contrary, each party is ordinarily required to pay its own attorneys' fees. *Alyeska Pipeline Service Co. v. Wilderness Society,* 421 U.S. 240, 247–62 (1975).

Further, the American Rule traditionally applies in all cases, including those in which the government has waived sovereign immunity and consented to suit. Consequently, "a general waiver of sovereign immunity should not be construed to extend to attorney's fees unless Congress has clearly indicated that it should." *Fitzgerald v. United States Civil Service Commission,* 554 F.2d 1186, 1189 (D.C.Cir.1977). Rather, in addition to a general waiver of immunity, Congress must in some way expressly indicate its intent to depart from the general rule that each party is to pay its own fees.

In light of these principles, the appropriate scope of our inquiry is whether Congress, in addition to a general waiver of sovereign immunity, has "clearly and unequivocally," *Lehman [v. Nakshian,]* 453 U.S. [156,] 162 [(1981)], by "specific and explicit" statutory provision, *Alyeska,* 421 U.S. at 260, provided for the recovery of attorneys' fees by a federal employee who successfully prosecutes an ADEA claim at the administrative level. To answer this question, "the starting point for our analysis must be the plain language of the [ADEA] itself." *United States Marshals Service v. Means,* 741 F.2d 1053, 1056 (8th Cir.1984) (en banc).

As originally enacted, the ADEA was not applicable to federal employees. In 1974, however, Congress amended the ADEA for the specific purpose of including federal employees within the scope of the Act. To accomplish this purpose, Congress, rather than simply incorporate federal employees within the existing provisions of the ADEA, adopted a new provision applicable only to federal employees.

This provision, section 15, 29 U.S.C. § 633a, authorizes federal employees to challenge potentially discriminatory decisions both administratively and judicially. And, with respect to the remedies available to federal employees who have been discriminated against, section 15 authorizes this court to award "such legal or equitable relief as will effectuate the purposes of [the ADEA]." *Id.* § 633a(c).

Significantly, however, while authorizing this court to award both legal and equitable relief, section 15 does not make explicit provision for the recovery of attorneys' fees. In fact, neither the language of section 15 nor the sparse legislative history accompanying section 15 makes any reference whatsoever to the availability of attorneys' fees. Further, if attorneys' fees are to be available, authorization must flow from section 15 itself since "[s]ection 15 ... is complete in itself," H.R.Rep. No. 527, 95th Cong., 1st Sess. 11 (1977), and is intended to be "self-contained and unaffected by the other sections [of the ADEA]." *Lehman,* 453 U.S. at 168.

The absence of any attorneys' fees provision in section 15 is particularly highlighted by the express inclusion of such provisions in other antidiscrimination legislation enacted by Congress. For example, in the ADEA itself, Congress specifically adopted an attorneys' fees provision applicable to claims brought by nonfederal employees. See 29 U.S.C. § 626(b) (incorporating by reference the attorneys' fee provision of 29 U.S.C. § 216(b)). Further, under Title VII of the Civil Rights Act, Congress specifically authorized attorneys' fees both for nonfederal employees, 42 U.S.C. § 2000e–5(k), and for federal employees, *id.* § 2000e–16(d) (incorporating by reference the attorneys' fees provision of 42 U.S.C. § 2000e–5(k)). In each of these three cases, Congress saw fit to include express attorneys' fees provisions despite the presence of broad remedial language similar to that adopted in section 15.

Additionally, like the ADEA, Title VII initially did not cover federal employees. However, when Title VII was amended to include such employees, 42 U.S.C. § 2000e–16, express provision was made for the awarding of attorneys' fees, *id.* § 2000e–16(d). By contrast, when Congress amended the ADEA to include federal employees, section 15 contained no attorneys' fees provision even though section 15 was patterned in part on key provisions of the federal employees' section of Title VII.

π's Arg.

Despite the absence of a statutory provision expressly authorizing an award of fees, Palmer contends that congressional intent to allow such fees may be gleaned from the broad "will effectuate the purposes" language of section 15, 29 U.S.C. § 633a(c), coupled with the remedial policies underlying the ADEA as a whole. Because we conclude that Palmer's position is inconsistent with controlling Supreme Court precedent, we reject it.

In *Alyeska,* the Supreme Court emphasized that courts are not authorized to ignore the American Rule and award fees simply because they believe "the public policy furthered by a particular statute important enough to warrant the award." *Alyeska,* 421 U.S. at 263. Rather, it is for Congress, by "specific and explicit" statutory provisions, *id.* at 260, to determine "the circumstances under which attorneys' fees are to be awarded and the range of discretion [to be exercised by] the courts in making those awards," *id.* at 262. Thus, absent such authorization, this court has no authority to award fees, and each party will be required to pay its own attorneys' fees.

Very simply, section 15 contains no provision specifically providing for an award of fees. Further, even assuming an express attorneys' fees provision is not absolutely required under *Alyeska,* the legislative history accompanying section 15 is equally devoid of the kind of unequivocally expressed intent necessary to authorize an award of fees against the government. While Palmer would have this court construe the broad language of section 15 to authorize an award of fees in this case, to reach such a result would require this court to ignore the mandate of *Alyeska* and to imply a remedy not expressly provided for by Congress. This we have no authority to do.

We conclude that this court is not authorized by the ADEA to award fees to someone in Palmer's position. While Palmer advances many policy considerations that arguably would justify such an award, these arguments are more properly addressed to Congress rather than this court. Our obligation is clear, and we have no choice but to deny Palmer's request for fees.

The decision of the district court dismissing Palmer's complaint is affirmed.

■ HEANEY, CIRCUIT JUDGE, dissenting.

I respectfully dissent. In my view, the majority opinion ignores the intent of Congress to give individuals who have been discriminated against because of their age the same remedies that they would have had if they had been victims of race or sex discrimination. It will also discourage settlement of cases at the administrative level and will lead to an increased filing of ADEA cases in the federal courts.

Although the ADEA does not expressly state that an agency may award attorneys' fees, it does state that "the Equal Employment Opportunity Commission is authorized to enforce the [federal employee section of the Act] through appropriate remedies ... as will effectuate the policies of this section." 29 U.S.C. § 633a(b). * * *

Further, the ADEA is intended to give administrative agencies limited opportunities to resolve problems of employment discrimination and thereby to make resort to federal relief by victims of the discrimination unnecessary. Denying recovery of fees would encourage complainants to wait out the thirty-day deferral period and focus only on obtaining judicial relief. Only the authorization of fee awards ensures incorporation of administrative procedures as a meaningful part of the ADEA enforcement scheme.

Finally, if the logic of the majority opinion is to be accepted, then there would be no basis for allowing attorneys' fees to federal employees who are victims of age discrimination who establish the validity of their claim in a judicial proceeding. Yet, the government cites no case in which such attorneys' fees have been disallowed. At least three district courts have specifically authorized attorneys' fees in this context. And these Courts have done so without relying on specific statutory language. The fact is that there is no specific provision in the ADEA which authorizes the payment of attorneys' fees in a judicial proceeding. The right to such a fee is inferred from 29 U.S.C. § 633a(c): "Any person aggrieved may bring a civil action in any Federal district court of competent jurisdiction for such legal or equitable relief as will effectuate the purposes of this chapter." The majority fails to explain how we can infer the right to attorneys' fees in a judicial proceeding and not infer it in an administrative proceeding from section 633a(b). A conclusion that the purpose of the ADEA is to make plaintiffs who participate in a judicial proceeding whole but those who participate in an administrative proceeding something less than whole is anomalous and is not supported by the language, history or structure of the act, or by logic.

Notes and Questions

1. During the past thirty-five years, there has been a huge proliferation of statutes providing for shifting attorney's fees from losing parties to winning parties and an attendant explosion in attorney's fee litigation. The essential treatise on this subject remains the three-volume set of Mary Frances Derfner & Arthur D. Wolf, *Court Awarded Attorney Fees* (2004). However, while new provisions for awards of attorney's fees in litigation have emerged with regularity, the traditional and general rule—called the "American Rule"—remains that each party bears its own legal expenses. Moreover, in the context of awards of fees against the federal government, the doctrine of sovereign immunity remains always in the background.

As we begin to survey the law of attorney's fee-shifting in general and awards of fees against the federal government in particular, you should ask a series of questions in each case:

1. *Exception to the American Rule:* Is there an exception to the American Rule, that is, is there a statutory or recognized common law basis for the award of attorney's fees against an opposing party?

2. *Waiver of Sovereign Immunity:* Is there a statutory waiver of sovereign immunity making an exception to the American Rule specifically applicable against the federal government?

3. *Eligibility :* What are the standards for determining whether a party is eligible for a fee award under that particular statute? Must a party have merely prevailed in the lawsuit? What degree of success is necessary to qualify as a prevailing or a substantially prevailing party? Is eligibility for fees limited to certain types of parties?

4. *Entitlement:* Assuming the fee claimant is *eligible* for a fee, is he or she also *entitled* to a fee? Are there additional requirements for entitlement beyond eligibility under the particular statute? If so, what are the standards for entitlement? Must the fee petitioner establish that the government acted unreasonably? Must the court consider additional factors, such as the benefit to the public interest derived from the case or the commercial benefit to the plaintiff?

5. *Measuring Fees:* What is the measure of an award of fees? How does the court determine the basic fee? May or must that basic fee be adjusted to reflect degree of success on the merits, the quality of the work, the contingent nature of the case, etc.? Does an attorney's specialization in a legal practice factor into the calculation? Does a different calculus apply when the federal government is the target of the fee application?

See generally Gregory C. Sisk, *A Primer on Awards of Attorney's Fees Against the Federal Government,* 25 Ariz. St. L.J. 733, 738–69 (1993). These issues will be addressed in the context of several specific fee-shifting statutes in this chapter.

2. In *Palmer v. General Services Administration,* what obstacles must the fee petitioner overcome to even assert a claim for attorney's fees against the federal government? What does the court find missing and thus fatal to the claim for a fee award? How could the missing element be supplied? The dissenting judge points out that some courts had assumed or implied the availability of fee awards against the federal government in Age Discrimination in Employment Act (ADEA) cases that reach the courts on the merits. This judge then complains that the majority's analysis denying a fee award in ADEA administrative disputes would logically extend to judicial proceedings. But isn't that right? Should the availability of fees be implied for ADEA cases brought in court, if not for cases at the administrative level? Why would the analysis differ?

Subsequent to *Palmer,* the United States Courts of Appeals for the First and Fifth Circuits also have held, applying the American Rule and strict construction of a waiver of sovereign immunity, that Section 633a of the Age Discrimination in Employment Act (ADEA) does not authorize an attorney's fee award against the federal government. *Boehms v. Crowell,* 139 F.3d 452, 462–63 (5th Cir. 1998); *Nowd v. Rubin,* 76 F.3d 25, 27 (1st Cir. 1996) However, while agreeing with the Eighth Circuit in *Palmer* that the ADEA itself does not authorize a fee award against the United States, the First and Fifth Circuits noted that an alternative fee-shifting provision is available. The Equal Access to Justice Act (EAJA) does create an entitlement to a fee award in favor of prevailing ADEA claimants and against the federal government. (The fee claimant in *Palmer* apparently did not make an argument based on the EAJA.) Under Subsection (b) of the EAJA, 28 U.S.C. § 2412(b), the United States is liable for attorney's fees "to the same extent that any other party would be liable under * * * the terms of any statute which specifically provides for such an award." Thus, the First and Fifth Circuits concluded, because the ADEA allows fee awards against private defendants, the EAJA empowers the courts to award fees against the federal government on the same basis. *Boehms,* 139 F.3d at 463; *Nowd,* 76 F.3d at 27–28. In sum, it is well-established today that a successful age discrimination plaintiff indeed may recover attorney's fees against the federal government, even though not directly through the ADEA. *See also Villescas v. Richardson,* 145 F.Supp.2d 1228, 1230–31 (D. Colo. 2001) (holding that the EAJA "serve[s] as an explicit waiver of the United State[s's] sovereign immunity as to the ADEA attorney fee provision"); *Craig v. O'Leary,* 870 F.Supp. 1007, 1009 (D. Colo. 1994) (holding that either the ADEA itself authorizes an attorney's fee award against the United States or that the ADEA provision is incorporated against the United States through the EAJA). The EAJA as a special fee-shifting statute in federal government cases is discussed in Chapter VII.B.5.

---

2.   TITLE VII OF THE CIVIL RIGHTS ACT OF 1964

42 United States Code § 2000e–5(k)

In any action or proceeding under this subchapter the court, in its discretion, may allow the prevailing party, other than the Commission or the United States, a reasonable attorney's fee (including expert fees) as part of the costs, and the Commission and the United States shall be liable for costs the same as a private person.

Copeland v. Marshall

United States Court of Appeals for the District of Columbia Circuit.
641 F.2d 880 (D.C.Cir. 1980) (en banc).

ON REHEARING EN BANC

■ McGOWAN, CIRCUIT JUDGE:

The court *en banc* has before it for review an order of the District Court awarding an attorney's fee of $160,000 for the successful prosecution of a gender-discrimination class suit against the United States Department of Labor.[1] A panel of this court earlier reversed the District Court's award and remanded for reconsideration under the novel standards described in its opinion (*Copeland I*).[2] The panel denied rehearing, but issued a second opinion (*Copeland II*) clarifying the first. We granted rehearing *en banc*.

At issue in this appeal are (1) the standards to be applied in awarding attorney's fees in Title VII suits against the government, and (2) the reasonableness of the District Court's fee award in this case. For the reasons set forth below, we affirm the District Court's award.

I

We cannot determine whether the District Court's fee award was reasonable without examining in some detail the history of this employment discrimination litigation. This chronicle is necessarily lengthy because the lawsuit involved numerous and complex proceedings and maneuverings. We think the very intricacy of the litigation—which was a product, in part, of the government's vigorous and long-continued resistance to the claim asserted against it—is highly relevant to the reasonableness of the fee award.

A.   *Copeland's Administrative Complaint*

Appellee Dolores Copeland, a black woman trained in data processing, joined the Department of Labor (the Department) in 1967. She worked for several years in the Department's Directorate of Data Automation and its predecessor unit (the Directorate) as a GS–13 computer specialist. Copeland thought that her supervisors were unfairly denying her training, promotions, and interesting work. Moreover, she believed that other female Directorate employees were treated similarly.

Pursuant to regulations, Copeland explained her suspicions to a Department Equal Employment Opportunity (EEO) counselor in April, 1973, but no action was taken. She therefore formally complained of discrimination in June. * * *

Assistant Secretary Fred G. Clark submitted his proposed disposition of the complaint in June, 1974. That disposition would have removed all adverse references from her personnel file, but it proposed no other significant relief.

Copeland, still dissatisfied, requested a formal hearing. Her file was sent to the Civil Service Commission for that purpose, but no hearing was

---

1. The representation of plaintiff Copeland was undertaken *pro bono publico* by the Washington, D.C., law firm of Wilmer, Cutler & Pickering (now Wilmer & Pickering). In prior cases in which this firm sought and obtained a fee as the prevailing party in a pro bono case such as this, the firm has contributed the fee to a public interest organization "committed to furthering the kind of public interest involved in the particular litigation."

2. *Copeland v. Marshall,* 594 F.2d 244 (1978).

held. The file was returned to the Labor Department without explanation.
* * *

* * * [T]he Department issued its final decision on November 7, 1974. The final decision conceded "that a pattern of sex discrimination exists" in the Directorate, and that such discrimination "manifests itself in the lack of leadership responsibility assignments given to qualified women professionals." The decision, however, denied that the Department's refusal to promote Copeland resulted from sex discrimination and asserted that Copeland's personal disagreements with her supervisors were the true cause of her grievances.

The Department in its decision agreed, *inter alia,* to (1) consider her fairly for future work assignments; (2) clarify her responsibilities and objectively assess her performance of them, (3) expunge adverse evaluations from her personnel file, and (4) monitor future promotion decisions to insure fair treatment for her and other minority employees and women. The Department did not, however, offer retroactive promotion and back pay, or priority consideration for future promotions.

The Department sent Copeland a copy of its decision. However, Copeland's attorneys were not served with a copy, in violation of Department regulations.

B. *Litigation in the District Court*

Copeland filed this class suit in the District Court on December 13, 1974. The complaint, as amended, alleged three gender discrimination counts, namely, violations of (1) Title VII of the Civil Rights Act of 1964, (2) Executive Order 11478, and (3) rights under the first and fifth amendments to the constitution and 42 U.S.C. section 1985. The complaint also alleged a count of race discrimination under the first and fifth amendments and 42 U.S.C. sections 1981 and 1985.

1. *The Government's Motion for Judgment on the Pleadings*

The government promptly moved for judgment on the pleadings under a variety of theories. Judgment on the Title VII count was sought because the suit was filed 31 days after Copeland received notice of the final agency decision, not within the 30–day period established by statute. See 42 U.S.C. § 2000e–16(c) (1976). The District Court held, however, that the government's failure to serve Copeland's attorneys with the agency decision tolled the running of the 30–day period.

2. *The Government's Opposition to Class Certification*

Copeland next moved that she represent a class of all past, present, and future female data processing employees in the Directorate. The government, however, moved to remand the case to the Civil Service Commission for additional hearings and, in the alternative, opposed class certification for a variety of reasons.

The District Court denied the motion to remand. The court also certified the case as a class suit, covering all females employed by the Directorate in data processing positions after June 11, 1971.

3. *Discovery Skirmishes*

Copeland's attorneys meanwhile had propounded a congeries of discovery requests, including interrogatories and requests for production of documents. These discovery requests prompted an acrimonious flurry between the plaintiff class (plaintiff) and the defendant.

The government initially did not comply with these requests. Plaintiff moved to compel discovery. The government then answered some of the interrogatories, but objected to certain others that it thought called for privileged information. The government, accordingly, opposed the motion to compel.

Plaintiff pointed out to the court that the Department had destroyed certain relevant documents and that, in any event, the government's responses to many interrogatories were inadequate. The question of the adequacy of the government's response to discovery requests generally was ultimately resolved by negotiation.

Meanwhile, the government had initiated discovery of its own. The government propounded interrogatories, requested documents, and took depositions. Plaintiff continued the discovery battle by noticing the deposition of an Assistant Secretary of Labor. The government moved for a protective order; this motion was denied.

Discovery continued for several additional weeks. Plaintiff answered defendant's numerous interrogatories, served additional interrogatories of its own, and noticed further depositions. The government again sought a protective order; the District Court ordered the government to supply any requested documents and information that were relevant and nonprivileged. * * *

Plaintiff orally complained to the court on January 26 about additional discovery difficulties. Plaintiff alleged that the government failed to identify and produce certain highly relevant documents, and requested that the court grant judgment on the merits as the sanction for nondisclosure.

The District Court noted:

> Plaintiff has ample ground to complain. Her systematic discovery efforts initiated months ago have been impeded unnecessarily and she has been forced to expend time and effort to fill in gaps in the proof which the documents would have largely avoided had they been produced as they should have been.

The court nevertheless denied the motion for sanctions, without prejudice, "as representing too extreme a sanction on the basis of facts presently available." The parties at this point continued to plan for a February 16 trial.

4. *The Government's Concession of Liability*

Instead of going to trial, however, the parties settled the liability issue. Now three years after Copeland first complained of discrimination, the government finally conceded that the Directorate had

> subjected [Copeland] and the other members of the class to sex-based discrimination in assignments, training, performance evaluations, promotions and working conditions, all in violation of Title VII. . . .

The government also agreed to develop and put into effect a court-approved affirmative action program.

The stipulation provided for a trial on relief to each of the individual plaintiffs. In those trials, the government would carry the burden of proving that the conceded sex discrimination had not "monetarily or otherwise" affected the particular plaintiff.

5. *Trial on Copeland's Claim for Retroactive Promotion and Back Pay*

Shortly after the government stipulated it had discriminated on the basis of sex, a six-day trial ensued on the relief vel non due plaintiff Copeland. The government contended that Copeland in any event would not have been promoted to GS–14, because Copeland's failure to receive promotions and training was attributable to her poor work, lack of qualifications, and personality problems.

The District Court found, however, that the government had failed to prove that sex discrimination did not play a part in Copeland's lack of advancement. The court, accordingly, awarded her a promotion to GS–14 and $6,169.80 in back pay. The court also ordered the Department to provide Copeland with training and assignments commensurate with her position.

6. *Litigation Before a Special Master on Retroactive Promotion and Back Pay for Other Class Members*

The parties stipulated to the appointment of a Special Master to receive evidence and report to the District Court on the relief due the other members of the class. * * *

After * * * substantial additional discovery, the parties settled the remaining individual claims. The settlements generally required promotions, back pay, the opportunity to participate in a training program, or some combination of the above. Approximately $33,000 in back pay was obtained.

7. *The Affirmative Action Program*

Meanwhile, the parties haggled over the terms of the affirmative action program. The government proposed a plan; plaintiff criticized it as inadequate. The District Court held a hearing to discuss problems with the government's plan.

Plaintiff later proposed its own affirmative action program. The government criticized it, and the District Court held another hearing. The following day, the District Court ordered the parties to negotiate a mutually satisfactory plan, using defendant's draft as the starting point, but incorporating various modifications sought by plaintiff. On August 1, 1976, the District Court approved a 36–page affirmative action plan negotiated by the parties.

8. *Plaintiff's Application for an Attorney's Fee*

On November 30, plaintiff filed a documented request for costs and an attorney's fee. The documentation revealed that plaintiff's attorneys had spent 3,602 hours on the case and that, if that time were billed at the law firm's customary hourly rates, the legal fee would be about $206,000. In papers filed December 20, 1976, the government opposed "an[y] award even approaching" $206,000. Apparently content to submit the attorney's fee issue to the judge on the papers, the government did not ask the District Court to hold a hearing.

On January 6, 1977, the District Court entered an order awarding a $160,000 fee, an amount approximately 22% less than that envisioned by plaintiff's papers. The order was accompanied by a four-page memorandum analyzing the fee request. The District Court wrote, in pertinent part:

> The Secretary apparently believes a fee award in a case of this type should be based primarily upon the monetary results achieved. This is an erroneous approach to the fee problem. While the actual cash awards to individual members of the class were in this instance relatively small in relation to the total fee claim, this was basically an equity action which was intended to and did achieve benefits that cannot be measured solely in monetary terms. The judgment, which has not been appealed, among other things established an entirely new pattern of training and promotion for female employees in an important segment of the Department of Labor which had blatantly discriminated against women. The benefits of the litigation will be felt for many years to come.

> * * *

> While the Secretary now suggests that there were really no serious issues at stake, this is not borne out by the facts. The litigation went forward in a relatively civilized manner but it was hard fought. The Government offered firm, persistent resistance throughout the litigation and concessions developed only as it became apparent there was little prospect of Government success. Indeed, the Government moved to dismiss at the outset, and it opposed discovery. There were many difficulties encountered during the discovery process which were caused, in part, by the Department's inadvertent destruction of certain records contrary to Court direction and the intentional withholding of other documents by some officials of the Department of Labor, as well as by the complexity of the issues.

The 3,602 hours were logged almost entirely by associates of the firm with varying degrees of experience. The average rate of $57.17 an hour is well within the local range for associates of larger firms.... What plaintiffs' counsel lacked in seasoned trial experience was offset by other factors. They were always well prepared, effective and knowledgeable. No time was deliberately wasted and counsel proceeded with full recognition of the congressional directive to expedite litigation of this type.

Billing for legal services, however, should not be a merely mechanical exercise. Where a fee is sought from the United States, which has infinite ability to pay, the Court must scrutinize the claim with particular care. When an application such as this is filed by a large law firm computing a proposed award by use of "customary rates," the firm has obviously made little, if any, effort to exercise billing judgment. Thus an important ingredient is lacking. A reasonable fee can only be fixed by the exercise of judgment, using the mechanical computations simply as a starting point to reach a higher or lower figure. The Court must perform this function.

In considering what is a reasonable fee in this instance a number of factors deserve special mention. The proposed fee absorbs not only expensive overhead such as rent and secretarial services, but no charge has been made for what was undoubtedly a substantial amount of time spent by paralegals who play such a useful role in large documentary cases. On the other hand, there was practically no partner time expended on this case and the associates lacked experienced trial direction. The Court must also take into account the fact that not all of the work proved productive. Some issues which were joined in the complaint were dropped, as were some individual defendants. * * * [T]he Court has concluded that a reasonable fee in this litigation, weighing the results achieved, the novelty of the issues, the difficulties encountered and the effectiveness of the excellent representation given is $160,000.

II

Title VII of the Civil Rights Act of 1964 allows the prevailing party to receive from the loser a reasonable attorney's fee in addition to other relief. The statute provides:

In any action or proceeding under ... [Title VII] the court, in its discretion, may allow the prevailing party, other than the [Equal Employment Opportunity] Commission or the United States, a reasonable attorney's fee as part of the costs, and the Commission and the United States shall be liable for costs the same as a private person.

42 U.S.C. § 2000e–5(k) (1976).

The availability of an attorney's fee encourages individuals injured by discrimination to seek judicial redress. As the Supreme Court explained:

When the Civil Rights Act of 1964 was passed, it was evident that enforcement would prove difficult and that the Nation would have to rely in part upon private litigation as a means of securing broad compliance with the law. A Title II suit is thus private in form only.... If [a plaintiff] obtains an injunction, he does so not for himself alone but also as a "private attorney general," vindicating a policy that Congress considered of the highest priority. If successful plaintiffs were routinely forced to bear their own attorneys' fees, few aggrieved parties would be in a position to advance the public interest by invoking the injunctive powers of the federal courts. Congress therefore enacted the provision for counsel fees not simply to penalize litigants who advance arguments they know to be untenable but, more broadly, to encourage individuals injured by racial discrimination to seek judicial relief....

Newman v. Piggie Park Enterprises, Inc., 390 U.S. 400, 401–02 (1968).

Confronted by the explicit language of the statute and its accompanying legislative history, the government in the instant case concedes that plaintiff is entitled to an attorney's fee. Indeed, the parties so stipulated during the course of the lawsuit. At issue in this appeal is whether the District Court's fee award was reasonable.

The Court of Appeals for the Fifth Circuit explained, in general terms, how the fee should be calculated under Title VII in *Johnson v. Georgia Highway Express, Inc.,* 488 F.2d 714 (1974). In *Johnson,* the court suggested that district courts base fee awards on the following criteria: (1) the time and labor required; (2) the novelty and difficulty of the questions; (3) the skill requisite to perform the legal services properly; (4) the preclusion of other employment; (5) the customary fee in the community for similar work; (6) the fixed or contingent nature of the fee; (7) time limitations imposed by the client or the circumstances; (8) the amount involved and the results obtained; (9) the experience, reputation, and ability of the attorneys; (10) the undesirability of the case; (11) the nature and length of the professional relationship with the client; and (12) awards in similar cases. *Id.* at 717–19. * * *

Simply to articulate those twelve factors, however, does not itself conjure up a reasonable dollar figure in the mind of a district court judge. A formula is necessary to translate the relevant factors into terms of dollars and cents. This is particularly true because the twelve factors overlap considerably. For example, largely subsumed under the factor "time and labor required" is an assessment of the "difficulty of the questions." That is so because the more difficult the problem, the longer it will take adequately to solve it. Similarly, the customary hourly fee (*Johnson* factor #5) is likely to be influenced by (#3) the level of skill necessary to perform the services, (#6) whether the fee is fixed or contingent, (#7) time limitations, (#8) the amount to be obtained, (#9) the reputation of the attorneys, and (#10) the undesirability of the case.

For these reasons, scholars have noted that the twelve *Johnson* factors, without more, cannot guarantee a rational setting of fees. One commented:

The fundamental problem with an approach that does no more than assure that the lower courts will consider a plethora of conflicting and at least partially redundant factors is that it provides no analytical framework for their application. It offers no guidance on the relative importance of each factor, whether they are to be applied differently in different contexts, or, indeed, how they are to be applied at all.

Berger, *Court Awarded Attorneys' Fees: What is "Reasonable"?,* 126 U.Pa. L.Rev. 281, 286–87 (1977) (footnotes omitted).

District court judges for this reason have had difficulty applying the *Johnson* factors. A common, yet understandable, fault is for the trial judge to make the conclusory statement, "After considering each of the twelve factors in *Johnson,* I find that a reasonable fee is X dollars." This very often leads to reversal and remand.

Appellate courts have recognized that the *Johnson* factors, despite their substantial conceptual value, also are imprecise. Some courts, therefore, have incorporated the twelve factors into an analytical framework that can be easily applied by trial courts and that will make possible meaningful appellate review.

Any fee-setting formula must produce an award sufficient to fulfill the primary purpose of awarding fees in Title VII cases, namely, "to encourage individuals injured by . . . discrimination to seek judicial relief." *Piggie Park*, 390 U.S. at 402. An award of fees provides an incentive to competent lawyers to undertake Title VII work only if the award adequately compensates attorneys for the amount of work performed. The Court of Appeals for the Third Circuit was the first to develop a fee-setting formula that reflects this principle. In *Lindy Bros. Builders, Inc. v. American Radiator & Standard Sanitary Corp.,* 487 F.2d 161 (1973) (*Lindy I*), and its successor case, *Lindy II,* 540 F.2d 102 (1976) (*en banc*), the Third Circuit articulated a formula that considered all the relevant factors but eliminated the redundancy and imprecision that many have identified in other fee-setting schemes.

Lindy recognized that the starting point in fee setting—what it characterized as the "lodestar" fee—should be computed by multiplying a reasonable hourly rate by the number of hours reasonably expended on the lawsuit. 487 F.2d at 167. Adjustments in this figure are appropriate, the court recognized, but the "lodestar" provides "the only reasonably objective" starting point for awarding a fee. *Id.* * * *

Myriad cases involving court-awarded fees continue to come before the district court judges and, ultimately, before this court. We therefore take this opportunity *en banc* to elaborate, to a greater extent than we have in the past, on the appropriate mechanism for calculating an attorney's fee pursuant to statutes like Title VII.

A. *The "Lodestar"*

Any fee-setting inquiry begins with the "lodestar": the number of hours reasonably expended multiplied by a reasonable hourly rate. The figure generated by that computation is the basic fee from which a trial court judge should work. We examine below some of the problems that arise in calculating the "lodestar."

1.   *Hours Reasonably Expended*

The fundamental purpose of the fee award is to compensate the attorney for his efforts. The first task for the trial court judge, therefore, is determining the amount of time reasonably expended.

When a law firm seeks a fee, it should document the amount of work performed. The District Court then will be able to do more than merely lump together all the hours spent by the various attorneys associated with the enterprise; the judge instead can segregate into categories the kinds of work performed by each participating attorney. This project need not be unduly burdensome:

> It is not necessary to know the exact number of minutes spent nor the precise activity to which each hour was devoted nor the specific attainments of each attorney. But without some fairly definite information as to the hours devoted to various general activities, *e. g.,* pretrial discovery, settlement negotiations, and the hours spent by various classes of attorneys, *e. g.,* senior partners, junior partners, associates, the court cannot know the nature of the services for which compensation is sought.

Lindy I, 487 F.2d at 167.

Compiling raw totals of hours spent, however, does not complete the inquiry. It does not follow that the amount of time actually expended is the amount of time reasonably expended. In the private sector, "billing judgment" is an important component in fee setting. It is no less important here. Hours that are not properly billed to one's client also are not properly billed to one's adversary pursuant to statutory authority. Thus, no compensation is due for nonproductive time. For example, where three attorneys are present at a hearing when one would suffice, compensation should be denied for the excess time. Similarly, no compensation should be paid for time spent litigating claims upon which the party seeking the fee did not ultimately prevail.

At this point in the computation, the District Judge might usefully construct a table that looks something like this example.

Attorney & Type of Work	Hours
Senior Partner: Court appearances	17.3
Senior Partner: Review of pleadings	39.2
Junior Associate: Research & drafting	87.6
Junior Associate: Depositions	35.5

2.   *A Reasonable Hourly Rate*

The remaining element in fixing a "lodestar" fee is the reasonable hourly rate.

The reasonable hourly rate is that prevailing in the community for similar work. As we noted a reasonable hourly rate is the product of a

multiplicity of factors[:] * * * [T]he level of skill necessary, time limitations, the amount to be obtained in the litigation, the attorney's reputation,
and the undesirability of the case. It follows that there may be more than
one reasonable hourly rate for each of the attorneys, and for each of the
kinds of work, involved in the litigation. After receiving documentation and
other submissions, and perhaps holding a hearing, the trial judge might
complete the fee table in the following manner.

Attorney & Type of Work	Hours	Rate	Total
Senior Partner: Court appearances	17.3	$95	$1,643.50
Senior Partner: Review of pleadings	39.2	$85	$3,332.00
Junior Associate: Research & drafting	87.6	$40	$3,504.00
Junior Associate: Depositions	35.5	$40	$1,420.00
			$9,899.50

Thus, the "lodestar" fee in this hypothetical is $9,899.50.

B. *Adjustments to the "Lodestar"*

The "lodestar" fee may be adjusted to reflect other factors. We discuss
herein those applicable in Title VII and similar fee-setting cases. The
burden of justifying any deviation from the "lodestar" rests on the party
proposing the deviation.

1. *The Contingent Nature of Success*

Under statutes like Title VII, only the prevailing party is eligible for a
court-awarded fee. An attorney contemplating representation of a Title VII
plaintiff must recognize that no fee will be forthcoming unless the litigation
is successful. An adjustment in the lodestar, therefore, may be appropriate
to compensate for the risk that the lawsuit would be unsuccessful and that
no fee at all would be obtained.

It is important to recognize that the contingency adjustment is designed solely to compensate for the possibility at the outset that the
litigation would be unsuccessful and that no fee would be obtained. Contingency adjustments of this sort are entirely unrelated to the "contingent
fee" arrangements that are typical in plaintiffs' tort representation. In tort
suits, an attorney might receive one-third of whatever amount the plaintiff
recovers. In those cases, therefore, the fee is directly proportional to the
recovery. Such is not the case in contingency adjustments of the kind we
describe herein. The contingency adjustment is a percentage increase in the
"lodestar" to reflect the risk that no fee will be obtained. The contingency
adjustment is not a percentage increase based on the amount of recovery.
* * *

The delay in receipt of payment for services rendered is an additional
factor that may be incorporated into a contingency adjustment. The hourly
rates used in the "lodestar" represent the prevailing rate for clients who

typically pay their bills promptly. Court-awarded fees normally are received long after the legal services are rendered. That delay can present cash-flow problems for the attorneys. In any event, payment today for services rendered long in the past deprives the eventual recipient of the value of the use of the money in the meantime, which use, particularly in an inflationary era, is valuable. A percentage adjustment to reflect the delay in receipt of payment therefore may be appropriate.

To the district court judge falls the task of calculating as closely as possible a contingency adjustment with which fairly to compensate the successful attorney. We have not, however, lost sight of the fact that this adjustment is inherently imprecise and that certain estimations must be made. For example, it is difficult in hindsight to determine the risk of failure at the commencement of a lawsuit that ultimately proved to be successful. Thus, we ask only that the district court judges exercise their discretion as conscientiously as possible, and state their reasons as clearly as possible.

2.   *Quality of Representation*

Next, the "lodestar" may be adjusted up or down to reflect "the quality of representation." It is important to make clear precisely the analysis that must accompany such an adjustment. A quality adjustment is appropriate only when the representation is unusually good or bad, *taking into account the level of skill normally expected* of an attorney commanding the hourly rate used to compute the "lodestar." In other words,

> the court must recognize that a consideration of "quality" inheres in the "lodestar" award: counsel who possess or who are reputed to possess more experience, knowledge and legal talent generally command hourly rates superior to those who are less endowed. Thus, the quality of an attorney's work *in general* is a component of the reasonabl[e] hourly rate; this aspect of "quality" is reflected in the "lodestar" and should not be utilized to augment or diminish the basic award under the rubric of "the quality of an attorney's work."

> *Lindy I,* then permits an adjustment to the "lodestar"—up or down-based on the all-around performance of counsel in the specific case: "Any increase or decrease in fees to adjust for the quality of work is designed to take account of an unusual degree of skill, be it unusually poor or unusually good." 487 F.2d at 168. By this is meant simply that the district court may determine that the lawyer discharged the professional burden undertaken with a degree of skill above or below that expected for lawyers of the caliber reflected in the hourly rates.

Lindy II, 540 F.2d at 117–18 (emphasis in original).

Until now the calculations have entirely ignored the results of the litigation. Success was a threshold inquiry relevant to the entitlement *vel non* to a fee, but the amount or nature of recovery was not considered in setting the "lodestar." These latter factors should be considered now, under the rubric of "quality of representation."

Where exceptional results are obtained—taking into account the hourly rate commanded and number of hours expended—an increase in fee is justifiable. However, it is important again to emphasize that a huge dollar recovery does not itself justify a huge fee award. The "lodestar" itself generally compensates lawyers adequately for their time. An upward adjustment for quality is appropriate only when the attorney performed exceptionally well, or obtained an exceptional result for the client. For example, if a substantial monetary judgment was to be *expected,* that expectation normally is reflected in the hourly rate used to compute the "lodestar," and no further adjustment would be necessary.

Quality adjustments may be upward or downward. Thus, if a high-priced attorney performs in a competent but undistinguished manner, a decrease in the "lodestar" may be necessary under the "quality of representation" rubric because the hourly rate used to calculate the "lodestar" proved to be overly generous.

III

Copeland I and *Copeland II,* however, took an entirely different view from that expressed in this opinion. The fee approach we have described roots on compensating attorneys for the market value of services rendered. The panel had the notion that, at least where the government is the losing defendant, the fee should be the amount representing the "actual cost to the law firm plus a reasonable and controllable profit" for the legal work done. *Copeland II,* slip op. at 5 (emphasis deleted).

We think, however, that the approach articulated earlier in this opinion represents the proper formula for the setting of fees regardless of the defendant's identity. We explain below why we think that fees should be calculated no differently when the government (rather than a private party) is the losing defendant. We then explain the difficulties we have, in any event, with the panel's "cost-plus" approach.

A.   *Fee Awards Against the Government*

The panel opinions suggested that, where the government is the losing defendant, a fee award should be subject to greater scrutiny—*i. e.,* the fee should be lower—than one against a private defendant. We agree that a judge setting any award should scrutinize the amount with care. But we do not think that the amount of the fee should depend on the identity of the losing party. Our conclusion is based on both the language of the statute and the policies that underlie it.

Our starting point, of course, is the statutory text. The attorney's fee section provides that, in any Title VII action,

> the court, in its discretion, may allow the prevailing party . . . a reasonable attorney's fee as part of the costs, *and the . . . United States shall be liable for costs the same as a private person.*

42 U.S.C. § 2000e–5(k) (1976) (emphasis added).

The language of the statute indicates that the calculation of the fee should not vary with the identity of the losing defendant, and the policies underlying the attorney's fee provision are fully consistent with this plain language. Those policies, as we have seen, are two. The primary purpose is to help persons obtain competent counsel with which to vindicate civil rights through litigation. Nothing in the statute suggests that the incentive to ferret out discrimination, provided by the prospect of an attorney's fee, should be any less when the government is the defendant. * * *

A second policy also underlies fee awards. As we have noted, the prospect of liability for an attorney's fee may help deter discrimination and thereby obviate litigation. We do not think that the incentive for the government to refrain from discrimination should be any less than for private employers. * * *

In sum, we agree with the panel opinions that the government has a "deep pocket" and that any fee request should be examined with care. But we think, for the reasons stated above, that fees should be neither lower, nor calculated differently, when the losing defendant is the government.

B.   *Difficulties with the "Cost–Plus" Approach*

The panel opinions in any event suggested that the "cost-plus" method of calculating fees might usefully be applied in all cases, regardless of the identity of the defendant. *See Copeland II,* slip op. at 18–19. The panel opinions, in brief, thought that a fee should be based on "the sums paid out to [the] attorneys as personal income and to defray overhead costs attributable to the maintenance of the attorneys in the firm," plus a "reasonable and controllable margin for profit." *Copeland I,* 594 F.2d at 251.

We think, however, that the standards we discussed earlier in this opinion are those that should govern all fee-setting cases under the statute. The "lodestar," or "market value," method of fee setting has the virtue of being relatively easy to administer. We do not want

> a district court, in setting an attorneys' fee, [to] become enmeshed in a meticulous analysis of every detailed facet of the professional representation. It ... is not our intention that the inquiry into the adequacy of the fee assume massive proportions, perhaps even dwarfing the case in chief.

Lindy II, 540 F.2d at 116. We fear that the proposed "cost-plus" method of calculating fees would indeed become the inquiry of "massive proportions" that we strive to avoid. * * *

In sum, the "cost-plus" system poses considerable administrative difficulties. But our rejection of its thesis does not depend on administrative inconvenience alone. We think the theoretical basis of "cost-plus" is fundamentally inconsistent with Congress' purpose in providing for statutory fee-shifting. A fee should be based on the market value of services rendered, not on some notion of "cost" incurred by the law firm. That is the conclusion both of the courts that have spoken on the issue, and also Congress itself. * * *

More fundamentally, nothing in the panel opinions explains why, in the typical case, rates established by the pressures of the market mechanism will differ from those resulting under "cost-plus." If "cost-plus" is simply another method of reaching the same result as under "market value" calculations, the added administrative burden seems not worth the candle. On the other hand, if "cost-plus" somehow produces different results from those obtaining under "market value" calculations, "cost-plus" is inconsistent with the wishes of Congress and the overwhelming view of courts that have considered the matter.

The one circumstance in which "cost-plus" almost certainly will yield a different fee from that under "market value" is where the successful plaintiff was represented by a "public interest" law firm. Such groups often represent their clients for low fees, or for no fee at all. Consequently, the individual attorneys at those organizations typically are compensated at rates far below those prevailing in the marketplace. "Cost-plus" calculations, focusing as they do on lawyers' salaries rather than on the value of services rendered, in this instance will yield lower fee awards than those under a "market value" system.

Copeland II argued that this result was entirely reasonable. The opinion pointed out that a fee-setting mechanism that awarded a firm its costs, plus a reasonable profit, could not be condemned as penurious because any such amount, almost by definition, provided the attorneys the same compensation that they normally received. We think, nevertheless, that the proper focus is the market value of services rendered, regardless of the notion of "costs" that the panel seemed to think so important. * * *

* * * First, Congress has indicated that public interest lawyers in these sorts of cases should be compensated by using a market value approach. The Senate Judiciary Committee, in its report endorsing the 1976 fees act, draws no distinction in awarding fees between public interest law firms and private attorneys. S.Rep. No. 1011, 94th Cong., 2d Sess. 6 (1976). * * *

Second, the purpose of the legislative scheme of the Civil Rights Act of 1964 will be served by computing fees based on a "market value" approach. The purpose of Title VII's fee award provision, as we have seen, is to encourage the private enforcement of the civil rights laws. While some lawyers would assist in the private enforcement of Title VII for a reduced fee, Congress has recognized that payment of full fees will provide greater enforcement incentives. Full fee awards to public interest law firms help finance their work, both in the instant case, and in others. Indeed, fee awards (paid by proven discriminators) may help reduce the subsidies (paid from the public fisc) that some of these organizations receive.

Third, to compute fees differently depending on the identity of the successful plaintiff's attorney might result in two kinds of windfalls to defendants. The incentive to employers not to discriminate is reduced if diminished fee awards are assessed when discrimination is established. Moreover, where a public interest law firm serves as plaintiff's counsel (a law firm that, under the panel's approach, will not obtain the full value of its services from the losing defendant) the defendant will be subject to a lesser incentive to settle a suit without litigation than would be the case if a high-priced private firm undertook plaintiff's representation. That is so because the marginal cost of each hour of continued litigation would be reduced. Defendant's counsel could inundate the plaintiff with discovery requests without fear of paying the full value of the legal resources wasted in response. We do not think that Title VII intended that defendants should have an incentive to litigate imprudently simply because of the fortuity of the identity of plaintiff's counsel.

Fourth, we note that the vast majority of courts that have considered this issue agrees with us that attorney's fees should not be based on the costs of the successful party. Instead, fees should be based on the market value of the legal services rendered. * * *

Nor is it relevant that a law firm, as in this case, originally undertook representation *pro bono publico.* We see "nothing inconsistent in prosecuting a case in the public interest, agreeing not to charge one's own client a fee and thereafter seeking fees" from the losing *defendant. Keyes v. School Dist. No. 1,* 439 F.Supp. 393, 406–07 (D.Colo.1977) (emphasis in original). Similarly, the fee calculus does not change simply because the law firm representing plaintiff in this case, may choose to donate its fee to a "public interest" law entity.

For all these reasons, we decline to adopt the panel's "cost-plus" method of calculating fees.

IV

The preceding explication of the proper criteria for awarding an attorney's fee permits us now to consider the District Court's award in this case.

A. *Scope of Review*

It is common learning that an attorney's fee award by the District Court will be upset on appeal only if it represents an abuse of discretion. We customarily defer to the District Court's judgment because an appellate court is not well situated to assess the course of litigation and the quality of counsel. The District Court judge, by contrast, closely monitors the litigation on a day-to-day basis. The Supreme Court long ago observed that a trial judge "has far better means of knowing what is just and reasonable than an appellate court can have." *Trustees v. Greenough,* 105 U.S. 527, 537 (1882). Accordingly, we think "it is better to have th[e] discretion [to award fees] exercised by the court which has been most intimately connected with case."[38]

---

38. *Cuneo v. Rumsfeld,* 553 F.2d 1360, 1368 (D.C.Cir.1977).

In this case, for example, the District Court Judge was intimately familiar with the barrage of pleadings, memoranda, and documents filed, and he observed the proficiency of counsel in court. Our inspection of the cold record cannot substitute for his first-hand scrutiny. Under these circumstances, we are most hesitant to upset the product of his judgment.[39]

B. *The District Court's Fee Award*

It is readily apparent that the District Court's fee-setting calculations do not precisely conform to the procedures identified in earlier cases and elaborated upon in this opinion. We do not believe, however, that it would be productive now to remand this case for new computations. * * *

Our own examination of the fee award in this case leads us to believe that the award is fully justifiable and that affirmance of the award, under the special circumstances of this case, therefore would not be inappropriate. Accordingly, we affirm.

1. *Calculation of the "Lodestar"*

Plaintiff's attorneys submitted the following materials documenting their fee request:

(1) a memorandum reviewing the history of the litigation;

(2) affidavits revealing that they spent 3,602 hours on the case;

(3) statistics revealing that the firm's normal hourly rates for these attorneys ranged from about $52 per hour to about $90 per hour;

(4) a letter from the Lawyers' Committee for Civil Rights Under Law stating that the typical fee charged by large Washington firms on employment discrimination cases ranged from $35 to $100 per hour; and

(5) an itemization of the back pay awards obtained by the lawsuit.

The average hourly rate, weighted for the number of hours spent by each attorney, was $57.17. A "lodestar" fee, computed by multiplying $57.17 by the 3,602 hours spent, would be $205,916.50.

The District Court properly inquired whether that hourly rate was reasonable, and whether all the hours were reasonably expended. It found that, although the rate was indeed reasonable, some of the hours were nonproductive. The District Court noted that "the firm has obviously made little, if any, effort to exercise billing judgment.... [T]here was practically no partner time expended on this case and the associates lacked experienced trial direction."

With this analysis we can find no fault. Our review of myriad attorney's fee cases demonstrates that the $57 average hourly rate certainly is

---

39. That we defer to the trial judge's familiarity with a lawsuit does not, of course, imply that we abandon our duty to review fee awards. It is axiomatic that we cannot identify an unreasonable award unless it is accom-panied by a statement of reasons. Thus, a remand may be necessary where the District Court awards a fee without adequately artic-ulating underlying reasons or bases its deci-sion on improper factors.

within the bounds of reasonableness. We think, also, that the District Court properly refused compensation for nonproductive hours. Hours may be disallowed as nonproductive for at least two reasons. First, no compensation should be given for hours spent litigating issues upon which plaintiff did not ultimately prevail. Also not allowable are hours that simply should not have been spent at all, such as where attorneys' efforts are unorganized or duplicative. This may occur, for example, when young associates' labors are inadequately organized by supervising partners.

It is true that the District Court in this case did not identify precisely the hours, or types of work, for which no compensation could be paid. Instead, it simply decreased the "lodestar" by a substantial fixed amount from the $206,000 proposed starting point. Under the special circumstances of this case, this practice cannot be condemned. The reduction in fee resulted primarily from the expenditure of unnecessary time by relatively inexperienced lawyers. It is neither practical nor desirable to expect the trial court judge to have reviewed each paper in this massive case file to decide, for example, whether a particular motion could have been done in 9.6 hours instead of 14.3 hours. * * *

This approach is particularly appropriate in a case such as this. A pleading-by-pleading examination of the copious files in this case would be unnecessarily burdensome. We think that the District Court Judge in this case—recognizing, as he did, that some duplication or waste of effort had occurred—did not err in simply reducing the proposed "lodestar" fee by a reasonable amount without performing an item-by-item accounting. * * *

2.   *Adjustments to the "Lodestar"*

A "lodestar" fee may be adjusted, as we have seen, to compensate for the possible contingent nature of success, and in recognition of the quality of representation.

a.   *Contingency*

The "lodestar" fee may be increased to reflect the possibility that the litigation would not be successful and that no fee ultimately would be obtained. The District Court in this case made no contingency adjustment, nor was it requested to do so.

b.   *Quality*

None of the factors that we must consider under this rubric suggests that the District Court's fee award need be disturbed.

The District Court recognized that plaintiff's attorneys were inexperienced. It found, though, that they were "excellent"; what they "lacked in seasoned trial experience was offset by other factors. They were always well prepared, effective and knowledgeable." Our examination of the record in this case confirms the appraisal of the trial judge.

Another of the important elements in assessing the quality of counsel is the benefit of counsel's efforts: the success of the litigation. The government points out that the fee award was vastly disproportionate to the monetary relief obtained, and contends that the fee award should be reduced accordingly.

The District Court, however, observed that where, as here, the primary purpose of a lawsuit is to obtain equitable relief, the fee award should not necessarily be reduced simply because monetary relief was small. Moreover, the court found that the nonmonetary relief achieved in this case—an affirmative action program for training and promoting women—was important, and "will be felt for many years to come."

We think that the District Court has accurately summarized both the benefits produced by this lawsuit and the law governing the award of fees in cases that produce primarily nonmonetary relief.

Title VII provides various sorts of remedies once discrimination has been found. Relief can be in form of back pay, promotion, and other prospective equitable relief such as affirmative action programs. This case involved each category of relief. Some $33,000 in back pay for 13 of the plaintiffs was paid. That amount is not insubstantial, but it does not represent the principal relief obtained. Some class members received promotions to the GS–14 level. Others received specialized training and guaranteed promotions upon completion of that training. The prospective value of this kind of relief far exceeds the back pay awarded.

Probably the most important relief obtained by this litigation was the affirmative action plan. The plan, which was broadly aimed at eliminating the "blatant discrimination" the District Court found to have existed in the Directorate, offers substantial prospective relief for the class. The plan provides significant training opportunities for women, including accelerated training for management positions. It requires that work assignments be made on a nondiscriminatory basis. It also establishes goals, timetables, and an annual reporting system to measure the Directorate's progress in remedying the effects of past discrimination.

Plaintiff's efforts also produced intangible benefits that flow from the elimination of discrimination. Since women no longer should be denied advancement because of their gender, the sense of inferiority resulting from the discrimination will be eliminated. Moreover, the exposure of discrimination in one portion of the Department of Labor may lead to heightened awareness of, and intensified efforts to eradicate, possibly discriminatory treatment throughout the Department.

The government insists, nevertheless, that the absence of a substantial monetary recovery ought to preclude a fee award on the order of magnitude of that given by the District Court. The panel agreed, concluding that the existence of a $160,000 fee to obtain about $33,000 in back pay establishes "at least a *prima facie* case that *something* is wrong with the previously constructed standards." *Copeland II,* slip op. at 20. (emphasis in original).

We disagree. That this litigation sought and obtained substantial equitable relief is highly relevant to the award of a large fee. We have noted that the primary purpose of the fee provision is to give persons victimized by discrimination the resources to vindicate their rights through litigation. Where, as here, the relief sought is generally nonmonetary, a substantial fee is particularly important if that statutory purpose is to be fulfilled. It is relatively easy to obtain competent counsel when the litigation is likely to produce a substantial monetary award. It is more difficult to attract counsel where the relief sought is primarily nonmonetary. For this reason, fee awards in cases that produce substantial nonmonetary benefits must not be reduced simply because the litigation produced little cash. * * *

For these reasons, no reduction in fee was appropriate after considering the relevant factors in the category of "quality of representation."

C. *Conclusion*

The District Court considered all the relevant factors in awarding an attorney's fee. Although its discount of the proposed "lodestar" amount could perhaps have been computed with greater specificity, that discount was quite substantial however it may have been measured. It was an exercise of judgment informed by both experience and direct observation of what had transpired in the course of the litigation.

We therefore find it unnecessary now to remand the matter for further inquiry, and affirm the District Court's attorney's fee award.

It is so ordered.

■ MacKINNON, CIRCUIT JUDGE.

I join in the court's opinion. In my view both the market value and the cost-plus standard can at times lead to exorbitant fees; but I view the market value approach as being more time honored and hence easier of application nationwide where all lawyers do not keep detailed records of overhead costs and other relevant expenditures. The bench and the bar are accustomed to market value in the area as representing reasonable attorney's fees and I believe that standard, when properly applied, includes within it its own elements of reasonableness. The only admonition I would include would be the caveat that the attorney's fee in the ordinary case must bear some *reasonable* relationship to the amount of money and equitable benefits that are involved. Attorneys in such cases should be forced to be mindful of the monetary and equitable benefits that are being sought and should not be permitted to run up bills that are greatly disproportionate to the ultimate benefits that may be reasonably attainable.

■ CIRCUIT JUDGE ROBB concurs in the foregoing opinion.

■ WILKEY, CIRCUIT JUDGE, joined by TAMM, CIRCUIT JUDGE, dissenting:

In our colleagues' "lodestar" opinion, the path of attorney's fees in Title VII litigation is easy to discern. It is Up, Up, and Away! It is *Per Calculos Ad Astra.*

Before going to the extraordinary *calculos* of the majority opinion, it would be well to point out the areas in which we have no disagreement and what precisely we think the issue is. We have no quarrel, of course, with the findings of the trial court, reiterated in exquisite detail by the majority opinion, regarding the labors of the young attorneys who worked for the plaintiff on this case. We have no quarrel with the regular hourly rates charged by this distinguished law firm to its regular corporate clients for the labors of its senior partners, its junior associates, or these particular junior associates. The issue is not whether they shall be paid; as attorneys for the prevailing party, they are rightly entitled to be paid. The issue is not, on this appellate level, even how much they shall be paid. The issue here is only—but unfortunately not simply—the formula by which these attorney's fees should be calculated by the trial court.

This question has required much time and effort on the part of this court to attempt to resolve. All members should have come to grips with the obvious fact, as we analyzed and dissected this particular case, that previous precedents in the field, even in our own circuit, rested on contradictory, overlapping, disharmonious, even spurious and irrelevant "factors." This incoherent melange provides no consistent rationale for a conscientious trial judge to apply, at least in a case in which the Government is the paying defendant; the effort to do so here has highlighted the inadequacies and inapplicability of previous precedents.

Judge McGowan's opinion for the majority is the most strenuous effort so far to pull a basically incoherent rationale (even if of some service in the private sector) together, to smooth putty into the visibly widening cracks of logic and to cover with the lacquer of a polished style. We in the dissent cannot buy the product. Over many months of pondering the arguments for importing the market value hourly rate fee into government Title VII litigation—this is the first case in this circuit—we are more than ever convinced that the market value concept is unworkable where there is no true market, that the effort to apply it inevitably leads to distortions and excesses, far away from the "reasonable attorney's fee" which was Congress's *only* avowed standard and intent.

First we delineate the differences which, on thoughtful analysis, are necessarily implicit in the setting of a "reasonable attorney's fee" according to the statute, where the Government as contrasted with a private party is the paying defendant and no true market exists. Next we take up the obvious flaws in the applicability of the majority's private sector theory to this case of the Government as defendant—the redundant contingency factor, the care and feeding of lawyers rather than injured plaintiffs, and the evasion of testing the majority formula in this case. Finally we describe the actual cost plus a reasonable and controllable profit method of determining a "reasonable attorney's fee."

I. DIFFERENCES IN THE ROLE OF THE GOVERNMENT AND PRIVATE PARTIES AS DEFENDANTS IN TITLE VII LITIGATION

* * *

C. *How the Attorney's Fee Incentive Operates in Government Litigation*

When a large firm knows that eventual success will bring it compensation at its customary rate for all relevant hours of work, the firm has a tremendous incentive to expand the pretrial stages of the case to the point where it becomes overwhelmingly in the Government's interest to settle, whether the Government is in the wrong or not. In private litigation the incentive to expand the discovery and pretrial motion stages is counterbalanced by the high cost that this will inflict on the client, because victory does not normally bring a recovery of the litigant's own attorney's fees from the other side. Not so in a case of this sort against the Government, where the law deliberately encourages the litigation by holding out the carrot of attorney's fees—but only to successful plaintiffs.

Furthermore, in private litigation the high cost of extensive discovery serves as an incentive for both sides to settle. But in Title VII cases against the Government, the incentives become entirely lopsided, because expanded litigation costs for plaintiff not only increase his chance of winning, but also greatly increase the sum his lawyer stands to gain if he does win. At the same time, each expansion of the litigation effort will pose a risk of higher and higher liability for the Government. The end result is that the Government faces overwhelming incentives to give in to claims, however unjust, before expanded litigation doubles or triples or quadruples the size of eventual Government liability. When attorney's fee levels come to dwarf the actual monetary amount in controversy, as in the present case, the structure of these incentives is magnified further. In deciding whether to settle a case like this one, the Government is not primarily considering whether its case is strong enough that it should risk an eventual $31,345 judgment to plaintiffs; instead, if Government attorneys are rational they must primarily consider whether their case is strong enough to risk the much greater possibility of a $200,000 plus eventual attorney's fee award.

D. *Failure of Attorney's Fees to Deter Discrimination by the Government*

Attorney's fees are meant to serve some purpose of deterring discrimination. They doubtless do in the private sector. But when attorney's fees come straight out of the United States Treasury, as in the present case, they exert no deterrent effect whatsoever against the persons responsible for the discrimination. In the private sector there is a justifiable punitive element. Attorney's fees impact on the profit picture of the corporation; the same executive management which is responsible for tolerating or encouraging discrimination are the same executives who are responsible for the profit of the corporation, so they are penalized in the pocketbook. No such deterrence applies to the Government, *i. e.,* the Labor Department budget was never touched, will never be touched, by the award of Judge Gesell in this case. Both the back pay and the attorney's fee come out of the general taxpayer contributed funds of the U. S. Treasury. By their strict analogy to the private sector, the majority has validated deterrent or punitive action against the U. S. taxpayer.

E. *"Reasonable" Private and Government Attorney's Fees in Government Litigation*

The Government operates in a universe of attorney's fees lower than that prevailing in the world of wealthy corporate clients. If the Government were pressing the Title VII case rather than defending, its legal costs would not approximate private "market value." Government legal counsel, whether on the plaintiff or defendant side, traditionally simply have never been compensated at the same scale as in private practice. The young associate makes slightly more than the young Government attorney; the margin becomes really vast when partner status in a prestigious law firm is compared even with the Attorney General of the United States. Since the Government willy-nilly is financing these Title VII suits both by plaintiffs who succeed and do not succeed (giving effect to a contingency factor), Government counsel defending and plaintiffs' counsel bringing the suits should have compensation of roughly the same amplitude.

There is a logical symmetry in this principle. When the Government as a defendant prevails, it has asked for and received only its actual costs, the salaries of the attorneys working on the case plus overhead costs attributable to their work—*not* the market value going hourly rate of the private sector. It is undeniably the same litigation, vindicating the rights of employees discriminated against, whether the Government wins or loses. The work on the facts and the legal issues is of the same complexity on both sides. Indeed, if the Government were not the defendant employer, the private attorneys would not be bringing a *pro bono publico* lawsuit as private attorneys general. What the private attorneys are doing is essentially Government legal work. Recognizing this, why should the private attorneys be compensated on a scale other than actual costs (salary and overhead) plus a reasonable profit to encourage them to continue accepting employment in this type of litigation? The purpose of Title VII attorney's fees would be fully vindicated by such a policy.

F.   *The Majority's "Market Value" Fee Where No Market Exists*

With reference to attorney's fees in Title VII litigation against the Government, the fundamental verities overlooked by our colleagues are these: first, there is no market in which fees are set by market value forces; second, whatever fee-paying mechanism there is exists as the total creation of the Government itself.

To the latter point, we must remember that the Government need not consent to be sued by its own employees or anyone else. No lawsuit, no lawyer's fee. In almost any other country in the world government employee complaints are adjudicated through the administrative process, as indeed was thought perfectly proper in the United States until 1972, when Congress decided it was more just to give government employees the same rights in court as private employees. Our role is not to choose between administrative or judicial relief; it is to give effect to that selected by Congress. And so we point out that if the majority's pathway to the stars formula for attorney's fees is applied often enough, there may be a popular demand to take government employee Title VII litigation out of the court system altogether and limit employees to administrative relief as previously.

As matters stand now, the Government as defendant pays the cost of its own lawyers in court, the Government pays attorney's fees for those plaintiffs who prevail, and the Government—because it pays not only the true cost of the specific suit but also a contingent factor for attorney's costs in other suits in which the plaintiff does not prevail—pays attorney's fees indirectly for plaintiff lawyers who lose. The Government—*the American taxpayer*—*is financing BOTH sides of ALL Title VII litigation against the Government.* This is the chosen mechanism; the court's role is to determine how the fees are to be calculated.

So we now return to the first point above: the Government is financing this litigation under circumstances in which *there are no market value forces to restrict or to set "reasonable attorney's fees";* fundamentally, because *there is no market.* We all recognize that the government employees who become plaintiffs in Title VII cases do not have the financial resources to bid in the marketplace for attorney's services. Copeland and fellow plaintiffs could never have contemplated this litigation, resulting in a suggested fee of $206,000, and an award of $160,000 plus $12,000 expenses. To vindicate the rights of persons discriminated against, Congress has realistically appraised the situation and recognized that attorney's fees must be taxed to the losing defendant, if there is to be any Title VII litigation brought by the injured persons. We in dissent obviously have no quarrel with this whatsoever; we realistically recognize, however, as our colleagues do not, that here there is no market, and that necessarily there must be a different method of setting a "reasonable attorney's fee" if there are no market forces to determine a "market value" fee.

Whatever the usual merit of "market value," it is anomalous where Congress has specifically sought to complement the market for legal services in Title VII cases with an alternative mechanism for allocating attorney's fees. Rather than relying on the parties in privity—the client and his or her lawyer—*to agree* among themselves to the value of the services *to be rendered,* Congress has provided that a trial court, in its discretion, may *assign* the burden of legal expenses *incurred* by the winner to the loser.

The emphasized points in this last sentence should underscore the substantial incongruity between market and judicial determinations of the cost of legal services. Furthermore, the market works so well because it works invisibly, almost effortlessly; even the most astute of judges can only mock the market concept when the judge seeks to replicate market results where none exist. Emulating the market, effective as it is, is worthless to the extent that market factors—supply and demand, agreement among market-makers, prospective not retrospective assessments of marginal utility—are more conjectural then real.

So it is plain, then, that attorney's fees in the Title VII context cannot be assigned according to market values because there are quite simply *no buyers* for the services rendered. Without clients who agree to pay at certain (bargained for) rates, there can be no market. There is missing an *a priori* pecuniary relation between the legal services undertaken and the willingness of any beneficiary to pay for them. Therefore, charging a losing defendant for the prevailing party's legal expenses at "market" rates which no one would ever have voluntarily assumed is to destroy the market concept by purporting to respect it.

Another inconsistency of the majority's "market value" approach when compared with *bona fide* markets is with regard to risk. In a market, *i. e.,* a real market, risk is a negative factor which *diminishes* the "expected value" of the beneficiary's lawsuit *to the client.* A rational client, the beneficiary of legal services, would pay less to pursue relatively riskier litigation because his anticipated recovery must be discounted for that risk. Naturally, lawyers who will be paid only upon the contingency of success would appreciate and demand a risk premium for their services. Only a true market, of course, could allocate the burden of risk accurately between lawyer and client. This the private sector does every day. In Title VII litigation against the Government we have placed this burden on the judge.

This is indeed a situation which, if recognized in its true proportions, is so completely different from private litigation that it is obvious that the same concepts of market value fees cannot be employed. Instead of the free play of the market of private clients we have the Government consenting to be sued, financing all successful litigation against itself, and also financing all unsuccessful litigation against itself by enlarged fees on a contingent basis. If this is what is to be done, and it is what is to be done by both the majority's concept and ours, *then the Government is entitled to put down some rules and regulations on the cost of the legal services,* which by the system designed by statute the Government is going to finance in totality. If the Government is going to finance the whole mechanism in totality, then the concept of actual cost plus a reasonable profit to the attorneys is about the only concept that can hold attorney's fees down to a *reasonable* level.

The tendency toward abusively high fees in this sort of case is real, yet the majority opinion offers absolutely nothing to cope with this problem. We believe there are indeed ways by which we can try to solve this problem, rather than throw up our hands and permit attorney's fees in Title VII cases to continue up to the stars. Two of these factors can be found listed in the *Evans* case: (1) limiting fees to a level commensurate with awards in similar cases, and (2) limiting fees to a level commensurate with the amount in controversy and results obtained. * * *

II.   THE MAJORITY OPINION FORMULA—FAULTY ANALYSIS PRODUCES SKEWED RESULTS

In its rigid interpretation of the statute as calling for precisely the same *method* of calculating attorney's fees in both the public and private sectors the majority errs, and then compounds that error by applying its own formula in a way which precludes ascertaining the congressionally directed "reasonable attorney's fee." Both errors stem from the majority's failure to appreciate the inapplicability of fee setting, as done by the market in private practice, to fixing a reasonable fee in the very different situation when the Government is the defendant. * * *

* * * [W]e have a fundamental disagreement with our colleagues as to the philosophy underlying the award of attorney's fees to prevailing litigants.

It is plain that our nation's policy—both legislative and judicial—is to promote the efforts of so-called "private attorneys general" who vindicate our civil rights laws by seeking legal redress for Title VII plaintiffs' injuries. It is necessary, then, that litigation expenses constitute *no barrier* that discourages these private plaintiffs from bringing their grievances before the courts. Eliminating the *barrier* of attorney's fees encourages plaintiffs to assert their legal and civil rights.

But *encouraging injured plaintiffs* is a goal distinct from that of *encouraging lawyers* with the lure of attorney's fees bonanzas.[32] The majority's philosophy appears to be solicitous of the "sellers" of legal services beyond the needs of the "buyers" of these services. The majority appears to believe that its "market value" formula must award attorney's fees which match the petitioning lawyers' *highest opportunity costs*. Neither lawyers nor other purveyors of products and services operate on the basis of achieving highest opportunity costs most of the time; by definition, the usual—and entirely satisfactory—reward is less. It seems clear that the mandated encouragement to plaintiffs is achieved by granting the lawyers a sum reflecting their actual cost plus a reasonable profit, as opposed to an award which reflects the highest rates of return that alternative applications of legal manpower and resources could command.

It is simply *not* invidious to conclude that the fee schedule acceptable to General Motors when confronting a possible billion dollar liability is not necessarily applicable in Title VII attorney's fees determinations. Our "cost-plus" method brooks no disservice to Title VII "private attorneys general." On the other hand, *overcoming the legal expense barrier for these private plaintiffs requires no windfall for lawyers—only that it be worth their lawyers' while.* This is what our view of attorney's fees awards accomplishes: service for the plaintiffs without the need for lawyers to sacrifice. The inevitable existence of some other opportunities for lawyers to gain relatively higher remuneration does not mean that *all* legal services—including purported *pro bono* work—must be compensated at the very highest figure discoverable. * * *

---

32. Our colleagues have noted the statement of the law firm involved here that in previous *pro bono* cases the firm has contributed the fee to a public interest organization "committed to furthering the kind of public interest involved in the particular litigation."

This might be characterized as the Robin Hood approach, taking from rich Uncle Sam to benefit attorneys for the deserving poor, as selected by the private firm. While charity is to be commended, we thought Robin Hood's fame rested on his romantic appeal, not his contribution to precedential jurisprudence. And, Robin Hood gave to the poor, not to their lawyers.

We suggest a more orderly and more constitutional approach would be to let Congress decide which public interest organizations are to be subsidized by taxpayer funds, not to do it indirectly and undirected through inflated attorney's fees in Title VII cases.

III.   "A REASONABLE ATTORNEY'S FEE"—ACTUAL COST PLUS A REASONABLE AND CONTROLLABLE PROFIT

In considering how to achieve the statutory goal of "a reasonable attorney's fee," we have delineated the undeniable distinctions inherent in levying fees against private employers as compared to the Government, where in the latter situation there is no market and therefore no market value constraints on fees, but on the contrary the entire mechanism of affording relief to aggrieved Government employees is created by and financed by the Government on both sides. We have seen how the unthinking utilization of the "market value" fee as the "lodestar" or basic fee results in gross escalation of fee awards against the taxpayers, far from the "reasonable attorney's fee" mandated by statute. Now we turn to outline the actual cost plus a reasonable and controllable profit method of fixing a reasonable fee, first enunciated in our panel opinion for the court, pondered and refined in the light of comment and discussion during the almost two years since our first opinion issued. We are convinced that the cost-plus formula is likely better to achieve the statutory goal then any other method yet proposed, and no case is apt better to illustrate this than the case at bar.

Returning to the specific facts of this case, putting the matter in perspective, the labors of the two young attorneys (plus some hours of partners' time) resulted in a promotion to a higher GS level and back pay of $4,169.80 for the plaintiff Copeland. In addition, following the negotiation of a settlement, remaining members of the class secured several promotions and back pay awards totaling $27,175.71. The law firm "suggested" a fee of $206,000, plus $12,602.59 in costs. District Judge Gesell awarded a flat $160,000 in fees and $11,567.11 in costs.

A.   *The Need for Additional Guidelines for the District Court*

As witness this case, the application of the existing standards led to a claim of $206,000 by a responsible law firm and an intelligent, experienced judge fixing a fee of $160,000 on a $31,345 monetary benefit to all members of the class. To state the matter this baldly is to make out at least a *prima facie* case that *something* is wrong with the previously constructed standards—when applied to fix a fee award in a Title VII case against the Government.

Previous Title VII attorney's fees cases before this court have involved private party defendants. While the statute provides that "the United States shall be liable for costs the same as a private person," it is rather likely that awards of attorney's fees against a private company, found guilty of race or sex discrimination, have contained a certain amount of a punitive element and have been scrutinized less sharply than awards against the Government (all taxpayers) should be. Hence, the panel of this court believed that it should give careful scrutiny not only to this particular award but to the standards which were to be followed subsequently in attorney's fees cases against the Government.

* * * [W]e examined at some length the unique factors affecting attorney's fees in Title VII litigation against the Government, an analysis which is an elaboration and development of thoughts set forth in our first panel opinion. At that time it was readily apparent that something was needed as a substitute for the commercial fee basis; hence, the court's original opinion suggested that actual cost plus a reasonable and controllable profit be substituted instead of the market value rate as the initial starting point for the district court's calculation.

B. *Rationale*

We pointed out the rather surprising fact that when law firms assert the value of their work to their clients—itself a rather nebulous concept, as witness the claim here of $206,000 plus expenses versus the $31,345 in back pay plus promotions awarded—the firm "never reveals the value of the attorneys' work to the firm, *i.e.,* the value of the gross income brought to the firm by the attorneys in the ordinary course of business, as compared with the sums paid out to those attorneys as personal income and to defray overhead costs attributable to the maintenance of the attorneys in the firm."[44] It seemed only reasonable to us that where a firm *is ostensibly performing a* pro bono publico *service, its reimbursement for that service should bear a direct relationship to the actual costs incurred by the firm* and, in fact, that this was the best possible reference point, at least in the initial calculation.

We therefore stated: "Thus the trial court should give consideration to abandoning the traditional[ly] claimed hourly-fee starting point for its calculations in favor of *a principle of reimbursement to a firm for its costs, plus a reasonable and controllable margin for profit.* Such a principle can be applied through separation of the several hidden components of the usual attorney's fee."[45] * * *

To the extent that the cost-plus formula and the other factors mentioned in the opinion might result in a lower than commercial fee, government legal services—and here the private law firm is acting as a private attorney general in a *pro bono publico* suit—have always been paid less than those in the private sector. For example, Justice Department lawyers do not start at the beginning salary paid at large law firms in Washington, D.C. The very top Justice Department lawyers do not even approach the earnings of partners in large firms such as that involved here. Government legal work has never been expected to pay the same as the top private legal work. What the law firm here and other large law firms, or public interest law firms, are doing is *government legal work*—on the other side of the issue in these cases from the government employer itself. * * *

What our "cost plus a reasonable and controllable profit" guideline does is to return the actual out-of-pocket cost to the firm for its attorneys' legal services and all overhead, plus a reasonable and controlled profit. *How much more* should a private law firm receive for its legal services? *How*

---

44. 594 F.2d 244, 251 (D.C.Cir.1978).   **45.** *Id.* (emphasis added).

much more than cost plus a reasonable profit can it be entitled to? How much more than cost plus a reasonable profit would this court be justified in awarding against the Government and its taxpayers?

C. *Application*

The petitioning law firm conjures up enormous difficulties of application by the court and of prying into confidential firm matters. We see absolutely none of this, if the proposed cost plus reasonable profit formula is applied on any sensible basis. If the trial court understands what it is doing, there should be no substantial additional evidentiary burden on the trial court. The basic figures are simple and simple to arrive at, as discussed below.

The three general components we identified in our opinion were salary, overhead, and profit.

1. *Salary*—The starting salary for young lawyers with the large firms in Washington, New York, and many other large cities is almost a matter of public record. The "going rate" for hiring is strictly competitive and well known to both the law firms and the young lawyers coming in. Furthermore, even the raises for the first few years are standardized.

And, of course, while our opinion talked in terms of the salary actually paid the individual lawyers involved in the case, it would be entirely satisfactory if the law firm merely furnished information on *the average* salary paid young lawyers in that firm with the same number of years' experience. (In the instant case, both associates were assigned this matter in their first year of employment at the firm.)

With regard to partners' "salary," our opinion deliberately put this on the basis of an extrapolation from the highest associate's salary. We recognize that the income of partners in the same firm may vary widely, even more widely between firms, and a partner's share may very well be thought of as confidential. Typically, in Title VII cases, the share of the fee claimed for partners' labors is usually very small, as in the instant case.

2. *Overhead*—The firm knows this at least annually, or it is not computing its income tax correctly. If the firm is well managed, it should know its overhead factor quarterly or even monthly. Every firm surely makes a calculation as to the average overhead factor for its individual fee-producing lawyers.

One of the preposterous arguments, but strongly made, is that most firms now make no accounting of costs, overhead, and profit on an attorney-by-attorney basis, and that a mountain of details will be called for. This rests totally on a misinterpretation of our opinion. It is the *average* overhead cost per attorney to which the opinion refers.

It may be that partners in fact develop more overhead cost for the firm than do associates (bigger offices, more luxurious furnishings, etc.), but this could be taken care of by an average overhead figure for associates and a different figure for partners.

In any given city, there is probably no great difference in the overhead per lawyer of similar sized firms in similar practice; hence, there are no great secrets to be revealed. If there are great differences in firm overhead, the firm management claiming a higher overhead factor is out of line and should know about it.

The claim is made that since the cost-plus formula allows all overhead costs to be shifted to the losing party, this cuts down the incentive to keep overhead costs low. Unless the firm is engaged virtually exclusively in Title VII work, this would not be so at all. The overhead cost average would reflect all of the work done by all attorneys in the firm on all type cases.

3. *Profit*—Our opinion made no suggestion to the trial court as to what is a reasonable profit. This is a calculation involving many factors, including the attorneys' usual profit return to the firm, the social benefits, the direct gain to the litigants, the skill demonstrated in the particular case, and the degree of contingency involved.

D.   *Substantive Inequities Feared from the New Method*

1.   *Special Problems with Small Firms and Solo Practitioners*

a.   The argument is made that small law practices will not be able to prove expenses as high as those of better established practices or larger firms, and thus will not be able to secure equivalent fees for the same work.

This may or may not be true (small firms frequently have higher per lawyer overhead), but the question of course arises: Is there any alternate work in which such firms would have been engaged in which they would get greater fees? The answer is that these firms, perhaps composed of younger lawyers, will get just as good fees as any alternative work they could possibly do, and probably *better* at this stage of their careers.

A more fundamental answer is that if both small and large firms obtain a *full return* of their *actual expenses,* plus a reasonable profit, there can be *no* inequity in the treatment of large and small firms.

b.   It is alleged that the formula is inapplicable to a solo practitioner, because there are no guideposts as to his "salary" from his associate's salary or his partner's income.

Perhaps the solo practitioner is a case in which a fairer award can be made without using the cost-plus formula, and there is nothing in our opinion which mandates the cost-plus formula in every case. However, it would be possible to take the going salary rate of several firms for lawyers of the same years of experience, extrapolate if need be, and award the solo practitioner a fee based on that plus his overhead and a reasonable profit.

2.   *Similar Problems for the Public Interest and Civil Rights Bar*

A similar claim is made for these specialists, alleging that the public interest and civil rights firms operate under far lower salary, overhead, and profit margins than others in private practice. The argument is made that somehow cost plus reasonable profit penalizes these firms.

The answer is the same as to a small firm or solo practitioner. They will be guaranteed a reasonable profit above their actual costs. We are not aware that public interest and civil rights firms usually receive more than this. However, the trial court could—and, in our view, *should*—evaluate the special skills which a public interest or civil rights firm may bring to bear among the other quality factors which the court applies to the actual cost plus reasonable profit figures. If the attorneys are specialists in Title VII cases, and thus may have been able to do the work at a high standard with a minimum of hours expended, then their "profit" in the total compensation awarded should indeed be higher than it otherwise would. * * *

We in dissent are convinced that the traditional customary commercial fee approach to billing the Government for attorneys' fees in a Title VII case is not adequate and is likely to lead to grossly excessive fees. A new approach is necessary. We have suggested that the trial court apply an actual cost plus reasonable profit formula in this case. Our analysis, in our original opinion and herein above, indicates that this formula would provide a much more precise and equitable basis, both to the Government and the private attorneys engaged in Title VII practice, for the award of attorneys' fees. We have not ruled out any other innovative methods which may commend themselves to the trial court. Since the trial court has yet to hold a hearing in this case, we think it should do so, and that in adducing evidence it should do so along the lines necessary to provide a foundation for the application of the actual cost plus reasonable profit formula. Then the trial court will have the opportunity to apply the actual cost plus reasonable profit formula to the established facts of a comparatively complex attorneys' fees case. The courts and all litigants engaged in Title VII litigation will benefit.

———

Notes and Questions

1. The case of *Copeland v. Marshall* is so rich and at least mentions, if not addresses, so many of the issues that may arise in a fee-shifting case, that one practically could teach an entire course on awards of attorney's fees using this single case as the text. The case does double-duty service in providing both an excellent survey of the law concerning the awards of attorney's fees in general *and* discussing the particular issue of such awards against the federal government.

2. *Availability of Fees.* After familiarizing yourself with the factual and litigation background to the case, what are the very first questions to be asked with respect to any request for attorney's fees against the federal government? (Look back at the notes following the previous case.) How are those questions answered here? What precisely in the text of Title VII of the Civil Rights Act of 1964 directly and affirmatively answers both threshold questions?

3. *Eligibility.* The next question to be resolved is that of eligibility for fees. Although eligibility is not disputed in *Copeland,* the court adverts to

the basic standard that a party must have prevailed in the litigation to be eligible for a fee award. *See generally* Gregory C. Sisk, *Litigation With the Federal Government* § 7.07(b), at 438–41 (ALI–ABA, 4th ed., 2006).

To qualify as a "prevailing party," the party seeking fees must have attained "some relief on the merits of his claims." *Hanrahan v. Hampton,* 446 U.S. 754, 757 (1980) (per curiam). In *Texas State Teachers Association v. Garland Independent School District,* 489 U.S. 782, 792 (1989), the Supreme Court rejected a test for prevailing-party status that would have required a party to prevail on the "central issue" in the litigation and not merely upon significant secondary issues. The Court instead adopted a general rule that, to be a prevailing party under fee-shifting statutes, a litigant need only succeed on "any significant issue in [the] litigation which achieves some of the benefit the parties sought in bringing the suit." *Id.* at 789. (However, while limited success, or success on only some of multiple claims, may not prevent a party from being *eligible* for a fee, the degree of success remains important to the *measurement* of what constitutes a reasonable fee in terms of amount.)

Finally, the case need not have gone to trial and resulted in a judgment before attorney's fees may be awarded. A party obtaining a favorable settlement that is approved and enforceable by the court has prevailed for purposes of fee eligibility. *Maher v. Gagne,* 448 U.S. 122, 129 (1980). However, in *Buckhannon Board & Care Home, Inc. v. West Virginia Dept. of Health & Human Resources,* 532 U.S. 598, 603 (2001), the Supreme Court emphasized that to qualify as a "prevailing party," the party must have been awarded some relief by a court. The Court, by a 5–4 vote, rejected the "catalyst theory," whereby a plaintiff was regarded as prevailing if the lawsuit brought about a voluntary change in the defendant's conduct. *Id.* at 603–05. The Court majority explained that "[a] defendant's voluntary change in conduct, although perhaps accomplishing what the plaintiff sought to achieve by the lawsuit, lacks the necessary judicial *imprimatur* on the change." *Id.* at 605. Accordingly, as a prerequisite to an award of attorney's fees, there must be a court-ordered change in the legal relationship between the plaintiff and the defendant, such as a judgment on the merits or a settlement agreement enforced through a consent decree. *Id.* at 604.

4. *Measurement of Fee.* After determining the availability of and eligibility for a fee award, and assuming there are no additional entitlement requirements (and there are none under Title VII), the next step is to calculate a reasonable fee:

a. *Standard.* What is the standard for an award under *Copeland*? What are the *Johnson* factors? What is the *Lindy* rule? Which does the *Copeland* court adopt? Why? (Like the *Copeland* court, most courts have gravitated toward the fee-setting formula known as the *Lindy* or "lodestar" rule. Do you see the practical advantage of the rule?) What is the "lodestar"? What steps are involved in calculating the lodestar?

b. *Hours.* How does the court determine what number of hours were reasonably expended by the plaintiff's counsel? How should a fee petitioner document those hours? The *Copeland* court suggests that the documentation required is not particularly burdensome and indicates that information about general activities is sufficient. However, the author of this casebook has written:

> [J]ust as private clients are increasingly demanding that attorneys specifically account for the time devoted to legal representation, courts likely will expect greater specificity in time records submitted to support a fee petition.[112] With the advent of the personal computer, detailed time records by individual attorneys are more easily maintained and thus will come to be the required standard. Inadequate documentation and failure to designate the nature of work performed is a common basis for reduction of a fee award.

---

112. *See, e.g.,* H.J. Inc. v. Flygt Corp., 925 F.2d 257, 260 (8th Cir.1991) (criticizing as inadequate documentation such vague time entries as "legal research," or "trial prep," or "met w/ client"); *In re* Meese, 907 F.2d 1192, 1204 (D.C.Cir.1990) (holding that time records are inadequate "where no mention is made of the subject matter of a meeting, telephone conference or the work performed during hours billed") * * *.

Gregory C. Sisk, *A Primer on Awards of Attorney's Fees Against the Federal Government,* 25 Ariz. St. L.J. 733, 749–50 (1993); *see also Role Models America, Inc. v. Brownlee,* 353 F.3d 962, 970 (D.C. Cir. 2004) (holding that fee petitioner "has the burden of establishing the reasonableness of its fee request * * * and supporting documentation must be of sufficient detail and probative value to enable the court to determine with a high degree of certainty that such hours were actually and reasonably expended") (internal quotation marks omitted).

After documenting the hours, the *Copeland* court says an attorney must exercise "billing judgment." What is "billing judgment?" What are some examples of non-productive time? How did the district court apply billing judgment considerations in this case to reduce the fee requested?

At this stage, the district court also will consider whether compensation should be granted for time spent litigating claims upon which the party seeking the fee did not ultimately prevail (or claims for which a fee award is not available). (The "additional claims" issue did not arise in the single-claim context of *Copeland.*) The courts generally have been reluctant to segregate claims in determining an appropriate fee unless there is a clear line of demarcation between detached parts of a single case. In *Hensley v. Eckerhart,* 461 U.S. 424 (1983), the Supreme Court stated:

> Where the plaintiff has failed to prevail on a claim that is distinct in all respects from his successful claims, the hours spent on the unsuccessful claim should be excluded in considering the amount of a reasonable fee. Where a lawsuit consists of related claims, a plaintiff who has won substantial relief should not have his attorney's fee reduced simply because the district court did not adopt each contention raised. But where the plaintiff achieved only limited success, the district court

should award only that amount of fees that is reasonable in relation to the results obtained.

Id. at 440. Accordingly, if there is a significant overlap or relationship between successful and unsuccessful claims, a plaintiff may properly recover for time spent on those related claims when substantial relief overall was obtained. The court will eliminate hours devoted to unsuccessful components of a case only if there are "distinctly different claims for relief that are based on different facts and legal theories." *Id.* at 434. If the case involves what is essentially a single claim arising from a common nucleus of operative fact, and the plaintiff advances separate legal theories that "are but different statutory avenues to the same goal," then all of the time should be compensable. *See Paris v. United States Dept. of Hous. & Urban Dev.,* 988 F.2d 236, 239–40 (1st Cir.1993) (discussing prevailing party status). *See generally* Gregory C. Sisk, *Litigation With the Federal Government* § 7.07(d)(2), at 446–49 (ALI–ABA, 4th ed., 2006).

c.   *Hourly Rate.* Next the court must determine what constitutes a reasonable hourly rate. What is the standard as explained in *Copeland?* What factors should be evaluated in arriving at the appropriate rate under this standard? In general, fee petitioners present evidence on the appropriate rate in the form of affidavits from other attorneys not affiliated with the case. What should those affidavits say?

d.   *Adjustment of Lodestar.* Finally, under the original *Lindy* rule, the last step was to consider an adjustment—upward or downward—of the lodestar figure. What bases for adjustment are identified by the *Copeland* court? Consider the continued viability of those purported justifications, particularly for upward adjustments, in light of the law review article excerpt immediately following these notes.

What about an enhancement for delay in receipt of the fees? Footnote 181 to the following article excerpt states that compensation for delay is generally available when awarded against private parties, but *not* in federal government cases. Why not? Hint: Look back at *Library of Congress v. Shaw,* 478 U.S. 310 (1986) (see Chapter II.C). Is such an adjustment now permissible, even against the federal government, in the particular context of Title VII? See Chapter II.C. On fee enhancements for delay, see generally Gregory C. Sisk, *A Primer on Awards of Attorney's Fees Against the Federal Government,* 25 Ariz. St. L.J. 733, 763–64 (1993).

5.   *A Different Measurement for Awards Against the Federal Government?* In *Copeland,* the dissenting judges from the en banc decision (who had constituted the majority on the original three-judge appellate panel hearing this case) contend that a different calculus should be used for measuring attorney's fee awards against the federal government. In what ways does the dissent believe the federal government is different and thus that the measurement of a fee should be different? What is the en banc majority's response? How would the lodestar approach address or fail to address these differences?

What about the dissent's contention that the majority mistakenly adopts a market-rate approach to measuring a fee award in a context where there is simply no market for reference? The very purpose of a fee-shifting provision such as that found in Title VII is to create an incentive for attorneys that the market does not provide. The statute thus supplements the market to encourage attorneys to take cases that private economic forces would not promote. Is this a fatal flaw in the majority's lodestar approach? Since there are no actual and willing buyers of such legal services in the private market, does the court indulge in speculation when purporting to award fees at a non-existent "market rate"?

What is the alternative to a market-rate fee that is devised by the dissent? Outline each of the components of the dissent's approach. Why is the majority dissatisfied with the dissent's alternative? What objections would a law firm likely raise to this alternative approach?

In the typical case, shouldn't the "cost-plus" approach advocated by the dissent produce the same result as the market-rate approach adopted by the majority? Wouldn't the market rate for an attorney already include the attorney's costs together with a reasonable profit margin?

The one circumstance in which the cost-plus approach would yield a very different fee from the market value approach is where a plaintiff is represented by a public interest, not-for-profit organization. Lawyers for such organizations typically are paid lower salaries, and these organizations depend upon public funds or private contributions rather than profitable activities. In *Blum v. Stenson,* 465 U.S. 886, 892–96 (1984), the Supreme Court held that public interest attorneys should be compensated at the same market rates as private attorneys. The Supreme Court's ruling in this regard would seem to lay the cost-plus method to a final rest. Thus, the cost-plus approach was both born in and died with the *Copeland* case.

Gregory C. Sisk, A Primer on Awards of Attorney's Fees Against the Federal Government

25 Arizona State Law Journal 733, 756–762 (1993).

* Upward Adjustments to the Lodestar (Multipliers)

Under the *Lindy* rule, once the court determined the lodestar amount, the court could adjust the final figure upward or downward based upon certain factors.[158] This adjustment was sometimes called a "multiplier," as the calculation commonly involved multiplying the lodestar amount by a certain number, usually between 1 and 2. First, an upward adjustment might be made to compensate for the contingency risk that the lawsuit would be unsuccessful and that no fee at all would be obtained. Second, the

---

158. Lindy Bros. Builders, Inc. v. American Radiator & Standard Sanitary Corp., 540 F.2d 102, 116–18 (3d Cir.1976) (en banc) (*Lindy II*).

lodestar might be adjusted upward or downward to reflect the quality of representation.

Although the lodestar concept that originated in the Third Circuit's *Lindy* line of cases has taken firm hold in fee-shifting jurisprudence, the Supreme Court has largely—but not completely—rejected the additional element of an upward adjustment or multiplier. Today, the lodestar is generally the beginning and the end of the calculation process.

The Supreme Court first cast a disapproving eye on the multiplier concept in *Blum v. Stenson*.[161] The Court specifically declined to hold that an upward adjustment was never permissible, but the *Blum* decision became the first in a line of cases that have uniformly rejected the application of a multiplier. In every case brought before it, the Court has adhered to the lodestar figure as the touchstone of a reasonable fee.

In *Blum,* the Court ruled that the novelty and complexity of the issues presented in a lawsuit could not justify an upward quality adjustment in the fee award because those factors presumably were reflected in the number of hours included in the lodestar calculation. Although the special skill and experience of an attorney may require the expenditure of fewer hours of legal services even on novel and complex issues, the Court held that the attorney's experience and skill should be reflected in the reasonableness of the hourly rate. Additionally, the Court held that the quality of representation provided by the attorney could not justify a departure from the lodestar because this factor is generally accounted for in the setting of the reasonable hourly rate. Finally, the Court rejected an upward adjustment based upon the results obtained in the litigation, saying that this factor also is generally subsumed within the lodestar and that the benefits achieved do not normally provide an independent basis for increasing the fee award.

In *Pennsylvania v. Delaware Valley Citizens Council for Clean Air,*[168] the Supreme Court rejected an adjustment for superior quality of representation in an environmental case, reiterating that adjustments to the lodestar are permissible only in "rare" and "exceptional" cases. The Court emphasized that the lodestar is "more than a mere 'rough guess' or initial approximation of the final award to be made;" it is presumptively the reasonable fee. Because the lodestar method uses a reasonable hourly rate and compensates for a reasonable number of hours, it leaves

> very little room for enhancing the award based on [the attorney's] post-engagement performance. In short, the lodestar figure includes most, if not all, of the relevant factors constituting a 'reasonable' attorney's fee, and it is unnecessary to enhance the fee for superior performance to serve the statutory purpose of enabling plaintiffs to secure legal assistance.[171]

---

161.   465 U.S. 886 (1984).

168.   478 U.S. 546 (1986).

171.   *Id.* at 565–66.

In its most recent discussion of the issue, in *City of Burlington v. Dague*,[172] the Supreme Court ruled that the lodestar may never be adjusted upward to compensate for the contingent risk of loss. At the outset, the Court reasoned that an enhancement for contingency "would likely duplicate in substantial part factors already subsumed in the lodestar." Because the risk of loss in any particular case depends in substantial part upon the difficulty of successfully establishing the merits, the Court held that the lodestar already provides adequate compensation by including a higher number of hours expended as required by the difficulty of the litigation or a higher hourly rate assigned to the attorney qualified to handle the matter.

Moreover, the *Dague* Court feared that enhancing the lodestar award for contingency would "provide attorneys with the same incentive to bring relatively meritless claims as relatively meritorious ones." By alleviating the risk of loss through a contingency enhancement, the attorney would be encouraged to pursue weak claims in the hope of scoring victory in a lucky case and then receiving an adjustment of the lodestar sufficient to compensate for defeat in other cases. The Court also reasoned that paying an attorney a contingency enhancement allows the attorney to "pool[ ] the risks presented by his various cases: cases that turn out to be successful pay for the time he gambled on those that did not." The Court thus viewed payment of a premium for risk of loss as effectively and inappropriately compensating the attorney for lost cases. Finally, the Court believed that contingency enhancements "would make the setting of fees more complex and arbitrary, hence more unpredictable, and hence more litigable."

In light of these decisions, the Supreme Court apparently has adopted the lodestar, without upward adjustments or multipliers,[181] as the sole measure of attorney's fees under fee-shifting statutes. Although the Court has declined to foreclose the possibility of a justifiable enhancement in a "rare" or "exceptional" case, the Court has never found such a case and probably never will.

* Downward Adjustment Based Upon Degree of Success

Although the Supreme Court apparently has closed the door on upward adjustments of the lodestar, the Court emphatically has retained the option of adjusting the fee downward to reflect a plaintiff's limited success. Indeed, the Court has said that the degree of success obtained is "the most critical factor" in determining the reasonableness of a fee award.[184] Unfortunately, the Court has provided little guidance on when less than perfect success triggers an adjustment or on how partial success should affect the

---

172. [505 U.S. 557] (1992).

181. * * * [T]here is one significant exception of sorts to the Supreme Court's general censure of upward adjustments to the lodestar. With respect to fee-shifting against non-governmental entities, the Court has approved compensation to the party for the delay between the date on which legal services are performed and the ultimate receipt of a fee award. An upward adjustment of the lodestar is one of several possible mechanisms for compensating for the delay in payment.

184. Farrar v. Hobby, [506 U.S. 103, 114] (1992); Hensley v. Eckerhart, 461 U.S. 424, 436 (1983).

lodestar figure. The Court has sent mixed messages on the when and the how of a limited success adjustment.

In *Hensley v. Eckerhart*,[186] the Supreme Court ruled that "[w]here a plaintiff has obtained excellent results, his attorney should recover a fully compensatory fee," and further stated that "the fee award should not be reduced simply because the plaintiff failed to prevail on every contention raised in the lawsuit." Moreover, the Court firmly resisted reduction of the lodestar according to a mathematical ratio that compares the number of issues upon which the plaintiff actually prevailed with the total number of issues in the case. Success in a case is not a mathematical, but rather a qualitative question, requiring an evaluation of not only the number of claims or issues but also the nature and significance of the relief.

In *City of Riverside v. Rivera*,[189] the Court rejected the theory that the amount of attorney's fees awarded must be directly proportionate to the amount of monetary damages obtained on the merits. The plaintiffs, who prevailed in a civil rights action against the city and police officers for using excessive force in making arrests, were awarded $33,350 in compensatory and punitive damages. The plaintiffs sought and were awarded $245,456.25 in attorney's fees—some seven times the amount of damages awarded. The Supreme Court affirmed the fee award. The plurality opinion recognized that money damages cannot be the only measure of success in litigation, especially in civil rights cases, because "a civil rights plaintiff seeks to vindicate important civil and constitutional rights that cannot be valued solely in monetary terms." * * *

However, when the sole purpose of a lawsuit is indeed to obtain damages, the Supreme Court has directed some comparison between the amount of damages awarded and the amount of attorney's fees sought. In *Farrar v. Hobby*,[197] the plaintiff sought $17 million in compensatory damages against Texas public officials for allegedly illegal actions in closing a private school operated by plaintiff and his son. The jury concluded that one state official had deprived plaintiff of a civil right, apparently by urging an investigation of the school in a press release, participating in an inspection of the school, and attending a hearing that led to a temporary injunction against the school, but that this conduct did not proximately cause any damages suffered by plaintiff. Ultimately, the district court awarded nominal damages of one dollar.

Under those circumstances, where the sole relief sought was damages and the recovery was purely nominal, the Court ruled that "the only reasonable fee is ... no fee at all." The *Farrar* ruling may be limited, however, to cases in which money is the only aim and thus the only possible measure of success. Justice O'Connor, whose vote was necessary to form a Court majority, stated in a concurrence that the relevant indicia of success involves not only the extent of relief, but also "the significance of the legal issue on which the plaintiff prevailed, and the public purpose

---

186. 461 U.S. 424 (1983).   **197.** [506 U.S. 103] (1992).
189. 477 U.S. 561 (1986).

served." However, Justice O'Connor found no public purpose served by the litigation in that particular case.

Thus, while the lodestar is the presumptive measure of the reasonable fee, at some unspecified breaking point a plaintiff's success may fall to a level where a reduction of the overall fee is appropriate. Plainly, a plaintiff need not aspire to perfection to avoid a reduction; an "excellent result" is sufficient to assure a full fee recovery. On the other end of the spectrum, when the plaintiff has attained a mere technical victory without corresponding public benefit, the fee applicant may expect a significant reduction or total disallowance of the fee. In between, however, there would seem to be a wide range of possible outcomes, ranging from cases of rather substantial success on most claims or issues to cases of distinctly "partial or limited success." Determining the point at which full compensation ceases to be reasonable when mixed results are achieved in a case and what reduction should be assessed against the lodestar under those circumstances has been left to the largely unfettered discretion of the district court.

———

3. FREEDOM OF INFORMATION ACT

5 United States Code § 552(a)(4)(E)

(E) The court may assess against the United States reasonable attorney fees and other litigation costs reasonably incurred in any case under this section in which the complainant has substantially prevailed.

———

Church of Scientology v. Harris

United States Court of Appeals for the District of Columbia Circuit.
653 F.2d 584 (D.C.Cir. 1981).

■ MacKINNON, CIRCUIT JUDGE:

The Church of Scientology of California ("Scientology") appeals from an opinion and order of the district court which denied its request for an award of attorney's fees and litigation costs under section 552(a)(4)(E) of the Freedom of Information Act ("FOIA"), 5 U.S.C. § 552(a)(4)(E). The district court concluded that Scientology was not *eligible* for such an award because it had not "substantially prevailed" within the meaning of that section. We find that Scientology did substantially prevail and direct the district court on remand to determine whether Scientology is *entitled* to the fees and costs it seeks.

I.

By letters dated December 3 and December 19, 1974, Scientology made a formal request under FOIA for all records in the possession of the

Department of Health, Education, and Welfare ("HEW") relating to the Church of Scientology or its founder, L. Ron Hubbard. HEW responded on December 30, 1974 that "[n]o materials pertinent to your request could be located in the Department's Central Files Section." Scientology subsequently submitted a supplemental request on November 5, 1975, which provided additional names under which relevant files might be located, and which noted that "[t]here exists within the organizational structure of DHEW several major offices and components thereof, apparently now encompassed by the records examination undertaken by your Department in compliance with my earlier request(s)." HEW replied on December 2, 1975 that "[c]opies of your request were circulated to components of the Department except for the Food and Drug Administration and the Alcohol, Drug Abuse, and Mental Health Administration as requested in your letter." HEW stated that three card references to Scientology had been found in the files of the Office of Investigations and Security, but asserted that these references were exempt from disclosure. HEW also explicitly declared that "[n]o other component of the Department was able to locate any records pertaining to the Church of Scientology or any of the organizations listed in your request."

Scientology filed an administrative appeal. In its final agency action, by a letter dated February 17, 1976, HEW reversed in part the initial denial of the three card references, and disclosed portions thereof. HEW also explained that these cards referred to documents which originated in other agencies—the FBI, the Civil Service Commission, and the FDA—and stated that the request for these documents had been transmitted to the originating agencies.

Dissatisfied with this result, Scientology filed a complaint under FOIA in the district court on June 9, 1976 seeking *de novo* review of HEW's actions. On August 4, 1976, Scientology served HEW with its first set of interrogatories. In its answers to interrogatories, HEW revealed for the first time that an unspecified number of additional documents encompassed by Scientology's request existed in the files of HEW's Office of General Counsel. These documents were said to concern "litigation and other relationships between HEW and the Church of Scientology or its affiliates", and to be exempt from disclosure under 5 U.S.C. § 552(b)(5). The only explanation given for withholding the documents was that

> Ms. Sisk [an attorney in the OGC] knew that all records in the division's files were either documents of which Joel Kreiner [a Scientology attorney] had copies ... documents subject to the attorney-client privilege and exempt from disclosure under the Freedom of Information Act ... or duplicates of documents from the files of the Food and Drug Administration.

In an effort to obtain further information, Scientology noticed and took the deposition of Ms. Joanne Sisk, who was the individual identified in HEW's answers to interrogatories as having searched the Office of General Counsel's files in response to Scientology's FOIA request. At the deposition, Ms. Sisk confessed that she had not conducted an actual search of the

Office of General Counsel's files until around the time that her deposition had been noticed, and that HEW's administrative response to Scientology's FOIA request and HEW's answers to interrogatories had not been based upon an actual search of the files but upon an assumption as to their contents. An internal HEW memorandum also disclosed that Ms. Sisk had been aware that the Office of General Counsel's files contained documents responsive to Scientology's FOIA requests at the time the requests were being processed administratively.

The belated search of the files of the Office of General Counsel produced approximately 230 responsive documents. Ms. Sisk's deposition resulted in the release of 116 documents to Scientology, all but eight of which were copies of envelopes, transmittal memos, or telephone message slips. It also resulted in the preparation of a *Vaughn* index[6] for the remaining documents which were claimed to be exempt from disclosure. On February 25, 1977, Scientology renounced its claims to 44 of the withheld documents. In June, 1977, HEW released 31 of the withheld documents following a letter by Attorney General Bell to the heads of all federal agencies informing them of new policies concerning FOIA.[7] Thus, at the time the district court ruled on the parties' cross-motions for summary judgment on February 28, 1978, 47 documents remained in dispute. The district court granted HEW's motion for summary judgment as to 45 of the documents, ordered partial disclosure of 2 documents, and directed HEW to provide additional information on three other documents.

On April 25, 1979, Scientology petitioned the district court for an award of attorney fees and litigation costs pursuant to section 552(a)(4)(E) of FOIA. The district court denied the motion on December 19, 1979. After reviewing the history of the litigation, the district court stated:

> In summary, the Church obtained release of 150 documents in litigation, but of this number, 108 documents were copies of envelopes, transmittal slips and the like, and 31 others were released as a result of Attorney General Bell's letter. The Church received just fourteen documents comprising 34 pages, excluding envelopes and transmittal slips, as a result of its FOIA suit.
>
> * * *
>
> In this case, plaintiff only obtained through the discovery process an insubstantial part of what was sought. While the Court does not accept the defendants' argument that the plaintiff must win a majority of what is at stake in order to substantially prevail for purposes of receiving attorney's fees, the Church was largely unsuccessful in its

---

6. *See Vaughn v. Rosen,* 484 F.2d 820 (D.C.Cir.1973), cert. denied, 415 U.S. 977 (1974). [*See also supra* Chapter III.D, which includes the *Vaughn* opinion.]

7. In this letter, the Attorney General stated that the government should not withhold documents unless it is important to the public interest to do so, even if there is some arguable legal basis for the withholding. He also declared that in order to implement this policy, the Justice Department will defend FOIA suits only when disclosure is demonstrably harmful, even if the documents technically fall within the exemptions in the Act.

efforts to obtain release of the withheld material. The uncovering of documents, unaccompanied by any substantial release, either voluntarily or by court order, is insufficient to demonstrate in this case that the plaintiff has substantially prevailed within the meaning of 5 U.S.C. § 552(a)(4)(E).

The failure to search files completely on receiving the initial FOIA request and to disclose the existence of the documents once they were discovered is inexcusable. This failure required the Church to resort to two sets of interrogatories and a deposition. However, HEW's actions are mitigated here by the existence of considerable other FOIA litigation by the Church, which led the agency to assume reasonably that the documents were duplicates of those available to the Church in other suits. Once defendants located this material in the Office of General Counsel, through plaintiff's discovery efforts, some material was released and a *Vaughn* index was prepared for the rest. Under these circumstances, HEW's delay in disclosing the existence of the documents, while regrettable, does not of itself justify an award of attorney's fees.

The Court recognizes that the "fundamental purpose of Section 552(a)(4)(E) is to facilitate citizen access to the courts to vindicate their statutory rights," but for that purpose to have any meaning, the statutory prerequisite that the plaintiff substantially prevail in the case must first exist. Since the plaintiff has not substantially prevailed, there is no need to reach the question whether an exercise of the Court's discretion to award reasonable attorney's fees and expenses is appropriate.

Scientology appealed.

II.

As the district court recognized, analysis of a section 552(a)(4)(E) motion for fees and costs requires that two questions be asked and answered. 1) is the plaintiff "eligible" for such an award, and if so, 2) is it "entitled" to such an award?

A FOIA plaintiff is eligible for a section 552(a)(4)(E) award if it has "substantially prevailed". Our cases have established that this is largely a question of causation—did the institution and prosecution of the litigation cause the agency to release the documents obtained during the pendency of the litigation? *See e. g., Cox* [*v. United States Department of Justice*], [601 F.2d 1 (D.C.Cir.1979)]; *Nationwide Building Maintenance, Inc. v. Sampson,* 559 F.2d 704 (D.C.Cir.1977). As we observed in *Cox* :

It is true that a court order compelling disclosure of information is not a condition precedent to an award of fees, but it is equally true that an allegedly prevailing complainant must assert something more than post hoc, ergo propter hoc. Instead, the party seeking such fees in the absence of a court order must show that prosecution of the action could reasonably be regarded as necessary to obtain the information, and that a causal nexus exists between that action and the agency's surrender of the information. Whether a party has made such a showing in a particular case is a factual determination that is within the province of the district court to resolve. In making this determination, it is appropriate for the district court to consider, *inter alia* whether the agency, upon actual and reasonable notice of the request, made a good faith effort to search out material and to pass on whether it should be disclosed. We have elsewhere had occasion to note both the plethora of Freedom of Information Act cases pending before federal agencies at any given time, and the time-consuming nature of the search and decision process. If rather than the threat of an adverse court order either a lack of actual notice of a request or an unavoidable delay accompanied by due diligence in the administrative processes was the actual reason for the agency's failure to respond to a request, then it cannot be said that the complainant substantially prevailed in his suit.

Cox, supra, 601 F.2d at 6.

The history of the instant litigation makes clear that Scientology substantially prevailed, for it shows not only that the institution and prosecution of this case was "necessary" to obtain the 150 documents ultimately released by HEW but also that a powerful "causal nexus" exists between the litigation and HEW's surrender of these documents. Throughout the administrative processing of Scientology's FOIA request, HEW maintained that only three card references and three documents fell within the scope of the request. After Scientology filed suit and began discovery, HEW disclosed that over 200 responsive documents existed in the files of the General Counsel, and during the course of the litigation released approximately two-thirds of those documents. There is absolutely no indication in the record that HEW would have actually searched the General Counsel's files or released any of the contents thereof in the absence of this litigation. This is clearly not a case where the agency, "upon actual and reasonable notice, made a good faith effort to search out material and to pass on whether it should be disclosed." *Cox, supra,* 601 F.2d at 6. On the contrary, it is a case in which the agency, upon actual and reasonable notice, decided to act upon an assumption as to the nature of certain material and was then obliged to release most of that material when the light of litigation exposed the error of its assumption. That, in our opinion, is the critical point—*but for the institution and prosecution of this suit, the documents ultimately obtained by Scientology would never have been identified and therefore would never have been released.* Under these circumstances, it is clear that the suit was necessary and causally linked to the release of the documents obtained.

The district court nevertheless found that Scientology had not substantially prevailed because it "only obtained through the discovery process an insubstantial part of what was sought" and "was largely unsuccessful in its efforts to obtain release of the withheld material". The basis for these comments appears to be the district court's conclusion that Scientology received "just fourteen documents" as a result of its suit. The premises underlying this conclusion in turn appear to be twofold: 1) the court's ruling that the 31 documents released in June, 1978 should be excluded from the tally of documents obtained, and 2) the court's subjective belief that the 108 envelopes and transmittal slips were too insignificant to be included in that tally. We think both of these premises are erroneous.

The district court discounted the 31 documents released in June 1978 because it found that they "were released as a result of Attorney General Bell's letter" and not as a result of the litigation. We accept this finding, to the extent that it acknowledges that the Attorney General's letter in the last analysis precipitated release of the documents and was *a* cause of their release. The initiation and prosecution of this litigation, however, was in our opinion the direct cause of their disclosure, for absent this litigation, following the unsuccessful administrative request, the General Counsel's files would never have been searched, the 31 documents would never have been identified as falling within the scope of Scientology's FOIA request, and the documents would never have been evaluated to determine whether they should or could be released under the guidelines set forth in the Attorney General's letter. The timing of the Attorney General's letter does not eliminate the fact that if the litigation had never been brought the documents would never have been disclosed. It was the litigation that *produced* the 31 documents, not the letter.

The government argues that release of these 31 documents should be discounted because to hold otherwise would "punish" HEW for making disclosures more liberal than commanded by FOIA. We disagree. To the extent that HEW is "punished", it is not because the agency released documents whose disclosure FOIA did not require, but because the agency failed to comply with its basic duty to search its files in response to a proper request. Indeed, we think we might be punishing Scientology if we discounted documents whose disclosure, in a very important and fundamental sense, was brought about only as a result of its lawsuit, and only after this lawsuit forced HEW to comply with the requirements of the Act.

We also think that there is no reason in law or logic to discount the significance of the 108 envelopes and transmittal slips in determining whether Scientology substantially prevailed. FOIA mandates that an agency disclose all identifiable agency "records" in response to a proper FOIA request unless the documents fall within one of the Act's specific exemptions, See 5 U.S.C. §§ 552(a)(3), (B). It is not contended that the envelopes and buck slips are not "records" within the meaning of the Act, nor that they are exempt or even arguably exempt from disclosure. Since disclosure of the envelopes and buck slips was required by FOIA, nothing in the Act in general, nor in section 552(a)(4)(E) in particular, suggests that their disclosure should be ignored or discounted in evaluating the relative success of appellant in this litigation. * * *

In sum, both the 31 documents released in June, 1978 and the 108 envelopes and transmittal slips must be recognized by the district court as having been released as a result of the litigation in determining whether

Scientology substantially prevailed. When such circumstances are considered, we find that the litigation caused the release of 150 documents, approximately two thirds of the documents at issue. Given these facts, there can be no doubt that Scientology prevailed in its suit, and prevailed to a substantial degree. Scientology is thus eligible to apply for an award of attorney's fees and litigation costs under section 552(a)(4)(E).

III.

A plaintiff, however, is not automatically "entitled" to an award under section 552(a)(4)(E) merely because it is eligible for such an award. Rather, the decision as to whether to award fees and costs to an eligible party rests in the sound discretion of the district court. Our decisions have touched upon some of the factors the district courts should consider in exercising their discretion, and these include (1) the benefit to the public if any, derived from the case; (2) the commercial benefit to the plaintiff; (3) the nature of the plaintiff's interest in the records sought; and (4) whether the government's withholding of the records had a reasonable basis of law. We have also reminded the district courts that, in determining whether an eligible plaintiff is entitled to an award, they must

> always keep in mind the basic policy of the FOIA to encourage the maximum feasible public access to government information and the fundamental purpose of section 552(a)(4)(E) to facilitate citizen access to the courts to vindicate their statutory rights. Each of the particular factors ... must be evaluated in light of these fundamental legislative policies. *The touchstone of a court's discretionary decision under section 552(a)(4)(E) must be whether an award of attorney's fees is necessary to implement the FOIA.*

Nationwide Building Maintenance, Inc., supra, 559 F.2d at 715 (emphasis added).

Because the district court in this case determined that Scientology had not substantially prevailed and thus was not eligible for an award of fees and costs under section 552(a)(4)(E), it did not reach the question whether Scientology was *entitled* to such an award. Scientology nevertheless requests that we direct the district court to award it fees and costs, on the grounds that the district court's refusal to do so on remand would constitute a gross abuse of discretion in light of HEW's "recalcitrant and obdurate conduct, both at the administrative level and during the course of this litigation".

We agree that the propriety of the government's conduct is an important factor to be considered in determining Scientology's entitlement to the award it seeks. We also believe, however, that we are not presently in a position to pass on what would or would not constitute an abuse of discretion given the facts of this case. The propriety of the government's conduct is but one variable in the section 552(a)(4)(E) equation, and a section 552(a)(4)(E) award must be based upon a reasoned consideration of "all relevant factors". *Nationwide Building Maintenance, Inc., supra,* 559 F.2d at 705; *see also id.* at 714 (district court must consider all factors, and must be careful not to give any particular factor dispositive weight). The record before us is simply insufficient for us to evaluate all the relevant factors, especially since it does not reveal the nature, content or significance of the documents released to Scientology. More importantly, however,

> in this area where, as we have continually emphasized, Congress has relied on the broad discretion of the courts, it is better to have that discretion exercised by the court which has been the most intimately associated with the case.

Id. at 716. Accordingly, we remand the case to the district court for consideration of whether Scientology is entitled to an award under section 552(a)(4)(E) and if so to determine the amount thereof.

Reversed and remanded.

————

Notes and Questions

Under the Freedom of Information Act (FOIA), a successful litigant who petitions for an award of attorney's fees must demonstrate not only *eligibility* for, but also *entitlement* to, a fee. Consider the requirements for each of these separate showings:

1. In terms of *eligibility,* what is required for a fee petitioner under FOIA? How must the fee petitioner demonstrate that he or she (or it) has "substantially" prevailed within the meaning of the statute? How does the court analyze this eligibility question in *Church of Scientology v. Harris*? What is the nature of the "causation" question—what action must have caused what result? What is the effect in terms of causation of the government's initial failure in this case to properly search the records? What about the Attorney General's subsequent adoption of a new liberal policy, encouraging disclosure even when not required by the FOIA?

Note that the statute requires that a FOIA fee petitioner not merely have prevailed, but have *substantially* prevailed. Thus, the court must also consider the degree of success in determining whether a party is eligible for a fee award. Under most other fee-shifting statutes, such as we've seen with Title VII of the Civil Rights Act of 1964, the pertinent question on eligibility is whether a party has succeeded on any one of his or her claims for relief. As long as the plaintiff has succeeded on some significant issue, he or she is eligible for a fee award even if most of the claims proved unsuccessful. By contrast, under FOIA, the eligibility question is whether that party has substantially prevailed in the case as a whole.

As the Court of Appeals for the District of Columbia Circuit has explained, the governing standard in FOIA cases is whether the plaintiff has "substantially prevailed as to his *overall* request." *Weisberg v. Department of Justice,* 745 F.2d 1476, 1497 (D.C.Cir. 1984). In other words, in FOIA cases, the court must consider the plaintiff's degree of success on the merits at the outset of the fee litigation to determine eligibility, as well as later giving consideration to the extent of success in the measurement of the fee award. Thus, as the court later explained in *Oil, Chemical & Atomic Workers Int'l Union v. Department of Energy,* 288 F.3d 452, 455 (D.C. Cir. 2002) "a FOIA plaintiff may seek thousands of documents but wind up with a judgment providing only a handful of insignificant documents," such that "[o]ne might say this plaintiff was a prevailing party, but nevertheless not say that the plaintiff substantially prevailed." *See also Union of Needletrades, Industrial & Textile Employees v. U.S. Immigration & Naturalization Serv.,* 336 F.3d 200, 208 (2d Cir. 2003) (noting, in dictum, that analysis suggests that "the term 'substantially' as used in FOIA's fee-shifting provision alters the *amount* or *degree* of recovery necessary to achieve fees") (emphasis in original). *See generally* Gregory C. Sisk, *A Primer on Awards of Attorney's Fees Against the Federal Government,* 25 Ariz. St. L.J. 733, 773 (1993).

In *Oil, Chemical & Atomic Workers Int'l Union v. Department of Energy,* 288 F.3d 452 (D.C. Cir. 2002), the D.C. Circuit extended to the FOIA context the limitation on eligibility for attorney's fee awards articulated by the Supreme Court in *Buckhannon Board & Care Home, Inc. v. West Virginia Dept. of Health & Human Resources,* 532 U.S. 598 (2001). In *Buckhannon,* the Supreme Court held that, to qualify as a prevailing party, the party must obtain some judicial approval of the outcome, through either a judgment on the merits or a settlement enforceable by the court through a consent decree. *Id.* at 603–05. The Court thus rejected the catalyst theory, which had characterized a plaintiff as prevailing if the lawsuit caused a voluntary change in the defendant's conduct. *Id.* Applying the *Buckhannon* analysis to a request for fees in a FOIA case, the D.C. Circuit in *Oil, Chemical & Atomic Workers* overturned prior court precedent following the "catalyst theory", which had permitted attorney's fees under FOIA if the litigation substantially caused requested documents to be released by the government. *Oil, Chemical & Atomic Workers,* 288 F.3d at 454–57. Henceforth, in FOIA cases as well, a plaintiff may become eligible for a fee award only if some relief is granted by a court. *Id.* at 457. The court of appeals then ruled that the FOIA-requestor was not a prevailing party, because the case had been settled by a stipulation that the union had received enough documents from the agency to forego continuation of the FOIA suit. *Id.* at 457–59. Although the stipulation had been endorsed by the district court, the D.C. Circuit held that it was not the equivalent of a court-ordered settlement because it was not a decision on the merits and did not meaningfully alter the legal relationship of the parties or leave the court with anything to oversee. *Id.* A dissenting judge, while agreeing that the Supreme Court's *Buckhannon* decision requires a judicially-sanctioned change in the legal relationship between the parties, questioned the majority's conclusion that only a judgment on the merits or a consent decree embodying a settlement could confer prevailing party status, and further argued that the court-endorsed stipulation provided the necessary judicial imprimatur, akin to a consent decree, so as to make the union eligible for a fee award under FOIA. *Id.* at 459–66 (Rogers, J., dissenting). Subsequently, the Second Circuit followed the D.C. Circuit's lead on this question. *See, e.g., Union of Needletrades, Industrial & Textile*

Employees v. U.S. Immigration & Naturalization Serv., 336 F.3d 200, 205–06 (2d Cir. 2003) (holding, with citation to *Oil, Chemical & Atomic Workers*, that while the plaintiff "may have accomplished the objective it sought to achieve by initiating this FOIA action, its failure to secure either a judgment on the merits or a court-ordered consent decree renders it ineligible for an award of attorney's fees under *Buckhannon*").

2. What additional showing must a fee petitioner make under FOIA to move beyond eligibility and also establish *entitlement*? What additional factors are to be considered?

Under these entitlement factors, with the emphasis upon whether the litigation has produced a public benefit, genuine scholars and journalists generally are accorded preferential treatment under the FOIA and ordinarily will be awarded attorney's fees when they substantially prevail—although entitlement is not automatic even for such preferred requesters. *Tax Analysts v. United States Dept. of Justice*, 965 F.2d 1092, 1096 (D.C.Cir. 1992). By contrast, "when a litigant seeks disclosure for a commercial benefit or out of other personal motives, an award of attorney's fees is generally inappropriate." *Id.* at 1095. The Freedom of Information Act "was fundamentally designed to inform the public and not to benefit private litigants," a purpose that must be weighed in determining entitlement to a fee award. *Cuneo v. Rumsfeld*, 553 F.2d 1360, 1368 (D.C.Cir. 1977). However, despite the court's statement in *Church of Scientology* that the entitlement question should be considered in light of the basic policy of FOIA of encouraging the right of public access to government information, one commentary has found that the burdens of establishing both eligibility and entitlement have meant that a successful petition for a fee award under FOIA is "the exception, not the rule." Alfred C. Aman, Jr. & William T. Mayton, *Administrative Law* 658 (2d ed., 2001). *See generally* Sisk, *supra*, at 774–75.

One judge on the D.C. Circuit has urged the court to take another look at whether to continue to apply the four-criteria test for entitlement to an award of fees under FOIA. *Burka v. United States Dept. of Health & Human Services*, 142 F.3d 1286 (D.C.Cir. 1998) (Randolph, J., concurring). Judge Randolph observed that the four criteria are not found in the actual text of the statute and that certain factors, such as the public benefit of the FOIA suit, cannot be applied objectively. *Id.* at 1293–94. Accordingly, he would eliminate the requirement that a successful FOIA plaintiff make any additional showing of entitlement to fees based upon the public interest. *Id.* Judge Wald, however, filed a special concurrence in *Burka* to defend the entitlement criteria, including the evaluation of whether any public benefit arose from the plaintiff's FOIA request. *Id.* at 1292 (Wald, J., concurring specially). She stated that the multi-factor entitlement test, although not included in the text of the statute, is "deeply rooted in the legislative history of FOIA." *Id.* at 1293. Moreover, she argued, parties who have a sufficient private motivation, such as a commercial interest, in obtaining government information do not need the additional incentive of recovering fees. Therefore, fees should be reserved to the party who acts, in effect, as a private attorney general to seek information under FOIA for a public purpose. *Id.*

Judge Randolph's doubts about the validity of the four-factor entitlement test were echoed in an even more recent D.C. Circuit decision, which rejected extension of those entitlement criteria to requests for awards of attorney's fees to parties prevailing in Privacy Act (5 U.S.C. § 552a) litigation regarding government files containing personal information. *Blazy v. Tenet,* 194 F.3d 90, 97 (D.C.Cir. 1999). The *Blazy* opinion quoted Judge Randolph's *Burka* concurrence and said that "Judge Randolph's arguments [against demanding that the petitioner show a public benefit to the litigation] have even greater force with respect to claims arising under the Privacy Act, because of the undisputedly private nature of these claims." *Id.*

However, the *Blazy* decision did not purport to overturn the application of these entitlement factors in the FOIA context and the courts of appeals continue to apply the four-criteria standard to FOIA fee applications. *See, e.g., Judicial Watch, Inc. v. U.S. Dept. of Commerce,* 470 F.3d 363, 369 (D.C. Cir. 2006); *GMRI, Inc. v. Equal Employment Opportunity Comm'n,* 149 F.3d 449, 452 (6th Cir. 1998); *Gowan v. United States Dept. of Air Force,* 148 F.3d 1182, 1195 (10th Cir. 1998) (upholding four-factor entitlement test for both FOIA and Privacy Act fee claims); *Klamath Water Users Protective Ass'n v. United States Dept. of Interior,* 18 Fed. Appx. 473, 474 (9th Cir. 2001) (in unpublished decision, applying four-factor test in FOIA case).

---

4. EQUAL ACCESS TO JUSTICE ACT

28 United States Code § 2412

(a)(1) Except as otherwise specifically provided by statute, a judgment for costs, as enumerated in section 1920 of this title, but not including the fees and expenses of attorneys, may be awarded to the prevailing party in any civil action brought by or against the United States or any agency or any official of the United States acting in his or her official capacity in any court having jurisdiction of such action. A judgment for costs when taxed against the United States shall, in an amount established by statute, court rule, or order, be limited to reimbursing in whole or in part the prevailing party for the costs incurred by such party in the litigation.

(2) A judgment for costs, when awarded in favor of the United States in an action brought by the United States, may include an amount equal to the filing fee prescribed under section 1914(a) of this title. The preceding sentence shall not be construed as requiring the United States to pay any filing fee.

(b) Unless expressly prohibited by statute, a court may award reasonable fees and expenses of attorneys, in addition to the costs which may be awarded pursuant to subsection (a), to the prevailing party in any civil action brought by or against the United States or any agency or any official of the United States acting in his or her official capacity in any court having jurisdiction of such action. The United States shall be liable for such fees and expenses to the same extent that any other party would be liable under the common law or under the terms of any statute which specifically provides for such an award.

(c)(1) Any judgment against the United States or any agency and any official of the United States acting in his or her official capacity for costs pursuant to subsection (a) shall be paid as provided in sections 2414 and 2517 of this title and shall be in addition to any relief provided in the judgment.

(2) Any judgment against the United States or any agency and any official of the United States acting in his or her official capacity for fees and expenses of attorneys pursuant to subsection (b) shall be paid as provided in sections 2414 and 2517 of this title, except that if the basis for the award is a finding that the United States acted in bad faith, then the award shall be paid by any agency found to have acted in bad faith and shall be in addition to any relief provided in the judgment.

(d)(1)(A) Except as otherwise specifically provided by statute, a court shall award to a prevailing party other than the United States fees and other expenses, in addition to any costs awarded pursuant to subsection (a), incurred by that party in any civil action (other than cases sounding in tort), including proceedings for judicial review of agency action, brought by or against the United States in any court having jurisdiction of that action, unless the court finds that the position of the United States was substantially justified or that special circumstances make an award unjust.

(B) A party seeking an award of fees and other expenses shall, within thirty days of final judgment in the action, submit to the court an application for fees and other expenses which shows that the party is a prevailing party and is eligible to receive an award under this subsection, and the amount sought, including an itemized statement from any attorney or expert witness representing or appearing in behalf of the party stating the actual time expended and the rate at which fees and other expenses are computed. The party shall also allege that the position of the United States was not substantially justified. Whether or not the position of the United States was substantially justified shall be determined on the basis of the record (including the record with respect to the action or failure to act by the agency upon which the civil action is based) which is made in the civil action for which fees and other expenses are sought.

(C) The court, in its discretion, may reduce the amount to be awarded pursuant to this subsection, or deny an award, to the extent that the prevailing party during the course of the proceedings engaged in conduct which unduly and unreasonably protracted the final resolution of the matter in controversy.

(D) If, in a civil action brought by the United States or a proceeding for judicial review of an adversary adjudication described in section

504(a)(4) of title 5, the demand by the United States is substantially in excess of the judgment finally obtained by the United States and is unreasonable when compared with such judgment, under the facts and circumstances of the case, the court shall award to the party the fees and other expenses related to defending against the excessive demand, unless the party has committed a willful violation of law or otherwise acted in bad faith, or special circumstances make an award unjust. Fees and expenses awarded under this subparagraph shall be paid only as a consequence of appropriations provided in advance.

(2) For the purposes of this subsection—

(A) "fees and other expenses" includes the reasonable expenses of expert witnesses, the reasonable cost of any study, analysis, engineering report, test, or project which is found by the court to be necessary for the preparation of the party's case, and reasonable attorney fees (The amount of fees awarded under this subsection shall be based upon prevailing market rates for the kind and quality of the services furnished, except that (i) no expert witness shall be compensated at a rate in excess of the highest rate of compensation for expert witnesses paid by the United States; and (ii) attorney fees shall not be awarded in excess of $125 per hour unless the court determines that an increase in the cost of living or a special factor, such as the limited availability of qualified attorneys for the proceedings involved, justifies a higher fee.);

(B) "party" means (i) an individual whose net worth did not exceed $2,000,000 at the time the civil action was filed, or (ii) any owner of an unincorporated business, or any partnership, corporation, association, unit of local government, or organization, the net worth of which did not exceed $7,000,000 at the time the civil action was filed, and which had not more than 500 employees at the time the civil action was filed; except that an organization described in section 501(c)(3) of the Internal Revenue Code of 1986 (26 U.S.C. 501(c)(3)) exempt from taxation under section 501(a) of such Code, or a cooperative association as defined in section 15(a) of the Agricultural Marketing Act (12 U.S.C. 1141j(a)), may be a party regardless of the net worth of such organization or cooperative association or for purposes of subsection (d)(1)(D), a small entity as defined in section 601 of Title 5;

(C) "United States" includes any agency and any official of the United States acting in his or her official capacity;

(D) "position of the United States" means, in addition to the position taken by the United States in the civil action, the action or failure to act by the agency upon which the civil action is based; except that fees and expenses may not be awarded to a party for any portion of the litigation in which the party has unreasonably protracted the proceedings;

(E) "civil action brought by or against the United States" includes an appeal by a party, other than the United States, from a decision of a contracting officer rendered pursuant to a disputes clause in a contract with the Government or pursuant to the Contract Disputes Act of 1978;

(F) "court" includes the United States Court of Federal Claims and the United States Court of Appeals for Veterans Claims;

(G) "final judgment" means a judgment that is final and not appealable, and includes an order of settlement;

(H) "prevailing party", in the case of eminent domain proceedings, means a party who obtains a final judgment (other than by settlement), exclusive of interest, the amount of which is at least as close to the highest valuation of the property involved that is attested to at trial on behalf of the property owner as it is to the highest valuation of the property involved that is attested to at trial on behalf of the Government; and

(I) "demand" means the express demand of the United States which led to the adversary adjudication, but shall not include a recitation of the maximum statutory penalty (i) in the complaint, or (ii) elsewhere when accompanied by an express demand for a lesser amount.

(3) In awarding fees and other expenses under this subsection to a prevailing party in any action for judicial review of an adversary adjudication, as defined in subsection (b)(1)(C) of section 504 of title 5, United States Code, or an adversary adjudication subject to the Contract Disputes Act of 1978, the court shall include in that award fees and other expenses to the same extent authorized in subsection (a) of such section, unless the court finds that during such adversary adjudication the position of the United States was substantially justified, or that special circumstances make an award unjust.

(4) Fees and other expenses awarded under this subsection to a party shall be paid by any agency over which the party prevails from any funds made available to the agency by appropriation or otherwise.

(e) The provisions of this section shall not apply to any costs, fees, and other expenses in connection with any proceeding to which section 7430 of the Internal Revenue Code of 1986 applies (determined without regard to subsections (b) and (f) of such section). Nothing in the preceding sentence shall prevent the awarding under subsection (a) of section 2412 of title 28, United States Code, of costs enumerated in section 1920 of such title (as in effect on October 1, 1981).

(f) If the United States appeals an award of costs or fees and other expenses made against the United States under this section and the award is affirmed in whole or in part, interest shall be paid on the amount of the award as affirmed. Such interest shall be computed at the rate determined under section 1961(a) of this title, and shall run from the date of the award through the day before the date of the mandate of affirmance.

———

Gregory C. Sisk, The Essentials of the Equal Access to Justice Act: Court Awards of Attorney's Fees for Unreasonable Government Conduct (Part One)

55 Louisiana Law Review 217, 220, 223–226 (1994).

In 1980, Congress embarked upon an experiment in "curbing excessive regulation and the unreasonable exercise of Government authority" by directing that attorney's fees be awarded in favor of private parties who resist unjustifiable government conduct in litigation.[1] The Equal Access to Justice Act (EAJA)[2] expanded the federal government's liability for awards of attorney's fees beyond the traditional realms of civil rights laws and open government laws, and broadly waived the sovereign immunity of the United States with respect to payment of attorney's fees in any civil action in which the position of the federal government is found to be without substantial justification. While Congress had previously enacted attorney's fee award statutes to encourage private enforcement of important statutory policies, the EAJA blazed a new path by adopting fee-shifting as an instrument to monitor government regulation and to deter unjustifiable government policies and enforcement actions.[6]

* Summary of the EAJA

The Equal Access to Justice Act * * * contains three fee-shifting provisions; two provide for awards in court proceedings and one applies to certain administrative proceedings:

The first fee-shifting provision in the statute, Subsection 2412(b), subjects the United States to liability for attorney's fees "to the same extent that any other party would be liable under the common law or under the terms of any statute which specifically provides for such an award."[20] Under the "American Rule" on attorney's fees, each party in litigation must bear its own legal expenses, unless there is an express statutory authorization for shifting fees or one of the narrow common-law exceptions to the rule applies. Subsection (b) makes the federal government liable for attorney's fees under common-law and statutory fee-shifting exceptions to

---

1. H.R. Rep. No. 1418, 96th Cong., 2d Sess. 12, *reprinted in* 1980 U.S.C.C.A.N. 4984, 4991; S. Rep. No. 253, 96th Cong., 1st Sess. 7 (1979) (same).

2. Equal Access to Justice Act, Pub. L. No. 96–481, Title II, 94 Stat. 2325–30 (1980) (codified at 28 U.S.C. § 2412 and 5 U.S.C. § 504).

6. *See* Risa L. Lieberwitz, *Attorneys' Fees, the NLRB, and the Equal Access to Justice Act: From Bad to Worse*, 2 Hofstra Lab. L.J. 1, 43 (1984) (arguing that the EAJA effects "a complete upheaval of the historic theoretical justification for fee shifting legislation" because, while "Congress has previously authorized fee-shifting in order to en-course private enforcement of important statutory public policies," the EAJA "for the first time will be using fee shifting to deter governmental enforcement of public policies"); Susan G. Mezey & Susan M. Olson, *Fee shifting and public policy: the Equal Access to Justice Act*, 77 Judicature 13, 13 (1993) (the EAJA "represents the intersection of two independent trends that developed during the late 1970s: the deregulation of business and the use of statutes shifting the costs of litigation to further public policy").

20. Equal Access to Justice Act, 28 U.S.C. § 2412(b).

the American Rule on the same basis as any other party. In effect, the statute places the government on "equal footing" with private parties in terms of liability for attorney's fee awards.[22] Subsection (b) waives the sovereign immunity of the federal government, but "does not create any new substantive rights to attorney's fee awards."[23] To collect a fee, the litigant must still identify another statute or common law doctrine that provides an exception to the general bar on fee-shifting per the American Rule.

The second fee-shifting provision found in the EAJA, [is] Subsection 2412(d)[25] * * *. Subsection (d) not only waives the sovereign immunity of the United States, but also creates a new basis for an award of attorney's fees beyond other common-law or statutory exceptions to the American Rule. Subsection (d) is broad, in that it applies to most civil actions, but it is also limited in that it allows an attorney's fee award only when the government's position is found to be unreasonable.

Under Subsection (d), in addition to court costs, the court must award attorney's fees to any party who meets specified eligibility qualifications (generally excluding wealthy individuals and large organizations) and who prevails in a non-tort civil action against the federal government, "unless the court finds that the position of the United States was substantially justified or that special circumstances make an award unjust." * * * Subsection (d) places a specific cap on the amount of permissible fee awards, directing that fees "shall not be awarded in excess of $75 per hour unless the court determines that an increase in the cost of living or a special factor, such as the limited availability of qualified attorneys for the proceedings involved, justifies a higher fee."* An applicant for a fee under Subsection (d) must file an application for fees "within thirty days of final judgment in the action."

Finally, a third fee-shifting provision created by the EAJA, which is separately codified,[35] authorizes a prevailing party in an "adversary adjudication" before an administrative agency to obtain an award for legal expenses in the administrative proceedings under the same terms as Subsection (d)—that is, when the government's position is not substantially justified. The statute defines an administrative proceeding as "adversarial" if it involves an adjudication under Section 554 of the Administrative Procedure Act in which the United States is represented by counsel or otherwise. * * *

---

22. H.R. Rep. No. 1418, 96th Cong., 2d Sess. 9 (1980), *reprinted in* 1980 U.S. Code Cong. & Admin. News 4984, 4987.

23. [Gregory C. Sisk, *A Primer on Awards of Attorney's Fees Against the Federal Government,* 25 ARIZ. ST. L.J. 733,] 784 [(1993)].

25. Equal Access to Justice Act, 28 U.S.C. § 2412(d).

* [Note: The $75 per hour rate cap was raised to $125 in 1996. Pub. L. No. 104–121, § 232 (1996) (codified at 28 U.S.C. § 2412(d)(2)(A)).]

35. Equal Access to Justice Act, 5 U.S.C. § 504(a)(1).

* Purposes of the EAJA

Through the Equal Access to Justice Act, "Congress presumably sought to achieve three inter-connected goals: to provide an incentive for private parties to contest government overreaching, to deter subsequent government wrongdoing, and to provide more complete compensation for citizens injured by government action."[39]

First, Congress intended to "reduce[] the disparity in resources between individuals, small businesses, and other organizations with limited resources and the federal government,"[40] thereby "encourag[ing] relatively impecunious private parties to challenge unreasonable or oppressive government behavior by relieving such parties of the fear of incurring large litigation expenses."[41] The Preamble to the EAJA expresses this purpose "to diminish the deterrent effect of seeking review of, or defending against, governmental action."[42] As one court colorfully put it, by "discourag[ing] the federal government from using its superior litigating resources unreasonably," the EAJA is "an 'anti-bully' law."[43]

Second, Congress sought to deter wrongful behavior by federal officials and regulators, "anticipat[ing] that the prospect of paying sizable awards of attorneys' fees when they overstepped their authority and were challenged in court would induce administrators to behave more responsibly in the future."[44] By encouraging judicial challenges to administrative decisions, Congress also hoped to refine the administration of federal law and "help assure that administrative decisions reflect informed deliberation."[45] At the same time, however, Congress did not want the prospect of paying attorney's fees to "chill public officials charged with enforcing the law from vigorously discharging their responsibilities."[46] Accordingly, rather than prescribing mandatory fee awards against the government whenever it lost a case, the EAJA adopts the "middle ground" approach of authorizing a fee when the government's position is found to be without substantial justification.[47] The "substantial justification" standard "balances the constitutional obligation of the executive branch to see that the laws are faithfully

39. [Harold J.] Krent, [*Fee Shifting Under the Equal Access to Justice Act—A Qualified Success,* 11 Yale L. & Pol'y Rev. 458,] 458 (1993).

40. *See* H.R. Rep. No. 120, 99th Cong., 1st Sess. 4 (1985), *reprinted in* 1985 U.S.C.C.A.N. 132, 133.

41. Spencer [v. National Labor Relations Bd.,] 712 F.2d [539,] 549 [(D.C.Cir. 1983)] (citing statute and legislative history), [*cert. denied,* 466 U.S. 936 (1984)].

42. Act of Oct. 21, 1980, Pub. L. No. 96–481, Title II, § 202(c)(1), 94 Stat. 2325, 2325 (uncodified).

43. Battles Farm Co. v. Pierce, 806 F.2d 1098, 1101 (D.C.Cir. 1986), *vacated,* 487 U.S. 1229 (1988).

44. Spencer v. National Labor Relations Bd., 712 F.2d 539, 550 (D.C.Cir. 1983), *cert. denied,* 466 U.S. 936 (1984).

45. H.R. Rep. No. 1418, 96th Cong., 2d Sess. 12, *reprinted in* 1980 U.S.C.C.A.N. 4984, 4991.

46. *See* H.R. Rep. No. 120, 99th Cong., 1st Sess. 10, *reprinted in* 1985 U.S.C.C.A.N. 132, 139.

47. H.R. Rep. No. 1418, 96th Cong., 2d Sess. 14, *reprinted in* 1980 U.S.C.C.A.N. 4984, 4993.

executed against the public interest in encouraging parties to vindicate their rights."[48]

Finally, although the legislative history focuses upon the first two purposes as primary, Congress also undoubtedly intended to compensate parties who had been wronged by the government, thus allowing "those injured by the government to receive complete compensation for their injuries, including litigation expense."[49] Thus, the EAJA serves "a salutary function in creating the appearance of fairness" by providing more complete compensation to those who have suffered a breach of the public trust through the arbitrary and unreasonable use of government power.[50]

Note

In 1996, Congress added a fourth fee-shifting provision—an "Excessive Demand" provision—to the Equal Access to Justice Act. Pub. L. No. 104–121, 110 Stat. 847, 862–63 (1996). Traditionally, and under the other three fee-shifting provisions of the EAJA, a party is not eligible for an award of attorney's fees unless the party first prevails in the litigation against an opponent. However, under the 1996 amendments to the EAJA, fees may be awarded to a *non-prevailing* party in litigation with the federal government, under certain narrow circumstances. *See* 28 U.S.C. § 2412(d)(1)(D) (which is included in the statutory excerpt set out above). (A parallel provision was added to the administrative EAJA. *See* 5 U.S.C. § 504(a)(4).)

Under the 1996 amendment, if "in a civil action brought by the United States, * * * the demand by the United States is substantially in excess of the judgment finally obtained by the United States and is unreasonable when compared with such judgment, under the facts and circumstances of the case, the court shall award to the party the fees and other expenses related to defending against the excessive demand, unless the party has committed a willful violation of law or otherwise acted in bad faith, or special circumstances make an award unjust." 28 U.S.C. § 2412(d)(1)(D). This Excessive Demand provision applies when the United States is the party initiating litigation as plaintiff, typically in an action to enforce a statute against a private actor or seek civil penalties. In the Senate debate about the legislation, one senator illustrated the new provision in this way: "So, if the Government sought $1 million to settle the case, and the judge or jury awarded, for example, $1,000 or $5,000, the defendant should be able to recover his fees." 142 Cong. Rec. S2156 (daily ed. Mar. 15, 1996) (remarks of Sen. Bumpers). Thus, the provision is directed to the situation where the government, although prevailing in the lawsuit by obtaining some recovery against the civil defendant, nonetheless overreached by demanding substantially more in penalties or damages than the adjudicator concludes is actually merited by the facts and circumstances of the case.

----

48. *Id.* at 10, 1980 U.S.C.C.A.N. at 4989.

49. Krent, *supra*, at 477.

50. [*Id.*] at 478

By amendment to the EAJA's definition of "party" in 28 U.S.C. § 2412(d)(2)(B), this Excessive Demand provision may be asserted only by a "small entity" as defined in 5 U.S.C. § 601. Section 601 of Title 5 describes what constitutes small business concerns, small organizations, and small government jurisdictions (such as smaller cities). The other restrictions on fee awards under Subsection (d) of the EAJA, including the hourly rate cap, apply as well to this new "Excessive Demand" fee-shifting provision. For thorough analyses of the 1996 fee-shifting amendment, its legislative history, and the interpretive issues arising under the new provision, see generally Judith E. Kramer, *Equal Access to Justice Act Amendments of 1996: A New Avenue for Recovering Fees From the Government,* 51 Admin. L. Rev. 363 (1999); and James M. McElfish, Jr., *Fee Simple? The 1996 Equal Access to Justice Act Amendments,* 26 Env't L. Rep. Cases (BNA) 10569 (1996). For a sharp critique of the policies behind this provision, as arguably providing undue advantages to small businesses and creating disincentives to government enforcement of regulations, see Melissa A. Peters, *The Little Guy Myth: The FAIR Act's Victimization of Small Business,* 42 Wm. & Mary L. Rev. 1925 (2001).

Pierce v. Underwood

Supreme Court of the United States.
487 U.S. 552 (1988).

■ JUSTICE SCALIA delivered the opinion of the Court.

Respondents settled their lawsuit against one of petitioner's predecessors as the Secretary of Housing and Urban Development, and were awarded attorney's fees after the court found that the position taken by the Secretary was not "substantially justified" within the meaning of the Equal Access to Justice Act (EAJA), 28 U.S.C. § 2412(d). The court also determined that "special factors" justified calculating the attorney's fees at a rate in excess of the $75–per-hour cap imposed by the statute. We granted certiorari to resolve a conflict in the Courts of Appeals over important questions concerning the interpretation of the EAJA.

I

This dispute arose out of a decision by one of petitioner's predecessors as Secretary not to implement an "operating subsidy" program authorized by § 236 as amended by § 212 of the Housing and Community Development Act of 1974, formerly codified at 12 U.S.C. §§ 1715z–1(f)(3) and (g) (1970 ed., Supp. IV). The program provided payments to owners of Government-subsidized apartment buildings to offset rising utility expenses and property taxes. Various plaintiffs successfully challenged the Secretary's decision in lawsuits filed in nine Federal District Courts. See *Underwood v. Pierce,* 547 F.Supp. 256, 257, n. 1 (C.D.Cal.1982) (citing cases). While the Secretary was appealing these adverse decisions, respondents, members of a nationwide class of tenants residing in Government-subsidized housing, brought the present action challenging the Secretary's decision in the United States District Court for the District of Columbia. That court also decided the issue against the Secretary, granted summary judgment in favor of respondents, and entered a permanent injunction and writ of mandamus requiring the Secretary to disburse the accumulated operating-subsidy fund. See *Underwood v. Hills,* 414 F.Supp. 526, 532 (1976). We stayed the District Court's judgment pending appeal. *Sub nom. Hills v. Cooperative Services, Inc.,* 429 U.S. 892 (1976). The Court of Appeals for the Second Circuit similarly stayed, pending appeal, one of the eight other District Court judgments against the Secretary. Two of those other judgments were affirmed by Courts of Appeals, and we consolidated the cases and granted the Secretary's petitions for writs of certiorari to review those decisions. Before any other Court of Appeals reached a decision on the issue, and before we could review the merits, a newly appointed Secretary settled with the plaintiffs in most of the cases. * * * The present case was then transferred to the Central District of California for administration of the settlement.

In 1980, while the settlement was being administered, Congress passed the EAJA, 28 U.S.C. § 2412(d) * * *. The District Court granted respondents' motion for an award of attorney's fees under this statute, concluding that the Secretary's decision not to implement the operating-subsidy program had not been "substantially justified." The court determined that respondents' attorneys had provided 3,304 hours of service and that "special factors" justified applying hourly rates ranging from $80 for work performed in 1976 to $120 for work performed in 1982. This produced a base or "lodestar" figure of $322,700 which the court multiplied by three-and-one-half (again because of the "special factors"), resulting in a total award of $1,129,450.

On appeal, the Court of Appeals for the Ninth Circuit held that the District Court had not abused its discretion in concluding that the Secretary's position was not substantially justified. 761 F.2d, at 1346. The Court of Appeals also held that the special factors relied on by the District Court justified increasing the hourly rates of the attorneys, but did not justify applying a multiplier to the lodestar amount. It therefore reduced the award to $322,700.

We granted the Secretary's petition for certiorari on the questions whether the Government's position was "substantially justified" and whether the courts below properly identified "special factors" justifying an award in excess of the statute's $75–per–hour cap on attorney's fees.

II

We first consider whether the Court of Appeals applied the correct standard when reviewing the District Court's determination that the Secretary's position was not substantially justified. For purposes of standard of review, decisions by judges are traditionally divided into three categories, denominated questions of law (reviewable *de novo*), questions of fact (reviewable for clear error), and matters of discretion (reviewable for "abuse of discretion"). The Ninth Circuit treated the issue of substantial justification as involving the last of these; other Courts of Appeals have treated it as involving the first.

For some few trial court determinations, the question of what is the standard of appellate review is answered by relatively explicit statutory command. For most others, the answer is provided by a long history of appellate practice. But when, as here, the trial court determination is one for which neither a clear statutory prescription nor a historical tradition exists, it is uncommonly difficult to derive from the pattern of appellate review of other questions an analytical framework that will yield the correct answer. See Rosenberg, Judicial Discretion of the Trial Court, Viewed from Above, 22 Syracuse L. Rev. 635, 638 (1971) (hereinafter Rosenberg). No more today than in the past shall we attempt to discern or to create a comprehensive test; but we are persuaded that significant relevant factors call for an "abuse of discretion" standard in the present case.

We turn first to the language and structure of the governing statute. It provides that attorney's fees shall be awarded "unless *the court* finds that the position of the United States was substantially justified." 28 U.S.C. § 2412(d)(1)(A) (emphasis added). This formulation, as opposed to simply "unless the position of the United States was substantially justified," emphasizes the fact that the determination is for the district court to make, and thus suggests some deference to the district court upon appeal. That inference is not compelled, but certainly available. * * *

We recently observed, with regard to the problem of determining whether mixed questions of law and fact are to be treated as questions of law or of fact for purposes of appellate review, that sometimes the decision "has turned on a determination that, as a matter of the sound administration of justice, one judicial actor is better positioned than another to decide the issue in question." *Miller v. Fenton,* 474 U.S. 104, 114 (1985). We think that consideration relevant in the present context as well, and it argues in favor of deferential, abuse-of-discretion review. To begin with, some of the elements that bear upon whether the Government's position "was substantially justified" may be known only to the district court. Not infrequently, the question will turn upon not merely what was the law, but what was the evidence regarding the facts. By reason of settlement conferences and other pretrial activities, the district court may have insights not conveyed by the record, into such matters as whether particular evidence was worthy of being relied upon, or whether critical facts could easily have been verified by the Government. Moreover, even where the district judge's full knowledge of the factual setting can be acquired by the appellate court, that acquisition will often come at unusual expense, requiring the court to undertake the unaccustomed task of reviewing the entire record, not just to determine whether there existed the usual minimum support for the merits determination made by the factfinder below, but to determine whether urging of the opposite merits determination was substantially justified.

In some cases, such as the present one, the attorney's fee determination will involve a judgment ultimately based upon evaluation of the purely legal issue governing the litigation. It cannot be assumed, however, that *de novo* review of this will not require the appellate court to invest substantial additional time, since it will in any case have to grapple with the same legal issue on the merits. To the contrary, one would expect that where the Government's case is so feeble as to provide grounds for an EAJA award, there will often be (as there was here) a settlement below, or a failure to appeal from the adverse judgment. Moreover, even if there is a merits appeal, and even if it occurs simultaneously with (or goes to the same panel that entertains) the appeal from the attorney's fee award, the latter legal question will not be precisely the same as the merits: not what the law now is, but what the Government was substantially justified in believing it to have been. In all the separate-from-the-merits EAJA appeals, the investment of appellate energy will either fail to produce the normal law-clarifying benefits that come from an appellate decision on a question of law, or else will strangely distort the appellate process. The former result will obtain when (because of intervening legal decisions by this Court or by the relevant circuit itself) the law of the circuit is, at the time of the EAJA appeal, quite clear, so that the question of what the Government was substantially justified in believing it to have been is of entirely historical interest. Where, on the other hand, the law of the circuit remains unsettled at the time of the EAJA appeal, a ruling that the Government was not substantially justified in believing it to be thus-and-so would (unless there is some reason to think it has changed since) effectively establish the circuit law in a most peculiar, secondhanded fashion. Moreover, the possibility of the latter occurrence would encourage needless merits appeals by the Government, since it would know that if it does not appeal, but the victorious plaintiff appeals the denial of attorney's fees, its district-court loss on the merits can be converted into a circuit-court loss on the merits, without the opportunity for a circuit-court victory on the merits. All these untoward consequences can be substantially reduced or entirely avoided by adopting an abuse-of-discretion standard of review.

Another factor that we find significant has been described as follows by Professor Rosenberg:

> "One of the 'good' reasons for conferring discretion on the trial judge is the sheer impracticability of formulating a rule of decision for the matter in issue. Many questions that arise in litigation are not amenable to regulation by rule because they involve multifarious, fleeting, special, narrow facts that utterly resist generalization—at least, for the time being.

> · · ·

> "The non-amenability of the problem to rule, because of the diffuseness of circumstances, novelty, vagueness, or similar reasons that argue for allowing experience to develop, appears to be a sound reason for conferring discretion on the magistrate.... * * * " Rosenberg 662–663.

We think that the question whether the Government's litigating position has been "substantially justified" is precisely such a multifarious and novel question, little susceptible, for the time being at least, of useful generalization, and likely to profit from the experience that an abuse-of-discretion rule will permit to develop. * * *

It must be acknowledged that militating against the use of that standard in the present case is the substantial amount of the liability produced by the District Judge's decision. If this were the sort of decision that ordinarily has such substantial consequences, one might expect it to be reviewed more intensively. In that regard, however, the present case is not characteristic of EAJA attorney's fee cases. The median award has been less than $3,000. We think the generality rather than the exception must form the basis for our rule.

In sum, although as we acknowledged at the outset our resolution of this issue is not rigorously scientific, we are satisfied that the text of the statute permits, and sound judicial administration counsels, deferential review of a district court's decision regarding attorney's fees under the EAJA. In addition to furthering the goals we have described, it will implement our view that a "request for attorney's fees should not result in a second major litigation." *Hensley v. Eckerhart,* 461 U.S. 424, 437 (1983).

III

Before proceeding to consider whether the trial court abused its discretion in this case, we have one more abstract legal issue to resolve: the meaning of the phrase "substantially justified" in 28 U.S.C. § 2412(d)(1)(A). The Court of Appeals, following Ninth Circuit precedent, held that the Government's position was "substantially justified" if it "had a reasonable basis both in law and in fact." 761 F.2d, at 1346. The source of that formulation is a Committee Report prepared at the time of the original enactment of the EAJA, which commented that "[t]he test of whether the Government position is substantially justified is essentially one of reasonableness in law and fact." H.R.Conf.Rep. No. 96–1434, p. 22 (1980). In this petition, the Government urges us to hold that "substantially justified" means that its litigating position must have had "some substance and a fair possibility of success." Respondents, on the other hand, contend that the phrase imports something more than "a simple reasonableness standard"—though they are somewhat vague as to precisely *what* more, other than "a high standard," and "a strong showing."

In addressing this issue, we make clear at the outset that we do not think it appropriate to substitute for the formula that Congress has adopted any judicially crafted revision of it—whether that be "reasonable basis in both law and fact" or anything else. "Substantially justified" is the test the statute prescribes, and the issue should be framed in those terms. That being said, there is nevertheless an obvious need to elaborate upon the meaning of the phrase. The broad range of interpretations described above is attributable to the fact that the word "substantial" can have two quite different—indeed, almost contrary—connotations. On the one hand, it can mean "[c]onsiderable in amount, value, or the like; large," Webster's New International Dictionary 2514 (2d ed. 1945)—as, for example, in the statement, "He won the election by a substantial majority." On the other hand, it can mean "[t]hat is such in substance or in the main," *ibid.*—as, for example, in the statement, "What he said was substantially true." Depending upon which connotation one selects, "substantially justified" is susceptible of interpretations ranging from the Government's to the respondents'.

We are not, however, dealing with a field of law that provides no guidance in this matter. Judicial review of agency action, the field at issue here, regularly proceeds under the rubric of "substantial evidence" set forth in the Administrative Procedure Act, 5 U.S.C. § 706(2)(E). That phrase does not mean a large or considerable amount of evidence, but rather "such relevant evidence as a reasonable mind might accept as adequate to support a conclusion." *Consolidated Edison Co. v. NLRB,* 305 U.S. 197, 229 (1938). In an area related to the present case in another way, the test for avoiding the imposition of attorney's fees for resisting discovery in district court is whether the resistance was "substantially justified," Fed.Rules Civ.Proc. 37(a)(4) and (b)(2)(E). To our knowledge, that has never been described as meaning "justified to a high degree," but rather has been said to be satisfied if there is a "genuine dispute," Advisory Committee's Notes on 1970 Amendments to Fed.Rule Civ.Proc. 37(a)(4), 28 U.S.C.App., p. 601.

We are of the view, therefore, that as between the two commonly used connotations of the word "substantially," the one most naturally conveyed by the phrase before us here is not "justified to a high degree," but rather "justified in substance or in the main"—that is, justified to a degree that could satisfy a reasonable person. That is no different from the "reasonable basis both in law and fact" formulation adopted by the Ninth Circuit and the vast majority of other Courts of Appeals that have addressed this issue. To be "substantially justified" means, of course, more than merely undeserving of sanctions for frivolousness; that is assuredly not the standard for Government litigation of which a reasonable person would approve.[2]

Respondents press upon us an excerpt from the House Committee Report pertaining to the 1985 reenactment of the EAJA, which read as follows:

> "Several courts have held correctly that 'substantial justification' means more than merely reasonable. Because in 1980 Congress rejected a standard of 'reasonably justified' in favor of 'substantially justified,' the test must be more than mere reasonableness." H.R.Rep. No. 99–120, p. 9 (1985).

---

2. Contrary to Justice Brennan's suggestion, our analysis does not convert the statutory term "substantially justified" into "reasonably justified." Justice Brennan's arguments would have some force if the statutory criterion were "substantially correct" rather than "substantially *justified.*" But a position can be justified even though it is not correct, and we believe it can be substantially (*i.e.,* for the most part) justified if a reasonable person could think it correct, that is, if it has a reasonable basis in law and fact.

If this language is to be controlling upon us, it must be either (1) an authoritative interpretation of what the 1980 statute meant, or (2) an authoritative expression of what the 1985 Congress intended. It cannot, of course, be the former, since it is the function of the courts and not the Legislature, much less a Committee of one House of the Legislature, to say what an enacted statute means. Nor can it reasonably be thought to be the latter—because it is not an explanation of any language that the 1985 Committee drafted, because on its face it accepts the 1980 meaning of the terms as subsisting, and because there is no indication whatever in the text or even the legislative history of the 1985 reenactment that Congress thought it was doing anything insofar as the present issue is concerned except reenacting and making permanent the 1980 legislation. (Quite obviously, reenacting precisely the same language would be a strange way to make a change.) This is not, it should be noted, a situation in which Congress reenacted a statute that had in fact been given a consistent judicial interpretation along the lines that the quoted Committee Report suggested. Such a reenactment, of course, generally includes the settled judicial interpretation. Here, to the contrary, the almost uniform appellate interpretation (12 Circuits out of 13) *contradicted* the interpretation endorsed in the Committee Report. Only the District of Columbia Circuit had adopted the position that the Government had to show something "slightly more" than reasonableness. We might add that in addition to being out of accord with the vast body of existing appellate precedent, the 1985 House Report also contradicted, without explanation, the 1980 House Report ("reasonableness in law and fact") from which, as we have noted, the Ninth Circuit drew its formulation in the present case.

Even in the ordinary situation, the 1985 House Report would not suffice to fix the meaning of language which that reporting Committee did not even draft. Much less are we willing to accord it such force in the present case, since only the clearest indication of congressional command would persuade us to adopt a test so out of accord with prior usage, and so unadministerable, as "more than mere reasonableness." Between the test of reasonableness, and a test such as "clearly and convincingly justified"— which no one, not even respondents, suggests is applicable—there is simply no accepted stopping-place, no ledge that can hold the anchor for steady and consistent judicial behavior.

IV

We reach, at last, the merits of whether the District Court abused its discretion in finding that the Government's position was not "substantially justified." Both parties argue that for purposes of this inquiry courts should rely on "objective indicia" such as the terms of a settlement agreement, the stage in the proceedings at which the merits were decided, and the views of other courts on the merits. This, they suggest, can avoid the time-consuming and possibly inexact process of assessing the strength of the Government's position. While we do not disagree that objective indicia can be relevant, we do not think they provide a conclusive answer, in either direction, for the present case.

Respondents contend that the lack of substantial justification for the Government's position was demonstrated by its willingness to settle the litigation on unfavorable terms. Other factors, however, might explain the settlement equally well—for example, a change in substantive policy instituted by a new administration. The unfavorable terms of a settlement agreement, without inquiry into the reasons for settlement, cannot conclusively establish the weakness of the Government's position. To hold otherwise would not only distort the truth but penalize and thereby discourage useful settlements.

Respondents further contend that the weakness of the Government's position is established by the objective fact that the merits were decided at the pleadings stage. We disagree. At least where, as here, the dispute centers upon questions of law rather than fact, summary disposition proves only that the district judge was efficient.

Both parties rely upon the objective indicia consisting of the views expressed by other courts on the merits of the Government's position. Obviously, the fact that one other court agreed or disagreed with the Government does not establish whether its position was substantially justified. Conceivably, the Government could take a position that is not substantially justified, yet win; even more likely, it could take a position that is substantially justified, yet lose. Nevertheless, a string of losses can be indicative; and even more so a string of successes. Once again, however, we cannot say that this category of objective indicia is enough to decide the present case. Respondents emphasize that every court to hear the merits (nine District Courts and two Courts of Appeals) rejected the Government's position. The Secretary responds that the stays issued by the Court of Appeals for the Second Circuit and by this Court reflect a view on the merits and objectively establish substantial justification; and that it is "unlikely that [this] Court would have granted the government's petitions [for certiorari in two cases to review this issue] had the Secretary's argument" not been substantial. Respondents reply that neither the stays nor the grants of certiorari are reliable indications of substantial merit. We will not parse these arguments further. Respondents' side of the case has at least sufficient force that we cannot possibly state, on the basis of these objective indications alone, that the District Court abused its discretion in finding no substantial justification.

We turn, then, to the actual merits of the Government's litigating position. The Government had argued that the operating-subsidy program was established in permissive rather than mandatory language: the Secretary is "*authorized* to make, and contract to make" operating-subsidy payments. 12 U.S.C. § 1715z–1(f)(3) (1970 ed., Supp. IV) (emphasis added). This contrasts with the mandatory language Congress used when creating a related housing subsidy program: the Secretary "*shall* make, and contract to make." § 1715z–1(f)(2) (emphasis added). * * * Finally, the Government contended that because Congress had not authorized sufficient funds to conduct the operating-subsidy program as well as two related subsidy programs, the Secretary had discretion to suspend the operating-subsidy program.

Respondents argued in rebuttal that other statutory language made clear that the operating-subsidy program was mandatory: "[T]here shall be established an initial operating expense level ... [which] shall be established by the Secretary not later than 180 days after August 22, 1974." 12 U.S.C. §§ 1715z–1(f)(3), 17152z–1(g) (1970 ed., Supp. IV). The "project owner shall ... pay to the Secretary all rental charges collected in excess of the basic rental charges [and] excess charges shall be credited to a reserve fund to be used by the Secretary to make additional assistance payments." § 1715z–1(g). * * * They also pointed out that the most direct precedents at the time the Government took its position in the present case were the nine adverse District Court decisions. Finally, respondents argued that the Secretary did not need an additional authorization because the reserve fund from excess rental charges had accumulated tens of millions of dollars which could be used only for operating-subsidy payments.

We cannot say that this description commands the conclusion that the Government's position was substantially justified. Accordingly, we affirm the Ninth Circuit's holding that the District Judge did not abuse his discretion when he found it was not.

V

The final issue before us is whether the amount of the attorney's fees award was proper. Here it is well established that the abuse-of-discretion standard applies.

The EAJA provides that attorney's fees "shall be based upon prevailing market rates for the kind and quality of the services furnished," but "shall not be awarded in excess of $75 per hour unless the court determines that an increase in the cost of living or a special factor, such as the limited availability of qualified attorneys for the proceedings involved, justifies a higher fee." 28 U.S.C. § 2412(d)(2)(A)(ii).* In allowing fees at a rate in excess of the $75 cap (adjusted for inflation), the District Court relied upon some circumstances that arguably come within the single example of a "special factor" described in the statute, "the limited availability of qualified attorneys for the proceedings involved." We turn first to the meaning of that provision.

If "the limited availability of qualified attorneys for the proceedings involved" meant merely that lawyers skilled and experienced enough to try the case are in short supply, it would effectively eliminate the $75 cap—since the "prevailing market rates for the kind and quality of the services furnished" are obviously *determined* by the relative supply of that kind and quality of services. "Limited availability" so interpreted would not be a "special factor," but a factor virtually always present when services with a market rate of more than $75 have been provided. We do not think

---

* [Note: The $75 per hour rate cap was raised to $125 in 1996. Pub. L. No. 104–121, § 232 (1996) (codified at 28 U.S.C. § 2412(d)(2)(A)).]

Congress meant that if the rates for all lawyers in the relevant city—or even in the entire country—come to exceed $75 per hour (adjusted for inflation), then that market-minimum rate will govern instead of the statutory cap. To the contrary, the "special factor" formulation suggests Congress thought that $75 an hour was generally quite enough public reimbursement for lawyers' fees, whatever the local or national market might be. If that is to be so, the exception for "limited availability of qualified attorneys for the proceedings involved" must refer to attorneys "qualified for the proceedings" in some specialized sense, rather than just in their general legal competence. We think it refers to attorneys having some distinctive knowledge or specialized skill needful for the litigation in question—as opposed to an extraordinary level of the general lawyerly knowledge and ability useful in all litigation. Examples of the former would be an identifiable practice specialty such as patent law, or knowledge of foreign law or language. Where such qualifications are necessary and can be obtained only at rates in excess of the $75 cap, reimbursement above that limit is allowed.

For the same reason of the need to preserve the intended effectiveness of the $75 cap, we think the other "special factors" envisioned by the exception must be such as are not of broad and general application. We need not specify what they might be, but they include nothing relied upon by the District Court in this case. The "novelty and difficulty of issues," "the undesirability of the case," the "work and ability of counsel," and "the results obtained," are factors applicable to a broad spectrum of litigation; they are little more than routine reasons why market rates are what they are. The factor of "customary fees and awards in other cases," is even worse; it is not even a routine reason for market rates, but rather a description of market rates. It was an abuse of discretion for the District Court to rely on these factors.

The final factor considered by the District Court, "the contingent nature of the fee," is also too generally applicable to be regarded as a "special" reason for exceeding the statutory cap. * * *

We conclude, therefore, that none of the reasons relied upon by the District Court to increase the rate of reimbursement above the statutory was a "special factor."

* * *

We affirm the award of attorney's fees, but as to the amount of the award we vacate the judgment and remand for proceedings consistent with our opinion.

It is so ordered.

■ Justice Kennedy took no part in the consideration or decision of this case.

■ Justice Brennan, with whom Justice Marshall and Justice Blackmun join, concurring in part and concurring in the judgment.

I agree that an award of attorney's fees under the Equal Access to Justice Act (EAJA) was appropriate in this case, and I agree that the courts below did not adhere to the statutory hourly cap on fees. Therefore, I concur in the Court's judgment affirming the decision to award fees and remanding for a new determination as to the amount. I disagree, however, with some of the Court's reasoning. While I agree that appellate courts should review district court EAJA fee awards for abuse of discretion, in my view the Government may not prove that its position was "substantially justified" by showing that it was merely "reasonable." Therefore, although I join Parts I, II, and IV of the Court's opinion, I do not join Part III. Further, because I believe that the Court's interpretation of the predicate showing for a party to obtain a fee award exceeding the statutory cap—that there existed "a special factor, such as the limited availability of qualified attorneys for the proceedings involved"—is stingier than Congress intended, I do not join Part V of the Court's opinion.

I

Concerned that the Government, with its vast resources, could force citizens into acquiescing to adverse Government action, rather than vindicating their rights, simply by threatening them with costly litigation, Congress enacted the EAJA, waiving the United States' sovereign and general statutory immunity to fee awards and creating a limited exception to the "American Rule" against awarding attorneys fees to prevailing parties. S.Rep. No. 96–253, pp. 1–6 (1979) (S.Rep.). Consequently, when a qualified party (as defined in the Act) prevails against the United States in an adversarial proceeding not sounding in tort, the EAJA prescribes that "a court shall award . . . fees and other expenses . . . unless the court finds that the position of the United States was substantially justified or that special circumstances make an award unjust." 28 U.S.C. § 2412(d)(1)(A). In this, our first EAJA case, we are called upon to consider the phrase "substantially justified."

The Court begins, as is proper, with the plain meaning of the statutory language. The Court points out that "substantially" is not a word of precise and singular definition. Indeed, the word bears two arguably different relevant definitions: " 'considerable in amount, value, or the like; large' "; and " 'in substance or in the main.' "See also Webster's Third New International Dictionary 2280 (1976) ("considerable in amount, value, or worth"; and "having a solid or firm foundation . . . being that specified to a large degree or in the main"). The Court concludes, and I agree, that, to the extent they are different, Congress intended the latter meaning.

Unfortunately, the Court feels duty bound to go beyond the words enacted by Congress and to fashion its own substitute phrase using what it perceives to be a more legally precise term. The test upon which the Court alights is initially the "reasonable basis both in law and fact" standard, adopted by the courts below. While this phrase is often mentioned in the legislative history as the explication of "substantially justified," this alternative phraseology is inherently no more precise than the statutory language. In fact, it may be less so, for the Court equates it with "the test of reasonableness," a standard rejected by Congress and significantly more forgiving than the one actually adopted.

The Senate Judiciary Committee considered and rejected an amendment substituting the phrase "reasonably justified" for "substantially justified." S.Rep., at 8. Clearly, then, the Committee did not equate "reasonable" and "substantial"; on the contrary, it understood the two terms to embrace different burdens. "Reasonable" has a variety of connotations, but may be defined as "not absurd" or "not ridiculous." Webster's New Third International Dictionary 1892 (1976). Even at its strongest, the term implies a position of some, but not necessarily much, merit. However, as we have seen, "substantial" has a very different definition: "in substance or in the main." Thus, the word connotes a solid position, or a position with a firm foundation. While it is true "reasonable" and "substantial" overlap somewhat (substantial at its weakest and reasonable at its strongest) an overlap is not an identity. Therefore, although Congress may well have intended to use "substantial" in its weaker sense, there is no reason to believe, and substantial reason to disbelieve (as I will discuss below), that Congress intended the word to mean "reasonable" in *its* weaker sense. * * *

My view that "substantially justified" means more than merely reasonable, aside from conforming to the words Congress actually chose, is bolstered by the EAJA's legislative history. The phrase "substantially justified" was a congressional attempt to fashion a "middle ground" between an earlier, unsuccessful proposal to award fees in all cases in which the Government did not prevail, and the Department of Justice's proposal to award fees only when the Government's position was "arbitrary, frivolous, unreasonable, or groundless." S.Rep., at 2–3. Far from occupying the middle ground, "the test of reasonableness" is firmly encamped near the position espoused by the Justice Department. Moreover, the 1985 House Committee Report pertaining to the EAJA's reenactment expressly states that "substantially justified" means more than "mere reasonableness." H.R.Rep. No. 99–120, p. 9 (1985). Although I agree with the Court that this Report is not dispositive, the Committee's unequivocal rejection of a pure "reasonableness" standard in the course of considering the bill reenacting the EAJA is deserving of some weight.

Finally, however lopsided the weight of authority in the lower courts over the meaning of "substantially justified" might once have been, lower court opinions are no longer nearly unanimous. The District of Columbia, Third, Eighth, and Federal Circuits have all adopted a standard higher than mere reasonableness, and the Sixth Circuit is considering the question en banc.

In sum, the Court's journey from "substantially justified" to "reasonable basis both in law and fact" to "the test of reasonableness" does not crystallize the law, nor is it true to Congress' intent. Instead, it allows the Government to creep the standard towards "having some substance and a fair possibility of success," a position I believe Congress intentionally avoided. In my view, we should hold that the Government can avoid fees only where it makes a clear showing that its position had a solid basis (as opposed to a marginal basis or a not unreasonable basis) in both law and fact. That it may be less "anchored" than "the test of reasonableness," a debatable proposition, is no excuse to abandon the test Congress enacted.

II

I also disagree with the Court's discussion of the circumstances supporting a fee enhancement beyond the $75–per–hour (adjusted for inflation) cap set by Congress, although I do agree that the lower courts' judgment in this regard cannot stand. The statute states that courts may not award fees in excess of this cap unless "a special factor, such as the limited availability of qualified attorneys for the proceedings involved, justifies the higher fee." 28 U.S.C. § 2412(d)(2)(A)(ii). * * *

* * * [O]ur job is to decide the meaning of the term: "a special factor, such as the limited availability of qualified attorneys." The Court begins with the single expressed special factor, the "limited availability of qualified attorneys." It holds that this phrase refers to an attorney with a required, articulable specialization, and does not refer to the limited availability of attorneys experienced or skilled enough to handle the proceedings involved. The Court reasons that allowing an enhancement for extraordinary skill or experience, even if required, would render the cap nugatory, since those factors merely set the market rate. This tidy analysis is too simplistic.

The most striking aspect of the Court's holding in this regard is its willingness to ignore the plain meaning and language of the exception. After all, in the rare EAJA case where highly experienced attorneys are truly required, a neophyte lawyer is no more "qualified ... for the proceedings involved" than a nonpatent lawyer is to handle a patent case. * * *

Second, the phrase "limited availability of qualified attorneys," read in conjunction with "special factor," reflects a congressional judgment that if the price of lawyers generally exceeds the cap, that trend alone will not justify an increase. Therefore, awarding an enhancement in cases where extraordinary experience or skill is required does not write the cap out of the statute. * * *

Therefore, the Court is simply wrong when it asserts that if we allow a showing of extraordinary skill or experience (in the rare case where it is required) to justify an enhanced award, then the cap will be rendered meaningless. Far from it. The same logic supporting a "patent lawyer" exception—that when only a fraction of the bar is qualified to handle a case, those attorneys may charge a premium for their services—supports an enhancement for skill or experience.

Equally troubling is the Court's requirement that a "special factor" must not be "of broad and general application." We are given no explanation of or for this limitation, beyond the declaration that it is necessary to preserve the efficacy of the cap. Further, while the Court is willing to say what is *not* a special factor—everything relied upon below—we are given no example of anything that is a special factor other than the subject-matter specialization already considered as falling within the "limited availability of qualified attorneys for the proceedings involved" example. Having rejected the lower courts' list of factors in its entirety, it seems as if the Court leaves nothing remaining.

Such a strained interpretation, apparently reading the words "such as" out of the Act, is unnecessary. A "special factor" may be readily analogized to the factors we identified in *Blum* to enhance the lodestar figure under § 1988. In *Blum,* we held that the lodestar amount (the reasonable hourly rate multiplied by the number of hours billed) is "presumably" the reasonable fee. However, we also held that an upward adjustment may be appropriate "in the rare case where the fee applicant offers specific evidence to show that the quality of service rendered was superior to that one reasonably should expect in light of the hourly rates charged and that the success was exceptional." 465 U.S., [886,] 899 [(1984)]. Analogizing to the EAJA context, the lodestar would be calculated by multiplying the reasonable rate (as capped) by the number of hours billed. That amount would presumably be the proper award. However, where a factor exists that would justify an enhancement of the lodestar amount under § 1988, an enhancement of the EAJA award might also be appropriate. Unlike the lower courts' approach, this rule would not read the cap out of the statute, for as we predicted in *Blum,* a lodestar enhancement would be appropriate only in "the rare case."

Although the *Blum* enhancers constitute more than the situation where there is a limited availability of qualified counsel, the statute expressly allows more to be considered. The Court's miserly refusal to accede to this statutory command is unjustified and unwarranted. I therefore concur only in the judgment as to the fee calculation.

■ JUSTICE WHITE, with whom JUSTICE O'CONNOR joins, concurring in part and dissenting in part.

I agree with the majority's interpretation of the term "substantially justified" as used in the Equal Access to Justice Act (EAJA), 28 U.S.C. § 2412(d). However, because I believe that a district court's assessment of whether the Government's legal position was substantially justified should be reviewed *de novo* and that the attorney's fees award in this case could not be sustained under that standard of review, I dissent from Parts II and IV of the majority's opinion.

I

The majority acknowledges that neither the language nor the structure of the EAJA "compel[s]" deferential review of a district court's determination of whether the Government's position was substantially justified. In fact, the statute is wholly silent as to the standard under which such determinations are to be reviewed. This congressional silence in the face of both the general rule of *de novo* review of legal issues and the EAJA's special purpose of encouraging meritorious suits against the Government suggests a different result than that reached by the majority.

The Congress that adopted the EAJA certainly was aware of the general rule that issues of law are reviewed *de novo* while issues of fact are reviewed only for clear error. Congress would have known that whether or not a particular legal position was substantially justified is a question of law rather than of fact. The historical facts having been established, the question is to be resolved by the legal analysis of the relevant statutory and decisional authorities that appellate courts are expected to perform. As the District of Columbia Circuit has observed, "the special expertise and experience of appellate courts in assessing the relative force of competing interpretations and applications of legal norms makes the case for *de novo* review of judgments [of whether the Government's legal position was substantially justified] even stronger than the case for such review of paradigmatic conclusions of law." *Spencer v. NLRB,* 229 U.S.App.D.C. 225, 249, 712 F.2d 539, 563 (1983), cert. denied, 466 U.S. 936 (1984). It is thus most likely that Congress expected that the courts of appeals would apply the same *de novo* standard of review to a district court's assessment of whether the Government's interpretation of the law was substantially justified for purposes of the EAJA as they would apply to a district court's assessment of whether the Government's interpretation of the law was correct in the underlying litigation.

De novo appellate review of whether the Government's legal position was substantially justified would also foster consistency and predictability in EAJA litigation. A court of appeals may be required under the majority's "abuse of discretion" standard to affirm one district court's holding that the Government's legal position was substantially justified and another district court's holding that the same position was not substantially justified. As long as the district court's opinion about the substantiality of the Government case rests on some defensible construction and application of the statute, the Court's view would command the court of appeals to defer even though that court's own view on the legal issue is quite different. The availability of attorney's fees would not only be difficult to predict but would vary from circuit to circuit or even within a particular circuit. Such uncertainty over the potential availability of attorney's fees would, in my view, undermine the EAJA's purpose of encouraging challenges to unreasonable governmental action.

Finally, the Federal Courts of Appeals have concluded with near unanimity that "close scrutiny," or *de novo* review, should be applied to district courts' assessments of whether the Government's legal position was substantially justified. This weight of appellate authority reinforces my view that whether or not the Government's interpretation of the law was substantially justified is an appropriate question for *de novo* review.

II

I do not believe that the District Court's conclusion that the Government's position in this litigation was not substantially justified could withstand appellate scrutiny under a *de novo* standard of review.

The housing statute at issue in this case provided for three subsidy programs: a "deep-subsidy" program, an "interest-reduction" program, and an "operating-subsidy" program. It was the Secretary's failure to implement the last of these programs that was challenged by respondents.

The statute provided that the Secretary was "*authorized* to make, and contract to make" operating-subsidy and interest-reduction payments. 12 U.S.C. §§ 1715z–1(f)(3), 1715z–1(a) (1970 ed., Supp. IV) (emphasis added). In contrast, the statute stated that the Secretary "*shall* make, and contract to make" deep-subsidy payments. § 1715z–1(f)(2) (emphasis added). In 1974, after concluding that Congress had not authorized her to commit funds sufficient to operate all three subsidy programs, Secretary Hills decided to devote the available funds to the more clearly mandatory deep-subsidy program (and to certain pre-existing commitments under the interest-reduction program) rather than to spread the funds among all three programs.

Whether or not the courts might differ with Secretary Hills on the scope of her discretion to decline to implement the operating-subsidy program, given the statutory language and the existing case law, her conclusion was not without substantial justification. The statutory provisions instructing the Secretary to make deep-subsidy payments, but merely "authorizing" her to make operating-subsidy payments, could reasonably be construed as vesting the Secretary with some discretion over the implementation of the operating-subsidy program. If Congress had intended to give the Secretary no choice in the matter, it is defensible to believe that Congress would have directed that the Secretary "*shall* make, and contract to make" operating-subsidy payments. * * *

Because I would conclude upon de novo review that the Secretary's refusal to implement the operating-subsidy program was substantially justified, I would reverse the award of attorney's fees under the EAJA.[4]

Notes and Questions

1. Most of the attorney's fee litigation flowing from the Equal Access to Justice Act proceeds under Subsection (d)—the provision directing the award of fees against the federal government unless it can demonstrate that its position was "substantially justified." (The next most commonly-cited provision in litigation is Subsection (b), which authorizes fee awards against the federal government under the same circumstances as against a private party. Subsection (b) is explored in the context of the case of *Perales v. Casillas,* the last case in this chapter of the casebook.) *Pierce v. Underwood* was the Supreme Court's first decision to construe EAJA Subsection (d). And it remains the Court's most important EAJA decision because it interprets the central language in the statute and establishes

---

4. The Court concludes that the amount of the award must be reconsidered. I agree in this respect and hence join Part V of the Court's opinion.

many of the key principles for application of this fee provision. As you read the *Underwood* decision, review the pertinent text of the EAJA as set out beforehand in this casebook. What are the limitations on a fee award? Who is eligible? Under what circumstances is the government liable for a fee? What special rules govern measurement of a fee award?

2. The first issue the Supreme Court addresses in *Pierce v. Underwood* is the appropriate standard of appellate review, a subject that too often is overlooked or quickly passed over in law school courses. The district court generally will be the first to rule upon a petition for fees after disposition of a case on the merits. When a fee petitioner appeals the denial of an EAJA fee or the government appeals the grant of a fee, how should the appellate court approach the dispute? Should any deference be given to the district court's disposition? Or should the court of appeals look at the matter afresh? In general, what are the three basic standards of appellate review and to what types of questions or issues is each ordinarily applied? Which one of these standards of review best suits the question of whether the government is liable for fees under EAJA? Does the choice of a standard of review really make any difference? (Read Justice White's dissent in *Underwood* to answer this last question.) On the standard of appellate review for EAJA determinations, see generally Gregory C. Sisk, *The Essentials of the Equal Access to Justice Act: Court Awards of Attorney's Fees for Unreasonable Government Conduct (Part Two)*, 56 La. L. Rev. 1, 78 93 (1995).

One of the reasons given by the *Underwood* majority for adopting an abuse-of-discretion standard of review is the fear that de novo appellate review of the EAJA substantial justification determination would establish precedential law in the appellate courts in a "peculiar, second-handed fashion." What does the Court mean by this? Read this part of the majority opinion carefully. Think about the effect that a de novo appellate decision concerning substantial justification for purposes of the fee petition might have on the evolution of law with respect to the merits of a legal issue. How does an abuse of discretion standard mitigate this concern?

3. The substantial justification question arises at the entitlement stage, after a fee petitioner has been found eligible for an EAJA award (by prevailing and falling within the net worth and employer size eligibility limitations of the statute). What does "substantial justification" mean? Compare Justice Scalia's majority opinion on this point with Justice Brennan's concurrence. How does each approach the language of the statute? How does each use or disregard legislative history? What use is made of similar language in analogous statutes or codes?

How does the Court majority then apply the substantial justification standard to the government's position in this particular case? Do you agree with the result? Did the government's argument reflect a reasonable interpretation of the statute? The Court applies a deferential standard of appellate review, which removes the Court one step away from directly passing upon the reasonableness of the government's position. Would you have reached the same conclusion if you were the district court addressing this question in the first instance? Applying a de novo standard of review, what result would Justice White in dissent have reached? On the subject of substantial justification and its application in a wide variety of settings in government litigation, see generally Sisk, *supra,* at 5–78.

4.   The final question is the proper measurement of the fee award. Under what circumstances may a court exceed the then–$75 (now–$125) hourly rate cap in calculating the proper fee? What is a "special factor" that would justify exceeding the rate ceiling? The *Underwood* decision is more notable for explaining what is *not* a "special factor" than what *is.* Why does it exclude so many considerations as possible "special factors"? The hourly rate cap and its exceptions are central as well to the resolution of the next two cases in the casebook.

Pirus v. Bowen

United States Court of Appeals for the Ninth Circuit.
869 F.2d 536 (9th Cir. 1989).

■ WILLIAM A. NORRIS, CIRCUIT JUDGE:

Appellant Sidell Pirus brought a class action against the Secretary of the Department of Health and Human Services, challenging the Secretary's decision to deny social security benefits to her and the class she represented. After the district court granted Pirus' motion for summary judgment, Pirus petitioned the court for attorney's fees under the Equal Access to Justice Act (EAJA), 28 U.S.C. § 2412(d). The district court granted Pirus' petition, holding that the Secretary's original decision to deny benefits to the class and then to defend that position through litigation was not "substantially justified" within the meaning of the EAJA. The court also determined that "special factors" justified awarding fees in excess of the $75 per hour cap mandated by the Act. The government challenges both the award of attorney's fees and the fee enhancement. We affirm the district court with respect to both issues.

I

At age 63, after many years of marriage, Sidell Pirus was divorced from a wage earner covered by the Social Security Act. Four years later she remarried. Soon afterwards, her former spouse died, and Pirus applied for benefits as the divorced wife of a deceased wage earner. Although the divorced spouses of deceased wage earners cannot normally receive these benefits after they remarry, 42 U.S.C. § 402(e)(1)(A), those divorced spouses who remarry *after age 60* are excepted from this general rule pursuant to 42 U.S.C. § 402(e)(3)(A), as amended by Congress in 1983. It was under this exception that Pirus applied. The Secretary, however, denied her claim; under the Department's regulations interpreting the amended section, a divorced spouse was not entitled to benefits if she remarried after age 60 *but before the covered spouse died.* 20 C.F.R. § 404.336(e)(4). After seeking administrative relief, Pirus filed suit on behalf of herself and a class of similarly situated individuals, challenging the Secretary's decision to deny benefits to spouses whose remarriages predated their former spouses' deaths.

During the litigation the Secretary took the position that when Congress amended § 402(e)(3)(A) to cover divorced spouses as well as widows who remarried, Congress did not intend to give benefits to those individuals who, like Pirus, remarried before the death of the covered wage earner. The Secretary sought support for this position in the language and legislative history of the 1983 amendment to the Act. The Secretary also took the position that Pirus' class action suit was barred on *res judicata* grounds. The Secretary contended that because a similar class action, *Bowen v. Owens,* 476 U.S. 340 (1986), had been brought by surviving divorced spouses who remarried after age 60, challenging the Secretary's earlier decision to deny them benefits during the period prior to the 1983 amendment, the specific claims at issue in this case could have been raised in *Owens.* Since those claims were not raised, the Secretary argued, Pirus' class was estopped from bringing them in a separate suit. The district court rejected both these arguments and granted summary judgment to the class. The district court also granted Pirus' petition for attorney's fees under the EAJA, awarding fees above the statutory cap of $75 per hour. The district court's award of these fees is the only issue before us on this appeal.

II

* * * To determine whether the Secretary's position was substantially justified within the meaning of the Act, the district court applied a reasonableness standard which has since been approved by the Supreme Court. *Pierce v. Underwood,* 487 U.S. 552 (1988). At the outset, the district court determined that the Secretary had not established that it was reasonable to adopt the regulation in the first instance. The court found that the regulation embodied a "forced statutory construction," which could not be reconciled with plaintiffs' facial entitlement under the plain terms of the section. Nor, found the district court, did the regulation make sense in light of the legislative history of the amendment, which revealed a general intent on the part of Congress to extend coverage to elderly claimants and not to penalize them for remarrying. Moreover, the Secretary's failure to provide any economic findings to support his decision to exclude the plaintiff class further indicated to the district court that the Secretary's decision to enact the regulation lacked a reasonable basis.

Turning to the government's litigation position, the district court found it to be equally untenable. Because neither the language of the statute nor the legislative history supported the Secretary's decision to exclude the plaintiff class from § 402(e)(3)(A)'s exception, there was no reasonable ground on which to defend the regulation when Pirus challenged it. Further, the district court found the government's *res judicata* argument completely implausible because the plaintiff class could not have had a full and fair opportunity to litigate its claim in *Owens* since the disputed regulation was not even *in existence* when the *Owens* case was decided by the Supreme Court.

III

The Supreme Court in *Underwood* held that an appellate court may review a district court's decision that the government's position was not substantially justified only under an abuse-of-discretion standard. Even when the district court's decision on the question of substantial justification "involve[s] a judgment ultimately based upon evaluation of the purely legal issue governing the litigation"—as is the case here—the deferential abuse-of-discretion standard must be applied. 487 U.S. at 568.

The Secretary advances several arguments to support the position he took in adopting the regulation and defending it in the district court. The Secretary argues that the language of § 402(e)(3)(A) is ambiguous, particularly when read together with other portions of the act. Specifically, when the amendment is compared to § 416(d)(2) of the Act, which defines "surviving divorced wife" as a woman divorced from an individual who had *died,* the regulation appears to be a reasonable, if not a required, interpretation of the section. The Secretary also seeks support for his interpretation in the legislative history of the amendment. Portions of the House and Senate reports on the amendment, the Secretary argues, indicate that Congress' primary concern in enacting the amendment was to protect elderly Social Security recipients from the hardship of having their benefits terminated *after they had come to depend upon them.* Since members of the Pirus class had never received any benefits prior to remarrying—they could not receive benefits until the wage earner died—they were not subject to the hardship of disentitlement that Congress intended to remedy. Finally, the Secretary argues that the district court should have given more weight to the fact that the government conduct in question here involved the interpretation of a new statute; the government should not be penalized, through the imposition of attorney's fees, for advancing a plausible interpretation of a new statute.

Were we deciding whether the government's position was "substantially justified," we might be inclined to reach a different result from that reached by the district court. *Underwood,* however, forecloses us from exercising independent judgment on the reasonableness of the government's position. We may not substitute our view of what constitutes substantial justification for that of the district court; our review is limited to assuring that the district court's determination has a basis in reason.

In finding that the Secretary's position lacked substantial justification, the district court focused on several weaknesses in the Secretary's reasoning. First, the district court noted that on its face § 402(e)(3)(A) does not require that the marriage take place before the covered wage earner dies. Had Congress intended to exclude the Pirus class, the court reasoned, Congress most probably would have included language to that effect, especially since the general purpose of the statute was to increase benefits to elderly persons. The only real support that the Secretary advanced for his position to the contrary was the legislative history of the amendment, which the district court correctly concluded was ambiguous. While several persons who testified before Congress in support of the amendment did talk about the special hardship for the elderly of having benefits taken away, that isolated testimony reveals little about the general legislative intent behind passage of the amendment. Moreover, other portions of the legislative history indicate that Congress passed the amendment to remove any disincentive that elderly people faced when considering remarriage. Since the disincentive existed whether or not the wage-earner was still alive—the divorced spouse could decide not to remarry for fear of not receiving benefits when the former spouse ultimately died—the purpose behind the amendment was served even if the marriage took place before the wage-earner died. Consequently, the district court rejected the Secretary's argument that the legislative history supported his interpretation of the amendment.

Based on these findings, the district court concluded that the Secretary's position lacked substantial justification. Given the highly deferential standard of review mandated by *Underwood,* we cannot say that it was an abuse of discretion for the district court to have concluded that a reasonable person would not have accepted the Secretary's position. Accordingly, we affirm the district court's ruling that the government's position was not substantially justified and that Pirus was therefore entitled to recover attorney's fees under the EAJA.

IV

The final issue before us is whether the amount of the fee award was proper. The EAJA provides that attorney's fees "shall be based upon prevailing market rates for the kind and quality of the services furnished," but "shall not be awarded in excess of $75 per hour unless the court determines that an increase in the cost of living or a special factor, such as the limited availability of qualified attorneys for the proceedings involved, justifies a higher fee." 28 U.S.C. § 2412(d)(2)(A)(ii).* The district court awarded fees in excess of the $75 per hour statutory cap. Most of the increase was intended to compensate for cost-of-living increases. Part of the increase, however, was attributable to the presence of several "special factors." First, Pirus' attorneys were expert in the field of social security law. Second, the court found that there were no lawyers in the community willing to undertake this case at the statutory rate. Finally, the court noted that Pirus' lawyers were uniquely situated to handle her case because of their recent experience litigating a similar case, *Bowen v. Owens,* all the way to the Supreme Court.

The Secretary now appeals the district court's decision to award fees in this case above the statutory hourly rate. We review the district court's decision to award fees in excess of the statutory cap for abuse of discretion. [*Underwood,*] 487 U.S. at 571.

---

* [Note: The $75 per hour rate cap was raised to $125 in 1996. Pub. L. No. 104–121, § 232 (1996) (codified at 28 U.S.C. § 2412(d)(2)(A)).]

In *Underwood,* the Supreme Court considered what Congress meant by a "special factor" that would justify fees at an hourly rate higher than $75. The "special factor" suggested by Congress as an example—"the limited availability of qualified attorneys for the proceedings involved"—received considerable attention. In this regard, the Court concluded that it is not enough to simply say that "lawyers skilled and experienced enough to try the case are in short supply." *Id.* The fact that prevailing hourly rates in a community might dissuade attorneys from taking a case at a $75 hourly rate was not the type of "limited availability" that Congress had in mind, since implicit in the language of § 2412(d) was a Congressional determination that "$75 an hour was generally quite enough public reimbursement for lawyers' fees, whatever the local or national market might be." *Id.* at 572. Congress instead intended for courts to deviate from the statutory cap only if there was limited availability of "attorneys having some distinctive knowledge or specialized skill *needful for the litigation* in question." *Id.* (emphasis added). As examples of the type of lawyers who possess the distinctive knowledge or skill that would justify deviation from the $75 cap, the Court described lawyers who have "an identifiable practice specialty such as patent law," or those who have knowledge of "foreign law or language." *Id.* "Where such qualifications are necessary, and can be obtained only at rates in excess of the $75 cap, reimbursement above the limit is allowed." *Id.*

The Court in *Underwood* thus recognized that lawyers who develop a practice specialty acquire distinctive knowledge and skills which may be necessary to a particular case. Although patent law was the only specialty identified by the Court, there is no reason to believe the Court intended the universe of such specialties to be limited to patent law alone. In the instant case, Pirus' attorneys had developed a practice specialty in social security law. Having litigated various class actions challenging provisions of the Act, they had extensive knowledge of the Act, its legislative history, and the development of the Social Security Administration's regulations. The expertise and skills that they developed are in many ways akin to those developed by a patent lawyer: expertise with a complex statutory scheme; familiarity and credibility with a particular agency; and understanding of the needs of a particular class of clients—in this case, the elderly—and of how those needs could best be met under the existing statute and regulations.

It is not enough, however, that the attorney possess distinctive knowledge and skills. Those qualifications warrant additional fees only if they are in some way needed in the litigation and cannot be obtained elsewhere at the statutory rate. In this case the district court ruled that the special expertise of the attorneys was necessary because the litigation involved a highly complex area of the Social Security Act, with which plaintiff's attorneys had already developed familiarity and expertise. The court noted that Pirus' class action was no routine disability case; it required substantial knowledge of the legislative history of the "widow's insurance" provisions of the Act. The court also found, as *Underwood* requires, that these skills could not be obtained at the statutory rate; indeed, the court determined that there were no lawyers in the Los Angeles area besides Pirus' attorneys who possessed the skills necessary to the case who would take the case for $75 an hour.

In sum, while the district court did not have *Underwood* for guidance when it considered Pirus' petition for attorney's fees, its decision to exceed the hourly rate cap was based on the same kind of factors as the *Underwood* court identified—Pirus' attorneys' extensive knowledge of social security law, their unique familiarity with the plaintiff class's entitlement to benefits because of the *Owens* case, and the fact that these necessary qualifications could not be obtained elsewhere except at rates in excess of the $75 cap. We cannot say that these findings were clearly erroneous, nor that it was an abuse of discretion for the district judge, on the basis of these findings, to award fees in excess of the statutory cap. * * *

The judgment of the district court is AFFIRMED. The case is RE-MANDED to that court for a determination of the amount of attorney's fees to be awarded Pirus for this appeal.

Notes and Questions

The *Pirus v. Bowen* case well illustrates the typical kind of statutory disputes that characterize federal government litigation, as well as the kind of cases in which EAJA fee petitions frequently arise. On the crucial question of whether the government's position on the merits was substantially justified, outline and compare the opposing arguments. Do you agree with the district court's conclusion? Was the government's position on the merits at least plausible (i.e., reasonable), even if it is not correct? Does the United States Court of Appeals for the Ninth Circuit hint that it might disagree with the district court's determination on the substantial justification question? If so, why does the court of appeals nonetheless affirm the district court?

On the question of when a court may exceed the hourly rate cap for EAJA Subsection (d) awards, read *Pirus* in tandem with the next case, *Perales v. Casillas*. We'll consider the issue further in the notes following that case.

Perales v. Casillas

United States Court of Appeals for the Fifth Circuit.
950 F.2d 1066 (5th Cir. 1992).

■ GARWOOD, CIRCUIT JUDGE:

This is an appeal from the second round of litigation initiated by several individual plaintiffs and a class of illegal aliens (hereinafter collectively referred to as plaintiffs). Plaintiffs brought a class-action lawsuit against the Immigration and Naturalization Service (INS) and several individual officials (defendants) requesting declaratory, injunctive and mandamus relief requiring the INS to change its method of considering petitions for voluntary departure and employment authorization for certain categories of illegal aliens. Plaintiffs were successful in the district court; however, on appeal to this Court, the challenged portions of the injunction were vacated. *Perales v. Casillas,* 903 F.2d 1043, 1053 (5th Cir.1990) (*Perales I*). While the appeal was pending, plaintiffs were awarded attorneys' fees under the Equal Access to Justice Act (EAJA), 28 U.S.C. § 2412. Defendants have appealed the award of fees in light of their successful appeal of the merits portion of this case. We vacate and remand the fee award for recalculation in light of our decision in *Perales I.*

Facts and Proceedings Below

All plaintiffs are married to United States citizens who filed initial immigration petitions on their behalf. Approval of these petitions does not entitle the aliens to visas, however. Because the aliens entered the United States illegally, additional approval from the United States Consulates abroad is required, 8 U.S.C. § 1255a(c), which can take many months. One key requirement for consular approval is a showing that the aliens are not likely to become "public charges." 8 U.S.C. § 1182(a)(4). While awaiting permanent residence status, the aliens are placed in limbo for as long as three years during which time they are subject to deportation by the INS.

The INS has historically followed a general pattern of allowing qualified aliens to remain in the United States under a grant of voluntary departure. In keeping with that policy, the San Antonio INS office (officials of which are defendants herein) routinely granted requests prior to 1984 for voluntary departure and employment authorization. At times, employment authorization was issued automatically even if the alien did not request it. For reasons undisclosed, however, between August 1984 and May 1987 the office failed to adjudicate requests for voluntary departure, and thus effectively also denied all requests for employment authorization, for which voluntary departure status is a prerequisite. Compounding the aliens' distress was the passage in 1986 of the Immigration Reform and Control Act, which makes it unlawful for employers to hire undocumented workers. 8 U.S.C. § 1324a. In the wake of this legislation, plaintiffs faced something of a legal "Catch–22": without documentation, plaintiffs found it difficult to lawfully support their families until visa applications were approved; moreover, without employment, plaintiffs faced denial of their visa applications and exclusion from the United States because of their inability to prove that they were not likely to become public charges.

Plaintiffs filed suit in 1986, seeking declaratory, injunctive and mandamus relief against the INS and several officials. The thrust of plaintiffs' claims was that the INS's failure to act on their requests for voluntary departure and employment authorization violated the Administrative Procedure Act (APA), 5 U.S.C. § 551 *et seq.,* and the Fifth Amendment. Class certification was granted on January 6, 1988.

On November 14, 1988, after a two-day bench trial, the district court issued a lengthy order granting permanent injunctive relief. After first rejecting several jurisdictional arguments raised by the INS (mootness, sovereign immunity and standing), the court announced that it was awarding relief under the APA rather than the Fifth Amendment. The court then issued a four-part permanent injunction providing: (1) All requests for voluntary departure shall be adjudicated within 60 days, * * * and applications for voluntary departure and employment authorization shall be considered jointly; (2) all denials of voluntary departure shall be made in writing, * * *; (3) defendants shall be prohibited from denying requests for employment authorization and voluntary departure on certain enumerated grounds;[4] and (4) the INS shall be prohibited from initiating deportation proceedings against class members in retaliation for their requests for relief. The court then concluded that the defendants' position in the lawsuit was not "substantially justified," and thus the plaintiffs were accordingly entitled to attorneys' fees under the EAJA. Plaintiffs correspondingly filed a motion for attorneys' fees on December 5, 1988.

Subsequently, on January 13, 1989, defendants appealed parts 3 and 4 of the injunction to this Court. Vacating the challenged portions, this Court held that courts may not circumscribe the discretion granted to the INS in setting factors for reviewing requests for employment authorization and voluntary departure; further, the injunction prohibiting retaliation against all class members was determined to be overbroad.

Meanwhile, pending the appeal on the merits, the district court referred the application for attorneys' fees to a United States Magistrate, pursuant to 28 U.S.C. § 636(b)(1). On March 14, 1990, the magistrate issued a lengthy order focusing primarily on the amount of the award, stating, "[T]hat the government's position was not substantially justified, is clear from the District Court's findings." Addressing an award of fees under the EAJA, the magistrate first observed the two-pronged aspect of the statute. Where the plaintiff prevails and the government's position was not "substantially justified," an award of fees of $75 per hour is permitted; this rate is intended to be a maximum, and may be increased only for cost of living changes or special factors. 28 U.S.C. §§ 2412(a), (d)(1)(A), (d)(2)(B). However, if the government acted in bad faith, "reasonable fees" (i.e., fees not limited by a specified maximum rate) may be awarded. 28 U.S.C. § 2412(b). The magistrate determined that an award of fees under section 2412(b) was warranted because defendants had acted in bad faith by: continuing to refuse to adjudicate requests for voluntary departure for over a year into the litigation; agreeing to change the policy, and then reneging; and attempting to deport class members in retaliation for the lawsuit. Consequently, the magistrate concluded that an award of fees at

---

4. The district court enjoined the INS from considering "economic need," the impact of an alien's employment on the job market, the manner of entry (as a sole basis for denial of relief), the alien's willingness to leave the United States, the condition of the alien's spouse, collateral asylum requests, and the absence of economic necessity or humanitarian concerns.

the market rate of $125 per hour was appropriate. The magistrate *alternatively* addressed fees under section 2412(d), and concluded that an enhancement to the statutory base rate of $75 per hour for cost of living increase was appropriate, and further, that the adjustment should be made as of the date of the award, and not historically (i.e., per year as the services were rendered). An overall rate of $95 per hour was determined to be appropriate under section 2412(d). Additional enhancements based on special expertise and limited availability of attorneys were rejected, however. After resolving the issues of which hours were to be compensated and which expenses were to be reimbursed, the magistrate ordered an award of $111,631.25 in attorneys' fees (893.05 hours at $125 per hour), $12,180.10 in costs, and $2,745.45 in expenses. * * *

Defendants now bring the present appeal, claiming that their success on the merits in *Perales I* decisively proves that they were "substantially justified" below; further, if they were "substantially justified," they could not have acted in bad faith. Accordingly, defendants request this court to vacate the award of fees. In the alternative, defendants request a remand for recalculation in light of plaintiffs' diminished degree of success. Plaintiffs challenge the alternate award under section 2412(d), claiming that the district court erroneously failed to grant an enhancement based on the attorneys' specialized skill and limited availability.

Discussion

I. Preserving Rights to Appeal: Objections to Magistrate's Report

[The court concluded that the government's failure to timely object to the magistrate's order awarding attorney fees did not result in waiver of the right to appeal, because the magistrate failed to inform the parties of the filing deadline for objections.]

II. Plaintiffs' Entitlement to Attorneys' Fees

A. Bad Faith

Although the litigants focus their attention on 28 U.S.C. § 2412(d) and the "substantial justification" issue, the district court affirmed the magistrate's award of fees to plaintiffs under *section 2412(b)* of the EAJA, which permits an award of fees against the government "to the same extent that any other party would be liable under the common law." 28 U.S.C. § 2412(b). We thus first consider whether the district court abused its discretion in awarding fees under this provision.

Section 2412(b) incorporates the "American rule" for fee-shifting, which permits a fee award only when the losing party acted "in *bad faith, vexatiously, wantonly, or for oppressive reasons.*" *F.D. Rich Co. v. United States ex rel. Industrial Lumber Co.,* 417 U.S. 116 (1974) (emphasis added). The court may consider conduct both during and prior to the litigation, although the award may not be based solely on the conduct that led to the substantive claim. Therefore, defendants' failure to adjudicate voluntary departure and employment authorization requests, in and of itself, does not implicate section 2412(b). The district court awarded fees at the market rate of $125 per hour under this provision based on the magistrate's following findings of bad faith: (1) the INS used inappropriate factors to adjudicate requests for relief; (2) the INS retaliated against class members through deportation proceedings; and (3) the INS failed to timely adjudicate requests for relief after promising to change this policy.

In opposition to plaintiffs' claims of bad faith, defendants merely rest on the laurels of their victory in *Perales I,* 903 F.2d at 1053, which they claim vindicated their position and vitiated any finding of bad faith. Such an argument may read *Perales I* too broadly. However, in light of "the district court's superior understanding of the litigation," *Hensley v. Eckerhart,* 461 U.S. 424 (1983), and because the district court was unaware of plaintiffs' ultimate degree of success at the time it passed on plaintiffs' request for fees, we remand for the district court to reevaluate its determination of bad faith in light our holding in *Perales I.* In that regard, we offer the following observations. As plaintiffs point out, the injunction against class-wide retaliatory deportation was struck down as overbroad and not as necessarily entirely unwarranted: "[t]he district court's fundamental error is the attempt to issue a class-wide restraint on the basis of a quintessentially individual problem." *Perales I,* 903 F.2d at 1053. Thus, the magistrate's finding that deportation proceedings were instituted (although not completed) against certain *individuals* was not reversed in *Perales I,* and might arguably still support a finding of bad faith. Moreover, although defendants' disregard of INS regulations was a basis for the suit, the fact that the regulations were still disregarded well over a year into the lawsuit, in contravention of the opinion of the INS Deputy District Director, also might support a finding of bad faith. Finally, the magistrate noted that defendants agreed to change their policy, then again slipped back into inaction without justification. Viewing these actions in the aggregate, the magistrate concluded that "[t]his blatant abuse of the immigration process and flagrant disregard of this judicial proceeding constitutes bad faith and warrants an award of attorneys' fees at the market rate under Section 2412(b)."

B. Substantial Justification

Plaintiffs alternatively based their claim for fees on 28 U.S.C. § 2412(d), which provides that the district court may award fees to the prevailing party when the government's position was not "substantially justified" and there are no other special circumstances that would otherwise make a fee award unjust. Plaintiffs were awarded $95 per hour under this provision. A finding that defendants did *not* act in bad faith does not resolve the "substantial justification" issue, because the standards are different. However, if on remand the district court upholds the finding of bad faith, then it need not address this issue since plaintiffs received the higher market rate of $125 per hour under the alternative provision, section 2412(b).

Eligibility for a fee award under the EAJA requires, at a minimum, that the claimant be a "prevailing party"; that the Government's position was not "substantially justified"; that no "special circumstances make an award unjust"; and that any fee application be submitted to the court within 30 days of final judgment and be supported by an itemized statement. *Commissioner INS v. Jean,* 496 U.S. 154 (1990). Only the application of the "substantially justified" condition is at issue here.

Defendants claim that this Court's ruling in *Perales I* indicates that their actions were substantially justified. Although defendants do not contest plaintiffs' status as the prevailing parties, they argue that plaintiffs were victorious on only the insignificant portions of their claim. Therefore, viewing the case as an "inclusive whole," defendants argue that plaintiffs are entitled to no fees. Plaintiffs, on the other hand, argue that even if portions of defendants' litigation position were substantially justified, their underlying actions were not. Accordingly, plaintiffs seek affirmance of fees for the entire litigation.

The district court's determination of whether the government's position was "substantially justified" is reviewed for abuse of discretion, *Pierce v. Underwood,* 487 U.S. 552 (1988); however, underlying conclusions of law are reviewed *de novo* and conclusions of fact are reviewed for clear error. In *Underwood,* the Supreme Court interpreted "substantially justified" as meaning " 'justified in substance or in the main'—that is, justified to a degree that could satisfy a reasonable person." *Id.* at 565. This definition, concluded the Court, comports with the "reasonable basis both in law and fact" adopted by the vast majority of circuit courts, including the Fifth Circuit.

Defendants rely heavily on *Jean, supra,* which they claim establishes a "holistic" approach to the "substantially justified" determination. Because plaintiffs' residual success was mandated by amendments to the immigration regulations passed during the pendency of the litigation, defendants contend that plaintiffs' victory does not defeat a finding of substantial justification. Rather, defendants argue that their successful appeal of the "more onerous" portions of the injunction demonstrates that they were "substantially justified" overall. Defendants read *Jean* too broadly. In *Jean,* the Supreme Court held that the government could not avoid fees for litigating the fee dispute ("fees for fees") by claiming that, although it lost below, its position in the fee litigation was substantially justified. Rather, the Court concluded, a "substantially justified" determination properly focuses on the governmental misconduct giving rise to the litigation, as well as on the government's litigation position. *Jean,* 496 U.S. at 165.

Under *Jean,* then, defendants' success in *Perales I* is not necessarily determinative of the "substantially justified" issue; the underlying misconduct giving rise to the suit must be also evaluated. In fact, the district court did evaluate that misconduct at length, concluding that "it should be abundantly clear that it is the finding of this Court that defendants' position in this lawsuit was not substantially justified." However, at the time of its decision, the district court did not have the benefit of our opinion in *Perales I.* Despite our favorable ruling for defendants in *Perales I,* we cannot say as a matter of law that defendants' position both prior to and during the litigation was substantially justified so as to deprive plaintiffs of attorneys' fees entirely. Therefore, we are compelled to return this case to the district court for reevaluation of the substantial justification issue in light of plaintiffs' diminished degree of success. In that regard, we observe that, despite defendants' cries of victory, plaintiffs are still the prevailing parties; their lawsuit changed the operations of the INS, producing a significant benefit for the members of the class.

III. Apportionment of Fees

If the district court determines on remand that plaintiffs are still entitled to fees under the EAJA, the next question the district court must address is whether plaintiffs are entitled to fees for the entire litigation, or whether the fees should be apportioned based on plaintiffs' diminished degree of success as a result of *Perales I*. In *Hensley v. Eckerhart,* 461 U.S. 424, [434–35] (1983), the Supreme Court announced that the district court should focus on the significance of the overall relief obtained by the plaintiff in relation to the hours reasonably expended on the litigation. In particular, the Court offered the following guidance:

> "Where the plaintiff has failed to prevail on a claim that is distinct in all respects from his successful claims, the hours spent on the unsuccessful claim should be excluded in considering the amount of a reasonable fee. Where a lawsuit consists of related claims, a plaintiff who has won substantial relief should not have his attorney's fee reduced simply because the district court did not adopt each contention raised. But where the plaintiff achieved only limited success, the district court should award only that amount of fees that is reasonable in relation to the results obtained." *Id.* [at 440].

Because the district court did not have the opportunity to properly consider the relationship between the extent of plaintiffs' ultimate success and the amount of the fee award, we are unable to affirm the decision below. Accordingly, if on remand the district court finds plaintiffs are entitled to fees under the EAJA, the court must still recalculate plaintiffs' fees in light of our opinion in *Perales I* and following the teachings of *Hensley.*

IV. Adjustments

If on remand plaintiffs are found entitled to fees but a market rate fee is found inappropriate under a bad faith theory, the district court must then consider plaintiffs' requests for adjustments under section 2412(d) of the EAJA. Generally, in determining the amount of attorneys' fees, the district court enjoys discretion. *See Underwood, supra,* 487 U.S. at 571. The EAJA limits that discretion, however, mandating that an award not exceed $75 per hour "unless the court determines that an increase in the cost of living or a special factor ... justifies a higher fee." 28 U.S.C. § 2412(d)(2)(A).* The amount of the cost-of-living increase is keyed to the

---

* [Note: The $75 per hour rate cap was raised to $125 in 1996. Pub. L. No. 104–121, § 232 (1996) (codified at 28 U.S.C. § 2412(d)(2)(A)).]

base year, which is 1981.** *Baker v. Bowen,* 839 F.2d 1075, 1084 (5th Cir.1988).[9] In this case, after adjusting the $75 an hour statutory rate for the then-current year, taking into consideration the testimony of several expert witnesses, the magistrate, in determining the alternate award, arrived at an adjusted rate of $95 per hour for all hours "whenever expended." The district court declined, however, to further adjust the rate based on the special expertise or limited availability of plaintiffs' counsel.

A.   Cost-of-Living Adjustment

Defendants do not now contend that a cost-of-living increase is not warranted, or that the rate selected by the district court is excessive. Rather, defendants focus on the timing of plaintiffs' attorneys' work. Defendants argue, as they did below, that a blanket fee for all hours expended is not appropriate, and contend that the cost-of-living increase should be calculated from 1981 for each year, separately, since the hours began accumulating in 1985 ("historic rates"). Hence, defendants contend that in setting a cost-of-living adjustment, the court may consider only inflation that occurred prior to the attorneys' performance and may not consider increases that occurred subsequent to the work performed. In support of this contention, defendants rely on *Library of Congress v. Shaw,* 478 U.S. 310 (1986), which held that the United States is immune from an interest award, absent express congressional consent. Justifying current rather than historic rates because of delay in relief, defendants contend, is tantamount to awarding interest.

Defendants correctly construe *Shaw* as holding that principles of sovereign immunity dictate, as a general proposition, that interest awards against the United States are prohibited. However, we have recognized that this general rule admits of several exceptions, only one of which is potentially relevant in this case; namely, where the United States has expressly consented to such an award, sovereign immunity does not bar interest. The focus of this exception is whether the legislation giving rise to the cause of action expressly subjects the government to interest payments.

In analyzing whether Congress has waived the immunity of the United States in a particular statute, we must construe the statute strictly in favor of the sovereign, and not enlarge any waiver found therein beyond what the language requires. The no-interest rule provides an added gloss of strictness upon these usual rules of construction. Driving home the point of explicit waiver, the Supreme Court admonished in *Shaw:*

** [Note: With the increase of the hourly rate ceiling to $125 in 1996, the base year for future cost of living adjustments to this higher cap will be 1996.]

9. The EAJA was originally enacted in 1981. In 1985, the EAJA was reenacted to remove the sunset provision; the $75 per hour statutory maximum remained unchanged. Despite the amendment, the courts recognized that the intended effect of the reenactment was to treat the act as if it had never expired. *See Baker v. Bowen,* 839 F.2d 1075, 1084 (5th Cir.1988). On this basis, the majority of federal courts have held that the cost-of-living adjustment should be measured from the date of enactment of the EAJA in 1981 and not from the reenactment in 1985. *Id.*

"[T]here can be no consent by implication or by use of ambiguous language. Nor can an intent on the part of the framers of a statute or contract to permit the recovery of interest suffice where the intent is not translated into affirmative statutory or contractual terms. The consent necessary to waive the traditional immunity must be express, and it must be strictly construed." [*Shaw,* 478 U.S. at 318.]

Underscoring its point, the Court observed that "[w]hen Congress has intended to waive the United States' immunity with respect to interest, it has done so expressly." *Id.*

We conclude that this is an issue of first impression in this Circuit.[12] Initially, we recognize that many courts have awarded a cost-of-living adjustment under the EAJA based on the current Consumer Price Index (CPI) without regard to the year in which the services were performed. The apparent motivating factor behind each of these decisions was a desire to compensate the attorney for the delay between performance and payment. None of these courts, however, addressed the question of whether such awards impermissibly required the United States to pay interest.

Turning to the language of the EAJA, as mandated by *Shaw,* we observe that it does expressly provide for the award of *post-judgment* interest, but only in certain circumstances.[13] Moreover, although the EAJA does not use the phrase "prejudgment interest," it does allow the $75 maximum rate to be increased based on the cost of living or special factors. * * *

* * * The Supreme Court could not have more clearly stated that waivers of sovereign immunity must be strictly construed; therefore, the presumption is against allowing interest awards. Moreover, we cannot simply side-step this difficult question by calling the award a "cost-of-living adjustment" rather than an interest award. "[W]hether the loss to be compensated by an increase in a fee award stems from an opportunity cost or from the effects of inflation, the increase is prohibited by the no-interest rule." *Shaw,* 478 U.S. at 322. Accordingly, we look not to whether Congress *precluded* a current adjustment for all hours, but whether Congress *expressly allowed* such awards. We find no language in the EAJA authorizing fees at current adjusted rates for all hours whenever expended. The narrowest reasonable construction of the cost-of-living provision in the EAJA leads us to conclude that this was an attempt to allow the statute to be self-updating in light of the modern realities of inflation. This purpose is accomplished through the award of historic rates; anything more treads

---

12. * * * In *Missouri v. Jenkins by Agyei,* 491 U.S. 274, 281 n. 3 (1989), the Supreme Court made clear that the "no-interest" rule applies only when the liability of the federal government is at issue. Outside the context of federal immunity, the Court stated that "we see no reason why compensation for delay cannot be included" within attorneys' fee awards. *Id.* * * *

13. With regard to postjudgment interest, the EAJA provides:

"If the United States appeals an award of costs or fees and other expenses made against the United States under this section and the award is affirmed in whole or in part, interest shall be paid on the amount of the award as affirmed." 28 U.S.C. § 2412(f).

impermissibly across the line and is tantamount to interest. Therefore, in keeping with *Shaw*'s mandate of not enlarging the waiver of sovereign immunity "beyond what the language requires," we hold that cost-of-living adjustments under the EAJA must be made to reflect the appropriate rate in the year in which the services were rendered.

A simple example illustrates the logic of what may seem to be a nice distinction. If an attorney provides services in 1991 and is compensated in that same year, adjusting the $75 statutory rate based on increases in the cost of living between 1981 and 1991 provides no concerns of prohibited interest. The adjustment operates simply to update the EAJA's statutory rate; delay is not a consideration. Suppose instead the attorney provides services in 1988 and the appropriate adjusted rate is then $100 per hour; however, because of the delays normally attendant on litigation, the fee award is not made until 1991. An award of $100 per hour for those services is expressly permitted under the EAJA. If the court goes further and awards the attorney $110 per hour to compensate for inflation not only between 1981 and 1988, but also between 1988 and 1991, then the court has in effect awarded interest for the three-year delay in payment. We do not find that the EAJA expressly countenances such a result. Accordingly, following the teachings of *Shaw,* we conclude that cost-of-living compensation of attorneys under the EAJA merely for the delay in payment is a prohibited award of interest against the United States.

Turning to the issue of whether special factors may independently justify departing from the historic rates rule, we note that we have previously recognized, albeit in *dicta,* that delay in payment may be a special factor within the meaning of the EAJA. *Baker v. Bowen,* 839 F.2d 1075, 1082–83 (5th Cir.1988). However, in *Baker* we also observed that such a factor will arise only rarely and will be unique to the fact situation of the particular case. In this case, the magistrate determined that the delay anticipated by plaintiffs before receipt of the award "cannot be considered normal delay." This determination was based on the already protracted nature of the litigation and on the anticipation that defendants would continue to appeal the merits to the Supreme Court and appeal the fee award to this Court, creating a delay of at least a year or more before plaintiffs would receive the award. Accordingly, he recommended that the adjusted rate be applied to all of plaintiffs' hours, whenever expended.

Despite our passing recognition in *Baker* that delay may justify increasing the EAJA's statutory rate, we have not had the occasion to define the boundaries of delay *vis-à-vis* the EAJA's "special factor" provision. Several courts have concluded that the "special factor" provision in the EAJA allows an increase in the statutory cap to compensate parties for prolonged delay in payment. Even after the Supreme Court's sweeping prohibition in *Shaw* of interest awards against the United States, the D.C. Circuit adhered to this view, noting that the EAJA expressly gives the courts leeway to adjust the statutory maximum in the presence of a "special factor." *Wilkett v. ICC,* 844 F.2d 867, 876 (D.C.Cir.1988). However, the court made clear its position that routine delay alone does not justify increasing the fee.

We agree that some forms of delay may justify enhancing the statutory base rate under the EAJA. However, we recognize, as did the court in *Wilkett,* that some delay in payment of fees is and has long been nearly always inevitable. Therefore, the normal delay attendant on litigation of a fee request can hardly be called a "special factor." Nor will we permit an increase in the cap in every instance of complex litigation where the delay is unusually long. Instead, we believe that delay will become a special factor only when it is truly exceptional and not attributable to negligence or improper conduct of the prevailing party.

We do not find the delay in this case to have been truly exceptional. Any delay in payment experienced by plaintiffs in this case has been caused merely by the complexity of the litigation and defendants' appeals to this Court. Were we to conclude that such delays are "exceptional," we would remove any real meaning from the term "*special* factor." Accordingly, we hold that the district court, in its alternate award, abused its discretion in compensating plaintiffs' attorneys above the properly adjusted per hour statutory maximum because of delay in payment.

B.   Enhancement of Fees: Specialization and Availability

Plaintiffs argue in respect to the alternative award under section 2412(d) that the district court abused its discretion when it refused to enhance the section 2412(d) fee due to the attorneys' expertise and limited availability. Plaintiffs point to the attorneys' fluency in Spanish, as well as their board certification in immigration law as evidence that the attorneys possessed special expertise. Additionally, plaintiffs assert that few attorneys are willing to engage in this sort of litigation; thus, there is limited availability. These special factors, contend plaintiffs, warrant an increase in the base fee. The magistrate considered these arguments at length, evaluating the testimony of numerous experts, but ultimately rejected them.

In *Underwood, supra,* the Supreme Court interpreted these special factors as referring to attorneys qualified

> "in some specialized sense, rather than just in their general legal competence. We think it refers to attorneys having some distinctive knowledge or specialized skill needful for the litigation in question—as opposed to an extraordinary level of the general lawyerly knowledge and ability useful in all litigation. Examples of the former would be an identifiable practice specialty such as patent law, or knowledge of foreign law or language." *Underwood,* 487 U.S. at 572.

Defendants concede that patent law appropriately represents a specialized area because of the specific technical training required of members of the Patent Bar.[15] However, defendants argue that immigration law is no more

---

15. Patent lawyers must have certain scientific and technical qualifications, which make them uniquely qualified to render a valuable service. *See Sperry v. Florida,* 373 U.S. 379 (1963). In addition, the Patent and Trademark Office administers a separate ex-a specialty than family law, or bankruptcy, or numerous other areas of the law. Further, defendants point out that the magistrate found no showing of a lack of attorneys able to handle this type of litigation.

Although at least one court has apparently recognized that immigration specialty can constitute a "special factor" under the EAJA, *Ramon-Sepulveda v. INS,* 863 F.2d 1458 (9th Cir.1988) (dicta), we believe that the Supreme Court in *Underwood* intended to distinguish nonlegal or technical abilities possessed by, for example, patent lawyers and experts in foreign law, from other types of substantive specializations currently proliferating within the profession. In a sense, every attorney practicing within a narrow field could claim specialized knowledge. Although the district court found that "[i]mmigration law is a specialty area requiring an extensive and current knowledge of applicable statutes and regulations," such is true for virtually any area of law, particularly those involving the intricate federal statutory schemes that typically give rise to awards under the EAJA.

In *Baker v. Bowen,* 839 F.2d 1075, 1084 (5th Cir.1988), we considered whether attorneys specialized in social security litigation merited an enhancement to the statutory rate. In remanding to the district court for further findings, we warned that the

> "district court must be careful to distinguish the limited availability of attorneys from the special expertise of certain attorneys or the mere unattractiveness of the field. . . . [T]he ultimate issue is whether there is reason to believe that social security claimants with colorable claims will actually be disadvantaged by denial of access to the courts because of lack of available representation." *Id.* at 1084–85.

Thus, *Baker* teaches that an increased rate should be awarded for special expertise/limited availability only if: (1) the number of competent attorneys who handle cases in the specialized field is so limited that individuals who have possibly valid claims are unable to secure representation; and (2) that by increasing the fee, the availability of lawyers for these cases will actually be increased.[16]

The district court below conceded that plaintiffs' attorneys possessed skill in immigration practice as well as useful fluency in Spanish. The court also considered testimony from several attorneys who testified that increasing the fee would increase the availability of lawyers willing to handle this type of litigation. However, the court found no limited availability of qualified attorneys to handle immigration cases, noting that the problem is not that the attorneys would not work for $75 per hour, but that they often could not collect *any* fee from their indigent clients. The court also found

amination for admission to the Patent Bar, further restricting the pool of potential attorneys.

16. Plaintiffs urge this Court to treat special expertise and limited availability as separate "special factors." Such a position, however, would contradict our holding in *Baker.* Furthermore, the enhancement of fees under the EAJA is not designed to reward certain attorneys for possessing unique skills, but rather to encourage attorneys in areas of high demand to represent claimants covered by the EAJA. Accordingly, limited availability is an essential element of the special expertise factor.

that plaintiffs' experts were unable to identify any persons with colorable claims that remained unrepresented. Accordingly, the district court rejected an increase based on expertise or limited availability.

We conclude that the district court's findings under the *Baker* test are not clearly erroneous. We therefore hold that the district court did not abuse its discretion by refusing enhancements based on specialization or limited availability in respect to its alternative award under section 2412(d).

Conclusion

The Supreme Court in *Hensley, supra,* admonished that a "request for attorney's fees should not result in a second major litigation." *Hensley,* [461 U.S. at 437]. Nevertheless, because of the unusual posture of this dispute, we are compelled to vacate the award of fees to plaintiffs' attorneys and return this case to the district court for reconsideration consistent with our holding in *Perales I* and the guidelines given here.

On remand, the court should determine first whether defendants' conduct prior to and during the litigation was such as to sink to the level of bad faith within the meaning of 28 U.S.C. § 2412(b). If it is determined that defendants are not shown to have acted in bad faith, then the district court must evaluate whether defendants' success on the merits entitles them to a finding of substantial justification for the litigation as a whole or in part. In the event the district court determines that plaintiffs are entitled to at least partial fees, the district court, consistent with the teachings of *Hensley, supra,* must apportion those fees based on plaintiffs' degree of success. With respect to enhancement of fees under section 2412(d), we hold that the district court erred in applying a current cost-of-living adjustment to all hours, and instruct the court, to the extent any award on remand may be based on section 2412(d), to segregate the attorneys' hours by year and apply the appropriate cost-of-living adjustment on an annual basis, if such adjustment is determined to be warranted in the court's discretion. Finally, we find no error in the district court's denial of enhancement of the alternative award based on the attorneys' expertise and availability.

For the reasons stated, the judgment of the district court is

VACATED and the cause is REMANDED for further proceedings consistent herewith.

———

Notes and Questions

1. With *Perales v. Casillas,* we are exposed to Subsection (b) in (at least potential) action. The United States Court of Appeals for the Fifth Circuit provides a good description of what Subsection (b) does accomplish and what it does not, in terms of making a fee award available. What, beyond Subsection (b), must be present before fees may be awarded against

the federal government? Consider again the opinion in *Palmer v. General Services Administration,* 787 F.2d 300 (8th Cir. 1986), set out in Chapter VII.B.1, and the notes following that case. What element does Subsection (b) supply and what additional element must be supplied from another source of law? How is that additional element arguably provided in the *Perales* case? Why is the case remanded on the Subsection (b) question? What evidence would be sufficient to justify a fee award under Subsection (b) fee on remand?

Why does the fee petitioner in *Perales* even raise Subsection (b) given the alternative of EAJA Subsection (d)? After all, Subsection (d) has a somewhat easier threshold to satisfy for a fee award than a "bad faith" claim presented through Subsection (b) (lack of substantial justification in the government's position versus bad faith in handling of the litigation). What advantage does Subsection (b) afford to a fee petitioner that would make it preferable to Subsection (d)? (Hint: Look at 28 U.S.C. § 2412(d)(2)(A).)

2. Turning to Subsection (d), the court also remands the case on the substantial justification question. Why? With respect to Subsection (d), the court of appeals focuses primarily on how a fee should be calculated if the government is found on remand to have lacked substantial justification:

a. *Cost of Living Adjustment.* The hourly rate cap under Subsection (d)—which was $75 per hour at the time of the *Perales* decision and is now $125 per hour (since 1996)—should be adjusted periodically to account for changes in the cost of living since the base year (which then was 1981 as the date of the original enactment of the EAJA with a $75 per hour rate ceiling, and which now is 1996 as the date on which the rate cap was raised to $125). In *Perales,* the government argues that the cost of living adjustment applies only to increases in the cost of living from the date of EAJA's enactment to the date the work was performed, but not beyond to the later date of the actual fee award. The court of appeals accepts this argument. Why? How does the court separate the permissible cost of living adjustment from impermissible compensation for delay in award of the fees? Why is this necessary? May delay ever be a basis for enhancing a fee award under EAJA Subsection (d)? How and when? On cost of living adjustments to the hourly rate cap and enhancement for delay, see generally Gregory C. Sisk, *The Essentials of the Equal Access to Justice Act: Court Awards of Attorney's Fees for Unreasonable Government Conduct (Part Two),* 56 La. L. Rev. 1, 128–45, 171–75 (1995).

For examples of decisions by other courts of appeals that apply the EAJA Subsection (d) cost-of-living adjustment consistent with *Perales,* see, *e.g., American Wrecking Corp. v. Secretary of Labor,* 364 F.3d 321, 329 (D.C. Cir. 2004) (explaining that "the court must calculate any cost-of-living increase according to the year in which the service was performed, not the year in which the fee is recovered"); *Sorenson v. Mink,* 239 F.3d 1140, 1147–49 (9th Cir. 2001) (holding that the court should use cost-of-living adjustments that apply to the years in which the hours were actually expended, rather than the cost-of-living index for the year in which judgment is entered, because the latter adjustment improperly "compensates a lawyer for a delay in payment and is the functional equivalent of prejudgment interest"); *Kerin v. United States Postal Service*, 218 F.3d 185, 194 (2d Cir. 2000) (holding that "[u]sing a single cap reflecting the cost of living in [the judgment year] for all nine years [of the litigation] to calculate the amount of attorney's fees would result in a *de facto* award of pre-judgment interest, which would constitute an abuse of discretion").

b. *Special Factor Enhancement.* Compare and contrast the Fifth Circuit's analysis in *Perales v. Casillas* of the "special factor" basis for departing from the hourly rate cap in the context of a practice specialty, with that of the Ninth Circuit in the *Pirus v. Bowen* decision we studied just previously. Both opinions refer for guidance to the Supreme Court's example in *Pierce v. Underwood* of patent law specialization as a special factor that would justify exceeding the EAJA rate cap. But the Fifth and Ninth Circuits draw very different conclusions from this patent law example. How do these two courts differ in analysis? What does each court view as distinctive about patent law practice? How broad is the Ninth Circuit's *Pirus* test for qualifying practice specialties as a "special factor" that justify a higher hourly rate? How narrow is the Fifth Circuit's *Perales* test?

Subsequent to *Pirus*, the Ninth Circuit ruled that an attorney's expertise in environmental law also warranted an enhancement under the EAJA. *National Wildlife Federation v. Federal Energy Regulatory Commission*, 870 F.2d 542, 547 (9th Cir. 1989). The court explained that the key criterion for a special factor enhancement was the attorney's "mastery of a technical subject matter gained by the investment of time and energy." *Id.* The Ninth Circuit confirmed this analysis in *Love v. Reilly*, 924 F.2d 1492, 1496 (9th Cir. 1991), where it explained that "[e]nvironmental litigation is an identifiable practice specialty that requires distinctive knowledge." Judge Wallace dissented in *Love*, saying that classifying "such a broad legal field" as environmental law as a special factor "strays too far from the limiting constraints" placed by the Supreme Court in *Underwood* on the definition of a special factor so as to preserve the integrity of the hourly rate ceiling. *Id.* at 1498–99 (Wallace, J., concurring in part and dissenting in part).

By contrast, the Fifth Circuit's approach in *Perales* appears to limit special factor specialties to "nonlegal or technical abilities possessed by, for example, patent lawyers and experts in foreign law." *See also Estate of Cervin v. Commissioner*, 200 F.3d 351, 353–55 (5th Cir. 2000) (rejecting claim of specialization in tax law and state community property law as basis for enhancing fee rate in case involving attorney's fee provision in Internal Revenue Code that parallels EAJA Subsection (d), and further stating that if *Perales* and other circuit precedent "left any room for doubt about whether the 'special factor' analysis requires 'nonlegal or technical abilities,' [the court] now conclude[s] that it does so require"). The District of Columbia Circuit has also suggested that a special factor for purposes of departing from the EAJA hourly rate cap requires "technical or other education *outside* the field of American law." *Waterman S.S. Corp. v.*

Maritime Subsidy Board, 901 F.2d 1119, 1124 (D.C. Cir. 1990); *see also In re Sealed Case,* 254 F.3d 233, 235–36 (D.C. Cir. 2001) (reiterating *Waterman* ruling that technical or other education outside the field of American law is required for an EAJA special factor enhancement and rejecting argument that higher fees were necessary to hire specialists in federal election law, observing that the field is not beyond the grasp of a competent practicing lawyer); *F.J. Vollmer Co. v. Magaw,* 102 F.3d 591, 598–99 (D.C.Cir. 1996) (holding that specialized training in a technical field, not mere practice experience in administrative law involving a technical industry, was required for a special factor enhancement under EAJA).

The Seventh Circuit has taken a middle road toward the issue, rejecting a liberal standard that would permit routine enhancement above the hourly rate cap whenever an attorney claims a practice specialty, but also resisting the narrow view that only nonlegal attributes may qualify as a special factor. In *Raines v. Shalala,* 44 F.3d 1355, 1359–62 (7th Cir. 1995), the court rejected social security law specialization as a special factor. As the standard for a special factor enhancement, the Seventh Circuit said the question is whether the attorney possesses distinctive legal knowledge or other specialized skills, needful for the litigation, that surpasses what could "be easily acquired by a reasonably competent lawyer." *Id.* at 1361.

The Seventh Circuit's "reasonably competent lawyer" approach appears to be gaining more adherents among the other circuits. *See, e.g., Healey v. Leavitt,* 485 F.3d 63 (2d Cir. 2007) (holding that "a case requires 'specialized expertise' within the meaning of the EAJA only when it requires some knowledge or skill that cannot be obtained by a competent practicing attorney through routine research or legal experience," and rejecting expertise in Medicare statutes and regulations as justifying an enhancement); *Hyatt v. Barnhart,* 315 F.3d 239, 249–43 (4th Cir. 2002) (holding that, even if a fee enhancement is permitted for something other than a speciality requiring technical or other education outside of the field of American law, no special factor enhancement was permitted in this case because "expertise in social security law would be of the type that is possessed or easily acquired by reasonably competent attorneys licensed to practice law"); *Atlantic Fish Spotters Ass'n v. Daley,* 205 F.3d 488, 491–92 (1st Cir. 2000) (rejecting the government's argument that specialists in fields of law, such as fisheries law, are automatically excluded from an EAJA special factor enhancement, but holding that the crucial question is not whether an attorney's special expertise was "helpful or productive but whether it is essential for competent representation" and further observing that in most cases of administrative law, "an otherwise competent lawyer can—albeit at the cost of some extra time—learn enough about the particular controversy to litigate in the area adequately, although perhaps not as well as a long-time specialist"); *Chynoweth v. Sullivan,* 920 F.2d 648, 650 (10th Cir. 1990) (stating that a special factor enhancement is permissible under EAJA in the unusual case that requires "specialized training and expertise unattainable by a competent attorney through a diligent study of the governing legal principles").

———

CHAPTER VIII

THE UNITED STATES AS PLAINTIFF

In most of the litigation and under most of the statutes examined thus far in this course, the United States is the target of a claim and thus has played the involuntary role of a defendant. However, although the United States is the defendant in more than two-thirds of the civil cases to which it is a party, the sovereign federal government is also a frequent-flying plaintiff in the federal courts. When the United States is the initiating party of court action, certain additional questions arise:

First, as addressed in Section A below, we must determine when the interests of the United States are sufficiently at issue, such that the federal government may institute a lawsuit, either on its own behalf or as a surrogate for the public at large or some segment of it. How do we define the government's interest? What kind of stake must the government have in a dispute before it may intervene in court, rather than leaving the prosecution of the claim to the private party most directly involved?

Second, as covered in Section B below, we must consider time limitations on filing suit by the sovereign. Is the federal government bound by statutes of limitations in the same manner as private parties? In the absence of a federal statute of limitations, may a state limitations period be borrowed and applied to the United States? Does the equitable concept of laches apply to the federal government as it does to other litigants?

Third, as studied in Section C below, when the United States files suit as a plaintiff, a defendant may wish to respond with a counterclaim against the government. Does the government's initiation of civil litigation open the door—fully, part way, or not at all—to counterclaims, even in the absence of an express statutory waiver of sovereign immunity?

———

SECTION A. POWER TO SUE

As a civil plaintiff, the federal government may seek judicial relief (1) to uphold its own interests as an entity, or (2) to safeguard the rights of its citizens (at least when authorized by statute):

First, the United States has the right to bring action to protect and advance its own interests as a property owner, party to a contract, employer, etc. Indeed, the United States as a body politic arguably does not require specific congressional authorization to enforce its own rights in the federal or state courts, so long as it shows a direct governmental interest in bringing suit. Thus, for example, the Attorney General on her own general statutory authority may institute suit for trespass to government property or for common-law torts against the government. *See, e.g., United States v. California*, 332 U.S. 19 (1947); *United States v. San Jacinto Tin Co.*, 125 U.S. 273 (1888). And, whether necessary or not, Congress has specifically granted the government authority to commence certain legal actions to recover debts owed to it or obtain reimbursement for expenses it has borne. A substantial portion of the government's affirmative litigation in the federal courts (and an equally substantial portion of its resources devoted to civil litigation) involves debt collection. *See generally* Gregory C. Sisk, *Litigation With the Federal Government* § 8.05, at 517–19 (ALI–ABA, 4th ed. 2006). As another example, under the Medical Care Recovery Act, 42 U.S.C. §§ 2651–53, the federal government may recover the reasonable value of the medical treatment provided by the government to those (such as military servicemembers) injured by third parties. *See generally United States v. Trammel*, 899 F.2d 1483 (6th Cir. 1990); Michael F. Noone, *The Federal Medical Care Recovery Act*, 55 A.B.A.J. 259 (1969).

Second, the federal government regularly plays a visible role as an advocate for public interests. Thus, as examples from the employment discrimination and labor relations fields of law, the Equal Employment Opportunity Commission may initiate anti-discrimination litigation against private employers on behalf of individual employees, 42 U.S.C. § 2000e–5(f)(1), and the National Labor Relations Board may petition the courts to enforce its orders concerning labor-management relations, 29 U.S.C. § 160(e). While the substance of such litigation sometimes may be controversial, the authority of the federal government to prosecute these kinds of suits is confirmed by statute and occasions little controversy.

By contrast, when explicit congressional consent to legal action is absent, the authority of the Executive through the Department of Justice to institute litigation on behalf of the primary interests of third parties is uncertain and controverted. That controversy is illustrated by the next case.

————

United States v. City of Philadelphia

United States Court of Appeals for the Third Circuit.
644 F.2d 187 (3rd Cir. 1980).

■ Aldisert, Circuit Judge.

The primary question in this appeal is whether the United States has implied authority to sue a city and its officials for an injunction against violations of the fourteenth amendment rights of individuals. The government argues that both the criminal provisions of the Civil Rights Acts of 1866 and 1870, 18 U.S.C. §§ 242 and 241, and the fourteenth amendment itself give rise to an implied right of action. We also must decide whether the government has stated a claim for relief under the Omnibus Crime Control and Safe Streets Act of 1968, 42 U.S.C. § 3789d, or the State and Local Fiscal Assistance Act of 1972 (the "Revenue Sharing Act"), 31 U.S.C. § 1242. In a pair of published opinions, the district court held that the Attorney General has no standing to advance the civil rights of third persons absent an express statutory grant of the necessary authority, and that the complaint did not allege claims under the two funding statutes with sufficient specificity; and accordingly it dismissed the complaint. *United States v. City of Philadelphia,* 482 F.Supp. 1248 and 1274 (E.D.Pa. 1979). We affirm.

I.

Because the case comes before this court on appeal from orders of the district court dismissing the complaint, we assume that all well-pleaded allegations of the complaint are true, and we set out the facts alleged in the light most favorable to the appellant.

The government's theory is that the appellees, the City of Philadelphia and numerous high-ranking officials of the City and its Police Department, have engaged in a pattern or practice of depriving persons of rights protected by the due process clause of the fourteenth amendment. The allegations of the complaint can be conveniently divided into two categories. First, it alleges that Philadelphia police officers have engaged in a widespread practice of violating the rights of persons they encounter on the streets and elsewhere in the city. In particular, it charges that officers have stopped automobiles and pedestrians without probable cause and physically abused or illegally arrested those who protested, arbitrarily closed public areas and responded to protests or resistance with physical abuse and unwarranted arrests, conducted illegal searches and seizures, detained persons without probable cause or for excessive periods, denied them access to counsel or to medical care while detained, physically abused arrested persons, extracted information and confessions by means of physical brutality, subjected individuals to verbal abuse (including racial slurs), filed unwarranted criminal charges, and engaged in unnecessary use of deadly force, such as shooting criminal suspects who offer no realistic threat to the safety of police officers or other persons.

Second, the United States alleges that the appellees have deliberately encouraged these illegal practices through the policies and procedures they have established for investigating complaints of illegal police activity. It charges that the appellees discourage victims of abuse from complaining, suppress evidence that inculpates police officers, accept implausible explanations of abusive conduct, harass complainants and witnesses, prematurely terminate investigations, compile reports that justify police officers' conduct regardless of actual circumstances, refuse to discipline police officers for known violations, and protect officers from outside investigations. It also charges various appellees with pursuing inadequate training practices, resulting in a pattern of police abuses, and with engaging in surveillance and harassment of critics of the police department.

The United States also alleges generally that some or all of the appellees have deliberately endeavored to encourage police violations of civil rights. It charges that these practices have been implemented with the intent and the effect of inflicting abuse disproportionately on black and Hispanic persons. And finally, it alleges that the foregoing practices have been implemented by police department personnel whose activities are funded in part by federal grants dispensed for the purpose of improving police procedures.

In its prayer for relief, the government asks for a declaration "that the acts, practices, policies and procedures alleged herein violate the Constitution and laws of the United States." It also asks the court to enjoin "the defendants, their agents, employees, successors in office, and all those acting in concert or participation with them" from engaging in the conduct alleged, "from failing or refusing to correct the effects" of that conduct, "from failing or refusing to ensure" that such conduct will not recur, "and from receiving, expending, or failing to make restitution for previously expended federal funds, unless and until defendants cease such acts, policies, practices, and procedures and correct their effects."

II.

We first address the contention that the two criminal statutes, 18 U.S.C. §§ 241 and 242, implicitly grant the United States a right of action for injunctive relief. These statutes provide:

§ 241.   *Conspiracy against rights of citizens*

If two or more persons conspire to injure, oppress, threaten, or intimidate any citizen in the free exercise or enjoyment of any right or privilege secured to him by the Constitution or laws of the United States, or because of his having so exercised the same ...

. . .

They shall be fined not more than $10,000 or imprisoned not more than ten years, or both; and if death results, they shall be subject to imprisonment for any term of years or for life.

§ 242.   *Deprivation of rights under color of law*

Whoever, under color of any law, statute, ordinance, regulation, or custom, willfully subjects any inhabitant of any State, Territory, or District to the deprivation of any rights, privileges, or immunities secured or protected by the Constitution or laws of the United States, or to different punishments, pains, or penalties, on account of such inhabitant being an alien, or by reason of his color, or race, than are prescribed for the punishment of citizens, shall be fined not more than $1,000 or imprisoned not more than one year, or both; and if death results shall be subject to imprisonment for any term of years or for life.

The Attorney General relies principally upon *Wyandotte Transportation Co. v. United States,* 389 U.S. 191 (1967), and *Cort v. Ash,* 422 U.S. 66

(1975), as authority for inferring a civil cause of action from the two criminal statutes. These and subsequent decisions of the Supreme Court, * * * establish comprehensive standards for inferring rights of action. Under these decisions the "central inquiry" and the "ultimate question" is congressional intent. *Touche Ross [& Co. v. Redington,]* 442 U.S. [560,] 578 [(1979)]. * * *

We reject the argument that *Wyandotte* established a different standard for inferring rights of action in favor of the government than the standard applicable to private litigants. *Wyandotte* relied on "cases involving civil actions of private parties," 389 U.S. at 202, and *Cort v. Ash* subsequently cited *Wyandotte* in developing further the test for inferring private rights of action. More important, however, we think that *Wyandotte* represents merely one step in the development of the current standards for inferring rights of action and that the unrefined analysis employed in *Wyandotte* is no longer an accurate statement of the law. In *Wyandotte* the Supreme Court seemed to operate on the basis of a presumption that a civil damages remedy ordinarily should be inferred from a penal statute in the absence of "some persuasive indication" that "Congress must have intended the statutory remedies and procedures to be exclusive of all others." 389 U.S. at 200. We would be blind to subsequent developments in a dynamic area of the law, however, if we failed to recognize that in recent years the Court has been far more reluctant to infer rights of action for silent statutes. Instead of the presumption employed in *Wyandotte*, that statutory silence indicates congressional intent to create a cause of action by implication, the Court now adheres to the "elemental canon of statutory construction that where a statute expressly provides a particular remedy or remedies, a court must be chary of reading others into it." *Transamerica [Mortgage Advisors, Inc. v. Lewis]*, 444 U.S. [11,] 19 [(1979)]. The analysis employed in the later cases is plainly inconsistent with the generous attitude of the *Wyandotte* opinion. Therefore, we must reject the government's argument that *Wyandotte* would require us to infer a right of action from congressional silence and an absence of "adequate" remedies to redress the wrongs at issue.

Even if we were to accept the suggestion that a lack of adequate remedies requires recognition of an implied right of action, however, we could not find a federal right to sue for an injunction in this case. Congress has created numerous mechanisms for the redress of denials of due process. Persons denied constitutional rights may sue state officials for damages or injunctive relief under 42 U.S.C. §§ 1981, 1982, 1983, and 1985. Those suits may be filed as class actions under Rule 23, Fed.R.Civ.P., and prevailing litigants may recover attorneys' fees under 42 U.S.C. § 1988. A private litigant may obtain damages or an injunction against a city itself in certain situations. Private injunctive actions have been maintained successfully against "widespread" violations committed by local law enforcement officials. In *Wyandotte,* by contrast, the United States was forced by an emergency situation to remove a negligently sunken barge loaded with a dangerous cargo from the bottom of the Mississippi River, and it had no mechanism to recover its expenses other than a personal action against those responsible for the sinking.

In addition, the United States can initiate criminal prosecutions under §§ 241 and 242, and it has successfully prosecuted Philadelphia police officers for unconstitutional conduct. The Attorney General argues nonetheless that the criminal process is inadequate, because he would rather rely on a massive "single civil action" than to "continue repeated use of the criminal process." Brief for Appellant at 19. In short, although numerous express remedies exist, the Attorney General, stretching *Wyandotte* beyond recognition, invites this court to create another. We decline the invitation on this record. * * *

III.

* * * The government argues that it has a "duty" under §§ 241 and 242 to prevent violations of constitutional rights * * *. This "duty" analysis begs the fundamental question presented by this appeal. Although we might concede that in some abstract and metaphysical sense the government has a "duty" to its citizens to enforce the criminal statutes, even that concession would leave us far from accepting the government's position. It may be also that § 5 of the fourteenth amendment would authorize Congress to impose on the Executive a generalized duty to prevent violations of the Constitution. Congress has not created such an obligation, however, either in §§ 241 and 242 or elsewhere, and this court does not have authority to impose the "duty" the government so eagerly seeks to assume. * * *

[We next consider] whether there is any indication of legislative intent, explicit or implicit, either to create such a remedy or to deny one. The government argues that this factor is neutral because the legislative history of the Reconstruction-era Civil Rights Acts does not reveal that Congress considered providing a civil remedy for the United States.

Between 1865 and 1871 Congress drafted the thirteenth, fourteenth, and fifteenth amendments and enacted a comprehensive statutory scheme for their enforcement. It gave extensive consideration to the creation of remedies to enforce the amendments. It provided several criminal and civil actions. * * * The Attorney General discusses the legislative history at length, but he fails to draw the obvious inference: that the extensive congressional consideration of the problem of enforcement and the comprehensive legislative program that it developed simply foreclose the possibility that it implicitly created an additional remedy without ever mentioning its existence in either the statutes or the debates. There certainly is no evidence of congressional intent to create an additional remedy with the incredible breadth and scope of this one. The responsible answer to this question, and indeed, the overarching answer to this appeal, is that Congress never intended to grant a civil action to the Attorney General.

The same conclusion is supported by an examination of three express refusals of modern Congresses to grant the Executive general injunctive powers in this field, which not only demonstrates explicit congressional intent not to create the power claimed here by the Attorney General but also reveals an understanding, unanimously shared by members of Congress and Attorneys General, that no such power existed. * * *

[This legislative history] demonstrates that Congress, even at the time it was taking dramatic and important steps toward the goal of protecting civil rights, was unwilling to grant the Attorney General more than a very limited power to interfere by injunction in the activities of state and local governments. Congress had three opportunities between 1957 and 1964 to authorize the Attorney General to bring lawsuits of the type that we now consider. It refused on each occasion because this authority would permit a dramatic and unnecessary shift of power from state and local governments to the Attorney General. The government now argues that this history is irrelevant to this case because two of the proposals were more limited than the authority it now claims. This view not only depends on a non sequitur, but also overlooks the fundamental objections raised by the opponents of each of the three proposals, that they would grant the Attorney General excessive authority over state and local governments.

We conclude, therefore, that the history of the Reconstruction era legislation reveals an implicit legislative intent, and that the modern history demonstrates an explicit intent, to deny the government the right of action asserted here. * * *

The Attorney General argues that the federal government has a central role in protecting individuals from violations of the Constitution. This argument is facially appealing because the protection of federal rights clearly is a federal concern. However, the argument blurs the distinction between the roles of the federal courts, the federal legislature, and the federal executive. It also ignores the reverse side of the same coin: this lawsuit represents an attempt by the federal executive to intervene on a grand scale in the workings of a local government, an area that is manifestly the concern of the states and not the federal government. Federal courts must be "alert to adjust their remedies" to grant relief for invasions of federally protected rights, *Bell v. Hood,* 327 U.S. 678, 684 (1946), but they are equally bound to give proper recognition to the principles of federalism that underlie the very structure of the Constitution, from which the federal courts and the federal Executive alike derive their authority. * * *

IV.

The Attorney General's second theory for maintaining this lawsuit rests on the fourteenth amendment itself and on the President's duty under Article II, § 3 to "take Care that the Laws be faithfully executed." His premise is that because the national government is the "guarantor" of the rights of individuals, we must provide him with a remedy under the Constitution. * * * [H]e argues that he has a right of action even though Congress has not exercised its power under § 5 of the fourteenth amendment to create one. * * *

* * * Recognition of the asserted right of action would violate the constitutional scheme of separation of powers as exemplified and embodied in § 5 of the fourteenth amendment and would trample on important constitutional principles that underlie and give life to our federal system.

Section 5 of the fourteenth amendment confers on Congress, not on the Executive or the Judiciary, the "power to enforce, by appropriate legislation, the provisions of this article." The Supreme Court has repeatedly recognized the central role of Congress in establishing appropriate mechanisms to enforce the fourteenth amendment. "It is not said the judicial power of the general government shall extend to enforcing the prohibitions and to protecting the rights and immunities guaranteed.... It is the power of Congress which has been enlarged." *Ex parte Virginia*, 100 U.S. 339, 345 (1879). Congress has exercised its power to "enforc[e] the prohibitions" on many occasions, but it has refused to grant the Executive and the Judiciary the authority that now is asserted. In our view, it would be entirely inappropriate for a federal court to overrule the explicit decisions of Congress not to increase federal executive and judicial authority over state and local governments in this manner.

In addition, the Supreme Court in the last decade has repeatedly recognized the importance of a proper respect for the independent roles of state and local governments in our federal system. Judge Ditter wrote eloquently and persuasively for the court below that to permit this action to proceed "would be to vest an excessive and dangerous degree of power in the hands of the Attorney General":

> The point is that the power which the Attorney General claims in this case is simply not compatible with the federal system of government envisioned by the Constitution. This power, in essence, would permit the Justice Department to bring a civil suit against any state or local administrative body merely because the Attorney General and his subordinates have determined that the defendant's operating policies and procedures violate any one of the civil rights guaranteed to citizens by the Constitution and laws of the United States. The purpose of such a lawsuit would be to obtain an injunction altering the challenged procedures. Quite literally, there would be no end to the local and state agencies, bureaus, offices, departments, or divisions whose day-to-day operating procedures could be challenged by suit, and changed by injunction. * * *

United States v. City of Philadelphia, 482 F.Supp. at 1268. We agree that judicial recognition of the asserted right of action would violate important principles of federalism and separation of powers. * * *

The Attorney General's apparent (albeit oblique) response is that the asserted right of action will be limited to "exceptional" cases involving "widespread and continuing" violations, for which the remedies expressly provided are not "adequate." *See* Brief for Appellant at 31, 41–42, Reply Brief at 10. There are several problems with this argument. First, the asserted standards are so vague as to lack real content. Second, the fundamental objection is to permitting the federal executive to assume authority over state and local governments. If that power is once granted, it will take an active judiciary indeed to confine it within principled limits. Third, even if the government's authority could be confined to "exceptional" cases, judicial assertion of the power to compel drastic and far-reaching changes in local governments would be inconsistent with a proper division of power in a federal system.

We hold, therefore, that the fourteenth amendment does not implicitly authorize the United States to sue to enjoin violations of its substantive prohibitions.

V.

Our conclusion, that neither §§ 241 and 242 nor the fourteenth amendment create in the government a right to maintain this action for an injunction, is bolstered by an additional consideration: the longstanding and uniform agreement of all concerned that no such right of action has ever existed. Our discussion of the modern legislative history in part III B, *supra,* demonstrates that neither Attorneys General nor Congress between 1956 and 1964 believed that either Congress or the Constitution had created this power sub silentio. Those officials did not act out a meaningless charade, debating whether to create what they believed already existed, but in a serious and responsible manner decided for reasons of constitutional principle and sound public policy not to create new federal authority over state and local governments.

The same understanding, that the United States may not sue to enjoin violations of individuals' fourteenth amendment rights without specific statutory authority, has been shared by almost every court that has had the opportunity to pass on the question. In *United States v. Mattson,* 600 F.2d 1295 (9th Cir.1979), and in *United States v. Solomon,* 563 F.2d 1121 (4th Cir.1977), the courts of appeals affirmed district court decisions and held that the Attorney General may not sue to vindicate the constitutional rights of institutionalized mentally retarded citizens without express statutory authority. * * * Three Justices of the Supreme Court have expressed their opinion that the United States does not have authority under either the fourteenth amendment or §§ 241 and 242 to seek an injunction against state corrections officials. *Estelle v. Justice,* 426 U.S. 925, 928–29 (1976) (Rehnquist, J., joined by Burger, C. J., and Powell, J., dissenting from denial of petition for certiorari). To our knowledge, the only decision that has held squarely that the United States may sue to enjoin "large-scale denials of due process" is a much criticized district court decision, *United States v. Brand Jewelers, Inc.,* 318 F.Supp. 1293, 1299–1300 (S.D.N.Y. 1970). We agree with the numerous critics of that decision, and we think it is significant that the United States does not rely on it here. * * *

In sum, the Attorney General argues that he possesses implied authority under the Civil Rights Acts and under the fourteenth amendment to request far-reaching mandatory injunctions, notwithstanding three separate refusals of Congress to grant him this authority and a widely-shared understanding that the authority does not exist. He also has looked to the courts, and applications similar to this have been rejected in the fourth, seventh, and ninth circuits. Unabashed, he has continued to shop for a forum that will lend its ear. He will not find it here.

We think that what he asks is unnecessary, because other avenues of relief are available. What he seeks is a grant of unbridled authority that does violence to the delicate balance of power among the legislative, executive, and judicial branches of government. What he requests strikes at the heart of fundamental comity between federal and state governments. Finally, what is sought—government by injunction—is anathematic to the American judicial tradition, succinctly and eloquently described by Justice Marshall:

> The Constitution provides that Congress shall make laws, the President execute laws, and courts interpret laws. . . . It [does] not provide for government by injunction in which the courts and the Executive Branch can "make law" without regard to the action of Congress. It may be more convenient for the Executive Branch if it need only convince a judge to prohibit conduct rather than ask the Congress to pass a law, and it may be more convenient to enforce a contempt order than to seek a criminal conviction in a jury trial. Moreover, it may be considered politically wise to get a court to share the responsibility for arresting those who the Executive Branch has probable cause to believe are violating the law. But convenience and political considerations of the moment do not justify a basic departure from the principles of our system of government.

New York Times Co. v. United States, 403 U.S. 713, 742–43 (1971) (Marshall, J., concurring) (citation omitted).

VI.

Appellant's remaining claims rest on allegations of racial discrimination in the administration of certain federally funded programs. The district court held that the Attorney General has explicit statutory authority to bring suit against discriminatory administration of federal funds, but it subsequently granted appellees' motion to dismiss these claims for failure to plead with sufficient specificity. * * *

[The court of appeals affirms the district court's dismissal of the racial discrimination claims on the grounds that the complaint did not set out the factual grounding for those allegations with sufficient specificity. The Third Circuit's ruling in this respect, which is beyond the scope of this course as it was applicable generally to private civil rights plaintiffs as well as the federal government, was one of a series of lower court decisions imposing a heightened pleading requirement in civil rights cases. In *Leatherman v. Tarrant County Narcotics Unit,* 507 U.S. 163 (1993), the Supreme Court held that the requirement of more specific pleading by civil rights plaintiffs could not be reconciled with the liberal system of "notice pleading" set up by the Federal Rules of Civil Procedure. Thus, the Third Circuit's ruling on this particular point has been superseded.]

VII.

The judgment of the district court will be affirmed in all respects.

SUR PETITION FOR REHEARING

■ Before SEITZ, CHIEF JUDGE, and VAN DUSEN, ALDISERT, GIBBONS, HUNTER, WEIS, GARTH, HIGGINBOTHAM and SLOVITER, CIRCUIT JUDGES.*

■ ALDISERT, CIRCUIT JUDGE.

The petition for rehearing filed by Appellant in the above entitled case having been submitted to the judges who participated in the decision of this court and to all the other available circuit judges of the circuit in regular active service, and no judge who concurred in the decision having asked for rehearing, and a majority of the circuit judges of the circuit in regular active service not having voted for rehearing by the court in banc, the petition for rehearing is denied.

■ GIBBONS, CIRCUIT JUDGE, dissenting from an order denying rehearing.

Rule 35 of the Federal Rules of Appellate Procedure provides that rehearing by the court in banc "will not be ordered except (1) when consideration by the full court is necessary to secure or maintain uniformity of its decisions, or (2) when the proceedings involve a question of exceptional importance." This case, in which the United States petitions for rehearing of a panel decision affirming the dismissal of its complaint, more clearly meets both criteria of Rule 35 than any of those which we have heard in banc in the eleven years of my service on this court. * * * [I]t is inconsistent with a long line of authority in the Supreme Court respecting the authority of the Department of Justice to conduct litigation in the public interest. It is flabbergasting, considering the trivial uses to which Rule 35 has been put in this court, that five votes are unavailable to authorize consideration of this case. Not only is it a case which amply satisfies the criteria of Rule 35, but the panel decision and the decisions in the district court are patently wrong.

I.   FACTS

This suit grows out of an eight-month Justice Department investigation into police brutality in Philadelphia. Following the failure of private plaintiffs in *Rizzo v. Goode,* 423 U.S. 362 (1976), to convince the Supreme Court of a sufficient factual nexus between particular acts of brutality and official collusion in condoning the conduct of or obstructing the disciplining of police officers, and system-wide deprivations of civil rights, the Justice Department undertook to establish that connection. Its investigations into police files of citizen complaints, and review of internal police department training and disciplinary procedures revealed a pervasive pattern or practice of verbal abuse (often involving racial epithets), physical abuse, false arrests, compounding of charges to cover up false arrests or to discourage

---

* Judge Adams did not participate in the consideration of this matter.

the filing of complaints, illegal searches and seizures, and unlawful detainments. * * *

[In parts of the opinion omitted here, Judge Gibbons describes the district court's opinions and the procedure below. He further argues that the district court applied too stringent a standard for pleading in dismissing the counts of the government's complaint asserting racial discrimination as not alleged with sufficient factual specificity. As noted above, the Third Circuit's opinion on this point was subsequently superseded by the Supreme Court's decision in *Leatherman v. Tarrant County Narcotics Unit,* 507 U.S. 163 (1993), which rejected a "heightened pleading" approach in civil rights cases.]

V.   SOURCES OF EXECUTIVE AUTHORITY TO BRING SUIT

Article II section 3 of the Constitution charges the Executive to "take care that the Laws be faithfully executed." Independent of any explicit statutory grant of authority, provided Congress has not expressly limited its authority, the Executive has the inherent constitutional power and duty to enforce constitutional and statutory rights by resort to the courts. When Federal courts have upheld executive standing without explicit congressional authority, they have looked to other provisions of the Constitution, such as the commerce clause and the fourteenth amendment, and to a general statutory scheme defining federal rights but lacking the specific remedy of executive suit. In addition, 28 U.S.C. § 518(b) affords the Attorney General statutory authority to "conduct and argue any case in a court of the United States in which the United States is interested." The Supreme Court has held that this statute confers on the Executive general authority to initiate suits "to safeguard national interests."[11] Moreover, the Supreme Court has held that the Executive's general constitutional duty to protect the public welfare "is often of itself sufficient to give it standing in court."[12]

A review of the caselaw construing executive authority to bring suit helps set this suit in context. Prior cases show that the district court's arguments for denying standing because of congressional inaction to afford explicit standing or because of a threat of abuse of executive power have already been rehearsed and rejected.

From the beginning of the nineteenth century, the Supreme Court has recognized the nonstatutory authority of the executive to sue to protect the United States' contractual and proprietary interests.

After the civil war, with the creation of the Justice Department, An Act to Establish the Department of Justice, 16 Stat. 162 ch. 150 (June 22, 1870), the scope of the Attorney General's statutory and nonstatutory authority to conduct litigation in which the United States had an interest expanded. The 1870 Justice Department Act, part of the Reconstruction Congress' efforts to implement and to secure enforcement of the 13th, 14th and 15th amendments, *see generally,* H. Cummings & C. McFarland,

---

11. *United States v. California,* 332 U.S. 19, 27 (1947).

12. *In re Debs,* 158 U.S. 564, 584 (1895).

Federal Justice, 218–249 (1937), broadened the Attorney General's authority to appear in federal court to present the interests of the United States.

The 1870 Justice Department Act added the provision now found at 28 U.S.C. § 518(b)

> When the Attorney General considers it in the interests of the United States, he may personally conduct and argue any case in a court of the United States in which the United States is interested, or he may direct the Solicitor General or any officer of the Department of Justice to do so.

Whether this statute, along with other Reconstruction Era enactments, in effect creates explicit congressional authority for the executive to seek declaratory or injunctive relief in civil rights cases, is perhaps debatable. Nonetheless, in the vast expansion of federal law and of the activities of federal lawyers that occurred after the Civil War, the nature of suits brought by the Attorney General without explicit statutory authority also widened. The Justice Department Act, if it did not automatically grant standing (a latter-day concept with which the legislators of 1870, accustomed to practice under the Process Act, would hardly be familiar), did authorize the Attorney General, or his designees, to sue in the lower federal courts. *See United States v. San Jacinto Tin Co.*, 125 U.S. 273, 278–79 (1888).

In *United States v. San Jacinto Tin Co., supra,* the Attorney General sued to revoke a fraudulently obtained land patent. Although the United States had a proprietary interest in the action, for if the patent were revoked the land would have reverted to the United States, the Court's concerns focused more on protecting the integrity of the land patents scheme than on any pecuniary interest of the United States. * * *

It is important to note that this early non-statutory action afforded the Supreme Court the opportunity to reflect on, and to reject, the argument that executive resort to the courts without congressional authority threatened the balance of power among the coordinate branches of the federal government.

> We are not insensible to the enormous power and its capacity for evil thus reposed in that department of the government. Since the title to all of the land in more than half of the States and Territories of the Union depends upon patents from the government of the United States, it is to be seen what a vast power is confided to the officer who may order the institution of suits to set aside every one of these patents; and if the doctrine that the United States in bringing such actions is not controlled by any statute of limitations, or governed by the rule concerning laches be sound, of which we express no opinion at present, then the evil which may result would seem to be endless as well as enormous. But it has often been said that the fact that the exercise of power may be abused is no sufficient reason for denying its existence, and if restrictions are to be placed upon the exercise of this

authority by the Attorney General, it is for the legislative body which created the office to enact them.

125 U.S. at 284. * * *

In *In re Debs,* 158 U.S. 564 (1895), the Attorney General sought an injunction against the activities of Eugene V. Debs and other leaders of the Pullman railway workers. Several grounds were available to confirm the Executive's nonstatutory right to bring the suit. The Pullman strike prevented the passage of the mails through Chicago. The unanimous Court observed that the United States' proprietary interest in the mails would afford a nonstatutory right of action. The Court continued, however:

> We do not care to place our decision upon this ground alone. Every government, entrusted, by the very terms of its being, with powers and duties to be exercised and discharged for the general welfare, has a right to apply to its own courts for any proper assistance in the exercise of the one and the discharge of the other, and it is no sufficient answer to its appeal to one of those courts that it has no pecuniary interest in the matter. The obligations which it is under to promote the interest of all, and to prevent the wrongdoing of one resulting in injury to the general welfare, is often of itself sufficient to give it a standing in court.

Id. at 584. The Court reviewed its decisions in [earlier cases, including *San Jacinto*], concluding:

> It is obvious from these decisions that while it is not the province of the government to interfere in any mere matter of private controversy between individuals, or to use its great powers to enforce the rights of one against another, yet, whenever the wrongs complained of are such as affect the public at large, and are in respect of matters which by the Constitution are entrusted to the care of the Nation, and concerning which the Nation owes the duty to all the citizens of securing to them their common rights, then the mere fact that the government has no pecuniary interest in the controversy is not sufficient to exclude it from the courts, or prevent it from taking measures therein to fully discharge those constitutional duties.

Id. at 586.

Thus, the Attorney General's nonstatutory right of action derived from the constitutional duty to protect the public from injury to the general welfare. The Pullman strike impeded commerce, obstructed the highways, and in effect, represented a nuisance whose removal the executive was obliged to effect. While one might attempt to limit *Debs* to its facts of extreme crisis, or to suggest that extensive congressional regulation of interstate commerce made *Debs* * * * an example of filling in remedial interstices, the Court's express language goes well beyond these interpretations. While in 1895 there might have been differences in the Court as to the appropriate standard of conduct, even then the Court would not have suggested that the interests protected by the thirteenth, fourteenth and fifteenth amendments were less "entrusted to the care of the nation" than were those protected by the commerce clause. * * *

The Supreme Court's treatment of Executive standing thus outlines four grounds of the Attorney General's authority to initiate suit despite the absence of express congressional directive to bring particular kinds of actions. 28 U.S.C. § 518 affords a general statutory source of standing when the United States' interests, and particularly its federal sovereign interests, are at stake. Moreover, without referring to that statute, the Court has declared a general federal right to protect Government property, and to supply an additional remedy to effect a general statutory scheme, as well as a constitutional obligation to protect the public welfare.

More recently, the civil rights movement of the late fifties and early sixties also occasioned nonstatutory executive resort to the federal courts. Courts in the Fifth Circuit, addressing the activities of the Ku Klux Klan against the "freedom riders," and segregation in bus and airline terminals, applied the *Debs* precedent to hold that the Executive had a nonstatutory right of action to sue to enjoin burdens on interstate commerce. While some of these decisions find statutory standing under interstate commerce acts and under the Federal Aviation Act, all explicitly also ground the Attorney General's right of action in the duty to enforce the commerce clause of the Constitution. It must be acknowledged that between 1877 and the late fifties, instances of Executive Branch civil actions to enforcement of rights protected by the post Civil War amendments cannot be found. The reason, however, is not lack of standing. Any kind of Executive Branch enforcement of those amendments was almost non-existent. The question was not lack of standing, but lack of initiative.

In *United States v. Brand Jewelers, Inc.*, 318 F.Supp. 1293 (S.D.N.Y. 1970), Judge Marvin Frankel, relying on *Debs* and its Fifth Circuit progeny, held that the Attorney General had nonstatutory authority to sue to enjoin the New York "sewer service" practice. Brand Jewelers and similar operations sold on credit to impecunious customers, then filed a suit to collect, employing process servers who never delivered the summons but filed an affidavit of service. Armed with the affidavit, Brand would obtain a state court default judgment, and would garnish the wages of the hapless and unnotified defendants. In addition to the burden on interstate commerce this practice engendered[,] Judge Frankel found the practice resulted in "large-scale denials of due process," 318 F.Supp. at 1300. The court held "the United States may maintain this action because it has standing to sue to end widespread deprivation (i. e. deprivation affecting many people) of property through 'state action' without due process of law," *id.* at 1299. * * *

Judge Frankel reviewed and rejected defendants' argument that the Executive's nonstatutory suit threatened abuse, and that Congress' failure to confer standing meant Congress intended to deny the Attorney General a right of action.

Defendants warn that the power claimed by the Government in this case is "overwhelming" and "awesome" a power that "can readily become a terrible engine of oppression." This is a little hyperbolic to describe the peaceable submission of the United States that it should be permitted to sue in court and pray for judgment on behalf of thousands of people alleged to have been cheated in ways that deny their constitutional rights and burden the nation's commerce. At the same time, defendants have a point when they urge that it is no small matter for anyone to have the resources of the Federal Government drawn up against him in a lawsuit. In the end, however, the potential of imaginable horrors is not a pointedly useful test. Possible abuses by the Attorney General are subject to the control of Congress. Still more immediately, the whole matter is in court, where the Attorney General submits for judicial judgment all questions of propriety, possible excess, scope and limit.

318 F.Supp. at 1299 (Citation omitted)

Judge Frankel continued:

It is said that Congress has on occasion given to the Attorney General power to sue for enforcement of individual rights, but has declined to grant by statute the standing now claimed: expressio unius, as the saying runs, est exclusio alterius. But the range and effectiveness of that canon are in general somewhat limited. It was available, mutatis mutandis, in *Debs* and other cases in the line. The failure of Congress to take positive action, sometimes a matter of moment, is hardly the equivalent of a negation. It seems especially dubious to fashion a prohibition from Congressional inaction in a case like this one, where both Congress and the courts are conceded by the executive to have veto powers, on the issue of standing as well as on the merits.

318 F.Supp. at 1300. * * *

VI.   THE EXECUTIVE AS PLAINTIFF–INTERVENOR AND AS PARTY IN CHARGE OF THE CONDUCT OF THE SUIT

In addition to initiating suits to protect the public from "large-scale deprivations of due process," burdens on interstate commerce, and fraud, and to assert its federal sovereign interests, the Executive has successfully intervened in civil rights actions. In *Faubus v. United States,* 254 F.2d 797 (8th Cir.1958), the court invited the United States' nonstatutorily authorized intervention to secure the enforcement of school desegregation orders in Little Rock, Arkansas, when the governor of that state had called out the local national guard to prevent the attendance of black children in white schools. In *Bush v. Orleans Parish School Bd.,* 191 F.Supp. 871 (E.D.La.) (3 judge court), *aff'd per curiam,* 367 U.S. 908 (1961), the Court invited the Attorney General's participation as amicus curiae. The court had already declared plaintiffs' right to attend desegregated schools, but the injunction had yet to be enforced. The court rejected defendants' argument that congressional failure, in the Civil Rights Acts of 1957 and 1960, expressly to permit the United States to initiate civil rights actions, denied the Attorney General standing to intervene. * * *

VII. FEDERALISM

The district court went on at some fulminating length about federal interference in local government. The district judge found it most unseemly that the United States would seek by injunction to enforce the civil rights of residents of Philadelphia. In what might be termed an expression of the "dog pound theory," the judge envisioned massive and unwarranted federal infiltration into every level of local authority, even down to canine administration, and concluded that the "very threat" of executive action to enforce the civil rights laws "could alter the conduct of local policy makers," 481 F.Supp. at 1269. The Court did not consider whether the fourteenth amendment itself was not designed to affect local policy. Instead, the court seemed to assume that local policy should be insulated from federal law, at least when that arm of the federal government constitutionally charged with enforcing the law in fact seeks to enforce it. * * *

The fourteenth amendment and the civil rights statutes present the threat to local authority. The Executive's injunctive action merely compounds, or perhaps makes good, that threat. * * *

VIII. SEPARATION OF POWERS

Separation of powers afforded a second ground for the district court's bewailing of nonstatutory executive activity. Because Congress had thrice declined to grant the Attorney General explicit authority to seek an injunction, the district court concluded it must therefore have meant to prohibit such an action. For the Executive nonetheless to resort to the courts would thus represent an abuse of executive power. There are several flaws in this argument. First, * * * congressional failure explicitly to approve executive action does not equal congressional prohibition.

Second, Supreme Court precedent provides that the Executive has implicit statutory authority to seek an injunction to fill in the remedial interstices of a general statutory scheme. * * *

Third, in this Circuit, the United States would have standing to participate in this action as plaintiff-intervenor. * * *

Fourth, while neither the Supreme Court nor, with the exception of the Southern District of New York in *Brand Jewelers,* the lower federal courts, have squarely held the fourteenth amendment affords the Executive nonstatutory standing, all courts which have considered the question have held the commerce clause confers nonstatutory authority to sue to remove obstructions and burdens on interstate commerce. Neither the Supreme Court nor the federal courts perceived a threat to separation of powers in the Attorney General's suit to enforce the commerce clause. To the contrary, they saw the suit as implementing the constitutional scheme that the Executive enforce the laws. The government has alleged in its complaint in this case that the practices of Philadelphia police and city officials impose burdens on interstate commerce. The government has had no opportunity to demonstrate the interstate commerce impact, and while a trial on the merits may fail to substantiate that claim, the claim itself afforded standing to the Attorney General.

Fifth, * * * executive action to secure an injunction is by its nature not an overweening exercise of power. A suit for an injunction is not a naked exercise of executive authority. Unlike the steel seizure in *Youngstown Sheet & Tube,* the Executive can do nothing here without the concurrence of the federal judiciary. And, because the United States is in effect suing as class representative for the citizens of Philadelphia, the Executive is entitled to no more relief than would be accorded the class members.

Sixth, despite its fear that this action would violate separation of powers, the district court failed to articulate a congressional purpose or intent that the Executive's nonstatutory action would undermine. What are the identifiable congressional interests this action threatens? Congress cannot intend to insulate defendants from enforcement of the fourteenth amendment. At most, Congress might prefer that Justice Department energies and resources be expended in some other way. Congress has not so declared, however, and were it to announce such an intent, an attempt to enforce it might itself implicate separation of powers. While the Executive may not decline to follow a congressional mandate within its proper legislative competence, it is questionable, to say the least, whether Congress may compel the Executive not to enforce the fourteenth amendment or the commerce clause. The Executive's Article II § 3 duty to enforce the laws may override certain congressionally imposed limitations on executive authority. But in any event, because Congress has not here attempted to forbid the Executive from carrying out its constitutional obligations, the question whether such an endeavor would violate separation of powers need not be reached.

Finally, the general problem of suits by the Executive to protect the public welfare should be confronted. While the potential of unbridled executive initiation of suits in the "national interest" understandably may evoke visceral fears of executive power run rampant, careful analysis of the Attorney General's action in this case reveals those fears to be baseless. It is true that phrases like "the public welfare," "the national interest," and "cases in which the United States is interested," can have a formless, and perhaps dangerously expansive quality. Before any court upholds the exercise of executive resort to it without explicit statutory standing, however, the court should determine what kind of right the Executive is seeking to enforce. Is the Executive endeavoring to protect its contractual and proprietary rights? To fill in the remedial interstices of a statutory scheme? To enforce a judicially recognized constitutional right? Or is the Executive instead attempting to create a new right that may conflict with statutory or judicial precedent? When, as here, the Attorney General can substantiate the "national interest" and "public welfare" by reference to clearly articulated legislative policies or judicial precedent, the danger of untoward exercise of executive power is fanciful. Thus viewed, this case does not pose a threat of limitless definition of executive authority to bring suit. In this action, the Attorney General seeks to enjoin the pattern or practice of police brutality in Philadelphia. The Attorney General can point to at least four statutes specifically enacted to prohibit concerted and official deprivations of civil rights by physical abuse, 42 U.S.C. §§ 1983 and 1985 and 18 U.S.C. §§ 241 and 242. In addition, the Attorney General has invoked a host of other statutes guaranteeing civil rights, as well as the fourteenth amendment. Thus, this action does not involve the creation of new rights conflicting with legislative and judicial precedent in the "national interest." Rather, it falls comfortably into the category of decisions upholding nonspecific statutory authority to supply a new remedy for an established scheme of rights. * * *

* * *

* * * Whatever else the fourteenth amendment and the Civil Rights Acts protect, they do not protect state and local governments from federal interference. Quite the contrary. Their very purpose is such interference. At least here the panel concedes, grudgingly, that the protection of federal rights is a federal concern. Not, apparently, a concern of the federal Executive, however. Somehow if the Attorney General asks a federal court to give the same declaratory or injunctive relief that it plainly is authorized to give in a suit by private parties, the pillars of the republic will be so shaken that "the very structure of the constitution" will be endangered. This sort of hyperbole has been often enough heard in Senate filibusters. It has not been taken seriously there, except as a filibustering tactic, since Webster's reply to Hayne in 1829, though it has often since been effective in delaying legislation. That it should surface in an opinion of a court that once had a reputation for deep interest in the protection of civil rights is astounding. As noted in Part VII above, the fourteenth amendment and the Civil Rights Acts are what intervene in the workings of local government. They were intended to intervene. The relief which the federal Executive seeks is nothing more than the fourteenth amendment and the Civil Rights Acts require if what is alleged in the complaint is true.

CONCLUSION

I would grant the petition for rehearing.

Judges Higginbotham and Sloviter, for the reasons expressed in this opinion, would also grant rehearing.

Because Chief Judge Seitz believes that Judge Gibbons' opinion demonstrates the existence of issues worthy of in banc consideration, he joins his dissent from the denial of the petition for rehearing in banc.

———

Notes and Questions

1. In *United States v. City of Philadelphia,* what interest does the Attorney General assert to give the United States standing to pursue the action? Why does the three-judge court panel (which was unanimous)

conclude that the Attorney General does not have the authority to bring suit against the City of Philadelphia for these claims? Why does the dissent from the denial of rehearing en banc conclude differently? From what opposing presumptions do the court panel and the dissent begin (and conclude)? At the time of this decision, had Congress authorized a civil suit by the federal government to enforce the constitutional rights of citizens against police brutality and other abuses by law enforcement? Does the presence or absence of an express statutory mandate matter (and should it)? Why in the court panel's view should there be restrictions on the government's standing to initiate litigation? How does the dissent respond? From your reading of these opinions, do you think that the nature of the underlying case, a civil rights complaint alleging police brutality, influenced the outcome of the court panel or opinion of the dissenters?

More than a decade after the *City of Philadelphia* decision, Congress acted in the wake of the Rodney King beating by Los Angeles police officers and the Los Angeles riots and conferred authority on the Attorney General to file a civil suit seeking equitable and declaratory relief against deprivations of rights by law enforcement officers. Violent Crime Control and Law Enforcement Act of 1994, Pub. L. No. 103–322, tit. XXI, 108 Stat. 2071 (1994) (codified at 28 U.S.C. § 14141). For a discussion of the background to this legislation, which includes the *City of Philadelphia* decision and the Rodney King incident, see generally Marshall Miller, Note, *Police Brutality,* 17 Yale L. & Pol'y Rev. 149, 149–64 (1998); James P. Turner, *Police Accountability in the Federal System,* 30 McGeorge L. Rev. 991, 1012–13 (1999). Does the enactment of this legislation mean that the *City of Philadelphia* court was wrong? Why or why not?

2.   The United States Court of Appeals for the Third Circuit in *United States v. City of Philadelphia* is not alone in refusing to grant standing to the United States to bring suit to defend the civil or constitutional rights of third persons without express statutory authorization. As the Third Circuit notes in its decision, the Fourth and Ninth Circuits both held that the Attorney General lacked the right, without statutory authorization, to bring suit seeking equitable relief against state officials for alleged violations of the civil rights of mentally retarded individuals confined in state hospitals. *United States v. Mattson,* 600 F.2d 1295 (9th Cir. 1979); *United States v. Solomon,* 563 F.2d 1121 (4th Cir. 1977). These two courts of appeals, citing separation of powers concerns, ruled that absent congressional direction, the United States lacked standing to sue on behalf of third persons against state governments. *Id.* Subsequent to both of those decisions, Congress enacted the Civil Rights of Institutionalized Persons Act to expressly grant the federal government the power to institute legal action in the name of the United States to uphold the civil rights of institutionalized persons against state or local officials. Pub. L. No. 96–247, § 3, 94 Stat. 349, 350 (1980) (codified at 42 U.S.C. §§ 1997a–1997j).

However, the United States has not always failed in its attempts to advance civil rights through litigation, even without explicit statutory authorization. In a case with significant similarities to *City of Philadelphia,* the United States Court of Appeals for the Fifth Circuit refused to grant a writ of mandamus to eject the United States from a civil rights lawsuit against a state prison system, although three members of the Supreme Court subsequently raised substantial doubts about the legitimacy of the federal government's intervention in the litigation. In *In re Estelle,* 516 F.2d 480 (5th Cir. 1975), a civil rights action was brought by state prison inmates against the Texas Department of Corrections alleging inadequate medical treatment and housing and other abuses in violation of their constitutional rights. The district court ordered the United States to appear as amicus curiae to investigate the prisoners' complaints and to fully participate in the case; the United States then moved to intervene, which the district court granted. The Texas Department of Corrections moved to dismiss the United States, contending that the federal government lacked an interest sufficient to be a party to the lawsuit. When the district court denied that motion, the department petitioned the court of appeals for a writ of mandamus. A majority of the Fifth Circuit panel concluded that the extraordinary remedy of mandamus was not justified and that the issues raised by the government's participation could properly be reviewed upon later appeal in the ordinary course from a final judgment. *Id.* at 483–84 (majority opinion), 487–88 (Godbold, J., concurring in part). Judge Tuttle further stated his view that the United States was entitled to seek civil relief based on the scope of protection guaranteed by analogous criminal statutes that prohibit deprivations of constitutional rights. *Id.* at 486–87 (Tuttle, J., separate views). Where criminal prosecution is difficult or criminal penalties would be ineffective, Judge Tuttle concluded that the congressional intent behind the criminal statute may be effected by allowing the government to pursue a civil remedy. *Id.* at 487.

The Supreme Court denied certiorari, but three justices—one short of the number necessary to grant review—dissented. *Estelle v. Justice,* 426 U.S. 925 (1976) (Rehnquist, J., dissenting from denial of certiorari). (This dissent is mentioned by the court panel in the excerpt of the *City of Philadelphia* opinion in this casebook.) Justice Rehnquist believed the district judge's order directing the United States to intervene raised "issues of sufficient moment, regarding both the relationship between the federal judiciary and the Executive Branch of the Federal Government and that between the federal judiciary and the States," and therefore that the Supreme Court should review the matter. *Id.* at 928. The dissent further opined that "the United States surely has no claim of its own under the Fourteenth Amendment" against the state prison system and did not appear to have any statutory basis for intervening into a civil rights dispute between private citizens and a state government. *Id.* Justice Rehnquist questioned the government's assertion that the United States has some form of inherent standing to sue to prevent widespread and severe deprivations of constitutional rights. *Id.* In sum, the dissent from the denial of certiorari in *Estelle* parallels the analysis subsequently applied by the Third Circuit in the *City of Philadelphia* case. (By the time the *Ruiz v. Estelle* case came up again in the regular course of appeal, Congress had enacted the Civil Rights of Institutionalized Persons Act mentioned above, and thus the Fifth Circuit found it unnecessary to decide whether the United States would have had the inherent authority to file suit at the time it intervened into the lawsuit. *Ruiz v. Estelle,* 679 F.2d 1115, 1134–36 (5th Cir. 1982), *amended in part, vacated in part,* 688 F.2d 266 (5th Cir. 1982), *cert. denied,* 460 U.S. 1042 (1983).)

3. Consistent with what appears to be the judicial trend, Professor Henry Monaghan contends that while there is a presidential power "to preserve, protect, and defend the personnel, property and instrumentalities of the national government," the power to sue without statutory authorization is narrowly limited to such concerns. Henry P. Monaghan, *The Protective Power of the Presidency,* 93 Colum. L. Rev. 1, 61, 66 (1993); *see also* Gregory C. Sisk, *Litigation With the Federal Government* § 8.02, at 504 (4th ed. 2006) ("The United States as a body politic arguably does not require congressional authorization to enforce its rights in the federal or state courts, so long as it shows a direct governmental interest in bringing suit."). Thus, in Professor Monaghan's view, the Executive possesses an inherent power to initiate litigation only to protect a direct governmental interest—that is, the sovereign or proprietary interests of the United States government itself—but not to advance the interests of third persons, such as citizens suffering constitutional deprivations. He thus agrees with the decisions "holding that, absent statutory mandate, the President has no standing to enforce Fourteenth Amendment rights against the states." Monaghan, *supra,* at 70 n.334.

Professor Larry Yackle, although acknowledging the conventional wisdom that the United States may not file suit for alleged constitutional infringements suffered by third persons without congressional permission, aims to "rekindle a debate" and "revive the controversy." Larry W. Yackle, *A Worthy Champion for Fourteenth Amendment Rights: The United States In Parens Patriae,* 92 Nw. U. L. Rev. 111, 111 (1997):

> The executive branch of the federal government in the person of the Attorney General or a surrogate, advancing the interests of the United States itself as well as the interests of individual citizens, has constitutional authority, at least in the absence of an express statute to the contrary, to institute civil lawsuits in federal court to enforce Fourteenth Amendment rights—including the "public rights" typically asserted affirmatively by class plaintiffs in "institutional" litigation and the procedural rights typically asserted defensively by individual defendants in state criminal prosecutions.

Id. So understood, he argues the federal Executive would be free to champion a progressive vision of constitutional rights, such as pursuing legal challenges to state limitations on affirmative action. *Id.*

(Is that what lies at the bottom of the debate about the federal government's power to sue without express statutory mandate—conservative versus liberal perspectives on political or constitutional rights and about resort to the courts to resolve controversial questions? Does that philosophical or ideological division explain the disagreement between the court panel and the dissent from the denial of rehearing in *City of Philadelphia*?)

4. The question of whether the federal government has a sufficient interest in a particular matter or has been given adequate statutory authorization to initiate suit is especially likely to arise when the political administration holding the Executive Branch wishes to pursue a legal strategy in the courts on an issue of pressing concern to it, but on which the Legislative Branch has not yet cooperated by affirmatively and unambiguously permitting judicial action. For a recent example in a non-constitutional context, having been unsuccessful in achieving its anti-tobacco agenda in the legislative arena, the Clinton Justice Department instead turned to the courts to seek damages and other restraints against tobacco companies based upon injuries to health suffered by smokers over the past generation. Some Clinton Administration officials also advocated filing a government suit against the manufacturers of handguns, asserting manufacturers' liability for injuries to victims of gun violence by failing to take more effective measures to ensure that firearms were not sold to individuals who could not legally own them. In both instances, serious questions have been raised as to whether the federal government—in contrast with individual smokers or victims of handgun violence—has an adequate stake to justify pursuit of these lawsuits in the name of the sovereign United States.

a. *Tobacco Litigation* In 1999, the Department of Justice filed a multi-billion dollar suit on behalf of the United States in federal district court against a number of tobacco companies, alleging that the federal government was entitled to recover damages to reimburse it for the costs of health benefits in treating smoking-related illnesses. Complaint for Damages and Injunctive and Declaratory Relief, United States v. Philip Morris, Inc. (D.D.C. Sept. 22, 1999). In support of its suit, the government asserted claims under health care benefit and racketeering statutes.

Prior attempts by third parties to sue the tobacco companies as surrogates for millions of smokers have met with mixed success. In 1998, the tobacco companies settled lawsuits filed by the state attorneys general, agreeing to pay billions of dollars to 46 states in compensation for health care costs incurred by smoking. However, similar suits by insurance companies or their insureds, union health funds, and hospitals against the tobacco companies have been rejected by the federal courts of appeals, holding that they lacked standing to assert injuries actually suffered by individual smokers. *See, e.g., Perry v. American Tobacco Co.*, 324 F.3d 845 (6th Cir. 2003); *Association of Washington Public Hospital Districts v. Philip Morris, Inc.*, 241 F.3d 696 (9th Cir. 2001); *Allegheny General Hospital v. Philip Morris, Inc.*, 228 F.3d 429 (3d Cir. 2000); *Texas Carpenters Health Benefit Fund v. Philip Morris, Inc.*, 199 F.3d 788 (5th Cir. 2000);*Laborers Local 17 Health & Benefit Fund v. Philip Morris, Inc.*, 191 F.3d 229 (2d Cir. 1999); *Oregon Laborers–Employers Health & Welfare Trust Fund v. Philip Morris, Inc.*, 185 F.3d 957 (9th Cir. 1999); *Steamfitters Local Union No. 420 Welfare Fund v. Philip Morris, Inc.*, 171 F.3d 912

(3d Cir. 1999). In light of the Supreme Court's refusal to review appellate decisions upholding dismissal of these suits, at least one prominent anti-tobacco advocate admitted that the "death knell" likely has been sounded for these types of third-party lawsuits. Richard Carelli, *Cigarette Makers Win Significant Legal Victory*, Des Moines Register, Jan. 11, 2000, at 6A (quoting anti-tobacco advocate).

The Department of Justice during the Clinton Administration was determined to buck the judicial trend. Interestingly, just two years before, in 1997, Attorney General Janet Reno testified before Congress that "the federal government does not have an independent cause of action" against the tobacco companies; another Justice Department official confirmed that the health care statutes did not confer standing on the government to recover from the tobacco industry the costs of treating the ill health effects of smoking. Kenneth Smith, *Smoke and Sue*, WASH. TIMES, Aug. 5, 1999, at A19; Jacob Sullum, *Following Suit: Clinton Wants to Stick It to Smokers Again*, REASON, Apr. 1, 1999, at 67. Moreover, Frank Hunger, then Assistant Attorney General for the Civil Division, and career attorneys within the Department of Justice reportedly were hostile to the litigation plan, believing there was no statutory basis for a government suit against the cigarette manufacturers. Alissa J. Rubin & Henry Weinstein, *Tobacco Suit Represents Quick Reversal*, L.A. TIMES, Sept. 25, 1999, at A13; David S. Cloud, Gordon Fairclough & Ann Davis, *Justices Reverses: Lobbying Effort Wins Turnabout on Tobacco Suit*, WALL ST. J., Sept. 24, 1999, at B1. But a promise by President Clinton in his 1999 State of the Union address to bring a federal lawsuit against the cigarette manufacturers, a concerted lobbying campaign on the Department of Justice by anti-smoking activists and legal academics, and the success of the states in procuring a huge monetary settlement from the tobacco companies, prompted a reversal of position at Main Justice.

However, in response to a motion by the tobacco companies to dismiss the federal government's lawsuit, the district court (consistent with the disposition by other federal courts of claims against the tobacco companies by health insurers and hospitals as discussed above) rejected those counts of the complaint seeking recovery of the government's costs in providing government health care benefits for smokers suffering tobacco-related illnesses. *United States v. Philip Morris, Inc.*, 116 F.Supp.2d 131, 135, 138–46 (D.D.C. 2000). The court concluded that the Medical Care Recovery Act was designed to allow the government to recover from third-party tortfeasors only when it directly furnished medical care or benefits to its own employees, particularly military servicemembers. *Id.* at 138–44. Indeed, in language pertinent to our study at this point in the casebook, the court noted that while "Congress * * * may not have adopted the aggressive, pro-consumer and pro-health stance that many activists have continually fought so hard for," the executive branch could not overcome congressional inaction by seizing upon a statute designed for a limited purpose and wielding it as an economic and regulatory weapon against the tobacco industry. *Id.* at 144. The district court further held that the Medicare Secondary Payer provisions of the Social Security Act serves to allow government recovery from other insurance plans or funds and was not intended by Congress as "an across-the-board procedural vehicle for suing tortfeasors" who had harmed third persons who then received federal statutory medical care benefits. *Id.* at 135; *see also id.* at 144–46. (The district court later rejected the federal government's attempts to resuscitate these counts, through motions to amend or modify the court's decision or by filing an amended complaint. *United States v. Philip Morris, Inc.,* 156 F.Supp.2d 1 (D.D.C. 2001); *United States v. Philip Morris, Inc.,* 153 F.Supp.2d 32 (D.D.C. 2001).)

Should the federal government's lawsuit to recover health care costs expended for citizens with smoking-related illnesses have survived the motion to dismiss? Applying the legal standards set out in the *United States v. City of Philadelphia* decision, and assuming that no specific statute directly authorizes such an action by the government (the government contends that certain health care statutes can be read to permit the suit, but they have never been so applied), does the federal government have an adequate interest to bring suit on behalf either of its own interests in having expended funds for health care or on behalf of the members of the public who have suffered smoking-related illnesses? Or do you conclude that the executive branch was improperly attempting to bypass the democratic process to obtain a result in the courts—punishing monetary damages against the tobacco companies and more stringent restrictions on tobacco marketing—that it could not persuade the Congress to grant?

In *United States v. Philip Morris, Inc.,* the district court did preserve the claims of the United States under the Racketeer Influenced and Corrupt Organizations Act (RICO), which alleged that the tobacco companies conspired to deceive the public about the health effects of tobacco products and the addictive nature of nicotine. *United States v. Philip Morris, Inc.,* 116 F.Supp.2d 131, 134–38, 146–55 (D.D.C. 2000). Through this RICO count, the government sought various forms of relief, including disgorgement of tobacco industry profits as an equitable remedy. *Id.* at 135. Interestingly for our purposes, this surviving RICO claim was the one in which the government's position most closely approaches the traditional governmental role of regulation and law enforcement, as contrasted with the dismissed claims in which the government essentially sought to stand in shoes of third parties, that is, smokers who suffered ill health effects from tobacco. Moreover, in contrast with the claims for reimbursement of health care benefits where the federal statutes cited by the government at best offered implicit authority to file the lawsuit, the government is expressly authorized under RICO to seek judicial relief against fraudulent behavior by commercial enterprises, although the question remained as to whether confiscation of all tobacco company profits was available as an equitable remedy.

In early 2005, while the trial was underway in the District Court, the United States Court of Appeals for the District of Columbia Circuit held by a divided panel in *United States v. Philip Morris USA, Inc.,* 396 F.3d 1190 (D.C. Cir. 2005), that disgorgement of $280 billion in tobacco companies profits was not an available remedy under the civil provision of RICO, which instead permits only forward-looking remedies that prevent and restrain violations of the statute. The appellate court's ruling thus dramatically reduced the damages available against the tobacco companies. In August, 2006, the district court issued a 1,653 page opinion, finding that the defendant tobacco companies had devised and executed a scheme to defraud consumer and potential consumers by falsely denying, distorting, and minimizing the significant adverse health effect of cigarette smoking, as well as in other ways. *United States v. Philip Morris USA, Inc.*, 449 F.Supp.2d 1, at * 1–2, 125 (D.D.C. 2006). Granting final judgment for the United States on most of its RICO claims, the court granted future-oriented equitable remedies designed to prevent and restrain future RICO violation, specifically enjoining use of market terms suggesting that certain brands of cigarettes are less hazardous to health, ordering defendants to issue corrective statements in the media, and requiring defendants to disclose their disaggregated marketing data to the government. *Id.* at *1–2; *United States v. Philip Morris USA, Inc.*, 449 F.Supp.2d 1 (D.D.C. 2006). As this edition of the casebook was being completed, the district court judgment was pending on appeal.

b. *Proposed Handgun Litigation.* Although the Department of Justice pressed ahead with its suit targeting the tobacco companies, news reports indicate the department drew the line against the Clinton Administration's plan to sue firearms manufacturers on a products liability theory. According to the report, Housing and Urban Development Secretary Andrew Cuomo urged the government to file suit directly against the gun manufacturers, asserting a government interest through federal financing of public housing, whose residents have been disproportionate victims of gun violence. This proposed action would have demanded substantial damages and likely would have sought as well to exact concessions from the firearms industry regarding the future production, design, and sale and marketing of handguns. However, one official was quoted as saying that "there was unanimous opinion [within the Department of Justice] that the federal government did not have a legal basis to sue." Sam Skolnik, *DOJ Reined in Cuomo on Gun Litigation,* Legal Times, Dec. 13, 1999, at 17. A *Washington Post* editorial appears to capture the general sentiment in and outside the government at the time, when it argued in favor of comprehensive federal gun control legislation but said that because "Congress has not been willing to do so is no license for the administration to use the courts as an alternative policymaking vehicle." *See also* Editorial, *The HUD Gun Suit,* Wash. Post, Dec. 17, 1999, at A40.

———

SECTION B.   TIME LIMITATIONS—STATUTE OF LIMITATIONS AND LACHES

As we've seen earlier in our studies (see Chapters II.C and III.A.2), the United States contends that time limitations incorporated within various statutory waivers of sovereign immunity be enforced rigorously and without exception against those making claims against the government. Although the government as defendant has not always been successful in convincing courts to strictly apply limitation periods, the government has been rather consistent in insisting that others be held to definite time prescriptions in commencing suit. Nonetheless, when the federal government is the plaintiff (and thus the shoe is on the other foot), it sometimes attempts to avoid time constraints that would bar its own arguably stale claims from being pressed in court.

There is no question that the federal government is bound when a statute of limitations is specified by Congress for a particular cause of action. Congress has enacted specific statutes to limit the time for commencing many causes of action that may be asserted by the federal government. Moreover, in 1966, Congress enacted a general six-year statute of limitations for actions commenced by the United States alleging, inter alia, money owed by contract, trespass on government lands, and conversion of government property, as well as a three-year limitations period for torts committed against the United States. 28 U.S.C. § 2415. However, this general statute of limitations although broad, is not all-inclusive. The universe of possible causes of action that could be asserted by the federal government is not encompassed by the list of claims in Section 2415.

For both private party plaintiffs and the federal government, there remain federally-created rights of action to which Congress, for whatever reason, has not seen fit to attach a limitations period. "When Congress has created a cause of action and has not specified the period of time within which it may be asserted, the [Supreme] Court has frequently inferred that Congress intended that a local [that is, state] time limitation should apply." *Occidental Life Ins. Co. v. EEOC*, 432 U.S. 355, 367 (1977). For example, Section 1983 of Title 42, enacted shortly after the Civil War, authorizes a federal cause of action against any person who, acting under color of state law, deprives another of rights secured by federal law or the United States Constitution. However, the Reconstruction Civil Rights Acts do not contain a specific statute of limitations for such actions. Accordingly, the Supreme Court has directed courts to borrow the forum state's personal injury statute of limitations, as most analogous, for Section 1983 claims. *Wilson v. Garcia*, 471 U.S. 261, 276–80 (1985). Should the courts likewise seek out and apply a borrowed statute of limitations when the sovereign United States asserts a cause of action for which Congress has specified no commencement limitation? Or, on such occasions, should the federal government be left absolutely free from *any* time constraint for filing suit?

When initiating an action against a private person or entity, should the federal government be obliged to faithfully adhere to the same rules of timely filing that apply to other litigants? Do statutes of limitations or the equitable concept of laches restrict the government's recourse to court in the same manner as for private persons? At least when the government is acting in a non-sovereign capacity, such as by assuming the rights of private parties, should it not likewise be held to the same time constraints that would have applied to those private parties?

———

Dole v. Local 427, International Union of Electrical, Radio & Machine Workers (AFL–CIO)

United States Court for the Third Circuit.
894 F.2d 607 (3d Cir. 1990).

■ A. LEON HIGGINBOTHAM, JR., CHIEF JUDGE.

This appeal arises from an action filed by the Secretary of Labor on behalf of the United States of America ("the Government") pursuant to sections 104 and 210 of the Labor–Management Reporting and Disclosure Act ("LMRDA" or the "Act"), 29 U.S.C. §§ 414 & 440. The Government sought to enjoin a local union from refusing to permit one of its members to review collective bargaining agreements between the union and employers other than her own. The district court granted the defendant union's motion for summary judgment and dismissed this action on the grounds that it was barred by the statute of limitations. In so doing, the district court imported the six months statute of limitations of § 10(b) of the National Labor Relations Act ("NLRA") ("section 10(b)"), 29 U.S.C. § 160(b), since section 104 of the LMRDA is silent as to any statute of limitations. We hold that no statute of limitations should apply to suits of this type brought by the Government under section 104 of the LMRDA.

I.

The essential facts of this case are undisputed. In a letter dated June 18, 1986, Hortensia Colmenares, a member of Local 427, International Union of Electrical, Radio and Machine Workers, AFL–CIO ("Local 427" or "the union"), requested a copy of the collective bargaining agreement entered into between Local 427 and her employer, Keene Corporation. In this letter, she also asked to review the collective bargaining agreements that Local 427 had entered into with employers other than Keene Corporation. * * * However, by a letter dated August 22, 1986, Local 427 informed Ms. Colmenares that it would not permit her to inspect its collective bargaining agreements with other employers. In explaining its refusal to permit review of these other agreements, the union asserted that Ms. Colmenares' request was a "fishing expedition" which threatened to reveal employers' confidential information "in a process which could expose them to non-union or other competition."

Shortly after receiving this information, on September 8, 1986, Ms. Colmenares filed an official complaint with the Department of Labor. Representatives of the U.S. Department of Labor and counsel for the union attempted unsuccessfully to resolve the dispute through correspondence. However, at no time during these communications did Local 427 indicate that it might change its position in this matter.

On September 1, 1987, the Secretary of Labor, pursuant to her authority under section 210 of the LMRDA,[2] commenced this action in the district court. The Secretary of Labor filed for summary judgment on substantive grounds that are not before us now. The union filed for summary judgment both on substantive grounds and based on the assertion that the suit was barred by the statute of limitations. The district court granted the defendant union's motion for summary judgment on the grounds that the suit was time-barred and accordingly dismissed the plaintiff's suit. This appeal followed.

II.

In general, the structure of the LMRDA contemplates enforcement both by private citizens * * * and also by the Secretary of Labor * * *. Section 104 of the LMDRA, the section at issue in the case before us now, provides both for private suits by union members and for suits brought by the Secretary of Labor. Congress thus conceived of Government suits as an integral part of the enforcement mechanism of section 104. Title I of the LMRDA makes no reference to a statute of limitations within which an action enforcing any of its sections must be brought.

The issue in this case is which statute of limitations, if any, is most appropriately applied to Title I of the LMRDA, and whether under that limitations period, the action filed by the Secretary is time-barred or timely. Because the district court dismissed the Secretary's claim as time-barred, the court had no occasion to rule on the substantive validity of the Secretary's claim. Accordingly, the statute of limitations question is the only issue before us now. We have plenary review of this issue of law.

III.

* * * As a general matter, no statute of limitations will be applied in civil actions brought by the Government, unless Congress explicitly imposes such time limitations. *Guaranty Trust Co. v. United States,* 304 U.S. 126, 132 (1938). This principle, expressed in the maxim, *nullum tempus occurrit regi* (time does not run against the king) was settled as early as 1840 in *United States v. Knight,* 39 U.S. (14 Pet.) 301, 315 (1840). In that case, the court recited the general rule in England governing limitations running against the Crown.

> [W]here an act of parliament is made for the public good, the advancement of religion and justice, and to prevent injury and wrong, the king shall not be bound by such act, though not particularly named therein. But where a statute is general, and thereby any prerogative, right, title or interest is divested or taken from the king, in such case he shall not

---

2. Section 210 of the LMRDA, 29 U.S.C. § 440, provides as follows:

Whenever it shall appear that any person has violated or is about to violate any of the provisions of this subchapter, the Secretary may bring a civil action for such relief (in-cluding injunctions) as may be appropriate. Any such action must be brought in the district court of the United States where the violation occurred or, at the option of the parties, in the United States District Court for the District of Columbia.

be bound; unless that statute is made, by express words, to extend to him. It is a settled principle, that the king is not, ordinarily, barred, unless named by an act of limitations.

Id. at 315. The doctrine continues to have vitality on public policy grounds "that the public interest should not be prejudiced by the negligence of public officers, to whose care they are confided." *Id.*

Another line of authority extends this principle to include those situations where the Government sues to enforce public rights. In *United States v. Summerlin,* 310 U.S. 414, 416–17 (1940), where the Federal Housing Administrator filed a claim against an individual's estate, the Court held that the Government is not bound by a limitations period when suing in its Governmental capacity whether the action is filed in state or federal court. In *Summerlin,* the court reasoned that "[w]hen the United States becomes entitled to a claim, acting in its governmental capacity, and asserts its claim in that right, it cannot be deemed to have abdicated its governmental authority so as to become subject to a state statute of limitations." *Id.* at 417. * * *

The cases we have cited express the abstract principle that in certain situations, no statute of limitations runs against the Government. However, the factual situations described in these cases, are different from the facts in the present case. Accordingly, we must factually analyze and distill the instant case to determine whether it is appropriate to apply the principle to the present action. Thus, this case involves what thoughtful scholars call "the anatomy of [a] precedent."[7] While in the case at bar, we think that this general principle tilts strongly in the Government's favor, we recognize that all of the cases cited by the parties (or the concurrence) involve different factual situations or statutory settings. Many of the cases cited in the concurrence do not involve the Government as a litigant and some of the cases which we cite involve statutes which have legislative histories different from that of the LMRDA. In fact, we are dealing with what Justice Cardozo has called the interstitial spaces of the law.[10] Though we find the concurrence somewhat myopic in its reading of the most analogous cases, the position taken is plausible.

In our view, the deficiency of the concurrence is the great weight it gives to those cases involving a dramatically different factual or statutory setting, its reliance on these cases to conclude that the Government's role here is akin to a private action suit, and its conclusion that there is no public interest at risk. The critical issue here—for both the majority and the concurrence—is whether the Government was "acting in its Governmental capacity" and "asserting its claim in that right" or whether the Government was acting in what the concurrence claims was nothing more than a "dispute between two [private] parties, Ms. Colmenares and Local 427." In determining whether this litigation involves a public or private issue, the concurrence relies primarily on *U.S. v. Beebe,* 127 U.S. 338

---

7. *See* R. Aldisert, *The Judicial Process* 777–861 (1976).

10. *See* B. Cardozo, *The Nature of the Judicial Process* 103, 113–14 (1921).

(1888). In *Beebe,* the Attorney General brought a suit in equity allegedly on behalf of the United States to set aside and cancel certain patents for about 480 acres of land issued in favor of Roger Beebe, who had died "many years ago." *Id.* The suit was commenced 45 years after the cause of action arose.

In *Beebe,* the Government admitted that the United States "did not own the land embraced in [the land patents] but that on the contrary, said land was legally appropriated by other persons and was therefore segregated from the public domain." *Id.* at 339. *Beebe* involved nothing more than a private dispute as to which of two families owned the land—the Philbrook heirs or the Beebe heirs. No basic issue of public policy or democracy was involved; it was indistinguishable from thousands of cases to settle a title as to who owns Blackacre. Nevertheless, even in that private setting, the court felt compelled to note first that

> [t]he principle that the United States are not bound by any statute of limitations, nor barred by any laches of their officers, however gross, in a suit brought by them as a sovereign government to enforce a *public right,* or to assert a *public interest,* is established past all controversy or doubt.

Id. at 344 (emphases added). The Court recognized a narrow exception to the general rule against subjecting actions by the federal Government to statutes of limitation when such actions do not assert any public right or protect any public interest, title or property. After a careful review of the intricacies of this land dispute, the court stressed that

> this case stands upon a *different footing,* and presents a *different question.* The question is, are these defenses available to the defendant in the case where the government, although a *nominal complainant party,* has *no real interest* in the litigation, but has allowed his name to be used therein for the *sole benefit of a private person?*

Id. (emphases added).

The concurrence draws an analogy between the present action by the Secretary on behalf of Ms. Colmenares, and the problems of the Philbrook heirs in a land dispute and concludes that the issue here merely involves the "assertion of Colmenares's private rights". To rely on the *Beebe* case as the foundation of one's analysis, and to assume that the Government is a "nominal complainant" who has "no real interest in the litigation" is to rely on an analogy which does not possess a high degree of similarity between the situations compared.

We differ completely with the concurrence's minimization of such an important aspect of union democracy and its reduction of the issue here to merely one of a private right. Even though suits under the LMRDA frequently have specific private as well as public beneficiaries, the touchstone remains the fact that public policies are served and the public interest is advanced by the litigation, and the fact that the litigation has private beneficiaries as well does not detract from the public nature of the suit. Instead, what is involved here is a classic example of a "public right" and a "public interest." The legislative history of the LMRDA repudiates the concurrence's position. The public significance Congress attributed to the Act is revealed in the well known terms it used in debating the merits of the legislation, such as "democracy" and "Bill of Rights," which have always had a public interest imprimatur.

The debates on the Labor–Management Reporting and Disclosure Act reveal Congressional concerns about the prevalence of undemocratic procedures in some American labor unions and the impact of these practices on the public. The Senate's Report on the legislation noted a substantial public interest intertwined in the internal problems of the labor unions. *See* S.Rep. No. 187, 86th Cong., 1st Sess. 6, *reprinted in* 1959 U.S.Code Cong. & Admin.News 2318, 2323. When speaking on the Senate floor in 1959, then Senator John F. Kennedy explained that a bipartisan select committee was established to look into improper activities in the labor or management fields, "because of recurring reports of abuses of power on the part of both labor and management to the detriment of the welfare of employees, employers, and the public." 105 Cong.Rec. 5983 (1959). Senator Ervin of North Carolina, a member of the McClellan committee which investigated the union abuses, viewed the legislation as an attempt to correct the illegal practice of "corrupt union leaders and equally corrupt management ... enter[ing] into agreements under which the union leaders had 'sold down the river' those whom they were supposed to represent." 105 Cong.Rec. 6410 (1959).

Accordingly, Congress enacted the LMRDA, to curb "breach[es] of trust, corruption, [and] disregard of the rights of individual employees" in the American labor movement. 29 U.S.C. § 401(b). One of the means chosen by Congress to avert these abuses is to expose union operations to the scrutiny of union members and the public. To that end, the LMRDA requires unions and union officers to disclose a variety of financial and other information concerning union activities. In the case at bar, the Secretary of Labor, on behalf of Ms. Colmenares was seeking to obtain information concerning her union's activity. * * *

For the foregoing reasons, we hold that where, as here, the Secretary sues to enforce Title I rights of access to information or freedom of speech that foster a democratic labor movement, the public purpose doctrine applies and no statute of limitation runs against the Secretary. Accordingly, the Secretary's action should not have been dismissed as time-barred.

* * * [W]e leave open the question of whether laches can apply as a defense against the Government suing to protect such public interests. The defendant is free to argue in the district court that the Secretary was dilatory and that it suffered actual prejudice thereby, the test in this circuit for laches. We express no opinion as to the outcome of such an argument.

V.

The judgment of the district court dismissing the plaintiff's action as time-barred will be reversed, and this case will be remanded for further proceedings consistent with this opinion.

■ GARTH, CIRCUIT JUDGE, concurring:

I.

Although I reach the same result in this case as my colleagues, I disagree totally with the "no statute of limitations" analysis they have adopted. It is because of the importance of this issue to the bench and to the bar, i.e., what statute of limitations is to be employed in cases brought under the Labor–Management Reporting and Disclosure Act ("LMRDA"), 29 U.S.C. § 401 *et seq.*, that I have been compelled to write separately.

A.

* * * I agree with my colleagues that the Secretary of Labor's suit on behalf of Ms. Colmenares is, under the given facts, not time barred: it falls within New Jersey's two-year statute of limitations for personal injury. Alternatively, the alleged breach involved here may be construed as contractual, in which case New Jersey's six-year statute of limitations for contract claims applies.

B.

In either event, however, I find no support here for a holding of *no* statute of limitations. The Secretary's evocations of the lofty goals and flowery language of the LMRDA, do not themselves a "public purpose" make. * * *

I suggest that the majority opinion has erred in straining to transform the present dispute between two private parties—Ms. Colmenares and Local 427—into a "public purpose" exercise of sovereignty, such as may be raised without regard to any statute of limitations. *See U.S. v. Beebe,* 127 U.S. 338, 346–47 (1888). * * *

C.

In *U.S. v. Beebe, supra* the Attorney General, on behalf of the United States, sought to set aside certain property patents that had been issued in favor of Beebe. Among the defenses raised against the United States was the defense of a statute of limitations. In affirming the dismissal of the action, the Court, in language that is exceedingly relevant here, stated:

> ... an inspection of the record shows that the Government, though in name the complainant, is not the real contestant party to the title or the property in ... controversy. It has no interest in the suit, and has nothing to gain from the relief prayed for, and nothing to lose if the relief is denied. The bill itself was filed in the name of the United States, and signed by the Attorney General on the petition of private individuals, and the right asserted is a private right, which might have been asserted without the intervention of the United States at all.

> * * *

> We are of the opinion that when the Government is a mere formal complainant in a suit, not for the purpose of asserting any public right

or protecting any public interest, title, or property, but merely to form a conduit through which one private person can conduct litigation against another private person, a court ... will not be restrained from administering the equities existing between the real parties by any exemption of the Government designed for the protection of the rights of the United States alone. The mere use of its name in a suit for the benefit of a private suitor cannot extend its immunity ... to said private suitor ... nor stop the court from examining into and deciding the case according to the principles governing courts ... in like cases between private litigants.

Beebe, 127 U.S., at 346–47.

In the instant case, following *Beebe's* instruction, the majority's flight into "public purposes/rights/interests" pieties, is unjustified and flawed. The proper inquiry must lead us to apply, at the least, New Jersey's two-year statute of limitations for personal injury or, at the most, New Jersey's six-year statute of limitations for contractual actions. In either event, the district court's decision cannot be sustained because the action is not time barred. To that extent, and to that extent only, I concur in the majority's judgment.

II.

* * * In order to settle upon the most appropriate statute of limitations, the most suitable analogy is to be found in those Supreme Court cases that have steadfastly applied state personal injury statutes of limitation whenever a statutory violation of 42 U.S.C. §§ 1981, 1983, or 1985 has occurred.

But even if I am in error in selecting the personal injury statute—and I do not think I am—the alternative is not "no statute of limitations" as espoused by the majority, but rather New Jersey's residual contract statute of limitation of six years. Because the union/union member relationship is essentially a contract, a union may, for example, seek to enforce its rules against members and may assume that contractual mutual reliance operates between a union and its members. In the instant case, it could be argued that Ms. Colmenares's right to copies of her union's various contract agreements with other companies may be inferred from her contractual rights as a member of her union.

What is not possible, however, is for this court suddenly to introduce a "public right" or "public interest" or "public purpose" into a union/union member contract relationship—just by virtue of a suit being brought in the name of the Secretary of Labor. * * * The majority's analysis that, where a statute is silent, no statute of limitations bars an action brought by the government, must necessarily lead to individual plaintiffs foregoing individual claims in favor of claims asserted by authorized government officials. But [Supreme Court decisions do not suggest] such an improbable and anomalous result.

Because no legitimate or rational "public purpose" has been, or can be, identified with the assertion of Colmenares's private right, it is immaterial for statute of limitations purposes whether the action was filed by Ms. Colmenares in her own right, or by the Secretary, to vindicate Ms. Colmenares's right. * * *

Notes and Questions

From *Dole v. Local 427,* and the key precedents cited therein, what is the general rule for application of a limitations period against the federal government when it initiates a legal action for which there is no specific federal statute of limitations? Why should it be treated differently from any other plaintiff seeking a hearing in court? Is there any exception to this general no-statute-of-limitations rule for the federal government? How do the majority and the concurrence understand this exception and its relevance to the case? How do they justify their different conclusions? In the end, what *is* the statute of limitations applied by the majority in this case? By contrast, where would the concurrence find a limitations period? After reading the next case and the accompanying notes, consider again whether a *state* statute of limitations or an equitable substitute for a statute of limitations, like laches, may ever bind the federal government and, if so, under what circumstances.

United States v. Robbins

United States District Court for the Eastern District of Michigan.
819 F.Supp. 672 (E.D.Mich.1993).

■ NEWBLATT, DISTRICT JUDGE.

Pending before the Court are cross motions for summary judgment on a claim by the United States to collect a defaulted student loan payment. Defendant acknowledges that unless she has a valid defense, she owes a debt of $986.20 from two National Direct Student Loans that she obtained in 1980 while attending Ferris State University in Big Rapids, Michigan. The university issued the loans in 1980. They became due October 1, 1981, nine months after the defendant ceased carrying a half-time academic [course] load. The university declared Ms. Robbins in default on the loans and assigned payment to the United States on June 30, 1985.

Defendant claims that the United States is barred by laches from collecting the debt. In particular, defendant contends that she left the university because of racial discrimination by the university. This discrimination, she contends, would constitute a defense to payment of the loan. Defendant claims that she was unaware of collection efforts by the university, and that because the university waited five years prior to assigning the loan, and the government waited seven years to file suit, she is unable to prove her defense of discrimination due to a decline in her memory of events.

Analysis

The motion is before the Court on summary judgment, and the familiar standard of Fed.R.Civ.P. 56 applies. Defendant has not argued that the statute of limitations has passed, and that argument, if it existed, is now waived as it was not affirmatively pled.

The statute of limitations is certainly no bar to collection, however, because Congress amended the Higher Education Act of 1965 ("HEA" or "the Act") in 1991 to abrogate the six-year limitations period that formerly applied to debt collection cases under the Act. 20 U.S.C.A. § 1091a(a).

I. **Can laches apply as a defense to a legal action under a federal statute where Congress has abrogated the statute of limitation?**

A. **No state statute of limitation is available.**

Laches is an equitable doctrine and, as a general rule, remains inapplicable to legal claims for damages. Usually, cases brought at law are limited by statutes of limitation. However, Congress does not always provide a statute of limitations for federal claims, and federal courts often borrow analogous state statutes of limitation in these cases.

In the Sixth Circuit, as well as others, there is a strong presumption that a plaintiff's delay in bringing an action under federal law is reasonable so long as the analogous state statute of limitations period has not elapsed.

In the case of the statute at issue in the case at bar, however, Congress has expressly proscribed the application of a state statute of limitation to the suit for collection * * * .

The present version of 20 U.S.C. § 1091a states in pertinent part:

§ 1091a. Statute of limitations

(a) In general

(1) It is the purpose of this subsection to ensure that obligations to repay loans and grant overpayments are enforced without regard to any Federal or State statutory, regulatory, or administrative limitation on the period within which debts may be enforced.

(2) Notwithstanding any other provision of statute, regulation, or administrative limitation, no limitation shall terminate the period within which suit may be filed, a judgment may be enforced, or an offset, garnishment, or other action initiated or taken by—

(A) an institution that receives funds under this subchapter . . .

* * *

(D) the Secretary, the Attorney General, . . .

This language clearly prohibits application of any limitations period.

B.   Determination of the Applicable Standard.

In those situations where no statute of limitations is applicable, courts have sometimes applied equitable barriers to recovery. To examine whether that course is available in this case, however, this Court must determine whether such a step is consistent with federal policy. *County of Oneida v. Oneida Indian Nation of New York State,* 470 U.S. 226, 240 n. 13, 244 n. 16 (1985).

In *County of Oneida,* an Indian tribe sued a New York county on a claim for ejectment based on land that was taken 175 years earlier. The suit was brought under federal common law in which no statute of limitations was applicable. The plurality found for the Oneida tribe and refused to rule on the county's defense of laches, holding that the defense had not been properly raised on appeal. The plurality noted, however, that laches appeared inapplicable because the claim was brought at law, and laches also violated federal policy with regard to Indian land rights. *Id.,* at 244 n. 16.

Justice Stevens, writing in dissent for Chief Justice Burger and Justices White and Rehnquist, found that the issue had been properly raised and would have applied laches to bar the claim. *Oneida,* 470 U.S. at 262 (Stevens, J., dissenting). The dissent agreed, however, that "the application of a traditional equitable defense in an action at law is something of a novelty." *Id.* The Oneida tribe's claim was distinguishable from other common law claims because "common-law real property principles were often tempered by equitable considerations...." *Id.*

Justice Stevens also argued that because the case arose under federal common law, "the Court would not risk frustrating the will of the legislature [Footnote 12] by applying this familiar doctrine of equity." *Id.* Footnote 12 stated, "In deference to the doctrine of the separation of powers, the Court has been circumspect in adopting principles of equity in the context of enforcing federal statutes."

While the *Oneida* dissent is only a dissent, it did represent the views of four justices. Since the plurality did not decide the laches issue, and the dissent's reasoning was sound, this Court finds the *Oneida* dissent's analysis should be considered in determining whether laches is applicable to a federal claim for which no statute of limitations is applicable.

C.   Application of *Oneida* dissent's reasoning to the higher education technical amendments of 1991.

The Court must consider whether applying laches is inconsistent with the Congressional intent in amending the HEA. The former statute of limitations clause provided the United States with six years from the date that the collection was assigned to the Department of Education from the educational institution.

The new statute stated that its "purpose" is to "ensure that obligations to repay loans ... are enforced without regard to *any* ... statutory, regulatory or administrative limitation." 20 U.S.C. § 1091a(a)(1) (emphasis added). This language is broad and, when read with the understanding that the previous limitations period was six years, suggests that Congress fully intended to open the courts to recovery on older debt claims.

On the other hand, Congress listed three types of limits that it did not wish to limit recovery: "statutes" "regulations" and "limitations," and it could have listed "equitable defenses" as well. However, because debt collection on a contract is a legal claim, Congress might well have thought such language superfluous. *See County of Oneida,* 470 U.S. at 244 n. 16 ("application of the equitable defense of laches in an action at law would be novel indeed."). * * *

Congress might also have considered that direct student loans are not collectable after the disability or death of the student. This provision places an outside limit on the government's ability to pursue the debtor and prevents the open-ended claim that was the basis of the *Oneida* claim, "the Court has always presumed that *some* principle of limitation applies to federal causes of action." *Oneida,* 470 U.S. at 258 (Stevens, J., dissenting).

The Court finds that while there is evidence on both sides, the best reading of the statute is one that comports with the direction of the amendment, to eliminate barriers to recovery. To read the statute in such a manner ensures that the courts maintain the greatest respect for Congressional intent and separation of powers. Moreover, because student loan collection claims are barred at the date of the debtor's death or disability, there is no danger of condemning a debtor's heirs "for his forefathers' misdeeds." *Id.,* at 273.

Nor can one reasonably argue that the effect of removing equitable defenses "will upset long-settled expectations." *Id.,* at 272. Indeed, it is reasonable to infer that a purpose of the amendment eliminating the statute of limitations is to ensure that all borrowers should expect to repay their loans.

For all these reasons, the Court finds that laches cannot be applied to contract actions brought to recover student loans that are subject to 20 U.S.C. § 1091a(a).

D. Even if laches could otherwise apply as a defense to a contract action subject to 20 U.S.C. § 1091a(a), does sovereign immunity bar its application?

Even if laches were otherwise available as a defense to a student loan contract, the government argues that laches cannot be asserted against the United States on the grounds of sovereign immunity. *Costello v. United States,* 365 U.S. 265, 281 (1961); *United States v. Summerlin,* 310 U.S. 414, 416 (1940). While this rule originated with the notion of royal privilege, twentieth century courts attribute it to the policy of preserving public rights and property against the negligence of public officers. *Guaranty Trust Co. v. United States,* 304 U.S. 126, 132 (1938). The Ninth Circuit recently applied the *Summerlin* rule to bar the defense of laches in a student loan collection case. *United States v. Menatos,* 925 F.2d 333, 335 (9th Cir. 1991).

Furthermore, because the government filed suit within seven years after it received assignment of the debt, when the repealed statute of limitations had been six years, the government acted in a sufficiently timely manner to bar laches against it.

2.   Lack of Diligence by the University

The evidence before the Court of the university's lack of diligence in attempting to collect on the loans is the defendant's affidavit that the university did not contact her for repayment of the loans. The government presented no evidence to the contrary of specific acts performed by the university, such as the sending of a collection letter. The government did submit, however, a statement signed by a university official, M.E. Witbeck, on the form assigning defendant's loan collection to the Department of Education. That form contains the statement, "This loan is now in default despite completion of due diligence on the part of the institution."

The Court finds that the present record is insufficient for a ruling under Fed.R.Civ.P. 56 as to whether the university exercised due diligence. A trial would not be required, on a possible future remand, however, because the second condition of laches is clearly not present.

B.   Undue Prejudice

Defendant cannot show that she suffered prejudice. Assuming *arguendo,* that defendant is correct, and that the university committed a tortious act of discrimination against her, that act would not serve as a defense to the debt, nor would it constitute a compulsory counterclaim under Fed. R.Civ.P. 13(a) either. *See United States v. Olavarrieta,* 812 F.2d 640, 643 (11th Cir.1987), *cert. denied,* 484 U.S. 851.

In *Olavarrieta,* the court denied a student loan debtor the right to file a third party complaint against the university for breach of contract or fraud on account of the university's failure to award the debtor a J.D. degree as promised. The court found the debtor's claim against the university to be a "separate and independent action from the government's action against him." *Id.* Therefore, for the same reasons as in that case, the court finds no prejudice to defendant resulting from the delay in filing suit.

Since laches does not apply, the debt plus interest plus collection costs must be paid.

Judgment for Plaintiff in the amount of $986.20.

SO ORDERED.

————

Notes and Questions

1.   In addition to a statutory limitations period, the equitable concept of "laches" traditionally has been applied when a plaintiff delays unreasonably in pursuing a claim to the prejudice of the defendant, usually when the request is for an equitable remedy. The doctrine of laches "is based upon

the maxim that equity aids the vigilant and not those who slumber on their rights. It is defined as neglect to assert right or claim which, taken together with lapse of time and other circumstances causing prejudice to adverse party, operates as bar in court of equity." *Black's Law Dictionary* 787 (5th ed. 1979).

With reference to *United States v. Robbins,* and the precedents relied on in that case, do laches apply against the federal government? (One of the key precedents relied on in *Robbins* is the Supreme Court's decision in *United States v. Summerlin,* 310 U.S. 414 (1940), which is discussed further in Note 2 below.) Or is the government exempt from this equitable time constraint? Describe the argument made by the defendant in *Robbins* that the federal government is not immune from laches in this particular case because of the type of claim involved and because of the manner in which the government assumed possession of that claim. Is the argument plausible? Why does it not succeed? (In this regard, see also the discussion in Note 2 about the government's assertion of assigned claims and about the nature of government lending programs.) Aside from sovereign immunity, would the application of laches in *Robbins* be consistent with the governing statutory provisions? What did Congress intend with respect to the government's collection of defaulted student loan debts?

In the years subsequent to *Robbins,* the federal courts, while occasionally suggesting that laches might attach in an exceptional case of egregious delay, have rather uniformly refused to allow the defense of laches to restrict the government's efforts to collect upon defaulted student loans. *See, e.g., United States v. Distefano,* 279 F.3d 1241, 1245 n.2 (10th Cir. 2002); *United States v. Lawrence,* 276 F.3d 193, 196 (5th Cir. 2001); *United States v. Durbin,* 64 F.Supp.2d 635, 636 (S.D.Tex.1999); *United States v. Dwelley,* 59 F.Supp.2d 115, 118 (D.Me.1999); *United States v. McLaughlin,* 7 F.Supp.2d 90, 92–93 (D.Mass.1998); *Sibley v. United States Dept. of Educ.,* 913 F.Supp. 1181, 1189 (N.D.Ill.), *aff'd,* 111 F.3d 133 (7th Cir. 1997) (table); *United States v. Smith,* 862 F.Supp. 257, 262 (D.Haw.1994); *cf. United States v. Phillips,* 20 F.3d 1005 (9th Cir. 1994) (holding, without specifically mentioning laches, that Congress intended to eliminate all time limitations on government actions to recover on defaulted student loans and to revive all claims that otherwise would be time-barred).

2. In *United States v. California,* 507 U.S. 746 (1993), the Supreme Court considered whether a *state* statute of limitations should be applied against the federal government when it has assumed a right from a private party and there is no controlling federal limitations period. In that case, the federal government had retained a private contractor to manage oil drilling operations on government land. Under the contract, the contractor was paid an annual fee and was reimbursed for its costs. The State of California assessed certain taxes against the contractor, which were paid by the contractor under protest with funds provided by the United States. After the 90–day period for filing a tax refund claim had passed, the United States filed a declaratory judgment action in federal court contending that the taxes had been wrongly assessed under California law. The government

argued that it was not bound by a state statute of limitations. The Supreme Court disagreed, due to the particular circumstances of this case. Quoting *United States v. Summerlin,* 310 U.S. 414, 417 (1940), the Court agreed with the government that " '[w]hen the United States becomes entitled to a claim, acting in its governmental capacity, and asserts its claim in that right,' "it is immune from state limitations periods. *United States v. California,* 507 U.S. at 757. (Recall that *Summerlin* was relied upon in both *Dole v. Local 427* and *United States v. Robbins* to preclude application of a time bar—whether by statute of limitations or laches—to the government in those cases.) However, the Court noted that the government had become entitled to the tax refund claim in *United States v. California* only by indemnifying a private contractor's state-law debt. Accordingly, the Court ruled that the "Government [was] in no better position than as a subrogee of its contractor" and must stand in the place of the one whose claim was paid. Under traditional subrogation rules, because the contractor's tax refund rights had lapsed, the government's claim was also barred. *Id.* at 752, 756.

In sum, under *United States v. California,* if the government becomes subrogated to a private party's claim by operation of state law, then its claim remains subject to state procedural rules, including state statutes of limitations. But if the government is "proceeding in its sovereign capacity" or if "the right at issue was obtained by the Government through, or created by, a federal statute," rather than by state law, then the *Summerlin* no-limitations rule apparently still governs. *United States v. California,* 507 U.S. at 757.

What then of a case, like *United States v. Robbins,* in which the government is trying to collect upon a contract debt that was assigned to it by a private lender after the borrower defaulted? Similarly, what if the government makes the loan directly, without an intermediary lending institution, and thus creates an immediate lender-borrower contractual relationship? When the government sues to collect the loan, is it acting in a mere proprietary or individual capacity, like any other commercial lender or debt collector, so that it should be bound by a state statute of limitations or at least some other constraint upon delay like laches? Or is the government proceeding in a sovereign capacity, when it possesses or is assigned the right to collect defaulted loan debts by virtue of federal statutes providing for government issuance, guarantee, or insurance of certain types of loans (such as those for students, small businesses, or farmers)?

Two federal courts of appeals have concluded that the government when acquiring the right to collect a debt pursuant to a federal lending program, which was enacted to enhance the security and economic well-being of the nation, is indeed acting in a sovereign or governmental capacity under established precedent. *United States v. Peoples Household Furnishings, Inc.,* 75 F.3d 252, 253–56 (6th Cir. 1996); *Farmers Home Administration v. Muirhead,* 42 F.3d 964, 964–67 (5th Cir. 1995). Accordingly, in light of the Supreme Court's apparent affirmation of the *Sum-*

merlin rule in *United States v. California,* these courts held that the government's collection efforts may not be restrained by state statutes of limitations or laches. *Peoples Household Furnishings,* 75 F.3d at 253–56 (permitting the United States to sue on a 15–year–old money judgment to collect on a business loan guaranteed by the Small Business Administration, notwithstanding state ten-year limitations period for actions founded upon judgments); *Muirhead,* 42 F.3d at 964–67 (permitting the United States to foreclose upon property liens nearly a decade after default on the underlying farm loans, where there was no federal limitations period for foreclosing mortgages). However, while believing themselves bound by established precedent, both courts argued that, at least for federal lending programs, the *Summerlin* case ought to be reconsidered and the government should be held to the same timetables as everyone else:

> The government's central proposition—that limitations may not run against the sovereign—seems quite inappropriate in the context of federal loan programs. * * * [T]he ancient attribute of sovereignty asserted by the federal government is far more appropriate to essential sovereign functions than to the federal government's role as a lender to veterans, small business owners, farmers, and disaster victims among others. That the attribute is ancient does not make it sensibly applicable to the government's role in commercial transactions.

Muirhead, 42 F.3d at 967; *Peoples Household Furnishings,* 75 F.3d at 256 (quoting *Muirhead*). Do you agree?

3.   Chief Judge Posner of the United States Court of Appeals for the Seventh Circuit, although finding it unnecessary to resolve the question in the particular case before the court, has suggested that "the question of the existence and scope of a defense of laches in government suits" remains unsettled and that prior decisions suggest three possible bases for application of laches against the United States:

> One possibility * * * is that only the most egregious instances of laches can be used to abate a government suit. Another would be to confine the doctrine to suits [involving] the government in which * * * there is no statute of limitations. * * * Still another possibility * * * is to draw a line between government suits in which the government is seeking to enforce either on its own behalf or that of private parties what are in the nature of private rights, and government suits to enforce sovereign rights, and to allow laches as a defense in the former class of cases but not the latter.

United States v. Administrative Enterprises, Inc., 46 F.3d 670, 673 (7th Cir. 1995); *see also Cayuga Indian Nation v. Pataki,* 413 F.3d 266, 278–79 (2d Cir. 2005) (a divided court held, relying upon Judge Posner's analysis in *Administrative Enterprises, Inc.,* that the United States was barred by laches from intervening in an Indian land claim based on events occurring two hundred years ago, where no statute of limitations applied to the claim under 150 years after it accrued, and where the government intervened to vindicate the interest of an Indian tribe which itself was bound by by laches), *cert. denied,* ___ U.S. ___, ___, 126 S.Ct. 2021, 2022 (2006).

Several courts of appeals have applied laches against the federal government where there is no applicable statute of limitations. For example, Title VII of the Civil Rights Act of 1964 contains no statute of limitations constraining the Equal Employment Opportunity Commission (EEOC) from initiating suit against an employer alleged to have violated anti-discrimination laws. *Occidental Life Ins. Co. v. EEOC*, 432 U.S. 355, 358–73 (1977) (holding that no statute of limitations applies to claims brought by the EEOC to enforce Title VII and interpreting congressional silence as precluding the borrowing of state law limitations for claims brought by the federal government). Thus, several courts have permitted assertion of laches against the EEOC in Title VII cases. *See, e.g., EEOC v. Watkins Motor Lines, Inc.*, 463 F.3d 436, 440 n.1 (6th Cir. 2006); *EEOC v. Vucitech*, 842 F.2d 936, 942 (7th Cir. 1988); *EEOC v. Dresser Industries, Inc.*, 668 F.2d 1199, 1201–02 (11th Cir. 1982); *Boone v. Mechanical Specialties Co.*, 609 F.2d 956, 959 (9th Cir. 1979); *EEOC v. Liberty Loan Corp.*, 584 F.2d 853, 856 (8th Cir. 1978); *see also Herman v. South Carolina Nat'l Bank*, 140 F.3d 1413, 1427 (11th Cir. 1998) (explaining that, while the United States generally is not bound by laches, "this circuit permits laches to bar an EEOC suit only because Title VII contains no statute of limitations"). Can this line of cases be reconciled with the no-laches rule adopted in *Robbins* and with the precedents cited by that court?

Section C.   Counterclaims Against the United States

As you well know by this point in our study, whenever a person seeks to initiate an affirmative court claim against the federal government, he or she must plead an express statutory waiver of sovereign immunity. Does that rule change when it is the federal government that initiates a civil lawsuit as plaintiff? When the government starts the lawsuit, may the defendant respond with a counterclaim regardless of the existence of a pertinent statutory waiver of sovereign immunity for that cause-of-action and the defendant's compliance with all procedural and substantive limitations imposed by the statutory waiver on such a claim? In sum, may a defendant avoid the constraints of sovereign immunity by framing the request for relief against the federal government as a counterclaim to a government-instituted suit?

United States v. Shaw

Supreme Court of the United States
309 U.S. 495 (1940).

■ Mr. Justice Reed delivered the opinion of the Court.

In 1918 Sydney C. McLouth contracted to construct nine tugs for the United States Shipping Board Emergency Fleet Corporation. On May 24,

1920, the contract was cancelled and the parties entered into a settlement agreement providing that McLouth was to keep as bailee certain materials furnished him for use in building the tugs and that the Fleet Corporation was to assume certain of McLouth's subcontracts and commitments. Among the commitments assumed was a contract of McLouth's to purchase lumber from the Ingram–Day Lumber Company. The Lumber Company obtained a judgment against McLouth for $42,789.96 for breach of this contract, and, McLouth having died in 1923, filed its claim on the judgment in the probate court of St. Clair County, Michigan. Subsequently the Unites States obtained a judgment of $40,165.48 against McLouth's administrator, representing damages for the conversion of the materials left with McLouth as bailee, and claim on this judgment was filed in the probate court. The administrator, respondent here, having presented without success the Lumber Company's judgment to the General Accounting Office, sought to set off that judgment against the judgment of the United States. The probate court allowed the claim of the United States and denied the set-off, but its ruling as to the set-off was reversed on appeal to the Michigan Supreme Court. The administrator then petitioned the probate court to grant statutory judgment of the balance due the estate. The court found that the claim of the United States, with interest, amounted to $49,442.41 and the Lumber Company's claim to $73,071.38 and "ordered, adjudged and ascertained" that the United States was indebted to the estate for the difference, $23,628.97, "and that such indebtedness be and the same is hereby allowed as and determined to be a proper claim which is owing to said estate by the United States of America." The probate court's judgment was affirmed on appeal.

On this certiorari we are concerned with the question whether the United States by filing a claim against an estate in a state court subjects itself, in accordance with local statutory practice, to a binding, though not immediately enforceable, ascertainment and allowance by the state court of a cross-claim against itself.

Because of different views of other federal courts as to the decisions of this Court in the important federal field of cross-claims against the United States, we granted certiorari. * * *

The state procedure for the determination of the balance against or in favor of an estate, which was employed here, was the recognized method of closing an estate at the time of the probate judgment. * * * The order entered was a final determination of the amounts due the estate by the United States on this claim and cross-claim if the probate court had jurisdiction to render the order against the petitioner.

Whether that jurisdiction exists depends upon the effect of the voluntary submission to the Michigan court by the United States of its claim against the estate. As a foundation for the examination of that question we may lay the postulate that without specific statutory consent, no suit may be brought against the United States. No officer by his action can confer jurisdiction. Even when suits are authorized they must be brought only in designated courts. The reasons for this immunity are imbedded in our legal philosophy. They partake somewhat of dignity and decorum, somewhat of practical administration, somewhat of the political desirability of an impregnable legal citadel where government as distinct from its functionaries may operate undisturbed by the demands of litigants. A sense of justice has brought a progressive relaxation by legislative enactments of the rigor of the immunity rule. As representative governments attempt to ameliorate inequalities as necessities will permit, prerogatives of the government yield to the needs of the citizen. By the act of March 3, 1797, and its successor legislation, as interpreted by this Court, cross-claims are allowed to the amount of the government's claim, where the government voluntarily sues. Specially designated claims against the United States may be sued upon in the Court of Claims or the district courts under the Tucker Act. Special government activities, set apart as corporations or individual agencies, have been made suable freely. When authority is given, it is liberally construed. As to these matters no controversy exists.

Respondent contends this immunity extends, however, only to original suits; that when a sovereign voluntarily seeks the aid of the courts for collection of its indebtedness it takes the form of a private suitor and thereby subjects itself to the full jurisdiction of the court. The principle of a single adjudication is stressed, as is the necessity for a complete examination into the cross-claim, despite attendant dislocation of government business by the appearance of important officers at distant points and the production of documents as evidence, to justify the allowance of an offset to the government's claim It is pointed out that surprise is not involved as no cross-claim may be proven until after submission to and refusal by the government accounting officers. * * *

It is not our right to extend the waiver of sovereign immunity more broadly that has been directed by the Congress. We, of course, intimate no opinion as to the desirability of further changes. That is immaterial. Against the background of complete immunity we find no Congressional action modifying the immunity rule in favor of cross-actions beyond the amount necessary as a set-off. * * *

The suggestion that the order of the probate court is in reality not a judgment but only a "judicial ascertainment" of credits does not affect our conclusion. No judgment against the United States is more than that. But such an entry, if within the competence of the court passing the order would be res judicata of the issue of indebtedness. The suggestion springs from the opinion in *United States v. Eckford*.[35] These words there appear:

> "Without extending the argument, we adopt the views expressed by this court in the case of *De Groot v. United States* (5 Wall. 432), decided at the last term, that when the United States is plaintiff and the defendant has pleaded a set-off, which the acts of Congress have authorized him to do, no judgment can be rendered against the government, although it may be judicially ascertained that, on striking

35. 6 Wall. 484, 491.

a balance of just demands, the government is indebted to the defendant in an ascertained amount."

The Court had just written that no action could be sustained against the government without consent and that to permit a demand in set-off to become the foundation of a judgment would be the same thing as sustaining the prosecution of a suit. The language quoted above means no more than that no judgment may be entered against the government even though the court has ascertained, through its processes that the government is actually indebted to the defendants. The judgment should be limited to a dismissal of the government's claim. * * *

Reversed.

■ MR. JUSTICE MCREYNOLDS took no part in the decision of this case.

Notes and Questions

1. With *United States v. Shaw,* the casebook ends on the same note that has been sounded throughout our study—with the concept of sovereign immunity and its continuing constraint on the amenability of the federal government to judicial action. Why does the assertion of what we today generally would call a counterclaim (what the *Shaw* court refers to as a "cross-claim") so plainly implicate sovereign immunity? Consider what the consequence would be if a defendant were permitted to assert an unlimited counterclaim against the United States without an express congressional waiver of sovereign immunity. However, as illustrated in the *Shaw* case, while a counterclaim for an affirmative judgment is not permitted (absent an independent statutory consent to suit), a "set-off" is allowed. What are the differences between an offensive counterclaim and a defensive set-off?

2. Subsequent to *Shaw,* the courts generally have interpreted the implicit consent to a set-off by the defendant as limited to counterclaims that are both defensive in nature and related in substance to the government's affirmative claim. As a leading Federal Courts casebook explains: "Despite some broad language in dictum in United States v. Shaw * * * that 'cross-claims are allowed to the amount of the government's claim, where the government voluntarily sues', the courts have permitted a defensive claim in recoupment, which arises out of the same transaction, while refusing to permit a counterclaim (including a set-off) that arises from a distinct transaction." Richard H. Fallon, Daniel J. Meltzer & David L. Shapiro, *Hart and Wechsler's The Federal Courts and the Federal System* 1004–05 (4th ed. 1996). Thus, the equitable recoupment exception to sovereign immunity is restricted to a set-off that both is limited by the amount of the government's claim and is in the nature of a compulsory counterclaim related to the same transaction or occurrence upon which the government's claim is grounded. *See, e.g., Miller v. Tony and Susan Alamo Foundation,* 134 F.3d 910, 916 (8th Cir. 1998) (ruling that "when the

United States brings a claim in court, it 'waives immunity as to claims of the defendant which assert matters in recoupment—arising out of the same transaction or occurrence which is the subject matter of the [G]overment's suit' "); *EEOC v. First Nat'l Bank of Jackson*, 614 F.2d 1004, 1008 (5th Cir. 1980) ("To state a claim in recoupment, a counterclaim must assert a claim arising out of the same transaction or occurrence which is the subject matter of the government's suit and seek relief only to the extent of diminishing or defeating the government's recovery."); *Frederick v. United States*, 386 F.2d 481, 488 (5th Cir. 1967) ("when the sovereign sues it waives immunity as to the claims of the defendant which assert matters in recoupment—arising out of the same transaction or occurrence which is the subject matter of the government's suit, and to the extent of defeating the government's claim but not to the extent of a judgment against the government which is affirmative in the sense of involving relief different in kind or nature to that sought by the government or in the sense of exceeding the amount of the government's claims"); *United States v. American Color and Chem. Corp.*, 858 F.Supp. 445, 451 (M.D.Pa.1994) ("A recoupment claim can be asserted only when the plaintiff is seeking damages for a defendant's actions and the defendant counterclaims seeking to reduce any potential damage award because of the plaintiff's actions.").

Moreover, Federal Rule of Civil Procedure 13, which generally authorizes pleading of counterclaims in federal court, emphasizes that "[t]hese rules shall not be construed to enlarge beyond the limits now fixed by law the right to assert counterclaims or to claim credits against the United States or an officer or agency thereof." Fed. R. Civ. P. 13(d). Thus, the rules of sovereign immunity and the restrictions established by other statutes on suits against the United States, including designation of the forum for suit, are not abrogated. For example, as explained by the United States Court of Appeals for the Second Circuit:

> While any action for damages against the government on an express or implied contract may be brought in the Court of [Federal] Claims, such a suit may be brought in a district court only if it seeks recovery of $10,000 or less. 28 U.S.C. §§ 1346, 1491 (1976). Counterclaims are subject to the same limitation. Apart from contract counterclaims for $10,000 or less, a defendant sued by the government in district court may have a setoff to the extent of the government's claim, but the principle of sovereign immunity deprives the court of jurisdiction to award a counterclaim against the government beyond the amount of the setoff. *United States v. Shaw*, 309 U.S. 495 (1940).

United States v. Bedford Associates, 618 F.2d 904, 917 (2d Cir. 1980); *see also United States v. Cushman & Wakefield, Inc.*, 275 F.Supp.2d 763, 775–76 (N.D. Tex. 2002). Therefore, even when there is an independent waiver of sovereign immunity that otherwise would permit the defendant to assert an offensive claim against the United States for more than the amount of the government's claim, the defendant's claim must be pursued according to the procedures established, subject to the exceptions delimited, and in the forum designated by that statute; the fact that the defendant asserts the claim as a counterclaim to a suit by the government does not excuse or waive these requirements or limitations (unless the statute expressly contemplates exceptions for counterclaims). On set-offs against the United States, see generally Gregory C. Sisk, *Litigation With the Federal Government* § 8.13, at 536–37 (ALI–ABA, 4th ed. 2006).

More than thirty years ago, the American Law Institute (ALI) proposed that, when the United States has commenced an action in a court, that court would be authorized to grant an affirmative judgment on a counterclaim against the United States arising from the same transaction or occurrence, if "any court of the United States would have jurisdiction" over such a suit against the government. American Law Institute, *Study of the Division of Jurisdiction Between State and Federal Courts* 38–39, 257–59 (1969). Thus, a court hearing the government's affirmative claim would be authorized to fully adjudicate related claims, including a defendant's counterclaim that requested relief in an amount above the government's claim, provided only that a statutory waiver of sovereign immunity authorize such a suit against the federal government in some federal court. For example, under the ALI's proposal, if the federal government initiated legal action in a district court, and the defendant responded with a transactionally-related Tucker Act counterclaim that both sought more than the government's claim and more than the $10,000 jurisdictional limit for Little Tucker Act claims in district court, the district court nonetheless could grant judgment on the Tucker Act counterclaim without transferring it to the Court of Federal Claims. *See id.* at 258. Congress, however, has never acted on that recommendation. Do you think it should? What do you suppose would be the impact on the Court of Federal Claims docket if such an exception to exclusive Tucker Act jurisdiction in that court were created?

———

INDEX

FEDERAL OFFICERS AND EMPLOY-EES, SUITS AGAINST—Cont'd

Constitutional claims (*Bivens* claims): —Cont'd

Immunity—Cont'd

Qualified immunity, 701–706

Specificity, level of, 706–709

Standard defined, 704, 706

Indemnification by government of employee, 687

Judicial implication, legitimacy of, 685, 696

Law enforcement, tort suit against as alternative, 685

Military servicemembers, claims by generally not permitted, 697–698

Motive of defendant officer as element of affirmative claim, 710–712

Private bill as alternative, 698

Private entities, constitutional claims against not implied, 720–721

Representation by Department of Justice:

Generally, 687

Limitations on, 687

Special factors, counseling against recognition of claim (See Alternative remedy by statute *supra*)

State law, color of, liability for constitutional violation when acting under, 684–685

United States or agency, constitutional claims against not implied, 716–721

United States, suits against as alternative (policy arguments), 717–721

Westfall Act, constitutional torts excluded, 670, 685

Damages relief, claims for, 639–721

Equitable relief, claims for:

Generally, 412–413, 579–591, 632–638

Administrative Procedure Act, 412–413, 579–591, 633–634

Mandamus, 634–638

Non-statutory suits, 589–590, 632–633

Immunity (See Constitutional claims *supra*; and Common law claims *supra*)

Mandamus (See Equitable relief *supra*)

Non-statutory suits against officers (See Equitable relief *supra*)

Sovereign immunity, when exception to, 121–122, 125, 131, 134, 572, 589–590, 633

Westfall Act (See Common law claims: Immunity: Statutory immunity *supra*; and **FEDERAL TORT CLAIMS ACT:** Substitution of United States as defendant)

FEDERAL TORT CLAIMS ACT

Abuse of process exception, 284

Administrative claim requirement:

Generally, 176–188, 675–676

Claim, description of, 186–187

Commencement of suit, 177–180

Denial of:

FEDERAL TORT CLAIMS ACT—Cont'd

Administrative claim requirement:—Cont'd

Denial of:—Cont'd

Generally, 188

Notice, proper, by government of, 188

Notice, adequacy of:

Generally, 186–187

Notice-pleading, comparison to, 186

Power of attorney and, 187

Premature lawsuit, void, 177–180

Prerequisite to filing suit, 177–180, 182, 185

Proper agency, delivery to:

Generally, 185, 187

Transfer if delivered to wrong agency, 187

Represent, authority to, and, 187

Settlement, for purpose of, 179, 182–183, 185–186

Standard form, 181

Substitution of United States in federal employee suit, 675–676

"Sum-certain" requirement, 180–184, 185–186

Admiralty claim exception (See also **SUITS IN ADMIRALTY ACT** and **PUBLIC VESSELS ACT**), 297, 349–351, 353

Agencies, exclusive remedy for tort claims against if claim cognizable under, 398, 713–714, 718

Aliens as claimants, 314

Assault and battery exception, 284–295

Attorney's fees, limitations on (see **ATTORNEY'S FEES, LIMITATIONS ON**)

Cause of action, state-law, 206–207, 713–714, 718

Choice-of-law, 200–206

Children as claimants, 314

Claimants excluded from coverage:

Federal Employees Compensation Act coverage as exclusive:

Generally, 314–321, 775–776

Statute of limitations for FECA claim, 320–321

Unreviewability of Secretary's determination of coverage, 319–321

Military servicemembers in active duty (*Feres* doctrine):

Generally, 314, 321–341

Civilian, government tortfeasor, included, 327–330

Benefits, alternative veterans, as rationale for, 323, 329, 337–338

Federal nature of military, as rationale for, 324–325, 328–329

Implied exclusion, 314, 339–341

Incident to military service, defined, 325–326, 338–340

Military discipline, impact on, as rationale for, 329–330

Veterans' Benefits Act (See **VETERANS' BENEFITS**)

Constitutional torts as outside scope of, 206, 296

†